Handbook of Decision Making

edited by
Göktuğ Morçöl
Penn State University
Harrisburg, Pennsylvania, U.S.A.

Taylor & Francis
Taylor & Francis Group
Boca Raton   London   New York

CRC is an imprint of the Taylor & Francis Group,
an informa business

PUBLIC ADMINISTRATION AND PUBLIC POLICY

A Comprehensive Publication Program

Executive Editor

JACK RABIN
Professor of Public Administration and Public Policy
School of Public Affairs
The Capital College
The Pennsylvania State University–Harrisburg
Middletown, Pennsylvania

Assistant to the Executive Editor
T. Aaron Wachhaus, Jr.

1. *Public Administration as a Developing Discipline,* Robert T. Golembiewski
2. *Comparative National Policies on Health Care,* Milton I. Roemer, M.D.
3. *Exclusionary Injustice: The Problem of Illegally Obtained Evidence,* Steven R. Schlesinger
5. *Organization Development in Public Administration,* edited by Robert T. Golembiewski and William B. Eddy
7. *Approaches to Planned Change,* Robert T. Golembiewski
8. *Program Evaluation at HEW,* edited by James G. Abert
9. *The States and the Metropolis,* Patricia S. Florestano and Vincent L. Marando
11. *Changing Bureaucracies: Understanding the Organization before Selecting the Approach,* William A. Medina
12. *Handbook on Public Budgeting and Financial Management,* edited by Jack Rabin and Thomas D. Lynch
15. *Handbook on Public Personnel Administration and Labor Relations,* edited by Jack Rabin, Thomas Vocino, W. Bartley Hildreth, and Gerald J. Miller
19. *Handbook of Organization Management,* edited by William B. Eddy
22. *Politics and Administration: Woodrow Wilson and American Public Administration,* edited by Jack Rabin and James S. Bowman
23. *Making and Managing Policy: Formulation, Analysis, Evaluation,* edited by G. Ronald Gilbert
25. *Decision Making in the Public Sector,* edited by Lloyd G. Nigro
26. *Managing Administration,* edited by Jack Rabin, Samuel Humes, and Brian S. Morgan
27. *Public Personnel Update,* edited by Michael Cohen and Robert T. Golembiewski
28. *State and Local Government Administration,* edited by Jack Rabin and Don Dodd
29. *Public Administration: A Bibliographic Guide to the Literature,* Howard E. McCurdy
31. *Handbook of Information Resource Management,* edited by Jack Rabin and Edward M. Jackowski
32. *Public Administration in Developed Democracies: A Comparative Study,* edited by Donald C. Rowat
33. *The Politics of Terrorism: Third Edition,* edited by Michael Stohl
34. *Handbook on Human Services Administration,* edited by Jack Rabin and Marcia B. Steinhauer

36. *Ethics for Bureaucrats: An Essay on Law and Values, Second Edition,* John A. Rohr

37. *The Guide to the Foundations of Public Administration,* Daniel W. Martin

39. *Terrorism and Emergency Management: Policy and Administration,* William L. Waugh, Jr.

40. *Organizational Behavior and Public Management: Second Edition,* Michael L. Vasu, Debra W. Stewart, and G. David Garson

43. *Government Financial Management Theory,* Gerald J. Miller

46. *Handbook of Public Budgeting,* edited by Jack Rabin

49. *Handbook of Court Administration and Management,* edited by Steven W. Hays and Cole Blease Graham, Jr.

50. *Handbook of Comparative Public Budgeting and Financial Management,* edited by Thomas D. Lynch and Lawrence L. Martin

53. *Encyclopedia of Policy Studies: Second Edition,* edited by Stuart S. Nagel

54. *Handbook of Regulation and Administrative Law,* edited by David H. Rosenbloom and Richard D. Schwartz

55. *Handbook of Bureaucracy,* edited by Ali Farazmand

56. *Handbook of Public Sector Labor Relations,* edited by Jack Rabin, Thomas Vocino, W. Bartley Hildreth, and Gerald J. Miller

57. *Practical Public Management,* Robert T. Golembiewski

58. *Handbook of Public Personnel Administration,* edited by Jack Rabin, Thomas Vocino, W. Bartley Hildreth, and Gerald J. Miller

60. *Handbook of Debt Management,* edited by Gerald J. Miller

61. *Public Administration and Law: Second Edition,* David H. Rosenbloom and Rosemary O'Leary

62. *Handbook of Local Government Administration,* edited by John J. Gargan

63. *Handbook of Administrative Communication,* edited by James L. Garnett and Alexander Kouzmin

64. *Public Budgeting and Finance: Fourth Edition,* edited by Robert T. Golembiewski and Jack Rabin

67. *Handbook of Public Finance,* edited by Fred Thompson and Mark T. Green

68. *Organizational Behavior and Public Management: Third Edition,* Michael L. Vasu, Debra W. Stewart, and G. David Garson

69. *Handbook of Economic Development,* edited by Kuotsai Tom Liou

70. *Handbook of Health Administration and Policy,* edited by Anne Osborne Kilpatrick and James A. Johnson

71. *Handbook of Research Methods in Public Administration,* edited by Gerald J. Miller and Marcia L. Whicker

72. *Handbook on Taxation,* edited by W. Bartley Hildreth and James A. Richardson

73. *Handbook of Comparative Public Administration in the Asia-Pacific Basin,* edited by Hoi-kwok Wong and Hon S. Chan

74. *Handbook of Global Environmental Policy and Administration,* edited by Dennis L. Soden and Brent S. Steel

75. *Handbook of State Government Administration,* edited by John J. Gargan

76. *Handbook of Global Legal Policy,* edited by Stuart S. Nagel

78. *Handbook of Global Economic Policy,* edited by Stuart S. Nagel

79. *Handbook of Strategic Management: Second Edition,* edited by Jack Rabin, Gerald J. Miller, and W. Bartley Hildreth

80. *Handbook of Global International Policy,* edited by Stuart S. Nagel

81. *Handbook of Organizational Consultation: Second Edition,* edited by Robert T. Golembiewski

82. *Handbook of Global Political Policy,* edited by Stuart S. Nagel

83. *Handbook of Global Technology Policy,* edited by Stuart S. Nagel
84. *Handbook of Criminal Justice Administration,* edited by
    M. A. DuPont-Morales, Michael K. Hooper, and Judy H. Schmidt
85. *Labor Relations in the Public Sector: Third Edition,* edited by Richard C. Kearney
86. *Handbook of Administrative Ethics: Second Edition,* edited by Terry L. Cooper
87. *Handbook of Organizational Behavior: Second Edition,* edited by
    Robert T. Golembiewski
88. *Handbook of Global Social Policy,* edited by Stuart S. Nagel and Amy Robb
89. *Public Administration: A Comparative Perspective, Sixth Edition,* Ferrel Heady
90. *Handbook of Public Quality Management,* edited by Ronald J. Stupak
    and Peter M. Leitner
91. *Handbook of Public Management Practice and Reform,* edited by Kuotsai Tom Liou
92. *Personnel Management in Government: Politics and Process, Fifth Edition,*
    Jay M. Shafritz, Norma M. Riccucci, David H. Rosenbloom, Katherine C. Naff,
    and Albert C. Hyde
93. *Handbook of Crisis and Emergency Management,* edited by Ali Farazmand
94. *Handbook of Comparative and Development Public Administration:*
    Second Edition, edited by Ali Farazmand
95. *Financial Planning and Management in Public Organizations,*
    Alan Walter Steiss and Emeka O. Cyprian Nwagwu
96. *Handbook of International Health Care Systems,* edited by Khi V. Thai,
    Edward T. Wimberley, and Sharon M. McManus
97. *Handbook of Monetary Policy,* edited by Jack Rabin and Glenn L. Stevens
98. *Handbook of Fiscal Policy,* edited by Jack Rabin and Glenn L. Stevens
99. *Public Administration: An Interdisciplinary Critical Analysis,* edited by
    Eran Vigoda
100. *Ironies in Organizational Development: Second Edition,*
     Revised and Expanded, edited by Robert T. Golembiewski
101. *Science and Technology of Terrorism and Counterterrorism,* edited by
     Tushar K. Ghosh, Mark A. Prelas, Dabir S. Viswanath,
     and Sudarshan K. Loyalka
102. *Strategic Management for Public and Nonprofit Organizations,* Alan Walter Steiss
103. *Case Studies in Public Budgeting and Financial Management: Second Edition,*
     edited by Aman Khan and W. Bartley Hildreth
104. *Handbook of Conflict Management,* edited by William J. Pammer, Jr.
     and Jerri Killian
105. *Chaos Organization and Disaster Management,* Alan Kirschenbaum
106. *Handbook of Gay, Lesbian, Bisexual, and Transgender Administration*
     and Policy, edited by Wallace Swan
107. *Public Productivity Handbook: Second Edition,* edited by Marc Holzer
108. *Handbook of Developmental Policy Studies,* edited by
     Gedeon M. Mudacumura, Desta Mebratu and M. Shamsul Haque
109. *Bioterrorism in Medical and Healthcare Administration,* Laure Paquette
110. *International Public Policy and Management: Policy Learning Beyond*
     Regional, Cultural, and Political Boundaries, edited by David Levi-Faur
     and Eran Vigoda-Gadot
111. *Handbook of Public Information Systems, Second Edition,* edited by
     G. David Garson
112. *Handbook of Public Sector Economics,* edited by Donijo Robbins
113. *Handbook of Public Administration and Policy in the European Union,*
     edited by M. Peter van der Hoek
114. *Nonproliferation Issues for Weapons of Mass Destruction,* Mark A. Prelas
     and Michael S. Peck

115. *Common Ground, Common Future: Moral Agency in Public Administration, Professions, and Citizenship*, Charles Garofalo and Dean Geuras
116. *Handbook of Organization Theory and Management: The Philosophical Approach, Second Edition,* edited by Thomas D. Lynch and Peter L. Cruise
117. *International Development Governance,* edited by Ahmed Shafiqul Huque and Habib Zafarullah
118. *Sustainable Development Policy and Administration,* edited by Gedeon M. Mudacumura, Desta Mebratu, and M. Shamsul Haque
119. *Public Financial Management,* edited by Howard A. Frank
120. *Handbook of Juvenile Justice: Theory and Practice,* edited by Barbara Sims and Pamela Preston
121. *Emerging Infectious Diseases and the Threat to Occupational Health in the U.S. and Canada,* edited by William Charney
122. *Handbook of Technology Management in Public Administration,* edited by David Greisler and Ronald J. Stupak
123. *Handbook of Decision Making,* edited by Göktuğ Morçöl
124. *Handbook of Public Administration, Third Edition,* edited by Jack Rabin, W. Bartley Hildreth, and Gerald J. Miller
125. *Handbook of Public Policy Analysis,* edited by Frank Fischer, Gerald J. Miller, and Mara S. Sidney
126. *Elements of Effective Governance: Measurement, Accountability and Participation,* edited by Kathe Callahan

Available Electronically

Principles and Practices of Public Administration, edited by Jack Rabin, Robert F. Munzenrider, and Sherrie M. Bartell

CRC Press
Taylor & Francis Group
6000 Broken Sound Parkway NW, Suite 300
Boca Raton, FL 33487-2742

International Standard Book Number-10: 1-57444-548-0 (Hardcover)
International Standard Book Number-13: 978-1-57444-548-0 (Hardcover)

Library of Congress Cataloging-in-Publication Data

Handbook of decision making / edited by Göktug Morçöl.
    p. cm. -- (Public administration and public policy ; 123)
    Includes bibliographical references and index.
    ISBN-13: 978-1-57444-548-0 (alk. paper)
    ISBN-10: 1-57444-548-0 (alk. paper)
    1. Public administration--Decision making. I. Morçöl, Göktug. II. Series.

JF1525.D4H36 2006
302.3'5--dc22
                                  2006008933

Visit the Taylor & Francis Web site at
http://www.taylorandfrancis.com

and the CRC Press Web site at
http://www.crcpress.com

Dedication

—————

To my parents,
Remzi and Melahat Morçöl

Preface

When this book project began with an encouragement by Jack Rabin, the editor of this series, in early 2003, there was a lull in the publication of books about decision making. That was perhaps because the series of books published in the 1980s and early 1990s, which I cite in my overview chapter, had saturated the market. Or, perhaps, the challenge of assembling a comprehensive volume on a topic as complex as decision making was daunting to potential editors. I took on the challenge with a mixture of trepidation and excitement. My aim was not to replicate what the predecessors of this book did, but to build on their accomplishments, with a particular emphasis on the nonmainstream and more recent theoretical approaches.

The theories and methods of neoclassical economic/utilitarian decision making, as well as their behavioral/organizational critiques and alternatives, have evolved over the last half century and found extensive coverage in the earlier books on decision making. The implications of the contemporary evolutionary theories, network theories, or complexity theories have not been explored systematically, however; also neglected in the mainstream discussions was the collective wisdom of the long theological and philosophical traditions of human societies. My aim was to include in the volume as many of these contemporary and ancient perspectives as possible, in addition to the more traditional and mainstream theories. I should mention that the coverage of the theories of decision making in Part II of this book is far from being exhaustive, partly because of my personal inability to locate potential contributors and partly because some of the authors I approached were unable to contribute due to their other obligations.

I also wanted to include chapters on decision making in different contexts. I believe that no single theory is comprehensive enough to capture the complexity of decision making, because it takes place in a variety of contexts. Common patterns can be identified—that is what theories try to do—but variations should also be recognized. The chapters in Part III of this volume do not cover all possible contexts of decision making, obviously—many colleagues whom I approached to write on some other contexts were unable to do so—but they give a sense of the variations in decision making styles and processes that different contexts may generate.

The chapters in Part IV describe a few of the methods devised to facilitate decision making. Once again, the coverage of the methods is not exhaustive, but the spectrum of methods discussed reflects the goal I set out for the book: not only the mainstream and well-known methods (experimental methods, cost–benefit analysis, linear programming, and queuing), but also others that are based on alternative philosophies and perspectives (geographic information systems, Q methodology, narrative policy analysis, and the methods of creative thinking and conflict management) are included.

I want to express my gratitude to all the contributors of this volume who toiled together with me in this long journey. Some of them applied their expertise in an area—decision making—they had not written about before. All of them patiently endured the review processes, and some of them had to put up with my editorial intrusions into their manuscripts. This book is truly a collective product of all the contributors.

The reviewers of the chapters in this book also deserve recognition and appreciation. Without their keen insights, the final product would be of less value. Their names and institutional affiliations are as follows in alphabetic order:

Roger T. Ames, University of Hawaii, U.S.A.
Tanya Augsburg, Arizona State University, U.S.A.
Eric Austin, Western Michigan University, U.S.A.
Nick Avdellas, LMI Government Consulting, U.S.A.
Frank Baumgartner, Penn State University, U.S.A.

Brady Baybeck, University of Missouri at St. Louis, U.S.A.
Peter Bogason, Roskilde University, Denmark
Geoffrey Brennan, Australian National University, Australia
Mine Çağlar, Koç University, Turkey
Ron Carlisle, Oglethorpe University, U.S.A.
Bret W. Davis, Loyola College of Maryland, U.S.A.
John Dixon, University of Plymouth, United Kingdom
John Forester, Cornell University, U.S.A.
Diana Fuguitt, Eckerd College, U.S.A.
Odelia Funke, Environmental Protection Agency, U.S.A.
Robert V. Gates, U.S.A.
Robert Geyer, University of Liverpool, United Kingdom
Jeffrey Goldstein, Adelphi University, U.S.A.
Charles Goodsell, Virginia Tech, U.S.A.
Akhlaque Haque, University of Alabama at Birmingham, U.S.A.
Richard Heeks, University of Manchester, United Kingdom
M. Curtis Hoffman, Grand Valley State University, U.S.A.
Mark Imperial, University of North Carolina at Wilmington, U.S.A.
Bryan Jones, University of Washington, U.S.A.
Kwang Sik Kim, Sungkyunkwan University, South Korea
Mark W. Lipsey. Vanderbilt University, U.S.A.
James March, Stanford University, U.S.A.
Clifford McCue, Florida Atlantic University, U.S.A.
Bruce Mckeown, Westmont College, U.S.A.
Jack Meek, University of LaVerne, U.S.A.
Kenneth Meier, Texas A & M University, U.S.A.
Hugh Miller, Florida Atlantic University, U.S.A.
Lisa Marie Napoli, Indiana University, U.S.A.
William H. Newell, Miami University, Ohio, U.S.A.
Ceyda Oğuz, Koç University, Turkey
Elinor Ostrom, Indiana University, U.S.A.
Charles S. Reichart, University of Denver, U.S.A.
Allen Repko, University of Texas at Arlington, U.S.A.
James Rhoads, Westminster College, U.S.A.
John Rohr, Virginia Tech, U.S.A.
Edella Schlager, University of Arizona, U.S.A.
Brian Schroeder, Rochester Institute of Technology, U.S.A.
Richard Stillman, University of Colorado at Denver, U.S.A.
Rick Szostak, University of Alberta, Canada
Aaron Wachhaus, Penn State University at Harrisburg, U.S.A.
Amanda Wolf, Victoria University of Wellington, New Zealand
Tracy Yandle, Emory University, U.S.A.
Ulf Zimmermann, Kennesaw State University, U.S.A.

And most important, I want to express my gratitude to Jack Rabin for his vision for this project and his confidence in me to carry it out.

Editor

Göktuğ Morçöl is an associate professor of public policy and administration at the Pennsylvania State University at Harrisburg. His research interests are complexity theory applications in public policy and governance, particularly metropolitan governance and the methodology of public policy research. He is the author of *A New Mind for Policy Analysis* and a coeditor of *New Sciences for Public Administration and Policy*. His work has appeared in *Administrative Theory & Praxis, International Journal of Public Administration, Politics and Policy, Policy Sciences, Emergence: Complexity and Organization*, and others.

Contributors

Robert Agranoff is a professor emeritus, School of Public and Environmental Affairs, Indiana University-Bloomington, where he continues to specialize in federalism and intergovernmental relations, public management, and community economic development. Since 1990 he has also been affiliated with the Instituto Universitario Ortega y Gasset in Madrid, Spain. He is currently chairperson of the Research Committee on Comparative Federalism, International Political Science Association. Among his many publications is a recent book with Michael McGuire, *Collaborative Public Management: New Strategies for Local Governments,* published by Georgetown University Press, winner of the 2003 Louis Brownlow Book Award of the National Academy of Public Administration. Agranoff is also the 2005 recipient of the Daniel Elazar Distinguished Scholar Award for career-long research achievement in Federalism and Intergovernmental Relations from the American Political Science Association, Section on Federalism and Intergovernmental Relations.

Ian A. Birdsall is a consultant for LMI Government Consulting, a nonprofit, public service research organization in McLean, Virginia, and an adjunct professor at Virginia Tech in Blacksburg, Virginia. At LMI, Dr. Birdsall specializes in logistics technology applications to track assets through the logistics pipeline, such as automatic identification, radio frequency tags, microelectromechanical sensors and satellite communications. Dr. Birdsall was a logistics officer in the Air Force, retiring in 1995 with twenty-two years of service. His research interests include public strategy formulation and implementation; the history and philosophy of strategy; the history of public administration, particularly during the Revolutionary and Civil Wars; and project management in the public sector. Dr. Birdsall is a graduate of Georgia Tech, the State University of New York, and Virginia Tech.

Steven R. Brown is professor of political science at Kent State University, where he teaches personality and political psychology, methodology and empirical theory, group dynamics, policy sciences, and statistics and experimental design. He is the author of *Political Subjectivity: Applications of Q Methodology in Political Science* and more than a dozen book chapters and sixty scholarly articles on Q methodology, including a recent application to empowerment (published by The World Bank, 2005). He is also coeditor of *Science, Psychology, and Communication*, a *Festschrift* honoring the inventor of Q methodology. His interest in experimentation is reflected in his coauthored *Experimental Design and Analysis.* He has served as executive director of the International Society of Political Psychology, past editor of *Policy Sciences* and of *Operant Subjectivity* (the official journal of the Q Methodology Society), and is manager of the Q-Method electronic discussion list.

Thomas J. Catlaw is an assistant professor in the School of Public Affairs at Arizona State University in Tempe, Arizona. His research interests include the history of public administration and political and social theory. Among other places, his work has appeared in *Administration & Society* (forthcoming), *The Public Manager,* and the *Journal for the Psychoanalysis of Culture & Society.* He received his Ph.D. in public administration from George Washington University in 2003.

Enamul Choudhury is assistant professor in the Department of Political Science at Miami University (Ohio). Previously he has taught at the University of Cincinnati, Wright State University, and the Indiana State University. He has published several articles in journals such as *International Journal of Public Administration, American Behavioral Scientist,* and *Journal of*

Public Affairs and Issues. He has served as the president of the Greater Cincinnati chapter of the American Society for Public Administration. His research interest lies in administrative theory, budgeting, and ethics. He earned his B.S. degree (1983) in public administration, his M.A. (1986) in urban studies, and his Ph.D. (1991) in public administration and public policy from Virginia Polytechnic Institute and State University, Blacksburg, Virginia.

Linda F. Dennard is a senior research fellow and director of the ETHOS project on Governance, Complexity, and Civic Arts at University College, Cork, Ireland. The consortium of international scholars is engaged in research and praxis projects related to new forms of administrative practice and citizen dialogue informed by the new sciences of complexity. She is a member, among other organizations, of the Society for Chaos Theory in Psychology and Life Sciences. She holds her doctorate in public administration from Virginia Tech Center for Public Administration and Public Policy.

John W. Dickey is a professor emeritus at Virginia Tech, where he continues his research and outreach activities in the Center for Public Administration and Policy and in the Department of Urban Affairs and Planning. His degrees are in civil engineering (transportation). He has worked on projects with a wide variety of firms and public agencies in over thirty countries around the world and given international academic presentations before groups in twenty countries. He has directed about 200 management/planning workshops and given congressional testimony. He has authored twelve books and a similar number of software packages. His major areas of interest include information technology management, creative problem solving and innovation support, policy analysis, transportation planning, artificial intelligence in planning and management, and programs and projects to aid the poor. He currently is pioneering a project to "map" the "Public Administration Genome."

Dan W. Durning is director of the International Center for Democratic Governance, which is part of the University of Georgia's Carl Vinson Institute of Government. He holds a Ph.D. in public policy from the University of California, Berkeley, and has taught policy analysis at Duke University and the University of Georgia. His research interests include policy issues on subnational levels of government, postpositivist methods of policy analysis, and comparative public policy. Durning has served as book review editor of *Policy Sciences* and *State and Local Government Review*. His research has been published in the *Journal of Policy Analysis and Management*, *Public Administration Quarterly*, the *Journal of Public Affairs Education*, and other journals.

Dipak K. Gupta is the Fred J. Hansen Professor of World Peace in the Department of Political Science at San Diego State University. He is also the director of the International Security and Conflict Resolution (ISCOR), a multidisciplinary undergraduate program. In 1997, he was awarded Albert W. Johnson Distinguished Lecturer, the highest research award for the university and was the "Professor of the Year" in 1994. His areas of expertise include ethnic conflict, terrorism, and public policy analysis. Professor Gupta is the author of seven books, including *Path to Collective Madness: A Study in Social Order and Political Pathology* (Praeger, 2001); *Analyzing Public Policy: Concepts, Tools, and Techniques* (Congressional Quarterly Press, 2001); *Decisions by the Numbers: An Introduction to Quantitative Techniques for Public Policy Analysis and Management* (Prentice-Hall, 1994); and *Economics of Political Violence: The Impact of Political Instability on Economic Growth* (Praeger, 1990). He has also authored over eighty monographs, book reviews, and articles published in scholarly journals and newspapers.

Akhlaque Haque, Ph.D., is an associate professor of government and director of graduate studies in public administration at the University of Alabama at Birmingham. His area of research is in public information technology and management and democratic decision making. His work has been published widely in reputable national and international journals. His current book manuscript is titled *Information and Surveillance Society*.

Michael Hayes (Ph.D., Indiana University) is professor of political science at Colgate University. He has written three books: *The Limits of Policy Change: Incrementalism, Worldview, and the Rule of Law* (Georgetown University Press, 2001); *Incrementalism and Public Policy* (Longman, 1992); and *Lobbyists and Legislators: A Theory of Political Markets* (Rutgers University Press, 1981). He also coedited *Inside the House: Former Members Reveal How Congress Really Works* (University Press of America, 2001) with Lou Frey, Jr. His journal articles include "Incrementalism as Dramaturgy: The Case of the Nuclear Freeze" (*Polity*, Spring 1987); and "The Semi-Sovereign Pressure Groups: A Critique of Current Theory and an Alternative Typology" (*Journal of Politics*, February 1978), which won the Jack Walker Award in 1991. His most recent article, "The Republican Road Not Taken: The Foreign Policy Vision of Robert A. Taft," appeared in the Spring 2004 issue of *The Independent Review*.

Tanya Heikkila is an assistant professor at Columbia University's School of International and Public Affairs, where she teaches courses in environmental policy and public management. Her research interests are in the fields of institutional theory, natural resource management, and water governance issues. Her recent research has focused on the organization of collaborative institutions and cross-scale institutional linkages in water resource management in the United States, as well as the relationship between governance structures and water management outcomes. She has published in the *Journal of Policy Analysis and Management*, *The American Review of Public Administration*, *Water Policy*, and *Natural Resources Journal*. Heikkila holds a master of public administration degree (1998) and a Ph.D. in management from the University of Arizona, School of Public Administration and Policy (2001).

David Jones is the director of the Center for the Development of Asian Studies in Atlanta and an associate professor of philosophy in the university system of Georgia. His publications are mostly in the areas of Chinese and Greek philosophy. His current book project, *The Fractal Self: Intimacy and Emergence in the Universe* (with John L. Culliney), is a cross-fertilization study between complex biological systems and ancient Greek, Daoist, Confucian, and Buddhist approaches to self-nature relationships. In addition, he has edited *Text and Contexts: The Art of Infusing Asian Culture and Thought* (with Ellen Klein, State University of New York Press, 2004), *A Feast of Logos* (with Jason Wirth and Michael Schwartz, Georgia Philosophy Series), and *Contemporary Encounters with Confucius* (under contract with Open Court). His work has appeared in *Zygon: Journal of Religion and Philosophy*, *Journal of Philosophy and Culture*, *Philosophy East–West*, *Education About Asia*, *Dao: Journal of Comparative Philosophy*, *Interlitteraria*, *Journal of Asian and African Studies*, *Asian Culture Quarterly*, *Journal of Chinese Philosophy* and numerous book chapters including *New Sciences for Public Administration and Policy: Connections and Reflections* (Göktuğ Morçöl and Linda F. Dennard, editors). He is the founding editor of *East–West Connections: Review of Asian Studies* (the journal of the Asian Studies Development Program of the East–West Center). In 2004, he was the recipient of the East–West Center's Distinguished Alumni Award. He received his Ph.D. in comparative philosophy from the University of Hawaii at Manoa.

Michael Kenney is assistant professor of public policy at the School of Public Affairs, The Pennsylvania State University, Harrisburg. Dr. Kenney has held research fellowships with the Center for International Security and Cooperation at Stanford University and the Center for International Studies at the University of Southern California. His research interests include the Colombian drug trade, counter-narcotics law enforcement, transnational terrorism, intelligence, and organization theory. His published work has appeared in *Survival*, the *International Journal of Intelligence and Counterintelligence, Transnational Organized Crime*, and the *Wall Street Journal*. Dr. Kenney recently completed a book on drug trafficking enterprises, terrorist networks, and government law enforcement agencies.

Erik-Hans Klijn is associate professor at the Public Administration Department of the Erasmus University, Rotterdam, and visiting professor at the School of Public Policy, University of Birmingham. His research focuses on complex decision making in networks, network management, institutional design, and trust in networks. His research mainly concentrates on the field of infrastructure and housing. He has published in journals such as *Public Administration, Administration and Society, JPART, PAR,* and *Public Management Review*. Recent books include *Managing Complex Networks* (with W. J. M. Kickert and J. F. M. Koppenjan, 1997) and *Managing Uncertainties in Networks* (with J. F. M. Koppenjan, 2004).

Joop F. M. Koppenjan is associate professor of public management, Faculty of Technology, Policy, and Management, Delft University of Technology. His research topics are policy networks; decision making and implementation; and privatization and public–private partnership, especially in the field of public infrastructures, safety, and sustainability. Recent publications include *Managing Complex Networks: Strategies for the Public Sector* (with W. J. M. Kickert and E. H. Klijn, eds., Sage, 1997), "The Formation of Public Private Partnerships, Lessons from Nine Transport Infrastructure Projects in The Netherlands" (*Public Administration,* 2005), and *Managing Uncertainties in Networks* (with E. H. Klijn, Routledge, 2004).

Alfred A. Marcus is the Spencer Chair in Technological Leadership and Strategic Management at the University of Minnesota Carlson School of Management, where he teaches courses in strategic management, business ethics, and business and the natural environment. He holds a Ph.D. from Harvard University and earned his undergraduate and masters degrees from the University of Chicago. He is the author or editor of twelve books, including *Big Winners and Big Losers: Four Secrets of Long-Term Business Success and Failure* (Wharton School Press, 2005) and *Reinventing Environmental Regulation* (with Donald Geffen and Ken Sexton, published by Resources for the Future in 2002. His articles have appeared in such journals as *Academy of Management Journal, Strategic Management Journal, Academy of Management Review,* and *The Journal of Forecasting.*

Melvin M. Mark is professor of psychology at Penn State University. He has served as editor of the *American Journal of Evaluation*, and is now editor emeritus. He is president of the American Evaluation Association for 2006. Dr. Mark's interests include applied social research, the theory and methodology of program and policy evaluation, and the intersection of social psychology and evaluation (e.g., theories of influence). Among his books are a recent *Handbook of Evaluation* (with Ian Shaw and Jennifer Greene, Sage) and *Evaluation: An Integrated Framework for Understanding, Guiding, and Improving Policies and Programs* (with Gary Henry and George Julnes, Jossey-Bass, 2000), as well as forthcoming books *Exemplars of Evaluation* (with Jody Fitzpatrick and Tina Christie, Sage) and *Social Psychology and Evaluation* (with Stewart Donaldson and Bernadette Campbell, Guilford).

Jack W. Meek is professor of public administration at the College of Business and Public Management at the University of La Verne, where he researches collaborative public administration and metropolitan governance, including the emergence of administrative connections in local government, regional and local collaboration and partnerships, and policy networks. Since 2003, he has also held the position of Visiting Senior Research Scholar working with Professor Terry Cooper and the Civic Engagement Initiative at the University of Southern

California. Professor Meek holds a Ph.D. in international relations from the Claremont Graduate University, and a bachelor of arts degree from the University of La Verne.

Ofer Meilich is currently an assistant professor at California State University, San Marcos. He received his Ph.D. in strategic management and organizational theory from the University of Southern California. His current research interests include business-level strategies, management of technology, organizational learning, and research methods. He has taught graduate and undergraduate level courses in business strategy and organization theory. Prior to pursuing his doctorate, Dr. Meilich has been an aeronautical engineer and a project manager in high technology.

Jennifer Mills earned a B.A. in psychology from Elizabethtown College in Elizabethtown, Pennsylvania. She is currently a graduate student in the social psychology program at The Pennsylvania State University. She primarily studies the application of social science research to policy and program evaluation. Her other research interests include power, stereotyping and prejudice, gender, social justice, and political psychology. She has actively participated in a number of politically oriented clubs and organizations, and recently attended Stanford's Summer Institute in Political Psychology.

Matthew S. Mingus (Ph.D., Colorado) is associate professor and doctoral director at Western Michigan University's School of Public Affairs and Administration. He is a Fulbright scholar and a Harry S. Truman scholar who earned his M.P.A. from the University of Victoria, British Columbia. His research is focused on comparative public administration, U.S.–Canada relations, and the foundations of American public administration. He is published in the *International Journal of Public Administration*, *Journal of Comparative Policy Analysis*, *Journal of Borderlands Studies*, *Administrative Theory and Praxis*, *Public Administration Quarterly*, and elsewhere.

Göktuğ Morçöl is an associate professor of public policy and administration at The Pennsylvania State University at Harrisburg. His research interests are complexity theory applications in public policy and governance, particularly metropolitan governance and the methodology of public policy research. He is the author of *A New Mind for Policy Analysis* and a coeditor of *New Sciences for Public Administration and Policy*. His works appeared in *Administrative Theory & Praxis, International Journal of Public Administration, Politics and Policy, Policy Sciences, Emergence: Complexity and Organization*, and others.

Tevfik F. Nas is a professor in the economics department and the Master of Public Administration program at the University of Michigan-Flint. His primary academic research is in the areas of international economics, macroeconomics and cost–benefit analysis. His recent contributions include *Cost–Benefit Analysis: Theory and Application;* two edited books (*Liberalization and the Turkish Economy,* and *Economics* and *Politics of Turkish Liberalization);* and a number of articles on macroeconomic and public policy issues published in various journals, including *American Political Science Review* and *Contemporary Economic Policy.*

William H. Newell is professor of interdisciplinary studies at Miami University in Oxford, Ohio, where he has taught in the School of Interdisciplinary Studies since its founding in 1974. He was the founding president of the Association for Integrative Studies in 1979 and has served as its executive director since 1992. In addition to directing the Institute in Integrative Studies in which he trained over 130 faculty members from other institutions in interdisciplinary curriculum development and teaching, he has been a consultant or external evaluator on interdisciplinary higher education over 100 times at colleges and universities in the United States, Canada, and New Zealand. He has published three books and over thirty articles or chapters on interdisciplinary studies, complex systems theory, public administration, and economic history.

Paul Nieuwenburg studied political science and philosophy at the universities of Leiden and Bologna. He wrote a Ph.D. thesis on Aristotelian ethics. He has worked as a postdoctoral researcher in the Department of Public Administration and as an associate professor of legal philosophy in the Faculty of Law. He currently is associate professor of political philosophy in the Department of Political Science at Leiden University. He has published widely on ethical issues, on practical reasoning, on Aristotle, and on subjects of political philosophy. In 2004 he received the Public Integrity Award for the Best Scholarly Essay of 2003. He is currently working on monographs on Aristotle and government ethics.

Steven A. Peterson is director of the School of Public Affairs and professor of Politics and Public Affairs at Penn State, Harrisburg. His areas of research interest include American politics, public opinion and voting behavior, biology and politics, and public policy (AIDS policy and education policy). He has authored or coauthored nearly twenty books, among which are *Darwinism, Dominance, and Democracy; Political Behavior: Patterns in Everyday Life; The World of the Policy Analyst; Human Nature and Public Policy,* and over 100 publications. He has served as president of the New York State Political Science Association and the Northeastern Political Science Association. He has served as an officer in the Association for Politics and the Life Sciences (APLS) and Research Committee #12 (Biology and Politics) of the International Political Science Association.

Susan Summers Raines is an associate professor of conflict management at Kennesaw State University, Atlanta, Georgia, where she teaches an executive master's program in conflict management. Her research includes investigations into the relative utility of various mediation techniques, the comparison of violent and nonviolent social movements, and the use of facilitated dialogues for public decision making. In addition to her teaching and research, she has mediated more than 5,000 civil and domestic disputes, designed and evaluated ADR programs for state and federal agencies, facilitated public meetings, and regularly leads negotiated rulemaking processes. She is the 2006 president of the Georgia chapter of the Association for Conflict Resolution (ACR).

Kurt A. Richardson is the associate director for the Institute for the Study of Coherence and Emergence (ISCE) and is director of ISCE Publishing, which specializes in complexity-related publications. He has a B.Sc. in physics, an M.Sc. in astronautics and space engineering, and a Ph.D. in applied physics. His current research interests include the philosophical implications of assuming that everything we observe is the result of complex underlying processes, the relationship between structure and function, analytical frameworks for intervention design, and robust methods of reducing complexity, which have resulted in the publication of over twenty-five journal papers and book chapters. He is the managing/production editor for the international journal *Emergence: Complexity & Organization* and is on the review board for the journals *Systemic Practice and Action Research, Systems Research and Behavioral Science,* and *Tamara: Journal of Critical Postmodern Organization Science.* He is also editor of the recently published *Managing Organizational Complexity: Philosophy, Theory, Practice* (Information Age Publishing, 2005) and coeditor of the forthcoming books *Complexity and Policy Analysis: Decision Making in an Interconnected World* and *Complexity and Knowledge Management: Understanding the Role of Knowledge in the Management of Social Networks.*

Scott E. Robinson is an assistant professor of political science and public affairs at the University of Texas, Dallas, where he researches the management of public organizations and the dynamics of public policy. His public management research focuses on the methods by which organizational decision makers deal with demands for change and conflicting values. Currently, Dr. Robinson is developing a large-scale research project investigating patterns of collaboration between schools and other public organizations in the context of emergency preparedness.

Emery Roe is a practicing policy analyst working on science, technology, and environmental controversies. He specializes in better understanding management strategies in large technical systems for the provision of critical services, such as electricity and water. He is author or coauthor of many books and articles, and during his career has helped design and direct initiatives on, among others, agriculture and urban sprawl in California's Central Valley, indicators of ecosystem health in the San Francisco Bay-Delta region, campus/community partnerships in underserved urban minority neighborhoods, and research on issues at the intersection of global population growth, natural resource utilization and the environment.

Eva Sørensen is professor of public administration and democracy at Roskilde University in Denmark. She has written extensively on empirical as well as theorietical subjects related to the institutionalization of new forms of governance and democracy. Recent publications are "Network Governance and Post Liberal Democracy" (*Administrative Theory and Praxis,* 2005) and "The Democratic Anchorage of Governance Networks" (*Scandinavian Policial Studies*, in press), both coauthored with Jacob Torfing.

Jason M. Wirth is an associate professor of philosophy at Seattle University. His recent books include *The Conspiracy of Life: Meditations on Schelling and His Time* (SUNY, 2003) and the edited volume *Schelling Now* (Indiana, 2004). He is currently finishing a book on Milan Kundera and coediting a volume on continental approaches to the Kyoto School.

Mete Yıldız is a lecturer at the Public Administration and Political Science Department of Hacettepe University in Ankara, Turkey. He worked as an associate instructor (2001–2003) and a visiting lecturer (2003–2004) at the School of Public and Environmental Affairs at Indiana University, Bloomington. His research focuses on the policy-making processes in government information and communication technology (ICT) projects, policy (social) networks, digital divide (especially the potential role of Internet cafes and cell phones in bridging it) and teaching ICT-related classes in public administration programs. Yıldız was the cofounder (with Jon Gant) and the organizer of the E-government Workshop at Indiana University. During his stay at Indiana University, Yıldız attended the NSF-funded WebShop at the University of Maryland (Summer 2002), and worked as the managing editor of *The Information Society* journal (2001–2002). He holds a master's degree in public administration from the University of Southern California, Los Angeles, and a Ph.D. in public affairs from Indiana University, Bloomington.

Table of Contents

Preface ix

Contributors xiii

Part I
Overview and Introduction. 1

Chapter 1   Decision Making: An Overview of Theories, Contexts,
and Methods 3
Göktuğ Morçöl

Part II
Theories of Decision Making 19

Chapter 2   The Contribution of Public Choice Analysis to Decision Making
Theories in Public Administration: Past, Present, and Future 21
Tanya Heikkila

Chapter 3   Policy Making through Disjointed Incrementalism. 39
Michael Hayes

Chapter 4   Bounded Rationality and Organizational Influence:
Herbert Simon and the Behavioral Revolution. 61
Matthew S. Mingus

Chapter 5   Practical Reasoning and Action: Simon's *Administrative
Behavior* in Context 81
Paul Nieuwenburg

Chapter 6   Discourse, Decision, and the Doublet: An Essay on the Crisis of
Modern Authority 99
Thomas J. Catlaw

Chapter 7   Evolution, Cognition, and Decision Making 119
Steven A. Peterson

Chapter 8   Punctuated Equilibrium Models in Organizational
Decision Making 133
Scott E. Robinson

Chapter 9   Democratic Theory as a Frame for Decision Making: The
Challenges by Discourse Theory and Governance Theory 151
Eva Sørensen

Chapter 10 Governing Policy Networks 169
Erik-Hans Klijn and Joop F. M. Koppenjan

Chapter 11 Complex Systems Thinking and Its Implications
for Policy Analysis. 189
Kurt A. Richardson

Chapter 12 The New Sensibilities of Nonlinear Decision Making: Timing,
Praxis, and a Feel for Relationship 223
Linda F. Dennard

Chapter 13 Decision Making in Interdisciplinary Studies. 245
William H. Newell

Chapter 14 Foundation of Confucian Decision Making 265
David Jones

Chapter 15 Decision: Nishitani on Time and Karma 289
Jason M. Wirth

Chapter 16 Theology and Decision Making: Judaism 299
Alfred A. Marcus

Part III
Contexts of Decision Making. 317

Chapter 17 Decision Making in Public Management Networks 319
Robert Agranoff and Mete Yıldız

Chapter 18 Political Decision Making within Metropolitan
Areas. 347
Jack W. Meek

Chapter 19 The Rules of Drug Trafficking: Decision Making in Colombian
Narcotics Enterprises 361
Michael Kenney

Chapter 20 Information, Technology, and Decision Making. 371
John W. Dickey and Ian A. Birdsall

Chapter 21 Decision Making Models Used in E-Government
Projects: Evidence from Turkey 395
Mete Yıldız

Chapter 22 Budgeting as an Institutional Practice: Modeling
Decision Making in the Budget Process 417
Enamul Choudhury

Chapter 23   Strategic Planning and Decision Making 433
Ofer Meilich and Alfred A. Marcus

Part IV
Methods of Decision Making 457

Chapter 24   Experiments and Quasi-Experiments for Decision Making:
Why, How, and How Good? 459
Melvin M. Mark and Jennifer Mills

Chapter 25   Cost Benefit Analysis 483
Tevfik F. Nas

Chapter 26   Linear Programming and Integer Programming:
Choosing the Optimal Mix of Alternatives 491
Dipak K. Gupta

Chapter 27   Queuing Theory and Simulations 511
Dipak K. Gupta

Chapter 28   Decision Making in Geographic Information Systems 525
Akhalaque Haque

Chapter 29   Q Methodology and Decision Making 537
Dan W. Durning and Steven R. Brown

Chapter 30   Methods of Assessing and Enhancing Creativity for
Public Policy Decision Making 565
Göktuğ Morçöl

Chapter 31   Participatory Decision Making: Using Conflict Management
Theories, Methods, and Skills to Overcome the Rational and
Irrational Sources of Conflict 587
Susan Summers Raines

Chapter 32   Narrative Policy Analysis for Decision Making 607
Emery Roe

Index 627

Part I

Overview and Introduction

1 Decision Making: An Overview of Theories, Contexts, and Methods

Göktuğ Morçöl

CONTENTS

1.1 The Ghost in the Middle 3
1.2 The Rational Comprehensive Model and Its Critics 5
1.3 Contextuality of Decision Making 8
1.4 Aggregation of Individual Decisions 8
1.5 Chapters of the Book 10
    1.5.1 Theories 10
    1.5.2 Contexts 14
    1.5.3 Methods 15
References 17

1.1 THE GHOST IN THE MIDDLE

No single volume, no matter how thick, can cover all aspects of decision making. Like its predecessors (e.g., Edwards and Tversky, 1967; Ungston and Braunstein, 1982; Nigro, 1984; Hogarth and Reder, 1986; Pennings, 1986; Zey, 1992), this book presents only a partial account of the theories, contexts, and methods of decision making. There were attempts to formulate a universal theory of decision making in the past. The assumption was that the "rational individual" could make decisions in a purely logical fashion (without the interference of values or any other distractions) and with the complete knowledge of the problems to be solved and the consequences of his or her actions. This notion, which is largely regarded as a myth today (some see it as a convenient myth, however) is the basis of the so-called "rational comprehensive model of decision making."[*]

The rational comprehensive model is an abstraction. Or, perhaps, it is a ghost, which has no material existence; it has no direct applications in any real-life situations, nor does it have any strong proponents. Some consider it a useful approximation, but no serious theoretical perspective assumes that individuals are (or can be) purely "rational" decision makers. Yet, the rational model is invoked again and again in theoretical debates on decision making. It is a ghost in the middle of the debates—a ghost that refuses to go away, despite the fact that it was criticized to death and

---

[*] Other names are used, somewhat interchangeably, for this model and the general theory of rationality it represents, and some of them can be seen in the chapters of this book. Some of the more-commonly used names are "economic rationality" (Simon, 1997), the "classical theory of omniscient rationality" (Simon, 1997), the "economic man assumption" (Edwards, 1967), and the "rational man assumption" (Etzioni, 1992).

buried, particularly in the second half of the 20th century. The reader will notice the ephemeral existence of this ghost in the chapters of this volume; some authors refer to it directly, others invoke some aspect of it in their critiques.

It is significant that the theorists of decision making cannot help but do so. This phenomenon can be explained partially with the deep historical and cultural roots of the notion of rationality, particularly in Western societies. (Other and more specific explanations for this phenomenon will be discussed later in this chapter.) Aristotle thought that rationality was the feature that distinguished human beings from animals, and that rational thinking was a close companion of empirical inquiry. The emergence of the Newtonian science in the 17th century provided scientists with a new methodology of empirical scientific investigation and buttressed the notion of empirically verifiable rational thinking. The Enlightenment philosophers, such as Hume, articulated a worldview that emphasized the decontextuality (universality) of scientific (rationally generated) knowledge and the quantifiability of rational thinking. The logical positivists of the early 20th century codified the Enlightenment principles of scientific investigation and turned it into a system of logical and mathematical operations. In the lineage of thought from the Enlightenment to logical positivism, rationality was equated with scientificity (as a result, it gained a high cultural status), universality, and decontextual logical thinking. This worldview (science = rationality = formal logic = quantification of knowledge) was subjected to devastating criticisms by phenomenologists in the late 19th and early 20th centuries and by critical theorists, social constructionists, post-structuralists, and others in the second half of the 20th century. And yet, as the reader will see in the chapters of this book, the notion of rationality promoted by the Enlightenment and logical positivism is still a major frame of reference in the theoretical discussions in the early 21st century.[*]

Then what specifically is the rational comprehensive model and the notion of rationality it represents? Because of its ethereal existence, it is somewhat tricky to nail down the assumptions and propositions of the rational comprehensive model, but the following can be deduced from the arguments of its critics and qualified supporters (i.e., those who think that it is a useful approximation). It has two core, and related, assumptions. First, individual decision makers are rational in the sense that they are capable of obtaining full information about the problematic situations they face and the consequences of their actions, and they can make their choices on the sole basis of factual evidence and logical calculations. Second, these characteristics of rationality are universal; all decision making can potentially be fully informed, solely factual, and logical, regardless of the historical and cultural contexts of individual decision makers.

Although nobody believes in these two core assumptions fully, two theoretical traditions can be identified as their closest supporters: the neoclassical economics/rational choice paradigm, which gained popularity particularly in the second half of the 20th century, and the rational comprehensive planning tradition of the mid-20th century. The former is more important, because it is a more sophisticated and elaborate approximation of the rational comprehensive model and because of its ascendancy in the academic discourse and policy applications of recent decades. The rational choice theorists believe in the universality of the self-interested and utility maximizing ("rational") individual decision makers. However, this core assumption is modified and qualified in many versions of rational choice.[†] Particularly, the institutional rational choice theorists (e.g., Ostrom, 1990, 2005) emphasize the role of social structures (institutions) in constricting the rationality of individual choices and behaviors. A common problem for rational choice theorists is whether or not, or to what extent, individual rational choices are aggregated into rational (or desirable) collective outcomes. The rationality of individual decisions and the aggregation of individual choices into

---

[*] For a more extensive discussion of the history of the scientific/rational worldview and its critiques mentioned in this paragraph, see Morçöl (2002).

[†] For in-depth discussions of the assumptions from rational choice perspectives, see Heikkila's chapter on "public choice"—a term that is used interchangeably with rational choice or to refer to its applications in public policy and administration—in this volume and Lichbach (2003); MacDonald (2003).

collective outcomes are the two main areas of theoretical development and debate, both among rational choice proponents and between rational choice theorists and their opponents. These discussions are summarized in the sections below.

Before that, however, a brief note on the rational comprehensive planning tradition is in order here. This tradition manifested itself in the central planning systems of the socialist and statist regimes in the 20th century, as well as in the Planning Programming and Budgeting System (PPBS) of the United States in the 1960s. Although the planning models were different in these systems, they all shared implicitly the Enlightenment assumption that societies could be governed rationally (based on scientific knowledge) by collective decisions makers. This notion of collective rationality is obviously different from the rational choice assumptions that individuals make self-interested rational choices and that these choices aggregate into collective outcomes. However, these two theories of rationality are similar in their assumptions that rational decision makers (either individually or collectively) are capable of obtaining full information about problematic situations and the consequences of their actions, and that the rational decision making model is universally applicable, regardless of the context of a particular decision.

The following sections summarize the discussions and debates in three areas: rationality of decision making (the rational comprehensive model), contextuality (or decontextuality) of decision making, and aggregation of individual choices to collective outcomes.

1.2 THE RATIONAL COMPREHENSIVE MODEL AND ITS CRITICS

At the core of the rational comprehensive model of decision making are two assumptions about the nature of decision making individuals: (1) that they are atomistic entities who are self-interested and whose interests and preferences are set prior to decision making situations, (2) that they are capable of clearly identifying and rank-ordering their decision criteria (preferences, goals, values, or "utility functions") and alternative courses of action and are able to predict the outcomes of their actions with certainty.[*] Again, no serious theoretical perspective fully adopts these assumptions, but some use them as useful approximations. The assumptions of neoclassical economists and rational choice theorists are the closest to those of the rational comprehensive model, but even they concede that not all individuals are capable of ranking their decision preferences systematically and consistently throughout the decision making process and that not all the consequences of all possible decision alternatives are predictable in their entirety (Tversky and Kahneman, 1986). The institutional rational choice theory goes further and asserts that institutions constrict the expression of self interest or shape it to varying degrees and that individual decision makers are not fully, but only "boundedly" rational (see Ostrom, 2005, 116–119).

These theorists may qualify their endorsements of the rational comprehensive model, but the belief in the self-interested rational human behavior is still at the core of theories. They may recognize the institutional, moral, or cultural constraints of rational behavior, but these are considered only as external constraints. They may limit rationality, but do not constitute (shape or determine) human interests or behavior. The primacy of individual choice is so deeply ingrained in the theory, that many neoinstitutional economists argue that institutions should be designed to accommodate (or reflect) the needs of individual rational decision makers. Russell (1979) for example, argues that we should define institutions to take account of self-interested behavior (3 and 18–19).

One reason why the rational comprehensive model maintains its "ghostly existence" as a reference point in the academic discourse on decision making is the popularity of neoclassical economics and rational choice theory in academia and public policy applications in recent decades. Another reason is that there is no coherent and comprehensive alternative to it, despite the fact that

---

[*] For more detailed versions of these assumptions, see Edwards (1967) and (Zey 1992, 2–3).

it has been shown to be defective and unrealistic (Schwartz, 1998, p. xv). Etzioni (1992) argues that the rational man assumption offers a "clear, concise, and simple conception of human nature" and until there is an alternative that offers a parsimonious explanation, it will maintain its central position in theorization and debates (90).[*] Simon (1979) cites another reason. He points out that although it was shown to be false empirically, the "classical theory of omniscient rationality" has been revived as a result of the spread of computers and the development of mathematical models. The new generation of researchers maintains its core assumptions, but also recognizes the uncertainties in decision making; the developments in the statistical decision theory and game theory helped them incorporate uncertainties into decision making models as probabilities.

Then what were the criticisms of the rational model that demonstrated its deficiencies and falsehoods? The reader will see some of these criticisms in the chapters of this book, particularly in the chapters in Part II. A brief preview here may help clarify the context of these discussions. The earlier and closest critique of the rational model came from the behavioral cognitive psychologists. Herbert Simon's work contributed in a major way to demonstrating the deficiencies of the rational comprehensive model as well. He also developed the alternative conceptualization of "bounded rationality." Simon's work may be considered as part of the behavioral and cognitive psychological critique of the rational model (it does have serious overlaps and parallels with these critiques), but he deserves to be mentioned separately, because his critique and conceptualization are major reference points in the literature on decision making. Three chapters in this book discuss Simon's work (Mingus', Nieuwenburg's, and Catlaw's), ably and elaborately, from different perspectives. Morçöls' will be a brief preview.

Behavioral and cognitive psychological researchers aimed at finding out how people actually make decisions. The behavioral and cognitive psychological literature takes the assumptions of the rational model as a their main reference frame and cites the "deviations" from it, or the human "biases" in decision making (with the implicit assumption that the rational model would be the "unbiased" behavioral model). Ward Edwards, Amos Tversky, Daniel Kahneman, and Robin Hogarth are among the earlier theorists who significantly contributed to the behavioral understanding of decision making, particularly economic decision making.[†]

Summaries of the research findings of behavioral and cognitive psychologists can be found in Halpern (1996, 288–299) and Schwartz (1998, 47–69). Psychologists who studied economic behaviors observed that the decision making process was influenced by a multitude of factors: motivation, values and norms, information processing capabilities and heuristics, attitudes in judging other persons and ides, social comparisons of one's output with others,' learning from past experiences, emotional factors, bargaining processes (rules and institutions), and expectations. The motivational factors include the need for achievement, locus of control, sensation seeking and risk taking, altruism, time preference, cognitive system, and lifestyle. Researchers also showed that individuals' "biases" affect their decision making styles and capabilities. According to this research, biases may occur in the acquisition and processing of information. In the acquisition phase, the following are important factors: the "availability" of information for human perception (e.g., dramatic events are more available to perception), the "selectivity" of perceivers (e.g., people with different cultural backgrounds or political beliefs may filter information about political events differently), the ease in perceiving absolute frequencies (e.g., sharp spikes, rather than seminal long-term trends, are more easily perceived), and the ease in perceiving "concrete" information (as opposed to "abstractions"). Information processing is also biased. Among the biases in information processing are people's tendencies to overvalue certainty over uncertainty (e.g., preference for certitude in policy positions and "moral clarity"), to find illusory (spurious) associations between

---

[*] In this piece, Etzioni offers a parsimonious alternative that he calls the "normative/affective actor."

[†] For original writings by these authors and other behavioral theorists, see Edwards and Tversky (1967) and Hogarth and Reder (1986).

phenomena and to draw linear inferences from them, to apply judgmental standards inconsistently (cognitive dissonance), to use simplifying heuristics (rules of thumb), to assume that a small group of events or behaviors by a person is representative of the whole, to engage in wishful thinking, and to fall into logical fallacies (e.g., gambler's fallacy). Psychologists also observed that learning may help improve decision making (i.e., it may reduce its biases), but because people have different methods of learning, and the learning process is not linear or perfect, they may end up with less than perfect cognitive skills and habits or even learn socially destructive habits.

Simon's works inspired and contributed to this research by showing some of the limitations of the human mind and demonstrating that the assumptions of the rational model—that the human mind could be objectively and fully rational—were not realistic. He theorized that the human mind was only "intendedly and boundedly rational," because of its limitations. The theory of bounded rationality was a product of his earlier works, particularly his *Administrative Behavior* (1997; originally published in 1945). In another earlier work, Newell and Simon (1972) described the mechanisms of decision making and problem solving as dynamic processes. According to Newell and Simon, individuals use personal problem spaces and individual heuristics to organize complex and massive incoming stimuli to make decisions. Personal problem spaces change as the experiences, and thus the aspiration levels, of individuals change. Simon's model of "bounded rationality" describes a process in which decision makers engage only in a limited search for alternatives within the dynamics of their personal problem spaces. In this model, decision makers "satisfice," not optimize, in their selection of choices: They select the first satisfying choice, rather than comparing all possible choices.

Some of his critics refer to Simon's theory of bounded rationality as a merely "revisionist" version of the rational model. The case can be made that Simon's theory goes beyond a mere revision of the rational model. In particular, his assertions in his later works, that the limitations of the human mind are "ineradicable" and that decision making takes place within contexts, have implications that go beyond a mere revisionism. Simon (1979) highlights the "neoclassical shift" in the "classical theory of omniscient rationality," which, he argues, occurred as a result of the developments in computer technologies and mathematical modeling. The neoclassical theorists, according to Simon, maintained the core assumption of objective rationality, but they also incorporated the notions of subjectivity and uncertainty into their models. The notion of "subjective expected utility" became the basis of a renewed rational decision making theory.[*] A major implication of this revised conceptualization is the recognition that the rational actor may not be able to pick the best possible decision alternative because of the uncertainties in predicting future states of affairs. The notion of "expected utility" signals the abandonment of the notion of perfect maximization in decision making, but, Simon stresses, it also helps keep up the hope that actual decision making processes can still approximate the ideal state of rationality. The implicit assumption is that the "imperfections" in the decision process could be alleviated. However, Simon argues, his and others' studies showed that such "imperfections" are in fact ineradicable because of the way the human mind works.

Simon et al. (1992) stress that the theory of subjective expected utility ignores not only the limits of human rationality, but also the complexity of the world. According to Simon (1997) psychological limitations and social and organizational factors together constitute the context of decision making. Social and organizational environments control decision choices or even impose certain types of behaviors. Therefore, Simon (1986) argues, the rationality of a certain behavior can be judged only in the context of its premises or "givens," which include its social situation, the goals of the decision maker, and the computational means available to him or her.

---

[*] Simon (1979) cites linear programming, integer programming, and queuing theory among the methods of the neoclassical shift. See the Gupta's descriptions of these methods in his chapters in this volume.

1.3 CONTEXTUALITY OF DECISION MAKING

Many critics of the rational model point to its presumption that all rational individuals can (or should) make decisions in the same way. This notion that rational decision making has universal rules and outcomes is criticized by those who argue that decisions are culturally embedded (e.g., Zey, 1992, 79) and that rationality takes meaning in a social context (e.g., Arrow, 1992). As Zey puts it, decision makers do not make decisions independent of their environments; decision making is context dependent.

The importance of cultural influences on economic behaviors has long been emphasized by sociologists. Max Weber was one of the first to highlight the importance of culture, particularly the religious beliefs of Protestantism, in the development of capitalism (Schwartz, 1998). More recent cross-cultural studies also highlight the importance of culture in understanding the differences in economic behaviors between the West and Eastern Asia. Schwartz cites a 1950s study that identified the different ways in which Koreans and Westerners react to economic incentives. He also cites studies that contend that Confucianism and other Eastern theologies play important roles in Eastern Asians' economic behaviors (6).[*] The importance of cultural differences in economic behaviors is recognized also by the World Bank, which has recently made particular efforts to understand different "governance factors" that affect different countries (7).

More specific research on decision making in sociology shows that people are not born with preferences; preferences are shaped by family, friends, religious institutions, and larger communities (Schwartz, 1998, 42). A recent example is Granovetter's (1992) thesis of "embeddedness of economic action in structures of social relations." He argues that economy has not become autonomous in modern market societies, contrary to what Adam Smith and his neoclassical and neoinstitutional economist followers believe. Economic activities are still embedded in social structures. Neither the atomistic individual of Smith's and his followers' theories, nor the "anonymous markets" they imagine exist. Individuals do not act as atomistic utility maximizers all the time. Granovetter argues that it is a fallacy that institutions must be built on this assumption about human behaviors.

Etzioni (1992) not only criticizes the notion of the atomistic individual decision maker, but also offers an alternative model. He argues that the criticisms of the rational man conception of the neoclassical paradigm have not been successful, because they do not offer clear or concise alternatives. He offers his "normative-affective actor model" as such an alternative. In his model, decision makers do not make decisions based on "logical-empirical" considerations, but on emotions and normative commitments. He admits that there is actually a continuum from the "logical-empirical" considerations to the "normative-affective" considerations in decision making. In some cases, emotional and normative choices dominate, and in others logical and empirical ones. However, the latter cases are exceptional, according to Etzioni.

The contextuality of decision making is a major theme in this book. The chapters in Part III illustrate how decisions are made in different contexts. Some of the chapters in Part II (Jones', Wirth's, and Marcus') demonstrate that the contexts created by theological/cultural belief systems are important for decision making. Obviously, much more research and theorization need to be done on the contextuality and contexts of decision making, but the chapters of this book give a glimpse of the possibilities for the future.

1.4 AGGREGATION OF INDIVIDUAL DECISIONS

Even if we assume that individuals are fully rational decisions makers, à la the rational comprehensive model, and that all decisions could be made in the same manner, regardless of the context, a question remains: do the results of individual rational decisions aggregate to rational collective

---

[*] Two of the chapters in this book (Jones' and Wirth's) discuss Eastern theories and decision making.

outcomes (outcomes that are beneficial to all concerned, or outcomes that would maximize the collective utility)? As Coleman (1992) puts it, in the neoclassical economic theory the aggregation problem is posed within an idealized system. In this system, actors are independent, goods exchanged are private, tastes are fixed, there are no barriers to inhibit information exchange, and there are no interdependencies among actors (268).

Whether or not one agrees with the assumptions of the neoclassical or rational choice theories, the ways in which individual decisions (whether rational or otherwise) influence, or aggregate to, collective outcomes is a major intellectual and practical policy problem. Even the proponents of rational choice, who are most comfortable with the rational comprehensive model, see this as a problem. Fiorina (1979, 47) points out, for example, that the game theory has shown that rational individual decisions do not automatically aggregate to rational collective outcomes.

The problematic nature of aggregation was convincingly demonstrated first by Kenneth Arrow (1963). He showed particularly that the preferences of decision makers in a democratic society could not be aggregated in such a way that the collective decision would meet the requirements of the economic rationality model. In other words, individual rational choices could not be aggregated through voting into the best choice for all voters. He also pointed out that the only model that could approximate the rational actor model at the collective level was actually the autocratic model of decision making. This key insight of Arrow's has been cited frequently by neoclassical economic and rational choice theorists, as well as by their critics. The former still maintain the rational individual choice assumption (Arrow did not refute that), but acknowledge the problematic nature of the aggregation process. The latter, expectedly, see Arrow's theory as yet another demonstration of the falsehood of the rational model.[*]

Some of the critics see aggregation as an intellectual and practical policy problem. Simon et al. (1992) see the "aggregation problem" as a major area of future research on decision making. Coleman (1992) criticizes neoclassical economists for trying to solve the aggregation problem in an idealized conceptual system, but gives them a credit for pointing it out. The aggregation problem, Coleman thinks, is the "central intellectual problem of the social sciences" (269). He argues that a good theory of aggregation must take into account systemic effects on individual decisions.

One area in which the aggregation problem has been studied is organization theory. As Zey (1992, 256) points out, some neoclassical economists assume that under market conditions organizations act as if they were rational individuals. In other words, in this conceptualization, there is no aggregation problem; organizations are seen as unified individuals with rational decision making capabilities. There is some research that has shown that this is not the case. In his case study of the Cuban missile crisis, Allison (1971) for example, demonstrated that many organizational decisions, in fact, do not follow the "rational actor" model. They emerge as results of organizational processes or bureaucratic-political bargaining games in organizations.

James March's works on organizational decision making also showed that the social, cultural, or political contexts of decisions matter in the aggregation of individual decisions. March and Shapira (1992) summarize the findings of his line of research. Organizations do not have preference functions; their preferences are imprecise, inconsistent, and ever-changing. Organizational information is not clear or rationally ordered; it is tainted and exaggerated. Organizations are arenas of symbolic action; information functions as a symbol more often than as a signal. Organizations are not orderly in a linear or hierarchical sense, but order arises in "garbage cans" and loosely coupled relationships. Organizational change occurs in unanticipated ways as a result of organizational learning, which is not a linear or orderly process. Organizations learn experientially and through evolutionary selection.

---

[*]In his later writings (e.g., Arrow, 1992, 75), Arrow makes it clear that he too is quite critical of the rational individual decision maker assumption of the rational model and points out that he is in agreement with Simon's theory of bounded rationality.

1.5 CHAPTERS OF THE BOOK

The predecessors of this book (Edwards and Tversky, 1967; Hogarth and Reder, 1986; Nigro, 1984; Pennings, 1986; Zey, 1992; Ungston and Braunstein, 1982) covered in detail many of the issues that were raised in the previous section and many others that were not. This book includes chapters whose contents overlap with those of its predecessors, but it also differs from them in major ways. First, it takes a more comprehensive approach to decision making. In addition to covering the traditional topics and perspectives in the discussions on decision making (e.g., public choice, incrementalism, bounded rationality, budgeting, and strategic planning), it also includes chapters that look at decision making from perspectives that are not covered in the mainstream decision making theories or research (discourse theories, evolutionary theories, network theories, complexity theories, and different philosophies and theologies). It also includes chapters on the different contexts of decision making, from public management networks, to metropolitan areas, drug trafficking, information and communication technology, E-government projects, budgeting, and strategic management. A group of decision making methods are also described and discussed in the book. The methods included in the volume (experiments, cost-benefit analysis, linear programming, queuing, geographic information systems, Q methodology, creativity methods, conflict management methods, and narrative policy analysis) represent different theoretical and methodological approaches.

The volume is organized into three parts: theories, contexts, and methods. It must be emphasized that this division is not categorical. A categorical division would be somewhat artificial. Different decision making theories obviously emerge in different contexts (e.g., the Confucian and Buddhist theories emerged in East Asian societies), and different theories prefer different methodological approaches. The context chapters also reflect a variety of theoretical approaches. Methods are based on theories.

1.5.1 THEORIES

Public choice theories, which Tanya Heikkila discusses in her chapter ("The Contribution of Public Choice Analysis to Decision Making Theories in Public Administration"), are the closest in their assumptions to the rational comprehensive model. As Heikkila points out, public choice theorists assume that individuals are rational and seek to maximize their self-interests, not only in economic activities, but also in politics and bureaucracy. After demonstrating the considerable influence of public choice shown in studies on voting behavior, bureaucratic decision making, and metropolitan governance, Heikkila discusses the revisions and adjustments in public choice theories. A number of public choice scholars have acknowledged the limitations of rationality in human decision making and adopted Simon's bounded rationality perspective; they have also incorporated institutional influences on individual decision making into their models. She concludes that by applying the logic of methodological individualism to explain political and organizational outcomes, public choice has enhanced our understanding of individual behaviors and decision making in institutions.

One of the earlier alternatives to the rational comprehensive model of decision making was Charles Lindblom's *incrementalism* (or *disjointed incrementalism*). Lindblom argued that the rational comprehensive model could be applied only under ideal conditions and offered incrementalism as both a better description of the actual decision making situations and a prescription for better decision making. In his chapter ("Policymaking through Disjointed Incrementalism"), Michael Hayes, a major contributor to the literature on incrementalism, first reviews the rational comprehensive model and its limitations and then lays out the elements of the incremental model as an alternative. He points out that the ideal conditions assumed in the rational comprehensive model are unrealistic, as Lindblom demonstrated earlier. Then Hayes discusses to what extent Lindblom's model accounts for the way policies are actually made. He argues that incrementalism avoids the problem of assuming abstract and ideal conditions; instead, it focuses on concrete problems to be alleviated. He concludes the chapter with a discussion of whether or not incrementalism really is the best way to make public policies. Hayes points out that incrementalism may not describe accurately all policymaking conditions, but it does many conditions. He critiques the "ideologues," such as neoclassical economists, who attempt to apply the rational model to all conditions, and argues that incrementalism is superior to the rational model because the former is "quintessentially pragmatic" and "anti-utopian," not ideological.

Herbert Simon's critique of what he called the "classical theory of omniscient rationality" and his alternative model of "intended and bounded rationality," arguably, has been more influential, and controversial, than Linblom's incrementalism. Three chapters in this volume directly address Simon's theory and its implications. In his chapter ("Bounded Rationality and Organizational Influence: Herbert Simon and the Behavioral Revolution"), Matthew Mingus discusses Simon's contributions to our understanding of individual and organizational decision making. According to Mingus, Simon contributed mainly with his three insights: People "satisfice" decision criteria, rather than optimizing them; human rationality is bounded by the limitations of the mind; and facts and values can still be separated in decision making. Mingus points out that Simon shifted the focus from studying organizational structures toward studying decision making in organizations and developed a linguistic and conceptual base for scientific analyses of organizations. Mingus argues that Simon's work, which spanned the entire second half of the 20th century, is still relevant now.

In his critical analysis of Simon's theory, Paul Nieuwenburg ("Practical Reasoning and Action: Simon's *Administrative Behavior* in Context") shows that it has its roots in the "practical reasoning" and "instrumental rationality" traditions of Aristotle and Hume. Nieuwenburg finds evidence of Aristotelian and Humean thinking in the distinction Simon makes between fact and value elements in decisions. He also argues that Simon's analysis of decision making is a "twentieth-century logical positivist version of the practical syllogism pioneered by Aristotle in his theory of prudence or practical wisdom." According to Nieuwenburg, Simon's fact/value distinction, which also constitutes the basis of the logical positivist conception of rationality, follows the Humean tradition of making a fundamental distinction between the functions of factual and ethical terms. Nieuwenburg points out that he does not aim to discredit instrumentalist practical reasoning, or its Aristotelian and Humean tradition. Rather, he wants to show that instrumental rationality is not the only form of rationality, or that instrumental reasoning is not the only way to reason.

Thomas Catlaw ("Discourse, Decision and the Doublet: An Essay on Crisis of Modern Authority") agrees with Mingus's assessment that Simon's legacy has endured, but he points out that Simon's concession that human beings cannot be comprehensively rational is far from being satisfactory for our times. In his post-structuralist critique, Catlaw argues that Simon conceded very little and that he retained the "technicist" attitude of the rational comprehensive model. The problem of decision making is not individual cognitive failure, according to Catlaw, nor is it "how to make good, instrumental decisions in the face of uncertainty and complexity in order to realize individual and collective projects." Catlaw argues that Simon's concessions conceal the core problem of our postmodern world, which is that "we continue to act and speak *as if* there were an underlying order (be it subject or object) to the world that could serve as a firm referent or ground for identity and decision while the institutions and mechanisms that sustained this fiction erode." Instead, we should try to understand the "conditions under which the construction of the experience of self, or subjectivity, and the cultivation of individual difference can constitute a dynamic and collective end in itself." According to Catlaw, decision making should be understood as a discursive and authoritative process. As such, it is constitutive of the boundaries of the domains of sensibility, which are generative and productive.

Steven Peterson's chapter ("Evolution, Cognition, and Decision Making"), addresses the issue of the biological bases of decision making by humans. Peterson argues that the rational comprehensive model of decision making not only overestimates the intellectual capacities of human beings (as Lindblom and Simon demonstrated), but also ignores the findings of evolutionary biologists and cognitive psychologists. These scientists have shown that human beings, like other species, developed, over the course of their evolution, brain functions and structures that "lead us to live in distinct worlds." In this sense, there is no "real world" out there, but there "is an array of worlds depending upon a species' unique sensory capabilities." Among these sensory capabilities are the heuristics (shortcuts) that we use in decision making under the conditions of uncertainty. These heuristics are part of the human biology.

Punctuated equilibrium theory, which Scott Robinson discusses in his chapter ("Punctuated Equilibrium Models in Organizational Decision Making"), emerged out of the debates and discussions in two distinct literatures, the dynamics of policy change and the dynamics of species change. The theory provides a model that explains the existence of long periods of stability with occasional, but infrequent, dramatic change. In his chapter, Robinson traces the development of punctuated equilibrium models in paleontology and policy theory and the incorporation of this approach into research on budgetary policy making. He then discusses the empirical implications of these models and makes suggestions for research into punctuated equilibrium processes.

Like Catlaw, Eva Sørensen ("Democratic Theory as a Frame for Decision Making") offers a discursive critique, but the focus of her critique is broader and somewhat different from Catlaw's. She argues, from a governance theory/discourse theory perspective, that the notion of "rational decision making" is irrelevant in understanding the actual processes of democratic decision making. She challenges the rationalist notions embedded in the traditional theories of representative democracy, which assume that non-political and bureaucratic mechanisms of decision making and implementation exist. There is no such thing as smooth and rational decision making, according to Sørensen; decision making is actually a political and discursive process. The "messy" processes of democratic decision making involves not one, but multiple rationalities. She also argues that democratic decision making should not be understood as aggregation or as consensus-oriented deliberation.

Erik-Hans Klijn and Joop F. M. Koppenjan ("Governing Policy Networks") also critique the rational and hierarchical theories of decision making from a network theory perspective. Decisions are not made, or problems are not solved, in social vacuums by "the autonomous cognitive-analytical exercises of central actors," according to Klijn and Koppenjan. Instead, they come out of complex interactions among large numbers of interdependent actors. Network (or network governance) theories aim to describe the mechanisms of such interactions and their products. Klijn and Koppenjan provide a summary of the developments in network theories, which describe the strategic games that actors play, the rules that facilitate these games, and the roles of power and conflict in governance networks. They emphasize that network governance is a complex and dynamic process and that its processes and products are not entirely understandable or predictable.

The complexity of the decision making process is the common theme of the following three chapters as well. In his chapter ("Complex Systems Thinking and its Implications for Policy Analysis"), Kurt Richardson argues that because all reality is inherently complex (i.e., all systems and phenomena are the result of complex, underlying, nonlinear processes), all understanding is incomplete and provisional. However, this does not mean that we cannot make any informed (or rational) decisions. This means that we need to develop a critical and pluralistic understanding of the complex, nonlinear, and evolving nature of reality. Rational interventions into this reality are possible, but, according to Richardson, such interventions have to be "boundedly" and temporarily rational. Because of the limitations of our understanding and rationality, we need to take a pluralistic approach in decision and policy making.

Like Richardson's, Linda Dennard's chapter ("The New Sensibilities of Non-linear Decision Making") is an argument from the perspective of the "new sciences of complexity." Dennard points out that the traditional view of decision making requires rational actors who play predictable games in environments in which causes and effects can be identified with high degrees of certainty. Because complexity sciences demonstrate that these are unrealistic expectations, we need to take a different approach, according to Dennard. As an alternative, she proposes "administrative praxis"—the process of learning from and with the organization and its adaptation to its environment and of encouraging individual capacity to make adaptive choices in "harvesting the possibilities of system dynamics, rather than seeking merely to control them." She suggests that the complex decision maker should not be the engineer of the ideal organization, but an "aware and ethical participant in the emergence of a stable and creative society."

Like Richardson and Dennard, William Newell ("Decision Making in Interdisciplinary Studies") finds his inspiration for a decision making theory in complexity sciences. He posits that interdisciplinary studies are the most effective approach to decision making for complex systems. He also points out that an examination of decision making within interdisciplinary studies ought to be informed by the sciences of complexity. Like Richardson, he proposes a pluralistic perspective. Newell offers an idealized model for individual interdisciplinary decision making about complex issues. He stresses that the idealized model described in the chapter is a challenge to "privileging any one perspective and its claim to transcendent truth"; instead, it validates using multiple perspectives in decision making.

The last three chapters in the theory part of the book are on philosophical and theological perspectives on decision making. The first two of these chapters present East Asian perspectives, the last one a Jewish perspective.

David Jones ("Foundations of Confucian Decision Making") makes the case that "Western decision making" (which is epitomized in the rational comprehensive model) is a product of a particular sense of self that was introduced to the world by the Enlightenment. This "integrity self" values choice over consensus, "right to think" over "right thinking," and decision making agency over the context of the decision made. Jones contrasts this Western sense of self with "intimacy self," which is the traditional sense of self in Asia, Africa, and the Pacific. Jones explains intimacy self in the example of the "Confucian project," which is "most concerned about human relations and the emergent human condition from the matrix of social relations." Confucius sees self in relational and conditional terms and orients and "proffers a different view of what constitutes society and how we attend to our decision making." Jones argues that the Western integrity self is not capable of understanding how judgments and decisions are made in those societies where intimacy self is the foundation for understanding the world.

Jason Wirth ("Ecstatic Decision") takes on "decision theory" (which rests on the fundamental assumptions of the rational comprehensive model of decision making) from the perspective of Buddhism. Wirth points out that decision theory construes a decision as an action that produces, accomplishes, or actualizes something. Actions are "causes that bring forth effects, which, in their turn, are judged according to their utility." This view of decisions avoids the fundamental ontological question: what is it that we bring forth, or what is action? This question is fundamental, because a decision is what confronts an ethical agent who must choose the ethically correct option, either at the level of intention or consequence. In his chapter, Wirth thinks through the question from the perspective of an old tradition, the Buddhist account of karma.

In his chapter ("Theology and Decision Making"), Alfred Marcus describes the decision making philosophy and practices in the rabbinic period in Jewish history and draws conclusions for today's decision makers. Rabbinic sages governed the Jewish people and made many significant decisions that determined the people's collective fate. Marcus points out that their decision making was a dialectical process that was informed and inspired by a strong written tradition as well as an oral tradition, and that it happened under historical and material conditions. The sage balanced the practical with the ideal by reconstructing and reinterpreting religious texts, rather than by supporting their literal meanings. "He relied on insights, reasoning, and logic. He was tugged and pulled by the needs of the moment and the needs of eternity and learned how to balance the two." The decision makers of today, Marcus argues, can learn from the decision making styles of rabbinic sages.

1.5.2 CONTEXTS

The chapters in Part III of the volume discuss decision making in a variety of contexts. These chapters illustrate the fact that decisions are not made in vacuums. As the contexts of decisions vary, so do the styles of decision making.

The Agranoff and Yıldız chapter ("Decision Making in Public Management Networks") discusses decision making in the context of public management networks. They ask: how can public management networks effectively use information and communication technologies for decision making? To answer the question, the authors present the findings in the e-government literature and in their own study on 14 public management networks. Their account of the networks illustrates a core insight of the network governance literature (see the Sørensen and Klijn and Koppenjan chapters) that decision processes in networks are not uniform or linear. Agranoff and Yıldız show the variations in decisions making processes among public management networks but also make some generalizations. They identify six different "pre-decision modes," or learning strategies that administrators engage in decision making, and distinguish networks by their propensities to exchange information, build capacity, blueprint strategies, and make policy and program adjustments.

In his chapter ("Political Decision Making within Metropolitan Areas"), Jack Meek shows that the social and political changes in metropolitan areas are changing the way local decisions are made. Drawing upon insights from complexity theory (see the Richardson, Dennard, and Newell chapters), the author addresses the question: how are administrative, political, and policy decisions formed in complex metropolitan environments? The emergence of a variety of social and political interactions—such as administrative conjunctions, neighborhood councils, business improvement districts, and sub-regional associations—require a new way of understanding decision making. Meek compares and contrasts two mindsets (or traditions) in understanding decision making: the rational tradition, which sees decisions in terms of objective reality, causality, and instrumental choices (i.e., the "logics of consequences"), and the tradition that takes into account the context of a decision and its appropriateness within that context (the "logics of appropriateness"). Meek argues that it is this second tradition that offers a better understanding of the self-organizing and adapting natures of complex metropolitan systems.

Most researchers have focused their attention on decision making in formal organizations or officially sanctioned market or network situations. The research Michael Kenney conducted among drug traffickers was an exception. In his chapter ("The Rules of Drug Trafficking"), Kenney describes how drug traffickers make decisions in their clandestine operations. Kenney observes that facing conditions of profound ambiguity and uncertainty, drug smuggling networks developed centralized, short, and routinized decision making hierarchies. These hierarchies are not necessarily bureaucratic, however. Traffickers often base their decisions on "logics of appropriateness" rather than "logics of consequence"; decision making is often rule-based, rather than choice-based.

Two chapters discuss the implications of information and communication technologies for decision making: John Dickey and Ian Birdsall's chapter ("Information, Technology, and Decision Making") and Mete Yıldız's chapter ("Decision Making Models Used in E-Government Projects"). Dickey and Birdsall describe a complex process when information and communication technologies are involved in decision making. The authors present three case studies to illustrate that large numbers of variables are involved in decision making situations that involve information and communication technologies. They conclude that the information pertinent to any one decision is usually beyond our individual capabilities to retrieve and analyze, and that "we had better learn how to adapt more quickly as decision making situations diverge from the expected but ill-informed paths."

Mete Yıldız presents the results of his research in Turkey; he concludes that E-government decision making is a highly political process. Multiple actors—public administrators, politicians, information and communication technology vendor firms, academicians, members of non-profit organizations, and international agencies—play important roles in the decision making process. Citizens are left out of the process, however. Yıldız finds the garbage can model and incrementalism (see the Hayes chapter in this volume) as the descriptions for E-government decision making in Turkey. According to Yıldız, opening windows of opportunity is critically important, as the garbage can model suggests. He also observes that decisions are made incrementally at the policy formulation stage. He concludes that because large amounts of public money are spent for E-government projects, and therefore public interest is at stake, it is important to expose the non-technical and political nature of the E-government decision making processes.

Public budgeting is an area in which decision making processes are complex and contextual. Enamul Choudhury ("Budgeting as an Institutional Practice") shows that public budgeting is multi-functional, multi-dimensional, and multi-disciplinary. He also argues that budget practices display a coherent pattern of collective decision making enacted through multiple decision rules. Choudhury points out that budgetary decisions are continuous and they are characterized by a variety of constraints such as time, politics, organizational relationships, fiscal environment, process requirements, and professional standards. He takes the position that we need to understand budgetary decision making from both the institutional and instrumental perspectives. In this dual perspective, decision making practices are seen as the rules, roles, and routines that coordinate the different stages of the budgetary process. As such, both the coherence and complexity of the budgetary process can be captured.

In their chapter ("Strategic Planning and Decision Making"), Ofer Meilich and Alfred Marcus argue that although it is no panacea, strategic planning can be used to make decision processes more rational. They contrast the strategic planning perspective with the garbage can perspective, which suggests that the decision making process is random. The authors define strategic planning as a formal system designed to support strategic decision making. Strategic decisions are integrative, competitively consequential, and hard to reverse. They involve considerable resource commitments and may affect organizational health and survival. Strategic planning cannot ensure complete rationality, but it can "move intendedly rational organizations closer to such an ideal," according to Meilich and Marcus. They point out that strategic decision making involves rational, incremental, and political processes, and that these three elements co-exist in various combinations. Meilich and Marcus conclude that strategic planning is no substitute for good judgment, but when used judiciously, it is better than no planning in organizations.

1.5.3 METHODS

A variety of decision making methods have been developed and used. Each method has its own explicit or implicit theoretical assumptions about decision making. Some of the methods were developed for particular contexts or purposes; others were designed as general-purpose methods. The methods described in this part of the book are by no means exhaustive, but among them are some of the more commonly used methods, and they illustrate the range of theoretical assumptions that helped shaped decision making methods. The first group of methods—experiments and quasi-experiments, cost benefit analysis, linear and integer programming, and queuing and simulations—are either direct implementations of the assumptions and principles of the rational comprehensive model of decision making or are highly compatible with them. Other methods—geographic information systems, q methodology, methods of assessing and enhancing creativity, narrative policy analysis, and conflict management methods—diverge from the assumptions and principles of the rational model at different degrees.

Melvin Mark and Jennifer Mills ("Experiments and Quasi-Experiments For Decision Making") point out that decisions people make depend, at least partly, on the causal inferences they make; actions are chosen because of their anticipated consequences (see the chapters critical of this perspective in this volume, particularly Wirth's essay on actions and decisions). Mark and Mill suggest that experiments and quasi-experiments may play important roles in decision making because of their ability to identify cause/effect relationships. They discuss and illustrate how experimental and quasi-experimental methods can contribute to decision making. They argue that these methods can play valuable roles in decision making when used together with thoughtful judgment.

Cost benefit analysis is considered by many to be the primary method of rational decision making. Its methodological assumption is that the costs and benefits of all clearly defined alternative paths of action can be expressed in quantitative terms, and the best alternative path can be identified. In his chapter ("Cost Benefit Analysis"), Tevfik Nas points out that this method draws heavily on the principles of welfare economics and public finance and that its methodology is rigorous and sophisticated. He also argues that when it is mastered and consistently used by an analyst, cost benefit analysis is likely to lead to optimal resource allocation decisions. A distinguishing characteristic of cost benefit analysis is that it requires that all values (costs and benefits) should be expressed in monetary terms. Nas provides an overview of its general methodology and its conceptual assumptions. He also summarizes the typical steps in an analysis and the practical rules for its implementation that were devised by the United States Office of Management and Budget.

In his chapter ("Linear Programming and Integer Programming"), Dipak Gupta compares the logic of these methods with that of cost benefit analysis. Whereas the latter assumes that one best alternative can be chosen, the former focuses on finding an "optimal mix" of alternatives. He points out that linear programming is one of the most sophisticated tools of operations research. It can be used to solve problems that involve maximization of some specific goals given the limitations of inputs or minimization of costs with the specification of some minimum levels of benefits. This method is capable of factoring in political considerations, as long as political authorities are able to articulate their preferences. Gupta also mentions that that the method has its limitations; primarily, as its name suggests, it processes information in a linear fashion, and hence it may miss non-linear relationships.

Queuing theory reflects some of the assumptions of cost benefit analysis and linear programming: it factors in costs and benefits and aims to find an optimal solution. It incorporates the notion and methods of probability into cost-benefit and optimization calculations. Dipak Gupta ("Queuing Theory and Simulations") tells the story of how queuing methods originated in gambling, where uncertainty is inherent. The probability models used for gambling were later developed and applied to problems such as optimizing the number of check-out lines at stores. The advances in computer technology facilitated the wider use of queuing theory in economics and operations research. Also with the advances in computer technology, simulations methods were developed for more complex problems. Gupta discusses the general methodological principles of queuing and simulations with examples in his chapter.

Akhlaque Haque ("Decision Making in Geographic Information Systems") points out that geographic information systems have opened a new path to better decision making by taking advantage of cutting edge information technology. Geographic information systems do not seek optimal solutions; instead they allow diverse participants to engage in decision making. Haque sees geographic information systems as methods that combine technocratic and pluralistic approaches in problem solving and decision making. The collaborative nature of these methods enables community participation in a variety of public policy areas. This is due to the different nature of computer technology used in geographic information systems, according to Haque. The geographic information systems technology is not just a set of applications, he points out, but it offers a new way of understanding, managing and displaying data; its users do not need to learn the technical aspects of the data they use, which makes it easier for them to directly participate in the process.

Q methodology, which Dan Durning and Steven Brown describe and discuss in their chapter ("Q Methodology and Decision Making"), is another approach that utilizes computer technology in a participatory manner. Q methodology is aimed at eliciting the subjectivities (values, preferences, opinions) of individuals and displaying them to facilitate participatory decision making. Durning and Brown describe the procedures used in Q methodology, contrast its logic and procedures with R methodologies (traditional statistical methods), and discus how Q methodology can contribute to decision making. The main contribution of Q methodology to decision making is in providing a means for "a systematic accounting of the outlooks, values, and thinking of actors as they strive to achieve desired outcomes," according to Durning and Brown. Thus, Q methodology enables us to examine human intentionality and rigorously incorporate it in decision making.

The methods of creativity Göktuğ Morçöl discusses ("Methods of Assessing and Enhancing Creativity for Public Policy Decision Making") have similarities with q methodology, both in their theoretical bases and applications. The premise of using methods of creativity in decision making and problems solving is that public policy problems are complex, and complex problems require creative solutions. Morçöl discusses the findings of the psychological research on creativity and describes a group of methods for facilitating and enhancing creativity, focusing particularly on the methods that are developed from George Kelly's repertory grid methodology. As in the cases of geographic information systems and q methodology, the advances in computer technology have enabled the development and application of the methods of creativity described in the chapter.

Susan Raines ("Participatory Decision Making") argues that the rapid growth of conflict management methods in recent decades is an implicit challenge to the assumptions of the economic/utilitarian (rational comprehensive) methods of decision making. Conflict management is a challenge, because it recognizes the messiness of decision making processes that involve "egos and other psychological biases, potentially clashing communication styles, leadership inadequacies, economic and non-economic incentives, and limitations on the ability of individuals and groups to obtain and process information." In her chapter, Raines discusses the literature in economics, psychology, communications, political science, and negotiation to demonstrate that economic/ utilitarian theories are inadequate in explaining decision making behaviors. Then she describes and illustrates conflict management methods and skills that can be used to improve decision making in group environments.

Like Thomas Catlaw and Eva Sørensen, Emery Roe ("Narrative Policy Analysis for Decision Making") sees decision making as a discursive process. Roe discusses decision making in the context of policy analysis and describes a method he developed for analyzing policy narratives. He points out that because policy issues are uncertain, complex, incomplete and conflicted, policy narratives—rules of thumb, arguments, scenarios, and other accounts about how policy can and should proceed—are needed to make sense of and to act on them. Roe discusses his general methodological approach and the specific steps of his narrative analysis method.

REFERENCES

Allison, G. T., *Essence of Decision: Explaining the Cuban missile Crisis*, Little, Brown and Company, Boston, 1971.

Arrow, K. J., *Social Choice and Individual Values*, Wiley, New York, 1963.

Arrow, K. J., Rationality of self and others in an economic system, In *Decision Making: Alternatives to Rational Choice Models*, Zey, M., Ed., Sage, Newbury Park, CA, pp. 63–77, 1992.

Coleman, J. S., Introducing social structure into economic analysis, In *Decision Making: Alternatives to Rational Choice Models*, Zey, M., Ed., Sage, Newbury Park, CA, pp. 265–271, 1992.

Edwards, W., The theory of decision making, In *Decision Making: Selected Readings*, Edwards, W. and Tversky, A., Eds., Penguin Books, Middlesex, UK, pp. 13–64, 1967.

Edwards, W. and Tversky, A., Eds., *Decision Making: Selected Readings*, Penguin Books, Middlesex, UK, 1967.

Etzioni, A., Normative-affective factors: toward a new decision-making model, In *Decision Making: Alternatives to Rational Choice Models*, Zey, M., Ed., Sage, Newbury Park, CA, pp. 89–110, 1992.

Fiorina, M. P., Comments, In *Collective Decision Making: Applications from Public Choice Theory*, Russell, C. S., Ed., Johns Hopkins University Press, Baltimore, pp. 46–51, 1979.

Granovetter, M., Economic action and social structure: the problem of embeddedness, In *Decision Making: Alternatives to Rational Choice Models*, Zey, M., Ed., Sage, Newbury Park, CA, pp. 304–333, 1992.

Halpern, D. F., *Thought and Knowledge: An Introduction to Critical Thinking*, 3rd ed., Lawrence Erlbaum, Mahwah, NJ, 1996.

Hogarth, R. M. and Reder, M. W., Eds., *Rational Choice: The Contrast between Economics and Psychology*, The University of Chicago Press, Chicago, 1986.

Lichbach, M. I., *Is Rational Choice Theory all of Social Science*, The University of Michigan Press, Ann Arbor, MI, 2003.

MacDonald, P. K., Useful fiction or miracle maker: the competing epistemological foundations of rational choice theory, *American Political Science Review*, 97(4), 551–565, 2003.

March, J. G. and Shapira, Z., Behavioral decision theory and organizational decisions theory, In *Decision Making: Alternatives to Rational Choice Models*, Zey, M., Ed., Sage, Newbury Park, CA, pp. 273–303, 1992.

Morçöl, G., *A New Mind for Policy Analysis: Toward a Post-Newtonian and Postpositivist Epistemology and Methodology*, Praeger, Westport, CT, 2002.

Newell, A. and Simon, H. A., *Human Problem Solving*, Prentice Hall, Englewood Cliffs, NJ, 1972.

Nigro, L., *Decision Making in the Public Sector*, Marcel Dekker, New York, 1984.

Ostrom, E., *Governing the Commons: The Evolution of Institutions for Collective Action*, Cambridge University Press, Cambridge, UK, 1990.

Ostrom, E., *Understanding Institutional Diversity*, Princeton University Press, Princeton, NJ, 2005.

Pennings, J., *Decision Making: An Organizational Behavior Approach*, Marcus Wiener Publishing, New York, 1986.

Russell, C. S., Applications of public choice theory: an introduction, In *Collective Decision Making: Applications from Public Choice Theory*, Russell, C. S., Ed., The Johns Hopkins University Press, Baltimore, pp. 1–25, 1979.

Schwartz, H., *Rationality Gone Awry: Decision Making Inconsistent with Economic and Financial Theory*, Praeger, Westport, CT, 1998.

Simon, H. A., Rational decision making and business organizations, *The American Economic Review*, 69(4), 493–513, 1979.

Simon, H. A., Rationality in psychology and economics, In *Rational Choice: The Contrast between Economics and Psychology*, Hogarth, R. M. and Reder, M. W., Eds., The University of Chicago Press, Chicago, pp. 25–40, 1986.

Simon, H. A., *Administrative Behavior: A Study of Decision-Making Processes in Administrative Organizations*, 4th ed., The Free Press, New York, 1997.

Simon, H. A. et al., Decision making and problem solving, In *Decision Making: Alternatives to Rational Choice Models*, Zey, M., Ed., Sage, Newbury Park, CA, pp. 32–53, 1992.

Tversky, A. and Kahneman, D., Rational choice and the framing of decisions, In *Rational Choice: The Contrast between Economics and Psychology*, Hogarth, R. M. and Reder, M. W., Eds., The University of Chicago Press, Chicago, pp. 67–93, 1986.

Ungston, G. R. and Braunstein, D. N., Eds., *Decision Making: An Interdisciplinary Inquiry*. PWS-Kent Publishing Company.

Zey, M., Ed., *Decision Making: Alternatives to Rational Choice Models*, Sage, Newbury Park, CA, 1992.

Part II

Theories of Decision Making

2 The Contribution of Public Choice Analysis to Decision Making Theories in Public Administration: Past, Present, and Future

Tanya Heikkila

CONTENTS

2.1 Introduction..21
2.2 Emergence of Public Choice and Convergence with Public Administration 22
    2.2.1 Classic Studies in Public Choice...22
    2.2.2 Public Choice Analyses of Bureaucratic Structures and Outcomes..........................23
        2.2.2.1 Classic Public Choice Studies of Bureaucracy...23
        2.2.2.2 New Institutionalist Theories of Bureaucracy 25
    2.2.3 Public Choice Analysis of the Structures
        and Outcomes of Local Government 27
        2.2.3.1 Local Public Economies and Public Service Industries 28
2.3 Critiques of Public Choice 29
2.4 Conclusions and Future Directions 31
References...34

2.1 INTRODUCTION

Public choice analysis involves the application of economic principles to the study of non-market or political behavior. The most basic of these principles is the reliance on methodological individualism, or a model of decision making that assumes individuals are rational and seek to maximize their self-interest (Friedman, 1996). Public choice often is viewed as part, or sometimes the foundation, of a larger branch of social science known as political economy, which includes both empirical and theoretical research using economic models to explain political phenomena. This chapter considers how the field of public choice has evolved and evaluates how the literature has shaped the understanding of decision making in the field of public administration.

Over the past fifty years, a wide array of literature has developed in the field of public choice. An entire journal, *Public Choice*, is dedicated to this field, as are hundreds of books, textbooks, and edited volumes (see, e.g., McNutt, 2002; Mueller, 1979, 1989, 1996; Rowley, 1987; Shughart and Razzolini, 2001). Scholars have applied public choice analyses to topics as diverse as voting behavior, bureaucratic regulation, judicial behavior, government growth, interest group behavior, monetary policy, and constitutional choice (McNutt, 2002). Instead of reviewing the extant literature in public choice, which is too vast for a single paper,[*] this chapter focuses on describing what public choice analysis offers scholars of public administration. Specifically, how does public choice inform our understanding of decisions about the design of public organizations, and how do structural choices affect the behavior of public administrators, managers, policymakers, and even citizens? The next section provides a brief overview of the foundations of public choice theory and describes how the field spawned the new institutionalist theories of bureaucracy and studies of metropolitan governance. This chapter then summarizes major critiques of these public choice theories and concludes by identifying recent scholarship that addresses some of the limitations of the field.

2.2 EMERGENCE OF PUBLIC CHOICE AND CONVERGENCE WITH PUBLIC ADMINISTRATION

2.2.1 CLASSIC STUDIES IN PUBLIC CHOICE

To understand the impact of public choice literature on decision making theories in public administration, one should begin with a brief look at the origins of this field of study. The precursors to the field of public choice established the theoretical underpinnings for applying rational choice models to the study of political behavior. They explicitly focused on the logic of individual choice underlying collective decision making and the limitations of voting rules in effectively aggregating individual choices. The literature that inspired much of the early thinking in public choice came out of voting theory and social choice, dating back to the late 1940s (McNutt, 2002; Mueller, 1989). Kenneth Arrow's (1951) social choice theory, which is about the political processes through which social choices are aggregated, is considered foundational to the emergence of public choice. He argued that no voting mechanism could satisfy a reasonable set of normative social criteria for collective choice. That is because democratic voting rules produce instabilities or unsatisfactory outcomes for society.

Voting theorists in the mid-twentieth century complemented social choice research by identifying the consequences of majority voting rules on the outcomes of collective decision making. Duncan Black (1948a,b; 1958) theorized that under simple majority rules, committees would always choose the preferences of the "median" voter. Anthony Downs's *An Economic Theory of Democracy* (1957) later evaluated how simple majority rules shape the incentives of rational voters in participatory democracies. In mass democratic elections, the probability of one voter influencing an outcome becomes increasingly small. Therefore, under a simple majority rule system, Downs argued, the costs of voting will usually exceed the perceived benefits of voting, implying that people have little incentive to vote. In observing that people still vote under these systems, he coined the phrase, "the paradox of voting." Downs further applied assumptions of individual economic rationality to explain how party leaders and politicians use party ideology as part of the competitive process to obtain votes. Party ideologies, he assumed, reduce information costs, saving politicians time in providing information to voters and saving voters time and effort in acquiring information about politicians. This research has spawned a substantial subfield of scholarship that attempts to identify theoretically and empirically why people do or do not vote (see, e.g., Riker and Ordeshook, 1968; Ferejohn and Fiorina, 1974; Kelley, 1985; Palfrey and Rosenthal, 1985; Nicholson and Miller, 1997; Kanazawa, 1998).

---

[*] For a comprehensive set of essays on modern public choice theory and research see Shughart and Razzolini, Eds., *The Elgar Companion to Public Choice* (Cheltenham: Edward Elgar, 2001).

Like other classic public choice books, Buchanan and Tullock's *The Calculus of Consent* (1962) sought to evaluate voting mechanisms using economic models, but their work delved more deeply into the connection between individual rationality and government choices. They considered the types of rules that rational individuals should collectively agree upon, given the uncertainties about their futures. The optimal decision rule for individuals making collective choices would minimize both decision making costs (gathering information, negotiating, etc.) and the external impacts of a particular decision on the welfare of the minority (at the expense of the majority). Optimal decision making rules, they contended, will vary depending on the situation and number of voters. Some decisions have external costs which are so great that they require near unanimity because of fear that the majority will always impose its will. Not knowing when one will be in the majority and when one will be in the minority in the future leads voters to the conclusion that a unanimity rule at the constitutional level of decision making would be optimal for rational individuals. Thus, two of the key contributions of Buchanan and Tullock were demonstrating the underlying motivations for constitutional choice, and showing how majoritarian politics can impose high costs on minorities. Moreover, Buchanan and Tullock raised awareness to ways that voting rules can lead to unintended outcomes like vote trading and logrolling.

In addition to voting and constitutional choice, some of the early works in public choice studied political coalitions (Buchanan and Tullock, 1962; Riker, 1962) and interest group formation (Olson, 1965). The use of game theory in this work was introduced as a formalized approach using rational choice assumptions of individual behavior to explain collective outcomes. Olson became particularly influential in the public choice field with his model that postulated that the pursuit of individual self-interest can lead to a suboptimal collective outcome because of the potential for individuals to free ride off the efforts of others. He further highlighted the importance of institutions for overcoming free riding in large groups, given that rational individuals are not likely to pursue collective interests unless the group is small.

The theoretical advancements of early public choice scholars helped clarify the relationship between institutional structures and collective decision making. Despite their explicit focus on public (versus market-based) decisions, public choice theories of voting and interest groups had a limited connection to the field of public administration and the study of organizations. Building on theories of political coalitions and assumptions about the self-interest of political actors, public choice scholarship later developed theories of bureaucracy and the provision of public goods that influenced the field of public administration.[*]

2.2.2 PUBLIC CHOICE ANALYSES OF BUREAUCRATIC STRUCTURES AND OUTCOMES

2.2.2.1 Classic Public Choice Studies of Bureaucracy

Early public choice theories of bureaucracy generally sought to explain bureaucratic pathologies, based on the assumption that bureaucrats are utility-maximizing, rational actors. For example, agency capture theory assumes that bureaucrats respond to pressure from industry and other business groups when devising and enforcing regulations (Becker, 1983; Peltzman, 1976; Stigler, 1971). This theory draws on the concept of rent seeking, which occurs when interest groups spend money and time on political lobbying (especially industries that push for regulations to produce higher prices) rather than productive market activity (Tullock, 1980). Buchanan and Tullock (1962) provided the foundations for agency capture and rent seeking theories by examining how government responds to the demands of interest groups by overproducing goods, which then encourages other interest groups to form. These concepts later fed into a more fully developed

---

[*] These inroads were also assisted by Herbert Simon's research in public administration and organization theory that looked more closely at the role of individual incentives in shaping organizational outcomes. Simon's focus on bounded rationality contrasted with the neoclassical rational choice model used by many public choice scholars.

interest group theory of government, which considers the influence of interest groups on policy choices and political decision making more broadly. It emphasizes how political actors transfer benefits or sources of wealth across groups in society to maximize their own political support and how politicians control bureaucratic budgets to ensure that support (Becker, 1983; McCormick and Tollison, 1981).

Public choice scholarship on bureaucratic pathologies has also examined how agencies amass excessive budgets (Niskanen, 1971). Bureaus are seen as monopoly suppliers to legislators who sponsor the budgets. Budget-maximizing bureaucrats can escape legislative controls that might constrain budgets because asymmetric information exists between legislators and agencies. In proposing budgets to Congress, bureaucrats provide information that inflates their budgetary needs. The assumption is that legislators do not have the capacity to ascertain the agency's true needs, and thus have no choice but to supply what the agency demands. Regulatory capture fits neatly with this theory implying that the benefits of bureau budgeting are concentrated among a select group, while the costs are distributed among a large group. This permits excessive budgets to gain political approval. The implications have been relatively simple: bureaucrats are beholden to interest groups who seek to control bureaucratic decisions, and bureaucrats also can take advantage of uninformed legislators during the budgetary processes to ensure that they get what they want. Presumably, these budget-maximizing and career-maximizing bureaucrats promote the excessive growth of bureaucracies and discourage bureaucratic adaptation to changing conditions (Tullock, 1965).[*]

The early public choice theories of bureaucratic decision making differed markedly from public administration research of the early twentieth century, which focused on identifying how bureaucratic structural characteristics, such as hierarchical control and unity of command, could produce effective administration (Ostrom, 1973). Public choice theories of bureaucratic capture and growth provided little in the way of understanding how internal agency structures affected bureaucratic outcomes. Indeed, as a result of their reliance on the rational choice model, early public choice scholars were able provide insights into the types of factors that are likely to maximize a bureaucrat's utility function, but the analysis of internal agency behavior was often limited to the explanation of the preferences of bureaucrats. Niskanen's seminal work, *Bureaucracy and Representative Government* (1971) for instance, implies that bureaucrats seek to maximize factors such as salary, public reputation, power, patronage, and increased budgets. In terms of public organization decision making, such theories of bureaucracy sought to connect the incentives of decision makers directly to what the bureaucracy produced, ignoring what happened inside bureaucracies.

Among the founders of public choice, Tullock (1965) and Downs (1967) offered notable departures from other classic public choice theories by analyzing the choices of bureaucrats in relation to the internal organization of bureaucracies. Tullock, for instance, considered how relationships between superiors and subordinates in an agency can perpetuate inefficiencies and, more generally, how the structure of bureaucracies can distort information and lead to poor decision making. Downs, on the other hand, looked explicitly at defining how different types of bureaucrats respond to specific decision making incentives. Like Tullock, Downs viewed bureaucracy as a social setting that could attract individuals who wish to further their prestige and power, thus pushing for growth in their organization. Yet he did not assume that all bureaucratic decision makers had the same goals. For example, he categorized "climbers" as being motivated by power and prestige; "conservers" as being motivated by security, "zealots" as loyal to narrow policies, "advocates" as loyal to a broader set of policies, and "statesmen" as loyal to society as a whole. The type of official is determined by psychological predisposition, the nature of the position, and the probability of attaining the

---

[*] The premise that there is a demand and supply side of budgetary inflation has promoted more generalized theories about government growth (McNutt, 2002).

desired goals. Given these types of officials and the defining characteristics of bureaus, the basic problems facing bureaus, Downs suggested, was how to maintain control over subordinates while also addressing the dynamics of organizational rigidity, organizational change, goal consensus, and communicating ideology.

2.2.2.2 New Institutionalist Theories of Bureaucracy

Despite these early attempts to use public choice models to explain the relationships between internal organizational factors and bureaucratic functions, the evolution of public choice scholarship focusing on bureaucracy remained most concerned with understanding how external governmental institutions shape bureaucratic outcomes (Moe, 1991). In particular, these theories have emphasized the decision making incentives created by the dyadic relationships between bureaus and other political institutions, particularly the legislature, the President, and courts (Chang, de Figueiredo, and Weingast, 2001). This branch of public choice literature has paid particular attention to "principal–agent" models in studying the relationships between bureaus and other governmental institutions. The basic premise of the relationship between bureaus and legislatures is that information asymmetry exists in the "contractual" relation between the two, where the principal (the legislature) lacks certain knowledge that the agent (the bureau) has; this makes it difficult to ensure that the agent will act in accordance with the principal's interest. Some of the recent research using principal–agent models has considered how Congress can control bureaucracy, through, for instance, congressional oversight of committees (Weingast and Moran, 1983) or the use of administrative procedures (McCubbins, Noll, and Weingast, 1987), and how presidential appointments can control bureaucratic choices (Moe, 1987; Grier, 1987). These principal–agent models differ from earlier works, such as Niskanen's (1971) model of bureaucracy, which implied a principal–agent model where bureaucrats essentially controlled the budgetary choices of legislators (Moe, 1984).

The body of literature that emerged from the public choice tradition of applying principal–agent models to explain how external political institutions control bureaucracies has also been called "the new economics of organization" (Moe, 1991), or new institutionalist theories. This literature has been deemed "a new way of thinking about American politics and about bureaucratic performance in particular: the modeling of political choice as a function of an integrated separation-of-powers system" (Chang, de Figueiredo, and Weingast, 2001, 276). It focuses on one of the topics central to public administration: the structure of public organizations and the influence of this structure on political outcomes. Scholars have used insights from principal–agent models to explain the formation and structure of bureaucratic institutions given the incentives rational political actors face within a political system (Horn, 1995; Moe, 1984; 1990a; Wood and Waterman, 1994). This research also draws upon contract theories of organizational relations and transaction cost economics to better explain the underlying factors shaping the choices of political actors (Moe, 1984).

New institutionalist theories have moved beyond the traditional approach of public choice by acknowledging the complexity of institutional interests that shape bureaucratic structures and outcomes, rather than just focusing on how self-interested individuals produce inefficient outcomes. Horn (1995) for example, evaluates the design of new public agencies by legislatures and considers how the cost of decision making, commitment problems, principal–agent relations, and uncertainty among legislators can shape the structure and organization of public agencies. In general, he notes: "The key to understanding institutional design in the public sector is to put the relationship between legislators and their constituents at center stage and to recognize that constituents will exercise intelligent foresight," and the "inability of legislators to commit their successors—and, to a lesser extent, the costs of legislative uncertainty—play an important role in shaping institutional design" (Horn, 1995, 183). Legislatures are likely to commit to more enduring administrative structures, and thus serve the demands of constituents, by ensuring that future legislatures have limited control over those decisions.

New institutional theorists do not focus solely on the role of legislatures in shaping bureaucracies. Various institutional actors (or principals) can influence the design of bureaucracies, including interest groups, politicians (congressional and executive), and courts (Banks and Weingast, 1992; Ferejohn and Shipan, 1990; Hammond and Knott, 1996; Moe, 1984; 1990a). Most notably, Moe (1984; 1990a,b) considers the effects of different political actors on the structure of bureaucracy as *ex ante* controls, given uncertain information about the political future. Interest groups, he argues, are likely to select a structure that constrains bureaucratic behavior, to ensure future opportunities to present their interests to bureaucrats. Legislators, on the other hand, are likely to avoid alienating constituents, favoring specific controls that allow them to intervene quickly or influence bureaus on behalf of special interests. Presidents, unlike the other principals, are most likely to be concerned with the organization of the bureaucracy as a whole (Moe, 1990b). They are more likely to encourage discretion and flexibility among bureaus, while subordinating them within the structure of the executive department. The underlying idea is that bureaucratic structural choice involves planning for the future interests of the principal. In addition, multiple principals are likely to conflict with one another and struggle to maintain bureaucratic control by building in monitoring and control systems.

In explaining how political interests impose structures and rules on bureaucracies to constrain future decision making, new institutional theorists also provide explanations of why public bureaucracies either act inefficiently or are perceived as inefficient (Horn, 1995; Moe, 1984). New institutional scholars thus pay heed to questions about bureaucratic efficiency posed by early public choice theorists like Tullock (1965) yet focus more on the institutional setting as a source of inefficiencies, rather than self-interested bureaucrats. For example, Johnson and Libecap (1994) studied how civil service reforms like merit-based hiring have produced widespread bureaucratic inefficiencies and argue that Congress and the President initially pushed for these reforms as a way to reduce the costs of monitoring a growing bureaucracy under the patronage system. In addition, new institutional scholars show how the perception of bureaucratic inefficiency can depend upon the perspective of the principal; Congress, the President, courts, and interest groups all push to constrain and control bureaucracies, yet their interests often diverge (Moe, 1984). Thus, when a particular institutional arrangement to control bureaucracy appears to satisfy the interests of one principal it may create monitoring or control problems for other principals.

The focus on institutional structure as the source of bureaucratic inefficiencies does not mean that new institutionalists ignore the role of self-interested bureaucrats in explaining bureaucratic outcomes. Central to new institutionalist theories is the notion that information asymmetries exist in principal–agent relations, which explains why bureaucrats are able to make decisions that diverge from their principals. Institutional reforms may attempt to reduce these information asymmetries, or at least lower the transaction costs of monitoring agents, but they cannot eliminate information asymmetries. Moreover, bureaucrats can play a role in the design of institutional reforms and may sometimes push for reforms that enhance information asymmetries. As Johnson and Libecap (1994) argue, over the course of the twentieth century, bureaucrats aggressively pushed for stronger civil service laws and employee unions, which led to the increase in merit based hiring, tenure, and job security for government employees. In other words, bureaucrats also have opportunities for structuring the institutional setting governing bureaucracy to meet their goals and interests.

New institutional theories clearly have shaped the study of the structure of federal bureaucracy, building from the basic assumptions that public choice scholars introduced nearly 40 years ago. Although the literature has taken on new labels, this field of research still fits squarely within the public choice paradigm (Chang, de Figueiredo, and Weingast, 2001). New institutional theories rely on methodological individualism and, like their predecessors, are concerned with understanding why individuals choose certain institutional structures under conditions of uncertainty and the effects those structures have on the choices of bureaucrats and other political actors.

2.2.3 PUBLIC CHOICE ANALYSIS OF THE STRUCTURES AND OUTCOMES OF LOCAL GOVERNMENT

Another stream of public choice scholarship has been concerned with explaining the structure of political institutions and their outputs. Rather than focusing on the federal government, this stream of public choice literature has described and analyzed public service provision in metropolitan regions. Public choice literature on metropolitan governance developed, in part, as a normative response to public choice conclusions about the inefficiencies of federal bureaucracies. As Tullock (1965) finds, one of the solutions for many of the pathologies of federal bureaucracies, such as capture by interest groups and uncontrolled agency growth, is to reduce the size of government and rely more on local governments for service provision.

The logic behind the normative assumption that local governments can provide services more effectively than federal bureaus is not based solely on the perceived pathologies of bureaucratic capture and growth. What public choice scholars in the 1960s noted is that deciding the appropriate level of government should be based on the geographical connections among groups sharing similar service preferences. As Tullock finds:

> Geographical contiguity is a basic characteristic of almost all such areas where we would choose collective provision. The distinction between any economy of scale which can be obtained only if the customers are located next door to each other and an economy of scale which can be obtained without this type of contiguity is fundamental. (Tullock, 1969, 197)

In other words, determining the appropriate provision of a good or service, according to this perspective, depends on the collective demands of groups of individuals who live in close proximity.

The idea that citizens group together to provide services at a scale appropriate to their service demands was complemented by public choice observations that in metropolitan regions, many small-scale, fragmented jurisdictions exist, sometimes overlapping one another, to provide various goods and services (Ostrom, Tiebout, and Warren, 1961). Ostrom and his colleagues assume that when multiple units of public service provision offer similar services in geographically defined spaces, these jurisdictions can then compete for citizens. Such competition would theoretically push local governments to supply goods and services more efficiently and effectively. The expectation of competition is based on the assumption that citizens "vote with their feet" and will treat alternative local governments like providers in a market, choosing to live in those jurisdictions that best meet their needs (Tiebout, 1956; Tullock, 1994). The notion that competition in the government marketplace is tied to government efficiency became a key tenet of the public choice literature (Mueller, 1989).

In terms of contributing to our understanding of public administration and government decisions, public choice scholarship has since offered more than just normative conclusions about efficiency, thanks in large part to Vincent Ostrom's book, *The Intellectual Crisis in Public Administration* (1973). Ostrom took issue with the traditional theories of public administration that asserted that centralization and hierarchy are most efficient for organizing the provision, production, and distribution of public goods and services. He argues that this scholarship concluded that centralized public service provision is more efficient than fragmented or decentralized service provision without engaging in sufficient empirical testing. Ostrom further suggested that such conclusions contradict the founding principles of American democracy. Citing Hamilton and Madison's Federalist Papers, and Tocqueville's analysis of American democracy, Ostrom notes that the constitutional foundations of government in the United States were intentionally devised to support alternate majorities, with "a system of administration which is thoroughly imbedded in a complex structure of democratic decision making" (Ostrom, 1973, 90). Therefore, Ostrom argues, public administration scholars need to develop a broader theory of administration that focuses on multi-organizational arrangements within the institutional context of democracy.

2.2.3.1 Local Public Economies and Public Service Industries

Ostrom's work spawned a significant body of theoretical and empirical research on the organization and benefits of public service provision in overlapping political systems, particularly in metropolitan areas (ACIR, 1987; Oakerson, 1999, 2004; Oakerson and Parks, 1988; Ostrom, 1997; Park, 1997; Parks and Oakerson, 1989, 1993, 2000). One of the key contributions of this literature is that it distinguishes between production and provision of public goods and services (Oakerson, 1999). Provision occurs through the efforts of "collective consumption units," or groups of individuals clustered within geographic boundaries, who impose taxes or other public funding requirements on themselves to supply a good or service (Ostrom and Ostrom, 1977). Provision jurisdictions, for example, can include municipal governments, public authorities, special districts, voluntary associations, or any other collective group. The members of provision units make decisions about the amount and/or quality of a public service or good to acquire or produce, as well as how to distribute the funding costs. Provision units sometimes produce or deliver the public services that they fund. Alternatively, they may contract with other government agencies and/or private firms for the production of all or part of the service, thus separating provision from production (ACIR, 1987; Ostrom and Ostrom, 1977). In such settings, jurisdictions also have the opportunity to coordinate the production of a good or service to achieve economies of scale through inter-jurisdictional coordination or the creation of special purpose districts (Heikkila, 2004).

Studies on public service provision in metropolitan areas have referred to the collection of overlapping jurisdictions that supply and produce various public goods and services in a community as "local public economies" (ACIR, 1987; Oakerson and Parks, 1988; Oakerson, 1999). In addition, this research has described the collection of overlapping jurisdictions that coordinate to provide and/or produce specific goods or services within a particular sector of the public economy, such as water supply or police protection. Overlapping jurisdictions that comprise a particular service sector are referred to as a "public service industry" (Ostrom and Ostrom, 1991).

To understand what the local public economy (and public service industry) literature offers decision making theory, it is useful to consider some of the studies on police provision conducted under this theoretical framework. For example, an empirical comparison of police provision in centralized versus decentralized systems of governance shows that community-controlled police agencies, generally found in smaller-scale jurisdictions, are more likely to be responsive to citizen needs and effective at controlling crime than large, citywide police jurisdictions (Ostrom, 1976; Ostrom and Whitaker, 1973). What this research implies is that public decision makers are responsive to citizens when institutional arrangements exist to ensure transparency and accessibility to public decision makers. Such responsiveness encourages public entrepreneurship among decision makers in systems of complex overlapping jurisdictions (Oakerson and Parks, 1988). Public entrepreneurs are likely to strive to find more efficient ways of performing and organizing services (Schneider and Teske, 1995).

The empirical research on metropolitan governance that has led to descriptive theories of the structure of polycentric systems also has clear normative implications for decision making in the public sector. One of the major conclusions reached in this field is that

> polycentric systems of government allow for more open governance structures that include greater "civic space," defined as the set of opportunities for nongovernmental actors to enter productively into the governance process by producing general benefits for a community. By contrast, monocentric systems engender less open governance structures more apt to be dominated by "insiders," who compete to enjoy privileged access to governmental authority for the purpose of obtaining selective benefits. (Oakerson, 2004, 22)

The implication of this conclusion in understanding decision making is that the way institutions are structured affects the capacity for citizens and public officials to communicate. If officials are too distant from citizens in large-scale bureaucracies, as would be the case in consolidated systems of government, then citizens are less able to monitor the decisions of policymakers and bureaucrats. In polycentric systems, the theory presumes, citizens actually have more opportunities to participate in local government, as well as more opportunities for checks on government decisions, which can enhance government accountability (Oakerson, 2004).

In summarizing the stream of public choice literature focusing on local government, two facets of the literature appear: (1) descriptive theories of how the production and supply of public services is organized at the municipal level, and (2) normative implications about the advantages of polycentric governance in shaping the decision making choices of individual citizens and bureaucrats. Although bureaucratic decisions are not addressed as directly as in the public choice studies of federal bureaucracy, it is clear that the local government literature suggests that bureaucrats are likely to respond more democratically and effectively when they know citizens are monitoring them in polycentric governance systems. Ultimately, what this branch of public choice explains about public decision making is that in fragmented systems of governance, individual citizens act as consumers and as participants in self-government, which in turn supports more efficient and effective choices by policymakers and public managers.

2.3 CRITIQUES OF PUBLIC CHOICE

Public choice theories of bureaucracy and metropolitan governance are the two of the most prominent research programs within the vast theoretical realm of public choice. These literatures have received their shares of criticism, both as separate theoretical streams and as components of the public choice school. This section examines the basis for some of the positive and normative criticisms of public choice in general, and the theories of bureaucracy and metropolitan governance in particular. In doing so, the section identifies ways in which these critiques have helped to advance the field and our understanding of decision making in the public sector.

Many criticisms of the classic public choice literature are based on the fact that the predictions about bureaucratic choices are either inaccurate empirically or not logically tied to the theory's assumptions. For example, the theory of capture, which drives much of the public choice assumptions about bureaucratic growth, does not always hold true for regulatory agencies in the U.S. federal government. Regulatory agencies certainly have been subject to capture by business interests, but consumer groups and environmental interest groups have large influences over regulation as well (Mitchell, 2001). Others note that even though some bureaucracies continue to amass their budgets or expand their capacities, it is not evident whether or not this expansion is actually related to legitimate increases in demand for services or tied to the incentives of utility-maximizing bureaucrats (Rockman, 2001). Moreover, some critics argue that bureaucratic growth conclusions simply cannot be based on the assumptions of utility-maximizing bureaucrats. Not only is it unlikely that a bureaucrat's self-interest is concerned only with budget maximization, but bureaucrats also have many ways of acting in their own interests to shape the organization other than maximizing budgets (Udehn, 1996).

The sharp criticism against the early public choice studies on bureaucratic behavior has been tempered somewhat by the more nuanced approaches of the new institutionalists' bureaucratic analyses. These scholars clearly recognize that the complex institutional settings within which bureaucrats operate shape their incentives for choice, and that those incentives are created by external agency controls. The new institutionalism, therefore, provides a more sophisticated view of bureaucratic decision making. As Moe (1984, 773) recognizes, "there is a legitimate inclination to assume away as many of these complications as possible" as much of the bureaucracy research has done, but new institutionalist theories in bringing in multiple principals and agents are "more representative of political reality." Despite this attention to multiple driving forces of political behavior, the new institutionalism can still be criticized for its lack of generalizability to various political settings. Most new institutionalists draw conclusions that are limited to the

U.S. federal system (Rockman, 2001), with Horn (1995) being one exception. Thus, although new institutional theories may be more accurate representations of political behavior than earlier public choice studies, or at least more plausible, the decision making context they consider is limited.

Perhaps even more problematic is the possibility that the underlying new institutionalist assumptions about what drives bureaucratic behavior are, like their antecedents, empirically inaccurate. Although the focus of the new institutionalism has moved into explaining bureaucratic structure, rather than bureaucratic choices per se, it is that very structure that theoretically drives bureaucratic choices. Yet, empirical research of principal–agent relations in bureaucracies has shown that bureaucratic decisions actually may be driven by organizational norms and culture, as well as citizen input (Brehm and Gates, 1997). These types of factors, of course, have been widely recognized by sociologists and organization theorists who study the internal institutional forces driving organizational behavior (March and Olsen, 1989).

The public choice literature on metropolitan governance has also been criticized as being empirically inaccurate. Critics point to problems underlying the assumptions about how citizens are likely to act in decentralized or polycentric municipal settings. Their argument is that in reality, fragmented systems do not provide greater opportunities for democratic governance and accountability than centralized systems (Lyons and Lowery, 1989; Lyons, Lowery, and DeHoog, 1992). Critics also argue that polycentric or decentralized local governments can often obscure accountability and democratic choice (Golembiewski, 1977), particularly due to the difficulties of acquiring information about local governments (Lyons and Lowery, 1989). Some scholars conclude that even when dissatisfied, citizens do not exhibit a propensity to "vote with their feet" in decentralized systems; this is supported by empirical evidence showing that people do not clearly differentiate among the service packages provided by overlapping jurisdictions (Lowery and Lyons, 1989; Stein, 1987). Public choice scholars have countered these criticisms by offering alternative empirical evidence showing that citizens do move in response to both the cost and the quality of local government services, particularly education services, which can put pressure on communities to be competitive (Teske et al. 1993, 710).

In addition to the criticisms against the predictions and underlying assumptions of the polycentric model of local government, some scholars claim that the policy prescriptions for decentralized municipal governments coming from the public choice approach present a number of normative problems. For instance, Lyons and Lowery (1989) argue that polycentric systems can make it difficult for citizens to be informed and thus participate in government, or that services may be stratified due to income sorting in highly polycentric systems. This stratification of services may then promote racial and social segregation (Lowery, 1999). Even assuming that income or service disparities can be addressed through redistribution, Lowery (2000) contends, political bargaining and negotiation costs can make such redistribution difficult across decentralized communities.

Underlying most of the critiques of public choice literature are concerns with the use of rational choice assumptions (i.e., methodological individualism) in explaining political decision making. The ongoing debates in the social science literature on methodological individualism (Friedman, 1996; Green and Shapiro, 1994; Udehn, 1996) are beyond the scope of this paper, but two general problems with rational choice assumptions should be noted. First, empirical research has shown that people are not myopically self-interested and will often work to ensure collectively optimal outcomes, rather than individually optimal outcomes (Ostrom, Gardner, and Walker, 1994). Second, there is an extensive literature on choice that has identified numerous cognitive and environmental factors that prevent individuals from rationally understanding and evaluating options presented to them (Jones, 2001). Among these many factors are incomplete or uncertain information from the environment, limited computational capacity to evaluate options, and the alteration of perceptions of choices due to issue framing. What these findings may suggest is that public choice theories describing the structure and outcomes of public organizations are fundamentally flawed because the behavioral assumptions about human decision making upon which they are based are inaccurate. As Rockman (2001, 16) argues, "if the conclusions remain stable while the foundations of the theory crumble, then either the conclusions were not uniquely derivable from the foundations or perhaps they merely depict a constructed reality compatible with its author's policy preferences."

Rockman's suggestion that scholars' policy preferences may drive public choice theorizing underscores the normative criticisms of using rational choice assumptions as the basis for theories in public administration and policy. For instance, the tendency to view political actors as being motivated by myopic self-interests can lead scholars to devise policy prescriptions based on these assumptions, despite their inaccuracies in many settings. In addition, some have noted that the democratic implications of public choice theories are actually self-perpetuating because when "institutions and public policies are designed as if self-interest is the motivating factor, then such designs not only legitimate this behavior, but actually encourage and produce it" (Schneider and Ingram, 1997, 50).

A number of public choice scholars acknowledge the limitations of using strictly rational models of individual decision making and use more relaxed assumptions of individual rationality. A few, in fact, never fully subscribed to the strictly rational model of individual behavior. For example, Downs (1967, 2) described bureaucratic behavior based on the assumption that officials "act in the most efficient manner possible given their limited capabilities and the cost of information," and that they "have a complex set of goals including power, income, prestige, security, convenience, loyalty (to an idea, an institution, or the nation), pride in excellent work, and desire to serve the public interest." Ostrom (1973) and other scholars of polycentric metropolitan governance rely heavily on Herbert Simon's work, which set forth the model of "boundedly" rational individuals, recognizing that people have limited information processing capabilities and often ill-defined preferences, yet still act purposively in their own self-interest. New institutional theories of bureaucracy also commonly rely on the boundedly rational model of decision making (Horn, 1995). Even when public choice scholars relax their assumptions to reflect more complex or broader utility functions, some critics contend, this effort is not enough because the social and normative drivers of human behavior are often still ignored. Yet another argument is that a broader view of self-interest makes public choice less analytically tractable because it is difficult to identify the underlying aspects of self-interest that actors will pursue (Golembiewski, 1977).

Even among the critics of public choice there is little doubt that individuals do act under conditions of bounded rationality to achieve self-interested goals in many contexts. The general conclusion of the critics of rational choice scholarship, as well as many leading rational choice scholars, is that to advance political theories, researchers need to clarify those settings in which people do act under the assumptions of rational behavior, versus those settings in which other motivations of human decision making, such as norms and altruism, come into play (Ostrom, 1998). In addition, scholars need to pay more careful attention to how self-interested behavior interacts with other motivations in political decision making (Green and Shapiro, 1994). The laboratory and field research on collective action and human cognition has begun to identify possible answers to some of these criticisms, leading to what Elinor Ostrom calls "second generation models of rationality" (Ostrom, 1998). The development of these models and their application within scholarship on decision making in public organizations is still in its infancy.

2.4 CONCLUSIONS AND FUTURE DIRECTIONS

The field of public choice has had a tremendous influence on the study of public organizations and policy choices. As this chapter has shown, public choice is not a theory per se. It is a methodological approach that relies on economic assumptions of rationality to develop theories of a wide range of political behavior, such as constitutional choice, voting, rent seeking and government growth. The areas of public choice scholarship emphasized in this analysis are federal bureaucracy and the organization of metropolitan governance in the United States—two areas of research that have been more closely tied to public administration research than other public choice theories.

Classic works in public choice sought to explain the inefficiencies in federal bureaucracy by looking at the incentives of self-interested bureaucrats, but provided a somewhat limited and pessimistic view of bureaucratic decision making. Tullock (1965) and Downs (1967) offered some exceptions to the classic public choice studies of bureaucracy by identifying some of the organizational incentives that drive bureaucratic behavior. More recently, the new institutionalist theories of bureaucracy, which have built upon the rational choice foundations of public choice, have continued to advance our understanding of decision making in public bureaucracies by moving beyond simplified assumptions that self-interested bureaucrats alone are responsible for bureaucratic outcomes. This research has looked at how the principals who create and shape bureaucracy (politicians, presidents, courts, or other interest groups) impose structures and rules on bureaucracies that protect their own self-interest (or the interests of their constituents) into the future. In doing so, the new institutionalist literature has also helped to explain how bureaucratic decision makers are constrained by multiple principals, whose interests often conflict or diverge. These conflicts, in turn, can lead to bureaucratic inefficiency or ineffectiveness, depending on the perspective of the principal. Thus, unlike the classic public choice theories of bureaucratic capture and growth, such outcomes are not solely a result of choices by utility-maximizing bureaucrats.

The literature on metropolitan governance, on the other hand, has built upon Ostrom's (1973) reliance on methodological individualism to explain the benefits of polycentric political jurisdictions (or local public economies) for providing public goods and services. Like the public choice theories of federal bureaucracy, this research program has advanced substantially over the last nearly 30 years (Oakerson, 2004). The early emphasis on explaining the benefits of local government competition has spurred scholars to develop more sophisticated descriptive and normative explanations about how governments are organized and how they can support democratic governance. This research has identified how decision makers have more opportunity to make efficient choices about the production of a service when multiple service providers are available. It also explains how citizens have more opportunities to communicate directly with decision makers in polycentric systems of governance, thus facilitating more responsiveness by decision makers—and ultimately producing public services more effectively.

Although public choice literature on federal bureaucracy and the literature on the organization of metropolitan governance certainly diverge from the classic works in public administration, they do have close ties to the models of individual decision making that have been used in the organizational behavior research coming out of the Herbert Simon school of bounded rationality. A number of public choice scholars have acknowledged that decision makers are boundedly rational and have incomplete information and limited information processing. They also have been concerned with understanding how institutional structure and design ultimately shape choices and thus more closely relate to our understanding of what drives the administration of public services and the settings in which they are likely to be more or less efficient. As such, these theories may fall into what Vincent Ostrom (1997, 89) has described as the "peripheries" of public choice. Yet, arguably, it is among the theories on the periphery where "important advances at the frontier are most likely to occur" (Ostrom, 1997, 89), because they are stretching the theoretical landscape and integrating assumptions of human behavior that more closely reflect reality. Of course, continued advances cannot occur without more empirical testing of theories and comparisons against alternative explanations of political organizations and outcomes.

In addition to theory testing, researchers of federal bureaucracy and metropolitan governance need to look toward theoretical advancement in areas that are less well-developed if this research is to be of value to scholars and students of public administration, as well as policy-makers. For example, public choice analyses offer clear theoretical insights about the choices of politicians and the structure of institutions, but they are less lucid in explaining the day-to-day choices of public managers within the complexity of public organizations or how managers are limited by the institutional structures shaping bureaucracy. Public organizations are often viewed as "black boxes" by public choice theorists who focus more on the decision making incentives created by the relationships between bureaus and legislators or bureaus and interest groups (Chang, de Figueiredo, and Weingast, 2001). Chang and her colleagues describe this as the "Wilson" challenge. Wilson (1989) has sought to describe and explain bureaucratic behavior and outcomes by focusing on the characteristics of organization structure and goals, and the types of individuals working in an organization—in other words, returning more to the internal focus that Downs (1967) raised. The real challenge Chang and her colleagues pose is to better explain the intersection between institutional analysis, which looks at the relationship between agency decisions and the incentives placed on them from external institutions (such as Congress, the courts, and the executive branch), and public administration, which relates agency outcomes to internal organizational incentives.

The new institutional economists have done this to some extent by focusing on the organizational and policy outcomes of bureaucracies. Related work has looked even more explicitly at the impact of bureaucratic institutions on the operational decisions of managers (Wood and Waterman, 1994). This scholarship has begun to consider the range of decision making incentives that influence public administrators. Banks and Sundaram (1998) for example, have identified how the incentives for career advancement or the renewal of one's position in public bureaucracy can be a way for principals to ensure civil servant commitment when other institutional or rule-based incentives fail. Miller (1992) similarly has addressed commitment problems that arise in hierarchies, when rational individuals face incentives to shirk in producing team outputs, noting the importance of organizational leadership in instilling collaborative institutional norms (Miller, 1992). Focusing on the connection between public management and public choice, Hammond and Knott (1999) have recently evaluated how political institutions shape or place limitations on the choices that public managers face. It is this type of research that is likely to produce some of the most fruitful insights in the near future for public administration scholars interested in decision making and institutions.

The literature on metropolitan governance can also better address internal management questions and challenges. One area that is ripe for more integration with public administration and management research is in the study of how overlapping jurisdictions collaborate or coordinate to provide certain services. For instance, scholarship in the "new public management" over the past decade has begun to identify how inter-organizational networks can be managed to better provide public goods and services (O'Toole, 2000). The metropolitan governance literature can certainly learn from the inter-organizational network and new public management studies in explaining how to coordinate the production of particular public services in political settings with multiple and overlapping service providers or producers. Ostrom, Parks, and Whitaker (1978) did present an empirical analysis of the of the inter-organizational relationships of police provision agencies in a number of metropolitan areas nearly 30 years ago, identifying a range of network structures across different types of policing services and across different local public economies. Given the growing sophistication of network analysis methodologies over the past decade, it would be worthwhile to consider how this research can support the modern integration of network analyses and local public economy research. Likewise, the public choice literature certainly can inform the new public management literature's network studies by providing theoretical foundations for understanding where and why networks arise.

Finally, public choice scholars also need to confront the move toward greater reliance on the second generation of rational choice models, which Ostrom (1998) calls for. A few scholars of public administration and policy (e.g., Jones, 2001) are now beginning to try integrating the science of human choice and psychology with social science explanations of institutions based on bounded rationality. Additionally, recent scholarship that integrates institutional theories from the rational choice tradition and those from organizational theory and sociology has been used to explain operational outcomes in the provision of public services (Heikkila and Isett, 2004). To move the field of public choice beyond its critiques and limitations, it would certainly help to draw further connections between rational choice theories of decision making in public organizations and other theories of organization, to build upon models of bounded rationality, and to develop more accurate models of human cognition.

Although the field of public choice still has some room for advancement, one cannot say that public choice has failed to contribute to our understanding of political and organizational decision making. Applying the logic of methodological individualism to explain political and organizational outcomes, this field has enhanced our understanding of why individuals choose certain institutional structures to govern themselves, and in turn, how those institutions can shape human choices. The future contributions of public choice will depend upon the extent to which scholars can continue to refine and evaluate the assumptions of rational choice models, and the extent to which they can continue to empirically test the explanatory power of public choice theories. Through such testing, public choice scholars will be able to more firmly acknowledge the conditions under which their assumptions of human decision making ring true, and where the predictions that arise from those assumptions accurately apply.

REFERENCES

Advisory Commission on Intergovernmental Relations (ACIR), *The Organization of Local Public Economies*, Advisory Commission on Intergovernmental Relations, Washington, DC, 1987.

Arrow, K. J., *Social Choice and Individual Values*, Wiley, New York, 1951.

Banks, J. S. and Sundaram, R. K., Optimal retention in agency problems, *Journal of Economic Theory*, 82, 293–310, 1998.

Banks, J. S. and Weingast, B. R., The political control of bureaucracies under asymmetric information, *American Journal of Political Science*, 36(2), 509–524, 1992.

Becker, G., A theory of competition among pressure groups for political influence, *Quarterly Journal of Economics*, 98(3), 371–400, 1983.

Black, D., On the rationale of group decision making, *Journal of Political Economy*, 56(1), 22–34, 1948a.

Black, D., The decisions of a committee using a special majority, *Econometrica*, 16(3), 245–261, 1948b.

Black, D., *The Theory of Committees and Elections*, Kluwer Academic Publishers, Repr. Boston, 1958.

Brehm, J. and Gates, S., *Working, Shirking, and Sabotage: Bureaucratic Response to a Democratic Public*, University of Michigan Press, Ann Arbor, 1997.

Buchanan, J. M. and Tullock, G., *The Calculus of Consent: Logical Foundations of Constitutional Democracy*, University of Michigan Press, Ann Arbor, 1962.

Chang, K. H., de Figueiredo, R. J. P., and Weingast, B. R., Rational choice theories of bureaucratic control and performance, In *The Elgar Companion to Public Choice*, Shughart, W. F. and Razzolini, L., Eds., Edward Elgar, Cheltenham, pp. 271–292, 2001.

Downs, A., *An Economic Theory of Democracy*, Harper & Row, New York, 1957.

Downs, A., *Inside Bureaucracy*, The Rand Corporation, Santa Monica, CA, 1967.

Ferejohn, J. and Fiorina, M. P., The paradox of not voting: a decision theoretic analysis, *The American Political Science Review*, 68(2), 525–536, 1974.

Ferejohn, J. and Shipan, C., Congressional influence on bureaucracy, *Journal of Law, Economics, and Organization*, 6(1), 1–43, 1990.

Friedman, J., Introduction: economic approaches to politics, In *The Rational Choice Controversy: Economic Models of Politics Reconsidered*, Friedman, J., Ed., Yale University Press, New Haven, pp. 1–24, 1996.

Golembiewski, R. T., A critique of "democratic administration" and its supporting ideation, *The American Political Science Review*, 71(4), 1488–1507, 1977.

Green, D. P. and Shapiro, I., *Pathologies of Rational Choice Theory: A Critique of Applications In Political Science*, Yale University Press, New Haven, 1994.

Grier, K., Presidential elections and federal reserve policy: an empirical test, *Southern Economic Journal*, 54(2), 475–486, 1987.

Hammond, T. H. and Knott, J. H., Who controls the bureaucracy? Presidential power, congressional dominance, legal constraints, and bureaucratic autonomy in a model of multi-institutional policymaking,
Journal of Law, Economics, and Organization, 12(1), 119–166, 1996.

Hammond, T. H. and Knott, J. H., Political institutions, public management and policy choice, *Journal of
Public Administration Research and Theory*, 9(1), 33–85, 1999.

Heikkila, T., Institutional boundaries and common-pool resource management: a comparative analysis of
water management programs in California, *Journal of Policy Analysis and Management*, 23(1),
97–117, 2004.

Heikkila, T. and Isett, K. R., Modeling operational decision making in public organizations: an integration of
two institutional theories, *The American Review of Public Administration*, 34(1), 3–19, 2004.

Horn, M. J., *The Political Economy of Public Administration: Institutional Choice in the Public Sector*,
Cambridge University Press, Cambridge, 1995.

Johnson, R. N. and Libecap, G., *The Federal Civil Service System and the Problem of Bureaucracy:
The Economics and Politics of Institutional Change*, University of Chicago Press, Chicago, 1994.

Jones, B. D., *Politics and the Architecture of Choice: Bounded Rationality and Governance*, University of
Chicago Press, Chicago, 2001.

Kanazawa, S., A possible solution to the paradox of voter turnout, *The Journal of Politics*, 60(4), 974–995,
1998.

Kelley, R. C., Independent voting behavior and its effects on rational social choice, *The Western Political
Quarterly*, 38(3), 377–387, 1985.

Lowery, D., Race and the fragmented metropolis: updating the social stratification-government inequality
debate, *Public Management*, 1(1), 7–26, 1999.

Lowery, D., A transactions costs model of metropolitan governance: allocation versus redistribution in urban
America, *Journal of Public Administration Research and Theory*, 10(1), 49–78, 2000.

Lowery, D. and Lyons, W. E., The impact of jurisdictional boundaries: an individual-level test of the Tiebout
model, *The Journal of Politics*, 51(1), 73–97, 1989.

Lyons, W. E. and Lowery, D., Governmental fragmentation versus consolidation: five public-choice myths
about how to create informed, involved, and happy citizens, *Public Administration Review*, 49,
533–543, 1989.

Lyons, W. E., Lowery, D., and DeHoog, R. H., *The Politics of Dissatisfaction: Citizens, Services, and Urban
Institutions*, Sharpe, Armonk, 1992.

March, J. G. and Olsen, J. P., *Rediscovering Institutions: The Organizational Basis of Politics*, Free Press,
New York, 1989.

McCormick, R. E. and Tollison, R. D., *Politicians, Legislation, and the Economy: An Inquiry into the Interest-
Group Theory of Government*, Martinus Nijhoff, Boston, 1981.

McCubbins, M. D., Noll, R. G., and Weingast, B. R., Administrative procedures as instruments of political
control, *Journal of Law, Economics, and Organization*, 3(2), 243–277, 1987.

McNutt, P. A., *The Economics of Public Choice*, 2nd ed., Edward Elgar, Cheltenham, 2002.

Miller, G. J., *Managerial Dilemmas: The Political Economy of Hierarchy*, Cambridge University Press,
New York, 1992.

Mitchell, W. C., The old and new public choice: Chicago versus Virginia, In *The Elgar Companion to Public
Choice*, Shughart, W. F. and Razzolini, L., Eds., Edward Elgar, Cheltenham, pp. 3–32, 2001.

Moe, T., The new economics of organization, *American Journal of Political Science*, 28(4), 739–777, 1984.

Moe, T., An assessment of the positive theory of congressional dominance, *Legislative Studies Quarterly*, 12,
475–520, 1987.

Moe, T., The politics of structural choice: toward a theory of public bureaucracy, In *Organization Theory*,
Williamson, O., Ed., Oxford University Press, Oxford, pp. 117–153, 1990.

Moe, T., Political institutions: the neglected side of the story, *Journal of Law, Economics, and Organization*,
6(1), 213–254, 1990.

Moe, T., Politics and the theory of organization, *Journal of Law, Economics, and Organization*, 7(1), 106–129,
1991.

Mueller, D. C., *Public Choice*, Cambridge University Press, Cambridge, 1979.

Mueller, D. C., *Public Choice II*, Cambridge University Press, Cambridge, 1989.

Mueller, D. C., *Constitutional Democracy*, Oxford University Press, Oxford, 1996.

Nicholson, S. P. and Miller, R. A., Prior beliefs and voter turnout in the 1986 and 1988 congressional elections, *Political Research Quarterly*, 50(1), 199–213, 1997.

Niskanen, W. A., *Bureaucracy and Representative Government*, Aldine-Atherton, Chicago, 1971.

Oakerson, R. J., *Governing Local Public Economies: Creating the Civic Metropolis*, ICS Press, Oakland, CA, 1999.

Oakerson, R. J., The study of metropolitan governance, In *Metropolitan Governance: Conflict, Competition, and Cooperation*, Feiock, R. C., Ed., Georgetown University Press, Washington, DC, pp. 17–45, 2004.

Oakerson, R. J. and Parks, R. B., Citizen voice and public entrepreneurship: the organizational dynamic of a complex metropolitan county, *Publius: The Journal of Federalism*, 18, 91–112, 1988.

Olson, M., *The Logic of Collective Action*, Harvard University Press, Cambridge, 1965.

Ostrom, E., Size and performance in a federal system, *Publius: The Journal of Federalism*, 6(2), 33–73, 1976.

Ostrom, E., The comparative study of local public economies. Paper presented at the Acceptance Paper for the Frank E. Seidman Distinguished Award in Political Economy, Rhodes College, Memphis, TN, 1997.

Ostrom, E., A behavioral approach to the rational choice theory of collective action, *American Political Science Review*, 92(1), 1–22, 1998.

Ostrom, V., *The Intellectual Crisis in American Public Administration*, University of Alabama Press, Tuscaloosa, 1973.

Ostrom, V., *The Meaning of Democracy and the Vulnerability of Democracies: A Response to Tocqueville's Challenge*, University of Michigan Press, Ann Arbor, 1997.

Ostrom, E. and Whitaker, G. P., Does local community control of police make a difference? Some preliminary findings, *American Journal of Political Science*, 17(1), 48–76, 1973.

Ostrom, E., Gardner, R., and Walker, J., *Rules, Games, and Common-Pool Resources*, University of Michigan Press, Ann Arbor, 1994.

Ostrom, E., Parks, R. B., and Whitaker, G. P., *Patterns of Metropolitan Policing*, Ballinger Publishing Company, Cambridge, MA, 1978.

Ostrom, V. and Ostrom, E., Public goods and public choices, In *Alternative for delivering public services toward improved performance*, Savas, E. S., Ed., Westview Press, Boulder, pp. 7–49, 1977.

Ostrom, V. and Ostrom, E., Public goods and public choices: the emergence of public economies and industry structures, In *Public Goods and Public Choices: The Emergence of Public Economies and Industry Structures*, Ostrom, V., Ed. *In The meaning of American federalism, ed. Ostrom, V.*, 163-197, Institute for Contemporary Studies Press, San Francisco, pp. 163–197, 1991.

Ostrom, V., Tiebout, C., and Warren, R., The organization of government in metropolitan areas: a theoretical inquiry, *American Political Science Review*, 55, 831–842, 1961.

O'Toole, L. J., Different public managements? Implications of structural context in hierarchies and networks, In *Advancing Public Management: New Developments in Theory, Methods, and Practice*, Brudney, J. L., O'Toole, L. J., and Rainey, H. G., Eds., Georgetown University Press, Washington, DC, pp. 19–32, 2000.

Palfrey, T. R. and Rosenthal, H., Voter participation and strategic uncertainty, *The American Political Science Review*, 9(1), 62–78, 1985.

Park, K., Friends and competitors: policy interactions between local governments in metropolitan areas, *Political Research Quarterly*, 50(4), 723–750, 1997.

Parks, R. B. and Oakerson, R. J., Metropolitan organization and governance: a local public economy approach, *Urban Affairs Quarterly*, 25(1), 18–29, 1989.

Parks, R. B. and Oakerson, R. J., Comparative metropolitan organization: service production and governance structures in St Louis (MO) and Allegheny County (PA), *Publius: The Journal of Federalism*, 23, 19–39, 1993.

Parks, R. B. and Oakerson, R. J., Regionalism, localism, and metropolitan governance: suggestions from the research program on local public economies, *State and Local Government Review*, 32(3), 169–179, 2000.

Peltzman, S., Toward a more general theory of regulation, *Journal of Law and Economics*, 19(2), 211–240, 1976.

Riker, W. H., *The Theory of Political Coalitions*, Yale University Press, New Haven, 1962.

Riker, W. H. and Ordeshook, P. C., A theory of the calculus of voting, *American Political Science Review*, 62, 25–42, 1968.

Rockman, B. A., Theory and inference in the study of bureaucracy: micro- and neoinsitutionalist foundations of choice, *Journal of Public Administration Research and Theory*, 11(1), 3–27, 2001.

Rowley, C. K., Ed., *Democracy and public choice: essays in honor of Gordon Tullock*, Basil Blackwell, Oxford, 1987.

Schneider, A. L. and Ingram, H., *Policy Design for Democracy*, University Press of Kansas, Lawrence, 1997.

Schneider, M. and Teske, P., *Public Entrepreneurs: Agents for Change in American Government*, Princeton University Press, Princeton, 1995.

Shughart, W. F. I. and Razzolini, L., Ed.s., *The Elgar Companion to Public Choice*, Edward Elgar, Cheltenham, 2001.

Stein, R. M., Tiebout's sorting hypothesis, *Urban Affairs Quarterly*, 23, 140–160, 1987.

Stigler, G. J., The theory of economic regulation, *Bell Journal of Economics and Management Science*, 2, 3–21, 1971.

Teske, P., Schneider, M., Mintrom, M., and Best, S., Establishing the micro foundations of a macro theory: information, movers, and the comparative local market for public goods, *American Political Science Review*, 87(3), 702–713, 1993.

Tiebout, C., A pure theory of local expenditures, *The Journal of Political Economy*, 64(5), 416–424, 1956.

Tullock, G., *The Politics of Bureaucracy*, Public Affairs Press, Washington, DC, 1965.

Tullock, G., Problems in the theory of public choice: social cost and government action, *The American Economic Review*, 59(2), 189–197, 1969.

Tullock, G., Efficient rent seeking, In *Toward a Theory of the Rent Seeking Society*, Buchanan, J. M., Ed., Texas A&M University Press, College Station, pp. 97–112, 1980.

Tullock, G., *The New Federalist*, The Fraser Institute, Vancouver, BC, 1994.

Udehn, L., *The Limits of Public Choice: A Sociological Critique of the Economic Theory of Politics*, Routledge, London, 1996.

Weingast, B. R. and Moran, M., Bureaucratic discretion or congressional control: regulatory policymaking by the Federal Trade Commission, *Journal of Political Economy*, 91, 765–800, 1983.

Wilson, J. Q., *Bureaucracy: What Government Agencies Do and Why They Do It,* Basic Books, New York, 1989.

Wood, D. B. and Waterman, R. W., *Bureaucratic Dynamics: The Role of Bureaucracy in a Democracy*, Westview Press, Boulder, 1994.

3 Policy Making through Disjointed Incrementalism

Michael Hayes

CONTENTS

3.1 Incrementalism as an Alternative to Rationality..40
    3.1.1 The Breakdown of Rationality..40
    3.1.2 How Incrementalism Works Where Rationality Is Paralyzed.................................40
3.2 Incrementalism as a Descriptive Model...43
    3.2.1 Is the Policy Process Typically Incremental?...43
    3.2.2 Rationality as a Prerequisite for Effective Nonincremental Change........................45
    3.2.3 Nonincremental Change and the Life Cycle of Issues...48
3.3 Incrementalism as a Prescriptive Model...49
    3.3.1 Ideologues vs. Pragmatists...49
    3.3.2 Who Likes Incrementalism?..53
    3.3.3 Conditions for the Effective Operation of Incrementalism 57
Further Reading..58
References...58

The rational-comprehensive method of decision making evokes a vision of policy makers clearly defining objectives and making value-maximizing choices after a thorough examination of relevant alternatives. Unfortunately, this ideal is usually unattainable. Inherent obstacles to rational decision making prompted Charles E. Lindblom to advance his model of disjointed incrementalism as an alternative method of policy making (Dahl and Lindblom, 1953; Lindblom, 1959; 1965; 1979; Braybrooke and Lindblom, 1963).

According to Lindblom (1965), policy making is less a matter of rational decision making than a process of mutual adjustment among various actors driven by different self-interests and divergent conceptions of public interest. Participants typically disagree on objectives and may start off from very different ideas of the problem at hand. Incomplete knowledge and time constraints limit attention to a short list of politically feasible alternatives differing marginally from previous policies. This focus on incremental alternatives, combined with the necessity for compromise, makes incremental outcomes virtually inevitable. Major policy change will occur gradually, if at all, as experience with newly enacted policies gives rise to demands for modification or expansion in subsequent policy cycles.

To Lindblom, incrementalism offers both a descriptive and a prescriptive model of the policy process. As a descriptive model, incrementalism provides a plausible explanation for the functioning of the policy process in most cases. However, the model describes so well how the process works because it consistently produces better outcomes than the rational-comprehensive ideal, given the constraints under which that method must operate most of the time.

This chapter is divided into three major sections. The first section reviews rationality and its limitations and then lays out the elements of the incremental model, showing how it departs from the rational method on all points. The second section focuses on incrementalism as a descriptive model, exploring the extent to which Lindblom's model accounts for how policy is actually made. The third section focuses on incrementalism as a prescriptive model by asking whether increment-alism really is the best way to make public policies, as Lindblom asserts.

3.1 INCREMENTALISM AS AN ALTERNATIVE TO RATIONALITY

In an ideal world, policies would result from a rational analysis culminating in a value-maximizing choice after a thorough examination of all relevant alternatives. Unfortunately, this approach breaks down on a variety of fronts.

3.1.1 THE BREAKDOWN OF RATIONALITY

The model begins by assuming that policy makers perceive and accurately define public problems. It further assumes that they rank potential public problems in order of priority, with the most serious reaching the agenda first. In reality, there is no guarantee that problems will be perceived at all; in fact, items that do reach the agenda are often priorities because they have attracted political support from organized interests or the mass public. In addition, there is not a guarantee that all actors will define public problems in the same way or even agree on what distinguishes legitimately public problems from private concerns.

Second, the model requires agreement on national objectives. This means policy makers must not only share the same goals, they must also share the same priorities. Finite resources force shared values into conflict. For instance, dollars spent on defense, which everyone favors in the abstract, are not available to be spent on education, which is also favored by all in the abstract. All participants must agree on how to make trade-offs among objectives; for example, they must decide exactly how much should be spent on education, how much on defense, and how much environmental damage they are prepared to accept to increase their energy independence and so on. Clearly this demanding condition is rarely satisfied.

Third, rational analysis presumes a capacity to estimate accurately the consequences of all alternatives. To forecast what will happen—exactly—if one option is chosen over another, issues must to understood extremely well. The variables that impinge on the outcome must be known and the cause and effect relationships among them must be understood. This degree of understanding of most public policy issues has not been achieved. Often, there is disagreement on what variables are important and how they are related.

The problem of inadequate knowledge base is not limited to problems involving highly tech-nical or scientific issues. Public policies often alter the incentives facing individual citizens. To the extent that people are self-interested and act rationally, new public policies can generate a wide variety of unanticipated consequences (Dexter, 1981; Merton, 1936). For example, laws passed in the wake of Watergate to regulate campaign finance led to a flood of corporate money in campaigns, and limits on what political action committees could contribute to individual candidates led to the very large problem of "soft money" contributions to political parties.

3.1.2 HOW INCREMENTALISM WORKS WHERE RATIONALITY IS PARALYZED

Incrementalism departs from the rational method on all points. It is much less demanding than the rational method, requiring neither comprehensive information nor agreement among policy makers on objectives. Consequently, incrementalism permits action where the rational ideal is paralyzed, often yielding no guidance to policy makers.

The rational method begins by identifying objectives. In practice, this means specifying trade-offs among shared objectives until a mix of positive values is identified. [*]Alternatives are evaluated in terms of their ability to satisfy the preestablished value mix. Where society cannot agree on tradeoffs among values, it is no longer possible to say which alternative is best, and the rational ideal breaks down completely, yielding no guidance whatsoever to policy makers.[†]

Incrementalism avoids this problem entirely by focusing on concrete problems to be alleviated (for example, unemployment) rather than on abstract ideals to be attained such as self-actualized citizenry. The process moves away from problems rather than toward ideals that can never be specified with sufficient precision to permit rational analysis. Lindblom terms this element of the model remediality (Braybrooke and Lindblom, 1963).

Moreover, within incrementalism, ends and means are typically considered simultaneously. Because different alternatives embody different trade-offs among values, as policy makers debate which of several alternatives should be adopted, they also consider—albeit implicitly—what trade-offs should be made among values. Indeed, ends and means cannot be separated as called for by the rational model, with a decision on values preceding any decision on alternatives. Any decision among alternatives is inherently and necessarily a decision about values. Lindblom terms this element of the model the adjustment of objectives to policies (Braybrooke and Lindblom, 1963).

Policy makers are not typically faced with a given problem (Lindblom, 1980). To the contrary, affected publics bring problems to government through the social fragmentation of analysis (Braybrooke and Lindblom, 1963). No single actor needs to possess comprehensive information on the problem. Rather, each participant brings to the table some portion of the knowledge that is required to analyze the problem. The dispersal of essential knowledge throughout the system makes some form of social fragmentation of analysis inevitable. Different individuals are the best judges of their own self-interests. No policy maker or supercomputer can accurately specify the varying value preferences of different individuals or assess the impact of policy proposals on different groups without some input from these groups. Because disagreements can be accommodated through bargaining, one may act on problems without ever being fully defined.

Perhaps the most fundamental way in which incrementalism departs from the rational-comprehensive ideal lies in its rejection of the idea of policy outcomes as the product of a decision process. According to Lindblom, policies are not the products of rational choice but rather the political results of interaction among various actors possessing different information, adhering to different values, and driven by different individual or group interests. The policy process necessarily generates mutual anticipation and adaptation among these many actors, a phenomenon that Lindblom terms partisan mutual adjustment (Lindblom, 1965).

Constraints on time and information preclude a comprehensive examination of all alternative solutions. Policy makers must somehow limit their attention to a manageable number of options. In practice, they accomplish this by limiting their focus to incremental alternatives (Braybrooke and Lindblom, 1963). Restricting attention to proposals differing only marginally from existing policies can be justified on several grounds. First, major policy departures are unlikely to be enacted. Most established policies will have acquired powerful supportive constituencies opposed to any significant changes in policy, and the need to make numerous concessions to build a winning coalition almost guarantees that outcomes will ultimately be incremental. Thus prolonged consideration of nonincremental policy proposals is likely to be a waste of time.

---

[*]This mix of values is what economists term a social welfare function. Value-maximization means moving to the highest social indifference curve that is attainable given resource constraints. Where a whole society must maximize utility, problems of collective decision making make it impossible to construct social indifference curves at all. This is a fatal problem for the rational ideal (Arrow 1951).

[†]Some critics of incrementalism object that it is insufficiently goal-oriented. They do not make clear how decision-makers are supposed to be goal-oriented when they disagree on objectives (Weiss and Woodhouse 1992, 258–260).

Second, policy makers gain experience with existing policies over time, building up a reservoir of knowledge they will be reluctant to throw away by moving in an entirely different direction. Existing policies were the products of a good deal of deliberation, constituting the best response previous policy makers could make to the problems they faced at the time. It makes more sense to build on this foundation than to begin again from the ground up.

Finally, focusing on incremental alternatives is more consistent with the scientific method, which is to say it is a more efficient way to acquire reliable knowledge. Scientists gain knowledge by developing falsifiable hypotheses and conducting experiments to see whether they are disconfirmed. It is impossible to determine whether a change in one policy has had a desirable effect if that change is accompanied by similar changes in a variety of other policies at the same time (Popper 1994, 88). If positive consequences do, in fact, follow these changes, should they be attributed to the change in Policy A, the change in Policy B, the change in Policy C, or some combination?

For example, in 1981 President Ronald Reagan succeeded in getting Congress to pass two major initiatives. One involved major tax cuts phased in over a three-year period designed to address serious problems of inflation and unemployment. The other was a major increase in defense outlays. Confronted with this potentially inflationary combination of tax cuts and spending increases, the Federal Reserve Board (FRB) significantly reduced the rate of growth of the money supply. Thus three major economic policy changes were adopted more or less simultaneously: a major tax cut, a major spending increase, and a change in the money supply. A severe recession resulted in the short term, followed a year or two later by a sustained economic recovery. Not surprisingly, Democrats attributed the recession to Reagan's tax and spending policies and credited the subsequent economic growth to the monetary policies adopted by the FRB that was chaired by a Democrat appointed by former President Jimmy Carter. Republicans attributed the recession to misguided FRB policies and the subsequent upturn to the effects of the Reagan tax cuts. Who was correct? Where so many major policy changes are made simultaneously, it becomes impossible to know.

In comparing incremental alternatives, policy makers make no attempt to identify all the potential consequences associated with each alternative. There is no need to because the policy process is serial, or repetitive (Braybrooke and Lindblom, 1963). Adjustments can be made to policies in subsequent policy cycles, spending a little more or a little less or giving administrators new statutory powers or different marching orders. Unanticipated consequences are not a serious problem for incrementalism; they merely generate new problems to be dealt with at a later date.[*]

Policy makers further reduce the costs of analysis by focusing on the increments by which various proposals differ from one another and from past policies. Lindblom terms this process *margin-dependent choice* (Braybrooke and Lindblom, 1963, 83–88). In the budgetary process, for example, legislators normally make no attempt to evaluate federal policies comprehensively. Rather, they focus on the increments by which spending will go up or down for various programs under different proposals. Focusing on margins permits an intelligent comparison of proposals where a comprehensive analysis of the various competing policies would not be feasible.

Because the failure of a given policy to completely solve a problem merely gives rise to subsequent rounds of policy making, it is not necessary to make a single, comprehensive decision that will solve the problem once and for all. Rather, polices are modified in subsequent iterations of the policy cycle through a process Lindblom calls seriality. The same actors who disagreed over values, tradeoffs, and even problem definition initially will typically be central participants in the

---

[*] Some critics of incrementalism have charged that it is ill-equipped to deal with policy consequences that show up suddenly, when a threshold is crossed, or very late in the implementation process, when sleeper effects may suddenly show up that were not apparent until a commitment to a course of action had become irreversible. While incrementalism is vulnerable to these effects, it is no more vulnerable to them than other decision-making methods, including the rational ideal. The chances of avoiding threshold effects and sleeper effects would seem to be enhanced rather than reduced by a policy process that proceeds gradually. (See the authors reviewed and critiqued in Weiss and Woodhouse, 1992, 264–266.)

subsequent process of policy evaluation and change. Thus policy evaluation is not a straightforward process of rational policy analysis, but rather a political process characterized by fragmentation, conflict, and imperfect knowledge.

Lindblom emphasizes the tendency to converge on a solution as policy makers narrow their differences through the gradual accumulation of experience with the policy. Problems are considered unsolved as long as some publics continue to express dissatisfaction with existing policies. By the same token, a policy may be regarded as solved when it finally disappears from the agenda, crowded off by other problems now considered more pressing (Wildavsky, 1984).

3.2 INCREMENTALISM AS A DESCRIPTIVE MODEL

How well does incrementalism describe how policies are actually made? This section of the chapter is divided into three subsections.

The first subsection will argue that normal incrementalism is less prevalent than Lindblom thought. Lindblom saw rational decision making and nonincremental policy making as precluded most of the time by conflicts over objectives and an inadequate knowledge base. However, these two conditions are not inevitable. Sometimes there will be agreement on values and/or an adequate knowledge base. When these two preconditions for rational decision making are treated instead as variables, recognizing that they may actually be satisfied at least some of the time, four distinct policy environments may be identified, each of which exhibits its own distinctive policy process. While incremental outcomes are associated with three of these four environments, the process by which these outcomes emerge is different for each cell. In the fourth policy environment, where agreement on values is combined with an adequate knowledge base, both rational decision making and nonincremental policy departures are possible.

Where the conditions for rational decision making are unmet, efforts at nonincremental policy change will be futile. This is the primary theme of the second subsection. While mass public arousal may pressure policy makers to take dramatic action, failure to meet one or more of the conditions for rational decision making virtually compels policy makers to engage in some variant of incremental policy making. Some way must be found to engage in bargaining and compromise out of public view, and the tangible outcomes will typically be incremental.

The third subsection will explore the circumstances under which the conditions for rational decision making and *effective* nonincremental change are most likely to occur. We will see that all policies move through a life cycle. The conditions for rational decision making are most likely to be attained, or at least approximated, in the final stage of the life cycle, after policy makers have acquired a great deal of experience with the policy area.

3.2.1 IS THE POLICY PROCESS TYPICALLY INCREMENTAL?

Lindblom identified two preconditions for rational decision making: agreement among participants on objectives and the possession of a knowledge base sufficient to permit accurate estimation of the consequences associated with various alternatives. In Lindblom's view, incrementalism describes how policy is made under normal circumstances because these two conditions are unmet almost all the time.

Nevertheless, the breakdown of these two dimensions of rational decision making should not simply be assumed. Rather, these two conditions must be treated as variables rather than as constants. For example, participants may agree on values without engaging in a comprehensive review of alternative value mixes. The attainment of consensus on objectives changes the policy process significantly even where it results from the failure of policy makers to examine any other goals or the inability of interests with contrary values to mobilize.

Second, policy makers may understand some problems well, or at least think that they do. While a complete understanding of cause and effect relationships requires comprehensive theories of behavior that are greedy for facts and constructed only through a great collection of observations, as Lindblom observes, there are nevertheless issues for which participants have achieved a high degree of understanding and a consensus on basic facts. Robert Rothstein (1984) has termed this condition *consensual knowledge*:

> ...a body of belief about cause-effect and ends-means relationships among variables (activities, aspirations, values, demands) that is widely accepted by the relevant actors, irrespective of the absolute or final "truth" of these beliefs (736).

As with consensual objectives, the policy process is fundamentally altered whenever policy makers reach agreement on how the world works for a given issue whether this shared understanding of cause and effect relationships is ultimately vindicated or disconfirmed.

Combining these two dimensions produces a typology of policy making environments as shown in Table 3.1 (Hayes, 1992, 137). Where issues fit within the typology is properly determined by their placement on the underlying dimensions and not by the names attached to the categories. Thus initial placement of a particular issue within one of the four cells in no way precludes its movement over time into one of the other cells. Issues will move from one category to another whenever the degree of agreement on values or the adequacy of the knowledge base is affected by events.

As this typology will show, incrementalism as a policy process, as described by Lindblom, is confined to only one of the four quadrants. Rational decision making—e.g., policy making as a more or less rational choice among alternatives rather than a pluralistic process of partisan mutual adjustment—will be the norm in another quadrant. The other two quadrants describe important policy processes Lindblom failed to identify in his analysis.

Where the policy process is characterized by conflictual objectives and conflictual knowledge, as in Cell A, normal incrementalism is virtually inevitable. As Lindblom predicts, problems here are complex and poorly understood. Conflict over important values and tradeoffs necessitates majority building through a process of partisan mutual adjustment, and outcomes will typically be incremental. Any nonincremental alternatives receiving consideration would necessarily be watered down in the course of the legislative process.

By contrast, Cell B consists of what might be termed pure problems of value conflict. While policy outcomes are likely to be incremental at best in this cell, the process by which these outcomes are determined will be much more conflictual than Lindblom envisioned for normal incrementalism. Where problems are poorly understood, as in normal incrementalism, the self-interest of various participants will be complex. To the extent that consequences of various policies for different groups cannot be predicted with certainty, conflict will be tempered (Bauer et al., 1972). By contrast, where problems are well understood, either because they are relatively straightforward or because the participants have acquired long experience with the issue through repeated policy cycles, the clarity of the stakes for all involved will intensify conflict. Reform of social security in recent years provides a good example here. Social Security is a difficult issue for policy makers because all reforms have immediate and readily understood redistributive consequences. The fight is over who will bear the costs of fixing the system.

TABLE 3.1

A Typology of Decision Environments

	Conflictual Objectives	Consensual Objectives
Conflictual Knowledge	(A) Realm of normal incrementalism	(C) Pure problems of knowledge base
Consensual Knowledge	(B) Pure problems of value conflict	(D) Realm of rational decision making

The policy process will be different again for pure problems of knowledge base (Cell C). Here, a consensus on objectives exists and only an inadequate understanding of the problem precludes rational policy making. Policy making here will conform to cybernetic models of decision making that emphasize the capacity for systems with stable goals to monitor information from the environment and adapt to changing circumstances through feedback. Under such circumstances, it might be profitable to look upon government somewhat less as a problem of power and somewhat more as a problem of steering (Deutsch, 1966).

Finally, where consensual knowledge is combined with consensual objectives, as in Cell D, rational decision making is attainable. While many of the issues for which these two conditions are satisfied may involve relatively small technical or administrative problems, as Lindblom has suggested (Braybrooke and Lindblom, 1963, 61–79), nonincremental policy departures are also possible here. Large change may not always be value maximizing, but it is at least possible within this cell.

The commitment by President Kennedy in 1961 to put a man on the moon provides an instructive example here (Schulman, 1975). Decision makers could not let diminishing returns determine resource commitments. While the president's strong commitment to the overarching objective made this a pure problem of knowledge base initially, the 10-year time frame placed on the project permitted NASA to gradually expand the knowledge base through research and testing. The best available scientific and engineering talent was attracted both by the challenge inherent in the problem itself and by the very magnitude of the undertaking.[*]

3.2.2 RATIONALITY AS A PREREQUISITE FOR EFFECTIVE NONINCREMENTAL CHANGE

Nonincremental policy changes are unlikely to be sustained or produce desirable results where both conditions for rational decision making are unmet. Charles O. Jones's case study of the Clean Air Amendments of 1970 provides an instructive case. Jones concluded that nonincremental policy outcomes can result where mass public opinion is aroused on an issue, forcing policy makers to satisfy a pre-formed majority. Although incrementalism provided a good description of policy making on the air pollution issue from 1941 to 1967, the increased salience of the issue in 1970 produced a very different kind of policy process, necessitating the development of an alternative model to describe events (Jones, 1974; 1975).

Normal majority-building incrementalism, as understood by Jones, has four elements. These relate to issue areas, institutions, decision making, and policy outcomes. According to Jones, there is no consensus on what constitutes the public interest for most issue areas. Instead, a multiplicity of narrow interests is mobilized on various sides of the issue seeking to influence policy. Mass public opinion is typically inattentive and ill-informed, leaving the field to organized interest groups.

The dominant institutions for most issues are policy communities, consisting of congressional committees or subcommittees with jurisdiction over the issue, executive agencies with responsibility for administering laws within the issue area, and clientele groups with a stake in the policies developed by these policy communities. For most issues most of the time, policy development is centered within these policy communities, and active involvement is limited to a small number of members of these communities.

While in the normal case policy formulation takes place within these policy communities, the full House and Senate must pass new laws and the president must sign them. The need for bargaining and compromise as bills work their way through multiple veto points virtually

---

[*] Although Schulman presents the lunar landing case as an instance of nonincremental policy-making, it may instead be another instance of incrementalism. Braybrooke and Lindblom cite a similar example—conversion from a peacetime to a wartime economy in the late 1930s and 1940s—as an instance of incremental policy-making inasmuch as the large change involved occurred through a gradual sequence of small, albeit more-or-less rational, decisions (Braybrooke and Lindblom, 1963, 755–777).

guarantees that proposals will emerge weaker than they were initially. Jones terms this process "tapering demands from the optimal down to the acceptable."

It follows that policy outcomes will normally be incremental, representing fairly small changes from existing policy. Accordingly, policy entrepreneurs often eschew nonincremental policy proposals as unrealistic—although sometimes proposing a major policy change may be good strategy to provide room for policy concessions later on in the legislative process.

The policy process departed from this model on all four points in 1970. In 1970 various public opinion polls pointed to a dramatic rise in public concern over the pollution issue. The apparent rise in salience was reinforced by the formation of many new interest groups representing environmental interests. This public pressure for dramatic federal action to address the problem constituted a kind of pre-formed majority, obviating the normal need for tapering down.

The sharp increase in public concern created a kind of bandwagon effect. Policy makers who had shown little interest in the issue before, saw it as having electoral potential. Although the institutional components of the policy community had not changed in any formal way, the sudden emergence of mass public concern over the environment drew in new and significant players from outside the community—including the president, who made a strong clean air bill one of the major items in his State of the Union Address.

This expanded circle of policy makers scrambled to satisfy the highly aroused, pre-formed majority. In distinct contrast to the normal legitimation process, air pollution legislation grew stronger as it moved through the House and Senate, through a process Jones termed "policy escalation."

The end result, according to Jones, was a nonincremental policy change: Congress gave the federal government sweeping new authority and set technology, which forced health-based air quality standards. However, this nonincremental departure was not the product of any expansion in the scientific knowledge base available to policy makers but rather was driven primarily by the need to appease an aroused mass public. For this reason, Jones characterized the 1970 policy outcome as legislating beyond capability.

While Jones's study of the 1970 clean air case suggests that an aroused mass public can contribute to nonincremental policy change—albeit change that goes beyond the available knowledge base—subsequent research on a similar issue calls this conclusion into question (Hayes, 1987; 2001, 72–98). The emergence of the nuclear freeze issue in 1981–1982 exhibited many of the same qualities Jones observed for the Clean Air Case. First, public opinion polls confirmed a sharp increase in mass public concern over the prospects of nuclear war or a serious arms race. In addition, this mass public concern manifested itself organizationally in the formation of a large number of new anti-nuclear arms groups calling on Congress to pass some form of freeze on the production of nuclear weapons. The emergence of this pre-formed majority also triggered a bandwagon effect, just as Jones's model would have predicted. The policy community lost control of the issue, as a variety of new players were attracted to the issue, including the president.

The stage seemed to be set for policy escalation and a nonincremental outcome. What followed instead, however, resembled normal incrementalism much more than public satisfying. The House of Representatives passed a very much tapered down freeze resolution urging, but not requiring, the president to consider a nuclear freeze along with any other approaches to arms control he might choose to advance. The passage of a watered down resolution by only one house of Congress could hardly be considered a nonincremental outcome. What was going on?

An alternative model, which may be termed "dramaturgical incrementalism," is necessary to account for events on the nuclear freeze issue (Hayes, 1987). In the nuclear freeze case, mass public arousal created real pressure on policy makers to take dramatic action without producing the conditions for rational policy making. Within the policy community, both conflictual objectives and conflictual knowledge characterized the process, making incrementalism inevitable. The problem facing policy makers was how to engage in normal bargaining and compromise on an issue that had become so salient and alarming for the mass public. The solution was to stage a highly public drama over the nuclear freeze while a small number of key players bargained with the White House in private. This was facilitated in this case by the fact that the two major issues in dispute were moving along simultaneously on separate legislative tracks. The nuclear freeze issue fell within the jurisdiction of the House International Affairs Committee and the Senate Foreign Relations Committee. By contrast, the development of the MX missile—a new weapons system the president desperately wanted that would have been blocked by a binding nuclear freeze—fell within the purview of the House and Senate Armed Services committees. It thus became possible to stage a highly public drama on the nuclear freeze issue—a highly symbolic, nonzero sum issue on which it was possible for all participants to profit simultaneously—while conducting private negotiations over the MX missile that went completely unnoticed by the mainstream media. In the end, the House passed a toothless freeze resolution symbolically repudiating the president. At the same time, the president got the MX missiles he wanted in return for his pledge to make some key wording changes in his arms control proposals and a commitment to support development of a single warhead missile system (the Midgetman) that some members of the policy community felt would eventually help stabilize the arms race between the United States and the Soviet Union.

This dramaturgical model can be applied to the 1970 Clean Air Act as well (Hayes, 2001, 72–98), leading to a very different understanding of that case. First, as in the nuclear freeze case, mass public arousal on the clean air issue in 1970 failed to eliminate conflict within the policy community over central issues. There were still substantial disagreements over the proper tradeoffs between energy production and the environment as well as between environmental protection and economic growth. Moreover, there were no major developments in the scientific knowledge base between 1967 and 1970 that would have warranted the kind of nonincremental policy departure under consideration. Mass public arousal made it difficult, however, to call for more realistic standards without seeming to be in favor of dirty air. The mass public seemed to be demanding a dramatic response by the federal government, and policy makers scrambled to appease this pre-formed majority, just as Jones predicted.

On closer analysis, however, policy escalation was confined to those provisions of the legislation establishing ambient air quality standards. Legislating technology-forcing air quality standards did not guarantee that the air would get dramatically cleaner. Rather, actual changes in air quality would result from state implementation plans (SIPs) laying out the specific actions that would be taken to reduce air pollution. These SIPs, to be drafted over the next two or three years, would be the product of consultation between state-level environmental protection agencies, industries, and other groups attracted to participate in the public hearings process. Thus SIPs provided for bargaining and compromise among a multiplicity of interests with different estimates of what was desirable, practically attainable, and economically feasible long after the clean air issue had lost its salience for the mass public. As in the nuclear freeze case, there would be two distinct conflicts: one highly public conflict involving a large number of participants (the symbolic battle over air quality standards) and one smaller and more private conflict over SIPs. In the latter conflict, members of the policy community would engage in normal incrementalism outside the glare of mass public arousal.

Properly understood, these two cases (clean air in 1970 and the nuclear freeze in the early 1980s) reaffirm the generalizations derived from the typology of policy environments reviewed earlier. Nonincremental policy change is unlikely to be adopted and almost certain to be unsustainable where the conditions for rational decision making are unmet. Where the policy process is characterized by conflictual objectives and/or conflictual knowledge, nonincremental outcomes are virtually precluded. Presidents or legislators may attempt nonincremental departures under such circumstances, but they are usually doomed to failure. The attempts by presidents Nixon and Carter to enact a negative income tax to reform welfare would constitute examples here (Hayes, 1992, 169–194), as would President Clinton's attempt at health care reform in 1993 (Hayes, 2001, 123–147). Where mass public arousal compels a legislative response, as in the clean air and nuclear freeze cases, the conflicts remaining within the policy community merely force the participants to find some way to shift normal incrementalism out of public view.

3.2.3 Nonincremental Change and the Life Cycle of Issues

If nonincremental change is unlikely to occur, and virtually certain to be ineffective, where the conditions for rational decision making are unmet, when will these conditions be satisfied? The preconditions for rational decision making are most likely to be attained, if at all, late in the life cycle of policies.

In understanding the life cycle of policies, it is important to distinguish between new problems and old, familiar problems. According to Lindblom, policy makers typically build on past policies and favor incremental change. This presumes the existence of previous policies to build on. Most policy problems have indeed been around for many years, taxing the capacities of policy makers and resisting any final solution. For example, welfare reform did not reach the agenda in 1995–1996 as a brand new problem. To the contrary, federal programs providing aid to the poor date back to the Social Security Act of 1935 and have been modified countless times since then. And, of course, anti-poverty policies existed at the state and local levels before the federal government was forced to take up the issue during the Great Depression.

However, old, familiar problems were all brand new problems at some point in time. The federal government was forced, by events or political movements, to take on new responsibilities. The Social Security Act of 1935 is a case in point. Not only did that act mark the beginning of Social Security as it is currently known, it also created the foundation for the modern welfare state by establishing federal grant programs to assist the states in providing for various categories of poor people. Building on the earlier research of Lawrence D. Brown (1983), the legislative enactments establishing new federal responsibility federal role are referred to as *breakthrough policies*. This is the first stage in the life cycle of policies.

Over time, policy communities develop around these new programs. Congressional committees are assigned responsibility for legislative oversight or budgetary control, executive agencies are given statutory authority to administer the new law, and affected interest groups establish close ties with these legislators and administrators. A great deal is learned over time about how well these programs work through periodic legislative re-authorization and the annual budget process. Because new problems are unlikely to be well understood or to generate consensual goals, policy making will typically exhibit characteristics of normal incrementalism for many years. Brown termed policies aimed at reforming or improving government programs already in existence "rationalizing policies." Because such rationalizing policies tend to exhibit the characteristics of normal incrementalism for many years, due to the fatal combination of conflictual objectives and conflictual knowledge, the second stage of the life cycle is called the stage of incremental rationalizing policies.

This will be the final stage in the life cycle for many policies. For at least some policies, however, workable solutions to problems may emerge after many years. As policy makers come to understand problems better over time, a consensus on both objectives and knowledge base may develop. Where this occurs—and this stage may never be reached for many policies—we may term this phenomenon a rationalizing breakthrough. Such initiatives are rationalizing policies because they seek to reform existing government programs, but they also constitute breakthrough policies of a very special sort inasmuch as they represent a dramatic shift in thinking and policy design that permits effective action in addressing enduring problems.

This life cycle of policies sheds new light on two critically important questions: (1) When will the policy process depart from normal incrementalism to yield nonincremental policy departures? Furthermore, (2) when will the policy process depart from normal incrementalism to permit rational decision making? The realm of normal incrementalism, as described by Lindblom, is confined to the second stage of the life cycle, the stage of incremental rationalizing policies. Because so much policy making involves reform of existing programs, and because so much policy making is characterized by a combination of conflictual objectives and conflictual knowledge, Lindblom's model of disjointed incrementalism has a great deal of explanatory power.

However, there are two other stages in this life cycle, both of which can be characterized as involving nonincremental change, albeit of very different types. In the first stage, federal role break-throughs mark the acceptance by the federal government of new roles or new responsibilities. According to Brown, the legislative struggles preceding these breakthroughs tend to be intensely conflictual, and passage of a law establishing the new federal role can take decades. The outcome of this legislative struggle can be characterized as nonincremental, even where the initial statute is vague or weak, because it represents a movement from nothing to something—from a world in which the federal government had no responsibility for addressing the problem in question to one in which the federal government takes on a new obligation. However, these initial federal role breakthroughs will not typically be characterized by rational decision making. To the contrary, where problems are new and unfamiliar, conflict over objectives and knowledge base is virtually inevitable.[*]

The development of consensual objectives and consensual knowledge is a slow process, one that often takes decades. E. E. Schattschneider described this life cycle many years ago:

> Every statute is an experiment in learning. When Congress attempts to deal with a new problem it is likely to pass an act establishing an agency with vague powers to do something about it. The new agency investigates, issues some literature about its functions, invites comments by interested parties, assembles a library of information, tries to find some experts, tries to get people to do something about the problem, and eventually recommends some revisions of the statues Congress. Thereafter the problem is passed back and forth between Congress, the president, the agency, interested people, and the public. It is debated, criticized, reviewed, investigated. The statute is revised, over and over again, sometimes for years before a policy is evolved (Schattschneider, 1969, 89).

Thus the conditions for rational policy making are more likely to emerge at the end of the life cycle than the beginning. Nonincremental policy change will be most effective and lasting where it constitutes a rationalizing breakthrough in the final stage in the life cycle of an issue. Policies do not reach this final stage without going through the two prior stages, however. As Schattschneider observed, all effective federal policies began as experiments in learning.

3.3 INCREMENTALISM AS A PRESCRIPTIVE MODEL

This section will ask whether incrementalism really is the best way to make public policies. Unfortunately, there can be no single, universally accepted answer to this question. One's evaluation of incrementalism will necessarily reflect underlying assumptions regarding what it is in fact possible to achieve through politics.

3.3.1 IDEOLOGUES VS. PRAGMATISTS

In this regard, a very important distinction can be made between ideologues and pragmatists.[†] Ideologues and pragmatists make very different assumptions regarding what it is possible to achieve through politics. Pragmatists view policy issues as too complex to be fully understood by any one policy maker or captured by any one theory. By contrast, ideologues believe the world can be understood in terms of some overarching vision of reality that the ideologue has

---

[*] However, the life cycle of policies may be circumvented through the diffusion of innovations from other political systems. Development of the Medicare program, eventually passed in 1965, benefited from the experience of various European nations with national health insurance programs (Crocker, 2000).

[†] While I am primarily indebted to Russell Kirk for this distinction (Kirk, 1969, 153–171; Kirk, 1993, 1–14), I have modified his definition here. In Kirk's view, pragmatists recognize the existence of God and see human sin and fallibility as axiomatic, making prudence the highest political virtue. Ideologues, by contrast, are secularists who believe there are no limits on what man can achieve. Ideologies thus represent misguided attempts to design secular utopias.

discovered (Minogue, 1985, 59–60).[*] Accordingly, ideological visions may be defined as deductive belief systems about the world or some aspect of the world. As such, they tend to be abstract, highly generalized, and internally consistent (Steinbruner, 1974, 131–136).

Ideologues and pragmatists differ on how human knowledge is acquired and applied to address social problems in at least four ways. First, ideologues and pragmatists differ in their approach to trade-offs among values. Second, ideologues and pragmatists differ in their receptivity to empirical evidence. Third, ideologues and pragmatists differ on how many interests should be represented in the policy process. Finally, ideologues and pragmatists differ profoundly on the proper form of the political community.

First, ideologues assume away value conflicts while pragmatists recognize the existence of trade-offs. Sowell emphasizes the inevitability of trade-offs across values and identifies a defining characteristic of ideologues in their tendency to deny the existence of such trade-offs:

> Perhaps the most fundamental difference between those with the tragic vision and those with the vision of the anointed [Sowell's terms for the two worldviews that are being defined here] is that the former see policy making in terms of trade-offs and the latter in terms of "solutions." This is not merely a difference in words or in optimism, but a difference in procedures. To those with the vision of the anointed, the question is: What will remove particular negative features in the existing situation to create a solution? Those with the tragic vision ask: What must be sacrificed to achieve this particular improvement? (Sowell, 1995, 135)

In practice, ideologues typically avoid dealing with tradeoffs in one of two ways. Often they focus exclusively on a single value and deny the importance of alternative values (Steinbruner, 1974, 131). For example, at least some economists exhibit an almost religious faith in the superiority of free markets, rejecting virtually all forms of government intervention or regulation. However, while markets are extremely good at promoting economic efficiency where certain conditions are met (perfect information, perfect competition, and so on), economic efficiency may go hand in hand with high levels of income inequality. There is thus a trade-off between efficiency and equality.

While government action to reduce inequities typically forfeits some economic efficiency, there are good reasons why society might be willing to give up some efficiency to reduce income inequality (Okun, 1975). For example, allowing oil prices to rise during an energy shortage is economically efficient, inasmuch as it encourages both conservation and additional oil exploration. However, the distribution of oil under a price system will inevitably reflect not just differences in consumer preferences but also differences in ability to pay the higher prices—e.g., while the rich adjust easily to higher oil prices, the poor may find them devastating. These differences in ability to pay may be addressed through price controls on oil or through policies designed to redistribute income. Economists opposed to such interventions, termed "free market fundamentalists" by Jerold Waltman (2000), value economic efficiency more than equity. Many would deny any importance to equality as an alternative value: "…the market and justice are synonymous. If the market assigns a certain value to a good or service, then it has that value, objectively and morally" (18). This is a central tenet of neo-liberalism (see Palley, 2004, 1).

By contrast, where ideologues do in fact recognize the importance of more than one value, they may simply deny the reality of a trade-off relationship. It is not necessary to give up some of one value to obtain more of another if the values in question are independent and can be pursued

---

[*] This definition of ideology differs not only from Kirk's, as described above, but from Minogue's as well. To Minogue, ideologies always involve domination and exploitation. This domination stems from some structure (capitalism, patriarchy, etc.) that must be removed to liberate those oppressed under this structure from those profiting under this structure. Because ideologues of this sort, by definition, see domination as stemming from structural causes, they necessarily eschew incremental or piecemeal reform in favor of holistic changes in entire social structures (Minogue, 1985, 8–40). By contrast, my definition of ideology in this chapter is closer to what, Steinbruner (1974, 131–136) terms "theoretical thinking."

simultaneously. Steinbruner terms this the "separation of values" (1974, 103–109). To return to an earlier example, in 1981 the Reagan administration pursued two major legislative initiatives: a major tax cut (ten percent per year for three consecutive years) and a major defense spending increase. While President Reagan was strongly committed to both these initiatives, he also wanted to reduce the budget deficit he had inherited from the Carter administration. However, cutting taxes significantly while sharply increasing federal spending led to massive structural deficits, much greater than those Reagan had inherited from the previous administration. While this may not seem surprising in retrospect (and it seemed predictable enough to Reagan's critics at the time), the president and many of his economic advisers sincerely believed such deficits would not occur because they accepted a previously untried economic theory, "supply-side economics," that associated economic sluggishness with high marginal tax rates. According to this theory, reducing marginal tax rates would generate a sharp increase in economic growth, resulting in increased federal tax revenues sufficient to pay for the defense spending increases sought by the president.[*] Supply-side economic theory thus treated tax cuts, spending increases, and balanced budgets as independent values that could be achieved simultaneously.[†]

Second, ideologues and pragmatists differ in their receptivity to evidence that challenges their preconceptions. Because pragmatists believe most policy issues are too complex to be captured adequately by any one theory, they believe the value of competing ideas must be judged on the basis of their observed consequences. It follows that theories must be subjected to empirical test and discarded if disconfirmed (Popper, 1994). By contrast, ideologues tend to believe they have already discovered the truth. Consequently, they see little value in a competition of ideas, and they often dismiss or ignore evidence that disconfirms their theories, preferring instead to search for evidence that supports their theories.[‡]

As Steinbruner (1974, 132) notes, such true believers in a theoretical system are often termed "theologians" by other participants in the policy process because their worldviews are sustained by faith and impervious to evidence. Waltman critiques the free market fundamentalist in precisely these terms. His analysis of free market fundamentalists is worth quoting at length:

> The great power of this extreme form of neoclassical economics is that it is both a science and a religion. It has a timeless framework based on natural laws. At the same time, it predicts exactly how the world works. Logically, of course, one should not be able to have it both ways. If the system is a science, it needs to be subject to invalidation through the ordinary process of inquiry. There are really only two ways to go about disconfirming such a model: show the assumptions on which it is built are false or demonstrate that the hypotheses generated by it do not accord with reality. The first can be circumvented if one is prepared to rely on the power of the propositions. That is, if the model is predictively powerful, it may not be relevant that the assumptions are simplifications or even false. Market fundamentalists,

---

[*] Sorting out the exact effects of these various policies is complicated, and economists still debate the merits of the Reagan program. The effects of these various policies in combination would depend, in ways neglected here, on their timing and relative magnitudes. More specifically, the supply-side tax cuts may indeed have increased federal revenues to some degree, as their proponents contend and as Keynesian tax cuts sometimes do. This in no way guarantees, however, that the resulting revenue increases would be sufficient to offset the relative size of the defense spending increases Reagan achieved. What branded the supply-side advocates as ideologues rather than pragmatists, discrediting them in they eyes of their mainstream critics, was their apparent disinterest in addressing issues of timing and magnitude with any real precision. To the supply-side true believer, cuts in marginal tax rates would trigger economic growth and increased tax revenues. If a little tax cutting was a good thing, more tax cutting would be even better. For a good example of such thinking, see Wanniski (1978).

[†] The 2003 American war with Iraq provides a more recent example of denial of trade-offs by ideological policy makers. Following Sowell, the pragmatist would focus on what would need to be sacrificed to achieve regime change in Iraq; the Bush administration consistently dismissed skeptics who raised such concerns. A political undertaking of great complexity was assumed to be not just possible but almost painless.

[‡] In Popper's (1994) view, scientific knowledge advances by formulating hypotheses specific enough to be falsified and testing them empirically. Counter-intuitive as it may seem, hypotheses are not tested by searching for confirming evidence; to the contrary, they are tested by searching for, and failing to find, disconfirming evidence.

however, have not been noticeably eager to reexamine their model when reality stubbornly refuses to go along with their predictions…If the system is a religion, then different criteria apply. The evaluative criteria should be drawn from philosophy and theology, and it must be laid alongside other value systems and judged accordingly. In the meantime, though, if one claims to have found the key to both normative and empirical truth, these criticisms do not register. Consequently, to its adherents, free market fundamentalism remains both inspiring and irrefutable. (Waltman, 2000, 18–19)

The economics of the minimum wage provides a good illustration here, according to Waltman. In theory, the operation of supply and demand within labor markets should determine both the quantity of labor employed and the prevailing wage. Where a minimum wage rate is set above the market rate, workers whose labor is not worth the minimum wage will be laid off. While workers fortunate enough to retain their jobs will be better off earning the minimum wage, their gains come directly at the expense of those laid off as a result of the policy.

However, empirical research does not provide consistent support for this theoretical conclusion (Waltman, 2000, 111–123). While this leads empirically oriented economists to develop alternative models that better fit the data, free market fundamentalists hold fast to the doctrine that increases in the minimum wage must produce increases in unemployment, regardless of what the empirical evidence may say, because the standard model says they will (Waltman, 2000, 115).

Ideologues and pragmatists process incoming information differently. In the short-term, ideologues appear to have the advantage over pragmatists. Because they interpret events through an integrated, overarching framework, ideologues can assimilate new information quickly, formulate coherent explanations for complex events, and act decisively while pragmatists are still struggling to understand events. In the long run, however, ideological thinkers are more likely to have problems. Whenever policies fail to produce anticipated results, ideologues are thrown off balance. Disconfirming evidence is particularly threatening to ideologues inasmuch as it calls into question not just a particular policy but a whole conceptual apparatus that gave rise to the policy (Steinbruner, 1974, 132). This explains why ideologues are so resistant to negative evidence, as Sowell (1995, 64–103) documented.

By contrast, while pragmatists may be disappointed when policies fail, they are not threatened by disconfirming evidence in this same way. Because pragmatists judge the value of ideas by their practical consequences, they view the implementation of policies as experimental in a way the ideologues do not. They expect learning to proceed by trial and error and are not surprised when policies fail to work out as planned. The failure of one idea is not fatal where policy making is understood as a competition of ideas (Popper, 1994).

Third, ideologues and pragmatists differ on how many participants should be included in the policy process. Pragmatists believe that good policy is most likely to result from good process that requires inclusion of a full range of points of view. In E. E. Schattschneider's (1960) classic formulation, pragmatists view the socialization of conflict (e.g., the expansion of the scope of conflict on an issue to include more participants) as a precondition to good policy. Pragmatists would favor checks-and-balance systems, not only to minimize the potential for tyranny but also to increase the number of participants with some degree of effective leverage over the final decision.

By contrast, ideologues tend to believe they have already discovered the truth and see less reason to assure representation of dissenting views. To the contrary, ideologues often favor procedures that exclude dissenters or place them at a disadvantage. To draw on Schattschneider's terminology once again, ideologues tend to favor the privatization of conflict, restricting the decision making circle as much as possible to those holding similar views. On the positive side, restricting the circle of players in this way facilitates rational-comprehensive decision making by limiting participation to those holding the same values and the same beliefs about consequences of various policy options. At the same time, however, such elitist decision making increases both the likelihood of serious mistakes and persistence in misguided policies by excluding potentially valuable information and dissenting viewpoints.

Fourth, ideologues and pragmatists differ profoundly on the role of government within society. Michael Oakeshott (1991, 438–461) makes an important distinction between two distinct conceptions of society that he terms purposive associations and civil associations. Within purposive associations, citizens are related to one another through their pursuit of some shared purpose, and they derive their identity as citizens from this common enterprise. While the first purposive associations were religious, with the state acting as guardian and promoter of orthodox beliefs, religion is not the only basis for purposive associations. A society becomes a purposive association any time it defines itself in terms of some common enterprise, whether that enterprise involves the maximization of economic efficiency, the pursuit of social justice (however defined), the spread of democracy throughout the world, or some other objective.

By contrast, within civil associations there is no common, overarching purpose to unite people into a shared enterprise. To the contrary, people are free to pursue their own individual purposes as long as they do not interfere with the rights of others to do likewise. The bases for identification within civil associations are territorial boundaries and a commonly accepted set of rules governing people as they pursue their own happiness in individual ways (Oakeshott, 1991, 454–457). In Hayek's (1973) terms the social order is spontaneous rather than planned or centrally directed.

Ideologues necessarily view societies as purposive associations because they see politics as an arena for pursuing utopian visions. As Oakeshott (1991) made clear, ideologues approach politics with a vision of human existence "from which the occasion of conflict has been removed, a vision of human activity co-ordinated and set going in a single direction and of every resource being used to the full" (426). Within such a worldview, the proper objective of politics is "to turn a private dream into a public and compulsory manner of living" (426). Where society is organized around a single common purpose, the power of the state will tend to expand until the state becomes indistinguishable from society, inevitably subordinating individual liberties to the pursuit of the shared purpose (Popper, 1994, 67).

By contrast, pragmatists tend to view societies as civil associations. While many pragmatists see a large role for the state in addressing social, economic, or political problems, they expect to do little more than mitigate or ameliorate problems that never fully go away. In large part, this is because pragmatists see conflict over important values as normal. They also see policy making as a competition of ideas in which no one actor possesses a monopoly on knowledge. To the extent that politics involves the elevation and resolution of such conflicts, pragmatists see politics as a central activity within civil associations, which is to say among free people. By contrast, ideologues envision an end to politics through the disappearance of value tradeoffs and imperfect information (Minogue, 1995, 110).

3.3.2 WHO LIKES INCREMENTALISM?

It should be clear by this point that ideologues tend to reject incrementalism for a variety of reasons. Ideologues prefer coherent, overarching, internally consistent theoretical visions to the muddled compromises that tend to emerge from pluralistic political processes. Moreover, ideologues eschew piecemeal and gradual social reforms in favor of holistic institutional transformations that are both sweeping and rapid (Popper, 1994). Finally, ideologues would decisively reject any strategy for building on and incrementally modifying a status quo they view as inherently flawed.

By contrast, pragmatists are much more likely to embrace incrementalism. Certainly pragmatists would applaud incrementalism's core tenet that good policies result from good processes in which a wide variety of viewpoints are represented. While there would surely be disagreement among pragmatists over the advantages to be gained by focusing exclusively on incremental policy proposals, all pragmatists would endorse incrementalism's stress on learning through trial and error and the achievement of significant and effective policy change through seriality.

While there will never be complete agreement on the virtues of incrementalism, I believe the pragmatists are right and the ideologues are wrong. Ideological thinking is dangerous to the extent that it rejects dissenting views, often resulting in imprudent and ill-advised policies. To make matters worse, having made bad decisions through a poor policy process, ideologues are also highly resistant to evidence calling their plans into question. Finally, and perhaps most important of all, ideologues by their very nature hold elitist views that must, sooner or later, subordinate individual liberty to the pursuit of their utopian visions.

Critics have charged that incrementalism is inherently a conservative process to the extent that it eschews fundamental changes in the status quo and focuses instead on gradual policy change through incremental steps (Weiss and Woodhouse, 1992, 260–262). Admittedly, it makes a degree of sense to view political utopianism as essentially a liberal phenomenon because of its expansive and optimistic view of what it is possible to achieve through politics. Similarly, pragmatists might be characterized as conservative to the extent that they are more skeptical regarding what it is possible to achieve through politics.

However, a simple, dichotomous distinction of this sort is misleading for two reasons. First, as outlined below, there are ideologues on both the left and the right. In the same way, pragmatists are not all conservative; room must be made for pragmatic political reformers in our classification scheme. And second, the terms conservative and liberal are poorly defined and thus used by different people to mean very different things. The typology of four distinct worldviews developed below thus represents an attempt to clarify the meaning of these popular and important terms.

It is not enough to distinguish between ideologues and pragmatists as defined above. We must also differentiate advocates of social reform from those concerned instead with preserving or restoring some aspect of society inherited from the past (Cropsey, 1965, 43). Here the distinction is between "progressives," who view society as a work in progress and thus see political reforms as likely to improve upon the inheritance, and "preservers," who revere existing institutions and practices and seek to protect them from erosion by one or more forces of modernity. When these two dichotomous dimensions are combined, the result is a typology of four worldviews, as shown in Table 3.2.

From the above typology, two distinctively different types of ideologues may now be identified. Utopian visionaries are Minogue's ideologues. They believe their vision identifies the systemic causes of exploitation and discontent—capitalism as a form of economic organization, male-dominated social systems. Positive change can only come through the kind of sweeping changes in whole social, economic, or political institutions that Popper terms holistic social engineering Incremental tinkering will not do. It should be clear that utopian visionaries envision society as a purposive association, as defined earlier.

Nostalgic conservatives are every bit as ideological as utopian visionaries, but they want change to move in a very different direction. Where utopian visionaries are intellectual innovators

---

TABLE 3.2

Typology of Worldviews

	Ideologues	Pragmatists
Progressives: Forward-looking reformers	Utopian Visionaries: Ideological innovators who seek to impose a common purpose on society in accordance with an ideological vision they have formulated	Meliorative Liberals: Pragmatic reformers who view change as desirable but best achieved through incremental or piecemeal social engineering
Preservers/Restorers: Backward-looking conservers	Nostalgic Conservatives: Restorers who seek to return to a way of life shown to be desirable by past experience or revelation	Adaptive Conservatives: Seek to preserve cherished institutions; accept the need for some reforms to preserve what is truly precious from the past

seeking brave, new worlds that were previously unimaginable, nostalgic conservatives are reactionary. They want to restore a way of life that has been shown to be desirable by past experience or revelation. In general, nostalgic conservatives view this lost way of life in utopian terms, viewing it as a kind of golden age undermined by the onset of modernity, however defined. These reactionary ideologies may center on secular as well as religious concerns. One common variant of this worldview advocates a return to a more religious age, in which the bulk of society is thought to have accepted the existence of God and worshiped Him in the same way (e.g., properly, as defined by the particular ideologue).

A second, more secular variant seeks a return to the pre-New Deal era during which the federal government intervened much less in the national economy. The free market fundamentalists fit here, calling for a minimalist state that does little more than enforce contracts and guard against fraud. For nostalgic conservatives, no less than utopian visionaries, society is necessarily conceived as a purposive association rather than a civil association.

The typology likewise identifies two distinctively different types of pragmatists. While people in both these categories would embrace incrementalism, they do so for somewhat different reasons. Whereas one of these two worldviews may accurately be termed conservative, the other cannot.

First, meliorative liberals are pragmatic reformers. Whereas the adaptive conservatives cherish aspects of the inheritance and will do whatever it takes to preserve it, including reform, meliorative liberals regard it as the product of fallible men. Because meliorative liberals view man as fallible, they suspect he is incapable of designing or discovering the perfect political or economic system. Accordingly, human institutions can always be improved and should not be viewed as sacred or inviolate simply because they are the products of tradition. At the same time, however, meliorative liberals—in distinct contrast to the utopian visionaries, with whom they share a disposition towards reform—believe society is too complex to be fully understood by any one individual or captured fully by any theory or model. Thus meliorative liberals believe that knowledge advances through the pluralistic competition of ideas.

With its emphasis on policy making through partisan mutual adjustment and policy change via a steady succession of small steps, incrementalism holds obvious appeal to meliorative liberals. In fact, as I have argued elsewhere, both Charles Lindblom and Karl Popper fit unambiguously within this category, and incrementalism can be properly understood as a clearly formulated strategy for pursuing meliorative liberalism (Hayes, 2001, 36–41).

But meliorative liberals are not the only group that embraces incrementalism. Adaptive conservatives do so as well, albeit for different reasons. Like nostalgic conservatives, adaptive conservatives cherish some aspect of the political, economic, or social inheritance. In distinct contrast to the nostalgic conservatives, however, adaptive conservatives are prudential and pragmatic rather than ideological. While adaptive conservatives do not embrace reform and almost never initiate it, they can be persuaded to accept reform where it can be shown to be essential to the preservation of what they regard as precious about the inheritance. Meyer (1996) best expressed the critical distinction between the nostalgic and adaptive conservative viewpoints:

> In any era, the problem of conservatives is to find a way to restore the tradition of civilization and apply it in a new situation. But this means that conservatism is by its nature two-sided. It must at one and the same time be reactionary and presentist. It cannot content itself with appealing to the past. The very circumstances that call conscious conservatism into being create an irrevocable break with the past (188).

On one level, the appeal of incrementalism to adaptive conservatives is readily apparent; if change must be accepted, then let it be as gradual as possible. On another level, however, adaptive conservatives follow Edmund Burke in making an important distinction between innovation and reform. Burke, a quintessential adaptive conservative, criticized the French Revolution for its devotion to radical innovation dictated by abstract ideology. The spirit of innovation, in Burke's view, sees nothing of value in inherited institutions. By contrast, the prudent statesman would recognize the complexity of society, the proven value of inherited institutions, and the difficulty of designing reforms that would reliably represent improvements. Where the French Revolution over-turned existing institutions in the name of utopian innovation, the British Revolution of 1688 was a conservative revolution designed to protect the existing British constitution from encroachments by the crown.

> A man full of warm, speculative benevolence may wish his society otherwise constituted than he finds it but a good patriot, and a true politician, always considers how he shall make the most of the existing materials of his country. A disposition to preserve, and an ability to improve, taken together, would be my standard of a statesman…(Stanlis, 1963, 602)

Thus while adaptive conservatives join with meliorative liberals in embracing increment-alism as the best method of policy making, they differ from meliorative liberals in their attitude toward reform and innovation. Although building on past policies is a central element of incrementalism, meliorative liberals and adaptive conservatives take a very different view of the inherited policy legacy. As noted earlier, meliorative liberals see all human institutions as the product of fallible men and thus subject to potential improvement. They build on past policies less because they like past policies than because they feel nonincre-mental innovation is inefficient—e.g., it generally moves faster than is warranted by human capabilities and the available knowledge base. While I defined meliorative liberals earlier as pragmatic reformers, they may be better understood as chronic or perpetual innovators who believe that innovation occurs more effectively where it proceeds incrementally. It must always be remembered that one of the defining characteristics of meliorative liberals is a progressive desire for change or reform. While they would pursue change more slowly than utopian visionaries, their project is ultimately the same.

Adaptive conservatives, by contrast, are preservers, not progressives. As such, they have an abiding affection for existing institutions that is simply not present in meliorative liberals. While Burke (Stanlis, 1963, 522) recognized that: "A state without the means of some change is without the means of its conservation," he also drew a clear distinction between reform and innovation:

> It cannot at this time be too often repeated, line upon line, precept upon precept, until it comes into the currency of a proverb-To innovate is not to reform. The French revolutionists complained of everything; they refused to reform anything; and they left nothing, no, nothing at all, *unchanged* (675). [Emphasis in original]

Thus the distinction between ideologues and pragmatists, although valuable, is insufficient by itself. Ideologues come in two varieties: utopian visionaries and nostalgic conservatives. Both reject incrementalism decisively for a variety of reasons. By contrast, pragmatists are much more likely to embrace incrementalism. However, pragmatists also come in two varieties, adopting distinctively different favorable views of incrementalism. As an academic model, incrementalism was developed and advanced by two meliorative liberals, Popper and Lindblom, and can be viewed as a self-conscious strategy for pursuing meliorative liberalism. While meliorative liberals embrace inno-vation, they pursue change gradually through pluralistic politics and the steady accumulation of incremental policy changes. Adaptive conservatives, by contrast, are Burkean. Unlike meliorative liberals, they place a premium on preserving cherished institutions. They view reform as a necess-ary means of preservation, but they never confuse reform with innovation. Adaptive conservatives, following Burke, are incremental reformers. Meliorative liberals are pragmatic, incremental *innovators*.

3.3.3 CONDITIONS FOR THE EFFECTIVE OPERATION OF INCREMENTALISM

For incrementalism to yield good public policies, two conditions must be met. First, all interests with a stake in policy issues must be effectively represented. Lindblom was optimistic on this point:

> In a society like that of the United States in which individuals are free to pursue almost any possible common interest they might have and in which government agencies are sensitive to the pressures of these groups, the system described is approximated. Almost every interest has its watchdog. (Lindblom, 1959, 85)

Unfortunately, there are good reasons to doubt that this optimistic assumption will be satisfied (Hayes, 2001, 51–71). The free rider problem prevents many groups from mobilizing and creating a systematic bias to the group universe that favors small groups over large, diffuse groups (Olson, 1970). There is also a socioeconomic bias to all forms of political participation, including voting and membership in organized interest groups: the more economically disadvantaged the group, the less likely it will be to mobilize. Finally, institutions of all sorts will have longer life spans than membership groups of all sorts (Salisbury, 1984). For groups dependent upon a membership base for financial support, the free rider problem never goes away.

Second, for incrementalism to yield good public policies, there must be a rough balance in the resources available to different groups as they seek to influence policy makers. Unfortunately, this assumption is also violated in practice most of the time. Organized interests possess a variety of advantages over unorganized interests, and corporations will occupy something approaching a privileged position within capitalist societies (Miliband, 1969; Lindblom, 1977; 1982; Hayes, 1992, 63–79; Hayes, 2001, 54–62).

The failure of incrementalism to operate perfectly all the time, or even some of the time, does not invalidate the basic argument advanced here: that the rational-comprehensive ideal is unattainable and that good policy tends to result instead from a pluralistic political process in which as many interests as possible are represented. In advancing his case for incrementalism, Lindblom (1959) never asserted that incrementalism would operate perfectly, only that it would outperform the rational ideal: "Without claiming that every interest has a sufficiently powerful watchdog, it can be argued that our system often can assure a more comprehensive regard for the values of the whole society than any attempt at intellectual comprehensiveness" (85).

If incrementalism were advanced as a kind of perfectly competitive, self-correcting political market, the case for incrementalism would degenerate into just another form of ideological thinking. But, as I have tried to argue here, the case for the relative superiority of incrementalism over rational-comprehensive analysis is quintessentially pragmatic rather than ideological. Properly understood, it is anti-utopian in every respect. Accordingly, it might be profitable to mitigate the flaws observed in incrementalism, even as it is recognized that the method will never function ideally. In this regard, I have elsewhere suggested two broad categories of reform (Hayes, 2001, 161–166). First, we should take any steps we can, including direct subsidies or changes in the tax code, to encourage the mobilization of currently unrepresented interests. And second, we should strive to ameliorate disparities in resources across mobilized groups. Here, some form of public financing of congressional elections would seem warranted to reduce the enormous financial advantage business possesses over all other actors in the political system (Schlozman and Tierney, 1986). Both these reforms should be viewed as meliorative rather than utopian, however. No matter how hard we try to encourage the mobilization of unorganized interests, some groups will always be left out of the equation, and any success we might achieve in reducing the corporate advantage in the campaign finance system will only go part way towards equalizing effective influence. As both Lindblom and Miliband emphasized, the privileged position of business within capitalist societies rests as much or more on intangible resources than it does on tangible resources like money.

FURTHER READING

Lustik, I., Explaining the variable utility of disjointed incrementalism: four propositions, *American Political Science Review*, 74, 342–353, 1980.

Premfors, R., Review article: Charles Lindblom and Aaron Wildavsky, *British Journal of Political Science*, 11, 201–225, 1981.

REFERENCES

Arrow, K. J., *Social Choice and Individual Values Political Science Quarterly*, Wiley, New York, 1951.

Bauer, R., Pool, I., and Dexter, L. A., *American Business and Public Policy: The Politics of Foreign Trade*, 2nd ed., Aldine-Atherton, Chicago, 1972.

Braybrooke, D. and Lindblom, C. E., *A Strategy of Decision: Policy Evaluation as a Social Process*, Free Press of Glencoe, New York, 1963.

Brown, L. D., *New Policies, New Politics: Government's Response to Government's Growth*, Brookings Institution, Washington, DC, 1983.

Crocker, L. Medicare and nonincremental innovations. Unpublished senior honors thesis, Colgate University, 2000.

Cropsey, J., Conservatism and liberalism, In *Left, Right, and Center: Essays on Liberalism and Conservatism in the United States*, Goldwin, R. A., Ed., Rand McNally, Chicago, pp. 42–59, 1965.

Dahl, R. A. and Lindblom, C. E., *Politics, Economics, and Welfare: Politico-Economic Systems Resolved into Basic Social Processes*, Harper, New York, 1953.

Deutsch, K. W., *The Nerves of Government: Models of Political Communication and Control*, Free Press, New York, 1966.

Dexter, L. A., Undesigned consequences of purposive legislative action: alternatives to implementation, *Journal of Public Policy*, 1, 413–431, 1981.

Hayek, F. A., *Law, Legislatio, and Liberty (Rules and Order)*, Vol. 1, University of Chicago Press, Chicago, 1973.

Hayes, M. T., Incrementalism as Dramaturgy: The Case of the Nuclear Freeze, *Polity*, 19, 443–463, 1987.

Hayes, M. T., *Incrementalism and Public Policy*, Longman, New York, 1992.

Hayes, M. T., *The limits of Policy Change: Incrementalism, Worldview, and the Rule of Law*, Georgetown University Press, Washington, DC, 2001.

Jones, C. O., Speculative augmentation in federal air pollution policy-making, *Journal of Politics*, 36, 438–464, 1974.

Jones, C. O., *Clean Air: The Policies and Politics of Pollution Control*, University of Pittsburgh Press, Pittsburgh, 1975.

Kirk, R., *Enemies of the Permanent Things: Observations of Abnormality in Literature and Politics*, Arlington House, New Rochelle, NY, 1969.

Kirk, R., *The Politics of Prudence*, ISI Books, Wilmington, DE, 1993.

Lindblom, C. E., The science of "muddling through", *Public Administration Review*, 19, 79–88, 1959.

Lindblom, C. E., *The Intelligence of Democracy: Decision Making Through Mutual Adaptation*, Free Press, New York, 1965.

Lindblom, C. E., *Politics and Markets: The World's Political-Economic Systems*, Basic Books, New York, 1977.

Lindblom, C. E., Still muddling, not yet through, *Public Administration Review*, 39, 520–526, 1979.

Lindblom, C. E., *The Policy-making Process*, 2nd ed., Prentice Hall, Englewood Cliffs, NJ, 1980.

Lindblom, C. E., The market as prison, *Journal of Politics*, 44, 324–336, 1982.

Merton, R. K., The unanticipated consequences of purposive social action, *American Sociological Review*, 1, 894–904, 1936.

Meyer, F. S., *In Defense of Freedom and Related Essays*, Liberty Fund, Indianapolis, IN, 1996.

Miliband, R., *The State in Capitalist Society*, Basic Books/Harper Colophon, New York, 1969.

Minogue, K., *Alien Powers: The Pure Theory of Ideology*, St. Martin's Press, New York, 1985.

Minogue, K., *Politics: A Very Short Introduction*, Oxford University Press, New York, 1995.

Oakeshott, M., *Rationalism in Politics and Other Essays*, New and expanded ed., Liberty Fund, Indianapolis, 1991.

Okun, A., *Equality and Efficiency: The Big Tradeoff*, Brookings Institution, Washington, DC, 1975.

Olson, M., *The Logic of Collective Action: Public Goods and the Theory of Groups*, Schocken Books, New York, 1970.

Palley, T. I., From Keynesianism to neoliberalism: Shifting paradigms in economics. FPIF special report. Silver City, NM and Washington, DC. http://www.fpif.org/papers/2004keynesianism.html (accessed 5th May, 2004).

Popper, K., *The Poverty of Historicism*, Routledge and Kegan Paul, London, 1994/1957.

Rothstein, R. L., Consensual knowledge and international collaboration: some lessons from the commodity negotiations, *International Organization*, 38, 733–762, 1984.

Salisbury, R. H., Interest representation: the dominance of institutions, *American Political Science Review*, 78, 64–77, 1984.

Schattschneider, E. E., *The Semi-Sovereign People: A Realist's View of Democracy in America*, Holt, Rinehart, and Winston, New York, 1960.

Schattschneider, E. E., *Two Hundred Million People in Search of a Government*, Holt, Rinehart, and Winston, New York, 1969.

Schlozman, K. L. and Tierney, J. T., *Organized Interests and American Democracy*, Harper and Row, New York, 1986.

Schulman, P. R., Nonincremental policy making: notes toward an alternative paradigm, *American Political Science Review*, 69, 1354–1370, 1975.

Sowell, T., *The Vision of the Anointed: Self-Congratulation as a Basis for Social Policy*, Basic Books, New York, 1995.

Stanlis, P. J., *The Best of Burke: Selected Writings and Speeches*, Regnery Gateway, Washington, DC, 1963.

Steinbruner, J. D., *The Cybernetic Theory of Decision: New Dimensions of Political Analysis*, Princeton University Press, Princeton, NJ, 1974.

Waltman, J., *The Politics of the Minimum Wage*, University of Illinois Press, Urbana, 2000.

Wanniski, J., *The Way the World Works*, Simon and Schuster, Touchstone Books, New York, 1978.

Weiss, A. and Woodhouse, E., Reclaiming incrementalism: a constructive response to the critics, *Policy Sciences*, 2, 255–273, 1992.

Wildavsky, A. B., *The Politics of the Budgetary Process*, 4th ed., Little, Brown, Boston, 1984.

4 Bounded Rationality and Organizational Influence: Herbert Simon and the Behavioral Revolution

Matthew S. Mingus

CONTENTS

4.1 Introduction..61
4.2 Simon's Basic Model..62
    4.2.1 Satisficing..62
    4.2.2 Bounded Rationality...64
    4.2.3 Decision Making Premises...66
    4.2.4 Organizational Influence on Behavior..68
4.3 Modern Treatment and Continuing Relevance..71
    4.3.1 Treatment in Current Public Administration Textbooks...................................72
    4.3.2 Two Modern Challenges...73
    4.3.3 An Interesting Extension of Simon's Research...75
4.4 Conclusion 76
References...77

4.1 INTRODUCTION

Harlan Elison's *"Repent Harlequin!" Said the Ticktockman* (1974) depicts an utterly efficient world being destroyed by people who are occasionally late, driven to the point of absurdity as represented in the Harlequin. He has lost so many minutes of his life that the Ticktockman must find him to revoke his cardioplate. Rather than dangling in the realm of the implicit, Elison brings us head-on with the ultimate conundrum in society—should society serve the individual or should the individual serve society?

Ayn Rand has an ultimately simplistic answer to his question in *Atlas Shrugged* (1957) whereas C. Wright Mills treats this puzzle as a penetrable yet unanswerable question in *The Sociological Imagination* (1959). For Rand, the best society unleashes the power of the individual. Self-interest writ large spurs entrepreneurial creativity, thus generating societal efficiency. For Mills, the impact of the individual is largely limited within his *milieu*, where there is hope he may solve personal problems. Larger issues of institutions and society are beyond the problem-solving scope of the individual.

Here, amidst the behavioral revolution, we find Nobel Laureate Herbert Simon, toiling in the trenches to understand better how humans make decisions and how organizations may affect these decisions. He lived to be 84 years old and published in academic forums in seven different decades. This chapter explores the basic Simon model by discussing (1) satisficing, our decision making criteria; (2) bounded rationality, the scope we decide is relevant; and (3) decision making premises, the values and facts we apply when making decisions. An important contribution is Simon's focus on individuals. In his view, organizations cannot make decisions. However, organizational leaders have the ability to impact individual decision makers in each of these three areas and must use their power to achieve the desired outcomes of the organization.

Following this discussion we will explore (1) how Simon's work shifted the focus from organizational structure toward decision making, (2) how Simon is treated in current public administration texts, and (3) how modern researchers are extending Simon's ideas. Simon was extremely prolific and so much of his research is unavoidably excluded in favor of focusing on the collective theme of this volume—decision making. Other chapters in this *Handbook* provide a critique of Simon's work (see particularly the chapters by Nieuwenburg and Catlaw), while the primary goal of this chapter is to create a clear understanding of his basic model. Care has been taken to write this in an informal and accessible style; the reader should be able to understand these ideas without having read Simon's work but will need to read Simon's work to grasp the ample detail contained therein.

4.2 SIMON'S BASIC MODEL

It is no coincidence that Skinner's *The Behavior of Organisms* (1938) and *Science and Human Behavior* (1953) were published at the same time that Herbert Simon's research career was developing. Both researchers focus on the behavior of organisms within their environment and both apply scientific principles to argue that environments may alter behavior. In many ways, Simon changed the study of organizations by developing a linguistic and conceptual base for scientific analysis in the same way that Barry Bozeman recently developed concepts and language to enable scientific study of organizational red tape (2000). So why did he do this? In brief, Simon had already bought into logical positivism, as established by the Vienna Circle, and followed rapidly in the footsteps of Chester Barnard to bring these ideas into the field of public administration. Simon agreed, to a point, with Barnard's concept of organizations as systems of exchange. While Barnard conceptualized organizations as open systems, Simon closed them a bit with the fact-value dichotomy (Cruise, 1998, 281). In open systems theory, one could not "carve out" such a value-free subsystem. Both theorists, however, agreed that organizations prescribe the alternatives that individual decision makers can choose. Barnard's empiricism relied on direct observation and experience, but he was not committed to logical positivism, as was Simon (Cruise, 1998). In fact, Barnard was accepting of intuition and hunches as managerial tools, while Simon was more committed to intellectual ability and academic training.

Simon's view of logical positivism involved four principles: (1) the truth of any complex statement depends on simple statements that may be sensed, (2) only propositions that can be given meaning verifiably by scientific methods can be either true or false, (3) statements reveal the contents of our ideas rather than reporting truth about the world, and (4) statements of value are expressions of attitude and are neither true nor false (Cruise, 1998). The influence of these ideas on Simon should become clear in the following discussion of his core ideas of satisficing, bounded rationality, and decision making premises.

4.2.1 SATISFICING

A critical component of Simon's model for administrative behavior is the concept that people rarely optimize when they make decisions; instead, they satisfice. In contrast, the scientific management approach and the economic man model assume that decision makers are optimizers. Optimizers must study all available alternatives to determine which ones are most efficient or most likely to achieve the desired ends.

To accomplish this shift in thinking, Simon discusses multiple aspects of rationality rather than continuing the belief that "rationality" equals "comprehensively rational." Rationality, according to Simon, can be subconscious or conscious, objective or subjective, unintentional or deliberate, organizational or individual, and, ultimately, comprehensive or bounded: "Roughly speaking, rationality is concerned with the selection of preferred behavior alternatives in terms of some system of values whereby the consequences of behavior can be evaluated" (Simon, 1976, 75).

So what exactly is satisficing? Satisficing means that individual decision-makers have a minimally acceptable set of criteria, specified or unspecified, that they are looking for when seeking to solve a particular problem. In examining the set of alternative solutions, the first solution that appears to meet the set of criteria is usually accepted. Further examination of other alternatives is curtailed. In fact, individuals may not even make a list of the alternative approaches—a critical step in the rational-comprehensive approach—and instead may simply proceed from one possible alternative to the next until one satisfies the required criteria. This approach makes the "satisficing man" a sequential information processing system.

The model of the all-knowing, comprehensively rational, "economic man" succumbs to the satisficing man, who, lacking the wits or resources to find an optimal solution, seeks to find a satisfactory alternative. Satisficing man is not, however, simplistic. For example, if an acceptable solution comes too easily, it may be rejected or held at bay pending the analysis of another alternative. In addition, the level of effort put into finding a satisfactory solution is varied based on the perceived significance or lasting impact of the decision that must be made. For example, satisficing man would devote more time and resources to developing criteria and studying options for buying a house than for purchasing an automobile. What makes this a scientific process is that administration should be based on systematic, empirical analysis instead of casual observation, and decisions should result from an accumulation of empirical evidence rather than intuition.

This concept had an impact on the development of policy sciences, where three basic decision making approaches developed: incremental, rational comprehensive, and mixed scanning. In brief, the incremental approach is a conservative approach where existing policies are preferable to drastic changes, thereby making minor modifications of the status quo the path of change (see the chapter by Hayes in this volume for a detailed discussion of incrementalism). Such an approach is thought to be politically expedient as well as reducing the downside risk for decision makers. Such decision making is frequently associated with government more than the private sector, although it may be more accurate to say it is a common feature of bureaucracy, which is found in all large organizations. After all, most organizations applaud risk taking only after the fact. Chandler and Plano insist that Charles Lindblom "may have claimed too much for incremental decision making when he argued that small changes avoid making monumental errors. That would be true only if the status quo itself were sound and conditions affecting it remained static" (1988, 129). In today's fast paced environment, the former may be more common than the latter.

At the other extreme lies the rational comprehensive approach of systems analysts and many economists. In this approach, one would make decisions by clarifying the values, studying all possible means to the desired ends, and choosing the most effective and efficient means to that end through a comprehensive analysis (often, this is a cost-benefit analysis). Zero-based budgeting (ZBB) was an attempt to apply this model to the world of financial decision making. The ZBB approach required budget analysts to justify spending in a given budget cycle from the first dollar, rather than focusing the budget process primarily on changes from the prior budget. In addition, budgets consisted of various decision packages, each of which could be approved or denied independent of other policy or program budget packages. Such budgets were intended to enable prioritization and a sense of supporting packages that best achieved the desired ends.

This rational comprehensive approach tends to idealize decision making by assuming that one knows all relevant information, that one can see into the future when determining the consequences of each alternative decision, and that one can take a "brand new" policy or decision even though the status quo obviously is already in place. Only someone with a very long-term view of efficiency could argue that an extremely efficient new policy sufficiently justifies a disruption in the current way of doing things.

Between these two approaches lies Amatai Etzioni's mixed scanning model, published in 1967. Along with Simon, Etzioni "recognizes the limited human capability to secure purely rational decisions" and argues that decision makers "intentionally truncate the scope of their review" (Chandler and Plano, 1988, 129–130). Etzioni's model combines the idea that scanning for alternative solutions will occur at various levels and provides a set of criteria to determine which level(s) to emphasize in different situations. Comparable to incrementalism and the rational-comprehensive approach, the two extreme levels of scanning *include* "truncated" and "full detail" (Etzioni, 1967).

It is difficult to comprehend how Etzioni could publish this model more than 20 years after Simon's *Administrative Behavior* without making a single reference to Simon's works. While he seems to embrace Simon's model overall, in one spot he critiques the model:

> The structures within which interactions among actors take place become more significant the more we recognize that the bases of decisions neither are nor can be a fully ordered set of values and an exhaustive examination of reality. In part, the strategy followed [in mixed scanning] is determined neither by values nor by information but by the positions of and power relations among the decision-makers. (Etzioni, 1967, 391)

At once this seems to question Simon's focus on decision premises and pushes the focus beyond the behavioral revolution and toward the postmodern concern for relationships and interconnectedness. Specifically this can be seen in the focus of postmodern policy analysts on dialogue, discourse, participation, and democracy.

Frequently confused with bounded rationality, satisficing refers to the desired ends rather than the decision making process. If one is seeking the best possible outcome, then one is optimizing. If one is looking for a solution that meets a set of acceptable standards, then one is satisficing. In one of his more technical articles, "A Behavioral Model of Rational Choice," Simon even goes so far as to suggest that what might satisfice at one time might not satisfice at other times: "The models thus far discussed are dynamic only in a very special sense: the aspiration level at time t depends upon the previous history of the system (previous aspiration levels and previous levels of attainment)" (1955, 113). In other words, during the satisficing process, past experiences deemed relevant to a new situation drive human perceptions.

4.2.2 Bounded Rationality

Simon's work is part of the behavioral revolution—part of his fundamental quarrel with the structuralists of the 1930s—given his belief that "Decisions are made *in the mind*. Mental choices are decidedly limited because complete and absolute knowledge of all the data in a given situation is seldom available" (Chandler and Plano, 1988, 155). To Simon, it is simply impossible for managers to make decisions with a high degree of rationality because information requirements for comprehensive rationality are too high, and human analytical capabilities are too low. In Simon's words,

> the task is to replace the global rationality of economic man with a kind of rational behavior that is compatible with the access to information and the computational capacities that are actually possessed by organisms, including man, in the kinds of environments in which such organisms exist. (1955, 99)

Simon never abandoned the goal of rational decision making in his research. In fact, he won the Nobel Prize in Economics in 1978 for his revelations about how humans actually make decisions in organizational settings. Decision making, he argued, although quite rational, is far from comprehensive. Rational theories of decision making assume external factors such as cost, time, and available technology constrain individual choices. Occasionally choices may be limited by legislative or legal constraints. In contrast, bounded rationality includes factors such as poor memory, inadequate human or computer analytical power, the tendency of individuals to satisfice, and the differential importance of necessary decisions. As Simon notes:

> The central concern of administrative theory is with the boundary between the rational and the nonrational aspects of human social behavior. Administrative theory is peculiarly the theory of intended and bounded rationality—of the behavior of human beings who satisfice because they have not the wits to maximize. (Simon, 1976, xxviii)

Three specific limits of objective rationality include the incompleteness of knowledge, the difficulty of anticipating or predicting what will occur in the future (and the value we will attach to future events when they occur), and the inadequate scope of alternative behaviors that are considered or analyzed (Simon, 1976, 80–84). Counterintuitively, incomplete knowledge likely will impose a bigger limit on rationality in the "information age" than it did in the past. Though knowledge may more likely exist in greater quantities, a decision maker will be less likely to be able to sift through all the existing information and identify and analyze what is relevant. In regard to this dilemma, Simon insists that one will focus on "only those factors most closely connected with the decision in cause and time," and that rational choice becomes feasible "to the extent that significant indirect effects are absent (1976, 82–83).

The second limit—difficulties in anticipation—probably has not changed much over time because it concerns not the theoretical ability to predict the consequences of our behaviors, but the ability to understand the emotions that we will attach to future events (i.e., anticipated pleasure). Looking at risky behavior, for example, Simon stated, "It is not so much that the experience of loss leads to attaching a higher probability to the occurrence of loss [after a risky venture fails to succeed] as that the desire to avoid the consequences of loss has been strengthened" (1976, 83).

Human procreation provides an example because rationality essentially fights against the "hard wired" biological imperative to continue the species, the reality of the aging process, and the emotional dynamics of relationships, all of which limit our rationality. In short, the anticipation of sexual experience and the experience itself fail to align with great regularity. Perhaps, for this reason, literally millions of men not suffering from impotence use pharmaceuticals such as Viagra, Levitra, and Cialis, while millions of other men purchase their herbal "equivalents," which are mass marketed primarily *via* electronic mail and web site advertising. In this case, men who would like their actual experiences to be the same as their anticipated or imagined experiences are spending literally billions of dollars. Rationality, based on their own empirical experiences, should suggest to them that what they believe to be anticipation is actually their imagination. The imagination drives them (i.e., is biologically hard wired) to procreate and will always exceed the rewards of their lived experience. What we observe nowadays is the effect of extensive advertisement and internet-based pornography fueling the natural imagination. Humans fail to be rational when they do not adjust their anticipation to their concrete experiences.

Simon also portrayed the third limit on rationality, failing to include all possible behaviors in the analytical process, as a failure of the imagination. Habit or organizational routine, for example, "performs an extremely important task in purposive behavior," and much training is designed to support the development of instantaneous habitual response patterns (Simon, 1976, 88). Actual behavior, as opposed to objectively rational behavior, is initiated by stimuli that channel attention in specific directions. The flip side of this is that many directions fail to be explored. The habitual responses are not necessarily irrational, but are highly unlikely to adapt to a dynamic environment, as habitual and dynamic are practically antonyms. Organizations often supply these stimuli to encourage individuals to make decisions in the interests of the organization.

Together, these limits on objectively rational behavior start to form Simon's concept of bounded rationality. This concept describes individual administrators' actual decision making in complex environments rather than some pathology of administration or bureaucracy. This approach differs significantly from Robert Merton's extension of trained incapacity and occupational psychosis into the bureaucracy (1940). While Simon does not negate Merton, Simon focuses on how people make decisions and how organizations, rather than personality, can impact this process. In short, the administrator will leave out all irrelevant factors by establishing boundaries that define the scope of problem solving in which the administrator will engage.

The word "establishing" does not imply that these boundaries are formalized or in writing. Rather, the process is formal and largely linear in the rational model, which features a decision maker who moves through preanalysis (problem definition), analysis, design (options are crystallized), choice (alternatives are evaluated and optimal choice is selected), and implementation (Denhardt, 2002, 128). These stages are performed deliberately and consciously in the rational model, whereas Simon argues that humans have cognitive limits and are more inclined to tackle meaningful subsets of problems (because humans are self aware and thus sense their own limits).

In organizational theory, Simon is associated with the decision-making approach rather than the classical or human relations approaches. Although he rejects comprehensive rationality, Simon still relies on human rationality by focusing on the premises people use to make decisions in pursuit of organizational goals.

4.2.3 DECISION MAKING PREMISES

The third key aspect of Simon's model introduces decision-making premises as units of analysis. Most organizational research has viewed individual managers, specific departments, specific decision, or entire organizations as the units of analysis Simon proposes instead that decision makers use two sets of premises to make decisions: one set grounded in facts that are empirically verifiable and another set grounded in values, which may be "good" or "bad" rather than "true" or "correct" (1976, 47). No evidence suggests that this tension existed prior to Simon's research (Glasman and Nevo, 1988, 20).

The days of scientific management focused explicitly on gathering the facts leading to efficient production, selecting employees based on skills and abilities, and training them to do the job "right" based on the collected facts. Picture Frederick Taylor with a stop watch, measuring five people doing the same repetitive task, over and over, until he could determine who was best at specific parts of the task, discern the optimal steps for completing the task, and, finally, train the others to adopt this "most efficient" approach to the task (Taylor, 1911). This era of scientific management assumed that efficiency was the core value while facts (i.e., objective information, analytically considered) were the means to achieve this value. The focus on management and decision making largely was based on the facts. In contrast, Simon argued that two types of decisions existed: rational or fact-based decisions and ethical or value-based decisions.

The two types of decisions do not represent a simplistic dichotomy for at least four reasons. First, the "ethical component" of decisions should not be confused with the use of judgment in decision making. Judgment may involve, for example, an unspecified knowledge based on decades of experience that lead one to make the best choice (Schmidt, 1993). This need not be about values or ethics because "factual" is a broadly defined concept—"a statement about the observable world is factual if, in principle, its truth or falsity may be tested. That is, if certain events occur, we say the statement was true; if other events occur, we say that it was false" (Simon, 1976, 50–51). The veracity of a factual premise, therefore, does not need to be known in advance to consider that the decision maker is making a rational choice. Time will tell if the decision premise was correct or not.

Second, ethical premises or propositions usually have factual components. This may go without saying, but for Simon, this duality marks the difference between intermediate and ultimate values. For example, does one study public administration because one values education or because one perceives it as a means to get a stable, professional job? Such "means-ends relationships" determine the values being pursued, and if the apparent value is an intermediate value then one ought to be able objectively to determine whether the apparent value acheives the desired end value. That is a factual conversation, whereas determining the value of such ultimate objectives is an ethical conversation. Because it is a factual conversation, one can utilize rational decision making by comparing alternative means for achieving the desired ends (Simon, 1976, 65).

Thirdly, means and ends are seldom neatly subdivided because one's "ends" depend on where one is in the organizational scheme of things. Many people tend to think of ends as values. Such a view is increasingly true today, when, for example, business consultants push an organizational mission statement as a clear articulation of the organization's overriding values and then argue that organizational subunits (departments, work teams, etc.), in turn, need their own values or mission statements. Subunits can best contribute by taking the organization-wide mission as the starting point for developing a statement of how the subunit will contribute to or implement the organizational mission. These subunit statements should include measurable objectives that can be factually demonstrated to contribute to the ultimate end. Put in another way, Simon states:

> There is, then, no essential difference between a "purpose" and a "process," but only a distinction of degree. A "process" is an activity whose immediate purpose is at a low level in the hierarchy of means and ends, while a "purpose" is a collection of activities whose operating value or aim is at a high level in the means-end hierarchy. (1976, 32)

Fourth, the role of legislatures, and the need for legislators to be reelected, thwarts the view that the fact-value distinction is a simple dichotomy. In theory the legislature would clearly spell out its decisions, which administrators would then use as their objectives. At the organizational level, senior managers would spell out the value premises, which others would then use in making decisions. In reality, Simon says the route to reelection often avoids clear-cut policy decisions, and such indecision is passed on to administrative agencies (1976, 58).

In the public administration literature, Simon is one of the key figures who dismantles the notion of the politics-administration dichotomy. He seeks to avoid simply replacing this dichotomy with the fact-value dichotomy by calling it the fact-value "distinction" and by stressing its complexites. Nevertheless, Simon also believes that the allocation of decisions to legislative bodies should depend on the relative importance of the factual and ethical premises of the decision (Simon, 1976, 58). He supports the notion that a professional technocracy should handle the scientific, factual decisions required to implement the value-based political decisions (Stillman, 1998).

In spite of these complexities, the notion that decision making entails the control of factual and ethical premises is an enduring impact of Simon's work. This analytical approach encourages one to view each decision as being driven by a number of premises, both factual and ethical, and to strive for rational decision making when only factual premises are involved.

Such an approach contrasts with Weber's version of rationality, which is generally viewed as a legalistic, rules-based rationality. While Weber outlines three forms of "legitimate domination," legal-rational authority is the basis for bureaucratic control, while traditional authority and charismatic authority are more common elsewhere in society (Schreurs, 2003). Petra Schreurs explains that the latter two are forms of "personal authority" rather than "objective, impersonal order." It seems logically possible for society to be ordered so that traditional authority and charismatic authority drive the decisions of political institutions, while legal rationality drives the bureaucracy. At the macro level, such an approach might resemble Simon's fact-value distinction, but Simon focuses more within the organization.

4.2.4 Organizational Influence on Behavior

Two minds are better than one. Depending on one's point of view, this adage points either to the difficulty of managing in the real world or to the inherently social nature of human beings. This saying rings true for anyone undertaking a complex task, such as building a house. If the architect were the only thinker on the job site, the house would remain in shambles. Yet, if others think outside their relevant boundaries the architect's work might be undone. For example, an architect's blueprints specify only the horizontal orientation of a window. The lead carpenter needs to know how high to place them off the floor. Blueprints also depend on other "systems" in which much of the thought is already done. For example, electrical codes determine where plugs and switches are installed in a house, except when the architect or contractor specifies otherwise. The architect presumes this knowledge will be utilized and thus needs only document departures from the norm.

So, are three minds better than two? Are ten minds better than three? Are a hundred minds better than ten? At what point do we either revert to the historical roots of administrations organized as hierarchical structures ruled by the unity of command or accept that inherently messy concepts of vision, participation, and even universal consciousness are more attuned to today's complex environment? (Mingus, 2006). The example of building a home suggests that coordination is key and that the mind at the top must rely on minds throughout the system to get the job done. Some of these minds must react according to previous training and specific written rules (i.e., like an electrician following the code). Other minds must simply do what is specified unless the departure from normal patterns warrants questioning authority (i.e., an experienced workman taking instructions from a lead carpenter will know when to ask, "Is this door really going to be five feet wide?").

A recent program solicitation on human and social dynamics from the United States National Science Foundation (NSF) notes, "Individuals often act through collective entities like organizations, which have interests and behave in ways that are distinct from and often not easily predicted by the behavior and interests of the individuals that constitute them" (National Science Foundation 2004, 8). The solicitation, among other things, encourages studies on the similarities and differences in individual and organizational motivations, the effects of organizational embeddedness on individuals, and the capacity of public and private organizations to assimilate information. Simon's view on this topic, as it relates to decision making, is that organizations control individuals by influencing their decision premises:

> Given a complete set of value and factual premises, there is only one decision, which is consistent with rationality. That is, within a given set of values, and a specified set of alternatives, there is one alternative that is preferable to others.... The behavior of a rational person can be controlled, therefore, if the value and factual premises upon which he bases his decisions are specified for him. (1976, 223)

He clearly would agree with the modern NSF perspective that the decision-making behavior of individuals is the key to understanding organizations. Simon's administrative man leaves out all irrelevant factors, including information that might help optimize rather than satisfice and information outside the bounds of the current decision, such as information on interrelationships that are too complex to grasp (Chandler and Plano, 1988, 5; Senge 1990, chapter 4). Such an approach is not a sign of Merton's bureaucratic pathologies, because humans do this even when they are making individual or personal decisions. In Simon's view this is simply a realistic portrayal of human decision making.

To unleash the power of organizations, managers must learn to control the way that the human mind seeks to simplify the complex environment. This is a natural part of involvement in organizations. Following Chester Barnard's view, "For Simon, it was necessary for individuals to lose autonomy if they were to function well in organizations. Losing autonomy means that the individual accepts authoritatively made decisions of the manager and organization as legitimate"

(Cayer and Weschler 2003, 106). This involves understanding satisficing, bounded rationality, and decision premises, and seeking to control them. Organizations provide roles that help members know how to act and react to particular situations, teach them how to reason, and explain to them what information is relevant for specific decisions. They push people to apply their normal processes in ways that will benefit the organizational mission. These processes of influence are discussed in more detail in March and Simon's *Organizations* (1958) which contains several chapters on motivational constraints.

Simon credits Barnard's *Functions of the Executive* (1938) as a highly influential source, which increased his belief that decision making was at the heart of administrative life and reinforced his belief that "Life in organizations is not very different from life elsewhere" (1991, 73). Bounded rationality, for example, is "not specifically an organizational concept. It applies as fully to individual decision making as to organizational decision making" (1991, 87).

People are going to satisfice. Managers may apply legitimate authority by setting high expectations for issues determined as "high priority" by the organization. In this way, natural satisficing on the most important issues will approximate optimization. By conveying to employees critical, important, and minor issues, managers can help them determine the level of effort and resources to apply when making decisions. In addition, employees must clearly understand the relevant time constraints for particular decisions. This is important to satisficing because, for example, a critical decision that must be made quickly may call for a more truncated search for a solution than an important decision for whose execution plenty of time still exists. In the longer term, tools such as job descriptions, employee evaluations, and subgoals may help communicate these ideas to employees. In the short term, managers need to communicate clearly with their employees rather than assume that employees will know how to prioritize all the decisions they need to make in a given period of time.

Organizations also can help control the application of bounded rationality. In both positive and negative ways, organizations bound the decisions that individual managers and employees will make. The familiar concept of groupthink is, in many ways, a negative form of bounded rationality. It is negative because it is generally an unconscious individual avoidance of possible alternative solutions—particularly the creative or risky ones—driven by the desire to "fit in" or "conform." This social principle seemingly would drive organizations to avoid new, creative, or risky solutions (i.e., those that are outside established boundaries or "past solutions") in favor of established or known solutions (i.e., inside perceived boundaries or the "status quo"). Groupthink may thus mean rationality is too narrowly bounded to promote a truly successful organization because the alternatives that get explored in the rational decision- making process may not include valuable new ideas.

This calls to mind an episode of *The West Wing*, a popular American television show that is set in the White House. In this episode, Palestinian terrorists allegedly kill an American general and two congressmen. The President calls a late night meeting with his top advisors and says he wants to hear new and crazy ideas for dealing with this situation. Meanwhile numerous Americans and congressional representatives are in a frenzy demanding immediate retaliatory bombings. A measure of executive persistence leads to the new idea that getting the Palestinian chairman to turn over the suspected bomber for trial in the United States might calm the situation and bring Israel back to the table for peace talks. This fictional executive enabled creative thinking among his staff by lifting the boundary of "political realism" for a short period of time. Similarly, real administrators have the ability to observe and alter the boundaries their employees use to narrow the search for decisions.

Finally, organizational leaders seek to control individual decision making by focusing on factual and value-based premises that are used by individuals when making decisions. As John Little understood it,

> The organization tries to influence the individual by supplying him with, at least some, decision premises. The most characteristic method for this is authority, which is the course of an organization's

formal structure… An organization's actions can be explained, even controlled, by identifying and understanding its decision premises. (Little, 1994, 75–77)

In *Mastering Public Administration*, Brian Fry goes a step further by saying that,

When the individual has decided to participate and produce, the organizational problem is reduced to one of providing the appropriate premises for individual decision making in the organization. For Simon, the primary responsibility for the provision of decision premises lies with the hierarchy…. Simon contends that hierarchy is the adaptive form for finite intelligence to take in the face of complexity. (Fry, 1989, 200)

Organizational structure is relevant, therefore, because a complex hierarchical organizational structure simplifies decision making by reducing the need for information transmission. Controlling the decision premises, from the manager's perspective, helps employees think like the manager thinks. Therefore, employees are more likely to make the same decisions as managers when confronted with the same information.

So how are premises formed and shaped by organizations? One way is through hiring processes. Organizations can hire people who share their existing premises, both value-based and factual, by hiring people with similar educational and professional backgrounds. Another way is through orientation and training programs, employee participation in planning processes, routine communication through newsletters and the like—strategies akin to ongoing propaganda. Likewise, the more critical certain classes of decisions are to an organization, the more the premises can be controlled through clearly spelled-out processes and procedures. For example, universities usually seek to control the quality of their output by having a program of study form, student advisors, and graduation audits. The program of study form, more or less, makes sure that the student understands the requirements for degree completion, allows advisors to ensure that students progress toward degree completion, and permits auditors to confirm or dispute that all requirements have been met. If all three groups were operating under different decision premises, chaos would reign.

In Simon's terms, the program of study form just described is a stimulus for repetitive decision making. This and similar stimuli-driven processes lead to programmed decision making that can allow the organization to focus more resources on making good decisions in areas where significant uncertainty exists. While other "nonprogrammed decisions are made in response to novel stimuli for which no structured response exists" (Fry, 1989, 204), search activities for these decisions still depend on premises that can be prescribed by the organization and its culture.

For example, organizations will nearly always search for solutions utilizing existing skills and talents before seeking outside assistance in the search for an appropriate decision. Likewise, because nonprogrammed decisions are related to novel problems, people will not search for structural solutions. In other words, people assume novel problems are transient problems rather than permanent problems; they may even deny the problem exists at all. Experience and judgment ultimately determine if a problem is novel or repetitive, and at some point, managers or staff must recognize new patterns and develop structural responses.

In Simon's model, organizations have the ability to influence individual decision making by helping individuals know how much to satisfice, by providing a sense of what boundaries should be applied in the search for solutions, and by identifying and reinforcing key value-based and factual premises that should be used when making decisions. Legislators in a government, managers in an organization, and maybe even parents in a family do have a sense of control in Herbert Simon's world and they need to understand the leverage points by understanding human decision making.

4.3 MODERN TREATMENT AND CONTINUING RELEVANCE

Perhaps more than any other figure in managerial, organizational, or administrative theory, Simon drove the shift from organizational structure to decision making. In effect, Simon created the decision-making approach within organizational theory at a time when the classical-rational and human relations approaches were dominant. While Little's (1994) interpretation of Simon's perspective was more critical than mine, he also agreed that Simon's view of administration became the dominant perspective within both public administration and mainstream organizational theory.

In fact, Gareth Morgan's *Images of Organization* (1998) is almost unique among organizational theory textbooks because it barely recognizes the impact of Herbert Simon. It is far more common to have a text like Richard Steers and Stewart Black's *Organizational Behavior* (1994) which devotes a chapter to individual and group decision making and puts Herbert Simon in the pivotal role of moving organizational theory beyond the strictures of the classical-rational model. They explain that Simon's views dominate with regard to programmed decisions and then cite nonprogrammed decisions as the area that flourished after Simon's ideas became mainstream.

Why was Simon able to play such a pivotal role? Part of the answer lies in the breadth of his understanding. He held academic positions in political science, public administration, psychology, informational science, and computer science, and had over 950 publications to his credit in these fields as well as in applied mathematics, statistics, operations analysis, economics, sociology, business administration, and others. Simon was the very definition of a multidisciplinarian and this quality allowed him to have a significant impact on the shift toward decision making across a wide spectrum of academic disciplines. Mie Augier and James March put it bluntly: "Simon was precociously inattentive to disciplinary and field boundaries" (2001, 399). He reportedly only chose to complete his doctoral studies at the University of Chicago in political science because their economics program required an accounting course, and then he gravitated toward the more applied research in public administration.

As with much new knowledge, Simon added a layer to organizational and administrative studies. Simon did not eliminate the need to think in terms of organizational structure because, as discussed earlier, that hierarchy was essential for organizations to impact the behavior of individuals. Hierarchy was addressed in Max Weber's early works on bureaucracy and falls firmly within the classical approach. Simon also steadfastly maintained a focus on efficiency, in keeping with Woodrow Wilson, Frederick Taylor, Leonard White, and so many of his predecessors in the field of public administration.

Nevertheless, this behavioral approach was significantly new and became the basis for the third American textbook in public administration, *Public Administration*, which Simon coauthored with Donald Smithburg and Thompson (1950). His *Administrative Behavior* grew in popularity through four editions and easily edged out all other books for the top spot in Frank Sherwood's assessment of the most influential books in 50 years of public administration (1990). James D. Thompson's *Organizations in Action* also made this list of books and extended Simon's focus on the role of organizations in decision making (Hall, 1991). Robert Golembiewski attributed much of Simon's success to his ability to establish the language that others eventually would use when discussing organizational decision making. As Simon had noted himself, "if you can set someone's vocabulary, you influence or even dominate that person's thought" (Golembiewski, 1988, 265–266). Golembiewski was not a believer in most of Simon's ideas, even arguing at one point that Simon failed to offer a new model (268), but he certainly believed in the impact those ideas had on public administration and organizational studies.

The lifelong impact and continued relevance of Simon's work is exemplified in two specific projects: (1) Robert Golembiewski's *two-issue symposium* for *Public Administration Quarterly* in 1988 and 1989 in recognition of the 40th anniversary of *Administrative Behavior* and (2) Peter Earl's edited collection, *The Legacy of Herbert Simon in Economic Analysis, Volumes I and II*

(2001). Neither project started out with two volumes in mind, but both projects served as excellent starting points to understand the depth and breadth of Simon's impact. Because of the continued relevance of Herbert Simon's model, the remainder of this section looks at the treatment of Simon's ideas in current public administration textbooks, discusses several modern challenges to Simon's work, and presents an interesting extension of Simon's research.

4.3.1 TREATMENT IN CURRENT PUBLIC ADMINISTRATION TEXTBOOKS

One might expect that Simon would be a major topic in introductory public administration texts, with his Nobel Prize and 65-year history of publishing in the field. However, a review of five leading introductory textbooks in public administration revealed minimal treatment of Herbert Simon and his ideas. While only one of them has extensive coverage of Simon, all of them mention Simon and provide some treatment of his ideas (Denhardt and Grubbs, 2003; Henry, 2001; Rozenbloom and Kravchuk, 2002; Shafritz and Russell, 2003; Stillman, 2000).

Richard Stillman states early on that "Herbert Simon's book... made, however, the most profound and original theoretical impact on postwar administrative sciences in the United States" (2000, 22). Earlier editions of this text included a reading coauthored by Simon, and the current edition mentions Simon's work in at least six places. Stillman incorporates one paragraph on his impact in general, one paragraph on the idea that administrative rationality depends on uniform value premises in the decisional centers of organizations, and over two pages on his work with Smithburg and Thompson, particularly focused on administrative communication and communication networks.

Shafritz and Russell use less space on Simon, but their text incorporates a heading, "Herbert A. Simon's Influence," under which they discuss the key themes of his life's work. This blurb seeks to explain bounded rationality and satisficing in one brief paragraph. Elsewhere in the text they have another paragraph on bounded rationality as a rejection of the rational comprehensive approach and one paragraph on his "The Proverbs of Public Administration" article (Simon, 1946).

Rosenbloom and Kravchuk grant Simon the key role in helping the field understand that Weber overstated the extent to which bureaucrats are able to behave rationally. They also grant him equal status with Dwight Waldo as the destroyer of "the intellectual underpinnings of the orthodox approach," yet state that neither theorist managed to replace the earlier theoretical paradigm (2002, 183). Importantly, when discussing decision making, Rosenbloom and Kravchuk explain that the traditional managerial approach accepts the reality of bounded rationality because the world is complex and consequences are frequently unknowable, and then attempts to "enhance rationality through specialization, hierarchy, formalization, and technical competence" (2002, 342). While not directly devoting much space to Simon, they devote extensive space to decision making and explain his impact in this area quite well.

This treatment seems more appropriate than Stillman's current treatment, which acknowledges Simon's pivotal role, yet devotes most of the discussion on Simon to the idea of communication networks. Stillman's purpose, however, was likely to show that network theory may be trendy, but is far from a new idea. By focusing on communication, however, he seems to leave out the point that Simon liked hierarchy precisely because it could transmit decision premises with far less communication than other organizational structures.

On this point, Denhardt and Grubbs hit the nail on the head by arguing that Simon's work helped counter "the field's dependence on a structural interpretation of organizational life," but failed to question the top-down pattern of organizational authority (2003, 310). In addition to this critical theory perspective, they present satisficing and bounded rationality in their chapter on decision making in organizations and again, more intensively, in their chapter on personal skills in public management. They conclude that the "satisficing model" is a more accurate description of how human beings make decisions than the rational decision-making model, which is really a prescription for how to make better decisions (2003, 382).

Unlike numerous textbooks, Denhardt and Grubbs pay far more attention to Simon's work than to Charles Lindblom's incremental model of decision making. Many texts simply use a sentence or two on Simon to show where Lindblom's ideas might have originated.

Henry's textbook is the only one of these five that treats the work of Herbert Simon in an extensive manner. He starts in a typical way by describing how Simon punctured the principles of public administration, but also suggests that Simon did replace the orthodox with a new paradigm:

> For Simon, a new paradigm for public administration meant that there ought to be two kinds of public administrationists working in harmony and reciprocal intellectual stimulation: those scholars concerned with developing "a pure science of public administration" based on "a thorough grounding in social psychology," and a larger group concerned with "prescribing public policy." (Henry, 2001, 34)

Henry presents the work of Simon and his colleagues in at least ten different places in his text, including several multi-page discussions. He associates Simon with the above-mentioned paradigm shift that has resulted in the nearly separate fields of public administration and public policy, with a synthesized model of organizations, with information processing and the rise of computers and automation, with organizational decision making, with the idea that power in organizations runs top-down and bottom-up (i.e., employees must choose to accept authority), with the figure of the administrative man as a bridge between the economic man and the psychological man, and with performance measurement. Henry's inclusion of Simon's entire career, as represented by this broad range of topics, makes his study by far the most comprehensive treatment.

While modern texts certainly should not treat Simon as the "do all, be all" of public administration theory, this coverage in five extremely popular introductory textbooks speaks to the need for supplemental readings for the serious student of public administration. These readings may find their way into the public administration curriculum in foundations courses, organizational theory and behavior courses, or public management courses. There are also accessible books like Brian Fry's *Mastering Public Administration: From Max Weber to Dwight Waldo* (1989) which includes Simon as one of eight key figures in the development of American public administration. Such biographical approaches offer much to students of administration and decision making in the same way that Robert Heilbroner's *The Worldly Philosophers* (1972) added life to the study of key economists since Adam Smith. In addition, Simon's ideas are still used to frame a great deal of active research in management, administration, and economics.

4.3.2 TWO MODERN CHALLENGES

Herbert Simon won the Nobel Prize in Economics for his revelations regarding how humans actually make decisions. Decision making, he argued, is quite rational, but far from comprehensive. Instead of using all available information, most human decisions are made within fairly tight constraints or parameters (i.e., bounded rationality). This focus on rationality—albeit redefined—has led to challenges from philosophical quarters and from the "new sciences."

On the philosophical front, Jay White's "Images of Administrative Reason and Rationality: The Recovery of Practical Discourse" clearly puts a dent in Simon's armor. White effectively explains that Simon's rationality is instrumental reasoning, effectively ignoring the use of interpretive and critical reasoning by public administrators. White equates the legal-rational mode of thought with instrumental reason and states that "Simon still clings to instrumental thought and action, but speaks of reason in terms of behavioral images of creativity and intuition…. Simon was aware that other modes of thought and action are involved in determining means and ends" (1990, 135–136).

Simon views reason as instrumental and understands that intuition and good judgment are needed to tell us where to go. Instrumentalism, however, can tell us how to get there. We might thus equate Simon's decisions based on factual premises with instrumental reason and understand that other forms of reason may be utilized for decisions based on value premises. White (1990, 137) would still insist that these "other forms" should be much broader than Simon's behavioral approach allows. In short, he suggests that the rational model "does not explain the logic of how decision makers recognize problems, identify goals and alternatives, and choose among different goals and alternatives" (White, 1990, 135).

On the interpretive side, White carefully explains that administrators interpret the intent of those who establish policies, and they also decide which past cases are relevant to current cases. On the critical front, he points to the process of self-reflection—deciding what needs to be done by looking inward for relevant norms and values. Both approaches frequently depend upon discourse, yet White is not making a theoretical argument for discourse like Habermas or Gadamer. Instead, he is explaining that these are two common non-instrumental approaches that administrators actually use to make decisions on a day-to-day basis.

Further evidence of Simon's instrumental leaning comes from his extensive mid-career focus on computer information and decision making systems in texts such as *The Sciences of the Artificial* (1969) and *The New Science of Management Decision* (1977). Evidence in learning theory and brain development suggests humans are becoming more visual and faster paced (or less patient), but does not suggest that overall capacity for handling information has increased in any way. Research on the young and the old and changes in television programming in recent years, for example, demonstrate the change in the pace of life. In general, younger people can take in information at a much faster pace than adults and the elderly, but this does not provide assurance that retention or analysis of the information will occur. This body of Simon's work, however, focuses largely on processing, and he views cognition in an organization as a group of individuals exchanging information within a system of roles or within prescribed decision premises (Boland, Tenkasi, and Te'eni, 1996, 247). Broader discussions of what "ought" to be done do not fit easily into Simon's way of thinking.

The second challenge to Simon's life work comes from the new sciences, not at all related to the "new science" of information systems referred to in his 1977 book title. In the beginning of American Public Administration, admittedly a narrow subset of public administration throughout the world, there were strong influences from the likes of Woodrow Wilson, Frederick Taylor, and Max Weber. Wilson argued that we must focus on governmental administration rather than constitution building, and intimated that administration should be a scientific study. Taylor filled out this idea with scientific management and Weber focused on an approach to organizational structure—the ideal-type bureaucracy—that resonated with Taylor's ideas. While these were not the only ideas available to scholars or practitioners at the time, Richard Stillman convincingly explains how they were embodied in Luther Gulick's POSDCoRB model to form a pre-World War II orthodoxy (Stillman, 1998).

Under the name of the "new sciences," these origins often have been grouped to indicate the origins of public administration or management in linear, Newtonian ways of thinking, which, as the next step of the argument often proceeds, are not supported by new sciences such as chaos theory in mathematics, quantum theory in physics, autopoiesis in biology, the emerging superstring theory or "theory of everything," and so forth. Margaret Wheatley made this argument at a broad level in *Leadership and the New Sciences* (1992) while Douglas Kiel, Euel Elliott, and colleagues provided the details in a series of books, including *Managing Chaos and Complexity in Government, Chaos Theory in the Social Sciences*, and *Nonlinear Dynamics, Complexity and Public Policy* (Elliott and Kiel, 1996; 1999; Kiel, 1994).

A few key ideas from the new sciences are in apparent conflict with Simon's thoughts. Self-organization, which implies that people in an organization will come to a collective sense of purpose or vision through the process of interacting, is much more a participatory concept than a hierarchical one. It fits White's notions of interpretive discourse far better than Simon's rational model. In fact, Simon warned against the habit of personifying organizations, insisting that only individuals can think, learn, or make decisions (Boland, Tenkasi and Te'eni, 1996). Next, the idea of quantum interconnectedness may mean that any boundaries established to help make decisions are potentially dangerous oversimplifications (Mingus, 2006). That creates an obvious conflict with bounded rationality because any boundary inherently ignores the system as a whole. Finally, participatory collusion—meaning that the observer has an impact on what is being observed—goes to the heart of the assumption that people will apply the decision premises promoted by their superiors. This idea suggests that employees may not be neutral implementers; they may pick and choose among available factual premises and even apply their own set of value premises in making decisions. Communication may go awry because employees may recognize premises that resonate with their own history and way of thinking, thereby severely limiting the ability of the organization to influence its members.

Simon represents the old Newtonian sciences—seeking solutions based on rationality and a largely top-down or mechanical process. His main break with the top-down approach entailed his recognition that an employee chooses whether or not to accept the legitimate authority of the organization—the so-called zone of acceptance. Simon weakens his argument by assuming that acceptance occurs only when people join organizations rather than every time a decision needs to be made. Either way, Simon's overall rational perspective would be difficult to reconcile with basic concepts derived from the new sciences.

4.3.3 An Interesting Extension of Simon's Research

The Center for Adaptive Behavior and Cognition in Berlin, ABC Research Group for short, has extensively studied decision-making heuristics. Heuristics are the building blocks humans use to make inferences, and, thus, decisions. Their work may yet prove to be the most exciting and meaningful extension of Simon's work to date.

In their edited book *Simple Heuristics that Make Us Smart*, Gerd Gigerenzer, Peter Todd, and the ABC Research Group (1999) make a strong case for how "fast and frugal" heuristics serve humans extremely well. Fast and frugal heuristics are a simplification on satisficing in that they "employ a minimum of time, knowledge, and computation to make adaptive choices in real environments" (14). They consider fast and frugal heuristics to represent bounded rationality in its purest form.

Many of the authors in this volume pay particular tribute to the work of Herbert Simon. Their collective research suggests that there are just four visions of rationality: the mythical, supernatural reasoning of (1) unbounded rationality and (2) optimizing under constraints, and the two forms of bounded rationality known as (3) satisficing and (4) fast and frugal heuristics.

An example of this later category is one-reason decision making such as, "I'll vote for John Kerry because George Bush got us into the war in Iraq" or "I'll vote for George Bush because it is not wise to change ships mid-stream." Such one-reason decision processes are required when multiple reasons cannot be converted into a single currency. If more complex reasoning is used, value conflicts will frequently lead to indecision or the decision of which value to rank first, thus leading back to one-reason decision making. Likewise, models of unbounded rationality might lead to the decision not to vote because the voter gets bogged down in analysis (i.e., commonly known as "paralysis by analysis"). Optimization under constraints, they argue, is a common misinterpretation of bounded rationality.

Another example of fast and frugal heuristics is the recognition heuristic. Name recognition is not everything, but it contains powerful, cumulative information. The ABC Research Group used name recognition as the criterion to test the performance of stock market portfolios. German laypeople selected a portfolio of American stocks that outperformed the top performing managed funds in the U.S. by a wide margin, and outperformed the picks of both German and American stock market experts. While American laypeople had a much lower recognition rate for German stocks, their picks also outperformed market averages (Borges, Goldstein, Ortmann, and Gigerenzer, 1999). A number of potential reasons exist for these outcomes, not the least of which is that information that is missing may frequently be more important than information at hand—the less is more approach.

Two types of rules must exist for simple heuristics: searching rules and stopping rules. Satisficing could have a sequential searching rule akin to "start with the next idea that comes to mind" and a stopping rule like "stop when these two criteria are met." In the stock market example, mere recognition was the binomial (yes/no) search rule for an individual, but portfolios were built in a variety of ways, such as including a stock when 90% of laypeople recognized the company name or selecting the ten companies with the highest name recognition. In contrast, optimization under constraints seeks to determine the optimum stopping point by calculating when the costs of further search exceed the likely benefits. This is really an application of unbounded rationality utilizing probability theory.

Part of the rationale behind their search for simple heuristics used in a variety of decision-making environments is that,

> If a different heuristic were required for every slightly different decision-making environment, we would need an unworkable multitude of heuristics to reason with, and we would not be able to generalize to previously unencountered environments. Fast and frugal heuristics avoid this trap by their very simplicity, which allows them to be robust in the face of environmental change and enables them to generalize well to new situations. (Gigerenzer, Todd, and ABC Research Group 1999, 18)

While chapters in their book focus on using heuristics for everything from selecting the right mate in life and playing chess (a favorite topic for Simon) to determining what heuristics people actually use. The end result is the beginnings of an adaptive toolbox with four classes of heuristics: ignorance-based decision making, one-reason decision making, elimination heuristics, and satisficing. Elimination heuristics are applied in most situations where more than two alternatives exist— one test at a time will be applied to each choice until only one choice remains standing. Satisficing is distinguished from the others because it can be applied when the decision-maker does not know all the possible outcomes. In these situations of uncertainty, both the search for possible alternatives and the search for information about each alternative must be limited by stopping rules (Gigerenzer, Todd, and ABC Research Group 1999, 360).

The work of this research group has expanded into exciting new territory by studying the accuracy of simple heuristic devices in making decisions that are bounded by limited time, incomplete knowledge, and insufficient computational resources. Their work would not have been possible without the advanced work of Herbert Simon. Much still remains to be done to determine how humans decide which heuristics to use, which heuristics perform best in specific environments, how the heuristics may be combined to make more complex choices, and what other classes of heuristics might exist. Nevertheless, what is exciting about this approach is the promise that human decision making processes may actually be much more simple than they frequently appear to be.

4.4 CONCLUSION

Together, these challenges and extensions demonstrate that Simon's work will live on for a long time in spite of his death on February 9, 2001. His critics and admirers alike stubbornly refuse to lose focus on his wealth of ideas and his approach to human decision making.

I had the honor to be present when Professor Simon delivered one of his last professional speeches, to the American Society of Public Administration's 58th National Conference (1997). He was, ironically, receiving the Dwight Waldo Award at the time. Simon made an impassioned argument that public choice theory and the new public management were taking public administration in the wrong direction because of their "badly flawed" assumptions that self-interest is the driving force of human behavior and Adam Smith's "invisible hand" best determines broad social needs. Instead, he argued that identification with groups—organizations, families, ethnic groups, nations—is the driving force. In light of this, at the very least, self-interest as "the" motivating factor had to be defined in non-economic terms. Identification with organizations and dedication to the goals of organizations, public or private, allows individuals to self-actualize in ways that are not possible in isolation.

He spoke eloquently of the need for a dispersion of power for democracy to thrive. Concentration of power in the corporate sector was a concern of his as was political corruption, which he interestingly described not just as the danger of an overly centralized government, but also as collaborative electoral corruption of the two major parties. On these issues he might have agreed with consumer advocate and perennial American presidential candidate Ralph Nader. Nader's key theme in the 2000 and 2004 presidential campaigns was that the United States has a one-party system—the corporate party. Both major parties, in his view, bend over backwards to meet the needs of the private sector because they have bought into the myth that citizens need the private sector more than the private sector needs citizens. Remarkably, Simon used the word "myth" in his speech when he said "the idea that there is an organization, the private corporation, with a unique capacity for efficiency and productivity, is simply a myth."

Finally, and most impressively, because of his decades of work with decision making and artificial intelligence systems, Simon appeared to have an incredible respect for the ability of individuals to absorb multiple streams of information and make good, timely decisions based on a combination of applying logic, following basic rules of thumb, and using adequate boundaries to guide the search process. I was a doctoral student at the time and had only minimal exposure to a few of Simon's earlier works. This conclusion of his life's study—his driving curiosity to understand what makes humans tick—surprised me immensely. I thought I had learned from *Administrative Behavior* and other works that humans are deeply flawed as decision makers. In 1997, Simon said clearly that we are both flawed and immeasurably powerful decision makers.

Recent understanding of the human brain may help to explain why developing a common vision is so difficult for organizations:

> Because limbic states can leap between minds [via facial expressions, posture, the eyes, vocal tone, etc.], feelings are contagious while notions are not. If one person germinates an ingenious idea, it's no surprise that those in the vicinity fail to develop the same concept spontaneously. But the limbic activity of those around us draws our emotions into almost immediate congruence. (Lewis, Amini, and Lannon, 2000, 64)

Whatever else it was, Simon's world was quite similar to that of Taylor, Gulick, Weber, and many others before him. It was deeply a world of ideas. He spent little time wondering how instantaneous conveyance of human emotions might trump his world of ideas. While he shredded the ideas of classical theorists in an effort to extend them into the world of individual decision making, his focus on how organizations could drive the behavior of individuals left a lasting impression.

REFERENCES

Augier, M. and March, J. G., Remembering Herbert A. Simon 1916–2001, *Public Administration Review*, 61(4), 396–402, 2001.

Barnard, C. I., *The Functions of the Executive*, Harvard University Press, Cambridge, 1938.

Boland, R. J., Tenkasi, R. Jr., and Te'eni, D., Designing information technology to support distributed cognition, In *Cognition within and between Organizations*, Meindl, J. R., Stubbart, C., and Porac, J. F., Eds., Sage, Thousand Oaks, CA, pp. 245–280, 1996.

Borges, B., Goldstein, D. G., Ortmann, A., and Gigerenzer, G., Can ignorance beat the stock market?, In *Simple Heuristics that Make us Smart*, Gigerenzer, G. and Todd, P. M., Eds., Oxford University Press, ABC Research Group, New York, pp. 59–72, 1999.

Bozeman, B., *Bureaucracy and Red Tape*, PrenticeHall, Upper Saddle River, NJ, 2003.

Cayer, N. J. and Weschler, L. F., *Public Administration. Social Change and Adaptive Management*, 3rd ed., Birkdale, San Diego, CA, 2003.

Chandler, R. C. and Plano, J. C., *The Public Administration Dictionary*, 2nd ed., ABC-CLIO, Santa Barbara, CA, 1988.

Cruise, P. L., Of Proverbs and positivism: the logical Herbert Simon, In *Handbook of Organizational Theory and Management. The Philosophical Approach*, Lynch, T. D. and Dicker, T. J., Eds., Marcel Dekker, New York, pp. 273–287, 1998.

Denhardt, R. B., Denhardt, J. Z., and Aristigueta, M. P., *Managing Human Behavior in Public and Nonprofit Organization*, SAGE, Thousand Oaks, CA, 2002.

Denhardt, R. B. and Grubbs, J. W., *Public Administration. An Action Orientation*, 4th ed., Thompson Wadsworth, Belmont, CA, 2003.

Earl, P. E., Ed., *The Legacy of Herbert Simon in Economic Analysis*, 2 Vol., Northhampton, MA: Edward Elgar, 2001.

Elison, H., "Repent Harlequin!" said the Ticktockman, In *Another Tomorrow; a Science Fiction Anthology*, Hollister, B. C., Ed., Pflaum, Dayton, OH, 1974.

Elliott, E. W. and Kiel, L. D., Eds., *Chaos Theory in the Social Sciences: Foundations and Applications*, University of Michigan Press, Ann Arbor, 1996.

Elliott, E. W. and Kiel, L. D., Eds., *Nonlinear Dynamics, Complexity and Public Policy*, Nova Sciences, Commack, NY, 1999.

Etzioni, A., Mixed scanning: a "third" approach to decision making, *Public Administration Review*, 275, 385–392, 1967.

Fry, B. R., *Mastering Public Administration. From Max Weber to Dwight Waldo*, Chatham House, Chatham, NJ, 1989.

Gigerenzer, G. and Todd, P. M., *Simple Heuristics that Make us Smart*, Oxford University Press, New York, 1999, ABC Research Group.

Glasman, N. S. and Nevo, D., *Evaluation in Decision Making*, Kluwer Academic Publishers, Boston, 1988.

Golembiewski, R. T., Perspectives on Simon's administrative behavior: stock-taking in the fortieth anniversary—part 1, *Public Administration Quarterly 12 (Fall)*, 259–274, 1988.

Hall, R. H., *Organizations: Structures, Processes, and Outcomes*, 5th ed., Prentice Hall, Englewood Cliffs, NJ, 1991.

Heilbroner, R. L., *The Worldly Philosophers. The Lives, Times, and Ideas of the Great Economic Thinkers*, 4th ed., Simon and Shuster, New York, 1972.

Henry, N., *Public Administration and Public Affairs*, 8th ed., Prentice Hall, Upper Saddle River, NJ, 2001.

Kiel, L. D., *Managing Chaos and Complexity in Government: A New Paradigm for Managing Change, Innovation, and Organizational Renewal*, Jossey-Bass, San Francisco, CA, 1994.

Lewis, T., Amini, F., and Lannon, R., *A General Theory of Love*, Vintage Books, New York, 2000.

Little, J. H., Administrative man faces the quality transformation: comparing the ideas of Herbert A. Simon and W. Edwards Deming, *American Review of Public Administration*, 241, 67–84, 1994.

March, J. G. and Simon, H. A., *Organizations*, John Wiley and Sons, New York, 1958.

Merton, R. K., Bureaucratic structure and personality, *Social Forces 18 (May)*, 560–568, 1940.

Mills, C. W., *The Sociological Imagination*, Oxford University Press, New York, 1959.

Mingus, M. S., Dotted lines: networks, quantum holism, and the changing nation state. *Public Administration Quarterly*, 29(4), 413–444, 2006.

Morgan, G., *Images of Organization. Executive Edition*, Berrett-Koehler, San Francisco, CA, 1998.

National Science Foundation, NSF 04-537: Human and social dynamics: Competition for FY 2004, http://www.nsf.org

Rand, A., *Atlas Shrugged*, Random House, New York, 1957.

Rozenbloom, D. H. and Kravchuk, R. S., *Public Administration. Understanding Management, Politics, and Law in the Public Sector*, 5th ed., McGraw Hill, Boston, 2002.

Schmidt, M. R., Grout: alternatives kinds of knowledge and why they are ignored, *Public Administration Review*, 536, 525–530, 1993.

Schreurs, P., The rule of rationality: Weber's concept of rationality in his writings on the bureaucracy, In *Retracing Public Administration*, Rutgers, M. R., Ed., JAI, Amsterdam, pp. 291–308, 2003.

Senge, P. M., *The Fifth Discipline: The Art and Practice of the Learning Organization*, Currency Doubleday, New York, 1990.

Shafritz, J. M. and Russell, E. W., *Introducing Public Administration*, 3rd ed., Longman, New York, 2003.

Sherwood, F. P., The half-century's "great books" in public administration, *Public Administration Review*, 502, 249–264, 1990.

Simon, H. A., The proverbs of administration, *Public Administration Review (Winter)*, 53–67, 1946.

Simon, H. A., A behavioral model of rational choice, *Quarterly Journal of Economics*, 691, 99–118, 1955.

Simon, H. A., *The Sciences of the Artificial*, MIT Press, Cambridge, MA, 1969.

Simon, H. A., *Administrative Behavior: A Study of Decision-Making Processes in Administrative Organization*, 3rd ed., The Free Press, New York, 1976.

Simon, H. A., *The New Science of Management Decision*, Prentice Hall, Englewood Cliffs, NJ, 1977.

Simon, H. A., *Models of My Life*, Basic Books, New York, 1991.

Simon, H. A., Donald C. Stone lecture. Paper presented at 58th national conference of the American Society of Public Administration, 28 July 1997, Philadelphia, PA.

Simon, H. A., Smithburg, D. W., and Thompson, V. A., *Public Administration*, Alfred A. Knopf, New York, 1950.

Skinner, B. F., *The Behavior of Organisms; an Experimental Analysis*, D. Appleton-Century, New York, 1938.

Skinner, B. F., *Science and Human Behavior*, Macmillan, New York, 1953.

Steers, R. M. and Black, J. S., *Organizational Behavior*, 5th ed., Harper Collins, New York, 1994.

Stillman, R. II., *Preface to Public Administration: A Search for Themes and Direction*, Rev. ed., Chatelaine Press, Burke, VA, 1998.

Stillman, R. II., *Public Administration: Concepts and Cases*, 7th ed., Houghton Mifflin, Boston, 2000.

Taylor, F. W., *Scientific Management*, Harper and Brothers, New York, 1911.

Wheatley, M. J., *Leadership and the New Sciences: Learning about Organization from an Orderly Universe*, Berrett-Koehler, San Francisco, CA, 1992.

White, J. D., Images of administrative reason and rationality: the recovery of practical discourse, In *Images and Identities in Public Administration*, Kass, H. D. and Catron, B. L., Eds., Sage, Newbury Park, CA, pp. 132–150, 1990.

5 Practical Reasoning and Action: Simon's *Administrative Behavior* in Context

Paul Nieuwenburg

CONTENTS

5.1 Introduction...81
5.2 Practical Reasoning and Deliberation..82
    5.2.1 Aristotelian Practical Reasoning: "Deliberation
        Is About Means Not Ends"..83
    5.2.2 Deliberation in the *Nicomachean Ethics* 84
    5.2.3 The Practical Syllogism 85
    5.2.4 (Sub-)Humean Practical Reasoning 87
    5.2.5 Internalism About Reasons for Action 88
5.3 Simon and Sub-Humean Practical Reasoning 89
    5.3.1 Politics and Administration...90
5.4 Davidson: Reasons, Causes, and the Practical Syllogism..........................92
    5.4.1 Deliberation Is of Means Not Ends 94
5.5 Conclusion 96
References...96

5.1 INTRODUCTION

In his *Reason in Human Affairs* Herbert Simon claims that "reason is wholly instrumental. It cannot tell us where to go; at best it can tell us how to get there. It is a gun for hire that can be employed in the service of any goals that we have, good or bad" (Simon, 1983, 7–8). This is a clear and provocative a commitment to instrumentalism, the doctrine that the predicate "rational" applies to our choice of means, but not our ends. In this conception, rationality consists in the effective and efficient achievement of ends that, so to speak, are given. Human beings exhibit rationality in selecting means to achieve those ends, not in preferring one end to another. As David Hume famously says, "Tis not contrary to reason to prefer the destruction of the whole world to the scratching of my finger" (Hume, 1986, 416).

Simon's metaphor of the gun aptly illustrates what some find objectionable in the idea of instrumentalism. It is a neutral device that can be recruited to devious purposes. However, instead of rejecting this idea, it is wiser to adopt Robert Nozick's view that instrumental rationality is the only theory of rationality that is not in need of justification. It is, in Nozick's terms, "the default theory." This, however, does not mean that it is the *only* theory of rationality, as Simon misleadingly suggests (Nozick, 1993, 133). [*]

This chapter is an inquiry into the nature of the relation between the Humean, or rather sub-Humean, picture of practical reasoning and Simon's specific project of founding the politics-administration distinction on the (more primitive) distinction between factual and value elements on decisions. [†] It should be stressed that in this contribution, the *philosophical* credentials of Simon's project will be central. As John Searle has pointed out, there is a "common thread" in Aristotle's dictum that deliberation is of means not ends (2001, 5), David Hume's claim that reason is the slave of the passions. This common thread can be shown to run through Simon's work. [‡]

The chapter has three parts. The first part provides the philosophical scaffolding for anchoring Simon's instrumentalism in a certain philosophical tradition of thinking about practical reasoning that, through Hume, goes back to Aristotle. The second part is a critical discussion of Simon's deployment of this tradition in his foundation of the politics-administration distinction in *Administrative Behavior*. The third part points to some of the more important recent philosophical developments of these themes.

5.2 PRACTICAL REASONING AND DELIBERATION

Theories of decision making are already present in ancient Greek philosophical writings. For instance, it is possible to construe parts of Aristotle's ethical theory as a systematic reflection on (instrumental) decision making. To be sure, it would be an anachronism to call the doctrine assembled from these parts a "theory of decision making." Philosophers prefer to call it "deliberation" or "practical reasoning." [¶] On the other hand, it is not absurd to attach the label to the theory either. For in effect, a theory of decision making is, in a quite literal sense, just what it sounds like—a theory telling us how to reach one species of decision (*krisis*), namely deliberate (or rational) choice (*prohairesis*) (Aristotle, 1926, 140–141). We shall return to the structure of Aristotle's theory presently.

"Practical reasoning" and "deliberation" are terms of art. They refer to reasoning that aims to find out *what to do*, as opposed to reasoning that aims to find out *why something is the case*. The latter kind of reasoning is, according to the classical Aristotelian distinction, theoretical reasoning. Thus, the difference between these forms of reasoning may be characterized by reference to their objects; where theoretical reasoning aims at understanding, practical reasoning aims at action. Admittedly, this is a rather slipshod way of clarifying the distinction, but it suffices for present purposes.

To forestall misunderstanding, it should be noted that in this connection the term "practical" is not synonymous with "concrete." By the same token, "theoretical" is not another word for "abstract." These are two different distinctions. In line with these distinctions, a body of statements can be (1) practical and abstract, (2) practical and concrete, (3) theoretical and concrete, and (4) theoretical and abstract. To take them in the reverse order, an example of (4) would be a treatise in meta-mathematics, of (3) a social-scientific case study, of (2) an advisory report directed to some particular organization, and of (1) a formal account of institutional design. This suggests that a case study of, say, a particular administrative agency, however, meticulous its recording of particular

---

[*] In the last section it will become clear why Nozick's position is plausible.

[†] The meaning of the prefix "sub" will be clarified in the subsection section titled "Sub-Humean Practical Reasoning."

[‡] In tracking down this common thread, I shall focus on the received, or traditional interpretations of the theories of Aristotle and David Hume, because these have had more of an impact on the history of the theory of practical reasoning than revisionist (but possibly more accurate) accounts.

[¶] For convenience, these terms are treated as synonyms.

facts, is not practical. What makes an account practical is not its concern with practical detail, but its *direction of fit.*[*]

Linguistic acts like statements and promises can have either of two directions of fit: word-to-world direction of fit and world-to-word direction of fit. Linguistic expressions that have a word-to-world direction of fit, such as an empirical proposition ("It's raining"), are supposed to match facts in an independently existing world (the fact that it is raining). By contrast, linguistic expressions that have world-to-word direction of fit, such as commands ("Close the door"), are not supposed to match an already existing fact, but to effect changes in the world so that the facts come to match the content of the expression (someone's closing the door as a result of my command).

If we suppose that reasoning is not just a public activity, conducted by means of spoken or written linguistic acts, but also a private form of thinking, then we may substitute "mind" for "word." Thus, we might say that the conclusion of theoretical reasoning is a proposition, or a system of propositions, with a mind-to-world direction of fit; it has to fit the facts in order for it to be an instance of theoretical reasoning. The conclusion of a piece of practical reasoning, like an intention or decision, has world-to-mind direction of fit; the facts have to be adapted to the intention. It would be patently absurd to intend to bring about a fact that one already knew to be in existence.

Practical reasoning, then, is simply the mental activity we engage in to figure out what to do. On this level of analysis, the concept is not mysterious. Things start to get more complicated when questions of motivation enter the fore. As we shall see, the picture of practical reasoning that Simon imports into his account of the politics-administration distinction, what shall be called (for reasons to be revealed shortly) the "sub-Humean" picture of practical reasoning, distinguishes itself by a peculiar motivational theory. First, however, let us discuss the theory of practical reasoning pioneered by Aristotle, for this can be seen as the prototype of the theory on which Simon's account of the science of administration is ultimately based.

5.2.1 Aristotelian Practical Reasoning: "Deliberation Is About Means Not Ends"

It is a matter of contingent fact that many theories of practical reasoning have traditionally been developed in the context of moral theory. The link between practical reasoning and moral theory is an obvious one. Because a moral theory is a theory about what one should do, and because a theory of practical reasoning is a theory of figuring out what to do, the two theories seem to be linked as product (decision) and process (decision making) (Millgram, 2001, 1). Most of the well-known theories of practical reasoning are therefore to be found in the great substantive ethical systems. For instance, a moral theory that tells us that we should always do those things that lead to the greatest benefit for the greatest number, such as a classical utilitarian moral theory, comes with a certain theory of how to make the decisions leading up to that end. Of course, the nature of the end of a substantive moral theory places important constraints on the way a moral agent is supposed to think about achieving it.

By the same token, a theory of practical reasoning, when developed independently of a substantive moral theory of what one should do, controls the repertoire of legitimate ends. Procedural theories of practical reasoning, such as Kantian-inspired theories, consequentially limit the ends of any associated moral theory. However, although the connection between practical reasoning and moral theory is obvious, it is by no means logically necessary. For instance, in instrumental or means-end practical reasoning, there is generally believed to be no necessary connection between the nature of the end that is given and the means for achieving that end. More particularly, if the

---

[*] For an illuminating discussion of the notion of direction of fit, see Searle (1983, 7–8).

means are *causal* means, any logical connection between (statements of) means and (statements of) ends is explicitly proscribed by many instrumentalists.[*]

Historically speaking, the most influential theory of practical reasoning embedded in moral theory is Aristotle's *Nicomachean Ethics,* (1926). We should therefore take a closer look at what is said about practical reasoning in that work.

5.2.2 DELIBERATION IN THE *NICOMACHEAN ETHICS*

The moral theory in which Aristotle's theory of practical reasoning is embedded gravitates toward two notions: happiness or well-being (*eudaimonia*) and virtue (*aretê*). Happiness is the final end of human life, and virtuous activity is the most important ingredient in such a life. For present purposes we need not enter into the complicated story of the exact relation between these concepts in Aristotle's ethics. However, if we want to expound Aristotle's theory of practical reasoning, we shall have to say something about his concept of virtue.

According to Aristotle, virtue is a disposition to act or feel in certain ways involving deliberate choice (*hexis prohairêtikê*) (1926, 94–95). There are two kinds of virtue, corresponding to the division of the human soul into a rational and a non-rational part. The non-rational part that harbors the emotions and non-rational desires can be made to obey the rational part or reason (*logos*). The virues of the rational part are called intellectual virtues, those of the non-rational part virtues of character. A virtue of character (*aretê êthikê*) is a disposition that comes into being by a process of habituation that is controlled by the experience and administration of pleasure and pain (reward and punishment). According to the traditional interpretation, virtues of character are responsible for the moral agent's conception of the end (*telos*) of life and of action, whereas the virtue of the practical intellect controls the agent's thinking about means to that end.

The traditional Aristotelian picture of the virtuous person, then, is that of an individual who has all the virtues of character telling him what to do and the intellectual virtue of practical wisdom (*phronêsis*) telling him how best to do it. Because Aristotle (like Plato) believes in the unity of virtue (in the sense that one cannot have only one, or some virtues, but that one either has none or all), he is capable of defining virtue in the general sense as a disposition involving deliberate choice; the *combined* effort of the virtue of character that makes the ends of action right, and of the intellectual virtue of practical wisdom that provides the agent with the right means, makes the individual a virtuous person. According to this interpretation, the positing of the end(s) is not a matter for reason to establish all on its own. According to the traditionalists, Aristotle (1926, 132–141) claims that deliberation is of the end (*telos*), not of the means (*ta pros to telos*).

With the general picture of Aristotelian virtue in place, we can take a closer look at the associated theory of practical reasoning. In Aristotle's theory an action always stems from a desire (*orexis*). There are three species of desire, two of them non-rational, one of them rational. The forms of non-rational desire are appetite (*epithumia*), or desire for what is or appears pleasant, and temper (*thumos*), or desire for revenge. The rational form of desire is wish (*boulêsis*), or desire for what is or appears good.[†] The concept of a rational desire may be somewhat counterintuitive to modern readers who are accustomed to a theory of the mind in which the cognitive and the conative are strictly separated; it is essential to Aristotle's theory. Only human beings have reason, and therefore only human beings have wish.

Wish is a general conception of the good. It is something that cannot be enacted immediately. For instance, if I think that my good consists in becoming immensely rich, there is, in normal circumstances, nothing I can do here and now to realize that end. In other words, I have to start figuring out how to achieve that end. This figuring out is deliberation (*bouleusis*, not to be confused

---

[*] See Section 5.3.

[†] This latter concept used to be construed as the will, *voluntas*.

with *boulêsis*). In Aristotelian terms, the end or *telos* is wealth, the means or *ta pros to telos* consists of the chain of actions I have to perform to procure wealth.

Aristotle describes this process as a linear quest. If wealth is what I want to achieve (that is, if wealth is a suitable interpretation of happiness), then I may rob a bank. If I want to rob a bank, I have to get a gun. If I want to get a gun, I have to go to the gun store and buy one. If I want to go to the gun store, I have to take the bus and so on, until I arrive at the final step of this chain, which is something in my power to do here and now, or at a determinate point of time in the future. If that time has come, I decide to act, and that decision is what Aristotle calls deliberate choice (*prohairesis*) which is a kind of decision (*krisis*). Schematically, the structure of Aristotelian practical reasoning is as follows:

Wish (*bouêlsis*) → Deliberation (*bouleusis*) → Deliberate choice (*prohairesis*) → Action (*proxis*)[*]

In summary, in the traditional interpretation of Aristotle's theory, deliberation or decision making is the process of finding the means with a given end. The gist of this theory is usually captured by the famous tag "deliberation is about means not ends."[†] So far, however, nothing has been said about what that interpretation holds to be the form Aristotelian deliberation takes. That form it takes to be *syllogistic*; the form Aristotelian deliberation or practical reasoning assumes is that of the *practical syllogism*. It is necessary to elaborate on this form of reasoning because one could say that Simon's analysis of decision making into decision premises is a twentieth-century logical positivist version of the practical syllogism pioneered by Aristotle in his theory of prudence or practical wisdom and in his writings on the explanation of animal movement in general and human action in particular.

5.2.3 THE PRACTICAL SYLLOGISM

To understand what a practical syllogism is, a brief exposition of the concept of syllogism is in order.[‡] The Greek term *sullogismos* means "argument" or "reasoning." However, in his logical treatises, particularly in the *Prior* and *Posterior Analytics*, which are concerned with theoretical reasoning aimed at scientific understanding, Aristotle gives the term a very specific sense. A syllogism is that form of reasoning that consists of, on the one hand, *two* premises, a major and a minor, and, on the other hand, a conclusion. Both premises and conclusion are *categorical* propositions, that is to say, propositions that affirm or deny a predicate of a subject. The relation between these three propositions is that of logical entailment. In other words, the conclusion is *necessitated* by the premises. To give the classical example:

All human beings are mortal (major)
Socrates is a human being (minor)
Therefore, Socrates is mortal (conclusion).

The propositions (both premises and conclusion) of a syllogism can be classified along two dimensions. They can be of universal or particular purport: "all humans beings are mortal," and "Socrates is a human being," respectively. And they can be affirmative or negative: "all humans beings are mortal," and "it is not the case that all humans beings are mortal." Within the theory of the syllogism, much depends on the middle term. In our example, the middle term is "human

---

[*] On Aristotle's theory, deliberate choice causes the action. The causal relation is important; see below.

[†] Aristotle actually says "deliberation is not about the ends, but about the means" (1926, 136–137).

[‡] To be precise, the term "practical syllogism" never occurs in that form in Aristotle's Greek. The expression most akin to it is "syllogism of things which can be done" (ho sullogismos tôn praktôn) (Aristotle, 1926, 368–369).

being," which links both premises. If the middle term is correctly placed, it disappears from the conclusion.

To make the logical structure more perspicuous, one may fill in symbols for each of the terms of the proposition, in the following way:[*]

MP
SM
Therefore, SP

where "M" stands for "middle term" (in this case "human being(s)"), "S", the minor term that is the subject of the conclusion (in this case "Socrates"), and "P" the major term, or the predicate of the conclusion (in this case "is (are) mortal"). In this form we may, as it were delete the M from both premises to obtain the conclusion:

~~M~~P
S~~M~~
Therefore, SP

As the example makes clear, the propositions of a deductively valid syllogism need not all be of universal scope; it is crucial to see that the introduction of the minor term ("Socrates") contaminates, as it were, the syllogism in the sense that it determines the scope of the conclusion. That is to say, a particular term is subsumed, by way of the middle term, under the major term. This, then, is what is understood by the syllogism as a *form* of reasoning.

Until the advent of modern symbolic logic in the nineteenth century, the syllogism provided the paradigm case of deductive reasoning. Meanwhile, what the theoretical syllogism was for theoretical forms of reasoning (logic, science), the practical syllogism was for practical reasoning. What, then, makes a syllogism practical?

At first sight, for Aristotle the distinction appears to lie in the *object*, not in the reasoning; it is not so much the specific nature of the reasoning that makes it practical, but what the reasoning is about: action (*praxis*). According to the standard interpretation, the conclusion of a practical syllogism is an action. But there are more ways in which the practical syllogism differs from its theoretical counterpart. In the first place, there is a difference with respect to what one might call their respective logical status. The major premise of a practical syllogism has *normative* purport; it is a (universal) statement of what is good. For instance, "It is good to do *x*," or "One ought always to do *x*." The normative purport of the major provides the main reason why the conclusion of a practical syllogism will be, not a statement, but an action. Another difference concerns the (scope of the) minor premise of the practical syllogism; the minor premise invariably is a particular statement of fact, for instance, "This is *x*." This stands to reason if the reasoning is to issue in action; action always occurs in particular circumstances, and for a general rule to be converted in action, it has to be *applied* to such circumstances. I can have knowledge of the universal injunction to help all people in need; if I am not capable, for whatever reason, of seeing that someone is in need, this rule will not be converted into an action of mine. Within Aristotle's philosophy, the term "seeing" should be taken literally. For particulars are grasped by perception. So the minor premise of a practical syllogism can be construed as the linguistic description of the intentional content of a perception. This is the significance of Aristotle's much quoted remark on virtue: "the decision lies in perception," meaning that we cannot give general rules for the application of our virtues in particular circumstances. Any attempt to do this would precipitate us into a vertigo of infinite regress.

---

[*] Note that in logic a term is not necessarily a single word; subject and predicate are terms, but may consist of many words.

Second, there are differences in *form*. Strictly speaking, the amount of premises need not be confined to two. This last point needs some highlighting. Take a syllogism like: "all human beings ought to help persons in need"; "this person is in need"; these premises result in an action, my helping this person. Logically speaking, the premises do not *formally* warrant the conclusion (or action). What is needed to consummate the syllogism is an additional premise, "I am a human being." The subject of the reasoning, however, does not usually state this premise. However, it needs to be stated if the form is to be formally valid (Anscombe, 1976). What is more, in his tract *On the movement of animals,* Aristotle gives examples of practical syllogisms that consist of more than two premises, even without the suppressed premise of self-attribution (Aristotle, 1978).

According to the traditional interpretation, then, Aristotelian deliberation or practical reasoning has the structure of the practical syllogism. With modifications, this is, by and large, the logical structure of administrative decision making as analyzed by Simon. Before we come to that analysis, let us complete our preliminary sketch.

5.2.4 (SUB-)HUMEAN PRACTICAL REASONING

While Aristotle, and ancient thinkers more generally (though not universally), believed that it was the task of reason to prevail upon a person's non-rational motivations, the Scottish philosopher David Hume turned things upside down.

Any adequate description of a Humean theory of practical reasoning has to take account of two of his most famous tenets. The first is the doctrine that human reason is a faculty for establishing matters of fact and logic, and that it is motivationally inert: "reason is, and ought only to be the slave of the passions, and can never pretend to any other office than to serve and obey them" (Hume, 1986, 415). Reason is "utterly impotent" when it comes to exciting passions, which in turn cause actions. In the Humean picture, ends are a matter of passion, things which affect us in a certain way. There is a very strong connection with (anticipatory) pleasure. According to many thinkers, beginning with Plato (for a clear statement see *Philebus* 32b–36c (Plato, 1945, 61–68)), the pleasure involved in thinking about p is integral to desiring that p.[*]

The second piece of Humean lore is that an "ought" can never be derived from an "is": "For as this *ought*, or *ought not*, expresses some new relation of affirmation, "tis necessary that it shou'd be observ'd and explain'd; and at the same time that a reason should be given. For what seems altogether inconceivable, how this new relation can be a deduction from others, which are entirely different from it" (Hume, 1986, 415, 457, 469). This is the *fons et origo* of the famous distinction between fact and value. For "is" stands for factual (indicative) statement and "ought" is shorthand for moral (which is one species of value) statement.

In a Humean view of practical reasoning, both of these tenets conspire to paint the picture of practical reasoning we ought to be familiar with by now. Motivation to action is not something reason can provide an agent with. What reason can do is, in the final analysis, engage in deliberation on how to fulfill certain desires an agent already has. The motivation to act is, as it were, preserved in the chain of considerations (notably related as means to a given end) ultimately issuing in an intention, or decision, to act. By this account, practical reasoning is of a fundamentally instrumental nature.

---

[*] It is important to draw a distinction here. What makes instrumentalism, viewed in this way, differ from hedonism? The important thing to note is that to desire that p, it is not necessary that (I believe that) p will cause me pleasure when p materializes. In terms of a distinction drawn by G.E. Moore in his criticism of utilitarianism, a thought of pleasure is not the same as a pleasant thought (Moore, 1965, 70). For hedonism the content (that p) has to be pleasure; for our view the mode (thought, imagination etc.) itself has to be pleasant, irrespective of its content. In Hume's example, if thinking of the destruction of the world, including myself, is a pleasant thought to me, then this suffices. This connection between pleasure and desire is by many philosophers thought to be of an essential nature: that is to say, the presence of desire entails that of pleasure and vice versa. On the other hand, there are also thinkers who connect desire with a painful state of deprivation, the classical examples being hunger and thirst (Locke, 1975, 229–233).

Ask a man *why he uses exercise*; he will answer, *because he desires to keep his health*. If you then enquire, why he desires health, he will readily reply, *because sickness is painful*. If you push your enquiries further, and desire a reason *why he hates pain*, it is impossible he can ever give any. This is an ultimate end and is never referred to any other object." (Hume, 1975, 293)

It is crucial to appreciate what is at stake in this picture. In the first place, the two Humean claims are not connected. In the Humean tradition, the *logical* distinction between fact and value is based on a more fundamental distinction between the *function* of factual and ethical terms. Thus, the impossibility of deriving a value statement from a factual statement is due to a divergence in the meaning of the terms around which those statements are built and which give them their inferential status. Ayer claims that the truth-value of factual statements can be ascertained by empirical verification. This is the brunt of the logical-positivist conception of rationality (and which is taken over, as we shall see, by Simon). Value statements, however, are not empirically verifiable, because the function of "normative ethical symbols" is not to describe, but to *express* moral sentiments: "the function of the relevant ethical word is purely 'emotive.' It is used to express feeling about certain objects, but not to make any assertion about them" (Ayer, 1990, 111).

This means that ethical terms, like "ought," "good," etc. are expressive of desires, among other things. If I say to you that "You ought not to take bribes," then I express a desire of mine. Whether you accept bribes or not is, in this picture, dependent on my speaking to a similar desire in your motivational makeup. Thus (and this is crucial) the non-derivability of propositions containing ethical terms from factual propositions is due to a difference in function of the key terms of those propositions.

Second, it contains strong suggestions of a commitment to what, in philosophy, is called "internalism" about reasons for action—to be discussed in the next section.

5.2.5 INTERNALISM ABOUT REASONS FOR ACTION

The controversy on internalism goes back to the fundamental opposition between the motivational theories of, at least, Hume and Kant (Korsgaard, 1986). Basically, this controversy has close connections with (without being identical to) the issue of the motivational power of human reason. Where Kant bases his account of practical reasoning on the assumption that the autonomous person is capable of rationally legislating to himself what it is his duty to do, Hume, as we have just seen, denies unassisted reason all motivational power. In brief, internalism about reasons for action means that reasons for action have to be traceable, via instrumental practical reasoning, to a desire of the person for whom they are reasons. A person cannot come to see a command, an injunction, or a piece of advice as a reason for action if that person does not already have some desire to which the command, injunction, or piece of advice speaks.

In recent times, the controversy has been stated in a slightly different way. The most influential proponent of the internalist thesis is Bernard Williams. His important essay "Internal and External Reasons" has set the terms of the current debate (1981). Williams frames the basic question of his essay in terms of *statements* about reasons for action.[*] The statement that someone has a reason to φ (where φ stands for a verb of action), or that there is reason for someone to φ, is subject to two different interpretations. In what Williams calls the "internal interpretation," a person has a reason to do something if that person has a *desire* which that action serves. If the person does not have such a desire, then the statement is false. In the external interpretation, this is not so. Thus, on the internal interpretation, if I have a reason to go to the supermarket, this means that I have some desire to which (I believe) going to the supermarket ministers. By contrast, in the external interpretation I need not have a desire to have a reason to go to the supermarket. It should be noted that, stated in

---

[*] Williams claims that "it is a matter for investigation whether there are two sorts of reasons for action, as opposed to two sorts of statements about people's reasons for action" (1981, 101).

this way, the controversy is *not* about whether *all* reasons for action are either desire dependent or not desire dependent. The externalist would duly substantiate his claim if he could point out that there are, or there is, in fact reasons which are desire independent.[*]

Williams posits as the "simplest model for interpretation" a "sub-Humean" model (which we shall encounter later, in the discussion of Simon). Williams calls the picture sub-Humean, because he thinks that Hume's views on practical reasoning are, in fact, more complex (Williams, 1981, 102). In Williams's more technical vocabulary, there must be an item in an agent's "subjective motivational set" or *S*, which the action serves. The items in this set may be construed as desires, but it should be kept in mind that the term "desire" is to be broadly construed, and rather resembles Davidson's category of pro-attitudes. This being the case, in the sub-Humean model, the action "has to be related to some element in *S* as causal means to end." The implication of this model is that, if an action is the upshot of deliberation or practical reasoning designed to further an element in *S*, then that element itself is not capable of being controlled by deliberation. This is an essential part of our Humean inheritance.

5.3 SIMON AND SUB-HUMEAN PRACTICAL REASONING

Admittedly, Simon never mentions David Hume, the philosopher who is arguably his most important intellectual ancestor. The line runs via the work of Alfred Ayer, with whose *Language, Truth, and Logic* (1990) Simon was well acquainted (1961, 46n1). In his *Administrative Behavior* (1961) Simon endorses the logical-positivist versions of the two Humean claims, which are central to his theory of practical reason(ing).

In *Administrative Behavior* Simon claims that this distinction "between the value elements and the factual elements in decision-making … is the basis for the line that is commonly drawn between questions of policy and questions of administration" (1961, 60). Simon almost literally takes over Ayer's logical-positivist conception of science, while suppressing one of its most important ramifications: the motivational theory informing the Humean tradition of practical reasoning. As we shall see, this has conceptually problematic consequences for Simon's project of founding the politics-administration distinction on Ayer's version of the fact-value distinction.[†]

Simon's first step consists in shifting the focus from the concept of action to the concept of decision or choice (1961, 1). Subsequently, the analysis of the concept of decision into two logically distinct elements permits him to isolate a class of *scientific* decision premises, which are empirically verifiable: the "factual" premises. Unsurprisingly, at least from a perspective of his commitment to logical positivism, Simon concentrates on this class of premises to hammer out an account of administrative decision making, which may by rights be called "scientific." The remaining class consists of "value judgments."

> Each decision involves selection of a goal, *and* a behavior relevant to it; this goal may in turn be mediate to a somewhat more distant goal; and so on, until a relatively final aim is reached. In so far as decisions lead toward the selection of final goals, they will be called "value judgments"; so far as they involve the implementation of such goals they will be called "factual judgments." (Simon, 1961, 5)

His indebtedness to the tradition of the practical syllogism is manifest. Aristotle's normative major is equivalent to Simon's value judgment, which is our central concern here. Value judgments are built around "ethical" terms like "ought," "good," and "preferable," which "are not completely reducible to factual terms." Essentially, they are neither true nor false, but, because they are

---

[*] This is nicely captured by the title of McDowell's article in Altham and Harrison (1995): "Might there be external reasons?" See also Hooker (1987) and Scanlon (1998).

[†] Before urging on, I should say that the issue here is not one between positivist and non- or post-positivist views of science. This is a debate that, by my lights, only accidentally touches upon the issue of practical reasoning.

"expressions of preferences," they have an *imperative* function. In other words, statements of value, because they enjoin to action, have world-to-mind direction of fit (Simon, 1961, 45–46, 248).

At this point, Simon acknowledges his debt to Ayer: "No attempt will be made here to demonstrate conclusively the correctness of this view toward ethical propositions; the justification has been set forth at length by logical positivists and others" (Simon, 1961, 46).[*] However, Simon cannot legitimately subscribe to the conclusions of (among others) Ayer and leave off the crucial part of what the latter has to say on ethical terms. Ayer's emotive mental states have been supplanted by the more neutral-looking term "preferences." To be sure, Simon suggests that the term "preferable" performs the same imperative function as "desirable" and that such terms play a role in the valuations entering into decisions, but he gets stuck at the level of linguistic *expression* (46). However, an *expression* of something is not identical with that something. A gesture may be an expression of an emotion, but it is not identical with that emotion. By the same token, a value judgment containing terms like "ought," "good," "preferable," or "desirable" may be *an expression of* a motivational state, but it is not that emotional state.[†]

In short, the primitive notion is not the expression, but the *expressed*: the motivation.[‡] Because of Simon's persistent talk about "decisions" (as if they were autonomously existing entities), this dimension virtually disappears from the textual surface of *Administrative Behavior*. Nevertheless, it is exactly on this precarious point that his project of grounding the distinction of politics and administration on the more primitive distinction of fact and value comes to grief.

5.3.1 POLITICS AND ADMINISTRATION

The argument runs as follows. If, as Simon holds, ethical terms are expressions of preferences (or desires), and if every decision contains an ethical element, then every decision is, at least in part, the expression of preference (or desire). But on account of the fact that Simon incorporates the emotivist view of the function of ethical terms into his theory, he actually says that each decision involves a motivational state, which is expressed in its contents. It is important to note that in this way, Simon places himself in the sub-Humean tradition of practical reasoning. Within this tradition, the tradition of (among others) rational choice theorists, "the norms governing practical reasoning and defining rational action are essentially instrumental norms, which derive their authority from intrinsically motivating preferences or desires" (Brandom, 2000, 31). This means (as already noted) that reasons for actions are always dependent on the presence of certain desires in the psychology of those who are to perform those actions.

The implications of this view for the idea of an administrative decision can now be spelled out. Within Simon's theoretical framework, the administrator must be *motivated* to implement a policy decision. But whence does his decision get its "imperative function" or, as I prefer to call it, its motivational efficacy? There seem to be, roughly, three possibilities:

1. *The internalist account*: the administrative decision *shares* the preferential or motivational efficacy with that of the policy decision.
2. *The externalist account*: this can be subdivided into:
   a. The administrative decision takes its preferential or motivational efficacy from other *agents*.

---

[*] The footnote with this passage contains a reference to Ayer (1990).

[†] Simon himself recognizes this in the very first pages of his book, when he uses the terms "choice" and "decision" (which he uses interchangeably), although in ordinary discourse they "carry connotations of self-conscious, deliberate, rational selection," this is not necessarily the case (1961, 4).

[‡] Of course, there are other sentiments that might be expressed by ethical terms, such as moral approval etc. Because we are talking about decision making, it is legitimate to focus on motivational states such as desires (or preferences).

b. The administrative decision takes its preferential or motivational efficacy from the *institutional context.*

None of these options is available within a framework grounding the distinction between policy questions and administrative questions on the more primitive distinction between (the functions of) fact and value components in decision making. But it is instructive to see why this should be the case.

Option 1 would, of course, place a heavy burden on the administrator. It would mean that he has to endorse to every policy decision he is to implement not only is this unrealistic, it also conflicts with the demand of neutral and nonpartisan administration. To be sure, the importance of this demand varies from culture to culture; but Simon's account of decision making is not just a local account geared to American practice of the 1940s. It has universal purport; "each" decision consists of an ethical and a factual part, not only decisions taken in the United States of the 1940s.

More important, however, is that by hypothesis this option capitalizes on a match of motivational efficacy across different decision makers, in this case policymakers and administrators. This means that administrators, in some way, have to "internalize" (cf. "motivational internalism") the preferences of others or (if we may hypothesize) of the organization in which they operate.[*] However, we should realize that for this notion of internalization to be available at all, the institutions must already be in place.

For instance, to internalize the imperatives captured by orders, commands, and instructions, these institutional items must be already in existence. For at least part of the explanation of the existence of these institutions would consist in the fact that administrators do *not* share the preferences of the policy makers. By the same token, the existence of the institution of promises, contracts, etc. is explained by the fact that people are *not* intrinsically motivated to practice what they preach. Thus, this option seems to be precluded to Simon, because it accords conceptual pride of place to institutional settings—but we should not forget that decisions, and by hypothesis motivation are conceptually *prior* to these settings.

In the case of option 2a, motivational efficacy is taken from another agent, and in this sense external. Of course, this option is by definition blocked from any internalist account. But let us see what happens if this constraint is neglected.

For instance, someone might say that the administrator simply decides on the basis of the expression of the preference *of some other person* (e.g., a superior). This will not do. The decision to implement that preference is still the *administrator's* decision, and because, on Simon's account, every decision has to have an ethical element, there has to be something in the administrator's decision that is expressive of *his own* motivational structure.

Suppose someone says, "Might the administrator not simply obey the instructions of a superior? And is not the imperative function of *that* decision reason enough for the administrator to make the appropriate decision?" This objector would simply fail to appreciate the Humean thrust implicit in Simon's account. For it is of the essence of a Humean account of motivation that instructions or prescriptions given by others, to motivate their receiver, have to speak to a desire *already present in the mental make-up of that receiver.* Of course, this does not mean that for every particular instruction there has to be a particular desire to follow up *that* instruction. A general motivation to obey orders of superiors is sufficient to do the work. But if so, then *that* motivation should figure as the value element in the description of the administrative decision.[†]

---

[*] This actually is the strategy Simon relies on in chapter 5 (1961).

[†] Simon seems to implicitly acknowledge this when he says that "if factual decisions are entrusted to the experts, sanctions must be available to guarantee that the experts will conform, in good faith, to the value judgments that have been democratically formulated" (1961, 57).

Hence, within the Humean framework, the "borrowed" prescription is given motivational efficacy by another expression of preference, and that expression has as much right to a place in the anatomy of the administrative decision as the prescription borrowed.

In the case of option 2b, the institutional context provides the motivational efficacy. To put it differently, it is simply wired into the institutional role of the administrator and his awareness of that role to execute preferences of others.

Part of the rejoinder to this option can be gathered from the discussions of the foregoing options. Thus, whether it belongs to an institutional role or not, if Simon is serious about his universal claim that *every* decision contains an ethical and a factual element, then a decision taken within an institution can be no exception to that rule. Of course, Simon is well aware that a (rational) decision need not *consciously* involve these elements (1961, 4); but the phenomenological structure of a decision says nothing whatsoever of its logical structure—and that is what Simon is interested in.

From a point of view of the politics-administration distinction, the most consequential point to be made here is the following. It should be noted that this option invokes what is conceptually posterior to account for what is conceptually prior. Within Simon's theory, it is not possible to have the *institutions* of politics and administration explain the structure of the decisions made within each of these institutions, because the structure of the decisions, to which the distinction between factual and value elements is essential, serves to explain the distinction between the specific questions these institutions deal with. In short, option 2b begs the question.

Naturally, Simon's adoption of the internalist Humean framework commits him to option 1. Thus, the externalist options are by definition not open to him. In Simon's account, however, *all* options invoke institutional factors (instructions, role descriptions etc.) to explain the administrator's motivation. We have seen that *motivation* is the primitive notion, underlying the peculiar version (Ayer's) of the fact-value distinction Simon incorporates into his account. But if motivation is dependent on a *prior* institutional distinction of politics and administration, his account has run full circle. My conclusion, then, is that for *conceptual* (not empirical) reasons, Simon's effort to ground the politics-administration distinction on the specific value-fact distinction fails.

5.4 DAVIDSON: REASONS, CAUSES, AND THE PRACTICAL SYLLOGISM

There is an obvious difficulty with desire-based conceptions of practical reasoning such as those of the sub-Humean stripe. For if the desire to φ is a psychological item a person happens to have, how can such a desire be a normative *reason* for φ-ing? How can the contingent fact of my having a desire to destroy the world be a normative reason to destroy it? The only answer available seems to be that it can be so only from the point of view of the person in the grip of the desire. To put it differently, even if a desire *causes* me to φ, how can it be a reason for φ-ing? These questions lead us to another important distinction in modern ethics, the distinction between reasons and causes and the related distinction between justification and explanation of action.

There is considerable disagreement about the purpose of the practical syllogism. In modern terms, is it a theory of practical reasoning, as it was traditionally taken to be, or is it a device for explaining action? Nowadays Aristotle's practical syllogism is usually seen as the prototype of what is also called the commonsense explanation of action rather than a, or the, vehicle for practical reasoning. The practical syllogism is, by some influential thinkers, thought to exemplify a mode of explanation that cannot be reduced to causal (law-like) explanation as it takes place in physics: explanation in terms of reasons. This idea was philosophically discredited during the years Simon was working on his *Administrative Behavior*, which also were the halcyon days of behaviorism in the sciences concerned with the explanation of human behavior.

One way to conceive of practical reasoning is in terms of justification. Justification, of course, is very different from explanation. Where the latter is a matter of descriptively giving the cause of a certain event, such as an earthquake or an eclipse, the latter is a normative affair: justifying something is giving reasons for that something on the supposition that that something is valuable. Justification and explanation, then, are mental activities that use two different kinds of building blocks: reasons and causes. If one engages in practical reasoning, one gives reasons for an action which one holds, for some reason or other, as a good (or the right) thing to do.[*]

The distinction between justification and explanation is based, it seems, on a more basic distinction between reasons and causes. There has been extensive philosophical debate on the nature of the difference between these concepts, which in colloquial English frequently run together. Some philosophers argue that whereas a cause is always an event, a reason never is (Searle, 2001, 97–134). In other words, causes and reasons belong in different ontological categories. If so, how can reasons ever impinge upon the world surrounding us, which is plainly governed by causes? Put in this way, the distinction between reasons and causes is a variety of a deeper metaphysical issue: the mind-body problem, the origins of which are frequently located in Descartes' distinction between two kinds of matter, material stuff (*res extensa*) and "thinking" matter (*res cogitans*). Another way of pointing to the difference (without making clear what the difference consists of) is by saying that a cause necessitates its effect, whereas a reason need not. I can have a very good reason not to drink that beer and nevertheless drink it. The event (or action) of drinking is caused by some other event, despite there being, for the agent, a reason for not drinking.[†]

During some time in the twentieth century, the claim that reasons for action could not be causes of action was orthodoxy among philosophers. In the decades of the mid-twentieth century, the heyday of behaviorism, philosophers like Ludwig Wittgenstein, Gilbert Ryle, Elisabeth Anscombe, and Stuart Hampshire started to doubt the ancient idea that actions can be adequately explained in terms of mental states (Mele, 1997, 4). This idea, which was not only deeply ingrained in philosophical analysis, but also in commonsense ways of explanations and attributions of actions to persons, was resuscitated in the 1960s. One of the principal vehicles for this resuscitation was Donald Davidson's famous essay "Actions, Reasons, and Causes" (1980; see also Davidson, 2004).

In his essay Davidson revives the desire-belief model, or the standard model of explaining action, in which one of the assumptions is that action is caused by beliefs and desires. Because Davidson's essay is one the most consequential interventions in the philosophy of action and has had a powerful impact on theories of practical reasoning, it is worth our while to take a closer look at his position.

Davidson calls an explanation of action in terms of its reason a "rationalization." Rationalizations consist of two elements: (1) a desire or, as Davidson would say, a pro-attitude towards actions of a certain type, and (2) a belief (or a more broadly cognitive attitude) to the effect that this particular action is of that type. When one lists (1) and (2) in answer to the question why an agent did something, one is giving a "primary reason." To see how a reason rationalizes an action, it is necessary and sufficient to give the primary reason of the action—and this primary reason is its cause (Davidson, 1980, 3–4). According to Davidson, a "transformation on the desire-belief couple" is required to form an intention to act: "The belief and the desire must be brought together; a course of action must be seen by the agent as attractive in the light of the fact that it promises to bring a desired state of affairs about. This transformation is what is usually called "practical reasoning, reasoning from the perceived value of the end to the value of the means" (Davidson, 2004, 106–107).

In view of what we are going to say about Simon, it is instructive to dwell for a while on one of the arguments Davidson deploys to rebut the thesis that reasons cannot be causes. Proponents of that thesis avail themselves of the claim that cause and effect have to be logically distinct. Because a reason for an action is not *logically distinct* from the action, a reason cannot be a cause. What they

---

[*] Therefore, justification of action need not occur after the fact.

[†] This is one way of describing the phenomenon the Greeks called akrasia, or weakness of the will: doing what one has decided not to do, all things considered.

mean by this is that one cannot explain an event *x* (say, raising my arm) by an event *y* (say, a desire to raise my arm), because there is a logical or conceptual connection between both items. This means that both explanandum and explanans refer to the same event under one description: raising my arm. For a valid and informative explanation of my raising my arm, I have to resort to a cause that avoids reference to raising my arm.

Davidson's rejoinder is simple but devastating. He claims that causation is a connection that holds between *events*, whereas a logical (or conceptual) connection holds between *descriptions* of events. An event, however, can be described in more than one way. So, the event of raising my arm can be described as "raising my arm" and "saluting." This means that the event that is a cause can also be described in more than one way. For instance, I may substitute "*x*" in the true causal statement "*x* causes *y*" with "the cause of *y*," yielding "the cause of *y* causes *y*." If I do re-describe the statement in this way, I violate the condition of logical distinctness. However, my violating it has no impact whatsoever on the *fact* that one event, *x*, causes another event, *y*. Therefore, the logical connectedness condition does not hold. It fails to distinguish causes from reasons in any definite way (Davidson, 1980, 13–15).[*]

Donald Davidson has been the chief exponent of this common sense position that has been the paradigm of the explanation of action. Its revival is important, because it (among other developments) has paved the way for the restoration of intentionalistic explanation of action to a respectable position in the social sciences thus being instrumental in the discrediting of behaviorism (Searle, 1995). The theory of practical reasoning itself, of course, is not concerned with *explanation* of action, but with justification. However, if it is the case that at least *some* reasons for action may be causes, then at least some reasons can figure in explanations of an action, which can also be justifications of that action. It is important to see that Davidson rehabilitates the idea that an agent's practical reasoning (that can be construed as the process of reason-giving for an action of a certain type) is capable of entering into the explanation of action. On the other hand, this does not mean that the practical syllogism coincides with an agent's practical reasoning: "The practical syllogism exhausts its role in displaying an action as falling under one reason; so it cannot be subtilized into a reconstruction of practical reasoning that involves the weighing of competing reasons. The practical syllogism provides a model neither for a predictive science of action nor for a normative account of evaluative reasoning" (Davidson, 1980, 16). If Davidson is right, this would seem to put the axe at the roots of Simon's project.

5.4.1 DELIBERATION IS OF MEANS NOT ENDS

One of the guiding assumptions of this chapter is that there is a common thread knitting together the theories of practical reasoning of (among others) Aristotle and David Hume on the one hand, and the conception of instrumental rationality of Herbert Simon on the other. In spinning this thread, I have relied on what I have called the traditional interpretation of the doctrines of these thinkers. One of the tags by which this thread is identified is "deliberation is of means not ends." Needless to say, this remark by Aristotle is one of the reasons for aligning him with Hume. However, although the guiding assumption is warranted in that the standard interpretations of these thinkers have exercised the most powerful influence, it would skew our view of them if we would leave it at that. This last section will briefly point to some difficulties with the received interpretation.

Some philosophers find the idea that one cannot rationally deliberate or practically reason about ends disconcerting. What obstacles are there to this possibility? Don't we, as a matter of fact, engage in deliberation about ends all the time? Of course, one might rejoin on behalf of the standard view that one can rationally deliberate about ends, if there are means that are considered, within

---

[*] Simon's grip on the possibility of re-description of events is shaky. For instance, he takes moving one's fingers as a means to an end, namely typing. Davidson would say that "typing" is just another way of describing the event of moving one's fingers (Nieuwenburg, 2003, 230).

the scope of a certain deliberative project, as ends, but that actually subserve another, final end. That final end need not consciously enter into our deliberations. The question, then, reproduces itself at the ultimate level: for why is it not possible to set *final* ends by rational deliberation? The first problem, then, seems to be that there is some kind of danger of regress. It seems to follow from the concept of an end that the chain of practical reasoning stops there. If we take reasoning as deducing, then there is nothing from which a final end can be deduced. This is the practical counterpart to the first principles or axiom from which theoretical reasoning begins. These cannot themselves be established by theoretical reasoning, but, in the classical foundationalist view, have to be acquired inductively by empirical observation or intuition.

Another objection lies in the function Hume ascribed to reason: the establishing of matters of fact and logic. Reason is concerned with ascertaining the truth of beliefs or statements of beliefs, but desires cannot be true or false. That is why Hume could rule out rational criticism of desires such as that aimed at the destruction of the world. The motivational corollary of this Humean point of view is that the passions or emotions guide reason; they provide motivation and direction. Reason cannot do this alone. "The passions get instrumental reasoning—reasoning from end to means—going" (Richardson, 1997, 14). However, according to Simon Blackburn, Hume is not describing "bureaucratic" or "instrumental" reasoning: Hume's theory makes it possible (or leaves room for) the notion that I may deploy some of my ends to criticize and reason about others. This way of reasoning would only be impossible if there were one single final end for me, with all other ends being means to that single end (Blackburn, 1998, 239–240).

What happens when ends conflict? We seem to have arrived, coming from another direction, at Davidson's point: practical reasoning "involves the weighing of competing reasons" for action. Jon Elster points out that "beliefs and desires can hardly be reasons for action unless they are consistent. They must not involve logical, conceptual or pragmatic contradictions" (Elster, 1983, 4). His point is that if practical rationality is a matter of logic, the system cannot possibly put up with inconsistency. However, proponents of this conception of instrumental rationality have to account for the contingent fact that the lives of human beings are replete with conflicts among ends.

The pluralist thesis points to another task of deliberation, a task already signaled by Max Weber.[*] For deliberation, with its original reference to "weighing" (the Latin word *libra* meaning "scales") refers to the process of choosing among different ends.

In instrumental reasoning I may have to choose between two means of achieving a certain final end; but this is not what is meant here. There may be situations in which it is a matter of weighing and comparing two ends in terms of another. This poses the issue of *commensurability*, or whether the conflicting ends can be rationally compared in terms of a value. The theory of value pluralism, which denies this possibility, holds that there is no ultimate single value in terms of which a choice between ends can be rationally made.[†] However, that may be, even if there is more than one final end, and even if among this plurality of ends there may be conflict and inconsistency, this does nothing in itself to detract from the relevance of instrumental practical reasoning to secure each of those ends.[‡]

It is apposite to close this chapter by mentioning another kind of theory of practical reasoning that has gained currency by reflection on Aristotle's tag. This type of theory is sometimes referred to by the name "specificationism" (Millgram, 2001, 10). One of the standard objections against instrumentalism (an objection also endemic to the theory of bureaucracy) is that ends are usually too vague or definite to be capable of getting means-end reasoning going. For instance, it is all very well to say that, happiness is a human being's final end, but we shall need a specific interpretation of

---

[*] Interestingly, Weber's concept of Zweckrationalität, which is often (and misleadingly) rendered "instrumental rationality," explicitly acknowledges that this kind of rationality also serves to "weigh" ends against each other (Weber, 1972, 13).

[†] This has serious and subversive implications for an agent's practical reasoning, see Nieuwenburg (2004).

[‡] On value pluralism, see Berlin (1969), Raz (1986), Crowder (1994), Kekes (1993) and Galston (1999).

happiness to begin reflecting on ways of achieving it. Does happiness for me consist in becoming a university lecturer, or a professional soccer player, or in founding a family? Instrumentally reasoning about how to achieve happiness, then, will be contingent on an adequate specification of my final end, happiness.

Some attribute to Aristotle an instrumentalist position on the basis of his claim that deliberation is of ends and posit specificationism as an alternative to that position.* Others deny that Aristotle was an instrumentalist, but that the traditional interpretation of the tag is wrong: David Wiggins claims that Aristotle himself was a specificationist (Wiggins, 1998).† Of course, specifying may have to occur at more than one step in the chain of instrumental reasoning. Richardson points out that specifying may be a remedy against an apparent conflict of ends: many conflicts between ends disappear upon adequate specification (Richardson, 1997).

5.5 CONCLUSION

In view of these justified criticisms of instrumentalism we may finally revert to Nozick's position that instrumental rationality is the default theory of rationality, without being the only theory. It should be pointed out that these criticisms are not designed to discredit the concept of instrumental practical reasoning. They are leveled at the tendency of instrumentalists to reserve terms like "reason" and "rational" to instrumentalist practical reasoning. What these criticisms intend to show is that there is no monopoly to be claimed here, not that instrumentalism itself is mistaken or should be jettisoned.

REFERENCES

Altham, J. E. J. and Harrison, R., Eds., *World, Mind, and Ethics*, Cambridge University Press, Cambridge, 1995.

Anscombe, G. E. M., *Intention*, 2nd ed., Cornell University Press, Ithaca, 1976.

Aristotle, *Nicomachean Ethics*, Harvard University Press, Cambridge, 1926.

Aristotle, In *Aristotle's De motu animalium*, Nussbaum, M. C., Ed., Princeton University Press, Princeton, 1978.

Ayer, A. J., *Language, Truth, and Logic*, Penguin, London, 1990.

Berlin, I., *Two Concepts of Liberty Four Essays on Liberty*, Oxford University Press, Oxford, pp. 118–172, 1969.

Blackburn, S., *Ruling Passions*, Oxford University Press, Oxford, 1998.

Brandom, R. B., *Articulating Reasons: An Introduction to Inferentialism*, Harvard University Press, Cambridge, 2000.

Cooper, J., *Reason and Human Good in Aristotle*, Harvard University Press, Cambridge, 1975.

Crowder, G., Pluralism and liberalism, *Political Studies*, 42, 293–305, 1994.

Davidson, D., *Actions, Reasons, and Causes Essays on Actions and Events*, Oxford University Press, Oxford, pp. 3–19, 1980.

Davidson, D., *Problems in the Explanation of Action Problems of Rationality*, Oxford University Press, Oxford, pp. 101–106, 2004.

Elster, J., *Sour Grapes*, Cambridge University Press, Cambridge, 1983.

Galston, W. A., Value pluralism and liberal political theory, *American Political Science Review*, 93, 770–783, 1999.

Hooker, B., Williams' argument against external reasons, *Analysis*, 47, 42–44, 1987.

Hume, D., *Enquiries Concerning Human Understanding and Concerning the Principles of Morals*, Oxford University Press, Oxford, 1975.

Hume, D., *A Treatise of Human Nature*, 2nd ed., Oxford University Press, Oxford, 1986.

---

* See Kolnai's famous article in Millgram (2001, 259–278).

† Much hangs on the interpretation of the Aristotelian term ta pros to telos. It has traditionally been rendered "means," but in fact means "things towards the end," including things also (partly) constitutive of the end (Cooper, 1975, ch. 1).

Kekes, J., *The Morality of Pluralism*, Princeton University Press, Princeton, 1993.

Korsgaard, C., Skepticism about practical reason, *The Journal of Philosophy*, 83, 5–25, 1986.

Locke, J., *Essay Concerning Human Understanding*, Oxford University Press, Oxford, 1975.

Mele, A.R., Ed., *The Philosophy of Action*, Oxford University Press, Oxford, 1997.

Millgram, E., Ed., *Varieties of Practical Reasoning*, The MIT Press, Cambridge, 2001.

Moore, G. E., *Principia Ethica*, Cambridge University Press, Cambridge, UK, 1965.

Nieuwenburg, P., Public administration and practical reasoning, In *Retracing Public Administration*, Rutgers, M. R., Ed., Elsevier, Amsterdam, pp. 209–240, 2003.

Nieuwenburg, P., The agony of choice, *Administration and Society*, 35, 683–700, 2004.

Nozick, R., *The Nature of Rationality*, Princeton University Press, Princeton, 1993.

Plato, *Plato's Philebus*, Cambridge University Press, Cambridge, 1945. Translated by R. Hackforth.

Raz, J., *The Morality of Freedom*, Oxford University Press, Oxford, 1986.

Richardson, H. S., *Practical Reasoning About Final Ends*, Cambridge University Press, Cambridge, 1997.

Scanlon, T. M., *What We Owe to Each Other*, Harvard University Press, Cambridge, 1998.

Searle, J. R., *Intentionality*, Cambridge University Press, Cambridge, 1983.

Searle, J. R., *The Construction of Social Reality*, Penguin, London, 1995.

Searle, J. R., *Rationality in Action*, MIT Press, Cambridge, 2001.

Simon, H., *Administrative Behavior*, 2nd ed., Macmillan, New York, 1961.

Simon, H., *Reason in Human Affairs*, Stanford University Press, Stanford, 1983.

Weber, M., *Wirtschaft und Gesellschaft*, Mohr, Tübingen, Germany, 1972.

Wiggins, D., *Needs, Values, and Truth*, 3rd ed., Oxford University Press, Oxford, 1998.

Williams, B. A. O., *Moral Luck*, Cambridge University Press, Cambridge, 1981.

6 Discourse, Decision, and the Doublet: An Essay on the Crisis of Modern Authority[*]

Thomas J. Catlaw

CONTENTS

6.1   Introduction: Simon's "Concessions"...99
6.2   "Tradition" and Authority...101
6.3   Authority, Language and Social Grammar...103
6.4   Representation and the Relocation of Modern Authority..................................105
6.5   The Logic of Foundational Authority, or the Order of Things...........................105
6.6   The Structure of Political Authority: The People..108
6.7   Authority in Social Relations: The Man of Reason 110
6.8   Thought Becomes Unhinged..111
6.9   Exclusion and the Failure of Institutions...112
6.10 The Lingering World of "As-If"...114
References..115

6.1 INTRODUCTION: SIMON'S "CONCESSIONS"

The enduring legacy of Herbert Simon has demonstrated to mainstream administrative and organizational thought the limits of rationality and instrumental action. It has also rendered "decision" as the primary object of analysis. Simon's now famous formulations of "bounded rationality" and "Satisficing Man," who has "not the wits to maximize," articulated an intellectual framework within which to understand the conditional and environmental constraints of decision making. He thus exposed the highly stylized, spurious assumptions of the comprehensively rational, utility maximizing, individual. Of course, the terms of Simon's "concessions," or what Harmon (1989) calls "artful caveats," have been widely influential throughout the social sciences. Indeed the idea of bounded rationality has been taken up by some whose theoretical commitments initially may not even suggest an affinity with Simon's work (Scott, 1998; Touraine, 1992).

Simon's critics counter that his concessions, in fact, concede very little. Fundamentally, Simon retains a "technicist attitude," i.e. the attempt to control consciously and purposefully direct human behavior through technical means (Denhardt, 1981; Farmer, 1995b; Miller, 2002; White and McSwain, 1990). It remains grounded in the same series of problematic dualisms (e.g., fact-value,

---

[*] This project was generously supported by a 2003–2004 Dean's Incentive Grant, College of Public Programs, Arizona State University.

thinking-doing, means-end) that characterize the comprehensive variant of rationality (Harmon, 1989). The practical implications of Simon's concessions, then, amount to an unspoken disavowal of the alleged critique. On this reading Simon's message is: "We know very well that we are boundedly rational and live under conditions of uncertainty, yet we shall nevertheless carry on *as if* this were not the case and assume that we can rationally and consciously adjust a set of means to bring about some specific end."[*] The practice of decision making does not change. Instrumental rationality and the technicist attitude remain firmly in place, perhaps more deeply entrenched, given the concessions' rhetorical "inoculation" against criticism (Barthes, 1972).

The usual counter to these critiques of Simon's concessions reveals what is really at stake. The critique of technicism, the counter argument goes, leaves us with nothing concretely to do and, more seriously, without *hope*, collectively, for making the world better, and personally, for improving our own lives. Absent the affirmation of the instrumental, conscious attitude, the response continues, we resign ourselves to contingency and anonymous structural or biological forces over which we have no control. This is thought to be profoundly pessimistic, not to say nihilistic. Absent a clear alternative mode of action the manifold arguments against technicism and instrumental rational decision making ultimately seem to run into a dead end.

Post-structuralist discourse theories attempt to advance beyond the terms of these critiques and counter-critiques by focusing directly on the dynamic ways in which social worlds are produced, reproduced, and how we are constituted by our inventions (Farmer, 1995b; Fox and Miller, 1995; McSwite, 1997; Sorensen, 2002). They thereby displace the subjectivist–objectivist ontological divide that underpins the debate over technicism. That is, for discourse theory, the problem lies not in the particular answers that one provides to questions about, for example, agency, decision, and purposive action, but rather the way in which the question itself has been constructed. Discourse theorists emphasize that underlying theoretical presuppositions "shape understandings, the propositions that stem from those understandings, and the possibilities for action that may then be imagined" (Fox and Miller, 1995, 8). These presuppositions and relationships, implicit and explicit, are discourses. Though discourses are restrictive in the sense that not everything is visible, imaginable, or possible, they are *constitutive* of what is visible, thinkable and possible. Simply put, without discursive limits, there is no meaning, no identity; no viable human world at all. Change occurs through modification and re-articulation of the patterns and rules of discourse (McSwite, 2000). By shifting these boundaries new relationships, objects, thoughts, identities, and possibilities emerge. Others retreat. Thus the creation of viable human worlds through discourse entails the imposition of limits, and in this imposition some elements are left on the other side of the boundary. Something must be excluded. This is the "price" we pay for sense: an inherent, unavoidable ambiguity, opacity, and incompleteness in sense itself. This is a distinctive ontology of the social world that attempts to account for the objectivity of the social world and objectifies the objectifying relationship we have with the world. In other words, it proposes to take seriously the active, subjective moment in objectification and to cultivate a reflexive attitude with regard to the structures and limits that "make us up."

From the ontological perspective of discourse, the preliminary question of action that emerges is: by what mechanisms are these limits and objectifications constructed? And, as a corollary, by what operation is a "decision on the exclusion" made? What formal, institutionalized arrangements grow around the dominant mode of deciding? As I will suggest in this chapter, these are historical and theoretical questions that basically turn on the question of authority. For what authority does, on one level, is to ground and legitimate a decision on the exclusion. Different modalities of authority, however, constitute these boundaries, decide on the exclusion in distinct ways, and institutionalize

---

[*] Simon's "as if" theory of decision places him squarely in the tradition of Kant, who acknowledged the inherent limits of reason and yet continued to carry on "as if" we were not subject to the limits (Pinkard, 2002; Vaihinger, 1935). Zizek (1989) calls this "as if" a "fetishistic disavowal," the form of which is, "I know very well, but nevertheless [I still believe]…"

those processes in historically specific ways. However, more critically, *authority as discourse* is generative of the human world itself. Drawing broadly on post-structuralist discourse theory,[*] I will explore the modality of authority and its distinct grounds for a decision on the exclusion in modern societies and identify how these grounds manifest themselves in institutions and social relations. Critically, I consider the problems modern authority produces for itself by virtue of these grounds and consider the effects of the contemporary rapid disintegration of the modern mode of deciding on the exclusion. The central practical problem in the contemporary moment is not, as Simon's "reformed" technicism suggests, how to make good, instrumental decisions in the face of uncertainty and complexity or to realize or abandon individual and collective projects but rather to articulate conditions under which the construction of the experience of self, subjectivity, and the cultivation of individual difference can constitute a dynamic and collective end in itself. It is, as I hope to show, a problem of the modality of authority, the decision on the exclusion, and the collaborative production of viable contexts for effective action.

Before moving into the main body of the essay, I want to address one final, critical, point, that may appear as an anomaly. The juxtaposing of "post-structural" and "decision" initially might appear strange. Indeed one might argue that the enterprise of a post-structural account of decision making is hostile to the very premises of post-structuralism, particularly its radical critique of the human subject and teleology. Post-structuralism challenges both the presumptuousness of "deciding" and the causality and teleology implicit in the act of decision. However, to accept this argument is essentially to accept what Foucault (1984) called the "blackmail" of the Enlightenment: "you either accept the Enlightenment and remain within the tradition of rationalism...; or you criticize the Enlightenment, try to escape from its principles of rationality," and too readily accept the conflation of the question Enlightenment with the themes of humanism (43, 45). For Foucault, Enlightenment positively entails a specific "attitude" or philosophical ethos concerned with the historical and critical interrogation of limits; limits, of course, that are both limiting in the confining sense but, equally important, are also constitutive and generative. The interrogation of limits, however, is not undertaken to formulate a "science of limits" but rather "as a historical investigation into the events that have led us to constitute ourselves and to recognize ourselves as subjects of what we are doing, thinking and saying" (46). Foucault calls this a "critical ontology of ourselves" and it is performed precisely so that the historically imposed limits (and their institutionalized mechanisms for managing them; in this essay, the Man of Reason and presumptive We of the People) might be overcome (47). Thus to think "decision" through this lens is to "work on the limits" within which decision has been performed, in practice and thought, and the manner in which its attendant terms, such as autonomy and purpose, have been conceived (50). Thus, central to this essay is the attempt to think decision as other than instrumental and authority as other than representation. And more tangentially, to think action as other than goal attainment and autonomy as other than individualism. It is an effort to reconceptualize the modes by which limits themselves are imposed and the status and "purpose" that they are accorded.

6.2 "TRADITION" AND AUTHORITY

I begin this inquiry with a small observation: while extensive intellectual labor has been expended to understand decision making, scarce attention has been paid to the historical and theoretical

---

[*] Virtually no post-structuralist theorist identifies himself/herself as a post-structuralist. I use the term here following Mark Poster (1989, 4) who argues that that post-structuralism largely is the invention of American academics who have drawn "a line of affinity around several French theorists who are rarely so grouped in France and who in many cases would reject the designation." For discussions of the historical and intellectual issues involved in labeling this group of thinkers, see Harland (1987), Frank (1989), Caws (2000), Polkinghorne (1983) and Sturrock (1986). The term "postmodern" will be used to name efforts to describe and account for a certain historical periodization, a break between two historical epochs, as in the phrase "postmodern conditions" (Harvey, 1990; Jameson, 1984).

emergence of "decision" as a problem or subject of serious, indeed increasingly pressing, intellectual inquiry and political concern. Why has decision been such a prominent concern in political and administrative thought in the twentieth century (Allison, 1971; Beck, 1992; Etzioni, 1968; Lindblom, 1959; March and Olsen, 1976; Simon, 1997; Stone, 1997; Vickers, 1995)? And why, in the contemporary moment, has there been a veritable explosion of interest and self-help style advice on what we might call "everyday decision making" (Galotti, 2002; Hammond et al., 1999; Kidder, 1995; Lewis, 1997; McGraw, 2000; Murnighan and Mown, 2001; Robbins, 2004; Russo and Schoemaker, 2002; Schwartz, 2004; Sloan, 1996; Welch, 2001)? What has ushered in this "age of decision"?

I will argue that the emergence of decision as both a sociopolitical problem and an object of intellectual study is a function of the radical transformations in the structure and functionality of authority that have unfolded during the last 300 years; spurred on, in part, by the rhetorical universality of democracy and the closely aligned Enlightenment injunction *Sapere aude*! Have courage to use your own understanding (Kant, 1784/2004)! With the Enlightenment the ground of authority shifted from a positional, personal, and "embodied" authority to an essentially "representational" form in which authoritative speech found its force not in its connection with the past, tradition, or divine origins, but in the representation of either natural and scientific processes or a presumptive social consensus that justified the imposition of an overarching normative framework for decision and exclusion. Authority acquired its force not from its simple givenness but rather from its capacity to provide reasons that justify decision, grounded in what I will call, following Foucault, "the order of things" (Foucault, 1970). Gradually, as the ground for this authority has eroded, decision has been "decentralized," and in the process, a dramatic expansion of things to be decided upon has been generated as traditional orders, identities, and roles fall away and the possibility for generating alternative futures spreads.

As founding social theorists such as Marx, Durkheim and Weber noted, for much of human history, authority had been grounded in "tradition." There is, of course, an anthropological or sociological connotation in the word that suggests the rituals or activities of a given social group that have been practiced across generations. In a sense, any regularized practice, such as an "academic" or "scholarly" canon, can be seen as a tradition. However, consistent with modernity's rupture with its past, tradition has also been conceived as standing in opposition to "modern" societies. This is perhaps most lucidly and famously conveyed in Ferdinand Tonnies's (1957) distinction between *Gemeinschaft* and *Gesellschaft*. In the sense in which I use it, tradition names a specific attitude towards the present and the past and a particular ground for authority. More precisely, deference towards institutions and order of the present is grounded in its connection to the past. Human action is fundamentally oriented towards the preservation of that order (Arendt, 1958). Tradition, writes Hannah Arendt (1958, 111), was the "thread which safely guided us through the vast realms of the past, but this thread was also the chain fettering each successive generation to a predetermined aspect of the past." Critically, this linkage to the past constituted the foundation for authority, which was rooted in its connection with that which had come before it. "Authority," Arendt (1958, 112) continues, "resting on a foundation in the past as its unshaken cornerstone, gave the world permanence and durability which human beings need precisely because they are mortals."

Tradition in this sense served a number of critical social functions. First, it provided a foundation for social and political authority, rooted in its relationship with the past. The focus of society was, likewise, past-oriented and concerned with preservation. This marked tradition-based societies as deferential with regard to existing social forms and relations. Second, tradition, by providing a foundation for authority, also constituted a firm foundation for decision and choice. Third, and related to this, tradition was a distinctive mechanism for dealing with uncertainty and bounding the range of human thought and action. This was done in a couple of ways. Tradition, first, relied on a conception of what Giddens (1994, 64) calls "formulaic truth" to which only a certain subset of people had access. This access was furthermore determined by one's particular status in the social order. Thus authority, access and status collapsed into one another. At the same time, the past-oriented, preservative dimension of tradition made it less likely that this access would expand or shift. Traditional authority was self-referential: tradition grounded authority and, in turn, authority was grounded in tradition. The problem of what grounds authority was answered by its very existence.

Tradition also "managed" uncertainty with regard to thought and action. Because identities and roles were largely inscribed and prescribed by tradition in existing social relations, rituals and customs, individuals were inscribed in their "place" in society. Strict role prescription, in turn, restricted the scope of individual thought and decision, and the authority of tradition delimited the openness of the future to the terms and determinations of the past. Decision making was guided by traditional and historical precedent, and adherence was, perhaps literally, informed by the force of habit. As Weber (1946, 296) wrote, traditionalism rested largely on the belief "in the everyday routine as the inviolable norm of conduct." The everyday assumed the status of the sacred and, as such, became inviolable.

6.3 AUTHORITY, LANGUAGE AND SOCIAL GRAMMAR

In these two critical ways, tradition is a highly effective technique for managing uncertainty. From the perspective of a post-structural discourse, the deeper importance of tradition is that it confronts the problem of the instability of language and meaning in an effective way and, as such, successively produces constitutive boundaries and stable, meaningful worlds. In the language of post-structuralism, tradition stops the "sliding of the signifier" (Lacan, 1981). Beginning with the work of Ferdinand de Saussure (1972) and the development of the field of structural linguistics, the objective givenness of language and the correspondence among words, ideas, and things began to come into question. With Saussure language became viewed as a system of elements called "signs." These signs, in turn, consisted of two parts, a signifier (concept or idea) and a signified (sound image or word). It is unity of the sign that "points" to the object in the world. Perhaps the most crucial innovation of Saussure was his demonstration that the relationship between the signified and signifier was fundamentally *arbitrary*. In other words, there is no necessary or substantive relation between signifier and signified that derives from a reality more profound than social convention. Any word potentially will do to signify the idea of "dog," provided that a linguistic community agrees to it. As Saussure (1972, 68) writes, "It must not be taken to imply that a [signifier] depends on the free choice of the speaker. …the individual has no free power to alter a sign once it has become established in a linguistic community." Language is a certain set of relationships or *structure* among different signs established by convention (Caws, 2000; Sturrock, 1986). These relations themselves are arbitrary but, through usage, obtain a stability and objectivity.

The post-structuralists, who followed and extended Saussure, argued that Saussure had not fully appreciated the importance and implications of his own work. Saussure argued that there is a rigid distinction between the signified (the idea) and the signifier (the word), implying that one might be able to exist without the other (Howarth, 2000). Related to this, Saussure suggested that the signified takes precedence over the signifier, implying that ideas and objects preceded words. These positions were shown to be problematic. Indeed, as Saussure himself argued, one can orient oneself among signifiers only by reference to other signifiers. For example, when we look in a dictionary for the meaning of a word (signifier), what we find are other words that in turn refer to other words. There is no pure signified. This means that there is no clear distinction between the signifier and the signified. Because there is no clear distinction between the two elements, there is, perforce, no reason to view language, and more broadly, *structure* in the fixed, static way that Saussure did. Though he viewed language as conventional, Saussure arrested the play of meaning by arguing for the overall stability and permanence of a system of linguistic signs (Howarth, 2000).

Jacques Derrida (1974; 1978; 1982), among others, challenged the way in which Saussure fixed language and the process of the production of meaning. Sign or signification systems are not stable, as Saussure had suggested. Rather, as Madan Sarup (1989) writes, "signifiers and signifieds are continually breaking apart and reattaching in new combinations. ...The process is not only infinite but somehow circular: signifiers keep transforming into signifieds and vice versa, and you never arrive at a final signifier in itself" (35). The consequence of what the psychoanalytic theorist Jacques Lacan called the sliding (*glissement*) among signifiers and signifieds is that meaning (or signification) is itself also highly unstable—it will shift from context to context, moment to moment.

The nature of language makes the construction of meaning and sense rather paradoxical in that meaning is always *retrospectively* constructed along a chain of signifiers. For example, when I speak, the meaning of my sentence cannot be produced until I stop or complete my thought. Likewise, it would be difficult to read any text without punctuation. These stoppages and periods create meaning; an effect *in excess* of the signifiers. That is, meaning does not inhere in the words or syntax but insists in the chain as a kind of surplus produced by the stoppage. In post-structural thought, this has direct social implications because social relations are fundamentally ordered by the limits imposed by discourse. In society, too, some "social punctuation" is required to stop the sliding of the signifier and allow for the production of meaning and the creation of stable contexts. Authority and the formal and institutional discourses and practices that grow around it constitute a social grammar characterized by a dynamic of production of words and the authoritative imposition of punctuation (Follett, 1998, 31) that is generative of individual subjectivity and the objectivity of the social thereby producing a kind of homology among internal and external structures (Bourdieu and Wacquant, 1992). Anything that "impairs the dynamic balance of the linguistic process could constitute a dire threat. It could lead to nothing less than the failure to socially construct a reality that evokes effective action" (McSwite, 2004, 418). As I will argue later, it is precisely this balance that has become compromised in the contemporary moment.

In episodically punctuating the social world, authority in the form of discourse draws a boundary and so constitutes a sensible and intelligible domain for human activity. Three points should be repeated here. First, the boundary or punctuation, *constitutes* the domain of sensibility. It is not a function of individual cognitive failure, logistical limitations or other such "empirical" problems as Simon's position contends. The boundaries are generative and productive. Second, by virtue of this boundary or punctuation some element is left on the "other side" of the boundary; some form of *exclusion* is required. Exclusion is, in fact, constitutive of the sensible realm (Catlaw, 2005). Finally, decision making is first and foremost a decision on this exclusion, a decision on what shall be left out. This is fundamentally a discursive (authoritative) process.

In this context, tradition, and its unique organization of authority, can more fully be seen as one mechanism among others for facilitating a decision on the exclusion. It is one institutional manifestation of our attempt to grapple with the ontology of the human world. Tradition manages the fundamental instability at the core of the human world by arresting the play of the signifiers and accomplishing the identity-related bounding functions described above. We can conceive of tradition as a certain attitude towards the given and, in turn, accord it, and those that purport to speak for it, a certain status. We also can conceive of authority in a related, though more complex and expansive way. Though certainly having institutional and social personifications, authority stops the sliding of the signifier and creates contexts in which choice and action can take place. Tradition grants the instituted present a privileged relationship with an assumed fundamental order of reality. Authorities, such as kings, priests, or patriarchs, gain their authority through such access. Following modernity's usual self-narrative, one would be tempted to say that it is precisely this mode of authority that has been undermined by modern, democratic and scientific practices. However, this is not quite the case. We can understand the modality of modern authority by examining the continuities and discontinuities with tradition in its structure and presuppositions.

6.4 REPRESENTATION AND THE RELOCATION OF MODERN AUTHORITY

In Weber's (1978) influential formulation, traditional authority is contrasted with the legal-rational and charismatic forms of authority. Charismatic authority is always, Weber wrote, *in statu nascendi*: "It cannot remain stable, but becomes either traditionalized or rationalized or a combination of both" (246, 1148). Thus, Weber identifies only two *permanent* forms of authority. Legal-rational authority rests on a "belief in the legality of enacted rules and the right of those elevated to authority under such rules to issue commands" (215). However, as Carl Friedrich (1972) demonstrated, the lexicon of Weber's formulation is misleading in that while he acknowledges these forms of permanent authority, he counter-poses tradition and rationality, thereby making tradition appear *irrational*; stripping it of its own, distinct, rationality and structures that make sense in the human world. As suggested above, tradition clearly operates according to a specific and clear logic or rationality. Furthermore, when tradition is linked with the primitive, its invidious colonial implications become manifest. This move also conceals the way in which authority (in the sense outlined above) operates in this new legalist form.

The more constructive hint we can take from Weber's analysis of the legalist form of authority is its *impersonality* quality. This stands in contrast to what we might think of as the "embodied" quality of traditional authority (see Weber, 1978, 216, 227).[*] With tradition, authority is authority in the tautological sense described above. In the legalist form, authority is disconnected from those who speak in its name or symbolically *represent* it.[†] In other words, law, for example, derives its force from what lies "beneath" or "above" it—that is, from a higher truth, principle, or some underlying foundational process or logic. I call this disembodied form of authority *representation* because the artifacts of authority and those that speak in its name are distanced from the origin of their authority. They do not embody. They represent a silent, displaced origin. In modern societies choice and action express themselves as representations of this foundational ground.

The disembodied quality of representational authority generates several practical challenges. Most critically, the mode of representation separates the institutional representative from its origin. The origin, displaced from its representatives, becomes "invisible," though its material and positive objectivity is assumed. The invisibility of the origin presents an acute problem for authority. It also presents an exclusion that will rest on the capacity to speak for the invisible origin; the determination of which is always open to contest. I will elaborate the nature of this representational authority and the problems it produces by examining the paradoxical status of what the philosopher-historian Michel Foucault (1970) calls the "empirico-transcendental doublet" in the human and social sciences.[‡]

6.5 THE LOGIC OF FOUNDATIONAL AUTHORITY, OR THE ORDER OF THINGS

In *The Order of Things* (1970) Foucault's analysis centers on the double status of the subject and object of the human sciences that he calls "Man." Man [sic] is both the primary object of social and human scientific inquiry, as well as its inquirer. Man investigates himself and his products. This

---

[*] For a series of interesting articles on the relationship of embodiment and public administration, see the symposium edited by Patricia Patterson (2001) in *Administrative Theory and Praxis*.

[†] In his discussion of the uniqueness of modern social relations in *Authority*, Richard Sennett (1980, 43) argues along similar lines viz. the market: "The market idea, as Adam Smith proudly announced, banishes the authority of persons; it is a system of exchange which is legitimate only as a system." The invisible hand is an abstraction that is not attached to the physical body of any specific human being. The anonymous, impersonal quality of formal institutions is also conveyed in Hannah Arendt's (1970) argument that this decoupling of authority from the person entails "Rule by Nobody."

[‡] I am sidestepping an important, but unclear, distinction that Foucault draws between the human sciences and the "empirical sciences:" biology, linguistics and economics. These empirical sciences constitute the origins of the "models" from which the human sciences draw to ground themselves.

requires a certain abstracting movement from the very context under consideration, thus producing the anomalies identified at the outset. For example, the social scientist studies and analyzes objective social forces and the regularities they produce in human relations while simultaneously being momentarily exempt from those deterministic forces. That is, social scientific research, while perhaps being driven in the direction of certain research foci by funding sources or pressing social problems, is itself not determined by the social forces being studied. This attitude disavows its own self-referentiality; it disembodies itself from the social conditions in which it is embedded.

The structure of the doublet allowed for two possible lines of intellectual inquiry that, writes Foucault, "rest entirely on themselves:"

"Two kinds of analysis then came into being. There are those that operate within the space of the body, and—by studying perception, sensorial mechanisms, neuro-motor diagrams, and the articulation common to things and to the organism—function as a sort of transcendental aesthetic; these led to the discovery that knowledge has anatomo-physiological conditions, that it is formed gradually within the structures of the body, that it may have a privileged place within it, but that its forms cannot be dissociated from its peculiar functioning; in short, that there is a *nature* of human knowledge that determines its forms and that can at the same time be made manifest to it in its own empirical contents. There were also analyses that—by studying humanity's more or less ancient, more or less easily vanquished illusions—functioned as a sort of transcendental dialectic; by this means it was shown that knowledge had historical, social, or economic conditions, that it was formed within the relations that are woven between men, and that it was not independent of the particular form they might take here or there; in short, that there was a *history* of human knowledge which could both be given to empirical knowledge and prescribe its forms." (Foucault, 1970, 319)

In Foucault's description, we can identify the familiar distinctions between the empirical and the normative, the positive and the historicist. Positivism and so-called empiricism render Man as an object for analysis and scientific inquiry. The "model" of scientific inquiry is the object in the *present*. Historicist and normative theories reject the determinations of the present and proceed to formulate a projected or "retroflective" historical and eschatological account of Man, an essence either to be realized, displaced, or alienated by the forces of History itself. Though the doublet takes these two forms, they remain embedded in the same presupposition, namely that "there must, in fact, exist a truth that is of the same order as the object" and one, furthermore, that can be represented fully (made present) in language. In other words, rather than assuming, as did theology, that truth resided in a non-human divine realm, these new sciences of Man conceive of truth in terms of the "immanent" or as inhering on the same plane as Man itself. The truth of Man is not projected onto a divine being but exists in the same human order as Man, the object. In this way truth, its object, and its knowing subject exist in the same order; a truth, moreover, that can be *represented in language*. Truth becomes coincident with either true and exact discourse or the recognized capacity to utter the truth that is the truth of Man, either in positivistic, historicist, or eschatological terms.[*] Foucault is deeply concerned with understanding the rules that allow for the production of this true discourse (he uses the term *episteme* to describe them), and in *The Order of Things* he locates his analysis of the doublet in a historical periodization that outlines the continuities and discontinuities between the Renaissance, Classical, and Modern Ages.

There is one further dimension of this work that requires attention. It concerns *difference*. Foucault (1970) provides an account of how modernity and the age of Man (in the sense outlined above) confront and manage the question of difference itself. Foucault argues that with the modern age the ground of thought and action is immanent but not readily visible to the eye, nor is it readily

---

[*] There is no actual alternative here between the historicist and the positive in spite of their "radical contestation" within the human and social sciences. Foucault rather identifies the distinction as a "fluctuation" within the structure of the doublet. Again, this fluctuation is a consequence of the assertion that there is that position that is either not objectified or socially conditioned, or stands outside history itself. It can assess and define Man's normative shortfall.

accessible in thought; "order now belongs to things themselves and to their interior law" (Foucault, 1970, 313). Thought itself may only be rendered true by reference or *representation* of that other, invisible, realm that constitutes the conditions for thought and experience. Again this is the logic of the doublet: Man aims to render as an object of consciousness precisely that which constitutes the conditions for consciousness itself. To frame this differently, consider the well-known effort to cross the infamous subject and object divide and restore the identity of Man and his origins and "bring his consciousness back to its real conditions" (364). How does this bear on the question of *difference*? We saw above that action is oriented towards closing the gap between the "model" (either the past or future-to-come) and the present. The logic of modern thought, according to Foucault, is a drive to reduce what we might call "distances in thought" or overcome the gap between subject and object, the two moments of the doublet. Foucault calls this a logic of the *Same* or, more pointedly, the reduction of difference to identity. In a critical passage, he writes, "modern thought is advancing towards that region where man's Other must become the Same as himself," the "ever-to-be-accomplished unveiling of the Same" (1970, 328, 340).

To appreciate Foucault's point, let me make explicit a chain of associations that are operative in his critical assessment of modern thought. Same is linked to consciousness (*cogito*) and "alienation," and Other is linked with unthought and origin (Foucault, 1970, 326). This chain is saturated with political implications, as suggested in this passage:

> "For though the double may be close, it is alien, and the role, the true undertaking, of thought will be to bring it as close to itself as possible; the whole of modern thought is imbued with the necessity of thinking the unthought... of ending man's alienation by reconciling him with his own essence, of making explicit the horizon that provides experience with its background of immediate and disarmed proof, of lifting the veil of the Unconscious, of becoming absorbed in its silence, or straining to catch its endless murmur." (Foucault, 1970, 327)

In a generic sense, the modern project is an effort to reduce otherness and difference to the same and close the gap between subject and object. Its initial form is the reduction of the Unthought to a category of conscious thought.

A troubling paradox goes unacknowledged here. Whenever the origin is defined and determined, something slips away and retreats into the background. From a discourse perspective, this is perfectly sensible; exclusion is required for the production of sensibility. With symbolization and the entrance into language, something inexorably escapes; something is excluded. Foucault (1978, 330) writes, "It is always against a background of the already begun that man is able to reflect on what may serve for him as origin." These "background, taken-for-granted commitments and practices, precisely because [they are] unthought make action and thought possible, but [they] also [put] their source and meaning out of our control" (Dreyfus and Rabinow, 1983, 37). Modern thought denies this. It is locked in an impossible project to "reappropriate the background" that cannot succeed because the disclosure of those structures and conditions cannot emerge except against a displaced background, and the act of knowing and representing changes the ground upon which we know. Thus every time an origin or cause is asserted or posited, the origin is deferred, and the structured background itself changes and shifts as a consequence of the representation. The nature of knowledge and language—in the very ontological nature of the human world itself—is that the gap between consciousness and its unthought is never closed. *Indeed it is precisely because of the gap, this internal difference, that consciousness and meaningful thought are possible.*

Both the constructed, posited quality of the foundation and the paradoxical moment is dangerously disavowed in modern thought, which Foucault writes, sets "itself the task of restoring the domain of the original" (1970, 334). There is, then, a deep pathology or perversion at work in the heart of modernity because the constitutive background structures will never fully emerge in representation, yet the project of rendering them transparent continues. The order of things asserts that there is positive, substantial, foundation to the human world. Yet each articulation of the foundation is, in fact, a necessary but necessarily incomplete, limited, social construction; an abstract(ed) partial projection onto the world, which is nevertheless defended on the basis of its representation of the order of things.

In contrast, again to tradition, modern authority is representational and disembodied. This and the constructed foundationalism of modern thought render institutional representatives of the order of things both unstable and excessively rigid. To put it simply, authority is unstable because it is never what it says it is; its universal, foundational claims and determinations of the order of things are always open to contest. Its logic, then, is to attempt to incorporate more and more elements into the "definition" or more variables into the model of that order; to expand the boundary, to bring the "outside" in; to make it more complete. This is futile because the "real" of the background shifts and retreats precisely as consequence of and condition for the representations we make of it. It is not stable or fixed. Authority is excessively rigid because it dogmatically asserts itself as a disembodied representation of a static order of things, not for example, as a rough "virtual map" of the world (Levy, 1997). It is *as the order of things* that boundaries are created and sense produced. However, this modern modality of authority denies the constitutive necessity of exclusion and, by extension, the conditions of its own generation.

The particular danger lies in the implicit teleology or end state that "puts to use" knowledge to further these impossible ends; eternally displaced and altered. That is the projected, symbolic, representation of the foundation does not merely mistakenly "reify" itself. Rather it projects a vision of the world that orients selection and action concerned with realizing the symbolic representation. It attempts to either fabricate or produce its posited foundation. The positive foundation becomes an implicit normative orientation (Archer and Tritter, 2000) and the mode in which the world, including social relations and identities, is produced (see Bourdieu and Wacquant, 1992). Likewise, contest of the foundation is articulated by competing representations of the presumed positive foundation.

In the next two sections, I will examine two important ways in which this struggle to represent the order of things proceeds and how it enables decision and action to occur in modern societies. However, in anticipation of later sections, let me say that what the post-structural position, and arguably, contemporary social conditions suggest is that this modern *mode of thought* is no longer viable. What is challenged intellectually and politically is not the historical contest among various conceptions of the foundation (as Truth or the Good) and their particular content. Rather the dominant structure of thought itself is challenged; thought that conceives of the exclusion as a positive, displaced origin of the human world and the concomitant social relations and institutions that are constructed in and by this mode of thought.

6.6 THE STRUCTURE OF POLITICAL AUTHORITY: THE PEOPLE

Specific structures and practices grow up around the modern relocation of authority and constitute the primary "bounding" or excluding activity within which alternatives can be produced and sensible choices made. Let me first examine modern political representation, a form of government that ostensibly decouples power from the body of the monarch and invests sovereignty in the People. Though modern political authority disembodies authority, the structure of representational government and popular sovereignty, the People can be shown to be both continuous and discontinuous with traditional authority. As David Farmer (1995a,b) has suggested, not yet have we "killed the king." The political theorist Claude Lefort (1986, 303–304) has provided an elegant and justly famous description of the structure of the People:

> "The modern democratic revolution is best recognized in this mutation: there is no power linked to a body. Power appears as an empty place and those who exercise it as mere mortals who occupy it only temporarily or who could install themselves in it only by brute force or cunning. There is no law that can be fixed, whose articles cannot be contested, whose foundations are not susceptible of being called into

question. Lastly, there is no representation of a centre and of the contours of society: unity cannot now efface social division. Democracy inaugurates the experience of an ungraspable, uncontrollable society in which the people will said to be sovereign, of course, but whose identity will constantly be open to question, whose identity will remain latent. ...[W]hat emerges is the image of the people, which, as I observed, remains indeterminate, but which nevertheless is susceptible of being determined, of being actualized on the level of phantasy as an image of the People-as-One."

Lefort's description lucidly shows how representative political power is non-substantial. While the association of the sovereign People, the territorial integrity of the nation-state, and the famous image of the Hobbesian Leviathan suggest otherwise, the People as a body politic in fact lacks a *physical* body (Sorensen, 2002, 695). It is not a pre-given and pre-political material referent; rather the identity of the People is constructed through the processes of representation. Its authority is disembodied; its positivity is articulated.

Expanding on Lefort's work, political theorists Chantal Mouffe and Ernesto Laclau (1985) have described the way in which the People is *articulated* and given positive content through a process called *hegemony*. Hegemony effectively entails the coming of a particular element or constellation of the social into the empty, open, space of the People's throne.* Laclau writes, (2000, 58), "The universal is an empty place, a void which can be filled only by the particular, but which through its very emptiness produces a series of crucial effects in the structuration and destructuration of social relations." For Laclau, the battle for this empty position is termed a *hegemonic* struggle. Hegemony, then, is the mechanism whereby content for the People's empty throne is produced, the constructive positive foundation is generated and a context for meaning and intelligibility is defined. The "empty center" or signifier of power has no positive context or meaning associated with it. Representative government, therefore, does not institute "the rule of all by all" but rather a kind of "rotating monarchy" in which temporary kings are selected according to constitutional schedule. To borrow a phrase from Ulrich Beck (1992, 191), representative government is, in fact, *democratic monarchy*.

Despite the fact that the empty throne of power is exposed with the democratic invention, hegemony quickly closes it up. For what emerges in the wake of this revolution are discourses, practices and institutions that are structured around authoritative speech and action in the name of a substantive People. The People is mistakenly believed to be something real, a unity that exists in actuality. It is, though, precisely on the basis of this disavowal that representational, substantive, politics proceeds and, consequently, grounds authoritative selection and articulates a line for action. That is, the denial of actual people excluded from the People informs the fundamental project of representational politics. The contradiction of symbolic assertion and the heterogeneity of actual, living, people; the rhetorical ambiguity between the official representation of the People in the state; and the assertion of *real* people who are excluded from that representation, such as the poor or marginalized, becomes the terrain for governing (Agamben, 1998, 176–177). The goal is to realize the identity of the people and the People. Precisely in the manner described by Foucault, the project is to close the gap between these two peoples by reducing the latter to a category; attempting to manage their imaginary alterity; or, in the most horrific moments, eliminate the excluded element physically.

Slavoj Zizek (1998) describes the dynamic between these political elements of modern thought in terms of two dimensions of a "fantasy." Zizek calls these dimensions "fantasy$_1$" and "fantasy$_2$." Fantasy$_1$ is the illusion of a beatific, stabilizing dimension of the society without disturbance or breakdown. It is the fantasy of the People per se. This misrecognition is underwritten by an account of the failure to realize the fullness and harmony of the People, by a destabilizing fantasy$_2$, "whose elementary form is envy" (192). The affectivity of fantasy$_2$ accounts for and explains the failure of

---

*Exceptionally good, clear, accounts of Laclau and Mouffe's theory appear in Howarth (2000), Sorensen (2002), and especially Torfing (1999).

the impossible utopianism of fantasy₁. The most sinister example here, of course, is Nazism in which "the essential and constant 'by-product' of this operation is the production of an arch-enemy to be eliminated at all costs" (Stavrakakis, 1999, 107). But in a generic sense, fantasy₂ is the content of any political program insofar as it proposes to articulate a diagnosis of the failure to realize the positive harmony of the People. Indeed, most of our well-intentioned social programs have been driven similarly by an ethic of warfare and elimination: the elimination of poverty, cancer, terrorism, etc. (Foucault, 2003).

Here, as in the problematic of the human and social sciences, the dynamic of a representational political form establishes an impossible project precisely because the People as such do not exist. They "exist" only insofar as the first dimension of fantasy is provided with positive content through hegemonic articulation, and the inevitable and necessary "failure" of the People is located as an object for action in society. The People, in other words, are constituted through a *constitutive exclusion*. There can never be a fully realized People because the People exist only as a particular element (hegemonically) elevated to the level of the universal. Every articulation of "We the People" will be false insofar as it purports to speak for the People-as-One. The viability of representational government and the plausible legitimacy of its authoritative decisions and action depend, therefore, on the believability not simply of a given articulation, but on ongoing efficacy of the particular form in which the decision on the exclusion proceeds; the representational "social grammar" generatively in use. As representation fails, the capacity for governments to select and decide is correspondingly compromised.

From this perspective it appears that representational government today is encountering the limits of the rhetorical and symbolic (and always false) universality of its discourse and the necessity of exclusion; the possibility of deciding and acting on the foundation of an actually existing "We." Governmental illegitimacy, then, is not a function of legal status, constitutional values or performance but a consequence of the breakdown of a certain structural mode of social construction; it is the erosion of a specific social grammar, namely representation.

6.7 AUTHORITY IN SOCIAL RELATIONS: THE MAN OF REASON

A similar logic and structure plays out at the interpersonal and organizational level. Modernity installs its own cadre of high priests with their particular form of "formulaic knowledge." In *Legitimacy in Public Administration* (1997), McSwite presents the "Man of Reason" as the dominant administrative type. It is not only a type to be associated with public administration but also one produced as the resolution of a particular political deadlock in how to govern representationally. That is, it is a contextual iteration of the solution proposed by "the People" to manage the inherent instability of the order of things. McSwite argues that representational government institutionalizes a particular ontological conception of the world (i.e., the order of things) upon which a government is erected. The key elements of this ontology are (1) a static view of human nature (*any* human nature), (2) ambivalence about the division between values and facts, and consequently politics and administration, and (3) the presupposition of a collective mandate (50). The problem is that, while appearing altogether sensible and reasonable, these three basic elements are fundamentally irresolvable. Part of why they are unanswerable was illustrated in the nature of democratic authority and modern thought: the foundation or "throne" are *empty*. Positive content does not exist in any pre-given (or a priori) way; rather it must rely on specific techniques or "grammars" for the production of sense that presuppose the order of things.

Like the People, the Man of Reason appears as the ad hoc fix that "acknowledges but nonetheless finesses the theoretical questions and 'gets on with the program'" (McSwite, 1997, 51). It is the local manifestation of the "as if." In this reasoned world, structural indeterminacy requires the selection of reasonable leaders (the right men) who must be trusted to act and judge according to the terms of the People's interest. The "democratic process," primarily voting, and subsequently interest groups, issue networks, and policy networks, provides the venue for participation should leaders fail to represent fully (interestingly, though, as Theda Skocpol (1999) suggests, albeit not in these terms, these "participatory" strategies themselves replicate the form of the Man of Reason and the clashing objectivism of representations of the order of things). The process is, moreover, "democratic" in that theoretically anyone can become a Man of Reason so long as one concedes to the discourse of representation. Nevertheless, the inherent contingency of thought and sense is disavowed as the Man of Reason's fix entails a specific attitude or posture towards the world, "the key axiom of which is *submission to objective reality... a* reality that cannot be avoided and that must be acknowledged and respected." "[T]he emotional baseline of this posture is *deference to the object*" (233).

In other words, the presumption is that the world is fixed and that the Man of Reason merely acts as that world's disembodied, passive representative. The Man of Reason is, in the illustrative phrase of Jacques Lacan (1981) the *subject-supposed-to-know*. Like the high priest of tradition, the Man of Reason is the one who has access to sacred knowledge and, on this basis, can effectively resolve conflicting representations of the order of things or adjudicate competing factual and objective claims (Kemmis, 1990). Again, the efficacy of the Man of Reason's fix and his choices and actions depend upon the efficacy of its mode of decision on the exclusion. This means that objectively asserted claims must be generally accepted as such; as objective representations of the order of things and as not contrived rationalizations of power or, in the idiom of the moment, as "spin." This, as Zizek (2000) argues, requires an elementary disavowal at the level of the individual. When asked what I believe, my own eyes or the words of the institution, I accept the representations of the institution without hesitation. "They" must know something I don't. As I will argue below, both this disavowal and the modern institutional "fixes" to the contingency of the social world are becoming increasingly untenable.

6.8 THOUGHT BECOMES UNHINGED

The making of worlds and meaning in modern societies, while similarly structured to those processes in monarchy and traditional forms of authority, proceeds from a different position and toward different ends. Because the preservation of instituted power relations cannot be explicitly asserted, the replication of power relations assumes the form of the representation of the mute, displaced, and disembodied order of things. This takes the two dominant forms of the normative-eschatological and positive–objective that, in turn, are duly instituted and replicated by the People and the Men of Reason. Like the sovereign or royal authority, these are practices that bound modern societies and manage the "hole" at the center of the human world. They allow for the generation and sustaining of meaning and proceed from an original disavowal that the foundation is itself a construction or articulation.

The world holds only as long as institutions hold because they are the basic mechanism for generating boundaries that, in turn, quite literally *make sense* of the world and make the world meaningful. As McSwite (2003, 190) writes, "It is when institutions begin to fail, to lose legitimacy, that they become of concern. This starts to occur when authority begins to contradict itself and the vacancy on which is its founded becomes exposed." Exposure of this vacancy has occurred repeatedly throughout human history and has informed the dialectic of instituted authority and constituent power (Negri, 1999). Indeed this is precisely what happened when the modern world of representation displaced the divine right of kings. Yet there is reason to believe that the contemporary moment marks a determinate break with this dialectic. To be sure, to announce a "crisis of authority," is nothing new. Since the 1960s such has been widely observed and commented upon (Castells, 1997; Nisbet, 1975; Nye et al., 1997). Perhaps the deeper reason for the novelty of the present moment concerns a discernable transformation in the possibilities of thought.

In an important essay, "Structure, Sign, and Play in the Human Sciences," Jacques Derrida (1978, 278–294) analyzes an "event" in this history of the thought of structure. This event concerns the moment in human history when it became possible to think of what he calls the "structurality of the structure." Derrida provides a metacommentary on the concept of structure and describes the way in which we have historically thought about the very idea of structure itself. The thinking of structure itself, he argues, has been structured by the idea of the center, a fixed point of origin that provides assurance of certitude and the potential for mastery. Like the doublet, structure occupies an ambiguous position both inside and outside. It structures the empirical world, yet remains "outside" in that it is not subject to any structure itself. Derrida identifies several names for this structure or center: God, the Law, Truth, Telos, Man, Science, etc. Furthermore, it is generally thought that it is precisely this element that grounds or produces social order (or in normative, instrumental, terms towards which social order ought to tend). Derrida, however, looks past the specific historical names of this element to what these various names share, that is, a claim to represent and define the center or origin. In a generic sense, the center is the name of the foundation or of Truth. What concerns Derrida, though, is the center structure, not its many historical names or occupants.

For Derrida, the rupture occurs when structure becomes located in concrete social practices of the order of things. His paradigmatic example comes from the anthropology of Claude Levi-Strauss's work on the incest taboo. Levi Strauss claimed to have identified a "scandal" in that the incest taboo is a social construction, an artifact of culture because it is a system of norms, yet seemingly universal across human cultures and, in this way, *natural*. This blurring of the natural and the cultural, the constructed and the given, is destabilized and with it the plausibility of an unstructured, non-social, origin. The consequence is that there ceases to be a positive position outside of discourse and language; a position that is neutral or universal and that has positive content. We have seen that this has implicitly always been the case, but with the thought of the structurality of the structure it is not simply a specific claim of authority that comes into question, but rather the very capacity for authoritative representation. The sense-making function of authority and the decision and selection-making contexts that are created are conceived as effects of power and arrests on what Derrida calls the "play of difference." The hole in the world is fully exposed. There is no underlying anchor for the world; there is no one who *really knows* what is going on because there is no *position* outside of language from which to know; there is no way to know in any definitive way what the consequences of our actions will be. Yet, at the same time this rupture occurs, and, perhaps, because of it, the mechanisms for decision on the exclusion begin to be radically decentralized. As individuals, we are required to decide and act in increasingly broad and complex ways. This is the challenge of the contemporary world.

6.9 EXCLUSION AND THE FAILURE OF INSTITUTIONS

An important effect of the failure of formal institutions is the expansion of the scope of things upon which we as individuals are called upon to decide and choose. The breakdown of representational authority and the failure to produce a positive determination of the origin and the capacity for collective action under the terms of the order of things (e.g., the People) means that decisions will no longer simply be made for us on our behalf. With the erosion of traditional representations of authority, decision has been "decentralized" to the individual. Increasingly we must make them ourselves; allegedly as "sovereign individuals" (Thorne, 2004). The decentralization of decision, when viewed in light of the erosion of the prescriptive designations of tradition and instituting of a stable identity, are thought to open the individual subject to the manifold possibilities of constructing oneself. Decisions are not merely selections among alternatives (i.e., which is the better insurance plan) but in many cases hinge on the conscious construction of personal identity. For many living in industrialized nations, we now may choose our utility companies, our financial planners and retirement plans, and our health care providers (Schwartz, 2004). We also can decide about fundamental issues like how we want to look physically, what gender we prefer to be, and what sex we want our children to be. Bioengineering is the outer limits of this brave new world of choice.

This decentralization has the related effect of a breakdown in the plausibility of sacrificing for the "greater good." Sociologist Todd McGowan (2004, 3) writes that traditional society is basically concerned with the preservation and success of the whole. And "the individual must give up her or his dreams of wholly individual achievement and fit his or her abilities into the structure of the team" (McGowan, 2004, 3). Or, we can add, the People. The decentralization of decision shifts attention away from this goal, and people become more concerned with their own "narrow" individual concerns and less worried about the "greater good." It is "no longer requisite that subjects accept constant dissatisfaction as the price for existing within a social order [i.e., sacrificing for the sake of the greater good]" (McGowan, 2004, 3). While there is some truth in analyses that interpret these changes as the retreat from public life, it is incorrect to view this "subjective turn" solely as selfishness or an apathetic retreat from the social world (Putnam, 2000). Major transformations are occurring that destabilize the many ways in which the division between collective and individual goods is formulated.

For much of human history this distinction was managed by high priests and Men of Reason through their unique formulaic knowledge; orienting identities towards the preservation or actualization of "the greater good" and the reproduction of certain social relations, rules, or grammars. Traditional worlds were "found." Modern societies were collective projects fabricated according to the logic described above. The possibility of the sacrifice McGowan artfully describes was rooted in the efficacy of a certain modality of authority and its decision on the exclusion. In stark contrast, the projects undertaken in contemporary society concern the active production of one's singular subjectivity and identity, rather than the submission to falsely (indeed impossibly) collective or universal goals. These transformations are producing considerable anxiety and uncertainty in the individual, and impasse and disruption in "collective" institutions such as government.

Why is this potential moment of individual freedom producing such discomfort? First, the contemporary society proposes no alternative mechanism for managing the uncertainty at the core of the world. In other words, it has no distinctive account of authority, which it mindlessly "outsources" to the newly sovereign individual. Before, the important role tradition and modern institutions played was to stabilize social relations and produce worlds. With the destabilization of formal, modern institutions, we experience the *unbounded* proliferation of decisions and selections in our personal and professional lives and for which we are responsible but about which we cannot possibly foresee the consequences. This loss of a meaningful objective context for identity results in what Zizek (2000, 373) calls the "antinomy of postmodern individuality," i.e. "extreme individuation reverts to its opposite, leading to the ultimate identity crisis." The freedom to decide who you want to be beyond tradition and prohibition coincides with the anxiety of having lost one's identity. It is important to stress, though, that this predictive inability is not a problem of bounded rationality or imperfect information. In other words, it is not a problem of what we *know*. Information does not get us out of this bind. This is becoming manifestly clear as once-hidden disputes among experts become fodder for political and non-scientific debate (Beck, 1992), and the failure of professional and technical knowledge to make good on its promises of social engineering are more widely recognized (Power, 1997; Scott, 1998). Rather, what we encounter is a problem of the pervasive loss of a mechanism for the production of shared, meaningful contexts in which choices themselves can be made. There is a concomitant loss of *both* the objective and subjective. What remain are the eroding institutions and relations of representation and the decision on the exclusion.

The "postmodern" is, then, hardly a total break with the modern. Much of the anxiety that has met the shift into contemporary social relations can be accounted for by examining the *continuities* with the past. In addition to the advance of market capitalism two further continuities are quite evident. First, the production of identity and subjectivity is not yet viewed as a collective, social, process.

Rather, as suggested by the widespread laments over civic apathy, "personal development" remains subordinated to the execution of the ostensibly broader, increasingly ambiguous, "greater" goals of collective development, whose content is increasingly under-determined and contentious. We remain stuck in the eschatology of the order of things and the implausible objectivism of a representational politics of a We. Thus, subject and identity production generally is occurring in a distinctly atomized and distended context. To the extent that subject formation occurs in anything like a social or collective setting, it occurs, most visibly, through the homogenizing, disciplinary, mode of personalized consumption in the market or religious fundamentalism (Barber, 1995; Niedzviecki, 2004).

Second, in spite of the decentralization of decision, we still find ourselves dependent upon Men of Reason and continue to locate the solution to social and personal decision making in objective, factual knowledge. We can think of this as a movement towards "redependency" on Men of Reason. Precisely because so many of our important life decisions and choices are decentralized to us, we are confronted with necessity of hiring Men of Reason as advisors, consultants, etc., to help us steer our way through financial, legal, and health-related complexities. The selection we make is ultimately a decision concerning which expert to trust in the marketplace. The problem of the "hole" or constitutive exclusion is simply displaced onto a localized expertise and sovereign individual. The deeper problem in the shifting of uncertainty, however, turns on the market model that underlies it. This displacement is informed by a belief that "The Market" can resolve problems of uncertainty and decision once associated with formal representations and institutions of authority. Markets are advanced to resolve, or rather *avoid*, the problem of exclusion and the ontology of the social. Markets certainly disperse authority and decision and challenge the dominion of political representation, but they entirely neglect the other critical, generative functions that authority serves.

6.10 THE LINGERING WORLD OF "AS-IF"

The explosion of interest in decision and decision making is a symptom of our times. Yet, as a symptom, it is itself not the primary problem we face. Simon's concessions conceal the core problem at the same moment they appear to give much away. The core problem of our postmodern world is that we continue to act and speak as if there were an underlying order (be it subject or object) to the world that could serve as a firm referent or ground for identity and decision while the institutions and mechanisms that sustained this fiction erode. The lingering faith in this "as-if" is tearing our world apart and impeding the delicate and deliberate reconstruction of a way of living together beyond representation.

The fourfold "pitch" of the post-structural or discourse response to these critical matters is this. First, collectively, we need to confront the fundamental *undecideability* of the human world itself, the constitutive gap that modern, formal, institutions managed and finessed until quite recently. This entails beginning social construction from a distinctly new *ontological* position; decisions on the exclusion, contextual choice and a determination of action no longer proceed from the assumption that there is either a stable normative or positive referent that is itself unconstructed. Second, worlds are generated through the imposition of discursive limits or social grammars. In a restricted sense, all realities are "fictions" or "virtual realities." However, it is only through this virtual production that the world assumes any objectivity. This does not render the social transparent to itself; the basis of our being cannot be known; however, it always remains enigmatic and impossible by virtue of its very condition for possibility.[*] This raises the third, practical, political matter: How will these constructions proceed? How will we collectively "mind the gap?" The inability to assert

---

[*] Experimental psychology is, in fact, coming to this conception of the individual self; the self that is always a "stranger to itself;" just as, I argue here, human worlds remain enigmatic; something is always opaque to us (Wilson, 2002).

impositions based on positive foundations or traditions requires a serious and careful reconsideration of the function of authority and its role in social relations. What is required is an appropriate modality of authority and social grammar for our times.[*] Fourth, in thinking all these elements together, a new concept of democracy is required; a collaborative democracy oriented, primarily, towards the active construction of shared meaning and sense rather than toward the impossible realization of fantastic ends. This reconstitution of social worlds begins from the revelation of the Enlightenment's democratic invention and the doublet, yet it breaks from the attitude and grammar of representation that undermined the development of democratic social relations and civil discourse.

REFERENCES

Agamben, G., *Homo Sacer: Sovereign Power and Bare Life*. Trans. Daniel Heller-Roazen, Stanford University Press, Stanford, 1998.

Allison, G. T., *The Essence of Decision*, Little, Brown and Company, Boston, 1971.

Archer, M. S. and Tritter, J. Q., Introduction, In *Rational Choice Theory: Resisting Colonization,* Archer, M. S. and Tritter, J. Q., Eds., Routledge, London, pp. 1–17, 2000.

Arendt, H., What was authority?, In *Nomos I: Authority*, Friedrich, C., Ed., Harvard University Press, Cambridge, pp. 81–112, 1958.

Arendt, H., *On Violence*, Harcourt Brace & Company, New York, 1970.

Barber, B. R., *Jihad vs. McWorld*, Ballantine Books, New York, 1995.

Barthes, R., *Mythologies,* Translated by Annette Lavers, Hill & Wang, New York, 1972.

Beck, U., *The risk society: Towards a new modernity,* Translated by Mark Ritter, Sage, London, 1992.

Bourdieu, P. and Wacquant, L. J. D., *Invitation to Reflexive Sociology*, University of Chicago Press, Chicago, 1992.

Castells, M., *The Power of Identity*, Blackwell, London, 1997.

Catlaw, T. J. 2003. The biopolitical state: Public administration and the fabrication of "the People." PhD diss, George Washington University, Washington, DC.

Catlaw, T. J. 2004. The structure and role of administrative authority in the construction of the post-representational social bond: A commentary on critique short-circuited. Paper presented at the 17th Annual International Conference of the Public Administration Theory Network, June, University of Nebraska, Omaha.

Catlaw, T. J., Constitution as executive order: The administrative state and the political ontology of "We the People", *Administration and Society*, 17(2), 445–482, 2005.

Caws, P., *Structuralism: A Philosophy for the Human Sciences*, 2nd ed., Humanity Books, Amherst, NY, 2000.

Connolly, T., Arkes, H. R., and Hammond, K. R., General introduction, In *Judgment and Decision Making: An Interdisciplinary Reader*, Connolly, T., Arkes, H. R., and Hammond, K. R., Eds., Cambridge University Press, Cambridge, pp. 1–12, 2000.

Copjec, J., *Read my desire: Lacan Against the Historicists*, MIT Press, Cambridge, 1994.

Denhardt, R. B., *In the Shadow of Organization*, Regents Press of Kansas, Lawrence, KS, 1981.

Derrida, J., *Of grammatology,* Translated by Gayatri Charavorty Spivak, Johns Hopkins University Press, Baltimore, 1974.

Derrida, J., *Writing and difference,* Translated by Alan Bass, University of Chicago Press, Chicago, 1978.

Derrida, J., *Margins of philosophy,* Translated by Alan Bass, University of Chicago Press, Chicago, 1982.

Dreyfus, H. L. and Rabinow, P., *Michel Foucault, Beyond Structuralism and Hermeneutics*, 2nd ed., University of Chicago Press, Chicago, 1983.

Etzioni, A., *The Active Society: A Theory of Societal and Political Processes*, Free Press, New York, 1968.

Farmer, D. J., Kill the king: Foucault and public administration theory, *Administrative Theory and Praxis*, 17(2), 78–83, 1995a.

Farmer, D. J., *The Language of Public Administration: Bureaucracy, Modernity and Postmodernity*, University of Alabama Press, Tuscaloosa, AL, 1995b.

---

[*] I have begun to formulate a preliminary account of this problem. See Catlaw (2003, 2004).

Follett, M. P., *The New State: Group Organization, the Solution of Popular Government*, Pennsylvania State University Press, University Park, PA, 1998.

Foucault, M., *The Order of Things: An Archeology of the Human Sciences*, Vintage Books, New York, 1970.

Foucault, M., *The History of Sexuality An Introduction*, Translated by Robert Hurley, vol. I, Vintage Books, New York, 1978.

Foucault, M., What is enlightenment?, In *The Foucault Reader*, Rabinow, P. Ed., Pantheon Books, New York, pp. 32–50, 1984.

Foucault, M., *Discipline and Punish: The Birth of the Prison*, Translated by Alan Sheridan, 2nd ed., Vintage Books, New York, 1995.

Foucault, M., *"Society must be Defended": Lectures at the College de France, 1975-1976*, Translated by David Macey, Picador, New York, 2003.

Fox, C. J. and Miller, H. T., *Postmodern Public Administration: Toward Discourse*, Sage, Thousand Oaks, 1995.

Frank, M., *What is Neostructuralism?*, Translated by Sabine Wilke and Richard Grey, University of Minnesota Press, Minneapolis, MN, 1989.

Friedrich, C. J., Authority, reason and discretion, In *Nomos I: Authority*, Friedrich, C., Ed., Harvard University Press, Cambridge, pp. 28–48, 1958.

Friedrich, C. J., *Authority and Tradition*, Praeger, New York, 1972.

Galotti, K. M., *Making Decisions that Matter: How People Face Important Life Choices*, Erlbaum, Mahwah, 2002.

Giddens, A., Living in a post-traditional society, In *Reflexive Modernization*, Beck, U., Giddens, A., and Lash, S., Eds., Polity Press, Palo Alto, CA, pp. 56–109, 1994.

Hammond, J. S., Keeny, R. L., and Raifa, H., *Smart Choices: A Practical Guide to Making Better Life Decisions*, Broadway Books, New York, 1999.

Harland, R., *Superstructuralism: The Philosophy of Structuralism and Post-Structuralism*, Methuen, London, 1987.

Harmon, M. M., "Decision" and "action" as contrasting perspectives in organization theory, *Public Administration Review*, 49(2), 144–152, 1989.

Harvey, D., *The Condition of Postmodernity*, Blackwell, Oxford, 1990.

Howarth, D., *Discourse*, Open University Press, Philadelphia, 2000.

Jameson, F., Postmodernism, or the cultural logic of late capitalism, In *The Jameson Reader*, Hardt, M. and Weeks, K., Eds., Blackwell, Oxford, pp. 188–232, 1984.

Kant, I., 1784/2004. What is Enlightenment? http://www.english.upenn.edu/~mgamer/Etexts/kant.html (accessed June 1, 2004).

Kemmis, D., *Community and the Politics of Place*, University of Oklahoma Press, Norman, 1990.

Kidder, R. M., *How Good People Make Tough Choices: Resolving the Ethical Dilemma of Life*, Fireside, New York, 1995.

Lacan, J., *The Seminar of Jacques Lacan, Book XI: The Four Fundamental Concepts of Psychoanalysis*, Translated by Alan Sheridan, W.W. Norton, New York, 1981.

Laclau, E., Identity and hegemony, In *Contingency, Hegemony, Universality*, Butler, J., Laclau, E., and Zizek, S., Eds., Verso, London, pp. 44–89, 2000.

Laclau, E. and Mouffe, C., *Hegemony and Socialist Strategy: Towards a Radical Democratic Politics*, Verso, London, 1985.

Lefort, C., *The Political Forms of Modern Society*, MIT Press, Cambridge, 1986.

Levy, P., *Collective Intelligence: Mankind's Emerging World in Cyberspace*, Translated by Robert Bononno, Perseus Books, Cambridge, 1997.

Lewis, H. W., *Why Flip a Coin?: The Art and Science of Good Decisions*, Wiley, New York, 1997.

Lindblom, C., The science of muddling through, *Public Administration Review*, 19(2), 79–88, 1959.

March, J. G., and Olsen, J. P., *Ambiguity and Choice in Organizations*, Universitetsforlaget, Bergen, 1976.

McGowan, T., *The End of Dissatisfaction? Jacques Lacan and the Emerging Society of Enjoyment*, State University of New York Press, Albany, 2004.

McGraw, P. C., *Life strategies*, Hyperion, New York, 2000.

McSwite, O. C., *Legitimacy in Public Administration, a Discourse Analysis*, Sage, Thousand Oaks, 1997.

McSwite, O. C., On the discourse movement, *Administrative Theory and Praxis*, 22(1), 49–65, 2000.

McSwite, O. C., Now more than ever: refusal as redemption, *Administrative Theory and Praxis*, 25(2), 185–204, 2003.

McSwite, O. C., Creating reality through administrative practice: a psychoanalytic reading of Camilla Stivers' Bureau Men, Settlement Women, *Administration and Society*, 36(4), 406–426, 2004.

Miller, H. T., *Postmodern Public Policy*, State University of New York Press, Albany, 2002.

Murnighan, J. K. and Mown, J. C., *The Art of High Stakes Decision Making: Tough Calls in a Speed Driven World*, Wiley, New York, 2001.

Negri, A., *Insurgencies: Constituent Power and the Modern State,* Translated by Maurizia Boscagli, University of Minnesota Press, Minneapolis, 1999.

Niedzviecki, H., *Hello I'm Special: How Individuality Became the New Conformity*, Penguin Canada, Toronto, 2004.

Nisbet, R., *Twilight of Authority*, Oxford University Press, New York, 1975.

Nye, J. S., Zelikow, P. D., and King, D. C., Eds., *Why People Don't Trust Government*, Harvard University Press, Cambridge, 1997.

O'Malley, T., Risk and responsibility, In *Foucault and Political Reason: Liberalism, Neo-Liberalism and Rationalities of Government*, Barry, A., Osbourne, T., and Rose, N., Eds., University of Chicago Press, Chicago, pp. 189–208, 1997.

Patterson, P. M., Reinventing the public body: embodiment, feminist theories and public administration [Symposium], *Administrative Theory and Praxis*, 23(2), 175–251, 2001.

Pinkard, T., *German Philosophy The Legacy of Idealism 1760-1860*, Cambridge University Press, New York, 2002.

Polkinghorne, D., *Methodology for the Human Sciences*, State University of New York Press, Albany, NY, 1983.

Poster, M., *Critical Theory and Poststructuralism: In Search of a Context*, Cornell University Press, Ithaca, 1989.

Power, M., *The Audit Society: Rituals of Verification*, Oxford University Press, Oxford, 1997.

Putnam, R. D., *Bowling Alone: The Collapse and Revival of American Community*, Simon & Schuster, New York, 2000.

Robbins, S. P., *Decide and Conquer: Make Winning Decisions and Take Control of Your Life*, Prentice Hall-Financial Times, Upper Saddle River, 2004.

Russo, J. E. and Schoemaker, P. H. J., *Winning Decisions: Getting it Right the First Time*, Doubleday, New York, 2002.

Sarup, M., *An Introductory Guide to Post-Structuralism and Postmodernism*, University of Georgia Press, Athens, 1989.

Saussure, F. D., *Course in General linguistics,* Translated by Roy Harris, Open Court Press, La Salle, 1972.

Schwartz, B., *The Paradox of Choice: Why More is Less*, Ecco Press/HarperCollins, New York, 2004.

Scott, J. C., *Seeing Like a State: How Certain Schemes to Improve the Human Condition have Failed*, Yale University Press, New Haven, 1998.

Sennett, R., *Authority*, Knopf, New York, 1980.

Simon, H. A., *Administrative Behavior*, 4th ed., The Free Press, New York, 1997.

Skocpol, T., Advocates without members: the recent transformation of civic life, In *Civic Engagement in American Democracy*, Skocpol, T. and Fiorina, M., Eds., Brookings/Russell Sage Foundation, Washington, DC, pp. 461–509, 1999.

Sloan, T., *Life Choices: Understanding Dilemmas and Decisions*, Westview Press, Boulder, 1996.

Sorensen, E., Democratic theory and network governance, *Administrative Theory and Praxis*, 24(4), 693–720, 2002.

Stavrakakis, Y., *Lacan and the Political*, Routledge, New York, 1999.

Stone, D., *Policy Paradox: The art of Political Decision-Making*, W.W. Norton and Co., New York, 1997.

Sturrock, J., *Structuralism*, Paladin Books, London, 1986.

Thorne, K., The dangerous case of the sovereign individual: How should we cultivate the civic in global cyberspace? Paper presented at the Seventeenth Annual International Conference of the Public Administration Theory Network, June, University of Nebraska, Omaha, 2004.

Tonnies, F., *Community and Society: Gemeinschaft und Gesellschaft,* Translated by Charles P. Loomis, Michigan State University Press, East Lansing, 1957.

Torfing, J., *New Theories of Discourse: Laclau, Mouffe and Zizek*, Blackwell, London, 1999.

Touraine, A., Is sociology still the study of society?, In *Between Totalitarianism and Postmodernity*, Beilharz, P., Robinson, G., and Rundell, J., Eds., MIT Press, Cambridge, 1992.

Vaihinger, H., *The Philosophy of "as if": a System of Theoretical, Practical and Religious Fictions of Mankind,* Translated by C. K. Ogden, Routledge and Kegan Paul, London, 1935.

Vickers, G., *The Art of Judgement: A Study of Policy Making*, Sage Publications, Thousand Oaks, CA, 1995.

Weber, M., *The Social Psychology of the World Religions*, In *From Max Weber*, Gerth, H. H. and Mills, C. W., Eds., Oxford University Press, New York, pp. 267–301, 1946.

Weber, M., *Economy and Society*, University of California Press, Berkeley, 1978.

Welch, D. A., *Decisions, Decisions: The Art of Effective Decision Making*, Prometheus Books, New York, 2001.

White, O. F. and McSwain, C. J., The phoenix project: raising a new image of public administration from the ashes of its past, In *Images and Identities in Public Administration*, Cass, H. D. and Caytron, B., Eds., Sage, Newbury Park, pp. 23–59, 1990.

Wilson, T. D., *Strangers to Ourselves: Discovering the Adaptive Unconscious*, The Belknap Press of Harvard University Press, Cambridge, 2002.

Zizek, S., *The Sublime Object of Ideology*, Verso, London, 1989.

Zizek, S., The seven veils of fantasy, In *Key concepts of Lacanian psychoanalysis*, Nobus, D., Ed., Other Press, New York, pp. 190–218, 1998.

Zizek, S., *The Ticklish Subject: The Absent Centre of Political Ontology*, 1st paperback ed., Verso, London, 2000.

7 Evolution, Cognition, and Decision Making

Steven A. Peterson

CONTENTS

7.1   Introduction 119
7.2   Models of Decision Making 120
    7.2.1   Rational-Comprehensive Decision Making 120
    7.2.2   Rational Choice Theory 120
    7.2.3   Incremental Decision Making...121
    7.2.4   Bounded Rationality 122
7.3   Human Nature and Decision Making 122
    7.3.1   Schemata and Decision Making 122
        7.3.1.1   Defined 122
        7.3.1.2   Neurophysiological Bases of Schemata 123
        7.3.1.3   Evolutionary Bases of Schemata 123
    7.3.2   Heuristics and Decision Making...125
        7.3.2.1   Defined 125
        7.3.2.2   Neurophysiological Bases of Heuristics...125
        7.3.2.3   Evolutionary Bases of Heuristics 127
        7.3.2.4   Coda..127
7.4   Discussion 127
References 129

7.1 INTRODUCTION

One of the most important areas in the study of public administration and public policy is decision making, how decisions actually get formulated and made. There are a number of well-known models that have been developed. Many ways, not the least of which is being awarded an entire section in the massive *Handbook of Public Administration* (Rabin et al., 1998), exemplify the importance of decision making. The subject is covered in basic textbooks on both public policy (Anderson, 1997) and public administration (Rosenbloom and Kravchuk, 2005). In his well-known textbook, Thomas Dye speaks of various models of policy making (Dye, 1987).

This chapter addresses one issue not often addressed in standard works in public administration and policy—the biological bases of decision making by humans. The chapter begins by summarizing some basic models of decision making: rational—comprehensive decision making, incrementalism, bounded rationality, and rational choice theory. The models of human nature underlying each are discussed to demonstrate that the question of human nature is central to the study of decision making. While there are many other theoretical perspectives (such as garbage can models [Cohen et al., 1972], multiple streams theory [Kingdon, 1984], public choice theory [e.g., Niskanen, 1971], principal-agent theory [Moe, 1984], elitism [e.g., Mills, 1956], and pluralism [Dahl, 1962]), we focus on the preceding four to illustrate the basic point about the importance of human nature in exploring the underpinnings of decision making theories. The chapter, after all, is not meant to be an exhaustive survey of models of decision making; rather, it uses some common, illustrative models to examine basic conceptions of human nature underlying each. Then, this chapter moves on to outline the influence that biology has on humankind's decision making behavior, including the relevance of neurophysiology and evolutionary processes for evaluating the various models. Finally, some general implications are noted.

7.2 MODELS OF DECISION MAKING

There is a large array of theories of decision making, as already noted. This section, explores one subset of these theories beginning with rational-comprehensive decision making.

7.2.1 RATIONAL-COMPREHENSIVE DECISION MAKING

This is one of the most traditional approaches to decision making. It is normally perceived as a series of steps. Passage through these steps is assumed to produce the optimal decision(s) among all alternatives. While there are variations in the process, one standard view identifies the following stages:

1. Define the problem.
2. Determine the objectives of efforts to address the problem.
3. Identify all possible alternative policy options to meet objectives and, hence, address the original problem.
4. Select the single best option (or combination of options) by some objective process, such as cost-benefit analysis.
5. Implement the policy choice.
6. Evaluate the operation and effect of the policy option chosen.
7. Make any corrections in the original policy (including termination) based on feedback from the evaluative process.

Problems exist with this perspective. First, political reality may intrude. It is possible that government decision makers have already decided upon some course of action. Hence, the analytical results of the rational-comprehensive approach may well be shelved if these do not comport with decision makers' values (e.g., see Heineman et al., 2001). Second, as Lindblom points out (1959, 80), "It assumes intellectual capacities and sources of information that men simply do not possess...."

Underlying this perspective is a view of human nature in which one key assumption is that humans can objectively analyze a wide array of alternatives and conclude that one (or a set of these) is preferable. The validity of this assumption is explored below.

7.2.2 RATIONAL CHOICE THEORY

Heikkila's chapter in this volume discusses in detail the assumptions, principles, and different versions of *public choice theory* that is an application of rational choice in public policy and administration and politics. The following is a brief summary of the rational choice assumptions that are pertinent to the discussions in this chapter.

The essence of rational choice theory is quite straightforward (e.g., see Shepsle and Bonchek, 1997). The basic starting concepts include: (1) preferences that represent various of humanity's want and needs, and (2) self-interest, by which people behave. As Shepsle and Bonchek put it, "More often than not, individuals may not have an exact sense of how an instrument or behavior they might adopt relates to the outcomes they value" (18). Beliefs, another key concept, "... describe the hunches an individual has concerning the efficacy of a given instrument or behavior for obtaining something he or she wants...." (18). Beliefs, then, connect instruments to outcomes. When a person acts in agreement with both preferences and beliefs, the end result is "instrumental rationality."

For a rational choice theorist, any choice is rational if it is in agreement with one's preferences. People develop a preference ordering, with some preferences ranking higher than others. When a person uses higher ranking rather than lower ranking preferences to determine what action to take, the result is "maximization" of results. Shepsle and Bonchek (1997) put it thus:

> Making a decision under conditions of risk involves choosing from among alternative lotteries. A rational choice entails choosing the "best" lottery. The rule of rational choice is known as the *Principle of Expected Utility.* (34)

In essence, one would follow this principle by selecting the choice that maximizes payoffs in terms of one's preference ordering. Rationality calls for people to make decisions on the basis of expected utility. The key underlying assumption is that people can carry out analyses consistent with the principle of expected utility, engaging in a sort of rational means-ends analysis.

7.2.3 INCREMENTAL DECISION MAKING

Charles Lindblom formulated the theory of incremental decision making first in the 1950s. Since then, he and others have developed the theory. Hayes' chapter in this volume discusses the theory and developments extensively. Lindblom describes incrementalism as decision making by successive limited comparisons. He contends that, empirically, this describes how decisions are commonly made. Lindblom (1959, 81) summarizes the essence of the approach thus:

1b. Selection of value goals and empirical analysis of the needed action are not distinct from one another but are closely intertwined.
2b. Because means and ends are not distinct, means-ends analysis is often inappropriate or limited.
2c. The test of a good "policy" is typically that various analysts find themselves directly agreeing on a policy (without their agreeing that it is the most appropriate means to an agreed objective).
2d. Analysis is drastically limited:
    i. Important possible outcomes are neglected.
    ii. Important alternative potential policies are neglected.
    iii. Important affected values are neglected.
2e. A succession of comparisons greatly reduces or eliminates reliance on theory.

In the end, a satisfactory decision is made—not an optimal decision, but one that is good enough to meet immediate needs. There are, of course, problems with incremental decision making (e.g., see Rosenbloom and Kravchuk, 2005; and Hayes' chapter in this volume). For current purposes, the key point is the view of human nature underlying this model. The most basic point is that humans have inherent cognitive limitations in the extent to which they can engage in rational, analytic decision making.

7.2.4 BOUNDED RATIONALITY

Herbert Simon is associated most closely with the concept of bounded rationality (for an extensive discussion of this concept, see Mingus' chapter in this volume). A series of Simon's works developed this concept well enough to earn a Nobel Prize (e.g., Simon, 1957a,b; 1983). Discussion in decision making literature often focuses on Simon's works, particularly his concept of bounded rationality. Not surprisingly, many chapters in this volume refer to and discuss extensively Simon's concepts and works (see particularly the Mingus, Nieuwenburg, and Catlaw chapters).

For the purposes of this chapter, the most important aspect of Simon's work is that he confronted the image of rational decision maker that emerged from economic theory. This image represented humans as rational cost-benefit calculators, working to optimize/maximize self-interest. Gigerenzer (2001) portrays the view as "unbounded rationality," characterized as encompassing:

> "... decision making strategies that have little or no regard for the constraints in time, knowledge, and computational capacities that real humans face. For example, models that seek to optimize expected utility or perform Bayesian calculations often must assume demonic strength to tackle real-world problems." (38)

Simon contends that this is not an accurate portrayal of human decision making. He argues for "bounded rationality" as a better image for this process. Here, humans use their limited computation power to seek out a decision under conditions of uncertainty and incomplete information that is satisfactory—not optimal. Hence, the rule of decision making is satisficing (settling for a solution that is good enough), in which, as Gigerenzer puts it (2001, 38), we have "... *limited information search* that was terminated by a *stopping rule*." The implications for decision making are that humans' limitations are such that optimal decision making is not the normal mode of operation. Thus, inherent human abilities limit rationality and the exercise of reason (Selten, 2001). The view of human nature underlying Simon's conceptualization of bounded rationality is apparent: humans are not rational decision makers, as per the image of "Economic Man"; rather, humans have limited computational capacity and must limit their searches for solutions to satisficing options.

7.3 HUMAN NATURE AND DECISION MAKING

The following sections focus on two distinct processes in human cognition arising from our evolutionary background. The first process is the evolutionary and neurophysiological underpinnings of what is often termed "schemata". (For more detailed analysis, see Peterson, 1985; 1986; Peterson and Lawson, 1982). The second process examines the evolutionary and neurophysiological bases of the use of heuristics in decision making under conditions of uncertainty. (For more detail, see Peterson, 1985; 1986; Peterson and Lawson, 1982; 1984a,b; 1989). Both subjects begin to provide a perspective for exploring the validity of key assumptions of human nature underlying the four theories of decision making previously summarized.

7.3.1 SCHEMATA AND DECISION MAKING

7.3.1.1 Defined

Schemata help make sense of a complex world, a world producing a wide array of stimuli that impinge upon the individual. Morton Hunt notes:

"Our method of making categories has a simple and obvious biological rationale: it is the mind's way of representing reality in the most cognitively economical form. In the real world… traits occur in "correlational structures"; observable characteristics tend to go together in bunches…. We may not have innate ideas… but our minds filter and compile incoming data in such ways that we tend to form prototypes and categories without help or instruction." (1982, 173)

The basic idea of schema theory is that much of what people see and comprehend and understand about the world is more closely tied to the internal schema than to the external stimulus itself. As a theory of comprehension, schema theory states that people often understand only those events that are consistent with their schemata and that they either ignore or misunderstand those events that are not. As an orientation toward memory, schema theory states that enduring memory does not typically occur independent of schemata. If comprehension of things is guided and organized by schemata, so is memory.

7.3.1.2 Neurophysiological Bases of Schemata

The development and functioning of schemata are complex phenomena; few such behaviors are going to be localized in a single area within the brain. Uttal (1978) summarizes the implication well when he states that "… almost all complex behaviors can be affected by almost any part of the brain and that the sort of localization that occurs must be interpreted more in the form of a system of interconnecting nuclei than in terms of any theory of sharply demarcated functions of single 'centers'" (342).

Arbib et al. (1998) argue that the concept of the schema is central to linking brain function with brain structure. A schema is the brain's internal representation of "reality out there" that organizes and guides information processing.

Arbib et al. (1998) claim that their "… contribution has been to provide a schema theory that can bridge from the external characterization of function to the interactions of brain regions and the inner workings of neural circuitry" (35). They consider two categories of schema—a perceptual schema and the motor schema. Then in the process, they attempt to link perception and action. In the final analysis, they note that through the schema (344), "The brain 'models' the world so that when we recognize something, we 'see' in it things that will guide our interaction with it" (Pinker, 1997).

Ulric Neisser (1976) a leading cognitive psychologist, speaks generally of the psychobiological roots of schemata (the plural form of the term schema):

"From the biological point of view, a schema is part of the nervous system. It is some active array of physiological structures and processes: not a center in the brain, but an entire system that includes receptors and afferents and feed-forward units and efferents. Within the brain itself there must be entities whose activities account for the modifiability and organization of the schema: assemblages of neurons, functional hierarchies, Fluctuating electrical potentials, and other things still unguessed." (54)

G.J. Dalenoort (1982) suggests that cell assemblies underlie schemata. Representations are stored in dispersed cell assemblies in humans' long-term memory. The key implication is that certain values and beliefs affect how people perceive the world and structure their perceptions; people are, in a sense, incapable of seeing the world as it is. What one sees is affected by what one believes that they are seeing or will see.

7.3.1.3 Evolutionary Bases of Schemata

Long ago, Jacob Von Uexkull (1957) noted that each species has a sensory system designed by evolution to produce information relevant to its survival needs. Because different animal species inhabit distinct ecological niches and have varying survival needs, this translates into those species living in unique sensory worlds (the idea of the *Umwelt*). For instance, humans cannot hear higher pitched sounds that dogs do—thus living in a different auditory world. Humans might see a nearly pitch black room where vision is useless; cats, on the other hand, would move freely about because of their keener night vision—thus inhabiting a different visual world than humans.

The point? Across species, animals' senses lead to living in very distinct worlds. There is no "real world" of sense and perception; there is an array of worlds depending upon a species' unique sensory capabilities. This, of course, begins to say that one cannot directly perceive reality and process sensations because one misses potentially important aspects due to the configuration of people's sense mechanisms. People may live in a "human" *Umwelt*, but it is a world with fairly clearcut limitations on what can be perceived and sensed.

Schemata (internal, neural representations) help shape perceptions. Usually people do not have unmediated access to the world "out there." In short, a person's preexisting values, beliefs, expectations (schemata) shape what humans perceive their senses to have detected (Bloom, 1971; Pribram et al., 1985). Today many theorists accept the importance of schemata or internal neural representations in interpreting sensory input, but that does not mean that all is illusion, of course. Yet it does indicate that normally people do not apprehend directly the world around them in an unmediated form. In that sense, reality is—to a considerable extent—a psychobiological construction (Arbib, 1980; Changeux, 1985; Epstein, 1980; Gyr, 1980; Sloman, 1980; Ullman, 1987).

Kenneth Pope and Jerome Singer (1980) quote William James (1980), "thought is interested in some parts of these objects to the exclusion of others, continuously choosing from among them" (170). James' point, in turn, is tied to a contention by Pope and Singer, that "thought itself appears to deal with objects independent of itself" (170). Schemata are taken as the reality itself; thought and its referents are accepted as congruent even though schemata are representational and abstractions (often distorted) of the referent. Thus, schemata tend to structure people's perceptions and to what they will attend. Selective attention is, in part, a function of an individual's system of schemata.

Bryan Kolb and Ian Whishaw (2003) observe that people simply do not have the capability to process the plenitude of information in their environment. Because of this incapability, there must be some screening in processing inputs. An important aspect of this screening is that (Kolb and Whishaw, 2003, 384): "This selectivity is generally not conscious, for the nervous system automatically scans input and selectively perceives the environment" (384).[*]

Currently one major approach to applying evolutionary theory to human social behavior is sociobiology, the study of the evolutionary bases of social behavior (Dawkins, 1975; Wilson, 1989). A key concept for sociobiology is "inclusive fitness." For sociobiology, an underlying premise is that evolution has inclined living organisms to those modes of behavior most likely to maximize the number of his or her genes transmitted to the next generation. This transmission can be done in two different ways: (1) by passing along one's genes directly, usually referred as individual reproductive success, and (2) one can behave in such a manner as to increase reproductive success of one's relatives, with whom one shares genes. The combination of these two is termed "inclusive fitness," encompassing both the reproductive success of an individual *and* of that individual's relatives with whom, depending upon the degree of relatedness, the individual shares more or fewer genes (see Alexander, 1975; Barash, 1982; Dawkins 1989; Wilson, 1975).

What of the application of this perspective to schemata? As already noted above, individuals would be overwhelmed with raw data input without some sort of organizing and screening mechanism. This mechanism would be necessary for survival in a world rich with stimuli. Attending to some stimulants and not to others would be an important survival necessity.

---

[*] Also see Kandel (1991) on the same point.

As Immelman (1980) observes:

> "Each organism is at any moment confronted by a wealth of information from the environment ..., but only a small fraction is biologically significant for the animal. Hence, one of the most important tasks for the organism is the selection of those stimuli that should be followed by a reaction." (27)

Otherwise, the individual would be overwhelmed by raw data.

7.3.2 HEURISTICS AND DECISION MAKING

7.3.2.1 Defined

Humans must make a myriad of decisions under conditions of uncertainty; humans and their ancestors have had to do so for millions of years. One mechanism for accomplishing this is the use of decision making shortcuts, or "heuristics" (see Kahneman et al., 1982; Nisbett and Ross, 1980; Gilovich et al., 2002; Kahneman and Tversky, 2000; Gigerenzer and Selten, 2001). As Gigerenzer (2001) observes: "Humans and animals must make inferences about unknown features of their world under constraints of limited time, limited knowledge, and limited computational capacities" (37). Heuristics are "rules of thumb" that provide for decent and quick decision making; they are "fast and frugal," requiring little information (Gigerenzer, 2004; Gigerenzer and Goldstein, 1996; Todd, 2001).

A few examples illustrate these rules of thumb. One of these is the "representativeness heuristic." Anderson (1980) notes: "Humans have a powerful ability to detect covariations among stimulus events and to build schemas to embody these correlations" (15). Thus:

> "What is the probability that object A belongs to class B? What is the probability that event A originates from process B? What is the probability that process B will generate event A?" (Tversky and Kahneman, 1974 1124)

In human life, examples of this heuristic at work abound. For instance, a hunting-gathering band finds that at a certain place at a certain time of year, game is present for a successful hunt. The correlation of time, place, and successful hunt would be used the following year to guide their decision making.

Another heuristic is "Take-the-First." This is an example of "one-stop" decision making and has been demonstrated to generate reasonably good predictions (Goldstein et al., 2001, 177). Firefighters, pilots, and chess players often use this. In short, "... when faced with a problem to solve, often the best course of action to take is the first (or only) one that comes to mind" (Goldstein et al., 2001, 177). This heuristic is most successful when the actors are experts in a field; it is not as reliable in novel situations, where learning is difficult, or where there are low costs to making errors. However, it is a "fast and frugal" approach to decision making that works reasonably well under certain circumstances.

7.3.2.2 Neurophysiological Bases of Heuristics

Miller et al. (1960) many years ago argued that human cognition needed to be understood in terms of both images ("... knowledge of the world" [Miller et al., 1960, 17]; "... the accumulated, organized knowledge that the organism has about itself and the world" [17]) and plans (analogous to computer programs, these provide instructions so that decisions can be made or tasks carried out). Images, as Miller et al. refer to them, represent what are termed schemata in the previous section of this chapter. Also among the plans noted by the authors are heuristics. It warrants notice that these shortcuts work below the level of consciousness. As Davidson says: "This unconscious system of information processing is presumably comprised of certain neural structures whose function is to transform input according to certain rules or algorithms" (1980, 18). In short, schemata (images) organize knowledge, and heuristics (one example of plans) use that knowledge to help guide behavior.

Luria (1973) observes that "Man not only reacts passively to incoming information, but creates *intentions*, forms *plans* and *programmes* of his actions, inspects their performance, and *regulates* his behavior so that it conforms to these plans and programs; finally, he *verifies* his conscious activity, comparing the effects of his actions with the original intentions and correcting any mistakes he has made" (79–80). An important part of this dynamic for Luria is actually selecting a general plan for performing some particular task. Among these plans are heuristics designed to develop solutions to problems or answers to questions. Clinical studies suggest that heuristic thought takes place in or is called upon by the prefrontal lobes (see also Miller et al., 1960). Luria notes that frontal lobe lesions produce "… the disintegration of intellectual activity as a whole…" (339). Patients suffering from frontal lobe lesions cannot solve verbal-logical problems; they are unable to program the intellectual act, in other words, to adopt a problem-solving strategy (and see Smith and Jonides, 2000). They may not even see the problem with which they are confronted! Thus, use of heuristics is part of the larger process of the frontal lobes' formation of plans and programs to solve problems and make decisions (see also Luria, 1980).

The prefrontal areas have rich two-way connections with lower levels of the brain as well as with other cortical areas. Consequently, these areas are in peculiarly good position for synthesizing the complex system of afferent impulses from all over and organizing efferent impulses to regulate other structures. The prefrontal lobes seem to prepare an individual for action and to verify that he or she has taken the proper course. One basic function of the prefrontal lobes appears to be "… forming stable plans and intentions capable of controlling the subject's subsequent conscious behavior" (Luria, 1973, 198).* Clinical findings that suggest that lesions of the frontal lobes produce a loss of patients' "… ability to check… results [of actions carried out]" (210) reinforce this contention. Patients with such a condition cannot form and execute solutions to complex problems (see also Luria, 1980; Teuber, 1964; Milner, 1964; Penfield, 1975). General decision making, too, is impaired with deficits in the prefrontal cortex (Anderson et al., 2002).

Plans or heuristics help to shape decision making. This is not all though. Luria (1973) also claims that these programs organize perceptions of the sensory world. This, in turn, is facilitated by schemata (although Luria does not use that specific term). He describes the process in the following manner (1973, 230):

> It begins with the *analysis* of the structure perceived, as received by the brain, into a large number of components or cues that are subsequently *coded* or *synthesized* and fitted into the corresponding *mobile systems*. This process of selection and synthesis of the corresponding features is *active* in character and takes place under the direct influence of the *tasks* that confront the subject. It takes place with the aid of ready-made *codes* (and in particular the *codes* of language), which serve to place the perceived feature into its proper system and to give a *general or categorical* character; finally, it always incorporates a process of comparison with the original hypothesis, or, in other words, a process of verification of the perceptual activity.

> "During the perception of familiar objects, firmly established in past experience, this process is naturally contracted and takes place by a series of shortcuts, whereas during the perception of new and unfamiliar or complex visual objects, the process of perception remains full and uncontracted."

This process, as with problem-solving, Luria (1973) says, "… is *dependent on the role of the frontal lobes in particular*" (240).

Davidson (1980, 18) notes that, although conscious access to use of heuristics or algorithms in cognition is limited, the outputs (i.e., decisions or problem-solving) do get fed into systems in the

---

* On planning, see also Knight and Grabowecky (2000).

brain responsible for conscious representations. In other words, the products of non-conscious processes and sometimes distorted information processing become accepted as valid during conscious thought processes.

If Lumsden and Wilson (1981) are right, this mode of thinking is "species-typical," i.e., built-in "epigenetic rules." If so, the implications are profound. Physiological structures shape human cognitive processes. The end result, simply, is that people think as they do because of their very nature. There is no easy "escape" from heuristic decision making.

7.3.2.3 Evolutionary Bases of Heuristics

Lumsden and Wilson (1983) note that "Each member of the human species has to begin as a small child lost in a vast and complicated maze" (60). The complexity of the human environment as an individual develops from childhood to adulthood is a bewildering array of stimuli—some important for survival and others not. The authors contend that "a premium is placed on speed and efficiency [of handling environmental information] because the child is racing against other children in similar mazes, and the greatest rewards of the contest will go to those who reach the exact goal with the least hesitation" (60). Translated into the language of natural selection:

> "The maze is a metaphor for the problems facing a young child as he [sic] matures. The race is the image of evolution by means of natural selection. The growing mind must pick its way through a chaos of sensations and perceptions, quickly assembling them in a form that imparts a substantial degree of command over the environment into which it was born." (61)

Individuals' genes will "… equip the mind with specific rules and principles needed to learn the world quickly in an advantageous form" (62). Those humans who have been provided with these innate clues will master the complex social world into which they emerge at birth. Among these rules are, of course, heuristics (and see Maramatsu and Hanoch, 2005). Without such decision making shortcuts, individuals could not effectively handle the array of stimuli that condition needed decisions. Heuristics allow people to make decisions quickly and economically and thus would confer selection advantage (see also Lumsden and Wilson, 1981).

More specifically, related to "fast and frugal" heuristics, Gigerenzer (2001) speaks to the selection value of "the adaptive toolbox":

> "The ultimate goal of organisms, according to evolutionary theory, is reproduction, either of genes or some other units. The adaptive toolbox is designed to achieve proximal goals, such as finding prey, avoiding predators, finding a mate, and if a species is social or cultural, exchanging goods, making a profit, and negotiating status. The tools are means to achieve proximal goals and include learning mechanisms that allow an adjustment of tools when environments change…. The strategies in the adaptive toolbox do not try to optimize…. The general reason is that optimization is feasible in only a restricted set of problems, typically on the basis of simplifying assumptions." (40)

7.3.2.4 Coda

Thus, heuristics have biological bases. In that sense, they are a part of human nature. Next, this chapter turns to an analysis of which theories of decision making appear best to comport with the above picture of human nature.

7.4 DISCUSSION

The view of decision making underlying rational choice theory and rational-comprehensive decision making appears to be an Enlightenment-based perspective (see Morçöl, 2003; Wachhaus, 2004). Human nature is similar to that assumed by key Enlightenment thinkers.

This faith in human reason can be traced to the so-called "Enlightenment," itself a term indicating a lineage going back to Plato and his "Allegory of the Cave." Characteristics of the Enlightenment view are a faith in the powers of human intelligence and reason, the growth of knowledge and its ability to improve the quality of human life, and a belief in science as a means of ameliorating the human condition. Of the Enlightenment, Harmon (1964) says that it was a

"... movement which drew to its ranks the most able thinkers in a great many fields... Their heroes were the skeptic Bayle, the philosopher Locke, and the scientist Newton. The scientific discoveries of the seventeenth century had led to the belief that the universe was governed by orderly and discoverable laws and that men could understand them and improve their world through the use of reason." (293)

Immanuel Kant (1970) expressed a faith in humankind's powers of reason. Further, Kant explicitly linked these powers of reason to the political realm. In another essay, he used the concept of human reason as a basis for asserting that humans ought to live in peace rather than war (Kant, 1957). Another Enlightenment thinker was Pierre Bayle. He argued that humans are responsible for using their reason to try to find for themselves what they believe to be truth (Bayle, 1970). Then, they must use this understanding to guide their behavior. This, then, can be the basis, as Condorcet (1970) put it, for "... the doctrine of the indefinite perfectibility of the human race..." (227) based upon the fact that "... *man is a sentient being, capable of reasoning and of acquiring moral ideas ...*" (224).

Both rational choice theory and the rational-comprehensive decision making model assume that individuals use reason (however, imperfectly realized) to make decisions and reach conclusions. In rational-comprehensive decision making, analysts use logic and data to choose objectively from among a series of alternatives that best addresses the original problems and meets the desired objectives. In rational choice theory, individuals develop preference orderings and then use the principle of expected utility to make decisions. While their preferences may spring from non-rational underpinnings, their behavior consistent with the principle of expected utility is based on an assumption of rationality. In both instances, again, these approaches to decision making tend to exemplify Enlightenment thinking.

Recall Bayle's argument that humans should use reason to try to find for themselves what they believe to be truth; upon meeting that *desideratum*, they would then use this understanding to guide their behavior. This argument fairly accurately describes both perspectives just mentioned. Determine what the facts and objective conditions are and then use this as the basis for decision making. In addition, the rational-comprehensive model resonates especially with the Enlightenment perspective's belief in science and in human progress. The essence of rational-comprehensive decision making is that by using quantitative methods, we can determine what policy or mix of policies is going to address problems and then lead to amelioration of the underlying conditions generating the problems.

However, such an orientation does not appear to be consistent with how people actually make decisions. The discussion of schemata suggests that people tend to use schemata to screen data; thus, the immediate apprehension of stimuli is itself a construction of those preexisting values and beliefs. In that sense, decision making is biased from the start by such values and beliefs, making true rational decision making along Enlightenment lines most difficult. Decision makers cannot separate themselves from their values and beliefs. These values and beliefs will color their decision making—and even their perceptions and understanding of external stimuli—in ways not consistent with theories based on rationality.

Research and theory on heuristics also raises questions about such theories. Humans do not routinely make decisions by rational modes. The use of decision making shortcuts—as common among leaders as the mass of citizens (e.g., see Peterson, 1985; 1986)—cuts strongly against rational-comprehensive decision making and rational choice theory.

What of incrementalism and bounded rationality theory? Both appear to be more solidly grounded in the view of human nature discussed earlier. Both theoretical perspectives accept that humans have limited computational capacity and, consequently, make decisions that are good enough rather than optimal. Indeed, many essays in Gigerenzer and Selten (2001) begin their analysis of the evolutionary bases of heuristics with Simon's work. They make the explicit case that humanity's evolutionary background has led to the use of "fast and frugal" heuristics as a means of exercising competent decision making under conditions of limited information and uncertainty and based on humans' limited computational ability.

In an essay published many years ago, I noted that:

Perhaps our faith in [rational] political decision making is yet one more example of *hubris*, the cost of which can be very high. In the Exodus from Sophocles' *Antigone*, Creon says: 'Fate has brought all my pride to a thought of dust.' The Choragos closes the tragedy by commenting on the folly of *hubris*:

> There is no happiness where there is no wisdom;
> No wisdom but in submission to the gods.
> Big words are always punished,
> And proud men in old age learn to be wise. (Peterson, 1985: 515)

Theories of decision making should to be based on a modest view of human rationality, should not reflect the sin of *hubris*. Accepting theories based on fallacious views of human nature, over-estimating inherent capabilities and rationality, increases the odds of disastrous decision making in the realm of politics (e.g., see Peterson, 1985; 1986). Perhaps modesty is the best stance for analysts of decision making.

REFERENCES

Alexander, R., The search for a general theory of behavior, *Behavioral Science*, 20, 77–100, 1975.

Anderson, James E., *Public Policymaking: An Introduction*, 3rd ed., Houghton Mifflin, Boston, 1997.

Anderson, J. R., *Cognitive Psychology and its Implications*, W.H. Freeman, San Francisco, 1980.

Anderson, S. W., Bachara, A., Damasio, H., Tranel, D., and Damasio, A., Impairment of social and moral behavior related to early damage in human prefrontal cortex, In *Foundations in Social Neuroscience*, Cacioppo, J. T., Bernsson, Gary G., Sue Carter, Ralph Adolphs C., Davidson, Richard J., McClintock, Martha K., McEwen, Bruce S., Meaney, Michael J., Schacter, Daniel L., Sternberg, Esther M., Suomi, Steve S., and Taylor, Shelley E., Eds., MIT Press, Cambridge, pp. 333–344, 2002.

Arbib, M., Levels of modeling of mechanisms of visually guided behavior, *Behavioral and Brain Sciences*, 10, 407–436, 1987.

Arbib, M. A., Erdi, P., and Szentagothai, J., *Neural Organization: Structure, Function, and Dynamics*, MIT Press, Cambridge, 1998.

Barash, D. P., *Sociobiology and Behaviour*, 2nd ed., Elsevier, New York, 1982.

Bayle, P., Reason and tolerance, In *The Liberal Tradition in European Thought*, Sidorsky, D., Ed., Capricorn Books, New York, pp. 39–47, 1970.

Bloom, F. E., Lazerson, A., and Hofstadter, L., *Brain, Mind, and Behavior*, Freeman, New York, 1985.

Changeux, J.-P., *Neuronal Man*, Princeton University Press, Princeton, 1985.

Cohen, M. D., March, J. G., and Olsen, J. P., A garbage can model of organizational choice, *Administrative Science Quarterly*, 17, 1–25, 1972.

Condorcet, M., Reason and history, In *The Liberal Tradition in European Thought*, Sidorsky, D., Ed., Capricorn Books, New York, pp. 223–236, 1970.

Dalenoort, G. J., In search of the conditions for the genesis of cell assemblies, *Journal of Social and Biological Structures*, 5, 161–187, 1982.

Dahl, R., *Who Governs?*, Yale University Press, New Haven, 1962.

Davidson, R., Consciousness and information processing: a biocognitive perspective, In *The Psychobiology of Consciousness*, Davidson, J. and Davidson, R. J., Eds., Plenum Press, New York, pp. 11–63, 1980.

Dawkins, R., *The Selfish Gene*, 2nd ed., Oxford University Press, London, 1989.

Dye, T. R., *Understanding Public Policy*, 6th ed., Prentice Hall, Englewood Cliffs, NJ, 1987.

Epstein, W., Direct perception or mediated perception, *Behavioral and Brain Sciences*, 3, 384–385, 1980.

Gigerenzer, G., The adaptive toolbox, In *Bounded Rationality: The Adaptive Toolbox*, Gigerenzer, G. and Selten, R., Eds., MIT Press, Cambridge, pp. 37–50, 2001.

Gigerenzer, G., Fast and frugal heuristics: the tools of bounded rationality, In *The Blackwell Handbook of Judgment and Decision Making*, Koehler, D. and Harvey, N., Eds., Blackwell Publishers, Oxford, pp. 62–88, 2004.

Gigerenzer, G. and Goldstein, D. G., Reasoning the fast and frugal way: models of bounded rationality, *Psychological Review*, 103, 650–669, 1996.

Gigerenzer, G. and Selten, R., Eds., *Bounded Rationality: The Adaptive Toolbox*, MIT Press, Cambridge, 2001.

Gilovich, T., Griffin, D., and Kahneman, D., Eds., *Heuristics and Biases*, Cambridge University Press, Cambridge, 2002.

Goldstein, D. G., Gigerenzer, G., Hogarth, R. M., Kacelnik, A., Kareev, Y., Klein, G., Martignon, L., Payne, J. W., and Schlag, K. H., Group report: why and when do simple heuristics work?, In *Bounded Rationality: The Adaptive Toolbox*, Gigerenzer, G. and Selten, R., Eds., MIT Press, Cambridge, pp. 173–190, 2001.

Gyr, J. W., Visual perception is underdetermined by stimulation, *Behavioral and Brain Sciences*, 3, 386, 1980.

Harmon, M. J., *Political Thought*, McGraw-Hill, New York, 1964.

Heineman, R. A., Bluhm, W. T., Peterson, S. A., and Kearney, E. N., *The World of the Policy Analyst*, 3rd ed., Chatham House, Chatham, 2001.

Hunt, M., *The Universe Within*, Simon and Schuster, New York, 1982.

Immelmann, K., *Introduction to Ethology*, Plenum Press, New York, 1980.

Kahneman, D. and Tversky, A., Eds., *Choices, Values, and Frames*, Cambridge University Press, Cambridge, 2000.

Kahneman, D., Slovic, P., and Tversky, A., Eds., *Judgment Under Uncertainty*, Cambridge University Press, Cambridge, 1982.

Kandel, E. R., Perception of motion, depth, and form, In *Principles of Neural Science*, Kandel, E. R., Schwartz, J. H., and Jessell, T. M., Eds., 3rd ed., Elsevier, New York, pp. 440–466, 1991.

Kant, I., *Perpetual Peace*, Indianapolis, Bobbs-Merrill, 1957. Trans. L.W. Beck.

Kant, I., Enlightenment and progress, In *The Liberal Tradition in European Thought*, Sidorsky, D., Ed., Capricorn Books, New York, pp. 64–69, 1970.

Kingdon, J., *Agendas, Alternatives, and Public Policy*, Harper and Row, New York, 1984.

Knight, R. and Grabowecky, M., Prefrontal cortex, time, and consciousness, In *The New Cognitive Neurosciences*, Gazzaniga, M. S., Ed., MIT Press, Cambridge, pp. 1319–1340, 2000.

Kolb, B. and Whishaw, I. Q., *Fundamentals of Human Neuropsychology*, 5th ed., W.H. Freeman, San Francisco, 2003.

Lindblom, C. E., The science of "muddling through", *Public Administration Review*, 19, 79–88, 1959.

Lumsden, C. J. and Wilson, E. O., *Genes, Mind, and Culture*, Harvard University Press, Cambridge, 1981.

Lumsden, C. J. and Wilson, E. O., *Promethean Fire*, Harvard University Press, Cambridge, 1983.

Luria, A. R., *The Working Brain*, Basic Books, New York, 1973.

Luria, A. R., *Higher Cortical Functions in Man*, 2nd ed., Basic Books, New York, 1980.

Maramatsu, R. and Hanoch, Y., Emotions as a mechanism for boundedly rational agents: the fast and frugal way, *Journal of Economic Psychology*, 26, 201–221, 2005.

Miller, G. A., Galanter, E., and Pribram, K. H., *Plans and the Structure of Behavior*, Holt, Rinehart, and Winston, New York, 1960.

Mills, C. W., *The Power Elite*, Oxford University Press, New York, 1956.

Milner, B., Some effects of frontal lobectomy in man, In *The Frontal Granular Cortex and Behavior*, Warren, J. W. and Akert, K., Eds., McGraw-Hill, New York, pp. 313–334, 1964.

Moe, T. M., The new economics of organizations, *American Journal of Political Science*, 28, 739–777, 1984.

Morçöl, G., The rational actor assumption, complexity theory, and cognitive science. Paper presented at the Southeastern Conference for Public Administration, Savannah, GA, 2003.

Neisser, U., *Cognition and Reality*, W.H. Freeman, San Francisco, 1976.

Nisbett, R. E. and Ross, L., *Human Inference: Strategies and Shortcomings of Social Judgement*, Prentice Hall, Englewood Cliffs, NJ, 1980.

Niskanen, W., *Bureaucracy and Representative Government*, Aldine, Chicago, 1971.

Penfield, W., *The Mystery of the Mind*, Princeton University Press, Princeton, 1975.

Peterson, S. A., Neurophysiology, cognition, and political thinking, *Political Psychology*, 6, 495–518, 1985.

Peterson, S. A., Why policies don't work: a biocognitive perspective, In *Biology and Bureaucracy*, White, E. and Losco, J., Eds., University Press of America, Lanham, pp. 447–502, 1986.

Peterson, S. A. and Lawson, R., Cognitive psychology and the study of politics. Paper presented at American Political Science Association meeting, Denver, CO, 1982.

Peterson, S. A. and Lawson, R., The ethology of political cognition. Paper presented at Conference on Ethology and Politics, Tutzing, Germany, 1984a.

Peterson, S. A. and Lawson, R., Who's responsible anyway? Attribution and politics. Paper presented at Midwest Political Science Association, meeting, Chicago, 1984b.

Peterson, S. A. and Lawson, R., Risky business, *Political Psychology*, 10, 325–339, 1989.

Pinker, S., *How the Mind Works*, Norton, New York, 1997.

Pope, K. S. and Singer, J. L., The waking stream of consciousness, In *The Psychobiology of Consciousness*, Davidson, J. M. and Davidson, R. J., Eds., Plenum Press, New York, pp. 169–192, 1980.

Pribram, K., *Languages of the Brain*, Prentice Hall, Englewood Cliffs, NJ, 1971.

Rabin, J. W., Hildreth, B., and Miller, G. J., *Handbook of Public Administration*, 2nd ed., Marcel Dekker, New York, 1998.

Rosenbloom, D. H. and Kravchuk, R. S., *Public Administration: Understanding Management, Politics, and Law in the Public Sector*, 6th ed., McGraw-Hill, New York, 2005.

Selten, R., What is bounded rationality?, In *Bounded Rationality: The Adaptive Toolbox*, Gigerenzer, G. and Selten, R., Eds., MIT Press, Cambridge, pp. 13–36, 2001.

Shepsle, K. A. and Bonchek, M. S., *Analyzing Politics*, W.W. Norton, New York, 1997.

Simon, H., *Administrative Behavior*, MacMillan, New York, 1957a.

Simon, H., *Models of Man*, Wiley, New York, 1957b.

Simon, H., *Reason in Human Affairs*, Stanford University Press, Stanford, 1983.

Sloman, A., What kind of indirect process is visual perception?, *Behavioral and Brain Science*, 3, 401–404, 1980.

Smith, E. E. and Jonides, J., The cognitive neuroscience of categorization, In *The New Cognitive Neurosciences*, Gazzaniga, Michael S., Ed., MIT Press, Cambridge, pp. 1013–1022, 2000.

Teuber, H.-L., The riddle of frontal lobe function in man, In *The Frontal Granular Cortex and Behavior*, Warren, J. M. and Akert, K., Eds., McGraw-Hill, New York, pp. 410–444, 1964.

Todd, P. M., Fast and frugal heuristics for environmentally bounded minds, In *Bounded Rationality: The Adaptive Toolbox*, Gigerenzer, G. and Selten, R., Eds., MIT Press, MA, Cambridge, pp. 51–70, 2001.

Tversky, A. and Kahneman, D., Judgment under uncertainty: heuristics and biases, *Science*, 185, 1124–1131, 1974.

Ullman, S., Against direct perception, *The Behavioral and Brain Sciences*, 2, 401–422, 1980.

Uttal, W. R., *The Psychobiology of Mind*, Lawrence Erlbaum Associates, Hillsdale, 1978.

Von Uexkull, J., A stroll through the world of animals and man, In *Instinctive Behaviour*, Schiller, C., Ed., International Universities Press, New York, pp. 5–80, 1957.

Wachhaus, T. A., Hermeneutic features in bounded rationality. Paper presented at the Southeastern Conference on Public Administration, Nashville, TN, 2004.

Wilson, E. O., *Sociobiology*, Harvard University Press, Cambridge, 1975.

8 Punctuated Equilibrium Models in Organizational Decision Making

Scott E. Robinson

CONTENTS

8.1 Two Research Conundrums..134
    8.1.1 Lindblom's Theory of Administrative Incrementalism................................134
    8.1.2 Wildavsky's Theory of Budgetary Incrementalism...................................135
    8.1.3 The Diverse Meanings of Budgetary "Incrementalism".............................135
    8.1.4 A Brief Aside on Paleontology..136
8.2 Punctuated Equilibrium Theory—A Way Out of Both Conundrums....................136
8.3 A Theoretical Model of Punctuated Equilibrium Theory.....................................137
8.4 Evidence of Punctuated Equilibria in Organizational Decision Making...............139
    8.4.1 Punctuated Equilibrium and the Federal Budget.......................................139
    8.4.2 Punctuated Equilibrium and Local Government Budgets............................140
    8.4.3 Punctuated Equilibrium and the Federal Policy Process.............................141
    8.4.4 Punctuated Equilibrium and Organizational Bureaucratization...................142
    8.4.5 Assessing the Evidence...143
8.5 Frontiers of Punctuated Equilibrium Research..143
    8.5.1 The Statistical Challenges of Punctuated Equilibrium Research.................143
    8.5.2 The Theoretical Challenges of Punctuated Equilibrium Research...............145
8.6 Conclusion..148
References...148

Many literatures on decision making have involved heated debates over the capacity of people and organizations to make large changes. Scholars have argued about the capacity of decision makers to make substantial changes from prior decisions at the individual and the organizational levels. Those who argued that substantial change was rare pointed to the conservative nature of decision making in a variety of areas including budgeting and policymaking. In this view (that I will call the incrementalist view) stasis is the characteristic state of organizational and individual decision making. In the incrementalist view, there are strong disincentives to making decisions that depart substantially from the status quo (Lindblom, 1959). These disincentives make large departures rare and dangerous. Those who disputed this argument pointed to examples of large change. Many policy areas seemingly experienced large changes; popular examples included the space program and military budgets. For the most part, the debate raged as both parties talked past the others.

Out of this melee, punctuated equilibrium theory emerged as a way out of the dispute between incrementalists and their critics by providing a model that explains the existence of long periods of stability with occasional, but infrequent, dramatic change. This chapter traces the development of punctuated equilibrium models in paleontology and policy theory and the incorporation of this approach into research on budgetary policy making. This chapter then provides a detailed account of the theoretical structure of a punctuated equilibrium model and the empirical implications of these models. Finally, this chapter reviews the extant literature applying punctuated equilibrium models to organizational decision making and explores the frontiers of research into punctuated equilibrium processes.

8.1 TWO RESEARCH CONUNDRUMS

Two distinct literatures—the dynamics of policy change and the dynamics of species change—faced similar disputes over the speed of change processes. These two literatures eventually found a proposed resolution to the dispute in punctuated equilibrium theory. This reviews the challenges faced by scholars of policy and species change with special attention to the similarities between the academic debates in these disparate areas. This analysis will reveal the problems common to each research dispute and the factors that led to the common acceptance of punctuated equilibrium theory in each field.

8.1.1 LINDBLOM'S THEORY OF ADMINISTRATIVE INCREMENTALISM

Charles Lindblom's theory of incrementalism is discussed in detail in Hayes' chapter in this book, but a brief summary is needed here, as his theory has a direct connection to punctuated equilibrium theory. Lindblom (1959) was unsatisfied with traditional rational models of administrative decision making that assumed that decision makers possessed more information than they did. Lindblom sought to replace the assumptions of the rational choice model of decision making with more realistic alternatives. The result is a model of administrative decision making based on "successive limited comparisons."

Each decision must limit the consideration of alternatives. Individuals cannot consider all alternatives because searching for alternatives is a costly process in terms of both money and time. Real administrative processes cannot absorb the costs of a large, nearly comprehensive search. Instead, limited searches produce a small set of alternatives subject to consideration. In most cases, the limitations of the search process result in the consideration of local alternatives, those that are very similar to the status quo.

Once a small set of alternatives is defined, administrators interactively evaluate those alternatives with the goals of the decision process. Goals (or values) are not set in stone and are instead under constant reevaluation relative to the available alternatives. Means and ends of any process are considered simultaneously.

Additionally, administrators only consider a small number of values relative to each decision. Just as a search for alternatives is costly, the consideration of diverse values is costly. Considering diverse values increases the difficulty of reaching a consensus in a group decision process. While there are many possible ways to evaluate a policy, only a small number of considerations are used in any decision process, for example efficiency, environmental sustainability, or equity (Braybrooke and Lindblom, 1963).

The result of narrow search routines, interactive application of values, and limitation on the number of considerations is conservative administrative decisions. Administrative decisions change policy only slowly through time as "successive, limited comparisons" prevent radical change. To adopt the language of incrementalism, decisions occur only in small increments. The basis for these limitations is information. When searches for alternatives are costly, incrementalism will dominate. When searches are inexpensive and many alternatives are subject to consideration, comparisons need not be "limited." The result may be non-incremental change. Incrementalism will only change over time (or cross-sectionally) as levels of complexity change.

It is important to note that this theory of decision making applies to individual and organizational decision making. Both individuals and organizations must confront the costs of searching for alternatives. Organizations face the additional barriers to change when multiple people are involved in the decision process, complicating the consideration of relevant values. So while the theory predicts incremental decision making by individuals, the incremental processes are likely to be more pronounced in organizational settings.

8.1.2 WILDAVSKY'S THEORY OF BUDGETARY INCREMENTALISM

Aaron Wildavsky (1964; 1992) applied the logic of incrementalism to budgetary processes. Incrementalism takes on a specific manifestation in the context of budgetary processes. An incremental budgetary process defines all decisions in terms of change from the baseline. In many cases this baseline is the previous year's budget. Budget outputs consist of changes in increments around the baseline.

Wildavsky's theory of budgetary incrementalism results in a conservatism similar to that inherent in Lindblom's theory of incrementalism. Programs are never considered in their entirety. In general, programs should emerge and disappear slowly over time. Instead, each program will see very small changes in their budgets over time.

The consideration of budget increments provides a number of benefits. First, administrators only have to consider a small number of alternative budgets (in this case representing a small number of potential increases or decreases from the budgetary base). Second, consideration of increments prevents revisiting past political struggles. Past budgets represent past political struggles. To fight over a budget from the first allocated dollar would require one to revisit the political struggles that resulted in the previous budget. By considering only incremental change, you avoid these fights and avoid agitating political interests.

Wildavasky also argued that the regularity of budgetary processes leads to incremental decision making processes. As a decision becomes routine, the parties become regular participants with well-formed expectations. The regularity of the participants expresses itself in the regularity of the budgetary outputs. As budgetary processes are bureaucratized and institutionalized, one expects a greater degree of incrementalism.

Wildavsky's theory of budgetary incrementalism added two factors that increase our expectation of incrementalism to the Lindblom's theory, political conflict and bureaucratization. More so than Lindblom, Wildavsky acknowledged that the degree of incrementalism might vary over time and between decision processes. In so far as political conflict and bureaucratization vary across time and across processes (cross-sectionally), Wildavsky would predict that levels of incrementalism would vary. Incrementalism should be positively related to both increasing levels of political conflict and increasing degrees of bureaucratization.

8.1.3 THE DIVERSE MEANINGS OF BUDGETARY "INCREMENTALISM"

The previous discussion conceals a lack of consensus on the use of the term "incrementalism" by focusing attention on a couple of authors. The incrementalist research tradition included a diverse set of authors working with diverse definitions of incrementalism. William Berry (1990) identifies 12 major conceptions of the term "incrementalism." Sometimes incrementalism meant small average change magnitudes. Other times incrementalism was a procedural characteristic but could lead to any level of average change magnitudes. The diversity of meanings led to a literature that resembled ships passing each other in the night.

For the most part, the volumes of work on incrementalism in budgets got stuck in this dispute. Debates raged over methodological issues (such as the appropriate level of budgeting to test the competing explanations, the threshold of "small" and "large," etc.) but the literature progressed little. Because the meaning of incrementalism was so vague, few of the related propositions could be falsified. Each finding of large average change magnitudes or the existence of profound, fast changes in policy was met with a shift in definitions of incrementalism rather than with a rejection of any theoretical hypothesis. By the early 1990s, the debate over incrementalism in policy research had largely disappeared without a resolution. The ambiguity over the meaning of small changes left many dissatisfied and uninterested in the research question.

8.1.4 A BRIEF ASIDE ON PALEONTOLOGY

While the disputes between incrementalists and their critics raged among scholars of public policy, a similar debate occupied the attention of scholars in paleontology. The paleontological orthodoxy focused on the gradual nature of evolutionary changes. The Darwinian theory of evolution suggests that changes are the product of random genetic events (Gould, 2002, 750). This gradualist approach was challenged by scholars who pointed to instances of rapid change (in geological and paleontological terms) in species. To the opponents of the gradualist approach, the key changes in the history of species are large changes.

Note the similarity between this and the dispute between incrementalists and their critics. The gradualists focused on the theoretical arguments for the relative rarity of large change. Their opponents focused on the existence of large changes in the fossil record. Again, standards for the "largeness" of a change were controversial. The nature of the empirical evidence was disputed as debates between the gradualists and their opponents raged. Without clear standards of evaluation or a clear fossil record, the debate could see no resolution.

8.2 PUNCTUATED EQUILIBRIUM THEORY—A WAY OUT OF BOTH CONUNDRUMS

It was the paleontological literature that developed a theory to escape the endless disputes between those who argued that large change was rare and those who said that large changes exist. Essentially, the answer was that both groups of scholars are right. There is nothing inconsistent in arguing that large change is rare but does exist.

The resulting synthesis was called punctuated equilibrium theory (Gould, 2002). In punctuated equilibrium theory, species spend most of the time in a period of stasis. In stasis, small genetic differences are present but these changes do not greatly affect the structural characteristics of the organism. There are constant forces for change in these periods of stasis represented by genetic variation, but these forces do not overcome natural barriers to large changes, representing the difficulty of change.

These periods of stasis are interrupted by rare episodes in which the forces for change override the barriers to change. This generally happens when pressures from the environment combine with internal genetic pressures for change. A punctuation may occur when changes in the environment make change necessary and the genetic variation randomly creates a competitive adaptation. These periods are called punctuations. The resulting process combining stasis with rare punctuations is punctuated equilibrium. While this theory is still controversial in paleontological circles, it has gathered substantial support in part due to the consistency of the predictions (rare, but large, change) with the existing fossil record.

Baumgartner and Jones (1993) saw in punctuated equilibrium theories a solution to the problems plaguing the dispute between incrementalists and their opponents. When Baumgartner looked at the various policy histories, they saw periods of inattention and stasis interrupted by periods of dramatic change. This pattern had been discussed at great length in policy theory before, but lacked a central organizing metaphor and theoretical vocabulary to empower analysis. Baumgartner and Jones brought the theory of punctuated equilibrium to the study of policy change as a way to resolve the dispute between incrementalists and their critics. Consistent with the incrementalist argument, large change is rare in a punctuated equilibrium process. Most of the history of any given policy is probably spent in a period of stasis. Consistent with the critics of incrementalism, policies can experience periods of dramatic change. While these punctuations are rare, they can be important parts of the development of public policy. Certainly these punctuations are the periods in policy history that people tend to study most carefully and the periods in which the policy subsystem gets the most attention.

Baumgartner and Jones took advantage of the ideal-typical nature of the punctuated equilibrium process to easily transfer the theory from its home in paleontology to the study of policy processes. The ideal-typical nature makes it possible to appeal to a broad range of phenomena — in this case, phenomena as diverse as speciation and the disintegration of policy monopolies. The appeal of the approach is that it synthesizes the previous existing theories under one theoretical tent. As a single theory, the punctuated equilibrium theory predicts the incrementalist/gradualist observation that large changes are rare while also predicting the existence of large changes in rare periods of punctuation.

8.3 A THEORETICAL MODEL OF PUNCTUATED EQUILIBRIUM THEORY

While the empirical support for the punctuated equilibrium theory is clear, the utility of the theory is not as obvious. Applying the work to policymaking, the theory made a statement about the relative frequency of different magnitudes of change. Small and large changes were supposed to appear more frequently than one should expect. Moderate changes were supposed to appear less frequently than one should expect.

Baumgartner and Jones (1993) hypothesized that the punctuated equilibrium pattern of policy change was the product of feedback processes in political institutions. This linked the punctuated equilibrium theory to parallel theories related to increasing returns and path dependence (Arthur, 1994) as well as the incrementalist tradition discussed above. However, the early research in the punctuated equilibrium theory focused less on the factors that were supposed to create the punctuated pattern than to verify that observed policy outputs were consistent with the patterns predicted by a punctuated equilibrium model.

The first question for the theory to address is how to define the baseline for comparison. One must be able to answer the question "more frequently than what?" True et al., (1999) contend that the proper baseline is the normal distribution with the mean and standard deviation defined by the empirical distribution of the sample of changes one is studying. If changes were truly random and not subject to a punctuated equilibrium process, the frequency of change magnitudes should follow the normal distribution by the Central Limit Theorem. One would see the frequency of small, moderate, and large changes arranged symmetrically around the mean based on the familiar bell curve. With this as the baseline, the expectations of the punctuated equilibrium model are that frequencies of large and small changes will exceed the expectations based on the normal distribution while the frequencies of moderate changes will be lower than expected.

The characteristic distribution of a punctuated equilibrium process is generally easy to identify with a look at a histogram of the change magnitudes (see Figure 8.1).

Figure 8.1 illustrates a typical distribution of data consistent with the True, Jones, and Baumgartner expectations for punctuated equilibrium.[*] The graph shows the density of observations at various magnitudes of change. For comparison purposes, a normal curve (with the same mean and standard deviation as the sample) is overlaid on the empirical distribution. At the small levels of

---

[*] This figure represents yearly percentage changes in instructional spending per pupil by public school districts in Texas from 1989 to 2000. The figure omits districts with percentage increases greater than 100% for clarity. The data is available from the Texas Education Agency (www.tea.state.tx.us).

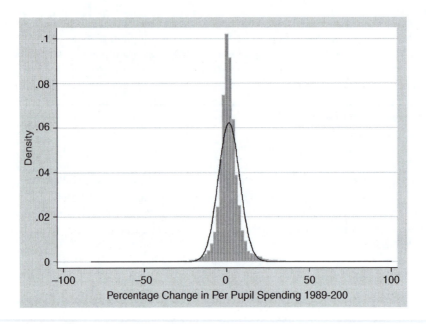

FIGURE 8.1 Percentage change in per pupil spending, 1989–2000.

change around zero percent (there is a small growth trend in the sample, so the distribution is centered just about zero) there are far more observations then expected based on a normal curve. Outside of the range of small range, there is a range of moderate change magnitude where there is lower than expected density. However, one sees spikes in the density function in the tails with much greater frequency than one would expect from the normal distribution. This empirical distribution of school district spending is illustrative of the general pattern that authors have found in areas as varied as stock markets and federal policy making institutions (Jones et al., 2003) and local government spending (Jordan, 2003).

The distribution is also easy to identify statistically with tests for the non-normality of a distribution. One simple test is to assess the kurtosis of the distribution (Rice, 1995). Kurtosis measures the frequency of observations at the tails and near the mean relative to the frequency in the middle range. The kurtosis is measured as:

$$k = \frac{\frac{1}{n}\sum_{i=1}^{n}(X_i - \overline{X})^4}{\sigma^4} \tag{8.1}$$

High values of k (higher than 3) represent an empirical distribution that has more observations at the peak and in the tails of the distribution than the normal distribution (which has a k of exactly 3). Distributions with high values of k are known as leptokurtic. Because kurtosis represents the relative frequency of low and high values of a frequency distribution, it serves as a test of whether a frequency distribution is shaped as one would expect from punctuated equilibrium processes.

The discussion of punctuated equilibrium theory in organizational decision making reveals an important limitation of the existing literature. While there is a lot said about the distribution of decision outcomes expected from punctuated equilibrium processes, little is said about the change processes themselves. While it may be clear that large change is rare, what mechanisms reinforce stasis to explain this rarity? What mechanisms lead to the rare periods of policy change?

Before venturing a theoretical model to address this lacuna in the literature, the next section will look at how the distributional theory has been tested and how hypotheses about the casual processes of punctuated equilibrium processes of organizational decision making emerged.

8.4 EVIDENCE OF PUNCTUATED EQUILIBRIA IN ORGANIZATIONAL DECISION MAKING

The argument that organizations (particularly policy making organizations) involve punctuated equilibrium processes has generated a lot of support but little testing. After the initial proposal of punctuated equilibrium models in Baumgartner and Jones (1993) few people tested the hypothesis. While many scholars felt the argument rang true, there was no clear way to falsify the claim. Any individual decision, whether representing a large or a small change, would be consistent with the theory. No individual observation can disconfirm the theory. This left many scholars frustrated with a theory that seemed true, but may be a truism. Other scholars forged ahead looking for falsifiable hypotheses generated by the punctuated equilibrium theory that could be falsified.

8.4.1 PUNCTUATED EQUILIBRIUM AND THE FEDERAL BUDGET

True et al. (1999) found a way to test the propositions of punctuated equilibrium theory by developing a falsifiable hypothesis. Developing the approach discussed in the previous section, True, Jones, and Baumgartner argued that punctuated equilibrium theory made falsifiable predictions about distributions of organizational decisions that could be falsified. The reputation for a lack of falsifiability came from the mistaken focus on individual decisions. While individual decisions were not sufficiently informative to test the expansive theory, assessments of large collections of observations could do so.

To test the punctuated equilibrium theory, True, Jones, and Baumgartner gathered data on budgetary decisions by Congress in the post World War II era. For each policy area, they observed the magnitude of program budgetary change in each year. For each year, the authors found the percentage change in the authorizations for 62 budgetary sub-functions in the federal budget. The authors then plotted a histogram of the changes and compared the empirical distribution of budget authorization to a normal curve with the mean and standard deviation of the empirical distribution.

What they found was consistent with the expectations of the punctuated equilibrium theory. There was a greater than expected number of authorization changes around zero and in the tails of the distribution. In particular, there was a far greater than expected number of authorization changes of greater than a 290% increase. There was also a lower than expected number of authorization changes in the moderate range (for both positive and negative changes) (True et al., 1999, 110). The authors observed the same pattern in budgetary functions at a higher level of aggregation, dividing the budget into seventeen functions, but the results were not at stark (109).

The results of the True, Jones, and Baumgartner study were initial confirmation that the punctuated equilibrium theory was plausible as a description of the outputs of an organizational decision process. Because the study only looked at the characteristic distribution, there was no evidence as to what factors led to this distribution. Within this descriptive statistic approach, one could not test opposing hypotheses about the causes of punctuated equilibrium (related to, say, the factors that increase the punctuated nature of the process). However, the initial test was strong confirmation that the outputs of the federal budgetary processes were more consistent with a punctuated equilibrium model than with assumptions of rational decision making.

8.4.2 Punctuated Equilibrium and Local Government Budgets

The early work on punctuated equilibrium served to confirm the plausibility of the descriptive prediction of punctuated equilibrium theory. However, there was little discussion of the factors that influenced the decision processes. This gap in the literature is starting to be filled. The first attempt to test hypotheses about the relative degree of punctuation (the relative non-normality of decision outputs) in the policy looked at the influence of the politics surrounding specific types of budget functions on the distribution of budgetary outputs (Jordan, 2003). Meagan Jordan studied the distribution of local government budgets and found that budget decisions about some functions were more consistent with punctuated equilibrium than others.

As opposed to the True et al.'s (1999) method of pooling all budget functions into a single sample of budgetary authorizations, Jordan sought to compare the behavior of different functions. Jordan (2003) argued that not all budget processes are the same. Borrowing a typology of budget functions from Peterson (1995), Jordan argued that some budget functions "neither hurt nor help the local economy" (350–352). She categorized these functions as allocational and included budgets for police, fire, and sanitation. Other functions are designed to spur economic development. She categorized these as developmental and included parks and recreation and public-building spending. Finally, some spending relies heavily on intergovernmental transfers of funding. She categorized these as intergovernmental and includes spending on highways.

Each of these types of budgets involves a different political environment.[*] The allocational budgets are supposed to involve low levels of conflict—and therefore will be more stable—because they represent "basic day-to-day services" (Jordan, 2003, 350). Jordan then tested whether allocational budgets are more stable than non-allocational budgets, with special attention to the relative probabilities of large changes.

To compare the relative probability of change magnitudes, Jordan defined upper and low thresholds for change. Jordan elected to define a specific percentage change as large. For negative change, a decrease in a budget of greater than 25% below the average change rate is considered a large negative change. For positive change, an increase in a budget of greater than 35% above the average change rate is considered a large positive change (Jordan, 2003, 352). Each policy then had different thresholds based on the sample mean percentage change—but the gap between the thresholds is the same for all functions.

Analysis of the results suggested that allocational budgets experience lower frequencies of punctuations than non-allocational budgets (Jordan, 2003, 354) and lower probabilities of punctuations (356). The probability results were not sensitive to tests using other gap distances between the lower and upper thresholds (357). Together the results suggested that the degree to which a budgetary decision process experiences punctuations is related to budgetary function—and maybe to the politics surrounding each functional type.

This research is a substantial improvement over the distributional tests in previous work. Jordan initiated the use of punctuated equilibrium theory as a subject of hypothesis testing. The tests described above split up the distribution to ask which decision processes are more likely to experience punctuations. The key strategy, one that will be picked up again later, was to compare different sub-samples. If a scholar can identify a factor that should influence the degree to which a decision process is likely to be a punctuated equilibrium process, a researcher can compare sub-samples where that factor is present to sub-samples where the factor is absent. The ability to compare decision processes with different characteristics allows hypothesis testing within the punctuated equilibrium framework and moved the literature past serial tests of the consistency of samples with punctuated equilibrium predictions.

---

[*] This way of thinking about the policy decision process is much like Lowi's (1964, 1972) famous statement that policies structure politics.

8.4.3 Punctuated Equilibrium and the Federal Policy Process

Around the time that Jordan (2003) published her hypothesis testing approach to the punctuated equilibrium model, Jones and his colleagues developed an alternative hypothesis testing approach. Jones et al. (2003) discussed the factors that make an organizational decision making process more characterized by punctuated equilibrium. Organizations face a number of obstacles to change. Jones and his colleagues contended that all organizations involve varying degrees of "institutional friction" (152).

This institutional friction can come from many sources. To discover relevant information for any decision, organizations may incur "informational costs." Once this information is available to the organization, the organization may pay "cognitive costs" to process the information. Once the information is processed, organizations may face "decision costs" representing the difficulty of reaching consensus within an organization on a decision. Organizations may also face "transaction costs" after a decision is made involving the costs of commitment, compliance, and oversight (Jones et al., 2003, 154).

These categories of costs have a broad range of potential application. The first two types of costs (information and cognitive) could affect individual decision as well as organizational decision making. The latter two types of costs (decision and transaction) can apply to just about any organizational decision. In this way, one could apply the friction theory of punctuated decision making to almost all decision processes. Linking punctuated equilibrium to this set of concerns integrates the theory of punctuated equilibrium decision making to broader concerns over bounded rationality and organizational decision making.

Jones et al. (2003) tested the general hypotheses that increased friction leads to increased punctuated equilibrium behavior by arranging a series of organizational decision outputs in an increasing order of friction (156–157). They argued that as one moves though the policy making process, a process that combines in parallel and serial fashion a variety of organizations, one should see increased punctuation equilibrium behavior. The list of organizational decision processes range from political input processes like the stock market, electoral outcomes, and media coverage to policy output processes like budget outlays, budget authority, and public laws (157).

Jones et al. (2003) used two methods for measuring the punctuated equilibrium nature of each of these decision processes. First, they measured the kurtosis of the output of each of the organizational processes, as in True et al. (1999). They found that political input distributions for elections, media attention, and the stock market had kurtosis measures ranging between three and ten. While this is an indication of leptokurtosis,[*] this is a low level of kurtosis compared to the previous studied budget distributions. Intermediate processes like hearings had kurtosis values in the 20 sec. Policy output processes had a wide range of kurtosis values with the public law distribution having a kurtosis of 24 and the budget distributions have kurtosis values in ranging from 60 to 85 (158).

The results of the kurtosis analysis were roughly consistent with Jones and his colleagues' expectations. With the notable exceptions of executive orders and public laws, the policy output processes had higher kurtosis values than the intermediary processes that in turn had higher values than the political input processes. The values of each group were statistically distinguishable from the sequentially prior group. The results were consistent with the institutional friction theory of organizational decision making.

There is not a lot known about the distribution of kurtosis statistics, so Jones et al. (2003) supplemented the analysis of the kurtosis of the various output distributions with other diagnostic tests. Jones and his colleagues tested the distributions against hypotheses that each distribution is normally distributed, exponentially distributed, and Pareto distributed. They found that the budgetary data were distributed along the heavy-tailed Pareto distribution as they expected while

---

[*] In all cases, the kurtosis of the distribution was greater than the normal distribution based on the asymptotic standard error of the kurtosis statistic.

other distributions were close to the moderately tailed exponential distribution (160). These distributional tests provided supporting evidence for the conclusions reached in the kurtosis analysis. Together the tests provided strong evidence linking the temporal order in the policy process to punctuations in organizational decision making.

Jones et al. (2003) played an important role in raising awareness of the punctuated equilibrium theory and proposing a theoretical framework within which one could employ the punctuated equilibrium theory. The theory of institutional friction linked the discussion of punctuated equilibrium to well-established literature on transaction costs, organizational decision making, and bounded rationality. At the same time, the hypothesis tests in the article were unsatisfying. The ordering of the organization processes along the lines of the policy process was not tied to institutional friction well. It was not clear that as one proceeds along the policy process that one necessarily encountered more friction. In fact, the outlier they observed (executive orders) was accounted for by reference to their relatively low friction (158). Furthermore, there was no way to sense the magnitude of institutional friction. If one accepted the rank order, one still had no sense of the magnitude of the changes in friction or the magnitude of the changes in punctuated equilibrium behavior. The article pointed in the direction of the relevant hypotheses to test within the punctuated equilibrium theory but did not itself provide a clear test.

8.4.4 Punctuated Equilibrium and Organizational Bureaucratization

Jordan (2003) and Jones et al. (2003) had pointed the way to hypothesis testing within the punctuated equilibrium model. Jordan provided a method of sub-sample comparison to facilitate hypothesis testing. Jones and his colleagues situated punctuated equilibrium theory in a broader tradition of bounded rationality thus creating a fertile ground of potential hypotheses. Robinson (2004) followed these leads to test hypotheses within the institutional friction theory of punctuated equilibrium using comparisons of sub-samples. In doing so, Robinson also addressed a large question looming over education policy debates for over a decade.

Earlier Chubb and Moe (1990) argued that bureaucratization reduced a school organization's capacity to respond to change. In their view, bureaucratization made change more costly and increased the influence of entrenched interests. The result was that bureaucratized school districts lacked the capacity to address changing problems in education and the districts' performance was lower than the performance of leaner, less bureaucratized districts.

While the microdynamics of Chubb and Moe's argument are not obvious, there is an assumed story about the effect of bureaucratization on schools and policy change. Chubb and Moe argue that bureaucratization represents the addition of new layers of management to schools. These new layers may include specialized curriculum directors or district liaisons. Each of these new layers adds either a veto point (a person who can stop change) or at least a delay point (a person who can slow down change by demanding to be consulted in the change process). The result is that as school districts become bureaucratized, they are unable to respond to new challenges. Each change in policy must work its way through all of these hands. The result is an organization that is slow to respond to demands for change.

Meier et al. (2000) countered that Chubb and Moe had the causal story backwards. Meier and his colleagues argued that poorly performing school districts developed response programs and thereby developed more extensive bureaucracy. Their analysis found that poor performance preceded bureaucratization and that low test scores did not follow bureaucratization. The authors interpreted this evidence to mean the bureaucratization was not the cause of low test scores but may serve as an instrument of change rather than an impediment to change.

A central point in this dispute is whether bureaucratization is a barrier to change or a tool increasing the capacity of an organization to change. Chubb and Moe's view of bureaucratization was that it represents institutional friction reducing the ability of the organization to change. Bureaucratization multiplied veto points and delay points in the system. Meier and his colleagues, view was that bureaucratization increases the organization's ability to overcome institutional friction. For Meier and his colleagues, bureaucratization represented an organization's efforts to increase its capacity to handle challenges. This may come in the form of new expertise or new information processing capacity. What neither study tested was how bureaucratization was related to rates of change in organizational policy.

Robinson (2004) addressed this conflict by looking at the relationship between bureaucratization and policy change. Robinson separated school districts into bureaucratized and non-bureaucratized sub-samples. He then compared the kurtosis values of the two sub-samples to see which exhibited greater evidence of punctuated equilibrium—a byproduct of institutional friction. The analysis revealed that bureaucratized school districts had a distribution of budgetary change with a substantially lower kurtosis than non-bureaucratized school districts. The bureaucratized school districts had a distribution of budgetary changes that more closely resembled the normal distribution (with lower levels of small and large change, larger levels of moderate change) than the non-bureaucratized school districts. Robinson interpreted the evidence to suggest that bureaucratization reduced institutional friction in school district budgetary processes. The result was that bureaucratized school districts exhibited decision outputs less consistent with punctuated equilibrium than non-bureaucratized school districts.[*]

8.4.5 Assessing the Evidence

The preceding studies illustrate the evolution of punctuated equilibrium research in the study of the policy process. In the early stages, scholars were limited to assessing whether aggregate distributions were consistent with the predictions of punctuated equilibrium theory. Recent developments have pushed the study forward toward hypothesis testing. Starting with Jordan (2003), scholars have begun to ask a new set of questions. Rather than assessing whether any distribution of decision outputs is consistent with the predictions of punctuated equilibrium theory, scholars now ask what factors make a decision process produce outputs more or less consistent with the predictions of punctuated equilibrium process. Jones et al.'s (2003) theory of institutional friction established an ambitious agenda for research. Researchers can now assess the specific contributors to punctuated equilibrium behavior such as information, cognitive, transaction, and decision costs, as Robinson did (2004).

8.5 FRONTIERS OF PUNCTUATED EQUILIBRIUM RESEARCH

For all of the strides in the study of punctuated equilibrium behavior in organizational decision making, a great deal of work lies ahead. This section will discuss some of the limitations of the existing approaches to studying punctuated equilibrium in organization decision processes. I will conclude with a short discussion of the opportunities punctuated equilibrium research presents to improve our understanding of decision making generally.

8.5.1 The Statistical Challenges of Punctuated Equilibrium Research

The study of punctuated equilibrium presents many challenges for those wanting to apply statistical tests to hypotheses. The primary challenges stem from the focus of the existing hypothesis testing procedures on the analysis of distributions of decision outputs. The Jordan (2003) research compared samples of local government budget expenditures. Jones et al.'s (2003) research compared samples of organizational outputs in the federal policy-making process (2003). The Robinson (2004)

---

[*] However, it is important to note that all of the samples Robinson analyzed exhibited a higher level of kurtosis than the normal curve and thus all samples were distributed as one would expect by punctuated equilibrium theory. The difference was in the degree of the punctuation behavior.

research compared samples of different types of school districts. In each case, the comparison was between samples of decision outputs.

The focus on sample characteristics severely limits the sort of hypotheses that scholars can test related to punctuated equilibrium. Rather than having to assemble sets of observations, researchers adopting the current hypothesis technology in the punctuated equilibrium literature have to assemble sets of samples. Each sample has to be sufficiently large enough to allow for the analysis of fourth moment characteristics—if not kurtosis than some other analysis of extremes. Each sample can be thought of as an observation of punctuated equilibrium behavior. In the largest set of comparisons to date, Jones et al. (2003) compared less than a dozen distributions. This is similar to a study with 12 observations. There is not much you can do with such a set of observations.

The focus on samples constrains researchers to univariate tests. The Jordan (2003) research focused on a univariate test of the effects of a dichotomous variable (policy type). Jones et al.'s (2003) research ranked the samples in order of institutional friction. The Robinson (2004) research compared two sets of school districts based on a dichotomous variable. The comparison of school district budget changes may be particularly illustrative of the limitations of the sample-based procedure. The independent variable under investigation was bureaucratization, measured as the percentage of resources devoted to administrative personnel. This original measure was actually a continuous variable. Robinson was forced to collapse the continuous variable into two categories to make a discrete comparison. One cannot analyze the effect of a continuous independent variable without transforming the variable into a discrete variable—with the associated loss of information.

The focus on samples also raises questions about the qualities one needs in the various samples under investigation. Jones et al. (2003) and Jordan (2003) sampled pool data across time. Jordan (2003) and Robinson (2004) sampled pooled data across space as well. The effects of these pooling exercises are not at all clear. The assumption of pooling across space or time was that the characteristic under study is constant across all of the units within the sample. In Jones and his colleagues' sample, for example, the authors assume that the kurtosis of the federal budgetary process is the same throughout the sample. The pooling across time assumes that there were no years that were any more likely to exhibit large changes than any other years. The data generating process (or the punctuation generating process) is assumed to be the same across all of the years in the sample. A similar problem lurks in the pooling across space. Jordan pooled all city budgets together. Jordan's pooling of city budgets assumed that all cities are as likely to experience punctuations in any given year as all of the other cities (within a specific policy type). The specter of omitted variable bias looms large. This is particularly problematic when the measurement or ordering of the independent variable is controversial.

The obvious solution to the focus on samples is to focus, instead, on individual observations. Focusing on individual observations (classified as small, medium, and large change) opens up a number of options. Most importantly, such a shift matches the empirical unit of analysis with the theoretical unit of analysis. The punctuated equilibrium theory focuses on individual decision making units and the individual outputs of the process. The focus of the theory is on the factors that make large, medium and small changes more and less likely. The theory does not focus on the distribution of outputs. The statistical test should similarly be focused on the size of the individual decision output.

Second, a switch to the individual unit of analysis allows one to test multivariate hypotheses including continuous independent variables. The sample focus limited the effective number of observations (for purposes of hypothesis testing specifically) to a small number. With samples of observations, one could not test multiple hypotheses simultaneously and could not test for the effect of continuous independent variables because the number of samples quickly becomes too small to serve as the basis for more advanced tests. As discussed above, continuous variables simply could not be tested using comparisons of discrete samples. Even if one wanted to test for the effects of multiple independent variables in the sample-focused system, the number of sub-samples need would proliferate quickly. If one were only testing for the effect of dichotomous variables, one would need 2^n sub-samples where n is the number of independent variables to be studied). As one can see, the demands on the data expand exponentially in the number of simultaneous variables.

An individual observation approach makes these sorts of tests realistic. Once one categorizes individual outputs as indicating small, medium, or large change, one can test for the effects of various independent variables using traditional regression technologies.[*] With the traditional regression framework, one can assess the effect of, say, bureaucratization (measured as a continuous variable this time) and organizational size simultaneously. The opportunities this hypothesis testing approach opens up are countless. With the regression framework, one can test for the effects of specific information, cognitive, decision, and transaction costs as well as comparing for the relative importance of each.[†]

Moving to the individual decision output level of analysis leaves a number of estimation problems. The first is the nature of timing in the theory of punctuated equilibrium. Many of the theories (as vague as they are) suggest that punctuations should reduce the stress on the decision system. The punctuation should return the decision maker to equilibrium with its environment. A key factor influencing punctuated behavior should be the history of the decision system. None of the tests have included history in the analysis. This is not just simply because of the rush to test so many other propositions. In part, this is because of the limited nature of the data available. In the sample-based studies, pooling of organizations across time prevented the inclusion of any time-based variable. Even a test using the individual decision as the unit of analysis is likely to find testing the historical hypothesis difficult. The large data sets that provide the scale of data needed to address questions of punctuated equilibrium have limited time periods. Ideally, one would need a data set with a large set of organizational decision outputs observed yearly for a long period of time. Not many data sets have these qualities.

The most fundamental problem facing the statistical testing of hypotheses derived from punctuated equilibrium theory is the difficulty of studying rare events. All of the most common statistical technologies focus on providing information about the central tendencies of observations. The reliability of such estimates becomes questionable when one starts to apply the results to the extreme values in the sample. However, punctuated equilibrium studies need to assess rare events—punctuations. Data sets have to be sufficiently large to provide some leverage on questions related to rare events. Every included independent variable increases the number of rare events one would have to observe to get leverage on the hypothesis. The result is a need for staggeringly large data sets. Furthermore, one needs data sets that are free of errors. An error may well turn up as a large change. If large changes are rare, each one will have substantial leverage on the results. In this case, errors may play a large role if determining the result if one is not careful in the analysis.

Together these challenges to the statistical testing of hypotheses related to punctuated equilibrium theory suggest the difficulty of such research, but not its impossibility. Researchers must be careful in designing the hypothesis tests of punctuated equilibrium hypotheses, but such tests are possible. More attention is needed on the hypothesis testing technologies available to researchers in this area of study, but the challenges are not insurmountable.

8.5.2 THE THEORETICAL CHALLENGES OF PUNCTUATED EQUILIBRIUM RESEARCH

Punctuated equilibrium theories face theoretical challenges in addition to the statistical challenges reviewed above. As may have been clear in much of the discussion above, there are a number of points where the theory of punctuated equilibrium is unclear. Many of the variables associated with punctuated equilibrium theory are unclear and difficult to make operational. Furthermore, the

---

[*] Jordan (2003) could have done just this once she created arbitrary cut points for small, medium, and large change. She stayed with the comparison of samples of observations by policy type-but she did not have to.

[†] For an example of the utility of this approach, see Robinson et al. (2004).

linkage between the variables and the decision processes are unclear. A clear theoretical model of punctuated equilibrium decision making would go a long way toward resolving some of the ambiguity.

The absence of a theoretical model stems from the descriptive orientation of some of the original work on punctuated equilibrium. The intuition of the punctuated equilibrium model was based on the observation of (rare) large changes and (common) small changes. This intuition does not provide an explanation for why one observes this pattern, but the pattern itself became evidence for the theory. Baumgartner and Jones' (1993) initial work suggested the sorts of mechanism that might be at play. They focused on the interplay of positive feedback and negative feedback. The negative feedback supported the equilibrium that emerged from the occasional episodes of positive feedback. Together, these feedback mechanisms hint at the causal mechanism behind punctuated equilibrium organizational decisions. However, the theoretical development has not progressed far from that point.

A strong attempt to elaborate a causal theory of punctuated equilibrium can be found in Jones' book *The Politics and the Architecture of Choice* (2001). Jones argues that punctuated equilibrium stems from systematic under-reaction and overreaction to environmental stimuli. Under-reaction is a product of negative feedback whereas overreaction is a product of positive feedback. This argument then focuses on the role that adaptation plays in decision making. While this provides some clarity on what can cause a positive or a negative feedback process, there is still a lot of work to be done to integrate the various factors discussed in the literature on punctuated equilibrium.

To take one example, the language of adaptation and feedback does not assist in sorting out the hypothesized effects of bureaucratization on decision systems. It is not clear whether to expect bureaucratization to create systematic under-reaction, as Chubb and Moe suggested (1990), or to expect bureaucratization to reduce under-reaction and overreaction processes, as Robinson found (2004). The limitations of the adaptation metaphor are clear in Jones et al. (2003) discussion of the institutional friction theory. While in some sense the institutional friction theory is an organizational version of the individual adaptation theory in Jones' earlier work (2001), the discussion of the sources of friction reveals how sparse the model is. There are four different potential sources of friction. Each of these sources of friction represents a large literature of research. There is no attempt to integrate the various components of friction or to model how they affect decision making—except to say that they make change costly and may lead to punctuated equilibrium.

Future theoretical work must take seriously the need for a model of punctuated equilibrium that integrates the various types of costs identified by Jones et al. (2003). This work should consider the components of each source of friction. What increases transaction costs? What decreases informational costs? How do the various costs tradeoff and interact? Are there nonlinear interactions of certain types of costs? All of these questions illustrate the need for theoretical development.

A threshold model of decision making may provide the starting point for such a synthesis. One can begin by imagining change as the product of some demand. That demand may be internal or external depending on the situation at hand, but without demand for change—change is unlikely. The metaphor of costs suggests that decision makers must overcome some barrier to change. That barrier may be the product of any of the four sources of costs discussed by Jones et al. (2003) As the costs of change go up, the barrier goes up. When the demand for change is below the critical threshold for change, nothing or very little happens. One can imagine that the organization changes only incrementally while demand is below this critical threshold. Once demand builds up to pass the threshold, positive feedback/overreaction mechanisms take over. Large changes are contemplated and likely chosen. Among organizations facing a demand for change that exceeds their critical threshold, the distribution of changes is likely to have very heavy tolls and may not have much probability mass around the zero change.

The threshold model provides a metaphor within which it is easier to theorize about the effects of bureaucratization, for example. Bureaucratization may play a role in raising the change threshold by increasing the number of people that must be consulted before any change can be enacted. The result would be longer periods of building demand during which change would only be incremental. Demand would have to reach a higher threshold to motivate a larger number of people (veto players or time-consuming players). Only after this higher threshold hold is reached is non-incremental change possible. This is very much the image that Chubb and Moe (1990) provide for bureaucratization in school districts.

Bureaucratization could have a different effect on the threshold. Bureaucratization may increase the organization's capacity to assess and respond to new demands. New bureaucrats may be able to collect more data and better assess the new data for the sorts of signals that should motivate non-incremental change. This is the motivation behind the reactive bureaucratization described by Meier et al. (2000). School districts seek more information to respond to initial signs of difficulties. If there is evidence of problems in math instruction, the districts may create a bureaucratic position that is supposed to collect information on math performance and design new math curricula. This informational capacity may lower the threshold by better assessing the demand for change when that demand exists. The result is a process that can more easily overcome the change threshold when needed.

The threshold model suggests that great attention should be paid to the exact change brought about by bureaucratization (or any factor hypothesized to influence the rate of change in an organization). Bureaucratization, for example, may increase veto players and it may increase demand-assessment capacity. The threshold model suggests that greater attention should be paid to the meaning of bureaucratization so that these faces of bureaucratization can be assessed separately. Scholars need to consider whether bureaucratization actually does increase the presence of veto players. They must also consider whether bureaucratization increases demand assessment capacity. Then, the scholars must consider the relative magnitudes of each.

The existing empirical research only assesses the aggregate effects of bureaucratization. The Robinson (2004) research, for example, suggests that the demand assessment influence is greater than the influence of any created veto players. This research, however, cannot assess the independent effect of each. There could be a strong veto player effect outweighed by a stronger demand assessment effect. There could be a weak veto player effect outweighed by a moderated demand assessment effect. Without disaggregation, such questions cannot be answered. The future lies in using a theoretical model of organizational change (like the threshold model of punctuated equilibrium) to figure out which aspects of an organization are likely to affect change processes (such as veto players, time-consuming players, and demand-assessment capacity) and match the measurement and testing to these aspects.

The threshold model, while a simple application of much of the verbal theory of punctuated equilibrium, suggests some very complicated dynamics. Any large sample of observations is likely to include a mixture of the pre-threshold incremental decision outputs and the post-threshold non-incremental decision outputs. Looking for characteristics of the sample as a single distribution (rather than as a mixture of distributions) may be problematic. Furthermore, this theory suggests that the relationship between any of the sources of institutional friction (which determine the threshold) and the size of the change will be nonlinear—may be dramatically so. The threshold model, in fact, suggests that the probability of a large change changes from nearly zero at a point just below the threshold to substantial (though still maybe small) at a point just the other side of the threshold. These nonlinear relationships may elude the linear assumptions of most regression-based approaches.

Still, the threshold-based approach provides a firmer grounding for theorizing about institutional friction (as well as a more realistic assessment of the difficulty in testing for the effects of the sources of institutional friction). Future researcher should consider what effect an organizational characteristic (like bureaucratization) or individual characteristics (like information processing capacity) will have on the threshold separating incremental from non-incremental response processes. Such a framework may provide a clearer model for future development of punctuated equilibrium theory.

8.6 CONCLUSION

While still in its infancy, punctuated equilibrium theory promises to offer insight into to decision making. Punctuated equilibrium theory provides a way out of the theoretical logjam between incremental and non-incremental decision theories. The model of decision processes as producing punctuated equilibrium focuses our attention on the factors that contribute to decision stasis and punctuation. Within various settings, theoretical and empirical work can advance as we begin to study the factors that contribute to the varying degrees of stasis and punctuation in different settings.

The existing research has focused on organizational decision making. It should be no surprise that it is in organizational decision making that the punctuated equilibrium has then had the greatest effect. The work of Jones et al. (2003) in particular has pointed to the potential contributions that punctuated equilibrium theory can have to a theory of organizational decision making. Their analysis illustrated the importance of institutional friction in shaping the distribution of organizational outputs. Though not studied directly in their research, Jones and his colleagues also linked punctuated equilibrium to broad areas of organizational decision making such as collective action, coalition building, and transaction costs. This suggests that punctuated equilibrium theory could potentially serve to integrate diverse fields of study in organizational decision making by focusing attention on the factors that affect the rate and magnitude of change in organizational behavior.

These contributions are most obviously relevant to the study of organizational decision making, but could also apply to individual decision making. While understudied to this point, many of the factors thought to affect organizational decision making could also affect individual decision making. While transaction and decision costs are not relevant to individual decision making, information and cognitive costs are key components of individual decision theories. The punctuated equilibrium theory suggests that as these costs rise, individual decision outputs should resemble the outputs of organizations facing institutional friction. This area is understudied, but could provide great insight to the punctuated equilibrium theory just as the punctuated equilibrium theory could serve to integrate models of change in individual decision making.

In both of these circumstances, the threshold model of decision making may provide assistance. Individuals and organizations are likely to stick with incremental decisions until the pressure to change passes some critical threshold. The factors affecting the level of this threshold may differ at the organizational and individual level, but the basic model may be helpful. The key to future development of this theoretical perspective is to identify the relationship between various individual and organizational characteristics and the threshold separating incremental from non-incremental decision processes.

REFERENCES

Arthur, W. B., *Increasing Returns and Path Dependence in the Economy*, Cambridge University Press, Cambridge, MA, 1994.

Baumgartner, F. R. and Jones, B. D., *Agendas and Instability in American Politics*, The University of Chicago Press, Chicago, 1993.

Berry, W. D., The confusing case of budgetary incrementalism: too many meanings for a single concept, *The Journal of Politics*, 52(1), 167–196, 1990.

Braybrooke, D. L. and Lindblom, C. E., *A Strategy of Decision*, The Free Press, New York, 1963.

Chubb, J. E. and Moe, T. M., *Politics, Markets, and America's Schools*, Brookings Institution, Washington, DC, 1990.

Gould, S. J., *The Structure of Evolutionary Theory*, Belknap Press, Cambridge, MA, 2002.

Jones, B. D., *Politics and the Architecture of Choice: Bounded Rationality and Governance*, University of Chicago Press, Chicago, 2001.

Jones, B. D., Sulkin, T., and Larsen, H. A., Policy punctuations in American political institutions, *American Political Science Review*, 97(1), 151–169, 2003.

Jordan, M. M., Punctuations and agendas: a new look at local government budget expenditures, *Journal of Policy Analysis and Management*, 23(3), 345–360, 2003.

Lindblom, C. E., The science of muddling through, *Public Administration Review*, 19, 79–88, 1959.

Lowi, T., American business, public policy, case studies, and political theory, *World Politics*, 16, 677–715, 1964.

Lowi, T., Four systems of policy, politics, and choice, *Public Administration Review*, 32, 298–301, 1972.

Meier, K. J., Polinard, J. L., and Wrinkle, R. D., Bureaucracy and organizational performance: causality arguments about public schools, *American Journal of Political Science*, 44, 590–602, 2000.

Peterson, P., *The Price of Federalism*, Brookings Institution, Washington, DC, 1995.

Rice, J. A., *Mathematical Statistics and Data Analysis*, 2nd ed., Duxbury Press, Belmont, CA, 1995.

Robinson, S. E., Punctuated equilibrium, bureaucratization, and school budgets, *Policy Studies Journal*, 32(1), 25–39, 2004.

Robinson, S. E., Caver, F. R., Meier, K. J., and O'Toole, L. J., Jr., Explaining policy punctuations: a multivariate model of the punctuated equilibrium theory of public agency budgets. Paper presented at the annual meeting of the American Political Science Association, Chicago, IL, September 2004.

True, J. L., Jones, B. D., and Baumgartner, F. R., Punctuated equilibrium theory: explaining stability and change in American policymaking, In *Theories of the Policy Process*, Sabatier, P., Ed., Westview Press, Boulder, CO, 1999.

Wildavsky, A., *The Politics of the Budgetary Process*, Little, Brown, Boston, 1964.

Wildavsky, A., *The New Politics of the Budgetary Process*, 2nd ed., HarperCollins, New York, 1992.

9 Democratic Theory as a Frame for Decision Making: The Challenges by Discourse Theory and Governance Theory

Eva Sørensen

CONTENTS

9.1   Introduction...151
9.2   The Traditional Approach to Democratic Decision Making...153
9.3   The Challenge of Discourse Theory..154
9.4   The Challenge from Governance Theory..157
9.5   Conclusion: Expanding the Scope of Democratic Decision Making..................................163
References...164

9.1   INTRODUCTION

As many political scientists have noted, democracy conquered the world in the twentieth century (Bellamy, 1987; Dahl, 1989, 2000; Holden, 2000; Shapiro and Macedo, 2000). It might be an exaggeration to say that democratic practices have become the dominant form of government, but democracy has, over the years, become a legitimate point of reference for political regimes and popular movements throughout the world. However, the concept of democracy is a heavily contested concept. The meaning that has been applied to the concept of democracy has changed throughout history, and different models of democracy have competed at any given moment of time (Bobbio, 1987; Dahl, 2000; Held, 1989; Holden,1993). Nevertheless, a rather distinct institutional model of democracy has obtained hegemony in the global community: representative democracy or, as Dahl and Lindblom (1953) term it, *polyarchy*. The main features of this institutional model for processing democratic decision making are competition between political elites, accountability through general elections, a free press, and a private sector based on a market economy.

The uncontested position of representative democracy as institutional framework for democratic decision making reached its peak with the collapse of the Eastern Block and the Berlin Wall in 1989 (Shapiro and Hacker-Cordón, 1999). The occasion caused Francis Fukuyama (1992) to proclaim that we had reached the end of history by fully realizing the utopia of market based liberal representative democracy. Later, it became clear that history had not come to and end. As the 1990s moved on, the loss of an outside enemy to democracy turned the critical attention inwards towards the shortcomings of representative democracy. Some theorists on democracy began to stress the need for minor reforms of the traditional institutions of representative democracy, yet others claim that radical transformations are needed (Barber, 1996; Benhabib, 1996; Cohen and Rogers, 1995; Connolly, 1995; Fung and Wright, 2003; Hirst, 1990; Hirst and Khilnani, 1996; Holden, 2000; Shapiro and Hacker-Cordón, 1999; Young, 2000). The many calls for a radical transformation of democracy are not only a result of the loss of a threatening "other" to democracy, because the construction of a new "other" to democracy in terms of terrorism and villain states has not led to a reduction in the criticism of representative democracy.

The aim of this article is to show that the calls for radical transformations of the traditional model of representative democracy is due to its narrow definition of what democratic decision making means, where and how it is exercised, and what issues democratic decision making should address. The narrow scope of the traditional image of democratic decision making has, in recent years, become still more visible for two reasons: (1) the development of a new discourse theoretical perception of the political, and (2) the emergence of new theories of governance that identify a large and growing distance between the democratic model and the actual processes of democratic decision making in the countries that are perceived as the strongholds of representative democracy.

Discourse theory suggests that the model of representative democracy takes its departure from a much too narrow definition of the political as an activity that has to do with rational reasoning and takes place within a predefined political sphere. From a discourse theoretical perspective, it is not possible to establish fixed boundaries between a political and a private sphere because the relationship between the political and the non-political is much too dynamic and is a matter of degrees of contestation and sedimentation. Because the model of representative democracy seeks to establish fixed boundaries between the political and the private sphere it is likely that decisions that are taken within what is being defined as the private sphere, escape democratic regulation even though they have important implications for the governing of society.

Also, the current strong wave of governance theories indicates that the traditional model of representative democracy only narrowly addresses the issue of democratic decision making (Bogason, 2000; Jessop, 2000; Klijn and Koppenjan, 2000; Mayntz, 1999; Pierre, 2000; Rhodes, 2000; Scharpf, 2000; Sørensen, 2002). Governance theorists argue that the distance between the traditional model and concrete processes of democratic decision making is widening. The model of representative democracy suggests that democratic decision making is performed at what we could denote two big authoritative moments of democratic decision making (D-decisions): (1) when the people elect a sovereign ruler on election day, and (2) when the sovereign pass laws and rule with reference to these laws. Governance theory insists that policy making takes place in a much wider range of moments of decision making in governing process, not least in phases of agenda setting and implementation. Because the model of representative democracy focuses solely on the big D-decisions, it fails to ensure that the many less visible and celebrated decisions (d-decisions) that are taken by other actors in the processes of agenda setting and implementation are regulated democratically, even though these small d-decisions have considerable impact on governance outcomes.

Although discourse theory and governance theory both criticise the model of representative democracy for defining democratic decision making too narrowly and for merely focusing on the tip of the iceberg, their critiques are different in their reasons and styles. What these theories indicate is that there is a need for developing a more inclusive theory of democratic decision making that takes into account the hidden parts of the iceberg to ensure that all and not only some political decisions are being regulated democratically. To uncover the hidden layers of the iceberg, I first describe democratic decision making as it is perceived by the traditional model of representative democracy. Then it is explained how discourse theory and governance theory challenge the traditional image of democratic decision making. Finally, I summarize the demands that discourse theory and governance theory direct towards a more inclusive model of democratic decision making.

9.2 THE TRADITIONAL APPROACH TO DEMOCRATIC
DECISION MAKING

It is, by definition, a dangerous task to construct images of the past because these constructions tend to become one dimensional and simplistic. Even so, in what follows, an ideal typical model of the traditional approach to democratic decision making will be constructed. Although the price to pay by this enterprise is sure to be a loss of complexity, a modelling that highlights the dominating features of the traditional approach to democratic decision making will help to clarify changes in perspective over time.

The approach to democratic decision making outlined in the model of representative democracy grows out of its path-dependent history of becoming. Historically, the model is born out of the effort to democratize various forms of sovereign rule in eighteenth- and nineteenth-century Europe. Hence, its implicit starting point is that governance must be performed by a sovereign ruler. Michel Foucault (1990, 92–98) argues that this historical approach to governance has produced a specific perception of power in modern societies. The main characteristics of this sovereign perception of power are that

1. Power can be possessed, and is a certain strength or resource that can be distributed amongst different agencies.
2. Power is often linked to authority conceived as the right to deploy one's strength and resources to achieve something.
3. Sovereign power is exercised from a sovereign centre and by an agent that was formerly an absolute monarchy, a prince or a king, but is today an elected government.
4. Sovereign power is repressive, draws in its wake a web of restrictions and repressions, and constitutes a guarantee that human needs and desires are curbed.
5. Power operates through prohibitions, injunctions, and taboos, delimits boundaries, and the law is its key medium.

The sovereign perception of power is deeply imbedded in the model of representative democracy. A main objective of the founders of the model (all the way from John Locke, James Bentham, and John Stuart Mill to Joseph Schumpeter, Giovanni Sartori, and Noberto Bobbio) has been to find ways in which the necessary, but at the same time repressive, centre of sovereign rule (the government) is controlled and restricted by the people. The solution is representative democracy that installs a parliamentary chain of governance according to which the people elect politicians who pass laws and appoint a government that implements the laws by means of a bureaucratically organized administration. The parliamentary chain of governance ensures that the sovereign ruler is accountable to the people, that political debates and decisions take place in publicly accessible parliamentary forums, and that the sovereign is capable of implementing the decisions by means of an efficient and neutral state apparatus.

Furthermore, representative democracy installs a sharp borderline between a public realm of collective decision making and a private realm of individual liberty. This private realm ensures that the repressive exercise of sovereign rule does not take control over all spheres of society. The insistence on a private realm derives, among other things, from John Locke's claim that the individual has a number of sacred human rights, not least private property rights that must not be violated (Locke, 1690/1988, 160). Accordingly, collective rule should be restricted to what is strictly necessary for society, even though it is highly disputed as to what is to be considered necessary and what is not.

The outcome of the sovereign perception of power, the image of democratic decision making as a parliamentary chain of governance, and the clear division of the public and the private provide a restricted view of democratic decision making. Democratic decision making has to do with ensuring that the people appoint, restrict, and control the sovereign ruler, and it is exercised at the big D-moments when (1) the people elect the sovereign, and (2) the sovereign passes laws as outlined in the formal constitution. From this perspective, the democratic decision makers are the voting citizens and the sovereign politicians in the representative bodies. Furthermore, there is a relatively clear borderline between the realm of sovereign rule and the private sphere (civil society) where individuals decide for themselves. Collectively binding decisions that are taken outside the D-moments of democratic decision making and outside the public realm are regarded as illegitimate, just as are other decision makers than the voting citizens and the sovereign politicians.

9.3 THE CHALLENGE OF DISCOURSE THEORY

A core feature of the diverse theories that are brought together under the heading "discourse theory" is their assertion of the contingency of all the aspects of social and political life that are taken for granted as unchangeable facts of life. Among others, Laclau and Mouffe (1985) argue that what are being perceived as objective facts are always conditioned by contingent discursive constructions of meaning and identity. These discursive constructions are outcomes of political battles for hegemony between competing discursive images of the world. Over time, a hegemonic discourse becomes sedimented and it appears as an uncontestable truth. Even though sedimented discourses do not appear as contingent political outcomes, their political impact is often huge because they are the condensed expressions of the power relations that brought them about. These sedimented discourses frame our being in the world, our images of who we are as social and political beings individually and as a society, our notions of possible and not possible futures, who we regard as our friends and enemies, etc.

Michel Foucault (1990, 92–98) and Sørensen and Torfing (2002, 3–4) argue that a discourse theoretical approach to the political leads to a notion of power that is radically different from the sovereign concept of power described above. First, discursive power cannot be possessed because it only exists in the concrete exercise of power. It is not the wilful deployment of an individual capacity to obtain a preferred outcome, but a set of discursive actions that act upon other action (Foucault, 1982). Second, power does not derive from a centre, but from everywhere. It is neither anchored in the economic, nor the political level in society, but it is present in all social relations, as the political force that constitutes and subverts social identity. Third, discursive power is both repressive and productive in the sense that it produces social identities and capacities. Because it always places social identities in specific relations of super-ordination/subordination, power is repressive. Fourth, discursive power is exercised by means of the institutionalization of local power technologies that discipline the body and normalize the mind.

The pressing question that springs to mind when approaching the question of democratic decision making from a discursive power perspective is how the complex processes that lead to the creation and changing of the premises of social and political action and the productive shaping of identities are made subject to democratic decision making. This question is not least a challenge because these complex processes take place in all corners of society.

One of the questions related to the shaping of the premises of social and political action that has been overlooked by the model of representative democracy is the political nature of the polity (Connolly, 1995; Hajer, 2003; Hansen and Sørensen, 2005; Tully, 2000). The tendency in most democratic theories to regard the polity as pre-given is most likely a result of the long lasting hegemonic position of the nation state that has made it appear as a pre-political fact of life that should not, in itself, be made subject to democratic decision making. Seen from a discourse theoretical perspective, this is problematic because the contingent scope of the polity is an outcome of politics and has political implications that appear as incontestable.

Discourse theory also challenges the implicit assumption behind the model of representative democracy, that it is possible to identify a universally valid set of democratic institutions. Discourse theory regards disorder and instability as the basic conditions of being. Order is created and institutionalized over short periods of time through the construction of discourses, but order is always threatened by dislocatory events that break down the sedimented symbolic structure (Torfing, 1999, 62ff). Hegemonic discourses and institutions produce moments of order and stability, but their survivals depend on their ability to adjust to changing conditions. The history of democratic thought is, in fact, in itself a classic example of a discourse with a strong potential of survival. The vague and ambiguous content of the concept of democracy has repeatedly, throughout history, paved the way for reinterpretations of what democracy might mean and, thus, made way for the necessary adaptation to new circumstances (Bobbio, 1987; Held, 1989; Macpherson, 1977). However, the transformability of the institutions of representative democracy has been markedly weaker. Hence, representative democracy has, in the twentieth century, obtained a hegemonic position as the institutional model of democracy per se.

From the perspective of discourse theory there is no such thing as the best democratic institutions, or, rather, that the best possible institutions are institutions that are capable of changing. If democracy is to survive, it must not only remain open for ongoing conceptual reinterpretation, but also for continuous institutional changes. As Glyn Daly (1994, 183) argues, democracy should not be seen as a fixed thing but as a dynamic or what he calls "writerly" form of governance that is constantly rewritten and reshaped. From this "writerly" approach to democracy, what is important is that the ongoing reinterpretation and reshaping of democracy is carried out through what is at any given time defined as democratic processes of decision making.

Another issue that has been neglected as a result of the hegemonic status of the model of representative democracy is the political character of social relations. This neglect is caused by the strict division between state and civil society. Discourse theorists claim that it does not make sense to refer to non-political areas of social life and insist on the primacy of the political (Torfing, 1999, 69ff). Discourse theory dismisses essentialist claims for a rationality that structures social life while itself escaping any structuration, and argues that all social relations are shaped in and through political struggles that partially fix social identity in the context of fluidity and undecidability. However, "social relations cease to be political when, over time, they become sedimented into an institutional ensemble of rules, norms, values and regularities, which we take for granted in our everyday lives" (Torfing, 1999, 70). What appears to be non-political is, in fact, frozen politics, and it also counts for well-established borderlines between the political and the non-political, as proposed in the model of representative democracy. But because the discursive and institutional structure that comes out of the political battle is always incomplete, it is constantly caught by moments of undecidability wherefore it is open for re-politicization.

Accordingly, discourse theory regards the relationship between the political and the non-political as both dynamic and asymmetrical. It is dynamic because what at some point of time appears as non-political can later become politicized, just as highly politicized issues might become depoliticized through a process of hegemonic sedimentation. It is asymmetrical because what appears to be non-political is a condensation of former political battles that have a political impact through the way they condition present political battles.

By insisting on the primacy of politics, discourse theory stipulates the impossibility of a non-political bureaucratic administration. The post-structuralist claim of discourse analysis for an incompleteness of structure undermines the idea that sovereign rule can be exercised exclusively by means of bureaucratic rule-following and law-implementation. Following Ludwig Wittgenstein, Laclau (1990, 29) argues that all rules are ultimately undecidable and open for reinterpretation. Rules can always be reformulated and given a new meaning and content in concrete governance processes, and are as such "in the last instance simply an instance of their usage" (Torfing, 1999, 64). For this reason, the ability of the sovereign ruler to control the state apparatus through a system of hierarchical rules and regulations becomes an illusion. Public administrators make political decisions—that is decisions in a structurally undecidable terrain—and if there is a failure to recognize this fact, then there is a failure to make these decisions an object of democratic decision making.

Furthermore, the impossibility of a non-political bureaucratic administration derives from the claim of discourse theory for the existence of a dynamic relationship between the political and the social. Due to this dynamism, attempts to establish a fixed distribution of labour between politicians and administrators are in vain. Hence, Max Weber's (1920/1971, 171) well-known claim that politicians determine the goals, while administrators define the means by which the goals are implemented must be given up. From a discourse theoretical perspective this division of labour does not make sense because goals can be sedimented and non-political, just as means can be highly contested and political. Because the relationship between the political and the non-political is dynamic, the distribution of labour between politicians and administrators must be just as dynamic.

The discourse theoretical claim for the primacy of the political challenges the idea first launched by John Locke (1690/1988) and later reinterpreted and expanded as an integrated part of liberal democratic thought that there is a set of pre-political individual rights which install a sacred private realm that should not be subjected to political intervention (Pagden, 2003; Søndergaard, 2003, 43ff). Discourse theorists speak against the essentialist argument for a sheltered realm by claiming that all rights are, in the end, politically defined, and that what is defined as private is an outcome of political decisions. The famous slogan of the women's movement, "the private is political," serves as a clear example of an attack on a specific sedimented hegemonic image of where the line is drawn between the political and the private by those who are disempowered by it. Seen from this perspective, the claim that a pre-politically defined private sphere exists represents a threat to democracy, and it should be seen as an attempt to escape political contestation by claiming that a particular political view is an incontestable fact of being. If, on the other hand, democracy is to be strengthened, the range of social phenomena that are made subject to discursive contestation must be expanded.

Finally, discourse theory raises a severe critique of the rationalist notions of democratic decision making imbedded in the traditional model of representative democracy. Two interpretations of rational reasoning compete in the model of representative democracy: (1) an aggregative calculus reasoning according to which democratic decision making is seen as a means of regulating conflicts between a plurality of self-interested actors with pre-given interests, and (2) an integrative communicative reasoning according to which democratic decision making leads to a shared perception of the common good. From the former perspective, majority rule is the only available means of reaching democratic decisions, while the latter perspective subscribes to deliberation. Despite these differences, the aggregative and the integrative perspectives share the image of democracy as a process in which individuals make collective decisions on the basis of rational reasoning.

Discourse theory suggests that what aggregative and integrative theories define as either particular interests or the common good do not result from rational reasoning, but from political battles for hegemony between competing discourses. The outcome of these power struggles can neither be described as instrumental aggregation, nor as reasoned consensus. Rather, it involves the establishment of contingent discursive perceptions of the common good that are constructed through a double movement whereby particular identities are universalized and universal values become particularized (Laclau, 1990, 171; Norval, 2004, 145; Torfing, 1999, 64–65). For that reason, democratic decision making should neither be seen as aggregation of particular interests nor as consensus oriented deliberation. Decision making is more correctly described as the establishment of negotiated agreements (Norval, 2004, 159). Such agreements are established through discursive battles for hegemony that create a common ground for agonistic battles between competing images of the common good (Mouffe, 1993).

Seen from a discourse theoretical perspective, there is no such thing as smooth and rational decision making. Decision making is a messy process partly because it involves political battles that lead to a discursive construction of the common good, and partly because its outcome is not determined through rational reasoning that leaves out other possibilities as irrational or impossible. Decision making might draw on different rationalities and involve reasonable motivation, but it will always involve the repression of other possible decisions.

As the claim for rational decision making is given up, it becomes clear that decisions are not external to the decision makers, but influence their self-perception and identity: "You become what you decide." Therefore, decision making is a painful business that involves the repression of former identities and the exclusion of alternative points of identification. And so, political decision making is far from cool rational reasoning—it is full of passion (Laclau, 2005; Mouffe, 2001; Torfing, 1999).

To sum up, discourse theory challenges the traditional approach to democratic decision making in a number of ways that all call for a more inclusive approach to democratic decision making. The discourse theoretical perception of the political raises a number of critiques against the traditional approach to decision making and calls for a more inclusive approach that regards the processes through which the premises of social and political action are created, maintained, and transformed as a central objective for democratic decision making. Some of the central premises for social and political life that must be taken into account are the scope of the polity, the way it is institutionalized formally and informally, and where the lines are drawn between the political and the non-political at a given point of time.

Discourse theory also challenges the rationalist approach to the content of democratic decision making and insists that democratic decision making should neither be seen as smooth aggregation nor as smooth integration, but as the construction of negotiated agreements. Furthermore, a central aspect of democratic decision making is the construction of the interests and identities of the involved actors. Hence, an inclusive approach to democratic decision making must focus on identity formation as a part of the outcome of the decision making process and keep in mind that because identity formation represents a long term outcome of democratic decision making, the outcome of decision making processes cannot always be measured.

In addition, discourse theory calls for a widening of the scope of what is to be regarded as legitimate behaviour in processes of democratic decision making. It is necessary to give up the idea that democratic citizens should either act as egoists who seek to maximize particular interests, or behave like angels who put particular interests aside and orient themselves towards the common good. If the claim for rational reasoning is given up, and it is underlined that politics involves passion, passionate forms of political argumentation are not ruled out in advance as anti-democratic.

9.4 THE CHALLENGE FROM GOVERNANCE THEORY

While discourse theory engages in a theoretical critique of the traditional approach to democratic decision making, the critique that is raised by governance theorists is more empirically oriented. Hence, governance theorists argue that there is a still more outspoken distance between the way decision making takes place in praxis in representative democracies, and the way decisions are to be taken according to the model of representative democracy. This critique is not new. Throughout the history of democracy, the tension between prevailing models of democracy and actual governance processes—between normative and descriptive approaches to democracy—has been a productive force in the development of democratic ideas and institutions (Bobbio, 1987, 18). Changes in the theoretical approach to democracy produce new descriptions of the world, while societal changes demand for changes in the theoretical models. Governance theorists tend to agree that the current emergence of governance theory is both caused by vast societal changes and incremental changes in the theoretical perspective on societal governance within the social sciences over the last forty years (Kooiman, 2000; Rhodes, 2000).

Surely the current critique of the distance between the model of representative democracy and concrete governance processes raised by the governance theorists did not pop out of nowhere. In fact, governance theory can be seen as the latest expression of a still more intensive critique of sovereign rule, representative democracy, and bureaucratic governance in the last part of the twentieth century both among state centred and society centred theories.

The state-centered critique of bureaucracy as a means to ensure sovereign rule was initiated as early as in the 1950s and 1960s, but did not become decisive until the 1970s when western democracies experienced what has been defined as an increasing ungovernability problem, that is their inability to solve defined policy problems (Habermas, 1975; Hanf and Scharpf, 1978; Mayntz, 1978).

In the effort to uncover the reasons for the ungovernability problem, the focus was initially turned towards the public administration. Public administration researchers set out to study where bureaucracy, contrary to the promises of Max Weber (1920/1971, 126), failed and how this failure could be remedied by other forms of public administration. This wave of research became known as implementation theory (Pressman and Wildavsky, 1973).

From this point on, a central issue for administrative theory was to examine why the big D-decisions taken by political leaders in parliament and government in many cases did not produce the intended outcomes. The research results form the first implementation studies raised serious doubts as to whether a bureaucratically organized administration was able to ensure sovereign rule through an efficient implementation of the sovereign's decisions. Among other things, the research indicated that the public administrators played a much more active political role in the implementation process than indicated in the parliamentary chain of governance (Cohen et al., 1972; Lindblom, 1979; Lipsky, 1980). Furthermore, research showed that a bureaucratically organized administration is often incapable of adjusting to a changing environment, and, therefore, easily becomes a barrier for an efficient implementation of policy goals (Teubner, 1983).

The implementation research gathered speed at the end of the 1970s and in the first half of the 1980s (Hanf and Scharpf, 1978; Hanf and Toonen, 1985; Hjern and Hull, 1984; Jones, 1980; Kaufman et al., 1986). The research was heavily inspired by the growing critique of Max Weber's model of rational organization within organization theory (Cohen et al., 1972; Dimaggio and Powell, 1991; Harmon and Mayer, 1986). These neo-institutionalist critics claimed that it was time to give up the image of an organization as a unified strategic actor with full information and replace it with an image of organizations as ambiguous institutional arenas.

The research that came out of the many implementation studies supported the growing scepticism towards the parliamentary chain of governance as a sound description of governance processes in Western democracies. The research further supported the claim that public administrators and professionals have a huge political impact on the outcome of governance processes. In addition, research indicated that political and administrative leaders often lack the necessary information and, thus, make "bad" decisions that cannot be realized in practise or do not address the problems that need to be solved (Bogason, 1986, 20; Elmore, 1985; Hjern and Hull, 1984, 198; Sabatier, 1986, 321). Finally, the implementation research concluded that efficient governance is often brought about in situations where goals and means are decided in close dialogue between the sovereign rulers and the actors that are directly involved in the implementation process (Hjern and Hull, 1984, 198; Sabatier, 1986, 321).

The implementation research paved the way for the "bottom-up theory" in the last part of the 1980s. It went one step further in the critique of sovereign rule by rejecting the very possibility of hierarchical top-down governance (Bogason, 1988, 1991; Hull and Hjern, 1987). The bottom-up theories claimed that organizations are unable to follow one single goal and act accordingly. Individuals act, not organizations (Bogason, 1988, 177; Hull and Hjern, 1987, 187). If individuals act together, it is because they have the same goals, but that cannot be taken for granted. The downgrading of the unity of the organization means that the image of a clear dividing line between an organization (the state) and its surroundings (society) that characterizes the traditional model of representative democracy must be given up (Hjern and Hull, 1984, 201). Individuals interact within organizations, but just as often they interact in networks that are across organizational boundaries (Hjern and Hull, 1984, 202–203, 207). In fact, efforts to solve concrete governance problems more often than not involve actors from more than one organization. Hjern and Hull (1984, 207) go so far as to say that policy processes are best described as network-like interactions between individual actors among which some represent formal organizations and their goals and others represent more informal groups.

In sum, the state-centered theories challenge the image of sovereign rule and the model of representative democracy in a number of ways. They claim that in concrete governance processes:

- Goal determination and implementation are interrelated activities
- The state is not a unitary actor
- It is difficult to draw a clear line between an organization (the state) and its surroundings (society), and hence between those who govern and those who are governed
- Governing processes are more precisely described as network-like processes, than as hierarchical sovereign rule

The attack on the traditional image of sovereign rule that was launched by the state-centered theories in the 1970s and 1980s was seconded by the development of society-centered theories. A common feature of these theories and the way they have developed from the 1950s onward is their interest in the interplay between state and society, and in the influence that private actors, such as interest organizations, have on the processes of public governance processes (Jordan and Schubert, 1992; Kenis and Schneider, 1991). The founding fathers of this body of theory were the American pluralists who were the first to challenge the idea that societal governance is being performed within the framework of a formally organized hierarchical state apparatus (Bentley, 1967; Dahl, 1961; Truman, 1971). Based on a number of empirical studies of policy processes, the pluralists claimed that governance (to a much wider extent than indicated by the model of representative democracy) is produced in horizontally organized interplays between politicians, public administrators, and a long list of interest organizations. The pluralists concluded that the state played a relatively weak and mediating role between the many competing interest groups. The weak position of the state did not trouble pluralists such as Dahl in any serious way. They concluded that the competition between different interests groups might, in the end, strengthen representative democracy because it would prevent the state from becoming too strong *vis-à-vis* society. Hence, pluralists launch both a descriptive and a normative critique of the traditional perceptions of liberal democracy and sovereign rule.

In the 1970s, the pluralist understanding of the relationship between state and society was challenged by the corporatists (Jordan and Schubert, 1992; Schmitter,1979). While the pluralists saw the interest groups as outside the state corporatists, they also claimed that a number of big interest organizations have been co-opted into the state apparatus. Furthermore, the corporatists argued that the state was much stronger and influential than indicated by the pluralists, and that the competition between different interest groups that seek to gain access to the state, was in reality very limited due to a strong sector organized monopolization of the available influence channels. Each sector is governed by a relatively stable network consisting of a few dominating interest organizations and a number of representatives from a highly segmented state apparatus. According to corporatism, networks play a central role in the formulation of policy goals (Jordan and Schubert, 1992, 10). The strong position of the state derives from its competence to decide which interest organizations should be given access to the negotiation networks and which should not.

The neo-corporatists and negotiation economists that emerged in the 1980s criticised corporatism for exaggerating the role of the state in the negotiation networks (Kenis and Schneider, 1991; Nielsen and Pedersen, 1988). They claim that even though the state has lost its sovereign position, it still holds the most important position in the networks (Kenis and Schneider, 1991, 28; Torfing, 1995, 34–35). However, at the same time, neo-corporatists argue that interest organizations do not only influence the policy formulation, but they also have considerable influence on the implementation of the policies. The negotiation economists agree on this and claim, in addition, that the state has lost its sovereign position in the governing of society and it simply should be seen as one out of many network actors (Nielsen and Petersen, 1989, 183).

The last step in the developmental ladder of the society-centered theories is policy network theory that surfaced in the end of the 1980s and the beginning of the 1990s (Jordan and Schubert, 1992; Kenis and Schneider, 1991; Marin and Mayntz, 1991; Marsh and Rhodes, 1992). The defining characteristic of a policy network is a self-governing group of actors who are linked together by the presence of interdependency and trust. Policy network theory claims that the role of the state in what they term policy networks differs because there are many different kinds of policy networks. Some networks consist of a small exclusive and stable group of actors and others are more open and dynamic. Accordingly, a main objective for the policy network theory became the development of a typology of policy networks (Marsh and Rhodes, 1992, 14).

In conclusion, one can say that the attack of the society-centered theories on the image of the sovereign state and the model of representative democracy becomes still more radical. In their theorizing of the relationship between state and society, the society-centered theories gradually downgrade the homogeneity and strength of the state and widen the number of private actors they perceive to take active part in the decision making processes. Although they do so with varying radicality, the theories agree that:

- The state is not sovereign, but must exercise its powers through horizontally organized network negotiations.
- The state has become heterogeneous and centreless due to a strong internal sectorialization of the state apparatus.
- A variety of interest organizations play a central role in the governance process.

From the beginning of the 1990s, the state-centered and society-centered theories have merged into what is being called governance theory. From different angles, they have reached the same conclusion namely that both the state in itself and the relationship between public and private actors have become highly complex, dynamic and diversified (Bogason, 2000; Jessop, 1998; Kickert et al., 1997; Kooiman, 1993, 2000; Mayntz, 1993; Peters and Pierre, 2000; Pierre, 2000; Rhodes, 1997; Scharpf, 1994, 1997). Jan Kooiman (1993) argues:

> "No single actor, public or private, has all [the] knowledge and information required to solve complex, dynamic and diversified problems; no single actor has [a] sufficient overview to make the application of needed instruments effective; no single actor has sufficient action potential to dominate uni-laterally in a particular governing model." (4)

In recent years, efforts to cope with this complexity, dynamism and diversity has led to three changes in the western world: increased political globalization (Greven and Pauly, 2000), a series of public sector reforms that aim to enhance the self-governing capacity of public actors, and an increased integration of private actors into the production of public governance (Milward and Provan, 1993). The globalization process has challenged the sovereign position of the state from above, while the heavy political and administrative de-centralization of public service delivery has challenged its sovereign position from below. The aggregated outcome of the globalization and decentralization processes is a still more multilevelled political system. In addition, the many internal reforms in the public sector have increased the fragmentation of the state apparatus that was already initiated by the sectorialized state. What is witnessed presently is the emergence of a differentiated and multicentered state apparatus consisting of a plurality of self-governing public institutions linked together either by contractual ties or by various forms of network interaction (Rhodes, 1997, 7–8; Jessop, 1998). Finally, many public sector reforms have aimed at integrating private actors directly in the production of public governance through various forms of self-governing, public-private partnerships and network constructions.

Governance theorists stress that the development of a multilevelled, differentiated political system based on self-governance does not indicate a goodbye to hierarchical rule. But, it does mean that hierarchical rule is exercised by a plurality of actors within the differentiated state and on different levels in the political system. Furthermore, the huge emphasis on self-governance means that hierarchical rule must be exercised in more subtle and indirect ways than through formal law and bureaucratic rule and regulation. First of all, hierarchical governing of the self-governing actors can be exercised indirectly through what Fritz Scharpf (1994) calls the shadow of hierarchy. According to Scharpf, the blank awareness of the self-governing actors that the state or another meta-governing body will take over if they do not deliver the expected outcomes is enough to influence governing outcomes (37). In addition, hierarchical governance can be exercised through various forms of meta-governance defined as the organization of self-organisation (Jessop, 1998, 42). The question of how to exercise meta-governance is one of the core prescriptive ambitions of many governance theorists (Jessop, 1998; Kickert et al., 1997; Scharpf, 1997).

Governance theory points to a number of ways in which meta-governance can be exercised. First, meta-governance can be performed through the framing of self-governing institutions and networks, which is through the shaping of the political, financial and organizational context within which self-governance is taking place. Framing affects self-governing processes through the shaping of institutional games that strengthen interdependencies and promote trust. Second, meta-governance can be exercised through story telling. Stories produce social and political meaning, wherefore they are a forceful means for influencing the formation of political strategies among a multiplicity of self-governing actors, without interfering directly in their strategy formulation. A third way of exercising meta-governance is through the facilitation of self-governing actors to promote self-governing activities among a certain group of actors (Rhodes, 1997, 56–57; Jessop, 1998, 42–43). The governance theorists claim that the core objective for the last twenty years of public sector reforms have, in essence, been to increase its capacity for exercising various forms of meta-governance (Kooiman, 1993; Pierre, 2000; Rhodes, 1997).

Even though meta-governance allows for hierarchical rule, it is not the same as sovereign rule that is exercised by means of law, instructions, and orders. Sovereign rule is exercised by a unitary actor with the full authority to govern all aspects of society, while meta-governance presupposes a distribution of authority between a number of meta-governing actors and a considerable autonomy for public and private institutions and networks.

The description that governance theory (inspired by the insights of the state and society centred theories of societal rule) gives of the way governance is performed and institutionalized in contemporary liberal democracies challenges the image of democratic decision making in the model of representative democracy. First, governance theory shows that governance is not performed within the limits of one unitary polity and that liberal democracies today are multilevelled, differentiated, and multicentered. From this perspective, it could be argued that an inclusive approach to democratic decision making must reflect on how and where it should be decided and at what level and in what centre governance decisions should be taken.

Second, governance theory undermines the idea that society can be democratically regulated by means of a parliamentary chain of governance. Hence, governance theory claims that political decisions are not only made at two big D-moments at election day and when politicians in parliament and government make sovereign decisions. Inspired by the state centred theories, governance theory portrays a governance process as a plurality of small d-moments that all contribute heavily to the shaping of governance outcomes. Small d-moments determine (1) what should be defined as policy problems and what should not; (2) what the possible solutions are to defined problems; (3) what, when, and with what priority issues should be placed on the formal political agenda; (4) what the overall policy objectives are; (5) how these broad policy objectives are to be transformed into concrete policy goals and governance initiatives; and (6) whether the governance outcome is satisfactory or not. According to this alternative image of the governance process, no one single sovereign actor governs, but a lot of more or less autonomous actors have some degree of influence on all these stages in the governing process. Although the traditional approach to democratic decision making would regard many of these small d-decisions as administrative or private, and accordingly irrelevant for considerations about democratic decision making, governance theory suggests that most of these decisions have considerable impact on governance outcomes and should, therefore, be regulated democratically (Hirst, 2000, 27; Jessop, 1998, 42; Jessop, 2000, 17; Kickert et al., 1997, 174; Rhodes, 1997, 21; Rhodes, 2000, 355). From this perspective, an inclusive approach to democratic decision making must relate to how all these small d-moments can be regulated democratically.

As already indicated by the state-centered theories, a theory of democratic decision making must look more closely at the role that public administrators are playing in the governing processes. Democratic theory has tended to treat public administrators as non-actors in the political process and has overlooked the active role they play and have always played in concrete governing processes. Max Weber's (1920/1971) and Woodrow Wilson's (1887) vision of the ideal typical bureaucratic administration has undoubtedly contributed to maintaining this image of public administrators as non-actors in processes of democratic decision making. Public administrators make decisions, but these decisions are administrative, not political, and should therefore not be made subject to democratic regulation. However, with the transformation of Western liberal democracies into multilevelled, differentiated, and multicentered political systems governed by means of the meta-governance of self-governance, considerations about the role of public administrators in processes of democratic decision making become more urgent than ever. This state of affairs places the question of the role of the public administrators high on the agenda of an inclusive approach to democratic decision making.

The uncovering of the governance process as a long row of small d-decisions also directs our attention towards the role that citizens play in the decision making process. Hence, small d-decisions taken in what was formerly perceived as the implementation phase do not only involve public administrators. Citizens tend to play an ever more active and institutionalized role in the processes that transform overall policy goals into outcomes. Voting is no longer the only way of obtaining influence. The increased space for local self-governance has brought with it new exit or voice oriented channels of influence for users of public services (Hirschman 1970; Hirst, 2000, 27; Klijn and Koppenjan, 2000, 115; Sørensen, 1997, 558). Increased opportunities of choice (exit) and participation (voice) in boards and voluntary organizations that cooperate with public institutions have become an efficient means to obtain influence on the formation of concrete governance outcomes. Due to these new channels of influence, the traditional image of democratic participation as voting is undermined and taken over by the image of the active self-governing everyday maker (Bang and Sørensen, 1999, 337). An inclusive approach to democratic decision making must reflect on how to ensure democracy in the interplay between street level bureaucrats and everyday makers in what governance theorists tend to describe as some sort of functionally oriented outcome democracy (Hirst, 2000, 28–29; Jessop, 2000, 14; Rhodes, 1997, 199).

In addition, an inclusive approach to democratic decision making must focus on the role that private actors play in the governance process both with regard to agenda setting and implementation in the governance process. Although traditional liberal theories of democracy do not count private actors such as firms and interest organizations as active participants in democracy, governance theory stands on the shoulders of the society centred theories in stressing the important role that private actors play in the governing process. Although pluralists tended to see the participation of various interest groups as a positive supplement to representative democracy, governance theorists are more in line with the other society centred theorists, from neo-pluralists, to policy network theorists, in arguing that the integration of private actors in the processes of public governance in many ways undermines the traditional institutions of representative democracy. Private actors should not only be seen as pressure groups that seek to influence government. They have substantial influence on many of the small d-decisions that takes place in the process of agenda setting and implementation of big D-decisions (Torfing, 2004). For this reason, an inclusive approach to democratic decision making must consider the role that private actors play and should play in processes of democratic decision making.

Finally, governance theory points to the need for developing a new role for politicians in a society governed through the meta-governance of self-governance. The traditional image of politicians—or at least the ministers—is one of the sovereign rulers. However, in a multilevelled, de-centered, and differentiated society, politicians are unable to exercise sovereign rule and must restrict themselves to exercising meta-governance to make up for self-governance. An inclusive approach to democratic decision making must consider what it means to be a meta-governing politician and not least how political influence should be distributed between the meta-governing politicians and the many self-governing institutions and networks (Klijn and Koppenjan, 2000; Sørensen, 2006). Furthermore, it must reflect on the strong and weak sides of various forms of meta-governance seen from a democratic perspective.

To sum up, governance theory calls for a more inclusive approach to democratic decision making that views governance processes as a long series of small d-moments that must all be regulated democratically. In addition, governance theory indicates the need for a more inclusive approach to who should be counted as democratic actors, and a reinterpretation of the role of these actors in processes of democratic decision making. Although traditional theories of liberal democracy narrow down the number of relevant actors to politicians and citizens, governance theory suggests that public administrators and private actors, such as firms and interest organizations, are just as important partakers in the governing of society. Also, governance theory calls for a reinterpretation of the politician role from that of being a sovereign ruler to that of a meta-governor, and a transformation of the voting citizen into a self-governing everyday maker.

9.5 CONCLUSION: EXPANDING THE SCOPE OF DEMOCRATIC DECISION MAKING

The hegemonic position of the model of representative democracy in the twentieth century has produced an image of democracy as a specific set of institutions organized along the lines of a parliamentary chain of governance. This model has resulted in a narrow approach to democratic decision making. A reading of discourse theory and governance theory points to a number of important issues that need to be taken into account in an effort to develop a more inclusive approach to democratic decision making. Discourse theory and governance theory do not dismiss the significant role of the big D-moments of democratic decision making when citizens elect politicians and when representative bodies pass laws and governments rule according to these laws, but insist that the scope of democratic decision making is larger than that.

Although discourse theory and governance theory have little in common as seen from an ontological and epistemological perspective, they both share the view that it is impossible in advance to identify a fixed realm of democratic decision making. Discourse theory makes clear that there is no such thing as the non-political. What appears to be non-political or social is sedimented politics that can always be re-politicized. The polity and the institutional set up of representative democracy have tended to appear as non-political facts of life that cannot themselves be made subject to democratic decision making. Even though sedimentation is necessary to establish some temporary order and meaning in the world, it is also problematic. Sedimented structures are never neutral because they embody former political battles and because they hamper necessary adjustments to new conditions. An inclusive approach to democracy must propose means to ensure an ongoing re-politization of the sedimented framings of political life.

Also, governance theory claims that it is difficult to demarcate the realm of democratic decision making. Hence, governance outcomes are affected by a multiplicity of small d-decisions that take place at all stages in the governance process, in all corners of society, and by a wide range of public and private actors. From this perspective, democratic decision making must be seen as a complex, dynamic and diversified process of meta-governance and self-governance that involves politicians, citizens, public administrators, and networks of public and private actors. One of the core objectives of an inclusive approach to democratic decision making is, therefore, to find ways in which to ensure a democratic exercise of meta-governance and enhance democratic decision making in the self-governing institutions and networks. A central task in relation to these objectives is to reformulate the roles of politicians, public administrators, citizens, and private actors in processes of democratic decision making.

Discourse theory and governance theory also share the view that democratic decision making should neither be understood as aggregation, nor as consensus oriented deliberation. Decision making most often takes the form of negotiated agreements between actors who perceive themselves as connected either through the shaping of a shared point of identification or through the existence of interdependencies or trust. Because processes of negotiated agreements can neither be regulated through aggregation processes, nor commanded to result in consensus, an inclusive approach to democratic decision making must focus on how negotiation processes within self-governing institutions and networks can be regulated in a democratic way.

Finally, discourse theory and governance theory suggest that a more inclusive approach to democratic decision making should regard the empowerment of the affected actors as a central outcome of democratic decision making. Discourse theory regards the construction of democratic identities—that is, citizens who regard each other as adversaries and not as enemies—as an important outcome of processes of democratic decision making. Governance theory regards the empowerment of self-governing actors as a prerequisite for efficient and democratic self-governance in the future.

In sum, the challenges to the model of representative democracy are considerable. Both the theoretical development within the social sciences and the huge societal changes has undermined the traditional model of democratic decision making. However, there is no reason to think that the current challenges to the traditional model of representative democracy will undermine democracy in general. With Benjamin Barber's (1996) words the call for change is exactly what keeps democracy alive and in good health:

"It is in the nature of democracy that it is a process, not an end; an ongoing experiment, not a set of fixed doctrines. Its ideals, unless we repossess them generation to generation, fossilise and become little different from any other ideology. The 'Open Society' is a society without closure, a society open to challenges and criticism. When a nation announces 'the work of democracy is finished it is usually democracy that is finished." (144)

REFERENCES

Bang, H. P. and Sørensen, E., The everyday maker: A new challenge to democratic governance, *Administrative Theory and Praxis*, 21(3), 325–341, 1999.
Barber, B. R., Three challenges to reinventing democracy, In *Reinventing Democracy*, Hirst, P. and Khilnani, S., Eds., Political Quarterly Publishing, Oxford, pp. 144–157, 1996.
Bellamy, R., Introduction, In *The Future of Democracy*, Bobbio, N., Ed., Polity Press, Cambridge, pp. 1–17, 1987.
Benhabib, S., *Democracy and Difference*, Princeton University Press, Princeton, NJ, 1996.
Bentley, A. F., *The Process of Government: A Study of Social Pressure*, Harvard University Press, Cambridge, MA, 1967.
Bobbio, N., *The Future of Democracy*, Polity Press, Cambridge, 1987.
Bogason, P., Cross-national problems in multi-level spatial planning: Theory and practice, *Scandinavian Housing and Planning Research*, 3, 13–24, 1986.
Bogason, P., *Organisation og beslutning*, Systime, Herning, Denmark, 1988.

Bogason, P., Guidance for whom? Recent advances in research on governmental guidance and control, *European Journal of Political Research*, 20, 189–208, 1991.

Bogason, P., *Public Policy and Local Governance: Institutions in Post Modern Society*, Edward Elgar, Cheltenham, UK, 2000.

Cohen, J. and Rogers, J., *Associations and Democracy*, Verso, London, 1995.

Cohen, M. D. et al., A garbage can model of organizational choice, *Administrative Science Quarterly*, 17(1), 1–25, 1972.

Connolly, W., *The Ethos of Pluralization*, University of Minnesota Press, Minneapolis, MN, 1995.

Dahl, R. A., *Who Governs? Democracy and Power in an American City*, Yale University Press, New Haven, CT, 1961.

Dahl, R. A., *Democracy and Its Critics*, Yale University Press, New Haven, CT, 1989.

Dahl, R. A., *On Democracy*, Yale University Press, New Haven, CT, 2000.

Dahl, R. A. and Lindblom, C. E., *Politics, Economics, and Welfare*, University of Chicago Press, Chicago, 1953.

Daly, G., Post-metaphysical culture and politics: Richard Rorty and Laclau and Mouffe, *Economy and Society*, 23(2), 173–200, 1994.

Dimaggio, P. J. and Powell, W., Introduction, In *The New Institutionalism in Organizational Analysis*, Dimaggio, P. J. and Powell, W., Eds., University of Chicago Press, Chicago, pp. 1–52, 1991.

Elmore, R. F., Forward and backward mapping: Reversible logic in the analysis in public policy, In *Policy Implementation in Federal and Unitary Systems*, Hanf, K. and Toonen, T. A., Eds., Martinus Nijhoff Publishers, Dordrecht, Holland, pp. 33–71, 1985.

Fukuyama, F., *The End of History and the Last Man*, Free Press, New York, 1992.

Foucault, M., The subject and power, In *Michel Foucault: Beyond Structuralism and Hermeneutics*, Dreyfus, H. L. and Rabinow, P., Eds., Harvester, New York, pp. 208–226, 1982.

Focault, M., *The History of Sexuality*, Penguin, Harmondsworth, UK, 1990.

Fung, A. and Wright, E. O., Eds., *Deepening Democracy*, Verso, London, 2003.

Greven, M. T. and Pauly, L. W., Eds., *Democracy Beyond the State*, Rowman and Littlefield, Lanham, UK, 2000.

Habermas, J., *Legitimationsproblemer i senkapitalismen*, Fremad, Copenhagen, 1975.

Hajer, M., Policy without polity? Policy analysis and the institutional void, *Policy Science*, 36, 175–195, 2003.

Hanf, K. and Scharpf, F. W., *Interorganizational Policy Making: Limits to Coordination and Central Control*, Sage, London, 1978.

Hanf, K. and Toonen, T. A. J., *Policy Implementation in Federal and Unitary Systems*, Martinus Nijhoff Publishers, Dordrecht, Holland, 1985.

Hansen, A. D. and Sørensen, E., Polity as politics: Studying the shaping and effects of discursive polities, In *Discourse Theory and European Politics*, Torfing, J. and Howarth, D., Eds., Palgrave Macmillan, London, pp. 93–116, 2005.

Harmon, M. M. and Mayer, R. T., *Organization Theory for Public Administration*, Little, Brown, Boston, 1986.

Held, D., *Models of Democracy*, Polity Press, Oxford, MA, 1989.

Hirschman, A. O., *Exit, Voice and Loyalty: Responses to Decline in Firms, Organizations and States*, Harvard University Press, Cambridge, MA, 1970.

Hirst, P., *Representative Democracy and its Limits*, Polity Press, Cambridge, 1990.

Hirst, P., Democracy and governance, In *Debating Governance: Authority, Steering and Democracy*, Pierre, J., Ed., Oxford University Press, Oxford, UK, pp. 13–35, 2000.

Hirst, P. and Khilnani, S., *Reinventing Democracy*, The Political Quarterly, Oxford, 1996.

Hjern, B. and Hull, C., Going inter-organizational: Weber meets Durkheim, *Scandinavian Political Studies*, 7(3), 197–212, 1984.

Holden, B., *Understanding Liberal Democracy*, Harvester Wheatsheaf, New York, 1993.

Holden, B., Ed., *Global Democracy: Key Debates*, Routledge, London, 2000.

Hull, C. and Hjern, B., *Helping Small Firms Grow*, Croom Helm, London, 1987.

Jessop, B., The rise of governance and the risks of failure: The case of economic development, *International Social Science Journal*, 50(155), 29–45, 1998.

Jessop, B., *The Network Society, New Forms of Governance, and Democratic Renewal*, Unpublished Paper presented at conference in COS, Copenhagen Business School, 2000.

Jones, G., *New Approaches to the Study of Central-Local Government Relationships*, Gower, Westmead, 1980.

Jordan, G. and Schubert, K., A preliminary ordering of policy network labels, *European Journal of Political Research*, 21, 7–27, 1992.

Kaufmann, F. et al., Eds., *Guidance, Control, and Evaluation in the Public Sector*, Walter de Gruyter, Berlin, 1986.

Kenis, P. and Schneider, V., Policy networks and policy analysis: Scrutinizing a new analytical toolbox, In *Policy Networks: Empirical Evidence and Theoretical Considerations*, Marin, B. and Mayntz, R., Eds., Max-Planck Campus Verlag, Frankfurt, pp. 25–59, 1991.

Klijn, E. H. and Koppenjan, J., Interactive decision making and representative democracy: Institutional collisions and solutions, In *Governance in Modern Society: Effects, Change and Formation of Government Institutions*, Heffen, O., Kickert, W. J. M., and Thomassen, J. J., Eds., Kluwer Academic, Dordrecht, Netherlands, 2000.

Kickert, W. J. M. et al., Eds., *Managing Complex Networks: Strategies for the Public Sector*, Sage, London, 1986.

Kooiman, J., *Modern Governance*, Sage, London, 1993.

Kooiman, J., Societal governance: Levels, models and orders of social-political interaction, In *Debating Governance: Authority, Steering and Democracy*, Pierre, J., Ed., Oxford University Press, Oxford, UK, pp. 138–166, 2000.

Laclau, E., *New Reflections on the Revolution of Our Time*, Verso, London, 1990.

Laclau, E., *Populist Reason*, Verso, London, 2005.

Laclau, E. and Mouffe, C., *Hegemony and Socialist Strategy*, Verso, London, 1985.

Lindblom, C. E., Still mudding, not yet through, *Public Administration Review*, 39(6), 257–264, 1979.

Lipsky, M., *Street-Level Bureaucracy: Dilemmas of the Individual in Public Services*, Russell Sage Foundation, New York, 1980.

Locke, J., *Two Treatise of Government*, Everyman's Library, London, 1690/1988.

Macpherson, C. B., *Life and Times of Liberal Democracy*, Oxford University Press, Oxford, UK, 1977.

Marin, B. and Mayntz, R., Eds., *Policy Networks: Empirical Evidence and Theoretical Considerations*, Campus Verlag, Frankfurt-am-Main, 1991.

Marsh, D. and Rhodes, R. A. W., *Policy Networks in British Government*, Clarendon Press, Oxford, 1992.

Mayntz, R., Interorganizational performance, In *Interorganizational Policy Making: Limits to Coordination and Central Control*, Hanf, K. and Scharpf, F. W., Eds., Sage, London, 1978.

Mayntz, R., Governing failures and the problem of governability: Some comments on a theoretical paradigm, In *Modern Governance: New Government-Society Interactions*, Kooiman, J., Ed., Sage, London, pp. 9–20, 1993.

Mayntz, R., *New Challenges to Governance Theory*, Working Paper, Max-Plank Institut für Gesellschaftsforschung, 1999.

Milward, H. B. and Provan, K., The hollow state: Private provision of public services, In *Public Policy for Democracy*, Ingram, S., Ed., Brookings Institution, Washington, DC, pp. 222–237, 1993.

Mouffe, C., *The Return of the Political*, Verso, London, 1993.

Mouffe, C., Democracy: radical and plural, *CSD-Bulletin*, 9(1), 2–5, 2001.

Nielsen, K. and Pedersen, O. K., The negotiated economy: Ideal and history, *Scandinavian Political Studies*, 11(2), 79–101, 1988.

Nielsen, K. and Pedersen, O. K., Fra blandingsøkonomi til forvaltningsøkonomi. Mod et nyt paradigmeskift?, In *Stat og marked: Fra Leviathan og usynlig hånd til forhandlingsøkonomi*, Klausen, K. K. and Nielsen, T. H., Eds., DJØF-Publishers, Copenhagen, p. 171–226, 1989.

Norval, A., Democratic decisions and the question of universality: Rethinking recent approaches, In *Laclau Reader*, Critchley, S. and Marchart, O., Eds., Routledge, London, pp. 140–167, 2004.

Pagden, A., Human rights, natural rights, and Europe's imperial legacy, *Political Theory*, 3(2), 171–199, 2003.

Peters, B. G. and Pierre, J., *Governance, Politics and the State*, Macmillan, London, 2000.

Pierre, J., *Debating Governance. Authority, Steering, and Democracy*, Oxford University Press, Oxford, 2000.

Pressman, J. and Wildawsky, A., *Implementation*, University of California Press, Berkley, CA, 1973.

Rhodes, R. A. W., *Understanding Governance: Policy Networks, Governance, Reflexivity and Accountability*, Open University Press, Buckingham, London, 1997.

Rhodes, R. A. W., The governance narrative: Key findings and lessons from the ESRC's Whitehall Programme, *Public Administration*, 78(2), 345–364, 2000.

Sabatier, P. A., What can we learn form implementation research?, In *Guidance, Control, and Evaluation in the Public Sector*, Kaufmann, F., Majone, G., and Ostrom, V., Eds., Walter de Gruyter, Berlin, pp. 313–326, 1986.

Scharpf, F. W., Games real actors could play: Positive and negative coordination in embedded negotiations, *Journal of Theoretical Politics*, 6(1), 27–53, 1994.

Scharpf, F. W., *Games Real Actors Play: Actor Centred Institutionalism in Policy Research*, West View Point Publishers, Oxford, 1997.

Scharpf, F. W., Interdependence and democratic legitimacy, In *Disaffected Democracies: What's Troubling the Trilateral Countries?*, Pharr, S. J. and Putnam, R., Eds., Princeton University Press, Princeton, NJ, pp. 101–120, 2000.

Shapiro, I. and Hacker-Cordón, C., Eds., *Democracy's edge*, Cambridge University Press, Cambridge, UK, 1999.

Shapiro, I. and Macedo, S., *Designing Democratic Institutions*, New York University Press, New York, 2000.

Schmitter, P. C., Still the century of corporatism, In *Trends Towards Corporatist Intermediation*, Schmitter, P. C. and Lehmbruch, G., Eds., Sage, London, 1979.

Søndergaard, J. T., *Ret, demokrati og globalisering: Om kosmopolitanisme og empirisme*, Jurist- og Økonom-forbundets Forlag, Copenhagen, 2003.

Sørensen, E., Democracy and empowerment, *Public Administration*, 75, 553–567, 1997.

Sørensen, E., *Politikerne og netværkssamfundet: Fra suveræn politiker til meta-guvernør*, DJØF-Publishers, Copenhagen, 2002.

Sørensen, E., Meta-governance: The changing role of politicians in processes of democratic governance, *American Review of Public Administration*, 36(1), 98–114, 2006.

Sørensen, E. and Torfing, J., Nordic studies of power and democracy: Towards a constructivist analysis of governance from below, *European Economic and Political Issues*, 6, 1–18, 2002.

Teubner, G., Substantive and reflexive elements in modern law, *Law and Society Review*, 17(2), 239–286, 1983.

Torfing, J., Organiseringen af relationen mellem stat og økonomi: neo-korporatisme, policy-netværk eller forhandlingsøkonomi, *Økonomi og Politik*, 69(3), 32–43, 1995.

Torfing, J., *New Theories of Discourse: Laclau, Mouffe and Zizek*, Blackwell, Oxford, 1999.

Torfing, J., *Det stille sporskifte i velfærdsstaten. En diskursteoretisk beslutningsprocesanalyse*, Aarhus universitetsforlag, Aarhus, Denmark, 2004.

Truman, D., *The Government Process. Political Interests and Political Opinion*, Knopf, New York, 1971.

Tully, J., *Freedom and Democracy: Unnoticed Aspects of Struggles over Recognition*, Paper presented at the Centre for Theoretical Studies, University of Essex, 2000.

Weber, M., *Magt og Byråkrati*, Gyldendals Norsk Forlag, Oslo, 1920/1971.

Wilson, W., The study of administration, *Political Science Quarterly*, 2, 197–222, 1887.

Young, I. M., *Inclusion and Democracy*, Oxford University Press, Oxford, UK, 2000.

10 Governing Policy Networks

Erik-Hans Klijn and Joop F. M. Koppenjan

CONTENTS

10.1 Introduction: Governance and Networks...169
    10.1.1 Governance, Public Management, and Network Management 170
    10.1.2 Three Models of Governance 170
        10.1.2.1 Model I: The Hierarchical Model 170
        10.1.2.2 Model II: The Multiactor Approach: Governance as Market 171
        10.1.2.3 Model III: The Network Model 171
    10.1.3 Focus of this Chapter...172
10.2 Network Perspective on Decision Making 173
    10.2.1 Theoretical Roots of the Policy Network Approach...173
    10.2.2 Implications of the Network Approach for Decision Making 174
    10.2.3 Decision Making in Policy Networks...174
10.3 Network Approach to Management 175
    10.3.1 "Classical" Management Versus Network Management 176
    10.3.2 Two Types of Network Management: Process Management
        and Institutional Design..176
10.4 The Network Approach as an Explanatory Model 178
    10.4.1 Process Variables as Factors for Success and Failure 178
    10.4.2 The Structure of the Network as Explanation 179
10.5 The Roles of Power and Conflict in Networks...180
    10.5.1 Power, Conflict, and Durable Relations 180
    10.5.2 Veto Power, Network Management, and Under-Privileged Interests 181
10.6 Evaluating Decision Making in Networks: The Search for Criteria 181
    10.6.1 The Impossibility of a Unilateral Substantive Criterion...................................181
    10.6.2 Assessment of Substance: Ex-Post Satisficing and Win-Win Situations...........182
    10.6.3 The Necessity of Process Norms...183
10.7 Conclusion 183
References...184

10.1 INTRODUCTION: GOVERNANCE AND NETWORKS

The wide consensus about the fact that government is not the cockpit from which society is governed and that policymaking processes are generally an interplay among actors, has resulted in a full-scale search for new steering methods and a discussion on governance and public management (Kooiman, 1993; Rhodes, 1996; Pierre, 2000). The discussion on these concepts is fused by the discussion on managerial reform in public administration and the adoption of business management techniques to implement these reforms, under the rubric of new public management (NPM) (Pollit, 1990; Kickert and Van Vught, 1997).

10.1.1 Governance, Public Management, and Network Management

Governance can roughly be described as "directed influence of societal processes." It covers all kinds of guidance mechanisms and stresses that guidance is a result of complex mechanisms, which do not only originate from public actors (Kooiman, 1993; Kickert and Koppenjan, 1997). Given the above statement on the nature of policy processes it is no surprise that the word "governance" has become a catchword and that it has been used with many different meanings (Rhodes, 1996; Pierre, 2000). There seem to be two different groups of meaning. On the one hand, governance stands for notions of reducing the state or making a difference between government and governance. In this sense, government is seen as something that should be reduced, or it should do more with less (Osborne and Gaebler, 1992). This meaning is strongly connected with the rise of what is called the new public management. On the other hand, the term governance is reserved for theories that argue that public guidance should take into account the interdependencies of public actors and (semi-)private actors. In this latter meaning governance stands for something like a self-organizing network. Theories of network decision making and network management, which are the focus of this chapter, fit in this latter meaning of governance.

Each meaning of governance offers different perspectives on public guidance and the role of government in society, and they draw their theoretical inspirations from very different sources. The "new public management" represents an attempt to translate managerial ideas from the private sector—such as contracting out, client orientation, and the introduction of market mechanisms—to public organizations (Pollit, 1990; Kickert and Van Vught, 1997; Pollit and Bouckaert, 2000). The "network management" theories offer alternative methods of guidance and focus on intermediating and coordinating interorganizational policy making. The theoretical basis for this alternative view is found in the network approach to policy, which has acquired a prominent position in policy science and public administration. This approach is illustrated in a number of publications on policy networks and network management in Europe (Wilks and Wright, 1987; Rhodes, 1988; Marin and Mayntz, 1991; Marsh and Rhodes, 1992; Glasbergen, 1995; Kickert, Klijn, and Koppenjan, 1997) and in the United States (Milward and Wamsley, 1985; Provan and Milward, 1995; O'Toole, 1997).

10.1.2 Three Models of Governance

The network approach may be considered an alternative to the hierarchical and market models of governance (Dahl and Lindblom, 1953; Hegner, 1986; Thompson et al., 1991). In this section we contrast these three models of governance—hierarchies, markets, and networks—to clarify the position of the network model. Of course, the models presented here are ideal types, which are used for the purpose of theoretical clarification. In practice the models will not be found in their pure, caricatured, forms; elements of these ideal types will be mixed.

10.1.2.1 Model I: The Hierarchical Model

The hierarchical model focuses on the relation between a central actor and objects of steering. The model takes the ambitions and goals of the central actor as a point of departure for analysis and evaluation. It can be qualified as a mono-actor model. It presupposes that the central actor has all the resources necessary to realize the policy objectives and to control steering and implementation processes. The hierarchical model is strongly inspired by the assumptions of the rational models of policy processes and decision making (Simon, 1957; Hogwood and Gunn, 1984; Parsons, 1995; Sabatier, 1999). In this model government is considered to be the central actor. This is justified in a normative way, by pointing out the democratic legitimacy of governments in Western democracies. According to this perspective, processes of public policy making and governance are characterized by the division between politics and administration. It also assumes that in the problem-definition phase a consensus is reached among the parties involved. Scientific knowledge is used to design policy measures and an implementation program. It is considered that decisions are made authoritatively and that implementation is a non-political, technical, and potentially programmable activity (Kickert et al.,1997; Thompson et al., 1991).

The criterion for success or failure is the attainment of the formal policy goals. The model suggests the following reasons for failure: incorrect assumptions about the causal relations between goals and means and the effectiveness of steering instruments, resistance from implementing bodies or target groups, lack of information about the goals of the policy, and lack of control. According to this model public policy making can be improved by clarifying policy goals, reducing the number of participants in the implementation phase, providing better information concerning the intentions of the policy, and more effectively monitoring and controlling activities. This model suggests that in situations involving a number of actors, coordination should be strengthened and, if necessary, previously autonomous actors should be brought under one central authority thorough reorganization.

Many authors have stressed the weaknesses of the hierarchical model. The model presupposes that the central steering agent has at his disposal the necessary information about existing public problems, preferences, and the available solutions—all impossible presuppositions, given the fact that agents have limited capacities and decision situations involve many uncertainties. The model neglects the values and interests of implementing bodies and target groups and disregards their strategies by labelling them as "uninformed" and as "conservative reactions to innovation." The hierarchical approach denies the political nature of governance and fails to utilize the resources and capacities of local actors.

The assumptions about the causes for failures and the prescriptions based on these assumptions reinforce the shortcomings of the model. The promotion of central coordination and central control furthers the bureaucratization of the public sector and therefore diminishes effectiveness, efficiency, and legitimacy (Van Gunsteren, 1976; Ostrom, 1990).

10.1.2.2 Model II: The Multiactor Approach: Governance as Market

A multiactor approach to governance is chosen in the market model of governance. It is assumed that public policy is made in a setting in which there is a multitude of autonomous actors: governmental, quasi-governmental, and private organisations. In this approach there is no governmental organization that has the knowledge or resources to steer societal development from the center. Instead, the emphasis is on the capacity of societal actors for self-regulation. Society is a marketplace in which autonomous actors make their own decisions. By mutual adjustment and the exchange of resources they succeed in satisfying their needs and realizing their goals. As long as there is a need for governance, governmental steering should be focused on creating the conditions for interaction (Kickert et al., 1997).

Public policies and governance are judged successful if they create discretional freedom and provide resources, which allow societal actors to make their own decisions. Governance fails when there is too much regulation, which makes it impossible for actors to operate according to their own preferences (Hanf and Toonen, 1985).

This model makes the following prescriptions: increasing the discretion freedom of local actors, providing them with more resources, and strengthening their autonomy (Osborne and Gaebler, 1992; Rhodes, 1996; Pollit, 1990). The model is a radical plea for decentralization, self-governance, and privatization, which in fact means the retreat of central government from the public domain.

10.1.2.3 Model III: The Network Model

The network approach suggests that public policymaking and governance take place in networks consisting of various actors (individuals, coalitions, bureaus, and organizations), none of which

TABLE 10.1
Three Perspectives on Public Policy Making and Governance

	The Hierarchical Model	The Market Model	The Network Model
Focus	Central ruler	Multiactor setting	Interactions among actors
Characterization of relations	Hierarchical	Autonomous	Interdependent
Policy process	Neutral implementation of ex-ante formulated policy	Self governance on basis of discrete decisions and mutual adjustment	Interaction processes in which information, goals and resources are exchanged
Successful governance	Attainment of goals of the formal policy	Goal attainment by actors	Realization of collective action
Causes of failure	Ambiguous goals, lack of information and control	Rigid policies, lack of discretionary freedom and resources	Lack of incentives for collective action, existing blockages
Recommendations for governance	Coordination and centralization	Deregulation, decentralization, privatization	Management of policy networks: improving conditions under which actors interact

Source: Adapted from Kickert et al., *Managing Complex Networks*, Sage, London, p. 10, 1997.

possesses the power to determine the actions of the other actors. The government is no longer seen as occupying a position superior to other parties, but as being on equal footing with them. Public policymaking within networks is about cooperation or non-cooperation among interdependent parties with different and often conflicting rationalities, interests, and strategies. Policy processes are not viewed as the implementation of previously formulated goals, but as an interaction process in which actors exchange information about problems, preferences, and means and trade off goals and resources (Kickert et al., 1997).

According to this model, a policy is a success when a collective action is undertaken to realize a common purpose or to avert common threats. This model assumes that policy failures are caused by the lack of incentives to cooperate and the existence of blockades to collective action. Proposed goals may be vague or not provocative. Important actors may be absent, while the presence of other actors may discourage the participation of necessary actors. Crucial information about goals, means, and actors may be lacking. Discretionary power may be absent. The absence of commitment of actors to the common purpose may also be a reason for failure (Klijn and Koppenjan, 2000).

Prescriptions are aimed at the improvement of the conditions for collective action. This requires network management: the management of the interaction processes within networks or the changing of the structural and cultural characteristics of the network (Agranoff, 2003; Mandell, 1990; 2001; Marsh and Rhodses, 1992; O'Toole, 1988).

Table 10.1 summarizes the three perspectives on governance.

10.1.3 FOCUS OF THIS CHAPTER

The aim of this chapter is to offer an overview of the network theory as a framework for the explanation, evaluation, and improvement of decision making in public policy. We first review the theoretical background and concepts of the network approach in the next section. We show that the network approach is solidly rooted in the theoretical history of policy science and organization theory and that it has a rather well developed set of concepts. In the following section, we try to systemize the explanations of interactions and outcomes of policy processes that the network approach offers. We try to strengthen the framework on the institutional level by introducing the concept rules and trust. Then we clarify the role of power and conflict in networks. After that, we address the problem of evaluation and the evaluation criteria in networks. Then, we elaborate upon the misunderstandings that surround the role of public organisations in networks and propose management strategies that help governments adequately operate under network conditions. In the last section, we address the issues in network theories that need further theoretical, empirical, and normative consideration.

10.2 NETWORK PERSPECTIVE ON DECISION MAKING

The network model offers a rather different perspective on decision making and the management of policy processes than, for instance, the hierarchical model. Before we discuss the implications of a network perspective for decision making, we will summarize the theoretical foundations of the network perspective.

10.2.1 THEORETICAL ROOTS OF THE POLICY NETWORK APPROACH

The use of the network concept in policy science dates back to the early 1970s. In implementation studies, especially in what has become known as the "bottom–up approach" (see Hjern and Porter, 1981), as well as in intergovernmental relations literature (see Friend et al., 1974; and the very influential work of Hanf and Scharpf, 1978), the concept has been used to map relation patterns between organizations and to assess the influence of these relations patterns for policy processes. In these two early uses of the network approach to policy one can find the influence of theoretical notions from inter-organizational theory and insights from the interactive perspective on public policy (Klijn and Koppenjan, 2000).

The interactive policy approach in policy science is visible in the work of authors such as Allison (1971), Cohen, March, and Olsen (1972), Lindblom (1965), Lindblom and Cohen (1979). In the work of these authors, policy appears as the result of an interaction among a multitude of actors. Conflicting interests characterize policy processes and problem definitions are dynamic and unpredictable.

The policy network approach builds on this process model because it also focuses attention on the interactions between interdependent actors and the complexity of objectives; it understands strategies as consequences of such interactions. An important difference with the process model is that in the network approach, more attention is given to the institutional context in which complex interactions take place. To develop an understanding of the institutional context of complex interaction processes, network theoreticians utilize the insights of interorganizational theories (Levine and White, 1961; Negandi, 1975; Aldrich, 1979).

The central starting point of the interorganizational approach is that the environment of organizations consists of other organizations. To survive, an organization requires resources from other organizations. These organizations engage in exchange relations with each other and a network of mutually dependent actors emerges. In interorganizational theory, a great deal of attention is paid to the links between organizations and the strategies used by organizations to influence the exchange processes (see e.g., Levine and White, 1961; Aldrich and Whetten, 1981; Benson, 1982; Cook, 1977).

As it has evolved, the policy network approach has developed its own, distinctive theoretical framework. The network approach assumes that policy is made in complex interaction processes among a large number of actors (i.e., networks of interdependent actors). These actors are mutually dependent; so, a policy can only be realized on the basis of their cooperation. This cooperation, however, is by no means simple or spontaneous, and it requires types of game management and network constitution. The central starting points of the network approach are elaborated below.

10.2.2 Implications of the Network Approach for Decision Making

The network approach assumes that actors are mutually dependent. Actors cannot achieve their objectives without resources that are possessed by other actors (Scharpf, 1978; Benson, 1982; Rhodes, 1988). Interaction patterns among actors emerge around policy problems and resource clusters, and these patterns acquire a degree of sustainability because of the limited substitutability of resources. In this way rules are developed to regulate the behavior of actors and resource distribution in the network. Resource distribution and rules of networks are gradually shaped in interactions, but they are also solidified and altered in these interactions (Giddens, 1984). Thus the created policy networks form a context in which actors act strategically and in which their strategies are confronted by the strategies of others.

As a consequence, decision making in social problem-solving processes has the characteristic of a strategic game that does not look at all rational. Rational policy models, also referred to as policy stage models, suggest a completely different course of the problem-solving process. Simon (1957) described the policy stage model concisely in three stages or phases: "intelligence" (What is the problem?), "design" (What solution or alternatives are there?), and "choice" (Which alternative is the best?).

One primary characteristic of the rational policy models is that the process of problem solving is regarded as an intellectual design process. The model places the individual decision maker and his or her decisions at the centre. Problems in terms of a gap between an existing or an expected situation and a norm are solved by first specifying the nature of the problem situation and its consequences and causes. Then the means that might be use to tackle these problems and objectives are defined. Alternatives are selected, implemented, and evaluated. Successful problem solving depends on the degree to which objectives are achieved or, better still, on the degree that the gap is narrowed. Problem solving in this perspective can fail as a result of insufficient information about the nature of the problem situation and the effects of solutions, lack of clear goals and specifications, failure to consider all options, and making assessments in a non-transparent way.

Complex societal problems, however, are not solved in a social vacuum, by the autonomous cognitive-analytical exercise of a central actor. Problem solving takes place in an arena in which mutually dependent actors mold and shape problem definitions and solutions. Network theory pays close attention to this feature of problem solving and decision making. In this perspective, problem solving and decision making is not so much an intellectual design activity aimed at taming substantive uncertainties, but rather a strategic game in a multiactor and multipurpose setting. In addition to the substantive uncertainties in decision-making contexts, involved parties experience strategic uncertainties. This arises from the unpredictability and uncontrollability of the strategic "moves" of other parties. Within these games, processes of problem solving develop; these are fundamentally different from what the policy phase models presume. Table 10.2 contrasts both approaches and shows that each leads to different descriptions, explanations, judgments, and recommendations.

10.2.3 Decision Making in Policy Networks

In a network perspective, problem solving and decision making occur in a series of interactions around (policy) issues within networks. These series of interactions are called games (Crozier and Friedberg, 1980; Rhodes, 1981; Scharpf, 1997). During the game, actors operate within the established resource distribution system and a set of rules, which are to a large extent framed by the network. In addition, they have to operate strategically to handle the given dependencies in the game so that they can achieve their own objectives. During this process, they interpret the existing rules that are, after all, ambiguous (March and Olsen, 1989; Klijn, 1996).

TABLE 10.2
Problem Solving as an Intellectual Design Process Versus a Strategic Game

	Problem Solving as Intellectual Design	Problem Solving as Strategic Game
Policy making	An intellectual design process that is sometimes interrupted by political decision moments	A political power game that is dominated by strategic considerations
Perspective	Central actor who solves problems in relative autonomy and whose stages are taken as the starting point for analysis and design	Mutually dependent actors who pursue a solution through negotiation and strife
Processes	Sequential processes that can be subdivided into stages or steps with a clear beginning and end	Zigzag and erratic processes in which information, means, and objectives are exchanged and a collective outcome is achieved in an incremental manner
Decision	A scientifically grounded answer to a well-defined problem, in which appropriate means are sought on the basis of a given objective	A political compromise where problems are sometimes found to fit existing solutions and the available means co-determine the choice of objectives
Uncertainties	Spring from a lack of knowledge and information about the nature of the problem and solutions	Come from behaviors of actors as grounded in their interests, positions, and preferences
Information	Emphasis on scientific knowledge gathering; knowledge use leads to better problem solving	Selectively used to support partisan arguments
Criterion for success	Decreasing the gap between the problem situation and criterion; achievement of ex-ante formulated objectives	Improving the position of those involved when compared to the existing situation
Fail factors	Lack of information about causal relations; lack of a clear framework for appraisal; inadequate planning, lack of means; too many actors involved	Inadequate processes of interaction and information exchange so that mutual solutions are not developed
Prescriptions	More information and research; clarification and prioritization of objectives; tighter planning and centralization; limiting and structuring participation	Improvement of conditions for cooperation and joint image building through facilitation, mediation and arbitration

Source: Adapted from Koppenjan and Klijn, in *Managing Uncertainties in Networks: A Network Approach to Problem Solving and Decision-Making*, Routledge, London, p. 46, 2004.

Thus the policy process can be seen as a game played by actors. In this game, each of the various actors has its own perceptions of the nature of the problem, the desired solutions, and of the other actors in the network. On the basis of these perceptions, actors select strategies. The outcomes of the game are a consequence of the interactions of strategies of different players in the game. However, these strategies are influenced by the perceptions of the actors, the power and resource divisions in the network, and the rules of the network. We will elaborate this in the next section.

10.3 NETWORK APPROACH TO MANAGEMENT

If decision making takes place in a setting in which there is no single central actor, but a network consisting of a number of interdependent actors, the central question is how to achieve joint action. Due to conflicts of interests, diverging perceptions, and the complex structure of collective interaction situations, cooperation and collaboration often do not come about easily. To arrive at collaboration among actors involved, interaction has to be facilitated and managed. Strategies aimed at the furtherance and improvement of cooperation among actors are called network management (O'Toole, 1988).

10.3.1 "Classical" Management Versus Network Management

Managing networks should not be confused with the "classical management approach," which is described in most management handbooks. In this approach, management is defined as composed of three main activities. Management involves setting out strategies for the future by the top of the organization (planning), (re)allocating resources to organizational subunits that fit the projected tasks (designing), and daily managing of the organization's interactions (leading). Note that the classical rational view on management is an exclusively intra-organizational view of management (Hunt, 1972; Robbins, 1980).

In a network situation, there is no single central authority, nor is there a single organizational goal. None of the actors has enough steering capacity to unilaterally control other actors. Network management is, in essence, an inter-organizational activity (Lynn, 1981; Mandell, 1990; Meier and O'Toole, 2001; Agranoff and McGuire, 2003). A top–down perspective of management is not likely to be very productive. If a central actor is missing, there can be no "system controller." There is no clear authority structure from which the manager can draw his or her steering resources (Mandell, 1990, 2001). This means that the manager has to handle complex interaction settings and work out strategies to deal with the different perceptions, preferences, and strategies of the various actors involved.

Network management thus aims at initiating and facilitating interaction processes among actors (Friend et al., 1974), and creating and changing network arrangements for better coordination (Rogers and Whetten, 1982; Scharpf, 1978). Table 10.3 shows the main characteristics of the "classical'" and network perspectives of management.

10.3.2 Two Types of Network Management: Process Management and Institutional Design

In the literature, a distinction is made between two types of network management strategies: process management and institutional design (for an extensive discussion, see Kickert et al., 1997; Koppenjan and Klijn, 2004).

Process management intends to improve the interactions among actors in policy games. In essence process management concerns steering strategies, which seek to solve the problem that various organizations, in having autonomously developed their strategy, are not automatically in concert with one another. In doing so, actors cannot unilaterally determine each other's strategy. The important point is that the strategies of process management assume that the structure and

TABLE 10.3
Two Perspectives on Management

	Classical Perspective	Network Perspective
Organizational structure	Single authority structure	Divided authority structure
Goal structure	Activities are guided by clear goals and well-defined problems	Various and changing definitions of problems and goals
Role of manager	System controller	Mediator, process manager, network builder
Management tasks	Planning and guiding organizational processes	Guiding interactions and providing opportunities
Management activities	Planning, designing, and leading	Selecting actors and resources, influencing network conditions, and handling strategic complexity

Source: Adapted from Kickert et al., In *Managing Complex Networks*, Sage, London, p. 12, 1997.

composition of the network is given. So, rules (formal or informal), resource divisions, and existing actors are treated as given. They are starting points for designing management strategies. Important process management strategies are:

- Selection and activation of actors (to take successful policy initiatives, actors with the necessary resources must be selected and motivated to participate) (Hanf and Scharpf, 1978; Friend et al., 1974)
- Improvement of mutual perception about an issue or solution (given the fact that actors have different perceptions on the problem, solutions, and existing situation, network management must be aimed at creating at some convergence of perceptions and creating packages of goals that are acceptable for a workable coalition of actors)
- Creation of temporary organizational arrangements among organizations (because coordination among different actors is not secured, organizational arrangements have to be created to sustain interactions and coordinate strategies)
- Improvement and supervision of interactions by means of process- and conflict-management (Mandell, 1990; Susskind and Cruikshank, 1987)

Institutional design is focused on realizing changes in networks. Based on the assumption that the institutional characteristics of a network also influence strategies and cooperation opportunities of actors, attempts can be made to change one or more of these characteristics (see Koppenjan and Klijn, 2004).

Institutional design strategies are usually aimed at changing formal or informal rules in networks, such as rules guiding the access to the network and the games within the networks and rules that specify the position and roles of actors and regulate the way they interact (see Ostrom, 1986; Klijn, 2001). Because rules are often formed gradually, or, in the case of formal rules, created in complex institutional arenas, it takes a long time to design and implement institutional strategies. As a result, newly designed rules are unsuitable for achieving changes in policy games that are already underway. In networks one can observe three types of strategies (Koppenjan and Klijn, 2004):

1. Strategies aimed at the *network composition*: These are strategies that focus on changing or influencing the composition of a network. This intervention is based on the premise that the composition of the network (and changes made in the composition) has an influence on the interactions occurring within it (and thus the outcomes of network activities). There are various ways in which the composition of the network may be changed. For example, there are strategies aimed at consolidating or changing actors' positions or adding new actors. However, strategies may also be aimed at changing the access rules for actors or at influencing the network as a whole by promoting network formation and self-regulation, or modifications to the system. The strategies range from relatively light interventions (like setting actors' positions that only confirm achieved and existing rules) to more encompassing interventions (like system modifications). An intervention, such as system modification, not only involves a larger variety of rules affected, but also influences more deeply the position and identities of actors, thus generally creating more resistance.

2. Strategies aimed at the *network outcomes*: These are strategies that try to influence the incentive structure within the network in such a way that actors will behave differently. The point of intervention here is not the actors, as in the previous set of strategies, but their choices (i.e., the sustainable influencing of actors' strategic choices and the outcomes resulting from them). The most important institutional design strategies in this category are strategies to change the payoff structure (financial or other rewards

that are connected to strategies and decisions), to change professional codes (standards by which actors see their professional activities and identities), to change evaluation criteria (standards by which actors judge achieved outcomes). The two last types of strategies are closely connected.

3. Strategies aimed at *network interactions*: These are strategies that try to influence the interactions among actors in a sustainable way. These strategies are thus aimed at influencing rules, which regulate the process in networks and in this way try to facilitate interactions. Strategies in this category include developing conflict settlement mechanisms (which regulate conflicts among actors) or introducing certain procedures into interactions (and thus fixing certain interactions or decision sequences in the interaction). Strategies such as certification (standards of quality attached to the characteristics of an actor or his or her relation to other actors) or influencing supervisory relationships also fall into this category.

The literature on the network approach emphasizes that network management is far from easy. Network management requires knowledge of the network and numerous skills, including negotiation skills, because network management strategies are conducted in a situation of mutual dependency. Thus a network manager is not a central actor or director, but rather a mediator and stimulator (Forester, 1989). This role is not necessarily intended for only one actor. Even though public actors often assume the role of network manager, other actors can do so as well. Which actor has the authority and possibility to fulfil the role of network manager is most certainly influenced by the strategic position of actors and the (behavioral) rules in use in the network (Ostrom, 1986; Burns and Flam, 1987).

10.4 THE NETWORK APPROACH AS AN EXPLANATORY MODEL

The cooperation problem is central to the policy network approach. Given the dependency of actors on each other's resources, policy can only be established when actors are willing to coordinate their actions and to invest their resources. In the network approach, explanations for the success or failure of decision making and public policy are sought in the extent to which cooperation in achieved. Explanations for the development of cooperation are found both in the characteristics of the interaction situation—the players, their stakes, and their strategies—and in institutional characteristics—the resources and the rules (Scharpf, 1997; Koppenjan and Klijn, 2004).

10.4.1 PROCESS VARIABLES AS FACTORS FOR SUCCESS AND FAILURE

The network approach assumes that policy outcomes are the result of interactions of strategies of various actors. Cooperation of actors necessary to the resolution of a joint problem is not ensured, however. Whether they will participate depend on their goals, perceptions, interests, and engagement in other affairs. Actors who possess resources that are crucial for problem solving can block interaction processes by withdrawing their resources; they have veto power. Replacement of these resources is not always possible; when it is, it might be costly and time consuming. The same can be said for attempts to coerce cooperation, for instance, by ordering a municipality to change its zoning plan if it does not do so of its own accord.

An important explanation for failing to realize concerted policy outcomes is the fact that actors are insufficiently aware of their external dependencies. They may assume that they can solve the problem alone or impose their solution on other actors. But even when actors are aware of their external dependencies, it is often quite an undertaking to bring the various goals and interests together. Differences and disagreements in perceptions among actors may cause conflicts and block the interaction. Only when actors are able to bring their perceptions together and formulate common goals and interests—or, more likely achieve packages of goals that serve multiple interests—will policy games lead to satisfactory outcomes. Learning processes are thus very important in policy games and process management seeks to stimulate these. Preferences of actors are not fixed (Weick, 1979; March, 1988). Discovering new goals that are interesting to actors can prevent stagnation.

In addition actors may also lose interest in policy games; then the interaction process will stagnate. These can be the consequence of the low priority that a policy problem has in the perception of one or more actors. Stagnation and blockades may also be a consequence of an undesirable balance between interaction costs and expected outcomes of policy games or of risks related to policy games as a consequence of unexpected strategies of others. Thus there is a risk that as soon as they have established profit in the interaction process, actors exit or threaten to exit, which leaves other actors empty-handed. This problem typically occurs when parties commit to transaction-specific investments that cannot easily be used for other transactions (Williamson, 1979; Barney and Hesterly, 1996). And then there is always the danger that outsiders may profit from the mutual efforts of a limited group, without making any contribution to the cause (the free-rider problem). In this case, network management should focus on the organization of interactions and the protection of interests of actors involved (De Bruijn, Ten Heuvelhof, and In 't Veld, 2002).

Concerted action thus requires that actors are able to assess their mutual dependencies and possibilities of cooperation and that the risks and costs involved are limited. Lack of awareness of mutual dependencies, conflicts of interests, interaction costs, and risks are important explanations for the failure of concerted policy. Conversely, the emergence of concerted action is explained through the acknowledgement of mutual dependencies, converging perceptions, the existence of incentives (which improve cooperation), and the limitation of interaction risks through the application of types of game management.

10.4.2 THE STRUCTURE OF THE NETWORK AS EXPLANATION

As we argued, explanations for the success or failure of interactions within networks can be based on both process variables and structure variables. In addition to the factors such as the goals, perceptions, and interest of actors and their choices of strategies (i.e., processes variables), there may be institutional (structural) factors at play. By identifying the two groups of factors, the interrelation between them can be analyzed.

Intensive interaction among actors creates a specific resource distribution that influences the functioning of the network. Actors recognize/acknowledge that certain resources are relevant or even necessary to the realization of policy outcomes. These resources provide actors with veto power. The resources enable them to veto interaction processes and they thus acquire a privileged position in the network and in the games within that network. The greater the veto power of an actor, the more indispensable the actor is to the policy games. The success of policy games is thus partially determined by the degree to which indispensable resources, and the actors who own them, are involved (Scharpf, 1997). Changes in the resource distribution in the networks are, therefore, reflected in the policy games.

The way actors interact is also influenced by the other games that take place at the same time and by the network rules that govern interactions (Ostrom, 1986; Burns and Flam, 1987). Especially when actors meet for the first time, or when they are members of different networks, interactions may be difficult because these actors are not familiar with each other and because there are few, diverging, or conflicting rules to regulate their interactions. In other words, institutionalized coordination mechanisms and trust are lacking. This results in higher interaction costs and strategic uncertainty, which hinders cooperation (Hindmoor, 1998; Koppenjan and Klijn, 2004).

Rules play an important role in the development of policy processes. Rules enable actors to depart from minimal institutional agreements in their interaction. This reduces transaction costs and simplifies collaboration (Scharpf, 1997; Hindmoor, 1998). It is difficult to arrive at general state-ments about the influence of rules on policy networks, because each network has its own rules. Rules are social constructions of actors in a network, and they differ from network to network. Research has shown, however, that rules of conflict management and mediation, as well as rules to protect autonomy and position, are important for determining the possibility of cooperation in general (Klijn, 1996; Scharpf, 1997). The stronger the territorial demarcations in a network and the weaker the rules for conflict management and mediation, the more difficult decision making will be. The lack of trust and useful sanctions make it difficult to prevent exploitative behavior on the part of actors.

These examples illustrate the structuring nature of rules in networks. They can improve or limit certain styles of interaction. Thus the lack of conflict-regulating mechanisms and trust will more quickly lead to non-cooperative outcomes. Although these mechanisms play an important role in preventing and reducing opportunistic behavior, it cannot eliminate it altogether. Scharpf (1997) concludes: "being able to trust, and being trusted, is an advantage—but exploiting trust may be even more advantageous" (89). Rules are one of the most important pillars of trust, but actors can violate rules, whether formal or informal, if this is attractive to them. In this sense, rules do regulate, but they not determine behavior, and they can be changed. Each analysis of decision making in networks must take this into account. Particular attention should be focused on the process of reformulation and (re)interpretation of rules as a consequence of circumstances external to the network and the strategic choices of actors.

10.5 THE ROLES OF POWER AND CONFLICT IN NETWORKS

Because of its focus on cooperation, network theory has received a lot of comments on the role of power. The critique was that cooperation is elevated to the norm and conflict and differences in power are insufficiently considered (Brans, 1997; De Bruijn and Ringeling, 1997). Indeed, co-operation is an important element of network theory, both with respect to the explanations of success and failure as well as for prescriptions. Networks reduce transaction costs and facilitate cooperation and thus create benefits for parties involved. But the impacts of cooperation are not always beneficial to all. And interactions are not always successful. So, network processes produce both internal and external benefits and costs. Furthermore, these benefits and costs are not equally distributed. No wonder power and conflict play an important role in networks and they should not be not excluded from consideration in network analysis.

10.5.1 POWER, CONFLICT, AND DURABLE RELATIONS

Without cooperation, actors who find themselves in situations of mutual dependencies cannot realize their objectives. This does not mean that cooperation is established without conflict. Nor does it mean that actors will manage to cooperate. Durable dependency relations do not necessarily mean that no conflict will emerge over the distribution of costs and benefits in concrete policy processes. As an example, one needs only to consider labor relations where employers and labor unions maintain a durable relationship characterized by both cooperation and conflict. It is exactly this tension between cooperation and conflict that needs to be resolved (Scharpf, 1997).

The lack of hierarchical relations does not imply that resources are equally distributed among actors (Knight, 1992). Actually power differences in network theory are closely connected to resource inequalities (just as is stated in inter-organizational theory; see e.g., Pfeffer, 1981). Also, rules may operate to the advantage of some actors, and to the disadvantage of others. This is implied by the fact that rules have been formed during earlier interactions. The inequalities resulting from earlier interactions are incorporated into the existing rules. A change of rules is thus also (but not exclusively) a battle for power among actors (Burns and Flam, 1987). In this sense the network approach has much attention for "invisible forms of power," traditionally known as "the mobilisation of bias" (Barach and Baratz, 1962), like rules that shape the problem definitions and entrées of the actors in games and networks.

In short, the differences in the distribution of resources matter; actors will use them to influence the process and the substance of the interaction. A project developer or a municipality will generally be able to wield more influence over building plans than citizens' organizations. Citizens lack the "know how" and organizational capacity to be present throughout the process and provide input (compare also Meier and O'Toole, 2004).

10.5.2 Veto Power, Network Management, and Under-Privileged Interests

Less powerful actors may still influence decision making. They can use their veto power and their ability to use resources for blocking decision making and thus create stagnation or blockade. Because stagnation and blockade result in extra costs—at the very least—more powerful actors need to consider their less powerful colleagues. To encourage actors not to use their veto power, some degree of convergence of perceptions must be achieved. This is also an important reason for the necessity of process management. Furthermore, and certainly as important, this also leads to the consideration of information and interests of other actors to enhance the quality and support of policy initiatives.

The starting point of process management is to enhance the learning capability of policy processes by including information and interests of various actors so that more complete policy initiatives can be developed. From a network approach, the involvement of actors is not only recommended for normative reasons, but also for reasons of effectiveness and efficiency. Expertise and knowledge for handling (policy) problems is not available in one place only and thus a confrontation of policy initiatives with information and interests of other actors is necessary. Power differences influence the way in which this process evolves. As long as actors hold veto power, they have influence.

A more serious problem occurs when actors have no veto power and/or are excluded from interaction by other parties. This can happen when interaction patterns among actors result in a certain degree of network insularity (Laumann and Knoke, 1987; Rhodes, 1988). Outsiders can only access the network if they familiarize themselves with the rules of behavior and the language of the network (Klijn, 1996). In the development of theory in network management, substantial attention is given to this aspect of networks and to the negative policy effects this may have for the environment. When formulating prescriptions, opportunities for dealing with the limitations of this closed nature are sought in network constitution and in the use of process norms. These issues will be clarified in the next section.

10.6 EVALUATING DECISION MAKING IN NETWORKS: THE SEARCH FOR CRITERIA

The network approach has consequences for the way in which success and failure are assessed in policy analysis. If the starting point is that various actors with different objectives are involved, it is unlikely that the process and outcome can be evaluated in terms of the objectives of one actor, even if this is a public actor. This type of rational top–down evaluation does not correspond with the network approach. Instead, criteria that consider the multiactor and dynamic character of interaction in networks are needed.

10.6.1 The Impossibility of a Unilateral Substantive Criterion

In rational policy approaches, success and failure of policy processes is measured in terms of goal effectiveness of a single (public) actor (Hogwood and Gunn, 1984). The justification for this norm lies in the notion that this actor represents the general interest and is the central steering actor in policy processes. We argue that this yardstick is not appropriate in the network approach for a number of reasons.

First, there is the problem of the "classic goal-achievement method," namely the accurate determination of the formulated objective. Actors in networks are relatively autonomous and there is no central, coordinating actor. Each actor has his or her own objectives so it is unclear whose objective should serve as the yardstick. The pragmatic choice for the public actor's objective is not helpful. Frequently, more public actors are involved in decision-making processes so that even "public interest" is hard to determine. The solution of defining general interest in terms of elected political representation is based on an unrealistic and naïve assumption about the accumulation of citizens' preferences that have long since been falsified by theory and research. A call upon the "general interest" is increasingly difficult in a fragmented society. Even if networks are explicitly established or redesigned to (better) accomplish governmental objectives, solely focusing on these formal goals neglects the intentions and interests of other actors involved and the fact that the network does more then just producing the outputs intended by government.

The problem of finding the right evaluation criterion is not solved by looking for a common problem definition or objective that is shared by actors involved (Glasbergen, 1995). It is unlikely that actors have a common perception of the problem or objective at the beginning of a process, given the large number of parties involved and their diverging perceptions and interests.

There is an additional problem with the use of objectives that are formulated ex-ante in the network approach. In interaction processes, actors adapt their perceptions and objectives based on the responses of other parties and events in the environment. As a result, they arrive at a conclusion through a goal-seeking process. Ex-ante problem formulation or objective setting as a yardstick, whether or not inter-subjectively established, does not take this into account. After all, the problem formulation and objective setting will change in the course of the process. If the evaluator only focuses on initial problem definitions or objectives, he or she will ignore an important element of interaction processes—namely that the perceptions of problems and solutions are subject to constant change—and he or she will evaluate learning processes negatively.

A final problem with evaluating success and failure by means of a prior and inter-subjectively accepted yardstick is the following: If parties do not participate in the interaction, the chances are high that their interests and preferences will not be served. The question of the degree to which the final solution furthers or jeopardizes their interests is not considered in the evaluation. In the network approach, the process along which a possible common problem formulation is established is critical.

10.6.2 ASSESSMENT OF SUBSTANCE: EX-POST SATISFICING AND WIN-WIN SITUATIONS

An adequate yardstick should consider the fact that various actors with diverging interests interact, that objectives are difficult to measure, that objectives shift, and that the interests of those involved may be overlooked. In the network management literature, the solution is found in the ex-post satisficing criterion (Teisman, 1995). This means that the starting point of the assessment of policy process outcomes is based on the subjective judgments of individual actors. The idea that various actors are interviewed about their satisfaction after the conclusion of the process solves several problems. When reaching a final conclusion, various actors have to determine how the outcome has benefited them, what the outcome has cost them, and how the outcome fits in the changing environment. In this assessment, both substantive and process elements are weighted, which is something that the researcher cannot possibly do. Because this is a judgement in retrospect, justice is done to the development of objectives and problem formulation during the process. Learning behavior receives the appreciation it deserves. One potential danger is that actors will, in retrospect, suggest rationalizations that mask possible loss. Comparing the subjective judgement of actors to achieved outcomes and to the interests of involved actors might alleviate this concern. Also, an assessment of learning effects should include the development of the substantive content of policy proposals. Policy proposals are better when they have been able to incorporate the various goals and desires of actors and have included or explicitly rejected criticism of earlier policy proposals. The ex-post satisficing criterion solves the problems of measurability, assessment, and dynamics.

What remains are the problems of inter-subjectivity and exclusion. The problem of inter-subjectivity refers to the fact that statements of actors may diverge strongly and will not directly lead to a general assessment of success and failure of the policy process. In other words, there is a need to assess the individual judgement of actors at a higher level. For this, the win-win situation criterion is used in the network approach. When actors have succeeded in establishing an outcome that represents an improvement from the earlier situation for all or when an undesirable situation is avoided through cooperation, we speak of a win-win situation (Dery, 1984; Kickert et al., 1997). The nature of the improvement may differ for the various parties. Also a party may have actually lost, but is compensated by others. A win-win situation can be assessed by aggregating the individual ex-post judgement of actors at a more collective level. It is also conceivable that the actors involved are given the opportunity to arrive at an assessment of the process and its outcome together. Here too, statements will have to be validated in relation to objectives formulated by actors and realized outcomes.

10.6.3 THE NECESSITY OF PROCESS NORMS

Not all forms of cooperation are of equal interest to all parties, nor are they always desirable from a wider perspective. It is conceivable that actors, who worked together on a problem, find themselves in a groupthink situation so that the interests of the outside world were insufficiently considered or not considered at all. Win–win situations may have been realized because other actors were excluded from the decision making or because the costs were placed elsewhere.

It is important to note that interaction processes are accessible to third parties, that careful assessments are possible, and that contact is maintained with the outside world. This means that in addition to the win-win criterion, process criteria such as openness, carefulness, reliability, and legitimacy are included when evaluating interaction processes in networks. Also, the external effects of these processes should be included (Majone, 1986; Kickert et al., 1997; Rhodes, 1997; Dryzek, 2000; Young, 2000).

Thus in the network approach, ex-post judgement of actors about the process and the outcome, in combination with process criteria and attention for external effects, are used to determine the success or failure of policy processes. These are considered to be better indicators for success and failure than the ex-ante formulated objectives of one actor.

10.7 CONCLUSION

In this article, we have presented the network perspective on decision making and problem solving. We have shown how it differs from rational approaches to problem solving and decision making. We discussed the main assumptions of network theory and what their implications are for how we look at decision making. We also discussed the notion of power and evaluation criteria.

We argued that the network approach refers to an empirical reality in which governments have to make decisions within a network setting. But this reality also has consequences for the way we look at decision making. The network approach offers a theoretical framework with which policy processes can be analyzed, explained, and evaluated. And it provides prescriptions for the design and implementation of strategies regarding game management and network structuring.

The nature of tasks with which governments in present complicated societies are confronted does not allow for command and control reactions. Because of the ambiguity and complexity of these tasks, governments will have to learn to adapt to the reality of network society (Castells, 2000). Network management strategies will have to become part of their standard operation procedures.

REFERENCES

Agranoff, R. I., *Leveraging Networks: A Guide for Public Managers Working Across Organizations*, IBM Endowment for the Business of Government, Arlington, VA, 2003.

Agranoff, R. and McGuire, M., *Collaborative Public Management: New Strategies for Local Governments*, Georgetown University Press, Washington, DC, 2003.

Aldrich, H. A., *Organisations and Environments*, Prentice Hall, Englewood Cliffs, NJ, 1979.

Aldrich, H. D. and Whetten, H. D. A., Organisation-sets, action-sets and networks: making the most out of simplicity, In *Handbook of Organizational Design*, Nystrom, P. C. and Starbuck, W. H., Eds., Vol. 1, Oxford University Press, Oxford, pp. 385–408, 1981.

Allison, G. T., *The Essence of Decision*, Little, Brown, Boston, 1971.

Bachrach, P. and Baratz, M. S., Two faces of power, *American Political Science Review*, 56(4), 947–952, 1962.

Barney, J. B. and Hesterly, W., Organisational economics: understanding the relationship between organisations and economic analysis, In *Handbook of Organisation Studies*, Clegg, S. R., Hardy, C., and Nord, W. R., Eds., Sage, London, pp. 115–147, 1996.

Benson, J. K., A framework for policy analysis, In *Interorganisational Co-ordination: Theory, Research, and Implementation*, Rogers, D. L. and Whetten, D. A., Eds., Iowa State University Press, Ames, IA, pp. 137–176, 1982.

Brans, M., Challenges to the practice and theory of public administration in Europe, *Journal of Theoretical Politics*, 9(3), 389–415, 1997.

Burns, T. R. and Flam, H., *The Shaping of Social Organisation: Social Rule System Theory with Application*, Sage, London, 1987.

Castells, M., *The Rise of the Network Society: Economy, Society and Culture*, 2nd ed., Blackwell Publishers, Cambridge, MA, 2000.

Cohen, M. D., March, J. G., and Olsen, J. P., A garbage can model of organisational choice, *Administrative Science Quarterly*, 17, 1–25, 1972.

Cook, K. S., Exchange and power in networks of interorganisational relations, *The Sociological Quarterly*, 18(1), 62–82, 1977.

Crozier, M. and Friedberg, E., *Actors and Systems: The Politics of Collective Action*, University of Chicago Press, Chicago/London, 1980.

Dahl, R. A. and Lindblom, C. E., *Politics, Economics and Welfare: Planning and Politico-Economic Systems*, Harper & Brothers, New York, 1953.

De Bruijn, J. A. and Ringeling, A. B., Normative notes: perspectives on networks, In *Managing Complex Networks*, Kickert, W. J. M., Klijn, E. H., and Koppenjan, J. F. M., Eds., Sage, London, pp. 152–165, 1997.

De Bruijn, J. A., Ten Heuvelhof, E. F., and In 't Veld, R. J., *Process Management. Why Project Management Fails in Complex Decision Making Processes*, Kluwer Academic Publishers, Dordrecht, 2002.

Dery, D., *Problem Definition in Policy Analysis*, University Press of Kansas, Lawrence, KS, 1984.

Dryzek, J. S., *Deliberative Democracy and Beyond: Liberals, Critics, Contestations*, Oxford University Press, Oxford, UK, 2000.

Forester, J., *Planning in the Face of Power*, University of California Press, Berkeley, CA, 1989.

Friend, J. K., Power, J. M., and Yewlett, C. J. L., *Public Planning: The Inter-Corporate Dimension*, Travistock Publications, London, 1974.

Giddens, A., *The Constitution of Society: Outline of the Theory of Structuration*, Macmillan, London/Berkeley/Los Angeles, 1984.

Glasbergen, P., Ed., *Managing Environmental Disputes. Network Management as an Alternative*, Kluwer Academic Publishers, The Netherlands, 1995.

Hanf, K. and Scharpf, F. W., Eds., *Interorganisational Policy Making*, Sage, London, UK, 1978.

Hanf, K. and Toonen, Th. A. J., *Policy Implementation in Federal and Unitary Systems*, Martinus Nijhoff Publishers, Dordrecht, The Netherlands, 1985.

Hegner, F., Solidarity and hierarchy: institutional arrangements for the coordination of actions, In *Guidance, Control, and Evaluation in the Public Sector*, Kaufmann, F. X., Majone, G., and Ostrom, V., Eds., De Gruyter, Berline, pp. 417–440, 1986.

Hindmoor, A., The importance of being trusted: transaction costs and policy network theory, *Public Administration*, 76, 25–43, 1998.

Hjern, B. and Porter, D. O., Implementation structures: a new unit for administrative analysis, *Organisational Studies*, 3, 211–237, 1981.

Hogwood, B. W. and Gunn, L. A., *Policy Analysis for the Real World*, Oxford University Press, Oxford, UK, 1984.

Hunt, J. W., *The Resultless Organization*, Wiley, Sydney, 1972.

Kickert, W. J. M., Klijn, E. H., and Koppenjan, J. F. M., Eds., *Managing Complex Networks*, Sage, London, 1997.

Klijn, E. H., Analysing and managing policy processes in complex networks: a theoretical examination of the concept policy network and its problems, *Administration and Society*, 28(1), 90–119, 1996.

Klijn, E. H., Rules as institutional context for decision making in networks: the approach to post-war housing districts in two cities, *Administration and Society*, 33(3), 133–164, 2001.

Klijn, E. H. and Koppenjan, J. F. M., Public management and policy networks: foundations of a network approach to governance, *Public Management*, 2(2), 135–158, 2000.

Knight, J., *Institutions and Social Conflict*, Cambridge University Press, Cambridge, UK, 1992.

Kooiman, J., Ed, *Modern Governance: New Government-Society Interactions*, Sage, London, 1993.

Koppenjan, J. F. M. and Klijn, E. H., *Managing Uncertainties in Networks: A Network Approach to Problem Solving and Decision-Making*, Routledge, London, 2004.

Laumann, E. O. and Knoke, D., *The Organisational State: Social Choice in National Policy Domains*, University of Wisconsin Press, Madison, WI, 1987.

Levine, S. and White, P. E., Exchange as a conceptual framework for the study of interorganisational relationships, *Administrative Science Quarterly*, 5, 583–601, 1961.

Lindblom, C. E., *The Intelligence of Democracy: Decision Making Through Mutual Adjustment*, Free Press, London, 1965.

Lindblom, C. E. and Cohen, D. K., *Usable Knowledge: Social Science and Social Problem Solving*, Yale University Press, New Haven, CT, 1979.

Lynn, L. E., *Managing the Public'S Business: The Job of the Government Executive*, Basic Books, New York, 1981.

Majone, G., Mutual adjustment by debate and persuasion, In *Guidance, Control, and Evaluation in the Public Sector*, Kaufmann, F. X, Majone, G., and Ostrom, V., Eds., De Gruyter, Berlin, pp. 445–458, 1986.

Mandell, M. P., Network management: strategic behaviour in the public sector, In *Strategies for Managing Intergovernmental Policies and Networks*, Gage, R. W. and Mandell, M. P., Eds., Praeger, New York, pp. 20–53, 1990.

Mandell, M. P., Ed, *Getting Results Through Collaboration: Networks and Network Structures for Public Policy and Management*, Quorum Books, Westport, CT, 2001.

March, G., The technology of foolishness, In *Decisions and Organizations*, March, J. G., Ed., Basil Blackwell, Oxford, UK, pp. 253–265, 1988.

March, J. G. and Olsen, J. P., *Rediscovering Institutions: The Organisational Basis of Politics*, Free Press, New York, 1989.

Marin, B. and Mayntz, R., Eds., *Policy Networks: Empirical Evidence and Theoretical Considerations*, Free Press, New York, 1991.

Marsh, D. and Rhodes, R. A. W., *Policy Networks in British Government*, Clarendon Press, Oxford, UK, 1992.

Meier, K. J. and O'Toole, L. J., Managerial strategies and behavior in networks: a model with evidence from U.S. public education, *Journal of Public Administration and Theory*, 11(3), 271–293, 2001.

Meier, K. J. and O'Toole, L. J., Desperately seeking Selznick: cooptation and the dark side of public management in networks, *Public Administration Review*, 64(6), 681–693, 2004.

Milward, H. B. and Wamsley, G. L., Policy subsystems, networks and the tools of public management, In *Policy Implementation in Federal and Unitary Systems*, Hanf, K. and Toonen, T. A., Eds., Martinus Nijhoff, The Netherlands, pp. 105–130, 1985.

Negandhi, A. R., Ed, *Interorganisation Theory*, University press of kansas, Kansas City KS, 1975.

Osborne, D. and Gaebler, T., *Reinventing Government: How the Entrepreneurial Spirit is Transforming the Public Sector*, Addison-Wesley, Reading MA, 1992.

Ostrom, E., A method of institutional analysis, In *Guidance and Control in the Public Sector: The Bielefeld Interdisciplinary Project*, Kaufman, F. X., Majone, G., and Ostrom, V., Eds., De Gruyter, Berlin, pp. 459–475, 1986.

Ostrom, E., *Governing the Commons. The Evolution of Institutions for Collective Action*, Cambridge University Press, Cambridge, 1990.

O'Toole, L. J., Strategies for intergovernmental management: implementing programs in interorganisational networks, *Journal of Public Administration*, 25(1), 43–57, 1988.

O'Toole, L. J., Treating networks seriously: practical and research-based agendas in public administration, *Public Administration Review*, 57(1), 45–52, 1997.

Parsons, W., *Public Policy: An Introduction to the Theories and Practices of Policy Analysis*, Edward Elgar, Chetterham, UK, 1995.

Pfeffer, J., *Power in Organizations*, Pitman, Boston, 1981.

Pierre, J., Ed, *Debating Governance: Authority, Steering and Democracy*, Oxford University Press, Oxford, UK, 2000.

Pollit, C., *Managerialism and the Public Services: The Anglo-American Experience*, Blackwell, Oxford, UK, 1990.

Pollit, C. and Bouckaert, G., *Public Management Reform: A Comparative Analysis*, Oxford University Press, Oxford, UK, 2000.

Provan, K. G. and Milward, H. B., A preliminary theory of interorganisational network effectiveness: a comparative study of four community mental health systems, *Administrative Science Quarterly*, 40, 1–33, 1995.

Rhodes, R. A. W., *Control and Power in Central—Local Government Relations*, Aldershot, Gower, UK, 1981.

Rhodes, R. A. W., *Beyond Westminster and Whitehall: The Subsectoral Governments of Britain*, Unwin Hyman, London, UK, 1988.

Rhodes, R. A. W., The new governance: governing without government, *Political Studies*, 44(4), 652–667, 1996.

Rhodes, R. A. W., *Understanding Government*, Open University Press, Buckingham, UK, 1997.

Robbins, S. P., *The Administrative Process*, Prentice Hall, Englewood Cliffs, NJ, 1980.

Rogers, D. L. and Whetten, D. A., Eds., *Interorganizational Coordination: Theory: Research and Implementation*, Iowa State University Press, Ames, IA, 1982.

Sabatier, P. A., Ed, *Theories of the Policy Process: Theoretical Lenses on Public Policy*, Westview Press, Boulder/Oxford, 1999.

Scharpf, F. W., Interorganizational policy studies: issues, concepts and perspectives, In *Interorganisational Policy Making*, Hanf, K. I. and Scharpf, F. W., Eds., Sage, London, UK, pp. 345–370, 1978.

Scharpf, F. W., *Games Real Actors Play: Actor Centred Institutionalism in Policy Research*, Westview Press, Boulder, CO, 1997.

Simon, H. A., *Administrative Behavior: A Study of Decision-Making Processes in Administrative Organization*, Macmillan, New York, 1957.

Susskind, L. and Cruikshank, J., *Breaking the Impasse: Consensual Approaches Resolving Public Disputes*, Basic Books, New York, 1987.

Teisman, G. R., *Complexe Besluitvorming; een Pluricentrisch Perspectief Op Besluitvorming over Ruimtelijke investeringen*, VUGA, The Hague, The Netherlands, 1995.

Thompson, G., Frances, J., Levacic, R., and Mitchell, J., Eds., *Markets, Hierachies and Networks*, Sage, London, 1991.

Van Gunstern, H. R., *The Quest for Control*, John Willey, London, 1976.

Weick, K. E., *The Social Psychology of Organizing*, 2nd ed., Random House, New York, 1979.

Wilks, S. and Wright, M., *Comparative Government Industry Relations*, Oxford University Press, Oxford, UK, 1987.

Williamson, O. E., Transaction costs economics: the governance of contractual relations, *Journal of Law and Economics*, 22(2), 233–261, 1979.

Young, I. M., *Inclusion and Democracy*, Oxford University Press, Oxford, UK, 2000.

11 Complex Systems Thinking and Its Implications for Policy Analysis

Kurt A. Richardson

CONTENTS

11.1 Introduction 190
    11.1.1 Aims and Background 190
    11.1.2 Themes in Complexity 191
        11.1.2.1 The Neo-Reductionist School 191
        11.1.2.2 The Metaphorical School 192
        11.1.2.3 The Critical Pluralist School 193
11.2 Nonlinear Science 194
    11.2.1 What Is a Complexity System? 194
        11.2.1.1 What Is Nonlinearity? 196
    11.2.2 The Complex Dynamics of Systems 197
        11.2.2.1 Simple Nonlinear Systems 197
            11.2.2.1.1 Multiple Qualitatively Different Behaviors 198
            11.2.2.1.2 (Quantitative) Sensitivity to Initial
                       Conditions–Deterministic Chaos 201
            11.2.2.1.3 Potential (Qualitative) Sensitivity to System
                       Parameters 202
            11.2.2.1.4 Qualitative Unpredictability—Riddled Basins 202
        11.2.2.2 Complex Nonlinear (Discrete) Systems—Networks 203
        11.2.2.3 Lessons from Structural Considerations 203
        11.2.2.4 Bringing Networks to Life 204
        11.2.2.5 Phase Space for Dynamical Boolean Networks 205
        11.2.2.6 Chaos in Boolean Networks 205
        11.2.2.7 Dynamical Robustness 207
        11.2.2.8 What is Emergence? 208
        11.2.2.9 From Boolean Networks to Agent-Based Models 209
        11.2.2.10 Computer Model Types 210
    11.2.3 What Are the Implications for Rational Intervention (Control)
         in Complex Networks? 211
11.3 Towards an Analytical Philosophy of Complexity 213
    11.3.1 On the Nature of Boundaries 213
    11.3.2 Complexity and Philosophy 214
        11.3.2.1 Justifying Pluralism 215

            11.3.2.2   Horizontal and Vertical Pluralism..215
        11.3.3   A Note on Ethics 216
11.4   Applying Complexity to Policy Analysis 218
11.5   Summary and Some Conclusions..218
References..219

11.1 INTRODUCTION

11.1.1 Aims and Background

What is complexity? A seemingly straightforward question perhaps, but as of yet no widely accepted answer is available. Given the diversity of usage it may prove useful to expand the question slightly. This can be done in a number of ways. What is complexity *theory*? What is complexity *thinking*? What are complexity *studies*? How is complexity *measured*? What is *algorithmic* complexity? Each of these alternative questions regards the notion of complexity in a different light. For example, according to Badii and Politi (1997, 6) "a 'theory of complexity' could be viewed as a theory of modeling…" whereas Lucas (2004) suggests that a theory of complexity is concerned with the understanding of self-organization within certain types of system. Baddii and Politi therefore point towards a philosophy of science whereas Lucas points towards a set of tools for analyzing certain types of system. A special issue of the international journal *Emergence* (2001) contained a collection of nine papers from nine different authors, each offering their answer to the question "What is complexity science?" in nine different ways. It is often said of postmodernism that there are as many postmodernisms as there are postmodernists—the situation regarding complexity is not so different.

Depending on whose book you pick up, complexity can be "reality without the simplifying assumptions" (Allen, Boulton, Strathern, and Baldwin, 2005, 397), a collection of nonlinearly interacting parts, the study of how "wholes" emerge from "parts," the study of systems whose descriptions are not appreciably shorter than the systems themselves (the system itself is its best model—from Chaitin's (1999a,b) definition of algorithmic complexity), a philosophy, a set of tools, a set of methodologies, a worldview, an outlook—the list is continuous.

Despite this diversity of opinion there does exist an emerging set of ideas/concepts/words/tools that do offer some approximate boundaries that delimit the field of complexity from everything else. Interestingly, the notion of incompressibility can be used to legitimate the inherent diversity within complexity, arguing that diversity (in all its forms, such as ideological, methodological, instrumental, etc.) is a feature of complexity rather than a flaw that needs to be ironed out.

The view taken in this chapter is that all that is real is inherently complex. All systems, all phenomena, are the result of complex underlying nonlinear processes, i.e., processes that involve intricate causal mechanisms that are essentially nonlinear and that feed back on each other. As will emerge in this chapter, just because every concept is defined as complex, it certainly does not follow that they all must be analyzed as if they were not simple. If the real is complex, the notion of a complex system is a particular conceptualization of the real—that wholes are comprised of nonlinearly interacting parts. To analyze these particular idealizations, a set of tools has emerged to facilitate the analyst—these tools or instruments form the science (used in a neo-reductionist sense) or theory of complex systems. The science of complexity, however, points to limits in our scientific view of complexity, and these indications can be used to construct a provisional complexity-inspired philosophy. As the real is complex (at the heart of this story is the assumption that the Universe is the only coherent complex system, or whole), then a philosophy of complexity is a general philosophy. Such a philosophy has implications for how we generate knowledge of the real, what status that knowledge has (i.e., its relationship to the real), and what role such knowledge should play in our decision-making processes.

This chapter is therefore divided into two broad sections. The first section is concerned with the science of nonlinearity, which is often regarded as synonymous with a complexity science. This will include a formal definition of a complex system, a presentation of the key characteristics of such systems, and a discussion on the analytical and planning challenges that result from the analysis of such systems. Rather than focus purely on technical detail this section will focus on the "so what?" question in regard to analysis. Section two considers the limitations of a science of complexity and briefly presents a philosophy of complexity. Such a philosophy, it will be shown, highlights the integral role of critical thinking in the analysis of the real, given that there is no such thing as an absolutely solid foundation on which to construct any knowledge claims about the real world. The philosophy of complexity developed also justifies the use of many tools and methods that are traditionally seen as beyond the scope of contemporary reductionist analysis.[*] Throughout the chapter, references will be made to relevant articles that provide the details necessarily omitted.

It should be noted that this chapter is meant as a general introduction to complexity thinking rather than its specific application in the policy arena (although general indications regarding implications for analysis are given). To provide the reader with links to specific current applications of complexity in policy analysis, a short annotated list of a subset of the growing "complexity and policy analysis" literature is included towards the end of the chapter. Until recently complexity science was regarded more as an interesting academic discipline rather than a useful body of knowledge to assist in the analysis of practical problems. This state of affairs is quickly changing.

11.1.2 THEMES IN COMPLEXITY

Before we delve into the details of what complexity is all about, it is important to briefly explore the different versions or schools in the study of complexity.

There are at least three schools of thought that characterize the research effort directed to the investigation of complex systems, namely, the neo-reductionists, the metaphorticians, and the philosophers (Richardson and Cilliers, 2001). It should be noted that, as with any typology, there is a degree of arbitrariness in this particular division, and the different schools are by no means independent of each other.

11.1.2.1 The Neo-Reductionist School

The first theme is strongly allied with the quest for a theory of everything (TOE) in physics, i.e., an acontextual explanation for the existence of everything. This community seeks to uncover the general principles of complex systems, likened to the fundamental field equations of physics (it is likely that these two research thrusts, if successful, will eventually converge). Any such TOE, however, will be of limited value; it certainly will not provide the answers to all our questions (Richardson, 2004a). If indeed such fundamental principles do exist (they may actually tell us more about the foundations and logical structure of mathematics than the "real" world) they will likely be so abstract as to render them practically useless in the world of policy development—a decision maker would need several PhDs in physics just to make the simplest of decisions. This particular complexity community makes considerable use of computer simulation in the form of bottom-up agent-based modeling. It would be wrong to deny the power of this modeling approach, though its limits are considerable (see, e.g., Richardson, 2003), but the complexity perspective explored in the second part of this chapter

---

[*] It is important to note that in this chapter whenever the term "science" is used, it is actually referring to reductionistic science. Many critiques of science are directed at reductionist science, and it is important to appreciate that the use of reductionist approaches (based on the assumption that the behavior of the whole can be explained in terms of the characteristics of its parts) is not the only way to do science. Science, as a general concept, is concerned with the rational objective interpretation of nature, and though this view has significant shortcomings, it is not necessarily reductionist.

suggests that the laws such nonlinear studies yield provide a basis for a modeling paradigm (or epistemology) that is considerably broader than just bottom-up simulation (the dominant tool of the neo-reductionists), or any formal mathematical/computer-based approach, for that matter.

The neo-reductionist school of complexity science is based on a seductive syllogism (Horgan, 1995):

Premise 1   There are simple sets of mathematical rules that, when followed by a computer, give rise to extremely complicated patterns.
Premise 2   The world also contains many extremely complicated patterns.
Conclusion   Simple rules underlie many extremely complicated phenomena in the world, and with the help of powerful computers, scientists can root those rules out.

Though this syllogism was refuted in a paper by Oreskes, Shrader-Frechette, and Belitz (1994), in which the authors warned that "verification and validation of numerical models of natural systems is impossible," this position still dominates the neo-reductionist school of complexity. The recursive application of simple rules in bottom-up models is certainly not the only way to generate complex behavior, and so it is likely that not all observed real-world complexity can be reduced to a simple rule-based description. It does not even follow that, just because a simple rule-based model generates a particular phenomena, the real world equivalent of that particular phenomena is generated in the same way as the modeled phenomena.

Despite all the iconoclastic rhetoric about reshaping our worldview, taking us out of the age of mechanistic (linear) science and into a brave new (complex) world, many complexity theorists of this variety have actually inherited many of the assumptions of their more traditional scientific predecessors by simply changing the focus from one sort of model to another. There is no denying the power and interest surrounding the new models (e.g., agent-based simulation and genetic algorithms) proposed by the neo-reductionists, but it is still a focus on the model itself. Rather than using the linear models associated with classical reductionism, a different sort of model— nonlinear models—have become the focus. Supposedly, bad models have been replaced with good models. The language of neo-reductionism is mathematics, which is the language of traditional reductionist science—although it should be noted that neo-reductionist (nonlinear) mathematics is rather more sophisticated than traditional reductionist (linear) mathematics.

11.1.2.2 The Metaphorical School

Within the organizational science community, complexity has not only been seen as a route to a possible theory of organization, but also as a powerful metaphorical tool (see, e.g., Lissack, 1997; 1999). According to this school, the complexity perspective, with its associated language, provides a powerful lens through which to see organizations. Concepts such as connectivity, edge of chaos, far-from-equilibrium, dissipative structures, emergence, epi-static coupling, co-evolving land-scapes, etc.,[*] facilitate organizational scientists and the practicing policy analyst in seeing the complexity inherent in socio-technical organizations. The underlying belief is that the social world is intrinsically different from the natural world. As such, the theories of complexity, which have been developed primarily through the examination of natural systems, are not directly applicable to social systems (at least not to the practical administration of such systems), though its language may trigger some relevant insights to the behavior of the social world, which would facilitate some limited degree of control over that world. Using such a soft approach to complexity to legitimate this metaphorical approach, other theories have been imported via the "mechanism"

---

[*] The interested reader will find introductory definitions of some of these terms at: http://www.psych.lse.ac.uk/complexity/lexicon.htm

metaphor into organization studies—a popular example being quantum mechanics (see e.g., McKelvey, 2001).

Though this discourse does not argue that new lenses through which to view organizations can be very useful (see Morgan, 1986 for an excellent example of this) the complexity lens, and the "anything goes" complexity argument for the use of metaphor has been abused somewhat. The instant concern is not with the use of metaphor per se, as it is not difficult to accept that the role of metaphor in sense making is ubiquitous and essential. Indeed, in Richardson (2005a) it is argued that in an absolute sense, all understanding can be no more or no less metaphorical in nature. However, the concern is with its use in the absence of criticism—metaphors are being imported left, right, and center, with very little attention being paid to the legitimacy of such importation. This may be regarded as a playful activity in academic circles, but if such playfulness is to be usefully applied in serious business then some rather more concrete grounding is necessary.* Through critique our metaphors can be grounded, albeit in an imperfect way, in the perceived and evolving context.

This school of complexity, which uncritically imports ideas and perspectives via the mechanism of metaphor from a diverse range of disciplines, can be referred to as the metaphorical school, and its adherents, metaphorticians. It is the school that perhaps represents the greatest source of creativity of the three schools classified here. But as we all know, creativity on its own is not sufficient for the design and implementation of successful policy interventions.

Neo-reductionism, with its modernistic tendencies, can be seen as one extreme of the complexity spectrum, whereas metaphorism, with its atheoretical relativistic tendencies can be seen as the opposing extreme. The complexity perspective (when employed to underpin a philosophical outlook) both supports and undermines these two extremes. What is needed is a middle path.

11.1.2.3 The Critical Pluralist School

The two previous schools of complexity promise either a neat package of coherent knowledge that can apparently be easily transferred into any context or an incoherent mishmash of unrelated ideas and philosophies—both of which have an important role to play in understanding and manipulating complex systems. Not only do these extremes represent overly simplistic interpretations of what might be, they also contradict some of the basic observations already made within the neo-reductionist mold; there are seeds within the neo-reductionist view of complexity that if allowed to grow, lead naturally to a broader view that encapsulates both the extremes already discussed as well as everything in between and beyond. The argument presented in the second part of this chapter makes use of these particular expressions of complexity thinking (particularly the neo-reductionist view), but focuses on the epistemological and ontological (and to some degree, ethical) consequences of assuming that the world, the universe, and everything is complex.

One of the first consequences that arises from the complexity assumption is that as individuals we are less complex than the "Universe" (The Complex System), as well as many of the systems one would like to control/affect, there is no way for one to possibly experience reality in any complete sense (Cilliers, 1998, 4). One is forced to view reality through categorical frameworks that allow the individual to stumble through a path in life. The critical pluralist school of complexity focuses more on what cannot be explained, rather than what can be explained—it is a concern with limits. As such, it leads to a particular attitude toward models, rather than the privileging of one sort of model over all others. And, rather than using complexity to justify an "anything goes" relativism, it highlights the importance of critical reflection in grounding our models/representations/perspectives in an evolving reality. The keywords of this school are open-mindedness and humility.

---

* This by no means suggests that the playful use of concepts is not an important activity in the making sense of complexity, but sooner or later a choice has to be made that best suits the perceived local needs of organization.

Any perspective has the potential to shed light on complexity (even if it turns out to be wrong; otherwise one would not know that it was wrong), but at the same time, not every perspective is equally valid. Complexity thinking is the art of maintaining the tension between pretending one knows something and knowing one knows nothing for sure.

11.2 NONLINEAR SCIENCE

The aim of this section is to provide an introduction to the science of complexity. It will introduce a loose description of a generic complex system and list some of the ways in which the behavior of such systems can be visualized and analyzed. The focus in this section is not on the technical details of bifurcation maps or phase spaces, but on answering the "so what?" question in relation to the rational analysis of such systems. Although this section is only concerned with simple nonlinear systems, most of the results can be carried forward to more complex nonlinear systems.

11.2.1 WHAT IS A COMPLEXITY SYSTEM?

Before attempting to define a general complex system and explore its behavioral dynamics, some context is needed. The view taken in this chapter is that it is the real that is complex; *every observable phenomenon* is the result of intricate nonlinear causal processes between parts (which are often unseen). This view is very similar to one recently stated by Allen et al. (2005) that true complexity is "just reality without the simplifying assumptions." Essentially, the underlying assumption is that the Universe at some deep fundamental level is well-described as some form of complex system, and that everything observed somehow emerges from that fundamental substrate. This may seem like too broad a scope, particularly when this discussion is actually concerned with the analysis of more everyday problems such as population growth or short-term financial strategy. This discourse is not intended to defend this starting point or even spell out the full implications of such an assumption. A comprehensive treatment, however, is outlined in Richardson (2004a,b). Nonetheless, it is important to at least be aware of the foundational assumption for this chapter.

Everything is the result of nonlinear (complex) processes. This does not mean, however, that anything examined in detail must, without question, be treated as if it were complex. Of course, if one demands perfect (complete in every detail and valid for all time) understanding, then of course there is no choice but to account for absolutely everything—a theoretical impossibility even if one somehow managed to scrape together the phenomenal resources to complete such an undertaking; demanding absolute knowledge is demanding far more than available tools will ever deliver. All understanding is, of course, incomplete and provisional. What one finds with complex systems is that, though over lengthy timescales they may only be profitably analyzed as complex systems, one can approach them as simple systems over shorter contingent timescales. The resulting understanding will be limited, but of sufficient quality to allow informed decisions to be made and actions taken. Sufficient quality means that the model/understanding captures sufficient detail to enable prediction over timescales during which one can meet (with a greater probability of success than failure) some limited goals. Of course, sometimes a complex-type analysis is necessary and the tools of complexity science offer a conceptualization of the real that is more sensitive to the demands of understanding certain aspects of reality. The challenge is recognizing when a simple representation is sufficient and when a more comprehensive (complexity-based) analysis is necessary. Unfortunately, the real world is not so easily understood. However, this discussion will come back to the analytical implications of assuming complexity later in this section, and especially in part two. The point to make here is that simple behavior is a special case of complex behavior, and so it seems appropriate to specifically consider the characteristics of complex systems—complex systems represent the general case, not special cases.

So what is a complex system? A definition might be given as:

A complex system is comprised of a large number of non-linearly interacting non-decomposable elements. The interactivity must be such that the system cannot be reducible to two or more distinct systems, and must contain a sufficiently complex interactive mixture of causal loops to allow the system to display the behaviors characteristic of such systems (where the determination of sufficiently is problematic).

A rather circular definition, perhaps. This just goes to show how difficult it is to definitionally pin down these seemingly commonplace systems. Cilliers (1998, 3–4) offers the following description of a complex system:

1. Complex systems consist of a large number of elements.
2. A large number of elements are necessary, but not sufficient.
3. The interaction is fairly rich.
4. The interactions themselves have a number of important characteristics. First, the interactions are nonlinear.
5. The interactions usually have a fairly short range.
6. There are loops in the interactions.
7. Complex systems are usually open systems.
8. Complex systems operate under conditions far from equilibrium.
9. Complex systems have a history.
10. Each element in the system is ignorant of the behavior of the system as a whole; it responds only to information that is available to it locally.

The majority of the above statements are concerned primarily with the structure of a complex system—they describe constitutive or compositional complexity. In the full description offered by Cilliers (1998, 3–4) vague terminology such as "fairly rich," "sufficiently large," "…are usually open," and "difficult to define" is used. Such usage is not a failure of Cilliers's above description/definition, but is a direct consequence of the many difficulties of pinning down a formal definition of complexity.

Statements nine and ten are of particular interest. Incompressibility, which is a technical term for the observation made in statement ten, asserts that the best representation of a complex system is the system itself and that any simplification will result in the loss of information regarding that particular system (i.e., all understanding of complex systems is inherently and inescapably limited). Statement nine basically asserts that the future of a complex system is dependent on its past. That past may be stored or memorized, at both the microscopic and macroscopic levels, i.e., at the level of the individual or the level of the whole that emerges from the interaction of these individuals.[*]

---

[*] Given that system history does not appear explicitly in the definition of a complex system given above (not Cilliers's description), it may seem inappropriate to arbitrarily introduce it here. However, history can be incorporated in at least three ways. First, one could mention it explicitly in a definition by suggesting that each non-decomposable entity retains some memory of its past. Second, one can recognize that the currently observed state (i.e., component states and overall structure) of any complex system is a direct result of its past and so in some sense the past is reflected in the current—this introduces the notion of a system level memory that is not explicitly coded into the system's components. Finally, one can recognize that nobody can ever actually have a direct and complete representation of any complex system and that it is the abstractions of a particular system that introduce the idea of local memory. In this case, and as strange as it may seem, memory is not a real feature of any complex system at the level of description offered by the definition above, but a useful concept to help create useful partial representations. Quasi-entities can emerge that can exhibit quite different properties from those exhibited by the system's fundamental components. These quasi-entities can behave in such a way as to appear as if they indeed have explicit memory. So, in short, even if memory is not included in the baseline definition of a complex system, a variety of memories can emerge from within the system in the form of sophisticated quasi-entities.

Statement four is the only statement above that comments specifically on the behavioral complexity of complex systems. "Non-linearity also guarantees that small causes can have large results, and vice versa" (Cilliers, 1998, 4). The next section explores the kind of dynamical behavior that can follow from nonlinearity. The key behavioral characteristics that are displayed by complex (constitutionally and behaviorally) systems are:

1. Sensitivity to initial conditions—commonly referred to as deterministic chaos
2. The potential for a range of qualitatively different behaviors (which can lead to stochastic chaos and catastrophes, i.e., rapid qualitative change)
3. A phenomenon known as emergence, or self-organization, is displayed

Behaviors one and two can be illustrated effectively in compositionally simple systems that exhibit complex behavior. The following section, therefore, shall list a few compositionally simple systems that display the phenomena listed above. It is not possible to fully present these systems within the limitations of a single chapter, but references will be given to these systems to allow the interested reader to explore further. A longer version of this chapter is available (Richardson, 2005b) that explores such systems in much greater detail.

What is of interest is that the phenomena exhibited by such simple nonlinear systems are also exhibited by complex nonlinear systems. There are of course differences (the ability to evolve qualitatively, for example, as well as the explicit role of memory/history), but one can learn a considerable amount about complex systems by analyzing simple, but still nonlinear, systems.

11.2.1.1 What Is Nonlinearity?

Before proceeding any further, it is important to clarify the meaning of nonlinearity just in case the linear–nonlinear distinction is not familiar to the reader. Figure 11.1 illustrates (a) some examples of linear relationships, and (b) some examples of nonlinear relationships. Basically, a linear relationship is where the result of some investment of time and energy is directly pro-portional to the effort put in, whereas in a nonlinear relationship, the rewards yielded are disproportionate to the effort put in. An important addition to this statement is that for particular contexts the relationship might actually be linear, even though, summed over all contexts, the relationship is nonlinear. This is a very important point, and again suggests that linearity (like simplicity) is a special case of nonlinearity (complexity), and that linear approaches to analysis are in fact special cases of nonlinear approaches. Mathematicians will be more than familiar with the techniques based on assuming local linearity to locally solve nonlinear problems.

When one thinks about real world relationships it is rather difficult to find linear relation-ships—nonlinear relationships tend to be the norm rather than the exception. The analyst must also bear in mind that it is not always obvious how to frame a particular relationship. Consider for a moment the exchange of money for goods. One might only be concerned with the monetary relationship, which in this simple scenario may well be regarded as linear given that it could be assumed that the value of the goods is the same as the value of the money. However, if one is concerned with the emotions involved in such a transaction, then there might be a situation whereby a collector has paid more than market value for an item needed to complete his/her collection. The trader might be quite pleased with making an above-market profit, whereas the collector may be ecstatic about completing a collection built over many years. It is clear that the function of the analysis determines how relationships are recognized and framed, and whether they can be approximated linearly or nonlinearly. It is safe to say that many of the problems that challenge policy analysts nowadays are characterized not only by the prevalence of nonlinearity, but also the great difficulty in recognizing what is important and

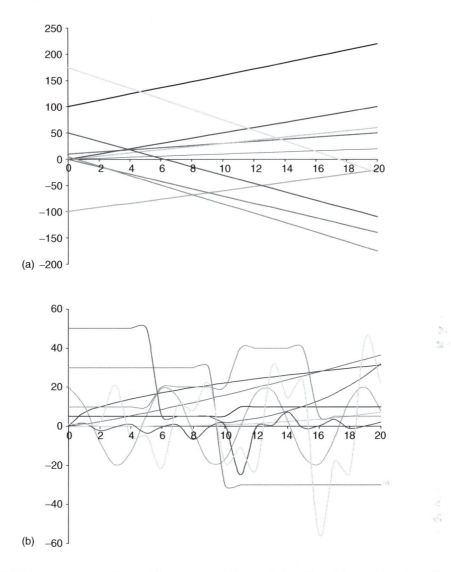

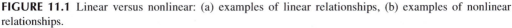

FIGURE 11.1 Linear versus nonlinear: (a) examples of linear relationships, (b) examples of nonlinear relationships.

what is not. The quasi-boundary-less nature of complex systems which reflects the high connectivity of the world creates some profound challenges for analysts and some fundamental limitations on just how informed decisions can be.

11.2.2 THE COMPLEX DYNAMICS OF SYSTEMS

11.2.2.1 Simple Nonlinear Systems

There are a number of behaviors that characterize simple nonlinear systems and ways of visualizing or measuring those behaviors. The following sections briefly describe the four main behavioral characteristics of simple nonlinear systems. Rather than presenting and illustrating these behaviors in detail, the focus is on the analytical implications of these behaviors.

There are a number of very simple systems that exhibit the behaviors listed above. These include:

- the logistics map (May, 1976; Ott, 2002, 32; Auyang, 1999, 238–242);
- the Lorenz system (Lorenz, 1963; Alligood, Sauer, and Yorke, 1997, 362–365);
- a simple mechanical system—a ball moving in a double well under the influence of gravity and a sinusoidal perturbation force (Sommerer and Ott, 1993).

There are many other simple nonlinear systems that yield complex dynamics and it is advisable to explore the detailed behavior of these systems. One can only really understand the complexity and subtlety of these systems' behaviors by interacting with them directly. There is only so much that can be gleaned from a chapter or book on the topic—complexity needs to be experienced.

There is a plethora of ways to visualize the dynamics of these systems. These visualizations include:

- time series: a simple plot of one or more variables against time;
- the phase space diagram: a plot of one system variable against one or more other system variables;
- the bifurcation diagram: a plot of all the minima and maxima of a particular time series against the value of the order parameter that generated that particular time series; the order parameter is adjusted and so the minima and maxima are plotted for a range of order parameters;
- the Lyapunov map: a map of the value of the largest Lyapunov exponent for a range of order parameter values. Lyapunov exponents (Wolf, 1986; Davies, 1999, 127–130) are a measure of divergence of two system trajectories/futures that start off very close to each other and can be used to test for chaotic behavior;
- the destination map: a plot showing the attractors to which a range of starting conditions converge; snapshots can be taken at different times to create a destination movie that shows how different basins of attraction intermingle.

Figures 11.2a and 11.2b show examples of most of these different visualization techniques. In a book format they are restricted to two dimensional representations and grayscale, but with a computer it is relatively easy to make use of a higher dimensionality. The visualization of complex high dimensional dynamics is a very active area of research, because it is through such visualization techniques that we develop an appreciation of the global dynamics of such systems.

The following several sections discuss the different phenomena that these simple nonlinear systems can display, with particular reference being made to the implications for the analysis of such systems.

11.2.2.1.1 Multiple Qualitatively Different Behaviors

The presence of nonlinearity, which is the norm in the real world rather than the exception, has a number of key consequences. The most important one is the potential for the same system to exhibit a range of qualitatively different behaviors depending upon how the system is initiated or how its trajectory is influenced from outside (in relation to the system of interest) forces. Constructing the phase space of any real system is no easy undertaking, simply because the abstraction process is so problematic for real world systems. However, assume for the moment that it is possible to reasonably abstract a real world system into a compositionally simple system like those listed above. The problem then becomes one of computation. A complete map of even the simplest system's phase space requires considerable computational resources, although of course, as processing power continues on its exponential path of growth it is simply a matter of time before ordinary desktop machines can construct the phase space of compositionally simple, yet nonlinear, systems with useful degrees of accuracy.

However, one need not only focus on computational methods for the construction of phase spaces. In a sense, soft systems approaches to scenario planning, like (extended) field anomaly

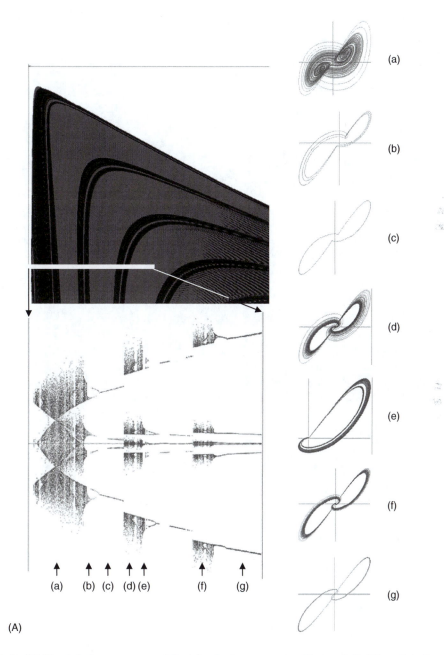

FIGURE 11.2 (A) Top-left: Lyapunov map (slice) for the Lorenz system. Bottom-left: bifurcation diagram for the Lorenz system. Phase portraits (a)–(g) illustrate the different phase trajectories that different areas of the bifurcation diagram correspond to. (B) The evolution of the destination map of a simple mechanical system showing the mixing of two qualitatively different basins of attraction.

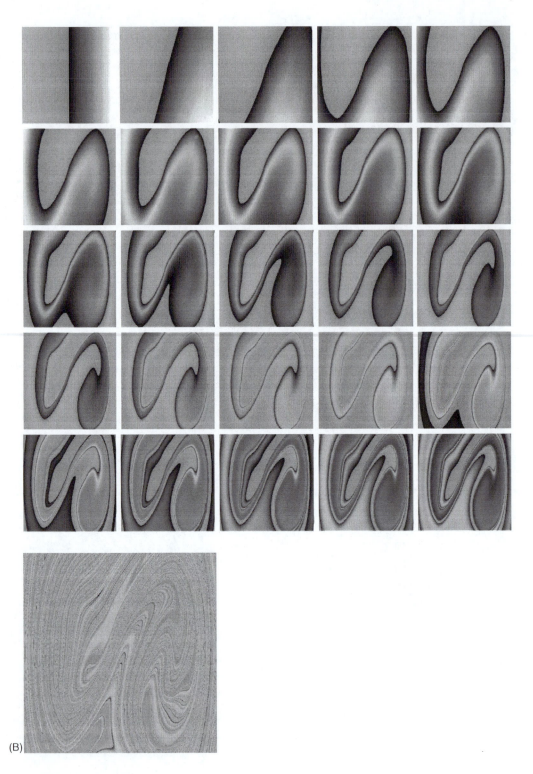

(B)

Figure 11.2 (*Continued*).

relaxation (Powell, 1997; Powell and Coyle, 1997) for example, are essentially indirect ways for constructing an approximate and provisional representation of a system's phase space. Each scenario can be regarded simply as a different qualitative mode. For real life compositionally complex systems, such methods may be the only feasible way of accessing the gross features of phase space. The use of mathematics and computation are by no means the only ways to construct an approximate representation of a system's phase space.

The existence of multiple modes poses challenges for the designers and implementers of policy interventions. First, multiple possibilities immediately suggest that a kind of portfolio approach to design must be taken so that the intervention strategy is effective in a number of scenarios, or basins of attraction. If policy interventions are tailored for only one attractor or encourage the system towards one particular future, then there is always the risk that even the smallest external (to the model) perturbation(s) will knock the system into an unplanned-for mode—which is especially true for systems with riddled basins (i.e., basins that are intimately mixed with each other). Of course, these are compositionally simple systems with no adaptation, and so phase space is fixed and change only occurs in the sense that the system's trajectory might be nudged towards a different attractor.

It might also be the case that there are a wide range of conditions that lead to the same attractor and so a solution might be found that is very robust to noise (perturbations) and, however hard one tries, the system follows the same mode persistently. This can work against the policy makers in the form of attractor lock-in, or institutionalism, in which it can be very hard to shake a system out of its existing state without it quickly "relaxing" back into familiar ways.

11.2.2.1.2 (Quantitative) Sensitivity to Initial Conditions—Deterministic Chaos

Deterministic chaos is mentioned a lot when presentations of complexity are made. It is not necessarily that important, and it is doubtful that any real world socio-technical system really displayed such behavior in a pure sense (because it assumes that the system representation, e.g., set of equations of motion, remain unchanged). If a system does indeed fall into a chaotic mode of operation, then quantitative prediction does become nigh on impossible over extended periods of time. However, the recognition that a system is behaving chaotically is useful information, especially if this can be confirmed through the construction of the system's "strange" attractor, or even better, a complete mapping of phase space which would show different operational modes (Lui and Richardson, 2005). If only the strange attractor is known then at least the analyst has information regarding the boundaries of the behavior, even if knowing where the system will lie between those extremes is not possible. Such information may still be used to one's advantage—one would immediately know that mechanical predictive approaches to policy development might not be very effective at all. If a map of phase space, which would include the relationship between different possible attractors was available, then it might be possible to identify a course of action that would nudge the system toward a more ordered attractor and away from the strange attractor.

Although long term quantitative prediction in a system behaving chaotically is not possible, this does not preclude the possibility for short-term, or local, predictions. The period over which useful predictions can be made about system behavior will vary tremendously from system to system, but short-term prediction certainly has value in the development and implementation of policy, perhaps suggesting a "punctuated equilibrium"-type approach to policy development in which each policy decision is seen as a temporary measure to be reviewed and adjusted on an ongoing basis (see McMillan, 2005; Van Eijnatten and van Galen, 2005 for examples of such evolutionary strategy development; also see the chapter by Robinson in this volume). Moreover, even though the system's trajectory (again talking about a qualitatively static system) will never exactly repeat itself, it will often revisit areas of phase space that it has been to before. If a successful policy decision was made at the previous point in the system's trajectory in the past, then it may well be successful again over the short term. So one can see, from the impossibility of long term quantitative prediction, that it by no means follows that various other kinds of prediction cannot be made and taken advantage of.

One note on language use; the term "chaotic system" is often used to describe systems that are behaving chaotically (bearing in mind that the term "chaos" is being used in a strict mathematical sense). However, this usage is a little misleading, as the same system will potentially have the capacity to behave non-chaotically as well. Chaos is a type of behavior, not a type of system. The systems listed above are static in that their definition/description (e.g., a set of partial differential equations) does not change in the slightest over time, new phase variables do not emerge, and the rules of interaction do not suddenly alter. They can behave chaotically under certain conditions and non-chaotically under many other conditions.

11.2.2.1.3 Potential (Qualitative) Sensitivity to System Parameters

As mentioned in point one, there are areas of phase space whereby a well-timed external nudge may effect a qualitative change in system behavior. These areas are close to the separatrices (basin boundary) that demark different attractor basins. The closer a system trajectory draws to a separatrix, the greater the chance that small disturbances might push the trajectory into the adjacent basin (sometimes called a catastrophe, although it is not necessarily a negative development despite the name). This can be of use to policy makers, but it can equally hinder them. Any policy design that pushes a system trajectory close to a phase space separatrix (whether intentionally or not) runs the risk of failing as the system falls into another basin as a result of a modest push. Of course, the same effect can prove useful in that if it can be recognized that the system is operating near a preferred attractor basin, then a very efficient policy might be designed to provide the extra push needed for the system to adopt that preferred behavior.

There is also insensitivity to system parameters. In situations in which the system's trajectory is moving through the middle of a basin, a large amount of effort might be required to push the system into a preferred basin of operation. Most attempts, short of overwhelming force, may likely lead to no long term change whatsoever.

There is always the possibility of instigating a deeper kind of change in which the phase space itself is redesigned and basin boundaries (separatrices) are deliberately moved around, for instance when a situation is created in which a new order parameter becomes relevant. However, to attempt such a move would require a deeper understanding of system dynamics than is often available to decision makers. Given the difficulties in carrying out such an analysis on real systems it might require an understanding that will always be beyond mere mortals.

11.2.2.1.4 Qualitative Unpredictability—Riddled Basins

Whereas chaotic behavior precludes long term detailed predictions, it does not preclude the possibility of making accurate qualitative predictions. The existence of riddled basins does however severely limit even gross qualitative predictions. It is still possible to make some assessment as to which qualitative modes might exist, but it is impossible to determine which modes the system will be in because it will be rapidly oscillating between different basins. Such behavior may appear to be quite random, but riddled basins are by no means random (as illustrated in Figure 11.2b).

In adaptive systems (systems whose constituent entities change qualitatively overtime—new types of entities come into being, and existing types disappear), severe limits are also placed on even long term qualitative predictions. However, it is interesting to note that even in simple systems whose ontology is permanently fixed (i.e., systems for which their definition/composition does not qualitatively change) can display qualitative unpredictability.

Though the situation for ontologically (compositionally) changing systems is more complex, in that prediction becomes even more problematic than for the simple systems described thus far, such changeable systems may still be effectively reduced and represented as simple systems, albeit temporarily and provisionally. One of the key observations of complexity theorists is the highly problematic nature of the abstraction process.

11.2.2.2 Complex Nonlinear (Discrete) Systems—Networks

Having considered the different behavioral characteristics of compositionally simple systems, it is time to look at compositionally complex systems. Interestingly, all the observations made in relation to the behaviors that can result from nonlinearity in simple systems can be extended almost without change to compositionally complex systems or networks. Complex networks also exhibit a phenomenon referred to as emergence, of which self-organization is an example. However, before moving on to consider network dynamics it is important to first consider the structure, or topology, of various networks, as there are a range of analyses available to policy makers even before they need concern themselves with network dynamics.

The following list provides some areas of interest when considering the structure of complex networks:

- Network topology exists in classifications such as ordered/regular, small-world (Watts and Strogatz, 1998), scale-free (Barabási and Albert, 1999), and random (Erdős and Rényi, 1959). It turns out, thus far at least, that there are four broad network types when we consider structure only. Of the four it is found that many natural and socio-technical systems are actually scale-free networks, which means that they contain a few nodes that are very well connected and many nodes that are not highly connected (see e.g., Adamic, 1999 for an analysis of the World Wide Web).
- Cluster co-efficient is a measure that indicates how "cliquey" a network is, or how many subgroups are contained within the same network.
- Path length is the shortest route between two nodes. In large networks it is found that the average path length is surprisingly low. For example, in Yook, Jeong, and Barabási (2001) the authors considered a subset of the Internet containing up to 6,209 nodes. The average path length was found to be only 3.76; to go from any node in the network to any other one requires no more than 4 steps on average.
- Degree distribution provides information concerning the distribution of nodes with particular densities of connections. Either the number of in-connections (indegree) or out-connections (outdegree) can be considered. It is through the plotting of such distributions that it is possible to determine if a particular network is regular, small-world, scale-free or random.
- Feedback loops refer to the number and size of feedback loops comprising a particular network. Different networks containing the same number of nodes but having quite different topologies can have very different feedback profiles.
- Structural robustness refers to how connectivity parameters, such as average path length and average cluster size, deteriorate as connections or nodes are randomly removed. Some network topologies are more robust than others. For example, if connections are removed at random, then a scale-free network tends to be more robust than a random network. However, if nodes are removed in order of number of connections then random networks are rather more robust than scale-free networks.

11.2.2.3 Lessons from Structural Considerations

Although not exactly an acknowledged subfield of complex dynamical systems theory, network theory does provide a range of analytical tools and concepts that can be usefully brought to bear on understanding the dynamics of such systems—and it should be noted that structure and dynamics are anything but independent. In dynamical systems there is a complex interplay between structure and dynamics that is barely considered at all in current network theories. However, having information about network characteristics such as path length, clustering, and structural robustness does offer potentially useful understanding (such as the identification of potent/impotent nodes), which could be used to support particular types of connectivity-based interventions.

Of course there are severe limitations to such an analysis, the first being the considerable challenges of even constructing an accurate network representation of a real system in the first place. Construction of such a map cannot occur without a purpose, otherwise one would simply end up with a network in which every node was connected to every other node. To apply these approaches usefully, the analyst must decide which types of interconnections need to be represented in the network model. For example, the analyst might only be concerned with financial transactions in which case a connection exists between two nodes that exchange money, or certain types of goods. Simply asking how a particular system is connected is a pointless question. To a great extent the intervention strategies available to policy makers will determine the sorts of questions that can be asked and therefore the type of network representation that can usefully be constructed. What sort of network representations would contain the World Trade Center as a dense node, for example? Whichever map is constructed, it is important to note that it is not an accurate representation of the real world network but a particularly biased abstracted slice through that network. As such, there is much more unaccounted for than there is accounted for.

Even if a usefully representative network map can be constructed, it can be no more than a static snapshot. This need not deny it of its usefulness, but the analyst must consider the timescales over which such a snapshot will remain valid and therefore useful. Real networks/systems evolve over time—the connections change, new nodes appear, existing nodes disappear or change their rules of interaction (through learning for example), etc., and so static network models cannot avoid being limited in their validity (like any model one can possibly construct of any real world phenomena, this is not a problem particular to network models!).

Lastly, and most obviously, there is no way to explore the dynamics of a real world system through such limited network analyses. There is no way to confidently understand the form of the relationship between connecting nodes, no way to understand how the various feedback loops interact, no way to construct a phase portrait of such a system to understand its qualitatively different modes of operation. One cannot even be sure that the highly connected nodes have the majority of the control/influence except as the result of a superficial first order approximation. In dynamical systems, a low-connected node can have widespread influence because of the multiple paths to every other node. However, such multi-order influence is far harder to consider without detailed simulation than the often overwhelming first-order control exhibited by dense nodes. Even then, following causal processes is by no means a trivial undertaking.

For further details on the statistical properties of complex networks please refer to Albert and Barabási (2002). For a more accessible general introduction to networks refer to Barabási (2002). To explore further how network analysis can lead to a better understanding of how organizations function, Cross and Parker's *The Hidden Power of Social Networks* (2004) may prove useful. This book also contains a detailed appendix on how to conduct and interpret a social network analysis.

11.2.2.4 Bringing Networks to Life

Of course, just because a system has a networked structure, it certainly does not follow that it is a complex system—computers are examples of very complicated networks and yet one would not consider them as complex systems (despite the fact that each node—transistor—responds non-linearly). In the networks discussed in the previous section, the only concern was whether or not a relationship, or "edge," exists between two nodes. The nature of that relationship has not yet been discussed. If the relationship is a linear one then the overall behavior of the system will be rather trivial. Such a system is often referred to as a complicated system as opposed to a complex system.

However, as already suggested above, just because linearity does not lead to any particularly interesting behavior, nonlinearity by no means guarantees chaos, multiple attractor basins, self-organization, etc. Nonlinearity, though, is a minimum requirement (although it is by no means a requirement that is particularly hard to fulfill in the real world).

In the following sections, dynamic networks containing nonlinear relationships, namely, complex systems, will be explored. As an example of a simple complex system we shall consider Boolean networks. For a treatment of Boolean networks, please refer to Bossomaier and Green (2000, 30–32), or Kauffman (1993, especially chap. 5), but basically, these networks are comprised of a number of nodes that can only take on one of two possible binary states. The way in which each node evolves, or the state its nodes adopt as time is stepped forward, is dependent upon how each node is connected to its neighbors—both by number of connections and how those connections are processed. The relationship between behavior and structure for any one particular network will depend on a complex interplay between the network connectivity and the details of each of those connections.

With potentially thousands of multi-dimensional nodes (in more sophisticated versions of the Boolean model) it becomes a nontrivial exercise to extract meaningful (emergent) patterns. The space–time diagram (which shows the state of each node over time) is a useful way to visualize the dynamics of Boolean networks, but even here the extraction of patterns can become very difficult indeed. Constructing the phase space of complex systems offers another way to get a handle on a particular system's overall dynamical behavior, but again, the computational resources needed to obtain an accurate representation become prohibitive for even modestly sized networks.

As mentioned above, finding different ways to visualize the dynamics of such high-dimensional systems is a real challenge and a very active area of research in complex systems. Ultimately, the rich dynamics of the system need to be reduced, through aggregation or some other means for them to be appreciated/interpreted to any degree. Such reduction removes detail for the sake of clarity, and must be handled with great care.

11.2.2.5 Phase Space for Dynamical Boolean Networks

Figure 11.3 is a complete representation of a particular Boolean network's phase space. It includes all transient information, namely, information regarding system's trajectories before they converge on a particular attractor, as well as attractor information. It is for this reason that it looks quite different from the phase space depicted in Figure 11.2A. In Figure 11.2A (a–g) all the paths to the attractor basins have been suppressed. Another way to visualize the phase space of a Boolean network is to color each point in phase space to correspond with the attractor that it finally converges on. This has been done in Figure 11.4. Figure 11.4 is equivalent to the phase portrait, for a continuous system, shown in Figure 11.2A (main image). Although the image does not look too good in grayscale, it is clear that there is structure there; the form of configurations of a particular shade (which correspond to a particular attractor basin) are certainly not distributed randomly. The phase space image of the Boolean network does seem to be rather more complex than that of the continuous system shown in Figure 11.2A. This is perhaps no surprise, as the Boolean network is very much more (compositionally) complex than the simple continuous system.

11.2.2.6 Chaos in Boolean Networks

As the phase spaces of discrete Boolean networks are finite, there really is no behavioral equivalent to chaos as all initial conditions will eventually fall onto a cyclic attractor. Not all cycles are created equal and quasi-chaotic behavior does indeed occur, which can be equated with the chaos exhibited in some continuous systems. The phase space of some Boolean networks contains cyclic attractors that have periods much larger than the size of the network. Attractors or

FIGURE 11.3 The complete phase space of a particular random network. The phase space is characterized as 2p1, 1p2, 1p5, 1p12, 1p25, 1p36 (XpY: X number of attractors with period Y)—a total of seven basins of attraction.

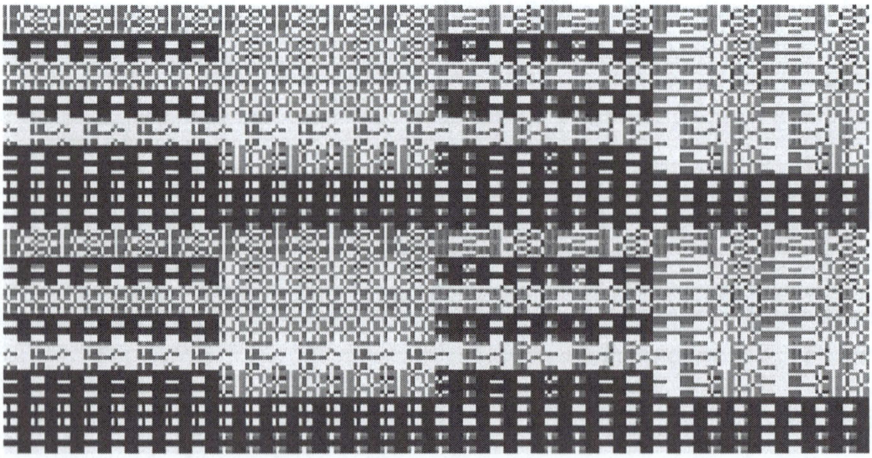

FIGURE 11.4 An example of the phase space of a simple Boolean network (note that Figure 11.3 and Figure 11.4 show data from two different networks).

periods much greater than network size are examples of quasi-chaotic behavior in discrete Boolean systems.

If one continues with this idea that chaotic behavior is no more than very complex dynamics then there are several ways in which these systems' behaviors can be characterized:

1. Transient length—larger networks can have astronomically long transients before an attractor is reached, which sometimes makes them look as though the system is behaving chaotically, although it might eventually converge on a point attractor
2. Long cycle periods—it is quite possible that chaotic behavior might simply be the result of cyclic attractors with astronomically long periods as is easily found in large discrete networks
3. Number of attractors—on average, the number of attractors in discrete Boolean networks of the sort discussed above grows linearly with the network size, N (Bilke and Sjunnesson, 2001)

These three aspects of dynamics each provide a different way of viewing a system's dynamics as being complex or not and should not be used in isolation from each other. For example, a system characterized by only one attractor may still exhibit astronomically long transient paths to that particular attractor, which would mean that the exclusion of transient data in developing an intervention would be inappropriate.

The existence of multiple attractors in phase space and the nontrivial way in which phase space is often connected leads us to another type of robustness: dynamical robustness.

11.2.2.7 Dynamical Robustness

Whereas structural or topological robustness is primarily concerned with the spatial connectivity of networks, dynamical robustness is concerned with the connectivity of phase space itself. Dynamical robustness is concerned with the probability that a system can be nudged from one basin into another by small external perturbations.

One would expect that on average, systems with large numbers of phase space attractors would have lower dynamical robustness than systems with lower numbers of phase space attractors, as there is a direct relationship between dynamical robustness and number of attractors. However, the size of the basins associated with different attractors are often different, as is the connectivity of phase space, and so dynamical robustness also contains the influence of these two contributions as well as the number of attractors.

The reason that dynamical robustness is of interest (and there are a number of ways to define it), is so that an analyst can get a "feel" (and it is not much more than that) for how stable a proposed solution might be. If the dynamical robustness of a solution is relatively low then we can readily assume that the chances that small perturbations will cause the system to deviate from our desired state are quite high. Richardson (2004c, 2005c) explores the impact of removing supposed organizational waste on the organization's dynamical robustness. It is found that as waste is removed, there is a tendency for the system to become less stable. This new found buffering role for supposed waste has significant implications for policy interventions that attempt to make the target organizations more efficient by making them "leaner."

The previous sections have introduced a number of tools, measures and definitions for understanding the behavior of complex (dynamical) systems. However, there is one area that has not been discussed, which is odd given that nearly all the literature of complex systems makes discussion of this particular concept central. This concept is called emergence. The reason it has not been discussed at length thus far is that it is a particularly slippery term that is not easily defined, much like complexity itself. The next section summarizes the key features of what the term emergence might refer to.

11.2.2.8 What is Emergence?

This brief discussion of emergence is not intended to be a thorough investigation. The interested reader may find Richardson (2004a) a useful discussion. The notion of emergence is often trivialized with statements such as "order emerges from chaos" or "molecules emerge from atoms" or "the macro emerges from the micro." It is quickly becoming an all or nothing concept, particularly in management science. The aforementioned paper explores how the products of emergence are recognized and their relationship with their "parts." The following statements summarize the argument offered therein:

- Emergent products appear as the result of a well-chosen filter—rather than the products of emergence showing themselves, we learn to see them. The distinction between macro and micro is therefore linked to our choice of filter.
- Determining what "macro" is depends upon choice of perspective (which is driven by purpose) and also what one considers as "micro" (which is also chosen via the application of a filter).
- Emergent products are not real, although "their salience as real things is considerable..." (Dennett, 1991, 40). Following Emmeche, Köppe, and Stjernfelt (2000), we say that they are substantially real. This a subtle point, but an important one, and relates to the fact that the products of emergence, which result from applying an appropriate filter—theory, perspective, metaphor, etc.—do not offer a complete representation of the level from which they emerged.
- Emergent products are novel in terms of the micro-description, that is, they are newly recognized. The discussion of emergent products requires a change in language—a macro-language—and this language cannot be expressed in terms of the micro-language.
- In absolute terms, what remains after filtering (the "foreground") is not ontologically different from what was filtered out (the "background"). What is interesting is that what remains after a filter is applied is what is often referred to as the real, and that which has been removed is regarded as unimportant.
- The products of emergence and their intrinsic characteristics, occurring at a particular level of abstraction, do not occur independently—rather than individual quasi-objects emerging independently, a whole set of quasi-objects emerge together.
- The emergent entities at one level cannot be derived purely from the entities comprising the level beneath, except only in idealized systems. What this means is that molecules do not emerge from atoms because atoms do not provide a complete basis from which to derive molecules (as atoms are emergent products of another level, and thus they are only partially representative). In this sense the whole is not greater than the sum of its parts because the parts are not sufficient to lead to the whole.
- Emergent products are non-real yet substantially real, incomplete yet representative.
- All filters, at the universal level, are equally valid, although certain filters may dominate in particular contexts. In other words, there is no universally best way to recognize emergence, although not all filters lead to equally useful understanding and despite there being no single way to see things, it does not follow that all ways of seeing things are legitimate.

The bullet points above might seem rather philosophical for a chapter on policy analysis. Other than the slippery nature of the term itself, there are other reasons to approach the discussion in this way. The language used thus far in this chapter has been rather positivistic in nature, which might inadvertently encourage some readers to assume that the tools and measures presented could be used in a systematic way to assist in the development of interventions in complex systems. This is certainly not the case. Intervening in complex systems is highly problematic and although there are opportunities for rational action the inherent limitations that arise from the problematic nature of activities such as problem bounding, system modeling, prediction and interpretation should not be overlooked. This philosophical attitude will be discussed further in the second part of this chapter. For now, it will suffice to suggest that the role of thinking critically about ideas and concepts is central to any complexity-inspired policy analysis—complexity science offers not only new tools, but also a particular attitude toward all tools.

The examples used thus far in this chapter—the simple nonlinear systems and the Boolean networks—may seem to some to be overly simplistic in their construction and therefore irrelevant to real-world policy analysis. The next section will extend the idea of complex systems to include complex adaptive systems that are more readily associated with real world social systems. It should be noted, however, that considering more complex systems (both topologically and dynamically) does not invalidate what has been said already. The interesting thing about nonlinearity is that most of what can be learned from simpler nonlinear systems can be readily applied to more complex systems as long as an awareness of their contextual dependencies is present. For example, we can readily construct the phase space of an adaptive system by making the simplifying assumption that what we have constructed is a snapshot that at some point (quite possibly in the short term, rather than longer term) will need to be updated.

There are very few, if any, universal principles in complexity theory (except perhaps that one!) that would hold for all systems in all contexts. However, there will often be contexts in one system for which results obtained through the study of another system will be applicable. There will not be a one-to-one mapping, but results are transportable even if only in a limited way. For this reason, the study of systems as seemingly trivial as Boolean networks can teach us a lot about more complex systems. Even the study of linear systems is not necessarily redundant.

11.2.2.9 From Boolean Networks to Agent-Based Models

Boolean networks are clearly relatively simple complex systems; they are less complex than agent-based models, and certainly less complex than reality. Their structure is static, as are the nodes' interrelationships. However, despite their simplicity, useful observations and analyses can be made that may be relevant for systems as potentially complex as real world socio-technical organizations, such as the multi-faceted role of waste, for example. There will be increased dimensionality with systems containing more complex nodes, or agents, whose interrelationships change with time and circumstance. For example, agent-based modeling is often seen as the state-of-the-art when it comes to complex systems modeling. Agent-based models are simply more complex Boolean networks, like the ones already discussed. (For examples of the agent-based modeling approach in policy analysis please refer to Bonabeau, 2002; Lempert, 2002a). The key difference is simply that the rules that define each agent's behavior are often more intricate than the simple rule tables for Boolean networks. The way in which agents interact is more context-dependent, and the underlying rules may actually evolve over time (as a result of a learning process for example—although there may be meta-rules that guide this process too). The state of any given agent will also be less restrictive than the two-state Boolean agents, and require greater dimensionality to describe it. Despite these differences, the basic observations made above still hold. The visualization techniques above still provide useful ways to explore the system's global dynamics, although the dimensionality of such constructions will be greater and will almost certainly evolve over time.

Peter Allen of the United Kingdom-based Complexity Society has developed a typology of models based upon increased model complexity, which is useful in helping us to understand the relationship between different model types.

11.2.2.10 Computer Model Types

When developing computer-based models of organizations, four modeling types are generally used. These are equilibrium models, system dynamics models, self-organizing models, and evolutionary models. The differences between these modeling approaches are the assumptions made to reduce the complex observed reality to a simpler and therefore more manageable representation. According to Allen (1994, 5) the two main assumptions (or, simplifications) made are:

1. Microscopic events occur at their average rate, average densities are correct
2. Individuals of a given type, x say, are identical

Essentially, these assumptions restrict the capacity of any modeled system to macroscopically or microscopically adapt to its environment. In some cases, assumption two is relaxed somewhat, and diversity in the form of some normal distribution is allowed. Combinations of these assumptions lead to different models. In addition to the above assumptions, another one is often made— that the system sufficiently rapidly achieves equilibrium. So, in addition to the model not being able to adapt macroscopically or microscopically, equilibrium is also achieved. The attraction of equilibrium modeling is the simplicity that results from only having to consider simultaneous and not dynamic equations. Equilibrium also seems to offer the possibility of looking at a decision or policy in terms of a stationary state before and after the decision. This is a dangerous illusion, although it does not deny that, as long as great care is taken, equilibrium models may provide useful, albeit very limited, understanding of complex systems.

Of course, if the assumptions imposed were true for a restricted (in time and space) context then the equilibrium model would be perfectly acceptable. What is found, however, is that in real organizations, none of these assumptions are true for any significant length of time. So, although the equilibrium model offers only a single possibility—that of equilibrium—it omits all the other possibilities that may result from relaxing one's modeling assumptions.

The following bullet points list the different models that result when different combinations of these assumptions are relaxed. Adjustments to the simple Boolean network model used earlier are also suggested that would turn them into the different sorts of models listed.

- Making assumptions one and two yields the nonlinear system dynamics model; discrete Boolean networks are examples of simple nonlinear system dynamics models—once they are initiated they move to one particular attractor and stay there even though the system's phase space may be characterized by many attractor basins. For these networks, the interconnections remain the same (i.e., topology is static) and the transition rules are also fixed.
- Making assumption two yields the self-organizing model; if one incorporated into each Boolean node a script that directed it to switch state (regardless of what the rule table said) under particular external circumstances (noting that the standard Boolean network is closed), then the system could move into different basins depending on different external contextual factors. Such an implementation could simply be that a random number generator represents environmental conditions and that for particular ranges of this random number a node would ignore its rule table and change state regardless.
- Making neither assumption yields the evolutionary model; for an evolutionary Boolean network, the network topology would change and the rule tables for each node would

also change. A set of meta-rules could be developed for each node that indicate the local conditions under which a connection is removed or added and how the rules would evolve—it is quite reasonable for these rules to be sophisticated in that they could include, and rely on, local memories. Another set of rules could determine when new nodes are created and how their connections and rule tables are initiated. This is essentially what the agent-based modeling approach is. This model is not truly evolutionary as we have simply created a set of meta-rules to direct change within the system. However, if we take evolutionary in such a literal way then no model can ever really be evolutionary.

Now that a summary of complexity science has been presented, some comments can be made regarding one's ability to rationally design interventions to achieve certain preset aims.

11.2.3 WHAT ARE THE IMPLICATIONS FOR RATIONAL INTERVENTION (CONTROL) IN COMPLEX NETWORKS?

Assuming that accurate representations of real world complex systems can be constructed, then what is the basis for rational intervention in such systems? If we assume that everything is connected to everything else (which is not an unreasonable assumption) and that such systems are sensitive to initial conditions (at the mercy of every minute perturbation) then, indeed, there would seem to be little basis for rational intervention. To take these assumptions seriously we would have to model "wholes" only, or, extend our modeling boundaries to the point at which no further connections could be found. This is more than an argument for wholes, and is really an argument that suggests that to be rational in any complete sense of the word, one must model the Universe as a whole. This is the holistic position taken to an absurd extreme. What is interesting is that from a complex systems perspective, no member of a complex system can possibly have such complete knowledge (point ten in the section titled "What is a Complexity System?"). Even if we could find wholes other than the entire Universe then the sensitivity to any small external perturbation would undo any efforts to intervene in a rationally designed way. Hopefully, the discussion presented thus far provides ample evidence to support the dismissal of such a pessimistic and radically holistic position—holism is not the solution to complexity.

As we have already seen, despite all the change in complex systems, there are many stabilities that can be identified and that can also provide a basis for rational intervention. First of all, one needs to recognize that asking for a basis for rational intervention does not mean absolute rationality. It means a bounded (Simon, 1945, 88–89; see the Mingus chapter in this volume) and temporary rationality, which has considerable limitations to it.

For example, if one is confident that a system dynamics-type representation of a real world system has merit, then identification of qualitatively different operating scenarios that would allow the development of policy strategies that succeed in a variety of future possibilities would be feasible. Another way of saying this is that it would be possible to develop a policy that was sensitive to a number of contextual archetypes. Possibilities that are known but could not easily be designed for might be dealt with as part of a risk assessment, and possibilities (unknown) outside the bounds of the model might be dealt with through contingency planning.

If a self-organizing model turned out to be appropriate then one could not only identify different possible operating scenarios, but also relevant elements, i.e., the elements/entities/nodes that are primarily responsible for the overall qualitative variation in the system. From such a reduced representation one has the possibility of more efficiently re-directing a system towards preferred futures. One can also grasp how robust solutions might be, and how one might allocate resources to achieve preferred policy aims.

Even if dynamical models are not used, one can construct static network representations that make available a wealth of other analytical techniques that would allow the assessment of topological characteristics such a path lengths, structural robustness, the presence of dense nodes, etc. that provide potentially useful information when it comes to developing intervention strategies.

It is clear that just because a system of interest is complex, it does not follow that analysts are necessarily impotent when it comes to developing robust intervention strategies. Although there are many possibilities for understanding certain aspects of complex systems, there are also important limitations to our ability to understand such systems. As one example, in complex systems, it is often the case that there is a delay between a particular cause and an observable effect—this delay can be such that it becomes very difficult indeed to associate a particular cause with a particular effect. Particular effects can have multiple causes (a phenomenon known as equifinality). This can work in one's favor, as there may be a number of ways to achieve the same goals. However, it is also a disadvantage in that there will likely be many ways to derail a particular strategy. Intervening in complex systems often changes them in nontrivial and unforeseen ways, which are difficult to account for in analyses. New entities/players/species also emerge that are near impossible to predict and that can totally change the phase space. Sometimes it can very much seem like trying to pin the tail on a fast moving donkey. Cilliers (2000a,b) discusses the limits of understanding concerning complex systems in greater detail.

Although there are many tools and concepts available to assist in the understanding of complex systems and to inform policymaking, it is also apparent that we need a strategy for managing the limits to what we can know about them. A naive realism that is overly confident in one's ability to represent complex systems is inappropriate regardless of how many analytical tools are developed to deal with complexity head-on.

Complexity theory can be used to help us understand the limits placed on developing knowledge of those same systems. For example, if one assumes that the real world system of interest is indeed a complex system (bearing in mind that the presupposed assumption is that all phenomena are the result of complex nonlinear processes) then what is the status of the resulting model of that system—even if it is a complex systems model—given that such a model will necessarily be an abstraction?[*] Focusing on the phenomenon of interest for a moment, if the boundaries inferred from perceptions of reality in order to form a model are a little bit off, or the representation of nonlinear interactions are inaccurate—even if only slightly—then there is always the possibility that the understanding developed from such a model is wholly inadequate because small mismatches can have serious consequences. Even a model that accounts for all observable data is still not entirely adequate. Given that nonlinear processes are operating at all scales, there is an infinite number of ways to build a model that generates what has already been seen (Richardson, 2003), and so one can never be sure that the model explains observables that have not yet been observed; applying the results of a model outside of the context in which it was developed is highly problematic. Another source of error, which is related to the first, is that all boundaries, or stable patterns, in a complex system are emergent, critically organized, and therefore temporary (and as already seen, they are not even real in any absolute sense but are the artifacts resulting from a filtering process).

Given these difficulties in even constructing a useful model in the first place—modeling is certainly not as straightforward as map-making traditionally is, which is what modeling really represents in the mechanistic view of the world—it is essential to have a theory of limits. Such an understanding informs a philosophy of analysis and this will be the focus for the third part of this chapter.

---

[*] This follows from the darkness principle in systems theory, which says that no system can be completely known (Skyttner, 2001, 93).

11.3 TOWARDS AN ANALYTICAL PHILOSOPHY OF COMPLEXITY

In the previous section it was suggested that complexity offers more than just a set of new tools—it also suggests a particular critical attitude toward all our instruments of understanding and the status of the understanding that those instruments give. Naively employing any of the tools of complexity in an unquestioning, unsophisticated way, without concern for their limitations, is little better than denying complexity in the first place. Complexity-based, or complexity-informed, analysis is as much to do with how analytical tools are used as it is to do with which tools are used.

The aim of the proceeding short section is to explore the philosophical implications of assuming that all real systems are complex or the result of underlying complex (nonlinear) processes. As mentioned above, just because all phenomena/systems are the result of complex, nonlinear processes it does not follow that simple, linear models are obsolete—aspects of complex systems can indeed be modeled as if they were simple, even if only approximately and temporarily. The result of acknowledging the inherent complexity of the real is a tentative critical philosophy of analysis. The exploration begins with probably one of the most fundamental questions: "What does it mean to exist?" In complexity terms this can be rephrased as "When is a pattern a real pattern?" or "When is a boundary a real boundary?" A major part of the process of analysis is the extraction of stable patterns, and so understanding the status of patterns in complex systems is key to developing an analytical philosophy to understand them.

11.3.1 ON THE NATURE OF BOUNDARIES

In Richardson (2004b) a detailed analysis is provided regarding the status of boundaries in a complex system, i.e., the emergence of objects and their ontological status. These arguments are summarized here.

The basic conclusion that the complexity-based argument given thus far leads to is that there are no real boundaries in any absolute sense (this by no way suggests that in certain instances assuming the existence of particular boundaries is inappropriate). How are we to derive knowledge of particular systems then, particularly if no systems really exist? This state of affairs is not as dire as it might immediately seem. There is no need to follow the radical holists to model the world, the universe and everything. From a complexity perspective, although there may be no real boundaries, there are resilient and relatively stable emergent structures, or patterns. In fact, there is a distribution of boundary stabilities. No evidence is given for what this distribution may actually be (the theory of self-organized criticality from Bak (1996) might suggest that such a distribution is in fact scale-free); it is simply argued that there is a distribution. Figure 11.5 illustrates a possible stability distribution which has no theoretical or empirical basis.

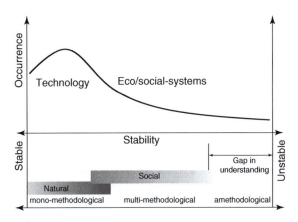

FIGURE 11.5 A possible distribution of natural boundary (structure) stability.

At one end of the stability spectrum there are boundaries/structures/patterns that are so persistent and stable that for most intents and purposes it can safely be assumed that they are in fact real and absolute. Boundaries that delimit the objects of science-based technology exist toward this end of the spectrum. Such long-term stability allows a "community of enquirers," for example, the scientific community, to inter-subjectively converge on some agreed principles that might actually be tested through experiment. Under such conditions it is quite possible to develop quasi-objective knowledge, which for most intents and purposes (but not ultimately) is absolute. The existence of such persistent boundaries allows for a something other than a radically holistic analysis—this may explain why the scientific program has been in many ways so successful when it comes to technological matters. In many circumstances reductionism is a perfectly valid, though still approximate, route to understanding complex systems. In short, what is suggested here is that scientific study depends upon the assumption that natural boundaries are static (in a qualitative sense), and that if one can prove that the boundaries of interest are in fact stable and persistent, then scientific methods, even reductionist methods, are more than adequate means to understand and interact with them.

At the other end of the stability spectrum is essentially "noise," in which the lifetime of apparent boundaries might be so fleeting as to render them unrecognizable as such and therefore unanalyzable. Under such circumstances, attempts to develop knowledge are strongly determined by the whims of the individual, with observed boundaries being more a function of our thirst to make sense, rather than an actual feature of reality. To maintain a purely positivistic position (i.e., a position that strives to attain absolute, complete, and unbiased understanding, and assumes that something called the scientific method is the route to such understanding), one would have to accept a radical holism and consider the entire universe (as the only way to have such perfect understanding is to model it all)—a practical absurdity and a theoretical impossibility as has already been suggested. This is the only method by which a robust understanding could possibly be derived.

Fortunately, a vast majority of the perceived Universe is not quite so nebulous. This does not mean, however, that boundary recognition and allocation is a trivial exercise. In fact, without the ability to not only determine the stability distribution, but also recognize where the objects of interest exist on the curve, it is very difficult to determine how to approach them. Radical positivists might argue that a rigorous implementation of the scientific method is appropriate across the board though such broad-brush positivism seems quite the opposite. It is likely that the social, or soft, sciences with their willingness to work with a plurality of (possibly incommensurable) methods and perspectives is better suited to deal with a state of affairs in which boundary recognition and allocation is deeply problematic. This position reflects Cilliers's (2001, 142) concern that "[i]n accepting the complexity of the boundaries of complex systems, we are committed to be critical about how we use the notion since it affects our understanding of such systems, and influences the way in which we deal with them."

11.3.2 COMPLEXITY AND PHILOSOPHY

Because boundaries are both emergent and temporary and their recognition is problematic, the need for critical thinking and paradigm/perspective/methodological pluralism comes to the fore. If there is no basis from which to unambiguously determine the best way to frame our models, then the importance of approaching the same problem from multiple directions becomes plainly apparent. If the validity of the understanding derived from one's models is potentially critically sensitive to the underlying assumptions, then the importance of critically reflecting on those assumptions also becomes equally apparent. So, in short, assuming that all phenomena are the result of complex nonlinear processes, causes one to recognize the central importance of both criticism and pluralism in analysis.

11.3.2.1 Justifying Pluralism

The first step in making an argument for a pluralist analytical philosophy is to justify pluralism (both ontological and epistemological/methodological). To some degree this has already been accomplished by highlighting the ambiguity of pattern recognition in complex systems, i.e., the considerable difficulties in recognizing an object as an object. The perception of the objects that form the basis of our models "appear" as a result of a filtering process, in other words, the objects of perceived reality are what is left over when a lot of background noise has been removed. The determination of what is the background and what actually is noise is a characteristic of the filter chosen. We say that these resulting (quasi-)objects are substantially real to make explicit the fact that there is a subjective element in their recognition, which necessarily changes the way in which we use them—if we assume their existence is objective and absolute then there is no reason to think about them critically and no reason to consider using different filtering processes.

Assuming an acceptance of pluralism as a key element of a philosophy of analysis, all the tools and concepts discussed in the previous section are of a particular sort—they are based on mathematical ideas and constructs. Even accepting that there are many ways to build a model of the same phenomenon, the tendency is still towards formal mathematical approaches and away from softer, seemingly less formal, approaches. However, in assuming pluralism, the restriction to mathematical approaches is an additional arbitrary assumption and what can be considered as a case of horizontal pluralism rather than pluralism in its truest sense. Here it can be seen that mathematical approaches to complexity offer evidence that these approaches are not necessarily the only, or best, way to manage complexity—this comes from the recognition that mathematics itself is not capable of explaining all there is to know about complexity.

11.3.2.2 Horizontal and Vertical Pluralism

Even though the above view has the capacity to allow the exploration of the same phenomena from different perspectives, all the perspectives are scientific, or mathematical, in nature. This view is exemplified by W.V. Quine's brand of ontological relativism: "Here the plurality consists in the possible existence of a range of alternative scientific worldviews, each empirically adequate to more or less the same degree, and none, even in principle, have privileged claim to provide a 'truer' description of the world" (Price, 1992, 389). Even "incompatible theories can explain the same facts equally well and make equally good predictions" (Masani, 2001, 279). Price (1992) goes on to argue that

> [t]here may be equally valid possible scientific worldviews, but all of them are scientific worldviews, and in that sense are on the same level of linguistic activity. In other words, this is what might appropriately be called horizontal pluralism. (389)

But why should pluralism be restricted to the horizontal? Why should pluralism be associated only with what might be called "discourse monism"? Traditional science has a knack for extracting particularly clear and long-lived patterns and expressing their form in an implementable way (generally through mathematics). What about everything else?

> If these [scientific discourses] are cases of horizontal pluralism, what would be a vertical pluralism? It would be the view that philosophy should recognise an irreducible plurality of kinds of discourse—the moral as well as the scientific, for example. This is the species of pluralism with which we ... [should] be most concerned. (Price, 1992, 390)

Price refers to this type of vertical pluralism as discourse pluralism. Here he has arrived at a description of what is meant by pluralism in a complexity-inspired evolutionary philosophy. This type of pluralism is not "irrealist" at all. It simply accepts that in the absence of a completely realist position, one may profit from the examination of a variety of other worldviews and discourses whose sensitivity to noise varies. Different scientific worldviews may be as useful as different moral world-views or different artistic worldviews (such as cubism or abstract expressionism), all of which are metaphors or caricatures of reality. This does not lead to an "anything goes" relativism, except maybe as a starting point. But how, if one is to make a decision one way or another, is one to untangle the pluralist web and agree upon, albeit temporarily and locally, a dominant worldview? The aim, after all, of analysis is generally to act in an informed way to achieve particular outcomes. Suggesting that one must approach every issue from every angle will quickly lead to paralysis from over-analysis.

The above discussion is included to show that it is not the case that to examine complexity one must use only the tools that have been developed by the complexity community. A complexity-inspired philosophy itself argues that all the tools for thought have the potential to provide insights, albeit provisionally and limitedly, concerning the operation of complex systems. It is not necessary to only use complexity tools as long as one's thinking is complex. Even linear models used appropriately can be very useful in temporarily understanding complexity. What is more, by maintaining a critical attitude towards these tools and their use, one can resist the possibility of becoming locked into a particular analytical attractor—complex systems evolve and one's thinking about them needs to evolve as well.

A number of "meta-methodologies" have been proposed that explicitly acknowledge that the recognition of complexity requires an alternative approach to policy analysis. These include total systems intervention (Flood and Jackson, 1991; Flood, 1995), system of systems methodologies (Jackson and Keys, 1984), group modeling (Vennix, 1996), systemic intervention (Midgley, 1997; 2000), and robust adaptive planning (Bankes, 2002; Lempert, 2002b), to name but a few.

11.3.3 A NOTE ON ETHICS

A critically pluralist decision making process has to come to an end at some point and a decision made. Literally, the concept of critical (vertical and horizontal) pluralism provides no end—the more one explores, using the mechanisms of critical thinking (critical systems heuristics, critical appreciation, and boundary critique, for example), the richer the understanding and presumably the better-quality the decision. This is, however, impractical.

Analysis is performed to provide insight into a particular problematic situation and has limited time and resources associated with it. Free unimpeded exploration does not and can not be sufficient on its own—one needs to recognize that an endpoint must be reached, which in so doing, limits exploration, and therefore limits the breadth and quality of the understanding developed. These shortfalls mean that something important might be missed, and so there are unavoidable risks associated with any decision process. This is where ethics becomes useful, but not as a way to specifically prescribe an endpoint.

By ethics it is not meant purely as some notion of altruism; conversely, in being unable to know it all (the darkness principle), one must accept the inevitability of choices that cannot be backed up scientifically or objectively (Cilliers, 2000a). This means that a judgment must be made that accepts that one has arrived at the best decision possible (given current capabilities), but it is not perfect as a decision can only be based on the insight developed through limited (bounded) effort. One must accept that decisions are based on incomplete analysis, and that potentially adverse outcomes might occur as a result of an inability to "see" everything. The analysis must be judged to be "good" by judging how it went about addressing the problem situation and how it critically appraised the determined boundaries. An analysis does not remove the responsibility from the decision maker (one cannot blame the plan if all goes wrong); the decision maker has the responsibility to ensure that the best possible exploration was performed. The decision maker must fully appreciate that the validity of the understanding derived depends wholly on the assumptions (both tacit and explicit) that were made (which may or may not be appropriate given the problematic situation despite

TABLE 11.1
Useful Complexity and Policy Analysis References

Title	Reference	Topic
Complexity and Healthcare: A View from the Street	Kernick, ed. (2004)	This book explores the application of complexity theory to healthcare with the aid of both theory and case-based analyses. Recently reviewed by Baskin (2004).
A New Mind for Policy Analysis	Göktuğ Morçöl (2002)	In this book the author argues for a new view of policy analysis that transcends the prevailing Newtonian approaches.
Systemic Intervention	Gerald Midgley (2000)	Although this book is not officially a 'complexity' book, the methodological discussions presented do resonate with those discussed herein and elsewhere in the 'complexity' literature.
Complexity Theory and the Social Sciences	Byrne (1998)	Introduces the central ideas which surround the chaos/complexity theories. It discusses key concepts and uses them to investigate the nature of social research.
Nonlinear Dynamics, Complexity and Public Policy	Elliott and Kiel, eds. (1999)	Introduction to the fields of nonlinear dynamics and complex systems, with particular application to a wide range of policy-related issues.
Managing Complex Networks: Strategies for the Public Sector	Kickert, Klijn and Koppenjan, eds. (1997)	Develops a network management approach to governance and public management, and shows how governments can manage policy networks to enhance policy performance and public service delivery.
Taking Complexity Seriously	Roe (1998)	Applies the policy analysis technique of triangulation to sustainable development in complex uncertain systems.
Complexity and the Economy	Finch and Orillard (2005)	Surveys conceptual approaches to understanding complexity as a key subject in evolutionary and political economy.
Managing Organizational Complexity	Richardson, ed. (2005)	Contains chapters concerning the philosophy, theory and application of complexity science to the understanding of human organisations.
Managing Complexity in the Public Services	Haynes (2003)	Argues that the complexity of the public policy process limits the usefulness of the "new public management" approach, and proposes alternative approaches that are based on an understanding of the disorder in the policy process.
Full Spectrum Analysis: Practical OR in the Face of the Human Variable	Mathieson (2004)	Explores the difficulties in understanding human systems and proposes that "full spectrum analysis," which is similar to critical pluralism, is needed to rationally intervene in such systems.
The Complexity of Concept Mapping for Policy Analysis	Trochim and Cabrera (2005)	Suggests that the use of concept mapping in combination with other types of human simulation provides a valuable methodological tool for studying complex human systems.
From Worst Slum to Best Example of Regeneration: Complexity in the Regeneration of Hulme— Manchester	Moobela (2005)	A case-based paper illustrating the application of complexity thinking to a regeneration project.
Facilitating Resource Decision Making in Public Organisations Drawing Upon Insights From Complexity Theory	Kernick (2005)	Explores how complexity insights can be used to facilitate resource decision making in public systems.
Robust Policy Analysis for Complex Open Systems	Bankes (2005)	Describes an approach to highly interactive decision support based upon using ensembles of alternative models, robust option analysis, and adaptive strategies.

considerable effort), and that it is provisional in that it is based upon current beliefs and perceptions. An awareness of both the contingency and provisionality of the analysis is far better than a false sense of security, the latter being a very risky state of affairs indeed. It is clear, though, that there are ethical implications for all boundary judgments.

This approach to ethics does not provide a definitive endpoint for the decision process (this point has to be negotiated between the process participants and reality) but it does provide guidelines as to which factors must be taken into account in determining whether or not an analysis has served its purpose. Essentially, an ethic must be developed locally, rather than falling back on a prescribed universal framework. However, a locally developed ethic may have to be defended non-locally. How might this defense be achieved? This is not a trivial issue, but will not be discussed further here.

11.4 APPLYING COMPLEXITY TO POLICY ANALYSIS

The aims of this chapter are far too ambitious to hope to achieve them in any complete way. The principal aim was to introduce a number of the ideas and developments in complexity theory and to explore in a general way only their implications for policy analysis. However, despite its introductory nature it would be remiss to not include references to actual applications of complexity thinking in policy analysis. Until recently, complexity thinking was regarded more as an academically interesting area of exploration rather than a body of knowledge that could be brought to bear on the solution (albeit non-optimally and provisionally) of real world policy-related problems. This state of affairs is changing rapidly, however, as the field matures. In an attempt to capture only a small part of these developments, Table 11.1 lists some key references in the application of complexity thinking to policy analysis. These references should provide useful points of departure for the reader keen to further explore the application of complexity thinking to policy analysis.

11.5 SUMMARY AND SOME CONCLUSIONS

Despite its length—which is due to its introductory nature—the main argument of this chapter is straightforward. There are many new tools available to policy analysts that can facilitate the job of comprehending complex systems, and intervening in them in a quasi-rational way. A subset of these tools and concepts was discussed in the first section. However, despite the widespread emergence of new tools, there is also a growing awareness of the limitations of any and all tools for understanding complex systems. Indeed, there is no way to fully comprehend a complex system and therefore no way to intervene in them in a totally risk-free way—taking action always means taking a step into the unknown, to some degree. An understanding of complexity requires an understanding of the limits to one's analyses. Such an understanding changes the way in which we regard these tools—not as accurate representations of reality, but as useful fictions to facilitate limited sense making. So complexity thinking is not only about the tools used, but also how those tools are used.

A complexity-inspired analytical philosophy does not privilege the accepted tools of complexity researchers as the only legitimate tools for understanding complexity, but argues that all tools have the potential to shed some light on the behavior of such systems. It is the maintenance of a critical stance that becomes essential so that analysts do not get locked into one particular analytical attractor. This shift from analytical lock-in, a pre-occupation with models and not the process of modeling, and an explicit recognition of limits is quite different from many traditional analysis departments. Complexity thinking not only has implications for how the analysis department operates, but also how that department interacts with the rest of an organization, and how that organization as a whole makes decisions if the position of critical pluralism is to be truly acknowledged. Such cultural considerations are difficult to implement given how resistant cultural lock-in is, but to effectively consider the analysis and intervention in complex systems, these cultural concerns are as important as, if not more important than, the analytical tools themselves.

REFERENCES

Adamic, L. A., The small world web, In *Proceedings of the Third European Conference, ECDL'99*, Springer-Verlag, Berlin, 443–452.

Albert, R. and Barabási, A.-L., Statistical mechanics of complex networks, *Reviews of Modern Physics*, 74(1), 47–97, 2002.

Allen, P. M., Evolutionary complex systems: models of technology change, In *Evolutionary Economics and Chaos Theory: New Directions in Technology Studies*, Leydesdorff, L. and van den Besselaar, P., Eds., St. Martin's Press, New York, pp. 1–17, 1994.

Allen, P. M., Boulton, J. G., Strathern, M., and Baldwin, J., The implications of complexity for business process and strategy, In *Managing the Complex: Philosophy, Theory and Applications*, Richardson, K., Ed., Information Age Publishing, Greenwich, CT, pp. 397–418, 2005.

Alligood, K. T., Sauer, T. D., and Yorke, J. A., *Chaos: An Introduction to Dynamical Systems*, Springer-Verlag, New York, 1997.

Auyang, S. Y., *Foundations of Complex-System Theories in Economics, Evolutionary Biology, and Statistical Physics*, Cambridge University Press, New York, 1999.

Badii, R. and Politi, A., *Complexity: Hierarchical Structures and Scaling in Physics, Cambridge Nonlinear Science Series*, 6, Cambridge University Press, New York, 1997.

Bak, P., *How Nature Works: The Science of Self-organized Criticality*, Copernicus, New York, 1996.

Bankes, S., Robust policy analysis for complex open systems, *Emergence: Complexity and Organization*, 7(1), 5–18, 2005.

Bankes, S. C., Tools and techniques for developing policies for complex and uncertain systems, *Proceedings of the National Academy of Sciences*, 99(suppl. no. 3), 7263–7266, 2002.

Barabási, A.-L., *Linked: The New Science of Networks*, Perseus Publishing, Cambridge, MA, 2002.

Barabási, A.-L. and Albert, R., Emergence of scaling in random networks, *Science*, 286, 509–512, 1999.

Bilke, S. and Sjunnesson, F., Stability of the Kauffman model, *Physical Review. E*, 65, 0161295, 2001.

Bonabeau, E., Agent-based modeling: methods and techniques for simulating human systems, *Proceedings of the National Academy of Sciences*, 99(suppl. no. 3), 7280–7287, 2002.

Bossomaier, T. R. J. and Green, D., *Complex Systems*, Cambridge University Press, Cambridge, UK, 2000.

Byrne, D., *Complexity Theory and the Social Sciences: An Introduction*, Routledge, London, 1998.

Chaitin, G. J., *The Limits of Mathematics*, Springer, Singapore, 1999a.

Chaitin, G. J., *The Unknowable*, Springer, Singapore, 1999b.

Cilliers, P., *Complexity and Postmodernism: Understanding Complex Systems*, Routledge, London, 1998.

Cilliers, P., What can we learn from a theory of complexity?, *Emergence*, 2(1), 23–33, 2000a.

Cilliers, P., Knowledge, complexity, and understanding, *Emergence*, 2(4), 7–13, 2000b.

Cilliers, P., Boundaries, hierarchies and networks in complex systems, *International Journal of Innovation Management*, 5(2), 135–147, 2001.

Cross, R. and Parker, A., *The Hidden Power of Social Networks: Understanding How Work Really Gets Done in Organizations*, Harvard Business School Press, Boston, 2004.

Davies, B., *Exploring Chaos: Theory and Experiment*, Perseus Books, New York, NY, 1999.

Dennett, D. C., Real patterns, *The Journal of Philosophy*, 88, 27–51, 1991.

Elliott, E. W. and Kiel, L. D., Eds., *Nonlinear Dynamics, Complexity and Public Policy*, Nova Science Publishers, Commack, NY, 1999.

Emmeche, C., Köppe, S., and Stjernfelt, F., Levels, emergence, and three versions of downward causation, In *Down Ward Causation*, Andersen, P. B., Emmeche, C., Finnemann, N. O., and Christiansen, P. V., Eds., Aarhus University Press, Aarhus, Netherlands, pp. 13–34, 2000.

Erdős, P. and Rényi, A., On random graphs, *Publ. Mathematical*, 6, 290–297, 1959.

Finch, J. and Orillard, M., *Complexity and the Economy: Implications for Economic Policy*, Edward Elgar Publishing, Cheltenham, UK, 2005.

Flood, R. L., Total systems intervention (TSI): a reconstitution, *Journal of the Operational Research Society*, 46, 174–191, 1995.

Flood, R. L. and Jackson, M. C., *Creative Problem Solving: Total Systems Intervention*, John Wiley & Sons, Chichester, UK, 1991.

Haynes, P., *Managing Complexity in the Public Services*, Open University Press, Milton Keynes, UK, 2003.

Horgan, J., From complexity to perplexity, *Science*, 272, 74–79, 1995.

Jackson, M. C. and Keys, P., Towards a system of systems methodologies, *Journal of the Operational Research Society*, 33, 473–486, 1984.

Kauffman, S. A., *The Origins of Order: Self-Organization and Selection in Evolution*, Oxford University Press, Oxford, UK, 1993.

Kernick, D., Facilitating resource decision making in public organizations drawing upon insights from complexity theory, *Emergence: Complexity and Organization*, 7(1), 175–184, 2005.

Kernick, D., Ed., *Complexity and Healthcare: A View from the Street*, Radcliffe Medical Press, Abingdon, UK, 2004.

Kickert, W. J. M., Klijn, E-H., and Koopenjan, J. F. M., Eds., *Managing Complex Networks: Strategies for the Public Sector*, Sage, London, UK, 1997.

Lempert, R. J., Agent-based modeling as organizational and public policy simulators, *Proceedings of the National Academy of Sciences*, 99(suppl. no. 3), 7195–7196, 2002a.

Lempert, R. J., A new decision sciences for complex systems, *Proceedings of the National Academy of Sciences*, 99(suppl. no. 3), 7309–7313, 2002b.

Lissack, M. R., Mind your metaphors: Lessons from complexity science, *Long Range Planning*, April, 294–298, 1997.

Lissack, M. R., Complexity: the science, its vocabulary, and its relation to organizations, *Emergence*, 1(1), 110–126, 1999.

Lorenz, E. N., Deterministic nonperiodic flow, *Journal of the Atmospheric Sciences*, 20, 130–141, 1963.

Lucas, C., *Complexity and Artificial Life: What are they?*, http://www.calresco.org/cal.htm/ (August 3, 2005), 2004.

Lui, H. and Richardson, K. A., Chaos-based principles for forecasting, In *Managing Organizational Complexity: Philosophy, Theory, Application*, Richardson, K. A., Ed., Information Age Publishing, Greenwich, CT, pp. 167–182, 2005.

Masani, P. R., Three modern enemies of science: materialism, existentialism, constructivism, *Kybernetes*, 30, 278–294, 2001.

Mathieson, G. M., Full spectrum analysis: practical OR in the face of the human variable, *Emergence: Complexity and Organization*, 6(4), 51–57, 2004.

May, R. M., Simple mathematical models with very complicated dynamics, *Nature*, 261, 459, 1976.

McKelvey, W., What is complexity science? It is really order-creation science?, *Emergence*, 3(1), 137–157, 2001.

McMillan, E., Encouraging strategic change by using complexity-based principles: A case study of the Open University, U.K., In *Managing Organizational Complexity: Philosophy, Theory, Application*, Richardson, K. A., Ed., Information Age Publishing, Greenwich, CT, pp. 505–520, 2005.

Midgley, G., Mixing methods: Developing systemic intervention, In *Multi-Methodology: The Theory and Practice of Combining Management Science Methodologies*, Mingers, J. and Gill, A., Eds., John Wiley & Sons, Chichester, UK, 1997.

Midgley, G., *Systemic Intervention: Philosophy, Methodology, and Practice*, Kluwer Academic, New York, NY, 2000.

Moobela, C., From worst slum to best example of regeneration: complexity in the regeneration of Hulme-Manchester, *Emergence: Complexity and Organization*, 7(1), 185–208, 2005.

Morçöl, G., *A New Mind for Policy Analysis: Toward a Post-Newtonian and Postpositivist Epistemology and Methodology*, Praeger, Westport, CT, 2002.

Morgan, G., *Images of Organization*, Sage, Newbury Park, CA, 1986.

Oreskes, N., Shrader-Frechette, K., and Belitz, K., Verification, validation, and confirmation of numerical models in the earth sciences, *Science*, 263, 641–646, 1994.

Ott, E., *Chaos in Dynamical Systems*, 2nd ed., Cambridge University Press, Cambridge, UK, 2002.

Powell, J. H., An application of a network-based futures method to strategic business planning, *Journal of the Operational Research Society*, 48, 857–872, 1997.

Powell, J. H. and Coyle, R. G., A network-based futures method for strategic business planning, *Journal of the Operational Research Society*, 48, 793–803, 1997.

Price, H., Metaphysical pluralism, *The Journal of Philosophy*, 89, 387–409, 1992.

Richardson, K. A., On the limits of bottom-up computer simulation: towards a nonlinear modeling culture, *Proceedings of the 36th Hawaiian International Conference on System Sciences*, California: IEEE, 2003.

Richardson, K. A., On the relativity of recognising the products of emergence and the nature of physical hierarchy, *Proceedings of the 2nd Biennial International Seminar on the Philosophical, Epistemological and Methodological Implications of Complexity Theory*, January 7th–10th, Havana International Conference Center, Cuba, 2004a.

Richardson, K. A., The problematization of existence: towards a philosophy of existence, *Nonlinear Dynamics, Psychology, and Life Sciences*, 8(1), 17–40, 2004b.

Richardson, K. A., Systems theory and complexity: part 2, *Emergence: Complexity and Organization*, 6(4), 77–82, 2004c.

Richardson, K. A., The hegemony of the physical sciences: an exploration in complexity thinking, *Futures*, 37, 615–653, 2005a.

Richardson, K. A., *Complexity thinking and policy analysis*, 2005b. Available at: http://kurtrichardson.com

Richardson, K. A., The role of "waste" in complex systems. Paper presented at the *1st International Workshop on Complexity and Policy Analysis*, Cork, Ireland, 2005c.

Richardson, K. A., Ed., *Managing Organizational Complexity: Philosophy, Theory, Application*, Information Age Publishing, Greenwich, CT, 2005.

Richardson, K. A. and Cilliers, P., "What is complexity science? A view from different directions, *Emergence*, 3(1), 5–23, 2001.

Roe, E., *Taking Complexity Seriously: Policy Analysis, Triangulation and Sustainable Development*, Kluwer Academic, New York, 1998.

Simon, H., *Administrative Behavior: A Study of Decision-Making Processes in Administrative Organizations*, 4th ed., The Free Press, New York, 1945.

Skyttner, L., *General Systems Theory: Ideas and Applications*, World Scientific, Singapore, 2001.

Sommerer, J. C. and Ott, E., A physical system with qualitatively uncertain dynamics, *Nature*, 365, 138–140, 1993.

Trochim, W. and Cabrera, D., The complexity of concept mapping for policy analysis, *Emergence: Complexity and Organization*, 7(1), 19–38, 2005.

Van Eijnatten, F. and van Galen, M., Provoking chaordic change in a Dutch manufacturing firm, In *Managing Organizational Complexity: Philosophy, Theory, Application*, Richardson, K. A., Ed., Greenwich, CT, Information Age Publishing, pp. 521–556, 2005.

Vennix, J. A. M., *Group Model Building: Facilitating Team Learning Using System Dynamics*, John Wiley & Sons, Chichester, UK, 1996.

Watts, D. J. and Strogatz, S. H., Collective dynamics of "small-world networks", *Nature*, 393, 440–442, 1998.

Wolf, A., Quantifying chaos with Lyapunov exponents, In *Chaos*, Holden, A. V., Ed., Princeton University Press, Princeton, NJ, pp. 273–290, 1986.

Yook, S., Jeong, H., and Barabási, A.-L., *Modeling the Internet's large-scale topology*, 2001. http://arxiv.org/abs/cond-mat/0107417/ (accessed 6th June 2006).

12 The New Sensibilities of Nonlinear Decision Making: Timing, Praxis, and a Feel for Relationship

Linda F. Dennard

CONTENTS

12.1 Introduction: Complexity and the Possibilities..224
    12.1.1 Decisions without Certainty...224
    12.1.2 Expressing the Full Potential of Complexity..224
12.2 Changing Perceptions..225
    12.2.1 New Rules for Decision Making in Nonlinear
            Systems and New Priorities...225
    12.2.2 The Systemic Pragmatism of Nonlinear Relationships....................................226
    12.2.3 Different Perceptions, Different Responses to Old Problems............................226
    12.2.4 Cause and Effect Only One Aspect of an Emerging Reality............................227
    12.2.5 Socially Responsible Administration Is Nonlinear and Relational....................227
12.3 Adaptation, Dichotomies, and Intention: Forming a New Relationship........................228
    12.3.1 What the Organization and Society Adapts to Is Affected
            by How Decisions Are Made and Implemented..228
    12.3.2 The Self-Organized Brain: The Chaotic Foreground of Intentionality.............228
    12.3.3 Simple Dichotomies Are Not so Simple..229
12.4 Relationship Dynamics..230
    12.4.1 Self-Organizaion and Intentionality..230
    12.4.2 Meaning Making...230
    12.4.3 Crisis Management that Becomes Habit..231
    12.4.4 Information Does Not Transform by Itself...231
12.5 Choosing What to Adapt To...232
    12.5.1 The New Adaptive Dynamics...232
    12.5.2 Increasing the Variables Available for Informed Decision Making..................233
    12.5.3 Choosing Something besides the Problem to Adapt To......................................234
    12.5.4 Equilibrium: Not the First Choice..234
    12.5.5 Emergence: Choosing to Participate...235
    12.5.6 Timing Is Everything..235
    12.5.7 Scaling and Boundaries..236
12.6 Choices that Matter: Nonlinear Ethics...237
12.7 Decision Making as Adaptive Choice Making..237

12.7.1   Marshalling Appropriate Resources: What Is Appropriate?...............................237
12.7.2   Eliminating Roadblocks or Learning from Them?..238
12.7.3   Increasing Capacity to Garner Future Resources: Doing More than
         One Thing at Once 238
12.7.4   Stabilizing a Productive and Ethical Work Force 239
12.8   Praxis: Coherence in the Details...240
       12.8.1   Stability Through Practice..240
       12.8.2   Meaning Making and System Coherence 240
12.9   Process Habits for Decision Making..241
12.10 Summary..242
References...242

12.1 INTRODUCTION: COMPLEXITY AND THE POSSIBILITIES

12.1.1 Decisions without Certainty

A good decision accomplishes several things simultaneously. It not only marshals the correct resources to achieve a certain outcome, but also eliminates the road blocks that seem to hamper goal achievement; and if it is a really superb decision, it increases the ability of the organization to garner future resources while stabilizing and strengthening a productive work culture that would be characterized by its capacity and will for participating fully in the emergence of the organization as a viable social institution. Conventionally, however, this definition of effective decision making both demands and assumes a high degree of certainty in the ability to identify the links between cause and effect in the workplace and in its broader environment. In turn, this perceived need for certainty has produced ample leadership studies that assume rational actors, playing predictable games to gauge how to manipulate the organizational landscape appropriately (Zinman, 2003). The new sciences of complexity, on the other hand, make this perception incomplete and somewhat less than rational.

Complexity sciences are defined here as the study of the behavior of collections of interactive units that possess the dynamic potential to evolve over time (Casti, 1994; Holland, 1995; Kauffman, 1995). As such, no distinction is made in this text between public and private organizations as each display this dynamic potential, and because each is seen as one element in a co-evolving system of social and political relationships. In essence, the concern here is not the intent of organizations, whatever their purposes, as much as it is the dynamic nonlinear decision-making processes by which intention emerges, is acted upon, and from which an ethical and democratic organizational culture might emerge.

12.1.2 Expressing the Full Potential of Complexity

The sciences of complexity have more relevance than the assistance nonlinear modeling provides managers seeking more control of wider networks of variables (Anthes, 2003). Agent-based modeling, for example, is being used in an increasing number of organizations to modify the behavior of individual, semi-autonomous agents acting according to simple rules—patterns identified by the new methodologies. The varied uses have been to "tighten supply chains, speed drugs to market, and even better design unmanned drones for the pentagon," among others (Mucha, 2002, 59).

As useful as these new methods are, however, they do not express the full potential of complexity sciences. In particular, they do not necessarily expand the focus of decision making by informing the joint achievement of management and social goals. This broader mandate for organizations cannot necessarily be realized only by engineering human behavior around specific short-term behaviors, historical bias, or by the strict adherence to either old or new methodologies.

What is proposed here is a more participatory approach than the application of methodology generally allows; one in which decision makers make choices that increase the capacity of the social landscape to sustain its institutions and individuals over the long haul of human experience, rather only seeking to solidify short-term efficiencies.

According to the principles of the sciences of complexity, for example, social events are influenced by sometimes random, dynamical,and nonlinear forces existing in the relationships among social actors that are not easily explained by simple motivations (for gain or the avoidance of loss), and that cannot be mapped in the long run as more than probabilities (Lewin, 1997). These "relationship dynamics" are not yet well understood and often are addressed in current management literature as simply another risk variable to manage and control to achieve a certainty of outcomes (Kiel, 1994; Schwartz, 1994). Again, however, simple risk management—even with new complexity tools such as agent-based modeling—does not necessarily meet both the challenge and the opportunity of emerging sciences of complexity. That is, new methodological tools do not free administrators from the need to make adaptively appropriate choices in response to newly discovered complexity.

For example, employing risk management as the dominant framework for decision making pulls attention to historical causes and their cures, and is therefore likely to increase organizational complexity as the organization adapts to new controls put in place as a response to the problem. With increased complexity, however, the opportunities for an increase in random behavior are as likely to emerge as a decrease in the level of risk. Another approach, one in which certainty is a secondary rather than a primary goal, is perhaps more pragmatic given our new knowledge of system complexity. What is proposed here is administrative "praxis"—where decision makers learn from and with the organization as it adjusts appropriately, ethically, and creatively to its environment, and where they encourage individual capacity to make adaptive choices that harvest the possibilities of system dynamics rather than seeking merely to control them.

12.2 CHANGING PERCEPTIONS

12.2.1 NEW RULES FOR DECISION MAKING IN NONLINEAR SYSTEMS AND NEW PRIORITIES

A system is linear when the *relationships* within or among systems can be described in strictly proportional terms (e.g., $y = 2x + 3$). From this perception, organizations are explainable as a set of identifiable variables that can be added or subtracted, encouraged or discouraged, according to simple transactions of time, money, or goods (Abramovitz, 1991, 95, 108). Further, the relationship among the variables is understood as primarily competitive—for time, space, and resources—and that it is this competition that produces the appearance of dynamism and innovation. Much of conventional management theory emerges from this belief that a linear cause and effect relationship exists between and among variables in the environment with the attendant belief that a manageable and often retroactive timeline of events between the first causes of a problem and its eventual resolution can be created. Further, organizational and social goals can be achieved by someone assuming the role of objective mediator to balance social conflict with the proportionate distribution of incentives and disincentives among those who are deemed to be either "the problem" or "the solution" (Rawls, 1999).

Using this linear equation as the conceptual framework for achieving certainty in decision making, however, creates a further perception that is especially problematic as the social landscape becomes more diverse—that complexity produces more conflict and conflict reduces the possibility of a certainty of outcomes. In this regard, the sciences of complexity, while not promising certainty, do offer a better conceptual framework for responding appropriately to a complex environment by changing our perception about what occurs in the relationship among variables beyond competition or the resolution of dichotomous relationships.

12.2.2 The Systemic Pragmatism of Nonlinear Relationships

Complexity mathematics provides visual representations of *nonlinear* relationships that occur when the output of one of the elements of a system is not proportional to its input. Nonlinear relationships, according to the new sciences, are the means by which a system adapts to changes in the environment, improves its capacity to remain stable overtime, and also produces innovation at certain degrees of complexity. This is accomplished in feedback loops (circuitous loops that are exponential in effect) of information, energy, and matter that create stable patterns, variations in those patterns, and innovation over time (Lewin, 1997).

Nonlinearity also implies that system "dynamics" are not simply the social tensions created by multiple demands on the environment or even the innovation that proceeds from the visceral urge to survive as a viable competitor. Rather, the system of nonlinear relationships, of which organizations are an element, is inherently both creative and pragmatic as it produces innovation as a way to handle an overload of information, and maintains the stability of the living organization within the broader, changing environment.

Nonlinearity produces a functional paradox in a system of relationships in this regard, one in which stability is maintained by continual and sometimes unpredictable change. Even as the identity and structure of the system strengthens in the persistence of information and energy feedback loops, for example, predictability of future system behavior decreases. The original causes are difficult to discern over time and perhaps no longer even exist in their original states as the system changes in repeated iterations (Rothman, 1997, 26, 29–31). Also, the iterations are not merely repeats of the same information, but rather extend from and to different variables each time, so each "loop" may therefore create a variation of some element in the system.

If certainty is not a realistic goal then decisions based on the need for certainty to achieve other goals also are probably fundamentally ineffective. The approach here, however, is not necessarily to undermine a desire for certainty as much as it is to realign decision making with the realities of a dynamic, nonlinear system. In this regard, decisions are probably better that address what the system is *adapting to* in the present as much as they concern themselves with eliminating historical causes of current conditions (Kiel, 1994). Adaptation can be a conscious *response to* a diverse aggregate of variables and their relationships in the current context rather than only being behavior forced by simple historical causes (Maturana, 2000).

12.2.3 Different Perceptions, Different Responses to Old Problems

The growth of what might be called the "crime ecology" is one example of how making decisions based only on the causes of a problem does not necessarily surpass that problem. The statistic that the United States imprisons more people per capita than any other developed country in the world often alarms both conservative and liberal thinkers, though perhaps for different reasons (UN Center for International Crime Prevention, 1999). For many people, the statistic feels like a social *imbalance* of either too many criminals or too harsh of laws. From a linear perspective the resolution of this imbalance would appear to be either an increase in the severity of the law to discourage criminals or conversely to reduce sentencing to keep prison populations down. From a complexity perspective, however, neither decision necessarily takes into account the social system's adaptive response to the regulatory nature of both approaches. The result is that a flux of a few degrees in the number of people in prison is likely to occur over time as one or the other of the viewpoints becomes dominant and then wanes. Yet regulation of crime in this manner—within the limits of this flux—has not eliminated it or reduced its presence in our lives. Rather crime, and violence in particular, has become woven into the fabric of society, producing a *patterning* of the problem in variations across the social landscape from the media to social policy. Prisons have become a sustaining part of local economies in a number of states. This patterning may be the result of a strategic response to crime that creates self-referential feedback loops that both originate from crime and extend back to it—rather than to more sustainable behaviors or emerging social relationships in the broader system.

This feedback may inhibit the emergence of a social system that has the fundamental capacity to leave crime behind as an evolutionary misfire and embrace other more sustaining behaviors. Instrumental adjustments to regulations or countermeasures framed as "prevention" do not necessarily support the social behaviors that would organize a society with a different future. Likewise, dichotomous approaches to social problems provide little space for recognizing the complex set of relationships from which any phenomena emerge. Nor is recognition of innovative solutions when they arise in new circumstances necessarily encouraged.

Conventional problem solving maintains the illusion that true social change is wrought by a simple adjustment of past circumstances. Yet neither correcting nor preventing historical causes of a problem like crime necessarily address the social imbalance created in its aftermath. Such an imbalance may require its own solutions, including those that are more responsive to the current context and less instrumental than those strategies employed to eliminate historical causes that tend to be both divisive and seem, given the state of the world, largely ineffective.

The patterning of crime—the propagation of cop shows and violent video games, firearms, the economy of prisons, and the proliferation of crime regulations—illustrates the nature of co-evolving social relationships in which elements of the same system adapt to each other. In particular, this widespread patterning illustrates the need for decision makers to consider more than historical causes in correcting the imbalances in society that the crime creates. What caused crime or even what prevents it may be less important than setting a different course for the future, one that is not merely an adaptation to what we hope to leave behind, but rather is an investment in those behaviors and sets of relationships that will create and sustain the kind of peaceful society aspired to.

12.2.4 Cause and Effect Only One Aspect of an Emerging Reality

For the record, the co-evolution of adaptive relationships does not mean that one cannot perceive a cause and effect, but only that the cause and effect do not represent the entire pattern of relationships to which a problem responds. For example, pushing the blue button on the CPU of a computer usually causes it to start. What this simple act does not prove, however, is that pushing the button is the only influence on the computer or that its obedience is the only effect. These are simply the most probable cause and effect and most probably because that is how the machine is engineered by the expectations of it. The issue of causality, however, becomes more complicated when it is applied to live complex environments in which the original causes of events are obscured in the constant iterations of information and feedback in changing and often random contexts. Further, although it is possible to engineer human behavior and outcomes by observing the dynamics of a market or politics, what is engineered, as with the prison example, may not be what we intend. The organization and its system of relationships, may adapt to the repeated acts of regulation and the administration of regulation so that what emerges is not the organization of social dreams, but rather one perfectly adapted to regulation and to the regulation of regulations (Ruhl, 1996; Ruhl and Ruhl, 1997).

12.2.5 Socially Responsible Administration Is Nonlinear and Relational

In conventional decision-making formats, the basis for social engineering is the control of individual behavior according to rules other than those that seem to actually govern the adaptive dynamics of social systems. A distinction is often made between linear administration and the nonlinear live environment so that the first is seen to control the risks inherent in the latter (Goodnow, 1967). Complexity sciences would suggest that a nonlinear and interactive relationship exists between administration and what it manages. Organizational and social behavior, therefore, may be engineered by administrative decisions and decision-making habits of the larger system as much as by the intent to achieve specific goals or behaviors.

12.3 ADAPTATION, DICHOTOMIES, AND INTENTION: FORMING A NEW RELATIONSHIP

12.3.1 WHAT THE ORGANIZATION AND SOCIETY ADAPTS TO IS AFFECTED BY HOW DECISIONS ARE MADE AND IMPLEMENTED

Developing the capacity to respond appropriately to a complex adaptive system is different than monitoring progress only with what is stored in human memory. It also involves being open to the unexpected. Indeed, the quality of adaptive choices must be sustained in each action and interaction in the system rather than only through periodic decisions that are subsequently strategically implemented. Achieving this quality of decision may require a fundamental adjustment in the kind of information sought to affect decisions, as well as an improved sense of timing of decisions to act or intervene. This quality also calls for an adjustment in how the processes by which the intent to act is formed, are interpreted.

The primary concern of Newtonian science reflected in conventional decision making models has been a limitation of information to support decision making to the "right" kind as a way to filter the often contradictory data coming from a dynamic environment (Goerner, 2001; Giddens, 1990; Peat, 2002). This process of filtering seems to be the first act of intentionality—one that creates the activating principles for subsequent iterations in administrative action. Intentionality, however, is limited by historical knowledge only because we choose to glean those elements of the landscape that fit already established models in our memory, not because more information and more diverse fields of options are not available to us.

For example, in suggesting that adaptation involves a response to the environment rather than a mere reaction, it is implied that adaptation can be a reasoned action involving, in particular, a conscious recognition of the relationship of the decision maker to the environment. From a complexity sciences perspective, however, the nature of the response necessarily involves more than simply applying static mental models to the selection of correct variables that support or deny our intentions. The changes in decision making theory, implicit in the new sciences, are perhaps best illustrated by current research in neurobiology.

12.3.2 THE SELF-ORGANIZED BRAIN: THE CHAOTIC FOREGROUND OF INTENTIONALITY

In the model that has dominated the conventional understanding of how decisions are made and executed, the human brain operates similar to a digital computer whose neurons operate as two-state, logical-decision elements organized into networks to compute simple geometric functions (Skarda and Freeman, 1987, 161). In this older computer metaphor, the individual acts as the system operator directing the brain to specific pathways through an implied command structure. Current research, however, characterizes both the brain and the Self as being less disembodied, but rather engaged in cooperative, system-wide nonlinear "chaos" that serves as a means to ensure continual access to previously learned sensory patterns *and* as a means for learning new ones.

The significance of these new findings with respect to decision making practice is that they invert the nature of the relationship between intentionality and information coming from the environment. In the computer model, the brain receives sensory information and then the individual, in a rational, intentional manner, filters out what is germane to the intended goal by applying stored memory and habitual methodological frameworks to how the information is both gathered and interpreted. Information, however, may be processed differently than previously imagined—as neurons fire across the landscape of the brain actively looking for information from which to create new meaning in new contexts, rather than methodically responding to implied demands to pull up data files to compare with the environment.

Neurobiologist Walter Freeman (2000, 209–235) makes a distinction between "passive" intentionality in models of linear causality and more active models suggested in the nonlinear *self-organization* of brain activity. According to Freeman, intentionality involves more than merely passively reacting to sensory information with static models—old or new. As a self-organizing structure, the brain is predisposed to respond to sensory and emotional cues by actively *searching* for new information in both memory and the environment from which intentionality is *then* formed as an act of meaning making (Freeman, 1997, 301). The significance of this distinction between passive and active perception is that it suggests that many management decisions have necessarily been based on counteracting the tendency of the human brain to explore the contextual significance of emotional and sensory information. That is, from a conventional framework, decisions to act are often preconditioned by the need to limit the information the body receives and, in effect, to "retrain" the brain to be rational as the capacity for reason is understood in the linear sciences of Descartes, Newton, and Leibniiz (Ralston, 1992). Modern institutions reflect this struggle of containment as disciplines adapt to linear models of reality and to linear methods for organizing information. As a result, decision makers often find diversity of actors and information contradictory and troubling because of the flood of new data, such diversity produces, and the perceived need to fit it into specific historical categories that may no longer fit the social realities of an evolving system.

12.3.3 Simple Dichotomies Are Not so Simple

From a conventional perspective, the various elements of the social landscape are usually organized into dichotomous relationships (for and against, rich and poor, good and bad, us and them). At first this seems a logical first step in decision making. For one, the presence of dualistic relationships seems to imply that there are clear, if contentious, lines of cause and effect among social actors. Therefore it also seems that good and bad behaviors can be manipulated with a high degree of certainty as to the outcome. Nonlinear science raises doubts as to whether such certainty is possible. Further, pursuing certainty may confine reason to habitual thinking without a true engagement of information flowing to the brain from simple sensory and complex emotional cues.

Decisions that seek to simply "enhance the good," while "eliminating the bad," for example, are not necessarily the most effective in a dynamic and emergent organization. Committing the majority of organizational resources to eliminating all unintended variables is likely to produce an organization defined by what controls these variables and not necessarily by the organization's aspirations. Likewise, creating a gravitational center for organizations from only historically "good" behaviors is likely to produce a rigid system whose virtues soon become obstructive vices in a diverse social landscape.

Newtonian science makes a poignant and dichotomous distinction between reason and emotion (Ralston, 1992). In contemporary neurobiology, however, emotion is identified as an essential property of intentional behavior (Freeman, 2000). This is so because emotional states are *anticipatory* of the need for action in the near future and *provoke* a search by the brain for information from which to determine action in the interplay between perceptions of both evolving conditions and historical memory. Further, this active response differs from instincts or drives that are perceived as *fixed* action patterns released by stimuli in the environment (Freeman, 2000, p. 214). Emotions and reason, therefore, are interdependent elements of one process of reasoning. This does not mean, however, that emotions necessarily define appropriate decisions. It does seem to mean that emotions clue the body and its brain into the presence of emerging patterns of relationship. As a result, blindly ignoring emotional cues marginalizes the brain's ability to initiate and collect a range of information that is both historical *and* contextual and that results in action appropriately situated in the emerging structure of a dynamic system.

Nonlinearity further suggests that related elements of a single, decision-making process cannot necessarily be placed in opposition to each other. Public and private are different realms in the structure of society with differing characteristics. Yet neither exists in isolation of the other. Nor can it be said that one does not affect the other. Likewise, both have equal importance because both provide information for forming goals and action that take the decision maker beyond merely adapting to the problem. Pre-sorting information as it is received according to historical models, bias, and preconceived goals, therefore, is not always the most effective way of gaining information about the broad sets of relationships a problem is attached to. From a complexity sciences perspective, a hyper-rational framework for decision making is replaced by a more thoughtful and direct *process* of goal formation in alignment with the realities of the live environment. Further insights of the sciences of complexity involve an understanding of self-organization, adaptive dynamics, emergence, and scaling.

12.4 RELATIONSHIP DYNAMICS

12.4.1 Self-Organization and Intentionality

Complex systems are said to be self-organizing. Like the brain, they form aggregate relationships and structures from feedback loops of information and energy. Further, there is an accommodation in this organizing as diverse elements and ideas find supportive niches in the evolving social structure. This occurs often without intent—vat least as the term is conventionally understood—as action set into motion by initiating a pre-existing architecture of thoughts and models.

At first glance the phenomenon of self-organization seems to imply an "automatic" society and that, in the course of time, all the elements of a system will achieve harmony as they accommodate each other in a perfect balance. In reality, the necessity of choice remains because a self-organizing system does not necessarily produce the optimal balance, but rather only the one that is dynamically possible given the restraints of contextual relationships and the limits of information available (Bak, 1999). However, the nature of decisions changes as decision makers seek *to optimize the dynamics* in the system, rather than proceeding from the starting viewpoint that a reduction of variables is necessary to produce certainty and ideal outcomes.

12.4.2 Meaning Making

Most healthy organizations recognize that survival is dependent on having up-to-date information about markets, products, policies, practices, and consumer and citizen needs. Conventionally, this need to be current is placed in tension with sustaining the historical order of organizational relationships. Change produced by a new influx of information often feels forced thereby, as if the demands of the environment are imposing discomfort on a stable working group; producing a struggle between maintaining order and the need to adapt. In particular, this is problematic if organizational learning is seen as only the accommodation of new information in conventional top-down or bottom-up structures; this is a view that lacks an attendant recognition of the dynamic processes of meaning making that occur in the transfer of information at and across all levels and in random events.

In considering the nonlinear processes of the brain, it may be said by extension that information is processed at all levels of the organizations—both personal and systemic—and also in each interaction, so that a meaningful congruence between the evolving structure of the organization and the organization's individuals emerge as both become more complex. This accommodation allows both to retain and to strengthen a sense of identity, while at the same time, making sense of and creating from new and often contradictory information. This meaning making is ostensibly more inclusive and therefore more sustainable than simply inculcating collective motivation through administrative channels or periodic pep talks (Finer, 1965).

However, decisions are often made in organizations that confound the nonlinear processes of meaning making and that force meaning to emerge in correspondence with largely unsustainable behaviors, such as fear, for example. At times, this is the result of placing artificial boundaries around what can be talked about in organizations to achieve control of short-term outcomes. Different organizing principles for decisions and action—such as sustainability or inclusion—would necessitate greater degrees of freedom to accommodate difference and to recognize those circumstances from which meaning is made.

12.4.3 Crisis Management that Becomes Habit

In a self-organizing system, information of any sort may ultimately strengthen organizational relationships as the increase in flow through established networks of feedback creates stable patterns and related variations in which to accommodate the new data into established systems of meaning (Mayor-Kress and Barczys, 1995; Johnson and Picton, 1996). An institutional leader might be imagined who introduces fear or paranoia into each decision as a way to manipulate behavior and guarantee outcomes through "crisis management." In time, however, it will become difficult to separate this fear from the day-to-day habits of the organization as fear becomes part of the evolving stable structure. That is, the stability of the organization and its relationships become deeply intertwined with fear or the presence of a crisis. The organization, therefore, becomes most adept at crisis management to the detriment of activities that are more focused on long-range outcomes and program stability.

The paradox perhaps is that a crisis may initially be very real, as is the fear. The challenge for decision makers, however, is not necessarily to drum out the causes of the crisis and eradicate them. The exact causes may be lost in the intricate interplay of nonlinear relationships over many years or even centuries. Rather, the challenge is how to respond to this new reality so that something besides the crisis and its historical antecedents provoke the organization of future relationships—that is, how to proceed to a different future from the new information provided by the break in equilibrium. These nonlinear decisions are crucial to aiding the emergence of an organization that does not collapse under the weight of noxious feedback loops that seem correct only because they are strong, or an organization that develops habits contrary to ethics and social responsibility or in defiance of social realities because it feels threatened by change that is chronically defined as a crisis.

12.4.4 Information Does Not Transform by Itself

The phenomena that more regulation seems to increase both the size of regulating agencies as well as the variation and resiliency of the problem regulated indicate that information alone will not transform an organization, a problem, or its system of relationships (Light, 1995; Ruhl and Salzman, 2003). More information will not necessarily create a more open organization if the primary organizing principle of decision making is survival of the fittest. Nor will innovation emerge if it is not the primary organizing principle of choice making rather than conflict resolution or the control of competition. The key decision involved in sustaining a robust organization in a dynamic environment, therefore, involves a clear choice about what the organization and its larger system of relationships are being given to adapt to and create from. In this way, coherence develops among the goals of the organization, the decisions that are being made, and the emergent nature of its relationships within the organization and across the adaptive field of the broader environment.

12.5 CHOOSING WHAT TO ADAPT TO

12.5.1 THE NEW ADAPTIVE DYNAMICS

An organization that refuses to adapt will not survive long in a dynamic and competitive environment. This is true, of course, but this maxim may be identifying the wrong choice for decisions makers and disregarding the fact that even a choice to ignore change is a response that frames the character of the organization. The choice for leadership is truly not whether the organization will adapt or not adapt. In a complex system, adaptation is the basis of self-organization as differing elements of the landscape accommodate each other around available information. An organization buried in the dark ages is adapting even if it is the minimalist response of "we're not them."

What would seem to be a more effective frame for decision making than "adapt or die" would be a clear expression of what conditions the organization *should* adapt to and further the ability to recognize these conditions when they appear in the normal course of social relationships. The issues may remain the same; a viable organization adapts to that which will sustain it and its environment while a more closed system chooses to adapt to habitual thinking that ultimately depletes the organization's relevancy and, therefore, survivability in a more robust landscape. However, there are other nuances to this choice making for sustainability.

Conventional decision making often narrows the possibilities of action to those that seem to keep organizational goals in approximate balance with a *hostile* environment. Innovation, ethical development, and the maturation of the organization and its individuals may be limited to what seems to maintain this uneasy balance with outsiders. The practice of ethics, for example, often seems to managers to be a good thing, but not one that necessarily has survival value. For ethical condut to be viable, it must have the ability to *organize meaning* in organizations in the way that survival of the fittest has shaped a particular sense of social responsibility and defined the boundaries of decision making in organizations.

The perception that adaptation is foreshadowed by the "survival of the fittest" reduces management decisions to strategic maneuvers for besting other organizations or for avoiding being swallowed up by the competition. The strength of these presumptions is that our experience tells us they are true. Yet, again this historical test of certainty is a passive response to an active environment and limits what administrators and society can intend. Complexity sciences suggest that an organization stands a better chance of optimizing itself in coherence with a broad and sustaining landscape by not limiting its reference only to competition or adapt or die scenarios (Ho and Fox, 1986; Kauffman, 1995; Jantsch, 1980).

Yet, both *coherence* and *optimizing* might suggest only another iteration of an old theme of Newtonian science—that what is being sought is predictability and, therefore, conformity for the sake of maintaining a straight and narrow path toward optimal performance or optimal profits. Indeed, nonlinear mathematical models are being used exactly for that purpose with a high degree of success in business in particular (Anthes, 2003). However, for purposes of mapping a more sustainable and ethical future for society, a different, less defensive disposition on the part of the decision maker is critical if the sciences of complexity are to provide anything new to the process of achieving social goals. From a complexity framework, the phenomenon of coherence allows us to imagine how social and individual goals might emerge together as each is accommodated in the wider and deeper weave of social history; for example, how a basic regard for human rights might co-evolve with administrative and social practice rather than being at odds with it.

In a similar vein, optimizing, as it is used here, implies that an evolutionary leap by an individual produces a response, a challenge, and opportunities across the entire system of relationships. This possibility, however, presents a challenge to decision makers to consider the uses of nonlinear modeling in ways that enhance human potential rather than only maximize short-term goals. What is distinctive about these phenomena—coherence and optimizing—is that they do not exist in isolation, but rather exist in the dynamics among the relationships of a shared, emergent complex system. These shared dynamics do not free individuals of choice making but rather seem to point to choices that take the shared dynamics into account.

Decisions at the leadership level in this regard could create the opportunities for individuals to consciously participate in social evolution by engaging emergence. In a system of dynamically interactive and interdependent relationships, mere profiteering may not sustain the individual any more than it sustains the larger social order. Yet, what is perhaps as problematic as individual greed is for decision makers to explain human behavior in a manner that limits the system's capacity to recognize or generate other behaviors that are not limited to just greed.

Humans do play reactive and habitual games that seem to reduce human capacity for social evolution to merely "avoiding pain" and "seeking pleasure" at the expense of other people. Even if this is a correct assessment of human nature at a particular moment in social evolution, the observation does not provide the possibility of a different future and different behavior. Complexity sciences suggest that adaptive behavior is a process of meaning making rather than only information processing. By allowing for this meaning making capacity, decisions can be made that seek to create the conditions in which evolutionary leaps in the quality of human relationships become possible in the future. The first decision may be to encourage awareness among workers and citizens that a wider range of choices are available other than those that simply defend a particular historical position, such as those that are closer to human aspirations and, therefore, more appropriate to sustaining an emerging system of interdependent relationships than rational-actor models derived from Newtonian science.

Social relationships are more than hostile exchanges tempered by fear, but rather are incidents of adaptation and co-evolution as individuals are accommodated into an evolving system. This adaptation as survival of what *fits* the evolving structure of relationships rather than of the "fittest" makes strategic competition somewhat irrational (Ho and Fox, 1986). Yet it is an enduring rationale for a free market economy that competition creates innovation by forcing organizations to create or die. From the perspective here, innovation appears at certain degrees of complexity as the symmetry of a prior order of thought is broken to accommodate difference in the environment. Complexity—from which resources and innovation emerge—can therefore be produced in countless ways in a system other than competition. The challenge is to learn to recognize and act on these other opportunities when they arise—a practice that contributes to the ongoing viability of the organization and its systemic relationships.

12.5.2 Increasing the Variables Available for Informed Decision Making

In a dynamic system, boundaries are formed by the choices that are made about what to adapt to. That is, feedback loops of information are initiated around certain organizing principles or initial conditions that thicken over time to produce a sense of disconnection between two elements in an emerging system. In making the assumption that emotions are contrary to reason, for example, western philosophy initiated modern management theory, limiting the intake of information to what sustained the boundaries of problem solving based on "objective" methodologies. These initial conditions for the development of complex management structures narrowly framed the meaning of rationality and rational actions resulting in widespread exclusion of "non-rational" actors and circumstances (Peat, 2002). This exclusion is a democratic and ethical issue, but it is also an important issue in sustainability as nonlinear adaptive systems increase their capacity for survivability, robustness, and innovation by accommodating difference.

By making competition the dominant organising principle for survival rather than it being only one of many possibilities, organizations are, in essence, choosing to adapt to what is weakest in other organizations. Further, they are asking an increasingly globalised planet to adapt to the same weak link. This decreases the capacity of the evolving social landscape to adapt to future contingencies—especially those that may be closer to democratic aspirations. The issue is not whether competition is a good or bad thing, but rather whether it is evolutionarily viable to make it the dominant organizing principle of all social organizations.

The adaptive response is often to engage what another organization is lacking to promote the self-image of innovation. What emerges are organizations that orbit each other; locked into trajectories regulated by the weakest components of each. An adaptive field is formed between and among various organizations in these orbits with each seeking to limit the other in some way; therefore narrowing the variables available for choice making to what seems to make this balance possible. Complexity is produced in the interactions in these adaptive fields, but it is likely to be increased complexity around the limitations and their regulations rather than true innovation.

12.5.3 CHOOSING SOMETHING BESIDES THE PROBLEM TO ADAPT TO

In the same manner that private organizations limit their adaptive fields by strategic competition, public service agencies may trap their agencies and their clientele in minimalist adaptive cycles by only seeking to instrumentally fix deficits in the social landscape, without also considering other non-problems that may provide both sustainable solutions and new paths of intent for society. A sustainable organization or institution, characterized by its ability to maintain its fitness (Kaufmann, 1995) in changing circumstances, would seem to require a more varied landscape and a broader diversity of choices to adapt to and gain resiliency from.

As in the case of prisons, attempts to control the environment and increase its predictability may force decisions that merely regulate problems, rather than surpass them. Further, as the focus of problem solving is repeatedly narrowed to finding and eradicating historical causes and their effects, other solutions, not necessarily casually linked to the problem, are marginalized even though these new solutions may be more sustainable in the current contexts. In fact, other non-related variables and behaviors in the landscape may be more expressive of what socially responsible managers want their organizations to become because they are unrelated to the causes of the problem.

Marginalizing these other behaviors or forcing them to conform to regulation meant to control the problem or its perceived causes, however, makes it difficult to imagine where the system of relationships, to which an organization belongs, might be going rather than only projecting where it has been. Indeed, it may appear to administrators that they have no choice but to focus all their attention on finding the causes of a problem. Like competition, the regulation of problems is believed to create a balance among conflicting interests in the environment. As responsible as this focus may appear to be, it often has the effect of creating *problem ecologies*—a system or systems of organizational relationships in which the elements most likely to survive and produce variations are those factors that create and sustain the regulatory framework of the problem (the problem and its variations, the identification and eradication of its causes, the regulation of deviance, research as to the problem, and media portrayal and recording of the problem), and not necessarily those behaviors and relationships that would leave the problem behind (Dennard, 2004).

12.5.4 EQUILIBRIUM: NOT THE FIRST CHOICE

An imbedded ideal in American political theory is that the market provides a non-violent process for achieving social equilibrium (Wolin, 1990). Derived from Newtonian science, the dominant belief has been that homeostasis is equilibrium and a fixed state of equilibrium is the optimal state for survival (Ross, 1922). Among the most profound of the insights from the sciences of complexity is that any system in a state of prolonged equilibrium is, in essence, a dead system. Homeostasis is not a fixed or ideal state but rather a *dynamic process* by which an emerging system of relationships remains viable in a dynamic environment. A system increases its stability by fluctuating between states at the *edge of chaos* and momentary equilibrium (Coveney and Highfield, 1995; Holland, 1995; Casti, 1994). This distinction suggests that decisions must also address the health of the dynamic process by which homeostasis is sustained, rather than only seeking a stable state as a fixed parameter for social action.

12.5.5 EMERGENCE: CHOOSING TO PARTICIPATE

Emergence implies that decision makers are participating in an ongoing act of creation as the organization learns and responds to a changing environment—fluctuating between states of equilibrium and non-equilibrium. At a minimum, emergence implies that decisions to act only on the temporal symptom of a longer and more complex stream of human activity are perhaps not among the wisest. These *crisis decisions* may be responding to the wrong variable in the emerging social landscape. The perceived crisis may not fully define what is happening in the broader set of system relationships. Instead, it may merely signal that *something* is happening. The decision may be premature as well, or it may fail to take into account that the offending behavior is the product of complex relationships that are not readily apparent and that are still affecting each other.

Emergence has been described as the appearance of unforeseen qualities from the self-organizing interaction of large numbers of objects that cannot be understood by studying any one object (Rogers, 1993, 1436). This condition of an emerging system has implications for how we perceive and react to individual behaviors in organizations and in civic culture. The strength of an organization is often thought to be related to its ability to change with respect to its initial intentions. This strength is dependent on the accumulation of information, power, and common and undisputed goals at all levels of the organization. Yet, the conventional dichotomy between weak and strong elements does not exist in reality because the characteristic of each element has a unique role in sustaining the evolving system. Nor is strict conformity by individuals necessarily a healthy state for organizations, that is, if we assume the need for inequality and conformity is likely to produce the opposite of what it desired, such as instabilities in an organization. Rigidity puts the organization out of balance with the rest of the system of relationships to which it belongs.

Further, the appropriate action is not necessarily to correct the instability by bringing it more in line with the rigid structure it is offsetting. It is likely that this action will increase the number of instances of instability because the initial conditions for its occurrence have not changed and indeed have become even more complex. This is what is meant when it is said that robust systems tend to operate in far-from-equilibrium states; that is, a stability in one part of the system will produce an instability in another as a functional way to keep the system stable by sustaining the system's capacity to accommodate change in the environment (Bak, 1999). A more reasoned response to instability, one in line with the dynamic realities of the system, may be to adjust the rigidity to minimize the degree of instability in the system by participating in the process of sustaining homeostasis rather than merely trying to create an artificial equilibrium.

Yet, this counter adjustment is not the only possible response and may not always be the most appropriate. The nonlinear dynamics that produce continual trade-offs between stable and unstable states suggest that the timing of decisions is also important. The information available to a decision maker, cued to nonlinear patterns and processes, includes knowledge of the dynamical state of the organization and its environment. A state of "chaos" in social relationships may signal less of a need to reinstate order, as it signals the emergence of multiple possibilities for new action from which sustainable social change may emerge.

12.5.6 TIMING IS EVERYTHING

The sun goes down every day and with remarkable predictability rises again in the morning. Events in society and its organizations are perhaps not so regular as the rising and setting of the sun, and yet, administrators do observe patterns of behavior over time that appear stable. But they are stable only because of continuing system dynamics. The challenge for decision makers, therefore, is not simply to decide where the stability is and then replicate it, as if time has suddenly come to a standstill, but rather to make appropriate adaptive choices at those frequent times of both uncertainty and opportunity when the system is reorganizing to accommodate change.

The phenomena of emergence and self-organization change the classic notion that organizations are stationary until set into motion by management action. The decision is not based on whether the organization decides to participate in change or to ride it out; instead, the decision is derived from the question: how do individuals within the organization participate meaningfully in an unfolding and often ambiguous set of circumstances? Participation in an emerging organizational landscape also creates the need for interventions that are timed carefully and with a full awareness of what is happening *dynamically* within the system.

The flux between states of temporary equilibrium and far-from-equilibrium states in a robust system is linked to the increasing complexity of the landscape. When more information is available to the system than it can accommodate, a symmetry break or bifurcation occurs; that is, a point in time when "in the same breath," so to speak, the system is "unorganizing" and re-organizing to accommodate the overload. It is at this juncture that variations occur (that may also be innovative), and also the point at which choices can be made about what the organization, and its system of relationships, is going to adapt to and what action might increase the vitality of the social landscape.

In the case of social problems like corruption, rigid controls made at bifurcation points that are usually identified as a crisis or as increased complexity around a problem, may force variations of the problem rather than an eradication of it (Dennard, 2004). This is the case because the choice to exercise zero tolerance at this sensitive stage of reorganization means the choice has been made to encourage the full system of relationships to adapt to the problem, rather than to some more sustaining behavior in the environment, or to emerging relationships that may move the enterprise beyond corruption rather than adapting to it. In many cases, this may involve decisions that are less of a response to the problem and more an expression of the intent to proceed along different pathways that are provided by the opportunity of bifurcation.

In a nonlinear system of interdependent relationships it may be counterintuitive to simply do the opposite as an adaptive response to a problem. To merely counter a widespread corruption with anti-corruption programs, for example, assumes that a self-organizing system makes choices between the differing sides of a perceived and philosophical dichotomy, rather than responding to information more generally. An intent to surpass corruption as a viable evolutionary behavior must recognize the inclusive nature of system dynamics and respond appropriately.

12.5.7 SCALING AND BOUNDARIES

An equally difficult challenge—aside from learning to recognize system dynamics—is to recognize that complex systems emerge through numerous bifurcations that, depending on what variable or variables initiate the reorganization, may result in a disconnection between the original purposes of the organization and subsequent growth in system complexity. Scaling represents the process by which systems maintain proportionality as they expand, while breaking into variations when the complexity cannot be sustained by the original structure (Bak, 1999; Kauffman, 1995). Without a conscious awareness of this process by which new information is managed in an emerging system, decisions makers can easily ignore boundaries that have formed between the original intent of the organization and those variations that emerge from its complexity.

The *administration* of regulations is easily disconnected from the original intent of surpassing social problems because the choice has been made to increase organizational complexity around the regulations and their compliance (Ruhl and Salzman, 2003). From a conventional perspective, the implementation of regulations constitutes the fulfillment of the original intent of the law. Therefore, it seems to make sense that, as regulations fail to achieve their intended purposes, we make them even more explicit and increase the administrative structure involved in their implementation and enforcement (Ruhl, 1996; Ruhl and Ruhl, 1997).

Instabilities in a system of regulation, however, are produced by *increased complexity* not necessarily only by an increase in non-compliance or because regulations are inadequate (Ruhl, 2003). Because the system is responding *to the complexity* and not to the specifics of the regulatory information, artificially increasing the numbers and severity of regulations to create certainty is likely to produce even more instability until the repeated response creates an imperative for both the problem and its regulation in the system. "How do we solve this problem" is perhaps a question that is best renewed at each bifurcation point as new information and new opportunities emerge.

12.6 CHOICES THAT MATTER: NONLINEAR ETHICS

Linear logic makes it seem impossible to address more than one aspect of an evolving culture at any given time without deviating from a selected path or goal. A tension between ethical behavior and the market has always existed as a result; such a tension where ethics are weighed against profit and the need to support a robust economy has, in essence, created a dichotomy between ethical practice and business imperatives. Complexity principles suggest both the possibility and the imperative for ethical practice in decision making in both public and private organizations.

A stable organization is one that achieves coherence within a larger set of emerging relationships. Yet coherence is achieved, renewed, and thereby sustained by participating in continuing cycles of change as a single process with stable and unstable characteristics. The practice of ethics would seem to require a similar coherence as normal administrative practice is brought in line with the aspirations for creating a responsible and responsive society. Organizational choices therefore cannot be segregated into "ethical" and "practical" decisions. Rather, each decision must be made by individuals who are cognizant of its ethical implications and who are aware of what manner of adaptive relationships the decision is spawning.

Nonlinear dynamics also seems to consider what constitutes ethical behavior in a system of emergent and adaptive relationships. Complexity ethics would seem to involve a concern, not only for individual behavior, but also for the aggregate effect of an organization and its practices on an environment, and indeed on the future capacity of the system to emerge and adapt appropriately. At a minimum, complexity ethics involves making choices that do not merely create tension among perceived opposites and then mediate its resolution, but which promote a creative dialogue among diverse elements seeking a meaningful niche in a shared system.

12.7 DECISION MAKING AS ADAPTIVE CHOICE MAKING

In the introduction, a good decision is defined in a rather linear way; that is, one that marshals the correct resources to achieve a certain outcome and that eliminates roadblocks that hamper goal achievement. Further, a good decision is one that increases the ability of the organization to garner future resources while stabilizing a productive and ethical work culture, one with both the capacity and will for compliance and innovation. This definition, however, takes on more vitality when placed within the dynamic framework of a complex adaptive system.

12.7.1 MARSHALLING APPROPRIATE RESOURCES: WHAT IS APPROPRIATE?

Time, materials, and money are resources that decision makers need to carry the flow of activity in an organization. However, this trinity is not the only flow possible nor does it exclude the possibility of co-existing with less linear resources that promote social goals. The possibility of coherence would imply that more predictable flows like money could emerge in correspondence with less measurable but equally present variables, such as a disposition towards human rights. The critical distinction would seem to be the willingness and capacity of decision makers to imagine and value this emerging coherence as a primary variable of social organization rather than certainty alone.

Yet employing complexity principles to redefine social coherence is an exercise in subtlety. The disposition of the decision maker and the willingness to provide citizens and employees with models for interaction (that do not simply reduce individuality and difference to produce an acceptable coherence in management practice) are elemental to opening up opportunities for greater freedom for individuals, stability for social relationships, and meaningful participation in the emergence of society that the insights from complex science may offer. Coherence may not be the appropriate strategic goal; instead, a more appropriate intent may be participating in and honoring the *process of emergence* from which coherence arises in acts that both strengthen society and create from its differences.

Indeed, long-term sustainability requires diversity in resources and, in particular, the capacity to recognize and act on new resources as they appear rather than being dependent only on old ones. Decisions that engage, rather than merely seek to control, a system's complexity, provide access to a broader range of choices and opportunities to produce new resources. Increasing flows of money may not be enough to ensure an organization's survival if the money has become disconnected from some more sustaining purpose, or if it results in marginalizing other behaviors that would produce more stable social relationships over time.

12.7.2 ELIMINATING ROADBLOCKS OR LEARNING FROM THEM?

Framing action according to the competitive relationship among dichotomous elements of a system may be counterproductive from a complexity perspective. For one, choosing to destroy the competition may not recognize the interdependent nature of organizations that share a common adaptive domain. Secondly, instrumental action often ignores the possibility that a roadblock may be an instability created by rigidity in another part of the system, so that its elimination is likely to produce more instability as the system responds. Thirdly, the organization may be forced to adapt to the roadblock to eliminate it—creating a system in which the roadblock has become part of a stable, evolving structure.

Eliminating a barrier to goal achievement therefore involves making choices that allow the system to move past a problem and learn from it without becoming attached to it. Broadening the parameters for decision making is perhaps the first step to achieving this—allowing ourselves to consider information that is not clearly linked causally to the problem, to listen to, not only differing opinions, but to differing sources of information, and being clear about what adaptive behavior our choices are likely to create in our system of relationships. This may mean giving up certain dichotomies, like the ones separating emotion and reason or politics and administration, for example, that limit our ability to see beyond the short and conflicted space between them.

12.7.3 INCREASING CAPACITY TO GARNER FUTURE RESOURCES: DOING MORE THAN ONE THING AT ONCE

Accruing current resources should also increase the capacity of the organization to garner resources in the future. In this regard, good decisions are multidimensional—they have a texture and quality to them that is enduring. But again, realizing such a decision requires not only the ability to see where the organization or institution has been, but also where it is going and what new landscapes are appearing on the horizon. In effect, it involves allowing the brain its full capacity to generate a meaningful response based on stored knowledge and a full gamut of new information.

12.7.4 STABILIZING A PRODUCTIVE AND ETHICAL WORK FORCE

The complexity of organizational relationships is mindboggling when first considered: individuals with divergent histories, cultures, personalities, and value structures converging somehow to accomplish a single goal. The effort implied in focusing all this conflicted energy for the purposes of the organization seems gargantuan. Indeed, it is a formidable task if the approach is to use a singular goal to minimize the differences among individuals so that the culture that emerges is essentially a bureaucratic one. For instance, this type of approach would include practicing those habits of interaction that pull people away from broader and deeper fields of knowledge and experience, and instead, focus them on the instrumental tasks involved in achieving a specific outcome. This approach limits, not only the development of individuals within the organization, but also the kinds of information available to the organization and the types of decisions that can be made about future action. Complexity cannot be rejected if leaders are to activate and sustain organizational and civic cultures that have the capacity for adaptive choice making, innovation, and social responsibility.

Decisions that seek only compliance are therefore inadequate in considering the possibilities of complexity, rather than only its limitations. Institutional stability, from a complexity perspective, depends no more on compliance with formal rules than it depends solely on boundary-spanning behavior. Dysfunctional extremes, for example, may emerge if a framework for management involves creating a dichotomy between "rational" and "irrational" actors in a system of adaptive relationships. Stability is in the ongoing dynamical relationship between innovation and the evolving character of the organization. It is therefore more important to sustain the dialogue between conventional and unconventional thinkers, rather than to set them in opposition to each other or to marginalize either one. A simple decision to punish deviance or reward creativity may be inadequate or even destructive to critical social relationships when the more important contribution to the viability of the organization is to maintain those relationships.

It is a common complaint among academics, for example, that when they begin their careers they are often pigeonholed according to their earliest successful theory and, as the years pass, it becomes increasingly difficult to escape the character they have been cast to play, to learn anything new, or to change their minds as a result of new knowledge (Boggs, 1983). Similarly, in organizations, a person may earn the role of "court jester," "rabble rouser," or a host of other niches that seem to fit some need of the organizational culture but limit the adaptive space of the individual. Ironically, when a person leaves the organization, the new replacement often gets assigned the same role. Hiring someone to shake up an organizational culture that is too conformist or too closed to promote innovation again ignores the adaptive dynamics of the broader system of relationships at work in the organization. That is, individual behavior never exists separately from the set of relationships to which it becomes attached.

For an organization to be open and responsive, with the capacity to make meaning and innovation from a perpetually changing adaptive landscape, it must possess the collective ability and consciousness to regulate its own processes. Again, this implies a more active and aware response to the environment than is possible if management is simply adjusting the ballast to maintain an orderly march toward compliance. In other words, there must be an emergent coherence between administrative practice and the emerging culture, not merely between administration and a disembodied goal whereby the culture is merely a means to an end.

By encouraging ongoing meaning making and the creative coherence it produces, decision makers align themselves with the evolutionary process by which both stability and innovation emerges—a feat not possible by the implementation of any rigid set of behaviors strategically enforced or manipulated through incentives. Incentives work, but what are usually stabilized are the incentives themselves, the need for them, and the unsustainable assumption that human nature demands a bribe—regardless of our intent otherwise.

12.8 PRAXIS: COHERENCE IN THE DETAILS

12.8.1 STABILITY THROUGH PRACTICE

Complexity sciences suggest a more direct approach to creating productive and cooperative working and civic conditions: to tap all the potential in the organization to both create and fulfill goals that are sustainable by the organization's emerging set of relationships. Goals are important as the means by which society and organizations form their identity and their relationships; however, goals emerging from the evolving character of the relationships among strongly defined individuals operating at full personal capacity are more sustainable than those merely implemented through behavioral controls.

Further, a lesson from recent advances in neurobiology indicates as well that allowing a high degree of freedom among individuals may promote the appearance of evolutionary leaps in innovation, problem solving, or personal development as each is granted the space to search among various networks of meaning and information not merely those that seem appropriate from a linear and historical perspective. The dynamic nature of the thought process indicates that it may be the nature of individuals to be constantly searching for meaning rather than being possessed only by a Hobbesian need for certainty.

Decisions therefore are most appropriate when they encourage organizational relationships that are not only open and communicative, but also forgiving. The new sciences of complexity provide decision makers the insight that certainty is not merely an unachievable goal, but one that, if instrumentally implemented, results in a distortion of system dynamics and a proliferation of those variables they seek to control. This insight, in turn, provides the opportunity for helping develop social and organizational relationships that are exploratory rather than defensive and that enhance both individual identity and the amount of talent and information flowing through the organization at all levels.

The maintenance of dynamic rather than reactive relationships is an ongoing consideration of a *complex decision maker*. Opportunities that would strengthen dynamic relationships are often missed because we wait for the big moment—the election or the crisis—to act although the phenomena of self-organization and emergence suggest that the conditions of the future can be considered in the most mundane of circumstances and in routine actions. The most productive opportunities for adding to the texture of organizational culture and its ability to make appropriate evolutionary decisions would seem to be those in which individuals are continuously engaged in making meaning out of ambiguous events rather than being forced into fearful corners by an expectation of certainty and conformity.

12.8.2 MEANING MAKING AND SYSTEM COHERENCE

Individuals process information by creating meaning from change. However, this does not imply that leadership is responsible for creating shared meaning that is thereafter inculcated through behavioral controls. Rather, from a complexity perspective, coherence is generated between the organization and individuals across many personal fields of history and contextual information. This coherence can be achieved perhaps in no other way except by individuals who seek a meaningful niche within the evolving system and by their personal ability to respond to changes, be transformed by them, and make meaning from them.

This meaning-making process by which coherence emerges among different elements of an evolving system suggests that nothing in the framework of an individual can be considered irrelevant or inappropriate. Because memory is a complex aggregation of countless experiences, one aspect of an individual's life cannot realistically be separated from another, just as a strand of thread cannot be pulled from a woven cloth without destabilizing its integrity. That is, for individuals to "fit" into the emerging social structure in a stable fashion the whole of their experience must be in continual adjustment at some level. Excluding differing aspects of individuals' experiences will, at some level, produce instability in the organization or the individuals as they struggle to either exclude or include the realities of their existence. The instabilities can be informative and produce openings for both deeper coherence and innovation—that is, if they are not stabilized as problems instead. The complexity of individuals implies several things for decision makers about the nature of information.

1. *All information is potentially useful.* Information available for decision making may not always be strictly on topic. Information appearing in social contexts may signal a process of meaning making or opportunities for coherence among dynamic actors and not simply be extraneous or emotional data. Given the nonlinear and dynamical relationship between emotions and reason, for example, an emotional display may not indicate inappropriate behavior on an individual's part but may, in circumstances where the response has not been assigned as an habitual role a person plays, be a cue for considering what rigidities exist in the system that would provoke this response. It may indicate the emergence of patterns that require both thought and action.

2. *Suppression of difference creates instabilities, not difference* itself (Teilhard, 1959). An individual's unconventional experience is not necessarily an impediment to goal achievement, but rather may provide another source of information—one with a different frame of reference than habitual logic. Further, attempting to marginalize difference in a dynamic, complex, and adaptive system that maintains its vitality by accommodating difference is likely to produce ongoing instability.

3. *Decisions can create more than one outcome.* Contemporary administrators are perhaps aware that decisions generally have good and bad outcomes. However, from a complexity perspective, any decision can produce adaptive change across multiple levels in the social system. It therefore seems possible that organizations can define goals in correspondence with the environment, affect these goals in an efficient manner while workers and citizens mature and develop within the adaptive dynamics of organizations—given that decisions made recognize this multidimensional possibility.

4. *Ambiguity is a good thing.* A sustainable work culture possesses the resiliency to accept ambiguity, recognizing it as the condition that often creates openings for diversity, new learning opportunities, and creative action. This creative resiliency is aided by decisions that recognize what individuals in the organization are being asked to adapt to. The structure of such a decision, in turn, depends on an awareness of opportunities present in the context for exceeding past behaviors—even if the new opportunities are not linked casually to the source of concern. This awareness allows decision makers to tap *local knowledge*—new solutions and new resources germane to real-time contexts (Kauffman, 1995). In turn, individual identity and evolutionary capacity are strengthened as they are asked to contribute a full range of gifts rather than only their problems.

12.9 PROCESS HABITS FOR DECISION MAKING

Complexity sciences provide decision makers a new framework for information gathering and for framing intent and action. However, the methodology for employing this new conceptual framework is necessarily less specific than it may have been with a more linear science. This is true because certainty is not a completely attainable goal and because the live, emerging, and dynamic environment is as important as historical memory in framing decisions. Therefore, decision makers must learn to process often-contradictory information, rather than glean out only that which fits a specific model. In this vein, complexity mathematics has produced some helpful observation tools for understanding system dynamics and gauging emerging patterns in complex systems like the market. As useful and illustrative as they are however, these new models do not free individuals from making evolutionary choices—those that involve more than calculating a risk to stability, program goals, or financial bets.

Process habits are perhaps one way to characterize the nature of complex decision making. Such habits may include:

1. Focusing on the process of change rather than only the problem and its historical causes
2. Keeping in mind that events, individuals, and organizational structures are emergent rather than fixed
3. Tending to emotional cues—neither responding too quickly nor suppressing them
4. Temporarily suspending judgment as to the quality and relevance of all information accepting the possibility that information may be historically irrelevant but contextually important because it expresses the current aggregation of relationships and further because it may provide a new pathway for action that moves society beyond its problems rather than adapting to them
5. Thinking without dichotomies so it is possible to see the dynamic nonlinear relationships among opposites
6. Looking beyond individual behavior for the dynamics of emerging relationships
7. Recognizing one's own intimate relationship with the emerging social environment

12.10 SUMMARY

Far from exasperating our need to make decisions and set goals for the future, complexity sciences provide a framework for producing more coherence between administrative action and the emergence of sustainable organizations and civic society through conscientious, ethical, and reasoned choice making.

Further, complexity principles suggest the possibility of creating goals in alignment with the broad set of human relationships rather than in opposition to it. Additionally, this coherence can be achieved in practice, rather than only through the implementation of strategic programs and regulations. This praxis is the process by which coherence is gained in the system by putting the transformative work of emergence and adaptation above the need for certainty.

The new sciences of complexity challenge decision makers, not only to become comfortable with uncertainty and also with experimentation, but also to lose their biases for selecting information from which to construct decisions. The complex decision maker is no longer the engineer of the ideal organization, operating according to fixed rules as a response to an unstable environment, but rather an aware and ethical participant in the emergence of a stable and creative society.

REFERENCES

Abramovitz, J., Valuing nature's sciences, In *State of the World 2001*, Brown, L. and Stark, L., Eds., Worldwatch Institute Books, London, pp. 95–125, 1991.
Anthes, G., Agents of change, *Computer World*, 37(4), 426–427, 2003.
Bak, P., *How Nature Works: The Science of Self-Organized Criticality*, Copernicus Books, London, 1999.
Boggs, C., *Intellectuals and the Crisis of Modernity*, State University of New York Press, New York, 1933.
Casti, J., *Complexification: Explaining a Paradoxical World Through the Science of Surprise*, HarperCollins, New York, 1994.
Coveney, P. and Highfield, R., *Frontiers of Complexity: The Search for Order in a Chaotic World*, Fawcett Columbine, New York, 1995.
Dennard, L., *Out of the Laboratory and into Complexity: The Limits of Regulation in Anti-Corruption Efforts. Paper Presented at Conference on Complexity and Global Governance*, Cork, Ireland, 2004.

Finer, H., Administrative responsibility, In *Bureaucratic Power in National Politics*, Rourke, F. E., Ed., Little & Brown, Boston, 1965.

Freeman, W., Nonlinear neurodynamics of intentionality, *Journal of Mind and Behavior*, 18(2–3), 291–304, 1997.

Freeman, W., Emotion is essential to all intentional behaviors, In *Emotion, Development and Self-Organization: Dynamic Systems Approaches to Emotional development*, Lewis, M. and Granic, I., Eds., Cambridge University Press, Cambridge, U.K., pp. 209–235, 2000.

Giddens, A., *The Consequences of Modernity*, Stanford University Press, Stanford, CA, 1990.

Goerner, S., *After the Clockwork Universe: The Emerging Science and Culture of Integral Society*, Floris Books, London, 2001.

Goodnow, F. J., *Politics & Administration*, Russell & Russell, New York, 1967.

Ho, M. and Fox, S. W., *Evolutionary Processes & Metaphors*, Wiley, Chichester, 1986.

Holland, J., *Hidden Order: How Adaptation Builds Complexity*, Addison-Wesley, Reading, MA, 1995.

Jantsch, E., *The Self-Organizing Universe: Scientific & Human Implications of The Emerging Paradigm of Evolution*, Pergamon Press, New York, 1980.

Johnson, J. and Picton, P., How to train a neural network, *Complexity*, 1(6), 13–16, 1996.

Kauffman, S., *The Origins of Order: Self-Organization and Selection in Evolution*, Oxford University Press, New York, 1995.

Kiel, D., *Managing Chaos and Complexity in Government*, Jossey-Bass Inc, San Francisco, 1994.

Lewin, R., *Complexity: Life at the Edge of Chaos*, University of Chicago Press, Chicago, 1997.

Light, P. C., *Thickening Government: Federal Hierarchy & the Diffusion of Accountability*, Brookings, Washington DC, 1995.

Mayer-Kress, G. and Barczys, C., The global brain as an emergent structure from the world wide computing network and its implications for modeling, *The Information Society*, 11(1), 1–28, 1995.

Maturana, H. 2000. Metadesign. http://www.inteco.cl/articulos/metadesign.htm (accessed April 20, 2004.)

Mucha, T., The wisdom of the anthill, *Business-2.0*, 3(11), 59–62, 2002.

Peat, F. D., *From Certainty to Uncertainty: The Story of Science and Ideas in the Twentieth Century*, Joseph Henry Press, London, 2002.

Ralston, J. S., *Voltaire's Bastards: The Dictatorship of Reason in the West*, The Free Press, New York, 1992.

Rawls, J., *A Theory of Justice*, Rev, Belknap Press, New York, 1999.

Rogers, W. H., Where environmental law and biology meet: of panda's thumbs, statutory sleepers, and effective laws, *University of Colorado Law Review*, 65(25), 1436–1453, 1993.

Ross, E., *Social Control: A Survey of the Foundation of Order*, Macmillan, New York, 1922.

Rothman, T., Irreversible differences, *The Sciences*, 26, 29–31, 1997, (July/August).

Ruhl, J. B., The fitness of law: using complexity theory to describe the evolution of law and society and its practical meaning for democracy, *Vanderbilt Law Review*, 49, 1407–1461, 1996.

Ruhl, J. B. and Ruhl, H. J., The arrow of the law in complex administrative states: using complexity theory to reveal the diminishing returns and increased risk the burgeoning of law poses to society, *UC Davis Law Review*, 30, 405–446, 1997.

Ruhl, J. B. and Salzman, J., Mozart & the red queen: the problem of regulatory accretion in the administrative state, *Georgetown Law Journal*, 91, 757–802, 2003.

Schwartz, John. Taking Advantage of Chaos to Find Stability and Maintain Control. Washington Post, (July 4): A3, 1994.

Skarda, C. A. and Freeman, W. J., How brains make chaos in order to make sense of the world, *Behavioral and Brain Sciences*, 10, 61–195, 1987.

Teilhard de Chardin, P., *The Phenomenon of Man*, Harper & Row, New York, 1959.

United Nations Office on Drug and Crime, Centre for International Crime Prevention, *Seventh United Nation Survey on Crime Trends and Operations of Criminal Justices Systems*, United Nations Publications, New York, 1999.

Wolin, S., *The Presence of the Past: Essays on the State and the Constitution*, John Hopkins University Press, Baltimore, 1990.

Ziman, J., The economics of scientific knowledge: a rational choice neo-institutionalist theory of science, *Interdisciplinary Science Review*, 28(2), 150–152, 2003.

Decision Making in Interdisciplinary Studies

William H. Newell

CONTENTS

13.1   Introduction...245
13.2   The Steps in the Interdisciplinary Process..248
      13.2.1   Defining the Problem..249
      13.2.2   Determining Relevant Disciplines...250
      13.2.3   Developing a Command of Each Discipline..253
      13.2.4   Gathering Disciplinary Knowledge, Studying the Problem,
              and Generating Insights..253
      13.2.5   Identifying Conflicts in Insights, Illuminating Their Source,
              and Evaluating Them...255
      13.2.6   Creating Common Ground 257
      13.2.7   Identifying Linkages among Disciplines...260
      13.2.8   Constructing and Modeling a More Comprehensive Understanding..................261
      13.2.9   Testing the More Comprehensive Understanding...262
13.3   Conclusion...262
References...263

13.1 INTRODUCTION

A few years ago, this chapter could not have been written. Definitions of interdisciplinary studies had not been operationalized with sufficient specificity to even identify the requisite types, styles, or processes of decision making involved. The field of interdisciplinary studies had an emerging consensus definition—"interdisciplinary studies may be defined as a process of answering a question, solving a problem, or addressing a topic that is too broad or complex to be dealt with adequately by a single discipline or profession... IDS draws on disciplinary perspectives and integrates their insights through construction of a more comprehensive perspective" (Klein and Newell, 1996, 393–394). But the process itself had not been adequately identified. Indeed, there is some opposition within the field to any greater specificity on the grounds that it might constrain freedom of activity or suggest objectivist modernism. Others, however, believe the field cannot advance or gain greater acceptance until it specifies how one draws on disciplinary perspectives and especially how one integrates their insights.

The nature of the debate over the definition of interdisciplinary studies shifted with the 2001 publication of my "A Theory of Interdisciplinary Studies," (Newell, 2001) along with responses from five prominent interdisciplinary scholars.[*] In that article, I advanced the claim that interdisciplinary study is mandated by complexity and proposed generic steps in the interdisciplinary process required to address that complexity. Since then, attempts to operationalize the interdisciplinary process, such as the interdisciplinary studies assessment instrument developed by Wolfe and Haynes (2003) for the Association for Integrative Studies, have made explicit use of the steps identified in the theory.[†] While readers should keep in mind that those steps may well undergo some alteration as the process is vetted within the professional literature on interdisciplinarity, the theory is as yet the only one available to explain the process and thus will form the basis for this chapter.

The literature on complex systems theory has, if anything, been even more fragmented than that on interdisciplinary studies. Certainly, no consensus definition of complexity has yet emerged, and the various sub-literatures have grown out of diverse disciplines (e.g., computer science, meteorology, mathematics, biology, chemistry) that lead theorists in different directions. Indeed, one might say the field itself is emerging. Even so, if interdisciplinary study is understood to focus on individual complex systems, then an examination of decision making within interdisciplinary studies ought to be informed by any available insights into complexity in general. The difficulty is that decision making is a distinctively human enterprise, yet the disciplines listed above from which complex systems theories emerged are all in the natural, not the social, sciences. Jack Meek and I have contended that this natural science legacy has shaped complex systems theory in ways that make it less than ideally suited to the human sciences (Newell and Meek, 1997). Worse, early attempts to apply the theory to humans and their institutions drew uncritically from the literature on complex systems, applying it directly instead of adapting it from theory designed for non-living systems or for living, non-human systems. A few years ago, I attempted to sketch out the applicability of complex systems theory to human systems in general (Newell, 2003). More recently, Elizabeth McMillan (2004) has published a compatible assessment of its applicability to human organizations in particular. It is primarily from these sources that the insights of this chapter into complexity in interdisciplinary decision making are drawn.

The complex systems characterizing the problems studied by interdisciplinarians (Klein, 2003) have many variables, typically organized into sub-systems (each of which is studied by a different discipline). The relationships between variables in different sub-systems are fewer, weaker, and more nonlinear, while relationships between variables within each sub-system are more numerous, stronger, and less nonlinear. The relationships between sub-systems are strong enough to make the behavior of each sub-system react to variables in the other, connected sub-systems—making the overall system unpredictable in the long-term—yet weak enough to give each sub-system some short-term stability and the overall system some limited short-term predictability. The resulting balance between order and disorder, consistency and novelty, and stability and change may shift over time and differ from one complex system to another, but all human systems that persist necessarily avoid both excessive fluctuations (else they end in revolution or disintegrate) and excessive rigidity (else they fail to adapt and become obsolete).

What is offered in this chapter is an idealized model for individual interdisciplinary decision making about such complex issues. It is a theory-based strategy for addressing any particular complex issue, not a description of current practice. It could hardly be otherwise, considering the current ad hoc approach to almost all decision making regarding actual complex issues. Some generalizations are starting to emerge from the literature on organizations as complex systems about how to approach complex systems in general, but that literature (hence the generalizations emerging from it) ignores the contributions of specialized expertise that disciplines provide. After all, that literature is inspired by complex systems theory, which deliberately ignores the distinctive characteristics of any particular complex system, as it critiques the discipline

---

[*] See responses in the same volume by Bailis, Klein, Mackey, Carp, and Meek as well as a reply by Newell.

[†] See also Meek's (2001) application to public administration.

of management. And while the management discipline engages in sporadic cross-disciplinary borrowing from disciplines such as psychology, economics, and sociology, it rarely undertakes a fully interdisciplinary examination of even the most complex managerial problem. None of these literatures makes use of literature on interdisciplinary studies. It is the contention of this chapter that interdisciplinary study, appropriately informed by complex systems theory, offers an effective approach to decision making regarding individual complex systems. Considering the prevalence of complex problems—in our lives, in business, in society as a whole, and in the international realm—decision making in interdisciplinary studies is as important as it is under-examined.

Idealized models in general are now under attack by postmodernists, postcolonialists, post-structuralists, critical theorists, feminists, etc., as obsolete relics of the modernist agenda (with its attendant white, male, capitalist, imperialistic biases), so some justification of my approach is in order. Interdisciplinary work is increasingly carried out by teams, and it is important to acknowl-edge and address the additional layer of challenges represented by power differences (e.g., North–South, male–female, hetero–gay, Caucasian–other races, able bodied–disabled) among participants in the interdisciplinary process. But it only muddies our understanding of interdisciplinarity to conflate such power differences with the cognitive challenges inherent in drawing critically on different "disciplinary" perspectives and integrating their insights into a more comprehensive, holistic understanding. The way to ensure they do not become conflated is to focus on the solo interdisciplinarian, as is done in this chapter. Even so, one's social location influences one's cognitive processes, hence the interdisciplinary work of even solo interdisciplinarians has a social as well as a cognitive component. But in principle one could look at the cognitive processes of different solo interdisciplinarians developing their own comprehensive models of the same complex problem and determine empirically the size and nature of the social influences on their models because those interdisciplinarians inevitably occupy different social locations. It is my contention that, once social location variables are held constant, we will discover that there are many similarities and probably a few notable differences in the decision making processes of interdisciplinarians. Those anticipated similarities are the focus of this chapter, though potentially significant differences are pointed out.

Another source of these critiques of idealized models is epitomized in Lyotard's (1984) state-ment: "Simplifying to the extreme, I define postmodern as incredulity towards metanarratives" (xxiv). The concern is with grand, all-encompassing stories, especially those that claim some kind of transcendent and universal truth, because they miss the heterogeneity of human experience. Such critics prefer small local narratives—what Lyotard calls "petit récits"—that validate multiple theoretical perspectives. Yet the idealized model set out in this chapter represents just such a challenge to privileging any one perspective and its claim to transcendent truth. Instead, the process described in the model gives both a rationale and a procedure for doing precisely what these critics wish: it validates multiple perspectives. And the more comprehensive understanding at which it arrives is small and local, in that it is temporary and tentative, and limited in time and space rather than universal because it focuses on a single complex problem. While one could argue that the model itself is a metanarrative, the same can be said of postmodernism itself (Habermas, 1985).

Finally, I should point out that one need not embrace complex systems theory, my minority view of disciplines as a reflection of the portion of reality they study, nor a constructivist realist ontology [see, for example, Varela and Harré (1996) and Cupchik (2001)] to utilize the steps in the interdisciplinary process and appreciate their implications for decision making in interdisciplinary studies. I provide the complex systems framework because it provides a rationale for best practice techniques that are widely accepted among interdisciplinarians. Many interdisciplinarians who believe that disciplines are more arbitrary than reflections of reality, or that reality is largely unknowable and cannot be seen even indirectly and "through a glass darkly," will agree with much of what is said here about interdisciplinary practice and decision making, even as they reject the complex system rationale.

13.2 THE STEPS IN THE INTERDISCIPLINARY PROCESS

The essence of the consensus definition of interdisciplinary studies mentioned above is that inter-disciplinary study is a two-part process: it draws critically on disciplinary perspectives, and it integrates their insights into a more comprehensive understanding. In the academy, public policy, and medicine, to name a few prominent settings, that process is appropriately used to understand an existing complex phenomenon. It can also be adapted to the creation of a new complex phenomenon such as a new product by a cross-functional team in business, an interdisci-plinary work of art in the fine and performing arts, or an intervention by social workers or therapists, again to name only a few applications. The focus of this chapter, however, will be on the use of the interdisciplinary process to understand an existing complex situation.

The steps listed in "A Theory of Interdisciplinary Studies" (Newell, 2001) are adapted from the work of Julie Klein (1990). They represent an elaboration of the two parts of the definition of interdisciplinary studies (see points 1 and 2 below). The steps below differ from the steps in that article only in that one two-part step (gathering all current disciplinary knowledge and searching for new information) is now split into two separate steps (gathering disciplinary knowledge, and identifying nonlinear linkages) and the latter step has been shifted from part 1 to part 2.

The Steps in the Interdisciplinary Process:

1. Drawing on disciplinary perspectives
   * *Defining* the problem (question, topic, issue)
   * *Determining* relevant disciplines (including interdisciplines and schools of thought)
   * *Developing* a working command of the relevant concepts, theories, and methods of each discipline
   * *Gathering* all relevant disciplinary knowledge
   * *Studying* the problem from the perspective of each discipline
   * *Generating* disciplinary insights into the problem.
2. Integrating their insights through construction of a more comprehensive understanding
   * *Identifying* conflicts in insights by using disciplines to illuminate each other's assump-tions, or by looking for different concepts with common meanings or concepts with different meanings, through which those insights are expressed
   * *Evaluating* assumptions and concepts in the context of the specific problem
   * *Resolving* conflicts by working towards a common vocabulary and set of assumptions
   * *Creating* common ground
   * *Identifying* (nonlinear) linkages between variables studied by different disciplines
   * *Constructing* a new understanding of the problem
   * *Producing* a model (metaphor, theme) that captures the new understanding
   * *Testing* the understanding by attempting to solve the problem.

A number of caveats are in order in evaluating these steps. First, separating a fluid process into discrete steps inevitably gives the misleading impression that the steps cannot overlap. They can and often do. Second, even though the steps are bulleted instead of numbered, there is still the implication that the sequence is monotonic (i.e., unidirectional). Nothing could be further from the truth. If anything, the process should be understood as iterative. While each step typically requires the completion of the previous steps, it often leads to a reexamination and redoing of earlier steps. Much like the steps in the "scientific method," these steps are heuristic rather than descriptive, idealized more than factually accurate. Third, as with the scientific method, practitioners are prone to leap ahead to later steps, but by spelling out the process, they at least realize they are getting ahead of themselves and will eventually have to go back and complete the steps they skipped over. Fourth, the process is simplified in that it assumes all of the disciplines are mined separately for nuggets of insight before any integration takes place, and when it does, the integration takes place all at once. Such an impression would be not only inaccurate but also undesirable. Interdisciplinarians tend to partially integrate as they go, reforming tentative syntheses as the insights of each additional discipline are incorporated. Fifth, one can enter the process at a number of different points—e.g., as a result of dissatisfaction with a single discipline's perspective or with its partial understanding—not just at the beginning, but eventually all the steps have to be taken. Finally, as mentioned earlier, the steps are subject to change as interdisciplinarians come to understand better the process that defines their profession.

These caveats notwithstanding, a close examination of how each step is carried out provides the best opportunity to identify the decision making ideally involved in interdisciplinary studies. What follows is a step-by-step assessment of the decision making implications of the interdisciplinary process.

13.2.1 DEFINING THE PROBLEM

The first decision faced by the interdisciplinarian is to determine if the problem is complex and thus requires an interdisciplinary approach to its solution. The following extended example should clarify what is meant here by a complex system:

> Think of a GIS (geographical information systems) overlay of maps for the same urban area, including not only one of street maps and neighborhoods taken from the road atlas, but also maps of water and sewer districts, fire districts, school districts, police precincts, rapid transit, regional planning administration, political wards, ethnic enclaves, the county, watersheds, soil profiles, water quality indicators, and many others. The typical large American city has several hundred administrative units, each charged with the responsibility for one of those maps. Each map represents a sub-system, which can be usefully studied in its own terms from a single perspective. But those sub-systems are connected by an intricate series of often-overlooked relationships that can be subtle, intermittent in their operation, and occasionally produce responses that are disproportionately large or small—in short, by a network of nonlinear relationships. The decisions of the school board about the location of a new school can have unanticipated effects on the ethnic distribution of neighborhoods and thus on voting patterns of wards or on traffic patterns, which in turn affect highway maintenance; the resulting political shifts and changing decisions about new highway construction can have unanticipated consequences for watersheds and water quality; and so on. Taken together, the sub-systems and their nonlinear connections form a complex system. (Newell, 2001, 8–9)

If the problem crosses boundaries *between* areas traditionally studied by different groups of disciplines (e.g., natural sciences, social sciences, humanities, fine and performing arts), then it is a highly complex problem. If it crosses boundaries (e.g., between social, political, economic, cultural, and geographical spheres) *within* an area traditionally studied by different disciplines (in this case, the social sciences), then it is complex as well but the order of complexity is lower. (The former is broadly interdisciplinary, the latter narrowly interdisciplinary; but both are still fully interdisciplinary because the problem is complex and its study therefore requires the full interdisciplinary process). Thus, one test of the complexity of a system is to ask if its sub-systems are typically studied by different disciplines. Alternatively, one can focus on the overall pattern of behavior of the system, asking if it occasionally exhibits major discontinuities or makes large responses to relatively small changes. System effects that are disproportionate to their causes, or sudden large shifts in the system's pattern of behavior, are also indicative of a complex system.

Having determined that the problem is complex, the interdisciplinarian needs to next decide on the scope of the problem. By taking too seriously the claim that "everything is connected to everything else," the problem can be conceived too broadly and become unmanageable. A problem can be narrowly defined and still be complex: the test of complexity is not breadth but the predominance of nonlinear linkages between sub-systems. The essential challenge is to include all sub-systems with strong nonlinear linkages in this problem-domain, while excluding those sub-systems with weaker linkages. Indeed, there are advantages to defining complex problems as narrowly as possible while still retaining their complexity. More time and resources can be available to: illuminate all of the subsystems; examine the concepts, theories, and methods utilized by each discipline in that illumination; and uncover, examine, and evaluate the assumptions underlying the perspective of each discipline.

Within the scope of the problem, the focus of the interdisciplinarian should be on the overall pattern of behavior that is problematic. Disciplines typically redefine a complex problem so they can address it using the tools at their disposal. They focus on an aspect of the problem and ignore the overall pattern of behavior (or at least those parts of the pattern that are inconvenient or outside the scope of phenomena studied by the discipline). To counteract this tendency, the interdisciplinarian needs to contextualize the contribution of each discipline within the overall complex system. In education, the topic of an interdisciplinary course should focus on a problem that requires the expertise and interest only of faculty assigned to teach it, and the illumination only of the disciplines mandated for inclusion in the course.

Once the scope and focus of the problem is established, the challenge is to decide how to word it in language that does not privilege any one of the disciplines. Avoid jargon, technical terms, or even non-technical terms that are characteristically used by one discipline. After all, disciplines see the overall pattern of behavior of the system from the unique vantage point of the sub-system they study, and their perspective is embedded in the language they use. The best strategy is often to start out stating the problem in everyday language: the resulting vagueness or imprecision may be an advantage, in that it admits of multiple interpretations. As subsequent steps in the interdisciplinary process call for reexamination of the definition of the problem, more precise wording (even newly minted terms) can be developed that is responsive to all the relevant disciplinary perspectives (Palmer and Neumann, 2002).

Finally, one must ask, "Problematic for whom?" Whose values and which ethical traditions were used in deciding that the pattern of behavior is a problem? (Szostak 2003). Is this problem more pressing than other problems? Are the interests of the most powerful disproportionately addressed in choosing to focus on this problem? Whatever the ethical standard employed, one must make the choice of the problem problematic. It is when one unquestioningly accepts a problem as self-evident that injustice can creep in.

These four decisions involved in identifying the problem—determining that it is complex, establishing its scope, choosing its focus, and determining its ethical appropriateness—require the interdisciplinarian to think systemically as well as comparatively across disciplines, to be alert to possible strong nonlinear relationships between sub-systems, to balance out the conflicting requirements of context and feasibility, to be sensitive to implicit disciplinary implications of the wording of the problem, and to be alert to whose interests are advanced by choosing this problem over others. More generally, the first step of the interdisciplinary process requires pattern recognition and mental flexibility in shifting back and forth between part and whole; breadth of knowledge and a feel for where knowledge is incomplete; judiciousness in reconciling competing claims; rhetorical analysis; and ethical sensitivity.

13.2.2 DETERMINING RELEVANT DISCIPLINES

The central decision here regards choosing which disciplines to bring to bear on the problem. In complex systems terms, this involves identifying which sub-systems comprise the complex system whose behavior is problematic (and thus contribute significantly to the overall pattern of behavior), and then identifying the discipline (or disciplines) that offers insights into each sub-system.

A couple of tests may help in identifying the appropriateness of a particular discipline: is the topic included in its professional literature, and do colleagues in that discipline see how it can be applied to the topic? In general, the rule of thumb is to err initially on the side of inclusiveness. After all, it may not be fully apparent even to those in a discipline how the sub-system they study contributes to the overall pattern of behavior of a system that is truly complex. If later steps reveal that a discipline has little of use to say about the topic, or it offers insights that overlap too much with those of another discipline, it can be removed from the study. Indeed, it *should* be removed at that point because the more researchers who end up on the research team or the more faculty members involved in developing the course, the greater the cost. Thus, inclusiveness should be favored in the early steps in the interdisciplinary process, but one should balance it against cost in later steps.

In evaluating the appropriateness of disciplines in the humanities (including the fine and performing arts), one must distinguish between the older traditional humanities and the newer critical humanities. The traditional humanities focus on the human culture sub-systems—the meaning, values, and significance (Davidson and Goldberg, 2004) of its art, literature, music, philosophy, religion, theatre, etc.—and fit well into the system-based approach to interdisciplinarity of this chapter. The critical humanities—feminist theory, critical theory, postcolonial theory, cultural theory, queer theory, postmodernist theory, post-structuralist theory, deconstructionist theory, etc.—on the other hand, focus not so much on human culture itself as on our knowledge of it, and on disciplinary knowledge in general. While these theories have much in common with interdisciplinarity, e.g., valuing multiple perspectives and seeing knowledge as constructed, they also have the potential of providing a critique of interdisciplinarity as well. After all, they offer fundamental critiques of disciplinary knowledge in which interdisciplinary studies are grounded.

"Discipline" should be understood here as an umbrella term that includes not only disciplines, sub-disciplines, and specialities, but interdisciplines and schools of thought. By "interdiscipline," I refer to an initially interdisciplinary field that has congealed into a kind of discipline with its own theories, journals, professional associations, and ultimately a new orthodoxy. Biochemistry, for example, has completed the transition from interdisciplinary study to interdiscipline, while women's studies is still seeking consensus on a new orthodoxy (though cultural, radical, and material feminists all agree on such key concepts as patriarchy and hegemony, on the need to distinguish between sex and gender, and on the political and gendered nature of ostensibly economic, social, and cultural behavior). By "schools of thought" (sometimes referred to as transdisciplines), I refer to groups of concepts, theories, and methods such as Marxism, structuralism-functionalism, and others listed in the preceding paragraph that cut across disciplinary lines. Like interdisciplines, they have their own core beliefs and approaches that form a sort of orthodoxy out of which a diverse array of positions can evolve, but their origin lies more in a rejection of disciplinarity than in interdisciplinary inquiry grounded in disciplines.

What disciplines, interdisciplines, and schools of thought all have in common is a characteristic perspective or worldview. Whether they are economists, biochemists, or Marxists, they share a distinctive, though often largely implicit, way of thinking. Members of each group can agree on what constitutes an interesting and appropriate question to study, what constitutes legitimate evidence, and what a compelling answer to the question should look like. They agree, again largely implicitly, on a surprising number of ontological, epistemological, and value assumptions (e.g., whether individual human beings are rational or irrational, whether the goal of research is explanation of commonalties or expression of particularities, and whether order or diversity, short-term or long-term, equality or freedom are more important).

Each perspective provides a unique vantage point from which to view the complex problem under study. Because each perspective illuminates a different facet of that problem (that may represent a different sub-system), the challenge is to identify as many relevant perspectives as possible so that all facets of the problem can be revealed. Indeed, the term "interdisciplinary" probably places too much emphasis on the disciplines and not enough on the other available sources of perspective. Were it not so infelicitous, one might better speak of "interperspectival studies" instead.

If the interdisciplinary process is being presented in a course and not applied in a research project, there are additional considerations involved in choosing which disciplines to include. In an interdisciplinary course in the social or natural sciences, the humanities can offer a hook that draws students into the topic by providing an empathetic feel for the topic, rich ("thick") description, and nuanced appreciation. They can also provide the basis for ethical analysis that goes beyond common sense. In an interdisciplinary science course, the inclusion of perspectives from the social sciences or humanities can help students see science as a human endeavor reflecting its social and cultural context, and bring out the imaginative, creative, or spiritual dimensions of the topic that are overlooked in science's focus on what is measurable. Conversely, the sciences can provide an empirical base that anchors humanistic speculations.

The decision about which disciplines to include has been presented here as a purely cognitive one, and for full-time interdisciplinarians I believe it can be, but disciplines have social, political, economic, and cultural as well as cognitive dimensions that can cloud the judgment of the unwary. Some disciplines are more prestigious than others (e.g., in the natural sciences physics held sway for centuries as the premier science—a position in the academic pecking order now usurped by biology). That prestige translates into more funding, more political clout, and more recognition in the larger culture. It can also translate into an unconscious bias towards its perspective in an interdisciplinary activity, especially when the decision is made by someone based in a discipline or new to evaluating the potential contribution of disciplines. Experienced interdisciplinarians, however, become familiar with the weaknesses as well as the strengths of each discipline, and come to reject disciplinary claims to privilege.

More problematic are the ideological differences between disciplines. Since its founding, sociology has been more liberal than economics, for example, and "studies" of any sort (e.g., women's, environmental, even religious) tend to be more liberal than their disciplinary counterparts. And individual scholars, interdisciplinary as well as disciplinary, typically have an ideological predisposition as well. Thus, it would not be surprising if left-of-center interdisciplinarians were to draw disproportionately from left-of-center perspectives. On the other hand, interdisciplinarians come to value diversity of perspective and seek out conflicting viewpoints; indeed, they revel in ambiguity (Davis and Newell, 1990). I see this tension at work in my seniors carrying out year-long interdisciplinary research projects. They become restive with the narrowness of individual disciplinary perspectives, yet they occasionally have to remind each other to look for ideological perspectives that are right-of-center. As with the earlier question, "Problematic for whom?," the best antidote for bias is awareness of its potential. Luckily, interdisciplinarians develop the habit of detached critical interrogation of *all* perspectives, making it easier to recognize their own biases and engage in self-examination of their own perspective.

Finally, it is not uncommon for the decision about which disciplines to include to lead to a reassessment of the problem; i.e., there is a feedback loop from choice of disciplines to problem identification. For example, once one recognizes that anthropology and religion have useful contributions to make to the debate among conservationists, preservationists, and restorationists, one may decide to recast more broadly what had appeared to be an economic, political, and scientific problem of overgrazing on public lands.

The decisions involved in determining relevant disciplines—identifying sub-systems and the disciplines focused on them, balancing inclusiveness and cost, determining the distinctiveness of a discipline's contribution, and checking for bias based on ideology or disciplinary prestige—require the interdisciplinarian to think systemically and comparatively, judiciously, and self-reflexively. More generally, this step in the interdisciplinary process requires breadth of knowledge of the relevant disciplines and the aspects of reality they illuminate; judiciousness in reconciling competing disciplinary claims; judgment of the significance of differences in disciplinary contributions; and strong-sense critical thinking (Paul, 1987) in which the critical gaze is turned inwards to one's own motivations.

13.2.3 Developing a Command of Each Discipline

The step of developing a working command of the concepts, theories, and methods of each discipline requires decisions about how much and what kind of knowledge to develop. These questions are particularly troublesome to those glancing at interdisciplinary studies from outside, especially from a discipline. Must one have a PhD in a discipline to make intellectually respectable use of it; if not, how much expertise is enough? How much depth and breadth in each discipline is sufficient? Which concepts, theories, and methods should be chosen? Is it even possible to do responsible interdisciplinary work as an individual, or must one collaborate with an expert from each of the other contributing disciplines?

At this point in the interdisciplinary process, the required breadth of knowledge in each discipline is quite modest: command of the few relevant concepts, theories, or methods from each discipline that are applicable to the problem under consideration, and a basic feel for how each discipline approaches such a problem. (However modest, the requisite knowledge of disciplines still has significant faculty development implications). How much depth (i.e., command) depends, just as it does for disciplinarians, on the characteristics of the problem, the goal of the activity, and the availability of collaborators and the nature of their collaboration. If the problem requires the collection and processing of large quantities of information, the use of specialized instruments or higher mathematics, or the use of advanced concepts and theories whose mastery requires a series of prerequisites, then more depth and collaboration is required. But if the problem can be illuminated adequately using a handful of introductory-level concepts and theories from each discipline, and modest information readily and simply acquired, then a solo interdisciplinary researcher or even a first-year undergraduate student can handle it. Luckily, one can get some useful initial understanding of most complex problems using a small number of relatively basic concepts and theories from each discipline.

If the goal of the interdisciplinary activity is the development of a course, then the level of the course largely determines the depth of mastery required. Introductory-level courses, whether in general education or an interdisciplinary major, require of faculty only an introductory-level familiarity with each of the contributing disciplines and a slightly more advanced knowledge of the actual concepts, theories, and methods drawn from them. Colleagues can be invaluable in identifying what their discipline has to contribute to an understanding of the problem, suggesting readings for students and additional background reading for faculty, and even giving guest lectures (Newell, 1992). The role of faculty in such courses is not to be an expert, but to serve as a coach, guide, mentor, and role model for how to draw on disciplines in which one is not an expert (Newell, 1994). Indeed, too much expertise can be a bad thing when teaching an interdisciplinary course: one needs enough knowledge for accuracy, but enough distance for detachment from the discipline.

Again, there is a feedback loop from developing a command of disciplines to determining the relevant disciplines. A discipline that initially seemed useful may not look so promising when the concepts, theories, and methods it has to offer are examined more closely. If the discipline doesn't provide the anticipated illumination of a particular sub-system, then one may need to look for another discipline or perspective that does.

Decisions involved in developing a command of disciplines—about how much and what kind of knowledge is required, and whether the disciplines chosen are still appropriate—require an assessment of the applicability of specific concepts, theories, and methods to the problem; an evaluation of the characteristics of the problem, the goal of the activity, and the availability of collaborators; and a reevaluation of the appropriateness of the disciplines selected. For one's own discipline, these decisions also require some detachment, the ability to step outside its comfortable perspective.

13.2.4 Gathering Disciplinary Knowledge, Studying the Problem, and Generating Insights

The steps of gathering relevant disciplinary knowledge, studying the problem from each disciplinary perspective, and generating disciplinary insights into the problem require decisions about the appropriate use of disciplines to shed light on the different aspects of the complex problem. In terms of complex systems theory, the challenge is to illuminate the sub-system underlying each aspect of the problem using the discipline focused on that sub-system. Those decisions determine how much and what kinds of information to gather, which concepts and theories to employ and how to use them, and how to interpret and evaluate the diverse insights generated. One consequence of these decisions is that earlier choices of disciplines, and even the problem itself, are re-evaluated.

Interdisciplinarians need a systematic overview of the available types of concepts, theories, and methods, Szostak (2003) points out, if they are to make informed choices. Much of his recent scholarship has been devoted to developing such typologies, which serve as a useful starting point in identifying the perspective of each discipline and identifying key theories and methods that characterize its approach (Szostak, 2004). More detailed overviews are available through a variety of library reference works such as the *International Encyclopedia of the Social Sciences* (1968); standard introductory textbooks for various disciplines give additional details. Starting with broad typologies and narrowing down systematically, with a little help from a librarian and then from relevant disciplinary departments, the interdisciplinarian can hone in not just on relevant disciplines, but on appropriate concepts and theories from each discipline.

The challenge to the interdisciplinarian interested in an entire complex problem is that each discipline focuses in on a particular aspect of the problem. When a discipline is brought to bear on a complex problem, it immediately redefines the problem more narrowly in a way that allows it to make use of its distinctive concepts, theories, and methods. The result is that each discipline offers powerful but limited and skewed insights into the overall problem. To make effective use of those insights, the interdisciplinarian must be fully aware of how each discipline redefines the problem to figure out the limitations and bias of its insights.

Because disciplines specialize in different sub-systems (that underlie different aspects of a complex problem), each discipline has its own distinctive strengths; the flip side of those strengths is often its distinctive weaknesses. A discipline such as psychology that is strong in understanding individuals, is thereby weak in understanding groups; its focus on parts means that its view of wholes is blurry. A discipline such as sociology that focuses on groups doesn't see individuals clearly; indeed, at the extreme it sees individuals as epiphenomenal—as little more than the product of their society. Empirically-based disciplines in the social and natural sciences cannot see those aspects of human reality that are spiritual or imaginative, and their focus on behavior that is lawful, rule-based, or patterned leads them to overlook human behavior that is idiosyncratic, individua-listic, capricious and messy, or to lump it into unexplained variance. Humanists, on the other hand, are attracted to those aspects and tend to grow restive with a focus on behavior that is predictable, feeling that it misses the most interesting features of human existence. Interdisciplinarians need to develop an appreciation of the strengths and concomitant limitations of each perspective, and to evaluate accordingly the insights of each discipline and its relevance to the overall problem.

Because the insights of a discipline are skewed by the way it redefines the problem, their relevance to the interdisciplinary understanding of the problem as a whole must be dispassionately evaluated. Insights from the discipline of economics that presume individuals are rational and self-interested may need to be reassessed when the problem involves social, religious, or cultural behavior that is based on other motivations as well. Otherwise useful insights from psychology into an environmental problem may lead the unwary interdisciplinarian to focus too much on the micro level at the expense of systemic factors. In using skewed insights, interdisciplinarians need to maintain some psychic distance from the disciplinary perspectives on which they draw, borrowing from them without completely buying into them.

It is not merely the insights of disciplines that are skewed, however, but also the factual information uncovered by the disciplines. One might think that facts are facts: how can they be correct and yet skewed? But facts are notoriously guilty of the sin of omission. They reflect what a discipline is interested in, and a pile of information on a particular topic makes it seem important even to someone outside the discipline. So interdisciplinarians need to be attuned to the subliminal messages of facts, and keep track of the complex problem that interests them without being side-tracked by the narrower, value-laden interests of the disciplines on which they draw.

Moving from one discipline to another involves more than moving from one set of concepts, theories, and methods to another; it means shifting from one perspective to another. The lenses of one discipline are taken off and the lenses of another discipline are put on in their place. The effect on the novice interdisciplinarian can be intellectual vertigo until one's eyes and brain can adjust and refocus. Experienced interdisciplinarians develop the mental flexibility to shift rapidly from one disciplinary perspective to another. I suspect the challenge is similar to shifting from English to Spanish to French: at first, it takes some time to get into using each new language and keeping them straight (I still find myself using Spanish in Quebec), but eventually one can move from person to person at a cosmopolitan cocktail party and shift effortlessly from one language to another.

As with the other steps in the interdisciplinary process, these typically lead the interdisciplinarian to revisit earlier steps. Once one sees precisely what insights the various disciplines have to offer, one may wish to add a discipline that might offer a missing perspective or remove one whose contributions overlap too much with others. One may discover the need to learn more about what a particular discipline has to offer. One might decide that the wording of the problem that once looked neutral now seems too much indebted to the perspective of one of the disciplines; and one might even realize that the very conception of the problem is overly reflective of that discipline's perspective.

Decisions involved in gathering relevant disciplinary knowledge, studying the problem from each disciplinary perspective, and generating disciplinary insights into the problem require the interdisciplinarian not only to take on the role of serial disciplinarian but also to address the consequences of disciplines, redefining as well as narrowing the problem. The cognitive challenges are to develop enough familiarity with each discipline to appreciate its strengths and apply its distinctive information, concepts, theories, and methods, while maintaining enough distance from the discipline (and focus on the complex problem) to recognize its weaknesses and avoid being distracted by its narrow, biased interests. Finally, the challenge is to recognize the implications of the disciplinary information and insights for decisions made at earlier steps, revisiting them if only to assure oneself that they still look correct though more often to revise them.

Looking back over the first half of the interdisciplinary process, it becomes apparent that Part A, drawing on disciplinary perspectives, involves decisions that are predominantly disciplinary: what concepts, theories, and methods to use; what information to collect; how much breadth and depth are required; what research strategies are feasible given the constraints, etc. However, it also involves decisions that are distinctively interdisciplinary: going back and forth between disciplinary part and complex whole; comparative evaluation of the various disciplines' strengths and weaknesses, and the narrowing and skewing that results from their respective redefinitions of the problem. Also evident should be a number of non-cognitive pitfalls that can bias the decisions of the unwary (and in some cases even the experienced) interdisciplinarian. But none of the decisions are particularly esoteric or exotic, even if the range and kinds of knowledge required may appear daunting.

Next, the steps involved in integrating disciplinary insights through construction of a more comprehensive understanding.

13.2.5 Identifying Conflicts in Insights, Illuminating Their Source, and Evaluating Them

The fundamental decisions in creating common ground among the disciplines on which to construct a more comprehensive understanding of the complex problem address the frequent conflicts among disciplinary insights. If it were not for these conflicts, common ground would already be established or merely await discovery. Integration would consist, as is too often supposed, of putting together a jigsaw puzzle. Instead, integration is more like discovering that many of the jigsaw pieces overlap, and worse, that the pieces seem to come from different jig saw puzzles and that many of the pieces are missing. The decisions one makes about how to modify the pieces determine if and how the puzzle can be sufficiently solved, in spite of the missing pieces, to make out the picture.

Conflict between the insights of different disciplines should not be surprising because the disciplines reflect the sub-systems in which they specialize. It is well known that the physical, chemical, geological, and biological spheres of the natural world follow different though apparently consistent laws. (While string theorists are the latest in a line of physicists intent on developing a physical theory of everything, most scientists recognize that biological principles are not reducible to underlying chemical laws, nor are chemical properties fully reducible to underlying physical laws, any more than plate tectonics from geology is reducible to more fundamental chemical and physical laws). In the human world studied by the social sciences and humanities, however, the different spheres of group existence follow rules that are not only irreducibly different but also conflicting. (Thus, the economy operates by principles that are partly at odds with the principles governing the social, political, or religious spheres). And the mental and imaginative world of humans (e.g., culture, fiction, art) follows principles that are not only irreducibly different and conflicting with those of the world of human behavior and institutions, but incommensurate with them as well. (They address what could or should be more than what *is*; and they value expression over explanation). The insights of different disciplines conflict because they reflect the irreducibly different, conflicting, or even incommensurate principles by which the sub-systems they study operate. And the nature and extent of the conflict in insights depends on whether they are drawn from the natural sciences, social sciences, or humanities.

While every discipline makes a number of assumptions, many of them are tacit. Experienced disciplinarians feel little need to scrutinize, much less justify, assumptions they share with others in their field (with whom they tend to communicate primarily). Novices in a discipline tend to pick up these assumptions unconsciously in graduate school, if not as undergraduates in their major, as part of the process of enculturation into the discipline. Interdisciplinarians can ferret out those assumptions by playing one discipline off another: they can use the critique of one discipline to illuminate contrasting assumptions of another discipline.

Insights from disciplines are expressed largely in language (though not entirely, as my colleagues in the fine and performing arts are quick to point out). So conflict in insights becomes embedded in terminology. Addressing differences in disciplinary terminology requires particularly nuanced decision making. To create common ground in the face of conflict, the inter-disciplinarian must address two types of situations—in which different disciplinary concepts mask common meaning, and in which the same concept masks different contextual meanings in the disciplines (Bromme, 2000). The operative decisions in both cases regard the extent and nature of the overlap in meaning (think Venn diagrams), and then the development of terminology that brings out the overlap in meaning while acknowledging the areas of conflict. The common ground will eventually be expressed in new technical terms or old everyday terms that scholars can agree to freight with new meaning. An additional challenge here is to decide which conflict is real but extraneous to the specific problem at hand, and which conflict makes a difference in this context.

Lying behind the language are assumptions that must be evaluated in the context of the problem at hand. Those assumptions reflect each discipline's time-tested perception of the principles governing the sub-system in which it specializes. They can be ontological (regarding the nature of the "reality"), epistemological (regarding the nature of knowledge of that "reality"), and value-based. For example, each social science makes an ontological assumption about the rationality of individuals—whether they are rational, irrational, rationalizing, etc.—that is one-size-fits-all in nature. Other ontological assumptions by the social sciences regard whether individuals are autonomous or a product of society, self-centered or other-regarding; assumptions about groups regard whether they are merely the sum of the individuals in them or take on a life of their own, and whether groups are characterized more by conflict or by order. Value assumptions are made by the social sciences about diversity, justice, truth, efficiency, and ideology. To a considerable extent, the conflict in insights of the disciplines reflects such differences in assumptions on which the disciplines are based: disciplines see what they are designed to see.

The interdisciplinarian can decide at any one moment whether to focus on redesigning the disciplines' concepts to best illuminate the complex problem at hand, or on determining the extent to which each blanket assumption is appropriate in the context of the problem at hand. Because assumptions underlie concepts and concepts reflect assumptions, focusing on one level has direct implications for the other level as well. Following the "principle of least action" from physics, conflicting disciplinary concepts or assumptions should be modified as little as possible to make them consistent in the context of the particular complex problem. (Specific techniques for modifying concepts and assumptions are discussed in the next section).

Decisions involved in addressing conflicts in disciplinary insights can be aided by becoming cognizant of implicit as well as explicit disciplinary assumptions and by assessing their appropriateness in light of the specific complex problem. Knowledge of the range of assumptions underlying each contributing discipline is more esoteric than that required in the first half of the interdisciplinary process. Disciplinarians are of disappointingly little help in identifying their own assumptions—they may even be reluctant to admit they make some of the assumptions that, logically, they must to arrive at the conclusions they do. Interdisciplinarians are only now joining experts from library and information science in compiling this information, though I expect it will be generally available within the next few years. For now, it can be extracted from a discipline by subjecting it to close scrutiny and logical analysis from other disciplines, though the cognitive skills involved—reasoning backwards from the concepts, theories, and methods underlying insights to infer the assumptions on which they must be based—seem difficult for most scholars.

Even more challenging is the assessment of the appropriateness of assumptions. As explained more fully below, that requires the interdisciplinarian to have a feel for the operation of complex systems, knowledge of the overall pattern of behavior produced by that particular complex system, familiarity with how sub-systems are typically connected through nonlinear linkages, a sense of the modifications in disciplinary assumptions typically required to identify the principles by which those linkages operate, and finally, movement back and forth between system and sub-systems. These are skills that even the most experienced interdisciplinarians are just starting to learn, skills that are far from the professional experience of most disciplinarians though some of these skills are familiar to computer modelers of complex systems.

Also challenging is the rhetorical and philosophical analysis of disciplinary concepts that mask some commonalty of meaning in different terms, or hidden contextual differences in meaning in the same concept when used by different disciplines. This task is rhetorical in that it requires an ear for the impact of language use, and philosophical in that it requires identifying fine gradations of meaning. The very flexibility, fluidity, and variegated nature of language itself (Frey, 2002; Lowy, 1991; Klein, 1996) make it difficult to achieve the requisite precision.

13.2.6 Creating Common Ground

The step of creating common ground requires decisions about how to bring out latent commonalties in the conflicting insights derived from the concepts, theories, or methods of different disciplines. As explained in the preceding section, this step can be carried out directly by modifying the concepts through which they are expressed, or indirectly by modifying the assumptions on which they are based and then reassessing the insights in light of the modified concepts or assumptions. In either case, the challenge is to decide how to modify concepts or assumptions as little as possible to bring out potential commonalties. Once common ground has been constructed, the modified insights can be integrated into a more comprehensive understanding of the complex problem.

Most of the literature on interdisciplinary studies has seen this step as a creative and therefore inexplicable act effectively taking place inside a black box. Spurred on by the recognition that interdisciplinary study would never be respected as rigorous as long as its defining feature of integration was unexamined and mysterious, I have attempted to identify the techniques of integration (Newell, 2000) in exemplary interdisciplinary scholarship. My focus has been on works that bring together the disciplines of economics and sociology because there is more head-on conflict between their assumptions than anywhere else in the social sciences—so much so that a Harvard economist once famously quipped, "Economics is all about how people make choices. Sociology is all about why they don't have any choices to make" (Duesenberry, 1960, 233). Because the development of common ground has been so poorly understood, the techniques of redefinition, extension, organization, and transformation that I identified so far are set out below in some detail.

Decisions about which techniques to use should be based on the nature and extent of the conflict. One possible situation is that concepts and assumptions do not conflict at all, though commonalty is still obscured by discipline-specific terminology or context. A second possibility is that concepts and assumptions of two disciplines are different but not opposing; they merely represent alternatives. A third possible situation is that concepts and assumptions are diametrically opposed. For most complex problems, the challenge of creating common ground confronts the interdisciplinarian with more than one of these situations; for problems that require input from the social sciences and humanities, all three are likely to be involved. Some techniques of integrations are useful in more than one situation, so the interdisciplinarian needs to understand the range of applicability of each technique.

The technique of *redefinition* can reveal commonalties in concepts or assumptions that may be obscured by discipline-specific terminology. This technique is useful whether or not disciplinary concepts and assumptions are in conflict. For example, when Kenneth Boulding (1981) tried to figure out how economics as well as sociology might contribute to an understanding of grants, he was faced with the fact that economic theory focuses on exchanges and there is no quid pro quo in genuinely altruistic grants, bequests, gifts, donations, etc. He created common ground by recognizing the commonalty of grants and exchanges, namely that they both involve a transfer: grants are one-way transfers while exchanges are two-way transfers. Because most disciplinary concepts and assumptions are couched in discipline-specific jargon, the integrative technique of redefinition is involved in most efforts to create common ground, in conjunction with other techniques of integration as well as by itself.

The technique of *extension* addresses differences or oppositions in disciplinary concepts or assumptions by extending the meaning of an idea beyond the domain of the discipline into the domain of another discipline. Robert Frank (1988) felt that economics could join sociology and evolutionary biology in the study of altruistic behavior, even though economics focuses on self-interested behavior and tends to reject claims of altruism as disguised self-interest. He came up with the idea of extending the meaning of self-interest from its short-term context in economics to the long-term for an individual, namely a lifetime. Because of the "commitment problem," he argued, some behavior that is self-interested in the short-run actually undermines long-run self-interest because it discourages others from entering into contracts with the person who has developed a reputation for placing short-run material self-interest ahead of honoring contracts or following a moral code. For the same reasons, behavior that would be termed altruistic in the short-run can actually enhance long-run self-interest. He then extended the meaning of self-interest even further to the long-term for the species as a whole, connecting it to ideas from evolutionary biology. Likewise, Kenneth Boulding (1981) used utility analysis from microeconomics to shed light on altruistic behavior by extending the concept of self-interest. Under his reformulation, an individual's utility (or amount of satisfaction) extends beyond the goods and services that an individual consumes to include the well-being of others towards whom the individual feels benevolence or malevolence. Thus, if A feels benevolent towards B and gives B a gift, A's utility will rise if

A perceives that B is better off. The integrative technique of extension can be used to create common ground by extending a concept or assumption not just in time (Frank) or across individuals (Boulding), but across the boundaries of cultures, races, ethnicities, genders, ideologies, nations, regions, classes, or any other classification.

Because interdisciplinary studies have a different focus than the disciplines on which they draw (namely they focus on a complex whole, not just on a part of that whole), interdisciplinary studies place disciplinary concepts in new contexts. Those contexts are likely to challenge the assumptions on which individual disciplines are predicated by extending beyond their range. By paying explicit attention to the definition of disciplinary concepts, the assumptions on which they are based, and the way the context challenges that definition and those assumptions, the interdisciplinarian can set up a redefinition or extension that creates the appropriate common ground for integration.

The integrative technique of *organization* not only identifies a latent commonalty in meaning of different disciplinary concepts or assumptions and redefines them accordingly; it then organizes, arranges, or arrays the redefined insights or assumptions to bring out a relationship among them. For example, Boulding (1981) recognized that both benevolent behavior (studied by sociologists) and malevolent behavior (studied by political scientists) can be understood as other-regarding behavior (positive and negative, respectively). He then arrayed them along a continuum of other-regarding behavior. The self-interested behavior studied by economists became the midpoint on that continuum because its degree of other-regarding behavior is zero. Thus, he set out a way to transform the debate about whether human nature in general is selfish or altruistic into a choice of where on the continuum of motivations people are likely to fall in the particular complex problem under study. By combining into a single continuum with self-interest the motivations of love and hate/fear that support or threaten the integrative mechanisms binding societies and polities together, Boulding used the technique of organization to integrate the differing conceptions of human nature underlying economics, sociology, and political science.

The integrative technique of organization can be expanded from individual concepts and assumptions to large-scale models, major theoretical approaches, and even entire disciplines. For example, Amitai Etzioni (1988) argued that there are several identifiable large-scale patterns of interrelationship between the "rational/empirical" factors studied by economics and the "normative/ affective" factors studied by sociology. One such pattern I call an envelope. Here the rational behavior studied by economists is bounded, limited, or constrained by the normative factors studied by sociologists. Thus, rational economic behavior functions within a normative sociological envelope. Another pattern might be called inter-penetration. Some sociological factors directly influence economic behavior, while some economic factors directly influence social behavior. Thus, social relationships can have an effect on how economic information is gathered and processed, what inferences are drawn, and what options are considered. And a third pattern can be referred to as facilitation. Etzioni points out that the "free individuals [studied by economists] are found only within communities [studied by sociologists], which anchor emotions and morals" (xi). Thus, sociological factors such as communities can actually facilitate individual economic behavior. Similarly, the anthropologist Dorothy Lee (1959) made the case that structure is freeing. Like their small-scale counterparts, these macro-level applications of the integrative technique of organization can bring out the relationship among commonalties of meaning within contrasting disciplinary concepts or assumptions.

The integrative technique of *transformation* is used where concepts or assumptions are not merely different (e.g., love, fear, selfishness) but opposite (e.g., rational, irrational). Etzioni (1988) believed that "dichotomies are the curse of intellectual and scholarly discourse" (203). He addressed the problem of opposite axiomatic assumptions by transforming them into continuous variables; e.g., opposing assumptions about the rationality (economics) or irrationality (sociology) of humans are resolved by changing a dichotomous assumption about rationality (that is exogenous to the model) into a continuous variable (that is endogenous to the model)—the degree of rationality. By studying the factors that influence rationality, one could then determine in principle the degree of rationality that is likely in the complex problem under study. Etzioni devoted an entire chapter to identifying factors that influence the degree of rationality in any given situation. Where feasible, those factors could even be measured in the context of the complex problem under study to determine empirically the degree of rationality. Likewise, Etzioni treated trust and governmental intervention as continuous variables whose determinative influences can be explored and estimated in any particular context, rather than as dichotomous assumptions to accept or reject. By transforming opposing assumptions into variables, then, we push back assumptions and expand the scope of the theory. The effect of this strategy is not only to resolve a philosophical dispute but also to extend the range of the theory. This integrative technique of transformation can be applied to *any* dichotomy or duality, and our culture is replete with them.

What typifies the decisions involved in the step of creating common ground is that they replace the either/or thinking, which is characteristic of the disciplines, with both/and thinking. Inclusive thinking is substituted for dualistic thinking. Because these decisions require abstract thought about shades of meaning, they have a philosophical character to them. And because they require the creation of new meaning, they epitomize the hackneyed managerial skill of "thinking outside the box." Indeed, intellectual flexibility and playfulness are more useful than logic at this step in the integrative part of the interdisciplinary process.

The goal of creating common ground is not to remove the tension between the insights of different disciplines, but to reduce their conflict. Differences will remain, reflecting the differences in principles by which the various sub-systems operate, but the commonalties that are brought out should reflect the principles according to which the system as a whole operates, in particular the non-linear linkages between variables in different sub-systems.

13.2.7 IDENTIFYING LINKAGES AMONG DISCIPLINES

The identification of linkages between variables studied by different disciplines involves decisions about what substantive information is missing about the complex problem under study. Interdisciplinarians need to be alert throughout the interdisciplinary process for unexamined linkages between disciplines and should identify as many as possible before attempting to construct a more comprehensive understanding. If integration is successful, the remaining linkages will be identified during the construction of a more comprehensive understanding.

It should come as no surprise that linkages between the variables of different disciplines are largely unknown and thus unexamined. Each discipline focuses on uncovering the linkages among its own variables, but no one (other than the interdisciplinarian) takes the responsibility to study behavior that falls between the disciplines or that transcends them. The divide-and-conquer strategy of disciplinary reductionism simply ignores cross-disciplinary linkages, yet they provide the glue that holds a complex system together and give it what coherence it has. Without these linkages, there would be no overall system, merely small independent systems studied by individual disciplines. So there would be no overall problem, merely separate problems adequately studied by separate disciplines. And the reductionist strategy of the disciplines would suffice, without the need for holistic thinking.

It is reasonable to expect that most of the linkages between the sub-systems studied by different disciplines will be nonlinear. Disciplines use simplifying assumptions that point scholars towards compatible (non-conflicting), complementary variables. And the tools (e.g., descriptive and inferential statistics, mathematics such as the calculus) typically used to determine the relationships among those variables work well when those relationships are orderly, simple, and linear, and tend to break down, yield messy results, or become insoluble when the relationships become too nonlinear. Disciplines are opportunistic and imperialistic, expanding their domain as far as their tools and theories permit. When they encounter behavior that cannot be explained using those tools and theories, or extensions and variants thereof, they stop their expansion. Thus, it seems likely that relationships that cross disciplinary boundaries are not linear, or at least more nonlinear than traditional disciplinary tools are designed to accommodate.

13.2.8 Constructing and Modeling a More Comprehensive Understanding

The decisions involved in constructing a more comprehensive understanding are about the connections between parts and whole, between partial theoretical insights and overall empirical information. The empirical information about the complex problem as a whole is examined to identify patterns of behavior of the complex system producing the problem. The partial theoretical insights come from the disciplines that study the various sub-systems of which the complex system is constructed. What little information that is available about the linkages between those sub-systems probably comes largely from interdisciplinarians. The general challenge in constructing a more comprehensive understanding is to develop a model of that complex system consistent with the theoretical disciplinary insights, with any available interdisciplinary insights into the linkages among sub-systems, and with the overall pattern of behavior of the complex system. That model should produce behavior consistent with observed overall patterns and emerge from the constituent sub-systems studied by individual disciplines. The interdisciplinarian goes back and forth between parts and whole, asking how disciplinary insights might be modified or postulating additional interdisciplinary linkages, so that the behavior they predict is consistent with the observed behavior of the complex system.

The challenge is complicated by the fact that the linkages between the sub-systems are typically nonlinear, so the system as a whole is complex, and complex systems are only partially ordered, determined, and predictable. Thus, it may not be readily apparent how the linked theoretical parts produce the observed whole, even if the sub-systems have been fully and accurately portrayed by the disciplines that study them, the linkages between sub-systems are all known and accurately characterized, and the overall pattern of behavior is fully and accurately observed. Because these conditions are unlikely to be fully met, the challenge of interdisciplinary integration is formidable indeed.

The more comprehensive understanding should be responsive to each disciplinary perspective, but beholden to none of them. That is, each discipline should contribute to that understanding, but no one disciplinary perspective should dominate it. The goal is to achieve a balance among disciplinary influences on the more comprehensive understanding.

The complex system modeled by the interdisciplinarian has at least some unity and coherence, or it would not be a system at all. One possible test of whether that unity and coherence has been captured in the more comprehensive understanding is to develop a metaphor that brings out the defining characteristics of that understanding without denying the remaining conflicts that underlies it. Metaphors are particularly useful in the humanities, where relationships are seldom usefully expressed by systems of simultaneous equations, computer simulations, or formal models, but the natural and social sciences make a surprising amount of use of metaphors as well (Lakoff and Johnson, 1980). If that metaphor is consistent with the contributing disciplinary insights as modified to create common ground, the interdisciplinary linkages found, and the patterns observable in the overall behavior of the complex system, then a more comprehensive understanding has been reached. Whether it is an *adequate* understanding, however, must be determined in the final step in the interdisciplinary process.

The decisions underlying the construction and modeling of a more comprehensive understanding are characteristic of business and politics more than of the academy. Playing both ends against the middle, balancing out conflicting constituencies, and reconciling expert advice with actual practice involve decisions associated more with expediting, logistics, policy-making and management than with scholarship and teaching. They are more characteristic of the real world than the ivory tower. Indeed, the challenge of integration requires the interdisciplinarian to confront real-world complexities that disciplinarians can partially avoid through the use of simplifying assumptions.

13.2.9 Testing the More Comprehensive Understanding

The decisions involved in the final step in the interdisciplinary process relate to the real-world application and pragmatic evaluation of the more comprehensive understanding. In interdisciplinary studies, the proof of the pudding is in the eating: does the more comprehensive understanding allow more effective action? Does it help solve the problem, resolve the issue, or answer the question? It is the interdisciplinarian who develops the more comprehensive understanding, but it is practitioners concerned with that particular complex problem, issue, or question who must decide if the more comprehensive understanding is useful to them. Thus, interdisciplinary study (the final step in the interdisciplinary process in particular) serves as the bridge between the ivory tower and the real world.

If pragmatic judgments of practitioners are that the more comprehensive understanding lacks utility, or that it has limited value because of a serious weakness, then the interdisciplinarian must correct the weakness by revisiting the earlier steps in the interdisciplinary process. While any step might contain the source of the inadequacy, the weakest step is usually the identification of linkages between disciplines because the least work was probably done on this step beforehand. As pointed out earlier, relatively little is known about linkages between disciplines because most scholars are disciplinarians and focus their scholarship on topics of interest to their discipline. The next most common source of failure or inadequacy is a missing perspective, either because a potential disciplinary contribution has been overlooked or because a discipline does not yet exist, or a phenomenon overlooked by the disciplines. In any case, a sub-system has remained unexamined. If the more comprehensive understanding is useful but has an identifiable shortcoming, the nature of the inadequacy may suggest which steps need to be reexamined.

Unfortunately for interdisciplinarians, as pointed out earlier, the complex nature of the problem means that even a model that is accurate and complete may produce a more comprehensive understanding that predicts less well than practitioners demand. The complexity of the problem means that it is only quasi-ordered, quasi-determined, and quasi-predictable; moreover, it may evolve unexpectedly to produce a new pattern of behavior. Thus, at best interdisciplinary studies may produce more comprehensive understandings that are of only limited utility. But the difficulty lies in the nature of the problems studied by interdisciplinarians, not in the process they use to study them. Interdisciplinary studies get the most utility possible out of the disciplines, but whether that utility is sufficient to usefully guide human decision making depends on the degree of complexity of the problem itself.

13.3 CONCLUSION

This chapter has set out the basic cognitive skills, strategies, sensibilities, and competencies underlying the decision making involved in the interdisciplinary process. While the nature and underlying characteristics of decisions have been identified for each step separately, there are some overall observations that need to be made about the process as a whole.

First, many of the decisions involved in the conduct of interdisciplinary inquiry are rather ordinary (though perhaps not customary); none of them are so esoteric that the entire enterprise seems infeasible. In short, interdisciplinary study is viable.

Second, the kinds of decision making vary widely. Some are familiar to disciplinarians, but many others go beyond the normal conduct of disciplinary inquiry. Thus, interdisciplinary study is far from "business as usual" in the academy.

Third, some decisions required by the interdisciplinary process, in particular those involved in integration, actually run counter to the disciplinary approach and thus to the academy as a whole.

The holistic, both/and, anti-dualistic thinking involved in interdisciplinary integration directly opposes the overall reductionist, divide-and-conquer strategy of the disciplines. But the interdisciplinary process is as much about drawing on disciplines as it is about integrating their insights. Thus, interdisciplinary study should be understood as complementary to the disciplines, as utilizing and then transcending but not rejecting them. Indeed, interdisciplinary study is best understood as a corrective to the disciplines; together, disciplinarity and interdisciplinarity produce a balance between reductionism and holism.

Finally, the decisions involved in interdisciplinary study are ultimately pragmatic. The test of the appropriateness of any one decision is whether it enhances the overall real-world utility of the more comprehensive understanding it produces. As such, interdisciplinary study constitutes a bridge between the academy and the rest of society.

REFERENCES

Boulding, K., *A Preface to Grants Economics: The Economy of Love and Fear*, Praeger, New York, 1981.

Bromme, R., Beyond one's own perspective: the psychology of cognitive interdisciplinarity, In *Practising Interdisciplinarity*, Weingart, P. and Stehr, N., Eds., University of Toronto Press, Toronto, pp. 115–133, 2000.

Cupchik, G., Constructivist realism: an ontology that encompasses positivist and constructivist approaches to the social sciences. *Forum: Qualitative Social Research* 2. (http://www.qualititative-research.net) (Accesed August 19, 2005).

Davidson, C. and Goldberg, D. Engaging the humanities, *MLA: Profession*, 42–62, 2004.

Davis, A. and Newell, W., Those experimental colleges of the 1960s: where are they, now that we need them?, In *Points of View on American Higher Education, Vol. 2: Institutions and Issues*, Barnes, S., Ed., Edwin Mellen Press, Lewiston, NY, pp. 38–43, 1990.

Duesenberry, J., *Universities-National Bureau of Economic Research, Demography and Economic Change in Developed Countries*, Princeton University Press, Princeton, 1960.

Etzioni, A., *The Moral Dimension: Towards a New Economics*, Free Press, New York, 1988.

Frank, R., *Passions within Reason: The Strategic Role of Emotions*, Norton, New York, 1988.

Frey, G., Methodological problems of interdisciplinary discussions, *RATIO*, 15(2), 161–182, 2002.

Habermas, J. and Lawrence, F., *The Philosophical Discourse of Modernity: Twelve Lectures*, MIT Press, Cambridge, MA, 1985.

Klein, J., *Interdisciplinarity: History, Theory, and Practice*, Wayne State University Press, Detroit, 1990.

Klein, J., *Crossing Boundaries: Knowledges, Disciplinarities, and Interdisciplinarities*, Charlotte, VA, University Press of Virginia, 1996.

Klein, J., History of transdisciplinary research. *Encyclopedia of Life Support Systems*, EOLSS Publishers, Oxford, U.K., (http://www.eolss.net) (Accessed August 29, 2005).

Klein, J. and Newell, W., Advancing interdisciplinary studies, In *Handbook of the Undergraduate Curriculum*, Gaff, J. and Ratcliff, J., Eds., Jossey-Bass, San Francisco, pp. 393–395, 1996.

Lakoff, G. and Johnson, M., *Metaphors We Live By*, University of Chicago Press, Chicago, 1980.

Lee, D., *Freedom and Culture: Essays*, Prentice Hall, Englewood Cliffs, NJ, 1959.

Lowy, I., The strength of loose concepts—boundary concepts, federative experimental strategies and disciplinary growth: the case of immunology, *History of Science*, 30(4), 371–396, 1991.

Lyotard, J.-F., Bennington, G., and Massumi, B., *The Postmodern Condition: A Report on Knowledge*, University of Minnesota Press, Minnesota, [1984] 1997.

McMillan, E., *Complexity, Organizations, and Change*, Routledge, London and New York, 2004.

Meek, J., The practice of interdisciplinarity, *Issues in Integrative Studies*, 19, 123–136, 2001.

Newell, W., Academic disciplines and undergraduate interdisciplinary education, *European Journal of Education*, 27(3), 211–221, 1992.

Newell, W., Designing interdisciplinary courses, In *Interdisciplinary Studies Today in New Directions for Teaching and Learning*, Klein, J. and Doty, W., Eds., Jossey-Bass, San Francisco, pp. 35–51, 1994.

Newell, W., Transdisciplinarity reconsidered, In *Transdisciplinarity: Recreating Integrated Knowledge—Advances in Sustainable Development*, Somerville, M. and Rapport, D., Eds., EOLSS Publishers Co, Oxford, U.K., pp. 42–48, 2000.

Newell, W., A theory of interdisciplinary studies, *Issues in Integrative Studies*, 19, 1–25, 2001.

Newell, W., Complexity and interdisciplinarity. *Encyclopedia of Life Support Systems*, EOLSS Publishers, Oxford, U.K., (http://www.eolss.net) (Accessed August 29, 2005).

Newell, W. and Meek, J., What can public administration learn from complex systems theory?, *Administrative Theory and Praxis*, 19(3), 318–330, 1997.

Palmer, C. and Neumann, L., The information work of interdisciplinary humanities scholars: exploration and translation, *Library Quarterly*, 72, 85–117, 2002, January.

Paul, R., Critical thinking the critical person, In *Thinking: The Second International Conference*, Perkins, D., Lochhead, J., and Bishop, J., Eds., Erlbaum Associates, Hillsdale, NJ, pp. 373–403, 1987.

Sills, D. L., Ed, *International Encyclopedia of the Social Sciences*, Macmillan, New York, 1968.

Szostak, R., How to do interdisciplinarity: integrating the debate, *Issues in Integrative Studies*, 20, 103–122, 2002.

Szostak, R., *A Schema for Unifying Human Science: Interdisciplinary Perspectives on Culture*, Susquehanna University Press, Selinsgrove, PA, 2003.

Szostak, R., *Classifying Science: Phenomena, Data, Theory, Method, Practice*, Springer, Dordrecht, Holland, 2004.

Varela, C. and Harré, R., Conflicting varieties of realism: causal powers and the problems of social structure, *Journal for the Theory of Social Behavior*, 26(3), 313–325, 1996.

Wolfe, C. and Haynes, C., Interdisciplinary writing assessment profiles, *Issues in Integrative Studies*, 21, 126–169, 2003.

14 Foundation of Confucian Decision Making[*]

David Jones

CONTENTS

14.1 Introduction...265
14.2 Integrity and Intimacy 266
14.3 Philosophical Foundation of the Integrity or Western Self.......................................270
14.4 Philosophical Foundations of the Intimacy or East Asian Self.................................272
14.5 The Confucian Self and Its Decisions 274
     14.5.1 Ren..281
     14.5.2 Junzi..284
14.6 In Sum..286
References...286

14.1 INTRODUCTION

Decision making—the method of making decisions and deciding important matters of economics, social organization, matters of government, and so forth—in Western culture is far from the objective process society is led to believe. The manner of approaching problems, or even defining what constitutes, for example, a good education in the twenty-first century, emerges from a deeper structural foundation of one's worldview. Considering one's sense of what characterizes a good educational system (the basis of training in making decisions), it becomes apparent that society's vision of education is based upon many tenets of the Enlightenment. In the past, knowledge was a goal of its own and was considered a good for its own sake; this knowledge was ultimately gained through education. This became the ideal of the liberal arts education. In contemporary society, however, knowledge has become more practical—one learns in order to become useful, that is, one does not learn to know; one learns to do. Hence, emphasis is now placed on skill acquisition and training rather than on some vague conception that knowing is what it means to be human. Nowadays, it is natural to question children about what they intend to do with their philosophy majors, art majors, or English majors. Business majors are exempt from such interrogation since it is clear they have acquired a set of skills that have trained them to go into the marketplace and make the "right" decisions in "correct" ways. Knowledge is now measured by its utility. Ends are valued over means and the indoctrination of training is venerated as being the role of education.

---

[*] Some of this chapter has appeared in earlier forms in Jones (2000); Jones and Crosby (2001); Jones and Culliney (1998); Jones and Sweeney (2005). I am grateful to Roger T. Ames for his thoughtful review of an earlier draft and helpful suggestions.

The influence of Western decision making has been vast. Its reach has extended throughout the world through imperialistic practices in such diverse places as China, Africa, India, Latin America, and the Pacific, though this general list is far from inclusive. European economic imperialism has reached Islamic, Asian, and African civilizations in the forms of mercantile imperialism (1400–1850) and the "New Imperialism" (1800–1950). In the West, Great Britain, France, Belgium, the Netherlands, Germany, and now the United States have been prominent players in the extension of their lands and utilization of the planet's vast resources to meet their own national needs and satisfy their ambition for political power. These imperialistic tendencies have brought the Western perspective to the world; now, in an age of globalization, traditional beliefs have been challenged through the West's hegemonic tendencies. The Chinese, for example, who never had a very established conception of "rights"—but who had a profound and superior conception of "rites" as being fundamental to a well-functioning civil society—now have discussions of human rights; they have even idealized the Statue of Liberty as a symbol for a more open China, and perhaps for a less civil Chinese society.

What has been imported to the world through the West's more imperialistic tendencies—Asia never colonized the world as Europeans did—is something more than just its economic and political might. A whole new sense of a self, a self that Thomas Kasulis calls an "integrity self," has been introduced to the world. This is the self of the liberal West that rises to the foreground of interactions and negotiations with other cultures. This self backgrounds what Kasulis refers to as an "intimacy self," which is the foreground self of many other cultures in the world. The difference between these two senses of self, the integrity self of the West and the intimacy self of Asia, and how decision making is conceived in these disparate cultural milieus is the focus of what follows. Although now in a postmodern moment, which often denies its intellectual heritage, the Western sense of self finds its apotheosis of expression in Enlightenment conceptions and is largely derived from philosophical moves by Descartes (1596–1650) when he makes his famous statement that changes the world: "*Cogito ergo sum*" or "I think therefore I am." What the West values, and how it goes about making its judgments and decisions about and in the world, emerges and manifests itself from this statement. A Self, a particular kind of self, is created and arises as specifically defined, encapsulated, as a bearer of rights, and affirms its willingness to be unaware of hidden motivations that drive it throughout the world. This Self will not understand the self of Asia, or Africa, or the Pacific, nor will it likely understand the self of the Middle East; this Self will remain opaque in its understanding of how judgments and decisions are made in those contexts of intimacy. This self will value choice over consensus, or what Randy Peerenboom (2002) calls the "right to think" instead of "right thinking." The agency of the one making decisions will be valued over the contexts in which those choices and decisions are made. Indeed, the value of the "right to think," of the integrity of the agent making decisions, will be esteemed and promoted over the situations and contexts of intimacy in which those decisions are made.

14.2 INTEGRITY AND INTIMACY

For years, scholars gained some territory on understanding cultural difference by focusing their attentions on the distinction between the individualistic and collective dimensions of cultural experience. Asians, especially East Asians, were seen as being motivated by some sort of collectivism whereas Westerners were rooted firmly in a foundation of individuality. This distinction gave rise to some understanding of cultural difference, but ultimately served a limited purpose in the earlier days of understanding Asia and its vast reach of difference among various Asian groups. However, the limited application and value of this distinction was quickly outgrown, albeit many continued to insist on using it, and some still do. In his recent book *Intimacy or Integrity: Philosophy and Cultural Difference* (2002), Thomas Kasulis offers a new heuristic in which the old models of collectivism and individualism are subsumed in the two more effective categories of "intimacy" and "integrity."

Kasulis rightly extends the boundaries of his discussion to traverse not only Asian/Western differences, but also variations between cultures and subcultures as well. This inclusion is pertinent in the process of decision making within the frameworks of any given culture. The thesis of *Intimacy or Integrity: Philosophy and Cultural Difference* addresses the too simplistic notion that Asians are simply more collectivist than their Western counterparts, and Kasulis' thesis applies to cultural differences within the structure of any culture's grand narrative. Put more directly, his thesis is that there are recursive cultural patterns that orient themselves in the two basic ways of "intimacy" and "integrity." These patterns reiterate themselves into complex theoretical manifestations through understandings of fact/value, what is and what-should-be (Kasulis, 2002, 11).

Being aware that he might easily fall into the same simplistic trap of "them and us," Kasulis is quick to point out that "it is unlikely that any culture is ever a perfect example of either an intimacy-dominant or integrity-dominant culture" (2002, 11). In other words, the terms "intimacy" and "integrity" are each positive terms (unlike collectivistic and individualistic) that continually, and recursively, foreground and background themselves in any given culture. For example, Americans, with their penchant for individuality and the benefits arising from this belief such as the notion of rights, also value and understand intimacy as a primary feeling of belonging either to a family, group, or being a citizen. To think there is no value whatsoever of individuality in Asia is just simpleminded and fundamentally wrong. Kasulis explores the different ways of relating from the cultural perspectives of intimacy and integrity and how those relations themselves narrate the key relations of self/world, self/other, knower/known, thing/thing, and so forth (2002, 13).

An important aspect of this approach, and one often overlooked by even philosophers themselves, is that philosophy, the mother discipline of all disciplines in the West, is both a product of culture and a producer of culture. This latter point will have serious bearing on cultural decision making as we proceed. Even if culture becomes a matter of philosophical discussion, it is often cast in terms of being a "philosophy of culture," that is, as a part of our understanding of the role culture plays in a more universal understanding of human existence (Kasulis, 2002, 13). Kasulis reminds us, however, of another (and perhaps an even more important) dimension of studying what he calls "cultural philosophy"—"philosophy itself is a cultural enterprise" (2002, 14). By viewing philosophy in this sort of way, philosophers can check their tendency to believe erroneously that philosophy is a discipline that can achieve a realization of, or even attempt to, search for universal, eternal, and transcultural truths (these are the truths of which an integrity self searches). Kasulis points out that this too is a "tendency… related to cultural conditions" (2002, 14) and hence, "philosophy and culture are in a symbiotic, dialectical, or mutually influential relation" (2002, 17).

Applied to the nature of self—and everything arising from any particular definition of self such as value judgments and how they play themselves out in our organizational and social decision making—it is necessary to be less intrepid with economic, political, and even more importantly perhaps, cultural imperialistic tendencies, especially since economic and political balances of power will invariably shift throughout the course of history. Living in a peaceful and harmonious world becomes increasing crucial as destructive means expand and continue to proliferate throughout what once was a large world. The world, through the process of globalization and technological advances, is now shrinking considerably.

Kasulis first outlines the fundamental characteristics of the intimacy orientation since it is less apparent to those in the Western world:

1. Intimacy is objective, but personal rather than public.
2. In an intimate relation, self and other belong together in a way that does not sharply distinguish the two.

3. Intimate knowledge has an affective dimension.
4. Intimacy is somatic as well as psychological.
5. Intimacy's ground is not generally self-conscious, reflective, or self-illuminating (Kasulis, 2002, 24).

In this same chapter, he outlines the integrity orientation *vis-à-vis* intimacy:

1. Objectivity as public verifiability
2. External over internal relations
3. Knowledge as ideally empty of affect
4. The intellectual and psychological as distinct from the somatic
5. Knowledge as reflective and self-conscious of its own grounds (Kasulis, 2002, 25).

As evidenced, the competing orientations of intimacy and integrity are far more complex than earlier predispositions to individual versus collective. And it is through this complexity that Kasulis offers us "heuristic generalizations" that serve as a gestalt that allows "one to focus on what each culture tends to consider central, authoritative, or mainstream" and that "also makes exceptions stand out more sharply" (2002, 25). Kasulis makes those harder distinctions necessary for a more in-depth understanding of cultural dynamics—the scope of which is fundamental in this rapidly changing world, which brings people together in unique ways never experienced before. This is one challenge of the considerations of decision making, since each decision moves throughout the system and affects it with unprecedented swiftness.

One of Kasulis' most crucial distinctions for our purposes is found in his "What is Intimacy?" chapter:

> In everyday life, people often justifiably trust intimate forms of knowing that cannot be publicly verified but are still, in a significant sense, objective. It is important to distinguish, therefore, between two species of objectivity. The objectivity of publicly verifiable knowledge is based on empirical evidence and logic—that is, on what is immediately available to anyone.... Intimate knowledge's objectivity, by contrast, is accessible only to those within appropriate intimate locus, those who have achieved their expert knowledge through years of practical experience. (Kasulis, 2002, 35)

In certain cases, (though one may do so unknowingly) a person realizes experience—especially expert experience—is more vital in many situations than rational knowledge; this is the case even though such knowledge is affective. This insight will be instructive in understanding the difference between Confucius' authoritative model for making decisions vis-à-vis an authoritarian model. Other important aspects of intimacy include matters of style, which are fundamental in developing intrinsic interconnectedness (Kasulis, 2002, 45) and the darkness or inscrutability of intimacy because it is often hidden even from those involved (2002, 47). As Kasulis concludes: "Intimacy is a human, not cultural, phenomenon. What is significant for our purposes, however, is that one can at least imagine a culture that places a primary, rather than secondary, value on the enhancement of intimacy. Furthermore, one might be able to deduce what kind of philosophical orientation would flourish in such a culture" (Kasulis, 2002, 51). This conclusion is precisely what so many forget when functioning in a different culture or dealing with someone from another culture in business and organization negotiations.

Regarding Asia, especially East Asia, the Western world has neglected to take into account its more integrity based projections. Keeping this point of placing intimacy as a primary mode of being in the world will allow a greater entrée into the sphere of Confucian decision making and how it differs from Western styles. When this point is forgotten, or when the Western world remains unaware of this difference, misunderstanding and confusion are bound to result. Furthermore, it will become shut-off from understanding the potential of intimacy as an effective way of succeeding in the respective spheres of commerce, production, and forms of public administration and policy making. With the dominance of the integrity model in place, there will be nothing to learn from those who have been subjected to the hegemony of the Western integrity orientation. They will be perceived as being inferior, underdeveloped (or developing), and third world. And this is a serious mistake in a "globalized" world.

The complexities that are brought to light in human negotiations—cultural, economic, political, social, organizational, and so forth—are more profound than they appear. Not recognizing and embracing these cultural differences and approaches presents epistemological, metaphysical difficulties as well as issues of analysis and argumentation, aesthetics, ethics, politics, and even what constitutes science such as the field of ecology. Without these heuristic devices of intimacy and integrity, Asian knowledge could be viewed as inferior (and in fact many have regarded it as such), but this would be to miss something very crucial born from Kasulis' analysis: "Integrity tends to think of the world as something external to be managed through knowledge" [and one can begin to see both the glories and the limits of such a view] whereas "intimacy... tends to see the self and world as interlinking—the goal being to develop a sense of belonging *with* the world, feeling at home in it" (2002, 102). Integrity has focused on the "out there" through its use of "concepts, principles, and words" and connects to the world through an external relation between "the polarities of knower and known." On the other hand, intimacy understands knowledge "to reside in the interface *between* self and world" (Kasulis, 2002, 103). This interface between self and world is given expression in the West by John Dewey. Speaking to the intellectual transformation effected by Darwinian logic, Dewey saw clearly that:

> Interest shifts from the wholesale essence back of special changes to the question of how special changes serve and defeat concrete purposes; shifts from an intelligence that shaped things once for all to the particular intelligences which things are even now shaping; shifts from an ultimate goal of good to the direct increments of justice and happiness that intelligent administration of existent conditions may beget and that present carelessness or stupidity will destroy or forego. (1910, 43)

Dewey's insights about developing a greater sensitivity and promotion of a more intimate self, one that is more *with* the world and feeling at home *in* it are anticipated by Confucius by over 2,000 years and have contemporary relevance.

When the distinctions of intimacy and integrity are employed by social and political scholars, policy makers, public administration theorists, and by philosophers to investigate questions of value found in society and its organizations, we soon see the range of this distinction. For example, whereas an integrity orientation will view art as a subjective addition to the world, the intimacy orientation will see the work of art as of the world and simultaneously in it, that is, objective and subjective at the same time. Where integrity will view the artist's creativity as belonging to individual expression, intimacy views creativity as arising from the interaction of self and world together. An integrity orientation will view the company, organization, and institution as a place of work to which employees go and are responsible for performing their duties as prescribed by job descriptions and contracts between parties. Intimacy selves will see such places with a sense of belonging and being definitive of who they are, and they will be inclined to be responsive to the ever-changing contexts they encounter. In an integrity orientation, one *ought* to preserve another's rights through application of one's abstracted universal principles and maxims based on one's external relation to others, but when coming from an intimacy orientation, this "ought" is a recognition and preserving of one's overlap with the other. As these examples suggest, there is a profound difference between discourses of responsibility (integrity) and responsiveness (intimacy) and the application of universal principles and maxims and developing discourses of love and compassion. As will be seen, such differences in the nature of these discourses is essential in developing a fuller, and more effective, theory of decision making.

14.3 PHILOSOPHICAL FOUNDATION OF THE INTEGRITY OR WESTERN SELF

The legacy of the Enlightenment continues today. The American Revolution clearly separated church and state (although to this day religion ironically plays a major role in politics and social organization as the election of George W. Bush has demonstrated) and the American forefathers seemed to place the tenets of the Enlightenment into human praxis with the period's move toward a more secular conception of society. The Enlightenment serves as a model for social, political, and economic liberalism where human beings are afforded rights and benefits simply because they are human.

The term "Enlightenment" refers exclusively to a specific intellectual posture toward reality and a particular conception of what constitutes a person. This is the posture and conception that Kasulis refers to as *integrity*; it was significantly placed into effect in Europe and the American colonies during the eighteenth century. Accordingly, Western humanity and its thinkers viewed themselves as transcending earlier periods of religiosity. Theirs was a new age defined by freedom from the darkness of ignorance because they were now enlightened by science, and held a special kind of reverence for humanity itself instead of only having a reverence for the Church—its papacy, saints, and some transcendent God. This new age was defined, and could only be defined, by reason alone.

Reason, however, had been around long before Enlightenment thinkers and social theorists. Rationalists of the seventeenth century such as René Descartes, Baruch Spinoza, Thomas Hobbes, and John Locke dominated Western thought on the social and political spectrum. Through the application of reason, new discoveries in science made certain there was a high value placed upon man's abilities and human nature to be rational. As the non-European world began to be explored more fully, advances in anthropological thinking led to a new spirit of cultural relativism. Such exploration manifested imperialistic tendencies and the superiority of Western man over those he encountered with "inferior" scientific and social practices and different ways of social organization. Western woman was still not on the radar screen of the rational and scientific man. The world of imperialism was a man's world and largely remains so to our day.

The philosophical roots of this imperialism are found growing in Renè Descartes, the Western world's rationalist *par excellence*. Although Descartes' method of universal doubt sounds foolish on first encounter, it actually was a novel way to ascertain the indubitable truth for which he sought—to doubt all there is and whatever is left over is by definition indubitable, an assured certainty. This methodology found a truth from which to build a philosophical and scientific system upon. When Descartes doubts away the physical world and the existence of his body because all could be nothing but a projection of his mind, a dream, or the evil activities of a devious demon, he arrives at the certain truth—that he is thinking. Since thinking always requires a subject (thinker), he reasons he has found his indubitable truth; therefore, he exists, but his assured existence is only as a mind. This rationalism will give Descartes a radical dualistic world of mind/body, self/other, appearance/reality, and subject/object. Social sciences, such as psychology, were created in order to address the issues emerging from his analysis—novel philosophical problems such as the mind-body problem and the problem of other minds. All of this is born from the application of the innate human ability to reason. The concern here is the rationalistic divide between self and other, and how it plays itself out in the creation of the integrity self.

Dualism was long present in Western thought from the time of the Greeks onward. In many ways, Descartes only completes Plato's project: that the philosopher is to care for his individuated soul by separating it from the body, which is his definition of death, and this "death" is what will propel the soul from the inferior realm of the senses and sensible objects to the intelligible realm where ultimate reality is found—to where the soul ultimately belongs. What is much different in Descartes' thinking, however, is the radical division between the mental and physical aspects of our reality and the radically dualistic nature of the self.

The affective is of the body, that is, the intimate self is of an inferior nature and should not be given any rule over the experiential politic of the self. Reason, which is of the mind and the objective realm, needs to dictate the decision making process from the outset. Hence, democracies become the absolute best form of governments without question because in these systems one can exercise his or her rights as a reasonably responsible citizen. Laws are created to litigate failures of responsibility and are viewed as being impartial, that is, objective and reasonable. Fellow "reasonable" citizens assess the merit of cases to insure fair and equal treatment because all members of society are viewed as having equal opportunity and absolute rights within the legal, economic, and political system. Ideally, these rights apply to everyone because individual rights supersede the corporate interests of the institution, company, or organization. The irony in this situation is that legal and political maneuvers are invented and implemented to protect either collective interests or the interests of investors, stockholders, boards of directors, or the elite controlling class. Generally in this type of political arrangement, which is based upon a certain conception of what constitutes a person, all citizens have a right to vote because they are potentially reasonable and responsible. This is the ideal born from such thinkers as Descartes and subsequently expanded upon by others such as John Locke who added the necessary aspect of private property into the mix. Thomas Hobbes even went so far as to develop a contractual arrangement with the sovereign to care for the people in exchange for their allegiance to an orderly system of governance vis-à-vis a life that is "short, nasty, and brutish." This contract is an external relationship developed between autonomous individuals and their sovereigns and is mutually beneficial to each party. From this orientation, intimacy will be viewed as compromising the impartiality and objectivity of decision making.

The inherent dualism in this way of looking at and being in the world lends itself to the creation of society as some sort of derived arrangement of the collection of autonomous individuals who assert their rights and realize their potentials in the fair field of the market place or society. Relationships with fellow citizens are external as exemplified by the common manner in which one appeals to the law in order to regulate behavior towards one another. How one is related to others and relates to others is determined by how one defines oneself. If one gains self-definition from a conception of atomic individuality as a possessor of inalienable rights—that the dominant characteristics of being a human being are independent from participation in society and social context—and if one perceives society as a means of realizing individual aims and ends, then society will take on the complexion of being a derived arrangement, and become an abstraction that hardly seems real. This loss of reality has deleterious effects because in the final analysis people not only need to live with each other in some kind of harmonious fashion, they also need to learn to affect some mutuality in relations with other groups. From this perspective, society is some vague conceptual notion that is "out there" and I am somehow "in here," that is, in my individuality; I am a self that is external to society; I am a self of integrity. My ethical comportment and decision making in such a situation will appeal to principles that ensure my rights and well-being and the rights and pursuits of pleasure of others. These appeals manifest themselves as contractual arrangements between others and me that are preserved and protected by laws, which are abstractly manifested as The Law. All relations are external to who I am fundamentally as a human being.

However, as we look more closely at individuals and how they relate in the Western context we find, along with Kasulis (2002, 54) that because "of its untouchable character, integrity might at first seem not to be a relational term." All human beings need to relate and have relationships with others, but even the English language betrays its sense of an integrity self by "having" relationships. "I *have* a relationship with her." "*In our* relationship, we *have* this problem." "We need to change this *in* our relationship." Relationships are perceived as external to the self, but the self is still in some profound sense relational. In other words, integrity "is a mode of relating to others, one that maintains the self-identity of the related persons even while they are being related…. I recognize a person's integrity only as I observe that person in relationships. This analysis of integrity suggests that a person of integrity is not simply an individual, but an individual-in-relation"

(Kasulis, 2002, 55). It is still the case, however, that my identity "remains inviolate *from* infringements by the other; such a person also does not, in principle, violate the other person's identity. The person of integrity maintains the individuality of others as well as his or her own" (2002, 55); the person of integrity is true to oneself, a person of principle. This idea of self and the identity of the self are different from the intimacy version found in many non-Western contexts.

An identity of integrity will give rise to a social contract model between self, society, government, or organization. Such a theory, as Kasulis notes, "claims that the nature of human beings leads to establishing certain appropriate kinds of external, contractual relations with others" (2002, 58). As organizations develop from this orientation, contracts of expectations and responsibilities are established between interested parties: employer/employee, supervisor/supervised, government/citizen, and so forth. Such contracts, whether written or assumed, create discrete entities that are connected with other discrete entities through the external relation of a contract that can be violated by either of the parties on the basis of infringements upon their rights. Although these entities function together, they always remain discrete from one another, and make their decisions accordingly. In times of trouble, attorneys are hired to protect their respective party's interests if contracts are somehow breached.

A serious pitfall of this system of decision making occurs when the integrity of any individual is valued over the health and well-being of the organization, that is, when authoritarianism prevails over authoritativeness; this is especially the case when someone of position has been promoted beyond her ability, or is simply incompetent. Often, these authoritarian types will seek legacy appointments after retirement. Even during their reigns, they will make certain there is always a circulation of elites in place to protect their authoritarian "leadership." At the integrity level all seems fine, even if the reach into the future is somehow thwarted by other factors emerging from the bottom up. In this context where there is a termination of the relationship, both parties maintain their integrity and "exist as unbroken, unviolated, wholes" (Kasulis, 2002, 60) because the relationship is external from the outset. However, terminating an internal relationship from an intimacy orientation "results in both relatents losing a part of their identity: the *a* and *b* become less themselves or at least less of what they had been" (Kasulis, 2002, 60).

14.4 PHILOSOPHICAL FOUNDATIONS OF THE INTIMACY OR EAST ASIAN SELF

In contradistinction to the autonomy and independence of the integrity self so prevalent in Western ways of being in the world is the interdependent orientation of the self of intimacy. This self is seen most vividly throughout East Asia, which will be the focus here, and African cultures. The extreme views of the selves of intimacy and integrity are most easily seen, as Kasulis (2002, 61) maintains, in the differences between Buddhism and existentialism. After setting out these extreme versions of the differences, our discussion will turn to the Confucian project because Confucius was most concerned about human relations and the emergent human condition from the matrix of social relations. This will give us a more direct way of understanding the foundation of intimacy in Chinese decision making.

It is well known that the project known as existentialism emphasizes human autonomy, freedom of choice, and the subsequent responsibility for those choices. The meaning of our existences is found in the integrity from which we comport ourselves with our fellow beings. The comportment of the existentialist is one of radical personal freedom that posits existence as preceding essence. For the existentialist, the radicality of this personal freedom is always, as Kasulis writes, "framed by 'facticity'—the external circumstances over which one has no control. Yet the existentialist maintains, no matter how restrictive the facticity, there is always room for some autonomy" (2002, 61). Although many Westerners would not totally buy into the existential project and its other themes of subjectivity, despair, melancholia, and absurdity as being definitive of the human condition, most of us are believers in the freedom of choice and responsibility. We concur that our lives are a series of choices and that we need to affirm our free wills to choose while facing the absurdity of things, that our choices may indeed result in negative consequences that may even hurt others, and that we must follow through on our decisions because if we do not, our lives are rendered meaningless. This affirmation of ours is a uniquely human one and gives a utilitarian value to a unique life. Because we are free to make decisions, we are completely responsible for the decisions we make. This freedom makes us responsible beings and through the exercise of our decision making, we ultimately choose ourselves. Although the realization that I am completely free, or as Sartre says "condemned to my freedom," may lead to feelings of profound anxiety, or *Angst*, I must not deceive myself—I need to embrace this realization. Only when I accept this responsibility can I live authentically, that is, only then can I have a meaningful life. This is the extreme version of the self of integrity, but one that is manifest in most Westerners.

The extreme version of the self of intimacy is found in Buddhism, especially in its doctrine of *anatman*, or no-self. The Buddhist understands the self to be radically relational, that is, it "entirely denies the existence of the 'I' or ego (*atman*) as an independent entity. [It] understands *every* aspect [of the self] to be conditioned by processes around him or her" (Kasulis, 2002, 62). The no-self doctrine resonates with a more fundamental theory of Buddhism, which is widely supported by new scientific discoveries and thinking such as chaos theory and complexity science, that everything in the world is conditioned by other things.[*] The Buddhist Theory of Interdependent Arising basically states, "When this comes to be, that comes to be; when this ceases to be, that ceases to be." In Buddhism, *Paticca sumuppada*, or interdependent arising, means that everything is constantly changing, impermanent, selfless; nothing exists separately by and of itself—every individual thing in the world conditions other things and is conditioned by them (Koller 1998, 151). This is the idea of *sunyata*, or emptiness. As the Madhyamaka philosopher Nagarjuna says in the *Mula-madhymakakarika* 24.18: "Emptiness is interdependent arising." From the Buddhist perspective, the affirmation of a separate reality of identity—the byproduct of conceptualizing after the fact of experience—is not subject to these conditioning forces; however, it is the greatest illusion and cause of *dukkha*, or trouble, and by extension, suffering—the affirmation of the not-self (*anatman*), that is, the self as an "interbeing" that emerges from the dynamic play of the conditioning forces of an unfolding world is to eliminate *dukkha* and affirm life. This affirmation of life reintegrates oneself continually and immerses the self into the dynamic structure and flow of the spontaneous, self-generating, organismic process continuum we call world. To borrow a term from Merleau-Ponty's Phenomenology of Perception (1962, 404), this world is really an *interworld* (*intermonde*). The interworld is continuous and dynamic. In its wholeness, the interworld is the only reality where everything, as Tu Wei-ming has emphasized, "is holistically integrated at each level of complexity"[†] (Ames and Callicott, 1989, 70).

According to Buddhism, "I am not a self-existent being who chooses with what or how I wish to relate to external circumstances [as does the existentialist]. I... am the nexus of a series of completely interdependent processes... and the processes of which I am part lead me to connect with other processes" (Kasulis, 2002, 63). Our identities then as persons are the unique overlapping of all the overlapping processes that constitute who we are and in the most fundamental ontological sense, we are completely without substantiality, without "any untouched nucleus" (2002, 62). From this type of cultural orientation, decision making, and what constitutes making good decisions, is radically different from the integrity view of the West and its legacy from the rationalists all the way

---

[*] This is often referred to as "coevolution" in these theories. For accessible reading on this coevolutionary connectedness see Lewin (1992, 81 ff.); Waldrop (1992, 288 ff.).

[†] Tu Wei-ming is writing here of Daoism, but what he says is applicable to the Buddhist project as well.

to the existentialists, which at first take appears to be completely antithetical. Confucius carefully articulates this type of intimacy view and applies it to human interactions in ways more socially oriented than Buddhism.

14.5 THE CONFUCIAN SELF AND ITS DECISIONS

If we apply our understanding of how a culture can give primary position to the intimacy view and secondary importance to the integrity view, we can begin to comprehend more fully the view of society and self Confucius puts forward. This view sees the self in the relational and conditional terms discussed, but will orient the self to its responsiveness to other selves, both living and dead, and proffer a different view of what constitutes society and how we attend to our decision making. In their book, *The Democracy of the Dead: Dewey, Confucius, and the Hope for Democracy in China* (1999). Roger Ames and David Hall offer a carefully referenced discussion on the Chinese sense of person as being "something that one *does* rather than *is*" (Hall and Ames, 1999, 190). Their discussion is framed by an analysis of two Chinese terms that are useful for our purposes here. The terms are *qi*, which they translate as "vital energizing field," and *xin*, "heart-mind." Their discussion is executed through a focus/field model "in which the individual is not considered a part of society to which he or she belongs, but a productive *focus* of the experiences and interactions constituting that society" (Hall and Ames, 1999, 191). In other words, the Chinese sense of self emerges from an intimacy cultural orientation, and all decision making taking place in the organizational and institutional fields is underwritten by that culture. Such decision making necessarily will be different from an integrity orientation where individuals view themselves as integral parts or components that at first stand outside the fields (as beings that *are*) and then participate in the particular contexts provided by organizations and institutions. The Chinese sense of self, on the other hand, is an emergent being (one that is because of what it *does*) from the context from which it surfaces. Any individual is a focus of overlapping vital energizing fields of *qi* that are interdependently related. In other words, the Chinese sense of self is more an event, an aggregated experience, than it is a disparate being standing outside its field of participation. The prototype for this aggregated field of interdependence is the family; the family is the sphere of influence for the consensual and is the governing metaphor for Confucian thinking and the Chinese cultural sensibility. Although there are fundamental roles in the family that must be recognized—fathers and mothers cannot act like sons or daughters to their children—and familial roles are by definition distinct from each other, healthy families promote consensus over the right of individual choice. Again, it should be noted that this is not an either/or division, but more a matter of foregrounding and backgrounding of the two cultural tendencies of intimacy and integrity.

To understand the dynamics of the way the Chinese conduct themselves in political, business, educational, and social decision making, which are often elusive to Westerners, it is necessary to look to the historical roots of their particular cultural orientation. To locate the roots of contemporary Chinese culture, one must have an understanding of and an appreciation for the role of Confucius' thinking.

Understanding Chinese thought and its cultural context represents one of the greatest challenges for Westerners. How can we come to understand adequately the longest continuous civilization on the planet and its success at surviving numerous challenges to its unified sense of being? And, more importantly, what is it we in the West might learn from the Chinese? Some understanding of China's cultural and philosophical heritage is necessary for the importation of Chinese ideas into our creative philosophizing, living, and making decisions about how we organize ourselves in the society today. By lifting ideas from the Chinese tradition *vis à vis* our own, we can gain a greater understanding of ourselves by looking at this ancient cultural *other* that has been more successful than anyone else in sustaining itself continuously throughout time in the face of many obstacles. One of the reasons for its sustained success is the Confucian sensibility to intergenerationality. The West understands the importance of China in the world today because of its political and economical stature, but what does this encounter with China ultimately mean to us in terms of how we go about comporting ourselves in a complex and rapidly change world and how we behave in our own social and organizational circumstances?

Let me suggest this encounter with the Chinese is curiously and ultimately the encounter with ourselves, because this encounter forces us to break through the dialogue of the silence of our solipsistic being and shows us our own face. The integrity self we have been discussing takes on a new dimension in this encounter; this new dimension is a new subjectivity; this new dimension is the self discovering itself to be a fuller self, a self of intimacy as well. This appropriation of giving more primacy to the intimacy self is the meaning of what Confucius says in the *Analects* 6.3 when he proclaims "in wanting to establish himself, he establishes others; in wanting to succeed himself, he helps others to succeed."*

By investigating some features of the Chinese philosophical tradition, we have greater opportunities to better understand ourselves, seek possible prescriptions for many of our social maladies, and come to terms with the awareness that "my" decisions are the decisions of others—that my decisions affect the entire range of those overlapping beings who fall within the scope of the intimate circle that is me. This intimate circle also includes our work places where we spend much of our lives and the institutions we create. The philosophy of Confucius is central to understanding Chinese thought and culture, and offers different ways, which are often novel to us in the West, of thinking about our individual lives and our relationship to the communities in which we participate. As we will see later, the Chinese have an enhanced sense of the constitution of community; this sense extends across generations. For us, the philosophy of Confucius is central in making a more inclusive and equitable democracy here at home and to living the good life that was heralded as the primary concern of those wise Greek philosophers who started us on our current course of integrity.

When we first approach the text of the Confucius' *Analects* we are confronted with what appears to be an assortment of unrelated sayings. Navigating through the *Analects* can be a daunting task for the initiate of Confucius' philosophy, but one of the easiest ways of gaining purchase on the *Analects* is to organize topically the text around key terms; such an approach reveals the conceptual structure and unity of Confucius' thought.† To bring the focus of the discussion into a more specific light, I will discuss some key terms and their relevant passages in the *Analects*, especially *li* (the rites or observing ritual propriety) and *ren* (human-heartedness or authoritative conduct). In addition, two other important terms are introduced: *junzi* (exemplary person) and *yi* (rightness, morality, or appropriateness). I discuss all of these terms in the revealing light of *wen*, or culture. This light reveals a different approach to decision making, whether it is about moral decision making, how we conduct ourselves in the marketplace, or how we comport ourselves in organizational settings.

The word *wen* means literally "to inscribe," "to embellish," and by extension means "culture" (Ames and Rosemont, 1998, 58). It is interesting to note the inference made here: those who can write and embellish are those with culture. In other words, humans are those beings within whom culture is present because we have a language that embellishes and inscribes. Confucius saw himself less a philosopher (not that he would have even had this conception) and more of an artificer of *dao*, or way. For him, "the way" is always the way of culture and it is through our cultural heritage that we become particular kinds of selves who make particular types of decisions about how we position ourselves in the collective context of culture. All cultures have social rituals.

---

* All translations from the *Analects* of Confucius are from the Ames and Rosemont (1998) translation unless otherwise noted. The book number will be given first followed by the passage number, for example, 6.3 (Book 6, passage 30). When book and passage numbers are given, page numbers in the Ames and Rosemont translation will not be cited. This translation is most readable. An excellent introduction and bibliography accompanies the translation and the translators are very sensitive to the nuances of Confucius' thinking and to philosophical issues in general.

† For a more detailed discussion on this approach to reading the *Analects*, see Jones (2000).

To understand Confucius is to understand his central thinking on *li*. For Westerners, the first encounter with *li*, the rites or observing ritual propriety, seems a bit odd. The centrality of *li* in Confucius's thought cannot be emphasized enough, however, as evidenced when Confucius says in the following passage on *ren*: "Do not look at anything that violates the observance of ritual propriety; do not listen to anything that violates the observance of ritual propriety; do not speak about anything that violates the observance of ritual propriety; do not do anything that violates the observance of ritual propriety" (12.1). Confucius might have added, "Do not ever make a decision unless it is in accordance with *li*. Why would Confucius accord such central prominence to *li*?"

As suggested above, Chinese philosophy appears as being far less abstract and dualistic than its European counterparts. Even the rationalistic tendencies in Chinese philosophy seem less abstract to us. On one hand, much of this tendency is a consequence of the concreteness of the Chinese language, but more central to our purposes is that the focus of the Chinese is on human relations (hence, a focus of intimacy), especially in Confucius' thought and the subsequent Confucian tradition. The overwhelming concern for Confucius is the relation of the human being with other human beings, which is maximized through a process of self-cultivation. While the Western philosophical tradition displays a strong abstract rationalistic disposition beginning with Plato and finding its fullest expression in Descartes' philosophy, Chinese philosophy is rationalistic in more concrete ways; exemplars of appropriate behavior and authentic responsiveness to others are preferred to universally applied doctrines. As we have seen, society in Western thought is viewed as a derived arrangement, or an abstraction, of atomic individuals, each of whom bears certain inalienable rights. The Chinese, on the other hand, traditionally view society as being the source for the circumscribing characteristics of the individual. Consequently, society becomes a repository of values, and is not seen as only an arena for actualizing human potential as it is often regarded in the West. For the Chinese, individuals become concrete exemplars of value, and ought to be emulated as instantiations of reasonableness. In this light, when one makes a decision from a position of authority, those decisions represent something more than just a course of action for which to be responsible. There is no qualification present that "we all make mistakes" and that "we can now make another decision" that will reorient the first course of action or rectify the consequences of the original decision. The authoritative decision of the one who is an authorized authority necessarily defines all those who are mapped in his or her sphere of influence and is an expression of traditional context that becomes an investment for future generations. Since the authority significantly defines the being and identity of others in the past, present, and future, it is requisite that he or she be exemplary. The underlying value here is respect and the promotion of productive harmony, not the assertion of individual rights.

Thinking about this difference in terms of intimacy and integrity and how they are ordered as either primary or secondary is helpful in understanding why the Chinese in their worldview privilege "rites" over "rights." The focus on humanity and the tendency for a concrete rationality lets us understand the central importance of *li* in the philosophy of Confucius. Once human beings as circumscribed participants in the social context are designated as the focus and locus of inquiry, it is easier to appreciate the centrality of *li* in Confucius' thinking. The word seems to have the root feature of a holy ritual or sacred ceremony (Fingarette, 1972, 6), which provides its historical dimension. This historical dimension is crucial for understanding Confucius' philosophy because the individual self, through the proper practice of *li*, extends into the social sphere and matrix of tradition. This extension into tradition has a magical quality to it that extends far beyond the original meaning of *li* as holy rite. As Fingarette points out, "the magical element always involves great effects produced effortlessly, marvelously, with an irresistible power that is itself intangible, invisible, unmanifest" (Fingarette, 1972, 4). When we think about *li* in the context of the *junzi*, or the exemplar of social value and virtue (an ideal for anyone in a position of authority), we find support for this claim of *li* having a magical, mysterious, and even heavenly power. If we read the following sections of the *Analects* together, we can see that the behavior of the *junzi*, the exemplary person, should and will prompt emulation that borders on the divine:

- The Master said: "Governing with excellence (*de*) can be compared to being the North Star: the North Star dwells in its place, and the multitude of stars pay it tribute." (2.1)
- The Master said, "Lead the people with administrative injunctions and keep them orderly with penal law, and they will avoid punishments but will be without a sense of shame. Lead them with excellence (*de*) and keep them orderly through observing ritual propriety (*li*) and they will develop a sense of shame, and moreover, will order themselves." (2.3)
- The Master said, "Learn broadly of culture (*wen*), discipline this learning through observing ritual propriety (*li*), and moreover, in so doing, remain on course without straying from it." (12.15)
- Ji Kangzi asked Confucius about governing effectively (*zheng*), and Confucius replied to him, "Governing effectively is doing what is proper (*zheng*). If you, sir, lead by doing what is proper, who would dare do otherwise?" (12.17)
- Ji Kangzi Tzu asked Confucius about governing effectively (*zheng*), saying, "What if I kill those who have abandoned the way (*dao*) to attract those who are on it?"

"If you govern effectively, "Confucius replied," what need is there for killing? If you want to be truly adept (*shan*), the people will also be adept. The excellence (*de*) of the exemplary person (*junzi*) is the wind, while that of the petty person is the grass. As the wind blows, the grass is sure to bend." (12.19) (Ames and Rosemont, 1998).

As the *junzi* looks, listens, speaks, and moves in accordance with *li*, others, as the above quotes suggest, follow his or her example without coercion or force; not only do they follow as the second quote suggests, they are self-ordering. Exemplary persons are given to what appears to us in the West as divine status. And it is this status from which the person of *ren* (authoritative conduct) is viewed because he also defines who and what we are as particular "vital energizing fields" (*qi*) emerging from the greater field of the context at hand. This context has also emerged from a series of ongoing, mutual influencing, and overlapping contexts that lead to future contexts that are either amplified or diminished (if not successfully congruent and reiterative) from the present one. In 15.5, we see this divine posture and magical power spoken by Fingarette (1972) reinforced:

The Master said, "If anyone could be said to have effected proper order while remaining nonassertive, surely it was Shun. What did he do? He simply assumed an air of deference and faced due south."

If the *junzi* acts and exercises appropriate (*yi*) decision making in accordance with *li*, effects of his or her actions follow in natural ways. Shun has nothing to do except be his excellent and virtuous (*de*) self, to be himself as an exemplar for others. This is the Confucian counterpart to the Daoist notion of *wuwei*, or non-directed and nonassertive action, where the sage does nothing and nothing is left undone. Such actions and their amplifying consequences arise from authoritative, not authoritarian conduct. The emanating appropriateness and goodness of the *junzi* is contagious and has amplifying effects as he or she moves throughout the overlapping circles of intimacy that are definitive of the authoritative decision maker. Decisions cannot be made purely in pragmatic terms where they are moved through as a list of prioritized options; they must be made with the cognizance that they create lives, are definitive of those very lives they create, and simultaneously contribute to the vigor of future generations. In other words, the *junzi* is the author of actions that commence a process that amplifies toward the manifestation of desired results for the well-being of the collective context, whether that context is a corporation, university, or government. Such expectation creates a ponderous duty on those in charge to be qualified and sensitive to the field of vital and energizing relationships, as well as sympathetically motivated to those affected by their decisions. In other words, this expectation creates a compassionate meritocracy of sorts where accomplishments are acknowledged within the greater meaning of the context of the organization. As Confucius says, "Authoritative persons establish others in seeking to establish themselves and promote others in seeking to get there themselves. Correlating one's conduct with those near at hand can be said to be the method of becoming an authoritative person" (6.30).

Both the sacred and magical dimensions of *li* lead ultimately to harmony and dynamic order, which are Confucius' goals. These goals ought to be the objective of any organizational structure defined by an intimacy cultural orientation because the emergence and development of *li* are not consciously driven or ordered by some external transcendent source such as God, the Platonic Idea of the Good, compliance with some abstract moral principle, or even a set of rules that stultify the dynamic process because they originate at the top and travel downward. *Li* are immanent patterns and emerge from their social context; *li* govern the patterns of social intercourse in any context where there is common purpose.[*] What makes *li* so magical is the "intangible," "invisible," "unmanifest" power of human interactions—*li*'s inherent emergent quality. The other side of the magic of *li* is its continuity, which often remains an unnoticed value in decision making in cultures influenced by Confucius' thought such as the economically successful China, Japan, and Korea. The continuity and (re)generation of *li* are necessary for "maintaining institutional and cultural continuity with a minimum of conscious intervention" (Hall and Ames, 1987, 22). *Li* are regenerated for the next generation and their children and this regeneration can be seen perhaps more accurately as a re-authorization of *li*. *Li* are continually authorized.

Our social conventions and customs are complex systems comprised from the connections of many interacting units. Each person in a society, or in its microcosmic version of an organization, has his or her own individual needs, desires, aspirations, ideas, and so on. Unlike democratic systems of government and social organization that base their development and structure on serving those needs of the atomic individual (or the collective needs of atomic board of investors, regents, or so forth), Confucian society ordered itself on the principle of the community being greater than any individual part or the sum of its parts, which includes past and future participants. Therefore, society is seen as an organic community emerging from the interaction of all its parts. The community is a complex system that is not so much created by any individual—even Confucius himself—but emerges as a result of individual transactions. Hence the individual is not defined by what he or she *is* but by what he or she *does*. Even corporations will often be viewed more like families where intimacy prevails than as places of contractual responsibilities between employees, employers, CEO's, and boards of investors. Accordingly, humanizing the workplace from a Confucian perspective creates more belonging, loyalty, continuity (a primary incentive of families), and commitment to common goals when employees define themselves as participants in the operations, activities, and practices that are solidly based on authoritative excellence as opposed to top-down authoritarian management.

Confucius did not invent *li*, nor did he actually design a society based on the socially therapeutic regimens of *li* (although he did try to influence rulers by asserting that his philosophy was a means of gaining social and political order). What makes Confucius such an important social thinker with relevance to any organization is that he affirms and articulates a natural development of the emergence of order from the possibility of chaos, and the possible slip of society over the precipice of that very chaos. Arising spontaneously, as Tony Cua (1971, 44) states, *li* defines "the conventionally accepted *style* of actions, i.e. the form and possibility of moral achievement within the cultural setting." Historically, no social group consciously decides its conventions—there is no convening. To borrow an example from Fingarette, conscious decisions to become either a bowing culture or a handshaking culture are never made. Such conventions emerge unconsciously. Depending upon the inherent interactions of the participants in any given social system, certain forms of customs, mores, conventions, and so forth emerge as natural consequences from systemic

---

[*] For a more developed discussion of this aspect of Confucius' thinking see Jones and Culliney (1998).

interactions and transactions. This emergent *li* is an expression and manifestation of the inherent values of the social system and its participants. Confucius merely looks at the interactions and the resulting manifestations of *li* and affirms the process as being essential to the establishment of social order. In fact, for Confucius nothing is more important than *li*, because as previously discussed, any participant in society or organization should: "not look,… listen,… speak,…[or] move unless it is accordance with the rites" (Lau, 1979, 112). In Confucius' thought there is a profound awareness that *li* has an organic aspect; it has the inherent ability for growth or diminution over time. The structure, sustainability, and orderly flow of information within any system can, and will change and Confucius is astutely aware of this when he suggests that observance and affirmation of this orderly flow is crucial to the preservation of society; to a great extent, the Chinese have accomplished this even under some rather adverse historical conditions. Such awareness can also be applied to any convening of people in any type of collective arrangement ranging from schools to corporations. If the social or organizational system's *li* are not responsive to the changing needs of the context, stability will surely be lost. Once lost, the fragile fabric of the society or organization comes one step closer to losing its pattern of order. Confucius knew that this step was a movement either toward the extinction of the social system as an orderly one or to a drastic change that may not be very desirable. Therefore, it is in any system's best interest to be adaptive; the alternative is chaotic extinction or abject authoritarianism, that is, the loss of appropriate authoritative decision making.

Hence, Confucius thus allows for variation in *li* over time, but this variance must be in harmony with the emergent order of the system. Tu Wei-ming makes this point when he addresses the problem of *li* as a process of humanization and "an authentic way of establishing humanrelatedness;" therefore, "*li* is understood as movement instead of form." According to Tu (1972, 194), *li* evolved from a "proper act of sacrifice to an authentic way of establishing humanrelatedness [*ren*]" and "the emphasis is on its dynamic process rather than its static structure." As Confucius himself says:

> The use of a hemp cap is prescribed in the observance of ritual propriety. Nowadays, that a silk cap is used instead is a matter of frugality. I would follow accepted practice on this. A subject kowtowing on entering the hall is prescribed in the observance of ritual propriety. Nowadays that one kowtows only after ascending the hall is a matter of hubris [that is, it's casual]. Although it goes contrary to accepted practice, I still kowtow on entering the hall. (9.3)

Fortuitous or forced changes—those changes that do not affirm the sustainability of the social system or genuinely appropriate the emergent spontaneity inherent within the system—will cast the system into unforeseen consequences, into a chaos similar to Confucius' day. Similarly, neither following the "party line," nor consistently rebelling against it without appropriate reason is to be avoided at all costs. These are some of the reasons why Confucius "had nothing to say about strange happenings [prodigies], the use of force, disorder, or the spirits" (7.21). Confucius' sense of the divine (*tian*, or heaven) is to be found in the emerging immanent patterns of human social behavior and conduct that continually present themselves. Changes that are not reasonable for the continuance, sustainability, and subsequent growth in Confucius' idea of a social system will pollute the system and subsequently cause its orderly flow of information to be disrupted sending it into the spiral of destructive change or even extinction. As Fingarette (1972, 20) has noted:

> The Confucian commitment to a single, definite order is also evident when we note that Confucius sees as the alternative to rightly treading the true Path: it is to walk crookedly, to get lost or to abandon the Path [*Dao*]. That is, the only "alternative" to the one Order is disorder, chaos.

This commitment to a single, definite order is an appropriation of the emergent spontaneity immanent in the process of the *li*'s becoming, which will mutate at the proper time for its—and the social and organizational organism's—health and survival. Ultimately, the survival of *li* is dependent on the continued life of its interacting cells, of cultured human beings, and the continuous life of human beings depends on the progression of *li*. This order to which Fingarette notes is not some transcendent independent order that is to be followed blindly, but is rather a participatory and emergent order that is immanent and dynamic. Confucius is aware, more than most of his Western counterparts, that any system seeks one constant goal: to perpetuate itself in the face of extinction. There are, however, forces at work in the system that are more self-promoting, selfishly motivated, and chaos driven. Many of these forces arise from integrity orientations where egos become more important than the health and well-being of a school, company, organization, or country. Such authoritarianism is divisive and ultimately destructive. Some organizations such as corporations may recover quickly with a change to appropriate leadership, but it will take others much longer given their particular contexts. Educational institutions, where change is often slower and more deliberate by nature, may take decades to fix. Even governments may be more responsive.

A virtue of Confucius' thought is his realization of the unknown immanent force that seeks emergence. This immanent force makes all life, not just human life (both biological and social), possible. As Ames and Hall (1987, 16) have said, "order is realized, not instantiated." The integrity approach instantiates order, imposing overlays of order onto things either through the application of universal principles, contracts, or laws. The intimacy approach will seek out the way of things. Confucius (as other potential exemplars should strive to become) is best seen as an artificer of *dao*, that is, one who skillfully crafts the way of natural phenomena (of which the human is seen as an intimate part) into human propriety. Confucius looked at the weakly interactive connectivity of his fellow beings, some of whom probably appeared arbitrarily impulsive to him, and designed his philosophy of *li*. When he viewed the emergent social order he saw a conditioned maximal information exchange, or the potential for that change, in the form of *li*. It was through the interactions and transactions of those human beings of the dissolved Zhou Empire that Confucius came to understand the need for societal order. Confucius is the first thinker to realize that human harmony can be achieved only when there is an appropriate vehicle through which it can gain expression. This vehicle, as Hall and Ames (1998, 259) describe, is the "repertory of those formal roles, practices, actions, and institutions that continue the living culture. [*Li*] are meaning-invested behaviors that, when properly enacted, conduce to communal harmony." This emergent vehicle of *li* is the creative force within the system.

Confucius was an astute observer when he regarded the interactions of his fellow beings. The exchanges he witnessed were often very subtle in nature. The flow of communication was not obvious, but it was present in very distinct and profound ways. Any resulting harmony from the acting through *li* had nothing much to do with the content of the act, but what emerged through the acting of the act. The vehicle for expression had already been convened unconsciously as the meaning for interaction. Any failure to respond appropriately within the context of the vehicle of *li* would violate the natural order of social relations. Either the imposition of excessive authoritarian control or the explosion of freewheeling impulsivity could render things frozen in complacency or totally chaotic. For Confucius, *li* occupies a narrow zone between failing to perceive appropriately the boundary of freewheeling impulsivity and pressing one's own advantage in an authoritarian way. From the Chinese viewpoint, balance is always crucial. Hence, Confucius was very concerned that *li* should be performed appropriately and with discipline; any person in power to make decisions, then, needs to be of such an excellent (*de*) quality that she will necessarily make decisions which will enrich lives, because those very decisions *are* the lives within the decision maker's own scope of self. As an exemplar for others, Confucius "would not eat food that was improperly prepared, or that was lacking the appropriate condiments and sauces. Even when meat was abundant, he would not eat it in disproportionate amount to staple foods. Only in his wine did he not limit himself, although he never got drunk" (10.8). Such disciplined authoritative comportment is necessary for harmonic relations and ultimately for sustained productivity.

Perturbations to any complex system, including social and organizational systems, need not be large to have immense impacts; potentially the addition or loss of a grain of sand may bring a mountain down. Similarly, casual, nonchalant, awkward, and unauthentic performances or denials of *li* can have devastating effects. This is the reason why Confucius continues the traditional practice of kowtowing on entering the hall as seen in 9.3 above. Modern society provides many examples of how contemporary culture is plunging into the cultural abyss of unauthentic ways of relating. We have forgotten how to apologize, express gratitude, and show respect for our fellow beings. Such failures are unfortunately the emergent values of the integrity based version of *li* where people are concerned primarily about themselves. The arbitrary, contemporary sense of community gives expression to this malaise: planned retirement, apartment, condominium complexes that are gated and equipped with private swimming pools, golf courses, handy mini-marts, and so forth. Being brought together in such soulless and artificial ways and being cordoned off from interacting with other communities is contrary to the natural drives and emergent possibilities that do not necessarily exclude others. Any number of possibilities existed for the development of *li* in China, but the various constituent parts of Chinese society interacted in such a way that ordered the apparent chaos to express itself in the way gleaned by Confucius.

Cultures consciously do not convene and decide what types of cultures they wish to be; nor do they decide what types of customs and mores are preferable over other options. *Li* are the emerging principles that give coherence and order to societies and any collective human endeavor; *li* are self-organizing evolutionary processes that are manifested through interaction and develop into networks of interdependence. These manifested and evolved networks of interdependence are the systemic basis of humanity. If harmony and order are primary goals, as they are in the traditional Chinese social and political context, authentic tradition is affirmed as necessarily having a sacred dimension. By extending oneself beyond the immediacy of one's life, one extends oneself back into the authentic tradition of the past where the emergent *li* express the manifest values of culture. For Confucius, what and who we are in the most profound sense is a product of this authentic tradition that separates us from the nonhuman. Our organizational structures, from Confucius' viewpoint, need to reflect this authenticity.

14.5.1 REN

The adage attributed to the Chinese that a picture is worth a thousand words is a good place from which to begin a discussion of *ren* because it affords some purchase on his social philosophy and its organizational implications. The everyday term *ren* simply means person: . Although the major Confucian virtue of *ren* is written a bit differently ; it is derived by adding the number two to *ren* . [*] What this *picture* suggests is that the highest virtue in Confucius' thought is achievable in relationships of only three or more, that is, only in families, organizations, and societal relationships. Asking what happens to relationships where a "third" is introduced, or about relationships of three or more leads to an immediate realization of the difficulty in attaining the life of excellence and virtue (*de*) because of the continuous attention needed for harmonious negotiations. Harmony is the central goal to cultures of intimacy, not self-actualization. As Ames and Hall (1998, 259) have remarked: "One cannot become *ren* in Descartes' closet."

Arthur Waley (1938, 27) points out that *ren* "in the earliest Chinese means freeman, men of the tribe, as opposed to *min*, 'subjects,' 'the common people'" and "the same word, written with a slight modification, means 'good' in the most general sense of the word, that is to say, 'possessing qualities of one's tribe.'" The extended meaning of this term according to Waley comes to be an accolade of kindness, gentleness, and humanity that ultimately distinguishes the "'human' as opposed to 'animal,' and [comes] to be applied to conduct worthy of a man, as distinct from the behaviour of mere beast" (Arthur Waley, 1938, 27). A.C. Graham (1989, 19) connects the

---

[*] See, Ames and Rosemont (1998, 48) for a discussion on two possible etymologies of *ren*.

commendation of *ren* more specifically to culture when he writes that "the noble, civilized, fully human, pride themselves on their manners and conventions [*li*], but above all on the virtues which give these meaning and which distinguish themselves from the boors and savages who do not know how to behave." In the *Analects*, *ren* means good in the most general sense (Waley, 28). For reasons that will be more apparent later, Waley's translation of *ren* as "Goodness" or "Good" or D.C. Lau's (1979) translation of *ren* as "benevolence" are unfortunate in some senses for Westerners. Although both translations have justifications for their renderings, they often mislead Westerners. The terms "Goodness" or "Good" often mislead those who have a Platonic understanding of universals, of the universal transcendent "Good", or those who simply prefer God. Likewise, the word "benevolence" is a word that has fallen out of use for most English speakers.

Rendering *ren* as "authoritative conduct" in the translation by Ames and Rosemont (1998) used in this essay requires the overcoming of certain connotations for those who distrust or dislike authority. Such a translation necessitates qualifying *ren* conduct as the type of authority commanded by the mere presence of an accomplished individual such as Barack Obama. When Obama gave his speech to the Democratic National Convention in 2004, it was done in bottom-up terms; by harkening back to heritage, and punctuating American individuality in terms of intimacy, he became a moving force for a future, healthier United States. *Ren* is always about accomplished individuals who continuously find themselves in some context, and who respond or become responsive by being appropriate (*yi*) in and to that context. These sage-like individuals augment *li* through their authoritative behavior and enhance *li*'s meaning by contributing to the complexity of *li*'s self-organizing and evolutionary processes. Making appropriate decisions by being responsive to the systemic flow around them, *ren* persons tip the process into greater levels of complexity necessary for healthier and more creative orders; they do so by being attentive and performing skillfully within their networks of interdependence.

It is clear from the *Analects* that there is nothing common about the attainment of *ren*. Confucius' sense of *ren* resonates with earlier meanings used by aristocratic clans during the Zhou to distinguish themselves from common people (Graham, 1989, 19), but there is something more profound operating here. Confucius' students are constantly asking him whether rulers or contemporary political figures have attained *ren*. His answer is always no. The attribution of *ren* is only ascribed to figures of China's mythic past. Not only is such an ascription assigned to root individuals more firmly in their authentic tradition, it is to create a goal as elusive as approaching and reaching the horizon. The emphasis for Confucius is placed on the self-cultivation of individuals emerging from their authentic tradition in light of their present social and organizational contexts. As Hall and Ames (1998, 171) suggest, "one is born into and constituted by an incipient nexus of relationships that then must be cultivated and extended. Although these inchoate relationships, and the ritual structures through which they are extended, are immediately interpersonal, their greater significance lies in their character of locating and integrating the particular human being in the larger world most broadly construed."

Even when Confucius' disciples entreat him about his own achievement of *ren*, he selfconsciously replies: "How would I dare to consider myself a sage (*sheng*) or an authoritative person [*ren*]? What can be said about me is simply that I continue my studies without respite and instruct others without growing weary" (7.34). This modest refusal and the ascription of *ren* to only quasi-mythical figures emphasize the on-going process of becoming human, not its ultimate achievement where one rests upon his or her laurels. The manager, boss, or leader must always be committed to working without respite, being an exemplar for others without growing weary, and putting *yi* (appropriateness) into practice by observing *li*: "the exemplary person gives first priority to appropriate conduct" (17.23).

Becoming a *ren* person, or becoming fully human, is considered a highly difficult attainment according to Confucius; nevertheless, this task is not impossible. In 4.6, Confucius seems to open the possibility of becoming *ren* regardless of rank when he asks and answers his own question: "Are there people who, for the space of a single day, have given their full strength to authoritative conduct? I have yet to meet them. As for lacking the strength to do so, I doubt there are such people—at least I have yet to meet them." The possibility of achieving, becoming, or being *ren* is a real option for everyone; becoming a *junzi*, an exemplary person, is a viable possibility for each and every one of us, but it is especially challenging for those placed in positions of authority.

Confucius' idea of *ren* can be analyzed by relating *ren* to two other important ideas in his philosophy. The "one continuous strand" that binds together Confucius's way (*dao*) is introduced in 4.15: "The way of the Master is doing one's utmost (*zhong*) and putting oneself in the other's place (*shu*), nothing more." One can look at *shu*, putting oneself in the other's place (also see 5.27) and *zhong*, doing one's best, as two fundamental ingredients of *ren*. When asked if there is "one expression that can be acted upon until the end of one's days," Confucius replies: "There is *shu*: do not impose on others what you yourself do not want" (15.24). This same point is emphasized in another passage:

> Zhonggong inquired about authoritative conduct (*ren*). The Master replied, "In your public life, behave as though you are receiving important visitors; employ the common people as though you are overseeing a great sacrifice. Do not impose upon others what you yourself do not want, and you will not incur personal or political ill will." (12.2)

The casting of the "Golden Rule" in the "negative" signifies the ongoing importance of discipline—restricting behavior and action always requires self-knowledge (understanding motivations and so forth) and summoning the strength to resist self-advantage over others. Moreover, such signification further restricts the ego's impulses by positioning the self in the context as emphasized in 6.30:

> Authoritative persons [*ren* persons] establish others in seeking to establish themselves and promote others in seeking to get there themselves. Correlating one's conduct with those near at hand can be said to be the method of becoming an authoritative person [*ren* person].

Those familiar with depth psychological ideas of projection can easily see that Confucius is recommending that individuals should not project their own needs and desires onto others, which is part of correlating one's conduct with those within one's immediate context. Reading 12.2 and 6.30 above with 7.22 and 4.17 demonstrates that Confucius even suggests people have a natural tendency to project their desires and needs onto others.[*]

> The Master said, "In strolling in the company of just two other persons, I am bound to find a teacher. Identifying their strengths, I follow them, and identifying their weaknesses, I reform myself accordingly." (7.22)

> 'When you meet persons of exceptional character think to stand shoulder to shoulder with them; meeting persons of little character, look inward and examine yourself.' (4.17)

Self-examination reveals the human tendency to project inadequacies onto others. Confucius enjoins us to redress this tendency; rectifying this tendency is a perquisite for becoming *ren*, having a sense of appropriate conduct (*yi*), and acting as a *junzi*. This too becomes the role for any manager, administrator, or anyone wanting to live a life of positive contributions.

Shu, putting oneself in the other's place, is the method of moving closer to the goal of *ren*. The movement towards becoming *ren* requires a substantial amount of energy that is requisite for putting the method in place. This energy is "doing one's utmost," or *zhong*.[†] The energy of *zhong* leads to the appropriate attitude for performing *li*. In the passage that began our discussion,

---

[*] The author wishes to thank Graham Parkes for these ideas.

[†] D.C. Lau (1979, 16) suggests this type of reading when he says, "*Chung* [*Zhong*] is the doing of one's best and it is through chung that one puts into effect what one had found out by the method of *shu*." See also *Analects* 1.4.

Confucius is asked about *ren*. In response he replies, "through self-discipline and observing ritual propriety (*li*) one becomes authoritative (*ren*) in one's conduct. If for the space of a day one were able to accomplish this, the whole empire would defer to this authoritative (*ren*) model. Becoming authoritative in one's conduct is self-originating—how could it originate with others?" To discipline the self is to caution against personal gain or profit; it is to discipline oneself to subtract self-interest and authoritarianism as a motive for action. Such discipline authenticates *yi*, or appropriateness, as a moral guide for productive and meaningful relationships in the overlapping spheres we call the self.

14.5.2 Junzi

If *li* are the coherent emergent order of humanity, *ren* is the spirit—the authentic heart-mind (*xin*), the human-heartedness, and authoritative conduct —we must bring to our ever-present *li*. As P.J. Ivanhoe (2000, 4) notes, *li* "were not intended merely to elicit particular kinds of behavior, the goal was to instill certain sensibilities, attitudes, and dispositions in the practitioner." The reflective practice of *li* makes us *ren*, which means to become an authentic human being. To be authentic in actions through the social mechanism of *li* is to become a *junzi*.*

The conventional way of translating *junzi* is "gentleman." Waley, Lau, and Graham translate the term this way. Others such as Tu Wei-ming ("profound person") and Roger Ames and Henry Rosemont Jr. ("exemplary person") have offered a variety of other translations. All of these translations are correct and give some sense for what Confucius means by the term. "Gentleman" is perhaps the most misleading for Westerners, especially for Americans. Lau (1979), and Waley (1938) chose this translation because of the relation between a gentleman, being gentle, the Latin root *gens*, and the Greek root *genus*, where the clan gives rise to the gentleman (Waley, 1938, 27). Unfortunately, so few people study Greek or Latin today that this connection is entirely lost. Although Tu's translation is accurate, being profound in English simply does not quite carry the practical connotations that seem necessary for grasping Confucius' thinking. For these reasons, either "consummate person" or "exemplary person" are preferable, but not without reservation because both are without the connotations of civility found in "gentleman"—and China is a culture of civility, not laws; also, each lack the philosophical strength of "profound person."

To reinforce the sense of the ongoing task of perfecting personal natures in becoming the *junzi* and moving toward the ever-withdrawing horizon of *ren*, one can begin with 7.33 where Confucius says that "as far as personally succeeding in living the life of the exemplary person (*junzi*), I have accomplished little." This passage resonates with 7.34 discussed earlier ("How would I dare to consider myself a sage (*sheng*) or an authoritative person? What can be said about me is simply that I continue my studies without respite and instruct others without growing weary."). These passages, and many others, reinforce the non-teleological character and process orientation of achievement found in the *Analects*. There are no divine realms beyond the magic of social intercourses, which means the challenge is to create meaningful lives through the process and maintain productive and useful organizations and institutions. The correlation between *ren* persons and the *junzi* is made in 4.5 where Confucius says: "Wherein do the exemplary persons (*junzi*) who would abandon their authoritative conduct (*ren*) warrant that name? Exemplary persons [*junzi*] do not take leave of their authoritative conduct even for the space of a meal." Even the most mundane experiences such as eating meals, conducting or participating in meetings, and performing job duties are infused with

---

* I have intentionally left out the various degrees or levels of *ren* achievement such as *daren* (persons in high station), *shanren* (truly adept persons), *chengren* (consummate persons), *renzhe* or *renren* (authoritative persons), *shi* (scholar-apprentices), *junzi* (exemplary persons), and *shen* or *shengren* (sages) for purposes of simplification. See Ames and Rosemont (1998, 60) for further discussion of the last three categories of *ren* listed above. From these distinctions, we can see Confucius has a whole set of criteria in mind to recognize the ongoing process and need for a disciplined praxis of *ren*.

the magical power of *li*. When approaching *li* in the spirit of *ren*, the apparently mundane or profane ways of acting are transformed into divine manifestations of *li*. The challenges of promoting such manifestations arise sharply in the workplace and at home.

The *junzi* is one who through disciplined practice sets in motion a sympathetic vibration for others to follow. The path others will follow will be the way of *yi*, appropriateness, rightness, or morality.* The way of *yi* will conflict with the mindless acquisition of wealth and the power of authoritarianism: "Exemplary persons (*junzi*) understand what is appropriate (*yi*); petty persons [*xiaoren*] understand what is of personal advantage" (4.16). And even more specifically: "To act with an eye to personal profit will incur a lot of resentment" (4.12) and "to eat coarse food, drink plain water, and pillow oneself on a bent arm—there is pleasure to be found in these things. But wealth and position gained through inappropriate means—these are to me like floating clouds" (7.16).† From Confucius' perspective, CEO's receiving bonuses in the millions while their corporations are failing to earn profits and laying-off workers would be inconceivable and the height of hubris.

There is, of course, a further downside to this intimacy model of "right thinking" where consensus is valued over choice. The possible misapplication of Confucian values can easily lead to the oppression of any minority by a tyrannizing majority. Morality in decision making can be reduced to the mere recitation of some sort of moral catechism. Authoritarianism, not legitimate authority, prevails and the dominance of the singular political voice—its will and power—will bring the system, the organization, or even an entire society into an uncreative and lethargic state. Just as the father can become the tyrannical ruler of the family (the Confucian model of society) if he fails to take into account the necessary and fundamental roles of all family members that are constitutive of families, the political ruler or the organizational president can become so besotted with his power that sameness reigns instead of harmony, suppression prevails over creativity, and self-abnegation ensues instead of personal connection. Such abrogation of the human potential to participate meaningfully in the greater context does not achieve the Confucian value of *ren*.

Achieving *ren* is not selfishly rewarded by creating an organization or institution in one's own image, experiencing some mystical union with the Idea of the Good (Plato), or finding a place in heaven, such as the promise of the Abrahamic traditions; neither is it the abrogation of another's self-cultivation. For Confucius, the reward is simply one of connection—of fitting in, finding one's place in society and the tradition from which one emerges, and being appropriately responsive to the context at hand. This harmony, which comes from finding one's place, is not simply some ritualized form of hollow external agreements between selves of integrity that promotes the *staus quo*. Harmony is always a creative act. As Hall and Ames (1998, 271) say, a "'making' of society… requires the investment of oneself, one's judgment, and one's own sense of cultural importances." The function of any organization and the responsibility of making decisions of how we live, work, and play with each other requires the same investment. As Confucius says in 13.23: "The exemplary person (*junzi*) seeks harmony (*he*) rather than agreement (*tong*); the small person does the opposite." The exemplary person must have the proprietorship of *yi*: "Having a sense of appropriate

---

* *Yi* is often considered a central term for the ethical dimension of Confucius' thought in the following ways: (1) When applied to a particular act, *yi* will usually mean "right" as in "that was the right action to take" or "that was the right thing to do." (2) In discussions about kinds of actions, *yi* means duty, the act that one ought to perform in a given particular situation. (3) When *yi* is applied to agents who perform a right act, *yi* means righteous, dutiful, or moral person. Further, given Confucius' sense of an intimate self, *yi* is usually used in reference to acts while *ren* is used to characterize persons (See Lau, 1979, 26–27). These distinctions of *yi*, however, fall under the governance of *yi* as appropriateness or fittingness and harmony (*he*)—one ought to find his or her proper place within a broader context. *Li* always provide this wider context. See Ames and Rosemont (1998, 53–55) for demarcating *yi* from a Western ethical understanding. See the following passages in the *Analects* for *yi*: 1.13, 2.24, 4.5, 4.10, 4.12, 7.3, 7.16, 12.10, 12.20, 13.4, 14.12, 14.13, 15.17, 15.18 16.10 16.11, 17.23, 18. 7, and 19.1.

† See also 14.1, 1.15, and 4.9.

conduct (*yi*) as one's basic disposition (*zhi*), developing it in observing ritual propriety (*li*), expressing it with modesty, and consummating it in making good on one's word (*xin*): this then is an exemplary person (*junzi*)" (15.18). Exemplary persons integrate all of these attributes into their being—they integrate themselves appropriately into the matrix of social relations and the authentic traditions from which they emerge; they infuse themselves into the robust present of the familial, organizational, and institutional and to their subsequent reiterations in the future; and, of course, exemplary persons make their decisions accordingly.

14.6 IN SUM

The twenty-first century provides challenges regarding how individuals go about making decisions that have vital effects on the present and future world. Such decision making is now understood in the light of different conceptions of the self from which decision making styles—and the resulting decisions—emerge. Routinely, such self conceptions create a blindness to various approaches that arise from diverse conceptions of self. Confucius gives the contemporary world—a world locked into the ideas of "integrity," the "right to think," and social contract theory where autonomous selves define themselves in external terms with each other—insights into self conceptions of intimacy, right thinking, and the situational over agency, and gives us an understanding of ourselves in the naturalness of the interdependence of the family. The family is the prototype for all organizations, including society, where a self is seen as a fundamental participant in its aggregated field of interdependence, without which there could be no family, organization, institution, or society. The family is the sphere of influence for the consensual and is the governing metaphor for Confucian thinking and the Chinese cultural sensibility.

This Confucian sensibility recognizes fundamental roles founded upon basic differences that form any collective arrangement of members of any species into a unit. Healthy families, as well as healthy organizations, institutions, and societies, will promote consensus over the right to choose, harmony over order, authoritative conduct over authoritarianism, selflessness over selfishness, modesty over hubris, and community over individuality.

Such a sensibility must be enacted with the requisite discipline and put into practice with much care, for not to do so leads eventually to its opposite—a besotted authoritarianism that pursues its imperialistic tendencies in a shrinking world. No species, as Confucius was aware, can afford to eliminate the diversity requisite for a healthy environment. And in decision making, authoritative conduct and comportment is not only appropriate, it is indispensable.

REFERENCES

Ames, R. T. and Callicott, J. B., *Nature in Asian Traditions of Thought: Essays in Environmental Thought*, State University of New York Press, Albany, NY, 1989.

Ames, R. T. and Hall, D., *The Democracy of the Dead: Dewey, Confucius, and the Hope for Democracy in China*, Open Court Publishing Company, Chicago, 1987.

Ames, R. T. and Rosemont, H., *The Analects of Confucius: A Philosophical Translation*, Ballentine Books, New York, 1998.

Cua, A. S., Concept of paradigmatic individuals in the ethics of confucius, *Inquiry*, 14(1), 44–55, 1971.

Dewey, J., *The Influence of Darwin on Philosophy*, Henry Holt, New York, 1910.

Fingarette, H., *Confucius—The Secular as Sacred*, Harper and Row, New York, 1972.

Graham, A. C., *Disputers of the Tao: Philosophical Argument in Ancient China*, Open Court, Illinois, 1989.

Hall, D. L. and Ames, R. T., *Thinking Through Confucius*, State University of New York Press, New York, 1987.

Hall, D. L. and Ames, R. T., *Thinking from the Han: Self, Truth, and Transcendence in Chinese and Western Culture*, State University of New York Press, Albany, NY, 1998.

Hall, D. L. and Ames, R. T., *The Democracy of the Dead: Dewey, Confucius, and the Hope for Democracy in China*, Open Court, Illinois, 1999.

Ivanhoe, P. J., *Confucian Moral Self Cultivation*, Hackett, Indianapolis, IN, 2000.

Jones, D., Teaching/learning through Confucius: navigating our way through the Analects, *Education About Asia*, 5(2), 4–13, 2000.

Jones, D. and Crosby, J., Review of democracy of the dead: Dewey, Confucius and the hope for democracy in China, *Education About Asia*, 6(3), 71–74, 2001.

Jones, D. and Culliney, J. L., Confucian order at the edge of chaos: the science of complexity and ancient wisdom, *Zygon: Journal of Religion and Science*, 33(3), 395–404, 1998.

Jones, D. and Sweeney, J., Review of intimacy or integrity: philosophy and cultural difference, *Philosophy East–West (October)*, October 603–607, 2005.

Kasulis, T. P., *Intimacy or Integrity: Philosophy and Cultural Difference*, University of Hawaìi Press, Honolulu, 2002.

Koller, J. M. and Koller, P. J., *Asian Philosophies*, Prentice Hall, New Jersey, 1998.

Lau, D. C., *Confucius: The Analects*, Penguin Books, New York, 1979.

Lewin, R., *Complexity: Life at the Edge of Chaos*, Macmillan Publishing Company, New York, 1992.

Merleau-Ponty, M. and Smith, C., *Phenomenology of Perception*, Routledge and Kegan Paul, London, 1962.

Peerenboom, R., Let one hundred flowers bloom, one hundred schools contend: debating rule of law in China. Perspectives, 3(5), 2002: http://www.oycf.org/Perspectives/17_063002/One_Hundred_Flower_Bloom. htm (accessed September 15, 2005).

Tu, W. M., Li a process of humanization, *Philosophy East and West*, 22(2), 194, 1972.

Waldrop, M. M., *Complexity: The Emerging Science at the Edge of Chaos*, Simon and Schuster, New York, 1992.

Waley, A., *The Analects of Confucius*, Vintage Books, New York, 1938.

15 Decision: Nishitani on Time and Karma*

Jason M. Wirth

CONTENTS

15.1 The Problematic..291
15.2 Case Study: Arjuna...293
15.3 Nishitani on Karma...294
15.4 Conversion and the Great Compassion: *Homo Ludens*...297
References...298

In 1946 Jean Beaufret wrote Heidegger a fretful letter about Jean Paul Sartre's lecture, *Existentialism is a Humanism* (1946). Sartre, famously arguing that existence precedes essence and that the human therefore becomes what she or he does, made Beaufret worry that this was an inadequate account of action, ethics, and humanism. Heidegger in his justly celebrated "Letter on Humanism" (1947) responded decisively. We have not yet begun to think action [*Handlung*]. Typically, we construe action as *Vollbringen*, as bringing something forth into its fullness, as production, as accomplishment, as actualization. As such, actions are causes that bring forth effects, which, in their turn, are judged according to their utility. Does this action accomplish what it is that we set out to accomplish? What should we *do*?[†] But this determination avoids altogether more fundamental ontological questions. Only what *is* can be brought forth, but of what do we speak when we speak of such a being (Heidegger, 311)?

Heidegger questioned the traditional ground of ethics and its protocols of decision making. Yet some might fear that such an interrogation is unduly disruptive. Would not a radical questioning of the essence of action not risk destroying some of the most productive modes of speaking when it comes to ethics? For example, one often laments that Heidegger did not have a real ethics, that this

---

[*] I would here like to thank Dr. Ron Carlisle (Oglethorpe University), Dr. Brian Schroeder (Rochester Institute of Technology), and Dr. Bret Davis (Loyola University, Baltimore) for their invaluable suggestions and commentary on this essay. Please note that throughout this essay, including the References, when listing Japanese names, I adhere to the East Asian practice of listing the family name first.

[†] Decision theory assumes this model. Despite the murkiness and complexity of real life applications, decision theory usually begins with assessing and articulating the problem at hand, discerning and providing the possible alternatives, and then offering an account of the best alternative. See, for example, the schematic account model provided by Christopher K. McKenna (1980, 5) In this sense, McKenna speaks of the production of "normative models" that "aim at finding 'the best' alternative—the best according to some previously identified criterion. This process is referred to as *optimizing*, and this type of model is referred to as *normative* or *prescriptive*" (11). This may be accomplished at the group or the individual level and may involve several irascible variables, but, in general, decision theory assumes, as does much of modernity, Heidegger's account of action as accomplishment (*Vollbringen*).

accounts for his poor political choices, and that these failings purportedly become evident whenever one follows Heidegger down such treacherous paths. And is not Heidegger symptomatic of the general decadence of our postmodern age, in which we flounder amidst such pervasive ethical incompetence? Does not such questioning enervate the ground and possibility of accountable decision making?

We have inherited ethics as a species of action in which we bring about ethical actions and thereby ethical ends. To *be* ethical is to *act* ethically, to *do* ethical things. There are competing accounts of how such ends are to be accomplished. Does one judge the quality of an ethical act by the quality of its intention or the quality of its result? In either account, what is fundamentally taken for granted is the situation of the ethical *decision*. A decision is what confronts an ethical agent—an acting subject must choose the ethically correct option, either at the level of intention (categorical imperative, classical Christian ethics) or consequence (utilitarianism, rational choice theory, virtue ethics by which ethical habituation brings about the consequence of my flourishing and the flourishing of others).

For Heidegger, the question of action is still a question that remains fundamentally unasked, a problem that remains inadequately problematized and investigated. Yet for the Buddhist tradition, as for some of the Hindu tradition that served as the womb of Buddhist heterodoxy, the question of action was decisive. There can be no decision theory unless one first addresses the more fundamental and elusive question of action. The word in these vast traditions that comes down to us in this context is the original Sanskrit word for action, namely *karma*.[*] This was a fundamental life question that, if left unresolved, rendered all ethics as lifeless dogma and mere self-delusion. Without resolving this question, decision, even with its most subtle "normative models," spins about the unexamined and troubling wheel of karma.

In what follows, I want to accept Heidegger's challenge to rethink more fundamentally the question of action. I shall do so, however, not by rehearsing the threads—implicit and explicit—that address this question in Heidegger's work. Rather my aim is to take up the question of action as a question, as a question whose decisiveness precedes any canonical account of ethics or decision theory.[†] It is a question more decisive than decision theory and hence decision theory itself rests on resurrecting a more *decisive decision*. I do not intend to pursue this question in a free and open-ended fashion. Rather, I will attempt to think what is more decisive than anything within the range of decision theory by taking up one of the oldest and most profound meditations on the question of action, namely the Buddhist account of karma.

Before I begin, however, I want to be clear about two things. First, this paper is not a dismissal of decision theory, but rather a reconsideration of its range by taking into account what is left fundamentally unsaid, uninvestigated—undecided—in decision theory. Second, it is not an account of the history of the idea of karma throughout Buddhism's vast lineages and traces. Indeed, I am of the conviction that there is no single thing called Buddhism. Although some practicing Buddhists would doubtless object, the Buddha's legacy has been expansive and complex, producing more of a Wittgensteinian "family resemblance" than an essential set of doctrines and practices. (This is not, however, to deny the centrality of certain teachings like nirvana, emptiness, and impermanence.) As Bernard Faure has recently argued, "Buddhism is itself double, hybrid, bastardized. On the one hand, it is a powerful intellectual system with tendencies both rationalist and abstract, almost structuralist and universalist. On the other, it is a form of local, pagan, quasi-shamanistic

---

[*] There are numerous accounts of karma in the Hindu and later in the Buddhist traditions. Some early Hindu accounts suggest that karma is a kind of residual effect of one's actions. I want to shy away from such accounts, concentrating rather on the root of all Buddhist and Hindu accounts, namely that karma, action, comes directly from *kr-*, which simply means to act. (See Klostermaier 1998, 95).

[†] Decision theory has classically sought *how* to decide, not to articulate fundamentally *what* a decision *is*. Again, it is not my intention to derail decision theory. I regard it as a necessary component of political life. Rather, I am attempting to allow another, more fundamental question to be heard.

thought. As the eminent Indianist Paul Mus has remarked, there are not just two, but at least a half dozen Buddhisms" (Faure, 2004, x).

I want rather to take the Buddhist problematic of karma seriously as a philosophical problematic—as a decisive consideration buried and often lost within the nether depths of the question of ethical agency and the varying accounts of its attendant decision theory. I will argue that the question of karma is a fundamentally *proto-ethical* consideration—a question that precedes and informs any ethical deliberation.

I will ground my investigation by considering the account of karma put forth by Nishitani Keiji, Nishida Kitarō's remarkable student and one of the seminal forces of what has become known and justly celebrated as the Kyoto School. Nishitani studied with Heidegger in Freiburg during the initial years of the latter's Nietzsche lectures. He also represents one of those rare creatures in the history of philosophy who moved with equal ease between the Continental philosophical tradition and the ancient Buddhist tradition, producing a way of thinking that allows both vast traditions to co-inform and co-illuminate each other in the service of addressing fundamental philosophical questions. Like Nishitani, I will not speak within an alleged doctrinal system of Buddhism and hence will not allow any Buddhist commitments to dictate automatically my philosophical decisions. Rather, and again like Nishitani, I turn to the Buddhist tradition in general, and to the Mahāyāna tradition in particular, for assistance in retrieving what is left undecided in decision theory. I will do so in the following four stages: First, I will delineate in general terms the problematic of karma. I will then turn to a brief analysis of Arjuna's plight in the *Bhagavad Gītā* as a test case by which to further account for the fundamental location of the problematic of karma. I will then discuss Nishitani's account of karma in his masterpiece *Religion and Nothingness*. Karma is something like a reactive relationship to *śūnyāta* (emptiness), which anxiously and exhaustedly renders it as nihility. I then conclude with Nishitani's solution to the problem of karma, namely conversion to the Great Compassion (*Mahā karunā*) of the *homo ludens*.

15.1 THE PROBLEMATIC

One might immediately ask how one could take karma seriously as a philosophical problematic. Is this not some anachronistic relic inherited from antiquated and exotic beliefs? Does this not commit one to a whole gamut of scarcely defensible, if not bizarre and idiotic propositions? We do live in an age in which there are those who are convinced that this really is a New Age, an age in which one should consume lots of herbs and smell lots of odiferous candles, constantly relax, and minimize the hold of karma on one's upper middle class spirituality. Is it not silly to think that instant karma is going to get us, as if John Lennon had anything illuminating to say about the Buddhist tradition?

Even if one eschews New Age culture, which I generally do, the difficulties and obscurities regarding the doctrine of karma nonetheless remain within the Buddhist tradition. In its more traditional trappings, does not an account of karma commit one to fantastical, anti-scientific accounts of reincarnation? For it was often claimed that it was the fruit of one's karma—even if it was good karma—that traps one in the endless cycle of *samsāra*, of death and rebirth. And since karma simply means action, how do our actions trap us? Are our actions somehow trapping agents, snaring us in *samsāra*? If so, how can an action be such a fantastical, lingering, and invisible physical force? In Japanese, the Chinese character for karma is read *gō* and one can find a phrase, similar in kind to such phrases in all languages of all Buddhist traditions, like *Gō ni hikareru*—to be drawn or pulled or led by one's karma or *gō*. How is one so led? Does not such drawing furthermore obviate free will and denigrate the ethical agent to the status of a karma slave?

Wanting to take the question of karma seriously, I will first claim that karma is not, in the Aristotelian sense, an efficient cause. It is not an action acting upon on another, making the acted upon react. Instant karma is not going to *get* you, for such getting falsely renders karma an efficient force. Second, if one were to speak of it as a positive force, for I think one must, it is more like what

Aristotle deemed a formal or eidetic cause, albeit in a context of dependent co-origination that obviates the possibility that something can contain its being within itself. We will turn to this later in the Buddhist account of *samskrita*, mutual forming and conditioning, but for now suffice it to say that karma includes the reactive, inert force of something's resistance to being otherwise than what it formally is. It is a thing's inert resistance to what threatens its eidetic integrity or, better, it is the propensity of something simply to be itself. This propensity, furthermore, is at odds with a thing's emptiness. Third, although one need not reject science and embrace reincarnation, one could at least say that a thing's eidetic propensity involves it in a massive causal nexus of interpenetration and interdependence that exceeds it both spatially and temporally. It is involved in the massive and dynamic web of *pratītyasamutpāda*, of dependent co-origination, which implicates a thing within the depths of the past and the obscurity of the future. In this, one could at least speak metaphorically of enlightened *samsāra* as a nexus of interdependence that robs each thing of its own integrity, of its completeness within its idea, by involving it within the inscrutable depths and heights of time.

Do these initial suggestions implicate karma within a doctrine of determinism and thereby vitiate agency, ethics, and decision theory? At this point, we have, in a preliminary fashion, arrived at our first decisive and fundamental issue. We tend to think of karma as a predicate that, if predicated of an acting human subject, subjugates the capacity of said subject to act. It does so because it would hinder or even eliminate another predicate of the human subject, namely freedom. Allow me to discuss these two issues in some detail.

It is one of the largely implicit assumptions of much of the Western philosophical and religious tradition that freedom, if it is at all, is a predicate that characterizes the human subject. Are we free? That is, can one characterize humanity as being free? Is this something that can be rightly attributed to humanity? Determinism argues that "freedom" cannot be predicated of the subject "human." The idea of humanity precludes such a predicate. Or there is no evidence to indicate the presence of such a predicate. Or the predicate is so ill defined that we do not even know what it is that we are attempting to predicate of humanity. Hence we conclude that human beings do not have free will, choice, etc.

Or a voluntarist concludes the opposite, namely, that freedom is compatible with the human subject and that there is evidence to support such predication. Or, needing, as did both Saint Augustine and Kant, each in their own way, to provide an account of moral responsibility, one argues that one *should* predicate freedom *as if* it were true of humanity. Without the capacity to decide, or to sin, how can I be held responsible for having made the morally salutary choice? In this context, karma could be read as either rendering freedom an illegitimate predicate of humanity or, if freedom is indeed a legitimate and even essential predicate, than karma is a predicate that hinders freedom from fully or even minimally actualizing itself. One cannot be free—and thereby be responsible or make compelling ethical decisions—until one sheds the manacles of karma. After all, the discourse in the Hindu tradition is of *mōksa*, of liberation, and in the Buddhist tradition of nirvana, of emancipation from *samsāra*. Does this mean that one must emancipate freedom from karma to enable the ground of decision theory?

These models, and other variations on the same themes, already assume, however, that the human being fundamentally is something, that it has its own being, and that it is the task of philosophical reflection and science to establish exactly *what* human being *is*. After all, one cannot have a proper ethics or politics unless one first adequately defines human nature. Yet what if such an assumption were not only incorrect, but a perversion of the human condition— ineluctable as it might be—by which karma emerges as a problem that constantly and urgently demands a solution? What if freedom were the subject—the groundless ground of all things, the infinite depths and heights of time—and humanity were its predicate? What then? Nishida (1987) the progenitor of the Kyoto School, had argued that "the absolute must relate to itself as a form of self-contradiction. It must express itself by negating itself " (68). The subject, in order to express itself, in order to self-predicate, simultaneously self-negates, remaining otherwise than *what* it is. It is the sovereign ground, the free subject, of the *facta bruta* of being. The sovereign subject of being—if one can even speak of it as a subject—is absolutely nothing, much like Krishna defined Vishnu, his own as well as all of being's groundless or phantom ground: "I pervade the entire universe in my unmanifested form. All creatures find their existence in me, but I am not limited by them. Behold my divine mystery!" (*Bhagavad Gītā*, chap. 9, verses 4–5).[*]

Freedom is the non-subject of being appearing as self-negated in the subject position of being. In this sense, karma initially names a perverted or upside down human relationship to freedom. In karma, the predicate humanity fights for its humanity as if it were its freedom. Humanity assumes itself as the subject position and freedom becomes a property that must be realized. In other words, humanity inverts freedom to the predicate position, as if freedom were *my* freedom. This is backwards. As such, Nishitani astutely argues that this mistake always implies that "karma is at all times *my* karma" (Nishitani, 1982, 246). In the *Gītā*, this means that the solution to the problem of karma—for *my karma* is rendered a pleonasm—involves the confrontation with *ahamkāra*, the perverse and pernicious fiction that it is *I who act*, I who decisively accomplish things.

15.2 CASE STUDY: ARJUNA

I turn now to a brief consideration of the *Bhagavad Gītā*, knowing full well that I am turning to one of the Great Hindu masterpieces to elucidate the Buddhist problem of action. I do so not because there is a paucity of Buddhist texts with which I could have pursued my analysis. I do so rather because this text is especially clear on the problem of karma and thereby affords us an initial entrance into Nishitani's more general analysis. Nonetheless, the *Gītā* is striving to articulate what Dōgen (1200–1253 ACE), claimed in the *Shinjin Gakudo* (*Body-and-Mind Study of the Dao*) about the study of the Dao, namely that "those who have rolled up this matter into wide-open eyeballs are two or three bushels. Those who have tampered with it by karma-consciousness [*gosshiki*] are thousands and millions of pieces" (Dōgen, 1985, 88). Until the problem of karma is solved, one is all over the place, in the agony of delusion.

The *Gītā*, which was originally a part of the great Hindu epic *The Mahābhārata* (1998) and assumes its dramatic setting, begins with the plight of Arjuna who is immobilized by melancholy. As soon as he blows the conch, an enormous battle begins. Fighting for the Pandavas against the Kurauvas, Arjuna is to lead his family and friends against the rancorous villainy of those who stole their home and all of their possessions, exiled them in a rigged gambling match, and humiliated the Pandavas ceaselessly, refusing again and again to relent. Yet the Kurauvas are the Pandavas' cousins and among the Kurauvas' forces are also friends and former teachers of the Pandavas. It is precisely at this point that Arjuna is brought to the limiting case of decision theory. What is his responsibility? What normative models could possibly serve him? Given that Arjuna is a noble warrior, what is the noble choice? Arjuna is in a quandary not unlike that of Sophie in Styron's *Sophie's Choice*. Either she must choose which of her two children shall live and thereby which of the two shall die, or the Nazi officer shall kill them both. Either she chooses murder or she chooses murder and if she chooses not to choose, she again chooses murder. This is also the quandary of the melancholy Dane, Hamlet, who finds himself immobilized by an impossible choice.

Arjuna, for his part, must choose either to fight and thereby murder family and friends or not to fight and thereby destroy the Pandavas. "How can I ever bring myself to fight against Bhishma and Drona, who are worthy of reverence? How can I, Krishna? Surely it would be better to spend my life begging than to kill these great and worthy souls! If I killed them, every pleasure I found would be tainted. I don't even know which would be better, for us to conquer them or for them to conquer us. The sons of Dhritarashtra [the Kurauvas] have confronted us; but why would we care to live if we

---

[*] Although I am consulting multiple editions of the *Bhagavad Gītā*, for the sake of simplicity, I will only refer to the Eknath Easwaran (1985) translation. To facilitate coalescence with other editions, I cite the chapter followed by the verse number.

killed them?" (*Bhagavad Gītā*, chap. 2, verses 4–6). What is the correct choice for Arjuna? There is none and thus Arjuna cannot act.

In his remarkable counsel to Arjuna, Krishna does not gather alternatives and provide normative models. There is no deliberation bent on producing optimization. In his efforts to prompt Arjuna to act, Krishna insists that the problem of action, of karma, must itself be solved. Famously, there are three prongs to Krishna's approach: the discipline or yoga by which one solves the problem of karma, the yoga of wisdom (*jñāna*), and finally the yoga of love and devotion, *bhakti*. In short, the wisdom by which the problem of action is solved results in the overcoming of oneself and a turning to the other in *bhakti*, in love. Krishna begins with the discipline by which one solves the problem of karma. One adopts a fundamental practice, a practice that also demands meditation, in which one cultivates a non-attachment to the fruits or consequences of one's actions, being equally well disposed to any outcome. "The awakened sages call a person wise when all his undertakings are free from anxiety about results; all of his selfish desires have been consumed in the fire of knowledge. The wise, ever satisfied, have abandoned all external supports. Their security is unaffected by the results of their action; *even while acting, they really do nothing at all*" (*Bhagavad Gītā*, chap. 4, verses 19–21, *emphasis mine*).

Bhakti, furthermore, emerged precisely when Arjuna received the mystery of mysteries, the royal secret, and has a vision of Krishna as *mahā kāla*, time, the world destroyer. In finding the absolute exteriority of death within his interiority, Arjuna converts towards the primacy of exteriority. The absolute alterity of death in its sovereign detachment is that which is always mine but therefore that which shows me that I was never primary. Arjuna clasps his hands in a prenom and defers to the Other. The origin, the ground, of action is not the self-enclosed agent. The Good of action is irreducible to *my* Good.

The way of *bhakti* exposes Arjuna's fundamental error: he was not living "beyond the reach of I and mine" (*Bhagavad Gītā*, chap. 12, verse 13). Arjuna's melancholy and consequent inability to act were born of his anxiety about *himself*, *his* goodness, and the *propriety* of *his* relations (friends, family, and teachers). Such anxiety becomes unbearable, if it is not always already unbearable, as soon I reach the limit in which the infinity and inexhaustibility and even incomprehensibility of the task of life reveals itself. In the face of such a revelation, there is only the collapse of action (its incipient inner movement brought to the light of day by the extremity of the situation) or the revolution of action occasioned by the renunciation of *ahamkāra*. As Georges Bataille later argued, albeit in the language of general economy: "To solve political problems becomes difficult for those who allow anxiety [*l'angoisse*] alone to pose them. It is necessary for anxiety to pose them. But their solution demands at a certain point the removal of this anxiety" (Bataille, 1967, 53–54; 1991, 14). By *angoisse*, Bataille means the desperate anxiety that manifests in relentless cares about *our* future.

15.3 NISHITANI ON KARMA

Karma for Nishitani (1982) is fundamentally a problem of time. As such, karma emerges within the essential all pervading *ambiguity* of time (219). On the one hand, time is the discontinuous succession of discontinuously new moments, without beginning and without end. The moment is the novelty of being's ceaseless natality, which therefore also implies being's simultaneously incessant fatality. Each new moment is newly new, emerging at the moment of the death of a now old new moment. Taken together, the natality and fatality of the moment is an experience of the impermanence of all beings.

The ambiguity of time carries within it the ambiguity of human temporality. This ambiguity emerges at the point of what Nietzsche once called the death of God, namely the demise of a trust in the assumption that there is an explanatory substratum or ground to human existence. One is no longer convinced that there is an illuminating bottom or beginning to the human being.

The ambiguity of human temporality emerges simultaneously with the dawning of human self-awareness as abyssal and non-foundational. One cannot get back to the beginning of oneself nor can one anticipate conceptually the end of oneself. Time as the meaning of being indicates the temporality of being absent from origin and always too early for one's end. Like the classic Mahāyāna articulation of karma as "since time past without beginning," time has no beginning, just infinite beginnings, and no end, just infinite endings. This is the recognition of an "infinite openness as the bottom of time" (Nishitani, 219) and an "infinite openness" that "displays an infinity of possibility" (220).

When the self reflects that it has never had itself, that it cannot complete itself within itself, that it is a moment (*Augenblick*) that does not own what came before or what comes after, it enters its own ambiguity. This ambiguity is the ambiguity of time itself: its reciprocal natality (incessant novelty) and fatality (the new is always new and therefore never permanent, never to be had or retained or owned). But, and here is what is critical for our appreciation of karma, *Dasein*, the self that knows itself in its reciprocal presence and infinite openness, is ambiguous ambiguously. That is to say, there are two inverse modes by which it "knows" its essential ambiguity.

Karma is the human experience of the ambiguity of temporality in the first of these two modes.[*] As such, it is perhaps important to stress that karma is not a property, an inalienable aspect, of *Dasein*'s identitarian nature. *Dasein* has no such nature. Rather it belongs to the ambiguity of human nature itself, the two-fold dynamism of essence. It is always already both present to itself and absent to itself simultaneously. Karma is a mode by which *Dasein* knows the impermanence and dependent co-origination of itself and all beings in a boundless nexus of interrelatedness. Karma does not become an issue until *Dasein* first becomes an issue for itself. Once *Dasein* becomes an issue for itself, karma is the first manner in which it is an issue for itself. In other words, karma as a problem demanding resolution does not occur until *Dasein* first fundamentally becomes a problem, until it becomes a question to itself, and a source of trouble. Or, if one were to be more Buddhist in one's manner of speaking, the problem of karma occurs when *Dasein* comes to know itself, as the noble truths instruct us, as a site of immense turmoil (*duhkha*) because of its insatiable ontological thirst (*trishnā*), its ceaseless and tormented craving to be itself.

To repeat: the karmic moment of the ambiguity of becoming ambiguous to oneself speaks to the manner in which one becomes ambiguous to oneself. *There are two ways to be two*, so to speak. Karma is a particular relationship to nothingness, a relationship in which nothing is in each case *my* nothingness (what Heidegger called *Jemeinigkeit* in *Being and Time*). This does not mean that nothingness is a predicate of *Dasein*, for nothingness takes *Dasein* to the point in which it realizes that it does not fundamentally own any of its predicates, that *Dasein* is without properties, without qualities to call its own. Rather one could say that nothingness renders Dasein a predicate without a subject, a sign that does not, as Hölderlin so beautifully phrased it in his late hymn *Mnemosyne* (c. 1803–1805), point anywhere. *Ein Zeichen sind wir deutungslos.*

Yet at this point, speaking in and between traditions, one might say that karma is something like what Nietzsche and later Nishitani call "reactive nihilism." One pushes against one's nothingness or, even more subtly, one nonetheless insists that this nothingness is *my* nothingness. This is precisely why Albert Camus (1955) located the problematic of absurdity in relationship to the problematic of suicide, "the one truly serious philosophical problem" (3). "In a universe suddenly divested of illusions and lights, man feels an alien, a stranger. His exile is without remedy since he is deprived of the memory of a lost home or the hope of a promised land" (5). Camus nonetheless argues for the tragic joy of the absurd human, of Sisyphus, condemned to actions that cannot be accomplished. Sisyphus is condemned never to be able to accomplish the task of pushing the rock successfully to the summit and thus realizing his action. Nonetheless, Sisyphus eschews suicide,

---

[*] For a helpful discussion of Nishitani on karma, see Abe Masao (1989).

opting rather to affirm with resigned happiness the ceaseless toil of a life that cannot be accomplished. "The absurd man says yes and his effort will henceforth be unceasing" (91).

The melodrama of Sisyphus is born of reactive nihilism and its heroic pretensions. Attempting to think beyond the reactivity of karma, Nishitani deployed a subtle and penetrating distinction between modes of nothingness, one particular to karmic consciousness and one particular to the Daoist tradition called *wei wu wei*, acting without acting.

Nishitani named the karmic mode of nothingness, nihility, a reactive and non-enlightened, nonvital mode of Zen mind (*mushin*).* Nihility is "always a nihility for self-existence, that is to say, a nihility that we contact when we posit ourselves on the side of the 'existence' of our self-existence. From this it follows that nihility comes to be represented as something outside of the existence of the self and all things, as some 'thing' absolutely other than existence, some 'thing' called nothingness" (Nishitani, 1982, 96). When I become a question to myself, nihility emerges as the nothingness of my ground, my inability to complete myself within myself. Yet we must stress that nihility is essentially *my* nihility just as karma is essentially *my* karma. (In fact the latter two formulations are simply pleonasms.)

In the ambiguity of karmic time, in the time of nihility, in the time in which I find myself attempting to act despite my awareness of the ambiguity of action and of myself, action becomes either an inexhaustible task or, as we saw with Arjuna, its infinity collapses into melancholy inaction. The task is too large! One becomes either the melancholy Dane, unable to act decisively, or one affirms with tragic joy the impossibility of action. We do nothing whatsoever or we exhaust ourselves with the futility of action. The "constant origination" of the abyssal infinity of time "gives us no rest, but pushes us ever forward. It makes us do things and tugs at us from within to keep turning us in new directions. This obligation to unceasing newness makes our existence an infinite burden to us" (Nishitani, 1982, 220).

It is not the case that *Dasein* has a particular task so large that *Dasein* cannot finish it. Rather Nishitani links this debt to *samskrita*,† to what Nishitani glosses as "being-at-doing" (220). We *are* the ceaseless obligation to act. We are not contained within our being but rather are drawn constantly beyond ourselves in the actions by which we constantly become ourselves. The task of being, that is, the obligation to act that is the irremunerable debt whose perpetual discharge is the task of being, knows no rest, only toil.‡ "To assure our own existence, we have to work off the burden imposed on it. The difference between us and the serf or convict is that the debt weighing on our existence cannot be attributed to someone other or something else. It is from the very beginning part of the essence of an existence that 'is' in the world of time" (239).

Samskrita as the karmic experience of one's being as "being-at-doing" reflects the ambiguity of human temporality. It speaks both to my longing for myself, to my restless search for myself, to my *trishna*, or, in the Latinate tradition, to my *cupiditas* and *concupiscentia*, to my greed for myself, to this "infinite, restless, forward drive within" (Nishitani, 1982, 221). Yet the natality of new beginnings is also the fatality that is the mortality of any being that has begun. There are no permanently abiding beginnings because there is the perpetual death of the old, the relentless

---

* *Mushin* and *mu* are, in this context, impossible to translate. *Mu*, which is basically the Japanese reading of the Chinese character *wu*, denotes *no* or *nothing*. But this character does not in the Zen context name a logical negation or designate the absence of something. *Mu* comes from the sayings of the great Chinese Zen (or Chan) patriarch Jōshū (Chinese Chao-chou) who posed the followed question, which often becomes the first kōan (Zen saying) in *dokusan* (kōan practice during Zen training). When asked if a dog had Buddha nature, he responded *Mu*! On the one hand, Buddhist doctrine holds that all things have Buddha nature and even an acolyte would have known this. This *mu* did not negate the doctrine nor affirm it. It is a no beyond yes and no. The heart and mind (Chinese, *shin*, Japanese *kokoro*) that realizes this is *mushin*, *shin* enlightened by the Zen experience of nothingness.

† *Samskrita* literally means "formed" or "conditioned" and is traditionally deployed in teachings about the interdependence and impermanence of all beings.

‡ Karma then is the "inability of the self to detach itself from the home-ground of its own transitory becoming—or, conversely, the self's being ever itself, while its being is nonetheless in constant change" (Nishitani 1982, 257).

cessation of what has been. In a way, I would argue that what the German Romantics, especially Friedrich Schelling, called *Sehnsucht*,[*] articulates the insatiable thirst of karmic desire. I do not have myself so I must look for myself but since no self has permanence or its own being, I can never have myself so I must ceaselessly look for myself anew. "The debt essential to existence is as elemental as existence itself. It is infinite because in doing something, that is, in the very act whereby we exhaust our debt, we sow the seeds of a new debt" (Nishitani, 239). I am looking for myself in all of the wrong places, that is, I know the ineluctable demand to act with the equally ineluctable fate that all action is futile and in vain (*Umsonst!* as Nietzsche said). I experience the hollow nothingness of myself as akin to Sisyphus's condemnation to the infinite task of the vanity of action. "In karma, the self is constantly oriented inward to the home ground of the self; and yet the only thing that it achieves by this is the constant reconstitution of being *qua* [*soku*] becoming in a time without beginning or end" (Nishitani, 248).

15.4 CONVERSION AND THE GREAT COMPASSION: *HOMO LUDENS*

The Great Compassion, born of the Great Death (the cessation of the primacy of the ego), which speaks to an event of a "fundamental conversion, the field of a change of heart" or "*metanoia (pravrittivijñāna)*" (Nishitani, 1982, 222), is the experience of the second mode of being an issue for oneself. Nihility is the ceaseless toil of *my* nihility. But I cannot speak of *my śūnyāta, my* emptiness. (Who is this *me* that would be empty?) It is the self-predicating qua self negating subject expressing itself as being, but not such that I preserve *śūnyāta* as something—even if it is the something that is nothing—for me, the anxious, toiling Sisyphus. "The stand point of karma, however, has to be abandoned to reach the standpoint of emptiness, a disengagement that signals a conversion from the standpoint of nihility to the standpoint of *śūnyāta*" (250). The latter is "the standpoint of radical deliverance from self-centeredness" (250).

At the moment of conversion, and here we can sense Nishitani also echoing Tanabe Hajime's masterpiece, *Philosophy as Metanoetics* (1986), we realize the radical negation that prompted Saint Augustine to confess the guilty innocence of the selfishness that had heretofore unconsciously governed his life. Augustine looked for God in all of the wrong places, ceaselessly toiling in karma, until a vast silent exteriority exposed Augustine's obsessive interiority (I toil for myself) as fallen. "What could be worse arrogance than the amazing madness with which I asserted myself to be by nature what you are?" (Augustine, 1991, 68).

In karma, exteriority is subjected to my interiority. It is *my* nihility. In the metanoetic turn towards *śūnyāta*, however, the ego repents itself and inverts what it has been. It is no longer an interiority that subsumes exteriority (*my* karma, *my* nihility, the endless toil of *my* Sisyphusian life). Rather exteriority now subsumes interiority. As Jean-François Lyotard argued in his masterful reflection in *The Confession of Augustine* (2002), "Placing your outside within, you [God, the wholly other] converted the most intimate part of him into his outside" (3).

The conversion to *śūnyāta* is a conversion within action such that work takes on the aspect of play; the latter does not confuse the changing of a tire or any other task for the ateleological play of the general economy of forces.[†] Our actions are "without aim or reason outside of themselves and become truly autotelic and without cause or reason, a veritable *Leben ohne Warum*"[‡] (Nishitani, 1982, 252). The endless toil of the *homo faber* converts to the endless play of *homo ludens* when I am *of śūnyāta*, when it is no longer an issue for me, but rather when it is freed in my abdication of myself. This is not to reduce our responsibilities to games, but rather to free action from the

---

[*] *Sehnsucht* speaks to the sickness and languor of ceaseless longing that cannot find the rest of accomplished action.

[†] This is an allusion to Georges Bataille: "Woe to those who, to the very end, insist on regulating the movement that exceeds them with the narrow mind of the mechanic who changes a tire" (Bataille 1967, 641; 991, 26).

[‡] "Life without why": this is an allusion to Meister Eckhart and to Angelus Silesius, who argued that the rose is without why.

tyranny of Grand Marches, of ceaseless missions, of the incipient melancholy and temptation to suicide of Sisyphus, a melancholy implicit in the inexhaustible task of being. "The labor imposed, without ceasing to be an imposition, is transformed into play by arising spontaneously in an elemental way" (254). It is the cultivation of what Nishitani called "dharmic naturalness"[*] and what Buddhism dubbed "playful samadhi" (Nishitani, 1982, 253). This is again what the Daoist tradition famously called *wei wu wei*, acting without acting.

In the playful mode of *śūnyāta*, finally, the burden of the other becomes my primary responsibility. I am every other. "In the elemental spontaneity appearing through that conversion, doing becomes a true doing, ecstatic of itself. This doing implies a responsibility to every neighbor and every other... It is a doing on the standpoint of non-ego, of the 'non-duality of self and other'" (Nishitani, 1982, 255). What, then, in the end, was most decisive in decision theory? It is the transcendence of action in the ongoing conversion to the emptiness that is my responsibility for the other in the spontaneity of dharmic naturalness.

REFERENCES

Augustine, *Confessions,* translated by Chadwick, H., Oxford University Press, Oxford and New York, 1991.
Bataille, G., *La Part Maudite*, Les Éditions de Minuit, Paris, 1967.
Bataille, G., *The Accursed Share,* translated by Hurey, R., Zone Books, New York, 1991.
Bhagavad Gītā, translated by Easwaran E., Nilgiri Press, Berkeley, CA, 1985.
Camus, A., *The Myth of Sisyphus and Other Essays,* translated by O'Brien, J., Random House, New York, 1955.
Dōgen, *Moon in a Dewdrop: Writings of Zen master Dōgen*, edited and translated by Tanahashi, K., North Point Press, San Francisco, 1985.
Faure, B., *Double Exposure: Cutting Across Buddhist and Western Discourses*, translated by Stanford, L. J., Stanford University Press, Stanford, CA, 2004.
Heidegger, M., *Wegmarken*, 2nd ed., Vittorio Klostermann, Frankfurt am Main, 1978.
Klostermaier, K. K., *A Concise Encyclopedia of Hinduism*, One World, Boston and Oxford, 1998.
Lyotard, J. F., *The Confession of Augustine,* translated by Beardsworth, R., Stanford University Press, Stanford, CA, 2002.
McKenna, C. K., *Quantitative Methods for Public Decision Making*, McGraw-Hill, New York, 1980.
Masao, A., Will, Śūnyāta, and History, In *The Religious Philosophy of Nishitani Keiji*, Taitetsu, U., Ed., Asian Humanities Press, Berkeley, CA, pp. 279–304, 1989.
Narasimhan, C. V., *The Mahābhārata*, rev. ed., Columbia University Press, New York, 1998.
Nishida, K., *Last Writings,* translated by Dilworth, D. A., University of Hawaii Press, Honolulu, HI, 1987.
Nishitani, K., *Religion and Nothingness,* translated by van Bragt, J., University of California Press, Berkeley, CA, 1982.
Sartre, J. P., *L'Existentialisme Est Un Humanisme*, Nagel, Paris, 1946.
Tanabe, H., *Philosophy as Metanoetics,* translated by Yoshinori, T., University of California Press, Berkeley, CA, 1986.

---

[*] Dharmic naturalness is "natural and spontaneous accord with the dharma" as in the child "who is never more earnest than when engaged in mindless play" (Nishitani 1982, 255).

16 Theology and Rabbinic Decision Making: Judaism[*]

Alfred A. Marcus

CONTENTS

16.1 Introduction..299
16.2 The Rabbinic Period...300
    16.2.1 The Sage 302
    16.2.2 The Sage's Authority 303
    16.2.3 The Context: Halacha..304
16.3 Seven Dilemmas (or Considerations) in Decision Making 307
    16.3.1 Consideration #1: The Plain Meaning of the Text Versus Actual
           Historical and Material Conditions 307
    16.3.2 Consideration #2: Reconstructed and Reinterpreted
           Meaning Versus Literal Meaning 308
    16.3.3 Consideration #3: Underlying Ethics Versus Strict Legality 309
    16.3.4 Consideration #4: Insights, Reasoning, and Logic Versus the Authority
           of the Past 310
    16.3.5 Consideration #5: The Needs of the Moment Versus Those of Eternity...........311
    16.3.6 Consideration #6: The Practical Versus the Ideal 312
    16.3.7 Consideration #7: The Conscience of the Sage Versus Majority Opinion.........313
16.4 Conclusion 314
References..314

16.1 INTRODUCTION

This topic is immensely complex. Let me begin by explaining what I am not going to do. I am not going to cover Jewish decision making during the classic or biblical era of the Jewish people. Nor am I going to cover Jewish decision making during the modern era per se (Chazan and Raphael, 1974; Graetz, 1891).[†] Rather, I am going to try to provide insights into the period that roughly corresponds to the destruction of the Second Temple to the French Revolution. This period might be referred to as the Rabbinic period in Jewish history, or the period when Rabbis as opposed to secular leaders were dominant. It is the period of the Diaspora, a period when then there was no independent state in the land of Israel, nor movement toward a state. It is the period during which the Jewish

---

[*] I would like to thank Ron Krebs of the political science department of the University of Minnesota for his kind and useful comments on an earlier draft of this paper. I also would like to acknowledge the assistance of Stephen Benin who is in the Jewish studies department of Memphis State.

[†] Though obviously dated, Graetz (1891) is still worth reading. Chazan and Raphael (1974) is a good source book on the modern period.

people and Jewish culture shifted from a preoccupation with issues surrounding those of state building, state governing, and state defending to issues of religious and spiritual preservation. The Jewish people were dwelling in domains that were frequently hostile and at best indifferent to their existence. The everyday life of the average Jew was threatened commonly by the severe hatred of neighbors in the countries where they lived, and by many outbreaks of violence and bloodshed that left entire communities devastated. Jews wandered from country to country and from land to land. Their dwelling places spread to just about every place in the known civilized world from Spain and Italy to Germany, Poland, the Ottoman Empire, and beyond—all of this wandering due to the desire to achieve some degree of safety, security, and tolerance.

The scope of this paper then is very broad. At the broadest level the model of decision making that I describe applies to Ashkenazic (European) and Sephardic (Spain and Arab countries) authorities. A finer grained analysis would examine how these major traditions in Judaism differed, if at all. It would go further to examine within the Ashkenazic world whether there were different models in Western Europe as opposed to Central and Eastern Europe. Other questions might be raised. For instance, how have particular institutional configurations, regarding the relationship between religious and secular authority shaped the process and principles of Rabbinic decision making? Throughout the Rabbinic period, Jews have been a minority, normally politically impotent. To what extent has this influenced Rabbinic decision-making styles and structures?

Strands from the very large middle period in Jewish history continue to exert their influence to this day, especially among religious elements of the Jewish people. The period dominated by the Rabbis was one when Rabbinic sages, or learned men, more or less governed the Jewish people and made most of the significant decisions that determined their fate. Their decision-making methods and styles are the topic that I will cover in this chapter. A somewhat idealized and paradigmatic view of Rabbinic decision making will be sketched. Whether decision making by the Rabbis in all instances and in each case conformed to this ideal view is beyond the scope of this paper.

The Rabbinic sage was subject to immense pressure in making decisions. The fate of the Jewish people—not only their physical fate but their spiritual state as well—hung in the balance. This tradition where the decision-making sage makes authoritative choices for the people in the religious sphere is still alive among the approximately 12 to 16 percent of the world Jewish population that continues to be orthodox today.

My understanding of the method and style of the Rabbinic sages comes mainly from modern orthodox sources (Berkovits, 1983; Sokol, 1992).[*] A word of caution to the reader—I am not a Rabbi. Thus, what I will say comes from the perspective of a knowledgeable, academic layperson.[†] In the very last section of this chapter, I will try to draw out some general implications from my discussion of the decision-making sage. The style and method of the decision-making sage, I believe, may be relevant to contexts outside of Jewish history and tradition.

16.2 THE RABBINIC PERIOD

I exclude the biblical and modern periods of Jewish history from this chapter for the following reasons.[‡] Both the biblical and modern periods involved movements toward Jewish sovereignty and an autonomous Jewish state. The charismatic liberator and lawgiver Moses would have to be considered. The ancient Jewish state had unique decision-making roles played by prophets, priests, judges, and kings. The modern period involved a revolutionary change in the condition of the Jewish people, the establishment of the state of Israel. The normalization of Jewish

---

[*] My approach is one that shows respect for the tradition but it is one that is also analytical and somewhat critical.

[†] I am a practicing modern orthodox Jew, whose remarks might be disputed by more knowledgeable and fundamentalist authorities and by secular and anti-religious scholars. I am also a business strategy and ethics professor.

[‡] Good sources on decision making in these periods include: Schreiber (1979); Walzer, Lorberbaum, and Zohar (2000).

TABLE 16.1
The Sage's Seven Decision Making Dilemmas

On the One Hand...	...And on the Other
The plain meaning of a text	Actual historical and material conditions
A teaching's literal meaning	A teaching's interpreted and reconstructed meaning
The Law's strict requirements	Underlying ethical principles
The authority of the past	The insights of reason and logic
The requirements of the moment	The needs of the future
Ideal solutions	Workable answers
The majority's point of view	The sage's conscience

existence in Israel meant the creation of a parliamentary system of governance not unlike that found in other western democracies. The modern period also was marked by extreme schisms among the Jewish people to the point where it would be hard to describe a single approach to decision making.[*]

In the Rabbinic period, which is my focus rather than the biblical or modern period, the Rabbinic sage dominated. What can a modern audience learn from Rabbinic decision making? A present-day decision maker often must draw on written law and inherited tradition in making a decision, but he must face up to many other factors including actual historical and material conditions, how law and inherited tradition have been interpreted, underlying ethical principles, the insights of reasoning and logic, the needs of the future, the requirement to find a workable answer to a concrete here-and- now problem, and his conscience. Similarly, the sage was at a crossroads between such forces (see Table 16.1) as: (i) the plain meaning of a text versus actual historical conditions, (ii) a teaching's literal interpretation versus its reconstructed and reinterpreted meaning, (iii) the law's strict requirements versus underlying ethical principles, (iv) the authority of the past versus the insights of reasoning and logic, (v) the requirements of the moment versus the needs of the future, (vi) a problem's ideal solution versus a workable answer, and (vii) the majority viewpoint versus the sage's conscience. In these ways, the sage's dilemmas are not that unlike those of modern-day decision makers in government and business. Think of a judge, civil servant, or businessperson who must decide how to adjudicate a case or carry out a law. There are parallels in this discussion of Rabbinic decision making.[†]

The emphasis in this paper is on flexibility and contingency in halakhic decision making, but what are the limits of this flexibility and contingency? A factor that could be further explored is the role of tradition, in particular personal transmission from one Rabbinic authority to another. How might flexibility and contingency interact with personal transmission and tradition? Where

---

[*] Jews have divided into separate orthodox, conservative, and reform movements. Many Jews are entirely secular. Jewish communal organizations in the United States and other countries of the Diaspora have their own structure, form of organization, and way of making decisions (Elazar, 1980). All of this is important and deserves separate in-depth consideration but is not relevant to the project undertaken in this chapter, to describe the dilemmas of the decision-making sage in the classic Rabbinic period.

[†] Shapiro (1981) is an excellent source on judicial decision making. He talks about courts as mediators among consent and authority signified by law and office. He discusses English courts, courts in imperial China, and courts in Islam. All of these could be used as points of comparison for this chapter. Shapiro makes a key distinction between the gradual development of case law and of systems dominated by case law like that of England and English law generally (i.e., the U.S. with the exception of Louisiana) and systems that have been codified starting with Roman law and extending in modern times to the French system. A very similar development from case law to codification took place in Jewish law. It is beyond the scope of this chapter but it would be fascinating to trace and compare codification in Jewish law with codification in the latter systems (see Shapiro 126–156 for a discussion of the process of codification).

do flexibility's limits come from and how far do they extend? Is the flexibility described in this paper more appropriate and indeed more needed in some times and places rather than others?

Thus, the argument that I wish to make here is that the Rabbinic sage was at the crossroads of numerous pressures and forces, often contradictory and paradoxical in their demands. He had to arrive at the best possible solution for his time and place and for all times and places; for he knew that the particular decisions he would make would form precedents that would be part of a chain of tradition that started at Sinai when the Jewish people received the Torah.

The term Torah itself has many connotations. First, it is the name given to the five books of Moses. Second, the Torah refers to the entire Old Testament including the five books of Moses, eight books of the prophets, and eleven books of other writings. These 24 books constitute the written law. However, there also is another sense in which the term Torah is used. It also applies to the oral law. A large part of this oral Torah, however, is found written in books such as the Mishna and Gemora. The Mishna was compiled by Rabbi Yehuda HaNasi in about 220 C.E. in the land of Israel. Material in the Mishna goes back more than 300 years. It records the voices of sages who long preceded Rabbi Yehuda. The Gemora was compiled by Rav Ashi in about 470 C.E. in Babylon. An earlier and separate Gemora was written in Israel, but it is not authoritative and is less studied. Together, the Mishna and the Gemora, which was assembled in Babylon, constitute the Talmud (or Learning). The Mishna, which precedes the Talmud historically and in the typical printed text is arrayed first, provides a brief outline of the Oral Law. The rabbis of the Gemora elaborate on this summary. They go to great length to examine what the Mishna says and explain its meaning in depth. But they often also go off subject and wander on their own in the area of story and legend. They move far away from strict legal discussion or dispute.

The Mishna and Germora are divided into six orders: (1) "Seeds" deals mostly with agricultural law. (2) "Holidays" discusses the laws of the Sabbath and festivals. (3) "Women" deals with marriage and family law. (4) "Damages" covers civil and criminal law and the court system. (5) "Holiness" is focused on the Temple. (6) "Purity" discusses the laws of ritual purity. The word Torah, then, encompasses all of this. Frequently the term is used to connote the entire body of Jewish teaching—both written and oral, the Old Testament and the Talmud. But the word Torah implies even more. It also consists of commentaries and codes based on the Old Testament and the Talmud. These commentaries and codes were written far after 470 C.E. and continue to be written now. Thus, the word Torah is very far-reaching. The term is used without reference to any of these specific books, but to the sum of knowledge found in all these works together and beyond in the entire corpus of Jewish philosophy, mysticism, and lore, both written and unwritten. In each generation the sage's job was to apply the wisdom and insights of the entire Torah broadly conceived to the practical problems of the day, to distill from this gigantic corpus of knowledge the essence by which an individual Jewish human being was to live. The sage operated in a context in which he felt himself to be a link in the chain of the Torah. Thus, he had to answer to the past and to unknown futures about which he could at best speculate.

The seven dilemmas the decision-making sage faced are discussed in some detail later in the chapter. To start with, it is important to understand who this sage was, the source of his authority, and the context in which he operated. In many ways these factors are not analogous to those faced by a modern day decision maker, as I shall show.

16.2.1 THE SAGE

Typically, the sage occupied a position of communal responsibility. In the medieval and early modern periods, the sage might have derived some of his authority from his being an agent of government authority. The Jewish community had a degree of autonomy over its internal affairs. Jewish self-government extended from domestic to civil, criminal, and business law. The sage might be part of a community *Beth Din* (court of justice). The community was usually taxed as a single body in return for the right to govern itself, and the sage might even play some role in tax collection. In these ways, the sage was an agent of the king or local lords as much as he was an agent of the Jewish people. His primary allegiance was to the Jewish people but he could not ignore the demands of these civil and secular authorities. In this way, the sage was no different from a modern day decision maker.

However, in each generation there also appeared a sage or a number of sages whose decisions approached the status where they might be considered binding in a broader way.[*] Such a sage might be directly elected by a community to serve as a Rabbi. He might be given a stipend to spend his time studying Jewish texts. In the former capacity, he can be seen as some type of judge or lawyer and in the latter as a scholar, perhaps an analyst at a research institute. The sage had to show a mastery of Jewish law and tradition well above the level of the community he served (Dubnow, 1916).[†] The sage might be known for his scholarship. Even prior to Guttenberg, the writings of an influential sage would spread far and wide. His opinions would be debated and his writings scrutinized.[‡] His oral or written decisions might be discussed in the entire Jewish community throughout the Diaspora. His reputation might even extend to non-Jews.

In these ways, an analogy can be made with a modern-day decision maker, but the sage not only would be known for his learning. The sage had to demonstrate saintly character. He also would be known for his piety.[¶] Tales of his piety might extend beyond the confines of his locality. Regardless of the position he occupied, the sage had to be regarded as a learned person whose opinions were worthy of deference, but scholarly learning in and of itself was not enough, and it had to be combined with purity of character.

16.2.2 THE SAGE'S AUTHORITY

These two factors—the Sage's learning and piety as well as the position he occupied—led the sage's decisions to have a binding character. In almost every instance, tales of mental genius and devotion to scholarship from an early age were combined with legends of piety, asceticism, and kind-heartedness. The sage had to have a profound and deep education in Jewish texts and had to be immensely learned in Jewish law, but he also had to be considered pious, upright, and of upstanding character. The sage owed his authority to his scholarship and character.

Others of his type, the community of sages, judged the sage. He normally did not act alone, but in consultation and subject to other sages' criticism. They were likely to share with him his learning and his dispositions. He derived his moral authority from how this group viewed his learning and

---

[*] This tradition has continued to modern times where a sage such as Rabbi Moses Feinstein of the lower East Side in New York was considered the main decision maker on matters of law for the majority of religiously adherent Jews. Rabbi Feinstein attained this status via his reputation for learning and piety and his upstanding character. He did not undergo a formal process of appointment. Although the sages' decisions approached the status of being binding, few sages went unchallenged. With the lack of a Rabbinic hierarchy and the absence of political sovereignty, and with the end of the Sanhedrin (the ancient Jewish court system), there was nothing that could be binding. Each sage had to earn the status of being the decider for his generation, and oftentimes this status was not earned without ongoing controversy.

[†] The Jewish lay public in certain periods in Jewish history—particularly the 16th and 17th centuries in Poland and Lithuania—was extremely learned. In some generations, for example, in the classic period of Polish Jewry in the 16th and early 17th century, when Jewish learning was widespread even among lay persons, the sage's immersion in and knowledge of Jewish texts had to be absolutely outstanding, for even the average Jew would have enough knowledge to challange his opinions.

[‡] The spread of the Rabbinic sage's influence was great even in the period before the printing press, when the production of manuscripts was a slow and painstaking process, and the dissemination of written texts was retarded by the primitiveness of the technology. Debates about what sages wrote were common throughout Jewish communities even prior to the appearance of the printing press. See, for instance, Twersky (1979).

[¶] A good question is the extent to which the purity of character to which I refer was actual. Was it more the stuff of myth than reality? Wise sages might or might not have had good character traits, but they also had to be portrayed as such in order to bolster the legitimacy of their rulings in the eyes of the community. Though I make this comment, I hesitate to challenge the mythology, which is likely to consist of a high element of truthfulness.

devoutness. He might be the author of important works of Jewish law or learning, but his fame could spread as well because of his piety and upright disposition. He also obtained standing and influence from the Jewish people, who voluntarily consented to abide by his decisions.

Jews of this period lived in generally small, tightly-knit and highly-organized communities that spread throughout the world. In almost every community and in almost every generation there was a sage or a number of sages who through moral influence, character, scholarship, and position had authority and made critical decisions affecting Jewish law and Jewish life. The Rambam (Maimonidies) is the outstanding example of such a sage; his authority was based almost entirely on his learning, to a degree on his character, but not by his official position.[*] His views spread rapidly and were debated vigorously throughout the Jewish world. His influence was very wide in Jewish and non-Jewish circles. Some of his views will be elaborated on in the sections that follow. The Rambam is the stellar specimen of the sage whose decisions concerning Jewish life, no matter how controversial they might be, were uniquely authoritative and determinative vis-à-vis Jewish fate and history (Twersky, 1995).

16.2.3 The Context: Halacha

The tradition within which the sage operated was that of other Halachic scholars. Thus, some words about Halacha are needed. Halacha means the "way." It is based on the teachings of the Torah. The adoration for Torah, incumbent upon the sage, does not find analogy in a modern context. Halacha is based on Torah, which is a combination of written and oral traditions. The oral tradition paradoxically also is written. It was written in order not to be forgotten. During the difficulties of Jewish history, the constant wanderings and persecutions, the Rabbis continually were anxious lest their oral discussions be forgotten. Writing the oral law down was controversial but it was felt to be a necessary compromise given the vicissitudes of Jewish fate.

The Talmud was the most important part of the oral tradition to be written down.[†] The Talmud discusses legal and practical problems in Halacha or the way of Jewish life. It also has fantastic stories about the Rabbis and their times. Some of these stories (they are called Aggadic material in contrast to Halachic material which is legalistic) contain clear, fairly straightforward moral lessons, but some are entirely mysterious.[‡] Their point is hard to fathom.

---

[*] Rambam (Rabbi Moses ben Maimon in Hebrew or Maimonides, the son of Maimon in Greek) was a physician, legal codifier, and philosopher of the highest order who lived in the Middle Ages (1135–1204). He was author of the *Guide for the Perplexed*. (A 1904 translation by M. Friedlander is reproduced in its entirety on the Internet; see http://www.sacred-texts.com/jud/gfp/gfp.htm). He dwelt successively in Cordoba, Spain, Fez, Morocco, and Cairo, Egypt. The Rambam was driven out of Spain by the fanatical Almohads who invaded Spain from North Africa and temporarily ended the tolerance Jews enjoyed.

[†] Today it is kept alive in Yeshivot (higher school of learning) where it is still intensively studied throughout the world. In fact, estimates have been made that more scholars today are sitting in Yeshivot and intensively studying the Talmud than at any time in Jewish history. The Talmud starts with an earlier layer called the Mishna. The Mishna is much shorter than the next layer, the Gemora. The Mishna is written in Hebrew. The Gemora is written in Aramaic. Rabbi Yehudah Hanasi (the Prince) compiled the Mishna in about 220 C.E. in the land of Israel. The Gemora, much more dense and discursive in nature, was compiled later in two versions at two points in time. The less authoritative Jerusalem Talmud, written in the land of Israel, was compiled somewhere in the fourth century C. E. Rav Ashi compiled the more authoritative Babylonian Talmud in about 470 C.E. But perhaps it was not completed till many centuries later. The Jerusalem Talmud has a shorter discussion of the same Mishnaic material as the Babylonian Talmud and the discussions in the Jerusalem Talmud are more cryptic. There may be different viewpoints expressed in the two Talmuds. They do not necessarily complement each other or complete each other.

[‡] Additional material of an Aggadic nature, called Midrash, is found in other books outside the Talmud. The Babylonian Talmud is studied deeply in Jewish Yeshivot today and was studied historically in Yeshivot in the Diaspora wherever Jews were found from Spain and North Africa to France, Germany, Eastern Europe, and the Middle East throughout the ages. It constitutes the centerpiece of Jewish learning. In many current Yeshivot it is the entire curriculum. Nothing else of note is studied and the students pour over the Talmud and its commentaries line-by-line day and night. Whatever else might be examined—whether it is a Biblical work, mysticism, or philosophy—is secondary and considered discretionary.

Not every discussion in the Talmud comes to a clear, definitive conclusion about the way a Jew or Jewish community should conduct itself. Opinions are given on various sides of an issue in debate that is often long, convoluted, and exacting (*Encyclopedia Judaica*, 1971; Elon, 1987).[*] The practical needs of daily life, however, require a resolution. Thus, organized, codified law books emerged in the medieval and early modern periods. The codification of Jewish law is analogous to the codification of law in other cultures. Codification was at first gradual. A Rabbi would put together a collection of authoritative opinions regarding a single issue but would not tackle the entire tradition. Writing down the oral tradition remained controversial and the ban against committing it to writing was strong. Only because of the needs of the moment, the vicissitudes of history, the fear that the Torah might otherwise be forgotten, were exceptions made.

But these exceptions built up and led to a period of codification. Four major figures took the lead in this effort. The first was Rabbi Yitzhak Alfasi. Born in Kila Chamad, Algeria, in 1013, Alfasi died in Lucena, Spain, in 1103.[†] His organization of the material was relatively primitive. It followed that of the Mishna and Gemora. He made no effort to recast the Mishna and Gemora in some other image. The great reformulator of the tradition, at least in how he organized the presentation of Jewish law, was the Rambam or Maimonidies. He created 14 volumes out of the six Mishnaic orders.[‡] His great compendium of Jewish law started with first principles and fundamental beliefs—recall that Rambam was a philosopher as well as Rabbi and physician—and covered everything a Jew had to know.[¶]

Rambam, however, was heavily criticized on many grounds.[§] A main fault was that he did not use footnotes. The next great figure in the codification of the Halacha was Rabbi Yaakov ben Asher, otherwise known as the Tur after his great compendium of Jewish law (Finkel, 1990; Lewittes, 1987). The Tur was born in Cologne, Germany in 1275 and died in Toledo, Spain in 1343. His father, Rabbi Asher ben Yehiel (1250–1337) had emigrated from Germany to become the chief Rabbi of Toledo after massacres of Jews took place in Germany. The Tur's father had compiled his own commentary on the Talmud. It summed up the state of the law as Rabbi Asher saw it in his time. Prior codifiers—the Rif, the Rambam, and the Tur's father—sometimes disagreed. The Tur's magnum opus was designed to arrive at definitive conclusions when disputes existed among these giants. His father represented the traditions of Ashkenazic (Germanic) Jewry. The Rif and the Rambam represented the traditions of Sephardic (Spanish) Jewry. The Tur's decision rule was to follow the majority. If there were no majority, he would analyze the issue as carefully as he could based on precedents and arrive at his own conclusions.

If this alone were the Tur's only accomplishment, it would be great, but he went further. He arrived at an entirely new organizing principle for Jewish law. Unlike the Rambam who arranged the laws starting with first principles, and his father and the Rif, who arranged them

---

[*] The Talmud itself may have some rule for deciding, for instance, that when Hillel or his students clash with Shamai or his students, the ruling, with some exceptions, always goes according the school of Hillel. Other rules of this nature exist. When Rav's views conflict with those of Shmuel's, Rav's views prevail in religious matters and Shmuel's views prevail in civil matters. A majority point of view, always signified in the Talmud by being that of the narrator and not that associated with a specific Rabbi or school of thought, wins out over a minority. In some cases, the Talmud will say which opinion holds. Rules for deciding did emerge over time in subsequent literature. See "Halakah" in *Encyclopedia Judaica* (1971), 1157–1167.

[†] He was known as the Rif after the initials of his name. His efforts to bring to light the resolution of Talmudic debate are still found in the back of most volumes of the Talmud.

[‡] The 14 volumes were as follows: (1) Knowledge, (2) Love of God, (3) Seasons, (4) Family Life, (5) Holiness, (6) Utterances, (7) Seeds, (8) Service, (9) Sacrifices, (10) Purity, (11) Torts, (12) Acquisitions, (13) Judgments, and (14) Judges.

[¶] Rambam's work of Halacha is called the Yad Hazakah or Strong Hand. The word Yad in Hebrew is equivalent to 14. His great compendium was also referred to as the Mishneh Torah, or Learning or Repetition of the Torah.

[§] Basically the challenges had to do with Rambam's boldness. How dare anyone commit all of Jewish teaching to writing? How dare anyone do so without providing the footnotes, for Rambam's work was almost entirely devoid of references.

according to Talmudic tractates, the Tur started with what a Jew had to do when he got up in the morning and proceeded with the laws that encompassed this person's obligations throughout the day, the year, and the seasons of his life including those that applied to all practical affairs and business.[*]

The final codifier was Rabbi Yosef Karo (Werblowsky, 1980). Born in Toledo, Spain in 1488, he was educated mainly in Istanbul where he settled after being exiled from Spain in 1492. At the age of 24, living in Adrianople, he began what was to be his life's work, a super commentary on the work of the Tur, which came to be called Bet Yosef, or the House of Yosef. In 1530, he moved to the Land of Israel, to the city of Safed, where a Jewish revival was taking place, which was fomented and forwarded by mystics and Kabbalists. Karo became a member of the Rabbinic court in Safed, established his own Yeshiva, spent time with Kabbalists like Rabbi Moshe Codoverro who studied in his Yeshiva, and completed his great legal work, a compendium called the *Shulhan Arukh* or Prepared Table. It was based on the scholarship he undertook in his super commentary on the Tur and organized according to the same format that the Tur used.

Karo passed away in Safed in 1575. A problem was that his work primarily reflected Sephardic custom. However, the Polish Rabbi, Moses Isserles (born in Cracow in 1520 and died there in 1572) provided a gloss that elaborated the Ashkenazic way of doing things. The *Shulhan Arukh* then became the authoritative rulebook for Jewry the world over. But even after, there were commentaries and super-commentaries.[†] These referred to each other and there were extensions, revisions, as well as deep and extremely learned critiques.[‡]

The books of Halacha were meant to be a bridge between the Torah that God gave the Jewish people on Mount Sinai and the actions that they were called upon to undertake on a daily basis.[¶] Based on this voluminous literature, the purpose of the Jewish sage in each community in every generation was to decide how the Halacha should be applied. In making his decisions, the sage was guided by the collective erudition of the Jewish sages that had preceded him. He had to be a master of this literature's ins and outs. He had to have devoted a considerable portion of his life to the study of it.

The Halacha was all-inclusive. It encompassed every aspect of life from marital relations to business, from how to behave when getting up in the morning to how to behave when going to sleep at night, from the right customs for holidays to the commands incumbent upon a person in his dealings with other human beings. The Jew was always required to fulfill a commandment (the Hebrew term is *mitzvah*). He had no right to waste any time (the Hebrew term is *bitul zeman*). If he had a free second, he had to study the Torah—the study of the Torah was considered like all the other commandments combined. In a situation of all-encompassing obligation, when numerous

---

[*] The four Turim or rows in his multi-volume compendium, which is called the Arbah Turim, are the book of (1) the Path of Life, (2) the Teacher of Wisdom, (3) the Rock of Assistance, and (4) the Breastplate of Judgment. The first volume deals with daily practices and holidays. The second volume treats dietary laws, oaths, family purity, ritual bathing, and mourning. The third volume focuses on marriage and divorce, and the final volume involves matters of business, disputes, damages and torts. Unlike the Rambam, the Tur only treated laws that applied in the current time. Hence, he eliminated anything having to do with sacrifices and the Temple service.

[†] The commentaries were composed mainly by Rabbis associated with Yeshivot in Poland and Lithuania, a great center of Jewish learning in the early modern period. These commentaries continued to be written until our day. See the Mishna Berurah or Clear Mishna of Rabbi Yisrael Meir Hakohen Kagan (The Chafetz Chaim or Seeker of Life), born in Zhetel, Lithuania in 1839 and died in Radin, Lithuania in 1933 (Finkel, 1990).

[‡] In each generation, there was a related literature of questions (shealot) posed to prominent Rabbis and the answers (teshuvot) that the Rabbis gave. This material went back to the early Middle Ages. It too was often collected and published (Finkel, 1990, 128).

[¶] There also were popularizers of Karo's great work, whose books also had substantial influence. The popular books, intended to be a guide to daily life for the average Jew, combined folk wisdom, superstition, high ethical philosophy, and law. See the Kitzur Shulhan Arukh or Short Prepared Table, an immensely popular book among Jews of Eastern Europe, which was written by Rabbi Shelomoh Ganzfried, who was born in Ungvar, Hungary in 1804 and passed away in that city in 1880 (Finkel, 1990, 124).

commandments might be binding and their specific application not always clear, it was necessary to consult a sage about how to act. In deciding how the Halacha should be carried out in daily life, the sage was guided by at least seven considerations.

16.3 SEVEN DILEMMAS (OR CONSIDERATIONS) IN DECISION MAKING

16.3.1 CONSIDERATION #1: THE PLAIN MEANING OF THE TEXT VERSUS ACTUAL HISTORICAL AND MATERIAL CONDITIONS

Between rigid conformity to objective morality and extreme subjectivity and chaotic individualism,[*] the Halachic system of decision making is based on dialogue between the will of God as reflected in texts passed down from generation to generation and the autonomy of the sage to interpret and apply these texts. The sage's applications are conditioned by time, place, circumstances, and personality. Rambam maintained that the Halacha required extensions and curtailments depending on case, location, what actually transpired, and the circumstances. Rabbi Abraham, his son, insisted that a sage's decision was "weak and wanting" if the decision only followed what was written and did not contain considerations of the decision maker's "own understanding."[†]

The decision maker was supposed to weigh each case according to the evidence before him. According to Rabbi Abraham, he should "develop branches from the roots," the branches being his own subjective contribution and the roots being prior decisions of a similar nature. Rabbi Abraham's idea of decision making is not a formalistic and absolute notion of the human will frozen outside of time, but a fitting and bending will appropriate to historical and material conditions. Decisions are contingent on time, place and subject. Rambam held that a court interprets rules as they appear "right" in its "eyes."[‡] A later court to whom another argument appears right can abolish a prior argument because a person in need of a decision must go to the judge of his days. A judge is judge in his time and place and not in all times and all places.

A sage does not make abstract, universal choices. A decision so thoroughly disembodied that it has no relation to actual historical and material conditions will not stick. Joseph Albo, another Medieval sage, wrote that the Torah is not "complete" such that it is "adequate for all times."[¶]

---

[*] The German philosopher and ethicist, Immanuel Kant (1989) presented humans with a uniform system of law that humans willingly acceded to as rational creatures. According to Kant, humans voluntarily subject themselves in an absolute sense. No exceptions are made to anyone or for any reason. The laws of reason are categorical in the sense that they are outside time and space and applied regardless of consequence or context. Human beings willingly subject themselves to self-imposed laws and act only in conformity with them. The laws are those that they will upon themselves. There is no outside authority in Kant's system. His system is a kind of circular absolutism, self-willed and self-imposed, seemingly within the realm of reason but with total subjection. Its assumptions about human rationality are great. The views about a singular, abstract human nature shared by all creatures may not be realistic. This universal person is at the center of Kant's doctrine, but where can this universal person be found? In reality, there are many humans with many separate wills. They have innumerable perspectives. Their values, systems, and basic orientations differ and as a consequence the laws to which they are willing to subject themselves also differ. A twentieth-century view such as that found in existentialism is that each human has his or her own unique values and is a creator of those values. Each person's values are personal and distinctive and not universal, abstract, and absolute.

[†] As cited by Berkovits (1983, 55) from Menahem Alon, *Hamishpat Ha'ibri*, 345.

[‡] As cited by Berkovits (1983, 57) from Maimonidies, *Mamrim II*:1.

[¶] As cited by Berkovits (1983, 71) from Yosef Albo, *Book of Principles III*, 23. Albo was born in Spain in 1380 and died there in 1440. He lived in the Saragossa district. He is best known for his *Book of Principles*, which tries to make Judaism more consistent with both logic and philosophy. See Finkel (1990, 209).

Instead, it consists of "general principles" upon which the sages of each generation are required to "deduce new particulars"—the new particulars of the law appropriate to the situation. The sage negotiates this tension between the Torah's static rules and the dynamic flow of events (Kirschenbaum, 1992). He balances the general with the specific and unique, he takes into account the demands of impartiality and individuality, considers both justice and mercy, and applies the law, which covers the majority of cases, to the unique angles in specific instances. In the application he modifies the law so that the law remains true to itself.

The work of the sage is to mediate between the formalism inherent in all legal systems and the flexibility required in a time and place. The Torah is part of the reality of daily life as it is actually lived. The sage's job is to make this connection between law and life. It is incumbent upon sages of each generation to interpret the Torah in a way that acknowledges the material and spiritual conditions of the real world. The sage has interpretive latitude in coordinating the revealed word of God with concrete human reality.

16.3.2 Consideration #2: Reconstructed and Reinterpreted Meaning Versus Literal Meaning

The deduction of particulars from general legal dictums is not based on a text's plain meaning, nor is it based on use of a strict logic. Theoretical reasoning in Halachic decision making is not of a compelling nature where A necessarily and absolutely follows from B. Reasoning is not mathematical or Cartesian. Results do not automatically follow from known premises and assumptions. Rather, the sage has a measure of independence to show creativity in interpretation. Creativity is encouraged provided that the sage accepts the idea that Halachic discourse is a continual process of reconstructing an original truth that has multiple layers of meaning. The sage is engaged in the difficult, demanding intellectual struggle to uncover and reveal these multiple layers in the text. The text's "indeterminancy" and "provisionality" allow for the plurality of interpretation (Kolbrener, 2004, 133; Benin, 1993).

Traditionally, interpretation of the Torah, biblical hermeneutics, was a process of uncovering four levels of meaning symbolized by the word *pardes*, or orchard (Finkel, 1990, 2). These levels were *peshat*, the text's literal meaning; *remez*, finding hints or allusions in the text to unrelated subjects; *derash*, a metaphoric interpretation; and *sod*, a mystical or secret revelation based on a hidden meaning. This kind of interpretive system gets things right, more or less. It does not get things right exhaustively, comprehensively, and with finality.

The sages thus have some interpretive relativism. Each generation has to engage in a process of creative reconstruction of the text, informed by the remembrance of Moses, who set in motion the process, by receiving the Torah at Sinai. The revelation at Sinai was a major event that allowed for this latitude (Kirschenbaum, 1992, 63–68). There were at least three ways in which this latitude might be manifest.

1. The *conservative* approach is that the original revelation was exhaustive. Thus, the sages are engaged in an act of rediscovery; novel interpretations are just ones that have been rediscovered. They already were revealed to Moses at Sinai.
2. The *explicative* approach is that the sages are authorized human agencies, loyal to tradition, who have the right, given to them at Sinai, to make choices provided that they follow received rules of interpretation. By means of these received rules, they can explicate the true intention of the revelation, which was not made plain at Sinai. A variant of this approach holds that the sages have power to make legitimate Halachic decisions even if not completely in line with the original intent of the

revelation at Sinai. It is in their power to develop ideas and principles that are latent in the texts.*

3. Yet a different approach is the *accumulative* approach. It holds that revelation is ongoing; the sages in every generation interpret the written material that they have acquired anew. This approach roughly corresponds to the mystics' conception that revelation has not ceased. It remains strong and goes on continuously.

All of these approaches insist on a human part in discovering and administering the word of God. There are numerous examples of how the sages intervened to modify biblical injunctions. An example would be the biblical injunction that a city should be utterly destroyed if its inhabitants are led astray by idol worship. The sages created stringencies so that this injunction *never* would be applied in actuality. The conditions they attached to the law meant it could not be fulfilled. A question was then posed: Why was this injunction commanded in the first place? To which the Rabbis answered, the command was given as a test for the intelligence and conscience of the sages. The Rabbis had a duty to reconstruct and reinterpret the text rather than rely on its literal meaning. To do so would be an abdication of their responsibility (Berkovits, 1983, 83).

16.3.3 CONSIDERATION #3: UNDERLYING ETHICS VERSUS STRICT LEGALITY

Tension between the written law and a "living conscience" meant that the sages had a dilemma. Given that they had freedom to choose, the sages were expected to take into account specifically ethical considerations. The interrelated practical and moral considerations that played an exceptionally strong role were justice, fairness, pleasantness, beneficence, goodness, peace, and goodwill (Kirschenbaum, 1992, 86; Spero, 1982). The Bible deplores the injustice done to the oppressed, whose tears must be regarded in making decisions. It calls on the sages to promote justice, to support the poor, to visit the sick, and to bury the dead (Berkovits, 1983, 23–28). They had to show respect for the feelings of the poor. They had to go out their way to make sure that they did not shame a person who had no means. They could not "shut the door" in front of borrowers. Leniency and generosity were to be shown toward fellow human beings. The sages had to prevent hatred, promote peace, and eliminate quarrels. They were obligated to protect the moral health of people. The honor that was due a person was so powerful that it could overrule a biblical command.

A sage demonstrated he was doing what was "right and good" by forgoing advantages that otherwise might accrue to a person from strict adherence to the law. Halacha insisted that a person should not be adamant about obtaining rights to which he was entitled by strict adherence to the law, but should forfeit these rights if doing so meant doing what was "right and good in the sight of the Eternal One, Your God" (Berkovits, 1983, 72; Spero, 1982, 178–185). With respect to doing what was "right and good," Rambam maintained that it would not be correct for the Torah to

---

* Nahmanidies, another Medieval sage, wrote that God gave the Torah to the sages even if they "erred" (as cited by Kirschenbaum, 1992, 65). Nahmanidies, or Rabbi Moshe ben Nachman was born in Gerona, Spain in 1195 and died in the land of Israel in 1270. He was Rabbi in Barcelona in 1263, when King James of Aragon forced him to hold a public religious dispute with the Jewish apostate Pablo Chistiani (Finkel, 1990, 11). Another Medieval sage, the Ritva, held that "the law was communicated as a series of options—a range of permissible outcomes for every case that requires a decision. The halachic process consists of selecting the most appropriate option. The final decision in any case is not preordained, but left to the Sages of each generation to whom the question is addressed. They must determine the law based on their opinion regarding the requirements of the times they live in. In so deciding, they are not innovating laws, but selecting among options included in the original Revelation" (as cited by Kirschenbaum). The Ritva was Rabbi Yom Tov ben Abraham of Seville who died in 1320. His date of birth is unknown (Finkel, 1990, 232).

command about these matters in detail (Berkovits, 1983, 57). It was necessary to go above and beyond the law to do what was "right and good."*

When the law led to morally unacceptable consequences, the sages could limit the law's applicability. Righteousness and the law were not perfect correlates. In matters of oppression, ethics could weaken the law and declare it inoperative. Deviation from the law was not seen as an annulment but an extension of the law's inherent meaning. Rashi, the great medieval commentator wrote that "at times one abrogates the laws of Torah to act for God... for it is written seek peace and pursue it."†
The sages also had the right to limit the applicability of a commandment to uproot wickedness. In addition, then could act against the law to prohibit evil practices. In addition, they could ignore the law for the sake of fulfilling the law, or the sake of avoiding the violation of another law. The sages were supposed to be informed by a more comprehensive sense of the law. That more comprehensive sense was rooted in the broadest of biblical commands, to "love your neighbor as yourself."

The ethical informed how the sages made use of the law. That the Torah's ways "are ways of pleasantness and its paths are peace" was a central guideline. The injunction to pursue peace was a built in control on excessive legalism and formalism.

16.3.4 CONSIDERATION #4: INSIGHTS, REASONING, AND LOGIC VERSUS THE AUTHORITY OF THE PAST

The literal meaning of the inherited tradition did not act like a straitjacket that took away the sage's discretion. The sage was to rely on insights, reasoning, and logic in choosing. The authority of the past was not so powerful as to remove the perpetual responsibility to rule according to what the sage's "eyes see."‡ The sage of every generation had to be guided by the empirical evidence. Disciples were not bound to follow a past sage's decisions but to use their own insight and reason based on what they observed. They were required to use their eyes to observe current customs, usage, and acts.

Reasoning was thus critically important. The sage had to act in accord with his understanding of the case before him. He had to rely on *svara* or human reasoning to understand that case. Tradition granted that any principle or idea that could be established by reason was sufficiently authoritative so as not to require biblical validation. Whenever a law or ruling could be established though logical reasoning there was no reason to rely on textual exegesis. *Sevara* or legal norms derived from natural reason had a very high status in the development, application, and perpetuation of Halacha. The Talmud ascribed to the logical thinking activity of the intellect, *sevara*, no less an authoritative role than Biblical text itself. Yehuda HaLevi, a Spanish poet and sage maintained that God could not allow anything in the Torah to contradict reason.¶

The sage had at least two decision-making aids for assisting him in making rational decisions (Landesman, 1995). First, there were highly developed methods for interpreting texts such as the "13 hermeneutical tools of Rabbi Ishmael." These included derivations based on comparisons such as a *kal* vachomer—an a fortiori assumption that if the known laws applying to X are more stringent than those that apply to Y, then the stringency that applies to Y is surely true of X.

---

* Ramban wrote: "Set your mind to do what is right and good... This is important. It is impossible to mention in the Torah the entirety of human conduct with friends and neighbors in business in the improvement of society and the state... but the Torah states that one should do what is right and good" (quoted in Berkovits, 1983, 72 from Nahmanidies, *Commentary on the Torah*, Deuteronomy chapter 6: verse 18).

† Quoted in Berkovits (1983, 66) Rashi (Rabbi Shelomoh Yitzhaki) was born in Troyes, France in 1040 and died there in 1105. He is considered the greatest Jewish commentator on the Torah. His commentaries simple and yet profound cover nearly all of the classic parts of Jewish literature including the Old Testament and the Talmud.

‡ From the Talmud, as quoted by Berkovits (1983, 53).

¶ Rabbi Yehuda HaLevi was born in Toledo, Spain in 1080 and died in the land of Israel in 1145. He was a philosopher and poet (Finkel, 1990, 200).

Another derivation based on comparison was the *gezarah shava* or use of analogy when the same term was found in separate cases. Other hermeneutical tools existed for reading texts. The sage was instructed about what he should do when a general statement was followed by specific examples, when specific examples were followed by general statements, and when a general category was followed by a specific example and then another general category.

The sage also had the right to rely on very broad principles of logic, less formalized than these hermeneutical rules. Some of the general rules of *sevara* included (Landesman, 1995, 141–151).

1. *Use of analogy.* If the laws of the Torah applied to one realm, it was likely they could be extended to another. Civil issues thus might be compared with religious ones.
2. *Relevant observations.* Halacha had to be consistent with how people actually behaved. The sages should observe people's behavior. Through their observations, they could formulate more appropriate decisions.
3. *Begin with the status quo.* The sages were instructed to assume inertia in a situation unless evidence was presented for change. For instance, if a person claimed another person's property, the burden of proof rested on the claimant so long as the property he wanted was not currently in his possession.
4. *Study behavior.* People's typical behavior was the starting point for logical inference. Statistical analysis therefore was relevant. The sage should try to find what applied in a majority of instances.
5. *Examine repeated occurrences.* Observed regularities were fitting points for estimating what was going on. What happened again and again was likely to continue to happen unless proven differently.

Indicative of the role of insights, reasoning, and logic was the tradition's insistence that when two sages disagreed, it was not a problem so long as each justified his position. The medieval commentator Rashi explained the tradition that said that "these as well as those are the words of the living God" as meaning that "at times, one reason is valid; at other times another reason, for reasons change in the wake of even only small changes in the situation."[*] So long as each sage gave a reason for his position it was possible to believe that both spoke the words of living God. Each point of view might have its day. In one example the sages might disregard the plain meaning of the text; in another they might uphold its literal meaning. They were not logically inconsistent. The insights, reasoning, and logic upon which they relied were not mechanical and impersonal. They were a function of the human intellect. The Torah, in the end, was not given to angels but to humans with unique minds struggling to use their reason to deal with concrete problems.

16.3.5 CONSIDERATION #5: THE NEEDS OF THE MOMENT VERSUS THOSE OF ETERNITY

The sage had to resolve the tension between the needs of the moment and those of eternity. Rambam's view was that the Torah was eternal and that it applied to all people and all times, but human beings and their behaviors change. So the sages established binding laws and pious precepts that that they derived from general principles. Their purpose was to keep the law the same and simultaneously to introduce such modifications as were needed (Sacks, 1992). By nature, the word of God was timeless, yet the sage of every generation had to take into account the needs of a changing human condition. The teachers of every generation had to take notice of the needs of the hour and modify the law in accordance with circumstances. Indeed, under some conditions, the law might not be applied because of weightier considerations.

---

[*] As quoted in Berkovits (1983, 66) from Rashi on Gemora Ketubot, 57a.

The story of Elijah, the prophet, as told in the Bible is an example. Elijah brought sacrifices on the mountain of Carmel in breach of the law—sacrifices only were to be brought at the Temple in Jerusalem—but the Rabbis justified this abrogation of the law because of the needs of the moment. Elijah's actions were needed to hedge off a situation that could become far worse. The Rabbis thus admitted to the possibility that breaking a law to prevent serious evil was permissible. Uprooting what was not permitted and temporarily allowing it could be permitted during an emergency and for the sake of God. Rambam was of the opinion that just as a physician might have to amputate a limb to save a person's life, so a court might have to temporary abolish laws in an emergency so that the laws themselves might survive. When evil practice had to be stopped or an immoral situation eliminated, the sages could suspend a law. The ends—protection of the law itself, bringing back multitudes to religion, and saving the people from general religious laxity—justified the means.

To seek and pursue peace also might justify suspending the law. The Rabbis, for instance, came to the conclusion that if a defendant was a person of violence "or of that ilk," they should be willing to suspend a basic rule (Kirschenbaum, 1992, 72–78). Don Isaac Abarbanel, the medieval Spanish Jewish statesman and commentator on the Bible, held that God allowed the sages discretion to set the law straight and correct it with regard to a specific matter.[*] Under the maxim that it was a "time to act for God," the sages might disregard a law to safeguard something of great national or social value. For moments of great or unique historical significance, Abarbanel believed that there was no prescribed law. In such moments, the sage had the right to create a "law of the hour." The Talmudic sage Resh Lakish commented, "At times the abolition of the Torah is its founding" (Berkovits, 1983, 69).

Even though the law forbids putting the oral teaching into writing, one of the reasons the sages did so was their belief that "it was a time to act for God." Conditions detrimental to the preservation of tradition were the determining factor. Severe troubles and the pressures brought about decreased understanding and a likely diminishment of the Torah unless extraordinary steps were taken. A time of urgency and great need was able to justify extraordinary actions. But taking extraordinary actions was not to be done lightly. Rambam in the *Guide for the Perplexed* cautioned against basic changes based on the "isolated" case.[†] Again using an analogy from medicine, he maintained that the decisions the sages made about the laws were not like those that physicians made about a patient's health. The latter were "dependent on changes in circumstances and times but governance of the Torah should be absolute and universal even if it does not meet the needs of each individual case."[‡]

16.3.6 CONSIDERATION #6: THE PRACTICAL VERSUS THE IDEAL

The sage's decisions were to be put to the test of pragmatic validity—did they apply to practical human needs, human nature, and the human condition. There was an important Talmudic adage upon which the sage could rely "Where it is possible, it is possible; where it is not possible, it is not possible" (Berkovits, 1983, 80). The sage had to do what was reasonable and feasible, paying attention to the practical and the morally possible. The sage was enjoined against making an edict if the majority of people could not obey. For instance, he was proscribed from creating serious economic problems for the people and warned against putting their livelihoods in jeopardy.

The Halacha thus had respect for the effective functioning of the market and for normal credit operations. The sage was not supposed to interfere because the "Torah treats protectively the money of Israel" (Berkovits, 1983, 17). Economic consequences had to be considered. Halachic decision making involved a wisdom of the feasible. In making decisions the sage was immersed in the

---

[*] Rabbi Yitzhak Abarbanel was born in Lisbon in 1437 and died in Venice, Italy in 1508.

[†] As cited by Kirschenbaum (1992, 74) from the *Guide for the Perplexed*.

[‡] As quoted by Kirschenbaum (1992, 74) from the *Guide for the Perplexed*.

practical problems of the day; he depended not only on the knowledge of the Torah, he also used the Torah as a pragmatic truth.

16.3.7 CONSIDERATION #7: THE CONSCIENCE OF THE SAGE VERSUS MAJORITY OPINION

Decisions were not made in heaven, but were in the hands of the majority of sages to decide. In the Talmud, a famous passage dealt with an oven's ritual purity. The passage was famous not because of the oven, but because of the decision rule that the passage affirmed. Rabbi Eliezer, the most revered sage of his generation, decided differently from the majority of sages. He brought as proof of his being right miracles, signs, and a heavenly voice, to which Rabbi Yehoshua as representative of the majority, said,

> The Torah already has been given to us from Sinai, we are not to listen to a heavenly voice in matters of halakhic decision. For has it not already been written for us at Sinai to make decisions in accord with the majority.[*]

After the death of Moses, decision making was by majority. Debate and disagreement were common and there were multiple interpretations of issues (Berkovits, 1983, 47–48).[†] A heavenly voice, mystic insight, or prophetic insight did not have privileged status over human interpretation and majority rule (Saks, 1992, 127–130).

The principle of rule by majority however, was qualified with exceptions. The rule of the majority might not be followed and the opinion of the individual upheld because of outstanding reasons given by the individual. Logic, not heavenly voices, then prevailed. If the individual could make a more convincing case, his view might be adopted. Instances existed where sound reasoning overruled both authoritative text and a majority. A consideration was who the majority was. Not all majorities were considered equal, as the later sage, Maharashdam, wrote, "Heaven forbid that we should accept the popular notion of strict majority rule regardless of who the majority is. True justice would suffer."[‡]

Rule by majority was not considered to be objective truth, but rather pragmatic truth. When the minority opinion was overruled, its view was supposed to be kept on record for a time when it might become logically convincing. Satisfied only with the pragmatic validity of the majority opinion, the sages believed that they had to treat holders of defeated minority reasons with respect. The Rabbis believed that the ideas of the sages, whether those of majority or minority, all originated in "One God" (Rosenzweig, 1992). The same God inspired some sages to forbid and others to permit, some to reject and some to accept. This underlying divinity meant all opinions were worthy of honor. The Rabbis had a tradition that all the individual souls of Israelites were present at Sinai to receive the Torah and that they received it in 49 paths or ways, all of these paths or ways being in their own way true and sensible.[¶] Thus, there were multiple truths and dissenting views by their very nature had inherent value. They could be rehabilitated as fallback positions under different occasions.

The belief in the inherent significance of the process of learning Torah, which necessarily included the exchange of conflicting opinions, reinforced the view that dissenting views not only were to be tolerated but encouraged and respected. There also was a sense in which the Rabbis

---

[*] Berkovits (1983, 47–48) citing the Talmud, *Bava Mezia*, 59B; also see Kolbrenner, 118 for additional discussion of this matter.

[†] According to Berkovits, the Rabbis took seriously the principle that the Torah was not in heaven, not in the province of the divine solely, but in the province of human persons, and that they had no need to have recourse to transcendental experience to recapture certainty.

[‡] As cited by Kirschenbaum (1992, 79).

[¶] As cited by Rosenzweig (1992, 109) the Maharshal introduction to *Yom Shel Shlomo on Bava Kama*. The Maharshal Rabbi Shlomoh Efraim of Luntchitz was born in that town in 1550 and died in Prague in 1619. He was Rabbi of Prague and author of a major commentary on the Talmud. For biographical details, see Finkel (1990, 23).

believed that truth could not be established without some measure of error. From analysis of error in a debate or discussion there would emerge critical nuances from which greater levels of truthfulness would be established.[*] Thus, rejected opinions had redeeming value both conceptually and didactically. The Halacha was open to rejected options.

Toleration of multiple perspectives, however, might be limited because of a pragmatic need to establish order. A "dissenting elder" was put to death if he broke the law by his own action or taught others to do so, but he was free to continue to teach and propagate his views even if they were contrary to majority rule (Rosenzweig, 1992). His actions were suppressed, not his opinions, because their time too might come. To the extent that pluralism and tolerance had a place, their origins were in the fact that despite loyalty to the same formal rules of interpretation, precedents, and authoritative texts, different sages arrived at different interpretations. They did not all decide the same. The Jerusalem Talmud thus maintained that it was necessary that there be "49 ways of affirming an opinion and 49 ways of opposing it" (Berkovits, 1983).

16.4 CONCLUSION

The sage who had authority to make decisions for the Jewish people in the classic, Rabbinic or middle period of Jewish history had to be both learned and righteous. The burdens on the decision maker were great, his responsibilities large. This learned and righteous sage was guided in his decisions by considerations discussed in this chapter. Jewish decision making was a dialectic between a strong written tradition, an oral tradition that was put into writing, and actual historical and material conditions. The sage balanced the practical with the ideal. He did so by reconstructing and reinterpreting text rather than just supporting its literal meaning. He relied on insights, reasoning, and logic. He used an understanding of underlying ethical principles and frameworks to guide him in making choices. He was tugged and pulled by the needs of the moment and the needs of eternity, and he learned how to balance the two. He was ruled by his conscience.

For decision makers in general there may be implications. A decision maker should be an erudite and scholarly individual but also a person of upstanding character and high moral standing. He should be well aware of precedent. He must have the creativity and creative license to reconstruct and reinterpret past precedents to make them current and relevant. He must investigate and understand the historical and material conditions around him. He must use empirical evidence and rely on insights, reasoning, and logic, but not in a mechanical way because he also must be guided by an underlying sense of ethical principles. He also must be sensitive to the needs of the moment as well as those of future. His decisions have to have a practical as well as ideal component. Ultimately, the decision maker must rely on his conscience regardless of the majority point of view. These are the lessons that can be garnered from an examination of Jewish decision making in the Rabbinic period.

REFERENCES

Benin, S., *The Footprints of God*, State University Press of New York, Albany, NY, 1993.
Berkovits, E., *Not in Heaven*, KTAV Publishing, New York, 1983.
Chazan, R. and Raphael, M., *Modern Jewish History*, Schocken Books, New York, 1974.
Dubnow, S., *History of the Jews of Russia and Poland*, Jewish Publication Society, Philadelphia, 1916.
Elazar, D., *Community and Polity*, Jewish Publication Society, Philadelphia, 1980.
Elon, M., Ed., *The Principles of Jewish Law*, Keter, Jerusalem, 1987.
Encyclopedia Judaica, Vol. 7., Keter, Jerusalem, 1971.

---

[*] As cited by Rosenzweig (1992, 102) from the introduction to *Netivot ha-Mishpat* on *Hoshen Mishpat*.

Finkel, A., *The Great Torah Commentators*, Jason Aronson, Northvale, NJ, 1990.

Graetz, H., *History of the Jews*, Jewish Publication Society, Philadelphia, 1891.

Kirschenbaum, A., Subjectivity in rabbinic decision making, In *Rabbinic Authority and Personal Autonomy*, Sokol, M., Ed., Jason Aronson, Northvale, NJ, 1992.

Kolbrener, W., The Hermeneutics of Mourning: Multiplicity and Authority in Jewish Law, Project Muse. http://muse.jhu.edu (Accessed July 26, 2004), 2004.

Landesman, D., *A Practical Guide to Jewish Learning*, Jason Aronson, Northvale, NJ, 1995.

Lewittes, M., *Principles and Development of Jewish Law*, Bloch, New York, 1987.

Rosensweig, M., Eilu ve-eilu divrei elohim hayyim, In *Rabbinic Authority and Personal Autonomy*, Sokol, M., Ed., Jason Aronson, Northvale, NJ, pp. 93–123, 1992.

Sacks, J., Creativity and innovation in Halakhah, In *Rabbinic Authority and Personal Autonomy*, Sokol, M., Ed., Jason Aronson, Northvale, NJ, pp. 123–169, 1992.

Schreiber, A., *Jewish Law and Decision Making*, Temple University Press, Philadelphia, 1979.

Shapiro, M., *Courts: A Comparative and Political Analysis*, University of Chicago Press, Chicago, 1981.

Sokol, M., *Rabbinic Authority and Personal Autonomy*, Jason Aronson, Northvale, NJ, 1992.

Spero, S., *Morality, Halakhah, and the Jewish Tradition*, KTAV, New York, 1982.

Twersky, I., *Rabad of Posquieres*, Jewish Publication Society, Philadelphia, 1979.

Twersky, I., *Maimonidies Reader*, Behrman House, New York, 1995.

Walzer, M., Lorberbaum, M., and Zohar, N., *The Jewish Political Tradition*, Yale University Press, New Haven, 2000.

Werblowsky, R. J. Z., *Joseph Karo*, Jewish Publication Society, Philadelphia, 1980.

Part III

Contexts of Decision Making

17 Decision Making in Public Management Networks

Robert Agranoff and Mete Yıldız

CONTENTS

17.1 Introduction...319
17.2 Network Management..321
    17.2.1 Knowledge Management..322
17.3 Types of Decisions Made by Networks...323
17.4 Network Agreement Process...328
17.5 Pre-Decision Modes: Learning Strategies..329
17.6 Information and Communication Technology Used in
    Network Decision Making..332
17.7 Value-Adding Through Network Decisions...337
17.8 Conclusion: A Network Decision Making Research Agenda...340
References..343

17.1 INTRODUCTION

In an era when the term "network" has taken on many meanings, public managers have entered the arena with both feet. Interorganizational networking is one of these endeavors; administrators exchange information, seek knowledge, and work out problems, programs, and policies across the boundaries of their agencies and their organizations. In addition to social networks, broadcast networks, transportation networks, manufacturing supply networks, and electronic intranets and internets, public management networks (PMNs) now bring together representatives of different agencies within a government, between levels of government, and with non-governmental organizations (NGOs) of the for-profit and non-profit sector.

These PMNs are collaborative structures that bring together representatives from public agencies and NGOs to deal with the knowledge, resource, and technological asymmetries that accrue when the public sector approaches its most pressing problems, for example, generational poverty, structural unemployment, metropolitan transportation, environmental protection, and community development. As such, these non-hierarchical organized entities need to have some established or patterned means of problem recognition and development of actions that are similar to those decisions made in hierarchical organizations. Indeed, the non-hierarchical nature of "decision making" in networks is a matter of fairly common agreement. Just exactly what the networks do to achieve similar states of agreement and how such processes unfold is relatively unknown territory. It is the terrain that we attempt to explore in this chapter.

PMNs as collaborative bodies involve managers seeking public value that they ordinarily cannot obtain by working exclusively within their organizations (Bardach, 1998; Moore, 1995). Koppenjan and Klijn (2004, 3) observe that:

> In doing their work and in solving problems, organizations of various different natures meet. These meetings are rarely non-committal. The organizations "want something from each other." They can no longer fulfill their task alone, whether they like it or not. Problems cannot be solved on their own.... The model of the 'lonely organization' that determines its policy in isolation is obsolete.

As a result, hierarchies are giving way to networks. They are normally thought of as policy entities, bodies that "connects public policies with their strategic and institutionalized context: the network of public, semi-public, and private actors participating in certain policy fields" (Kickert et al., 1997, 1). These activities are conducted in a non-hierarchical fashion.

Networks display some important public management differences from the hierarchical organizations that administrators spend most of their time in. First, participants in non-hierarchical bodies like PMNs are *partners* with other representatives, not superiors—subordinates. As partners, the actors are co-conveners, co-strategists, co-action formulators, co-programmers, and so on. Second, the public agency administrator as partner possesses neither exclusive legal authority nor technical or informational control over a program or effort. To the public manager, PMNs involve many stakeholders at the table, e.g., other administrators, program specialists, scientists, policy researchers, interest groups, and advocacy associations. Third, public agencies no longer have the monopoly of resources at their control as they once did. They are derived from the many collaborating partner organizations. Fourth, given the many loci of resources and information, resources and knowledge are not only more dispersed, but most government agencies increasingly try to engage in forms of governance to leverage investments and to broker program activities through other governments and NGOs (Kooiman, 1993). Fifth, the implementation of programs and concomitant decisions normally occurs not through some "superstructure" of the network administration itself, but through those same organizations that were involved in sharing knowledge/technologies, building collective capabilities, or in formulating strategies and policies. In other words, networks rarely have programming or "decision" implementation capabilities. As will be demonstrated, these differences have a substantial impact on both the processes and outcomes of decision making within networks.

This chapter focuses on the processes by which networks make decisions; for some it means to "take action" as collaborative bodies comprised of representatives of public agencies and NGOs. While there is very little research on the internal operations of these entities, we are fortunate to have empirical data from a grounded theory, or inductive study, of some 14 such networks. The chapter is launched with a brief introduction to management within networks. The important function of knowledge management for decisions within PMNs is next introduced. It then moves into an examination of the type of decisions/actions actually taken by the 14 networks, along with an overview of the decision processes from the perspective of study administrators. Next, as collaborative information seeking and processing bodies, we focus on networks as "learning organizations," identifying six distinct peer decision modes of problem solving. Then, the supportive information and communication technology used in network processes are explained. After the exploration of technology, the final substantive section turns to how deliberative network decisions/actions add public value, that is, their results or outcomes. The chapter concludes by eliciting a network decision-making research agenda and by comparing network decision making to decisions in today's constant learning knowledge/-information "conductive" organizations.

17.2 NETWORK MANAGEMENT

Because PMN research is relatively new and has not been highly focused on the internal processes of their operations, we know very little about the details of decision making. In most of the literature, the underlying issue is that networks are different venues than those of organizations. Normally comparison between how decisions are made in hierarchical organizations and these non-hierarchical bodies establishes a context of decision. The issue that one immediately faces is that, to date, no readily agreed-upon set of functional activities exists that serve as the hierarchical equivalent of POSDCORB, the well known acronym for planning, organizing, staffing, directing, coordinating, reporting, and budgeting.

Bardach (1998, 274) suggests that collaborative bodies are built on two platforms, (1) one of trust, leadership, and an interactive communication network, and (2) on creative opportunity, intellectual capital, existence of implementation programs and agencies, and advocacy groups. These two platforms, then, mutually build improved capacity to steer or guide the system toward objectives, which leads to the development of one of a network's operating subsystems, and to continuous learning.

Kickert and Koppenjan (1997, 47–49) identify network management as the process of steering interaction processes, comprising three elements: intervention in an existing pattern of relations, consensus building, and problem-solving. The major processes include: (1) *activation*, initiating interaction or games to solve particular problems or achieve goals; (2) *arranging interaction*, getting actors to participate; (3) *structuring*, building rules, norms, and a culture; (4) *brokering*, or guarded mediation and tapping and utilizing the diversity of ideas, insights, and solutions; (5) *facilitating interaction*, or building in processes that are conducive to the development of strategic consensus building. In a similar vein, McGuire (2002) brings together the network literature into the following stages: activation of players, framing tasks and issues, mobilizing to reach agreement and take action, and synthesizing the network by creating the environment and enhancing favorable conditions. These are among the activities that managers engage in as they try to figure out "what to do and how to do it." In effect, these are core network decision making processes.

Decisions made in networks therefore can be characterized as consensus-oriented but considerably more involved; they are deeply engaged in mutual learning processes. On the surface, the elements of a network decision appear similar to those in hierarchical organizations, for example, involving elements of consensus, accommodation, and shared learning processes. But more is at stake. Innes and Booher (1999, 3) suggest that a new mind-set is needed in networks to overcome long-standing habits of organizational routines, rules, and normative practices. It is one of producing specific agreements or actions. The interactive learning process needed in networks is similar to Senge's (1990, 3) characterization of the learning organization, "where people are continually learning how to learn together." He suggests that learning organizations require five core disciplines: personal mastery, mental models, shared vision, team learning, and systems thinking. Like learning organizations, networks require similar collective "cognitive capabilities" because "the intelligence of a network lies in the patterns of relationships among its members" (Lipnack and Stamps, 1994, 210).

Negotiation is a parallel "decision" support process. Bardach (1998, 232) refers to a "culture of joint problem solving" that includes an "ethos that values equality, adaptability, discretion and results." Part of this ethos is to overcome bureaucratic tendencies (hierarchy, stability, obedience, procedures) through a lively sense of creating possibilities. Bardach also suggests that "collaboration is a matter of exhortation, explication, persuasion, give and take. To collaborate is to negotiate" (238). Negotiations have to take into account all interests—personal and professional organizational interests as well as the collective interests (Galaskiewicz and Zaheer, 1999). Negotiations in networks seek consensus only after members have fully explored the issues and interests, and only after significant effort has been made to find creative responses to differences (Innes and Booher, 1999). Such processes are supported by accommodations and by the dualism manifested in the "agency delegate" to the network and the "network delegate" to the agency (both being the same person). Weiner (1990) concludes that when negotiating, such dual loyalty necessitates a totally new mind-set and value stance for managers who work within transorganizational systems.

These processes appear to be held together by similar behavioral science techniques to those employed in single organizations. Myron Weiner (1990, 456) suggests that in transorganizational (network) management, techniques similar to organization management are normally employed: group problem solving, force-field analysis, action planning, team building, process consultation, and others. But more is required in networks, Weiner suggests. First, in network management, empowerment on processes such as decisions is based on *information* rather than on authority. Second, when considering network management, the factoring in of organizational structures into decisions are to be regarded as *dependent* variables for networks as systems. The several organizations working together can be fashioned into new systems, using the flow of information to link decisions into transorganizational systems.

17.2.1 KNOWLEDGE MANAGEMENT

Just as contemporary organizations increasingly rely on information-based knowledge and decreasingly rely on physical labor, networks are organized structures that maximize knowledge. Davenport and Prusak (2000) consider knowledge to be "a fluid mix of framed experience, values, contextual information and expert insight that provides a framework for evaluating and incorporating new experiences and information" (5). Knowledge derives from information as information derives from data. Most importantly, they remind us that one of the reasons why we find knowledge to be valuable is that it is closer than data or information to action (6). In this knowledge era we have learned that (1) we must rely on both explicit or codified knowledge and tacit or intuitional or experiential knowledge, and (2) that we must collaborate to engender action. In regard to collaboration, Groff and Jones (2003) remind us that unlike warring invaders such as the Vikings, who knew if they shared their food and drink, their loss was another's gain, sharing knowledge is not a zero-sum game. "Unlike conventional assets, knowledge grows when it is shared. The main limitation to infinite knowledge growth is the currency of the information economy-attention" (20). Networks serve to maximize the organized knowledge experience between organizations.

Knowledge and information are deeply embedded in all forms of organized activity. In particular, the interorganizational network is formed to pool knowledge and experiences not held by single organizations (Alter and Hage, 1993). As decision makers, networks have become important venues for reflective discussion. Giddens (1990) observes that "the reflexivity of modern social life consists in the fact that social practices are constantly examined and reformed in the light of incoming information about those very practices, thus constitutively altering their character" (38). This process within organizations is described by Tsoukas (2005, 111–112) as part of the distributed knowledge systems of emerging organized structures:

> "Organizations are seen as being in constant flux, out of which the potential for the emergence of novel practices is never exhausted—human action is inherently creative. Organizational members do follow rules, but how they do so is an inescapably contingent-cum-local matter. In organizations, both rule-bound action and novelty are present, as are continuity and change, regularity and creativity. Management, therefore, can be seen as an open–ended process of coordinating purposeful individuals, whose actions stem from applying their partly unique interpretations to the local circumstances confronting them. Those actions give rise to often unintended and ambiguous circumstances, the meaning of which is open to further interpretations and further actions, and so on. Given the distributed character of organizational knowledge, the key to achieving coordinated action does not so much depend on those 'higher-up' collecting more and more knowledge, as on those "lower-down" finding more and more ways of getting connected and interrelating the knowledge each one has."

With fewer constrained or rule-bound actions, networks are designed to bridge the knowledge distribution issue as actors approach those intractable actions that single organizations do with greater difficulty.

Networks like the PMNs under analysis serve to provide the same kind of organized predictability that single organizations do for their participants. Just as within organizations, stability and predictability of knowledge and its application is necessary, so it is between them when more intensity and regularity than market conditions apply (Powell, 1990). The acquisition of "propositional knowledge" (Tsoukas, 2005, 87) is necessary while actors maintain certain levels of free will, autonomy, and creativity. Sustained and long-term efforts at knowledge development, both explicit and tacit, require some form of rationalized contexts. At the interorganizational level, networks can provide such vehicles of converting knowledge into decisions.

17.3 TYPES OF DECISIONS MADE BY NETWORKS

A major portion of the empirical data for this chapter is derived from a study of 14 PMNs in the U.S. Central States. The major purpose of the overall study is to examine the internal management processes of networks and to explore those managerial differences from single organization management that might accrue in networks (Agranoff, 2003a; Agranoff, under contract). Table 17.1 identifies each network's full title, its abbreviation in the text, and it contains a snapshot description and composition of each. A very essential part of this study includes three important dimensions of decision making: (1) what kinds of decisions networks actually make, (2) what media of decisions are employed within the network, and (3) what is the typical process of decision making. The research itself was to develop a grounded-theory study of network management (Strauss and Corbin, 1998). It is an inductive field study that includes focused discussions with over 150 public and NGO administrators who are involved in these PMNs.

The first issue was the kinds of decisions that networks made; this appeared to be critical because of their ascribed role in making policy and program adjustments. Among other questions, discussants were asked, "What processes does your network engage in order to reach agreement and ultimately decisions?" The responses proved to be very interesting. A notable number of responses, such as, "We don't make decisions, we exchange information," or "This body is responsible for metropolitan plan development and fund allocations," or "SCEIG does not make funding allocations or decisions; our Finance Committee guides small towns to find a way to solve their water problems," or "The Partnership assists its component organizations in becoming better at rural development," suggested that something different than administrative decision making was going on. Reflection and systematic coding of the qualitative data led to some very important information about what networks decide upon.

It turned out after subsequent coding that a form of scalable progression of decisions taken by the PMNs appeared that differentiated the various PMNs. The data that emerged from the coding is identified in Table 17.2, which identifies nine different types of decisions or agreements. In other words, it appeared that networks could be identified by the type of decisions, agreements, or actions they took.

One can easily see from Table 17.2 that not all networks make the kind of planning and policy decisions that the literature normally ascribes to them. In the lower range are three networks (Darby, Indiana Economic Development Council [IEDC], and the Lower Platte River Corridor Alliance [LPRCA]). They do not really make substantive decisions, but mainly are for information exchange and otherwise learning about partner actions. They make absolutely no policy decisions nor do they make program adjustments.

At the next level are four networks (Iowa Enterprise Network [IEN], Indiana Rural Development Council [IRDC], Partnership for Rural Nebraska [PRN], and the Iowa Geographic Information Council [IGIC]). They do make limited forms of decisions: those related to enhancing

TABLE 17.1
Networks Under Investigation

Name of Network	Purpose	Type	Enabling Authority	Primary Agencies
Access Indiana/Enhanced Data Access Review Committee (EDARC)	Sets policies for state web portal, reviews, modifies and approves agency agreements and private use	Action	State Government	SA, NGO, Cit, Media
Des Moines Area Metropolitan Planning Organization (DMMPO)	Transportation planning for metropolitan area	Action	Intergovernmental Agreement	CtyGov, CoGov, SA, FA, R/Met
Indiana Economic Development Council (IEDC)	Research consultant for state economic development	Informational	Not-for-profit 501C(3)	SA, Priv, NGO, Un
Indiana Rural Development Council (IRDC)	Forum to address rural issues, establish partnerships, enable partners to take action	Developmental	Intergovernmental Agreement/Not-for-profit 501C(3)	FA, SA, CoGov, CtyGov, Legis, NGO
Iowa Communications Network (ICN)	Operates a statewide, state administered, fiber optics network	Action	State Government	SA, FA, CtyGov, CoGov, Legis, NGO, Cit
Iowa Enterprise Network (IEN)	Supports home-based and micro enterprises	Developmental	Not-for-profit 501C(3)	FA, SA, NGO, Priv
Iowa Geographic Info. Council (IGIC)	Clearinghouse for coordinated systems and data sharing	Developmental	State Government	Un, FA, SA, R/Met CoGov CtyGov NGO, Priv
Lower Platte River Corridor Alliance (LPRCA)	Supports local efforts at water conservation; comprehensive and coordinated land use; promotes cooperation among Nebraska organizations	Informational	Intergovernmental Agreement	R/Met, SA, FA, Un
Partnership for Rural Nebraska (PRN)	Provide resources and expertise to enhance rural development opportunities	Developmental	Intergovernmental Agreement	SA, Un, FA, R/Met
Small Communities Environmental Infrastructure Group (SCEIG)	Assist small Ohio governments in their water and wastewater systems	Outreach	Non-formal group	SA, FA, Un, Priv, NGO, R/Met
The Darby Partnership (DARBY)	Share information and resources to address central Ohio watershed threats	Informational	Non-formal group	FA, SA, CoGov, CtyGov, R/Met, NGO
United States Department of Agriculture/Rural Development Nebraska (USDA/RD)	Outreach and assistance to leverage funds of other programs for public and private development	Outreach	Federal Government	FA, NGO, SA, R/Met, Un, CtyGov, Priv

(Continued)

Table 17.1 *(Continued)*

Name of Network	Purpose	Type	Enabling Authority	Primary Agencies
Kentuckiana Regional Planning and Development Agency (KIPDA)	Transportation planning for two-state Louisville metropolitan area	Action	Intergovernmental Agreement	CoGov, CtyGov, FA, SA, R/Met
Indiana 317 Taskforce (317 group)	Strategies for developmentally disabled community services	Outreach	Non-formal	NGO, SA, FA, Un, Cit, Priv

Notes: FA, federal government agency at regional or state level; Un, university, college, and community college; SA, state government agency; Legis, state legislature/congressional staff; CoGov, county government; NGO, non-governmental organization/advocacy group; CtyGov, city government; Priv, for profit business organization; R/Met, regional or metropolitan agency; Cit, citizen representative.

component partner organization's ability to work with one another, and in their respective fields. These decisions relate to the establishment of working groups, annual conferences, technical presentations, new skill sets, and the like. Only IRDC once became involved in a form of strategy development—a rural plan for the Indiana state legislature—but its impact was only advisory and only a portion of the recommendations were introduced into legislation.

A third group of networks, including the Small Communities Environmental Infrastructure Group (SCEIG), the U.S. Department of Agriculture/Rural Development-Nebraska (USDA/RD), and the Indiana 317 Group make decisions that relate to plan review, and most important, blueprinting strategies for other organizations to take action. For example, SCEIG helps small towns deal with drinking and waste water compliance in Ohio, and while it does not fund towns directly, its Finance Committee brings the multiple funding partners together to focus on that community.

The next group of four networks, Iowa Communications Network (ICN), Enhanced Data Access Review Committee (EDARC), Kentuckiana Regional Planning and Development Agency (KIPDA), and the Des Moines Area Metropolitan Planning Organization (DMMPO) are, as Table 17.2 indicates, the only networks that fill cells in decision categories 8–9, making policy and program adjustments, and are also involved in policy making. These bodies are essentially those that meet the literature criteria of what networks do.

What of the other ten study networks and others in the world that are similarly non-decision fashioned? Clearly, they should not be eliminated as networks because they do not meet some pre-determined (but perhaps empirically incorrect) criteria. They too are PMNs but of a different type, based on their primary type of function or types of decisions they make. Table 17.3 displays the subsequent typology formed from the four groupings. It proved useful to maintain these distinctions in the larger study. A number of subsequent analyses were conducted using the network typology for comparison (Agranoff, under contract).

Finally, the decision scale in Table 17.2 also reveals that a progression of sort occurs among the networks. Those networks at the higher end of the scale make virtually all of the decisions that those at the lower end engage. In other words, in terms of decision category, there is a "Guttmann scale,"[*]

---

[*] Guttman scales empirically test the cumulative unidimensionality of a set of items. If the items comprising the scale tap the same attitudinal dimension, they can be arranged so that there will be a continuum that indicates varying degrees of the underlying dimension (Frankfort-Nachamias and Nachamias, 1992, 438).

TABLE 17.2
Scaled Decision Types in Fourteen Networks

Network[a]	Network Information Exchange	Agendas/ Network Work Plans	Scientific Reports/ Studies	Forums/Member Enhancement and Assistance	Web Link Info. Systems development	Strategic Blueprint/Fund Leveraging	Plan Review	Mutual Policy/Program Adjustment	Network Policy Making
Darby (1–3)[b]	Quarterly meetings	Meeting locations agenda suggestions Dir., elec.	Partner reports Dir., print						
IEDC (1–3)	Economic conditions Dir.	Scope of research projects Dir.	Project reports Print, beh.						
LPRCA (1–3, 5)	District reports state of the river Print, elec.	Annual work plan Dir.	At district level only Print		Web-based GIS				
IEN (1–2, 4–5)	Annual workshop Dir.	Assistance work plan Print		Special topic forums one-to-one assistance Dir.	Website access to business assistance Elec.				
IRDC (1–2, 4)	Meeting briefings Dir.	Work group plans Dir.		Annual meeting water, community, visitation task forces Dir., print, elec.	Elec.	2002 Rural strategy (advisory only)			
PRN (1–5)	Annual institute Dir., elec.	Education/training agenda Dir., print	Nebraska rural poll Elec.	Joint training events Elec., beh.	Site for rural news reports Elec.	Print			
IGIC (1–5)	Biannual conference Dir., print	Work plan Print, elec.	New GIS applications Dir., beh.	Meeting demonstrations Dir., beh.	Over 30 different GIS applications Dir., print, elec. beh.				
SCEIG (1–3, 5–7)	Committee mtgs steering committee Dir., elec.	Research plans; new programs (e.g., appalacia program) Dir., elec.	Technology transfer committee Dir., elec.	Dir., print, elec. beh.	Training cmte. maintains website & materials Dir., elec.	Finance cmte. guides town strategies Dir.	Informal review of agency strategies Dir., elec.		

Network[a] (Range 1–9)[b]	1	2	3	4	5	6	7	8	9
USDA/RD (1–2, 5–7)	Informal only — Dir.	Annual coordination plan — Dir., elec.			USDA links — Elec.	Formally in water and wastewater project by project in others — Dir., elec.	Regularly on multiple funding projects — Dir., elec.		
317 Group (1–7)	Intermittent mtgs & special conferences — Dir.	Only when legislative amendments needed — Dir., elec.	Impact studies, waiting list studies — Dir., print, elec.	Futures session at IU decision laboratory — beh.	Through NGO policy groups — Dir., print, elec.	Through state govt. agency and contractors — Print, elec.	2003 Legislative audit, report — Dir., elec.		
EDARC (1–3, 5, 7–9)	At monthly meetings — Dir., print	User-driven — Print	Staff prepared market plans — Elec.		Manages state govt. web portal — Dir., elec.		On operation and use of state website — Print, elec.	Negotiations with agencies — Dir., elec.	Web portal use and fee structure — Dir., print elec.
KIPDA (1–3, 5, 7–9)	Monthly policy and technical committee mtgs — Dir., elec.	— Elec.	Special project reports — Print, elec.	To local governments — Dir., elec.	Extensive decision support data bases — Elec., beh.		Transp. imprvmntplan; special project plans — Dir., elec.	Continually for metro focus — Dir., print, elec.	Transp. Plan fund awards; targeted projects — Print, elec.
DMMPO (1–3, 5, 7–9)	Quarterly meetings — Dir., print, elec.	Policy and technical committees — Dir., print, elec.	Special reports — Print, elec.		Basic information only — Elec.		Transp. Imprvmnt plan; other if requested by community — Print, elec.	Continually for metro focus — Dir., print, elec.	Transp. Plan fund awards; targeted projects — Print, elec.
ICN (1–9)	Only one-to-one among users — Dir., print, elec.	Annual strategic plan — Elec., beh.	Technology report — Elec., beh.	Technical assistance to users — Dir., print, elec. beh.	Major point of public contact — Elec., beh.	Special: telemedicine emergency mgt.; public health; telejustice — Elec., beh.	By publicly supported board — Dir., print, elec.	With state and local govt users — Dir., elec., beh.	Network operations by a public board — Dir., elec., beh.

Notes: medium of decision: Dir., face-to-face, telephone, fax; Print, printed materials, printed reports; Elec., e-mail/web postings/electronic bulletin board; Beh., teleconferencing, electronic decision making, simulated electronic decision laboratory.

[a] Network, see Table 17.1 for full name and description of the network

[b] Range on Scale 1–9 in type of decisions

TABLE 17.3
Type of Networks Studied

Informational networks: partners come together exclusively to exchange agency policies and programs, technologies, and potential solutions. Any actions that might be taken are entirely up to the agencies on a voluntary basis.

Developmental networks: partner information and technical exchange are combined with education and member service that increases member capacity to implement solutions within home agencies or organizations.

Outreach networks: partners come together to exchange information and technologies, sequence programming, exchange resource opportunities, pool client contacts, and enhance access opportunities that lead to new programming avenues. Implementation of designed programs is within an array of public and private agencies themselves.

Action networks: partners come together to make interagency adjustments, formally adopt collaborative courses of action, or deliver services along with exchanges of information and technologies.

in this case based on empirical findings, a progression of decisions that indicate a similar underlying dimension. In this case it is network decisions.

It was these decision or agreement modes that led to the typology of networks presented. Table 17.2 breaks down the types of decision-related activities that led to the typology—that is, their agreements, agenda actions, strategies, or policy/program adjustments that they make in the normal course of PMN activities. They have been numbered in range from less involved exchanges and meeting agendas to the kinds of mutual program and policy adjustment attributed to networks in the literature. Thus, Table 17.2 provides a detailed look at the kinds of decisions networks actually make. These decision modes were then scaled into a typology, from 1 to 9, and categorized, as displayed in Table 17.3: informational, developmental, outreach, and action networks. The typology means, unfortunately for those who have defined network action accordingly, that not all networks make the kind of policy or program adjustments attributed to them. The others nevertheless are to be considered public networks.

The medium of decision is an additional entry into the matrix, network by network, in Table 17.2. Each type is placed into a four-fold classification: Dir. = personal contact (face-to-face meetings, telephone, fax); Print = written interaction (letter, print report, print materials); Elec. = electronic contact (e-mail, web postings, electronic bulletin board); Beh. = electronic conferencing (teleconferencing, electronic decision making, electronic simulated decision laboratory, or other behavioral means). A similar pattern or progression does not appear, although the PMNs that make more types of decisions clearly employ more modes. Most information exchanges are both personal and electronic, but many also retain the written mode. All fourteen have a website, which is a major means of letting non-partners know of their existence, and all interact electronically by e-mail, the virtually exclusive mode of transmitting decision making information among PMN partners. Few networks engage in electronic conferencing, for example, teleconferences or simulated behavioral electronic decision making. The notable exceptions are IGIC's use of the ICN closed circuit real time statewide television network for meetings and exercises, and the 317 group's use of an Indiana University electronic decision making laboratory for reaching "future" agendas. Perhaps the most interesting finding is that the widespread use of electronic networking—e-mail and web postings—has not markedly reduced the face-to-face mode of decision, although it has led to some reduction in written interaction. This mode will be examined further when the use of information and communication technology for decision making is taken up.

17.4 NETWORK AGREEMENT PROCESS

The typical process of decision making within the fourteen networks did prove to be quite close to the literature's observations regarding these entities as high consensus-based learning entities.

How are typical decisions made at meetings of most networks? They are brokered, as Bardach (1998) concludes. Clearly the partners work at achieving forms of consensus through joint exploration and discussion until agreement is at hand. Then another issue is brought to the table. A state official described the process this way: "Proposals are made by participating agencies; the staff there researches the proposal and does a market feasibility study; the report is distributed electronically before the meeting; at the meeting, discussion is held and questions are asked; if there are too many questions we table the issue until more research can be undertaken; in between meetings, phone calls, and one-to-one discussions ensue; the issue is brought back to the table; and if there are a lot of head nods in the yes direction, we consider it to be approved." A process like this, with lots of brokering, is followed in most of the networks, although normally "staff" research tends to be the partners; that is agency administrators themselves who go back to their own programs and work with their agency colleagues later bring the agency-derived research results to the network.

One partner described the network decision process as similar to "a rural community meeting." "You get the people out, connect them, let them identify the issues, and let them come up with a solution over time." Another said that beyond setting priorities on work, and allowing the staff to do some studies, "we let consensus rise to the top." Another said, "We have Robert's Rules in our by-laws, but only use them after we have reached agreement." Another network chair said: "Parliamentary procedure rules won't work—as a last resort when we are near consensus we may resort to informal Robert's Rules to move things along."

The learning process is very clearly and directly a parallel component of network decisions. "Once we agree that a problem is an issue we care to look into, we study it and discuss the results before any action is taken." "We try to get on the same technical page if we possibly can. That means someone or a work group has to study a problem, then we discuss it." "Our Technology Transfer Committee is charged with finding feasible small town water solutions used elsewhere; they then become the basis of Steering Committee discussions." "The Transportation Technical Committee is charged not only with looking at the feasibility of projects, but to advance state-of-the-art [transportation] programming to the Policy Committee agenda." These quotes from the discussants highlight the centrality of making the network a learning entity in the sense of Senge's (1990) learning organization.

One can then characterize the typical network decision process as involving joint learning that leads to brokered consensus. Because networks are self-organizing and non-hierarchical, they approach interactive decision processes carefully, whether it be to adopt an agenda or to take some form of action. Why the trepidation over parliamentary procedure or even in taking hard and fast decisions? Several reasons are apparent. First, these PMNs are rarely program bodies, but they more frequently exist to *exchange* information and explore knowledge and become aware of potential adjustments that the network actors can make in their own organizations (Alter and Hage, 1993). Second, most PMN members come to the table on a *voluntary* basis and the nature of this participation suggests some form of shared participation in decisions. Third, the partners come together from very *different organizational cultures*, and the risk of clashing styles is great if not managed. Fourth, in PMNs, as is the case in most networks, decisions come as a result of these *shared learning* experiences, in which the *product is the creative solution* that emanates from the discussion (Agranoff and McGuire, 2001a). Fifth, decisions that create winners and losers, most zero-sum situations, discourage involvement and *contribution* in networks. These concerns make clear why so few of the PMNs engage in the type of parliamentary decisions that membership organizations do, and clearly do not experience someone up the hierarchy to make the type of decisions that settle disputes in bureaucratic organizations.

17.5 PRE-DECISION MODES: LEARNING STRATEGIES

As entities heavily involved in the exchange of information and the discovery and adaptation of knowledge, PMNs need preparation for brokered consensus. This involves looking at a problem or issue in depth, conducting research into available technologies, tapping into or developing alternative databases, and, most important of all, finding information-based solutions. The latter involves discussions of legal, technical, financial, and political feasibility (Agranoff, 1986). These discussions are normally preceded by an information search that enhances the learning ability of the collaborative. These pre-decision modes reinforce the capacities of PMNs to seek and manage knowledge. In the study of the PMNs at least six different learning/knowledge modes can be identified.

The first mode is simply *group discussion* or exchange following a loose format where technical or legal and financial information is converted to knowledge. This process is conducted by the partners in the enterprise, a sort of shared diversity of expertise by those brought to the table. When networks follow this mode, the administrators almost always bring in their agency's relevant technical experts. Also, networks do a great deal of their work in groups (committees, taskforces). For example, PRN organizes its annual Rural Institute by bringing together program specialists from its federal and state government and NGO partners, along with a local/regional committee (the venue rotates) under the rubric of its Education Committee. In this way the latest in community and economic development ideas are brought forward and ultimately offered to the participants. In a similar fashion, IRDC has deployed community visitation teams to selected small communities, employing volunteer experts in business development, town planning, public works, market analysis, environmental management, and others to develop action plans. The teams spend one to two days in the community and near the end of the visit agree on conclusions and write a joint report. In other cases, the various PMN partners meet as a plenary to match technical information with potential solutions. Virtually every network employs this mode at one time or another.

A second mode involves high degrees of *political negotiations* when issues are sensitive and the network needs to invoke players that go far beyond the network. For example, when KIPDA began to research the location for a second bridge over the Ohio River to connect Louisville and Kentucky with the Indiana side, the data were somewhat swept aside as the Mayor of Louisville and the Chief Executive of Jefferson County (since merged) got into a city-suburbs battle. The ultimate result was two bridges, which deferred federal money for other projects for up to 25 years. In a similar fashion, the Darby Partners had to deal with a threatening issue when a congressional bill was introduced to make a section of its watershed a national wildlife refuge. Its organizing partner, The Nature Conservancy of Ohio, publicly supported the bill and in turn the area local government officials and landowners opposed it. Many of the state and federal administrators remained neutral. It took nearly two years for Darby to in effect "remove" or extricate this issue and transfer it to non-network politicians, and in fact, it did not die until the bill was unsuccessful. On the other hand, if there are minor political considerations involved, network partners can shift issues to political decision-makers to help solve a problem. One example was when IGIC was faced with a transition-related crisis when Iowa state government's new Chief Information Officer's support was withdrawn for its State GIS Coordinator. After negotiations between the Governor's office and Iowa State University Extension, the GIS Coordinator position moved to Extension. Again, many PMNs find the need to explore and ultimately invoke political negotiations from time to time.

A third mode involves the straightforward application of technology or pre-established formats that amount to decision rules to address a problem. Once a problem is discovered or a need is agreed upon, there is a proscribed *technical* or normative means of meeting the problem. In 2001 when there was a national airborne anthrax scare, ICN and the Iowa Department of Public Health immediately moved into the breach. Accessing an extant set of training videos and workbooks from the U.S. Federal Emergency Management Agency (FEMA) and the U.S. Public Health Service, an anthrax program for all of Iowa's 99 county health and county emergency management officers was put into place within 72 hours, transmitting it though ICN's fiber-optic system of real time television. This followed the established pattern of ICN partnering with government agencies. When the SCEIG Finance Committee meets to assist a small town, it normally reviews an established water system technology, transmitting established sets of eligibility and funding rules to local officials, plus program requirements. A simple example occurred when a tiny village appealed for help at a time when their water plant was flooded and they had no flood insurance. They needed $125,000 for cleanup and reconstruction. The representative of the Community Development Block Grant program suggested that they could loan up to $100,000 at 1.5% interest, for one of four approved mitigation approaches if they could get a match for the rest, citing the regulations. Next, the Ohio Public Works Commission partner related that this town was eligible for an emergency grant for the rest of the money; all they needed to do is fill out a one-page application and a decision would be made within ten days. Of course, very few of SCEIG's town water problems are this simple. Often finding a cost-effective approach and invoking the rules and regulations of three or four funding agencies, the example demonstrates how discussions and often interactive exchanges predicated proscribed technical practices.

A fourth mode is for a network to have pre-established or *formulaic* procedures to prepare partners for decisions. USDA/RD has a template of potential collaborators as its personnel follow its coordination plan. For example, in its many lending activities partnering with local banks and savings and loans, rural utilities (such as telephone and electric), development districts, and the State of Nebraska Department of Economic Development are standard. IEN has a set way of helping home-based and micro-businesses that include area Small Business Development Centers and volunteer assistance such as from retired executives, state agencies, and private credit institutions, in that order. A more complicated formulaic process is DMMPO's method of adopting individual community projects in its Transportation Improvement Plan. It is a protracted process that begins with Technical Committee screening for feasibility, and negotiated adjustments, followed by staff assignment of a priority number based on a rotation principle (population impact and time since last project), then informal negotiations among Policy Committee elected officials, and finally voting according to a predetermined weighted process based on feasibility, rotation, and population. The process is designed to enhance a metropolitan-wide perspective and reduce conflict between the City of Des Moines and the suburbs. A number of networks find that this method enhances partnering and facilitates consensus.

A fifth method is simply by using *data driven* means of producing decision making information. In other words, a core input into the learning and consensus process is research rooted in an existing database. EDARC meetings that set use rates for state government mailing lists always begin with a staff report that, in effect, is a market feasibility study of costs, number of potential users, type of potential users (e.g., for profit, non-profit), expected return rates for lists, and so on. The staff report normally contains a recommended rate structure and use policy. Committee discussions always begin with staff reports. As in the case with most transportation agencies (Metropolitan Planning Organizations) that bridge jurisdictions, KIPDA relies on its technical support staff that compile data from multiple sources and jurisdictions, including traffic counting, geographic information systems, mass transit route monitoring, maintenance and project management updates, socioeconomic data, crash data, bicycle and pedestrian facilities, and many others. This database is plugged into a travel model, which is an important basis of KIPDA knowledge-based decision process. The travel model is applied to all proposed plans and projects, which becomes the basic input for decisions made by the KIPDA Transportation Technical Committee and ultimately its Policy Committee. A number of other networks also follow this data-driven mode for some of their decisions, but none more than the four most policy/program involved action networks.

A sixth and final decision learning strategy is one that involves a *pre-decision simulation* or electronic decision making techniques. In these cases, network partners attempt to sort and sift large quantities of information and use a form of group technique to aid in learning and agreement when they actually arrived at the decision making stage. ICN constantly uses automatic feedback responses from its multiple public sector users to learn about systemic technical and operational problems, for extended programming uses, and for user/audience counts. LPRCA had a one-time experience with a *charette*, which is a data-assisted simulation for using on the status of a ten-mile stretch of the Platte River. The data and process then led to the partners coming up with a "mock solution" for remediation of this stretch. While the *charette* proved to be a successful demonstration of preparing LPRCA for making remediation decisions, it raised a great deal of anxiety and opposition among landowners and local government officials, despite its status as an exercise. It has not been repeated. The 317 Group has twice used an Indiana University computerized executive laboratory to build agendas for future meetings and issues related to updating its plans and to formulate a legislative agenda. The electronic exercise combines a commissioned research project with data supplied by the State of Indiana, Family and Social Services Administration. Also factored in are the individual agendas of the participating agencies and NGOs. Beyond these examples, few networks have engaged in this type of simulated activity, relying much more on data-driven, technical, or formulaic preparation.

These six approaches define the possible ways that PMNs organize their databases into useable knowledge/information to help reach agreement at their decision making or action sessions. Obviously these are explained as "pure types" for heuristic purposes; in actual situations one may prevail, but some combination of the others will also be employed. The six types represent different vehicles or opportunities for mutual exchange and have the potential to enhance learning on an interagency basis. Whether verbal or data based, the potential pool of information is derived from many different sources, most importantly from agencies that are brought together on the basis of some interdependency. Participating administrators are exposed to a great deal of information that they would not ordinarily access in their own agencies. They learn about the work of other agencies. In this way, managers' capabilities to engage in discussions and agreements involving disciplines other than their own are enhanced. It is through these media that technological, legal, financial, and political considerations are put on the table, and managers engage in and learn what Weiner (1990) identifies as transdisciplinary practice. Both group and individual learning curves increase, as one set of information and subsequent discussions build for future actions. Indeed, the decision-preparation process makes networks in many ways quintessential interactive information processing/knowledge seeking bodies.

17.6 INFORMATION AND COMMUNICATION TECHNOLOGY USED IN NETWORK DECISION MAKING

The current transformation of the public administration field and increasing use of public manage-ment networks can be partially explained as a reaction to increasing complexity and uncertainty due to either incomplete or scattered information about societal problems (Klijn, 1996, 152). The task, then, is to find and organize the information and the expertise that is scattered among different agencies/actors to overcome information and resource asymmetries (Agranoff and McGuire, 2003a, 92). Information and communication technologies (ICTs)[*] can be useful to achieve this purpose and help networks in becoming "exchange vehicles and learning entities" (Agranoff, 2003b, 3). Networks have been objects of academic research in the public management field for almost two decades. Their existence and functions; skills and techniques that public managers need to success-fully function in networks; the impact of networks on processes of decision making, policy outputs, and outcomes; and democratic governance were examined in depth (Berry et al., 2004, 542). Various uses of ICTs in networks, however, are not examined and explained in depth. The subset of public administration that deals with the use and impact of ICTs (e-government) is limited in its treatment of the topic. This is strange because it is "the emerging information or knowledge age [that] gives rise to the network, where persons link across internal functions, organization boundaries and even geographic boundaries" (Agranoff and McGuire, 2001a, 22). The treatment is usually at macro level as exemplified by Ho (2002) who highlights the existence

---

[*] The use of "information and communication technology" (ICT) is a deliberate choice over using "information technology" (IT). How the information is used for communication among various stakeholders in network operations is as important as how information is collected, stored, and shared among network members.

of a new paradigm for e-government that is unlike the traditional bureaucratic paradigm, which emphasizes collaboration, governments forming networks together with other government agencies as well as private firms and NGOs to solve public problems. It can be argued that the relationships between the network type of organization and ICTs are understudied in the public administration field. To this end, this section explains how using ICTs may offer several advantages to networks in organizing information and making decisions.

First, networks provide information to their members and interested parties at low cost via their pages on the Web. These web pages offer detailed and updated information about the network and the issue(s) that the network deals with to all network members and non-partners (all other interested parties) 24 hours a day, 365 days a year. Websites also offer networking opportunities by providing contact information for network members, which requires an extra effort for non-partners to find otherwise. The availability of member contact information is critically important for the network to grow to answer future needs of information and expertise.

Second, electronic communication decreases coordination costs because various ICTs such as e-mail, teleconferencing, Web site presence, and electronic document transfer ease coordination efforts. E-mail, for example, can be used as a "one-to-many medium,"[*] as opposed to telephone conversations or fax messages. Digital archiving opportunities are also advantageous over other media of communication.

Third, ICTs provide electronic decision making techniques that are less costly and more encouraging for open discussion of ideas within networks, as explained in detail below. Such techniques help network members overcome the barriers of time and distance. Some technologies such as groupware products also offer anonymity that enables network members to freely express their various concerns and different viewpoints without the pressures of dominant members or those of groupthink.

The fourth advantage of ICTs in network decision making is the existence of management information systems (MISs) supported by databases and software packages. Existence of web-based geographic information systems (GIS) that enable decision makers to make visual assessments of complex datasets before decision making is a case in point.

The questions being answered in this section are as follows: how can networks use ICTs for decision making? Which ICTs do the 14 networks mentioned in the study use and to what purpose? In order to answer these questions, first the literature that covers the intersection of ICT use in public administration (e-government) and network literature is examined. Second, the 14 networks are evaluated according to their use of ICTs to support information sharing and decision making.

How can networks use ICTs for decision making? Following Kickert and Koppenjan's (1997, 47–49) framework (see also Agranoff and McGuire, 2001a), ICTs can be instrumental in managing their five processes of network functioning. First, during the "activation" process, e-mail can be used in initiating interaction among members. Websites provide a virtual presence for the network from which members and other interested parties can learn about the network's structure and activities. Interactive decision making technologies can be used to create simulations that mimic actual problem-solving sessions. One thing that needs to be kept in mind though, is that simulations of specific problem-solving exercises should be planned very carefully in order not to upset some network members who may be very sensitive about their decision making authority, exemplified by some unfortunate events in the Lower Platte River Corridor Alliance (LPRCA) case where an intense, time-limited problem-solving simulation exercise was perceived by local governments and one district as a threat to their autonomy. Not only has the exercise not been repeated, it also has been replaced by less controversial socializing methods, such as airboat tours of the watershed and an annual golf tournament.

---

[*] The ability to reach many people/organizations simultaneously with sending one e-mail message.

Second, ICT use can help the process of "arranging interaction." For example, in developmental networks, seminars, conferences, and institutes are instrumental not only for the exchange of information. They are also important for the creation of knowledge within the network (Agranoff, 2003c, 9). This newly created knowledge may later be distributed to network members via e-mail communication and network websites.

Third, in the "structuring" process in networks that builds rules, norms, and culture, ICTs can play an important role by providing the feedback (communication) to network members from which they explicitly and implicitly learn the rules and norms of the network. The structuring process may be easier if network members belong to epistemic communities, social groups that transcend the boundaries of their agencies (Thomas, 2003, 35), as explained in detail above.

Fourth, decision making software can be used for the "brokering" process, as they enable network members to provide their feedback anonymously. Such an arrangement significantly reduces the social pressures that dominant network members have on others. The occurrence of groupthink, which may limit the flow of new ideas and viewpoints to the networks (Berry et al., 2004, 546), can be reduced because members using some groupware products may not be aware of the number of participants supporting a certain idea or the magnitude of their support. As mentioned above, the Indiana 317 Group's use of Indiana University Collaborative Work Lab[*] for reaching a futures agenda is a perfect example of electronic meeting facilitation. This lab provides an environment in which computer-supported, collaborative meetings can be organized. With the help of a facilitator, people in these meetings are able to use their computers to provide simultaneous and anonymous feedback, each person having a similar amount of time for his or her contribution.

Network members may also use e-mail as a brokering tool. For example, program administrators/specialists come to networks with less delegated authority than line managers/program heads do. E-mail communication can be used as a supplement to telephone conversations and face-to-face interactions between program administrators/specialists and their superiors about delegation of authority before a certain decision is made. One advantage of e-mail use in this process is its auto-archiving quality. The program administrators/specialists may prefer a written authorization that can be proved later.

Finally, in the "facilitating interaction" process, again, e-mail use provides a fast and cheap supplement or an alternative to traditional means of communication (Agranoff, 2003b, 15). E-mail is also superior to communication channels such as telephone and fax, as it enables one to communicate with many members simultaneously with one e-mail. For example, agency representatives in networks can forward e-mail messages coming from other network members to their colleagues and superiors in their home agency to spread the knowledge derived from the network in a very fast, cheap, easy, and visible way. As mentioned above, e-mail communication also works as an automatic archive of what is being discussed in the network and when they are discussed. Such an archive has the advantage of being decentralized (that is, stored by more than one network member) which serves as an excellent back-up mechanism. Video conferencing and similar technologies also encourage participation as they overcome the barriers of time and location. For example, Iowa Communications Network uses video conferencing very successfully in the areas of education, health, and justice among others, overcoming the problems geographical distance or bad weather conditions, and also reducing the cost of communication and coordination.

Which ICTs do the 14 networks use and to what purpose? The 14 networks examined in this chapter can be divided into three broad categories according to the nature of their ICT use. These three categories are not mutually exclusive. On the contrary, they build on each other. As seen in Table 17.4, the second category includes the first, and the third category contains the first and the second. Such a categorization is similar to Mandell and Steelman's (2003, 207–208) classification

[*] http://www.iidc.indiana.edu/cpps/cwlab.html

TABLE 17.4
Categorization of Networks According to Their Use of ICTs

Categories	ICT as a Tool of Communication	ICT as a Facilitator	ICT as an Outcome
Definition	1. ICT is only a tool for information exchange and dissemination	2. In addition to #1, ICTs facilitate decision making by providing decision-support systems/mechanisms	3. In addition to #s 1 and 2, ICTs themselves are outcomes of information exchange, dissemination, and decision making
Examples of ICT use	Networking, e-mail correspondence, providing data and contact information on network websites, teleconferencing, sharing technical, legal, or financial knowledge	E-mail correspondence, databases, simulations, decision making software, web-based GIS, teleconferencing, sharing technical, legal, or financial knowledge	The network processes increase ICT use and awareness, determine policies regarding ICT use, determine future uses and structures of those ICTs
Examples from networks	All 14 networks, such as rural news reports on PRN website, training committee materials on SCEIG website, links to NGO policy groups on 317 Group website, teleconferencing via ICN	Web-based GIS applications at LPRCA and IEDC, decision-support databases at KIPDA, teleconferencing via ICN, 317 group's use of Indiana University Collaborative Work Lab for reaching a 'futures' agenda	EDARC determining the prices of e-government services for the accessIndiana state government Web portal, IGIC increasing awareness and use of GIS, telemedicine and telejustice via ICN.

of complexity of purpose for interorganizational arrangements into four groups—(1) information-sharing, (2) limited joint problem-solving, (3) limited to complicated joint problem-solving, and (4) complicated joint problem-solving—within their typology of interorganizational institutional innovations.

The first group of networks use ICTs only as tools of information exchange and dissemination. ICT is employed in this manner by all of the study networks. Examples are the display of rural news reports on PRN website, training committee materials on SCEIG website, links to NGO policy groups on 317 Group website, and teleconferencing via ICN. Networking with current or prospective network members, e-mail correspondence among network members, providing relevant data about the history, structure, members, and objectives of the network (Agranoff, 2003b, 11), displaying contact information of network members on network websites, and teleconferencing are good examples to this kind of ICT use. However, one interesting detail indicated in Table 17.4 is that e-mail and website use do not significantly decrease face-to-face interaction.

A second group of networks use ICTs to facilitate decision making by providing decision-support mechanisms. Some examples of ICT facilitators include e-mail correspondence among and between network members and their hierarchical superiors for delegation of authority before the making of decisions, use of databases for better decision making and forecasting, availability of various computer-generated simulations, decision making software that enable anonymity and more effective use of time in decision making, and web-based GIS applications that help network members visualize data. Web-based GIS at LPRCA and IEDC; decision-support databases at KIPDA; ICN's use of GIS for local planning and zoning; global positioning system for transportation, land use, soil and agriculture, and environmental management issues (Agranoff, 2003b, 15), and finally 317 Group's use of Indiana University Collaborative Work Lab for reaching a futures agenda are cases in point.

For the third and the final group of networks, ICTs are not only tools of communication or facilitators of decision making, they are also the very outcomes of information exchange, dissemination, and decision making in networks. In such cases, network processes increase ICT use and awareness among all interested parties, and they determine policies regarding ICT use; they thus shape the future of that ICT. For example, the way that the Enhanced Data Review Committee determines the prices of e-government services for the Indiana state government web portal determines the technological and fiscal structure of state e-government efforts. Iowa Geographic Information Council's promotion of the awareness and use of GIS, and Iowa Communication Network's telemedicine applications and virtual court depositions are perfect examples.

The level and frequency of ICT use by network members may depend on several factors. The first factor is the heavy schedules of public managers (Agranoff, 2003b, 15) who take part in networks. Under these busy circumstances, sending one e-mail that reaches many network members simultaneously is much more easy, fast, and cost-effective than traditional methods of communication.

A second factor is whether network members perceive ICT use to be easy or difficult. This may partially be a generational issue (Agranoff, 2003b, 16). One may expect that, as a rule, the older a network member gets, the less likely that he or she uses ICTs regularly in network settings. Of course, there may be exceptions to this rule. Also, older network members may benefit from ICT use by the help of younger staff members who work for them in their home agencies.

A third factor is the issue of digital divide. Different network members might have unequal levels of access to and ability for the use of ICTs. The digital divide literature (Bikson and Panos, 1999, 31–41; Neu et al., 1999, xxii) tells us that geographical location, income, and educational level are important determinants of the level of ICT access and use. Therefore, it can be inferred that network members from remote areas and with less income (Agranoff, 2003b, 16) and education are more likely to experience the negative effects of digital divide, and less likely to fully benefit from ICTs during their experience with the network structure. This proved to be a very big problem in linking many of the home-based business persons whom state and federal government administrators tried to involve in Iowa Enterprise Network.

A fourth factor is the issue of power in networks, discussed in detail below with regard to the costs of involvement. Contrary to a common misperception about networks, network members are not equal in power. There are strong and weak members in networks, and some members even have extensive powers due to their strategic position or resources, which enable them to fill what Burt (1992, 67) calls "structural holes." Thus, the view of trust and cooperation at the surface may easily hide manipulation by strong members deep down (Agranoff and McGuire, 2001a, 315). As explained above, some groupware products may lessen the negative consequences of unequal power as reflected in the social pressures of dominant network members and groupthink. Use of such software provides anonymity and the ability of online simultaneous participation to network members during meetings, so that they would not know the number of participants supporting a certain idea or the magnitude of their support.

The final problem is that of bounded rationality due to complexity and uncertainty inherent in issues being dealt by networks. Agranoff and McGuire (2001a) argued that the wider participation and agreement that typically characterizes the decision making process in networks may partially overcome the bounded rationality problem and produce better or new alternatives to consider, which could not be produced by bureaucracies. ICTs may also help network members manage the problem of bounded rationality by summarizing and visually representing vast amounts of data with technologies such as geographical information systems, and by making connections between different sets of data easier for human beings to comprehend, such as use of global positioning systems for transportation, land use, soil and agriculture, and environmental management.

17.7 VALUE-ADDING THROUGH NETWORK DECISIONS

Whereas the literature on network decision making normally refers to the collective benefits of deciding for the whole (Kickert et al., 1997; Mandell, 1999), the process proved to be more dynamic in the PMN field study. To the network administrators, the rationale for investment in the network entails more than serving some collective public purpose, vaguely understood, such as facilitated transportation or rural development, but also includes certain advantages the network can bring to their organization's mission and functioning and to the managers as professionals involved in public programs.

An accounting of the different types of "values added" in the network study is summarized in Table 17.5. It is displayed from the standpoint of the (1) administrator/specialist, (2) participating organization, (3) network process, and (4) network outcomes. It becomes an accounting, of sorts, of the "outcomes" of network decision making. Perhaps the most overlooked dimension in the literature are benefits that accrue to the boundary-spanning individuals—the public managers as decision-makers—who represent organizations in networks. One exception is Craig Thomas's (2003) study of interagency collaboration in biodiversity preservation. While he dispels the notion that line managers are eternal turf and budget protectors, the desire to maintain autonomy over decisions and resources is real, not only because managers are convinced they know best, but also because of their desire for control over the tasks and outputs of their agencies (35). Program specialists or professionals more easily collaborate, Thomas suggests, because they belong to social communities that transcend agency boundaries. The professionals he studied belong to "epistemic communities" that "have similar values, believe in the same causal relationships, and have a common methodology for validating knowledge, all of which shape their formulation of best management practices" (41). This leads to similar decision outlooks. The Indiana 317 Group is comprised of program administrators who possess a depth of knowledge and contacts that improve the ability of program specialists and state administrators in dealing with the program challenges of deinstitutionalization of the mentally handicapped. They regularly work with one another across agencies, with NGOs, and with the federal government.

Those benefits of network decisions listed in the first column of Table 17.5 probably appear to be achieved more naturally to specialists, but also accrue to the managers of programs and agencies. For most involved, the act of networking broadens the scope of interaction beyond the organization's boundaries as new information is placed on agendas and communication becomes facilitated through established channels outside the organization. The individual's potential field of technical knowledge, that is the "expansion of possibilities," is broadened. Finally, and perhaps most important from the standpoint of network results, managers/program specialists expand their capacities to collaborate with critical elements upon which additional levels of capability to achieve collaborated results can accrue (Bardach, 1998, 274).

Those benefits and results of network decisions to participating organizations are deeply rooted in the literature on networking. Synthesizing the extant literature when the "age of the network" became visible, a number of baseline authors point to the need to network to expand information and access expertise from other organizations, pool and access financial and other resources, share risks and innovation investments, manage uncertainty, fulfill the need for flexibility in operation and response time, and assessing other adaptive efficiencies (Alter and Hag, 1993; Perrow, 1992; Powell, 1990). For example, although the Indiana Economic Development Council (IEDC) is reluctant to take positions as a collective, its research on economic trends and practices in other states accrue to the agencies most heavily invested in it, such as the Indiana Departments of Commerce and of Family and Social Services Administration, and the Indiana Small Business Development Center, providing them with expanded information and potential to pool resources or access adaptive efficiencies.

Many of these organizational decision benefits are revealed in column two of Table 17.5. The list makes clear that pooling and accessing knowledge and resources held by individuals

TABLE 17.5
An Accounting of the Value-Adding Functions of Network Decisions

Administrators/Specialists	Participating Organizations	Interagency/Interorganizational Processes	Interagency/Interorganizational Outcomes
Broadened external contacts	Technology awareness	Convening of stakeholders	Resource exchanges
Enhanced boundary spanning	Knowledge of other agency's actions	Problem depth awareness	Facilitated solutions
Increased technological awareness	Regularized interagency/interorganizational communication	Technology awareness	Program interfaces
Facilitated communications	Cross-training	Information exchange/technical information flow	Policy applications to "places"
In-depth technical knowledge	Access to staff and resources of other agencies	Mutual adjustment-trust	Interactive, cross-agency databases
Improved management through collaborated adjustment	Enhanced data access/exchange	Identification of potential problem solutions	Adapted technologies
Enhanced professional practice through knowledge cooperation	New tools for meeting internal problems	Access to external expertise	Enhanced knowledge infrastructures
Technical program information expansion	Knowledge of grant/funding opportunities	Group learning	Reciprocal programming
Increased collaborative capacities	Boundary adjustments with agencies/organizations on a systematic basis	Cross-training and development	Enhanced "governance" through data-driven area decisions
	Access to service and program innovations in other agencies	Comprehensive and strategic planning	Program and service innovations for difficult problems
	Access to flexible funding sources	Knowledge application	
		Technology application	
		Knowledge/Technology creation	

and other organizations is essential. The ability to learn about and acquire new technologies that can be put before and potentially adapted by the home organization is also essential. Also, more regular channels of interagency contacts, expanding the pool of decision making information, occur as a byproduct of network activity, a sort of substitute for the non-existent hierarchical decision channels. Finally, and most important for the home organization, networking provides formal and informal decision channels for critical problem-solving or program adjustment potential, either on a multi-party or bilateral basis.

Networks must be judged by their process benefits as well as by the products of their decisions (Klijn, 2003). Process outcomes are both similar and different from those of single organizations. Network processes are more collective than authority-based in regard to organizing, decision making, and programming, but in terms of the human resource dynamics of communication, leadership, group structure, and mechanisms of reaching collaborative agreements, they are more similar to those of single organizations (Agranoff, 2003a). As a process, network management is said to involve "steering" of interaction processes that sequences the following phases: activation, or initiating activation processes; guided mediation; finding strategic consensus; joint problem solving; and activities of maintenance, implementation, and adjustment (Kickert and Koppenjan, 1997, 47–51). The SCEIG network in Ohio follows a similar sequence, as it uses participant knowledge and contributed resources to explore and develop capacities in collaborating. Its strategic blueprints, that is, this network's equivalent of decisions, are virtually always the products of a clearly established process that engages its multiple actors from university, consulting, government, and non-government sectors.

Column three of Table 17.5 displays many of these outcomes of PMN decision processes from the perspective of study participants. The networks become important platforms for bringing together individuals who have potential resources and a stake in certain problems; they deepen and broaden the knowledge pool of technical information and to adapt it to immediate situations. The process presents opportunities for interagency processing and problem-resolution on a regular, channeled basis. Perhaps most important are those other collective benefits, including those decisions that relate to continuing interagency "group processing": information flows, new information channels, potential problem-solving avenues, mutual learning, training and development, comprehensive/strategic planning, and mutual understanding leading to increased trust. Without the constant massaging of these elements of group dynamics or applied behavioral science approaches, as directed to interagency activity (Weiner, 1990), tangible network decisions and outcomes are more difficult to achieve.

This leaves the tangible flows from network decisions, that is, the real world outcomes of network activity. As O'Toole (1997a, 46–47) indicates, networked solutions are needed to (1) try to solve the most difficult of policy problems that no single agency can tackle, (2) overcome the limitations on direct government intervention to solve real problems, (3) recognize that political imperatives usually demand broad coalitions of interests to solve problems, (4) capture second-order program effects (e.g., lack of employment opportunities in rural development) that generate interdependencies, and (5) cope with layers of mandates and requirements that invoke the involvement of many jurisdictions and organizations. In this respect, making those decisions that lead to tangible pubic performance is hard to directly measure in relation to networked solutions. Robert Behn (2001, 77) suggests, "the one-bill, one-policy, one-organization, one-accountability holdee principle doesn't work for performance." He reaches this conclusion because today most programs involve collaborative undertakings, which makes accountability problematic.

ICN may be a state-chartered program, but its legal requirements for competitive broadcast and service pricing means that it must serve many interests and functions in a way that "satisfies" numerous users, stakeholders, and public agencies. While originally providing extended education and telemedicine services, ICN now is heavily engaged in homeland security, economic development, information transmission, and intranet provision, among other processes.

Networks like the PMNs provide such decision venues, that is, those poised for collaborative solutions. The most important examples from the study are listed in the fourth column of Table 17.5. Clearly, the most important for some networks are the policy adaptations that they are able to reach, identified as "facilitated solutions," applications to "places" (e.g., a metropolitan area), reciprocal programming, enhanced governance, and program and service innovations. These outcomes represent the kind of adjustments that intergovernmental policy networks are designed to address (Agranoff and McGuire, 2001a; Kickert and Koppenjan, 1997; O'Toole, 1997a). Other outcomes relate to the end stages of the network decision process itself: exchanged resources, program interfaces, joint or collaborated data bases, mutually adapted technologies, and enhanced interagency knowledge infrastructures. While some of these "products" may fall short of the decision-driven policy solutions or new ways of programming (although their potential for subsequent solution should not be underestimated), we have made the case empirically that they are the only outcomes some networks can achieve.

The balance sheet of decision value-adding suggests that there is much more to network production than sheer policy adjustment. Whereas decisions that lead to or in effect are forged policy solutions might be the ultimate aim for some networks, it appears equally important that the acts of networking also add process and product value; they also help managers and professionals along with the agencies in which they work. Thus, for the network as a whole, many non-policy decisions are related to a whole series of "other" values that can be added within the collaboration mix.

17.8 CONCLUSION: A NETWORK DECISION MAKING RESEARCH AGENDA

There is clearly insufficient knowledge concerning how networks arrive at decisions/courses of action. Drucker's (1991, 70) observations concerning knowledge management applies: the question is not "How do we do the job?" which is a manual work concern. It should be "What should we do?" This is a new and rarely asked question. With regard to forging network courses of action, Drucker's advice regarding what needs to be done invokes some interactive dynamic of explicit and tacit knowledge. A number of these research issues with regard to how decisions are made within networks are analyzed in detail in Agranoff and McGuire (2001a, 2003a, 2003b). Rather than repeat these two accounts, some important concerns that emanate from this chapter are highlighted.

First, clearly how knowledge is converted to action is at the core of decision making within network discovery processes. In addition to the various fora for deciding, this chapter identifies six different "pre-decision modes" or learning strategies that administrators engage: group discussion, political negotiations, technical/normative proscription, formulaic process, data drivers, and pre-decision simulation. These emanated from the field study and they by no means complete the universe of explorations. More needs to be known regarding how explicit and tacit knowledge is converted to network decisions. As Tsoukas (2005, 136–137) maintains, "knowledge management is then primarily the dynamic process of turning an unreflective practice into a reflective one by elucidating the rules guiding the activities of the practice, by helping give a particular shape to collective understandings, and by facilitating the emergence of heuristic knowledge."

Second, the role of ICT by networks is in its infant stages. The empirical study revealed little use of electronic group simulated behavioral decision techniques, or even the non-electronic application of applied behavioral approaches to network decision making. But what it did reveal is extensive use of electronic communication for network interaction, structuring, brokering, and facilitating interaction. At the same time, face-to-face communication was not diminished by the overlay of ICT. Clearly more needs to be known about the role of such communication in the process of forging network action.

Third, the research reported here will hopefully contribute to the notion that in the public sector, network decisions add value to the professionals and managers, to participating agencies, to the interagency process, and to the larger problems of public policy. The linkage between interactive network decisions and public value is best encapsulated by Stone et al. (1999, 354) in their social production model:

> The alternative to such a social control model of power is a social production model. The social production model assumes that society is characterized mainly by lack of coherence, and by a single system of domination and subordination. Society is a loose network of institutional arrangements; many activities are autonomous with many middle-range accommodations instead of a cohesive system of control. In this kind of loosely joined society, 'the issue is how to bring about enough cooperation among disparate community elements to get things 'done.' This is 'power to' rather than 'power over.' Of course, there is a great deal of "power over" in society, and struggle and conflict are real, but one can acknowledge this dimension of power without positing an overall tight-knit system of social control.

These are typical network conditions. In terms of making decisions among disparate parties, preferences are not hard and fast. Loosely joined collections of parties have the ability to constitute new possibilities, often through fresh configurations: "As a concept, social production is simply a way of enabling people to see a larger range of possibilities" (355).

Fourth, an issue that is related to the benefits or values added by network decisions is that of costs. It is clear that networks exact some administrative, political, and behavioral "price" or decision costs that must be weighed against benefit. The most familiar cost in the literature is, of course, the energy expended and negative effects of administrators protecting agency "turf" or home organization autonomy (Bardach, 1998; Thomas, 2003). In the larger study of PMNs, six categories of concern proved to be real costs of deciding within networks: (1) time and opportunity costs that are lost to the home agency due to network involvement, (2) those time and energy costs experienced from protracted decision processing based on non-hierarchical, multi-organizational, multi-cultural human relations processes, (3) agreements not reached due to the exertion of organization power or the withholding of power (4) network gravitation toward consensus-based, risk-aversive decision agendas (5) resource "hoarding," or failure to contribute needed resources by agencies and (6) public policy barriers, that is, legislators' or other policy-makers' unwillingness to make needed changes, which in turn frustrate collaborative decisions (Agranoff, 2003b). These issues also deserve further investigation.

Fifth, the typology of networks employed in the larger empirical study was to a very great extent based on the types of actions they take. Following an earlier typology employed by Alter and Hage (1993) we distinguished networks by their propensity to exchange information, build capacity, blueprint strategies, and make policy and program adjustments. One resulting example is that networks take different types of actions. Consequently the type of value they may add is different, as are their internal processes. Further research on network decision making does not necessarily have to adopt this typology, but must recognize that networks are differentiated in structure, purpose, activities, and results (see also Bardach, 1998).

Sixth, the protracted decision processes of network involvement needs more detailed examination. It appears from our research, formulating network action involves a protracted process that takes the best efforts of stakeholder identification, mobilization, and agreement processes. Chrislip and Larson (1994) suggest the following elements of success: (1) good timing and clear need, (2) strong stakeholder groups, (3) broad-based involvement, (4) credibility and openness of process, (5) commitment or involvement of high-level, visible leaders, (6) support or acquiescence of elected officials and peak organization executives, (7) an ability to work through trust and skepticism, (8) achieving interim successes, and (9) an ultimate shift to broader concerns. Key actors must factor these dynamics into strategic or joint-decision-based abilities. Unlike strategy making in single organizations, which can capitalize on similar culture, standard operating procedures, a relatively well-understood division of labor, and overall network activity multiplies these decision forces. Many routines that are familiar in single organizations are not easily repeatable. They must blend these forces into some form of mutual agreement after researching and visualizing some larger picture. The routines and "big picture" seeking exercises that are unique to networks require greater understanding.

Seventh, the multiple decision complexity faced by the manager is real but little understood. Academics examine networks in a singular fashion. Practitioners do not enjoy such luxuries. For example, the reality of the manager sitting in city government is multiple and overlapping networks. Consider the vertical field of this public manager: it may include one or more regional agencies, one or more state agencies, or one or more federal government agencies. Their horizontal field is even more crowded, including county government, townships, non-governmental organizations, and in a policy field like economic development, financial institutions, developers, businesses, public-private partnerships, and more are included.

As a result, many ostensibly intergovernmental studies have examined "a network" or a series of overlapping networks in distinct intergovernmental settings (Agranoff and McGuire, 2001b; 2003a). If one applies a mental multiplier beyond economic development to human services, transportation, community development, and environmental policy, we understand the breadth of multi-organizational networks that exist in the various policy domains. To compound the confusion, the "silos" of policy domain overlap in the real world. For example, economic development and environmental policy networks intersect at many points. This reveals much more than the importance of networks and the need for public administration to come to grips with how they are managed. It also says that we must learn how to study how real complexity can be approached.

Finally, a research question suggested by network decision making relates to the ultimate venues of policy decisions made within networks versus governmental bodies. While not a central concern of this chapter, the larger study does focus on the degree to which networks alter the boundaries of the state, including its decision powers. Have the boundaries of government changed? Rhodes (1997) refers to the multiple influences of complex networks among other forces as differentiating the British polity. Loughlin's (2000) analysis of European regionalism suggests that the transformation from a welfare state to a neoliberal state to a communitarian state has changed government to an *enabling* state where decentralized public–private partnerships among other forces are diminishing government's hold. Frederickson (1999) points to the increasing disarticulation of the state, where there is an increasing gap between jurisdiction and program management.

On the other hand, authors like Paul Hirst (2000) and Sharpe (1986) caution us that government retains essential powers over decision and traditional normative and service roles. The important decision issue would appear to be to take the next, research-oriented step to examine just how and how much such network-generated complexity impacts what we have traditionally known as *government*. Do complexes of networks extend decision processes outward to non-governmental organizations?

Organized efforts of all types, organizations, dyadic connections, partnerships, consortia, as well as networks collaborate to use knowledge to improve action-decision and ultimately programs that improve performance (McGuire, 2000; Radin et al., 1996). In this sense, networks and organizations appear to be growing closer together despite formal distinctions regarding the two types of structures. This examination of decisional action in the study of PMNs suggests that networks appear much like the business-oriented "conductive" organizations that Saint-Onge and Armstrong (2004) identify: "An organization that continuously generates and renews capabilities to achieve breakthrough performance by enhancing the quality and the flow of knowledge and by calibrating its strategy, culture, structure and systems to the needs of its customers and the market place" (213). In this respect they underscore the need for leaders to ensure that the systems and structures are in place to enable collaboration, learning, and sharing of knowledge and in networks:

> "The capability to effectively manage complex partnerships is growing in importance as organizations are reconfigured. Organizations are becoming more and more involved in complex value-creation networks, where the boundaries between one organization and another become blurred and functions are integrated. It's becoming a critical organizational and leadership capability to be able to create and leverage participation in network-designed and -delivered solutions." (191)

In the same way, networks and network processes become extensions of the increasing number of conductive organizations that network partners bring to the process.

Within these emergent organizations and in networks, the process involves conversion of data to information to knowledge that can support decision/action. In the most basic of descriptions, this type of decision making involves shared learning, or perhaps even better, *joint learning systems.* Innes and Booher (1999, 3) conclude that in such systems a new mind-set is needed to overcome traditional notions of producing specific agreements and actions. This follows closely to Senge's (1990, 3) learning organization introduced and defined earlier in the chapter. Remember that Senge suggests that learning organizations require five core disciplines: personal mastery, mental models, shared vision, team learning, and systems thinking.

The most important consequences occur not at the end, but during the discussion process itself. In a network, a learning environment is created when partners follow principles of civil discourse, when all are listened to, and when conditions of sincerity, comprehensibility, accuracy, and legitimacy are met. Collaborative discussions involve creating shared meaning, pursuing mechanisms other than arguing and debating, bringing out added knowledge, and formulating ideas and processes of joint action that can result in "good answers through process" (Innes and Booher, 1999, 5). To repeat, "the intelligence of a network lies in the patterns of relationships among its members" (Lipnack and Stamps, 1994, 210).

In the networks under examination, it did not always follow that networks make the same type of "hard decisions" as those of public organizations with legal charges and a hierarchical structure. They do not, as O'Toole (1997b, 445) suggests, "have the formal wherewithal to compel compliance with such cooperative undertaking." Many of their joint conclusions are really agreed upon courses of action rather than decisions. As knowledge brokers, however, their managerial "decisions" emanate from similar processes to those engaged by learning organizations. Moreover, network agreements to take action are based on their conductive properties, as are an increasing number of knowledge-brokering organizations.

REFERENCES

Agranoff, R., *Intergovernmental Management*, State University of New York Press, Albany, NY, 1986.

Agranoff, R., *Leveraging Networks: A Guide for Public Managers Working Across Organizations*, IBM Endowment for the Business of Government, Arlington, VA, 2003a.

Agranoff, R., *A New Look at the Value-Adding Functions of Intergovernmental Networks*, Paper presented at the Seventh National Public Management Research Conference, Georgetown University, Washington, DC, 2003b.

Agranoff, R., *Is Managing within Intergovernmental Networks Changing the Boundaries of Government?* A Preliminary Report, Paper presented at the Second Annual Founders Forum, American Society for Public Administration 64th National Conference, Washington, DC, 2003c.

Agranoff, R., *Looking into Public Management Networks*, Georgetown University Press, Washington, DC, Under contract.

Agranoff, R. and McGuire, M., Big questions in public management network research, *Journal of Public Administration Research and Theory*, 11, 295–326, 2001a.

Agranoff, R. and McGuire, M., After the network is formed: process, power and performance, In *Getting Results Through Collaboration: Networks and Network Structures for Public Policy and Management*, Mandell, M. P., Ed., Quorum Publishers, Westport, CT, 2001b.

Agranoff, R. and McGuire, M., Inside the matrix: Integrating the paradigms of intergovernmental and network management, *International Journal of Public Administration*, 11, 1401–1422, 2003a.

Agranoff, R. and McGuire, M., *Collaborative Public Management: New Strategies for Local Governments*, Georgetown University Press, Washington, DC, 2003b.

Alter, C. and Hage, J., *Organizations Working Together*, Sage, Newbury Park, CA, 1993.

Bardach, E., *Managerial Craftsmanship: Getting Agencies to Work Together*, Brookings, Washington, DC, 1998.

Behn, R. D., *Rethinking Democratic Accountability*, Brookings, Washington, DC, 2001.

Berry, F. S. et al., Three traditions of network research: what the public management research agenda can learn from other research communities? *Public Administration Review*, 64, 539–552, 2004.

Bikson, T. K. and Panos, C., *Citizens, Computers and Connectivity: A Review of Trends*, Rand, Santa Monica, CA, 1999.

Burt, R., *Structural Holes: The Social Structure of Competition*, Harvard University Press, Cambridge, MA, 1992.

Chrislip, D. D. and Larson, C. E., *Collaborative Leadership*, Jossey-Bass, San Francisco, 1994.

Davenport, T. H. and Prusak, L., *Working Knowledge: How Organizations Manage What They Know*, Harvard Business School Press, Boston, MA, 2000.

Drucker, P. F., The new productivity challenge, *Harvard Business Review*, 69, 69–79, 1991.

Frankfort-Nachmias, C. and Nachmias, D., *Research Methods in the Social Sciences*, 4th ed., St. Martin's Press, New York, 1992.

Frederickson, H. G., The repositioning of American public administration, *PS: Political Science and Politics*, 32, 701–711, 1999.

Galaskiewicz, J. and Zaheer, A., Networks of competitive advantage, *Research in the Sociology of Organizations*, 16, 237–261, 1999.

Giddens, A., *The Consequences of Modernity*, Polity, Cambridge, 1990.

Groff, T. R. and Jones, T. P., *Introduction to Knowledge Management*, Butterworth Heineman, Amsterdam, 2003.

Hirst, P., Democracy and governance, In *Debating Governance*, Pierre, J., Ed., Oxford University Press, Oxford, pp. 13–35, 2000.

Ho, A., Reinventing local governments and the e-government initiative, *Public Administration Review*, 62, 434–444, 2002.

Innes, J. E. and Booher, D. E., Consensus building and complex adaptive systems: A framework for evaluating collaborative planning, *Journal of the American Planning Association*, 65, 412–423, 1999.

Kickert, W. J. M., Klijn, E. H., and Koppenjan, J. F. M., Introduction: a management perspective on policy networks, In *Managing Complex Networks*, Kickert, W. J. M., Klijn, E. H., and Koppenjan, J. F. M., Eds., Sage, London, pp. 1–13, 1997.

Kickert, W. J. M. and Koppenjan, J. F. M., Public management and network management: an overview, In *Managing Complex Networks*, Kickert, W. J. M., Klijn, E. H., and Koppenjan, J. F. M., Eds., Sage, London, pp. 35–61, 1997.

Klijn, E. H., Analyzing and managing policy processes in complex networks, *Administration and Society*, 28, 90–119, 1996.

Klijn, E. H., Governing networks in the hollow state: contracting out, process management, or a combination of the two? *Public Management Review*, 4, 149–165, 2003.

Kooiman, J., *Modern Governance: New Government–Society Interactions*, Sage, London, 1993.

Koppenjan, J. F. M., *Managing Uncertainties in Networks*, Routledge, London, 2004.

Lipnack, J. and Stamps, U., *The Age of the Network*, Wiley, New York, 1994.

Loughlin, J., Regional autonomy and state paradigm shifts, *Regional and Federal Studies*, 10, 10–34, 2000.

Mandell, M. P., Community collaborations: working through network structures, *Policy Studies Review*, 16, 42–64, 1999.

Mandell, M. P. and Steelman, T. A., Understanding what can be accomplished through interorganizational innovations: the importance of typologies, content and management strategies, *Public Management Review*, 5, 197–224, 2003.

McGuire, M., Collaborative policy making and administration: The operational demands of local economic development, *Economic Development Quarterly*, 14, 276–291, 2000.

McGuire, M., Managing networks: Propositions on what managers do and why they do it, *Public Administration Review*, 62, 426–433, 2002.

Moore, M. H., *Creating Public Value*, Harvard University Press, Cambridge, 1995.

Neu, C. R., Anderson, R. H., and Bikson, T. K., *Sending Your Government a Message: E-mail Communication Between Citizens and Government*, Rand, Santa Monica, CA, 1999.

O'Toole, L., Treating networks seriously: Practical and research-based agendas in public administration, *Public Administration Review*, 57, 45–52, 1997a.

O'Toole, L., The implications for democracy in a networked bureaucratic world, *Journal of Public Administration Research and Theory*, 7, 443–450, 1997b.

Perrow, C., Small firm networks, In *Networks and Organizations: Structure, Form, and Action*, Nohria, N. and Eccles, R. G., Eds., Harvard Business School Press, Boston, pp. 445–470, 1992.

Powell, W. W., Neither market nor hierarchy: Network forms of organization, *Research in Organizational Behavior*, 12, 295–336, 1990.

Radin, B. A. et al., *New Governance for Rural America: Creating Intergovernmental Partnerships*, University Press of Kansas, Lawrence, KS, 1996.

Rhodes, R. A. W., *Understanding Governance*, Open University Press, Buckingham, 1997.

Saint-Onge, H. and Armstrong, C., *The Conductive Organization*, Elsevier, Amsterdam, 2004.

Senge, P. M., *The Fifth Discipline: The Art and Practice of the Learning Organization*, Doubleday, New York, 1990.

Sharpe, L. J., Intergovernmental policy-making: the limits of subnational autonomy, In *Guidance, Control and Evaluation in the Public Sector*, Kaufman, F. X., Majone, G., and Ostrom, V., Eds., Walter deGruyter, Berlin, pp. 159–181, 1986.

Stone, C. et al., Schools and disadvantaged neighborhoods: The community development challenge, In *Urban Problems and Community Development*, Ferguson, R. F. and Dickens, W., Eds., Brookings, Washington, DC, pp. 339–380, 1999.

Strauss, A. and Corbin, T., *Basics of Qualitative Research: Techniques and Procedures for Developing Grounded Theory*, Sage, Thousand Oaks, CA, 1998.

Tsoukas, H., *Complex Knowledge*, Oxford University Press, Oxford, 2005.

Weiner, M. E., *Human Services Management*, 2nd ed., Wadsworth, Belmont, CA, 1990.

Thomas, C. W., *Bureaucratic Landscapes: Interagency Cooperation and the Preservation of Biodiversity*, MIT Press, Cambridge, MA, 2003.

18 Political Decision Making within Metropolitan Areas

Jack W. Meek

CONTENTS

18.1 Political Decision Making Traditions in Public Administration:
Rationality, Efficiency and Context 349
18.2 Emerging Practices of Decision Making: Forums
for Governance and Adaptation 352
18.3 Understanding Metropolitan Regions as Complex Systems..356
18.4 Summary..357
References..358

Interpreting metropolitan areas has taken on some exciting new advances. These advances come from a variety of scholars who offer potentially robust approaches for interpreting the dynamics of urban regions, such as regime theory (Stone, 1989), governance (Peters, 1996), citistates (Peirce, 1993), post-city (Savich and Vogel, 1996), and postmetropolis (Soja, 2000), among others. One characteristic of these insights is that social forces and public institutions within metropolitan environments are altering the patterns of local decision making from institutional to non-institutional and cross-institutional forms of governance. The result is that metropolitan environments are different places than they were decades before: they have transformed into more complex environments of diversified power centers with cross-jurisdictional issues and demands. In response to these demands, it seems clear that our metropolitan areas are full of very innovative organizing activities that capture the imaginations of citizens and governmental officials alike. Political decision making in this "regional mosaic" (Wikstrom, 2002) is no longer understood only as a series of local governments managed by civic and administrative leaders influenced by a set of skills and tools that are framed in an organizational setting designed to meet the needs of specific publics. Political decision making is now also understood as a set of skills and tools that are framed around collaborative efforts designed to meet the cross-jurisdictional and cross-boundary needs of both publics (Agranoff, 2003) and public and non-profit agencies (Linden, 2002).

Drawing upon insights from complexity theory (see the other chapters on complexity theory—or the science(s) of complexity—by Richardson, Dennard, and Newell in this volume), this essay offers some ideas that may provide a useful interpretation of the metropolitan context from which we can understand metropolitan environments and the way in which decisions are made within these environments. In particular, the essay will offer several examples of how our current metropolitan systems produce self-organizing patterns that can best be viewed as complex social systems. These patterns are described as "adaptive" in that these patterns are human inventions created to adapt to complex conditions from which issues arise. These complex issues present challenges that often surpass the ability, will, or capacity of traditional institutions to respond.

In addition to these self-organizing patterns, it should be noted that more traditional, top-down cross-jurisdictional strategies are also more prevalent in our metropolitan regions, and these include traditional institutions seeking coordination among local agencies. In some cases, traditional long-standing public institutions initiate these strategies. As such, those concerned about a new world of governance and decision making without a significant role for government or public administration should not be alarmed. In each of the emerging decision making forums addressed here—self-organizing and cross-jurisdictional associations—government and public administration play a central and significant role (Klijn and Koopenjan, 2000). Yet, the role of government is changing and involves expanded participation, which in itself changes how decision making is processed and implemented. Administrative decision making at the local level has transformed into various forms of political and policy making that are now referred to as governance.

The central question explored in this paper is *how are administrative, political, and policy decisions formed in complex metropolitan environments*? At the center of this question are two very different mindsets. The first mind-set is the deeply traditional frame of reference that relies on the oft-touted principles of rational decision making. Long a tradition in public administration, rational decision making theories are the bulwark of the field, and most approaches rely on the underlying principles and assumptions of rationality in conducting and understanding decision making in public administration. Under this mind-set, the emphasis of the quality of decisions is viewed as a result of a form of rationality that seeks to order policy decisions around the criterion of efficiency.

The second mind-set places emphasis on the very different question of who is involved in the decision process. This approach to decision is representative of what is referred to as post-positivist (Fischer, 2000), in which there is a reliance on expanding the decision frames of reference to improve policy and administrative deliberation. It is understood in this mind-set that expanding participation will lead to a more fully developed sense of understanding the problem at hand and a more fully committed response to the problem solution once meaningful involvement is achieved. In the first mind-set, it is understood that rationalist logics lead to a well-defined set of problem definitions and solutions that offer valuable ways to articulate the costs and benefits of decision options that serve decision makers. The second mind-set leads to a more defined community that is affected by and participating in the decision. It is this second mind-set that offers "adaptive" strategies based on decisions that include and expand community. It is this mind-set that offers self-organizing attempts at adaptation to complex environments and their attendant problems.

What follows is a review of the tradition of political decision making that stresses the reliance on rationality and efficiency in public administration decision making. The review emphasizes administrative decision making that is guided by the "logic of consequences" long held in high regard in public administration approaches to decision making (Frederickson and Smith, 2003). This is followed by a discussion of emerging practices of collective decision making that characterize metropolitan environments. These practices go beyond the familiar administrative decision processes that frame organizational decisions and actions. These collectivities embrace a broader range of participants that inform a more collective political decision making process, in which governments are critical but not the only center for political decision making. This review emphasizes the broader, more inclusive nature of administrative and political decision making in public administration, or what Frederickson and Smith refer to as the "logic of appropriateness" (2003). The chapter then offers an interpretation of the rise of these forms of political decision making as new forms of governance that, as a whole, characterize the metropolitan region as a complex system.

18.1 POLITICAL DECISION MAKING TRADITIONS IN PUBLIC ADMINISTRATION: RATIONALITY, EFFICIENCY AND CONTEXT

Decision making is a critical feature of public administration. Traditionally, of central concern to decision making in public administration is the degree to which the tenets of rationality can be applied, given the dynamic character of the public administrative environment. These tenets, derived from rational choice theory, embrace the notion of economic motivation as a centerpiece to both describe human actions and decision as well as to predict such actions. With this understanding, decisions can then be constructed within a framework of knowable costs and benefits that are weighed given individual values (Zey, 1998). Rational choice is more than a theory; it is a paradigm that has absorbed the assumptions of rational decision making models and neo-classical economics regarding human behavior (see the chapter on "public choice" theories by Heikkila in this volume, which covers the theories of rational choice that have been developed for politics, policy, and public administration). The question raised in the study and practice of public administration is whether one can arrive at rational choices when those choices and their consequences are politically motivated. For some, rational decision making provides a valuable compass from which decisions can be made and serves a community with equitable consideration and weighing of options. For others, equitable decision parameters are not possible, and the central tenets of rationality themselves are questionable guides for decision making in human communities.

According to John R. Gist (1989), in his review of the decision making literature, the initial concern of public administration decision making was with rationality, as evident in the works of Frank Goodnow (1900) and Woodrow Wilson (1941). The notions of Frederick Taylor's "scientific management" assisted the promotion of a public administration that would be separated from politics, where decisions would be made based on objective information and data that would seek efficiency in administrative tasks far removed from political influences. As a response to municipal corruption, the progressive era approach to decision making sought to separate legislative and executive and judicial concerns from the workings and functions of government. Rationality was the centerpiece of the "science of administration," and business models were welcome in public administration thinking. It was the function of the executive to develop a rational frame from which decisions could be derived. Perhaps the most well-known representation of this classical approach to the functions of the public executive was the work of Gulick and Urwich (1937), who offered the acronym POSDCORB as the basis to guide the public administrator in the decision making process.

Herbert Simon (1947) was one of the first scholars who identified the limits of rationality in public administration decision making. Known values, known preferences, and known costs of choices were all challenged as knowable certainties, and as a result, decisions were to be viewed as a product of "bounded rationality" (see the Mingus chapter in this volume for details). And it was Dwight Waldo (1952) who challenged the notion of efficiency—the central feature of rational decision making—as the highest value for decision making in a democratic society (Frederickson and Smith, 2003).

Thus, the "rational model," traditionally understood, had its shortcomings: there was a lack of adequate information of policy options, there were competing values to maximize (value prioritizing is difficult), there was the avoidance of values in developing decision options, there was the intertwining of means and ends, and there was the lack of time for proper data gathering and scrutiny of decision options. These were formidable challenges to rational decision making that lead James G. March and Herbert A. Simon (1958) to believe that decisions eventually defaulted to the lowest common standard of satisfaction for the public administrator, or what March and Simon termed as "satisficing" (see the Mingus chapter in this volume for details). As a result, decisions became "incremental" or were viewed as adjustments of past decisions. What Charles Lindbloom later called "muddling through" (1959) was a description of decisions that resulted from a process whereby vaguely formulated and simple goals are matched in a fragmented fashion with relatively few policy alternatives and which of course compels a repetition of the same unpredictable process. The consequences of such a process include: incremental decisions and change; simplified strategies and shortcuts; the inability to articulate clear alternatives; the inability to solve value conflicts; the scarcity of time, leading to decisions that are incremental; an attitude of, "Let's do what we did last year." Lindbloom (1965) in his later work pointed to the benefits of a muddling through process that he termed "partisan mutual adjustment," which was viewed as more comprehensive than simplified rationalist approaches that ignored the complicated realities of decision in public administration (see the Hayes chapter in this volume for a detailed discussion of Lindblom's incrementalism). And it was March, Cohen, and Olsen (1982) who articulated that decisions are best understood from the metaphor they labeled the "Garbage Can Model." In this model decisions are a result of the simultaneous availability of people, problems and solutions; decisions are not determined a priori systems, but are borne of the conditions of chaos. Decisions are not random processes but evolve from conditions of ambiguity, and the availability and existence of options that nears "satisficing."

It was Graham Allison's (1971) study of the Cuban missile crisis that offered three competing paradigms of decision making: rational, organizational process, and bureaucratic politics. Each paradigm pointed to different perspectives that could explain decision making and policy choice during the crisis. In the rational paradigm, analysts can explain and predict the behavior of national governments in terms of value-maximizing behavior. In the organizational process paradigm, the decision options are limited as a result of the existing organizational routines and physical capabilities that constitute the effective options open to address any particular problem. The bureaucratic paradigm points to decision options that are shaped by the leaders who sit on top of organizations, who in their own right are players in a central, competitive game (bureaucratic politics) characterized as bargaining along regularized channels among players positioned hierarchically within the government. In this model, government behavior is thus understood as outcomes of bargaining games.

In his study of the Bay of Pigs invasion, Irvin Janis (1972) coined the term "groupthink" as a way to refer to a mode of thinking that people engaged when there is a search to reach consensus and unanimity. The notion of "groupthink" overrode individual motivation to realistically appraise alternative courses of action. "Groupthink" refers to decision making outcomes that fall short of rationality and are more reflective of results that emerge from informal in-group pressures.

These versions of decision making contribute to a rich understanding of decision making interpretation in public administration. It is also clear that the standard rational choice approach enjoys an extensive utility in public administration decision making with the use of benefit costs analysis, PPBS, operations research, management by objectives, and management information systems. Indeed, public administration decision making can be characterized as leaning toward rationally based approaches where the overarching goal is efficiency. These strategies range from contracting out to the total replacement of government and are collectively viewed as tools of "new public management." Such reforms of government operations and decision making have received much favorable attention for assisting "reinventing government" (Osborne and Gabler, 1992). Proponents of these reforms argue that government, as a result of implementing these strategies, would be closer to the customer, more responsive and efficient, and not involved in affairs of citizens when they are best left alone.

Critics of the "new public management" abound. Some argue that government shedding simply shifts burdens to systems unprepared to provide proper services (Frederickson, 1998). Others argue that this new facilitative nature of government leads to a "hollow state" (Milward, 1993) and sets up public risks best predicted by agency theory (bureaucratic and agency outcomes versus public wants and wishes). Others argue that modern management strategies treat citizens as customers and separate government and citizens from meaningful relationships (King and Stivers, 1998). King and Stivers argue that for government and public administration to confront the problem of legitimacy, they need to recognize a deeper problem of failed human relationships. To do so, public administration must "shift attention in our field away from its fixation on efficiency, profession-alism, objectivity, and neutrality toward relationships" (1999, xiii). Others take aim at a public administration that relies so heavily on "technical rationality" that it excludes important and necessary information and acceptance, known as "democratic knowledge," at the expense of the entire social system (Fischer, 2000; Yankelovich, 1991). Others point to a need for a shift of focus in public administration that enhances the role of citizens (Fung and Wright, 2003), moving from the isolated role of customer to a participatory and more inclusionary role, captured by the phrase the "new public service" (Denhardt and Denhardt, 2003).

In a further clarification of the meaning of rationality, Etzioni (1988) attempts to improve our understanding of the difference between rational economic choice—based on the neo-classical tradition—and choice based on other factors that influence decisions. One central theme of the work of Etzioni is that traditional economic decision making aggregates motivation in decisions around the concept of self-interest and maximizing utility narrowly defined in terms of maximizing monetary returns. Etzioni's power is his ability to unpack the concepts of self-interest, utility, and others to be much more complex phenomena than described in neo-classical traditions. His argu-ment is that decisions are often couched within a broader context of the individual decision maker, such as that of a family or a community. These contexts have enormous influence on decisions that render simplified and misleading the characterization of decisions as self-interested.

In an assessment of the use of rationality in the study of organizational behavior, Mary Zey's (1998) argument is that organizational change and adaptation is best understood within the various contexts of organizations. Decision makers do not make decisions independent of their environ-ments. "The reason for this is that organizations are open systems with constant feedback from the external environment... the nature of their (the decision maker's) existence is context dependent, not context independent" (1998, 24). Later, Zey writes, "most social scientists agree that behavior can be judged only in the frame in which its takes place" (94). Thus, rationality is context-depen-dent and should be viewed as such. This understanding to examining organizations varies greatly from that outlined by rational choice theory. As Zey observes, the retreat of the welfare state and the dismantling of public bureaucracies is being replaced by organizations "subjected to economic analysis in attempts to make them accountable or productive or competitive" (88). Zey's concern is that we live in a period wherein individual utility maximization and cost accounting is pushing aside comforting human connections built on relationships.

The discussion above reveals, with regard to the public administration experience in decision making, two fundamental approaches to or traditions of decision making: those that rely primarily on the tenets of rationality as understood in terms of objective reality, causality, and instrumental choices, and those that reflect on a rationality that relies on an understanding of the decision context and its influence on rational decision making. Frederickson and Smith (2003) have carefully distinguished both of these traditions. They argue that both traditions are forms of "bounded" rationality, but each seeks a different end: one is the rational decision "logic of consequences," the other is the rational decision "logic of appropriateness." For Frederickson and Smith, those theories of decision that rely on logical-positivist assumptions of rational decision making are focusing on examining the anticipated and preferred outcome of decisions and their consequences. This tradition's focus is on results. Such strategies emphasis the use of quantitative approaches and information-structuring devices, such as cost-benefit analysis, performance measurement, and risk analysis, to enhance decision analysis. These decision strategies are closely associated with econ-omics and its concern for efficiency.

In the decision approaches concerned with the "logic of appropriateness," decisions are based on shared understandings of the decision situation. This tradition in public administration decision making is traced to the work of Waldo (1952), March and Olsen (1989), and March (1994), where it is understood that decision making is deeply contextual. Decisions in this approach are more attuned to the notions of social construction and sense making (Weick, 1995). It is to this tradition that we now turn.

18.2 EMERGING PRACTICES OF DECISION MAKING: FORUMS FOR GOVERNANCE AND ADAPTATION

With the examples that follow, we link our understanding of new forms of governance and decision making in metropolitan environments to the "logic of appropriateness" tradition in public administration. For Frederickson and Smith (2003), it is the recognition that decisions are made in a context of ambiguity and uncertainty wherein "this is not to be just a process by which the institution adapts to its environment, but a process by which the institution and the environment adapt to each other" (175). It is decision making by what is termed "loose coupling," meaning that "To deal with complex confusing, inconsistent and ambiguous environments, complex organizations decentralize, delegate, and contract out" (177). "What appears to be disorder, chaos, and highly unsystematic patterns of institutional decision making can, in fact hide deep patterns of order… the patterns reveal an underlying organizational symmetry… [and, they are]… primarily patterns of contextual adaptation." (180). It is to these patterns we can now turn.

Peters (1996) argues that we can view decision processes and choices from the broader perspective of governance systems (or models) and offers four possibilities: market, participative, flexible, and deregulated. He differentiates among each in terms of implications for management, policymaking, and public interest outcomes. For public administration, there are trade-offs outlined for each governance possibility. These alternative visions of governance assist in outlining choices available to governments. While each vision of governance has some ideological basis of support, there are meaningful consequences of which public administration officials need to be aware. Indeed, each system has merit, but each imposes costs to citizens and to the multiple actors in the governmental system. Such a view or perspective on systems helps us view governance as an option with costs and benefits.

From this "systems" perspective, the emergence of various forms of social and political interactions is having a significant effect on the management of metropolitan areas. The emergent

---

TABLE 18.1
Metropolitan Decision Making: Governance and Adaptation

Governance Focus	Decision Examples	Initiative	Issues Held in Common	Organizational Characteristic
Global	Economic Partnerships	Civic Leaders	Economic Competition	Informal
Region	Regional Planning	Federal Government	Transportation Improvement	Formal
Sub-Regional	Sub-Regional Planning	Civic Leaders Professional	Regional Marketing	Informal
	Administrative Conjunction		Inter-local Interests and Practices	Informal
Neighborhood	Business Improvement Districts	Either Public or Private Leaders	Service Enhancement	Formal
	Neighborhood Councils	Civic Leaders	Citizen Representation	Formal

Source: From Meek, J. W., Paper presented at the international symposium on public management in the 21st century: opportunities and challenges, In *Emerging Forms of Metropolitan*, Macau, China, January 9–10, 2004.

forms of interactions, such as administrative conjunction, neighborhood councils, business improvement districts, and sub-regional associations, influence metropolitan governance at the global, regional, sub-regional, and neighborhood levels (see Table 18.1 below). Combined, these emergent forms of interaction are contributing to an enhanced involvement of citizens and administrators as they strive to influence how services are decided upon and implemented in their jurisdictions and region. Arguably, these emergent forms influence the processes of decision making which then influence the nature of local governance. The forums of association fulfill a useful need in addressing problems and solutions that are not met by traditional, jurisdictionally based public administration and government. Interestingly, many of these forms of decision making include traditional governmental institutions as participants and often leaders of newly formed decision structures. As Table 18.1 below indicates, these forums of interaction have many different foci (ranging from global to local), are initiated from diversified sources (ranging from civic leaders to professional administrators), seek integrative or adaptive solutions to issues viewed to be held in common, and can have either formal or informal organizational characteristics.

At one level, one can identify an emergence of regional governance and decision making strategies that include a global focus. In this approach, citizens see themselves not only as a member of a neighborhood, a state, or nation, but also as member of an urban region. And there is economic and demographic rationale behind organizing around urban regions. Some metropolitan regions are so large they dwarf nation-states. For example, if California were a country it would be ranked fifth in the world as an economic unit. Figures indicate that Los Angeles County's economy would rank sixteenth in the world if it were a separate nation, with a gross product of $352 billion. For Neil Peirce (1993), these sizable demographic entities represent meaningful geographic units that make state and national boundaries seem arbitrary. The concept of the "Citistate" represents a cohesive unit that plans and coordinates civic capacity to compete globally and to solve regional problems. In this situation, what becomes a regional priority may compete with state and national priorities. More and more region-like networks are forming that make the "Citistate" a more likely representative of collective will. Thus, regional economic coordination is an informal network that embraces Neil Peirce notion of the city-state as an economic competitor in the global economy. Regional economic coordination is becoming more a necessity with the advent of global competition.

The critical observation offered by Peirce is that in addition to the traditional local administrative units, there are also emerging regional structures of decision making, and these are gaining in influence. Savich and Vogel (1996) found that metropolitan arrangements range from comprehensive to partial regional coordination. Miller (2002) found that such arrangements can be or characterized by various degrees of centralization or decentralization. The point of emphasis in this essay is that we can now identify a rather pronounced emergence of regional economic planning. With regard to comprehensive regional planning in transportation, the United States federal government initiated Metropolitan Planning Organizations (MPOs) to assist the coordination of regional planning. MPOs are mandated to coordinate planning with governmental authorities of various regional functions, such as transportation, environmental air quality, housing, and other issue areas deemed to have solutions that go beyond local jurisdictional boundaries. The MPO initiatives have consciously brought about a different way to operationalize needs facilitation within urban areas. One emerging form of regional governance is the relationship between a metropolitan planning organization (MPO) and a regional transportation organization (the Los Angeles Metropolitan Transportation Authority—MTA). In the Los Angeles region, the MPO created to coordinate regional and sub-regional transportation planning is the Southern California Association of Governments (SCAG). SCAG, formed in, 1964, is made up of county and city jurisdictions through a joint powers agreement.

In addition to the efforts are made for regional planning of transportation projects, there are examples of sub-regional efforts of focused collective action. Some notable successes "within" the region can be attributed to the growing efficacy of Councils of Government (COGs). And there is research that indicates that these sub-regional associations have had some success in providing the influence necessary to supply transportation solutions where larger metropolitanwide mechanisms have bogged down under the weight of competing interests (Hubler and Meek, 2005). While these solutions have their limits, they do represent region-like solutions that go between both local and supra-regional jurisdictions. These examples indicate a slow progress toward shared transportation planning in some areas. Such an outcome means that regional coordination is limited by local needs. Scott A. Bollens (1997) characterized the movement toward regional governance in Southern California as evolving, and where a form of "shadow governance" coordinates regional transportation policy.

In addition, there appears to be an emergence of sub-regional economic partnerships in metropolitan regions. There are several examples in the California region of local regional associations that include such civic leaders as members from city, business, commercial, health, public service, and non-profit agencies. The California Center for Regional Leadership, for example, has been established to "support, facilitate, and promote innovative regional solutions to economic, environmental, and societal challenges" (California Center for Regional Leadership, 2004). The Center works with approximately twenty-odd networks of regional organizations from throughout California. Examples of these regional networks include the San Gabriel Valley Economic Partnership, created in 1990, and the Inland Empire Economic Partnership, created in the mid-1990s. These partnerships are coalitions of public and private sectors working to sustain and grow the economic base of the Valley. Their goal is to attract more businesses, provide more jobs, and create a "business-friendly" region. Among the many products and services provided by the San Gabriel Partnership are: business retention, expansion, and attraction; regional workshops; and marketing campaigns to increase the profile of the Valley. These regional networks are examples of newly formed partnerships designed to influence the allocation of state and federal funds and seek agreements that would achieve trade concessions in their region. These networks seek state and national government support, but they act very independently and are often disappointed in the level of state support for their goals and objectives. Much of the success of these networks is in information sharing and service provision.

At the city level, a newly recognized form of inter-local governmental relationship—administrative conjunction (Frederickson, 1999)—evolves from local public administrators engaging others within the region. While city managers deal with a heavy dose of local responsibilities, it has become evident that they are quite aware of how their changing environments can affect the success of their functioning. According to some preliminary research, the amount of connectivity among city managers varies by region (Meek, 2001). In terms of time spent, it was found that city mangers spend the bulk of their time on city council relations and administrative management. These are clearly internally focused activities. And compared to surveys conducted fifteen years ago, this pattern remains unchanged (Frederickson, 1989). However, it was found that city managers do not see regional participation as conflicting with the goals of their local municipality. While participation with other regional municipalities is limited (eight to ten percent), a study of selected city managers in the Southern California region found regional connections beyond city jurisdictions were a central part of part the city manager's commitment of time and resources (Meek et al., 2002). Rich local associations with nearby communities—referred to as administrative conjunction—is where city mangers and some of the key city department heads were found to be deeply connected in the management of administrative units, especially when there was a perceived overlap of mutual interests. It was viewed by city managers that their work would not be successful if carried out in isolation. Their success would be achieved, in part, by understanding how their city was interdependent with the other cities within their region. It was also found that the degree of administrative conjunction varied in several areas of Southern California, largely a result of previous historical connections and traditions in planning and previous interchange.

To illustrate administrative conjunction, consider an example from the City of Irwindale, California.

In a brief period over 20 arson fires had been set and it became difficult to patrol due to major homeless encampments and trash. Jurisdictional uncertainties left it in "no man's" land. Drug use was apparent along with lewd acts, wild dogs etc. Assaults had occurred on parks employees and most importantly, citizens were not using the facilities.

A Task Force was created by Sgt. Falone (Irwindale) to address the problems using the SARA Model of problem solving. After a preliminary meeting with a few stakeholders it was apparent that the problem would impact many agencies and community based organizations. Some 16 federal, county and city agencies and two private companies agreed to meet to address the problem.

"Over a 6 month period a number of meetings with various combinations of the above agencies was conducted. Army Corp of Engineers obtained funding to aid in the clean-up, networking with Homeless advocacy services was positive, witnesses cam forward and identified the arsonist and cleanup was overall a success. This effort received awards from numerous associations, including by the International Association of Chiefs of Police." (DeLaurante, 2004)

Administrative conjunction is a real dynamic in metropolitan regions and reveals a remarkable trend of administrative officials working across boundaries.

There is evidence that citizens are now having more influence on administrative decision making in large cities. In the 1990s, a large number of participatory initiatives based on collaborative planning were implemented in American cities. Each of these programs represents new forms of citizen engagement. Examples include Neighborhoods First of Austin, Texas; Neighborhood Strategic Planning in Milwaukee, Wisconsin; and Philadelphia's Pennsylvania Neighborhood Transformation. Various metropolitan civic leaders are involving the citizens and neighborhoods in traditionally "governmental" functions, especially in areas such as service planning and service delivery. These efforts have gained so much momentum that some scholars celebrate "the Rebirth of Urban Democracy" (Berry, Portney, and Thompson, 1993). The power of the "neighborhood voice" and citizen participation is now taken seriously in cities like Portland, St. Paul, Birmingham, Dayton, and San Antonio.

The goal of the Neighborhood Councils is to establish a more direct community involvement in city government. The idea is to give residents more voice in city hall beyond what is represented in city council districts. Neighborhood council boards are elected and advise city council members and city administrative officials with regard to their community's concerns and interests, and there is modest hope that they can evolve into to stronger community relationships with the city (Musso et al., 2004).

There are a number of questions that remain regarding the formation of Neighborhood Councils, including how they are to interact with existing City Council representatives. In addition, Neighborhood Councils may be seen by current City Council leaders as a challenge to their authority and may seek to reduce or marginalize their influence. Neighborhood Councils represent a reduction or a narrowing of the scope of jurisdiction from previous city council jurisdiction. While serving political purposes, City Council districts and corresponding bureaucratic systems are seen as unresponsive under the current system. Neighborhood Councils offer a new level of citizen involvement and the promise it holds in the future of urban governance in metropolitan areas.

It is also worth noting how local public-private partnerships are influencing patterns of governmental relationships and decision making in metropolitan arenas. Lester Salamon (1989) has found that these newer forms of action for public administration involve elaborate partnership arrangements with non-governmental actors. These newer forms of action rely upon and utilize decentralized models of operation and the techniques of bargaining and persuasion. For Salamon, the shift from the government supply of goods and services to the set of public–private or third-party mixes of service delivery alters our conventional view of government (2002).

An example of such public and private partnerships is the appearance of business improvement districts (BIDs) as a tool to secure and focus service provision. These partnerships are forming within traditional local jurisdictional arrangements, and they are helping shape the metropolitan landscape. Among American states, California ranks first in hosting these entities (73 in 1999), which in total include some 404 (Houstoun, 2003). In addition to the rapid increase in their numbers, BIDs have also evolved into professionally run organizations. BIDs have both public and private characteristics. Viewed as a form of public–private partnership, BIDs are able to organize narrowed shared interests and influence local governments toward improving targeted service delivery. As such, they represent a possible strategy for enhanced public service delivery. They are viewed as complementary to local government and community interests (Meek, 2004). As these new partnerships continue to grow in numbers and size, they are setting new standards of service delivery and are likely to attract the full attention of traditional governmental authorities. The growing influence of BIDs in public service delivery also raises concerns about their accountability and responsibility, as well as the equity issues in their communities.

18.3 UNDERSTANDING METROPOLITAN REGIONS AS COMPLEX SYSTEMS

As metropolitan environments experience new forms of association—such as co-production social services, the creation of cross-jurisdictional administrative networks (Linden, 2002), and the formation of inter-organizational agreements—the interaction within the system as a whole swells with both traditional and new types of participation. As the levels of interactions intensify and diversify, the system becomes more complex. As mentioned earlier, some of the new collectives seek to confront what are viewed as mutual problems unmet by traditional local governmental administrative units. For H. George Frederickson (1997), these new forms of arrangements are a recognition of the inability of the state as government—organized through bureaucracies, and represented through increasingly meaningless geographic jurisdictions—to be responsive to citizen needs and the creation of social good. Simply stated, social problems have outpaced traditional solutions. For the purposes of this chapter, the development of new types of arrangements and the growth of cross-jurisdictional connections are *adaptations* that contribute to an intensity of interaction and connection that leads to a condition of complexity. As a result, metropolitan communities must be viewed in a new way.

To explicate the notion of metropolitan environments as complex systems, it is useful to provide a brief illustration. In the Los Angeles metropolitan region there are 16 million people and 184 cities and 5 counties. Population growth rates for the next 25 years are expected to be around 40%, with employment growth at 43% and household growth at 42% (Southern California Association of Governments, 2000). Given these enormous population pressures, governmental institutions face challenges in housing, transportation congestion, maintaining environmental quality, and public safety, each of which places pressure on current resources and capacities. In response, civic leaders, elected officials, and public administrators are searching for solutions both within and beyond their jurisdictions. Local governments are relying on an almost countless number of non-profit organizations to deliver social services. The local governments in the state have created special-purpose districts in many areas of service delivery (water, sanitation, business, pollution control, mosquito abatement, and others) to the degree that these entities now outnumber local governments in California ten to one. Some local governments are seeking to add many new special-purpose districts. What all these organizational assertions have in common is that the each is seeking a solution not easily defined by current jurisdictional boundaries; they are adaptations to existing institutions. What makes these new entities important is their potential for interaction, which results in the emergence of a complex system. In other words, civic leaders and officials are not only self-organizing, but they are also interacting in new ways that produce complex patterns of interaction.

Complexity theory, as described by Newell and Meek (2002); Morçöl (2002); McMillian (2004); Phenigo, Nehman, and Eve (1999), and Elliott and Keil (1999), offers a set of central tenets that can be applied to understand metropolitan governance systems. In complex adaptive systems:

- There are a large number of elements.
- These elements (while contradictory or conflicting) are held together and interact with high intensity within the system, and these interactions are dynamic.
- The interaction of these elements produces self-organizing patterns, referred to as attractors.
- These self-organizing patterns stimulate changes in the entire system.
- Self-organizing patterns are forms of "adaptation."
- The elements of the system can be viewed differently from different perspectives, which highlights their multifaceted nature.

These complex patterns are analogous to complex biological systems. Drawing on the work of Capra (1996), living systems are complex systems whose interactive sub-systems contribute to each other's production, maintenance, and development, as well as to adaptation to their environments. Thus, complex living systems are self-organizing, self-correcting, and self-replicating. Metropolitan systems are analogous to biological systems, yet complex metropolitan systems contain components—human beings and their institutions—that are capable of exercising free will. The patterns of interaction that emerge from new forms of interaction are indeterminate and are a result of human experience and interaction with their environment.

As Etzioni (1988) points out, humans are capable of exhibiting behaviors that reflect a deliberate balance of morals and values with various forms of self-interest (i.e., wealth, power, or prestige). They can imagine alternative worlds and select behaviors to promote the world they choose. After observing the behavior of systems in which they participate, they can learn to anticipate formerly unappreciated large-scale consequences of their actions and change their behavior to alter a systemic pattern. Thus, human components create further indeterminacy in a complex system by turning causal links into mere influences, by creating new feedback loops, and by responding to attractors to create new patterns or different forms of alignments and configurations (Newell and Meek, 2000).

Of most interest in relation to metropolitan environments, complexity theory offers insight into self-organizing patterns that can be viewed as adaptive strategies to complex conditions. Accordingly, complex adaptive systems have properties in which new forms of alignments among components are possible and changes in alignment have undetermined effects. The key features of complex adaptive systems is that they *learn* to adapt to changing circumstances in their environment and they are constantly reconsidering and reorganizing themselves as they gain experience McMillian (2004, 30–32).

18.4 SUMMARY

Modern metropolitan regions contain an array of coordinating activities and collective action that actively creates needed connections among administrative agencies. These coordinating activities are new forms of governance and effect decision making processes. Both the number and complexity of interactions among government and non-government organizations have increased.

From the perspective of complexity theory, metropolitan areas are witnessing the emergence new collectives that resemble complex adaptive systems in that they respond to changes in the environment and simulate changes within the metropolitan system. These organizational initiatives can be viewed as the efforts by the actors of metropolitan governance to adjust to complicated conditions and environments. There is no central controlling agent in metropolitan governance system; they are self-organizing. Metropolitan regions are characterized by multiple actors whose actions are decentralized; they are in constant motion, seeking ways to interact and learning how to meaningfully adjust their interests to the others in the system. For example, citizen engagement strategies diversify local government decision making input and coordination. Sub-regional economic associations, which include local governments as their members, exert new levels of influence and power in the regional, state, and national levels of decision making. Local governmental partnerships with businesses add value to well-defined districts and influence decision making on selective local public services.

For decision making, these emergent patterns represent a blurring public–private distinctions alter and enhance decision making by expanding participation in the decision process. Influence becomes more collectively shared, and the governmental role in decision making shifts from using technical rationality to facilitation and collaboration (Agranoff, 2003). There is a marked shift in the skills of managing local public administration, from one of managing hierarchies to that of managing multi-institutional networks of administration.

For public administration the implication is that metropolitan governance is to take place in a very dynamic and changing environment. Armed with newly formed groups seeking influence through various forms of participation decision making is enhanced and more challenging. Environmental stability, one of the key strong points of public administration, is dramatically altered in the metropolitan environments we experience today. This condition may threaten public institutions and legitimacy, as H. George Frederickson (1997) warns: "In a public administration as governance, it is essential that we do not diminish our institutions to such an extent that we lose our capacity to support the development of sound public policy" (94). As outlined in this chapter, the role of public administration has changed, particularly in how decisions are made and implemented: they involve expanded participation and are contextually embedded and guided by the "logic of appropriateness." As these changes take place, our concern for legitimate public institutions and the roles they play in legitimizing public processes and choices will remain paramount.

REFERENCES

Agranoff, R., *Leveraging Networks: A Guide for Public Managers Working Across Organizations*, IBM Endowment for the Business of Government, Arlington, 2003.

Allison, G. T., *Essence of Decision: Explaining the Cuban Missile Crisis*, Little, Brown, Boston, 1971.

Berger, P., *Pyramids of Sacrifice: Political Ethics and Social Change*, Anchor Books, Garden City, 1976.

Berry, J. M., Portney, K. E., and Thompson, K., *The Rebirth of Urban Democracy*, The Brookings Institution, Washington, DC, 1993.

Bollens, S. A., Fragments of regionalism: the limits of Southern California governance, *Journal of Urban Affairs*, 19(1), 105–122, 1997.

Capra, F., *The Web of Life*, Doubleday Anchor Books, New York, 1996.

City of Los Angeles Department of Neighborhood Empowerment, *Neighborhood Council Certification Status Report*, 2003.

California Center for Regional Leadership, www.calregions.org/about/index.html (accessed November 18, 2004), 2004.

Cohen, M., March, J., and Olsen, J., *A Garbage Can Model of Organizational Choice*, Administrative Science Quarterly, Vol. 17, pp 1–25, 1972.

Denhardt, J. and Denhardt, R. B., *The New Public Service: Serving, Not Steering*, M.E. Sharp, Armonk, 2003.

Elliott, E. and Keil, L. D., Nonlinear dynamics, *Complexity and Public Policy*, Nova Science Publishers, Commack, 1999.

Etzioni, A., *The Moral Dimension: Toward a New Economics*, The Free Press, New York, 1988.

Fischer, F., *Citizens, Experts and the Environment: The Politics of Local Knowledge*, Duke University Press, Durham, 2000.

Frederickson, H. G., Ed., *Ideal and Practice in Council-Manager Government*, International City Managers Association, Washington, DC, 1989.

Frederickson, H. G., *The Sprit of Public Administration*, Jossey-Bass, San Francisco, 1997.

Frederickson, H. G., City and community in American life, In *Emerging Public Forms and Governance: Adaptive Strategies of Public Organizations*, Meek, J. W., Ed., University of La Verne, Department of Public Administration, pp. 67–84, 1998.

Frederickson, H. G., The repositioning of American public administration, *Policy Science and Politics*, 32, 701–711, 1999.

Frederickson, H. G. and Smith, K. B., *The Public Administration Theory Primer*, Westview Press, Boulder, 2003.

Fung, A. and Wright, E. O., *Deepening Democracy: Institutional Innovations in Empowered Participatory Governance*, Verso, New York, 2003.

Gist, J. R., Decision making in public administration, In *Handbook of Public Administration*, Rabin, J., Hildreth, W. B, and Miller, G. J., Eds., Marcel Dekker, New York, pp. 225–252, 1989.

Goodnow, F., *Public Administration: A Study in Government*, Russell and Russel, New York, 1900.

Gulick, L. and Urwich, L., *Papers on the Science of Administration*, Columbia University, New York, 1937.

Haas, P. N., Introduction: epistemic communities and international policy coordination, *International Organization*, 46(1), 1–35, 1992.

Houstoun, L. O., *Business Improvement Districts*, 2nd ed., Urban Land Institute, Washington, 2003.

Hubler, P. and Meek, J. W., Sub-Regional Transportation Initiatives: Implications for Governance. *International Journal of Public Administration*, 28, 1081–1094, 2005.

Janis, I., *Victims of Group Think: A Psychological Study of Foreign-Policy Decisions and Fiascoes*, Houghton Mifflin, Boston, 1972.

Keil, D., Managing chaos and complexity in government: a new paradigm for managing change, Innovation and Organizational Renewal, Jossey-Bass, San Francisco, 1994.

King, C. S. and Stivers, C., *Government is U.S.: Public Administration in an Anti-Government Era*, Sage, Thousand Oaks, 1998.

Klijn, E. J. and Koopenjan, F. M., Public management and policy networks, *Public Management*, 2(2), 135–158, 2000.

Linden, R. M., *Working Across Boundaries: Making Collaboration Work in Government and Nonprofit Organizations*, Jossey-Bass, San Francisco, 2002.

Lindbloom, C. E., The science of muddling through, *Public Administration Review*, 19, 79–88, 1959.

Lindbloom, C. E., *The Intelligence of Democracy: Decision Making Through Mutual Adjustment*, Free Press, New York, 1965.

Luke, A., San Gabriel valley: council of governments and economic partnership, *Business Life*, Glendale, CA, pp. 6–8, 2001.

March, J., *A Primer on Decision Making: How Decisions Happen*, The Free Press, New York, 1994.

March, J. and Olsen, J., *Rediscovering Institutions*, The Free Press, New York, 1989.

March, J. G. and Simon, H. A., *Organizations*, John Wiley Sons, New York, 1958.

March, J. G. and Simon, H. A., *Organizations*, Blackwell Press, Oxford, 1993.

McGowan, R. P., Five great issues in decision making, In *Handbook of Public Administration*, Rabin, J., Hildreth, W. B., and Miller, G. J., Eds., Marcel Dekker, New York, pp. 253–276, 1989.

McMillian, E., *Complexity, Organizations and Change*, Routledge, New York, 2004.

Meek, J. W., Governance and Networks: Understanding the City-State. Paper presented at the annual meeting of the Public Administration Theory-Network Conference, University of Leiden, Netherlands, 2003.

Meek, J. W., Complementary Governments: Policy Management and Business Improvement Districts (BIDs) in California. Paper presented at the 2nd Sino-U.S. International Conference for Public Administration in Renmin University of China (RUC) Beijing, P.R. China, 2004.

Meek, J. W. and Newell, W. H., What can public administration learn from complex systems theory? In *New Sciences for Public Administration and Policy: Connections and Reflections*, Morçöl, G. and Dennard, L. F., Eds., Chatelaine Press, Burke, VA, pp. 81–106, 2002.

Meek, J. W., Schildt, K., and Witt, M., Local government administration in a metropolitan context, In *The Future of Local Government Administration*, Frederickson, H. G., Ed., International City/County Management Association, pp. 145–153, 2002.

Miller, D. Y., *The Regional Governing of Metropolitan American*, Westview Press, Boulder, 2002.

Milward, B. H., Implications of contraction out: new roles for the hollow state, In *New Paradigms for Government: Issues for the Changing Public Service,* Ingraham, P. and Romzek, B., Eds, Jossey-Bass, San Francisco, 1994.

Morçöl, G., *A New Mind for Policy Analysis: Toward a Post-Newtonian and Post Positivist Epistemology and Methodology*, Praeger, Westport, CT, 2002.

Musso, J. A., Ware, C., and Cooper, T. L., Neighborhood Council in Los Angeles: A Midterm Status Report. University of Southern California, Urban Initiative Report, 2004.

Newell, W. H. and Meek, J. W., Complexity re-conceptualized. Paper presented at the annual meeting of the Public Administration Theory-Network, Fort Lauderdale, FL, 2000.

Osborne, D. and Gaebler, T., *Reinventing Government: How the Entrepreneurial Sprit is Transforming the Public Sector*, Addison-Wesley, New York, 1992.

Peirce, N. R., *Citistates: How Urban America Can Prosper in a Competitive World*, Seven Locks Press, Washington, DC, 1993.

Peters, G., *The Future of Governing: Four Emerging Models*, University of Kansas Press, Lawrence, KS, 1996.

Phenigo, R., Lee, M., Nehman, G., and Eve, R. A., Environmental regulation vs. ecological self-regulation: implications of complex adaptive systems theory to regulatory policy, In *Nonlinear Dynamics, Complexity and Public Policy*, Elliott, E. and Keil, L. D., Eds., Nova Science Publishers, Commack, New York, pp. 81–95, 1999.

Salamon, L., *Beyond Privatization: The Tasks of Government Action*, Urban Institite Press, Washington, DC, 1989.

Salamon, L. M., Ed., *The Tools of Government: A Guide to the New Governance*, Oxford University Press, Oxford, 2002.

Savich, H. V. and Vogel, R. K., *Regional Politics: American in a Post-City Age*, Sage, Thousand Oaks, CA, 1996.

Simon, H., *Administrative Behavior*, The Free Press, New York, 1947.

Soja, E. W., *Postmetropolis: Critical Studies of Cities and Regions*, Blackwell Publishers, Malden, MA, 2000.

Southern California Association of Governments, *Regional Transportation Plan Update*, Los Angeles County Metropolitan Authority, Los Angeles, CA, 2000.

Stone, C. N., *Regime Politics: Governing Atlanta, 1946–1988*, University Press of Kansas, Lawrence, KS, 1989.

Waldo, D., Development of theory of democratic administration, *American Political Science Review*, 46, 81–103, 1952.

Weick, K. E., *Sensemaking in Organizations*, Sage, Thousand Oak, CA, 1995.

Wikstrom, N., The city in the regional mosaic, In *The Future of Loca Government Administration*, Frederickson, H. G. and Nalbandian, J., Eds., International City/County Management Association, Washington, DC, pp. 21–38, 2002.

Wilson, W., The study of public administration, *Political Science Quarterly*, 56, 197–222, 1941.

Yankelovich, D., *Coming to Public Judgement: Making Democracy Work in a Complex World*, Syracuse University Press, New York, 1991.

Zey, M., *Rational Choice Theory and Organizational Theory: A Critique*, Sage, Thousand Oaks, CA, 1998.

19 The Rules of Drug Trafficking: Decision Making in Colombian Narcotics Enterprises

Michael Kenney

CONTENTS

19.1 Introduction...361
19.2 Environments of Colombian Trafficking Enterprises 362
19.3 Centralized Decision Making...363
19.4 Short Decision Hierarchies..364
19.5 Roles in Smuggling Groups 365
19.6 Routines in Trafficking Organizations 366
19.7 Conclusion 369
References..369

19.1 INTRODUCTION

As we sat in his smartly-appointed study in a suburb of Atlanta, Arturo, the former Miami-based distribution manager for a Colombian cocaine network explained how decisions were made in his operation:

> Don 'José' called all the shots in Colombia, and I called all the shots here. He could not tell me what to do here. He could not tell me who to hire, he could not tell me what to sell… but he was my boss in the sense that he was the guy that got me started in the drug business. In a sense, though, I had more authority than him because I called all the shots here, but he was bigger in Colombia, which is what everyone knows. (Arturo [pseud.] 2000)

My aim in this chapter is to explore how Arturo and other drug smugglers make decisions. Traffickers, to be sure, are not the standard subjects of decision theorists, who for decades have focused their empirical inquiries on legally-sanctioned firms and bureaucracies. My research, in contrast, focuses on clandestine networks that operate outside the rule of law and beyond the purview of governmental authorities. Drawing on dozens of in-depth interviews with U.S. and Colombian law enforcers and several former drug traffickers, along with a range of secondary-source materials, I seek to understand how participants in Colombian smuggling organizations make decisions.

My exploration is complicated by the enigmatic and fluid nature of illegal drug markets, the diversity of collective forms that function in these markets, and the corresponding challenge of obtaining access to reliable data. While formidable, these obstacles are not insurmountable. From the empirical record it is possible to piece together a coherent—if incomplete—rendition of the malleable collectives that coordinate this transnational industry. Given the inevitable problems of validity and reliability that characterize research in deviant behavior, these data should be interpreted with caution. However, taken together they provide an intriguing portrayal of decision making in the Colombian trafficking groups I studied. The original subject of my research was the Colombian cocaine industry, hence my focus on Colombian traffickers.[*] Drug trafficking enterprises operate in dynamic and hostile environments characterized by hundreds of law enforcement agencies that seek to destroy them. To protect the integrity of their operations in these surroundings, many smuggling enterprises have developed centralized, short, and routinized decision making hierarchies. As Arturo suggests, decision making authority is concentrated in few heads, and decisions are profoundly influenced by participant's conception of what is "right" according to their role in the enterprise. Traffickers, it turns out, often base their decisions on what James March and his colleagues refer to as "logics of appropriateness" rather than "logics of consequence" (March, 1994; March and Olsen, 1989).

19.2 ENVIRONMENTS OF COLOMBIAN TRAFFICKING ENTERPRISES

Outside of warfare, and counter-terrorism, it is difficult to imagine a more hostile relationship than between trafficking groups and government drug enforcement agencies. narcotics agents or narcs exist to destroy *narcotraficantes* or *narcos* (narcotics traffickers), and the latter only survive to the extent that they can avoid, circumvent, or suborn the intentions of their government adversaries. Elite law enforcement units in the United States and Colombia monitor the telecommunications of suspected smugglers, run undercover sting operations, raid stash houses and residences, destroy drug processing laboratories, "flip" traffickers and business associates, and—on occasion—hunt traffickers down and kill them. Colombian trafficking groups monitor the telecommunications of police units; infiltrate law enforcement agencies through paid informants, corrupt police and military officials, prison authorities, public prosecutors, judges and politicians; kidnap and assassinate influential officials that can not be co-opted through bribery; and—sometimes—detonate car bombs at government offices.

Colombian narcos also confront numerous guerrilla and paramilitary groups in Colombia that tax drug production, protect smuggling routes, process drugs, or trade drugs for weapons, including the Revolutionary Armed Forces of Colombia and the United Self-Defense Forces of Colombia. Traffickers also interact with law firms, money launderers, accountants, computer analysts, and other professionals that provide them with specialized services; government agencies and politicians that create drug control policies and oversee enforcement programs; and—ultimately— several million consumers in the United States and elsewhere that purchase Colombian cocaine, heroin, and marijuana.

As this discussion suggests, Colombian narcos confront dangers from a variety sources. Hundreds of Colombian, U.S., and international law enforcement agencies strive to interdict their drug shipments, seize their illicit profits, arrest their members, extradite their leaders, and incarcerate both for as long as possible. Other smuggling organizations compete with them for resources and market share, and as this competition occurs outside the rule of law, adversaries are not restrained from using extreme measures to gain the advantage. Trafficking groups are vulnerable to rip-offs from customers, corrupt police officials, and even from their own members. They face the threat of kidnapping and extortion from guerrilla groups and criminal bands that specialize

---

[*] While the home office and top leaders were located in Colombia, many participants in these transnational enterprises, including Arturo, were not Colombian. Arturo and other U.S.-based participants were American citizens of varying ethnic backgrounds.

in these activities. Unfriendly neighbors, deceptive business associates, and undercover informants spy on them and report their activities to police authorities. Making decisions and conducting activities in such environments is inherently risky. To protect the integrity of their illicit operations and reduce their exposure to risk and uncertainty, many Colombian trafficking groups centralize, shorten, and routinize their decision processes.

19.3 CENTRALIZED DECISION MAKING

While no single organizational model fits all Colombian trafficking groups, many enterprises feature one or more leaders that exercise considerable decision making authority over participants. This model is true of small enterprises that contain only a few members, *ad hoc* groups that coordinate their activities for a solitary business deal, and large organizations that contain dozens of participants involved in multiple, complex transactions spanning across several countries. Many of these groups contain centralized authority structures, where leaders make almost all strategic decisions regarding production, marketing, and operational security. In these enterprises, leaders have final say on drug production levels, shipment size, methods of conveyance and concealment, wholesale prices, customers, money laundering and repatriating methods, along with a host of other business-related issues. Entrepreneurs also frequently become directly involved in the day-to-day problems that develop in the course of conducting clandestine narcotics transactions.

In some organizations, including several of the Medellín and Cali networks that dominated (but did not monopolize) Colombia's cocaine industry during the 1980s and 1990s, these decisions are largely made by the entrepreneurs in Colombia, whose orders are communicated directly to cell managers or other mid-level managers in charge of overseas operations. Max Mermelstein, the head of one U.S.-based smuggling ring that provided transportation and distribution services for a Medellín group, often received orders directly from network leaders in Colombia or through their Miami representative regarding the dates and quantities of cocaine shipments, the identities and contact information for specific wholesale customers, code words to be used when communicating with wholesalers, and methods for disbursing and repatriating drug profits (Mermelstein, 1990). John Thomas Johnson, a member of a Texas-based distribution group for one of the Cali trafficking networks testified in court that the orders for distributing cocaine proceeds came directly from Miguel Rodríguez Orejuela, the Colombian leader of the network, through the manager of Johnson's group Johnson (1993). Indeed, Rodríguez Orejuela was known among law enforcement authorities for his tendency to micro-manage many aspects of his vast criminal operations, including making decisions on such meticulous details as the best corner of a vegetable box for hiding cocaine (Reyes, 1999). In many trafficking groups, the tendency to micro-manage and centralize decision making is most pronounced in sensitive areas of operation, such as the distribution of wholesale shipments and the repatriation of drug profits, as several Drug Enforcement Administration (DEA) officials explained during my interviews with them.

Of course, not all Colombian entrepreneurs are such scrupulous managers. In some enterprises, upper-level participants, such an exportation manager or the chief of U.S. operations, may enjoy considerable decision making discretion. In these organizations, the entrepreneur may stay abreast on overall operations but step in only when problems develop. As Arturo explains, he enjoyed substantial decision making authority on the U.S. end of his network:

> The way the distribution group worked was that I made all the decisions in the U.S., from whom to sell to, to how to get to that person, to what house was to be rented as a stash house, to how the money was to be sent back to Colombia, to what price I agreed to on receiving end, all these things. (Arturo [pseud.] 2000)

While Arturo exerted greater authority than his counterparts in other trafficking networks, the decision making process in his operation was still centralized. Arturo concentrated decision making authority in his own hands. The people that worked for him made few decisions on their own without first seeking his approval.

Given the large sums of money entrepreneurs invest in their transnational drug shipments and the vulnerabilities facing transactions in hostile law enforcement environments, it is not surprising that Arturo and other leaders feel compelled to centralize decision making authority.[*] Concentration of decision making power is one way that entrepreneurs seek to avoid risk and uncertainty.

Ironically, centralization of authority probably better serves the interests of mid-level managers and low-level participants than it does network leaders. When entrepreneurs micro-manage their charges, as Rodríguez Orejuela did during the early 1990s, they expose themselves to greater risk from law enforcers by communicating with their underlings on a regular basis. Indeed, several DEA officials I interviewed stressed that Rodríguez Orejuela's decision making style eventually came back to haunt him once they were able to record incriminating phone conversations between the entrepreneur and his U.S.-based subordinates.

Moreover, when something goes wrong in a drug smuggling venture, a frequent occurrence in this high-risk profession, the centralization of authority allows participants to defer responsibility to their supervisors. It is more difficult to hold participants accountable, financially or otherwise, for problems that develop from simply following the boss' orders. Lower-level participants that face greater exposure to law enforcement efforts stand to benefit from closely following their supervisor's instructions, assuming that these directives do not place them in imminent danger. This may become counter-productive for network leaders if participants fail to adapt their day-to-day activities to the vagaries of drug enforcement, for fear of taking any action that may be perceived as subverting the interests and authority of their superiors. Managers try to offset this tendency by designing elaborate procedures for their participants to follow when performing sensitive operations, such as delivering drugs to independent wholesalers, a point to which I will return later in the chapter.

19.4 SHORT DECISION HIERARCHIES

Organizations that feature centralized decision making hierarchies are not necessarily bureaucratic. While decision making hierarchies in many Colombian trafficking enterprises are centralized, they also tend to be fairly short or "flat." In organizations with flat hierarchies, decisions flow through relatively few layers of management, often three or less, allowing for rapid decision-action cycles. Colombian trafficking organizations that contain flat, non-bureaucratic hierarchies include not only small groups that specialize in providing a single good or service, but also transnational, multi-task inter-organizational networks.

In smaller enterprises, decision hierarchies may contain just two or three levels: the leader that gives the orders and subordinates that carry them out. In some cases, intermediaries that serve as a communications link between the leader and workers also enjoy limited managerial and decision making authority, adding a third layer to this flat structure. Even in transnational networks, including the so-called cocaine cartels, hierarchies are often limited to three or four levels of "bureaucracy." These include the leader or entrepreneur, the cell manager/chief operator in consumer markets, assistant managers/cell section leaders, and cell or field workers. In some enterprises, there are no managerial roles below the cell manager: in these operations, field

---

[*] For example, in the early 1990s operating costs for producing cocaine and exporting it to the U.S. ranged between $2,000 and $4,500 per kilogram (Zabludoff, 1997, 43–44). Given these per kilogram expenses, shipping a ton of cocaine to the U.S. would cost a trafficking organization between $2 million and $4.5 million. While entrepreneurs could hope to double the return on their initial investment if the shipment succeeded, losses to government interdiction and robbery precluded guaranteed success. Per kilogram operating costs for producing heroin are generally even higher.

workers report directly to the cell manager. In other organizations, the entrepreneur adds a layer of insulation by designating an "exportation manager" in Colombia to serve as his representative to the cell manager.[*]

Whether the layers of management are three or four, the decision making hierarchies found in many Colombian trafficking groups analyzed in this research are short. Not only are these criminal organizations relatively non-bureaucratic, when necessary they can quickly implement the decisions of enterprise leaders. Because information flows through few channels, flat hierarchies allow trafficking organizations to make rapid operational changes with little distortion of the decision-maker's intent. Fast decision making is critical for organizations that operate in dynamic, hostile environments where the flow of novel and problematic situations is continuous. A DEA Group Supervisor interviewed for this research illustrates the importance of a rapid decision making-action-taking process:

> With the decision process in the company [trafficking organization], they can make this decision instantaneously and it will be translated in a day by everyone in the chain of command. It gets transmitted immediately. The kingpin can jump into the middle of it immediately and say, "Look, guys, for the same of business, for our own sake, this is what we will be doing." We have seen them do that. For example, we used to hit them a lot on AMTRAK, the train. In New York they would take the drug money, put it in suitcases with wheels, and they would have different old people transporting their suitcases. And no one [in law enforcement] would look at them. We actually popped some of these guys three or four times. It took them like a day to make this adjustment. Because down in Colombia they got the call from an attorney, say, in a particular state where we made one of the arrests and we have a narcotics trafficker jabbed in the middle because he just lost three or four million dollars in a day. So the kingpin says, "Look, do not put your ass on a train. If anyone is on the train with my papers [money], he will be killed." End of story. They cannot jump on the train. You cannot do that in traditional systems.[†]

19.5 ROLES IN SMUGGLING GROUPS

Participants in Colombian trafficking enterprises make decisions according to roles that outline behavioral expectations for task performance. Roles define the division of labor within smuggling groups, assigning participants to tasks that facilitate collective aims. Participants make decisions by matching their roles to situations that arise in their day-to-day activities. Someone involved in managing a stash house for storing cocaine pending wholesale distribution, for example, will make situational decisions according to his role in the enterprise, such as leaving the house in the morning to create the impression of being legally employed or contacting the distribution cell manager to report signs of police surveillance. Such decisions are more profoundly informed by a logic of appropriateness than consequences: the individual decision maker is more concerned about doing what is "right" under the circumstances as defined by his role than maximizing his expected utility. Of course, there are times when traffickers disregard role expectations in favor of satisfying their own interests, or fulfilling other roles, as when participants decide to steal from the enterprise or cooperate with law enforcers against their erstwhile colleagues.

Although the degree and formality of role specialization vary according to the size and task complexity of smuggling enterprises, even small groups assign participants to perform specific tasks. One small cocaine smuggling network described by Robert Sabbag (1990), 144–146 relied upon a system of human couriers and mail packages to ship between two and four kilograms of cocaine hidden inside specially prepared wooden handcrafts. This enterprise was active for several

---

[*] Interviews with U.S. and Colombian officials, February 15, 2000 and May 2, 2000; also see Fuentes, 1998; Natarajan, 2000.

[†] Interview with a DEA official, February 15, 2000.

years during the 1970s and included the following roles: a U.S.-based entrepreneur/investor, the coordinator of Colombian operations, a carpenter, several couriers, and the receiver of the merchandise in New York. Three people—the entrepreneur, the Bogotá-based coordinator, and the carpenter—formed the nucleus of the operation, with each one basing their decisions, in part, on the different functions they performed for the enterprise, including purchasing cocaine from suppliers, packing cocaine inside the handcrafts, and even writing "love letters" as a cover for postal shipments.

Larger organizations that transact in greater quantities of illicit drugs tend to develop more elaborate roles. One core-affiliated narcotics organization studied by Natarajan (2000, 275, 285–286) received and distributed hundreds of kilograms of cocaine per month in New York City. This enterprise contained approximately twenty-six members occupying a variety of positions. Several entrepreneurs oversaw the entire operation from Colombia. One person served as an administrative secretary to one of the entrepreneurs. A "chief operator" managed the organization's New York operations. A "special assistant" served as a link between the chief operator and two "assistant managers." Four separate assistant managers were responsible for different activities, including purchasing motor vehicles and other equipment, interrogating and punishing errant employees, and delivering narcotics and money. The enterprise also contained numerous lower-level workers that transported narcotics, delivered money, ran stash houses, and ran errands for the assistant managers and chief operator.

Many drug traffickers identify themselves according to the role(s) they perform in their enterprise. As clandestine organizations, individuals belong to smuggling groups not by virtue of signing a formal contract of employment, but by identifying themselves as participants with specific roles, and contributing to the activities of the group through performance tasks. Freckles, an informant interviewed by Colombian sociologist Darío Betancourt (1998, 159), observes, "I work for a mafioso as a cooker [cocaine processor]; we are a group of four people all well known, generally family members or old friends" (author's translation). Another former trafficker I interviewed for this research describes his importation and distribution group as follows:

> We had like thirty-five to forty members and yes, of course, we all identified ourselves as members. We all had our part, some supervised the merchandise, others the distribution, others the money. (Homero [pseud.] 2000; author's translation)

Both Homero and Freckles, who worked for separate organizations involved in different phases of the Colombian drug industry, identify themselves as part of a larger collective based on the roles they performed within their respective groups. Moreover, their identity as supervisors, distributors, and money launderers, in turn, informs the decisions they make on behalf of the enterprise.

19.6 ROUTINES IN TRAFFICKING ORGANIZATIONS

Routines represent a fundamental part of the social structure of Colombian trafficking groups. Rules and conventions provide specific prescriptions and proscriptions for action, while practices and procedures channel individual behavior into collective criminality. Colombian trafficking organizations develop routines to coordinate a variety of activities. Practices, procedures, and performance programs are used to recruit participants; process, transport, and distribute drugs; collect and launder illicit proceeds; communicate information; maintain records; respond to problems; plan activities; and assess responsibility for failed transactions.

These routines emerge over time and through repeated interactions among actors. As March and his colleagues have long emphasized, routines are repositories of organizational experience (e.g., see Levitt and March, 1988). This structure has two implications. First, trafficking organizations accumulate diverse repertoires of routines over time. An organization with ten years experience will likely have a greater variety of smuggling routes and shipping modalities available in its repertoire than an enterprise that has been around for only a few months. Second, successful trafficking organizations develop practices, procedures, and programs that allow them to achieve desired ends effectively, although not necessarily efficiently. Smuggling routes often pass through one or more transit points prior to reaching their final destination. For example, Colombian produced, U.S.-bound cocaine and heroin will frequently travel by way of Mexico, Central America, Canada, or numerous Caribbean islands, including Aruba, the Dominican Republic and Puerto Rico, prior to entering to entering the United States. These routes are designed to be secure rather than efficient, allowing traffickers to circumvent areas with greater law enforcement activity.

Over the years Colombian trafficking groups have developed a number of routines to minimize their exposure to law enforcement authorities and other adversaries. Examples of risk reducing practices and procedures include:

- Compartmentalizing organizational structures and communication flows
- Limiting the size of trafficking operations (both in terms of numbers of participants and the size and frequency of drug shipments)
- Recruiting family members and close friends as conspirators
- Requiring prospective employees to fill out application forms that list the addresses of immediate family members
- Pooling resources among multiple entrepreneurs and investors
- Providing insurance against interdiction losses
- Using multiple routes and shipping modalities simultaneously
- Incorporating transportation and delivery routines that minimize contact among lower-level participants
- Developing coded language and aliases to communicate details of impending transactions
- Gathering information about law enforcement activities,
- Corrupting strategically placed police, military and judicial officials
- Contributing to the electoral campaigns of Colombian politicians
- Lobbying government officials over impending legislation that is favorable or inimical to the political and economic interests of entrepreneurs
- Building grass-roots social support through philanthropy and public works
- Using threats and violence against those that threaten the security of the enterprise
- Carrying out bombing campaigns, kidnappings, assassinations and other violent acts against current and former government officials, their families, and innocent civilians

Some of these routines are reasonably simple, such as recruiting family members and life-long friends to join a trafficking group. Others are more complicated, involving a series of procedures combined into elaborate performance programs. These programs guide the decisions and coordinate the behavior of numerous participants into multi-step action sequences. Mermelstein provides a detailed description of one performance program used by his trafficking ring to store cocaine in "stash houses" prior to wholesale distribution. The action begins as Mermelstein and his immediate supervisor, Rafa, arrive at one of the organization's stash houses following the completion of separate performance programs for transporting the cocaine shipment from Colombia to the United States by general aviation aircraft and delivering the load by car to a stash house in south Florida:

> Even as we were walking in the front door, the two drivers were unloading their cars in the garage. They piled up the duffel bags on the floor of the adjacent laundry room… I followed Rafa through the dining room and kitchen to the laundry, where he began the process of unloading the duffel bags and counting and inspecting the packages one by one. Each individual one-kilo packet had a marking on the tape [to identify separate owners] and the bags were stacked neatly, separated into piles according to their

markings... Rafa was carrying a spiral notebook and he noted the number and code of each package. Then George Bergin made his count. He represented the pilots. He confirmed Rafa's count. This was an on-the-job training exercise, and Rafa handed me his notebook. On a clean page he had me count and note the codes of the bags of coke. Finally, since Chava was responsible for the stash house, she too counted the bags and noted the number and codes. She signed for delivery of them. Rafa co-signed with her. When it was determined that all of us had arrived at the same count we went on to the next phase of the operation. After they had been sorted and counted, all of us pitched in and moved the bags from the laundry to the empty rear b'oom with its one small window. There we stacked them on the floor and in the closet according to their markings. Despite the heavy plastic wrapping, you couldn't miss the hospital smell of ether and acetone. To combat the chemical stink generated by 440 pounds of pure cocaine, Chava place several bottles of vinegar in the corners of the room. Now the stash was complete and ready for delivery. (1990, 58–59)

The stash house routine Mermelstein describes is composed of several procedures that interlock the behavior of multiple participants by matching their individual decisions and actions to ongoing stimuli. For illustrative purposes, I diagram this performance program in Figure 19.1. In the diagram, two drivers (DD) deliver cocaine to the stash house and unload the vehicle. Rafa (R) responds to the visual cue of several cocaine-filled duffel bags lying on the laundry room floor by deciding to open the bags and inspect their contents, sorting and counting each kilogram package of cocaine. Rafa's decision changes the situation and provides the stimulus for Bergin (B) to re-count the packages himself and confirm Rafa's tally. Bergin's decision provides a stimulus for Mermelstein (M) to make his count, which in turn causes Chava (C) to conduct her count, record the packages, and sign for the delivery. And so on the stimulus-decision sequence continues among the six interlocked participants until the inventory is complete and the group is ready to begin

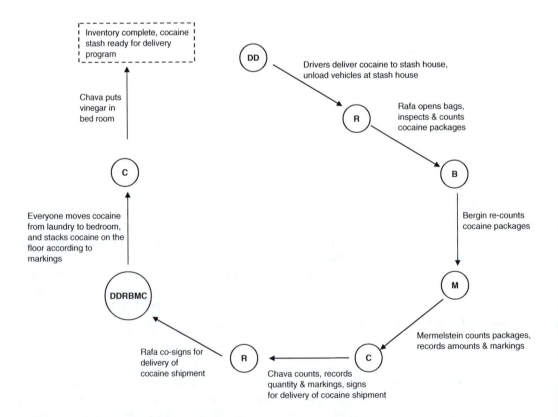

FIGURE 19.1 Stash house inventory routine.

the delivery performance program. At each step of the inventory routine, the decisions made by Rafa, Mermelstein, Bergin, and Chava are based on their roles in the performance program. Rafa, by virtue of his leadership role, initiates the program and provides cues for the other participants to enact their behavior according to their own roles. In matching their respective roles to the situation, each decision-maker intuitively follows the logic of appropriateness.

19.7 CONCLUSION

The empirical evidence presented in this chapter suggests that Colombian trafficking groups contain centralized, short, and routinized decision processes. Leaders based in either Colombia or the United States often concentrate authority in their hands, making decisions on smuggling methods, wholesale prices, delivery practices, code words, and stash house locations, among other day-to-day concerns. While leaders often seek to protect themselves from criminal investigations by communicating their decisions through intermediaries, their enterprises contain few management layers, allowing decisions to flow rapidly from top to bottom, with few opportunities for subordinates to distort or suppress their directives. To further protect their operations from law enforcers and other adversaries, traffickers develop elaborate practices and procedures for transporting shipments, distributing drugs among independent wholesalers, and repatriating their illicit proceeds. These routines emerge over time and repeated transactions, allowing traffickers to benefit from their experience by diversifying their repertoires and developing secure, if not necessarily efficient, performance programs.

One of the most interesting and surprising findings of this research is that decision making in the trafficking enterprises studied is often rule-based rather than choice-based. Contrary to popular images of gun-toting, drug-sniffing kingpins engaging in lawless, yet instrumental, rationality premised on satisfying their personal preferences, many smugglers pursue logics of appropriateness in making decisions. Traffickers operate outside the rule of law, but not the law of rules. Rules and routines are pervasive in smuggling enterprises, shaping the way members allocate resources, communicate information, perform tasks, and make decisions. Traffickers often determine their actions by matching situations to rules. They enact their identities as professional smugglers by following roles appropriate to circumstances that arise in performing their daily activities. These behavioral expectations are based on values, norms, and beliefs held by group members regarding how their enterprises should be organized and operate.

These social structures are well-suited for enterprises that seek to achieve satisfactory profits and avoid unnecessary risk in hostile environments. The trafficking groups studied in this research confront hundreds of law enforcement agencies that seek to dismantle their operations, along with dozens of illegal competitors eager to exploit their fall. That so many enterprises have managed to survive this environment, even as U.S. and Colombian authorities have intensified the "war on drugs" in recent decades, speaks to the fitness of centralized, short, and routinized authority structures and rule-based decision making in drug trafficking.

REFERENCES

Author interview with "Arturo" [pseudonym], former drug trafficker, Atlanta, Georgia, 29 August 2000.

Author interview with "Homero" [pseudonym], former drug trafficker, Federal Correctional Complex, Coleman, Florida, 19 September 2000 (my translation).

Betancourt Echeverri, D., *Mediadores, Rebuscadores, Traquestos y narcos: Las Organizaciones mafiosas del Valle del Cauca entre la historia, la memoria y el relato, 1890-1997*, Ediciones Antropos, Bogotá, Colombia, 1998.

Dye, R. T., *A Social History of Drug Smuggling in Florida*, PhD diss. Florida State, University, Tallahassee, FL, 1993.

Fuentes, J. R., *The Life of a Cell: Managerial Practices and Strategy in Colombian Cocaine Distribution in the United States*, PhD diss. City University of New York, New York, NY, 1993.

Johnson, J. T., Direct testimony of John Thomas Johnson. Trial Transcript in the United States of America vs. Harold Ackerman, *Pedro Gomez Fernandez, Carlos Giron, Gerardo Morales, Juan Jose Guel, Defendants*, Case No. 92-262 CR-DLG, Volume 14 (16 February), 1993.

Levitt, B. and March, J. G., Organizational learning, *Annual Review of Sociology*, 14, 319–340, 1988.

March, J. G., *A Primer on Decision Making*, The Free Press, New York, 1994.

March, J. G. and Olsen, J. P., *Rediscovering Institutions: The Organizational Basis of Politics*, The Free Press, New York, 1989.

Mermelstein, M., *The Man Who Made it Snow*, Simon and Schuster, New York, 1990. As told to R. Moore and R. Smitten.

Natarajan, M., Understanding the structure of a drug trafficking organization: A conversational analysis, In *Illegal drug markets: From Research to Prevention Policy*, Natarajan, M. and Hough, M., Eds., Criminal Justice Press, Monsey, NY, pp. 273–298, 2000.

Reyes, G., *Made in Miami: Vidas de narcos, santos, seductores, caudillos ysoplones*, Planeta Colombiana Editorial, Bogotá, Colombia, 1999.

Sabbag, R., *Snowblind: A Brief Career in the Cocaine Trade*, Grove, New York, 1990.

U.S. Drug Enforcement Administration. The illicit drug situation in Colombia: Drug intelligence report (November, DEA-93016). Washington, DC: Drug Enforcement Administration, Publications Unit, Intelligence Division, 1993.

U.S. Drug Enforcement Administration. The Cali cartel: The new kings of cocaine (November, DEA-94086). Washington, DC: Drug Enforcement Administration, Publications Unit, Intelligence Division, 1993.

Zabludoff, S. J., Colombian narcotics organizations as business enterprises, *Transnational Organized Crime*, 3(2), 20–49, 1997.

20 Information, Technology, and Decision Making*

John W. Dickey and Ian A. Birdsall

CONTENTS

20.1 The Process in this Chapter..372
20.2 Decisions...372
20.3 Decision Makers 373
20.4 Decision-Making Process 373
20.5 Information 373
    20.5.1 What Is Information? 374
    20.5.2 What Are the Sources of Information?...375
    20.5.3 How Much Information?..376
20.6 Information (and Communication) Technology 376
    20.6.1 Classification...377
    20.6.2 Extraordinary Examples of the Application of ICT 378
        20.6.2.1 Google...378
        20.6.2.2 National Security Agency 379
        20.6.2.3 Defense Advanced Research Project Agency......................379
        20.6.2.4 Cooperative Bacterial Networks 379
        20.6.2.5 DNA Microarray Technology for Tracking
                  Gene Expression 379
    20.6.3 Change over Time 380
20.7 ICT in Decision Making..381
20.8 ICT Implementation Factors in Decision Making 382
    20.8.1 Variables...382
    20.8.2 Relationships...386
20.9 Case: Joint Total Asset Visibility (JTAV) Project 386
    20.9.1 Force Field Theory 386
    20.9.2 Procedure 387
    20.9.3 Data Analysis..388
20.10 Final Thoughts..392
Acknowledgements..393
References..393

---

* We would like to give special thanks to John Levy, who always has a deep and balanced perspective to offer. Thanks also go to two groups: the many graduate students who ably interviewed ICT managers about their implementation experiences, and the 25 JTAV managers and former managers who were willing to spend time and dig thoughtfully and earnestly into the history of a very important and complicated project.

In this chapter we will attempt to do the impossible: say something intelligent and fairly exhaustive about three huge topics—information; information and communication technology (ICT); and their roles in decision making. The overwhelming success of the Internet makes it obvious that information and its associated technologies pervade every aspect of life, and that includes the decisions we make. Despite the overwhelming breadth and depth of the topics, we will try to approach them in a systematic way and at the same time highlight what may be some interesting cases and aspects that may not have been recognized heretofore.

It is important to mention that we could have adopted many ways of approaching information and information technology. For example, we could have approached it from a philosophical or social viewpoint, as Jacques Ellul did in *The Technological Society* (1964). Like Martin Heidegger did in *The Question Concerning Technology* (1977), we could have taken a theological view. Our strength, however, is more on the side of practice, especially in project/program management in the public sector. Thus we have selected a practical and managerial approach to the subject matter.

20.1 THE PROCESS IN THIS CHAPTER

The intent in the first part of this chapter is to talk sequentially and briefly about decisions, decision makers, and the decision making process. This will be followed by a look into the nature and extent of information in our lives and subsequently into the similar character of information and communication technologies (ICT). The task then will be to put these two components together. This will be done through a case study that shows how ICT and its information flows enter into the aforementioned decision making process. The last two sections also are case studies. The first case study focuses on the type and number of variables and relationships that might need to be entertained in a particular decision situation (specifically implementation of ICT itself). The last case study involves a larger example where an attempt is made to show the hierarchy and importance of the variables.

20.2 DECISIONS

Decision making can be complicated, and this Handbook presents many dimensions of this complication. We will begin with our version of the basics and grow from there. First is the decision itself. According to Heller (1998) a decision is "a judgment or choice between two or more alternatives, and arises in an infinite number of situations, from the resolution of a problem to the implementation of a course of action" (6).

While the first phrase is obvious, the second may not be so. A common supposition is that there is only one big decision to be made, with everything else falling into place after that. This could occur, but in our experience it is extremely rare. In a particular case there actually may be a myriad of decisions from all different levels of the many organizations that may be involved.

In *The Buckinghamshire and Milton Keynes Biodiversity Action Plan 2000–2010* (see reference list), one can find the variety of decisions inherent in the planning and implementation of a government program. The progam was prepared for a new town in central England—Milton Keynes—in the county of Buckinghamshire. Presently this plan deals with 13 species (e.g., the "Marsh Fern" and the "Hornet Robberfly") and 12 habitats (e.g., "Hedgerows" and "Chalk Rivers"). Each of the "action plans" created to deal with these species and habitats has 28 elements (e.g., "policy and legislation" and "site safeguard and management"). Each of these elements has about three sub-elements (e.g., "identify requirements for …" and "set standards for…") that in turn may have sub-elements of their own). Not even counting the last items, there are roughly $(13+12) \times 28 \times 3 = 2100$ decisions required in the plan.

20.3 DECISION MAKERS

There also may be numerous decision makers involved. In the planning exercise mentioned above there were 38 organizational partners involved (e.g., the Buckinghamshire Bird Club and the National Farmers Union), which would bring the total to around 50,000 decisions. Considering that biodiversity is only on of 360 goals identified for the well-being of cities in the future (Hall and Pfeiffer, 2000) and is also one of 325 environmental variables (Lo and Marcotullio, 2002), then the overall magnitude of the decision making tasks becomes more apparent. Moreover, there are currently almost 100 biodiversity action plans in England and Wales (UK Biodiversity Action Plan, see reference list) so an extension to the national level would involve a still greater order of magnitude.

To complicate matters even more, just a small portion of these decision variables mentioned above deal with the implementation process. A small example would be the interaction between the partners needed to agree on certain courses of actions. So we can start to see already the need for ICT, if for nothing else but to keep track of the decisions and the decision makers.

20.4 DECISION-MAKING PROCESS

Decisions usually come about as part of a decision making process. One such decision making process, fashioned, Heller's process (1998) uses questions:

1. Identify issues: What exactly has to be decided?
2. Identify choices: What are the alternatives?
3. Undertake analysis: What are the potential impacts?
4. Evaluate options: What are the benefits and costs?
5. Make decision: What alternative is the best?
6. Implement plans: What actions need to be taken?[*]

This process will be illustrated in more detail later in this chapter, but the preceding biodiversity plan can provide the basis for a simple, hypothetical illustration:

1. Issues: species to be studied and protected.
2. Choices: focus on "marsh fern" or "hornet robberfly"?
3. Analysis: marsh fern in greater danger of extinction.
4. Evaluation: cost of preservation higher for marsh fern
5. Decision: focus on marsh fern
6. Implementation: undertake relevant policy and legislative actions.

An important point to recognize here is that decisions actually are needed at every step along the way. Also information and possibly ICT are needed to gather and present that information.

20.5 INFORMATION

Three basic issues need to be addressed about information. First, it is important to differentiate it from other concepts, such as knowledge. Second, its general sources should be located. And third, the quantity involved should be determined.

---

[*] Please note that this approach to decision making is known as the rational model that is discussed and critiqued in the chapters in the first part of this book.

20.5.1 WHAT IS INFORMATION?

The first question to be addressed is, "What is information?" More broadly, "Is it just 'information' that is of interest?" These questions come up in many situations, and are the sources of much confusion. One of the main issues concerns the differences between data, information, understanding, and knowledge. Webster's dictionary (1987) offers the following definitions:

- Data: facts or figures from which conclusions can be drawn
- Information: something told or facts learned; data previously stored and then retrieved (assumedly with a particular purpose or query in mind)
- Understanding: to perceive the meaning of; to assume from what is heard; to know the nature/character of; to learn
- Knowledge: to be well-informed about; to be aware of; to recognize or distinguish; the body of facts accumulated by mankind; range of information or understanding

These distinctions help but still leave some confusion. For instance, information to one person may be knowledge to another. In fact, many organizations are undertaking to build "Knowledge Management Systems" (Davenport and Prusak, 2000), but these systems may contain everything from basic data to theoretical concepts. Of course, it is not our role to dictate our own definitions to the world. We can conclude here that there is much more to consider in decision making than just "information."

A part of an exercise at the Naval Surface Warfare Center (Dahlgren Division) to respond to an admiral's request to think about the nature of a knowledge-based aircraft carrier illustrates the need for some definitions. The request required the Navy to focus on the critical characteristics of a knowledge based operating environment. In turn, the Navy had to understand what they refer to as the *knowledge continuum* that contains elements such as "data, information, knowledge" and a higher level of understanding—"wisdom." To avoid confusion, from now on we will talk only about information, although this will be a surrogate for everything from data to wisdom.

Another aspect of information is that it is more than just a list of items. Information also can involve connections or relationships. Drug interaction databases, like *RxList* (see reference list), are good examples. They show a variety of drugs and how the drugs have been shown to react with others to cause some possibly undesirable health effects. The identification of these connections is of great value in decision making by doctors, pharmacists, and patients alike.

A more general set of relationships comes in the form of rules. The set in Figure 20.1 is a schematic for the determination of eligibility and benefits for the Food Stamp Program (FSP) in Virginia. The rules propagated in the *FSP Policy Manual* (see reference list) were the basis for the determination. There are 95 factors with 111 connections between them that enter into the determination. The diagram highlights the fact that many government (as well as private sector) programs are highly complicated, so that decisions have to be made very carefully with respect to changes that may have ramifications in unanticipated places.

Note that the rules only cover the eligibility and benefit amount determinations. They do not address a much bigger range of various decision behavioral rules affecting the FSP, like those of potentially eligible families to apply; of food stores to accept the Food Stamps (now in the form of credit cards); of banks to process the charges; of food banks to fill emergency voids; of local governments to pay the administrative costs; of the federal government to pay for all eligible food costs; of advocacy groups to push the program; and of politicians to create and approve of FSP policies and funding.

We have not investigated these decisions, but we have looked at many of the same types for the program of child daycare (CDC) subsidies for low-income, working families. We found 354 variables at work, with 899 bivariate relationships between them. It should be noted that the formal CDC program eligibility rules, like those represented in Figure 20.1, formed a fairly tight

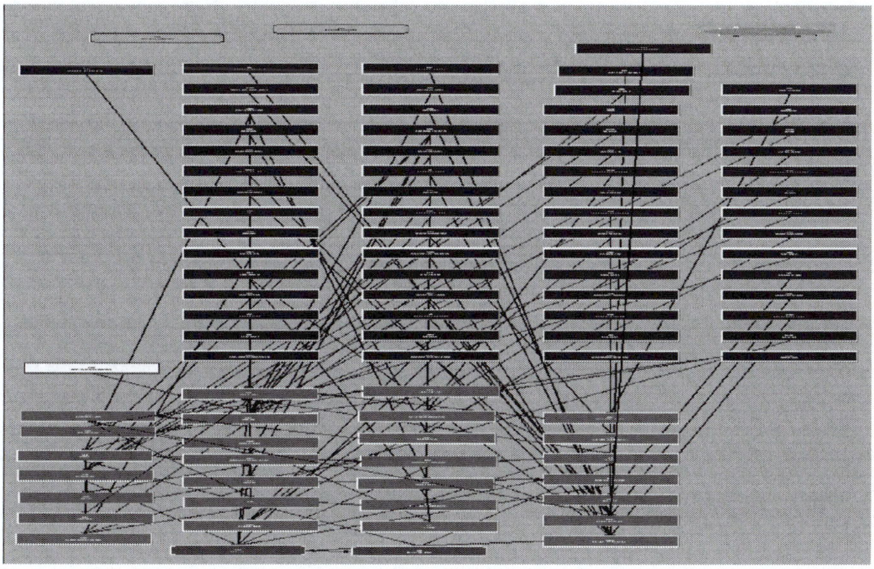

FIGURE 20.1 Schematic of the "rules" (variables and connections) in Virginia's food stamp policy manual.

network of relations, with almost all variables connected to one other. But many of the additional variables outside of eligibility were "unattached," meaning that there was still much to learn about the relationships before they could be identified and employed usefully in a decision making context.

20.5.2 WHAT ARE THE SOURCES OF INFORMATION?

The next question about "information" concerns its sources. There are at least six potential sources:

- Observation
- Authority (books, talks, experts)
- Induction (from specifics to generality)
- Deduction (from general to specifics, or to other generalities)
- Experience (guess, trial, error)
- Revelation

Much information comes from observation. This can be in the form of physical measuremant (e.g., meters or minutes) or direct observation (e.g., with TV cameras) or questionanaires (e.g., a population census or opnion poll).

Sometimes, information is taken from an authoritative source. It could emanate from an expert in the field such as a scholar, in which case the source may be a book or a presentation. The determination of what constitutes an "authority" is the purview of the person developing the theory. Of course, that person has the task of convincing others of the legitimacy of the authority.

Induction is another way information can be captured. For example, Newton supposedly was hit on the head with a falling apple (specific case), which subsequently led him to come up with perhaps the greatest generalities ever—the "law" (theory) of gravity. It has since been used in specific cases (like, say, in NASA's launch of space vehicles) to provide information (estimates) of the force of gravity at different phases of the launches.

Deduction is another method often used to provide information. Deduction uses a general case to arrive at conclusions for a specific case. For example, we can look at hurricane patterns over the last ten years (general case) and deduce a projected path for a hurricane under certain conditions (specific case). This process would provide information about the path of that specific hurricane based upon the general paths over the last ten years.

Personal experience naturally is a major information source. In this case, the experience is specifically related to the effort to discover information. We often test a few potential theories and based upon how the results fit with our experience (trial and error), determine if the resulting information is useful.

Revelation is a sixth way that information may be obtained. Revelation consists of a moment of inspiration when the resolution to a problematic issue becomes clear. The experience in this case is not directly related to the effort to discover information, rather the experience is an amalgam of previous experiences, some related and some not related, that are melded to provide the information.

20.5.3 How Much Information?

The School of Information Management and Systems (SIMS) at UC Berkeley has done periodic studies to estimate how much new information is generated worldwide in a year (UC Berkeley, 2003). The most recent data was for 2002, and that data was compared to the data for 1999. The investigations focused on information output obtained through multiple media: four electronic channels—telephone, radio, TV, and the Internet—and other non-electronic media, such as films, print, magnetic, and optical media.

The measure of the quantity of new information employed was the *exabyte*, which is 1 million *terabytes*. By means of comparison, the 19 million books and other printed material in the Library of Congress (LOC) at the time comprised about 10 terabytes, so an exabyte is equivalent to 100,000 LOCs.

Obviously it is not an easy task to estimate the amount of information obtained through all these media, but the findings from the study certainly can give an idea about the approximate range. The total for the four non-electronic storage media (films, print, magnetic, and optical media) was approximately 5 exabytes ($\sim$800 megabytes per person worldwide), and the total for the flow through the four electronic channels (telephone, radio, TV, and the Internet) was about 18 exabytes ($\sim$2900 megabytes per person worldwide). Of the non-electronic media, 92% is on magnetic media, mostly hard drives, and of the electronic channels, 98% was transmitted through telephone calls (including both voice and data).

Perhaps the most significant and overwhelming fact is that, compared to 1999, the stored information was essentially doubled in 2002 (increasing at about 30% per year). While no comparable figures were generated for information flows, it is interesting to note that the Internet (web only) was estimated to contain 167 terabytes, or about 17 LOCs.

The implications for decision making are staggering. There is a continuing worldwide request for information. Although this request seems to be answered, it appears that most of the information is now more specific and isolated, thus making it continually more difficult for stakeholders in a decision situation to speak the same language.

20.6 INFORMATION (AND COMMUNICATION) TECHNOLOGY

In the United States it is usual to think in terms of information technology (IT), but in most of the rest of the world IT is ICT, where the "C" stands for communication. The latter has been adopted here because it is more inclusive. Certainly it is not our intent to do the impossible by talking about all of ICT. Instead our goals are merely to show a sample classification to describe some extraordinary and highly sophisticated technologies that may not be that familiar to all our readers, and to take a peek into the future to see what technology may have in store for decision making.

20.6.1 CLASSIFICATION

For the ease of understanding we will begin to describe ICT by providing a taxonomy—to break the multitudinous technologies into categories or classes. One attempt is shown in Table 20.1, which was created to help determine the amount of infusion of ICT into the pre-service teacher education

---

TABLE 20.1
Taxonomy of Possible Technology Adoption in an Education Curriculum

3-d modeling	Animation systems
Assessment evaluation software	Assistive technology
Atlases	Audio tapes
Bar-code generators	Brainstorming software
Calendar makers	Certificate makers
Charting/graphing software	Clip art programs
Commercial curriculum software	Computer-aided design
Computer projection systems	Concept mapping tools
Data analysis tools	Data collection tools
Database software	Desktop publishing software
Dictionaries	Digital photography
Digital video disc (DVD)	Digitizing systems
Draw programs	Drills
E-books	Electronic calendars
Electronic encyclopedias	E-mail
Form makers	Gis software
Gradebooks	Graphics tools
Graphing calculators	Groupware products
Heuristic software tool	Hypermedia
Iep generators	Image programs
Instructional games	Interactive videodisc
Lesson planning tools	Materials generators
Microcomputer-based labs	Multi-media
Music editors	Optical character readers
Outlining tools	Paint programs
Planning and organizing tools	Presentation software
Print graphics packages	Problem solving
Puzzle generators	Reading tools
Reference tools	Research tools
Scanners	Schedule makers
Social skills software	Sound collections
Spread sheet software	Statistical software
Synthesizers	Teleconferencing
Test generators	Test question banks
Time management tools	Tools to support specific content areas
Tutorials	Video collections
Videoconferencing	Video development systems
Video tapes	Virtual reality
Voice recognition software	Virtual reality/3D programs
Word processing software	Worksheet generators
World wide web	Writing aids

---

curriculum at a university. It was done as part of a national program called Preparing Tomorrow's Teachers for Technology (PT3).

One use for such a classification, as noted, was to help measure infusion. Each designated course/section was reviewed relative to the list of technologies, which was updated periodically. A score was derived for each technology by taking the highest applicable value from the following scale:

0 = (NOT CONSIDERED): the technology is not considered in the course
1 = (AWARENESS): students are made aware of the technology (e.g., in lectures or demonstrations)
2 = (KNOWLEDGE): students are required to learn the basics of the technology without being asked to apply it (e.g., in readings and written tests)
3 = (GUIDED APPLICATION): students are required to apply the technology in an exercise with a specific outcome (e.g., "Use a word processor to type and print 'Now is the time for all good people to come to the rescue'.")
4 = (GENERALIZED APPLICATION): students are required to apply the technology in an exercise with a partially nonspecific outcome (e.g., "Use a word processor to type and print an essay on 'rescuing people'.")
5 = (PREREQUISITE): students are required to be able to use the technology as a condition for taking the course

If a new and different technology became apparent, it simply would be added to the list. The individual scores for each technology then were totaled. A mean subsequently was computed for all designated courses/sections in the semester and also in the academic year. Curiously, the overall score for all classes went down slightly from the initial year to the next, a finding attributed to the departure of one teacher who was particularly strong on technology use in her classes.

20.6.2 EXTRAORDINARY EXAMPLES OF THE APPLICATION OF ICT

As Table 20.1 shows, there are numerous information communications technologies. This list is only applicable to schools of education so it is far from complete. This section focuses on some of the more successful applications that have used a combination of the technologies in Table 20.1. These applications are somewhat unique and have already made, or might be expected to make, a big impact in the future.

20.6.2.1 Google

Google is a search engine well-known to many people using the World Wide Web (see Google in the reference list). It is employed mainly to find web pages that contain certain specified words, but it also is used for a variety of other purposes, including, for example, Google AdSense, which aids in the placement of highly targeted ads adjacent to its content.

One of the most impressive features of Google is the size of the information source upon which it draws. As of February 2004, Google had a 6-billion-item index, involving Web pages, images, and book-related information (ClickZ News, 2004). In August, 2003 this was broken down into 4.28 billion Web pages, 880 million images, 845 million Usenet messages, and "a growing collection" of book-related information pages.

However, all this information is not useful if it cannot be accessed appropriately. So perhaps the most impressive feature of Google is that it has a good "sense" of what the user is seeking. For example, if you enter "History of Google" vs. "Google History," the former will focus on the history of the company and the latter on the way in which Google (the process) keeps track of the web pages that have been accessed previously.

20.6.2.2 National Security Agency

While Google certainly is spectacular, it pales in comparison to what the National Security Agency (NSA) can do. It has been over 20 years since Bamford (1982) drew back the curtains so people could see at least a little of what was going on in the "Puzzle Palace." Later he showed (Bamford, 2001) a former signal corps and code-breaking agency that at the time had 50,000 employees and the technical capability to intercept almost every satellite-based message and phone call that went internationally and then to take that information back to its 12 acres of computers in Ft. Meade, Maryland. There it was decoded, translated, and searched for key phrases that might relate to national security. Even more astounding, from a democratic, judicial, and decision-making standpoint, is that NSA (along with the FBI) has its own "supreme court" (that is, a court of last appeal separate from the Supreme Court), called the Foreign Intelligence Surveillance Court (FISC), where those agencies can press their demands for warrants for domestic surveillance. J. Bamford's *Body of Secrets: Anatomy of the Ultra-Secret National Security Agency: from the Cold War through the Dawn of a New Century* offers a short history of NSA, highlighting what must be the most advanced ICT in the world.

20.6.2.3 Defense Advanced Research Project Agency

The U.S. Defense Advanced Research Project Agency (DARPA), generally given credit for initiating the Internet, has continued to innovate in many other arenas. One such innovation is the Advanced Logistics Project (ALP). The ALP involves the movement of personnel and materiel for both military and humanitarian purposes. Computer "agents" would go out, say every 15 min, to search databases of hundreds of customers (e.g., government agencies and commercial enterprises) to determine their spatial and temporal demand for various goods. The system then would search the databases of additional hundreds of transport providers to determine available personnel and equipment, and then within an hour or so automatically create an efficient plan to connect demand and supply. What is significant about ALP for decision making is that it is being automated across so many organizations, both in terms of accessing the data and acting on it.

20.6.2.4 Cooperative Bacterial Networks

Greg Bear, a well-known science fiction writer, in his book *Vitals* (2002) has envisioned a situation where the millions of bacteria in the human body can, with the proper stimulus, be controlled to cooperate with each other to accomplish a given task—perhaps to make somebody be gentle and kind to others or perhaps to kill them. Bear claims in the acknowledgements that the concept of bacterial cooperation is well established in the literature (see Shapiro and Dworkin, 1997 and Ben-Jacob, in reference list), although apparently it is just at the beginning stages. If bacteria can be thus trained, it would bring a whole new meaning to decision making (e.g., is the person making the decision in control of himself sufficiently, or is the decision being made by his network of bacteria?).

20.6.2.5 DNA Microarray Technology for Tracking Gene Expression

It has been over 50 years since human DNA was discovered. One of the great tasks in this period has been to map the human genome—that is, to identify all the genes that compose the DNA, variously estimated to be about 15,000 to 80,000 (Brown, 2002). Now one task is to see how the genes react (are expressed, that is, are turned on or off) under different external stimuli (like cold shocks). Microarrays and chips are technologies that allow the actions of many thousands of genes to be traced over a succession of time intervals. As of 2002, up to 125,000 polymorphisms (different arrangements) can be typed in a single experiment (Brown, 2002). If a similar type of methodology were developed for management decision making, the implications could be numerous and significant.

20.6.3 CHANGE OVER TIME

Ray Kurzweil (1999) who among other things invented much of the technology for optical character reading and speech-to-text, has put together a chart that shows the increases in the maximum computer power (and calculations per second) that can be bought for a thousand (constant) dollars at a series of points in time since 1900 (Figure 20.2). It certainly should come as no surprise that there is an upward trend, but notice that the scale is logarithmic (base 10). In other words, from 1900 to 2000, computer power increased 10,000,000,000,000 fold! It also is intriguing that the (log) trend is close to linear.

If this trend continues, and based on the last hundred years of experience there is no reason to doubt that it will, Kurzweil (1999) sees the following kinds of the impacts in the future:

By 2009:

- Communication between computers is mostly wireless
- Most standard business transactions (purchases, bookings, etc.) will connect a human client to a virtual server
- The majority of text will be created using continuous speech recognition
- Speech (language) will be translated over phones into speech in other languages

By 2019:

- Computers will be largely invisible and embedded everywhere—walls, chairs, bodies
- Three-dimensional virtual reality displays will be used routinely
- People can do virtually anything with anybody, regardless of location
- Learning will be conducted through intelligent, simulated, software-based teachers
- People will start to have relationships (lovers, caretakers) with automated personalities

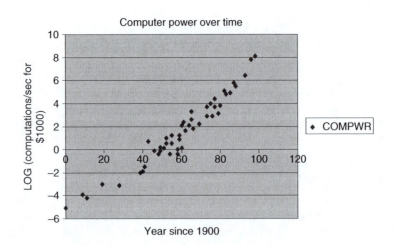

FIGURE 20.2 The rise of computer power since 1900. (Adapted from Kurzweil, R. *The Age of Spiritual Machines*, Viking, New York, 1999.)

By 2029:

- Automated agents will be learning on their own
- There will be almost no human employment in production, agriculture, and transportation
- There will be growing discussion about the legal rights of computers and what constitutes being human

Not too much further in the future:

- "Life expectancy" will no longer be a viable term in relation to intelligent beings.

20.7 ICT IN DECISION MAKING

An application of a real life situation to the six steps in the decision making process presented earlier in this chapter can illustrate the relationship of ICT to decision making. The real life situation comes from the annals of the National Security Agency (NSA). It is an older story of worldwide interest, dating to the 1950s. According to Bamford (2001) however, some interesting decisions were made that could have led to a war between the superpowers (the Soviet Union and the United States).

The essence of the story is that the U.S. was using U-2 airplanes (Area51ZONE, U-2 Spyplane, see reference list) out of Peshawar, Pakistan to fly intelligence reconnaissance missions deep into Soviet airspace at the time. The purposes of the missions, according to, Bamford (2001) were to pinpoint such things as radar locations, antiaircraft defenses, and nighttime space and missile launches (to determine inter-continental ballistic missile—ICBM—nuclear delivery abilities) (for a more detailed story, see About.com 2004, (see reference list)). The U-2 had the advantage that it could fly at 65,000 ft. and thus avoid all fighter jets and surface-to-air missiles at the time.

As it turns out, President Eisenhower played a central role in most of the decisions about whether the U-2 should fly a particular mission and sometimes about what route should be taken. On the day in question, the Soviet Union was to celebrate a major holiday (May Day). Unbeknownst to the U.S., they also had developed their surface-to-air missiles to the point where the missiles could reach the U-2. On that day, the U-2 was shot down, the plane wreckage was recovered, and the pilot (Francis Gary Powers) was captured alive. President Eisenhower and his senior officials were shuttled by helicopter from Washington, DC to a not-too-distant inner-mountain command center in case of a nuclear attack.

A big issue and decision was whether to admit that the president (also Commander in Chief of the military) was directly involved, which might lead the Soviets to consider the invasion of their air space as an act of war. The president decided not to admit his involvement, particularly because it was an election year. He also decided to order any administrators involved to lie to Congress and the press about his micromanaged participation, a secret that Bamford (2001, 58) recently discovered in previously classified documents.

Insofar as decision making was concerned, there were a whole series of smaller decisions about individual U-2 missions (our codename: MISSION) as well as a much larger one about whether to lie about the president's personal involvement (our codename: INVOLVE). These decisions can be viewed from the standpoint of the six-step decision making process presented earlier and are summarized in Table 20.2 (codename: MISSION) and Table 20.3 (codename: INVOLVE), respectively. Associated with each step is a sample of both the likely prominent information and communication technology (ICT) used and the resultant information forthcoming.

TABLE 20.2
Hypothetical Decision Making Process for MISSION Decisions

1. Identify issues: What exactly has to be decided?
   MISSION: Is getting needed information worth the risk?
       ICT: Computer-aided analysis of past missions.
       Info: Likelihood of getting information and not being exposed.
2. Identify choices: What are the alternatives?
   MISSION: "Go/No Go" on individual U-2 flights, and routes to take if Go.
       ICT: Weather forecasting; Soviet radar and missiles; U-2 and equipment.
       Info: Weather, defensive capability, possible reconnaissance data to collect.
3. Undertake analysis: What are the potential impacts?
   MISSION: Knowledge of ICBM capabilities vs. Soviet war reaction to flights.
       ICT: Computer-aided analysis of reconnaissance data.
       Info: ICBM knowledge; Soviet reaction to flights.
4. Evaluate options: What are the benefits and costs?
   MISSION: Value of knowledge vs. risk of "creating an incident."
       ICT: Computer-aided analysis; encrypted communication facilities.
       Info: Senior staff experiences, opinions, and advice.
5. Make decision: What alternative is the best?
   MISSION: "Go" on May-Day U-2 mission; fly deep into Soviet territory.
       ICT: Encrypted communication facilities.
       Info: Full description of selected alternative.
6. Implement plans: What actions need to be taken?
   MISSION: Plane prepared for mission. Transmission of decision to pilot.
       ICT: Encrypted communication facilities; U-2 plane and equipment.
       Info: Action plan for decision.

Of course, the first set of decisions (MISSION) has a high degree of ICT composition in it—one of the most technical kinds of decisions possible. It should come as no surprise that ICT shows up prominently in each step of the process. On the other hand, it also is interesting to find that ICT plays such a prominent role in the INVOLVE case, which deals with one of the most basic of human behaviors: doing almost anything in the quest for survival.

20.8 ICT IMPLEMENTATION FACTORS IN DECISION MAKING

We demonstrated earlier that some situations involve thousands of decisions and hundreds of decision makers. It also is true that there can be many hundreds, if not thousands, of factors to be considered in any given decision (or associated set thereof). This possibility is investigated here with respect to information and communication technology implementation (ICTI). The authors of this chapter have overseen a series of studies of ICTI, which were based on 1 to 2 h interviews with about 40 ICT managers, mainly in various US federal government agencies. The following is a summary of our observations.

20.8.1 VARIABLES

In the ICTI case, there were a substantial number of variables (a total of 914), which have a greater or lesser effect on ICTI. These variables were classified as follows:

- Strategy   281
- Time clock   1

TABLE 20.3
Hypothetical Decision Making Process for INVOLVE Decisions

1. Identify issues: What exactly has to be decided?
   INVOLVE: Should senior officials be asked to lie?
      ICT: Intelligence equipment.
      Info: Knowledge of actual U-2 downing event and outcome.
2. Identify choices: What are the alternatives?
   INVOLVE: "Lie/Not Lie" about president's role in U-2 flights and routes they took.
      ICT: Intelligence "listening" posts; encrypted communication lines.
      Info: Ideas about whom to blame and nature of lies to be made.
3. Undertake analysis: What are the potential impacts?
   INVOLVE: War; loss of presidency in election.
      ICT: Computer-aided analysis of intelligence data. Encrypted communications.
      Info: Soviet knowledge and reactions; likely reaction of public and Congress.
4. Evaluate options: What are the benefits and costs?
   INVOLVE: Truth; cost of war; "detriment" of change in political party.
      ICT: Computer-aided analysis.
      Info: Senior staff experiences, opinions, and advice.
5. Make decision: What alternative is the best?
   INVOLVE: Have everybody "lie" about involvement.
      ICT: Encrypted communication facilities.
      Info: Directions to officials on what false "stories" to tell.
6. Implement plans: What actions need to be taken?
   INVOLVE: Meet with Congressional investigators and committees.
      ICT: Encrypted communication facilities.
      Info: Action plan to make stories consistent.

- Intermediate   267
- Goal   99
- Reaction Time   25
- External Force   241

Some of these numbers of variables are surprisingly large. For example, it is difficult to imagine that there could be almost 100 different goal variables. Each goal variable has a marginal effect on the goals themselves, thus creating almost 100 variations (or more) of the goals. Likewise, there are more than 280 strategy variables. Much like the goal variables, each of these strategy variables has a marginal effect on the strategy which could conceivably create, in effect, 280 (or more) strategies.

Table 20.4 presents a sample list of variables that might be considered as bottom-line or goal-related. Some are fairly common (e.g., "Secure Network") while others may not be that obvious (e.g., the ICTI contribution, or not, to "Organized Anarchy" in the recipient agency). The list also emphasizes the fact that goals can and may be expressed at different levels of generality (e.g., from "Ease of Screen Manipulation" to "Scalability") and occasionally all at the same time. Thus, the different levels of generality for each goal provide an additional factor of complexity. For example, if each of the 99 goal variables has only three levels of generality, that would create 297 (99×3) variations of goals.

Similar comments can be made about the sample client "strategy" or decision variables in Table 20.5. What stands out the most in that list may be the wide variety of decisions and actions that can (and in many cases must) be undertaken to make ICT implementation successful. Some of these decisions and actions can be easy to overlook, as in the "Cataloging of Current System Applications." Much like the goal variables discussed previously, if each strategy variable had

TABLE 20.4
Sample of Goal Variables

Percent load vs. capacity of system
Cost to supplying agency of not upgrading
Employee abuse of IT systems
Acceptance by supplying agency
Acceptance by receiving agency
"Organized anarchy" in the agency
Archival requirements
Potential number of ICT bugs
Response time for customer satisfaction
Retrieval speed
Satisfaction with contractor
Scalability
Conformance with implementation schedule
Ease of screen manipulation
Secure network

only four levels of generality it would create 1124 (281×4) variations of strategies. The numerous combinations and permutations of the 914 variables demonstrate quickly the complexity of many administrative decision making endeavors.

We have created our own classification of the variables. This classification is useful when the variables are numerous, as in the 914 in the ICTI case at hand. The 914 call out for some means of simplification. As a consequence, we have placed them into 15 major categories (Table 20.6), which have been further subdivided into a total of 67 subcategories (a small portion of which are exemplified in Table 20.7). Although the categories amount to less than 10% of the original set of variables, the interesting dilemma is that even the $15 + 67 = 82$ categories/subcategories seem too numerous.

The lesson seems to be that many ICT managers have to deal with a much wider set of situational factors than might be commonly believed. A sample of several "interesting" variables that may be part of this set can be found in Table 20.8. The first variable—"Undocumented 'Band-Aid' Fixes"—is particularly intriguing, especially if these fixes might be actually parallel

TABLE 20.5
Sample of Client Strategy Variables

Mandate: budget must support strategic plan
Timing of training
Electronic bulletin board
Use of "business engineering"
Bypassing of intermediaries for decisions
Web site to track cases
Cataloging of current system applications
Standards for certification
Responsiveness to emerging requirements
Empowerment of employees to implement
Enforcement of policy deviation penalties
Identification of essential data bases

TABLE 20.6
Main User-Defined Categories of Variables

Client use, impacts
Organizational culture
Economics
Laws, regulations, and ethics
External forces
Finance/contracting
Information/data/knowledge
Information and communication technology (ICT)
General management
Organizational form and function
Personnel
Planning
Politics
Training
Values: personal and organizational

TABLE 20.7
Example Subcategories (of ICT Category)

Communication technology
Software
Hardware
Information flow
Legacy systems
Stability

TABLE 20.8
Sample of "Interesting" Variables

Undocumented "band-aid" fixes to ICT
Unofficial database systems created by end users
Standards: process for software development
Acceptance plan: vendor company
Amount of customization needed
Nature of people who frame the issues
"Churn" in the work environment
"Know it all" technicians: receiving agency

substitutes for the official system, which may be seen as too calcified. These alternate systems are mostly out of the purview and control of the ICT manager yet can have a significant impact on the time and cost involved in making changes in existing systems and/or putting new systems in place.*

---

*The complete, alphabetized list of variables, as well as one where they are divided into categories can be found at: www.cpap.vt.edu/cyberquest/ict-implement

20.8.2 Relationships

A continuing surprise and dilemma we have faced in our on-going research is that the number of relationships identified is very small, compared to the number of variables. An excellent example is the ICTI case. In the ICTI case only 342 bivariate linkages were found *vis-à-vis* the 914 variables. Thus the situation, unlike the one in Figure 20.1, is much more disconnected. Many variables are not even connected to any others. This makes it extremely difficult to trace causal paths between strategies (decisions) and goals, which naturally makes tracking of the impacts of decisions much more problematic and more subject to personal prejudices.

20.9 CASE: JOINT TOTAL ASSET VISIBILITY (JTAV) PROJECT

Birdsall (2004) performed a study of the forces acting on the decisions affecting implementation of strategy in the public sector to develop a conceptual framework of those forces. He used the implementation of Joint Total Asset Visibility (JTAV), a logistics automated information system in the U.S. Department of Defense (DoD) as his field study. JTAV provides combatant commanders, the military services, and their components with timely and accurate information about the location, movement, identity and status of units, personnel, equipment, and supplies. The inability to "see" both assets in the pipeline and the status of orders is the genesis of duplicate orders, unnecessary material shipped into theater, backlogs at aerial and water ports, and difficulty in prioritizing cargo backlogs. The JTAV capability is achieved by fusing data retrieved from over 700 systems throughout DoD that support logistics functional processes such as supply, transportation, and maintenance. The JTAV goal is to provide a capability that facilitates improvements in the performance of those logistics functional processes. For most of the 1990s, JTAV was considered to be DoD's number one logistics initiative.

Many forces are extant in the public arena, and some forces affect decisions regarding the implementation of strategy. Additionally some forces aid decisions and are seen as positive while others act to hinder decisions and are seen as negative. Thus, at times those forces may be pushing (or pulling) the strategy toward success and sometimes the forces may be pushing (or pulling) the strategy away from success.

20.9.1 Force Field Theory

A useful construct for analysis of these forces is Lewin's force field theory (Lewin, 1951; Marrow, 1969). This theory grew out of Lewin's psychological studies of how humans change attitudes and associated behavior. Force field theory emphasizes the fact that any event, such as a decision, is the result of a multitude of factors and the forces acting upon the decision makers. Force field analysis is the associated problem solving technique based on the concept that a change in any of the forces might alter the result or influence the change. The forces that help achieve change, or in our case a decision, are called driving forces, and the forces that work against the change are called restraining forces.

Force field theory not only helps to identify the driving and restraining forces, but also assists in determining multiple facets of the problem and in generating solutions. Force field analysis can be applied during each stage (definition, requirements, analysis, design, and development) of a project where decisions have to be made or where problems need to be solved. This technique enables the researcher to graphically display a problem, a goal situation and the forces that influence it (see Figure 20.3).

Birdsall (2004) borrowed the general concept of forces as outlined in the force field theory and applied it to decisions affecting implementation of public strategies for an information technology project.

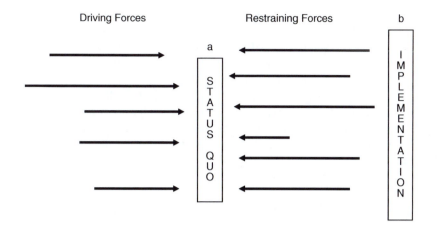

FIGURE 20.3 Conceptualization of force field theory.

20.9.2 PROCEDURE

The goal of the JTAV case study was to develop a framework (Argyres and McGahan, 2002; Miles and Huberman, 1994; Porter, 1980) of forces affecting strategy implementation decisions. Birdsall interviewed 25 people who had worked or were still working on the JTAV Project. Interviewees included current military officers, current DoD civilians, contractors who are retired military officers, and contractors with no military experience.

Two data analysis tools were employed in this study. *TextAnalyst2* (TA2) (Megaputer Intelligence, see reference list) was used initially to manipulate large quantities of data extracted from the interviews; *Quantitative Cyberquest* (QCQ) (Dickey, 1999) was used to assist in the categorization and comparison of data. TA2 is a text analysis software system that determines which concepts (individual words or phrases) in a given text are most important in terms of a numeric semantic weight. The semantic weight is a measure on a scale from 0 to 100 that is high when the concept is mentioned frequently, especially when it is in juxtaposition to other frequently mentioned concepts. QCQ is a program for developing analytical relationships and employing them to make forecasts. QCQ combines scientific research methodology, qualitative research, cause/effect questioning, regression, scenario generation, and forecasting. Although QCQ contains several unique features, such as checklists for concept identification and cause and effect analysis, the software was utilized primarily for its categorization function—to assist in classifying the concepts and developing a hierarchy of resultant forces.

In determining a framework, it is necessary to define categories at various levels of abstraction (Argyres and McGahan, 2002; Porter, 1980; Miles and Huberman, 1994). Two issues needed to be recognized in developing this framework. The first issue is that forces were identified at various levels of hierarchy in the strategy implementation environment. In other words, some forces were seen as very specific and detail oriented and others as broader. Second, forces were identified with various magnitudes or strengths. One of the purposes of the higher-level categories was to provide a context in which the forces could be related to each other in terms of hierarchy and magnitude.

A six-step process for making such a framework was created to deal with these two issues:

1. Develop the initial low-level forces. TA2 provided an initial analysis of interviews that assisted in determining primary themes and relationships of concepts. The concepts with the strongest relationships provided an initial working list of forces.

2. Subjectively refine that set of forces. This involved manual review of the interviews, comparing and contrasting the TA2 results. This step ensured that TA2 did not miss something that the author deemed important to the study. In addition, this comparison and contrast step required further re-categorization of factors. Thus, a refined list of forces emerged from this effort.
3. Identify driving and restraining forces on decisions from the interviews. One of the interview questions asked the specific question concerning driving and restraining forces.
4. Return to the interviewees and ask them to rate each force identified in steps 1 and 2 in terms of impact on the strategies on a 5-point Likert scale. In addition, they were asked to provide their judgment as to the overarching 5–10 driving and the overarching 5–10 restraining forces that could serve as "categories" of forces and could subsume other forces.
5. Establish a hierarchy of forces acting within the JTAV environment and use that hierarchy to continually map the lower level forces into the higher-level forces, adding and deleting categories at each level as necessary.
6. Use those results to develop the framework using force field theory as the basic construct.

20.9.3 Data Analysis

The first data analysis step was to specify the initial low-level forces identified in the interviews. That task was accomplished by using TA2. The initial analysis provided a list of 2839 concepts. There thus was a readily apparent need to determine the concepts with the strongest relationships. The preceding results subsequently were sorted based upon the 15 concepts with the highest frequency and any other concept with a semantic weight above 50. This provided a list of 260 forces. The list was reviewed and adjusted to eliminate obvious redundancies or words that were inconsequential (e.g., "many," "year," etc.) resulting in 75 low-level forces.

A manual analysis yielded 20 additional potential forces not included in the original list of 75. The original 75 were the result of a somewhat arbitrary trimming of the complete TA2 list so there naturally was a question of whether the 20 new concepts were part of the original TA2 list. As it turned out, the original list of 2839 concepts included each manually identified force, or a closely related concept. It is interesting to note that words or phrases such as "strategy," "success," "implementation," "timeline," "government," and "windows of opportunity" appear frequently in the interviews. Yet these words without their context do not shed very much light on the inquiry. Consequently, the next step was to analyze the interviews manually searching for context.

Each interview was examined in depth, and forces were identified from specific questions aimed at answering the research question. This step identified a list of forces within a contextual framework, thus providing forces at a higher level of abstraction than that provided by TA2. Interestingly, the 25 interviewees provided a total of 21 separate driving forces. Over half (62%) responded that one of the driving forces was the fact that JTAV was simply "a great idea." The next most popular single response (43%) was the "quality of the contractor support." Fifty-three percent of the respondents indicated that it was important to have some kind of advocacy, whether it was from the customer (warfighters), stakeholders, or merely a vocal advocate.

A total of 31 restraining forces were identified by the 25 interviewees. The most common single restraining force was "parochialism," mentioned by almost half of the interviewees. A closer review of the interviews indicated that all interviewees were talking about the parochialism of the components. In other words, the Army wanted to do JTAV but wanted all of DoD to do it their way. The Navy wanted to do JTAV but wanted the other services to do it their way. As one interviewee put it, "everyone wanted to do it his or her way. The 'not invented here' syndrome was very prevalent across the enterprise. It was without fail the dominant theme."

The fourth step was to return to the interviewees. They were asked to rate each force in terms of impact on a 5-point Likert scale designed as follows:

0 = No opinion
1 = Very weak impact
2 = Weak impact
3 = Moderate impact
4 = Strong impact
5 = Very strong impact

They were also asked to identify the forces that would serve as overarching concepts and encompass most of the other forces. Three forces stood out. "Leadership" was named on 17 surveys, and both the "great idea" and "support" (from the customers, stakeholders, and advocates) were named on 16 surveys. The results for the restraining forces were more diffused than for the driving forces. Three driving forces were mentioned on more surveys than the restraining force with the most mentions (parochialism). "Parochialism" and "change" were the only restraining forces to be on at least 50% of the surveys.

The fifth step was to place the forces in a hierarchy. Otherwise there can be no "higher" order. Three levels of forces have been identified. At the lowest are the individual forces identified via the TA2 analysis and the manual review of the interviews. At the next higher level are the driving and restraining forces identified by the interviewees in response to the direct question concerning driving and restraining forces. At the highest current level are the overarching forces identified by the interviewees at the time they were rating the strength of the forces. The current problem is to develop a fourth level of analysis, the highest order of forces present (see Figure 20.4), through a continuous process of comparing the lower forces with the next higher level by using the higher level topics as categories in which to place the lower level forces.

For example, the Level 4 forces identified by TA2 will be mapped to the Level 3 driving and restraining forces. Level 3 categories will be eliminated or added as necessary depending on the data. The same mapping procedure will be performed between Level 3 and Level 2. Finally, Level 2 categories will be mapped into draft Level 1 categories to be determined by a literature search. Thus the Level 1 categories of forces will be grounded in the literature yet primarily derived from the research.

Vinzant and Vinzant (1996) present an interesting framework for strategy implementation analysis. They posit that successful efforts to implement strategic decisions must address a complex mix of both internal and external factors. They note two primary external factors:

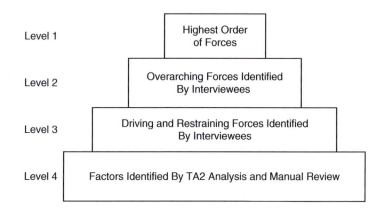

FIGURE 20.4 Hierarchy of forces.

organizational autonomy and stimuli. Organizational autonomy is nothing more than self-directing freedom or independence, while stimuli consist of crises which can produce either threats or opportunities. They also note four primary internal factors: human and behavioral issues, structural and technical factors, prior experience, and process design. Human and behavioral issues include leadership, management style, and organizational culture. Structural and technical factors include the size, design, and infrastructure of the organization. Prior experience primarily refers to experience in planning, budgeting, and other administrative areas. Process design encompasses the issues of who, what, when, and how in the strategic management approach.

The forces proposed by Vinzant and Vinzant, however, differ markedly from the Force Field concept in that the forces do not assume a positive (driving) or negative (restraining) value. Consequently, each of their proposed factors was established as both a driving and restraining force for the purposes of identifying draft Level 1 entities.

The Level 2 forces mapped somewhat neatly into the draft Level 1 categories although two new categories had to be added: *requirements* and *technical knowledge.* "Requirements" was added because Vinzant and Vinzant's categories provided no place for the forces associated with the problem, solution, or the technical requirements of the project. Interviewees were adamant that one of the greatest forces in JTAV's favor was that it was a great idea and potentially solved some serious long-standing logistics problems for DoD. Second, "technical knowledge" was added because Vinzant and Vinzant's categories did not provide a mapping home for contractor support (primarily technical knowledge), for the technical expertise on the DoD team, or for the technology itself.

One of Vinzant and Vinzant's categories (prior experience) was deleted from both the internal and external groups because none of the Level 2 forces mapped to it and the interviewees did not specifically call it out as an important force. This process left 14 total forces, 5 internal driving forces and 5 internal restraining forces and 2 external driving forces and 2 external restraining forces.

Force field theory requires not only that the forces be identified, but also the corresponding magnitudes. These were established using the strengths from the Likert Scale questionnaire, as rated by the interviewees. The average ratings for the Level 3 forces were summed and mapped into their associated Level 2 forces. The same procedure then was used to sum the Level 2 forces that mapped into the Level 1 forces. Therefore, the magnitude of a given Level 1 force is the sum of the Level 3 and Level 2 forces that map to it. The resulting Level 1 driving and restraining forces and their respective strengths, as determined by that method can be seen in Table 20.9. The difference is reflected as a positive number if it favors the driving force and a negative number if it favors the restraining force.

TABLE 20.9
Strength of Level 1 Categories of Forces

Number	Characteristic Force	Driving	Restraining	Difference
1	External: organizational autonomy	45	58	−13
2	External: stimuli	70	84	−14
3	Internal: human/ behavioral	199	141	58
4	Internal: process design	101	81	20
5	Internal: technical knowledge	66	105	−39
6	Internal: requirements	76	46	30
7	Internal: structural	63	69	−6
Total		620	584	36

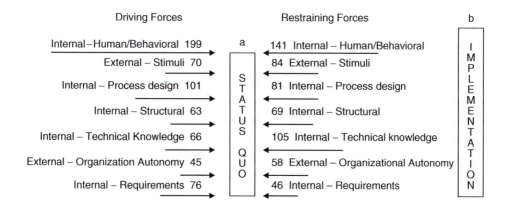

FIGURE 20.5 Level 1 driving and restraining forces in the JTAV environment.

The sixth step was to develop the actual framework using force field theory. Force field theory assists in describing the interrelationships between forces. In Figure 20.5 it is clear that a change, however so slight, in any of the forces would alter the equilibrium of the system and thus also alter the other forces involved. Force field theory may also help to explain why some aspects of a decision are completed successfully and other aspects are not. For example, in Figure 20.5, the driving and restraining forces appear to be equally applied because the status quo appears to move as a single entity.

The diagram is unable to capture the dynamic nature of the force field and the strategy implementation environment. If we allowed those vector arrows to actually push the status quo in the direction in which the force was the strongest (the difference between the forces), it might look like that in Figure 20.6.

Although still a snapshot, Figure 20.6 better represents the fluid nature of decision making. The forces are not equally applied Thus the status quo is at some points closer to success than it is at others. Some aspects of the decision are going well because the forces that drive it are stronger than the restraining forces. Other aspects of the decision are not going as well because the restraining forces are stronger than the driving forces.

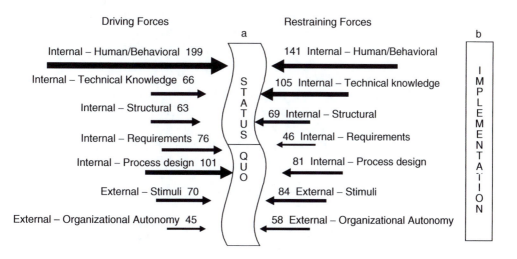

FIGURE 20.6 Effect of level 1 forces on the JTAV status quo.

20.10 FINAL THOUGHTS

As discussed in the beginning, the task set before us was basically an impossibility—to bring about a thorough amalgam of information, corresponding technology (ICT), and decision making. Many questions are left to be addressed (for basic background, see Heller, 1998). For example: Who decides? Who has responsibility (but perhaps no authority) for decisions? What is the hierarchy of decision makers? When to decide? Where to decide? How to decide? What decisions that have been made need to be "unmade" and/or "remade"?

Insofar as "information" is concerned, we have barely touched on such issues as lack of information, biased information, misinformation, and disinformation. All of these issues could have a substantial impact on some kinds of decisions.

A look at ICT shows, as an illustration, that the very important topic of the automation of decisions and decision making has not been addressed directly. The "Knowledge-Based Aircraft Carrier" endeavor and the "Advanced Logistics Project" both were examples of efforts to reduce manpower by automating as much of the related decision making as possible. But even on a smaller, more personal scale—say with washing machines and fire alarms—the grand automation of decision making becomes readily apparent.

The JTAV case study offers some interesting insights concerning the factors in decision making in the implementation of strategies. First, there are a large number of factors that have effects and serve as forces on decisions. Some of those factors are drivers toward a successful decision, and some factors serve as restrainers. Possibly the most interesting insight is that a single force can serve as both a driver and restrainer.

The study also underscores the difficulties in making a decision. One of the factors that makes decision making so difficult is an uncertain future. The future cannot be determined with certainty—until it is the past—and even then the truthfulness of the account is sometimes called into question. All actions in the future take place in an atmosphere of uncertainty—what Clausewitz (von Ghyczycgi, von Oetinger, and Bassford, 2001) referred to as the "fog of war." One of the key steps in decision making is to reduce that uncertainty as much as possible by gathering information. Regardless of the amount of information we gather, however, it is impossible to eliminate uncertainty from the future, thus all future actions will be based on incomplete, inaccurate or even contradictory information. This description of the future is a postmodern perspective (Powell 1998), yet the underlying premise of decision making is a classic rational idea. It is pure cause and effect; if decision A is pursued, event X should happen. Decision making is an attempt to impose a rational process on a non-rational environment—an apparent paradox.

In a related vein, decision making is integrative in nature. The formulation of decisions integrates divergent ideas, disparate concepts, and differing perspectives. The implementation of those decisions integrates money, processes, human nature, problems and solutions. This integrative nature of decision making is one of the reasons it has been so difficult for scholars to get a clear handle on a single foundational theory.

Another insight from the JTAV case is the fact that a decision can have serious problems yet still continues toward success. Figure 20.6 is an excellent example of this idea. While there are some significant issues that may be holding a decision back in some areas, there may also be others that are driving it to success. When viewed from a certain perspective the decision may appear to be doomed to failure, but when viewed from another perspective, the decision may be in relative good health.

Finally, the JTAV case study has confirmed that much like in human nature, a person's perspective on decision making is highly dependent on the job a person has and the roles he or she plays. The JTAV Resource Manager saw the decisions in terms of getting and managing more money. The software engineers saw JTAV decisions in terms of software releases. The functional analysts saw JTAV decisions in terms of improving the supply, transportation, and distribution processes. The warfighters saw the JTAV decisions in terms of increased combat capability.

Much of the effort in this chapter has been directed at "quantity" issues, which more often are being seen as centrally important. ICT has allowed for the expansion of the number of decisions, decision makers, information packets, and available technologies. As we mentioned earlier, in the early 1980s NSA could intercept and analyze practically all telephone and digital messages going in and out of the U.S. Now, despite all attempts to create the world's fastest computers, that is basically impossible. As Lt. Gen. Hayden, NSA's Director has been quoted as saying (Bamford, 2001):

"Forty years ago there were 5000 stand alone computers, no fax machines, and not one cellular phone. Today there are over 180 million computers — most of them networked. There are roughly 14 million fax machines and 40 million cell phones, and those numbers continue to grow. The telecommunications industry is making a $1 trillion investment to encircle the world in millions of miles of high bandwidth fiber-optic cable." (647)

There is no way that any one agency can keep up. The general continues by saying "the NSA is lagging behind."

And so it is for each of us. All the information pertinent to any one decision usually is beyond our individual capabilities to retrieve and analyze. The conclusion seems to be that we need to learn how to adapt more quickly as decision making situations diverge from the expected but ill-informed paths.

ACKNOWLEDGEMENTS

Some of the material in this chapter appeared in the Souvenirs (informal proceedings) for the Eighth and Ninth International Conferences (2002 and 2004) of The Chartered Institute of Logistics and Transport (India). The first author would like to express his appreciation to the organizer, Mr. N. M. Balasubrahmanyam, for the opportunity to participate in these events.

We would also like to acknowledge that the quote from p. 647 of Bamford (2002) originally was from a speech by Lt. Gen. Michael V. Hayden, USAF, Director, National Security Agency, Address to the Kennedy Political Union of the American University, 17 February 2000.

REFERENCES

About.com. Gary Powers and the U-2 incident: Demise of the Paris summit, http://americanhistory.about.com/library/weekly/aa061801a.htm (accessed June 5, 2006).

Area51ZONE: U-2 spyplane, http://www.area51zone.com/aircraft/u2.shtml (accessed June 5, 2006).

Argyres, N. and McGahan, A., An interview with Michael Porter, *The Academy of Management Executive*, 16, 43–52, 2002.

Bamford, J., *The Puzzle Palace: A Report on NSA, America's Most Secret Agency*, Houghton Mifflin, Boston, 1982.

Bamford, J., *Body of Secrets: Anatomy of the Ultra-Secret National Security Agency: From the Cold War through the Dawn of a New Century*, Doubleday, New York, 2001, http://history.sandiego.edu/gen/20th/nsa.html (accessed September 5, 2004).

Bear, G., *Vitals*, Ballantine Books, New York, 2002.

Ben-Jacob, E., http://star.tau.ac.il/~inon/baccyber0.html (accessed September 5, 2004, site now discontinued).

Birdsall, I., It seemed like a good idea at the time: The forces affecting implementation of strategies for an information technology project in the Department of Defense. Ph.D. diss., Virginia Polytechnic Institute and State University, 2004.

Brown, T. A., *Genomes 2*, 2nd ed., Wiley, Oxford, 2002.

ClickZ News, http://www.clickz.com/news/article.php/3313761 (accessed June 5, 2006).

Creswell, J., *Research Design: Qualitative and Quantitative Approaches*, Sage Publications, Thousand Oaks, 1994.

Davenport, T. H. and Prusak, L., *Working Knowledge: How Organizations Manage What They Know*, Harvard Business School Press, Cambridge, 2000.

Dickey, J. W., Cyberquest, http://www.cpap.vt.edu/cyberquest/products/qcq.htm (accessed June 5, 2006).

Dickey, J. W., QCQ2: The next version of an analytic discovery too, In *CUPUM '99: Computers in Urban Planning and Management on the Edge of the Millennium*, Rizzi, P., Ed., FrancoAngeli, 76 and attached CD-ROM, Milan, 1999.

Ellul, J., *The Technological Society*, Knopf, New York, 1964.

Google corporate information, http://www.google.com/corporate/history.html (accessed June 5, 2006).

Hall, P. and Pfeiffer, U., *Urban future 21: A Global Agenda for Twenty-first Century Cities*, Spon, London, 2000.

Heidegger, M., *The Question Concerning Technology*, Harper Colophon, New York, 1977.

Heller, R., *Making Decisions*, DK Publishing, New York, 1998.

Kurzweil, R., *The Age of Spiritual Machines*, Viking, New York, 1999.

Lewin, K., In *Field Theory in Social Science: Selected Theoretical Papers*, Cartwright, D., Ed., Harper & Row, New York, 1951.

Lo, F.-C. and Marcotullio, P. J., Eds., *Globalization and the Sustainability of Cities in the Asia-Pacific Region*, United Nations University Press, Tokyo, 2002.

Marrow, A. F., *The Practical Theorist: The Life and Work of Kurt Lewin*, Basic Books, New York, 1969.

Megaputer Intelligence, http://www.megaputer.com (accessed June 5, 2006).

Miles, M. and Huberman, A., *Qualitative Data Analysis: An Expanded Sourcebook*, Sage, Thousand Oaks, 1994.

Porter, M., *Competitive Strategy: Techniques for Analyzing Industries and Competitors*, The Free Press, New York, 1980.

Powell, J., *Postmodernism*, Writers and Readers, New York, 1998.

RxList, http://www.rxlist.com (accessed June 5, 2006).

Shapiro, J. A. and Dworkin, M., *Bacteria as Multicellular Organisms*, Oxford University Press, New York, 1997.

Sodhi, J. and Sodhi, P., *IT Project Management Handbook*, Management Concepts, Vienna, VA, 2001.

Tesch, R., *Qualitative Research: Analytic Types and Software Tools*, Falmer, New York, 1990.

Buckinghamshire and Milton Keynes Biodiversity Action Plan 2000–2010. UKBAP, http://www.ukbap.org.uk/asp/lbap.aspx?ID = 448 (accessed June 5, 2006).

UK Biodiversity Action Plan, UKBAP, http://www.ukbap.org.uk/ (accessed June 5, 2006).

University of California, Berkley, *How Much Information?*, University of California, Berkeley, School of Information Management and Systems Publications, Berkeley, 2003.

Vinzant, D. and Vinzant, J., Strategy and organizational capacity: Finding a fit, *Public Productivity and Management Review*, 20, 139–157, 1996.

Virginia Department of Social Services, FSP policy manual, http://www.dss.state.va.us/benefit/fsmanual.cgi (accessed June 5, 2006).

Von Ghyczycgi, T., von Oetinger, B., and Bassford, C., *Clausewitz on Strategy*, Wiley, New York, 2001.

Webster-Merriam, *Webster's New World Dictionary*, Webster-Merriam, New York, 1987.

21 Decision Making Models Used in E-Government Projects: Evidence from Turkey

Mete Yıldız

CONTENTS

21.1   Introduction...395
21.2   E-Government...397
21.3   A Study of E-Government Projects in Turkey...398
21.4   Models of Decision Making in E-Government Projects................................400
21.5   Cultural Factors in E-Government Decision Making...................................403
21.6   Factors that Influence Decision Making: A Force Field of Competing Forces...............405
21.7   Actors in Decision Making...408
          21.7.1   Vendors: Vendor Push...409
          21.7.2   Supra-National Organizations 410
21.8   Nature of Decision Making: The Role of Politics and Policy Networks.........411
21.9   Summary and Conclusions...412
References..414

21.1 INTRODUCTION

This chapter discusses the topic of e-government with illustrations from Turkish public administration. Turkey is selected as a case because e-government decision making research on developing countries such as Turkey is very rare, and these countries do not have large amounts of monetary or human resources to commit to ensuring the successful planning and implementation of e-government applications. Careful analyses of the decision making processes behind these projects is essential to making sure that resources are spent for projects with the highest priority, previous mistakes are not repeated, and gains are maximized, while minimizing resources spent.

Technology, specifically information and communication technologies[*] (ICTs), have penetrated every aspect of our lives and nearly every academic discipline. Public administration is no

---

[*] The use of "information and communication technology" (ICT) over "information technology" (IT) in this chapter is a deliberate choice. How the information is used for communication among various stakeholders in government operations is as important as how information is collected, stored, and shared among government agencies.

exception. For its early students, technology[*] use in government was a peripheral, rather than a core management function. The main objectives of technology use in government were to enhance the managerial effectiveness of public administrators and increase government productivity. Taylor's scientific management movement is a perfect example of this orientation (Waldo, 1955, 18–19). Technology was also seen as a means of managing the limitations of bounded rationality and providing the infrastructure for better decision making (Simon, 1976, 286). Perrow (1967) argued that technology is an important determinant of the structure and strategy of the organizations that use it.

Until the introduction of the Internet and widespread use of personal computers, the main use of technology in government organizations was the automation of mass transactions, such as financial transactions, using mainframe computers (Schelin, 2003, 121). ICTs were used for the automation of backroom operations and improvement of the efficiency of clerical activities (Zuboff, 1988). Ordinary government employees were not using ICTs in their regular daily routines. The resulting lack of connectedness between the technology departments and the other departments of the organization was, in particular, isolating government ICT professionals from functional and executive oversight (Holden, 2003, 56).

The proliferation of the use of personal computers in the 1980s provided many public administrators with a personal information technology system, and thus opened a new period of ICT use in government. At this point, technology management began to be decentralized in government agencies. Along with decentralization came the realization that ICT issues should be integrated into the core functions of government.

It can be argued that three research studies, and the subsequent publications, influenced public administration thinking on and the applications of the systematic integration of technology with governmental and administrative functions in the United States. The first is the URBIS (Urban Information Systems) project, which was conducted from 1973 to 1978 at the University of California, Irvine by a multidisciplinary team. This was the "first large, systematic, empirical study to focus specifically on policy and outcomes related to computer use in complex service organizations" (King, 2004, 97). It uncovered the "continuing social and political processes in which the technology is constrained—somewhat controlled and shaped—by its environment" (Danziger, Dutton, Kling, and Kraemer, 1982, 7). These researchers adopted an open systems theory perspective of technology and its environment, and emphasized the continuous interaction between government organizations and their internal and external environments (8). They argued, "computing will reinforce the power and influence of those actors and groups who already have the most resources and power in the organization" (18).

The National Association of Schools of Public Affairs and Administration (NASPAA) committee conducted another important study in 1985. The committee recommended that computing should be a main skill taught in Master of Public Administration programs (Northrop, 2003, 2). Bozeman and Bretschneider (1986) argued in their seminal article, published in the *Public Administration Review*, that technology was transforming the government, and that more academic attention had to be paid to this area. Even then, one had to wait for the widespread use of the Internet and the Web for the emergence of a full-fledged e-government concept. Before the use of the Internet and the Web, ICT use in government was primarily internal and managerial (Ho, 2002).

Together with the introduction of the World Wide Web in the 1990s, the "reinventing government" movement (Osborne and Gaebler, 1992) and the *National Performance Review* (1993) influenced the incorporation of ICT into government reform. The enactment of some very important legislation during this decade supported the reform movement and the use of ICT in government (Schelin, 2003, 122–123). The 1995 amendment of the 1980 Paperwork Reduction Act (PRA)

---

[*] The concept of "technology" is used rather loosely here. In addition to the meaning of "machines and sophisticated devices," technology also means the study of techniques or tasks. (Perrow, 1979, 162)

provided guidelines for government ICT investments and encouraged more cross-agency infor-mation sharing. The 1996 Electronic Freedom of Information Act (EFOIA) clarified the rules for the issuing of and public access to the government electronic records. The 1996 Personal Respon-sibility and Work Opportunity Reconciliation Act (PRWORA) mandated that social services agencies test the promise of e-government applications on the field at intergovernmental levels. The 1996 Clinger-Cohen Act created the position of Chief Information Officer in every agency, and encouraged the integration of ICT into the strategic planning process. All of these legislative efforts culminated in the enactment of the 2001 E-Government Act, which provided both the organiz-ational and financial infrastructure of widespread e-government applications (124).

The tragic events of September 11, 2001 increased the utilization of technology, ranging from the centralization and consolidation of government databases to the use of emerging technologies, such as biometrics, in efforts against terrorism.

21.2 E-GOVERNMENT

The term *electronic government*, or *e-government*, has recently become popular in public adminis-tration, and is used in reference to the applications of ICTs in government functions. In a joint report by the American Society for Public Administration (ASPA) and the United Nations, e-government is defined as "utilizing the Internet and the World-Wide-Web for delivering government information and services to citizens" (American Society for Public Administration (ASPA), and United Nations, 2002, 1). The term also includes other ICTs, such as "databases, networking, discussion support, multimedia, automation, tracking and tracing, and personal identification technologies" (Jaeger, 2003, 323). Fountain (2001) prefers to call e-government "digital government" or "virtual state":

> Digital government … is a government that is organized increasingly in terms of virtual agencies, cross-agency and public-private networks whose structure and capacity depend on the Internet and web. … The virtual agency, following the web portal model used in the economy, is organized by client. (4)

There is a need for a more decision making oriented research on e-government. E-government research can roughly be divided into three groups as output, outcome and process-oriented studies. As the titles suggest in Table 21.1, output and outcome-oriented e-government studies focus on a particular point in the development of e-government projects. They examine the output of e-government efforts, the artifacts, such as websites and online government services. Outcome oriented studies, on the other hand, explain which government performance indicator (i.e., cost, transparency, efficiency) is improved as a result of a particular e-government effort. The limited focus of these two types of studies is generally accompanied by the purpose of determining best practices for benchmarking. They examine e-government efforts through the eyes of a scientific observer who examines the products of e-government efforts (i.e., websites, online services) exter-nally and typically through secondary data. The objective is to find successful cases to emulate. Such external examination is a deductive, outside-in approach (Agranoff, 2004). These studies are by and large exploratory and descriptive. They do not tell us what is happening inside the black box of e-government.

Understanding the decision making models require the comprehension of e-government processes, in addition to the outputs and outcomes. Study of e-government processes is not a new type of research. The URBIS (Urban Information Systems) project conducted in 1970s at the University of California, Irvine produced some early process-oriented research (Danziger et al., 1982). More recently, Bellamy and Taylor (1998) and Fountain (2001) produced process-oriented studies. However, generally speaking, output and outcome-oriented research has dominated the e-government literature.

Process-oriented studies typically use primary data provided by extensive fieldwork. They use data collection methods such as interviews, participant observation and archival analysis to

TABLE 21.1
A New Categorization of E-government Research

	Orientation		
Dimensions	Output	Outcome	Process
Focus	Websites Online government services Front-office	How does an e-government application affect a certain variable, such as trust, accountability, transparency, corruption, government effectiveness, users perceptions of service quality	Processes of decision making, planning, implementation Back-office
Method	Content analysis Determining best practices Benchmarking Surveys Case studies Regression analysis	Content analysis Determining best practices Benchmarking Surveys Case studies	Interviews Archival analysis Discourse analysis Case studies
Data	Primary and secondary	Primary and secondary	Primary
Mode of Analysis	Outside-in, deductive	Outside-in, deductive	Inside-out, inductive
Outcome	Descriptive, exploratory	Descriptive, exploratory	Theory generation, explanatory
Examples	Bauer and Scharl, 2000; Cohen and Eimicke, 2001; Hernon, 1998; McNeal; Tolbert, Mossberger and Dotterweich, 2003; Stowers, 1999; West, 2004	Cullen and Houghton, 2000; Gant and Gant, 2002; Heeks, 1999; Hwang, Choi and Myoung, 1999; La Porte, De Jong and Demchak, 1999; Mahmood, 2004; Thomas and Streib, 2003; Torres, Pina and Acerete, 2005	Bellamy and Taylor, 1998; Fountain, 2001; Jonas, 2000; Yıldız, 2004

Source: From Yıldız, M. Peeking into the Black Box of E-Government Policy Making: Evidence from Turkey, Unpublished
doctoral dissertation, Indiana University, Bloomington, 195, 2004.

understand and explain the e-government processes and generate theory. One way is to ask people
who work for e-government projects to tell their stories to a researcher. The researcher transforms
their words into abstract concepts through systematic data gathering and analysis and triangulation.
This is an inductive, or "inside-out," process: "a spy-like strategy of getting inside the organization ...
to understand how the forces of operation transform 'inputs' into 'outputs'" (Agranoff, 2004, 3).
Among the examples cited in Table 21.1, mine (Yıldız, 2004) is an example I will discuss in some
detail, in the following section.

21.3 A STUDY OF E-GOVERNMENT PROJECTS IN TURKEY

Careful analyses of the decision making processes behind e-government projects are essential to
make sure that resources are spent appropriately, previous mistakes are not repeated, and costs are
minimized while gains are maximized. As Kraemer and Perry (1999) aptly state:

> In order to develop a more complete and grounded understanding of changes in computing in
> organizations, it will be necessary to identify the mechanisms, and not merely the stages, integral to
> the evolution of computing in public organizations. (14)

Only when the processes of decision making are understood properly, can one assess
e-government initiatives and modify them if necessary. Also, the central issues in e-government

are about democracy, not about economic efficiency; who makes the decisions in e-government development is important.

> Cost savings and the benefits of increased access to information and services … represent only a small subset of the promise of digital government. More important, however, is public dialogue about how digital government will be designed and implemented. The central issues are democratic in nature, rather than simply economic. … How will reliance on the public sector to design, implementation and management of digital government affect the traditional boundaries of between what is public and private? [There are] … pressing questions that move discussion of digital government beyond its economic importance to its broader implications for democracy. (Fountain, 2001, 247)

The main objective of my study was to understand what kind of decision making process decision makers use in e-government projects: rational (Allison, 1971, 10–14), incremental (Lindblom, 1959; Lindblom, 1979), or garbage-can model (Cohen, March, and Olsen, 1972), or some combination of these models. Before explaining the research design, let us review these decision making models briefly.

Lindblom's (1959) classic article describes the incremental, pluralist policy analysis method in contrast to a rational-comprehensive method. Lindblom begins with introducing two models of policy analysis. The first is a set of successive comparisons, which he calls "branch method." The second is the rational-comprehensive model that he names "root method."

In the rational-comprehensive "root" method, policy analysts first clarify values and the desired ends, and then find the most appropriate means to desired ends by taking into consideration all the relevant information. Thus, the test of good policy is to find the most appropriate means to desired ends. The analysis is comprehensive because every important factor is supposed to be taken into account. As a consequence, the policy analysts rely heavily on the theory. Lindblom asserts that this ideal root method—because of the bounded rationality of men, economic, political and time constraints—is not used in making the policy decisions. Moreover, the political systems of the democratic regimes encourage a step-by-step, incremental change process each time there are small variations from the status quo.

In the branch method, on the other hand, selection of means and ends are closely intertwined. Since means and ends are not distinct, means-end analysis is not fruitful. Branch method users assume that the test of good policy is the agreement on the policy itself instead of agreeing on the most appropriate means. Thus, administrators first decide on the policy, and then clarify the objectives. In this method, there is a systematic neglect of important values, potential policies and possible policy outcomes for the sake of reducing the amount of information down to humanly manageable limits. In this method, a succession of comparisons greatly reduces or eliminates the reliance of theory.

In conclusion, Lindblom argues that in spite of all the claims to the contrary, nearly all policy decisions are made by the branch method. This is because branch method is the only method which can deal with complex problems given the bounded rationality of men. He argues that the incremental model is also compatible with the democratic political systems with its limitation of radical change and the resulting chaos. The most important shortcoming of the incremental model, he argues, such as the systematic neglect of important values, potential policies and possible policy outcomes, are automatically solved by the pluralist nature of the political system which assigns "watchdogs" for nearly all interests.

Finally, Cohen, March, and Olsen's (1972) "garbage-can model of organizational choice" deals with the problem of organizational survival, as organizations deal with complex, even intractable and wicked problems—problems with only temporary and imperfect solutions (Harmon and Mayer, 1986, 9; Rittel and Webber, 1973)—that cut across agencies vertically and horizontally (Brown and Brudney, 2001, 33) within unpredictable political, economic and social environments. The model questions the assumption of coherent, rational and intentional structures of organizational decisions. The authors argue that, contrary to conventional wisdom, organizational goals are not consistent and well-defined; the processes to achieve these goals are not well-understood by the organizational members; and finally, participation in organizational decision making is not systematic to say the least. Most importantly, different components of the decision making process—problems, solutions and choices—do not necessarily follow each other in a linear fashion (such as defining a problem, seeking alternative solutions for it, choosing one solution over the others depending on its merits and implementing that solution), but rather a chaotic decision making process in which solutions and problems are dumped into "garbage-cans" by organizational participants, and then are matched/coupled under suitable conditions. In short, organizations are defined as "organized anarchies," a "collection of choices looking for problems, issues and feelings looking for decision situations in which they might be aired, solutions looking for issues to which they might be the answer, and decision makers looking for work" (Cohen et al., 1972, 2).

A major portion of the findings presented in this chapter comes from the study of seven e-government projects in the Republic of Turkey (see Table 21.2). The information about seven e-government cases were collected by conducting 50 in-depth interviews with project managers from government agencies, members of ICT vendor firms, non-governmental agency representatives, and ICT experts in the media. Interview findings were triangulated by conducting archival analyses of project documents and content analyses of the Turkish media's coverage of these projects. It was determined that these were seven of the most important e-government projects in Turkey. They represent a mix of different approaches and outcomes. The similarities and differences of these projects are summarized in Table 21.3.

21.4 MODELS OF DECISION MAKING IN E-GOVERNMENT PROJECTS

Which decision making models do e-government projects follow? Do they operate according to rational, incremental, or garbage-can models, or some combination of them? To answer these questions, one needs to analyze carefully the decisions made by important actors during the various stages of the e-government projects: emergence, agenda-setting, and policy formulation.

In the seven cases I studied in Turkey, in the agenda setting stage, the attributes of the garbage-can model were apparent. According to this model, problems, solutions and political receptivity to the proposed solutions (suitable political climates) are coupled when policy windows open (Kingdon, 1990). For example, in Local-Net, Accountancy-Net, Population-Net, and Foreign-Net projects, enterprising public administrators waited for the right time to promote their ideas by presenting a problem for the solutions that these agencies had in their possession for some time.

In Local-Net, the opportunity presented itself as funding from the State Planning Organization (SPO) became available. The Local-Net project management group also made a strategic decision by temporarily integrating the members of a small private ICT firm to its organizational structure as independent contractors. This structural arrangement and the use of open source software—thus, not paying any money for software licenses—enabled the Local-Net team to cut costs dramatically. In the Foreign-Net project, an enterprising public administrator, who later became the project manager, combined his continuing interest and accumulating experiences regarding ICT in diplomatic posts with the efforts of a reform-oriented group of people in the ministry. They found support in the higher echelons of the ministry, which was critically important for their success. The Population-Net project was first introduced in early 1970s. The lack of monetary resources and, more importantly, that of sufficient levels of technological capability allowed only little progress for the following two decades. A window of opportunity opened when World Bank funding became available in 1996. Finally, in Accountancy-Net, the project manager coupled his solution with a problem, as he used some available agency funds to launch a pilot project. The skillful use of the media and the strategic decision to implement the pilot project in the hometown of the minister provided the needed political support and created the window of opportunity for the project. It can be argued that different factors opened the windows of opportunity for each of the four projects.

TABLE 21.2
Sample E-Government Projects

Nickname[a]	Project Title	Description	Importance
Accountancy-Net	SAY2000i (National Public Accountancy Network)	Daily online control of public financial management	Control of public finance, fiscal discipline, less corruption, better use of government resources
Foreign-Net	Ministry of Foreign Affairs Network	Paperless transactions and information sharing throughout the ministry	Paperless Transactions, Network management
Justice-Net	UYAP (National Judicial Network Project)	Integrate all the courts and other organizations in the judicial system in Turkey and ease the transfer of judicial information among them.	Streamlined, more efficient and transparent judicial system, working better, faster and cheaper
Local-Net	YERELNET (Local Government Network)	Provide a data-sharing and discussion forum for Turkish local governments	Encourages better informed and coordinated local governments by disseminating information and encouraging transparency
Pension-Net	EMEKLI SANDIGI (Auditing of Health Benefits Project)	Centralizes online patient data for retired bureaucrats and controls the transactions at hospitals, pharmacies and opticians by running them through a database	Determines eligibility of individuals for health benefits and prescription, eliminates human error in the prescription process and prevents fraudulent use of the health benefit system
Population-Net	MERNIS (Ministry of Interior Centralized Population Management System)	Centralized Population Management System	Creates a central database of all population information, centralizes and automates all demographic information
Tax-Net	VEDOP (Automation Project of Turkish Tax Offices)	Improvement of tax collection and elimination of tax evasion	Better control of the tax system

[a] The cases are represented with nicknames in English to make it easier for the reader to recognize them when they are mentioned hereafter in the text.
Source: From Yıldız, M., Peeking into the Black Box of E-Government Policy Making: Evidence from Turkey, Unpublished Doctoral Dissertation, Indiana University, Bloomington, 3, 2004.

The garbage-can model helps explain the processes of agenda setting. Incremental models are more explanatory in the following stage. Once the project is initiated and placed on the public agenda, policies are formulated and day-to-day operational decisions are made incrementally. This change of models from garbage-can to incremental model in the policy formulation processes is illustrated below with examples from the projects studied and the reasons why the decision making process in the implementation of e-government projects is incremental.

I should mention that most of the e-government projects studied were the last stages of earlier technical modernization efforts. For example, in Foreign-Net, Population-Net, and Tax-Net

TABLE 21.3
Categories Across Cases

	Accountancy-Net	Foreign-Net	Justice-Net	Local-Net	Pension-Net	Population-Net	Tax-Net
Level	National & Local	National & Int'l	National & Local	Local	National & Local	National & Local	National & Local
Funding	Domestic (WB paid for the consultant)	Domestic & UNDP	Domestic	Domestic	Domestic	Domestic (WB paid for the consultant)	Domestic + WB
Software	Open-source (in part)	Proprietary	Proprietary	Open-source	Proprietary	Proprietary	Proprietary
Technical Support	Partly Outsourced	Partly Outsourced	Outsourced	In-House, contracted in	Partly Outsourced	Outsourced	Mostly outsourced
Decision-Support Systems	Being planned	Yes	Yes	Being planned	Yes	Yes	Yes
Paperless Office/ Document Mgmt. System?	No	Yes	No	No	No	No	No
Databank/ base	Yes	Yes	Yes, Document management system	Yes	Yes	Yes	Yes
Internet/Intranet	Both	Both	Both	Internet only	Both	Both	Both
Type	G2G	G2G, G2B, G2C	G2G, G2C	G2G, G2C, G2B	G2G, G2C, G2B	G2G, G2C	G2C, G2G, G2B
Began	1998	Circa, 1993 (PO-DMS) Late, 1990s (VE) 1999–2000 (pilot)	1999	1998	1994	1972	1995 (Earlier automation projects began in 1985)
Completed	2001	June 2001 2003	2005–2006?	2001, ongoing	2002	2003	2003?

Source: Revised from Yıldız, M., Peeking into the Black Box of E-Government Policy Making: Evidence from Turkey, Unpublished Doctoral Dissertation, Indiana University, Bloomington, 60, 2004.

projects, top managers of the agencies had been discussing technological modernization plans for at least a decade. However, due to the lack of entrepreneurial project managers, money, and most importantly technical means, limited progress had been made before the official starts of the projects in the late 1990s. The availability and increasing popularity of the Internet, along with the force field of competing forces[*] paved the way to the successful implementations of these projects.

Political uncertainties made the project managers progress only step-by-step. Turkey was governed by several coalition governments in the 1990s. This succession of governments was not conducive to creating a stable political and economic environment for the country, especially in the second half of the decade. Political support and monetary resources could not be secured for extended periods of time. Therefore, the best strategy for an e-government project manager was to use the resources when they were available. Project managers decided to implement the next step of the project instead of trying to accumulate the necessary amounts of monetary and political resources to finish the project completely.

There was also economic instability in the country in the 1990s. The closure of the oil pipeline coming from Iraq in 1991, after the first Gulf War, had devastating effects on the Turkish economy. At the same time, a strengthening Kurdish separatist movement in South-Eastern Turkey required a considerable increase in military spending. The frequent economic crises (in 1995, 1999, and 2001), together with the high levels of inflation and increasing foreign and domestic debt, further worsened the economy. In such an environment of high economic uncertainty and no central/national top-down project planning, incremental decision making made sense to e-government project managers. The successes of the pilot projects were critical for the successes of the following stages. In personal interviews, vendor firm representatives argued that showing the return of the investment for the e-government project in increments/steps was highly effective in persuading the bureaucrats to take the risk of accepting the projects' implementation. In other words, before implementing the next step in a project, bureaucrats wanted to learn which benefits would be produced by this step beforehand.

The models of decision making help us understand the black-box of e-government development process. They make visible the highly political nature of decision making with multiple competing stakeholders, who try to achieve different goals with the skillful use of tools such as the media and policy networks. The use of garbage-can model, for example, showcases the randomness inherent in the development of e-government projects. It becomes clear that an e-government project might have evolved towards a completely different direction if a window of opportunity—such as availability of a World Bank loan—had not been opened, or if the project manager had not been an enterprising public administrator who used the media to get the support of the politicians for a given project. Although agenda setting stage is dominated by the garbage-can model, policy formulation stage conforms to the incremental decision making model due to the impact of political and economic instability coupled with the rapid pace of change in technology.

21.5 CULTURAL FACTORS IN E-GOVERNMENT DECISION MAKING

Turkish administrative culture is a popular topic in academic studies. Caldwell (1968) criticized the negative aspects of Turkish administration, such as the politics of expediency, high levels of centralization and administrative control, little delegation of authority, lack of detailed rational planning, slow and inefficient decision making processes, inclination to secrecy, and lack of coordination. Aldemir, Albak, and Ozmen (2003) argued that Turkish work mentality has a

---

[*] Within the context of e-government, the concept of "force field of competing forces" is coined by Yıldız (2004, 127–131) to explain the emergence of e-government projects and the way(s) these projects are placed on the government's decision agenda. The main argument is that in a given project, there are multiple and competing forces that initiate a project and help it to get on the decision agenda. A detailed explanation of the concept is presented in the next sections of this chapter.

dilemmatic nature; historically, it has been a combination of Western-oriented characteristics (professional and rational work mentality) and indigenous ones (status-oriented, mystical and Hippocratic work mentality). In his attempt to construct a T (Turkish) model of management culture, Sargut (2001, 219–235) listed collectivism (versus individualism), strong leadership, determinism, low levels of tolerance for risk, high levels of resistance to change, and low levels of synergy and interpersonal trust, among other factors.

Cultural factors both facilitate and inhibit e-government decision making. The results of my study shows that the cultural factors that shape the e-government development in Turkey are (1) the value attributed to strong leadership, (2) secretive bureaucratic culture, and (3) fascination with technology. Some environmental factors that interact with these cultural factors are the generation gap between old and young civil servants and the values that government reform movements introduce to the bureaucratic culture. The following discussion explains these cultural and environmental factors in detail.

The first cultural factor that has a significant impact on e-government decision making is the value attributed to strong leadership. Strong leadership is perceived to be a crucial factor in the success of e-government projects. Project leaders/managers need to have internal and external organizational and political skills. The internal skills of organizing and motivating project teams, providing a shared vision for the project, and having knowledge and experience of technology are attributed to strong project leaders. The external skills of strong leaders are used for securing political support from organizational leaders or politicians (and thus securing funding), managing conflict with other departments and organizations, and persuading less technically competent stakeholders of the project that the outcome of the project will not threaten their statuses.

Strong leadership has its drawbacks. First, there is the risk of leaders slowing down project development due to their lack of knowledge of modern management concepts and latest technology. Typically leaders in public organizations do not want to delegate their powers to more technically knowledgeable staff, and thus they slow down the process. Second, too much dependence on leaders causes lack of institutionalization, which in turn causes delays in project implementation when managerial or technical leadership change. Such changes are quite common, particularly in times of political and economic instability, and they contribute to the incremental nature of the decision making and planning processes.

The second cultural factor that affects e-government decision making in Turkey is the secretive bureaucratic culture. The secretive culture causes lack of information sharing between projects, and thus it leads to poor project planning, coordination and integration, and turf wars between departments and agencies. Such a cultural trait has its roots in the Turkish-Ottoman history (Caldwell, 1968; Aldemir et al., 2003, 24), and it is perpetuated by the fears of modern-day public administrators. They fear that e-government projects will monitor their works and assess their job performances more closely, and thus make them more accountable and threaten their statuses. Such a cultural environment limits the applicability of rational planning and decision making models. Politicians and project managers of many e-government projects state that replacing this traditional secretive government culture with a citizen-centered, entrepreneurial culture as one of their most important objectives.

The third cultural factor is the fascination with technology. This factor has two dimensions. First, public administrators' fascination with technology is symbolic to an extent: They want to use cutting edge technology for its sake (i.e., because they perceive technology as a novelty, a "cool thing" to have). Second, Turkish people are enthusiastic and interested in new technologies. Project managers use this to justify the fairly large investments for e-government projects, even when there is a limited demand for a specific project. The underlying argument is that although there is not a significant demand for online government information and services in Turkey, "if you build it, they (the users of the services) will come." Providing supply before there is an adequate level of demand makes it difficult for planners and decision makers to use rational processes in their projects, and encourages an incremental, "plan/decide-as-you-go" model, or a garbage-can model.

The environmental factors that interact with the above-mentioned cultural factors are the generation gap between old and young civil servants and the values that government reform movements introduce to the bureaucratic culture. There is a generation gap between the "type-writer" and "personal computer" users. In a way, the frictions between the generations have been aggravated by the recent efforts to replace the secretive bureaucratic culture of the past with a more open culture—a culture of more information sharing, better coordination and planning, more transparency in government operations, and a more citizen-centered mentality. The older generation's cautionary attitude creates a process of incremental decision making and planning. Their lack of knowledge about technology creates an environment for garbage-can decision making processes.

The values that government reform movements introduced to the bureaucratic culture required a shift in the Turkish administrative practice and culture. These new values encourage the use of strategic planning, process reengineering, performance management, and better decision making via electronic decision making tools such as management information systems; they also require transparency and accountability. The reforms aimed to minimize the effect of the secretive culture, institutionalize e-government development (rather than the development being leader-driven), and resolve the generation gaps and resultant clashes. They also aimed to use the fascination of bureaucrats and citizens with technology to transform the way government does business with its citizens and other actors, such as businesses and civil society organizations. The implementation of these new values increases the probability of the use of rational models in planning and decision making.

21.6 FACTORS THAT INFLUENCE DECISION MAKING: A FORCE FIELD OF COMPETING FORCES

The variables that determine the emergence of e-government projects and the process of agenda setting form a force field of competing forces. The concept of "force field of competing forces" was developed by Kurt Lewin (1951). In his "field theory," Lewin describes a field as "the totality of coexisting facts which are conceived of as mutually interdependent" (240). One can observe a similar analysis in Graham Allison's (1971) analysis of the Cuban Missile Crisis.

I used the concept of force field of competing forces as used in the context of Turkish e-government projects to explain their emergence and the way(s) these projects are placed on the government's decision agenda. I did not compare different decision making models, as Graham Allison does, but emphasized different model attributes found in the cases under examination. My main argument is that there are multiple and competing forces that initiate a project and help it to get on the decision agenda. Several forces I identified during my field research are actual needs (problems for which an e-government projects are a genuine solution), government reform, administrative control, various kinds of isomorphic (normative, mimetic, coercive) pressures,[*] and

---

[*] DiMaggio and Powell (1983) assert that institutional theory is useful in explaining why organizations are so similar. In a similar fashion, Meyer and Rowan (1977) contend that formal organizational structures have symbolic as well as action-generating properties. They believe that the social evolution of organizations and their survival can rest on the observation of the formal structures. Therefore, it is possible that government organizations use ICTs in their operations and management because of the pressures of symbolic meanings (social legitimacy) and pressures to conform to commonly adopted action-generating properties (efficiency and productivity gains of using ICTs). There are three main types of isomorphic processes: coercive, mimetic, and normative (DiMaggio and Powell, 1983). Coercive isomorphism suggests that government organizations use ICTs either as the result of government mandates or by the informal pressures of other similar government and private organizations that already use ICTs successfully. Mimetic isomorphism suggests that government organizations model themselves after similar organizations, which they perceive to be more legitimate and successful. By imitating organizations that already successfully use ICTs; they enhance their legitimacy by demonstrating that the organization is at least trying to improve the conditions of its service or information provision. Normative isomorphism suggests that government organizations use ICTs because of the newly emerging professional norms of public service, such as online interactivity, virtual service, and transparency and accountability.

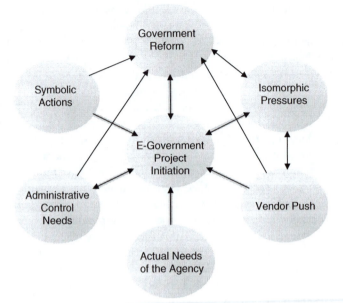

FIGURE 21.1 Force field of competing forces in E-Government project emergence (From Yıldız, M., Peeking into the Black Box of E-Government Policy-Making: Evidence from Turkey. Unpublished doctoral dissertation. Indiana University, Bloomington, 2004, 128).

vendor push and symbolic actions (see Figure 21.1). This model presents a set of working hypotheses, based on Turkish data, and is open to testing and development.

The combination and relative influences of the forces are determined by various environmental factors. The first factor is the urgency of the problem that needs to be solved by the e-government project. This factor is represented by "Actual Needs of Agency" in Figure 21.1. The second factor is the project's compatibility with the global standards and the rules and regulations of the European Union,* which is the greatest source of isomorphic pressures. Third is the nature and level of political support the project manager gets from his or her direct supervisor (usually the head of the agency), and from the minister of the ministry that oversees the agency.

The forces that play important roles and the outcome of the force field of competing forces for each project are both unique (Yıldız, 2004, 117–120). For example, in the Accountancy-Net project, the solution was the integration of public accountant offices throughout the country via secure Internet connection. The solution was coupled with the main problem that government revenue, expenditure and productivity information were not available for decision makers in great detail and in real time. The windows of opportunity opened when, first, the agency's special funds were provided with the seed money for a pilot project, and then, when World Bank provided the salary of a technical advisor. Then the project manager skillfully used the media to get political support for the project by launching the pilot project at the Minister's congressional district. Successful implementation of the pilot project brings in legitimacy.

There are three important dimensions of the force field of competing forces concept. The first dimension is the number of forces. It ranges from two to many. The second dimension is the

---

* At the time of the research, Turkey was candidate for membership in the European Union. The Turkish governments were striving to meet the membership requirements of the Union. Negotiations for Turkey's accession to the EU are scheduled to begin on October 3, 2005, and they are expected to continue for at least a decade.

outcome of the competition. It depicts the specific force (if any) that dominates the process, a process by which an e-government project emerges and is placed on decision agenda. Finally, the actors involved affect the outcome of competition between forces. Policy actors, who influence the number and magnitude of competing forces, are project managers, supranational agencies, private ICT vendor firm representatives, and politicians (usually ministers).

The relationships among the factors illustrated in Figure 21.1 are complex. Six issues are of concern here. First, some government reform needs are fueled by isomorphic pressures. Implementation of the reform creates local best practices, and therefore creates a wave of isomorphic pressures for projects to come. The two-way arrow in the figure symbolizes the two-way interaction between these variables.

Second, the emergence of e-government projects trigger new needs for government reform, as most e-government projects create an impact that goes beyond the agency that sponsors them. The majority of the projects, once implemented, force similar reform efforts in the agencies that are in their institutional environment. This impact is symbolized by a two-way arrow between project initiation and government reform in Figure 21.1.

Third, the existence of isomorphic pressures is an important argument used by vendors to persuade decision makers in government agencies. The vendor push concept and project emergence, in return, create mimetic pressures for implementing the same idea to other government agencies, in which the same vendor is used. This relationship is symbolized by a two-way arrow between vendor push and isomorphic pressures in Figure 21.1. A private ICT vendor firm representative explains this process:

> When I go to international conferences, sometimes I see a project implemented in a different country and say to myself "why cannot we implement such a project in Turkey?" So, I come back to Turkey and talk to the people I know in government about the benefits and feasibility of implementing a similar project. (Yildiz, 2004, 130)

Fourth, administrative control aspirations support arguments for government reform. The actual needs for controlling money, people, information, and government transactions are justified with more acceptable objectives, such as greater efficiency and accountability in government operations. Two technical consultants expressed their concerns about this "control function" of e-government projects in personal interviews. One told me that no one seems to be worried about the possibility of matching population census information with other kinds of information and the potential violations of personal privacy and human rights as an outcome. The other consultant admitted the claim of government officials that Turkey's e-government efforts are more advanced than those in many European countries. However, the reason for this, according to him, was that people living in those European countries were afraid of the misuse of governmental power. He was arguing that projects are implemented more easily and rapidly when there are no checks-and-balances over the power of the government, similar to the case in Turkey.

It should be noted that not all the results of the control are worrisome. One civil society representative underlines the positive aspects of control by saying "E-government projects constitute an infrastructure that would prevent misuse of government resources and [eventually] curb corruption" (Personal interview).

Fifth, it is a widespread phenomenon in Turkish public administration to use e-government as a symbol of being at the cutting edge and keeping up with the other agencies. One project manager explains the symbolic aspect of initiating e-government projects very vividly:

> Initiating an e-government project is like having a picture of Mustafa Kemal Ataturk [the founder of the Turkish Republic, a figure who has the combined significance of George Washington and Abraham Lincoln for the Turks] hanging next to your desk. Why is it there? Because, everybody else has an Ataturk picture on their walls. It is politically incorrect not to have one. Similarly, why do all agencies

have an e-government project? Because every other agency has its own e-government project, and not having a project of your own signals that you are left behind, you are missing out on something. (Personal interview).

Finally, the actual needs of the agency that initiate an e-government project are important. These needs are problems for which e-government projects are genuine solutions. Examples of actual needs of agencies are increasing cost-savings and efficiency and effectiveness (almost all), transparency (Local-Net, Accountancy-Net), and citizen trust in government (Justice-Net).

21.7 ACTORS IN DECISION MAKING

The main actors in the process of e-government decision making are the public administrators working in projects, vendor firm representatives, politicians, policy network members, and supranational organizations such as the World Bank and the United Nations Development Program (UNDP). Citizens are secondary actors. They very rarely, if ever, play an important role. In none of the cases I studied had citizens who would benefit from the projects been consulted directly for project design or management.

There are two main arenas in which policy actors interact with each other: policy networks and the media. The policy networks in Turkey are formed within and around the ICT-related non-government organizations. Two of the most influential of these policy networks are the Informatics Association of Turkey (TBD) and the Turkish Informatics Foundation (TBV). TBD is based in the capital city, Ankara, and it represents mainly current and retired government ICT personnel. TBV, on the other hand, is located in the commercial capital of the country, Istanbul, and it voices the concerns of the private ICT firms. It is the interaction between these two big policy networks and their sub-networks that influence a considerable part of the government decision making regarding ICT. Many government project managers and technical staff are members of these policy networks.

The membership structure of either policy network is far from being homogenous. Each network is subdivided into smaller networks of greater cohesion and objectives that may be different from those of the main network. A group under the roof of TBD, for example, endorses the use of open source software in e-government projects, although this is not an official TBD position.

Private ICT firm representatives use policy networks to influence politicians and public administrators in their decisions concerning government ICT investments. These networks provide the representatives of the private ICT firms with a platform to socialize with the government ICT personnel and to have their voices heard on the shaping of strategic decisions. Vendors support many activities of these policy networks, such as sponsoring ICT-related conferences and award ceremonies for successful e-government projects, publishing ICT magazines, and distributing these magazines to the policy network members to further increase the sustainability of these relationships.

The second major arena for the interaction of policy actors is the media, that is, the coverage of e-government projects in the news media. Media outlets, most of which belong to big corporations, which also own or occasionally partner with vendor firms and ISPs (Internet Service Providers), are used as effective promoters of e-government projects. Media serve a double purpose: First, the general public learns about the future benefits of the e-government projects from the media. Newspaper articles, television and radio programs and Internet-based newspapers' coverage shape the public perception of e-government projects. All these activities are aimed at creating citizen acceptance and demand for certain e-government projects. Second, the craving of politicians for media attention is used; through media coverage, a platform is created in which politicians endorse the projects. The endorsements by politicians send positive signals to other politicians and public administrators about the projects in question. A leading member of an e-government project management group explains the strategic use of media:

After the change in government, a new minister came into office. I was trying to make an appointment with him to get his permission and support for launching the [e-government] project. All my efforts provided no results. I decided to use the media [to obtain his support]. I decided to implement a pilot project in his [minister's] hometown and alerted the media to make sure that the event is well covered. The minister showed up at his hometown, using this opportunity to show his voters that he serves them well. He talked to the media correspondents in favor of the project. From that point on, I got his support. I have never had a problem to make an appointment with him again. (Personal interview)

Media coverage is also instrumental in reinforcing the communication patterns within and between policy networks. News on the media outlets can be used to influence the general public and lower-level members of the policy networks, praise the future benefits of e-government projects, signal political support (or the lack of it) for a certain project, or voice discontent about specific decisions regarding a project.

21.7.1 VENDORS: VENDOR PUSH

The vendor push concept argues that private sector IT firm representatives can influence the decisions of government officials because they know more about the technology and its application in other, non-governmental settings. The concept assumes the existence of information asymmetry between private sector and government IT officials, as explained below. Vendor firms use their employees in the ICT policy networks to influence the decision making process that leads to the creation of an e-government project and important policy decisions after the initiation of the project. For example, decision makers in Justice-Net and Population-Net projects consulted with other government agencies and ICT vendor firms before choosing the vendor that they worked with. In Local-Net and Pension-Net projects, vendor firm representatives and project decision makers already knew each other via some non-governmental organizations.

The reasons of vendor push are the information asymmetry problem discussed above, and the competitive pressures of increasing or defending a market share in an enlarging ICT market for government agencies. The main arguments used for the vendor push are of modernization and government reform (cost savings, increasing efficiency, increasing customer/citizen friendliness/ transparency) and isomorphism (i.e., conforming to the EU standards). The venues of the vendor push, identified in this study (Yıldız, 2004, 72), are membership in the same policy network or in the same civil society organization (sometimes they are one and the same), conferences and symposia and the media. Articles in the news media organizations, such as newsletters, newspapers, radios, televisions, and the Internet, underline the utmost importance and critical contributions of these projects. Important ICT-related media outlets are owned by the vendor firms themselves.[*]

The persuasion power of private ICT vendors on government decision makers originates, in part, from the existence of information asymmetry between the two. A vendor's push is more effective if information asymmetry exists between the vendor and the government agency regarding their knowledge about that technology, the former knowing more than the latter. The findings of my study (Yıldız, 2004, 72–73, 138–140) suggest that information asymmetry is made up of and maintained by monetary, cultural, and political factors. First, government lacks the monetary resources to hire, educate, and retain high-quality ICT experts. Private vendor firms employ highly trained and qualified ICT experts. Government ICT experts, on the other hand, with some exceptions, are relatively less qualified, under-trained and under-paid. Second, due to cultural factors, such as lack of ICT culture, limited vision of public managers, organizational ineptitude or inertia, turf wars, and secretive culture that discourages information-sharing, information

---

[*] Several vendor firms formed their own news media company (Interpro), and are publishing two IT newsletters (BTHaber and BTNet), both in print and online. Copies of these newsletters are distributed widely to the government decision makers. I observed that a copy of one of these newsletters was present in many of the offices I visited for the interviews. Policy networks, such as TBD and TBV, have their own newsletters.

asymmetry is culturally maintained and reproduced. Third, political factors, such as lack of political support for e-government projects, lack of motivation for process improvement and performance management among key public decision makers, sustain information asymmetry as they block any serious attempt to overcome it.

These conditions pave the way to the influence of private ICT firm representatives on government decision making. Having such an influence may be critical for the survival of some vendor firms, as one consultant argues: "there are [ICT vendor] firms in Turkey the existence of which depend on government ICT contracts [since they] could not compete in a free market worldwide" (Personal interview).

ICT vendor firm representatives approach government agencies with their ideas. Sometimes they are able to "sell" those ideas to the organization. This does not mean that all the projects initiated by private vendors are useless. On the contrary, some, if not most, of them are projects that may benefit both the government and its citizens. There are instances when vendor push does harm the interests of the government and the citizenry. In a personal interview, an ICT consultant gave an example of this when he told me about a project in which academicians argued for using new or emerging technologies, while private ICT firms argued for using obsolete technologies. In this case, private ICT firms had an important leverage over some bureaucrats, and they got it their way.

For some projects the initiators of the project are the private ICT firms, not the government representatives. The emergence of the Pension-Net project is a good example of this process: The vendor firm played a critical role in the emergence of the project and formulation of policies. The same processes work not only for the initial emergence e-government projects, but also for the decisions in later phases of the projects. One vendor firm representative explains this "idea-selling" process:

> We (vendor firms) know what our customers (government agencies) are doing. We use our knowledge about the international developments in the ICT world to propose them ideas regarding what else they can do. We tell them about the economic returns of their investments. (Personal interview)

Once public administrators are persuaded, it is relatively easy to persuade politicians, the real holders of the public purse. They quickly jump on the bandwagon, since e-government is a popular and "cool" development that creates political capital usable during elections and elsewhere. Availability of media coverage tempts them to comment—mostly favorably—about e-government projects.

21.7.2 Supra-National Organizations

The supra-national organizations that play important roles in e-government projects are the World Bank and the United Nations Development Program. Their role consists of providing money and expertise, via technical and managerial consultants, for the projects they find important. Importance of a project is in part derived from its contribution to the control function. Tax-Net, Accountancy-Net and Population-Net projects are partly funded by the World Bank to make it easier to control the Turkish government's fiscal transactions. Turkey has a very large foreign debt. Therefore, successful completion of the above-mentioned projects is critically important for IMF and the World Bank, because it is seen as a means to ensure the continuing financial stability of the country.

Supra-national actors are important because they are among the major providers of funds and technological/managerial support for e-government policy formulation and decision. They try to guarantee the sustainability of their continued involvement with Turkey, as they loan considerable amounts of money to the country. That is why the World Bank has chosen to fund projects that deal with government revenues and expenditures (i.e., Tax-Net and Pension-Net). It also provides funds for Population-Net project, which creates the backbone for the financial projects mentioned above.

Supra-national actors closely monitor these projects via paying the fees of the project consultants and thus receiving periodic progress reports.

The last supra-national actor of importance is the United Nations Development Program (UNDP). Foreign-Net is partially funded by the UNDP. This can be explained by two factors. First is the entrepreneurship of the project management group, who found the opportunity to come up with additional funding for the project and successfully used that opportunity. The second factor is that Foreign-Net is important both at domestic and international levels. Internationally, it connects Turkey to the outside word via online embassies. Therefore, it performs an important role in the integration of Turkey to the European Union and beyond. Domestically, it is a pioneer project in paperless office automation and providing citizens with online transactions within a customer-friendly environment. Therefore, to the international donor agencies, it appears reasonable to fund.

21.8 NATURE OF DECISION MAKING: THE ROLE OF POLITICS AND POLICY NETWORKS

What is the nature of the decision making processes in the agenda setting and policy formulation stages for e-government development? The results of my research show that rational model of decision making could not be followed because of the political nature of the overall processes, especially the funding structure. There are deals, side-processes, and negotiations that take place among multiple actors simultaneously. Project managers, ICT vendor firms, and international/supranational agencies are the primary actors and the ICT elite, and NGOs are secondary actors. ICT vendors are selected via their membership in policy networks.

An excellent example of policy networks trying to further their agendas by encouraging the use of certain products instead of others is the debate on using proprietary versus open source software in e-government projects. The proponents of open-source software constitute a group of academicians who are members or have tangential relations with the Informatics Association of Turkey (TBD). They argue that the availability of the source code for examination by the government is essential to understanding exactly what that software does for the government agency. According to this group, the security of sensitive government information is at stake when it is not possible to see the source code in proprietary software.

The second argument this group raises is that government agencies pay considerable amounts of license fees for proprietary software. Using open source software would save all this money, since it is free to obtain. Their third and last argument is that computers using open-source products crash less, and are much easier to maintain. The members of this group support their arguments by showcasing the developments in other countries such as Germany, Brazil, China, Japan, and South Korea (see Sum, 2003). The governments in these countries use open-source software in their e-government projects for the reasons already stated. All members of the project team in the Local-Net project and some members of the Accountancy-Net project share these views; they emphasize especially the cost savings.

The opposing group, supporters of proprietary software, is mostly made up of the vendors of these products. They argue that although open-source software has the initial advantage over their products of not paying license fees, it has a very big weakness. Technical support for open-source products is very limited. This argument understandably worries a lot of project managers because of the lack of high-level technical expertise in their agencies. As a reaction to the openness of the source code in the open-source model and its advantages regarding national security issues, producers of proprietary software such as the Microsoft Corporation decided to share their source code with foreign governments. Microsoft even argues that since the source code is open only to the government, but not to third parties as it is in open-source, this is even more secure for the government.

An important dimension of this debate is ideological. The underlying philosophy of the open-source movement is to develop the source by improving it and then share it with others to use and develop. This approach, which defies intellectual property rights, creates an alternative business model to that of proprietary software. Such an alternative worries software companies and threatens their existence. The open source software approach is characterized as "digital socialism" by some of its supporters and opponents. It creates uneasiness in politicians and project managers who do not want to be politically incorrect in a country with historically anti-communist governments.

The effectiveness of policy networks in furthering their causes is limited by various environmental factors. For example, the efforts of the open-source software policy network have not been fruitful so far. The lack of centralized ICT decision making capacity is an important reason that explains the lack of policy change on this issue. Individual agencies are reluctant to take the initiative on such a sensitive issue as open-source software in the absence of a decision by a central planning and decision making body. Technical (the risk of not finding an acceptable level of computer support) and ideological (perception that using open-source software is a sign of subscribing to "digital socialism") concerns also play a part in the limited adoption of open-source software in Turkish government.

21.9 SUMMARY AND CONCLUSIONS

In this study I identified a variety of ICT decision makers (public administrators, politicians, non-profit organizations, vendor firms, media outlets, policy networks, and international donor agencies) who participate in e-government decision making in Turkey. Decision-makers interact through news media outlets and policy networks. The political environments, both at the national and international level, create various forces that influence e-government policy making. On the one hand, such a variety in participants can be regarded as beneficial. For example, Shulock (1999) and Radin (2000, 186) argue that sophistication of policy analysis increases as the policy discussion becomes more inclusive with the participation of multiple stakeholders in the policy analytic process. Radin (1997) also emphasizes the evolving pluralist nature of policy analysis and decision making. As more people and organized groups engage in and reflect on issues of knowledge production and alternative courses of action, the more checks-and-balances are placed on the distortion of decision making processes.

On the other hand, the appearance that there is a variety of policy actors/decision makers may be deceptive. The distribution of power among decision makers also needs to be taken into consideration. For example, in Turkey's case, citizens have very limited say in e-government decision making processes, even though they are greatly impacted by the outcomes of e-government projects. It is obvious that some decision makers do have more power than others in determining the breadth and depth of policy options. They may be better positioned to promote their agendas over the agendas of other actors. Indeed, my findings show that vendor firms are using the news media outlets and their membership in influential policy networks to define the scope of discussion on ICT policy options, as in the issue of open-source software.

The results of the research presented in this chapter suggest that e-government decision making is a highly political process. The opening of policy windows during project initiation is best described with the garbage-can model. Once the e-government projects are initiated, formulation of policies can be best explained with incremental models of decision making. Incrementalism occurs due to the political nature of the process and the cognitive limitations of decision makers in general; economic and political instabilities being two such limitations in Turkey in particular.

Initiation of e-government projects is explained by coining the term, "force field of competing forces." The actual needs of government agencies, government reform, administrative control, isomorphic pressures, symbolic actions, and the vendor push factor constitute a field of competing forces for each e-government project. The outcome of this force field shapes each project in a unique way. This process also has a strong effect on that project's future evolutionary path.

Opening of windows of opportunity is critically important. The biggest policy window is Turkey's ambition to join the European Union. The struggle for membership is a driving force for both government reform and symbolic and isomorphic tendencies. In other words, the drive for EU membership is one of the biggest triggers of e-government development and decision making in Turkey. For example, integration with the European accounting, justice and taxation systems, and conforming to technical and procedural standards of the EU were important reasons for the initiation of Accountancy-Net, Justice-Net and Tax-Net projects. In addition to the standardization argument, the prospect of EU membership is one of the strongest forces behind the technical modernization of the country, closely tied to the other types (administrative, political and social) of modernization.

Decisions are made incrementally at the policy formulation stage. Incremental processes are dictated by several factors. First, many of these e-government projects are the continuation of earlier automation projects, which began before the introduction of new ICTs, such as the Internet. Using the new ICTs made these continuing projects work faster, better, and with more interaction among the various stakeholders.

Second, human resource quality and technical knowledge gaps lead to a problem of information asymmetry between government and private ICT experts. The information asymmetry problem—caused and maintained by financial, cultural, and political factors—is critical in understanding the influence of private sector ICT experts on those who work in the public sector. The information asymmetry problem causes the inability to plan ahead due to bounded-rationality. Government ICT experts do not have perfect or even near-perfect information about future political, technical, and economic developments, such as the degree of integration with the European Union, availability of government funds, advances in technology, and political support for e-government. In addition, government planners and decision makers were encouraged to engage in risk-averse incremental behavior because of continuous political and economic uncertainty, mainly stemming from the fact that unstable coalition governments ruled Turkey from the early 1990s to 2003.

Third, the nature of government budgeting, that is, project funding in annual increments and the limited amount of resources available to each project staff, contributes to the incremental nature of policy formulation. This problem is tied to the bounded-rationality problem, since the outcome of budgeting politics is uncertain; government decision makers know neither the exact amount of government funds, nor the amount of flexibility in their use of those funds.

Finally, the fast pace of change in technology encourages government decision makers to behave incrementally. Rapid technological changes quickly make the technical specifications in the planning phase obsolete. Consequently, frequent updates on technical preferences are needed before large-scale technological decision making. These technological updates are performed at each step of the incremental process.

As explained with the help of e-government projects in this chapter, it is essential for public administrators to understand the power relations hidden behind the production and dissemination of information (Gerth and Mills, 1946, 233; Stone, 1997, 27–28). Decision making in e-government projects requires a good understanding of the social and political environment of the organization(s) in question, the power relations among all stakeholders, and the individual project's technical nature and requirements (Cresswell and Pardo, 2001; Kling, 1999).

By exposing the non-technical and political nature of e-government studies, such as this one, help to protect the public interest when large amounts of money are being spent for e-government projects. This is a very similar procedure to the socio-technical approach that Kling and Lamb (2000) prescribe. When we understand the process of decision making, we can evaluate the true merits of e-government initiatives better. Moreover, such an understanding enables public administrators to make the technical, managerial, and political adjustments in decision making processes. An understanding of the political process in decision making can also help us take precautions against the abuses of power by private actors, and increase the transparency of the decision making processes and the accountability of non-governmental decision makers.

REFERENCES

Agranoff, R., *Inside the Operation: Building Grounded Network Theory*, Paper presented at the American Society for Public Administration National Conference, Portland, OR, 2004.

Aldemir, M. C., Arbak, Y., and Özmen, O. N. T., Türkiye'de işgörme anlayışı: Tanımı ve sorunları, *Yönetim Araştırmaları Dergisi*, 3(1), 5–28, 2003.

Allison, G. T., *Essence of Decision: Explaining the Cuban Missile Crisis*, Little, Brown and Company, Boston, 1971.

American Society for Public Administration (ASPA), and United Nations, *Benchmarking E-government: A Global Perspective*, U.N. Publications, New York, NY, 2002.

Bauer, C. and Scharl, A., Quantitative evaluation of web site content and structure, *Internet Research: Electronic Networking Applications and Policy*, 10(1), 31–43, 2000.

Bellamy, C. and Taylor, J. A., *Governing in the Information Age*, Open University Press, Buckingham, U.K., 1998.

Bozeman, B. and Bretschneider, S., Public management information systems: Theory and prescription, *Public Administration Review*, 46, 475–487, 1986.

Brown, M. M. and Brudney, J.L., *Achieving advanced electronic government services: An examination of obstacles and implications from an international perspective*, Paper presented at the National Public Management Research Conference, Bloomington, IN, 2001.

Caldwell, L. K., Turkish administration and the politics of expediency, In *The Turkish Administrator: A Cultural Survey*, Hopper, J. R. and Levin, R. I., Eds., US AID Public Administration Division Publications, Ankara, pp. 23–58, 1968.

Cohen, M. D., March, J. G., and Olsen, J. P., A garbage can model of organizational choice, *Administrative Science Quarterly*, 17, 1–25, 1972.

Cohen, S. and Eimicke, W., The use of internet in government service delivery, In *E-Government 2001*, Abramson, M. and Means, G. E., Eds., Rowman & Littlefield Publishers, Oxford, pp. 9–43, 2001.

Cresswell, A. M. and Pardo, T. A., Implications of legal and organizational issues for urban digital government development, *Government Information Quarterly*, 18, 269–278, 2001.

Cullen, R. and Houghton, C., Democracy online: An assessment of New Zealand government web sites, *Government Information Quarterly*, 17(3), 243–267, 2000.

Danziger, J. N., Dutton, W. H., Kling, R., and Kraemer, K. L., *Computers and Politics: High Technology in American Local Governments*, Columbia University Press, New York, 1982.

DiMaggio, P. and Powell, W., The iron cage revisited: Institutional isomorphism and collective rationality in organizational fields, *American Sociological Review*, 2, 147–160, 1983.

Fountain, J. E., *Building the Virtual State: Information Technology and Institutional Change*, Brookings Institution, Washington DC, 2001.

Gant, J. P. and Gant, D. B., *Web Portal Functionality and State Government E-Services*, Proceedings of the 35th Hawaii International Conference on Systems Sciences, 2002.

Gerth, H. H. and Mills, C. W., eds. and trans. *From Max Weber: Essays in sociology*. Oxford University Press, New York, 1946.

Harmon, M. H. and Mayer, R. T., *Organisation Theory for Public Administration*, Scott Foresman, Glenview, 1986.

Heeks, R., Information technology and the management of corruption, *Development in Practice*, 9(1–2), 184–189, 1999.

Hernon, P., Government on the web: a comparison between the United States and New Zealand, *Government Information Quarterly*, 15(4), 419–443, 1998.

Ho, A. T., Reinventing local governments and the e-government initiative, *Public Administration Review*, 62(4), 434–441, 2002.

Holden, S. H., The evolution of information technology management at the federal level: implications for public administration, In *Public Information Technology: Policy and Management Issues*, Garson, G. D., Ed., Idea Group Publishing, Hershey, PA, pp. 53–73, 2003.

Hwang, S. D., Choi, Y., and Myeong, S. H., Electronic government in South Korea: conceptual problems, *Government Information Quarterly*, 16(3), 277–285, 1999.

Jaeger, P. T., The endless wire: e-government as a global phenomenon, *Government Information Quarterly*, 20(4), 323–331, 2003.

Jonas, D. K., Building state information highways: Lessons for public and private sector leaders, *Government Information Quarterly*, 17(1), 43–67, 2000.

King, J. L., Rob Kling and the Irvine school, *The Information Society*, 20, 97–99, 2004.

Kingdon, J. W., *Agendas, Alternatives and Public Policies*, HarperCollins, New York, NY, 1990.

Kling, R., What is social informatics and why does it matter?, *D-Lib Magazine*, 5(1), 43–57, 1999.

Kling, R. and Lamb, R., IT and organizational change in digital economies: a socio-technical approach, In *Understanding the Digital Economy: Data, Tools and Research*, Kahin, B., Ed., MIT Press, Boston, pp. 134–157, 2000.

Kraemer, K. L. and Perry, J. L., Innovation and computing in the public sector: A review of research, *Knowledge, Technology and Science Policy*, 12(1), 3–18, 1999.

La Porte, T. M., De Jong, M. and Demchak, C. C., *Public Organizations on the World Wide Web: Empirical Correlates of Administrative Openness*, http://www.cyprg.arizona.edu/publications/correlat.rtf (accessed 30 April 2001), 1999.

Lewin, K., In *Field Theory in Social Science; Selected Theoretical Papers*, Cartwright, D., Ed., Harper and Row, NY, 1951.

Lindblom, C. E., The science of muddling through, *Public Administration Review*, 19(2), 79–88, 1959.

Lindblom, C. E., Still muddling, not yet through, *Public Administration Review*, 39(5), 17–26, 1979.

McNeal, R. S., Tolbert, C. J., Mossberger, K., and Dotterweich, L. J., Innovating in digital government in the American states, *Social Science Quarterly*, 84(1), 52–70, 2003.

Mahmood, R., Can information and communication technology help reduce corruption? How so and why not: Two case studies from South Asia, *Perspectives on Global Development & Technology*, 3(3), 347–373, 2004.

Meyer, J. W. and Rowan, B., Institutionalized organizations: Formal structure as myth and ceremony, *American Journal of Sociology*, 83(2), 340–363, 1977.

Northrop, A., Information technology and public administration: The view from the profession, In *Public Information Technology: Policy and Management Issues*, Garson, G. D., Ed., Idea Group Publishing, Hershey, PA, pp. 1–19, 2003.

Osborne, D. and Gaebler, T., *Reinventing Government: How the Entrepreneurial Spirit is Transforming the Public Sector*, Addison-Wesley, Reading, MA, 1992.

Perrow, C., A framework for the comparative analysis of organizations, *American Sociological Review*, 32, 194–208, 1967.

Perrow, C., *Complex Organizations: A Critical Essay*, 2nd ed., Scott, Foresman & Company, Dallas, TX, 1979.

Radin, B., The evolution of the policy analysis field: From conversation to conversations, *Journal of Policy Analysis and Management*, 16(2), 204–218, 1997.

Radin, B., *Beyond Machiavelli: Policy Analysis Comes of Age*, Georgetown University Press, Washington, DC, 2000.

Rittel, H. W. J. and Webber, M., Dilemmas in a general theory of planning, *Policy Sciences*, 4, 155–169, 1973.

Sargut, S., *Kültürlerarası Farklılaşma Ve Yönetim*, 2nd ed., İmge, İstanbul, 2001.

Schelin, S. H., E-government: An overview, In *Public Information Technology: Policy and Management Issues*, David Garson, G., Ed., Idea Group Publishing, Hershey, PA, pp. 120–137, 2003.

Shulock, N., The paradox of policy analysis: If it is not used, why do we produce so much of it?, *Journal of Policy Analysis and Management*, 18(2), 226–244, 1999.

Simon, H. A., *Administrative Behavior*, 3rd ed., The Free Press, New York, NY, 1976.

Stone, D., *Policy Paradox: The Art of Political Decision Making*, W.W. Norton, New York, 1997.

Stowers, G. N. L., Becoming cyberactive: state and local governments on the world wide web, *Government Information Quarterly*, 16(2), 111–127, 1999.

Sum, N. L., Informational capitalism and U.S. economic hegemony: Resistance and adaptations in East Asia, *Critical Asian Studies*, 35(3), 373–398, 2003.

Thomas, J. C. and Streib, G., The new face of government: Citizen-initiated contacts in the era of e-government, *Journal of Public Administration Research and Theory*, 13(1), 83–102, 2003.

Torres, L., Pina, V., and Acerete, B., E-government developments on delivering public services among EU cities, *Government Information Quarterly*, 22, 217–238, 2005.

West, D., E-government and the transformation of service delivery and citizen attitudes, *Public Administration Review*, 64(1), 27, 2004.

Waldo, D., *The Study of Public Administration*, Random House, New York, NY, 1955.

Yıldız, M., Elektronik devlet kuram ve uygulamasına genel bir bakış ve değerlendirme, In *Cagdaş Kamu Yonetimi-1*, Acar, M. and Ozgur, H., Eds., Atlas-Nobel Publications, Istanbul, pp. 305–327, 2003.

Yıldız, M., Peeking into the black box of e-government policy-making: Evidence from Turkey. Unpublished doctoral dissertation. Indiana University, Bloomington, Bloomington, IN, 2004.

Zuboff, S., *In the Age of the Smart Machine: The Future of Work and Power*, Basic Books, New York, 1988.

22 Budgeting as an Institutional Practice: Modeling Decision Making in the Budget Process

Enamul Choudhury

CONTENTS

22.1   Introduction..417
22.2   Budget Decision Making as an Instrumental Action.......................................419
      22.2.1   Logical Analysis..419
      22.2.2   Rational Actor...420
      22.2.3   Critique of the Instrumental View of Budget Decision Making.........421
22.3   The Evolution of Budget Decision Making...421
22.4   Decision Making as an Institutional Practice..422
      22.4.1   Institution and Institutional Practice..422
            22.4.1.1   Rule...423
            22.4.1.2   Role...423
            22.4.1.3   Routine...424
      22.4.2   Budget Decision Making as an Institutional Practice.........................424
      22.4.3   Stages of the Budget Process and the Integration of Rules,
            Roles, and Routines..425
            22.4.3.1   The Budget Pre-Preparation Stage....................................426
            22.4.3.2   The Budget Formulation Stage..427
            22.4.3.3   The Budget Approval Stage...428
            22.4.3.4   The Budget Execution Stage..428
            22.4.3.5   The Budget Audit Stage..429
22.5   Conclusion..430
References..430

22.1 INTRODUCTION

Public budgeting is multi-functional, multi-dimensional, and multi-disciplinary. All three terms convey the complex and contextual nature of budgeting. Budgeting is complex and contextual because it varies by the level of government, jurisdictional characteristics, environmental conditions, the use of analytical tools, as well as the behavior of budget and non-budget actors. The following description succinctly captures the variation in budget practices:

> While budgeting is done almost everywhere, nowhere is it done in quite the same way... Budgeting includes processes as diverse as those employed by Congress, Nebraska's unicameral legislature, and the most impoverished town board, as well as routines as complex as statistically sophisticated

computer-based workload increases and as simple as price changes in office supplies, figured on an accountant's spread sheet, in pencil, and under green eyeshade. (McCaffery, 1991, p. 112)

The variation in context and complexity makes conceptualizing the budget process difficult. In fact, the evolution of budgeting can be seen as a struggle to define budget practices and change them. For a long time, Verne Lewis's (1952) call for a predictive budget theory has shaped the struggle. However, contemporary students consider the pursuit not only far-fetched but also impossible (Rubin, 2000; Wildavsky, 1992; Keil and Elliot, 1992). In fact, the contemporary focus in budget research has been moving away from predictive theory to descriptive understanding (Grizzle, 1998; Rubin, 2000). One way to advance descriptive understanding is to account for budget decision making as an institutional practice.

Budget decisions are about resource allocation—where most decisions are continuous with the past while some register significant departures. Analyses generated both inside and outside the budget process support budget decision making. For instance, analyses to classify information, explore alternatives, and balance the technical with political criteria. Budget decision making is also characterized by a variety of constraints: time, politics, organizational relationships, fiscal environment, process requirements, and professional standards. However, the incidence and effect of these constraints are largely mediated by the way budget decision making is structured.

The budget calendar as established by law acts as the dynamo of budget action—as it structures most of the practices of budget decision making. In turn, these practices render budget decision making into a regular, repetitive, and cyclic process. However, the budget cycle operates on a staggered basis, which makes budget decisions to overlap consecutive cycles. Such overlap necessitates other practices, such as keeping different information streams separate and adjusting present decisions to past ones. The cycle also forces some decisions to be made more quickly than they otherwise would. This often results in the failure to integrate strategic plans with the priorities of annual budget decisions. Thus, the stages of the budget process are not only descriptive categories, but also exert a regulative influence on budget decision making.

In policy research, the stage approach was initiated to capture the dynamics of decision making in the policy process. The policy stages serve as a heuristic device to categorize policy practices and account for their variation (Brewer and DeLeon, 1983). Initially, researchers came to view the stages as disjointed and episodic—beginning with estimation, followed by implementation, then evaluation, and ending in termination. Later on, they came to understand the stages as inter-related, overlapping and continuous (DeLeon, 1999). In a parallel way, we can view budget decision making as sequenced in stages. In fact, a common theme in most descriptions of the budget process is the representation of budgeting in five stages of decision making: Pre-Preparation, Formulation, Approval, Execution, and Audit. Budget decisions in each stage not only overlap, but are also iterative and recursive. This makes budget decision making both sequential and experiential.

The following questions provide access to two very different ways to understand budget decision making as both sequential and experiential.

1. Whether budget decision making is the aggregation of rational decisions of discrete actors or it is a coherent pattern of collective decision making?
2. Whether budget decision making is structured by a single decision rule or multiple decision rules?

I argue in this chapter that, budget practices display a coherent pattern of collective decision making enacted through multiple decision rules. To support this position, I will discuss two contrasting approaches to budget decision making: instrumental and institutional. In the sections to follow, I will first discuss the meaning of budget decision making as an instrumental action, its historical evolution within budgetary studies and its consequences for understanding the budget process. This is followed with the discussion of decision making as an institutional practice in general, and of budget decision making as one such practice.

22.2 BUDGET DECISION MAKING AS AN INSTRUMENTAL ACTION

Despite the heterogeneity of budget contexts and the complexity of budget practices, the representation of budget decision making continues to be seen as reductive and unitary. The conception is premised on reducing all decision making to a single decision rule—the efficient allocation of financial resources. Here, the decision maker is considered a rational actor, who acts instrumentally following the logic stipulated in the decision rule. Furthermore, the assumptions of classical economics like the separation of facts and values, the ranking of preferences, and maximization of utility based on the ranked preferences are tacitly extended to describe budget decision making.

In the instrumental approach, budget practices are derived from applying the decision rule of either comprehensive rationality or marginal utility. In both approaches, the stages of the budget process function as a conveyor belt—instrumentally carrying forward decisions from one stage to the next, with the stages as such having no impact on budget decision making. This view of budget decision making as an instrumental action is supported by its two constituent elements: logical analysis and rational actor.

22.2.1 LOGICAL ANALYSIS

In the instrumental approach, decision making is based on the premise that the decision maker separates facts from values. Based on facts alone, the decision maker employs logical analysis to search, sort, evaluate, and then choose an alternative to act. From this perspective, budget decision making is also viewed as an instrumental action. This is because, budget actors carry out second order decisions to put into effect first order decisions of the political process, and also because each budget stage is understood to function as a component of a single decision rule.

The decision rule for instrumental action is derived from the model of synoptic decision making. The model depicts decisions to flow from the top with a clear knowledge of the goal. Decisions once made are not revisited unless information flaws are revealed through program or process evaluation. The decision rule of instrumental action can be depicted as follows:

- Identify the objectives, clarify the values that underpin them, and rank the objectives against the values that are made explicit;
- Identify all alternatives in relation to the objectives as ranked;
- Select the criterion to evaluate the efficiency payoff of each alternative;
- Choose the alternative that best satisfies the criteria that have been selected.

In budgeting, this logical approach was translated into the PPBS and ZBB reforms to structure decision making. The key tool in this structuring action was the choice of decision units: program, subprogram, program element, or cost-center. The units were taken to stand for budget authority and organizational boundary. Analyses across the units were then aggregated to arrive at the final allocation decision. Zero-based budgeting introduced an additional step in the aggregation process—forcing the rank ordering of program elements and generating alternative rankings to arrive at a final allocation decision.

Real world budget practices did not resemble this approach. In fact, the recognition of the limits of analysis became an alternate premise of understanding budget decision making. Consequently, the theory of bounded rationality amended the decision rule of comprehensiveness with the notion of satisficing (Simon, 1958). This shift offered a powerful means to understand budget practices in terms of decision making at the margins. The focus of logical analysis thus shifted to the behavioral facts of decision making—where actors use simplifying rules to reduce uncertainty in making efficient decisions.

22.2.2 RATIONAL ACTOR

In the instrumental action approach, the decision maker is viewed as a rational actor. The actor could be a legislative committee member, an executive authority, a budget analyst, or an auditor. Here, decision making is premised on rational actors making discrete choices that are constrained by their cognitive and contextual limits. Within these limits, the rational actors seek to reduce uncertainty and manage complexity by satisficing their stated goals (see the Mingus chapter in this volume for a detailed discussion of satisficing and bounded rationality). This depiction obscures the variety of interactive, joint, and collective decision making that make up the budget process.

In budget decision making, the marginal analyses of rational actors codified the decision rule of satisficing. Rational actors were seen primarily interested in increasing the size of increments in relation to their budget base—irrespective of the salience of their program areas in question (Wildavsky, 1964). However, research using sub-agency budget requests and discrete budget items reveal that, incremental choices prevail only when a budget action is not subjected to decision making, but is allowed to accrue on past decisions (Natchez and Bupp, 1973; Bailey and O'Connor, 1975). Furthermore, when a program area becomes the subject of decision making, then, depending on the strength of its clientele and legislative support, budget actors tend to pursue an assertive strategy (LeLoup and Moreland, 1978).

TABLE 22.1
Budget Decision Making as Instrumental Action

Formulation	Asks problem-solving questions on the efficient use of money. Here, the focus of analysis is on objectivity, reliability of forecasts, multi-year projections, accuracy, and consistency.
	Make requests on the basis of multi-year forecasting, planning, and critical paths.
	Provide objective specification of program inputs, outputs and their full cost. Explore the efficacy of the choices for alternative service delivery.
	Specify the performance targets in relation to the chosen alternatives
Approval	Asks attention-directing questions on programs and processes. Here, the criteria of analysis are completeness, explicitness, and consistency.
	Quantify the costs and benefits of alternative paths to service delivery.
	Hold legislative deliberations based on cost-efficient options.
	Make approval contingent on positive audit report.
	Assess agency requests for format consistency and content accuracy
Execution	Asks score keeping questions to relate program inputs and outputs. Here, the goal is to minimize the transaction cost of risk, cash, & procurement management.
	Apportion funds with the most efficient formula of allotment.
	Delineate clear program boundaries and responsibility.
	Link budget to cost centers.
	Continuous review to determine if planned objectives are being met.
	Prospective monitoring through analysis & crosswalk
Evaluation	Asks questions on the services being provided with regard to output and outcome.
	Objective evaluation of programs and budget process: For example, analysis of staff utilization.
	Audit of the controls in place, identify the need for additional controls. Specify the reasons for budget variances and propose corrective actions.
	Recommend program restructuring or program shedding options

Thus in the instrumental action approach, decision making is seen as a set of logical steps, carried out by rational actors making choices based either on complete or marginal analysis. A summation of the instrumental actions at each stage of the budget decision making process is listed in Table 22.1.

22.2.3 CRITIQUE OF THE INSTRUMENTAL VIEW OF BUDGET DECISION MAKING

Budget decision making not only involves the passive application of decision rules but also the active pursuit of institutional ends (Reed, 1986). Analyses include different forms of learning that budget actors cultivate in their positions—from experience, networks, and subject matter expertise. Thus, the act of decision making and the corrective understanding that is derived from collective learning are not merely instrumental but also relational (Forrester and Spindler, 2001). Bounded rationality does not go far enough to capture this feature of decision making, particularly, when it involves the constrained actions of multiple actors acting in multiple phases with multiple strategies.

Budget actors cope with the complexity of decision making not only by simplifying their cognition of problems, but also by procedural accommodation to and contextual adaptation of existing rules and roles. Also, they do not make choices in isolation but in relation to the anticipated decisions of other institutional actors, thereby, each adjusting to how others behave. The nature of such adjustments depends on the nature of the information, as well as the expectation and confidence one has in the other. Charles Lindblom's (1965) partisan mutual adjustment model offers a closer approximation of this aspect of budget decision making (see the Hayes chapter in this volume for a detailed discussion of Linblom's incrementalist approach). In this model, decision makers choose ends and means simultaneously. This allows agreement on decisions to continue even when actors hold conflicting values or allows disagreements to continue on the ground that the opportunity for a more favorable agreement can emerge at a later stage.

22.3 THE EVOLUTION OF BUDGET DECISION MAKING

Modern budgeting was born in the progressive reform movement with the aim that instrumental reasoning (such as the calculus of efficiency) can and should replace the entrenched institutional mores of decision making. Therefore, the budgetary practices that emerged from the reform movement are skeptical of institutional reasoning. In fact, over time, budgetary reforms show a sustained effort to replace practices based on institutional reasoning with new decision rules derived from instrumental reasoning.

In the rational decision making approach, decisions are held to occur prior to taking action. This temporal precedence necessitated the specification of decision rules to structure action. The search for such decision rules began with the rule of rational (efficient) allocation, which became the principal tool of theory development. Budgeting was seen as an instrument to exercise neutral competence by way of rational allocation. Attaining cost-efficiency thus became entrenched as the decision rule with which to structure budget decisions.

In this instrumental approach, the decision rule is considered robust while rule application is viewed as wanting. It follows that, when the decision rule fails to provide a positive outcome, then, the failure is attributed to some inadequate conditions of practice (for example, organizational capacity, inadequate authority of agents, miscommunication) or in some weaknesses of the agent (for example, opportunism, incompetence, ignorance). Efforts are then put to correct or remove these limitations through systematic controls and procedural reforms. The high hopes in introducing the PPBS approach stands as a classic example of using the logic of instrumental action to structure budget decision making. Furthermore, the failure of the PPBS stands as a testimony to the fundamental weakness of the instrumental conception to represent the contextual nature of budget decision making.

A reinvigorated search for a predictive budget theory emerged with the incorporation of bounded rationality to understand decision making. The criterion of efficiency was reconceived in terms of satisficing practices. Because instrumental rationality separates facts from values, the practice of satisficing (being a refinement of instrumental reasoning), in effect, reproduces this separation in terms of the logic of politics-administration dichotomy. The incorporation of boundedness opened up an autonomous space for instrumental action. However, the budget stages remained as a stand-alone context, having no effect on decision making other than accounting for the conditions of boundedness.

While the bounded rational conception of action strengthened instrumental reasoning by making it more contextual, the actual practices of budget decision making continued to be political and hence institutional. For example, Allen Schick's (1966) depiction of the stages of budget reform illustrates that the developments in budget theory are in fact reflections of the institutional changes that have occurred in politics. In a similar vein, Aaron Wildavsky's (1978) observation on why traditional budgeting lasts illustrates the staying power of politics embodied in institutional practices.

From both Schick's and Wildavsky's illustrations it follows that in the context of budget practice, institutional reasoning (as embodied in political practice) triumphed over instrumental reasoning (as embodied in analytical logic). In fact, successive budget reforms (The Congressional Budget and Impoundment Control Act of 1974, the 1990 Budget Enforcement Act, and the Balanced Budget Act of 1997) granted more power to the legislative process in the attempt to structure budget practices. This brought into being an entirely new stage in the budget process, which Schick (1986) labeled as "pre-preparation." The specification of a budget ceiling prior to the call for budget requests thus introduced a competing decision rule to that of cost-efficiency.

In terms of social science theory, developments in institutional analysis led to the view of decision making as an integrative and interpretive practice. Institutional analysis advanced beyond its earlier focus on structure to its contemporary focus on micro level practices. At this level, the understanding of decision making became further enriched by two developments in social theory: the social construction process, which sees decision making as enactments of meaning; and the interpretive process, which renders decision making as interpretive acts of situated actors. In both perspectives, budget decisions are described as relational processes among actors who enact conformance with key norms though multiple practices in different stages of decision making.

22.4 DECISION MAKING AS AN INSTITUTIONAL PRACTICE

22.4.1 INSTITUTION AND INSTITUTIONAL PRACTICE

The conventional understanding of institution refers to enduring organizational entities, like the U.S Congress. However, in contemporary social science theory, the meaning of institution is understood in broader terms. Although social science theories differ on the meaning of the term "institution," there seems to be a general agreement to view an institution as a set of formal and informal rules, norms and strategies that operate within and across organizations (Weimer, 1995; Ostrom, 1986; March and Olsen, 1984).

Through the internalization of norms, institutions shape practices within which role players form their preferences and attach meaning to their actions (March and Olsen, 1984). Because preferences are embedded in practices, it follows that decision making rests less on individual intentions and more on conserving, adapting, and continuing some core values that confer legitimacy to these practices (Stone, 2002). A practice is not simply the act of carrying out a decision. Instead, it involves acting appropriately for norm maintenance and adjustment. In budget decision making, such norms include fair share, fiduciary responsibility, accountability, and responsiveness.

The meaning of institution as rules that structure actions and interactions among individuals and organizations is significant for understanding decision making as an institutional practice.

This is because, it is in the context of these rules (i.e., expectations and constraints) that a person or an organization pursues goals and takes action in relation to these goals. Both formal and informal roles support the rules. Rules and roles in turn shape the routines, where expectations, constraints and norms become codified as practices. Therefore, institutional practice refers to a constellation of rules, roles and routines through which decisions are made in relation to the values that confer legitimacy to their use. A variety of institutional practices can be identified, for example, practices that symbolize core values and those that maintain the legitimacy of discretionary action.

In the institutional approach, both cognitive and organizational factors are taken into account to understand a practice. For example, Linder and Peters (1995) describe the focus on cognitive factors in decision making as the decisional approach, while the focus on the relational influence in decision making as the dialogical approach. Therefore, while institutional analysis draws upon the concepts of bounded rationality, information cost, and uncertainty, it also adds complex motivations, normative values, and contexts to our understanding of decision making. Decision making practices are viewed not simply as a functional response to a set of constraints, but also as a dynamic response based on patterns of information use and styles of interaction. One instance of such pattern is the structure of hierarchy regulating the way information is processed and alternatives are generated in complex organizations.

Because decision making rests on patterns of interaction, the continuation of these patterns and the learning that occurs in the process affect integration among multiple practices. Highlighting this integrative function of decision making, James Thompson (1967) writes:

> The basic function of administration appears to be co-alignment, not merely of people (in coalitions) but of institutional action—of technology and task environment into a viable domain, and of organizational design and structure appropriate to it. Administration, when it works well, keeps the organization at the nexus of several streams of action. [p. 157]

The integrative function of institutional practices rests on the interdependence among rules, roles, and routines that shape decision making. The meaning of each term, in general, and in relation to the budget process, are provided below.

22.4.1.1 Rule

A rule is a shared understanding that enforces the actions that are required, prohibited, or permitted (Ostrom, 1999). Rules can be explicit or implicit. When rules are implicit, actors may not be able to recognize them, particularly when they evolve over time—such as, the classification of items in a budget format. A variety of rules structure budget decision making. These rules include, expenditure initiation process, deadlines, program parameters, use of the base, political incentives and constraints, and strategies for program expansion or protection.

22.4.1.2 Role

A role is a behavioral expectation associated with a position, task, or profession. A role can be designated by functional expertise or problem solving style (Steckroth, Slocum, and Sims, 1980). Different roles converge in the budget decision making process. For example, the oversight role of legislative committee, program partisan, legislative staff, chief executive, agency head, budget office professional, accounting professional, and elected or appointed auditor. Roles can be classified in terms of the style of action—such as, "rational actor," "reactive actor," "budget-wise," or "wise-budget" (Lynch, 1995). In turn, these roles can be seen to facilitate different institutional practice—such as, spending, guarding, advocating, or cutting.

22.4.1.3 Routine

A routine is a prescribed and detailed course of action that is followed regularly. In organizational decision making, routines are the standard operating procedures used in rule application and regulating role performance. For example, following the budget calendar; funding the contingency reserve; issuing of standardized forms or using internal controls. Routines are highly structured information processing devices that are triggered in response to internal and external cues. Therefore, routines operate in terms of the timing of decisions and the interpretation of a situation. Routines also function as a means of embedding rules in role performance.

22.4.2 BUDGET DECISION MAKING AS AN INSTITUTIONAL PRACTICE

Given the backdrop of institutional analysis, budget decision making can be understood as a set of rules, roles, and routines that integrate the stages of the budget process. It was previously noted that, budget decision making is a sequential process with a variety of constraints and controls. Within the set of constraints, the stages frame the decisions of budget actors (Rubin, 2000). The constraints are institutional in nature because they remain operative across organizations and jurisdictions—for instance, the balanced budget rule or the budget balancing practices that enforce the rule across jurisdictions.

In this context, the concept of practice provides access to a more differentiated meaning of decision making. For instance, when researchers focused on how budget analysts function, they report that, analysts do not rely exclusively either on technical or political orientation but utilize both as the situation warrants (Willougby, 1993; Thurmaier and Gosling, 1997). Which type of analysis will be the norm of practice depends on whether the nature of the problem calls for immediate attention, the phase of the budget cycle where the analysis is necessitated, and the cues that are received from important stakeholders (Thurmaier, 2001).

Understanding budget decision making as an institutional practice is reflected in the information classification practices as well as in the presence of regulative norms in the budget process. In budgeting, information is classified in terms of decision rules that limit options to those alternatives that are considered viable and to group similar things together for comparison across decision levels and contexts—for example, the application of accounting rules for sorting expenditures by fund groups. There are also many informal rules that sort and select information. Regulative norms on the other hand conserve key values that underlie action. These norms function as rules of appropriateness by infusing standards in decision making—standards such as, regularity, credibility, and public support. The efficacy of budget decisions is assessed against these norms and not against any externally stipulated decision rule. For instance, the control over spending may stand as the meaning of efficiency rather than the optimal relation between inputs and outputs.

The use of budget formats and rainy day funds has also been found to operate according to the norms of appropriateness rather than fulfill some objective criterion. For instance, there is no substantial evidence showing that budget formats significantly influence organizational decision making, yet formats are dutifully followed in preparing the budget (Grizzle, 1986). Similarly, no significant relation has been found between the amount kept in rainy day fund and the level of fluctuation in revenue flow (Walcoff, 1987; Joyce, 2001), yet rainy day funds are maintained on a routine basis. Despite the apparent contradiction, these practices continue because they conserve important norms of public decision making, such as accountability and caution.

The practices that underlie agency budget success have been found to vary due to the selective adoption of analytical tools (Poister and Streib, 1989; Lee, 1997; Thurmaier and Gosling, 1997). For a jurisdiction, the selective adoption of analytical tools is often based on strengthening specific roles and routines, in order to sustain the norms that are considered critical for success.

For example, maintaining political support, reputation, and credibility (Duncombe and Kinney, 1987), or making a compelling case that is consistent with political priority (Abney and Lauth, 1993). The norm maintenance function of budget practices is also found to involve the use of strategic ambiguity (Meyers 1994), the use of strategic misrepresentation (Jones and Euske, 1991), and even the use of fiscal illusion to balance the budget (Giroux and Wiggins, 1994).

To view budget decision making as an institutional practice, both the rational and the behavioral approaches need to be considered (Bunch and Strussman, 1993). This consideration is needed for two reasons. The first reason is that, instrumental actions and institutional norms function jointly in budget decision making. For instance, Wildavsky (1992) notes that, the slack in the system provides considerable room for innovation without running into major political difficulties or introducing large-scale changes in the system. In fact, analyses may function as a strategy of responding to pressure as well as a means to optimize a given goal when possible.

The second reason is the culturally embedded character of budget practices. The political culture structures the meaning of budget decisions through rules and their interpretations (Wildavsky, 1988), such as the meaning of budget balance, budget deficit, and budget base. Political culture also exerts an independent impact on total spending as well as on spending priority (Koven, 1988; Koven and Mausolff, 2002). Analysis can also rest exclusively on institutional values. For instance, McCue reports that, the investment decisions of budget officials rest more on the pursuit of the public interest and less on their personal disposition towards risk (McCue, 2000). Therefore, budget decision making can be represented as the institutional embodiment of instrumental actions. These actions are derived not from a pre-given logic of rationality, but enacted through a set of rules, roles, and routines. The following section delineates the stages of the budget process that embody these rules, roles, and routines.

22.4.3 STAGES OF THE BUDGET PROCESS AND THE INTEGRATION OF RULES, ROLES, AND ROUTINES

A key feature of institutional practice that affects budgetary decision making is the sequential nature of the budget process. In contrast to the four stages of policy analysis, the budget process is constituted of five stages that tie the different decision making practices together to affect institutional ends. The stages determine who does what, when, and how, thereby, framing the decisions that can be made (Rubin, 2000). The framing is based on the relationship among participants and the sequencing of their decision making at each stage of the process (Rubin, 2000; Hildreth, 1996; Mikesell, 1995; Howard, 1983).

In each stage of the budget process, decision making takes on distinctive characteristics and assembles different sets of rules, roles, and routines. Although, in each stage, institutional actors employ their own criteria to decode what is important, they do so in relation to the actual and anticipated decisions of actors in other stages. Because of the effect of the stages, decision making becomes iterative—allowing some decisions to remain unchanged from the previous stage or even the previous cycle, and some other decisions to be quite different. Decision making thus becomes both forward and backward looking. This simultaneity, rather than resulting in inconsistent preferences, instead, allows the accommodation of contingent situations through anticipatory judgments. For instance, it allows for deploying counter strategies at a later stage to reverse a decision made at an earlier stage. In this context, building and maintaining confidence through mutual support stands as a more valued practice than being simply efficient or objective.

Thus, the stages of the budget process do not function as a conveyor belt but operate as a network of rules, roles, and routines, which draw from and contribute to each other. It is this coherence, which renders budgeting as an institutional practice. Table 22.2 summarizes the institutional practices that are characteristics in each stage of the budget process. This is followed with a delineation of the rules, roles, and routines that characterize each stage.

TABLE 22.2
Budget Decision Making as Institutional Practice

Pre-preparation	Establishing ceilings, freezing funds, and specifying targets based on fiscal policy and political compromise
	Delineating tax and spending limits
	Creating automatic spending mechanisms (for example, entitlements)
Formulation	Submitting spending requests within the specified deadline
	Complying with budget instruction and guideline, chart of accounts
	Complying with the regulation and standards of professional bodies
	Classifying requests in the line-item format
	Providing program justification to gain executive approval
	Consolidating requests by the budget office to reflect executive's policy goals
	Padding requests in anticipation of cuts
	Maintaining strategic ambiguity in ranking to preserve key stakeholder needs
	Bargaining, negotiating, and compromising on the numbers
	Establishing a set aside fund for rainy days
	Justifying the base (last year's appropriation)
	Adjusting the base to reflect changes in salary, benefit, and price
Approval	Accommodating to mandates and fiscal constraints
	Increasing, decreasing, eliminating or withholding spending based on negotiation and strength of justification
	Hearings, timing of meetings, and responding to comments
	Using current authority and amount as proxy means to fund programs if approval is not reached in time
	Exercising the Line-item veto
	Bargaining and determination of fair share
	Establishing norms to limit and channel competition
	Using strategies to protect programs that one prefers or cut programs that others prefer
	Following the committee rules to write appropriation bill
Execution	Using departmental structure and procedures to assign responsibility
	Using apportionment and allocation formula to regulate spending
	Using transfer and reprogramming procedures to make adjustments
	Complying with account codes and accounting norms
	Writing up budget report by month or quarter
	Establishing norms to flag variance
	Using encumbrance to control spending
Audit	Checking for fund balance and compliance with audit rules
	Checking the accuracy of accounting record and the use of budget authority
	Following professional standards
	Assessing the consistency with historical records
	Building confidence on internal controls
	Determining the legal use of funds
	Checking for fraud and abuse of authority

22.4.3.1 The Budget Pre-Preparation Stage

The process begins with setting restrictive norms prior to the preparation of the budget. The norms are based on making aggregate adjustments with macro-economic or ideological requirements (Schick, 1986; Wildavsky, 1992; Gosling, 1997). For example, establishing tax and spending limitations, ceiling, targets, funding freeze, and putting lids on new program creation and on existing program growth. Schick (1986) describes the institutionalization of this stage in the following terms:

> "Recent developments lack the fanfare that attended earlier waves of budgetary reform, but they may have a more lasting imprint. The reason for this is that the changes are animated by an internalized need to alter practices rather than by an external concept of good budgeting." (124)

Thus, key decisions are made even before agencies prepare their spending estimates. Budget decision making here is not premised on program objectives or detailed analysis, but on the politics of economic policy. The reason for normalizing the limits on spending is to restrict the growth of government, and to force the justification of the budget in terms of the legitimate role of government. The specification of the rules, roles, and routines for this stage is yet to be stabilized.

22.4.3.2 The Budget Formulation Stage

In this stage, administrative agencies form their request for funds, which is consolidated by the chief executive, who then sends it to the legislature for review and approval. Decision making involves the assessment of program expenditures for the current year and projecting the expenditure needs of the next fiscal year.

Rules:

- Official endorsement of expenditure requests (The chief executive generally decides what to recommend for funding as well as the form in which requests are to be presented to the legislature);
- Compliance with legislative intent and the fund structure;
- Adjusting requests to the limit set at the pre-preparation stage;
- Taking the budget base as a given until an institutional actor decides to alter it;
- Classifying funds as discretionary and nondiscretionary;
- Providing justification for requests (a variety of standard justifications are in use: workload, outcome, output, price change, method improvement or new service).

Roles:

- Executive advocacy for programs;
- Interpreting budget instructions and negotiating agency request;
- Being conservative by inserting systematic bias for adjusting requests;
- Framing requests as fair share for a program or agency;
- Tracking the decisions of prior participants;
- Program advocacy and deference to legislative priority. A variety of positive or negative roles can be deployed—being assertive in making budget request is one;
- Cultivating program support from constituency and legislative committee members;
- Embedding political reasons in requests to increase their chances of approval.

Routines:

- Submission of forms within deadlines;
- Using forecasting of prices and costs to structure requests;
- The use of line items or established account codes;
- Fitting agency needs within the categories of the standardized form;
- Padding budget requests;

- Formal and informal meetings to settle differences;
- The strategic use of justification.

22.4.3.3 The Budget Approval Stage

Decision making in this stage is centered on reviewing the submitted requests and approving or denying them. Approval is based on reviewing and negotiating priorities and by cutting some programs or adding new ones. Requests that are denied at a previous cycle can also be reactivated here under a different justification.

Rules:

- The writing and passing of the appropriation bill or bills and negotiating policy priorities;
- Separating the approval of spending amount from the approval of spending authority;
- Holding committee hearings to establish shared meaning and to avoid surprises;
- Establishing fair share for non-priority items with expectation of trade-offs;
- Saying no to requests that failed to emerge as a priority.

Roles:

- Different role requirements of legislative and executive officials (For example, the guardianship role for the legislative and responsive agent role for the executive);
- Agency culture regulates the meaning of neutrality;
- Inexperienced practitioners tend to change their recommendation with new information, while seasoned practitioners integrate multiple rationalities;
- Changes in process and technical rules affect role performance;
- Weighing both the political and economic factors in making decisions;
- Framing questions in order to direct the attention of legislative committee members.

Routines:

- Using hearings: briefing books, preplanned strategies, and even staging witnesses to build confidence in a program or in program officials;
- Deflecting attention with a variety of strategies (for example, proposing a study, showing dire consequences or requesting the cutter to pick the programs to cut);
- Deploying counter strategies (for example, the earmarking of funds or questioning the source to challenge a data base) as a way to demonstrate or stay in control;
- Structuring expenditures in conformity with the accounting system;
- Rounding up the numbers;
- Focusing on activities to be accomplished, rather than on the amount requested.

22.4.3.4 The Budget Execution Stage

This stage involves establishing internal controls through tracking expenditures in designated funds, making adjustments based on new and changing information, and delaying decisions to meet program and fiscal contingencies.

Rules:

- Interpreting the appropriation language forged in the approval stage;
- Allocating on the basis of historical patterns to prevent spending money prematurely;
- Separating accounting data from operational record keeping;
- Maintaining fund balance through tracking variance and restraining or stopping spending if gap exceeds a pre-established limit;

- Reviewing purchases or obligations over a limit to prevent fraud and limit spending;
- Intra-fund transfer between accounts to attend a contingency;
- Reprogramming within an account to balance fund;
- Showing a balanced budget on the basis of accounting records or justifying the reasons for a deficit or surplus.

Roles:

- Creating flexibility within the system of controls;
- Interpreting information to get an agreement or renegotiate it;
- Monitoring budget reserves;
- Accelerating spending to address a contingency;
- Juggling special funds;
- Pursuing productivity gains by increasing workload;
- Taking pressure off the general fund.

Routines:

- Creating contingency reserve or a rainy day fund;
- Entering the approved budget into the accounting system by following the accounts codes.
- Creating and closing accounts and funds;
- Creating and maintaining slack to balance funds (for example, by delaying hiring);
- Keeping mistakes in check through dual authorization;
- Maintaining separate bank accounts and serializing purchase orders;
- Flagging frequent transfers;
- Encumbering spending commitments and reporting variance.

22.4.3.5 The Budget Audit Stage

In this stage, decision making involves the determination of whether spending occurred in the amount that is recorded, and whether spending and its authorization are in compliance with laws, performance standards, and management policy.

Rules:

- Adopting professional guidelines and standards and their consistent application;
- Classification of spending;
- Legal use of authority in the disbursement process;
- Issuing penalties for violating fund use protocols;
- Issuing audit report.

Roles:

- Legal compliance with accounting principles and focusing on disclosure;
- Elected vs. appointed auditors, in-house vs. outside audit;
- The assessment of internal controls differs between internal and external actors (for example, assessments of finance officers tend to be more favorable than the assessments of external auditors);
- Shifting roles with changes in the political environment (for example, the number of suggested audit change has been found to increase with political competition).

Routines:

- Pre-audit to check the appropriateness of payment;
- Using established sampling procedure to focus audit;
- Using indicators to detect fraud (for example, focusing on the amount of petty cash or the maintenance of questionable accounts);
- Built in controls to flag disbursement (for example, signs of plugging gaps in figures with averages).

As the detailed enumeration of budget practices show, budget decision making does not follow the logic of instrumental action. Rather, the budget stages reveal the embodiment of a set of rules, roles and routines, which points more to budget decision making as an institutional practice.

22.5 CONCLUSION

In representing the budget process as complex and contextual, we face the choice between two very different understandings of the process: instrumental and institutional. The difference stems from how we account for budget decision making. In the instrumental approach, we see decision making as more logical but less embodied in practices. On the other hand, in the institutional approach, we see decision making as less logical but more embodied in organizational practices.

In the instrumental approach to budget decision making, we see that the budget decision making stands apart from budget practices. I argued in this chapter that we need to understand budget decision making in terms of both the institutional and instrumental perspectives. In this dual perspective, decision making emerges as a group of practices that is embedded in a sequential process—where instrumental analyses reinforces the rules, roles, and routines that coordinate the different stages of the process. Therefore, in this joint approach, we can account for the complex and fragmented as well as the coherent and integrated nature of decision making in the budget process.

REFERENCES

Abney, G. and Lauth, T., Determinants of state agency budget success, *Public Budgeting and Financial Management*, 5(1), 37–65, 1993.

Bailey, J. and O'Connor, R., Operationalizing incrementalism: measuring the muddles, *Public Administration Review*, 35, 22–41, 1975.

Brewer, G. and DeLeon, P., *The Foundations of Policy Analysis*, Brookes/Cole, Monterey, CA, 1983.

Bunch, B. and Strussman, J., State budgetary processes: The two faces of theory, *Public Budgeting and Finance*, 5(1), 9–36, 1993.

DeLeon, P., The stages approach to the policy process: What has it done? Where is it going?, In *Theories of the Policy Process*, Sabatier, P., Ed., Westview, Boulder, CO, pp. 19–34, 1999.

Duncombe, S. and Kinney, R., Agency budget success: How it is defined by budget officials in five western states, *Public Budgeting and Finance*, 7(1), 24–37, 1987.

Forrester, J. P. and Spindler, C. J., Budgeting theory through "relational learning," *International Journal of Organization Theory and Behavior*, 4(1&2), 107–131, 2001.

Giroux, G. and Wiggins, C., Information and municipal expenditures: Is monitoring effective in reducing overspending?, *Public Budgeting and Financial Management*, 6(4), 600–622, 1994.

Gosling, J. J., *Budgetary Politics in American Governments*, 2nd ed., Garland, New York, 1997.

Grizzle, G., Does budget format really govern the actions of budget makers?, *Public Budgeting and Finance*, 6(Spring), 60–70, 1986.

Grizzle, G., Budgeting and financial management: Propositions for theory and practice, In *Handbook of Public Administration*, Rabin, J., Hildreth, W. B., and Miller, G., Eds. 2nd ed., Marcel Dekker, New York, pp. 223–264, 1998.

Hildreth, W. B., Financial management: A balancing act for local government chief financial officers, *Public Administration Quarterly*, 20(3), 320–342, 1996.

Howard, S. K., The real world of state budgeting, In *Public Budgeting and Finance*, Golembiewski, R. T. and Rabin, J., Eds., 3rd ed., Marcel Dekker, New York, pp. 103–125, 1983.

Jones, L. R. and Euske, K. J., Strategic misrepresentation in budgeting, *Journal of Public Administration Research and Theory*, 1(4), 437–460, 1991.

Joyce, P. G., What's so magical about five percent? A Nationwide look at factors that influence the optimal size of rainy day funds, *Public Budgeting and Finance*, 21(2), 62–87, 2001.

Keil, L. D. and Elliot, E., Budgets as dynamic systems: Change, variation, time, and budgetary heuristics, *Journal of Public Administration Research and Theory*, 2(2), 139–156, 1992.

Koven, S. G., *Ideological Budgeting: The Influence of Political Philosophy on Public Policy*, Preager, New York, 1988.

Koven, S. G. and Mausoloff, C., The influence of political culture on state budgets, *American Review of Public Administration*, 32(1), 66–77, 2002.

Lee, R. D., A quarter century of state budgeting practices, *Public Administration Review*, 57(2), 133–140, 1997.

LeLoup, L. T. and Moreland, W. B., Agency strategies and executive review: The hidden politics of budgeting, *Public Administration Review*, 38(3), 232–239, 1978.

Lewis, V., Toward a theory of budgeting, *Public Administration Review*, 12, 43–54, 1952.

Lindblom, C., *The Intelligence of Democracy*, Free Press, New York, 1965.

Linder, S. H. and Peters, G., The two traditions of institutional designing: Dialogue versus decision?, In *Institutional Design*, Weimer, D. L., Ed., Kluwer, Norwell, MA, pp. 133–160, 1995.

Lynch, T. D., *Public Budgeting in America*, 4th ed., Prentice Hall, Englewood Cliff, NJ, 1995.

March, J. G. and Olsen, J. P., The new institutionalism: Organizational factors in political life, *American Political Science Review*, 79, 734–749, 1984.

McCaffery, J., The craft of budgeting, In *Doing Public Administration*, Henry, N., Ed., 3rd ed., Wm. C. Brown, Dubuque, Iowa, pp. 112–136, 1991.

McCue, C., The risk-return paradox in local government investing, *Public Budgeting and Finance*, 20(3), 80–101, 2000.

Meyers, R. T., *Strategic Budgeting*, University of Michigan Press, Ann Arbor, MI, 1994.

Mikesell, J. L., *Fiscal Administration: Analysis and Applications for the Public Sector*, 4th ed., Wadsworth Publishing Co, Belmont, CA, 1995.

Natchez, P. B. and Bupp, I. C., Policy and priority in the budgetary process, *American Political Sciences Review*, 67, 951–963, 1973.

Ostrom, E., An Agenda for the Study of Institutions, *Public Choice*, 48, 3–25, 1986.

Ostrom, E., Institutional rational choice: An assessment of the institutional analysis and development framework, In *Theories of the Policy Process*, Sabatier, P., Ed., Westview, Boulder, CO, pp. 35–72, 1999.

Poister, T. H. and Streib, G., Management tools in municipal government: Trends over the past decade, *Public Administration Review*, 49, 240–248, 1989.

Reed, S. A., The impact of nonmonetary performance measures upon budgetary decision making in the public sector, *Journal of Accounting and Public Policy*, 5, 111–140, 1986.

Rubin, I. S., *The Politics of Public Budgeting*, 4th ed., Chatham House, New York, 2000.

Simon, H. A., *Administrative Behavior*, McMillan, New York, 1958.

Schick, A., The road to PPB: The stages of budget reform, *Public Administration Review*, 26, 243–248, 1966.

Schick, A., Macro budgetary adaptations to fiscal stress in industrialized democracies, *Public Administration Review*, 46, 124–134, 1986.

Steckroth, R. L., Slocum, J. W., Jr., and Sims, H. P., Jr., Organizational roles, cognitive roles, and problem-solving styles, *Journal of Experiential Learning and Simulation*, 2(2), 77–87, 1980.

Stone, D., *Policy Paradox: The Art of Political Decision Making*, W.W. Norton, New York, 2002.

Thompson, J. D., *Organizations in Action*, McGraw Hill, New York, 1967.

Thurmaier, K. and Gosling, J., The shifting roles of state budget offices in the midwest: Gosling revisited, *Public Budgeting and Finance*, 17(4), 48–70, 1997.

Thurmaier, K., Decisive decision making in the executive budget process: Analyzing the political and economic perspectives of central budget bureau analysts, *Public Administration Review*, 55(5), 448–456, 1995.

Thurmaier, K., Budget rationality in a policy oriented state budget office, *International Journal of Organiz-ation Theory and Behavior*, 4(1&2), 133–161, 2001.

Walcoff, M., An evaluation of municipal rainy day funds, *Public Budgeting and Finance*, 7(2), 52–63, 1987.

Weimer, D. L., Institutional design: An overview, In *Institutional Design*, Weimer, D. L., Ed., Kluwer, Norwell, MA, pp. 1–16, 1995.

Wildavsky, A., *The Politics of the Budgetary Process*, Little Brown, Boston, MA, 1964.

Wildavsky, A., A budget for all seasons? Why the traditional budget lasts, *Public Administration Review*, 38, 501–509, 1978.

Wildavsky, A., A cultural theory of budgeting, *International Journal of Public Administration*, 11(6), 651–677, 1988.

Wildavsky, A., Political implications of budget reform: A retrospective, *Public Administration Review*, 5, 594–599, 1992.

Willoughby, K., Decision making orientations of state government budget analysts: Rationalists or incremen-talists?, *Public Budgeting and Financial Management*, 5, 67–114, 1993.

23 Strategic Planning and Decision Making

Ofer Meilich and Alfred A. Marcus

CONTENTS

23.1 The Concept and Its History...434
    23.1.1 Definitions...434
    23.1.2 Characteristics of Strategic Planning Systems.......................435
    23.1.3 A Historic Review..436
23.2 Tools and Techniques..437
    23.2.1 Business-Level Tools and Techniques.....................................438
        23.2.1.1 SWOT Analysis...438
        23.2.1.2 Five-Forces Analysis...438
        23.2.1.3 Stakeholder Analysis...438
        23.2.1.4 Value-Chain Analysis..438
        23.2.1.5 McKinsey's Seven-S Framework...............................439
        23.2.1.6 Industry Life Cycle...439
    23.2.2 Corporate-Level Tools and Techniques...................................439
        23.2.2.1 Portfolio Management Frameworks...........................439
        23.2.2.2 Value-Based Planning...440
        23.2.2.3 Economic Value Added...440
        23.2.2.4 Scenario Analysis..440
23.3 The Controversy over Strategic Planning..441
    23.3.1 Arguments for Strategic Planning..441
    23.3.2 Arguments against Strategic Planning......................................442
    23.3.3 Empirical Evidence—Does Strategic Planning Help
        Organizational Performance?..443
23.4 Resolving the Controversy Over Strategic Planning.......................445
    23.4.1 External Contingencies...445
        23.4.1.1 Environmental Uncertainty.......................................445
        23.4.1.2 Capital Intensity...447
        23.4.1.3 Strategic Discretion..447
    23.4.2 Internal Contingencies...447
        23.4.2.1 Organizational Size...448
        23.4.2.2 Strategic Orientation...448
        23.4.2.3 Other Internal Contingencies....................................448
23.5 The Future of Strategic Planning...449
    23.5.1 Alternative Perspectives on Strategic
        Decision Making...449
    23.5.2 Improving Our Understanding of Contingencies......................451

23.6   Conclusion...452
References..452

23.1 THE CONCEPT AND ITS HISTORY

23.1.1 DEFINITIONS

Strategic planning is a formal system for supporting strategic decision making (Steiner, 1979). Strategic decisions* are decisions that are integrative, competitively consequential, involve considerable resource commitment, and are hard to reverse (Mintzberg, 1994; Nutt, 2001). Such decisions have the potential to critically affect organizational health and survival (Eisenhardt and Zbaracki, 1992). Examples of strategic decisions are: restructuring, new product introduction, organizational change, joint venture and strategic alliance, acquisitions, divestments, new process technologies, new marketing venues, geographic expansion, diversification to other industries, capacity expansion, creating new facilities, fundamental revision of human resource policies, and engaging in quality initiatives (Dean and Sharfman, 1996; Sinha, 1990).

Planning is a "formalized procedure to produce articulated result, in the form of an integrated system of decisions" (Mintzberg, 1994). It clearly consists of future thinking and often is motivated by attempts to control what comes next. It means trying to design a desired future and identifying ways to bring it about (Steiner, 1979). It involves resource allocation, priorities, and actions needed to reach strategic goals (Griffin, 2006). Strategic plans are converted into action through organizational policies, procedures, and rules (DuBrin, 2006). Policies provide general guidelines for decision making and actions. Procedures provide customary ways for sets of activities. Rules are specific courses of actions.

Strategic planning is "an explicit process for determining the firm's long-range objectives, procedures for generating and evaluating alternative strategies, and a system for monitoring the results of the plan when implemented," (Armstrong, 1982, 198). It is based on a profile of the decisions and the predispositions of those who control the firm with respect to its environment, context, and structure (Shrader, Taylor, and Dalton, 1984). The process of strategic planning consists of determining the firm's mission, major objectives, strategies, and policies that govern the acquisition and allocation of resources to achieve the firm's goals. This process is formal in that it "involves explicit systematic procedures used to gain the involvement and commitment of those principal stakeholders affected by the plan" (Pearce, Freeman, and Robinson, 1987, 658). According to these authors, the process includes detailed formats, quantification of all inputs, and a rigid calendar of events. Grinyer and Norburn (1975) maintain that planning must be formal and systematic in its approach to formulating the firm's objectives and major policies as they affect its relationship with its environment. Planning is formal inasmuch as it involves a preordained flow and processing of information. This preordained flow has to be regular and scheduled.

According to Mintzberg (1994, 15) strategic planning "must be seen, not as decision making, not as strategy making, and certainly not as management, or as the preferred way of doing any of these things, but simply as the effort to formalize parts of them—through decomposition, articulation, and rationalization." Strategic planning supports, but it is not a substitute for, strategic thinking. Strategic planning supports strategic decision making both before and after such decisions are made. As input, strategic planning provides data and analysis. As output, it elaborates and operationalized strategic decisions (Mintzberg, 1994).

---

* The definitions of strategy in the field of strategic management are legion. For instance, Abraham (2006) lists sixty-six definitions of "strategy" according to strategic management textbooks, trade books, articles, and dictionaries. It is therefore clear that the definitions we provide are not the only ones available.

Other definitions of strategic planning include the following: Kallman and Shapiro (1978) maintain that it is a process of analyzing and understanding a system, formulating goals and objectives, assessing capabilities, designing alternative courses of action, evaluating effectiveness, choosing, initiating actions for implementation, and engaging in continuous surveillance. Kudla (1980) holds that it is a systematic process for determining goals and objectives for a number of years into the future and developing strategies to govern resource acquisition and use. Liedtka (2001, 79) sees it as a "mechanism for setting and reviewing objectives, focusing on choices of long-term significance, identifying options, allocating resources, and achieving coordination, monitoring, and control." And Hax and Majluf (1991) define it as a disciplined and well-defined effort aimed at establishing objectives and assigning responsibilities for execution.

23.1.2 Characteristics of Strategic Planning Systems

Strategic planning systems vary between firms and industries. Boyd and Reuning-Elliott (1998) note that there is remarkably little consistency in the operationalization of strategic planning. Based on an extensive literature review, they identify and test seven internally consistent indicators of strategic planning. These are the extents to which each of the following are emphasized: mission statement, environmental trend analysis, competitor analysis, long-term goals, annual goals, short-term action plans, and ongoing evaluation.

The role and realm of decisions are different across the hierarchical levels in the firm (Grant and King, 1982; Hax and Majluf, 1991). At the corporate level, strategic decisions and, hence, planning efforts are directed at integrating the variety of businesses the corporation operates and managing the trade-offs necessary to maximize the benefits to the whole organization. At the business level, efforts are made to achieve long-term competitive advantage over specific competitors and within a specific industry context, congruent with the general corporate direction and with the resources allocated to the particular business unit. Finally, functional strategic planning deals with the specific functional parts of each business (such as manufacturing, R&D, sales, marketing, logistics, and service) where the unique competencies of the business are developed and leveraged. Because functional strategies are both so heavily dependent on business and corporate decisions and very specific, they are rarely studied by strategic planning researchers.

At the business level, the sequence of strategic planning commonly progresses in four steps: (1) developing of firm's vision, mission, and goals, (2) performing external and internal analyses, (3) creating, evaluating, and choosing strategies, and (4) implementation, control, and feedback (Hill and Jones, 2004; Hitt et al., 2005; Marcus, 2005). In large, multidivisional corporations the typical annual corporate-level strategic planning cycle involves more steps. Grant (2003) for instance, describes nine steps: (1) planning guidelines, (2) draft business plan, (3) discussion with corporate headquarters, (4) revision of the business plan, (5) annual capital and operating budgets, (6) aggregate corporate plan, (7) board approval, (8) performance targets, and (9) performance appraisal.

Though most strategic planning systems share common core features, they must also be tailored to each firm's specific situations and needs. There are quite a few characteristics differentiating specific planning systems. In one of the classic studies in the field, Grinyer, Al-Bazzaz, and Yasai-Ardekani (1986) and, later, Yasai-Ardekani and Haug (1997) measure strategic planning systems according to six characteristics: (1) planning specialization (sophistication of techniques used, size of planning staff), (2) formality of planning activities (extensiveness of use of written documents, number of plans and areas reviewed on a scheduled basis), (3) delegation of planning activities and decision making to staff (such as triggering reviews, generating and evaluating alternatives, and controlling implementation), (4) involvement of top management team and of line managers (in terms of generation and evaluation of proposals and choice of alternatives), (5) length of planning horizon of plans, and (6) planning staff status within the firm (frequency of attending top level meeting, reporting level of head of planning). Kukalis (1991) notes that planning systems can have different flexibility, time horizons, and frequency of revisions. And in addition to flexibility, Rogers, Miller, and Judge (1999) list emphasis on accounting, control, and efficiency, extent of scanning activities, and concentration on broad versus specific issues.

23.1.3 A Historic Review

Though Ansoff (1965) and Steiner (1979) are credited with the establishment of strategic planning as a field within strategic management, the concept has earlier precursors. Interest in strategic planning in the United States started in the post-World War II era, when the American middle class ballooned and U.S. businesses were responding to a surge in demand and prosperity. This surge stimulated demand for new management concepts and tools (Bowman, Singh, and Thomas, 2002). Two management practices were the precursors to strategic planning: financial planning and long-range planning (Hax and Majluf, 1984). Financial planning was dominant during the 1950s and earlier. Its focus was on budgeting and financial control on an annual or bi-annual basis. Budgeting involves forecasting revenue, costs, and capital needs based on historical internal data (Sweeny and Rachlin, 1981; Welsch, 1964). Financial control distills key parameters as data and targets, aimed at efficient and effective use of financial resources. Such parameters are related to the business growth, assets, and financial ratios (such as return on assets, return on sales, and asset turnover). At that time, the concept of responsibility center (such as profit, revenue, and cost center) was developed. Though an important component of a firm's financial and accounting system, financial planning did not incorporate the strategic priorities of the firm. Long-range planning started to include strategic priorities.

Long-range planning dominated in the relatively placid corporate environment of the 1960s. Unlike financial planning, it was more externally oriented, involving projection of environmental trends, typically for five years into the future. The process started with a forecast of the firm's sales, from which plans for functional areas (such as manufacturing, marketing, and human resources) were derived, culminating with the aggregation of the projections into a financial plan (Kastens, 1976; Linneman, 1980; O'Connor, 1976). Though little more than budgets extended into the future, such an approach was viable during these times, as the post-war U.S. market was growing steadily and predictably. As much as this approach was an improvement on financial planning, it had some shortcomings: its concentration on sales instead of the total market, its assumption that the future progresses along historically-based trends, and its unsuitability for diversified companies operating in several industries (Hax and Majluf, 1984).

The 1960s also saw the first encompassing analytically based methods for strategic planning with the publication of Ansoff's (1965) book on corporate strategy and the Learned, Christensen, Andrews, and Guth (1965) text on business policy, later to be solidified by Steiner's (1979) book on strategic planning. These books, along with a myriad of others, have since proposed models and frameworks for conducting planning for businesses and corporations (several examples of these detailed models are presented in Mintzberg, 1994, 41–65). The basic model typically starts with objective setting, moves to external and internal analysis, strategic options evaluation, selection of strategies, programming them into action plans, and evaluating the effect of these strategies. Since then, strategic planning has gone through several stages as business environments have become less certain and corporations have became more complex. There are three discernable stages, running from the early days of business planning in the 1970s through strategic management in the 1980s and the uncertain, fast-paced 1990s.

The first stage, business planning, began in the 1970s as the growth of the American economy tapered down and rivalry was growing. At the same time, corporations were increasing in both size and diversity. At the core of this stage lies the concept of the Strategic Business Unit (SBU): "a separate business area with an external marketplace for goods and services, whose objectives can be established and strategies executed independently of other business areas" (Hax and Majluf, 1984, 15). As corporations (led by General Electric Corporation) started segmenting themselves into SBUs, business portfolio management tools began developing—the growth–share matrix (known as the Boston Consulting Group model), the industry-attractiveness-business strength matrix (developed by General Electric and McKinsey and Co.), and the product life cycle approach (developed by Arthur D. Little and Co.).[*] Yet, the solution to the problem of manageability of the multi-business corporation by breaking it down into a collection of SUBs created problems of over-decentralization, lack of a corporate identity, and the foregoing of cross-business synergies.

The second stage, strategic management, had dual thrusts—on one hand it incorporated more rigorous analyses at the SBU level, and on the other it represented an attempt to integrate and leverage the corporation's businesses around its core competencies. At the business level, Porter's (1980; 1985) concepts of industry analysis and generic strategies added considerable detail and sophistication to the analysis and strategic option evaluation steps of strategic planning. As such, Porter helped reorient corporate management away from the pitfalls of portfolio planning. Industry analysis reminded managers that moving in and out of lines of business was not a trivial matter. Porter's generic strategies framework highlighted the fact that profitability could be obtained not only via high market share and economies of scope but also through differentiation (i.e., high added value in limited market share niches). The second thrust rests on the resource-based view of the firm and the concept of core competencies. The resource-based view of the firm (Barney, 1986; Rumelt, 1984; Wernerfelt, 1984) deals with the development of unique resources for achieving sustained competitive advantage. Such resources help establish firm core competencies—activities that are central to the firm's competitiveness (Prahalad and Hamel, 1990). Core competencies allow a firm to dominate not only a single line of business but also to leverage them across a range of business, hence, integrating the corporation around these competencies.

The 1990s saw the start of a fierce attack on strategic planning. This attack was led by Mintzberg's (1994) influential book, *The Rise and Fall of Strategic Planning*. Mintzberg attacked the over-reliance on formal, bureaucratic planning process, highlighting planning's dysfunctional characteristics. A closely related issue was the appropriateness of formal strategic planning systems in the face of increased environmental uncertainty. The pendulum now shifted back to highlighting entrepreneurial spirit and managerial intuition, as management concepts such as community of practice and unmediated learning gained acceptance (Brown and Duguid, 1991; Lave and Wenger, 1991). An alternative perspective was offered by reference to complexity theory (Axelrod and Cohen, 1999; Brown and Eisenhardt, 1998), where planning is exhibited as the grand direction of the firm and coupled with establishing simple rules that permit adaptation within the grand direction (Grant, 2003).

It is important to note that firms today use a wide array of tool and techniques depending on their specific needs, situations, and aspirations. Therefore, previously dominant tools and methods are not necessarily abandoned; rather, these methods are employed under the current methods. We now proceed to discussing the major tools and techniques of strategic planning.

23.2 TOOLS AND TECHNIQUES

In this section, we briefly survey some of the more prominent tools and techniques used in strategic planning. Our focus here is on strategic analysis tools, as opposed to operationally oriented ones (such as scheduling, budgeting, and control tools). The section is divided into two broad topics, dealing first with single business tools and techniques, then with those related to corporate level.

---

[*] For a review of portfolio management techniques see Wind and Mahajan (1981) and Haspeslagh (1982).

23.2.1 BUSINESS-LEVEL TOOLS AND TECHNIQUES

23.2.1.1 SWOT Analysis

The goal of SWOT (Strengths, Weaknesses, Opportunities, and Threats) analysis is to develop strategies that exploit internal strengths and environmental opportunities while neutralizing external threats and avoiding internal weaknesses (Ansoff, 1965; Andrews, 1971; Hofer and Schendel, 1978). By now, SWOT analysis appears in virtually all textbooks in strategic management. SWOT analysis is one of the early methods to enhance a firm's fit with its environment. Mintzberg (1994) notes that, in particular, strengths and weaknesses must be assessed only in the firm's specific context by a learning process that tests whether a certain resource a firm has is indeed an asset or a liability.

23.2.1.2 Five-Forces Analysis

Porter (1980) five-forces model aims to determine the profit potential of an industry a firm might be in or one it is considering entering. The five forces determining the attractivity of an industry are: rivalry, new entry, buyers, suppliers, and substitutes. The weaker each of these forces is, the higher the profit potential of the industry. Having fewer and less fierce rivals and a lower risk of entry by new firms would allow incumbents to spend fewer resources on defending themselves. Strong buyers can demand that the industry accept lower prices or that it provide them products that are more expensive to produce. Strong suppliers demand higher prices for the inputs needed by the industry. Attractive substitutes limit the price the industry can charge before buyers switch to these substitutes. The model derives from industrial organization economics, incorporating concepts such as entry or exit barriers, economies of scale, switching costs, product differentiation, capital intensity, asset specialization, access to distribution channels, and ability of buyers and suppliers to integrate into the industry. The five-forces model is useful for forecasting trends in the industry (manifested as changes in the five forces), positioning to mitigate inherently negative forces, and choosing businesses to avoid unattractive industries.

23.2.1.3 Stakeholder Analysis

Stakeholder analysis examines both the competitive and cooperative relationships a firm has with various elements in its environment (Freeman, 1984). A stakeholder is any group that affects and is affected by the firm. Such analysis looks at both external stakeholders (such as rivals, customers, governments, local communities, and the media) and internal ones (such as shareholders, employees, and managers). According to stakeholder theory, a firm that obtains greater contributions from its internal and external stakeholders will be more successful than other firms. Attaining this level of contribution requires giving stakeholders appropriate incentives. The firm needs to provide a different type of incentive to each stakeholder group and in turn expects to obtain a different type of contribution from each group.

23.2.1.4 Value-Chain Analysis

Value-chain analysis was proposed by Porter (1985). A firm's functions constitute a chain of activities that transform inputs into outputs that customers value. This transformation process is composed of primary activities (like R&D, production, marketing and sales, and service) and support activities (such as infrastructure, information systems, material management, and human resources). Each activity has to be evaluated for its costs in comparison to the income it generates. Firms in an industry can compare the profit margin of its primary and support activities to those of their major competitors to detect signs of comparative strength or weakness. Moreover, not all activities must be done in-house. Some can be contracted to outside vendors. This examination of the rent-generating potential of each link in the value chain allows the firm to consider its investments in various links and to consider outsourcing or expansion of particular activities (Bowman, Singh, and Thomas, 2002).

23.2.1.5 McKinsey's Seven-S Framework

The seven-S framework was developed by McKinsey and Company's Peters and Waterman (1982). It draws attention to the integration and fit of strategy with six other important aspects of the firm: structure, systems, style, staffing, skill, and shared values. Structure is the extent to which an organization has a coherent form of dividing labor, allocating responsibilities, coordinating tasks, and ensuring accountability. Systems relate to how processes work and tasks are accomplished in critical areas within the firm. Style is the degree to which time, attention, and behavior of management and employees are aligned with the firm's real strategic needs. Staffing deals with the matching of management and employee skills with the tasks that have to be carried out, the extent to which the personalities in place are capable of working together, and the degree to which there is sufficient diversity among staff to allow opposing and dissenting voices to be heard. Skills relates to the extent to which the firm as a whole, as opposed to its employees, has the capabilities in place to compete and generate growth. Last, shared values are associated with the extent to which there is unity of purpose behind a common vision and culture in the firm.

23.2.1.6 Industry Life Cycle

The strategic options available to a firm, in terms of threats and opportunities, are closely related to the life cycle stage its industry is currently at (Anderson and Zeithaml, 1984; Hambrick and Lei, 1985; Hofer, 1975; Miles, Snow, and Sharfman, 1993). There are five major life cycle stages: embryonic, growth, shakeout, maturity, and decline. An embryonic industry is just beginning to develop, with typically growth rate below five percent (Abraham, 2006, 205). In the growth stage demand grows rapidly (above five percent). However, such growth cannot be sustained indefinitely, and once growth slows the industry enters the shakeout stage, where weak competitors drop out. Once growth drops below five percent the industry enters the mature stage. When growth is negative, the industry is in the decline stage. The challenges and key success factors are dramatically different in the various life cycle stages. In the embryonic stage much of the technology and industry infrastructure need to be developed. In the growth stage the major hurdles relate to the ability to attend to the larger customer groups beyond the early adopters and to establish sustainable first mover advantages (Moore, 1991). Firms in mature industries are concentrating on deterring new entrants and managing rivalry to avoid spiraling into price wars. Firms in declining industries must decide whether to stay in the industry and either dominate the industry or concentrate on specific niches or to leave the industry through divestment or to harvest (cutting off all new capital investment).

23.2.2 CORPORATE-LEVEL TOOLS AND TECHNIQUES

23.2.2.1 Portfolio Management Frameworks

Portfolio management frameworks attempt to allow corporate-level managers to evaluate the range of businesses at which the firm operates (Haspeslagh, 1982; Wind and Mahajan, 1981). Among the more well-known of such frameworks are the Boston Consulting Group (BCG) matrix, the GE/McKinsey matrix, and the Arthur D. Little (ADL) matrix. The BCG growth–market share matrix is a framework for managing a corporation's portfolio of businesses (Henderson, 1979). Strategic business unites (SBUs) are evaluated based on their relative market share and the growth rate of their industry. SBUs that are high on market share and growth rate are considered Stars. The strategy for these SBUs is to invest in them and increase their share of the corporation's overall business. Businesses that are high on market share but low on market growth are considered Cash Cows. The strategy in this case is to hold onto them and maintain them to extract the cash needed to invest in more promising businesses. SBUs that are low on market share but high on market growth rate are Question Marks. The strategy here is to selectively hold onto them, invest in the most promising, and increase their share of the company's overall business. SBUs that are low on both market share and growth rate are considered Dogs, and the strategy is to harvest or divest them. The GE/McKinsey industry attractiveness-business strength matrix is essentially an extension of the BCG matrix to a three-by-three framework where industry market growth rate is replaced by industry attractiveness and the business market share is replaced by business strength (Hax and Majluf, 1984). The Arthur D. Little matrix considers a business's competitive position within its industry and the industry's life cycle stage (Hax and Majluf, 1984). Similarly to the other two frameworks, a dominant business in a young, growing industry is to be developed and leveraged, while weak businesses in mature, aging industries are to be harvested, divested, or liquidated.[*]

23.2.2.2 Value-Based Planning

Value-based planning (VBP) assesses strategies in terms of their potential to create shareholder value (Rappaport, 1981; 1986; Fahey, 1988). VBP attempts to provide answers to such questions as: (1) Will, and how much will, the corporate plan create value for shareholders? (2) Which business units are creating value and which are not? (3) How would alternative strategic plans affect shareholder value? (Rappaport, 1981, 139). This method involves the examination of a few key financial measures such as sales growth, profit margins, investment requirements, taxes, and cost of capital. VBP requires the firm to consider the risk associated with strategic alternatives. It separates between the systematic risk (the risk affecting all firms in the economy, as reflected in the discount rate) and the risk specific to each business strategy (such as the variations in the rate a new product may sell).

23.2.2.3 Economic Value Added

Economic Value Added (EVA) is a methodology for assessing a firm's overall performance (Ehrbar, 1998; Stern, Stewart, and Chew, 1995; Stewart, 1991). EVA is defined as net operating profit minus the opportunity cost of capital. It measures how much better or worse a firm's earnings are than the amount investors could obtain by putting their money in alternative investments or comparable risk. EVA highlights the productivity of all factors of production, showing which activities inside the firm have an unusually high productivity. Essentially, EVA sets the cost of capital as the threshold for rate of return, below which performance is unacceptable.

23.2.2.4 Scenario Analysis

Scenario analysis was introduced by Royal Dutch/Shell Group planning department (Wack, 1985a; 1985b); (see also Georgantzas and Acar, 1995; Schoemaker, 1995). A scenario is essentially a story or plot that describes how a particular endpoint might be reached under certain conditions. Scenarios play out various "what-if" possibilities. Scenario analysis seeks to discover the implications for the strategic decisions and moves of the firm related to getting to that endpoint. The purpose of scenario creation is not to predict the future but to consider futures and to prepare or to rehearse for what they might bring. The analysis involve possible actions the firm can take to cope or even leverage the impact of a certain scenario, including a risk-return projection of these actions.

---

[*] See Hax and Majluf (1984) for a thorough discussion of the three portfolio management frameworks and their applications.

23.3 THE CONTROVERSY OVER STRATEGIC PLANNING

The value of strategic planning has been debated for decades now (Liedtka, 2001, 79). Indeed, as Brews and Hunt (1999, 889) note, "Few issues have attracted more attention in strategy research than the relationship between the mode of strategic planning adopted by the firm and the economic performance of the firm." And Ackoff (1981, 359) quips: "Most corporate planning is like a ritual rain dance: it has no effect on the weather that follows, but it makes those who engage in it feel that they are in control." In this section we first present the arguments for and against strategic planning and then review the empirical evidence to date.

23.3.1 ARGUMENTS FOR STRATEGIC PLANNING

Broadly speaking, strategic planning is expected to enhance organizational performance via two routes. One route is through uncertainty reduction, the other through increased coordination and control. Planning reduces uncertainty because, as opposed to a trial-and-error, it provides a structured approach to decision-making (Miller and Cardinal, 1994). The benefits are related to both the process of planning and to its results. The planning process helps to unify corporate direction and introduces a discipline for long-term thinking (Hax and Majluf, 1991). Planning, done by specialized staff in collaboration with line managers, draws attention to strategic issues (as opposed to operational matters) and builds analytic capability in the firm (Steiner, 1979). Planning activities such as environmental scanning for threats and opportunities, competitive analysis, and constructing and evaluating alternative strategic moves for their risk, benefit, and internal consistency, all aid the firm in adapting to its competitive landscape and even shaping it (Rogers, Miller, and Judge, 1999; Yasai-Ardekani and Haug, 1997). The label "strategic" is reserved for those decisions and actions that are consequential to the performance and even viability of the firm. Hence, activities that are aimed at systematic identification of potential sources of strategic threats and opportunities and ways to diffuse the former and leverage the latter should be directly related to firm performance.

Strategic planning also is expected to enhance coordination, commitment, and control within the firm and with entities outside it. Having a formal (usually written) plan facilitates communication and hence coordination. By formally including all involved stakeholders, planning facilitates a comprehensive view of the firm and prevents sub-optimization (Steiner, 1979). "Strategic planning systems are superb channels of communication by means of which people throughout an organization converse in a common language about problems of central importance to them and to the organization" (Steiner, 1979, 48). When plans are made formal, the plan becomes explicit, impersonal, and legitimate. Explicitness is reflected in the clear specification of policies, decision rules, and actions, making them readily available for all concerned members to draw upon. Impersonality means that guidelines and instructions are disembodied from both originator and receiver. This allows organizations to transcend time and space limitations (Giddens, 1984; Scott, 1998, 37), as codified information can be transmitted to multiple destinations a-synchronically at much lower cost than face-to-face communication. Legitimacy implies that formal standards and guidelines signal to members that these goals and behaviors are authorized by the organization. Planning also fosters commitment to the firm, its goals, and the plan itself. While the plan itself is formal, the planning process is highly interactive. As it involves multiple levels in the organization (Hax and Majluf, 1991), planning fosters commitment through the participation of organizational members in generating and evaluating alternative strategies (Armstrong, 1982). "The engaging communicational efforts, the multiple interpersonal negotiations generated, the need to understand and articulate the primary factors affecting the business, and the required personal involvement in the pursuit of constructive answers to pressing business questions are what truly make the planning process a most vital experience" (Hax and Majluf, 1991, 20). In addition, planning has a fundamental function as a control mechanism because it sets clear direction and goals that can be compared to what has been achieved to date, highlighting the gaps and prompting adjustments. Indeed, feedback following implementation is an integral part in nearly all models of strategic planning systems (e.g. Ansoff, 1965; King, 1983; Steiner, 1979). Mintzberg (1994) reminds us that control through plans crosses firms' boundaries in both ways—external elements such as markets, competitions, suppliers, and government agencies may be components in the plan, while outside influencers such as parent company or government entities can use their plans to control the firm.

23.3.2 ARGUMENTS AGAINST STRATEGIC PLANNING

In addition to its potential benefits, quite a few scholars have noticed that planning carries its own costs. Even Steiner (1979), one of the strongest proponents of strategic planning, notes that it is a costly activity, as it draws resources that may be otherwise used in a firm, and that it may encourage rigidity due to the channeling of behaviors. Hax and Majluf (1991) warn that planning may become an end in itself, transformed into a meaningless game of numbers. And Powell (1994, 125) notes that strategic planning "deludes managers into a false sense of control and security, and obscures outworn assumptions, producing the strategic 'blind spots' and complacency that leads inevitably to crises. These crises yield internal conflicts and create a confusing array of alternatives that cannot be rationally compared."

Yet, by far the most vocal critic of formal strategic planning has been Mintzberg (1994). The following quote gives the reader a flavor of Mintzberg's critique: "Take apart any model of strategic planning, box by box, and at the heart of the process where strategies are supposed to be created, you will find only a set of empty platitudes, not any simulation of complex managerial processes" (297). Mintzberg lists four pitfalls of planning and explicates why he declares the fundamental concepts of planning as fallacies.

The four pitfalls of planning, according to Mintzberg, are that it (1) does not foster commitment, (2) forces inflexibility on the firm, (3) incorporates a substantial amount of political behaviors, and (4) gives managers a false sense of control. Strategic planning may hinder commitment of line managers and employees because it seeks to take discretion away from them by prescribing what they need to do. Mintzberg notes that "commitment seems to grow out of personal control, a sense of ownership of a project… not deeply constrained by the specifics of formal plans or the detachment of so-called objective calculations" (172). Plans are by their nature inflexible. "A strategy is formulated to direct energies in a certain direction; momentum is, therefore, not only the inevitable result but the desired one… The price, of course, is the organization's ability to change when it must, sooner or later" (175). Moreover, because the planning process uses existing categories, it may not have room for novel ideas. While planning is supposed to rely on hard, objective data, it is infused with politics and parochial influences, from the naïve assumption that goals are unitary to suggested alternatives that naturally favor the planning staff and to what is measured and controlled. Mintzberg also maintains that planning is the organizational counterpart of the psychological mechanism of illusion of control. It gives managers the false impression that they actually control their environment even if they don't. Worse, the whole effort can turn into a systemwide public relations game to impress outsiders: "Presumably to be able to plan is tantamount to being able to spend money responsibly" (215).

Mintzberg goes even deeper in explicating the fundamental fallacies of strategic planning: predetermination, detachment, and formalization. Predetermination relates to the ability of planners and the planning process to predict the future. Here Mintzberg argues that planning fits closed systems that are controllable, while organizations are in reality open systems. Being such, they are strongly influenced by external factors. Mintzberg doubts the ability of forecasting to predict the future. He especially notes the great difficulty forecasting has with predicting discontinuities, because of the need to sift through and identify the importance of weak signals ahead of time. Mintzberg also discards the value of the Delphi technique and scenario planning and, more generally, all attempts at contingency planning. Such planning is futile according to Mintzberg because (a) not all contingencies can be foreseen, (b) inaction is encouraged due to a "wait and see" approach, and (c) the contingency plan may be activated just because it exists, out of expediency, not because it is the correct one.

Detachment is the ability to detach strategy making from daily operations, and of strategy formulation from implementation. While classical strategic planning prescribe such separation, Mintzberg argues that thought cannot be separated from action, "while thinking must certainly precede action, it must also follow action, close behind, or else run the risk of impeding it" (292). Because planners tend to be removed from operations, they rely on hard (quantified) data. The reliance on hard data is problematic for a variety of reasons—such data are limited in scope and may not include important but nonquantifiable factors; in the process of aggregation that hard data goes through, vital data may be lost; hard data takes time to compile, hence it is inherently historical; and, last, such information includes intentional and unintentional distortions. Detachment deprives decision makers from the tacit knowledge that exists at the line and leads to analytically correct but inappropriate decisions. Similarly, implementation is not separate from formulation. Therefore, formulation must be made in situ: "every intended strategy must be interpreted by a great many people facing a wide range of realities" (285).

Formalization relates to the purported superiority of formal analysis over intuition. Mintzberg agrees that formal systems can certainly process more hard information. However, even though they can consolidate it, aggregate it, move it about, they cannot internalize, comprehend, or synthesize it. Mintzberg argues that the process through which strategies are actually made is informal and intuitive. Strategy making is inherently a process of synthesis, which cannot be achieved through the analytical methods of formal planning. Analysis-based approaches tend to be convergent and deductive. They are better at finding similarities than differences, better at decomposition than design. In the rush to evaluate alternatives and reach closure, analysts tend to skip issue diagnosis and generation of alternatives. Mintzberg sums up what he terms as the grand fallacy: "analysis cannot substitute for synthesis. No amount of elaboration will ever enable formal procedures to forecast discontinuities, to inform managers who are detached from their operations, to create novel strategies. Ultimately, the term 'strategic planning' has proven to be an oxymoron" (321).

Though academics argue back and forth, businesses live and die by their strategic decisions. What does the empirical evidence that is related to the effect of strategic planning on firms' performance indicate?

23.3.3 EMPIRICAL EVIDENCE—DOES STRATEGIC PLANNING HELP ORGANIZATIONAL PERFORMANCE?

The pendulum has shifted back and forth with regard to the value of strategic planning. Early literature reviews found support for a positive effect on firms in general (Armstrong, 1982) and within the context of small businesses (Robinson and Pearce, 1984). Armstrong (1982) reviewed 15 studies done between 1970 and 1981. He found that formal planning was superior to informal in five studies (statistically significant at $p < 0.05$). Robinson and Pearce (1984) reviewed 12 studies of small businesses done between 1953 and 1982. Of these, 11 studies found positive relations between planning and performance.

Yet, two latter literature reviews had considerable doubts about the contribution of strategic planning to a firm's bottom line. Shrader, Taylor, and Dalton (1984, 154) concluded that "there is no clear systematic relationship between long-range planning and organizational performance." However, closer examination of their findings reveals a less grim picture. Shrader and his colleagues examined 56 relevant studies, ranging from 1956 to 1983. Formal strategic planning seemed to enhance performance in 25 of 31 studies. In 25 other studies that examined the effects of planning at different organizational levels, the results were similar: in 21 of the 25 studies strategic planning was related to enhanced performance. The effect was most pronounced at the corporate level (13 of 14 studies reported a positive relationship). At the business level the relationship was positive but not as strong (five out of eight studies).

Another literature review by Pearce, Freeman, and Robinson (1987) examined 21 samples in 18 studies published between 1966 and 1983. Of the 21 samples, ten demonstrated a positive relationship between formal strategic planning and performance, another ten did not have significant findings, and only one study exhibited a negative relationship. Though these findings were mostly positive, Pearce and his colleagues declared that "empirical support for the normative suggestions by strategic planning advocates that all firms should engage in formal strategic planning has been inconsistent and often contradictory" (671).

The controversy in the empirical literature did not abate. Three later studies used meta-analyses to quantify the overall relationship between strategic planning and performance. Boyd's (1991) study was the first systematic effort to employ this method. He incorporated planning-performance correlations from 29 studies, published between 1970 and 1988. Boyd determined the overall mean correlation to be 0.15 (considered to be a lower bound because method effects were not included). Additionally, he separated the analysis by specific performance measures and found the following mean correlations between strategic planning and performance: earning per share growth (0.28), sales growth (0.25; the most common measure), earnings growth (0.21), and price-earnings ratio (0.24). Among the various performance measures, growth in earning per share and price-earning ratio had consistently high correlations and little variation across the studies.

Schwenk and Shrader's (1993) meta-analysis concentrated on small businesses. They looked at 26 samples from 1982 to 1990. The effect of planning on performance measures (sales growth, return on assets, return on sales, and return on investment) was found to be positive and statistically significant (at $p < 0.05$) but small. No correlations were reported because the authors used different measures of association in their analyses.

The most recent study to date was that of Miller and Cardinal (1994). They included 26 studies in their sample, ranging from 1973 to 1991. They found that strategic planning had an overall positive effect on performance. More specifically, a mean correlation of 0.17 was calculated between planning and growth measures, and 0.12 between planning and profitability measures. Miller and Cardinal also found that the more carefully a study presented a period of time appropriate to what was being studied, the more positive were the correlations (by as much as 0.18).

We identified five additional studies since 1991 (the last year included in the latest meta-analysis of Miller and Cardinal, 1994) reported on the relationship between aspects of strategic planning and various measures of performance. All five reported a positive relationship between planning and performance. Capon, Farley, and Hulbert (1994) examined a sample of 113 of the Fortune 500 manufacturing firms. They found that an increase in corporate planning sophistication was associated with higher return on capital and higher survival rates. Hopkins and Hopkins (1997) found that the higher the intensity in which the 112 banks in their sample engaged in strategic planning, the better was their financial performance. Brews and Hunt (1999) analyzed the planning practices of 656 firms and found a strong effect of formal planning specificity on firm performance. Andersen (2000) found a positive relationship between strategic planning and a composite measure of return on assets and sales growth (he had a sample of 230 firms in three industries: food products, computer products, and banking). More recently, Delmar and Shanem (2003) found that business planning reduced failure rate and accelerated product development in their sample of 223 Swedish new ventures.

In summary, in contrast with Mintzberg (1994) who argued that "A number of biased researches set out to prove that planning paid, and collectively they proved no such thing" (134), recent meta analyses, reexamination of the literature reviews, and later studies, all indicate that strategic planning has a small but consistent positive main effect on organizational performance. Therefore, Brews and Hunt (1999) assert that "If anything, the dissatisfaction with formal strategic planning has surfaced the practices to be avoided in planning [such as detaching planning from line managers, and resisting mid-way adaptations], rather than providing support for the proposition that the remedy for bad planning is no planning" (904).

23.4 RESOLVING THE CONTROVERSY OVER STRATEGIC PLANNING

Setting rhetorical arguments aside, it is clear that we should not expect strategic planning to have the same effect on performance in all situations. Planning does not benefit every firm in every circumstance. Planning is a costly activity. There are opportunity costs associated with planning even if the general direction of the empirical results reported above are positive. There are direct human resources expenses. Planning takes staff time and effort away from normal duties; if external consultants are hired, not only are they typically expensive but there is the added issue of commitment of those not involved in the ongoing processes of the organization (Powell, 1994). There are also the dangers of misapplying strategic planning, leading to inertia and alienation of employees and line mangers.

Therefore, it is important to find the conditions that determine when strategic planning is likely to be more effective. Quite a few contingencies have been suggested in the literature about when planning's benefits outweigh the costs, and some have been tested.

Broadly speaking, the contingencies can be divided into two groups—external and internal. While external factors (such as uncertainty and capital intensity) are largely determined by the firm's environmental context, internal contingencies (such as size and strategic orientation) are more determined by the firm itself. Below, we review the contingencies that may be associated with the success of strategic planning and assess the empirical evidence related to them.

23.4.1 EXTERNAL CONTINGENCIES

By far, the most debated and researched contingency is that of environmental uncertainty (also termed as dynamism, turbulence, or instability). Other contingencies mentioned in the literature are capital intensity, and strategic discretion. These external contingencies are largely related to the uncertainty reduction role of strategic planning.

23.4.1.1 Environmental Uncertainty

Interestingly enough, there are two camps here. One maintains that planning is more crucial in situations of greater uncertainty. While the other camp, led by Mintzberg (1994), argues that strategic planning is more suitable in stable environments. The first camp's arguments hinge on the purported ability of strategic planning to reduce uncertainty. Environmental uncertainty has been defined as the absence of information about the environment (Huber and Daft, 1987). The need and benefit of such information is greater in more uncertain environments. Such information is used to cope with changes and make the future less unpredictable. Strategic planning involves environmental scanning, which may identify weak signals of impeding drastic changes in a firm's competitive landscape. Likewise, dynamic agenda setting requires trend analyses to determine if changes are transient or enduring.

The other camp posits that in unstable environments planning's costs outweigh its benefits. The wide diversity of possible future developments can severely tax the firm's scanning ability with little useful outcomes (Fredrickson and Mitchell, 1984). Worse, Fredrickson and Mitchell point out, in highly uncertain environments, firms lack cause-effect understanding related to key decision variables. Essentially, when environments change in rapid and unexpected ways, strategic planning may provide "tomorrow's solution to yesterday's problem" (Braybrooke and Lindblom, 1970, 121). By the nature of the planning and implementation processes, plans must be "frozen" to allow elaboration of strategies into tactical and operational actions (Steiner, 1979). Unless the environment is stable, the plan must be revised and updated so frequently that it never gets to be implemented, not to mention the obvious waste of resources involved in this effort (Mintzberg, 1994). For all these reasons, planning in uncertain environments is, according to the second camp, a futile exercise.

The empirical evidence seems to be in favor of the first camp, as, out of eleven study results, only three studies support the Frederickson-Mintzberg view, six indicate that strategic planning in more dynamic contexts is more effective than planning in more stable contexts, and two studies produce statistically non-significant results.

Fredrickson and his co-authors (Fredrickson, 1984; Fredrickson and Mitchell, 1984; Fredrickson and Iaquinto, 1989) studied the relationship between strategic decision making comprehensiveness and firm performance in two contrasting industries—paint and coating (a stable industry) and forest products (an unstable industry). Comprehensiveness was defined as "the extent to which an organization attempts to be exhaustive or inclusive in making and integrating strategic decisions" (Fredrickson and Mitchell, 1984, 402). It captures a key aspect of strategic planning. Fredrickson and his co-authors found in two study waves (1980–1982 and 1986) that the correlation between comprehensiveness and return on assets was positive in the stable industry and negative in the unstable one. An independent study that corroborated Fredrickson's findings is that of Hough and White (2003). These scholars found a negative interaction term between knowledge pervasiveness (how widely knowledge is held within a team) and industry dynamism on strategic decision quality in the context of a computerized business game.

Six other studies supported the opposite point of view. In chronological order, the first study is that of Kukalis (1991) who surveyed 114 of the 200 largest (by sales) manufacturing firms as of 1985. He found that firms who were above the median environmental complexity (a measure that included aspects of uncertainty) exhibited positive correlations between planning extensiveness and both return on equity and earning per share. On the other hand, the below median group (low complexity) had non-significant correlations. Glick, Miller, and Huber (1993) surveyed top managers of 79 Strategic Business Units (SBUs) from various industries and found that decision making comprehensiveness was positively related to profitability in turbulent environments but slightly negatively related in low turbulent environments. Miller and Cardinal (1994) in their meta-analysis (see description above), found that sub-samples classified as high turbulence had a positive mean correlation between planning and performance, while low turbulence sub-samples had a negative mean correlation. Priem, Rasheed, and Kotulic (1995) surveyed 101 manufacturing firms and found a positive interaction term of decision making rationality by dynamism when this term was regressed on self-reported return on sales and on sales growth. When they divided their sample into three groups, the high dynamism group had positive correlations between rationality and the performance measures, and there were non-significant correlations in the medium and low dynamism groups. Atuahene-Gima and Li (2004) investigated the moderating effect of market demand uncertainty on the relationship between strategic decision comprehensiveness and new product performance in 247 Chinese new ventures. They found that the interaction term of comprehensiveness by demand uncertainty had a positive effect on both sales growth and new product performance. Interestingly, the interaction term of comprehensiveness with technological uncertainty was negative. Atuahene-Gima and Li have argued that the difference lies in the analyzability of the two environmental aspects—while market conditions are amenable to analysis and hence uncertainty reduction, technology is much more complex such that planning activities cannot reduce the uncertainty associated with technology. The last study uncovered a more complicated relationship. Goll and Rasheed (1997) surveyed 62 of the largest manufacturing firms in the US. Their findings were based on a three-way interaction between environmental dynamism, munificence, and rationality. They found that decision making rationality correlated positively with return on assets and return on sales only when both environmental dynamism and munificence were high, while the three other combinations had non-significant correlations. Last, two other studies, Brews and Hunt (1999) and Powell (1994) found no significant differences in the effect of strategic planning on performance between more and less uncertain environments.

Because the evidence goes against the Frederickson-Mintzberg view, the question arises as to why Fredrickson's studies depict an effect opposite to most of the other studies. Priem, Rasheed, and Kotulic (1995, 925–926) have listed several possible reasons. First, Fredrickson's studies concentrated on two industries. The assumption that these differ only on the variable of interest is tenuous. Second, other environmental dimensions such as munificence and complexity were not incorporated (note Goll and Rasheed, 1997 above). Third, Fredrickson used specific hypothetical decision scenarios that may not be generalizable to other strategic decisions. Fourth, there were differences in the operationalization of the constructs of interest. Also note that the other study supporting Fredrickson (Hough and White, 2003) uses an even more extensively contrived scenario (a computerized business game) than Fredrickson's studies. We will provide another possible explanation for this discrepancy when we discuss alternative forms for conceptualizing contingencies in Section 23.5.

23.4.1.2 Capital Intensity

Capital-intensive industries are characterized by heavy investments that must be used for long periods to justify adequate return on investment (Miller and Cardinal, 1994). Typically, these investments are specialized and therefore, hard to adapt. Because the consequences of wrong choices are severe and nearly impossible to reverse, such strategic investments must be carefully examined as comprehensively as possible, and they typically require long gestation time from decision to implementation (Armstrong, 1982; Mintzberg, 1994). The penalty for not planning is expected to be much higher than in non-capital intensive situations.

Two studies examined the effect of capital intensity on the planning-performance relationship (both are described above, in the section dealing with uncertainty). Kukalis (1991) found that the correlations between planning extensiveness and both return on equity and earning per share were positive and significant for the high capital intensity group, while those for the low capital intensity group were not significant. On the other hand, Miller and Cardinal (1994) meta-analysis found no effect of capital intensity on either the correlations between planning and growth nor that between planning and profitability.

23.4.1.3 Strategic Discretion

Environments also differ in the extent to which they allow strategic discretion to firms and their managers (Hambrick and Finkelsein, 1987). In low discretion environments, managerial actions make little difference on organizational performance. Strategic discretion may be curtailed due to low environmental munificence (i.e., resources and opportunities) or due to strong external control such as having a parent company or institutional elements (Goll and Rasheed, 1997; Mintzberg, 1994).[*] Under conditions of low strategic discretion, planning activities are expected to be less effective and to have lower performance effects. Indeed, when discretion is low, planning activities detract from economic performance because they take away organizational resources. Empirically, Goll and Rasheed (1997) found a positive interaction term between decision making rationality and munificence (as a proxy for strategic discretion) regressed on both return on assets and return on sales, thereby supporting this aspect of strategic discretion.

23.4.2 Internal Contingencies

Among the internal contingencies are organizational size, strategic orientation, diversification mode, experience in planning, and the nature of a firm's operations. These internal contingencies are largely related to the firm's need for structured internal coordination.

---

[*] In the case of institutional pressures, planning has little effect on performance because it is used to gain legitimacy and social capital by impressing external elements on which the organization is dependent. Though in such cases planning has only symbolic value and it is arguably costly in the short run, it may also enhance long-term viability by securing the support of strong external entities. However, such business situations are rare and unique (Meyer and Zucker, 1989).

23.4.2.1 Organizational Size

Large organizations plan more than smaller ones (Al-Bazzaz and Grinyer, 1981). However, are the benefits from planning greater for larger firms? Mintzberg (1994) argued that larger organizations not only can afford planning activities and staff but they have a greater need for it as a way to coordinate and integrate their actions. Unlike small organizations, larger ones cannot rely on informal, face-to-face interactions due to their sheer magnitude. Large organizations can benefit from finer division of labor, leading to higher numbers of sub-units and, hence, to a greater need for coordination and integration, done in part through planning (Vancil and Lorange, 1975). This does not mean that small firms do not benefit from planning (see the reviews by Robinson and Pearce, 1984; Schwenk and Shrader, 1993). Rather, while both small and large firm benefit from the uncertainty reduction aspect of planning, only large ones can leverage the integrative aspect of planning.

The empirical evidence on the relationship between size and strategic planning performance is, however, scant and mixed. Three studies examined this contingency (mentioned earlier in the uncertainty sub-section). Powell (1994) found support for the argument above, as the large size sub-sample exhibited significant and positive correlations of planning with both profitability and growth while the small size sub-group had non-significant correlations. However, two other studies (Kukalis, 1991; Miller and Cardinal, 1994) did not find any significant differences in correlations between large and small firms.

23.4.2.2 Strategic Orientation

Chakravarthy and Lorange (1991) distinguish between two orientations that strategic planning systems may take—adaptive and integrative. These reflect the two roles of planning: an adaptive orientation emphasizes uncertainty reduction, while an integrative one emphasized the control and coordination aspect of planning. An adaptive orientation is more externally focused and geared to innovation in products and markets. Conversely, an integrative orientation concentrates on enhancing efficiency and exploiting a firm's current position. These two orientations are mirrored in the distinction between differentiators and low-cost leaders (Porter, 1980) and between Prospectors and Defenders (Miles and Snow, 1978). Therefore, it might be expected that differentiators and prospectors would benefit more from planning activities aimed at uncertainty reduction, while low-cost leaders and defenders would benefit more from planning activities geared toward internal control and coordination.

Only two studies investigated the moderating effect of strategic orientation on the planning-performance relationship. Contrary to the arguments above, Powell (1994) found that the correlation between planning and profits was positive for the low-cost subgroup and negative for the differentiators. Interpretation is somewhat hampered because Powell's planning scale was an amalgamation of 12 items that were generic in nature. The sample of Rogers, Miller, and Judge (1999) consisted of 157 banks. As expected, the regression coefficients of accounting control (predicting three performance measures) for Defenders were positive while these for Prospectors were negative. Conversely, the coefficients of scanning and of breadth of analysis were negative for Defenders and positive for Prospectors. The only result not in line with the arguments of Chakravarthy and Lorange (1991) was the effect of the variable related to integration and control; it had a negative sign for the Defenders and positive one for Prospectors. That is, Defender banks that emphasized integration and control produced lower performance while Prospectors benefited from such emphasis. Therefore, research has not yet provided a clear answer regarding this contingency.

23.4.2.3 Other Internal Contingencies

Several other contingencies have been proposed and tested—diversification mode, experience in planning, and the nature of a firm's operations. Kukalis (1991) suggests that corporations operating businesses in related industries require greater cross-businesses coordination than those operating several unrelated businesses (such as a holding company). Kukalis' results partially supported this argument. While the correlation between planning extensiveness and return on equity was positive for related corporations, it was not significant for the unrelated ones. However, for both sub-groups the correlations between planning and earnings per share were not significant. Brews and Hunt (1999) confirmed that experience in planning (measured as having four or more years' experience) improved the effectiveness of both planning ends specificity and means specificity. Last, Mintzberg (1994) offers anecdotal evidence that planning is more effective when a firm's operations are tightly coupled yet simple, such as in an assembly line or in airline operations. When operations are tightly linked, the whole system depends on the smooth interfaces between its parts; therefore, in such situations planning's contribution to coordination and control is most important and even vital. However, as Mintzberg notes, to allow tight coordination, operations must be easily compre-hended; otherwise, the formal, detached planning process will itself break down. Therefore, formal planning is expected to work best in systems that are highly complex (i.e. with many interacting parts) but not complicated.

23.5 THE FUTURE OF STRATEGIC PLANNING

The research evidence on the relationship between strategic planning and firm performance under various contingencies is mixed. Therefore, for strategic planning to advance as a tool of manage-ment additional research is needed. We end this review with a critique of strategic planning and suggestions for future research. This section is organized into two topics. We discuss alternative perspectives of strategic decision making and then concentrate on shortcomings in current con-ceptualizations of contingencies.

23.5.1 ALTERNATIVE PERSPECTIVES ON STRATEGIC DECISION MAKING

The rational planning, or "synoptic," perspective that has dominated both planning theory and research (Mintzberg, 1994) assumes that actors have preexisting and known goals and objectives, approach decisions comprehensively, compare a large array of alternatives, and choose the optimal course of action. The closer one gets to realizing this approach, the more rational is one's decision making process. In contrast, there exist at least three perspectives on how organizations make strategic decisions: the incremental, the political, and the Garbage Can perspectives (see Table 23.1).

The incremental perspective includes a variety of approaches such as the bounded rationality approach (Simon, 1976), the evolutionary approach (Nelson and Winter, 1982), and the emergent approach (Mintzberg, 1994).[*] All these approaches share the view that organizations are composed of individuals limited in their ability to comprehend and manipulate their environments. Organiz-ational action is focused on responding, adapting to, and leveraging environmental threats and opportunities. According to Chakravarthy and White (2002) if these assumptions are accepted then planning serves an important purpose. It "is not to create strategy; but to retrospectively reduce equivocality, to discern a pattern in past action and explain it as a strategy" (Chakravarthy and White, 2002, 191). The explanation is then extrapolated into the future and used as a guide to action. Organizations in this way are intendedly rational, but not fully so.

The political perspective envisions members of an organization as being rational and calcu-lating, but collectively, when all their separate calculations are brought together, the organization is

---

[*] Note that we define the incremental perspective somewhat differently from incrementalism, which is discussed in the Hayes chapter in this volume. Also note that our definition includes Simon's concept of bounded rationality, which is discussed in the Mingus chapter in this volume.

TABLE 23.1
Comparison of Strategic Decision Making Perspectives

Concept	Rational Planning	Incremental Perspective	Political Perspective	Garbage Can Perspective
Key contribution	Systematic, comprehensive analysis	Breakdown of perfect rationality	Breakdown of consistent organizational goals	Temporal logic rather than causal logic
Organization	Unitary, led by the top manager	Collection of people pursuing common direction	Coalition of people with competing interests	Organized anarchy
Participation	Complete	Depends on decision needs	Depends on interests, power	Fluid: depends on load and structure
Search and analysis	Comprehensive, to find best solution	Local, to find a solution	To justify view, to win	Not applicable
Goals	Consistent, integrative	Reasonably consistent or sequential attention	Conflicting, multiple	Ambiguous, shifting
Conflict	Nonexistent	Positive, but no attention to resolution	High, stimulates 'game' of politics	Not applicable
Choice process	Comprehensive, rational	Intendedly rational with cognitive limits and loops, intuitive	Conflict of interests dominated by powerful coalitions	Random collisions of problems, solutions, participants, and opportunities
Emphasis	Optimizing	Problem solving	Resolving conflict	Problem wandering
Key references	Ackoff (1970), Ansoff (1965), Steiner (1979)	Cyert and March (1963), Simon (1976), Nelson and Winter (1982), Quinn (1980)	Allison (1971), Baldridge (1971), Mintzberg (1983), Pfeffer (1981)	Cohen, March, and Olsen (1972), March and Olsen (1976)

Source: Adapted from Eisenhardt, K.M. and Zbaracki, M.J., *Strategic Management Journal* 13, 32, 1992.

not rational. Key to this perspective is the assumption that individual decision makers have conflicting goals. Strategic decisions are achieved through building coalitions and overcoming less powerful coalitions (Eisenhardt and Zbaracki, 1992). Though research in this area started in the non-profit sector, by now there is ample evidence that political behaviors exist in all organizations (Mintzberg, 1983; Pfeffer 1981). Examples of such behaviors by individuals and groups include manipulation and control of information channels, coalition formation, lobbying, cooptation, and controlling agendas (Eisenhardt and Zbaracki, 1992, 26). Interestingly, the use of power and politics in organizations need not be always dysfunctional (Chakravarthy and White, 2002); astute decision makers can leverage politics to induce organizational change and adaptation.

Another approach that is worth mentioning is the "garbage can" perspective (Cohen, March, and Olsen, 1972; March and Olsen, 1976). Those advocating this view suggest that some organizations operate under substantial internal and external ambiguity, leading to an essentially random process of decision making. As such, this perspective is the most removed from the rational one—neither individuals nor organizations act rationally. Goals and preferences are either nonexistent or inconsistent or shifting. There is no clear means-ends understanding. Participants' involvement in the decision making is irregular. Problems, goals, solutions, and participants are all mixed together in a virtual garbage can picked from it at random. "Thus, decision making occurs in a stochastic meeting of choices looking for problems, problems looking for choices, solutions looking for problems to answer, and decision makers looking for something to decide" (Eisenhardt and Zbaracki, 1992, 27).

It is clear that the rational perspective is an ideal one, but no organization or individual can be so heroically rational as this perspective maintains (Huff and Reger, 1987). However, planning certainly has the potential to move intendedly rational organizations closer to such an ideal. Eisenhardt and Zbaracki (1992) determined that the garbage can model is less relevant for strategic decision making because of its limited occurrence, primarily in government and education. This is good news for strategic planners, as the garbage can approach is antithetical to any planning attempts. On the other hand, Eisenhardt and Zbaracki do find support for the rational, incremental, and political perspectives, leading to the conclusion that strategic decision making involves rational, incremental, and political processes. This conclusion is corroborated by Brews and Hunt (1999) who find that both formal planning (i.e. rationality) and incrementalism contribute to firm performance. Rational, incremental, and political perspectives are not mutually exclusive—they co-exist in organizations in various combinations. The rational approach, meant to dominate strategic planning, intermixes with these perspective approaches in real organizations.

23.5.2 Improving Our Understanding of Contingencies

Referring to the early, prescription-based literature in strategic planning, Mintzberg (1994) stressed:

> "For nowhere in the planning literature has there been any indication whatsoever that efforts were made to understand how the strategy making process really does work in organizations ... In just plain ignorance of the strategy making process, they [traditional strategic planning advocates] proposed a simplistic set of steps as their 'one best way' to create strategy, claiming at their most naïve that it simulated intuition and at their most arrogant that it was superior." (226)

Truth be told, latter strategic planning researchers did make an effort to incorporate the effect of various contingencies on strategic planning and its effect on performance. However, much can be improved beyond sub-group analysis (the most common way contingency effects were operationalized) and moderated linear regressions (Aiken and West, 1991). As we have seen in the section dealing with the contingencies, the results are far from clear. A possible source of these inconsistencies lies in the simplistic, linear way the relationship between planning, performance, and the contingencies has been conceptualized (Rajagopalan, Rasheed, and Datta, 1993). We suggest the incorporation of curvilinear interrelationships in addition to the simple linear ones.

A curvilinear relationship depicts regions of shortage, optimum, and over-abundance of strategic planning. Like an inverted U-shape, prior to the optimal level, an increase in planning activity results in an increase in performance, which peaks at the optimal level of planning. Beyond this level, further increases in planning result in lower performance. Such a relationship is more realistic than assuming that linear relationships continue indefinitely. Recall that planning may have benefits, but it also taxes the firm. At minimum, it takes resources that can be utilized more productively elsewhere. And when over-applied it becomes nothing other than bureaucratic red tape. Therefore, even though it appears from the existing empirical literature that planning has an overall positive effect on performance, it cannot be assumed to have this positive effect at every level of planning. In turn, the contingencies determine the optimal level of planning. Take, for instance, the two central contingencies of environmental uncertainty and of organizational size.

Under stable environments and up to a moderate amount uncertainty, it is expected that planning will enhance performance due to its uncertainty reduction aspects. However, it is possible that beyond a certain point where uncertainty is extremely high, that planning efforts may detract from performance as the costs associated with information gathering and analysis may exceed the benefits of such activities. This is possible because when environments are highly uncertain, no amount of scanning and evaluation of long-term alternatives will help with an environment that is so unpredictable. Such environments may simply be not analyzable. Instead of wasting resources on planning, firms should take an incremental approach to strategy making (Mintzberg, 1994). Therefore, in stable and moderately unstable environments, the optimal level of performance is expected to be at a high level of planning, while in highly uncertain environments the optimal level of performance is expected to be at a low level of planning. This may resolve some of the contradiction between Fredrickson's studies (Fredrickson, 1984; Fredrickson and Iaquinto, 1989; Fredrickson and Mitchell,1984) and others (Atuahene-Gima and Li, 2004; Glick, Miller, and Huber, 1993; Goll and Rasheed, 1997; Kukalis, 1991; Miller and Cardinal, 1994; Priem, Rasheed, and Kotulic, 1995) regarding the contingent effect of environmental uncertainty on the relationship between planning comprehensiveness and performance. It is possible that the use of a contrived setting (scenarios in the case of Fredrickson, computerized simulation in the case of Hough and White, 2003) was able to achieve much higher levels of uncertainty than field studies. In such settings of elevated uncertainty, the optimal level of planning may have been reached very quickly, resulting in a negative slope for most of the range of the planning measure. Also note that this conceptualization does not constrain the peak performance level achieved in the optimal planning level. Therefore, it is possible that peak performance level under high uncertainty is higher than the peak performance possible in stable environments.

Similarly, regarding the effect of size, the evidence was found to be scant and mixed. One study found that large firms that plan more enjoy increased performance, while small firms do not enjoy a planning-performance relation (Powell, 1994). However, the other two studies found size not to exhibit such an effect. Because small firms, like large ones, benefit from planning's uncertainty reduction aspect but do not need planning's integrative aspect (Grinyer, Al-Bazzaz, and Yasai-Ardekani, 1986), it is possible that the optimal level of planning is low for small firms and high for large firms. These effects could have been masked because a curvilinear relationship between planning and performance was not incorporated (hence, constraining the analyses to linear correspondence). Again, even though peak performance appears at lower levels of planning, it is certainly possible that the effect of planning on performance is more pronounced for small firms (i.e. the same change in the level of planning may affect performance much more for small firms than for large ones).

23.6 CONCLUSION

The controversy over strategic planning's role is only likely to continue as firms grow and as they face even more fast-paced environments of hyper-change to which they must adapt quickly and effectively. How, and in what ways, should they and can they plan to meet these environments? How can they cope with them? Can they plan for the uncertainties that they introduce? Strategic planning will never be a substitute for good judgment. In this, Mintzberg (1994) is right in his critique. But the absence of planning also does not result in corporate nirvana. Planning must and can be judiciously used as a tool that has both its strengths and its weaknesses.

REFERENCES

Abraham, S. C., *Strategic Planning: A Practical Guide for Competitive Advantage*, South-Western College Publishing, Mason, OH, 2006.

Ackoff, R. L., *A Concept of Corporate Planning*, Wiley-Interscience, New York, 1970.

Ackoff, R. L., On the use of models in corporate planning, *Strategic Management Journal*, 2, 353–359, 1981.

Aiken, L. S. and West, S. G., *Multiple Regression: Testing and Interpreting Interactions*, Sage, Newbury Park, CA, 1991.

Al-Bazzaz, S. and Grinyer, P. H., Corporate planning in the U.K.: The state of the art in the 70s, *Strategic Management Journal*, 2, 155–168, 1981.

Allison, G. T., *Essence of Decision: Explaining the Cuban Missile Crisis*, Little, Brown, Boston, 1971.

Andersen, T. J., Strategic planning, autonomous actions and corporate performance, *Long Range Planning*, 33, 184–200, 2000.

Anderson, C. R. and Zeithaml, C. P., Stages of the product life cycle, business strategy, and business performance, *Academy of Management Journal*, 27, 5–24, 1984.

Andrews, K. R., *The Concept of Corporate Strategy*, Dow-Jones Irwin, Homewood, IL, 1971.

Ansoff, H. I., *Corporate Strategy: An Analytic Approach to Business Policy for Growth and Expansion*, McGraw-Hill, New York, 1965.

Armstrong, J. S., The value of formal planning for strategic decisions: review of empirical research, *Strategic Management Journal*, 3, 197–211, 1982.

Atuahene-Gima, K. and Li, H., Strategic decision comprehensiveness and new product development outcomes in new technology ventures, *Academy of Management Journal*, 47, 583–597, 2004.

Axelrod, R. M. and Cohen, M. D., *Harnessing Complexity: Organizational Implications of a Scientific Frontier*, Free Press, New York, 1999.

Baldridge, J. V., *Power and Conflict in the University: Research in the Sociology of Complex Organizations*, Wiley, New York, 1971.

Barney, J. B., Strategic factor markets: Expectations, luck and business strategy, *Management Science*, 42, 1231–1241, 1986.

Bowen, H. B. and Wiersema, M., Matching method to paradigm in strategy research: limitations of cross-sectional analysis and some methodological alternatives, *Strategic Management Journal*, 20, 625–636, 1999.

Bowman, E. H., Singh, H., and Thomas, H., The domain of strategic management: history and evolution, In *Handbook of Strategy and Management*, Pettigrew, A. M., Thomas, H., and Whittington, R., Eds., Sage, Thousand Oaks, CA, pp. 31–51, 2002.

Boyd, B. K., Strategic planning and financial performance: a meta-analytic review, *Journal of Management Studies*, 28, 353–374, 1991.

Boyd, B. K., Gove, S., and Hitt, M. A., Construct measurement in strategic management research: illusion or reality?, *Strategic Management Journal*, 26, 239–257, 2005.

Boyd, B. K. and Reuning-Elliott, E., A measurement model of strategic planning, *Strategic Management Journal*, 19, 181–192, 1998.

Braybrooke, D. and Lindblom, C. E., *A Strategy of Decision: Policy Evaluation as a Social Process*, Free Press, New York, 1970.

Brews, P. J. and Hunt, M. R., Learning to plan and planning to learn: resolving the planning school/learning school debate, *Strategic Management Journal*, 20, 889–913, 1999.

Brown, J. S. and Duguid, P., Organizational learning and communities-of-practice: Toward a unified view of working, learning, and innovation, *Organization Science*, 2, 40–57, 1991.

Brown, S. L. and Eisenhardt, K. M., *Competing on the Edge: Strategy as Structured Chaos*, Harvard Business School Press, Boston, 1998.

Capon, N., Farley, J. U., and Hulbert, J. M., Strategic planning and financial performance: More evidence, *Journal of Management Studies*, 31, 105–110, 1994.

Chakravarthy, B. S. and Lorange, P., *Managing the Strategy Process*, Prentice Hall, Englewood Cliffs, NJ, 1991.

Chakravarthy, B. S. and White, R. E., Strategy process: forming, implementing and changing strategies, In *Handbook of Strategy and Management*, Pettigrew, A. M., Thomas, H., and Whittington, R., Eds., Sage, Thousand Oaks, CA, pp. 182–205, 2002.

Cohen, M. D., March, J. G., and Olsen, J. P., A garbage can model of organizational choice, *Administration and Society*, 17, 1–25, 1972.

Cyert, R. M. and March, J. G., *A Behavioral Theory of the Firm*, Prentice Hall, Englewood Cliffs, NJ: CA, 1963.

Dean, J.W. Jr. and Sharfman, M. P., Does decision process matter? A study of strategic decision-making effectiveness, *Academy of Management Journal*, 39, 368–396, 1996.

Delmar, F. and Shane, S., Does business planning facilitate the development of new ventures?, *Strategic Management Journal*, 24, 1165–1185, 2003.

Dewar, R. D. and Werbel, J., Universalistic and contingency predictions of employee satisfaction and conflict, *Administrative Science Quarterly*, 24, 426–448, 1979.

Drazin, R. and Van de Ven, A. H., Alternative forms of fit in contingency theory, *Administrative Science Quarterly*, 30, 514–539, 1985.

DuBrin, A. J., *Essentials of Management*, 7th ed., Thompson South-Western, Mason, OH, 2006.

Ehrbar, A., *EVA: The Real Key to Creating Wealth*, Wiley, New York, 1998.

Eisenhardt, K. M. and Zbaracki, M. J., Strategic decision making, *Strategic Management Journal*, 13, 17–37, 1992.

Fahey, L., Linking product-market analysis and shareholder value, *Planning Review*, 16, 18–21, 1988.

Fredrickson, J. W., The comprehensiveness of strategic decision processes: extension, observations, future directions, *Academy of Management Journal*, 27, 445–466, 1984.

Fredrickson, J. W. and Iaquinto, A. L., Inertia and creeping rationality in strategic decision processes, *Academy of Management Journal*, 32, 516–542, 1989.

Fredrickson, J. W. and Mitchell, T. R., Strategic decision processes: comprehensiveness and performance in an industry with an unstable environment, *Academy of Management Journal*, 27, 399–423, 1984.

Freeman, R. E., *Strategic Management: A Stakeholder Approach*, Pitman, Boston, 1984.

Georgantzas, N. C. and Acar, W., *Scenario-Driven Planning: Learning to Manage Strategic Uncertainty*, Quorum Books, Westport, CT, 1995.

Giddens, A., *The Constitution of Society: Outline of the Theory of Structuration*, University of California Press, Berkeley, CA, 1984.

Glick, W. H., Miller, C. C., and Huber, G. P., The impact of upper-echelon diversity on organizational performance, In *Organizational Change and Redesign: Ideas and Insight for Improving Performance*, Huber, G. P. and Glick, W. H., Eds., Oxford University Press, New York, pp. 176–214, 1993.

Goll, I. and Rasheed, A. M. A., Rational decision-making and firm performance: The moderating role of environment, *Strategic Management Journal*, 18, 583–591, 1997.

Grant, J. H. and King, W. R., *The Logic of Strategic Planning*, Little, Brown and Company, Boston, 1982.

Grant, R. M., Strategic planning in a turbulent environment: evidence from the oil majors, *Strategic Management Journal*, 24, 491–517, 2003.

Griffin, R. W., *Fundamentals of Management*, 4th ed., Houghton Mifflin, Boston, 2006.

Grinyer, P., Al-Bazzaz, S., and Yasai-Ardekani, M., Towards a contingency theory of corporate planning: findings in 48 U.K. companies, *Strategic Management Journal*, 7, 3–28, 1986.

Grinyer, P. H. and Norburn, D., Planning for existing markets: Perceptions of executives and financial performance, *Journal of the Royal Statistical Society*, 138, 70–97, 1975.

Hambrick, D. C. and Finkelstein, S., Managerial discretion: a bridge between polar views of organizational fates, In *Research in Organizational Behavior*, Staw, B. M. and Cummings, L. L., Eds., 9th ed., JAI Press, Greenwich, CT, pp. 369–406, 1987.

Hambrick, D. C. and Lei, D., Towards an empirical prioritization of contingency variables for business strategy, *Academy of Management Journal*, 28, 763–788, 1985.

Haspeslagh, P., Portfolio planning: uses and limits, *Harvard Business Review*, 60, 58–73, 1982.

Hax, A. C. and Majluf, N. S., *Strategic Management: An Integrative Perspective*, Prentice Hall, Englewood Cliffs, NJ, 1984.

Hax, A. C. and Majluf, N. S., *The Strategy Concept and Process: A Pragmatic Approach*, Prentice Hall, Englewood Cliffs, NJ, 1991.

Henderson, B. D., *Henderson on Corporate Strategy*, Abt Books, Cambridge, MA, 1979.

Hill, C. W. L. and Jones, G. R., *Strategic Management Theory: An Integrated Approach*, 6th ed., Houghton Mifflin, Boston, 2004.

Hitt, M. A., Ireland, R. D., and Hoskisson, R. E., *Strategic Management: Competitiveness and Globalization*, 6th ed., South-Western, Mason, OH, 2005.

Hofer, C. W., Toward a contingency theory of business strategy, *Academy of Management Journal*, 18, 784–810, 1975.

Hofer, C. W., ROVA: a new measure for assessing organizational performance, In *Advances in Strategic Management*, Lamb, R., Ed., JAI Press, New York, pp. 43–55, 1983.

Hofer, C. W. and Schendel, D. E., *Strategy Formulation: Analytical Concepts*, West Publishing, St. Paul, MN, 1978.

Hopkins, W. E. and Hopkins, S. A., Strategic planning-financial performance relationships in banks: a causal examination, *Strategic Management Journal*, 18, 635–652, 1997.

Hough, J. R. and White, M. A., Environmental dynamism and strategic decision-making rationality: an examination at the decision level, *Strategic Management Journal*, 24, 481–489, 2003.

Huber, G. P. and Daft, R. L., The information environments of organizations, In *Handbook of Organizational Communication*, Jabin, F. M., Putnam, L. L., Roberts, K. H., and Porter, L. W., Eds., Sage, Beverly Hills, CA, pp. 130–164, 1987.

Huff, A. S. and Reger, R., A review of strategic process research, *Journal of Management*, 13, 211–236, 1987.

Kallman, E. A. and Shapiro, H. J., The motor freight industry—A case against planning, *Long Range Planning*, 11, 81–86, 1978.

Kastens, M. L., *Long-Range Planning for Your Business: An Operating Manual*, AMACOM, New York, 1976.

King, W. R., Evaluating strategic planning systems, *Strategic Management Journal*, 4, 263–277, 1983.

Kudla, R. J., The effects of strategic planning on common stock returns, *Academy of Management Journal*, 23, 5–20, 1980.

Kukalis, S., Determinants of strategic planning systems in large organizations: a contingency approach, *Journal of Management Studies*, 28, 143–160, 1991.

Lave, J. and Wenger, E., *Situated Learning: Legitimate Peripheral Participation*, Cambridge University Press, New York, 1991.

Learned, E. P., Christensen, C. R., Andrews, K. R., and Guth, W. D., *Business Policy: Text and Cases*, Irwin, Homewood, IL, 1965.

Lewin, A. Y. and Minton, J. W., Determining organizational effectiveness: another look, and an agenda for research, *Management Science*, 32, 514–538, 1986.

Liedtka, J. M., Strategy formulation: the roles of conversation and design, In *The Blackwell Handbook of Strategic Management*, Hitt, M. A., Freeman, R. E., and Harrison, J. S., Eds., Blackwell, Malden, MA, pp. 70–94, 2001.

Linneman, R. E., *Shirt-Sleeve Approach to Long-Range Planning for the Smaller, Growing Corporation*, Prentice Hall, Englewood Cliffs, NJ, 1980.

March, J. G. and Olsen, J. P., *Ambiguity and Choice in Organizations*, Universitetforlaget, Bergen, Norway, 1976.

Marcus, A. A., *Management Strategy: Achieving Sustained Competitive Advantage*, McGraw-Hill, Boston, 2005.

Meyer, M. W. and Zucker, L. G., *Permanently Failing Organizations*, Sage Publications, Newbury Park, CA, 1989.

Miles, G., Snow, C. C., and Sharfman, M. P., Industry variety and performance, *Strategic Management Journal*, 14, 163–177, 1993.

Miles, R. E. and Snow, C. C., *Organizational Strategy, Structure, and Process*, McGraw-Hill, New York, 1978.

Miller, C. C. and Cardinal, L. B., Strategic planning and firm performance: a synthesis of more than two decades of research, *Academy of Management Journal*, 37, 1649–1665, 1994.

Mintzberg, H., *Power in and Around Organizations*, Prentice Hall, Englewood Cliffs, NJ, 1983.

Mintzberg, H., *The Rise and Fall of Strategic Planning*, The Free Press, New York, 1994.

Moore, G. A., *Crossing the Chasm*, HarperCollins, New York, 1991.

Nelson, R. R. and Winter, S. G., *An Evolutionary Theory of Economic Change*, Harvard University Press, Cambridge, MA, 1982.

Nutt, P. C., Strategic decision-making, In *The Blackwell Handbook of Strategic Management*, Hitt, M. A., Freeman, R. E., and Harrison, J. S., Eds., Blackwell, Malden, MA, pp. 35–69, 2001.

O'Connor, R., *Corporate Guides to Long-Range Planning*, The Conference Board, New York, 1976.

Pearce, J. A. I., Freeman, E. B., and Robinson, R. B., Jr., The tenuous link between formal strategic planning and financial performance, *Academy of Management Review*, 12, 658–675, 1987.

Peters, T. J. and Waterman, R. H., Jr., In *Search of Excellence: Lessons from America's Best-Run Companies*, Harper & Row, New York, 1982.

Pfeffer, J., *Power in Organizations*, Pitman, Marshfield, MA, 1981.

Porter, M. E., *Competitive Strategy: Techniques for Analyzing Industries and Competitors*, Free Press, New York, 1980.

Porter, M. E., *Competitive Advantage*, The Free Press, New York, 1985.

Powell, T. C., Untangling the relationship between strategic planning and performance: the role of contingency factors, *Canadian Journal of Administrative Sciences*, 11, 124–138, 1994.

Prahalad, C. K. and Hamel, G., The core competence of the corporation, *Harvard Business Review*, 68, 79–91, 1990.

Priem, R. L., Rasheed, A. M. A., and Kotulic, A. G., Rationality in strategic decision processes, environmental dynamism and firm performance, *Journal of Management*, 21, 913–929, 1995.

Quinn, J. B., *Strategies for Change: Logical Incrementalism*, R.D. Irwin, Homewood, IL, 1980.

Quinn, R. E. and Rohrbaugh, J., A spatial model of effectiveness values approach to organizational analysis, *Management Science*, 29, 363–377, 1983.

Rajagopalan, N., Rasheed, A. M. A., and Datta, D. K., Strategic decision processes: critical review and future directions, *Journal of Management*, 19, 349–384, 1993.

Rappaport, A., Selecting strategies that create shareholder value, *Harvard Business Review*, 59, 139–149, 1981.

Rappaport, A., *Creating Shareholder Value: The New Standard for Business Performance*, Free Press, New York, 1986.

Robinson, R. B. Jr. and Pearce, J. A. I., Research thrusts in small firm strategic planning, *Academy of Management Review*, 9, 128–137, 1984.

Rogers, P. R., Miller, A., and Judge, W. Q., Using information-processing theory to understand planning/performance relationships in the context of strategy, *Strategic Management Journal*, 20, 567–577, 1999.

Rumelt, R. P., Toward a strategic theory of the firm, In *Competitive Strategic Management*, Lamb, R., Ed., Prentice Hall, Englewood Cliffs, NJ, pp. 556–570, 1984.

Schoemaker, P. J. H., Scenario planning: a tool for strategic thinking, *Sloan Management Review*, 36, 25–40, 1995.

Schwenk, C. R. and Shrader, C. B., Effects of formal strategic planning on financial performance in small firms: a meta-analysis, *Entrepreneurship Theory and Practice*, 17, 53–64, 1993.

Scott, W. R., *Organizations: Rational, Natural, and Open Systems*, 4th ed., Prentice Hall, Englewood Cliffs, NJ, 1998.

Shrader, C. B., Taylor, L., and Dalton, D. R., Strategic planning and organizational performance: a critical appraisal, *Journal of Management*, 10, 149–171, 1984.

Simon, H. A., *Administrative Behavior*, 3rd ed., The Free Press, New York, 1976.

Sinha, D. K., The contribution of formal planning to decisions, *Strategic Management Journal*, 11, 479–492, 1990.

Steiner, G. A., *Strategic Planning*, The Free Press, New York, 1979.

Stern, J., Stewart, G. B., and Chew, D., The EVA financial management system, *Journal of Applied Corporate Finance*, 8, 32–46, 1995.

Stewart, G. B., *The Quest for Value: A Guide for Senior Managers*, Harper Business, New York, 1991.

Sweeny, H. W. A. and Rachlin, R., *Handbook of Budgeting*, Wiley, New York, 1981.

Vancil, R. R. and Lorange, P., Strategic planning in diversified companies, *Harvard Business Review*, 53, 81–90, 1975.

Venkatraman, N., The concept of fit in strategy research: toward verbal and statistical correspondence, *Academy of Management Review*, 14, 423–444, 1989.

Wack, P., Scenarios: shooting the rapids, *Harvard Business Review*, 63, 2–14, 1985.

Wack, P., Scenarios: uncharted waters ahead, *Harvard Business Review*, 63, 73–89, 1985.

Welsch, G. A., *Budgeting: Profit Planning and Control*, Prentice Hall, Englewood Cliffs, NJ, 1964.

Wernerfelt, B., A resource-based view of the firm, *Strategic Management Journal*, 5, 171–180, 1984.

Wind, Y. and Mahajan, V., Designing product and business portfolios, *Harvard Business Review*, 59, 155–165, 1981.

Yasai-Ardekani, M. and Haug, R. S., Contextual determinants of strategic planning processes, *Journal of Management Studies*, 34, 729–767, 1997.

Part IV

Methods of Decision Making

24 Experiments and Quasi-Experiments for Decision Making: Why, How, and How Good?

Melvin M. Mark and Jennifer Mills

CONTENTS

24.1 Introduction..459
24.2 Why Might Experiments and Quasi-Experiments Be a Source
of Decision Making?...460
    24.2.1 The Technical Justification for Experiments.......................................461
        24.2.1.1 The Rationale for Quasi-Experiments.................................462
        24.2.1.2 Complementary Political and Personal Justifications........464
24.3 Methodological Ancillaries and Refinements 465
    24.3.1 Implementation Assessment 465
    24.3.2 Mediation and Moderation 467
    24.3.3 Other Ancillaries within a Single Experiment or Quasi-Experiment.................469
        24.3.3.1 Meta-Analysis..469
24.4 From Evidence to Decision Making..470
24.5 Challenges in Moving from Experimental Evidence to Decisions...................473
    24.5.1 Challenges in Measuring the Right Outcomes......................................473
    24.5.2 Challenges in Assessing Findings' Implications for
Decision Making...474
    24.5.3 Challenges in Weighing Findings against Other,
Non-Experimental Considerations..476
24.6 A Case Example..476
    24.6.1 Vioxx, Drug Studies, and the FDA...477
24.7 Conclusion..479
References...480

24.1 INTRODUCTION

Decision making often depends—and arguably, more often should depend—on inferences about cause-and-effect relationships. If a person with arthritis takes Celebrex or Vioxx, will it reduce joint pain—without causing a heart attack? If California funds universal pre-K, will this lead to children being better prepared for school, to better long-term educational outcomes, and eventually to reduced crime and poverty? How much, if at all, do highway fatalities drop because of an increase in the legal drinking age? Does the school-based Drug Abuse Resistance Education program (DARE) cause a decrease in students' use of illicit drugs? Do commercial leadership training programs lead to better leadership in companies, and does this translate into improvements in the bottom line?

24.2 WHY MIGHT EXPERIMENTS AND QUASI-EXPERIMENTS BE A SOURCE OF DECISION MAKING?

As the preceding and many other examples illustrate, the decisions people make may depend, at least in part, upon causal inferences. This is true of decisions people make as individuals (e.g., about whether to use a given medication), of decision making within organizations (e.g., in funding employee training within companies), and also of collective decisions made by governments on behalf of the public (e.g., to fund universal pre-K or change the drinking age). In short, actions are often chosen precisely because of their anticipated consequences, that is, because of presumptions about the causal effects of the action in question. If carried out successfully, experiments and quasi-experiments can provide relatively strong evidence about an intervention's effects; for this reason, and because cause-and-effect relationships often underlie action, experiments and quasi-experiments may play an important role in decision making.

Although experiments or formal quasi-experiments can contribute to strong causal inferences, they are not intrinsically required. Humans made causal inferences for countless centuries before the techniques of experimental design were developed. These causal inferences may even have been life saving, as when early humans learned that striking certain kinds of rocks can cause sparks that can start a fire. Indeed, because of the life-saving potential of causal inference, an evolutionary press may have existed for a natural human propensity to infer causality. In any event, people do not naturally wait for the results of experiments to make all causal inferences. Infants who have not yet learned any explicit formal rules of causal inference nevertheless assess cause-and-effect relationships. Even the most ardent contemporary advocates of experimental methods draw countless causal inferences in everyday life without benefit of experimentation.

Although experimental methods are not required for causal inference, they can be quite valuable. Experiments and their best approximations may be especially valuable in certain common circumstances: when multiple factors plausibly influence the outcome of interest; when change over time can occur in the outcome of interest because of factors other than the causal variable of interest; when people naturally vary on the outcome of interest; and when an effect is worth knowing about, even if it is not dramatic in size. Put differently, experiments and quasi-experiments may not be important when there are few plausible alternative explanations of an observed effect (Campbell and Stanley, 1966; Cook and Campbell, 1979; Shadish, Cook, and Campbell, 2002). You may not need an experiment to infer whether sticking a hairpin in an electric socket causes a painful shock, but if you are interested in questions such as whether an educational intervention is effective, experiments can be quite worthwhile. For example, assessing whether a new curriculum improves student achievement can be challenging, given that: student achievement is affected by numerous factors other than the new curriculum; student achievement is characterized by both change over time and differences across individuals; and people are likely to care about achievement improvements even if they are not so huge as to stand out dramatically against the complex causal background.

In light of the possible benefits of using randomized experiments (and their best quasi-experimental approximations), use of such methods has grown increasingly common in recent decades. An identifiable literature on social experimentation itself exists (e.g., Boruch, 1997; Greenberg and Shroder, 1997), as does a body of work on quasi-experimentation (e.g., Shadish,

Cook, and Campbell, 2002). Experiments are now a standard method in medicine, in conjunction with the evidence-based medicine (EBM) movement (Sackett, Rosenberg, Gray, Haynes, and Richardson, 1996). Experiments have also become typical in evaluations of various areas of social or psychological interventions, such as welfare reform and other employment initiatives (e.g., Friedlander, Greenberg, and Robins, 1997; Riccio and Bloom, 2002) and psychological therapy for depression and other affective disorders (e.g., Borkovec, 1997, 2004).

This is not to say that experiments and their best quasi-experimental approximations rule the land of decision making. Admittedly, even the evaluation of social and educational interventions can involve other methods (Donaldson and Scriven, 2003). In addition, experiments may still be underrepresented in some areas, as Cook (2001; 2003) has argued regarding educational research and evaluation. Despite such caveats, a considerable investment is being made in experiments and quasi-experimental approximations, in light of their potential contribution to decision making.

In the remainder of this chapter, we examine randomized experiments and quasi-experiments, with special attention to their potential for decision making. We examine the rationale for conducting experiments and quasi-experiments, including the rationale for their use in decision making. We discuss several additions to basic experiments, highlighting how these methodological ancillaries can contribute in important ways to decision making. We briefly examine alternative models of how the step from evidence to decisions can or should be taken. We discuss a set of challenges that arise when one attempts to move from experimental or quasi-experimental evidence to decisions. And we briefly examine one contemporary case that illustrates both the importance and difficulties of basing decisions on experimental evidence.

24.2.1 THE TECHNICAL JUSTIFICATION FOR EXPERIMENTS

In randomized experiments, individuals (or other units, such as classrooms) are randomly assigned to treatment conditions. For example, some individuals could be assigned at random—essentially, with a flip of a coin, or more likely, by random number table or computerized equivalent—to receive a new drug for arthritis pain, while other individuals are instead assigned at random to receive a placebo (or, alternatively, a currently available drug). As another example, some classrooms might be assigned at random to offer DARE, while others offer no substance abuse prevention program.

The benefits of randomized experiments can perhaps best be seen in relation to simpler alternatives, that is, to simpler kinds of research designs or informal comparisons on which one might base a causal inference. The benefits of randomized experiments can also be clarified by considering what Campbell and his colleagues (Campbell and Stanley, 1966; Cook and Campbell, 1979; Shadish, Cook, and Campbell, 2002) call "internal validity threats": generic categories of alternative explanations—alternatives to the claim that the treatment made a causal difference on the outcome variable, within the study itself.

For example, imagine that instead of conducting a randomized experiment, a researcher tried to estimate the effects of a new drug for arthritis pain by measuring pain before patients started taking the drug and then measuring pain again after patients had been taking the drug. In this example, other sources of change could easily obscure the true effects of the drug. For example, arthritis pain may typically increase over time. In the language of Campbell and his colleagues, such a naturally occurring change over time would be called *maturation*. A maturational pattern, whereby arthritis pain normally increases over time, could make an effective drug look ineffective in a simple before-and-after comparison. For this and a variety of other reasons,[*] one often would not get an accurate

---

[*] Among the other reasons, in the language of Campbell and his colleagues, are the validity threats of history, statistical regression, testing, instrumentation, and attrition.

answer about an intervention's effect simply by measuring the relative outcome variable (in this case, pain) before and after the treatment of interest (in this case, the drug).

As another example, imagine an evaluation of the effects of DARE on adolescents' drug use. In the absence of random assignment, one might compare drug use by students from schools that offer DARE with that of students at schools without DARE. Here the validity threat of *selection* would apply. That is, any observed difference between DARE and non-DARE students could easily result not from the prevention program, but from pre-existing differences in any of a number of variables. For example, the schools with DARE may differ from the other schools in terms of the demographic or economic circumstances of the children they serve, prevalence of drugs in the surrounding community, local social norms, and so on. These and other confounding variables could easily obscure the true effect of DARE.[*]

In contrast, random assignment effectively takes care of such selection problems (and, assuming the experiment is conducted successfully, other internal validity threats including maturation). If classrooms (or other units) are assigned to conditions at random, no bias will exist. This is not to say that random assignment guarantees that the two groups will be *exactly* equal prior to the treatment, but no systematic bias will exist. Moreover, any random differences between the two groups can be effectively accommodated with familiar hypothesis-testing statistics (Boruch, 1997). The ability to estimate treatment effects without bias, that is, without the systematic intrusion of selection, maturation, and other internal validity threats, provides the primary argument for randomized experiments.

24.2.1.1 The Rationale for Quasi-Experiments

Quasi-experiments are approximations of randomized experiments. Quasi-experiments, like randomized experiments, involve comparisons across two or more conditions, and they may include before–after or other comparisons. However, by definition, quasi-experiments lack random assignment to conditions.

If random assignment is so valuable, you might ask why quasi-experimental alternatives are ever used. In one sense, the answer is simple: experiments are not always feasible for practical or ethical reasons (Cook and Campbell, 1979). A slightly more nuanced, if perhaps more controversial answer, also exists (Boruch, 1997; Shadish, Cook, and Campbell, 2002): sometimes quasi-experiments, even relatively simple ones, can give compelling answers to cause-and-effect questions, because plausible alternative explanations are few or can be effectively eliminated by other kinds of evidence (e.g., Eckert, 2000); and in some cases, lower quality (and less costly) information may suffice for the particular decision at hand (Mark, Henry, and Julnes, 2000).

There are numerous possible quasi-experimental designs, including variants on basic designs (for detailed discussion of quasi-experiments, see Shadish, Cook, and Campbell, 2002). The present chapter focuses on the contribution of experiments and quasi-experiments to decision making, and does not discuss in detail the entire set of quasi-experimental designs and features. However, it will be useful to highlight briefly two quasi-experimental designs, one relatively strong, and the other relatively common.

The *regression-discontinuity design* is among the best quasi-experimental designs for causal inference (Shadish, Cook, and Campbell, 2002). The conditions necessary for this design are quite specific, and to date the design has been implemented rarely in practice. However, the design is explicitly mentioned in recent legislation and user guides in education (What Works Clearinghouse, 2005), and so may become more common. To use the design, assignment to conditions must be based on some eligibility criterion, with a firm cutoff such that people scoring on one side of the cutoff are assigned to one group (e.g., the treatment), while those on the other side of the

---

[*] More complex designs, combining a before-and-after (or as it is often called, pretest-posttest) comparison with comparison to other units not assigned at random, are briefly discussed subsequently in the section on quasi-experiments.

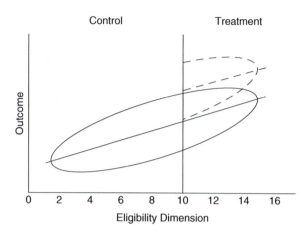

FIGURE 24.1 Findings from a hypothetical regression-discontinuty study.

cutoff are assigned to the other group (e.g., the control). For example, adjusted family income might be the eligibility criterion, with people scoring below the cutoff receiving food stamps and people above the cutoff not receiving them. In this case, the regression-discontinuity design might be used to study the effects of food stamps on health outcomes. As another example, the eligibility criterion might be average ratings, across reviewers, of grant proposals, with all proposals above some cutoff funded and all those below not funded. One might study the effect of receiving a grant from this funding source on subsequent productivity.

Figure 24.1 illustrates hypothetical findings from a regression-discontinuity study. At the bottom are scores on the eligibility criterion. The cutoff is indicated by the vertical line at 10. Scores on the outcome measure are represented on the left-hand side of the graph. The ellipse in the Figure represents the distribution of scores, with the line within the ellipse representing the regression of the outcome variable on the eligibility criterion variable.[*] If the treatment in fact makes no difference, the regression line (and the ellipse) should be continuous, as represented by the solid lines in Figure 24.1. In contrast, if there is a treatment effect, then the regression line (and ellipse) should be higher or lower (depending upon whether the treatment increases or decreases outcome scores); this is illustrated by the dotted lines in Figure 24.1.[†] The logic of the regression-discontinuity design is not always immediately intuitive. One way to think about it is: How likely is it that there would be a jump in scores on the outcome variable that coincides precisely with the cutoff on the eligibility criterion, unless there really is a treatment effect? It may also be helpful to ask yourself the question: Unless the treatment makes a difference, why would individuals who score 10 on the eligibility criterion be substantially different on the outcome from those who score 11, and why would this difference be so much greater than the difference between those who score 9 versus 10, or between those who score 11 versus 12, etc?

While the regression-discontinuity design is rare, the *non-equivalent comparison group design* (NECG) is among the most common quasi-experimental designs. As the name implies, a treatment and a control/comparison (or alternative treatment) group are compared. In an effort to control for global selection bias, a pretest and/or other relevant pre-treatment variables are measured. A key problem is that it is difficult to be certain that selection has been adequately controlled for by

---

[*] The slope of the regression line, upward or downward, indicates whether the criterion and the outcome variables are positively or negatively related.

[†] Traditionally, statistical analysis of the design has involved multiple regression analysis, with a dummy code for condition and the eligibility criterion variable (centered at the cutoff) as predictors, and with procedures to test for possible curvilinearity that otherwise could create spurious effects (see Trochim, 1984).

the pretreatment measures. For example, in an evaluation of DARE, imagine that pretest, as well as posttest, levels of drug use were measured. One might think that controlling for prior drug use would control for selection differences; but even youths who are predisposed to drug use, because of familial, psychological, and social factors, do not use drugs as much at early as at later ages. Thus, you might find more difference in drug use between two groups at the end of 8th grade than at the beginning of 6th grade, even in the absence of any treatment (this is called the "selection by maturation" validity threat). Of course, other control variables can be used, such as previously demonstrated risk factors for drug use. The difficulty lies in knowing that you have identified and effectively measured the variables that should be controlled for, and that the statistical model adjusts appropriately.

Much work has been done in recent years on alternative statistical control techniques that can be used in the NECG and similar designs. For example, the statisticians Rubin and Rosenbaum and their colleagues have developed an approach known as "propensity score" analysis (e.g., Rosenbaum and Rubin, 1983). In essence, one first develops a model predicting membership in the treatment and comparison groups. The results of this first step are then used to statistically adjust for selection bias when comparing the outcomes of the treatment and comparison groups. Shadish, Cook, and Campbell (2002) overview propensity scores and alternative forms of statistical analysis for the NECG, while Winship and Morgan (1999) give a more detailed comparison.

A few conclusions regarding decision making can be drawn from this brief discussion of quasi-experimental designs. First, quasi-experiments can vary greatly in terms of the strength of causal inference they allow. One should consider whether a particular design provides the level of confidence needed for a given decision. Second, when confident causal inferences are critical for sound decision making, the limits of weaker quasi-experiments provide a strong argument for randomized experiments or more rigorous quasi-experiments.[*] Third, for NECDs or similar designs, given the difficulty of ensuring adequate adjustment for selection bias, one should attempt to bracket the right answer with alternative analyses (Reichardt and Gollob, 1987; Reynolds and Temple, 1995) or employ "sensitivity analyses" that assess whether findings would change substantially under different assumptions about the statistical control model in use (e.g., Leow, Marcus, Zanutto, and Boruch, 2004). Fourth, although it goes beyond the current discussion, one can sometimes increase confidence by examining a more complex pattern of findings that should hold if there is a treatment effect (Reichardt and Mark, 1998; Trochim, 1984).

24.2.1.2 Complementary Political and Personal Justifications

To this point, the justification offered for experiments and their best possible quasi-experimental approximations is, first, that causal inference is often important for decision making and, second, that experiments have a special capacity for causal inference, especially when the plausibility of validity threats such as selection and maturation would impair simpler methods for inferring cause and effect. Further justification can and has been offered.

Focusing on governmental decision making, both Chelimsky (in press) and Henry (2001) suggest that the very nature of democracy calls for systematic means of investigating government actions and their consequences—including, but certainly not limited to, experiments and quasi-experiments. Henry emphasizes the self-correcting nature of democratic decision making. The effectiveness of any action undertaken by a government body (e.g., a new social program or policy) is not guaranteed. However, part of the genius of democracy, Henry and Chelimsky point out, is the capacity to examine the consequences of action, and to change course if needed.

---

[*] The current presentation, like most discussions of experiments and quasi-experiments, may seem to imply that there are impermeable boundaries between the two; however, there are potentially useful hybrids, as illustrated by Riccio and Bloom's discussion of combining random assignment with the interrupted time series quasi-experiment.

Further justification for experimental evidence (or the best available quasi-experimental approximation) can also be given for *individual* decision making. Consider, for instance, the evidence-based medicine (EBM) movement, which is founded on the premise that choices about medical procedures should be based on sound scientific evidence (e.g., Sackett, Rosenberg, Gray, Haynes, and Richardson, 1996). For example, EBM advocates argued that claims about the desirability of mastectomies versus lumpectomies for breast cancer patients should be based on randomized trials. The rationale in part is simply that more rigorous evidence should result in better decisions and, therefore, better outcomes. Part of the argument for EBM, however, is that it can empower individual patients. Prior to EBM, patients necessarily depended heavily on the recommendations (and thus the decision making) of their physicians — getting a second opinion was about the only alternative. In contrast, EBM has the potential to help create informed, empowered patients, especially in a world of Web searches and online articles. In principle, patients and their loved ones can educate themselves about the best available evidence regarding the effectiveness of potential medications or other treatments (Eysenbach and Jadad, 2001). In practice, however, questions have been raised about how informed consumers are if they obtain most of their information from 30- or 60-second TV ads, rather than benefiting from more comprehensive information.

24.3 METHODOLOGICAL ANCILLARIES AND REFINEMENTS

A great deal of work by statisticians and methodologists in recent decades can be seen as efforts to improve on experimental and quasi-experimental methods. As noted in this section, information from several key methodological ancillaries can have substantial implications for decision making that draws on experiments and quasi-experiments.

24.3.1 IMPLEMENTATION ASSESSMENT

In many early social experiments, the treatment, also known as the intervention, received almost no direct attention as an object of inquiry. Instead, attention was on estimating the effects of the treatment (whatever the treatment itself looked like in practice). Researchers were, of course, concerned about who was assigned to the treatment and comparison groups, because that information was needed to estimate the effects of the treatment. But early researchers typically did not observe the treatment to see how (and, indeed, whether) it was implemented.

Such inattention to the intervention can have major implications for decision making. Imagine, for instance, an evaluation of the effects of bilingual education in which actual educational practices did not differ between the so-called bilingual education schools and the so-called comparison schools. Without an actual treatment contrast between the two groups, the findings would have limited implications for action. Fortunately, since the early days of social research, it has become far more common for some form of implementation assessment to occur. Today, there are different approaches to implementation assessment. These different forms of implementation may each fit best with different types of interventions.

Perhaps the simplest form of implementation assessment involves measuring how much treatment participants received. This approach is alternatively labeled measurement of *compliance, dosage, treatment exposure,* or *treatment intensity.* For instance, in a drug study, one might measure whether participants took all the pills they were prescribed. In a study of psychotherapy or social services, the number of hours of services received might be measured. Not surprisingly, for many interventions, higher dosage is associated with more positive outcomes (see, for example, Cook and Poole, 1982). However, when participants self-select into higher versus lower exposure to the treatment, such findings are subject to selection bias (Mark, 1983). In many cases, empirical study of the effects of different levels of treatment exposure can employ statistical techniques such as propensity scores in an attempt to control for selection bias.

Two additional considerations deserve mention regarding the measurement of compliance or treatment intensity. First, equal vigilance is often called for in measuring treatment exposure in the comparison group. For instance, in an evaluation of DARE, what if other, similar substance abuse prevention programs took place in "control" schools? Similarly, in a study of the effects of coronary bypass surgery, it is important to find out how many patients who were assigned to the no-surgery control group actually had bypass surgery done by other physicians.

Second, measuring treatment exposure can also raise questions about appropriate statistical analyses. For instance, it is not uncommon for participants to receive less of the treatment than planned, and even to drop out of the treatment condition. When this happens, how should such participants be treated in the statistical analysis? One option is the so-called "intent-to-treat" analysis, which includes participants in the condition to which they were originally assigned, regardless of actual treatment exposure. In general, this will result in a conservative estimate of the treatment effect. Thus, one would usually be convinced the treatment is effective if the intent-to-treat analysis reveals a positive effect. Nevertheless, especially if treatment dropout is common, the preferable approach may be to conduct multiple analyses in an attempt to bracket the true treatment effect (Reichardt and Gollob, 1987).

A relatively recent approach to implementation assessment applies to programs that effectively offer a menu of services from which clients can select. For example, some welfare reform programs have offered clients various services, such as center-based childcare, subsidies for other childcare providers, high school equivalency training, various forms of job training, and job counseling and referral services. Because different clients may partake of very different mixes of services, an overall estimate of program effectiveness is more ambiguous than for programs that prescribe specific services each client should receive. One response has been to measure *client "uptake"* of various services, that is, the dosage received of each type of service offered (e.g., Yoshikawa, Rosman, and Hsueh, 2001). With uptake data, the researcher can then identify various patterns of service use. Gibson (2003) conducted a cluster analysis to identify different patterns of service uptake, and then used propensity score analysis to estimate the effects of these different patterns of service uptake. Notably, in these studies, subgroups with different types of service uptake often appear to differ in terms of program effects.

Measuring compliance or treatment intensity may suffice for interventions that are prefabricated, such as pills, or for those that are simple and easy to implement as intended. But for many social and educational interventions, questions can arise as to how well the treatment was implemented. For example, many substance abuse prevention programs have a prescribed curriculum, specifying precisely what material the teacher is supposed to cover, what exercises students are supposed to engage in and how, what sequence should be followed across different modules of the curriculum, and so on. Again, the implications for decision making can be considerable: An effective intervention might not appear to be effective, if most teachers don't follow the prescribed curriculum. For interventions where some a priori curriculum or protocol exists, *fidelity assessment* is typically the preferred way to examine implementation. As the name suggests, fidelity assessment involves observing the extent to which treatment implementation was faithful to the pre-existing treatment model or curriculum. Mowbray, Holter, Teague, and Bybee (2004) provide a thorough discussion of the methods for and uses of fidelity assessment. They also summarize studies showing that treatment effects are larger to the extent that well-planned interventions are implemented with fidelity.

In some instances, programs or other interventions are implemented without a clear a priori specification of what the intervention should look like. In such cases, fidelity assessment is not plausible. Instead, in these cases, an *inductive or bottom-up implementation assessment* is likely to involve more qualitative methods, with the objective being to describe the intervention as it was implemented. As with fidelity assessment, a variety of methods might be used, including direct observation, interviews with implementers (e.g., teachers) and/or service recipients (e.g., students), and review of program documentation or "artifacts" (e.g., teacher lesson plans, quizzes).

Implementation assessment, in whatever form, has important implications for decision making. The idea of implementation assessment reminds us to consider what precisely comprises an intervention. For example, was a new, experimental educational curriculum implemented with extensive training of teachers, or did teachers in the experiment have to implement the new curriculum without any assistance? A school board considering adoption of the new curriculum, based on experimental findings, should benefit from knowing what, if any, teacher training was involved in the experiment, and whether similar training would be available if they adopted the new curriculum.

More generally, experiments often involve rigorous controls of various kinds, with well-trained implementers whose work is monitored, inclusion and exclusion rules leading to a relatively homogenous group of participants, and other procedures that may increase the likelihood of positive effects. In contrast, when the intervention is implemented outside the experiment, it may be implemented by untrained staff, with no monitoring, wide variability in implementation, and participants of all kinds, all of which may result in lower effectiveness. In some literatures, this challenge is summarized as the distinction between efficacy and effectiveness studies, respectively, where efficacy refers to tests under highly controlled conditions and effectiveness to tests under messier, "real-world" conditions (see, e.g., Borkovec, 2004; Nathan, Stuart, and Dolan, 2000; Shadish, Matt, Navarro, Siegle, Crits-Christoph, and Hazelrigg, 1997). The efficacy-effectiveness distinction is one reason that questions can arise about the extent to which experimental findings apply to the specific setting(s) about which a decision is to be made. We return to this issue subsequently, when addressing various challenges in using experimental findings for decision making.

24.3.2 MEDIATION AND MODERATION

Implementation assessment offers a major advance, relative to experiments or quasi-experiments that do not specify what the intervention was or how it was implemented. Implementation assessment thus is sometimes described as a way to peer inside the "black box" of an intervention. Another important methodological development, the study of mediation, also can be characterized as going beyond the "black box" experiment.

A *mediator* is a variable that falls between two other variables in a causal chain, in this case, between an intervention and its outcome; the mediator also accounts for or is responsible for the relationship between the intervention and outcome. For example, now-controversial drugs Vioxx and Celebrex have been shown to reduce arthritis pain. What mediates this relationship? These drugs selectively block the Cox-2 enzyme, which otherwise would produce prostoglandins that in turn would trigger painful inflammation. As another example, certain kinds of anti-littering campaigns are mediated by what are called injunctive social norms; that is, the campaign announcements make it salient to listeners that people in general disapprove of littering (Cialdini, 2003). The announcement's effect on injunctive social norms in turn leads to reduced littering.

Mediational analyses are relatively common in experiments and quasi-experiments in some practice areas. For example, for many kinds of behavioral health interventions, a family of behavior change theories often guides mediational analyses (see, for example, Mullen, Hersey, and Iverson, 1987). Mediational analyses also play a key role in some developing traditions of social experimentation. In particular, theory-driven evaluation is a growing approach to program and policy evaluation, and includes mediational analyses as a routine methodology (Donaldson, 2003).

Certain kinds of statistical analyses predominate the study of mediation in many areas of social and educational interventions. For instance, structural equation modeling (SEM) is often used to test mediation (e.g., Ullman and Bentler, 2003). Such statistical methods are valuable, but not without limits (e.g., Freedman, 1987; Kenny, Kashy, and Bolger, 1998). Alternative statistical procedures for studying mediation exist; examples include a form of instrumental variables analysis (Riccio and Bloom, 2002) and simpler regression analyses (Baron and Kenny, 1986). In addition, other methods can sometimes be useful for studying mediation. In medical and other biological contexts (and occasionally in social contexts; Mark, 1986), it is sometimes possible to intervene directly on the mediator. For instance, imagine that some other drug exists that would block or stimulate Celebrex's effect on the Cox-2 enzyme; if so, then an experiment in which this agent was given to some Celebrex takers but not others would provide a strong test of the Cox-2 mediational model. In social and educational interventions, on the other hand, more qualitative procedures might sometimes be used in order to trace mediational pathways.

The study of mediation is important for decision making, for several reasons. First, mediational evidence increases confidence that an effect is causal. If the observed effect is spurious, or the result of some artifact, you would not expect mediational tests to reveal a meaningful mediational pathway. Second, knowledge of what mediates a relationship can sometimes lead to more effective or more efficient interventions. For example, if you discover that anti-littering campaigns work because of injunctive social norms, you might be able to develop new ads better designed to affect this mediator. Third, knowledge about mediators can also be helpful when making judgments about generalization to other settings, as noted methodologist Lee Cronbach (1982) argued. The basic idea is that, if you know why an effect occurs, you'll be better able to make reasoned judgments about whether that effect will occur in another circumstance. Fourth, and related to the preceding, evidence about mediation can also be helpful to efforts to adapt an intervention, for instance, by modifying it for some new types of clients. For example, when adapting a program to be culturally relevant, it should be easier to avoid eliminating effective aspects of the intervention if you have the right mediators in mind. Finally, when mediational tests are conducted, research has the capacity to contribute, not only to decision making, but also to the more general knowledge base. For example, evaluations of environmental interventions that test the mediational role of injunctive social norms contribute to the more general literature on social influence (Cialdini, 2003).

Moderation, in contrast to mediation, refers to circumstances in which the effect of an intervention on an outcome depends upon the level of some other variable (the moderator). For example, if participant age moderates the effect of Cox-2 inhibitors on arthritis pain, this would mean that the effect of these drugs is different for younger than older patients (as Dr. Pamela Palmer [cited in Wallis, 2005], medical director of the University of California, San Francisco's pain-management center, speculates may be the case). Using different terminology, one might say that participant age interacts with the treatment. Knowing about important moderators can have clear implications for decision making from experimental and quasi-experimental research. For example, if some medical technique is effective for younger but not older patients (or for men but not for women, etc.), you would not want physicians to recommend it for all patients.

It is relatively easy and uncontroversial to test whether a given variable (e.g., a participant's age or sex) moderates the effect of an intervention, when it is suspected in advance of being moderator. However, there is some danger in testing multiple variables post hoc to see if they might be moderators. As Stigler (1987, 148) has put it, "Beware the problem of testing too many hypotheses; the more you torture the data, the more likely they are [to] confess, but confession obtained under duress may not be admissible in the court of scientific opinion." That is, the likelihood of obtaining a significant moderator relationship *by chance* increases with the number of potential moderator variables tested. This creates something of a quandary. It's undesirable to have important moderator variables that are unknown; when this occurs, treatments may be given to those for whom they are ineffective or even harmful. On the other hand, it's also undesirable to think you have found a real moderator variable only because you tortured the data. The standard suggestion is to consider all unplanned tests of moderators as exploratory, and then to replicate any interesting findings. This, too, can be problematic for social experimentation and evaluation, because replication in a reasonable time frame may not be feasible, and decision making often cannot be delayed pending completion of a replication study. Mark and his colleagues (e.g., Mark, 2003; Mark, Henry, and Julnes, 2000) have suggested "principled discovery" as a possible solution. In essence, the idea is to conduct exploratory tests of moderators, and to seek quasi-replications with other data from the same study's data set. This approach is promising, but still relatively early in its development and application.

24.3.3 OTHER ANCILLARIES WITHIN A SINGLE EXPERIMENT OR QUASI-EXPERIMENT

There are numerous other methods that complement the basic experiment or quasi-experiment. These include: the use of procedures to try to reduce dropouts and maintain contact with participants (Ribisl, Walton, Mowbray, Luke, Davidson, and Bootsmiller, 1996); improved procedures for handling missing data (Graham, Cumsille, and Elek-Fisk, 2003); and exploratory data analyses procedures that, prior to hypothesis tests, can identify data quality problems and perhaps suggest possible moderator variables (e.g., Behrens, 1997). In general, the implication of these ancillaries for decision making is simple: studies that do not handle missing data appropriately, for example, may be weighted somewhat less heavily in decisions.

24.3.3.1 Meta-Analysis

Meta-analysis is an important ancillary that goes beyond the individual experiment or quasi-experiment. Meta-analysis refers to procedures for the quantitative synthesis of primary research. Prior to the advent of meta-analysis, efforts to summarize a literature typically involved narrative reviews, often with simple tallies of which studies' findings were statistically significant, in which direction, and which studies' findings were not significant. Meta-analysis offers numerous advances over the older narrative review. For example, especially when the original studies in an area have low statistical power, an effect might be important even if most original studies do not achieve statistical significance. Initial meta-analyses typically looked at relatively simple questions, such as the size and statistical significance of a treatment effect combining across the available studies. Recent meta-analyses are more likely to study possible moderators of the treatment effect, and perhaps even to examine mediational questions (see, e.g., Cook et al., 1992).

In general, meta-analyses cannot go beyond the shared validity limitations of the original studies. For example, if all of the studies of some job-training program are weak quasi-experiments that share the same selection bias, then this shared bias will affect the meta-analytic findings. On the other hand, if the studies in an area use different designs, then meta-analysis can be used to assess whether, in this particular substantive area, the different designs lead to different outcomes. For example, one can examine whether randomized experiments result in different effect sizes than do quasi-experiments.

Meta-analytic evidence can be especially valuable for decision making. Well-conducted meta-analyses can summarize the best available answer across multiple studies. While the results of a single study can be influenced greatly by arbitrary methodological choices (e.g., wording of a key survey item), meta-analyses are far less dependent upon the idiosyncrasies of any single study. Perhaps most importantly, meta-analyses can offer greater confidence about generalizing from research findings to the particular decision context at hand. Meta-analytic results can reflect findings from studies with different kinds of participants, carried out in varying kinds of settings, and at different points in time. If an intervention's effect is consistent across these multiple forms of heterogeneity, one typically can have greater confidence in generalizing to the specific circumstances for which the decision is to be made (see Shadish, Cook, and Campbell, 2002 on the ways meta-analysis can contribute to generalization). And, if the meta-analysis indicates that effect sizes are not homogenous (that is, the overall findings do not appear to hold across all the studies included in the meta-analysis), it may be possible to search for moderators and then base the decision on findings from those studies with circumstances most like those of the setting to which the decision will apply.

24.4 FROM EVIDENCE TO DECISION MAKING

It is one thing to conduct an experiment or a quasi-experiment and produce findings. It is quite another thing for those findings to translate into decision making. Just as methods for experiments and quasi-experiments have developed over time, so too has there been some evolution in the way advocates of experimental and quasi-experimental evidence think about its use in decision making. In some areas, there has been a notable recent change in decision making practices, as well.

One might characterize the implicit model underlying early advocacy of experimental and quasi-experimental methods for decision making as the "field of dreams" model. Rather than "Build it, and they will come," the idea seemed to be: "Do the experiment, and they will use it." In an extensive examination of the work of several key evaluation theorists, Shadish, Cook, and Leviton (1991) describe Donald Campbell and Michael Scriven as "Stage 1" theorists. According to Shadish and his colleagues, Campbell and Scriven emphasized the use of procedures to obtain the best possible answer, with an assumption that good answers would generally influence decision making. One of Campbell's many slogans, "servant to the experimenting society" (Campbell, 1971), captures his view of the relationship between experimenter/evaluator and decision makers. In this view, the values operationalized in the experiment (e.g., in the selection of some outcome variables versus other potential ones) come from others, presumably the decision makers (House, 1980, 1993). The researcher's role is in serving the information needs of — and as seen by — those who are to be involved in the decision at hand. Like a servant placing a meal in front of his employer, the experimenter places the experimental results in front of decision makers — with the hope that the results will be consumed.

There are plenty of case examples in which experiments or quasi-experiments have affected important decisions. For example, Chelimsky (in press) discusses a review of quasi-experimental studies of the effect of lowering the drinking age on driving fatalities. This review of quasi-experimental evidence was the subject of a congressional hearing. It was also cited in a Supreme Court ruling that upheld the constitutionality of a law that reduced federal highway aid to states that did not have a minimum drinking age of 21. Despite the existence of this and other cases in which experiments and quasi-experiments have influenced decisions, early experience gave way to a widespread sense of unused reports gathering dust on shelves.

Thus, the early history of social experimentation and program evaluation raised grave concerns about the "field of dreams" model of use. Consequently, what Shadish, Cook, and Leviton (1991) characterize as "Stage 2" evaluation theorists emerged. These scholars emphasized the complex and often inchoate processes through which decisions are made. Among the Stage 2 evaluation theorists, the work of Carol Weiss is especially noteworthy in terms of implications for the use of experimental and quasi-experimental evidence in decision making. Weiss (1977, 1979, 1988) drew on the work of scholars of organizational decision making, as well as her own and others' studies of whether and how evaluation and research findings were used by policy makers.

Weiss' work paints a picture quite unlike the implicit picture of decision making in Stage 1 evaluation theory. That earlier work appears to have assumed that there are identifiable decision makers, who make go/no-go decisions at discrete points in time, and who will be heavily influenced by high-quality information. According to Weiss, decisions often accrete. That is, they emerge over time out of numerous judgments by diffuse actors, rather than there being identifiable decisions made at a single point in time by specific actors. Weiss also emphasized the competition between research evidence and other influences on decisions, including values, politics, traditions, and the like. In part because of these multiple considerations, no study is likely to be able to answer all the questions and concerns that decision makers have. Weiss further pointed to the multiple channels of influence, including the media, issues networks, and advocates, further complicating the potential use of experimental evidence.

Given the complex and often distributed nature of decision making, perhaps it should not be surprising that direct, instrumental use of experimental evidence is infrequent. But Weiss and others have pointed to an alternative form of use, which she refers to as "enlightenment" and others label as "conceptual use." According to this perspective, findings may affect the conventional wisdom. They may influence the way policy makers and others understand a problem and its possible solutions. That is, findings can create more general learning rather than have immediate impact on decision making. Through these conceptual effects, findings can eventually influence decision making at later times or in other locations than where the research was conducted.

Since Weiss' original work, many practitioners of social experimentation and evaluation have taken on additional responsibilities for getting their results onto the agenda of decision makers. In large part, this has involved additional work on dissemination of findings, including: preparing multiple forms of reports, some user-friendly and others technical; briefing the press as well as identifiable decision makers; developing web sites on the study and its results; and including communication specialists on evaluation teams (or, more generally within research firms or foundations). In addition, those who conduct social experiments often are active within the issues networks that exist around various policy issues. Implicitly, such activities expand the "servant of the experimenting society" metaphor. Given the costs of experiments (including not only financial costs, but also the time and other burdens born by the study participants), there is an argument, if not an ethical mandate, that those who conduct social experiments should try to facilitate use, at the very least, through extensive dissemination (cf. Rosenthal, 1994).

More recently, notable changes in decision-making practices have occurred in selected areas, in an apparent attempt to increase the connection between experimental research findings and direct action. For example, Weiss, Murphy-Graham, and Birkeland (2005) have examined decisions about the continuation or discontinuation of the DARE program in a purposive sample of schools. Weiss and her colleagues studied decisions about DARE in a set of schools in which DARE had already been implemented, in four states where large-scale evaluations of the program had been conducted. In those and in other studies, some of which received considerable publicity, DARE had been found to be ineffective. Weiss and her colleagues found that the set of schools they studied retained DARE until a change in the Safe and Drug Free Schools and Communities Act (SDFSCA) stipulated that programs funded through the act must be research-based. Most of these schools subsequently chose replacement programs from the SDFSCA Office's recommendation list, to ensure there would be no loss of federal funds, even though this was not mandated. Weiss and her colleagues describe this as a kind of "imposed use," in the sense that the local school district's use of research findings was more or less mandated by the perceived stipulation that funding is contingent on implementation of programs that are research-based.[*]

The fundamental model of imposed use is not new in practice, however. Something like it presumably underlay the 1984 legislation cutting highway funding to states that did not adopt a drinking age of 21. A similar model of use also exists in third-party payment systems in the healthcare system. For example, insurance companies and other third-party payers often specify a "formulary" of approved drugs, as well as a list of approved medical procedures, in part based on experimental findings (but also on other considerations, particularly cost). As with SDFSCA, decision making at one level is meant to influence decision making at another level. In this case, the decisions of the third-party payer are intended to influence the decisions of individual consumers and physicians, by changing their costs and rewards. In short, what Weiss and her colleagues call "imposed use" exists in several domains, and we speculate that it may become more frequent.

---

[*] In related work, Gruner, Murphy-Graham, Petrosino, and Weiss (2005) contend that the quality of some programs recommended by the SDFSCA was as questionable as that of those not making the list.

For instance, it will be interesting to see whether and to what extent so-called imposed use comes to occur with the What Works Clearinghouse (WWC). The WCC was established in support of the No Child Left Behind Act of 2001, which mandates that "federal funds support educational activities that are backed by scientifically based research" (U.S. Department of Education, 2005). Initiated in 2002 through contracts with the American Institutes for Research and the Campbell Collaboration of Philadelphia, the WWC is meant to serve as a "decision making tool" that reviews and synthesizes research on a wide range of educational methods and programs (What Works Clearinghouse, 2005). The WWC identifies key topic areas important to education — such as adult literacy, character education, delinquent behavior interventions, dropout prevention, English language learning, math interventions, and reading interventions — and reviews numerous studies relevant to those topic areas against a set of criteria (What Works Clearinghouse, 2005). The highest ratings of validity are given to randomized studies and regression-discontinuity designs that did not experience attrition or disruption. Lower but passable ratings are given to quasi-experiments with equivalent groups that did not experience attrition or disruption, or to randomized studies and regression-discontinuity designs with some attrition or disruption (What Works Clearinghouse, 2005). The resulting reports are available on the WWC website (www.whatworks.ed.gov) for educators, researchers, and members of the public.[*] WWC reports are intended in part to be resources for educators involved in selecting scientifically sound interventions and methods.

With respect to decision making and use, an interesting question involves whether the WWC lists will come to be taken by educational decision makers as the approved lists of "imposed use." For instance, although NCLB does not dictate that funds from Reading First programs go only to programs endorsed by the WWC, some observers have suggested that educators and administrators are moving toward those programs in order to guarantee funding (Fletcher, 2004). Will presence on the WWC list become, for many schools, the operational definition of scientifically based evidence and the safest way to avoid the risk of loss of funds? Given the large amount of money invested in textbooks, curricula, and other educational interventions in the US, this is a high-stakes enterprise.

Imposed use, like other forms of use previously discussed (direct, instrumental use versus conceptual use/enlightenment), focuses primarily on the use of study findings. It is possible, however, for experiments or quasi-experiments to influence decision making, if indirectly, by their procedures as well. Expanding on Patton's (1997) concept of process use, we might call this "procedural influence."[†] For example, imagine that measures of children's well-being are added to several foundation-funded evaluations of welfare reform; the simple fact that children's well-being is examined as an outcome in these studies may increase its salience when policy makers think about welfare reform. In short, aspects of studies other than their findings — such as the outcomes measured, the nature of the comparison group's services or activities, and the mediators and moderators tested — can sometimes influence beliefs and actions.

In short, very different (often implicit) models exist representing the expected or proper relationship between experimental (or quasi-experimental) evidence and decision making. These ideas include the following:

---

[*] Critics have offered complaints about WWC reviews, primarily about the criteria that are applied, but also about some details of how they have been applied (Lederman and Flick, 2003; Viadero, 2004). The WWC, at present, is still something of a work in progress, and it will also be interesting to see how it evolves over time.

[†] Patton (1997) defined process use as "individual changes in thinking and behavior, and program or organizational changes in procedures and culture, that occur among those involved in evaluation as a result of the learning that occurs during the evaluation process" (p. 90). The idea of process use is here expanded to "procedural influence" because we are referring to effects of procedural attributes of the experiment or quasi-experiment (e.g., the outcome variables measured, or the details of the comparison condition), which can influence individuals who were not directly involved in the conduct of the evaluation.

- that experimental results are there for decision makers to use or not, as they prefer
- that, with the complexity of organizational decision making, enlightenment is more likely than direct use
- that, while direct use cannot be guaranteed, social experimenters have an obligation via dissemination and other professional activities to strongly encourage such use
- that "imposed use" can help shorten the path from evidence to action, through the creation at one organizational level of approved lists, as well as sticks or carrots, to influence decisions at lower levels
- that procedural aspects of social experiments, and not just findings, can influence decision making.

24.5 CHALLENGES IN MOVING FROM EXPERIMENTAL EVIDENCE TO DECISIONS

Regardless of how experimental evidence is supposed to contribute to decision making, and regardless of whether the decision making is individual, organizational, or governmental, challenges are likely to arise. In this section, we discuss concerns that go beyond the technical, methodological challenges of conducting high-quality, valid research. Instead, they involve challenges in measuring the right outcomes to feed into decision making; judging what implications a given experimental finding has for decision making; and incorporating experimental findings in decision making amidst other factors that may influence decisions.

24.5.1 CHALLENGES IN MEASURING THE RIGHT OUTCOMES

Imagine you are reading a review of different car models, in anticipation of buying a new car. To your dismay, the review provides no information about the thing that matters most to you; for example, you may be an environmentalist reading a review that says nothing about gas mileage. Similarly, experimental evidence may have limited import for decision making, if outcomes of great interest for the decision makers were not examined in the experiment. For instance, certain policy makers might discount evaluations that report on the economic consequences of welfare reform, but do not report effects on children's well-being. For cost and other practical reasons, experiments cannot measure everything; how then are investigators to try to make sure that they measure the outcomes most important for subsequent decision making? Historically, program goals have been a key guide in selecting outcomes to measure, but this approach is problematic, in part because stated goals may have more to do with the rhetoric of getting a program approved than with the views of varied stakeholders (e.g., House, 1980). Alternative approaches exist to aid in identifying and prioritizing among possible outcome constructs, with one recent suggestion being to conduct values inquiry, that is, the systematic study of what it is that various stakeholders value regarding a program and its outcomes (Mark, Henry, and Julnes, 2000).

Another common challenge is that the outcomes that are truly of interest often are long-term ones, well beyond the feasible timeline of the study. For example, universal pre-K may be justified in terms of its supposed impact on children's long-term developmental trajectories, including such delayed outcomes as crime and employment. But most studies will not be able to track children beyond a few years, and decision making usually cannot be deferred until long-term evidence is available. In practice, researchers measure shorter-term outcomes, especially those thought to be precursors of the long-term outcomes of greater interest. But then it also becomes quite important to consider the quality of the evidence about the link between the shorter-term and the longer-term outcomes. Further, it is no easy matter to incorporate into decision making the (imperfectly known) degree of uncertainty that exists about the extent to which the short-term proxy measures foretell longer-term outcomes.

Yet another challenge arises in terms of having information about the right outcomes: the case of side effects. If side effects (whether positive or negative) truly are unanticipated, the experiment will not contain systematic measurement of them. In addition, in at least some cases, important side effects are rare in occurrence. Studies that have adequate statistical power to test differences on the primary outcomes often will not have sufficient power to observe effects on most infrequent but important side effects.[*] If the intervention is subsequently adopted more widely, it should be easier to see side effects because the number of people exposed to the treatment will be greater; however, causal inference will be more ambiguous, because the experimental study design will no longer be operating.[†]

24.5.2 Challenges in Assessing Findings' Implications for Decision Making

Experimental methods, and to a lesser extent quasi-experimental approximations, provide relatively strong answers to questions about whether, and to what extent, a treatment affects a given outcome variable. Statistical analyses also can indicate whether the observed findings are unlikely to have arisen by chance. But knowing simply that a treatment affects some outcome of interest does not automatically and simply translate into a decision to adopt the treatment generally.

One question that arises in decision making is: How big an effect matters? If DARE were to reduce adolescent substance use by 10%, would this justify the cost of implementation and the loss of class time required to implement the program? One response to such questions is to suggest that experimental findings should feed into cost-benefit analyses or other formal or informal decision making techniques. However, an added complexity arises in the sense that not all experimental or quasi-experimental findings are readily interpreted, at least by non-technical audiences. There is typically little problem when the outcome measure is in a metric that is naturally meaningful. For instance, decision makers can easily make sense of findings indicating that in an experiment, participants using a nicotine patch smoke 10 fewer cigarettes a day, on average, than those with a placebo patch.

On the other hand, outcome variables are often measured with scales that do not have an everyday meaning. In some such cases, interpretability can be increased by converting the difference between groups on the arbitrary scale into a more meaningful referent. For example, in educational evaluations, researchers sometimes provide grade-equivalents (reporting, for example, that an intervention improved students' scores by half an academic year, relative to the comparison group). In other cases, standardized effect sizes are reported. These typically are defined as the mean difference between groups, divided by the pooled standard deviation. Standardized effect sizes allow comparison across outcomes measured in different scales, as well as comparisons across studies (and are typically used to aggregate findings across studies in meta-analyses). However, effect sizes themselves can be influenced by design choices the researcher makes (e.g., to study a relatively homogeneous vs. a more heterogeneous set of participants). In addition, researchers probably need to educate those who would use findings about how to interpret standardized effect sizes.[‡]

---

[*] Ironically, unanticipated side effects might well be noticed - though not confirmed statistically - if they are unusual and thus also rare. For example, if a drug causes hemorrhagic fever, which physicians rarely if ever see, this possible side-effect would likely be noticed more quickly than if the drug caused an increase in heart attacks, which are more commonplace.

[†] In at least some cases, the search for side effects could be facilitated by following experiments with more descriptive, but systematic reporting systems.

[‡] For helpful recommendations about how to report findings, as well as useful guidelines about several methodological matters, see Wilkinson and the Task Force on Statistical Inference (1999).

A second, and quite important, consideration arises when decision makers try to consider the implications of experimental (or quasi-experimental) findings. That is, what is the comparison standard, in the sense of what is occurring in the comparison condition? It is one thing to show that a new drug reduces pain relative to a placebo, but another thing to show that that same drug reduces pain relative to the leading available painkiller. When several alternative courses of action exist, implications for decision making are likely to differ when the comparison is something relatively ineffective (e.g., no treatment or even a placebo) than when the comparison standard itself is a relatively effective option.

Questions about how to aggregate across outcomes can also add complexity, as decision makers consider the implications of findings. For instance, a preschool evaluation might find positive effects on social outcomes, but no effect on academic outcomes. How should these differing findings be put together to reach an overall evaluative judgment? Technical procedures exist for aggregating across multiple criteria, as described elsewhere in this Handbook, and these can be applied to study findings. Alternatively, more informal deliberation might be undertaken, with dialogue among decision makers leading to judgments about how much they value each of the outcomes (for a recent approach to deliberative dialogue, see House and Howe, 1999). Similar considerations apply to conflicting findings across studies, which can sometimes be addressed meta-analytically if there are enough studies. Sometimes, however, conflicting findings across studies are more difficult to make sense of, because of trade-offs across study characteristics. For example, a randomized experiment might have lower power to detect a rare side effect, relative to a subsequent quasi-experiment, but might also be less susceptible to selection bias.

The question of generalizability is among the most challenging issues that arise as decision makers contemplate the implications of study findings. That is, will the results of the research apply to the specific individuals and the specific setting about which the decision has to be made? For example, bypass surgery might be effective on the average, but will it really help *me*? Could not DARE work in our school, even if it was not effective in the handful of other schools where it was studied? How well do studies of welfare reform in two states predict what would happen if similar changes were made in the country as a whole? The issue is essentially the same as that which Cook and Campbell (1979) call the question of the external validity: How correct are our inferences about the extent to which the conclusions of an experiment or quasi-experiment would apply to persons, settings, and times other than those examined in the study?

We have already noted several ways in which generalizability can be assessed and strengthened. First, meta-analysis can contribute substantially to generalizability, by providing estimates of the effects of a treatment that aggregate over the various samples, settings, and dates of the multiple studies. In addition, meta-analysis can provide statistical tests of whether the overall effect size applies to all the studies included (homogeneity tests). Second, tests of possible moderator variables can be quite important when judging whether experimental results will apply to a particular setting. For instance, if an experiment tests whether an educational intervention is moderated by family income level, the results, whatever they are, should be informative to those considering implementing the intervention in a particular school with a given economic profile. Third, the study of mediational models can also aid in judgments about generalizability. As Cronbach (1982) has suggested, knowing why an effect occurs will at least sometimes help in making judgments about whether it will occur in some new setting. And fourth, as noted previously, implementation assessment can aid in judgments about generalizability. In particular, with more detailed knowledge about how the treatment was actually implemented in practice in an experiment, it should be possible either to do a better job of implementing similarly or of assessing in advance whether similar implementation is possible in the decision makers' context.

24.5.3 Challenges in Weighing Findings against Other, Non-Experimental Considerations

It is important to keep in mind that decisions do not necessarily depend on cause-and-effect assessments. In evaluating new car models, for example, the attributes that matter to most people, such as safety, gas mileage, comfort, and repair record, are assessed without randomized experiments or other causal methods.[*] Decisions about personnel (who to hire, who to promote) can be quite important, but rely on methods other than experiments or quasi-experiments. Even in important policy-related evaluations, descriptive information, perhaps coming from "testing," may apply, rather than cause-and-effect information from experiments. For example, in evaluating the strategic nuclear triad, that is, the land, sea, and air legs of the US nuclear missile system, the methods used look more like product testing, policy analysis, and cost-accounting, rather than experiments or quasi-experiments (cf. Chelimsky, in press).

If researchers and others are doing reasonable planning, they will not undertake an experiment or quasi-experiment unless causal questions are of interest. A potentially more challenging situation exists when decisions should depend on both the causal and the more procedural characteristics of an intervention. For example, what people value about pre-K includes not only causal effects, such as pre-K's impact on school readiness, but also process considerations, such as safety (e.g., whether the pre-K center has adequate fire safety; see Henry, 2002). In one sense, integrating causal and non-causal criteria need be no more difficult than aggregating across multiple outcome constructs. However, when programs or other interventions are studied by experimentalists, the focus often is exclusively on measuring downstream causal effects. Attention may not always be given in experiments to equally careful assessment of important procedural characteristics (Mark, Henry, and Julnes, 2000). Systematic values inquiry, as illustrated by Henry (2002) may increase the likelihood that important procedural as well as causal questions are addressed when this is appropriate.

As a final comment on non-causal considerations, one should perhaps simply acknowledge that reasoned attention to the best available evidence about causal effects will not and should not overwhelm other considerations. As the work of Weiss and many others reminds us, policy decisions depend on politics and values at least as much as evidence; there are windows of opportunity that, once closed, diminish the potential contribution of findings to immediate decision making; and agendas can change with administrations, key personnel shifts, or for a variety of other reasons. There is a limit to how much experimenters can minimize the impact of such considerations. However, this is as it should be. Despite the important limits of democracies, collectively we probably prefer (and, in the long run, probably are better served by) democratic and individual decision making, rather than an experimental technocracy.

24.6 A CASE EXAMPLE

In this section, we present a brief description and analysis of a contemporary case in which experimental and quasi-experimental evidence is central to decision making. The case highlights some of the challenges and complexities that can arise when decisions are based on rigorous evidence about cause and effect relationships. Importantly, although the case we discuss comes from medicine, other cases could have been drawn from social and educational spheres, such as substance abuse prevention programs (Weiss, Murphy-Graham, and Birkeland, 2005), juvenile justice interventions (e.g., Lipsey, Cordray, and Berger, 1981), or education (U.S. Department of Education, 2005; What Works Clearinghouse, 2005).

---

[*] Even here, though, one might conceptualize the resulting comparisons across car models as a quasi-experiment or something close to it (C.S. Reichardt, personal communication, April 2005).

24.6.1 Vioxx, Drug Studies, and the FDA

On September 30, 2004, the pharmaceutical company Merck and Co., Inc. withdrew its prescription drug Vioxx from the market. This decision, which was not mandated by the Food and Drug Administration (FDA), came in response to findings from a large-scale experiment (the so-called APPROVE trial). These findings indicated that long-term use of the drug increased the risk of cardiovascular events, including heart attacks and "sudden cardiac death," in some patients (U.S. Food and Drug Administration, 2004). Both Merck and the FDA had some earlier indication of the cardiovascular risks of Vioxx via a 2000 trial (called VIGOR), which was not a randomized experiment.[*]

Less than two months after Merck pulled Vioxx from the market, the U.S. Senate Committee on Finance held a hearing that examined whether Merck and the FDA had the health and safety of the public in mind in their respective reactions to Vioxx study data (U.S. Senate, 2004). The most striking figure at the hearing was David Graham, Associate Director for Science and Medicine in the FDA's Office of Drug Safety (U.S. Senate, 2004). In his testimony at the Senate hearing, Graham referred to the way the FDA handled Vioxx as "a terrible tragedy and a profound regulatory failure." He indicated that this was not an isolated incident but, rather, was symptomatic of the overall inadequacy of the FDA "as currently configured" (U.S. Senate, 2004). In conjunction with Kaiser Permanente, Graham had previously performed an epidemiological (and quasi-experimental) study of Vioxx; Graham's conclusions were that "high-dose Vioxx significantly increased the risk of heart attacks and sudden death" and, therefore, "should not be prescribed or used by patients" (U.S. Senate, 2004, 3). These conclusions had not been embraced by the FDA, which initially refused to allow Graham to publish his findings.

In his Senate testimony, Graham described what he considered to be the FDA's fundamental limitations. He first implicated the structure of the FDA's Center for Drug Evaluation and Research. Under this structure, those who are responsible for approving a new drug are also accountable for any safety concerns that may appear after the drug has been marketed. This, according to Graham, creates an "inherent conflict of interest" (U.S. Senate, 2004, 4). Graham also sees the relationship between the FDA and the pharmaceutical industry as problematic. He argues that the FDA "views the pharmaceutical industry it is supposed to regulate as its client" (ibid., 5). Graham suggests this contributes to a focus in the Agency on new drug approval and to an inadequate emphasis on post-marketing regulation (U.S. Senate, 2004).

Some observers point to the 1992 Prescription Drug User Fee Act to explain what they see as the FDA's overemphasis on drug approval and as an unhealthy relationship with the pharmaceutical industry (Herper, 2005). This act allowed the FDA to charge pharmaceutical companies user fees — in 2004, these fees totaled $220 million — for expedited drug reviews (Peterson, 2005; Herper, 2005). Harvard Professor of Medicine Jerome Avorn states that dependence on the pharmaceutical industry for funding "changes the sense of who [the FDA is] accountable to and who's paying [their] salary" (cited in Peterson, 2005). The Agency's initiation of expedited reviews was the result of AIDS activists' protests against the once conservative, time-consuming review process that was then seen as an obstacle to "breakthrough drugs". Vioxx was among many recent drugs that underwent expedited review.

Among Graham's criticisms of the FDA are ones that reveal underlying differences he has with the Agency regarding standards for scientific research. Graham states the Agency's position is that "only randomized trials provide useful and actionable information," which led them largely to ignore both the results of the VIGOR trial (which was not randomized for ethical reasons) and his subsequent epidemiologic study (which was based on managed-care data) (U.S. Senate, 2004, 4). In her testimony at the Merck/FDA Senate hearing, Sandra Kweder, Deputy Director for the Office

---

[*]Following VIGOR, the FDA insisted that the labeling for Vioxx instruct physicians to take side-effects into consideration when prescribing the drug (2004).

of New Drugs, stated that studies such as Graham's are "difficult to conduct and interpret" because of their non-randomized designs (U.S. Senate, 2004, 3). However, as Bruce Psaty, Professor of Medicine at the University of Washington testified, the small number of patients and short duration of randomized clinical trials make them an inadequate way of assessing risks such as those associated with Vioxx (U.S. Senate, 2004). Psaty further argued that clinical trials and observational studies (quasi-experiments) should be considered together when investigating the effects of medication.

Graham also objects to the scientific standards of post-marketing that place the burden of proof on demonstrating that risks exist. When initially proving drug effectiveness, Graham argues, a standard of 95% certainty (technically, a 95% confidence interval) is appropriate, because it drastically limits the number of ineffective drugs given FDA approval. However, Graham contends that when this same standard is applied to risks, especially to side effects with low base-rates, this creates "an almost insurmountable barrier to overcome" (U.S. Senate, 2004, 5). The small number of patients in clinical trials rarely affords enough statistical power to demonstrate risk at 95%, and subsequent "observational studies" (quasi-experiments) are less sensitive and more ambiguous regarding causality (U.S. Senate, 2004). Moreover, statistically nonsignificant findings are largely disregarded by the FDA. Indeed, Graham's epidemiologic study was criticized by Anne Trontell, Deputy Director of the Office of Drug Safety, for focusing on "a nonsignificant finding" (Seligman, 2004).

The complete story of the FDA and Vioxx is much longer, and likely will continue well after this chapter has been published. An FDA advisory panel was convened to make recommendations, not only about Vioxx, but also about fellow Cox-2 inhibitor drugs Bextra and Celebrex. The panel recommended that Bextra and Celebrex stay on the market and that Vioxx be brought back. The panel also recommended "black box" warnings on drug packaging, as well as the end of TV ads. Research continues: studies are ongoing as to the mediational mechanism by which Cox-2 drugs may lead to heart attacks and strokes (which may be by suppressing prostacyclin, which normally prevents blood platelets from clumping together). In addition, various changes in FDA policies and practices have been adopted or proposed, and more are likely in the future (Gorman, 2005). The final fate of Vioxx and other Cox-2 inhibitors is not yet known.

Again, this brief case analysis highlights several issues raised earlier in the chapter.

- This case example dramatically highlights the challenges, as well as the importance of detecting side effects. As this case shows, it can be especially difficult to obtain conclusive evidence about those side effects that, like heart attacks, are relatively infrequent as an outcome of the treatment, and also occur for a variety of reasons other than the drug being tested.
- The VIOXX case also illustrates the challenges that arise when outcomes of interest may take longer to occur than the time frame of the study. The challenge of detecting coronary side effects is increased in part because these complications may not appear within the limited duration of the experiment(s) on which approval of the drug is based.
- The case demonstrates difficulty in aggregating evidence from randomized experiments (with lower power to detect side effects) with quasi-experimental evidence. Is the FDA's strong preference for randomized experiments simply good science? Or is it, as Graham contends, a choice that is dangerous for consumers, who may not be as quickly protected from potentially harmful medication?
- This case also raises questions about the criteria to use when deciding whether to base action on experimental or quasi-experimental evidence. The FDA appears to have relied on a conventional standard of statistical significance. Might different standards be appropriate under different circumstances? In particular, might the public health costs of approving a drug with a fatal side effect suggest that something other than the traditional 95% confidence interval be employed for such outcomes?
- Moreover, should the focus be on effect size rather than statistical significance?

- The case also raises questions about how to aggregate across multiple outcome variables. How should the FDA weigh the pain relief benefits, without gastrointestinal distress, for many patients, relative to the coronary risk that would affect far fewer?
- In the discussion to date, little attention has been given to the question of whose values and concerns should guide the selection of outcome variables to measure in drug tests. For example, many patients might ask whether quality of life should be measured.
- Although it has not been a major focus of most discussions of this case, the issue of mediation is important. Consider two alternative mediational pathways: (1) Vioxx increases the likelihood of heart attack and stroke by suppressing prostacyclin, versus (2) Vioxx, by alleviating joint pain, increases physical activity among patients who were previously inactive, and this increased activity leads to a temporary increase in cardiovascular events. The decision-making implications of these two alternative mediational pathways seem quite different.
- One can ask whether factors such as age, gender, and race moderate Vioxx's effects, both intended and unintended. If we knew that, for example, age moderates these effects, then decisions could be better tailored to the individual patient. But larger samples or more studies would be required to have the power to estimate effects for subgroups rather than on the average. Again, trade-offs exist.
- Issues of treatment implementation are not prominent in discussions of Vioxx, where dosage/compliance is the primary implementation concern. In contrast, implementation assessment might be a larger issue for many social or educational interventions, where fidelity (or more generally, the question of what the intervention consisted of) may be in question.
- FDA's drug approval process, in one sense, is a case of imposed use that preceded Weiss and her colleague's coining of that term. That is, based on research findings, the FDA's decisions constrain on physicians' and patients' actions. The Vioxx case reminds us that even when we can identify a case of imposed use, other important questions exist about the relationship between experimental or quasi-experimental evidence and decision making. We have already noted several questions about the FDA's decision-making process, involving, for example, side effects and aggregating across outcomes. We can also ask whether the individual empowerment expected by some advocates of EBM arises, or whether evidence such as that in the Vioxx case leaves individual consumers in a state of confusion (Wallis, 2005). Experiments and quasi-experiments can contribute to decision making, but they do not automatically lead to easy decisions. Indeed, sometimes their contribution might be to remove spurious certainty that would otherwise exist.

24.7 CONCLUSION

Experiments and quasi-experiments, especially strong ones such as the regression-discontinuity design, can provide valuable evidence about the effects of various interventions. Given that action is often based on presumptions about consequences, experiments and quasi-experiments can serve a valuable role in decision making. But experiments and quasi-experiments alone cannot be determinative of decisions. Substantial challenges exist to obtaining findings that meet the complex decision needs of varied individuals in multiple settings. Values and other considerations inevitably intrude, and judgments must be made, such as what strength of evidence is required (including issues related to confidence level, effect size, and experimental ancillaries). Despite such complexities, even an experiment that is imperfect in some way can contribute to thoughtful decision making, relative to alternative sources of causal information. In short, experiments and quasi-experiments should contribute to thoughtful judgment and decision making, not be a substitute for it.

REFERENCES

Baron, R. and Kenny, D. A., The moderator-mediator distinction in social psychological research: Conceptual, strategic, and statistical considerations, *Journal of Personality and Social Psychology*, 51, 1173–1181, 1986.

Behrens, J. T., Principles and procedures of exploratory data analysis, *Psychological Methods*, 2, 131–160, 1997.

Borkovec, T. D., On the need for a basic science approach to psychotherapy research, *Psychological Science*, 8, 145–147, 1997.

Borkovec, T. D., Research in training clinics and practice research networks: A route to the integration of science and practice, *Clinical Psychology: Science and Practice*, 11, 211–215, 2004.

Boruch, R. F., *Randomized Experiments for Planning and Evaluation: A Practical Guide*, Sage, Thousand Oaks, CA, 1997.

Campbell, D. T., Methods for the experimenting society, Paper presented at the American Psychological Association Annual Meeting, Washington, DC, 1971.

Campbell, D. T. and Stanley, J. C., *Experimental and Quasi-Experimental Designs for Research*, Rand McNally, Skokie, IL, 1966.

Chelimsky, E., The purposes of evaluation in a democratic society, In *Handbook of Evaluation*, Shaw, I., Greene, J., and Mark, M. M., Eds., Sage, London, in press.

Cialdini, R. B., Crafting normative messages to protect the environment, *Current Directions in Psychological Science*, 12, 105–109, 2003.

Cook, T. D., Sciencephobia: Why education researchers reject randomized experiments, *Education Next*, 1, 1, 62–68, 2001.

Cook, T. D., Why have educational evaluators chosen not to do randomized experiments?, *Annals of American Academy of Political and Social Science*, 589, 114–149, 2003.

Cook, T. D. and Campbell, D. T., *Quasi-Experimentation: Design and Analysis Issues for Field Settings*, Rand McNally, Skokie, IL, 1979.

Cook, T. J. and Poole, W. K., Treatment implementation and statistical power: A research note, *Evaluation Quarterly*, 6, 425–430, 1982.

Cook, T. D., et al., Eds. *Meta-Analysis for Explanation: A Casebook*, Russell Sage Foundation, New York, 1992.

Cronbach, L. J., *Designing Evaluations of Educational and Social Programs*, Jossey-Bass, San Francisco, 1982.

Donaldson, S. I., The theory-driven view of evaluation, In *Evaluating Social Programs and Problems: Visions for the New Millennium*, Donaldson, S. I. and Scriven, M., Eds., Erlbaum, Hillsdale, NJ, pp. 109–141, 2003.

Donaldson, S. I. and Scriven, M., Eds., *Evaluating Social Programs and Problems: Visions for the New Millennium*, Erlbaum, Hillsdale, NJ, 2003.

Eckert, W. A., Situational enhancement of design validity: The case of training evaluation at the world bank institute, *American Journal of Evaluation*, 21, 185–193, 2000.

Eysenbach, G. and Jadad, A. R., Evidence-based patient choice and consumer health informatics in the Internet age, *Journal of Medical Internet Research*, 3, E19, 2001.

Fletcher, G. H., Scientifically based research: Guidelines or mandates for product purchasing?, *The Journal*, 31, 22–24, 2004.

Freedman, D. A., As others see us: A case study in path analysis, *Journal of Educational Statistics*, 12, 101–128, 1987.

Friedlander, D., Greenberg, D. H., and Robins, P. K., Evaluating government training programs for the economically disadvantaged, *Journal of Economic Literature*, 25, 1809–1855, 1997.

Gibson, C. M., Privileging the participant: The importance of sub-group analyses in social welfare evaluations, *American Journal of Evaluation*, 24, 443–469, 2003.

Gorman, C., Can the FDA heal itself?, *Time*, 165, 58, 2005.

Graham, J. W., Cumsille, P. E., and Elek-Fisk, E., Methods for handling missing data, In *Comprehensive Handbook of Psychology (Volume 2)*, Schinka, S. A. and Velicer, W., Eds., Wiley, New York, pp. 87–114, 2003.

Greenberg, D. and Schroeder, M., *The Digest of Social Experiments*, 2nd ed., Urban Institute Press, Washington, DC, 1997.

Gruner, A., Murphy-Graham, E., Petrosino, A., and Weiss, C. H., The devil is in the details: Examining the evidence for "proven" school-based drug prevention programs, Unpublished manuscript, 2005.

Henry, G. T., How modern democracies are shaping evaluation and the emerging challenges for evaluation, *American Journal of Evaluation*, 22, 419–430, 2001.

Henry, G. T., Choosing criteria to judge program success: A values inquiry, *Evaluation*, 8, 182–204, 2002.

Herper, M., FDA fix no. 1: Pay up. *Forbes.com*., January 12. http://www.forbes.com/healthcare/2005/01/12/cx_mh_0112fda1.html (accessed January 13, 2005), 2005.

House, E., *Evaluating with Validity*, Sage, Thousand Oaks, CA, 1980.

House, E., *Professional Evaluation*, Sage, Thousand Oaks, CA, 1993.

House, E. R. and Howe, K. R., *Values in Evaluation and Social Research*, Sage, Thousand Oaks, CA, 1999.

Kenny, D. A., Kashy, D. A., and Bolger, N., Data analysis in social psychology, In *The Handbook of Social Psychology, Vol. 2*, Gilbert, D. T., Fiske, S. T., et al., Eds., 4th ed., Mcgraw-Hill, Boston, pp. 233–256, 1998.

Lederman, N. G. and Flick, L. B., Never cry wolf, *School Science and Mathematics*, 103, 61–63, 2003.

Leow, C., Marcus, S., Zanutto, E., and Boruch, R., Effects of advanced course-taking on math and science achievement: Addressing selection bias using propensity scores, *American Journal of Evaluation*, 25, 461–478, 2004.

Lipsey, M. W., Cordray, D. S., and Berger, D. E., Evaluation of a juvenile diversion program: Using multiple lines of evidence, *Evaluation Review*, 5, 283–306, 1981.

Mark, M. M., Treatment implementation, statistical power, and internal validity, *Evaluation Review*, 7, 543–549, 1983.

Mark, M. M., Validity typologies and the logic and practice of quasi-experimentation, In *Advances in Quasi-Experimental Design and Analysis*, Trochim, W. M. K., Ed., Jossey-Bass, San Francisco, pp. 47–66, 1986.

Mark, M. M., Program evaluation, In *Comprehensive Handbook of Psychology (Vol 2)*, Schinka, S. A. and Velicer, W., Eds., Wiley, New York, pp. 323–347, 2003.

Mark, M. M., Henry, G. T., and Julnes, G., *Evaluation: An Integrated Framework for Understanding, Guiding, and Improving Policies and Programs*, Jossey Bass, San Francisco, 2000.

Mowbray, C. T., Holter, M. C., Teague, G. B., and Bybee, D., Fidelity criteria: Development, measurement, and validation, *American Journal of Evaluation*, 24, 315–340, 2004.

Mullen, P. D., Hersey, J., and Iverson, D. C., Health behavior models compared, *Social Science and Medicine*, 24, 973–981, 1987.

Nathan, P. E., Stuart, S. P., and Dolan, S. L., Research on psychotherapy efficacy and effectiveness: Between Scylla and Charybdis?, *Psychological Bulletin*, 126, 964–981, 2000.

Patton, M. Q., *Utilization-Focused Evaluation: The New Century Text*, Sage, Thousand Oaks, CA, 1997.

Peterson, J., FDA approach tough pill for critics. Houston Chronicle.com January 8 http://www.chron.com/cs/CDA/ssistory.mpl/nation/2982886 [cached] (accessed January 13, 2005), 2005.

Reichardt, C. S. and Gollob, H. F., Taking uncertainty into account when estimating effects, *New Directions for Program Evaluation*, 35, 7–22, 1987.

Reichardt, C. S. and Mark, M. M., Quasi-experimentation, In *Handbook of Applied Social Research Methods*, Bickman, L. and Rog, D. J., Eds., Sage, Thousand Oaks, CA, pp. 193–228, 1998.

Reynolds, A. J. and Temple, J. A., Quasi-experimental estimates of the effects of a preschool intervention: Psychometric and econometric comparisons, *Evaluation Review*, 19, 347–373, 1995.

Ribisl, K. M., Walton, M. A., Mowbray, C. T., Luke, D. A., Davidson, W. S., and Bootsmiller, B. J., Minimizing participant attrition in panel studies through the use of effective retention and tracking strategies: Review and recommendations, *Evaluation and Program Planning*, 19, 1–25, 1996.

Riccio, J. A. and Bloom, H. S., Extending the reach of randomized social experiments: New directions in evaluations of American welfare-to-work and employment initiatives, *Journal of the Royal Statistical Society: Series A*, 165, 13–30, 2002.

Rosenbaum, P. R. and Rubin, D. B., The central role of the propensity score in observational studies for causal effects, *Biometrika*, 70(1), 41–55, 1983.

Rosenthal, R., Science and ethics in conducting, analyzing, and reporting psychological research, *Psychological Science*, 5, 127–134, 1994.

Sackett, D. L., Rosenberg, W. M., Gray, J. A., Haynes, R. B., and Richardson, W. S., Evidence based medicine: What it is and what it isn't, *BMJ*, 312, 71–72, 1996.

Seligman, P., August 12. FW. Cox-2 ipse poste: More comments. Publicly archived email. www.cbsnews/hrdocs/pdf/vioxxseligman.pdf (retrieved January 13, 2005), 2004.

Shadish, W. R., Cook, T. D., and Campbell, D. T., *Experimental and Quasi-Experimental Designs for Generalized Causal Inference*, Houghton Mifflin, Boston, 2002.

Shadish, W. R., Cook, T. D., and Leviton, L. C., *Foundations of Program Evaluation: Theories of Practice*, Sage, Newbury Park, CA, 1991.

Shadish, W. R., Matt, G. E., Navarro, A. M., Siegle, G., Crits-Christoph, P., Hazelrigg, M. D., et al., Evidence that therapy works in clinically representative conditions, *Journal of Consulting and Clinical Psychology*, 65, 355–365, 1997.

Stigler, S. M., Testing hypotheses or fitting models: Another look at mass extinction, In *Neutral Models in Biology*, Nitecki, M. H. and Hoffman, A., Eds., Oxford University Press, Oxford, pp. 145–149, 1987.

Trochim, W. M. K., *Research Design for Program Evaluation: The Regression-Discontinuity Approach*, Sage, Newbury Park, CA, 1984.

Ullman, J. B. and Bentler, P. M., Structural equation modeling, In *Comprehensive Handbook of Psychology (Vol. 2)*, Schinka, S. A. and Velicer, W., Eds., Wiley, New York, 2003.

U.S. Department of Education. http://www.ed.gov (accessed January 13, 2005).

U.S. Food and Drug Administration. (November 24, 2004). Vioxx (rofecoxib). http://www.fda.gov/cder/drug/infopage/vioxx/default.htm (accessed January 13, 2005). [NB: page now gives date created as April 6, 2005], 2004.

U.S. Senate., FDA, Merck and Vioxx: Putting patient safety first? (November 18) http://finance.senate.gov/sitepages/hearing111804.htm (accessed January 13, 2005), 2004.

Viadero, D., Researchers question clearinghouse choices, *Education Week*, 23, 30–31, 2004.

Wallis, C., The right (and wrong) way to treat pain, *Time*, 165, 47, 2005.

Weiss, C. H., Ed, *Using Social Research in Public Policy Making*, Lexington Books, Lexington, MA, 1977.

Weiss, C. H., The many meanings of research utilization, *Public Administration Review*, 39, 426–431, 1979.

Weiss, C. H., Evaluation for decisions: Is anybody there? Does anybody care?, *Evaluation Practice*, 9(1), 5–20, 1988.

Weiss, C. H., Murphy-Graham, E., and Birkeland, S., An alternate route to policy influence: How evaluations affect D.A.R.E, *American Journal of Evaluation*, 26, 12–30, 2005.

What Works Clearinghouse, http://www.whatworks.ed.gov (accessed January 13, 2005), 2005.

Wilkinson, L. and the Task Force on Scientific Inference, Statistical methods in psychology journals: Guidelines and explanations, *American Psychologist*, 54, 1999, 594–604.

Winship, C. and Morgan, S. L., The estimation of causal effects from observational data, *Annual Review of Sociology*, 25, 659–707, 1999.

Yoshikawa, H., Rosman, E. A., and Hsueh, J., Variation in teenage mothers' experiences of child care and other components of welfare reform: Selection processes and developmental consequences, *Child Development*, 72, 299–317, 2001.

25 Cost Benefit Analysis

Tevfik F. Nas

CONTENTS

25.1 Introduction..483
25.2 Stages of CBA 484
25.3 Identifying Costs and Benefits 485
25.4 Quantifying Costs and Benefits..486
25.5 Discounting 487
25.6 Project Selection 488
25.7 CBA in Real-World Applications 488
25.8 Conclusion 489
References..490

25.1 INTRODUCTION

Cost benefit analysis (CBA) draws heavily on the principles of welfare economics and public finance, systematically bringing the important criterion of efficiency into resource allocation decisions, and possibly considering distributional equity.[*] Its methodology, based on an economic way of thinking, is rigorous and sophisticated; but, when it is mastered and consistently used by an analyst, it is likely to lead to optimal resource allocation decisions.

The theoretical justification and the analytical detail CBA requires differ significantly from those of other evaluation formats, in particular from *financial* and *cost effectiveness* analyses.[†] In CBA, costs and benefits are defined on the basis of public interest, and evaluated in terms of their real output effects throughout the economy. In financial analysis, costs and benefits are considered from the perspective of private entities: Expected inflow of cash and revenues are regarded as benefits, and outflow of cash and payments made by the private entity as costs. Also, in financial analysis, third party costs and benefits, defined as externalities, are not taken into account, because they do not involve any compensation or cash payment to affected parties.[‡] In CBA, on the other hand, externalities must be carefully identified and included in the overall evaluation of a project. One other feature that distinguishes CBA from cost-effectiveness analysis is that, with CBA, both costs and benefits are expressed in monetary terms. Cost-effectiveness analysis, also used in public

---

[*] For references and further reading on many issues raised in this chapter, see Gramlich (1990), Nas (1996) and Tresch (2002). For more on welfare economics and the use of efficiency and equity criteria in CBA, see Nas (1996, Chaps. 1–2) and Tresch (2002, Chaps. 1–2, 23, 27).

[†] For a comparison of other evaluation methodologies, see Smith (1986).

[‡] Externalities are costs and benefits on non-consenting third parties. They are unintentional, and their effects are not conveyed through the price mechanism. In the case of external costs, the party causing the externality is not held accountable for the damage they cause, and individuals subject to the externality may not be compensated for the damage inflicted on them.

project evaluation, ranks project outcomes in simple ratios or index numbers when either benefits or costs are undefined or cannot be measured in dollar terms.

This chapter provides an overview of the general methodology used in cost benefit analysis. It begins with a review of two conceptual distinctions that need to be made throughout the analysis, followed by an outline of the main steps involved in a typical evaluation. The rest of the chapter summarizes the evaluation design included in the Circular that the Office of Management and Budget (OMB) sends out to the heads of executive departments in federal agencies, and provides practical rules to guide the analyst through the application process of project evaluation.

25.2 STAGES OF CBA

Developed specifically for the analysis and evaluation of public policy proposals, CBA provides a general framework within which a project's costs and benefits can be identified and assessed from society's perspective. Costs and benefits, quantified in dollar terms, are then enumerated for each period of a project's lifetime, discounted to their present value, and ranked on the basis of project selection criteria, such as net present value, internal rate of return, or benefit cost ratios. A typical evaluation design also involves a preparatory phase during which the evaluation model is framed, the primary real output of the proposed project is defined, and the boundaries of the target area and the population for which the project is to serve are determined.

To conduct a complete and theoretically consistent analysis, two conceptual distinctions need to be made. First, in assessing the net benefits of a project, the evaluator should rely on the *with/without* approach rather than the *before and after* approach. The with/without approach compares costs and benefits in terms of the net social gains that would have been incurred with and without the project. The before and after approach is based on data indicating what costs and benefits were before the project and what they would be after the project.

In a typical CBA, costs and benefits that would occur with the project are identified and measured as *incremental* changes over a *baseline scenario*, which is defined to be what would occur without the project. For example, in an analysis of expanding the lanes of a highway, the baseline scenario would be the existing set of lanes, and relevant costs and benefits would include only those that result from, and are therefore incremental to, modifying the lanes. The example of the difference between the number of criminal occurrences with a crime prevention project and the cases that would have been observed in the absence of the project, the baseline scenario, would be more accurate than comparing the project outcome to the number of incidents that existed prior. Using this method, the worth of the project will be unambiguous since the number of criminal acts is likely to change as a result of factors other than the project itself.

A second distinction is between the *real* and *pecuniary* effects of resource allocation. Real output effects are changes in total physical production possibilities that create welfare gains or losses in related sectors as a result of resource reallocation. These changes result from the actual use of resources due to the proposed project, and should carefully be assessed from the perspective of public interest. Unlike real output effects, the pecuniary effects are distributional and produce no real welfare changes. Such project outcomes result from price changes in both primary and secondary markets and have no impact on society's resource base. For example, the increase in market salaries of computer technicians as a result of increased demand for their services, a demand due to the implementation and expansion of information technology services in public universities, is pecuniary and should not be included as a benefit. The increase in salaries is a transfer of the benefit generated by the project, and to avoid double-counting, they should be excluded from the net benefit calculations. Improved educational efficiency and increased productivity in university operations as a result of the new technology, however, are real and should be properly identified and accounted for in the evaluation. Clearly, to avoid double counting only the real output effects of a project should be included but not the pecuniary effects.

25.3 IDENTIFYING COSTS AND BENEFITS

To identify costs and benefits it is important to start with a clear understanding of the primary real output of a given project. What seems to be an obvious project outcome may not be, which could inadvertently lead to erroneous and imprecise resource reallocation. The output could be unidentifiable or sometimes unnecessarily broadly or narrowly defined. For example, as is usually the case in most revitalization and urban renewal projects, the number of visitors to an amusement park, proposed as one of the revitalization projects in a region, may be too narrow a definition. Depending on the purpose of the project, other measures reflecting changes in overall economic activity in the community, such as retail sales or some measure of revitalization that could be converted into monetary terms, may be more appropriate. Thus, for these and similar types of proposals, a viable strategy is to define the purpose of the project, and identify the target population that the project is designed to serve. The project outcome could be identified as a *pure* or *quasipublic* good produced in such sectors as national defense, environmental protection, or higher education. The output could also be defined as *tangible*, such as increased agricultural output from a proposed irrigation facility, or *intangible*, including such project outcomes as improved time management, improved morale, number of human lives saved, and so on.

In addition to the direct real output effects, *external* effects, or, *externalities*, which also alter the total welfare of society, should be included in the analysis. External effects may be positive or negative, and to determine the true impact of a project they should be properly identified and accounted for. A common category of negative externalities includes costs related to environmental damage, originating from all sources of pollution, adversely impacting the wellbeing of the exposed population. Positive external benefits, on the other hand, are third party benefits typically emanating from education, health care, and urban renewal projects. For example, building an institute of fine arts in the center of a city may add to traffic congestion, which is a typical external cost. In addition to the direct benefit the institute is expected to provide for the attending population, it also generates external benefits in the form enhanced cultural enrichment to the community at large. As another example, the construction or expansion of a new highway could produce additional air and noise pollution due to generated traffic in the vicinity of the proposed site, while leading to improved environmental quality in areas from which the traffic is diverted. The omission of these and many other types of spillover effects, if they have not already been accounted for through market dynamics or internalized by the use of *Pigouvian* taxes and subsidies, is likely to result in the overestimation or underestimation of a project's net worth, and thus lead to resource misallocation.[*]

Another important identification issue is the question of how to define the boundaries of the target area and the population for which the project has been designed. Usually the boundary and the scope of the project are predetermined based on the priorities and preferences of the agency initiating or financing the project. If there are ambiguities in this respect, then the spillover effects to neighboring areas where the project is to be implemented should be identified as *outside effects*, and included in the evaluation depending on the financing arrangements. If the resources to be used in a project belong to a given jurisdiction, then only the *inside effects*, those that are within the boundaries of the jurisdiction, should be considered and not the spillover effects on other areas. Irrespective of the financing arrangements, however, all relevant outside effects should be acknowledged and appended to the final report even if they may not be entered into cost benefit calculations.

---

[*] Pigouvian adjustments are corrective fees and subsidies to internalize the externalities. Named after Cambridge University economist Arthur Pigou (1877–1959) these fees are assigned by government agencies to control external effects. Taxes are levied to minimize environmental damage in the case of pollution, and subsidies are provided to encourage socially desirable production. Other forms of corrective measures include setting production standards and auctioning marketable pollution permits.

25.4 QUANTIFYING COSTS AND BENEFITS

Once costs and benefits have been identified, they must be quantified in dollar terms. In the case of market items for which measures can be readily derived from observed prices, this is a straightforward procedure. The cost of supplies, capital equipment, labor, land, and all tangible inputs used in a project are easily measured by their prospective market prices.

Measurement problems could arise in the absence of competitive market conditions. The actual economic cost of the input may differ from market price because of price distortions due to labor market imperfections, government tax policies, and monopolistic practices. For example, in cases of unemployment or heavy presence of labor unions, the market wage might not reflect the opportunity cost of labor, which is what needs to be included in cost/benefit estimates. From a public project perspective, the cost of labor is the forgone output elsewhere in the economy as a result of employing the individual in the proposed project. Furthermore, in the case of market distortions, the observed market wage may not necessarily be representative of the forgone value. To adjust the observed market wage for the related market distortion, a *shadow wage*, which is the true scarcity value of labor, needs to be derived.

As shown in the following equation, the shadow wage, W^*, is the weighted sum of the market wage and the worker's evaluation of his or her marginal product.

$$W^* = W_m \frac{\Delta E}{\Delta L} + W_s \frac{\Delta U}{\Delta L} \qquad (25.1)$$

where W_m is the observed market wage rate, W_s is the amount of compensation that must be paid to induce workers to join the labor force, ΔL is the amount of labor required for the project, ΔE is the reduction in employment elsewhere as a result of the increase in demand for labor, and ΔU is the increase in the number of workers entering the labor market due to the project.

In real world applications, information needed for shadow price derivation is likely to be limited. For example, W_s is subjective and it is difficult to estimate since information about workers' preferences toward leisure and work is unavailable. Depending on the nature of unemployment, W_s could be any value between zero and the net of tax wage. As an approximate value, the net of tax wage could be used to estimate W_s for both voluntarily and involuntarily unemployed workers. The same formulation is used to derive shadow prices for all market items with observed prices deviating from their respective costs of production and the demand margin, the amounts the buyers are willing to pay.

Another category of costs and benefits includes non-market items, those for which market data do not exist. Project outcomes, such as time and lives saved, air pollution, and endangered species preservation, could make a difference in project selection. Their valuation is based on information obtained directly through surveys and indirectly from alternate markets. A direct evaluation technique that has been used increasingly in recent CBA projects to elicit information on use and nonuse values is the *contingent valuation method.*[*] The indirect methods include *the technique of averting behavior, hedonic pricing,* and *the travel cost method.*[†]

The contingent valuation method makes use of interviews, questionnaires, and experimental design to generate information on specific project outcomes. With this direct evaluation method, the respondents are asked to reveal their willingness to pay or to accept preferences regarding project

---

[*] In the case of use value, individuals benefit by deriving use from a resource. In the case on nonuse value, individuals reveal their preferences only for the existence of a resource even if they would not use it. The contingent valuation method is the only technique that has been increasingly used in estimating nonuse or existence values in evaluation of the natural environment. Endangered species preservation, for example, belongs to the category of a nonuse value for which individuals reveal their preferences by stating the amount that they will be willing to pay to secure the existence of such species.

[†] For detailed discussions of these methodologies see Cummings, Cox, and Freeman (1986); Cropper and Oates (1992); Mitchell and Carson (1989); and Smith (1993).

outcomes. The technique of averting behavior provides benefit estimation from observed responses to a change in environmental quality. These include health responses to a pollutant and activities or products used as substitutes to avoid or mitigate the effects of a pollutant. The hedonic pricing method values environmental quality variables that differentiate closely related markets, influencing values in property markets, for example. The travel cost approach uses the travel cost to a specific site as a proxy measure of improved environmental quality. All four methods of benefit and cost evaluation are used widely in empirical analysis of non-market benefit and cost assessment. Despite possible complications stemming from insufficient data and the joint product problems, these methods establish theoretically convincing linkages between non-market values and observed choices, and thus appear to meet policy making needs.

25.5 DISCOUNTING

In the third stage of project evaluation, costs and benefits are discounted separately or in the form of net benefits, to determine their present value. For private projects, the rate used as a discount factor is the market rate of interest, which is determined in financial markets. This practice is based on the assumption that the market rate of interest reflects both the private rate of time preference, and the rate of return to private capital investment. Thus it is suitable for private projects.

There are various views for what the theoretically acceptable discount rate for public sector projects should be, however. These include *social opportunity cost of capital (SOC)*, *social rate of time preference (SRTP)*, the *weighted average discount rate*, and *shadow price of capital*. When funds are diverted from alternative investment, SOC, which is the rate at which present consumption is converted into future consumption, may be used as a discount rate. If society's saving rate is relatively low, then the SRTP reflecting society's preferences between present and future levels of consumption may be used. The SRTP, which accounts for intergenerational equity preferences, may be especially appealing when the funds needed for a public project come at the expense of reduced consumption.[*]

If the needed funds are obtained from increased savings and partially crowd out other investment, then either the weighted average discount rate or shadow capital approach may be appropriate. The weighted average discount rate is essentially the market rate of return adjusted for market distortions. It is the sum of the consumption rate of interest, reflecting individuals' rate of time preference, and the rate of return to investment, weighted by the fractions of displaced consumption and reduced investment elsewhere in the economy. The shadow price of capital approach also combines the rate of time preference and investment rate of return, but does it somewhat differently. It converts all future cost and benefit streams into consumption equivalents, and discounts these streams at the rate of time preference. A project's cost in this approach is the future stream of consumption benefits that would have been expected from displaced private investment. These benefits, discounted by the rate of time preference, are then compared to the project's benefit, which are also expressed in consumption values and discounted by the rate of time preference.

It is difficult to present a strong argument for or against any rate. The shadow price approach has appealing properties theoretically, but it is difficult to apply. There are also problems of estimating the SRTP and identifying the relative weights for the two sources of funds used in a project. The current practice in public agencies also varies. But as we note later in the chapter, even though the analytically preferred method is the shadow price of capital, in practice for most public sector analyses a preset discount rate is used. One other practical approach may be to evaluate the net present value of a project over a range of discount rates, and to determine a sensitivity range with selected upper and lower bound discount rates.

---

[*] For more on the individual and societal perspectives of time preferences see Robinson (1990) and Nas (1996).

25.6 PROJECT SELECTION

In the final stage of cost benefit analysis, projects are ranked in terms of at least one of the three project selection criteria. These include the *benefit cost ratio* (*B/C*), the *net present value* (NPV), and the *internal rate of return* (IRR). A benefit cost ratio is used to rank projects during any given year or over a time span. It can be calculated by taking either the present value of future benefits over the present value of costs including investment and annual operating costs, or the present value of future net benefits over the one-time investment costs. In either case, the project is accepted if the benefit cost ratio exceeds one.

To calculate the NPV, the future streams of benefits and costs are reduced to a single present dollar value. The stream of benefits and costs, which might include recurrent costs, either separately or in the form of a net benefits stream, are discounted to find their present value. The general formula for calculating the NPV of a future stream of benefits is

$$\text{NPV} = -I_0 + \sum_{n=1}^{N} \frac{\text{NB}_n}{(1+r)^n}, \tag{25.2}$$

where I_0 is the initial investment cost, r is the discount rate, NB_n is the benefit stream that begins at year one and N is the project's lifetime.

The third method, IRR, is the discount rate that equates the present value of future net benefits with the initial investment costs. It is the specific discount rate that results in a zero net present value. The internal rate of return is a convenient decision rule that provides a quick reference to a project's ranking. It is calculated by using the following formula

$$0 = -I_0 + \sum_{n=1}^{N} \frac{\text{NB}_n}{(1-\pi)^n}, \tag{25.3}$$

where π is the IRR. By this rule, the project is accepted if π is greater than the market rate of return or any of the discount rates discussed in the preceding section.

Of these three decision rules, NPV is the most preferred. Excluding the possibility of inaccurate project ranking in the case of budget limitations, NPV usually provides a reliable ranking, and therefore it is widely used in practice. B:C ratios can be used consistently to rank competing projects only if projects are of equal size in terms of initial capital outlay. IRR may not be reliable when projects are of different sizes.

25.7 CBA IN REAL-WORLD APPLICATIONS

The decision making process of CBA, which has a long history of use in federal agencies in the United States, has been frequently and systematically utilized since the1960s. Since then, through periodic circulars sent to federal agencies, the Office of Management and Budget (OMB) in particular has been instrumental in developing and providing guidance for the economic and social evaluation of federal programs. As clearly stated in its latest updated version, OMB's Circular A—94 outlines the most essential steps and the rules of evaluation that federal agencies must follow (U. S. Office of Management and Budget, 2005). According to these rules, costs and benefits must be identified from the perspective of society rather than the Federal Government, costs and benefits can be either tangible or intangible, and real output effects rather than the pecuniary items and transfer payments must be included in cost benefit calculations. In measuring the costs and benefits the circular emphasizes both that the concept of *consumer surplus* must be employed and willingness to pay must be estimated directly and indirectly,[*] and that, in the presence of market failure and price distortions, shadow prices may have to be used.

The circular also states that, during the project selection stage, the decision whether to accept or reject a project must be based on net present value and an appropriate real discount rate. In practice, the pretax rate of return to private capital and the federal government's borrowing rates are referred to as appropriate discount rates. OMB considers the shadow price of capital approach as the analytically preferred method, but as stated in Circular A—94, a real discount rate of 7 percent is used as an approximation of the marginal pretax rate of return on average private investment in recent years.[†] Additionally, the treasury's borrowing rates are used as discount rates in cost-effectiveness, lease-purchase, internal government investment, and asset sales analysis. For the period February 2003 through January 2004, the rates ranged from 1.6 percent (three year) to 3.2 percent (thirty year).

25.8 CONCLUSION

We conclude this chapter with following guidelines to follow in a typical CBA design:

1. Before finalizing the evaluation design, conduct the necessary support and functional studies. These include market surveys and analyses of demographics and local characteristics in regions for which the project is designed. With the help of a literature survey, examine the circumstances surrounding the project and develop justification for its implementation. Identify areas where data collection is needed and select specific methodologies for the conceptualization and measurement of costs and benefits.
2. Upon completion of the preparatory stage, begin to focus on identifying, quantifying, and comparing the costs and benefits. The primary real output of the proposed project must be carefully and appropriately identified.
3. Use workable classifications and spreadsheets to distinguish between benefits and costs, real and pecuniary effects, and tangible and intangible outcomes. Even if some of these effects cannot be measured in dollar terms, they still need to be identified to show the impact areas of the project. Externalities, if they exist, must be included in the evaluation. Avoid double-counting by excluding pecuniary effects, financial transactions, and transfer payments.
4. To account for inflation, all benefits and costs and the discount rate used must be expressed in real terms. To make the necessary adjustment nominal cost and benefit items as well as the nominal discount rate must be converted to their real value, that is, constant dollar equivalents.
5. The evaluation could also include distributional weights to account for equity in income distribution and to incorporate sensitivity analysis testing procedures, or other techniques to factor in likely ambiguities that may result from risk and uncertainty.
6. Project selection and ranking should be followed by the evaluation results, explanations of limitations of the evaluation, and a discussion of policy implications and recommendations.

---

[*] Consumer surplus is a monetary measure of the maximum gain that an individual can obtain from a product at a given market price. Derived from an ordinary demand curve it measures an individual's willingness to pay for or accept a welfare change, and it is used to estimate the gains and losses from proposed public policy programs. For a detailed discussion and use of consumer surplus in CBA see Mishan (1988) and Nas (1996).

[†] The recommended real discount rate of 7 percent does not apply to water and related land resources projects. The discount rate for federal water resources planning for fiscal year 2004 is 5.625 percent. For details see *Federal Registry*, Vol. 69, No. 80 (April 26, 2004). Also, for the details of government's discount rate policy and rates used in various government agencies see Bazelon and Smetters (1999).

In closing, it should be emphasized that initiating and carrying out a cost benefit analysis requires well-coordinated teamwork. The main goal is to identify the true value of a project from the public interest perspective. In accomplishing this important task, it is essential to remember that the analyst's role is not making choices, but providing them.

REFERENCES

Bazelon, C. and Smetters, K., Discounting inside the Washington D.C. Beltway, *Journal of Economic Perspectives*, 4, 213–228, 1999.

Cropper, M. L. and Oates, W. E., Environmental economics: a survey, *Journal of Economic Literature*, 30, 675–740, 1992.

Cummings, R. G., Cox, L. A., and Freeman, A. M., General methods for benefits assessment, In *Benefit Assessment: The State of the Art*, Bentkover, J. D., Corvello, V. T., and Mumpower, J., Eds., Reidel, Dordrecht, Holland, pp. 161–191, 1986.

Gramlich, E. M., *A Guide to Benefit-Cost Analysis*, 2nd ed., Prentice Hall, Englewood Cliffs, NJ, 1990.

Mishan, E. J., *Cost-Benefit Analysis*, 4th ed., Unwin Hyman, London, 1988.

Mitchell, R. C. and Carson, R. T., *Using Surveys to Value Public Goods: The Contingent Valuation Method*, Resources for the Future, Baltimore, 1989.

Nas, T. F., *Cost-Benefit Analysis: Theory and Application*, Sage, Thousand Oaks, CA, 1996.

Robinson, C. J., Philosophical origins of the social rate of discount in cost-benefit analysis, *The Milbank Quarterly*, 68, 245–265, 1990.

Smith, V. K., A conceptual overview of the foundations of benefit-cost analysis, In *Benefit Assessment: The State of the Art*, Bentkover, J. D., Corvello, V. T., and Mumpower, J., Eds., Reidel, Dordrecht, Holland, pp. 13–34, 1986.

Smith, V. K., Nonmarket valuation of environmental resources: an interpretive appraisal, *Land Economics*, 69, 1–26, 1993.

Tresch, R. W., *Public Finance: A Normative Theory*, Academic Press, San Diego, CA, 2002.

U.S. Office of Management and Budget. Circular No. A—94 Revised. http://www.whitehouse.gov/omb/circulars/a094/a094.html#6 (accessed August 17, 2005).

26 Linear Programming and Integer Progamming: Choosing the Optimal Mix of Alternatives

Dipak K. Gupta

CONTENTS

26.1 History and Introduction 491
26.2 Facilities Planning: An Example..492
    26.2.1 Expressing Linear Programming in Algebraic Form 498
    26.2.2 Accommodation of Policy Considerations 499
    26.2.3 When Social Preferences Change 499
    26.2.4 Mathematical Solutions for Linear Programming Problems................501
    26.2.5 Shadow Price and the Dual Solution 501
    26.2.6 The Logic of Minimization Problems..503
26.3 Another Application of Linear Programming..504
    26.3.1 Prison Planning..504
    26.3.2 Discussion of the Results 507
26.4 Sensitivity Analysis 508
26.5 Integer Programming..508
26.6 Conclusion 509
References...510

26.1 HISTORY AND INTRODUCTION

Mainstream economics assumes that as rational individuals, we take our decisions on the basis of the relative costs and benefits of our action. The technique of cost/benefit analysis (discussed in chapter 25 in this volume) spells out in detail the problem of choosing the best from a number of alternatives. However, often the question of optimum choice does not involve accepting the best one over all others. Frequently we must determine the optimal mix—spread out our efforts or resources among a number of competing alternatives in a way that best serves our purpose. Thus, if we have a fixed amount of money that we want to invest in the stock market, we may not want to put all our eggs in one basket. Instead, we might want to spread the risk and choose an optimum mix of investments that would maximize our return by keeping within reasonable bounds our concerns for risk, uncertainty, and liquidity of assets.

The technique of linear programming grew out of similar concerns. Developed by a number of mathematicians and economists, linear programming is one of the most sophisticated tools of operations research. This technique lends itself to a wide variety of problem solving that involves maximization of some specific goals given the limitations of inputs or minimization of costs with the specification of some minimum levels of benefits.

Linear programming has a long illustrious history going back to the mid-1700s and the writings of a group of French Enlightenment philosophers and economists called the *Physiocrats* (which means "rule by Nature"). In 1758 François Quesnay, the most famous among the Physiocrats, published *Tableau Économique*—demonstrating the "zig-zag" pattern of income flows between economic sectors in what we would call today a matrix form. It became the founding document of the Physiocratic sect. The analytical insight that we can derive from such a clear depiction led to its wide use. Karl Marx used it to show income distribution among various economic classes. In 1930s, Russian economist Wassily Leontief formally developed the input-out model. In this model, the interdependence of the entire economy is presented in a matrix form, where the output of one industry is shown as the input of the others. Thus, the coal industry produces coal (its output), which is utilized in various proportions by the power plants, steel industry, and automobile manufacturers as inputs toward their production process. Similarly, the power plants produce electricity, which serves as input for the other sectors. The next two decades after its initial conceptualization saw the rapid development of the input-output models, thanks largely to the efforts of Leontieff and another prominent economist, Pierro Sraffa. The decades of 1950s and 60s were characterized by efforts by many states toward large-scale national planning. Leontief's input-output system found extensive use in this area and became instrumental in the formation of macroeconomic policies. He received a Nobel Prize for its development in 1973.

However, the technique of *Tableau Économique* was purely descriptive. Even its successor, the input-output model, initially served the same purpose. Yet, for it to become a powerful planning tool, it must have prescriptive capabilities; it must be able to identify the best course of action from a number of competing alternatives. This was accomplished by the parallel development of linear programming methods by some of the brightest economists and mathematicians of the time.

For example, in 1941, F. L. Hitchcock analyzed a "transportation type problem," where the method of choosing the optimum route of a bus was discussed. In 1945 Joseph Stigler studied the "diet problem" demonstrating the method of choosing the best combination of food for a dieter. In 1947, Tjaling Koopmans further developed the transportation problem for an optimal routing solution. In the same year, George Danzig developed the formal mathematical method of solving linear programming problems. His efforts were taken further by work of two eminent mathematicians, Tjalling C. Koopmans and Leonid V. Kantorovich. Although Dantzig was the initiator of the idea, all three scholars are credited with developing the *simplex method* by which linear programming problems are solved. However, in 1975 when the Noble Prize Committee announced its winners for developing linear programming, they chose to name only Koopmans and Kantorovich, leaving out Dantzig. This significant omission profoundly distressed Koopmans. He even suggested to Kantorovich that they jointly refuse the prestigious award. For Kantorovich, who was from the Soviet Union, this posed a significant problem, because without the Nobel Prize his work had little chance of getting recognition in his home country. So, the duo accepted the prize, and Koopmans donated $40,000, a share of the prize money, to the Austria-based International Institute for Applied Systems Analysis to carry out his joint work with Dantzig (Gass and Assad, 2004).

26.2 FACILITIES PLANNING: AN EXAMPLE

Linear programming is best understood with the help a concrete example. Suppose the director of facilities for a small college is planning the construction of dormitory units for the students. She is considering two types of units: single student units and married student units. A recent survey of student demand shows that there are 4,000 married and 6,000 single students seeking dormitory rooms. This situation is shown in Figure 26.1. On the vertical axis we measure the number of married students in units of 1,000. On the horizontal axis we plot the number of single students.

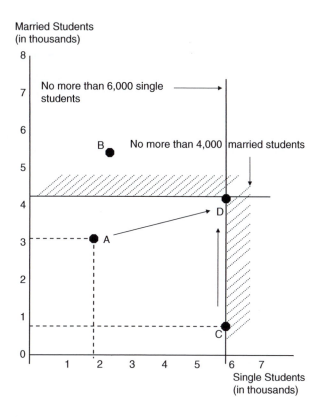

FIGURE 26.1 Demand constraints for the two kinds of housing.

Each point on the surface of this figure represents a specific combination of housing for the two groups of students. For instance, the point A represents a combination of 2,000 units of housing for the married students and 3,000 for the single students. Because there are 4,000 married students, we draw a straight line through 4 on the vertical axis. As there is no more demand for married student housing beyond this point, it would not make any sense to build at point B. Therefore, we etch out the area above the line showing 4,000 married students. We call this a constraint or a limitation, because our choice of combination of units will be limited by the demand for those units.

Similarly, we can draw another line showing the demand constraint for single student housing. Now consider the point C. This point shows a combination of 1,500 married student units and 6,000 single student units. Should we recommend that we build at that combination? Obviously not. By constructing at that point, we will leave a great deal of unmet demand from the married student population. Therefore, we should ideally construct accommodations for all 10,000 students at point D.

Alas, as with everything else in life, unconstrained choices are rarely available. Suppose we come across an additional constraint: space. Let us assume that single student accommodations require 700 square feet of land area per unit; married student units require 900 square feet. The college has 6,300,000 square feet of developable land for the project. To draw this constraint in our diagram, we need to find the extreme points on the two axes. That is, by utilizing all the available land, one can construct 9,000 single-student housing units (obtained by dividing the total available land by the square footage required per unit of single student housing, 700 square feet). This is the extreme point on the horizontal axis. Similarly, if all the space is allocated for married student housing, we can build 7,000 units (6,300,000/900 = 7,000). Having obtained these two points, we simply join the two with a straight line. By the laws of geometry, any point on this line represents a combination of the two kinds of units, which exhausts the total allocated space for the project.

In Figure 26.2, we have been able to etch out an area within the confines of which it is possible to construct the two types of housing units. Thus, we may build at any point within the bounded region, including points A, B, C, D, E, or G. As noted before, the point F falls outside this area, becausewe do not have enough space to build housing for every student. The area bordered by the three constraints is called the *feasibility zone*, as it is feasible to build any mix of housing within this area. All points outside this area are considered to be infeasible.

It is important for us to note that while constructing a linear programming model, we should always be aware of an important constraint. This is the *non-negativity* constraint. Because it is not possible to construct negative units of housing, we should be aware of the fact that the feasibility zone is bound by the two constraints which say that the total number of housing for the two kinds of students cannot be less then zero. Although it may sound like a trivial assumption, a quick look at the diagram will convince anyone of the need for making the feasibility zone completely bounded.

It is important at this point to understand three distinct features of linear programming. They are:

- All solutions should be within the feasibility zone.
- All the solutions should be on the boundary of the feasibility zone.
- The optimal solution must be located at the intersection of the constraints.

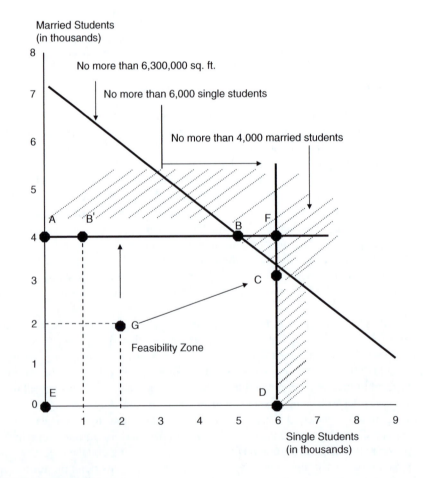

FIGURE 26.2 The feasibility zone.

We have discussed the fact that we cannot have a solution that is impractical or falls outside the feasibility zone. We should also note that the optimal solution cannot be an "interior point" and must be located on the boundary outlined by the constraints. Thus, although it is feasible to produce at an interior point such as G, it does not make sense to build at that combination, because at that point we have an excess capacity and can expand our production of housing units without any trouble. Therefore, the second feature of linear programming is that the optimal or the best possible combination should always be on the borders of the feasibility zone.

Furthermore, we should also note that while it is possible to build at a point on the boundary between points A and B or between C and D, it does not make sense to do so. This is because from that point, we can always move to another point, at which we will be able to achieve more of one good without having to give up any portion of the other. Thus, consider a combination between points A and B. Let us call that point "B". At this point, we are considering a combination of 4,000 married student housing units and 1,000 single student units. It is obvious from the figure that this combination would not utilize all the resources to the fullest, as we will still have space left over for more single student housing. We can move to the right of this point, until we bump against the space constraint at point B. Thus, the third feature of linear programming is that the optimal solution will always be located at the corner—at the points of intersection between at least two constraints. Hence, the possible corner solutions for our problem are: A, B, C, D, and E.

If we examine the corner points, we can see an interesting story. There is an important issue when it comes to the tradeoff between B and C. While moving from point A to B our choice is obvious. Because with that move we can get more single student units without any sacrifice in the married student units, we are going to prefer B over A. The same thing is true for a move from D to C. However, if we consider the relative desirability between B and C, we see that the tradeoff involves the sacrifice of one type of housing for the other. In other words, when we move from B to C we give up some married student housing for single student housing. Therefore, to judge which combination is preferable, we must know about our preference or the relative weight we place on the two products. The relative weight of the outcomes (type of housing) is a policy variable and is determined by the appropriate authorities. Thus, if the Facilities Planning Director, for whatever reason, attributes a greater weight to married student housing, then B will be the optimal choice. If the emphasis is on single student housing, then point C should be chosen. If the total number of housing units is the criteria for choice, then the two points should be evaluated for the total number of units constructed. The choice of relative weights is called *objective function* and we will discuss it in more details below.

It is a valid question to ask, if we are going to consider only the corner points on the boundaries of the feasibility zone, then would it not be trivial to consider the point E, although it satisfies both of the aforementioned criteria of being on the border and being a corner point? It appears to be so in this case, where one can visually inspect the diagram of an extremely simple example. However, when there are many more than two variables and constraints, it is impossible to plot them on a two-dimensional graph for a quick visual inspection. In such situations, the computer must go through the time-consuming iteration process of evaluating each corner point for the one that maximizes the objective.

Let us proceed further with our example and introduce a few more constraints. In this example, we have only considered the demand constraints and the limitations of available space. To be realistic, we must take into consideration the financial constraint. Suppose it costs $10,000 to build a unit of married student housing. A unit of single student housing costs $6,000. The total budget for the project is $ 60 million.

Linear programming is a versatile tool. It can also consider many other kinds of constraints. For instance, we can consider a couple of legal or policy constraints. Suppose the college has determined that we must build at least 1,000 units of married and 1,000 units of single student housing. Or, there may be a provision that at least 15 percent of the total units must be set aside for one type of housing. These kinds of constraints arise due to some government regulations or policy decisions within an agency to ensure a fair minimum or to place a ceiling for the allocation of resources among the competing groups.

In Figure 26.3, the budgetary constraint is drawn in the manner just described. We joined the two extreme points on the two axes to find out the maximum number of units of each kind that can be built by diverting the entire allocated sum to the production of one kind of housing only. Then, a connecting straight line would mark the constraint. The two policy constraints are the vertical and horizontal straight lines.

The rules of linear programming suggest that the optimal solution for our problem lies within the feasibility zone, and that it would be one of the corner points where two or more constraints intersect. By visually examining the feasibility set, we can determine that the optimal solution must lie on one of the points: A, B, C, D, or E.

Optimality of solution begs the question of the determination of desirability. Therefore, to choose among the various possible mixes, we must specify what we want. This clearly is a policy matter, which is often determined within an organization at a level higher than the analysts'. In technical terms, this is known as the *objective function*. We may specify it for our problem in

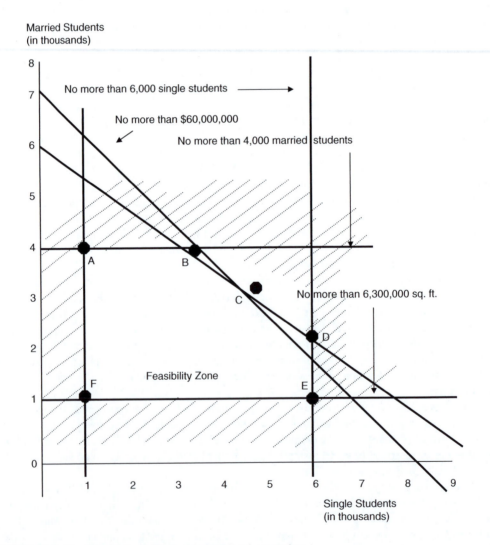

FIGURE 26.3 The introduction of budgetary and legal constraints.

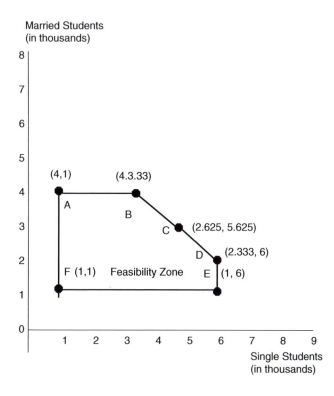

FIGURE 26.4 The feasibility zone.

many ways. Suppose we are not concerned about the relative desirability of building housing units for the two kinds of students, and instead are interested in maximizing the total number of units built. In such a case, we can look at the possible combinations of the two kinds of housing for each corner point and choose the one with the highest number of units built. This is shown in Figure 26.4.

The coordinate values for points A, E, and F are easily discerned by visually inspecting the graph. For other points, approximate values may be obtained if it is plotted on graph paper. However, these points are not going to be the exact values. Because we can see that the corner points are the points of intersection between two straight lines, we can obtain the exact values by solving simultaneously the equations for the two intersecting lines. By inspecting Figure 26.4, we can see that the five corner points suggest the following combination of housing units shown in Table 26.1.

TABLE 26.1
The Feasible Solution of the Comer Points of the Feasibility Zone

Corner Point	Married Student Units (in thousands)	Single Student Units (in thousands)	Value of the Objective Function
A	4.000	1.000	5.000
B	4.000	3.333	7.333
C	2.625	5.625	8.250
D	2.333	6.000	8.333
E	1.000	6.000	7.000
F	1.000	1.000	2.000

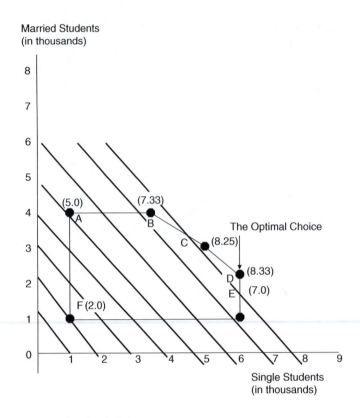

FIGURE 26.5 The process of optimal choice.

The values in Table 26.1 are given in the units of 1,000. Therefore, we can see that at point A we can build 4,000 units of married student housing and 1,000 units of single student housing. The figures for point B are 4,000 units of married student and 3,333 units of single student housing. From this table, one can see that the optimal mix of housing is reached at point D.

To demonstrate the logic of choosing the mix that maximizes the objective function graphically, we need to draw the indifference maps. Because we have assumed that the policy makers place equal value on the two types of units, we are able to draw a series of indifference maps by joining two equidistant points on the vertical and horizontal axes. This allows us to move in a 45° direction. By moving in this direction, one can see that the highest indifference curve touches point D in the feasibility zone. Therefore, this is our optimal choice and we would recommend that the college builds 2,333 units of married student and 6,000 units of single student housing. This situation is shown in Figure 26.5.

26.2.1 EXPRESSING LINEAR PROGRAMMING IN ALGEBRAIC FORM

In the previous section we discussed the process of setting up the linear programming problem. Once it is formulated, we can write it in algebraic terms as follows:

$$\text{Maximize } Z = M + S \qquad (26.1)$$

subject to the constraints

$$M \leq 4,000 \qquad (26.2)$$

$$S \leq 6,000 \tag{26.3}$$

$$900M + 700S \leq 6,300,000 \tag{26.4}$$

$$10,000M + 6,000S \leq 60,000,000 \tag{26.5}$$

$$M \geq 1,000 \tag{26.6}$$

$$S > 1,000 \tag{26.7}$$

$$M \geq 0 \tag{26.8}$$

$$S > 0 \tag{26.9}$$

where, M is married students and S is single students.

Let us examine the algebraic representation closely. The objective function, which we call Z, is equal to M + S. This implies that both kinds of housing carry an equal weight of 1. Therefore, both of these two types of units are equally important to us.

Now we look at the constraints. The first two constraints (26.2 and 26.3) represent the market limitations of demand for housing. They state that the total number of units to be constructed should be less than or equal to 4,000 for the married students and less than 6,000 for the single students.

The third and the fourth inequalities (26.4 and 26.5) represent the space and budget constraints for the project. The third constraint may be read as follows: It takes 900 square feet of land area for married student housing and 700 square feet for single student housing, with a total allocation of 6.3 million square feet of land area. The budget constraint implies that it costs $ 10,000 and $ 6,000 per unit of married and single student units, respectively, with a total allocation of $ 60 million.

The next two constraints (26.6 and 26.7) represent legal or policy constraints. They state that the optimal mix must contain at least 1,000 units of each type of housing. And finally, constraints (26.8) and (26.9) are introduced to ensure that we do not get a trivial optimal solution with negative values for the variables.

Note the analytical strength of linear programming. As long as the logical consistency of the formulation is maintained, linear programming is able to consider any kinds of disparate constraints, measured in units of money, time, weight, space, or any other quantifiable unit. It is also able to accommodate various kinds of legal and policy considerations, as long as they are articulated in numbers.

26.2.2 ACCOMMODATION OF POLICY CONSIDERATIONS

Policy considerations can be accommodated within the linear programming framework in two ways: through weights in the objective function or as constraints. We discussed policy constraints earlier and will introduce a few others later in this chapter. Let us look into the issue of other policy considerations introduced through the objective function. In popular discourse, it is often heard that the strict logical formulation of quantitative techniques of decision making is unable to consider the political aspects of decision making. However, as long as the political authorities are able to articulate their preferences, it is not a problem to include them within a logical construct. Of course, one may question the prudence of fully articulating the preferences of a political decision maker. In such a case, we may show the results of a change in the weights of the objective function on the optimal mix of housing units.

26.2.3 WHEN SOCIAL PREFERENCES CHANGE

Let us return to our example of facilities planning for our college. Let us now assume that for some reason—which may be political or simply reflective of the fact that the married students find it more difficult to find housing—the college has decided that it place a higher weight on married student housing, to the order of 3 to 1. That is, one unit of married student accommodation is valued three times more than a corresponding construction of a single student unit. This causes a rewriting of the objective function (26.1) as

$$\text{Maximize } Z = 3\,M + S$$

Reflecting this change of weight, we have redrawn the indifference curve in Figure. 26.6. Because we are placing more importance on married student housing, the optimal solution now turns out to be point B. Notice that because we are putting three times the weight on married student housing, we need to recalculate the value of the new objective function for each point by multiplying the number of married units times 3 plus the number of single units. Thus, the value of the objective function for point A is calculated by $3 \times 4 + 1 = 13$. We have recalculated the objective function value of each point in Table 26.2 and have shown them next to the corresponding points in Figure 26.6. In Table 26.2, we see that as a result of a change in the objective function, the new optimal point is B.

The preceding results point to the importance of proper specification of the objective function for arriving at the right optimal solution. For instance, if we change the weight to $Z = M + 1.5\,S$, we will see that D has become the most desirable mix of two kinds of housing. We can calculate the value of Z for this latest specification and verify the result.

Having discussed the effects of the direction of the objective function, we can go back to the question we raised at the beginning of this chapter: Why is it not possible to have an optimal solution in the middle of a trade-off line, such as between points B and C in Figure 26.2? The answer is simple. If the objective function is tilted with reference to this constraint, we will settle at

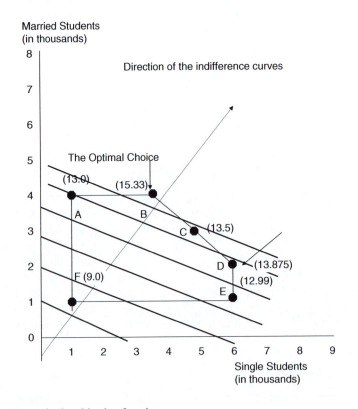

FIGURE 26.6 A change in the objective function.

TABLE 26.2
The Feasible Solution of the Comer Points of the Feasibility Zone: The Recalculated Values of the Objective Function

Corner Points	Married Student (in thousands)	Single Student (in thousands)	Value of the Objective Function
A	4,000	1,000	13,000
B	4,000	3,333	15,333
C	2,625	5,625	13,500
D	2,333	6,000	12,999
E	1,000	6,000	9,000
F	1,000	1,000	4,000

a corner solution. However, if the objective function is parallel to the constraint, there will be no unique solution, as the objective function will satisfy an infinite number of combinations.

26.2.4 Mathematical Solutions for Linear Programming Problems

In our example, we solved our linear programming problem by graphical means. There will rarely be a situation in real life when we will be able to obtain the solution to a problem graphically. The mathematical solution to problems of linear programming is obtained through the simplex method, developed by George Danzig. This method algebraically reaches the optimal point through iterations, as it searches for the optimal solution by calculating the values of the objective function for all corner solutions. It is an extremely laborious process, which, for most practical problems, can take weeks or even months to work out. Fortunately, we need not learn this tedious technique for our present purpose, as we can always summon the help of a computer.

Through the efforts of many scholars and practitioners, and spurred by progress in computer technology, linear programming with the simplex method has become one of the most widely used quantitative methods of decision making. However, the problem with the simplex method is that it is extremely time consuming, even for computers. If there is a situation in which there are large numbers of variables and constraints, the iterative process of a simplex method would require an enormous amount of computer time. Because computer time directly translates into money, efforts have been made to find a more direct and less time-consuming way of deriving solutions for linear programming models. In 1984, Narendra Karmarkar of Bell Laboratories developed an innovative approach which allows the computer to avoid evaluating all the corner points and move directly to the optimal solution from a given point within the feasibility zone (Karmarkar, 1984). However, because Karmarkar developed his technique for the Bell Laboratories, its exact algorithm remained proprietary. Furthermore, this technique was designed for extremely large problems and, therefore, it does not affect the developers of less sophisticated programs.

26.2.5 Shadow Price and the Dual Solution

Solutions to a linear programming problem provide a policy maker with a number of extremely useful insights into the complex problems at hand. For instance, government in its regulatory role frequently imposes constraints on economic activities. In our public debate, we often hear that "this added restriction will cost the consumers this much money." The lumber industry, for example, in response to a proposal for saving the natural habitat of the spotted owls in the northwestern states, warned consumers that this restriction would translate into higher prices for all kinds of wood products. The cable television industry, facing the imposition of new regulations to hold down costs, cautioned viewers that the regulations would do just the opposite of what they purported to do. Therefore, it is legitimate to ask: What is the cost of a particular constraint? Or, we may put the question a little differently: How much do we gain (measured in terms of an increase in the value of the objective function) if we were to allow the constraint value to go up by 1 percent? We are able to answer such questions within the framework of linear programming. The answer to this question is called the *shadow price* of a constraint (see the Nas chapter in this volume for a discussion of shadow prices). Shadow price is also known as the *opportunity cost* in the economic literature. This is the value of the best alternate use of a resource. In other words, a shadow price or an opportunity cost asks: If we did not use an additional input (in our example, space, money, etc.), what would have been its best possible alternate use?

For example, we may want to examine the shadow price of the space constraint in our facilities planning model: How much of a gain in the value of the objective function can be obtained by, say, a 1 percent increase in the space allocation? A 1 percent increase in total available space would give us 63,000 square feet of land area. The availability of this additional land would shift the constraint to the right, thereby allowing us to build more houses. We show the impact of this shift in Figure 26.7. As can be seen, the shift in the space constraint affects point D. At this point, we are already at the limits of the demand for married student housing. Therefore, as a result of this relaxation, we would be able to construct 90 additional units of single student housing.

Think of how useful this information can be to a policy maker. Because a single student unit costs $6,000, the construction of these additional 90 units would cost $540,000. The policy maker can then determine if it is worthwhile for the college to purchase the additional land to meet the

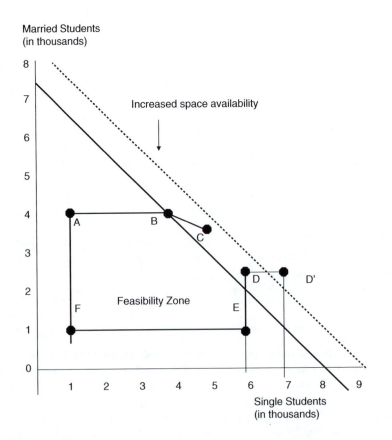

FIGURE 26.7 Shadow price.

residual demand. If the cost turns out to be less than the gain, then it is surely not worth it. On the other hand, if the cost is less than the gain, then it is desirable that he go ahead with the additional acquisition. Of course, in this particular example, there is no advantage to be had by increasing the single student housing because there is no more demand for single student housing. This is a case of zero shadow price, or a *non-binding constraint*. In other words, for the facility planners of the college, building space is not the constraint. The most desirable aspect of the calculation of shadow price is that it allows a decision maker to evaluate the relative costs of each constraint.

However, the calculation of shadow price by graphical method can be tricky. As we relax one constraint, we may run into some other constraint. In that case, this new constraint may become critical and not allow us to move beyond a certain point. If the relaxed constraint runs into another constraintthat was not critical before and had a zero shadow price, the new one will show a positive shadow price. However, almost all the computer-based linear programming algorithms are designed to give shadow prices for the constraints.

These shadow prices are calculated as part of what is known as the *dual solution*. The original problem, as we have posed it, is called the *primal* in linear programming literature. The dual solution of a maximization problem is a minimization problem. The solution of the dual problem does not provide any more information than the primal solution. However, by generating shadow prices, it places the imputed prices of the relevant constraints under sharper focus.

26.2.6 THE LOGIC OF MINIMIZATION PROBLEMS

Frequently, problems arise regarding determination of the optimal combination of variables that aim at minimizing cost rather than maximizing benefit, as shown in the previous example. The logic of the minimization problem is similar to that of the maximization problem. However, in this case, the direction of the preference is downward sloping. That is, we prefer the point that has the least value for the objective function. Minimization situations arise when we try to choose a mix that will provide us some minimum amount of benefit with the least amount of expenditure. The logic of a minimization problem is shown with the help of a hypothetical feasibility zone in Figure 26.8. As can be seen in this figure, the optimum point turns out to be A, which is tangential to the highest indifference curve indicating the least costly option.

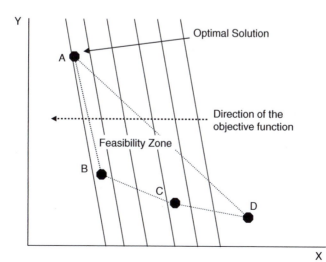

FIGURE 26.8 The logic of a minimization problem.

26.3 ANOTHER APPLICATION OF LINEAR PROGRAMMING

Linear programming is a versatile technique and lends itself to the analysis of a variety of problems [Walsh, 1985]. For instance, an airline may use linear programming to determine the shortest routes among a number of airports (Anderson et al., 1974). A hospital may use it for finding the least-cost diet program given a certain minimum level of nutritional needs. A farming industry may use linear programming for ascertaining the least cost method of raising various kinds of livestock (Beneke and Winterboer, 1973). There are numerous other cases in which linear programming can be of great help to decision makers. These may involve portfolio management (maximizing total return subject to risk constraints), personnel problems (finding the least expensive combination of personnel of various grades to complete a job), and scheduling problems (filling the slots of various shifts with the optimum number personnel), to name a few. Because there are so many possibilities, it is not feasible to discuss them all here. However, to show the versatility of the technique, we will discuss prison planning, which shows one possible use of linear programming in the public sector.

26.3.1 PRISON PLANNING

In crime-ridden parts of the United States the rising tide of prison population poses a significant problem for all levels of government. The governments face the problem of limited prison space, budgets, and other institutional constraints. Suppose a state's planners are considering the following problem. The state has three categories of inmates: the hardened criminals (or the most dangerous ones, requiring incarceration with maximum possible security), the violent criminals, and the nonviolent criminals. Because the hardened criminals require the maximum amount of security measures, they are the most expensive to incarcerate. The cost goes down for the violent criminals, and of course the nonviolent prisoners are the least expensive to accommodate within the prison system. Let us suppose that there are three state penitentiaries, A, B, and C. A is the minimum security prison, B is the medium security prison, and C is the maximum security prison.

While allocating the total population of convicted individuals, the state planners face a few more constraints. The first constraint is the capacities of the prisons. The maximum capacities of the facilities are: 3,000 inmates in prison A, 4,500 in prison B, and 5,200 in prison C. In algebraic form these three constraints can be written as:

$$X11 + X12 + X13 \leq 3,000 \tag{26.11}$$

$$X21 + X22 + X23 \leq 4,500 \tag{26.12}$$

$$X31 + X32 + X33 \leq 5,200 \tag{26.13}$$

where: X1 1 is hardened criminals placed in prison A,
X1 2 is violent criminals placed in prison A,
X1 3 is nonviolent prisoners placed in prison A,
X2 1 is hardened criminals placed in prison B,
X2 2 is violent criminals placed in prison B,
X2 3 is nonviolent prisoners placed in prison B,
X3 1 is hardened criminals placed in prison C,
X3 2 is violent criminals placed in prison C, and
X3 3 is nonviolent prisoners placed in prison C.

There are 1,500 hardened, 4,500 violent, and 10,000 nonviolent criminals who require incarceration in the state. Constraints (26.4), (26.5), and (26.6) show the total numbers of the three types of prisoners requiring accommodation:

$$X11 + X21 + X31 \leq 1,500 \tag{26.14}$$

$$X12 + X22 + X32 \leq 4,500 \tag{26.15}$$

$$X13 + X23 + X33 < 10,000 \tag{26.16}$$

Each individual prison facility also faces certain legal constraints. For instance, to keep the "minimum security prison" status of Prison A, the state planners cannot let the ratio of hardened criminals exceed 5 percent of its total inmate population. For symbolic expressions of this constraint, we need to do a bit of algebraic manipulation. Because the hardened criminal population in prison A ($X11$) cannot exceed 5 percent of its total inmate population ($X11+X12+X13$), we can write the constraint as:

$$X11 \leq .05(X11 + X12 + X13),$$

which can be rewritten as:

$$(X11 - .05\ X11) - .05\ X12 - .05\ X13 \leq 0$$

or:

$$.95\ X11 - .05\ X12 - .05\ X13 \leq 0 \tag{26.17}$$

There are other constraints as well. Let us assume that the state planners do not want the ratio of violent criminals to the total population to exceed 40 percent in a minimum security prison. Similarly, the medium security prison faces similar legal constraints on the distribution of its prison population. For these prisons, the planers do not want the more hardened criminal population to exceed 20 percent, or the violent prisoners to exceed 40 percent of its total. By following the logic used to derive constraint (26.17), we can write these three constraints as

$$-.4\ X11 + .6\ X12 - .4\ X13 \leq 0 \tag{26.18}$$

$$.8\ X21 - .2\ X22 - .2\ X23 \leq 0 \tag{26.19}$$

$$-.4\ X21 + .6\ X22 - .4\ X23 \leq 0 \tag{26.20}$$

Finally, there is budget constraint. Because the minimum security prison is not equipped to handle the hardened prisoners, it is quite expensive to place them there. The cost structure for a month is given in Table 26.3, with a total allocation of $100,000,000 million of the yearly state prison budget.

The budget constraint can be written as:

$$2,500\ X11 + 900\ X12 + 560\ X13 + 1,800\ X21 + 1,000\ X22 + 900\ X23$$
$$2,000\ X31 + 1,800\ X32 + 1,700\ X33 \leq 100,000,000 \tag{26.21}$$

Because the state places the utmost weight on the incarceration of the hardened criminals, and then on the violent ones, let us assume that the policy makers' preferences are translated into weights of 30 for the hardened criminals, 5 for the violent ones, and 1 for the nonviolent oness. The state does not have any preference for the relative desirability of the location of these inmates. Therefore, the linear programming problem is written as:

$$\text{Maximize Z} = 30\ X11 + 5\ X12 + X13 + 30\ X21 + 5\ X22 + X23 + 30\ X31 + 5\ X32 + X33$$

TABLE 26.3
Cost of Incarceration in State Prisons

Prison	Hardened Criminals	Violent Criminals	Non-violent Criminals
A (minimum security)	$2,500	$900	$560
B (medium security)	$1,800	$1,000	$900
C (maximum security)	$2,000	$1,800	$1,700

Subject to:

$$X11 + X12 + X13 \leq 3,000 \tag{26.11}$$

$$X21 + X22 + X23 \leq 4,500 \tag{26.12}$$

$$X31 + X32 + X33 \leq 5,200 \tag{26.13}$$

$$X11 + X21 + X31 \leq 1,500 \tag{26.14}$$

$$X12 + X22 + X32 \leq 4,500 \tag{26.15}$$

$$X13 + X23 + X33 \leq 10,000 \tag{26.16}$$

$$.95\,X11 - .05\,X12 - .05\,X13 \leq 0 \tag{26.17}$$

$$-.4\,X11 + .6\,X12 - .4\,X13 \leq 0 \tag{26.18}$$

$$.8\,X21 - .2\,X22 - .6\,X23 \leq 0 \tag{26.19}$$

$$-.4\,X21 + .6\,X22 - .4\,X23 \leq 0 \tag{26.20}$$

$$2,500\,X11 + 900\,X12 + 560\,X13 + 1,800\,X21 + 1,000\,X22 + 900\,X23$$
$$2,000\,X31 + 1,800\,X32 + 1,700\,X33 \leq 100,000,000 \tag{26.21}$$

The computer solution to this problem is given in Table 26.4. The slack values and the dual prices are given in Table 26.5.

TABLE 26.4
Optimal Mix of Prisoners in the Three State Penitentiaries

Prison	Hardened Criminals	Violent Criminals	Nonviolent Criminals	Total
A (minimum security)	0	1,200	1,800	3,000
B (medium security)	700	1,800	2,000	4,500
C (maximum security)	800	806	0	1,606
Total	1,500	3,806	3,800	

TABLE 26.5
Slack and Shadow Prices

Constraints	Description	Total Available	Optimal Allocation	Slack	Shadow Price
13.11	Space in the minimum security prison A[a]	3,000	3,000	0	.667
13.12	Space in the medium security prison B[a]	4,500	4,500	0	.309
13.13	Space in the maximum security prison C[a]	5,200	1,606	1,394	0.0
13.14	Total number of hardened criminals	1,500	1,500	0	24.44
13.15	Total number of violent criminals	4,500	3,806	694	0.0
13.16	Total number of nonviolent criminals	10,000	3,800	6,200	0.0
13.17	Ratio of hardened criminals in prison A[a]	5 percent	0 percent	5 percent	0.0
13.18	Ratio of violent criminals in prison A[a]	40 percent	40 percent	0	3.06
13.19	Ratio of hardened criminals in prison B[a]	20 percent	15.5 percent	4.5 percent	2.28
13.20	Ratio of violent criminals in prison B[a]	40 percent	40 percent	0	3.95
13.21	Budget constraint	$100 million	$100 million	0	2.78

[a] Policy variables for the prison planner.

26.3.2 DISCUSSION OF THE RESULTS

The computer solution to this linear programming problem provides us with some extremely interesting results. The optimal solutions in Table 26.4 suggest that we should not burden the minimum security facilities with inmates who are considered to be the most violent (hardened). It also suggests that, due to other constraints, the majority of the non-violent offenders should be placed in the medium security prisons. Perhaps, more importantly, the optimal allocation accommodates all the hardened offenders, but cannot find accommodation for 694 violent and 6,200 nonviolent criminals within the limited prison system. For them, the State must seek other accommodations. Or, alternately, placing them within the system will cause severe overcrowding and will violate some of the legislative or organizational mandates.

Table 26.5 gives us the shadow prices of the various constraints. By studying this Table, we can draw the following conclusions:

1 The space constraint is most critical for the minimum security prison, followed by the medium security facility.
2 The structural constraints of the mix of inmates within the three prisons are limiting, and efforts should be made to change them. Of these four constraints, the most critical are the provisions that the ratio of violent criminals must not exceed 40 percent of the total in the medium security facility and minimum security prison. Also, the rule that the ratio of hardened criminals cannot exceed 20 percent of the total prison population in the medium security prison should be reviewed.

3 Presently, because of the cost factor, the maximum security prison is running below capacity. Therefore, appropriate policies need to be developed.

26.4 SENSITIVITY ANALYSIS

Sensitivity analysis involves analyzing the results of the optimal solution by changing some of the important parameter values. In the example of the prison population distribution among the various facilities discussed above, we may not be satisfied with just the derived results. Instead, we may want to know the impact of cost changes and other policy changes on the optimal solution. Sensitivity analysis has become extremely useful tool as a result of increased computer capabilities. For a decision maker, it may be more useful to receive a series of optimal solutions corresponding to a number of probable scenarios than to be informed of a unique optimal solution.

For example, we may want to know what might happen if the minimum security facility is turned into a medium security prison. In that case, we would experiment with the possibility of housing more hardened criminals in that prison. Or, we may want to study the impact of the maximum security facility becoming a facility exclusively for the hardened criminals. If these are real concerns, sensitivity analysis is able to provide extremely useful answers for policy makers.

26.5 INTEGER PROGRAMMING

The optimal solution of a linear programming problem may come in fractions, but such answers may be meaningless. Consider, for example, our first problem in this chapter: planning to construct housing for two kinds of students. When we solved the linear programming problem, many of the corner solutions were in fractions. As it does not make sense to recommend the construction of, say, 2.93 units of housing, we merrily discarded the fractions (because by rounding we would go over the constraints). However, shedding the fractional part of a solution can give us misleading results. Therefore, we use *integer programming*, by which we place an additional constraint on the solution: We want the answer only in integers.

Let us consider a simple example. Suppose we are trying to maximize the following:

$$\text{Maximize } Z = X + 6Y$$

$$\text{Subject to} : 2X + 3Y \leq 11.5$$

and

$$X, Y \geq 0$$

We have drawn this problem in Figure 26.9. Because we have only one constraint, we can readily see that the two relevant corner points—ignoring the obviously inferior (0,0) point—are A and B. At point A, we have no X and 3.83Y, and at point B we have no Y and 5.75X. By inserting these values in the objective function, we can see that A has a value of 23, with 5.75 for B. This obviously makes A the optimal choice.

Suppose both X and Y are indivisible. Therefore, we cannot have a 3.83 amount of Y because we cannot round it off to 4, as it will exceed the limitation imposed by the constraint, we have to choose the integer 3 by ignoring the fractional part of the solution for A. Within the linear programming logic, this is done by introducing a new constraint: $Y - \leq 3$. This is called a cut. Therefore, we may recommend 3 Ys and no X, shown as point C in Figure 26.10. But we can readily see from Figure 26.10 that the choice of the point C would be a sub-optimal, interior solution, as from this point we can move to the border of the feasibility zone to obtain more X. In fact, by moving as far as possible within the feasibility zone, we can get 1.25 X (We get this by substituting

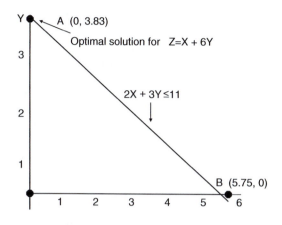

FIGURE 26.9 Integer programming problem.

2 for Y in the constraint $2X + 3Y = 11.5$, which gives us $X = (11.5 - 9/2) = 1.25)$. This is the point D in Figure 26.10. Still the problem remains that X also cannot be divided into fractions. Therefore, we introduce another cut or a constraint, $X \leq 1.0$, which gives us the optimal integer solution of $X = 1$ and $Y = 3$. Thus, by using appropriate technique, we can obtain meaningful solutions in integers.

26.6 CONCLUSION

Linear programming is an extremely powerful analytical tool. The strength of this elegant technique rests with its ability to consider various kinds of constraints and provide numerical answers to the questions posed by the decision makers. Furthermore, the results of the dual solutions (shadow prices) provide an extremely strong tool for a deeper understanding of the problem at hand.

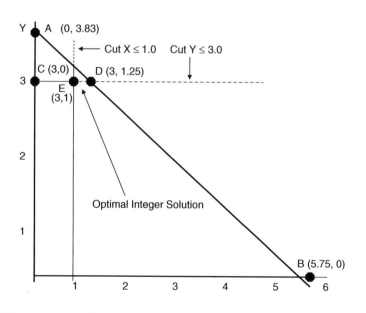

FIGURE 26.10 Integer programming solution.

However, like any other mathematical model linear programming is based on logical reasoning. Results obtained through techniques such as these are only as good as the formulation of the problem and the reliability of the data. From the discussion of linear programming, we can see that this technique can be useful in reaching an optimal mix of alternatives. However, apart from the data and the limitations of imagination of the researcher, the technique also carries some important shortcomings. First, as the name suggests, the objective function and the constraint are all linear. It is entirely possible that in reality they would be nonlinear. Indeed, in actual life, we seldom come across linear relationships. Consider, for example, that we are trying to determine the optimum size of the jurisdiction of a fire service department. As the size of the area increases, the per-household cost for obtaining fire protection goes down. However, after a certain point, as the department becomes too large, inefficiency creeps in, and as a result the price of providing fire protection goes up. This is clearly a non-linear relationship and is typical of many average cost functions. Linear programming is unable to consider such complexities, although for the most part actual relationships can be approximated with the help of a linear form.

However, when the nonlinearity of a relationship is strong and cannot be approximated by linear forms without a significant loss of information, we must resort to *nonlinear programming*. However, in non-linear programming the solutions are highly complex. In the 1960s and 70s, a great deal of enthusiasm was generated by the advancement of computer technology. Non-linear models were finding their applications in the areas of development economics and national planning (see, for instance, Intrelligator, 1971). However, these models turned out to be far more difficult to apply to real world situations than was originally anticipated. As a result, although linear programming is still being used, particularly in the private sector, enthusiasm for their more complex counterpart has definitely waned over time.

REFERENCES

Anderson, D. R., Sweeney, D. J., and Williams, T. A., *Linear Programming for Decision Making: An Applications Approach*, West Pub. Co., St. Paul, MN, 1974.

Beneke, R. R. and Winterboer, R., *Linear Programming Applications To Agriculture*, Iowa State University Press, Ames, IA, 1973.

Gass, S. I. and Assad, A. A., *An Annotated Timeline of Operations Research: An Informal History*, Kluwer, New York, 2004.

Intrelligator, M. D., *Mathematical Optimization and Economic Theory*, Prentice-Hall, Englewood Cliffs, NJ, 1971.

Karmarkar, N., A new polynomial-time algorithm for linear programming, *Combinatorica*, 4, 373–395, 1984.

Walsh, G. R., *An Introduction to Linear Programming*, Wiley, New York, 1985.

27 Queuing Theory and Simulations

Dipak K. Gupta

CONTENTS

27.1 The Problem...511
27.2 The Elements of a Queuing Model 512
    27.2.1 Solving a Queuing Problem 512
    27.2.2 The Diverse Structures of Queues..513
    27.2.3 A Deterministic Solution..514
    27.2.4 Queuing Theory in an Uncertain World 516
        27.2.4.1 Arrivals..516
        27.2.4.2 The Nature of the Queue 517
        27.2.4.3 Service Time...518
27.3 Theoretical Distributions in a Queuing Model 519
27.4 The Use of Simulations...521
    27.4.1 System Simulation..521
    27.4.2 Heuristic Simulation..522
    27.4.3 Game Simulation..522
    27.4.4 Monte Carlo Method 522
27.5 Conclusion 523
References..523

27.1 THE PROBLEM

The director of the youth summer employment program of a town must make a decision involving a significant number of variables. As part of the federal effort to provide urban youth with constructive activities during the idle summer months, the city has received funding to employ 1,500 young people. The program will attract a large number of applicants; as many as 8,000 are expected. The town wants to determine the optimal number of people to interview and hire the applicants, as well as to assist them with completion of the required forms. Estimates indicate that this process will take, on average, fifteen minutes per applicant. If the city opens only one booth, it will take $8,000 \times 15$ minutes $= 120,000$ minutes, or 2,000 working hours. One individual, operating one booth and working a 40 hour week, could process all of the applications in one year (-2 weeks vacation time). Fifty individuals operating 50 booths could complete the entire job within one week. The director requires a thorough analysis of the variables in order to make a decision on the optimum number of booths in terms of both time- and cost-efficiency.

27.2 THE ELEMENTS OF A QUEUING MODEL[*]

This problem is typical of queuing theory, which derives its name from the analysis of queues. The systematic analyses of probability arose from our need to manage the uncertainties of life. The history of operations research often starts with the sixteenth century work of a Milanese physician, mathematician, and an avid gambler named Girolamo Cardano. This is not surprising, because uncertainty is inherently imbedded in gambling. His book, *Liber de Ludo Aleae* (Book on Games of Chance) defined, for the first time, probability as the ratio between the number of desired outcome(s) and the total number of possible outcomes. Unfortunately for Cardano, by the time his book was published in the middle of the seventeenth century, renowned French scholars like Blaise Pascal and Pierre de Fermat had firmly established the mathematics of probability.[†] Pascal not only defined probability, but also provided the fundamental rule of calculating expected value by multiplying the probability of occurrence of a desired outcome by its reward.

In the 1930s, the pioneering study of Felix Pollaczek gave queuing theory its early form. Pollaczek was interested in developing a probability model for customers waiting in line and presented the formula for the mean waiting time, which served as the building block for queuing theory. Today the familiar notations used in queuing theory owes its origin to the path breaking work of another celebrated mathematician, David G. Kendall. His published work in 1953 completed the theoretical side of this new analytical technique (see Franklin, 2001).

However, the application of queuing theory had to wait for another important development: the Monte Carlo method. The advances in probability theory had always maintained its close ties to gambling and games of chance. The Monte Carlo method, by which a probability distribution is simulated by "playing" a hand over and over again, bears the name of the fabled European city known for its gambling casinos. Physicist Stanislaw Ulam worked out the problems of the Monte Carlo method while playing solitaire during an illness in 1946. A year later, along with another famous mathematician, John von Neumann, he presented a small paper to the American Mathematical Society, thereby nearly revolutionizing an entire field of study based on the new method. The invention of high-speed computers facilitated the wider use of the method in many areas of academic studies, including economics and operations research. By combining theories of probability with the functional ease of the newer computers, queuing theory received its final form. The method of queuing theory will now be discussed.

27.2.1 SOLVING A QUEUING PROBLEM

The process of choosing the optimum number of queues is conducted within the context of two separate costs. If the city wants to hire 50 individuals for this job, it could be done in a week, or if it wants to hire 100 persons, the processing would take only 2.5 working days. Therefore, the more people hired (or queues that are opened), the more smoothly and quickly the job will be completed. But hiring of personnel costs the city money. Hence, if too many people are hired, public funds would be wasted. On the other hand, nobody likes waiting in line. Making people wait in line has its own cost factor, especially in a democratic nation, to which elected officials and bureaucrats are sensitive. That is, the longer people have to wait, the greater will be their ire, and hence the cost to the organization. The optimum number of booths, therefore, will be at the point of intersection of these two cost curves. This is shown in Figure 27.1.

Figure 27.1 shows the equilibrium point at the intersection of the two cost curves. The cost of waiting in line is somewhat complex because it embodies two different factors. First, as discussed earlier, the cost of waiting in line is a positive function of the duration of wait: the longer a client has to wait in line, the greater the cost to the organization. Second, the extent of wait is inversely related

---

[*] Note that in this section, a simple model of queuing theory is presented. For a more rigorous discussion, see Mehdi (2003).

[†] For extensive histories of mathematics and probability, see Franklin (2001) and Hald (1990).

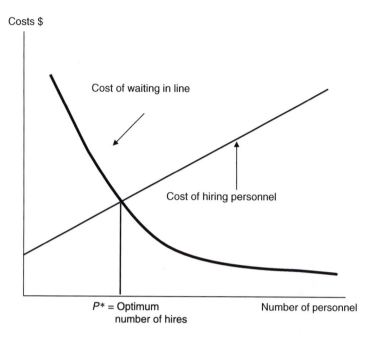

FIGURE 27.1 The optimal solution of a queuing problem.

to the number of personnel hired to service the clientele—the length of the waiting period goes down as more people are hired. This line is derived by combining these two factors. Specifically, this line is expressed as the cost of waiting in line as a function of the number of employees. One can see that when the number of personnel hired is low, the cost of waiting is high. This cost comes down as more people are brought in.

In contrast, the cost of hiring personnel is straightforward: the cost goes up as more people are hired. The point of intersection between these two curves is $P*$. At this point, the cost of waiting in line to the clients is the same as the cost of hiring workers for the city. To the left of this point, too few people are hired. At that point, because the benefit of hiring additional workers outweighs the cost of their hiring, the city should employ more people. To the right of this point, the costs of hiring exceed the benefit of lowering the waiting time.

27.2.2 The Diverse Structures of Queues

In queuing theory, the entire process, starting with the arrival of a client, waiting in line, getting serviced, and then exiting, is called the *queuing system*. The system consists of four elements: arrival, waiting, service, and exit. Another important concept in queuing theory is the *arriving unit*, defined as the smallest entity that is handled by the system at one time. This unit can be a teenage job applicant, as in our current example, or can be a family of six applying for a visa to visit a country. While designing a queuing model, the structure must be carefully defined because it will have a definite impact on the time of service.

If service is provided at a single point, it is called a *single-phase system*. For instance, the applicants get the necessary forms, fill them out, and get interviewed for a job in a single booth (as in "one-stop-shopping"). On the other hand, if there are multiple points at which service is provided, it is called a *multiple-phase system*. In designing a queuing model, the queue structure and the number of phases must be determined.

Figure 27.2 illustrates three of an infinite variety of queue structures. In this figure, the lines show the direction of the channel, the circles are the clients, and the shaded squares are the service

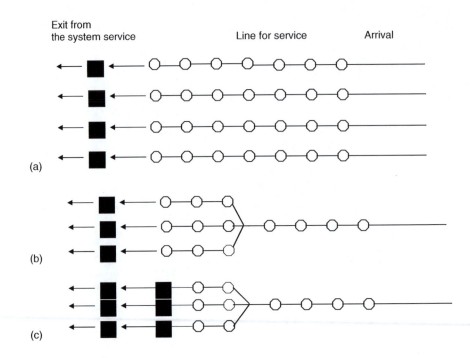

FIGURE 27.2 Examples of queuing structures.

areas. The most elementary form of a queue is shown in Figure 27.2a, where the queuing units stand in a single-channel, single-phase structure. Supermarket checkout counters are usually operated this way. Another common form of queue is where the clients form one line up to a certain point, beyond which they split among a multiple of booths for service (Figure 27.2b). Finally, Figure 27.2c illustrates a two-phase system, where service is provided at two separate points. The design of the queue determines the level of complexity in the theoretical analysis and can save clients a great deal of annoyance and minimize consequent costs to the service-providing organization.

27.2.3 A Deterministic Solution

The problem of choosing the optimum number of booths or queues can be simply solved if it is assumed that people are going to line up exactly on time, spacing themselves evenly in the line, like the bottles in an automated bottling plant, ready to be filled with mechanical precision. "Totally unrealistic," one might think, but the assumption is more useful than it first appears.

Going back to the example of the youth summer job program, let us assume that each working day the city expects 120 applicants to arrive. Assuming that they will arrive at regular intervals during the 8-hour day, (120/8 = 15) youths will arrive every hour. This pattern of arrival of 15 individuals per hour translates into one arrival every four minutes. It takes 15 minutes per applicant to provide the necessary service, and a single processor can serve (60/15 = 4) applicants per hour. Therefore, if only one window is open at the start of the day, then before the processing for the first client is completed, there will be a line of three. By the time the second person exits the system, the line will have extended to seven. With only one person in charge of serving the applicants, the second applicant in line would have to wait 11 minutes (15 minutes service time − 4 minutes of arrival delay). The third applicant, who arrives within eight minutes of the opening of the doors, would wait for 22 minutes [(15×2) − (4×2)]. If someone is unfortunate enough to arrive 30 minutes after the beginning of processing, she would have to wait 7.5 hours before being served. And, if she

TABLE 27.1
Calculation of Waiting Time with Two Windows Open

Applicant	Arrives at nth Minute	Goes to Window	Waiting Time
1	0	A	0
2	4	B	0
3	8	A	$15 - 8 = 7$
4	12	B	$(15 + 4) - 12 = 7$
5	16	A	$(15 \times 2) - 16 = 14$
6	20	B	$[(15 \times 2) + 4] - 20 = 14$
7	24	A	$(15 \times 3) - 24 = 21$
8	28	B	$[(15 \times 3) + 4] - 28 = 21$
61	240	A	$(15 \times 30) - 240 = 210$

happens to arrive during the middle of the day (four hour after the doors open), she will be the sixty-first person to arrive that day and will have to wait 13 hours for her turn at the booth!

The waiting time can be reduced significantly if there are two open windows. As the calculations presented in Table 27.1 show, the first two arrivals do not face any waiting time, because now two windows are open. The third person walks in at the eighth minute and has to wait until the first window is available, which is going to be in the fifteenth minute. Therefore, for this individual, the waiting time is $15 - 8 = 7$ min. The fourth applicant also has to wait for seven min. This is because, although window B gets free at the nineteenth min ($15 + 4 = 19$ min because the second applicant arrived in the fourth min), the applicant arrives in the twelfth minute. By following this logic, the luck of our mid-day arrival, the sixty-first applicant, is improving considerably as his waiting period has been cut to 210 min, or 3.5 h.

According to this logic, if the city hires three persons to process the applications, then the situation improves even more dramatically. Because the sixty-first arrival has been taken as the point of evaluation, calculations show that this individual will have to wait for (only) an hour. This number is reduced to zero (no waiting) if there are four windows open (because it takes 15 minutes to process each applicant, with four windows open and applicants arriving at regular intervals of four minutes, one window will always be open for the next arrival). The waiting time has been plotted against the number of open windows in Figure 27.3.

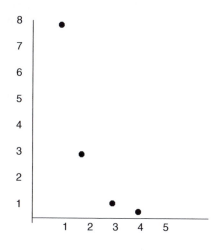

FIGURE 27.3 Waiting time and the number of windows.

27.2.4 QUEUING THEORY IN AN UNCERTAIN WORLD

To design the best configuration of queues, one must examine in detail the essential elements of the model: the arrival of the clients, the nature of the queues, and the service time.

27.2.4.1 Arrivals

Unless the arrivals can be completely controlled (which is scarcely seen in life), predicting the arrival of clients should be based on probability. That is, one should be able to plan on the basis of predictions, such as "the probability of 10 people showing up at the same time is 15%." The derivation of these probabilities must depend on the past experiences of arrivals. To obtain this information, data must be collected on actual arrivals in either of two ways.

The first possibility is to record the number of people coming through the door during a given time period (such as an hour, half an hour, or every 10 minutes, etc., depending on the nature of the operation). A substantial database can be built by observing the arrival pattern over a number of typical days. Suppose the arrival pattern has been observed on an hourly basis over a 40-hour work week. This information is shown in Table 27.2.

Alternately, data may be collected by the time between arrivals. Table 27.3 illustrates such a method of tabulating information. Note that the time interval of zero implies a simultaneous arrival. The length of the interval depends on the analyst's judgment. However, the shorter the interval, the more detailed the information. When calculating the average of grouped data, the midpoint of each interval is used; therefore, a long time interval would make the average less reliable. Suppose that with the help of a stopwatch and a counter the arrival pattern of 200 people during the course of a week has been recorded. These data are presented in Table 27.3.

Although the arrivals can take any shape, a number of studies indicate that actual arrival rates over a fixed period of time (as shown in Table 27.2) usually conform to a theoretical probability distribution called the *Poisson probability distribution*. On the other hand, if one does not simply look at the time of arrival, but calculates the time gaps (interval space) between arrivals, it follows another theoretical probability distribution called a *negative exponential*. Figure 27.4 illustrates the pattern of a Poisson distribution, and Figure 27.5 shows a negative exponential distribution.

The Poisson distribution assumes that the arrivals are random. This assumption of randomness implies that an arrival can occur at any time and that its probability is the same regardless of the length of the current waiting period. That is, the clients are not assumed to adjust their behavior based on some external factor. For example, people living around the international border of the United States and Mexico near San Diego have to contend with long lines at the border checkpoint, where at certain times waiting periods can extend to hours. Because there are several crossing

TABLE 27.2
Hypothetical Hourly Arrival Pattern within Hourly Intervals

Number of Arrivals	Frequency	Probability of Arrival (Frequency/40)
0–2	8	0.20
3–5	10	0.25
6–9	12	0.30
10–14	6	0.15
15–19	3	0.075
20–24	1	0.025
Total	40	1.00

TABLE 27.3
Hypothetical Data on the Space of Arrival within a Time Interval

Time Interval (Minutes)	Frequency	Probability (Frequency/200)
0–5	75	0.375
6–10	62	0.31
11–15	39	0.195
16–20	13	0.065
21–30	7	0.035
31–45	3	0.015
45–90	1	0.005
> Total	200	1.00

points along the border, the local radio stations periodically announce the length of current waiting periods. People frequently change their plans by either hurrying or delaying their departure to minimize waiting time. If this behavior substantially affects the traffic pattern, then it can be assumed that the arrivals at the border points are no longer random, as the future numbers are dependent on the current ones in the queue.

The arrival rate can also be calculated by looking at the interval space between arrivals. As Figure 27.5 illustrates, this pattern can often be approximated by a negative exponential curve.

The information that the arrival rates over a fixed period closely follow a theoretical probability distribution is of enormous value because this can simplify the calculations of the various results of a queuing mode.

27.2.4.2 The Nature of the Queue

The proper functioning of a queuing model depends to a large extent on the configuration and length of the line, and on the discipline of the clients in the line. For instance, Figure 27.2 shows

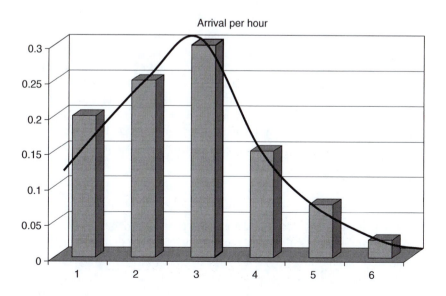

FIGURE 27.4 Poisson distribution.

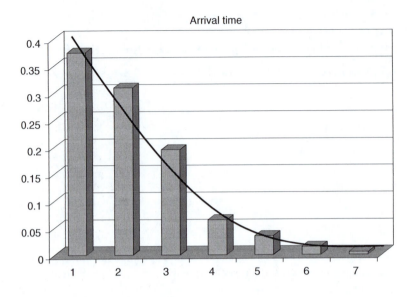

FIGURE 27.5 Negative exponential distribution.

a number of different types of queue structures. The choice of the most appropriate structure will reduce the waiting time to a significant extent. In contrast, an ill-conceived design will clog the system and cause nightmarish waiting periods for service delivery.

The length of the potential line can be an important consideration. For example, a service establishment that routinely creates a logjam of traffic waiting in line will be considered a nuisance by its neighbors. Such establishments may often be kept away from neighborhoods by zoning ordinances. If there is an artificial limit (imposed by the law), the mathematical queuing model will be able to handle it, but this will make the formulae quite complicated.

The final point about the queue is the clients' discipline. If those waiting in line keep order, both the service delivery and its proper planning can be greatly helped. If people tend to break the line, either because they are culturally not accustomed to standing in orderly lines (there are many places around the world where people are not used to standing in long, orderly lines) or because those who are in charge of running the operation routinely break the line to accommodate important persons, members of their own family and friends, or those who might offer a bribe, no amount of sophistication in model building will be of help.[*] Examples of smooth-functioning lines can be seen in large amusement parks, such as Disney World, where despite the huge lines, the park officials' experience in handling large crowds and the crowd's willingness to follow direction help considerably, even during the peak visiting periods. On the other hand, a small but rowdy and unruly crowd (such as people waiting in line to buy beverages at a college football game) can make service delivery inefficient.

27.2.4.3 Service Time

The time spent obtaining service can have a great degree of variability or can be totally fixed. At the one extreme are medical emergency rooms, where service delivery time can vary widely.

---

[*] An example of a legitimate breaking of the line is the operation of a medical emergency room. Similar line breaking can also be permitted in police work, fire prevention, and other emergency services, where need takes precedence over the time of arrival.

At the other extreme are services that are doled out with mechanical precision, such as our example of shows at Disney World and other large amusement parks. Having no fluctuations in duration of services helps the cause of planning with a queuing model immensely. However, even if the service varies in duration, one can find distribution patterns similar to those associated with the probability of arrival (Figure 27.4 and Figure 27.5). When such patterns are pronounced, prediction becomes easier and the use of a model becomes more precise.

27.3 THEORETICAL DISTRIBUTIONS IN A QUEUING MODEL

The logic of a deterministic queuing model was applied to the problem of processing applications for a youth summer job program. Because the assumptions of a deterministic model are totally unrealistic, realism can be introduced by assuming uncertainty in arrival and service delivery. The probability pattern of arrival can be safely assumed to follow a Poisson distribution, while service delivery time varies negative exponentially.

The most significant impediment to the use of a theoretical model is mathematics, which can be quite involved. Because the level of mathematics required is generally beyond the scope of this introductory book, a number of useful formulae are used without proof.

Recall the simple example of a single-channel, single-phase problem. It is assumed that the arrivals follow a Poisson distribution, while service delivery follows a negative exponential form. The use of a mathematical distribution requires the assumption of independence. That is, the current arrival rate is not influenced by the length of waiting in the previous period. The assumption of independence also implies an infinite, or at least a very large (8,000 youths in our example), source of arrival. No balking (not entering the queue because of its size), no reneging (leaving the queue before being served), and no limits on the length of the queues are also assumed. Finally, it is extremely important to note that for the queuing theory to operate such that a totally unrealistic situation is developed where the lines spiral to infinity, the mean arrival rate must be less than the service rate.

In queuing theory literature, the use of the following symbols is fairly consistent: A is the mean rate of arrival and S represents mean service rate. These two averages are calculated on the basis of their respective distributions. After they are calculated, the entire gamut of results can be calculated using this information.

The expected number in the system is given by:

$$\frac{A}{S-A} \tag{27.1}$$

The expected number waiting in line is:

$$\frac{A^2}{S(S-A)} \tag{27.2}$$

The expected time waiting in line is:

$$\frac{A}{S(S-A)} \tag{27.3}$$

The utilization factor, or the probability that when the next person arrives she or he will have to wait in line, is given by:

$$W = \frac{A}{S} \qquad (27.4)$$

and the probability that the system is idle is $(1 - W)$.

Going back to our example, assume that the mean rate of arrival of youths is 15 per hour ($A = 15$). Also, if there are four booths open, then the average service rate is 4 every 15 minutes, or 16 applicants per hour ($S = 16$). Armed with these two bits of information, the following results can be estimated:

The expected number in the system:

$$\frac{15}{16 - 15} = 15$$

The expected number of waiting in line:

$$\frac{(15)^2}{16(16 - 15)} = 14$$

The expected time waiting in line:

$$\frac{15}{16(16 - 15)} = 0.94 \text{ hours}$$

Probability that when the next person arrives she or he will have to wait in line:

$$\frac{15}{16} = 0.94$$

These numbers may be calculated for any number of windows, as long as there are more than three windows so that the arrival rate is less than the service delivery time. Note that, unlike the deterministic system, the waiting time does not go to zero because it is not known how these young men and women are going to come in. Therefore, as the number of windows is increased, the expected waiting time comes down drastically but does not become zero. Table 27.4 shows the results when four, five, and six windows are open for comparison.

Table 27.4 indicates that as the number of booths increases, the expected time spent in the line is reduced significantly, but at the same time, the probability that the system may be idle climbs steadily. As one can imagine, information such as this can be of great help to a decision maker trying to decide on the number of booths to open.

TABLE 27.4
Results of a Queuing Model Based on Probability Distribution

Number of Windows	Number Waiting in Line	Waiting Time in Hours (Minutes)	Probability of Waiting in Line	Probability of an Idle System
4	14	0.94 (56.4)	0.94	0.06
5	2.25	0.15 (9)	0.75	0.25
6	1.04	0.069 (4.14)	0.625	0.375

27.4 THE USE OF SIMULATIONS

The use of a mathematical model to derive the optimal solution works fine as long as the process is not terribly complicated. However, if there are complicated considerations, the mathematics can be harrowing and, indeed, may not even be solvable. For instance, the preceding example of solving a queuing model with Poisson distribution yielded quick results. After it was determined that this distribution most accurately described the arrivals, the two mean values were substituted into the equations to produce the optimal solution. Yet, for all its apparent convenience, the problem of a single-channel, single-phase model in real life may not require the use of complicated mathematics because the results may be obtained by a bit of logical thinking. On the other hand, if the problem at hand is more complicated (e.g., it has multiple lines and multiple phases, and the arrival pattern and service time does not conform to the theoretical distributions), then solving the system mathematically will be problematic. Therefore, in such cases, a better method of solving a queuing model is to employ a simulation model. Simulation models do not require a mathematical solution and are therefore flexible enough to accommodate any random pattern. However, they require tedious calculations, best performed by a computer. As computer technology has improved, so has the use of simulation models in policy analysis.

Although simulations are being discussed in the context of a queuing model, they have wide-ranging applications in policy analysis wherever there is an uncertain outcome. There are many kinds of simulations, which vary from simple to highly elaborate. However, they usually fall into one of four categories: system simulation, heuristic simulation, game simulation, or Monte Carlo methods.

27.4.1 SYSTEM SIMULATION

A system simulation attempts to reproduce the process with a number of equations. It is also known as a "what-if " simulation. For instance, a city-run electric company expresses the demand for its product as $R = a + pQ$, where R is total revenue, a is fixed amount of demand, p is price per kilowatt hour, and Q is quantity consumed. On the other hand, the cost curve for the production of electricity is $C = b + qQ$, where C is total cost, b is fixed cost of production, and q is variable cost of production.

Because the city has a mandate to run its production at a break-even point (with no loss or profit), the point of optimal quantity to be produced can be determined by setting total revenue equal to total cost, and then solving for the quantity:

$$a + pQ = b + qQ$$

$$qQ - pQ = b - a$$

$$Q = \frac{b-a}{q-p}$$

With this algebraic description of the process, the management of the plant can run various scenarios under which the various cost and revenue factors change, and then analyze their implications for the quantity to be produced. For example, the manager may ask, "If the fixed cost goes up by 20%, how much electricity should we produce?" This is a typical example of a simple system simulation. For a much more complex simulation, there can be many more equations of more complex forms. These are extremely useful tools for analyzing the impact of a new tax on the economy, or discerning the impact of the relaxation of a particular regulation on the market.

A system simulation can be applied to a queuing problem by describing the system algebraically and then finding the potential "choke" points, or the areas where the system can get clogged if there are an unexpected number of arrivals.

27.4.2 Heuristic Simulation

When a mathematical description is impossible because of extreme complexity of the system or the presence of a high degree of uncertainty about the relationships, a heuristic simulation may be the solution. A heuristic simulation involves expert judgment of various scenarios using rules of thumb instead of precise numbers. Although a mathematical model can aid a heuristic simulation, it is typically done as a process of subjective assessment.

27.4.3 Game Simulation

A situation of conflict (such as the prisoner's dilemma) can be effectively simulated with the help of a game model. These models are ideally suited for uncertain situations involving strategies to deal with a potential threat. Although game simulations are widely used in many areas, their usefulness to the analysis of a queuing problem is limited.

27.4.4 Monte Carlo Method

A Monte Carlo model (name taken from the island city in Europe famous for its gambling casinos) deals with the probabilistic process of using random values to explore the nature of relationships within a system. Because Monte Carlo models require repeated iterations with numbers generated through random processes, the proliferation of computers has seen their extensive use of such models in various fields of study, wherever there is a need to look into a stochastic or a probabilistic process. When dealing with a complex queuing problem for which a mathematical solution is problematic, a simulation based on a Monte Carlo model may provide the answer. This model is best described with the help of an example.

Recall the original example of the youth summer employment program. Table 27.3 provides us with results of the observation of actual arrival patterns for 200 applicants. These arrival data are expressed in terms of relative frequency or probability. The probabilistic arrival pattern can be generated by taking these probabilities.

Suppose, in a game, a person has to take a certain action if it rains. The game sets the chance of rain at 40%. To simulate the chance factors, imagine a bag filled with 10 balls, 4 of which will be, for instance, red. If a person draws a ball without looking, and it is a red ball, then assume that it has actually rained. By following this process, the chance of rain has been kept equal to its predicted value.

The Monte Carlo model uses this concept of simulation over and over again. As an example, in Table 27.5, the random data series have been added to the data presented in Table 27.3. In this table, numbers have been assigned from 1 to 1,000 to the cumulative probability measures for arrival time. By close examination, it can be observed that the probability that an applicant walks in the summer employment office within 10 minutes of the previous arrival is 0.685. The computer can now simulate random numbers between 1 and 1,000, and when it picks a number, 387 for instance, it is assumed that a client has arrived between 6 and 10 minutes. Although this is a tedious process if performed manually, the computer can keep generating such numbers and with the help of this data one can evaluate a queuing design. If it is getting clogged frequently, additional personnel may have to be hired to open a new window. If, on the other hand, there is a lot of slack time, a window may be closed and the worker reassigned to a different job.

TABLE 27.5
Simulating the Probability of Arrival Using Random Numbers

Time Interval (Minutes)	Probability Frequency	Cumulative (Frequency/200)	Probability	Random Numbers
0–5	75	0.375	0.375	000–374
6–10	62	0.31	0.685	375–684
11–15	39	0.195	0.880	685–879
16–20	13	0.065	0.945	880–944
21–30	7	0.035	0.980	945–979
31–45	3	0.015	0.995	980–994
45–90	1	0.005	1.000	994–999
Total	200	1.00		

27.5 CONCLUSION

The biggest advantage of queuing theory is its clarity. The technique can visually lay out the design of a system and demonstrate its potential strengths and weaknesses with the help of probability theory, which is at once sophisticated yet relatively easy to conceptualize and simple to use. In fact, there are many different applications, from banking to college registration, where queuing theory can be profitably used. However, despite its apparent simplicity, the queuing model can quickly become extremely complicated as multiple levels of services and other complexities are introduced. In such cases, a policy analyst should consult an expert in the application of this technique. Finally, it seems appropriate to mention that with the advent of computer technology, where students can register and patients can fill their prescriptions online, the domain of queuing theory has definitely shrunk. However, as long as there is the need for direct service delivery, this elegant technique will find frequent use.

REFERENCES

Franklin, J., *The Science of Conjecture: Evidence and Probability Before Pascal*, Johns Hopkins University Press, Baltimore, 2001.

Hald, A., *A History of Probability and Statistics and their Applications*, Wiley, New York, 1990.

Medhi, J., *Stochastic Models in Queuing Theory*, 2nd ed., Academic Press, Boston, 2003.

28 Decision Making in Geographic Information Systems

Akhlaque Haque

CONTENTS

28.1 Introduction..525
28.2 Background of GIS..526
    28.2.1 How GIS Works..526
28.3 Decision Making with GIS...528
    28.3.1 Using GIS for Problem Solving..529
    28.3.2 The Art of GIS-Cartography..530
    28.3.3 The Science of GIS—Geographic Information Analysis....................531
    28.3.4 Decision Making Players..531
28.4 Implications of GIS for Decision Making in Democracy..............................533
28.5 Conclusion...533
References...534

28.1 INTRODUCTION

Information Technology (IT) has become the central decision support tool for managers in the twenty-first century. Through faster information access, processing, and data management, they provide greater promises of efficiency, effectiveness, and control over human decision making capacity. For managers dealing with data tied to location, Geographic Information Systems (GIS)[*] have opened unprecedented opportunities and new avenues of decision making research (Longley et al., 2001; Rodriguez-Bachiller and Glasson, 2004; Craig, Harris, and Winer, 2002; Jankowksi and Nyerges, 2001). Dramatic increase in the use of GIS is becoming increasingly useful for decision makers who can routinely make use of digital maps and multidimensional graphical dictionaries to examine, for example, race and income characteristics of an urban area, or study the proximity relationships between crimes, drug use, and HIV clients in different locations within the region or in any part of the world. According to the e-government survey conducted by the International City/County Management Association and Public Technology, Inc., GIS is the fastest-growing e-government activity in local governments (ICMA, 2004). Unlike any other times in modern history, having disparate datasets in one organized system allows managers to have access to varied citizen information in their desktops or handheld devices.

By incorporating space into decision-making models and displaying the attributes of the space, GIS systems provide policy analysts with new tools and bring new challenges to citizens.

---

[*] Geographic Information Systems will be abbreviated as GIS. For readability, GIS will be used in the singular throughout the text.

Once a primary problem is identified, GIS can be used to create different scenarios (of maps) that any layperson could understand. Stakeholders with differing views can now be brought to the table for discussion, and they can visualize their stakes looking at a set of maps. For target-based marketing, GIS is recognized as the most effective decision making tool (Sliwinski, 2002; Thrall, 2002). GIS finds its most common use in solving complex problems with non-deterministic outcomes.

This chapter provides an overview of the role of GIS in decision making. The first section describes the background of GIS and issues in GIS applications. The following section describes the role of GIS in decision making, with an emphasis on the players involved and the skills required to execute effective decision making using GIS. The final section highlights the implications of decision making with GIS for a modern democracy.

28.2 BACKGROUND OF GIS

GIS is a computer-based system designed to aid the collection, maintenance, storage, analysis, output, and distribution of spatial data and information (Bolstad, 2002, 1). In simple terms, GIS allows the real world to be represented by maps, objects, and pictures in digital form over a computer screen. GIS is based on geographic information science and supported by the disciplines of geography, surveying, engineering, cartography, computer science, social and behavioral sciences, health sciences, and the law. GIS is a tool for all who are interested in analyzing data by space (geography).

Today GIS is one of the most widely used information technologies in government and is increasingly becoming a standard tool for information management, storage, and data interpretation (Haque, 2001; Huffman, 1998). According to Barrett and Greene (2001), among the new innovative IT applications used in local government "GIS are near the top of the list in terms of utility in almost every aspect of government from crime fighting to street cleaning" (173). About 80,000 local government agencies in the U.S. have been identified as using GIS technology (Masser, 1998, 73), and the federal government has given particular attention to the dissemination of GIS by creating the National Spatial Data Infrastructure (NSDI) and the Federal Geographic Data Committee (FGDC). Whereas in 1992, 40% of the local governments used GIS (Moll, 1999), in 2003, according to a survey sponsored by the US Department of Interior and conducted by Public Technology, Inc., 97% of the local governments with populations of 100 thousand and 88% of those with populations between 50 to 100 thousand use GIS technology. Such a dramatic increase is due to the promise of GIS that is increasingly being reflected in mainstream public administration literature (see, for example, Haque, 2001; Ventura, 1995; Nedovic-Budic and Godschalk, 1996; Brown and Brudney, 1998; Masser, 1998). By portraying real world data as maps, GIS provide unparalleled power to analyze social, economic, and political circumstances.

Table 28.1 shows a list of GIS uses by industries. Although GIS, like most other computer applications, can be used as a stand-alone application, to serve as an effective decision-support tool it must be used within a holistic framework (Berry, 1993). Such a framework should be based on an understanding of the institutional context in which GIS is to be used. The context determines who creates the map, how it will be displayed as a final product, and who and how it will be interpreted and applied. Therefore, the details of the decision-support mechanism must be fully conceptualized before a complete GIS operation can be performed effectively.

28.2.1 How GIS Works

Different supporting tools have always aided decision making as they evolved over time. In the 1970s mainframe computers became an important tool to run applications that aid in decision making. In the late 1980s desktop computers replaced mainframes to become the fastest growing technological application in modern history. In the process, numerous decision-support

TABLE 28.1
Use of GIS by Industry

Industry	Use of GIS
Forestry	Inventory and management of resources
Police	Crime mapping to target resources
Epidemiology	To link clusters of disease to sources
Transport	Monitoring routes
Utilities	Managing pipe networks
Oil	Monitoring ships and managing pipelines
Central and local government	Evidence for funding and policy e.g. deprivation
Health	Planning services and health impact assessments
Environment agencies	Identifying areas of risk e.g. flood
Emergency departments e.g. ambulance	Planning quickest routes
Retail	Store location
Marketing	Locating target customers
Military	Troop movement
Mobile phone companies	Locating masts
Land ReGIStry	Recording and managing land and property
Estate agents	Locating properties that match certain criteria
Insurance	Identifying risk e.g. properties at risk of flooding
Agriculture	Analyzing crop yields

Source: From Getting started with GIS. http://www.gis.rgs.org/10.html

applications have been developed, ranging from simple statistical software to more advanced programming languages, such as ORACLE, C++, Java, and internet-based programming. Since the 1990s, more computer information processing capacity (processing speed) has paved the way for GIS applications to run on desktops. The GIS software was dramatically different from other software applications because it provided the opportunity to display data as attributes of a location, thus giving life to data through colorful digital maps. In other words, data could be captured and portrayed on maps to reveal what the data look like when real objects are represented by symbols tied to specific locations.

To represent the real world, GIS software combines spatial data (such as a forest or highway) with the attributes of the spatial location (timber acreage or number of cars in a highway) within maps. Figure 28.1 shows a schematic diagram of a typical GIS operation as it relates to a data model obtained from the real world and expressed in digital format on a computer screen. For computer processing, the digital information is transformed to machine language (M1, M2).

The flexibility of digital information is an extremely powerful feature of GIS that can revolutionize the way decisions are made by managers. However, the flexibility has also increased the ease with which data can be manipulated, increasing the chances of making errors and misrepresenting the real world. The GIS technology places added responsibility on the shoulders of technocrats who are only interested in pointing-and-clicking. In this sense GIS is less a technical tool than a communication tool for better decision making. The GIS technology assists decision makers by deriving a map that indicates the set of alternative uses of competing outcomes. Once the information is displayed on a screen, decision makers can assess the patterns of conflicting uses and determine the allocation of resources. GIS also can assist by comparing different allocation scenarios and identifying areas of difference. Although GIS technology greatly enhances our decision-making capabilities, it does not replace them. According to Joseph Berry (1993) "GIS is both a tool box for advanced analysis and capabilities and a sandbox to express our creativity" (196).

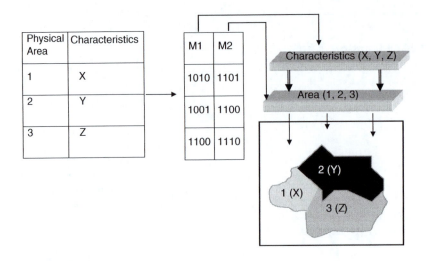

FIGURE 28.1 Schematic diagram of a digital data model of GIS.

Visual displays generated by GIS software augment decision making by giving added information to data. The quality of decision making is expected to be better not because GIS software generate more information, but because people can relate to the situation or problem in the real world through visual inspection. For example, data for school children by age and nutrition level for each city in a county can be mapped to reveal the neighborhoods where the problem of nutritional deficiency among children is prominent. The same analysis can be done for any neighborhood, and the decision maker can relate to his/her own neighborhood. Figure 28.2 shows areas of low, medium and high Black populations in three census tracts in downtown Birmingham, Alabama. The location of physician facilities is also plotted in the three tracts. Among the three census tracks the facilities are all concentrated in the areas with the lowest numbers of Blacks.

28.3 DECISION MAKING WITH GIS

In GIS the geography, or location, is used as the common denominator to link disparate data sets in one platform. Complex questions related to decision making can be answered when alternative scenarios are generated from the given data and problems are narrowed by using the peeling-the-onion method. By revealing scenarios of information in layers, GIS champions the target-based intervention planning (TBIP) method. TBIP can be described as a process of identifying areas that should be targeted for intervention given several competing options that meet varied requirements for future planning. For example, rather than employing resources in all parts of hurricane affected coastal areas, GIS provides the capability of identifying the areas most in need for allocation of resources for both short-term and long-term planning.

The classic demonstration of map-based decision making is Dr. Jon Snow's investigation of cholera in Victorian London in 1854 (for details, see http://www.ph.ucla.edu/epi/snow.html). Jon Snow plotted the locations of incidences of cholera against the location of water pumps, and noticed how the center of the epidemic seemed to focus on a certain neighborhood and was most concentrated in the households that clustered around the Broad Street water pump. Through the causal linkages, it was proven that when the contaminated pump was closed, the epidemic quickly came to a halt. Modern day epidemiology began when Jon Snow used mapping to identify the contaminated source. A map of just the water pumps or incidences of cholera would have been of little value. Following both the water pump network and the incidence revealed the contaminated source.

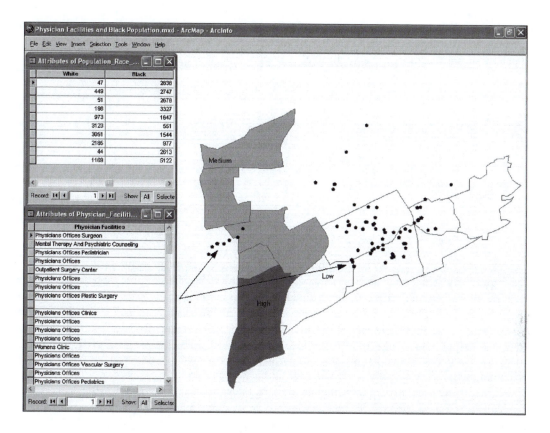

FIGURE 28.2 Black population and physician facilities by Census tracts, Birmingham, AL. Date source: US Census 2000 and 1997 Business Retention Survey, City of Birmingham. Map produced using ArcGIS 9.0 by ESRI.

Maps help us reveal relationships of spaces and objects that are in close proximity; as such, they give decision makers additional information, the best possible scenario of what may have been occurring in the real world. As Longley et al. observe, "By building representation [models using GIS], we humans can assemble far more knowledge about the planet than we could as individuals. We can build representations that serve such purposes as planning, resource management and conservation, travel, or the day-to-day operations of a parcel delivery service" (2001, 61).

28.3.1 USING GIS FOR PROBLEM SOLVING

GIS combines the science and art of decision making. If we perceive GIS as a communication tool, then how the information is communicated (visual presentation) can become more important than the underlying spatial reasoning (geographical information science). To make the most use of GIS capabilities we must learn the fundamentals of both the art and science of GIS. The art is described here as the final map for visual inspection by naked eye. For an effective use of this tool, it is not enough to have the knowledge of the data. Map analysis presupposes the availability of information about the characteristics of the area under investigation. Geographic information science, which is the science component of GIS, deals primarily with spatial reasoning. In most cases, however, how to create maps (technique) supersedes the underlying science behind map making (spatial analysis or spatial logic). For example, maps that show landfills in a neighborhood can be powerfully described with appropriate colors and schemes (map design and cartography). However, to determine the proximity of houses from the landfills, for example, would require some basic understanding of the science of GIS in addition to technique: digital maps have to be projected to the correct coordinate system, and the spatial attributes clearly delineated to reflect the correct measurement from the landfills. In other words, just like a social scientists who needs to hypothesize a model prior to his/her analysis (studying relationships using raw data), a GIS specialist needs to develop a geographic model to make a correct assessment of the real world phenomenon.

GIS users are a varied group ranging from high school students to NASA administrators. Similar to users of other tools, GIS beginners spend more time learning the art or technique of GIS using familiar software, than the underlying science behind the tool. Therefore, to describe the field of GIS in general, it would be more appropriate to categorize GIS by type of uses than the users. Here, for analytical simplicity, we can identify two broad uses of GIS: (1) cartography, and (2) geographic information analysis.

28.3.2 THE ART OF GIS-CARTOGRAPHY

Appearance gets the most attention at first. The last 8,000 years of mapping primarily dealt with the description of the objects on the surface of the earth. Cartographers aimed to place physical features precisely for navigation purposes. In the digital age, maps can also be prescriptive (what could be or what ought to be). For example, by changing the criteria of different data models (scenarios) we can visually compare the social and economic situation of areas under investigation, giving more emphasis to the underlying data behind the maps. What-if questions can be posed for creative thinking and to reach effective solutions to problems. Understanding and managing the data is an important part of cartography.

Cartography primarily works with drawings and graphics and aims to improve the visualization of maps so that they can easily be communicated. Cartography requires a certain amount of artistic skills so that maps can be presented in ways that are appealing and easy-to-understand, while ensuring the most accurate reflection of the real world phenomenon. Most cartographic models are temporally static, because they represent spatial features at a fixed point or points of time. Cartographic models are created according to their utility for specific uses. Such utilitarian maps tell the story in ways that help us understand our situation and surroundings in better ways. They facilitate a better understanding of the status quo (what is) and utilize that information to make strategic decisions (what could be).

In the tradition of utilitarian mapping, social scientists are using the ecological approach to solving social problems: GIS capabilities allow us to analyze relationships to nearby space and their characteristics and find creative ways of presenting the issues and identifying appropriate solutions. For example, using a descriptive map, we can ask the question of what is the neighborhood effect of high crime in a certain neighborhood. We can look at high crime areas (standardized by some measures, e.g., population density) and take note of other socioeconomic characteristics of the neighborhood (income, educational attainment, age of household, etc). We can visualize the neighborhood effects and compare them with similar "high crime" neighborhoods to reveal the commonality or the nuances that are important in understanding criminal behavior. We can take that information one step further and analyze it to answer questions such as: Do we need more police presence? What is the relationship between the crime rate and the quality of schools in the neighborhood? The GIS technology can be customized to create applications that routinely study these phenomena by updating existing data on a continuous basis. By analyzing the "hot-spots" overtime and showing them to stakeholders, we may be able to reach new strategic decisions for short- and long-term planning. By showing different scenarios in maps, GIS software can bring diverse group of stakeholders on one platform, and help develop innovative intervention plans to resolve conflicts effectively. Unlike in the ad-hoc approach to decision making and implementation, the GIS process will make decision making and implementation continuous, even simultaneous, and make final outcomes more effective and easier to interpret.

28.3.3 THE SCIENCE OF GIS—GEOGRAPHIC INFORMATION ANALYSIS

Geographic information analysis (or spatial analysis) involves the use of space as the primary denominator in decision making. A new scientific community of GIS users has emerged who works with digital images of the space (raster-based data) captured through satellites (satellite images and remote sensing data), and aerial photography. Although there is no clear way to distinguish a spatial analyst from a cartographer (both may be using the same GIS applications but for different purposes), the spatial analyst takes GIS at a different level of observation beyond discrete points of data (known as vector data), to continuous contours, or flow of points on space that form our geography of space (rivers, terrains, land, etc) and the objects on that space (buildings, trees, humans, etc). Such a level of geographic analysis requires that space be treated as a continuous variable as opposed to a discrete set of points (as in a snap shot). For geographic analysis the spatial models are dynamic in both space and time. These spatio-temporal models use spatially explicit inputs to calculate or predict spatially explicit outputs. They differ from cartographic models in that time is used explicitly as a variable that reflects changes in the spatial variables. For example, the dispersion of the debris in the ocean caused by natural or man-made disasters might be analyzed via a spatio-temporal model. These models can be best used to identify *processes* that lead to certain outcomes. We may predict the flooding of specific areas by a detailed spatial representation of the hydrologic cycle.[*] Intensity of rainfall can be studied for each raster cell.[†]

New areas have emerged within GIS; they aim to aid decision making better, using advanced spatial logic, such as optimum spatial decision making (OSDM), which uses fuzzy logic (see Zhou and Charnpratheep, 1996; Charnpratheep, Zhou, and Garner, 1997). In general, OSDM involves the analysis of factors and constraints that affect decision making. In contrast to conventional multi-criteria decision making analysis, spatial multi-criteria analysis requires information on criterion values and the geographical locations of alternatives in addition to the decision makers' preferences with respect to a set of evaluation criteria. This means analysis results depend not only on the geographical distribution of attributes, but also on the value judgments involved in the decision making process.

28.3.4 DECISION MAKING PLAYERS

According to Herbert Simon (1979) the process of developing a decision strategy consists of three broad phases: gathering intelligence on decision criteria, designing options to choose from, and choosing one of the options. Each phase is composed of four specific activities: gathering data (information), organizing the data, making selection based on said criteria, and reviewing the information. The GIS decision-making model follows the same logic described by Simon. However, the process for making decisions using maps is a collective endeavor and requires active participation by the group to make the best use of GIS decision-making capability. In this sense, GIS paves the way for a more horizontal approach, rather than a top-down approach to decision making. It commonly involves three categories of participants in the decision-making process: (1) stakeholders, (2) decision makers, and (3) technical specialists. The stakeholders (who directly or indirectly are affected by a decision) and the decision makers (who have the authority to execute the decision on behalf of the stakeholders) make up what can be named the GIS user group. The user group plays a critical role in formulating the plan for an effective decision. People who are primarily involved in creating maps form the support group (technical specialists). The support group's responsibility is critical in that they not only ensure the integrity of the map

---

[*] The circulation and conservation of earth's water is called the "hydrologic cycle".

[†] Raster data takes an evenly spaced grid (like a piece of graph paper) and places a value in each square, or cell, called raster cells. Aerial photographs and satellite images are examples of raster images used in mapping.

making system, but also determine how the real world could be accurately represented in the digital world. The support specialists can be divided into three broad groups: (1) database development technicians, who encode and maintain the spatial attribute databases; (2) data managers, who coordinate data integration and information flow, and maintain the GIS system; and (3) application specialists, who customize and facilitate development of specific spatial models (see Figure 28.3). Although the primary map users form the largest group, their participation may not contribute to better decisions unless they are familiar with the process of map making. Understanding the process builds confidence among the user group about the decision outcome. The art of using maps for better decision making lies in understanding the data reliability and in the integrity, reading, analysis and interpretation of the maps. GIS as a decision support tool is schematically explained in Figure 28.3.

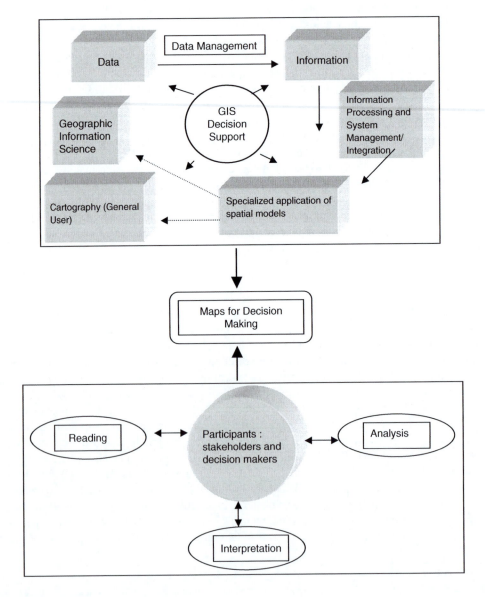

FIGURE 28.3 GIS Decision Support Process.

28.4 IMPLICATIONS OF GIS FOR DECISION MAKING IN DEMOCRACY

In the midst of complexity and uncertainty decision making can be seen as an attempt to impose a rational process on a non-rational environment. Decision making in a controlled environment (as is the case in the positivist approach) is notorious in imposing preconceived rational rules to social phenomena. Rather than investigating the whole phenomenon under consideration, a rational method would seek optimal solutions based on partial variables (mostly variables that are quantifiable). Such a controlled method is deemed inappropriate for conflict resolution because the problem must be addressed in context as a whole rather than in parts. Traditional decision-making models have focused on management options that search the technically optimal solutions. Yet in real life, the decisions dealing with social issues calls for social solutions. Non-quantifiable measures critical to conflict resolution, such as human values, attitudes, beliefs, judgment, trust, and understanding have a very limited (if any) presence in the traditional (rational) method.

GIS offers a new path to better, and rational, decision making, by taking advantage of the cutting edge information technology and having multiple stakeholders involved in the process. Instead of seeking an optimal solution to be generated by a small group of decision makers (primarily technocrats), GIS offers a computer-supported group approach: It engages diverse participants in problem exploration and negotiation. By using the branch method GIS allows making successive limited comparisons to adjust policy at the margins. In this sense, GIS promises a science of "muddling through," as it combines technocratic and pluralist approaches in social problem solving (Lindblom, 1959). GIS technology provides the means to alter social and political relationships through community participation in areas such as urban and environmental resource management planning and to make spatial information more adaptable for community use (Ghose, 2003; Elwood, 2001; 2002).

The collaborative nature of the GIS tools has attracted a new group of GIS practitioners who use them to have communities participate in decision making. Their approach is commonly known as the public participation geographic information systems (PPGIS). They use PPGIS methods to empower communities by enabling them to participate in critical decisions in housing, zoning, environmental equity, and sustainable developmental projects (Craig, Harris, and Winer, 2002). Because the most effective decision rules are made locally (in small groups), PPGIS explicitly recognizes local involvement in decision making, including the scale of analysis appropriate to the needs of the participant community, data products, and access to the information. PPGIS opens avenues for marginalized communities to take control of the decision making process before the technical details are finalized. The evolving technology of internet mapping and online multi-media capabilities will significantly contribute to PPGIS and further the empowering capacity of GIS.

It should be borne in mind, however, that the GIS technology only provides a set of tools that can be used in decision making to augment our capacity to make better decisions. It is not a substitute for either our cognitive abilities, or our responsibility in decision making. As with any other tool, we must balance its use—whether we use it to control and maintain the status quo (surveillance) or to change it, for example—with an understanding of the increasing socioeconomic complexities of the twenty-first century. Unlike the stand-alone applications of computer technology (e.g., word processors, spreadsheets, and statistical software) GIS technology is not just a set of applications; it offers a new way of understanding, managing, and displaying data. GIS users do not only need to learn the technical aspects of manipulating the data they use (e.g., type of data, and data storage and retrieval procedures), but also the new analytical concepts of spatial reasoning which form the basis of the transformation of real world data to computer screens in GIS applications.

28.5 CONCLUSION

The information technologies of the twenty-first century are empowering the government and the governed by giving access to information in unprecedented ways. New applications of information technology have great promises for decision makers but at the same time raise concerns about possible administrative abuses of power. Without self-conscious and socially conscious data management and interpretation and peer coordination, such technologies have the potential to misguide and harm us in ways that are yet unknown. Inappropriate uses of GIS in decision making could result from incorrect data manipulation and from misinterpretation of the data (Haque, 2003). The higher quality maps the GIS software can generate may be attractive to novice users, but they can be misleading and prevent them from making sound decisions. Important decisions affecting public policies will be left in the hands of technicians if decision makers do not learn how to process and display complex information.

REFERENCES

Barrett, K. and Greene, R., *Powering Up: How Public Managers Can Take Control of Information Technology*, CQ Press, Washington, DC, 2001.
Berry, J. K., *Beyond Mapping: Concepts, Algorithms, and Issues in GIS*, GIS World Books, Fort Collins, CO, 1993.
Bolstad, P., *GIS Fundamentals: A First Text on Geographic Information Systems*, Eider Press, White Bear Lake, MN, 2002.
Brown, M. M. and Brudney, J. L., A "smarter, better, faster, and cheaper" government, *PAR*, 58, 335–346, 1998.
Charnpratheep, K., Zhou, Q., and Garner, B. J., Preliminary landfill site screening using fuzzy geographical information systems, *Waste Management and Research*, 15, 197–215, 1997.
Craig, W., Harris, T. M., and Weiner, D., Eds., *Community Participation and Geographic Information Systems*, Taylor & Francis, New York, 2002.
Elwood, S., GIS and collaborative urban governance, *Urban Geography*, 22, 737–759, 2001.
Elwood, S., GIS in community planning, *Environment and Planning*, 34, 905–922, 2002.
Getting Started with GIS n.d. Who uses GIS and why http://www.gis.rgs.org/10.html (accessed August 9, 2005).
Ghose, R., Community participation, spatial knowledge production, and GIS use in inner-city revitalization, *Journal of Urban Technology*, 10, 39–60, 2003.
Haque, A., GIS, public service and the issue of democratic governance, *Public Administration Review*, 61, 259–265, 2001.
Haque, A., Information technology, GIS and democratic values, *Journal of Ethics and Technology*, 5, 39–48, 2003.
Huffman, L., More cities utilizing technology, *Government Technology*, 11(6), 44–49, 1998.
International City/County Management Association (ICMA), *Digital Government Survey*, ICMA/PTI, Washington, DC, 2004.
Jankowksi, P., Nyerges, T., Smith, A., Moore, T. J., and Horvath, E., Spatial group choice, *International Journal of Geographical Information Systems*, 11, 577–602, 1997.
Jankowksi, P. and Nyerges, T., *GIS for Group Decision Making*, CRP Press, New York, 2001.
Lindblom, C., The science of muddling through, *Public Administration Review*, 19, 79–88, 1959.
Longley, P., Goodchild, M., Maguire, D., and Rhind, D., Eds., *Geographic Information Systems and Science*, Wiley, New York, 2001.
Longley, P., Goodchild, M., Maguire, D., and Rhind, D., *Geographic Information Systems and Science*, 2nd Ed., Wiley, New York, 2005.
Masser, I., *Governments and Geographic Information*, Taylor & Francis, Bristol, PA, 1998.
Moll, G., Municipalities more than double GIS use, *Civil Engineering*, 69(6), 65–78, 1999.
Nedovic-Budic, Z. and Godschalk, D., Human factors in adoption of geographic information systems, *Public Administration Review*, 56, 554–568, 1996.
O'Looney, J., *Beyond Maps: GIS and Decision Making in Local Government*, ICMA, Washington, DC, 1997.
Rodriguez-Bachiller, A. and Glasson, J., *Expert Systems and Geographic Information Systems for Impact Assessment*, Taylor & Francis, London, 2004.
Simon, H., Rational decision making in business, *American Economic Review*, 69, 493–513, 1979.

Sliwinski, A., Spatial point pattern analysis for targeting prospective new customers, *Journal of Geographic Information and Decision Analysis*, 61, 31–48, 2002.

Thrall, G. I., *Business Geography and New Real Estate Market Analysis*, Oxford University Press, Oxford, 2002.

Ventura, S. J., The use of geographic information systems in local government, *Public Administration Review*, 55, 461–467, 1995.

Zhou, Q. and Charnpratheep, K., Fuzzy expert system and GIS for solid waste disposal siting in regional planning, *Geographical Information Sciences*, 2, 37–50, 1996.

29 Q Methodology and Decision Making

Dan W. Durning and Steven R. Brown

CONTENTS

29.1   Introduction...537
29.2   The Essentials of Q Methodology...538
    29.2.1   The Major Phases of Q Methodology..539
        29.2.1.1   Concourse..539
        29.2.1.2   Q-Sample Structure...540
        29.2.1.3   Q Sorting and P Sets...542
        29.2.1.4   Correlation...544
        29.2.1.5   Factor Analysis and Factor Rotation.................................546
        29.2.1.6   Factor Scores and Interpretation.......................................547
    29.2.2   Summary..548
29.3   Q Methodology to Study and Contribute to Decision Making.....................549
    29.3.1   Researching Decision Making with Q Methodology...........................549
    29.3.2   Types of Research to Identify Decision Structures............................549
        29.3.2.1   How Professionals Make Decisions...................................550
        29.3.2.2   Decisions Made by Specific Decision Makers...................551
        29.3.2.3   Decision Structures Related to Policy and Other Issues....552
        29.3.2.4   Decision Structures Using Single Cases 553
    29.3.3   Providing Information to Decision Makers 555
        29.3.3.1   Understanding a Decision Framework and Context...........556
        29.3.3.2   Identifying Competing Problem Definitions
                  and Related Solutions 556
        29.3.3.3   Identifying Solutions to Intractable Problems...................559
29.4   Conclusion...560
References...560

29.1 INTRODUCTION

The defining characteristic of decision making is that it involves freedom of choice. Choices are constrained to a greater or lesser degree, of course, but they exist within constraints—otherwise, no decision remains to be made. The exercise of choice reveals preferences, which are always *subjective* in the sense that from a decision maker's vantage point, one course of action is preferred over others, based on criteria with varying degrees of explicitness. Given the imperfect knowledge that characterizes most decisional situations, no objectively right answer can be known in advance; hence, discretion is intrinsic and ineradicable. However, traditional social science has generally been unable to understand acts of choosing and preferring because, as Morçöl (2002) suggested, it has been unable to shake a Newtonian tradition that lacks a way to qualify the subjectivity involved and looks instead for causes and contingencies that are objective and as unencumbered as possible by value considerations.

Q methodology is referred to as "the best-developed paradigm for the investigation of human subjectivity" (Dryzek and Holmes, 2002, 20). It provides a conceptual framework and systematic procedures for not only incorporating the participants' perspectives, but also placing them at the center of analysis. It has much in common with qualitative methods (Watts and Stenner, 2005), but it is more rigorous at the point of data analysis. Moreover, Q methodology runs parallel to quantum mechanics in mathematical respects and is in harmony with the post-Newtonian stance to which Morçöl (2002) refers.

Q methodology begins with decision makers' or stakeholders' thoughts and impressions typically expressed in their natural language—about Middle East peace, agricultural development, or any other topic that decision makers are called on to deliberate. Once gathered, the volumes of commentary comprising the concourse are reduced to a representative sample of assertions that participants use to represent their own individual views. The data are then correlated and the factors analyzed, and the resulting factors point to the various perspectives at issue. The factors that emerge implicate genuine divisions among decision makers and stakeholders, and they reveal a basis of cooperation as well as sources of conflict. Therefore, Q methodology can contribute to the study of decision making (i.e., to an understanding of why and how decisions are made) and can also assist in the pragmatics of making decisions by providing information to decision makers about such things as the points of confluence and division among stakeholders.

This chapter is concerned with both uses of Q methodology. How Q methodology can produce insights into decision making that are not available through traditional social science methodologies and how it can provide decision makers with information different from that generated by the usual analytic methods is explained. The following section introduces the essentials of Q methodology, explaining how Q-method research is structured and how it differs from the traditional statistical approach (referred to as *R methodology*). Next, the different ways that Q methodology has been used as a social science method to better understand decisions that have been made and as an analytic method that provides inputs into the decision making process are discussed.

29.2 THE ESSENTIALS OF Q METHODOLOGY

Researchers use R methodology, the statistical methods that dominate social science research, to identify the characteristics associated with such things as attitudes, opinions, or decisions of populations or samples. With these methods, they can find evidence that variables such as age, race, sex, and income do or do not have a statistically significant influence on a sample of Americans' decisions concerning their intention to vote. However, researchers cannot use these methods to enable a set of voters to reveal, in their full complexity, the preferences, values, and interests underlying their choices.

In contrast to R methodology, Q methodology provides researchers with the means to explore the complexity of thought leading to individual decisions such as whether or not to vote and if so, then for whom. It allows researchers to systematically investigate the subjectivity of individuals and to understand how individuals think about a topic. When the topic is a decision, Q methodology can identify the preferences, values, and interests of individuals or groups involved in making a decision or those likely to be affected by it.

Q methodology was invented in the 1930s by physicist–psychologist William Stephenson (1953) whose works have recently attracted renewed attention (Good, 1998, 2000, in press; Gross-wiler, 1994; Logan, 1991; Midgley and Morris, 2002; Smith, 2001, 319–343). Although initially used in psychology, it is now employed by researchers in many different disciplines. Research using Q methodology has been published in political science, sociology, anthropology, medicine, business, food science, and other journals across a variety of disciplines and professions.

In this section, details about the conceptual and technical sides of Q methodology as applied in concrete decisional situations are presented. In the next section, the use of Q methodology in research on decision making and in the production of analytic inputs into decision making is reviewed.

29.2.1 THE MAJOR PHASES OF Q METHODOLOGY

By way of preview, the volume of subjective communicability (i.e., what is being said or written) about any topic comprises the *concourse* for that topic, and from the concourse a *Q sample* is selected, which is a set of statements that is broadly representative of the contents of the concourse. Participants (referred to as a *P set*) are then asked to represent their viewpoints about the considered topic by ranking the statements in a *Q sort* from agree to disagree. The Q sorts are then subject to *correlation*, and the correlation matrix is *factor analyzed*, resulting in a typology of responses. The original factors are *rotated* to a meaningful solution, and *factor scores* are then calculated for each of the statements in each of the factors. These scores provide the basis for factor *interpretation.*[*]

29.2.1.1 Concourse

With regard to any event or topic, people express their opinions, views, beliefs, and feelings, and it this "subjective communicability" that is denoted by the term *concourse* (Stephenson, 1978). For instance, New Orleans' hurricane disaster of August 2005 spawned an outpouring of sentiment and commentary, such as the following, taken from newspapers across the U.S.:

- When local resources were overtaxed, the state of Louisiana should have stepped in with logistical help and manpower.
- New Orleans has played such a storied role in American life that anything less than full restoration is unthinkable.
- The commitment could easily reach $50 billion to recover from a disaster that could have been avoided with an investment of about $2 billion.
- The federal government was too slow to act.

Universes of opinion and sentiment such as those listed above are limitless and continue to grow, and they are distinguished from statements of fact such as "Katrina was a Category-5 hurricane at landfall," a fact that few would refute. Statements of fact are measured by barometers, wind-speed and rainfall instruments, humidity and dew point sensors, thermometers, and other meteorological devices as well as by the rating scales of social science. Statements that are conjectural at one point (e.g., that disease could bring a new wave of deaths) can become factual later just as accepted facts can lose their truth status in light of subsequent information.

Decision making situations are comprised of the same mixture of facts and opinions. For example, experts agree that approximately 660 wolves populated the Northern Rockies in 2002, but it is a matter of opinion whether the wolf should be removed from the list of protected species under the Endangered Species Act. Likewise, opinions proliferate concerning what to do about the wolf's predatory behavior (as it impacts ranchers' livelihoods), about who should be authorized to kill wolves, about what conditions are necessary for killing a wolf to be permitted, etc.

---

[*]For comprehensive statements on Q methodology, see Brown (1980) and Stephenson (1953). McKeown and Thomas (1988) provide a concise guide to the practical aspects of conducting a Q-methodological study.

The contours of problems as well as decisions about their solutions are contained in the concourse, which consists of all that can be thought and said about a situation, event, or phenomenon.

29.2.1.2 Q-Sample Structure

An ever-growing concourse can be of impractical magnitude when it comes to designing experiments because it can number into the thousands. Typically, it is desirable to take a sample from the concourse just as a geologist requires a rock sample or a pollster requires a respondent sample for more detailed study. Given the potentially limitless character of a concourse, however, it is not possible to define the boundaries of a statement universe (as can be done with a person population) as a prerequisite for statement sampling.

Rather than sampling statements randomly, Q methodology *models* a universe, using the experimental design principles advanced by Fisher (1935). As an illustration, Hall and Taylor (1996) articulated three different analytic approaches to new institutionalism—historical, rational choice, and sociological—and their article contains many conjectures such as those shown in the left-hand column:

From Hall and Taylor (1996):		Rephrased in Q sort as:
[*Historical*] Forces operating in a system are mediated by the contextual features of the given situation as inherited from the past, and institutions are central features of the historical landscape that push development along particular paths. (941)	→	The College and University context as well as the Department's own past are features of the landscape that are pushing them along their particular path.
[*Rational Choice*] Relevant actors have a fixed set of preferences or tastes; behave instrumentally so to maximize the attainment of these preferences, and do so in a highly strategic manner that presumes extensive calculation. (944–945)	→	Both students and faculty have preferences, and they calculate and behave in such a way as to maximize their preferences.
[*Sociological*] Institutions are not simply formal rules, procedures, and norms, but they are also symbol systems, cognitive scripts, and moral templates that provide meaning to guide human action. (947)	→	The Department is not simply a composite of rules and norms. It also contains subtle authority signals, cognitive scripts, and guides to appropriate conduct.

More than 100 such propositions were abstracted from this 20-page article, each assignable to one or another of the three varieties of new institutionalism. All of them were as general and abstract as those shown above. For practical purposes, Hall and Taylor's comprehensive coverage can serve as a concourse. In this case, 13 statements were selected from each of the three categories for a Q-sample size of $N = 39$. The aim of the exercise was more specific—to provide a Q sample that would be useful in describing the decision making context of a particular academic department—and so, as shown in the right-hand column above, each of Hall and Taylor's propositions was rephrased into more common terminology and rendered applicable to that department.

The institutionalism Q sample was structured in terms of the design shown in Table 29.1A. The Q-sample structure for a second study, focused on China–Taiwan relations, is in Table 29.1B, and it illustrates the more commonly used multi-dimensional factorial design. In this instance, the academic literature and popular press in China, Taiwan, and the U.S. were combed for salient statements, which were initially divided into pro-China and pro-Taiwan categories plus a residual category (unspecified) for those statements favoring neither side. To tie the study to a more comprehensive conceptual framework, the three categories of perspective were further subdivided into symbols (demand, identification, and expectation) explained by Lasswell and McDougal (1992, 352–353). Once categorized in the $3 \times 3 = 9$ cells, a set of $m = 3$ statements were drawn from each cell for a Q-sample size of $N = 27$ that was broadly representative of the issues involved in the Taiwan Strait.

TABLE 29.1A
Q-Sample Structure: New Institutionalisms

Main Effects	Levels		
Institutionalisms	(*a*) historical	(*b*) rational choice	(*c*) sociological

3 cells, $m = 13$ replicates per cell, $N = 3m = 39$ statements

TABLE 29.1B
Q-Sample Structure: Taiwan Strait Tensions

Perspectives	(*a*) China	(*b*) Taiwan	(*c*) unspecified
Symbols	(*d*) demand	(*e*) identification	(*f*) expectation

$(3)(3) = 9$ cells, $m = 3$ replicates, $N = 9m = 27$ statements

Statements representing one replication of the factorial design in Table 29.1B are as follows:

China	*Demand*: Although different living conditions exist between Taiwan and the Mainland, they should be overcome patiently so that unification is eventually achieved.
	Identification: If Chinese history since the Ming Dynasty is treated in the school curriculum as part of world history as proposed by some educational officials in the Chen Shuibian government, then this action would be intolerable. It would destroy the Chinese identity of the Taiwanese people.
	Expectation: Taiwan matters far more to China than it does to the U.S. Exactly how much blood and treasure China would be willing to expend is unclear, but it might be considerably more than the U.S. would be prepared to shoulder.
Taiwan	*Demand*: To master its own destiny, Taiwan needs to sever relations with Mainland China and establish a community with its own 23 million lives.
	Identification: For the past four hundred plus years, Taiwan has gradually developed its own historical and cultural identity, which is different from that of China. Taiwan has become a new nation.
	Expectation: Beijing's threat to use military force if the Taiwanese authority crosses the red line for independence as defined by Beijing, is an empty threat.
Unspecified	*Demand*: Both sides of the Strait should start by unifying economically and culturally, foster confidence, and seeking a new political framework that integrates the two.
	Identification: There are multiple understandings of the concept of One China that reflect the multiple races, ethnicities, and nationalities on both sides of the Strait.
	Expectation: War is inevitable in the Strait.

Just as persons comprise the sample in survey research, samples in Q methodology are comprised of statements or other measurable stimuli (i.e., samples are taken from domains of subjective expression).[*] This is an important point because critics often direct attention to the fact that Q methodology studies typically involve small numbers of cases, but "cases" in Q refer to statements rather than persons. In this regard, the function of Q-sample structures, such as the two shown in Table 29.1, is both pragmatic and theoretical. The ultimate goal is to obtain a set of statements that are *representative* of the concourse (stimulus domain) so that the Q sample used

---

[*] Q samples have also been comprised of political cartoons (Root, 1995; Trahair, 2003), photographs (Goldman, 1985), advertisements (Stephenson, 1994), country/western songs (Wacholtz, 1992), and even odors (Kim et al., 2003). In a practical decision making setting, a Q sample comprised of journal titles was presented to faculty who were asked to prioritize them (via Q sorting) as a way to determine which journals to retain and which to terminate in light of budgetary constraints (Dick and Edelman, 1993).

in obtaining participant perspectives contains the main features that are found in the statement universe in the same way that a sample of persons has features similar to those in the population. The Q-sample structure also enables the investigator to be theoretically explicit (e.g., about different kinds of institutionalism or about issues of demand and identification in China–Taiwan relations) and encourages thinking about the participant's Q sort in theoretical terms.

However, the Q-sample structure does not predetermine outcomes, nor does it depend on conventional issues of validity. In conventional scaling and questionnaire construction, the a priori meaning of items is often of great importance: There must be confidence that a scale such as the Decision Process Test (Brim, Glass, Lavin, and Goodman, 1962), actually measures what it is meant to measure. On the other hand, in Q methodology, it is of little importance whether a particular phrase can be properly considered rational choice rather than historical or socio-logical—or that a particular statement reflects a demand rather than an identification or expectation—because interest rests solely on the meaning attributed to the statement by the person who performs the Q sort rather than on a priori meanings imposed by social scientists. The actor's subjective understanding is of central importance, and no external criterion can serve to validate one point of view. Q-sample structures such as those in Table 29.1 are useful in providing criteria for selecting a sample of statements from a concourse and in providing some assurance that the sample contains diversity. Its purpose is not to impose iron-clad meaning that prevents the investigator from discovering how the participants actually think about the issues.

29.2.1.3 Q-Sorting and P Sets

After the Q sample is selected, each person included in a target set of individuals is asked to rank order the stimuli (usually statements comprising the Q sample) according to some *condition of instruction* (most often from agree to disagree). Table 29.2 is illustrative. This particular Q sort was provided by a member of a university department whose faculty had embarked on a self-study designed to provide suggestions for improving the department's research productivity. Table 29.2 displays the person's judgment about the relative utility of the $N = 40$ proposals nominated by the faculty during a brainstorming session. The 40 suggestions were printed one to a card, and each card was numbered randomly from 1 to 40. The person sorted them from beneficial ($+4$) to unbeneficial (-4) in the fixed distribution shown, to which all $n = 11$ faculty members adhered.[*]

It is unnecessary to provide details of this particular study, but the coherence of the Q-sort can be observed in those suggestions that are embraced and rejected by this person, *viz.*:

> *Most Beneficial (score +4)*: (1) Establish a faculty colloquium to share research and get feedback on pre-publication written work…, (3) Assign graduate assistants to those faculty members who publish the most…, (19) Permit faculty to teach overloads in the fall semester in exchange for light teaching loads in the spring so to increase research time…, (31) Maintain reduced course loads for the most productive faculty in the department.
>
> *Most Unbeneficial (score −4)*: (25) Do away with the category "in preparation" on vitae; focus on actual publications…, (26) Strive to publish monographs…, (29) Encourage the university to hire someone to spend time in DC pushing grant proposals…, (30) Establish a market in the department so that faculty can exchange teaching and research units.

---

[*] Hence, all Q sorts had the same mean ($\mu = 0.00$) and standard deviation ($\sigma = 2.46$). The so-called forced distribution underwent considerable criticism, virtually all of which has been based on the erroneous assumption that a quasi-normal curve, inasmuch as it is not natural to everyone, distorts some persons' responses. Actually, the distribution is a *model* (of the Law of Error) that is imposed on participants so as to induce them to make decisions that might otherwise be obscured. Statistically, the shape of the distribution has negligible effects on the results (Brown, 1980, 288–289).

TABLE 29.2
Strategic Planning Q sort

	Unbeneficial					Beneficial		
−4	−3	−2	−1	0	+1	+2	+3	+4
25	6	7	4	5	12	2	8	1
26	20	13	9	11	16	20	22	3
29	34	18	15	14	17	28	27	19
30	40	32	33	21	23	39	38	31
			37	24	35			
				36				

As is apparent, personal efficiency and departmental culture are of concern to this individual who wishes to be relieved of some undergraduate teaching burdens so to provide more opportunities for research. This person has little tolerance for intrusiveness, however: Note the downgrading of market mechanisms, of a dress code for vitae, and of privileging monographs. This person does not want the department to provide guidance, but to get out of the way. Normally post-sorting interviews take place to provide participants with the opportunity to elaborate on their choices, but in this instance, it was deemed more important to provide confidentiality so to induce more frankness. Therefore, identities were not revealed. It bears repeating that nothing in the above procedure leaves room for tests of validity. Q sorting merely provides the occasion for individuals to express their points of view in a formal and explicit way.

In the same way that statement samples are structured (see Table 29.1), person samples, or P sets, are also structured. In the preceding study of departmental decision making, it was both sensible and feasible to include all of the members of the organization (i.e., the entire population), but in most instances, the population is too large. It then becomes necessary to select a subset for study. Table 29.3 provides an illustration from a study of policy preferences concerning physician-assisted suicide (Newman, 2005). Three functional categories of actor were proposed: experts, authorities, and special interests. *Experts* are individuals who have special knowledge concerning an issue based on careful and prolonged study. In this case, care was taken to include as study participants persons who were academic philosophers with training in medical ethics or theology, physicians who deal with terminal illness (e.g., oncologists), and psychologists knowledgeable about depression. *Authorities* are persons who speak authoritatively because of their position in society such as members of the clergy, journalists, lawyers, and politicians. *Special interests* are those who have a stake in the outcome such as hospital administrators, hospice workers, people who are dying, and their relatives. Over and above interest, age (i.e., nearness to death) was also a factor

TABLE 29.3
P-Set Design

Effects				Levels				
Interests	(*a*) experts			(*b*) authorities			(*c*) special	
Age	(*d*) young			(*e*) middle			(*f*) elderly	
cells	ad	ae	af	bd	be	bf	cd	ce	cf

Source: From Newman, T. D., Links between ethics and public policy: A Q methodological study of physician assisted suicide and euthanasia. Doctoral dissertation, Kent State University, 2005, 173.

that was judged best not to leave to chance, so efforts were made to include individuals across the life span (young, middle-aged, and elderly).

These considerations gave rise to the $3 \times 3 = 9$ cells in Table 29.3. Hence, *ad* would be a young expert (e.g., a junior professor or doctoral student whose studies were focused on medical ethics), *ae* would be a person with the same kind of training but closer to mid-career, continuing down to *cf*, possibly an elderly person dying of cancer (*cd* could be a young person whose grandmother is dying), etc. The categories may be somewhat imprecise, but this is of little concern in Q methodology because these categories, unlike the demographics in conventional research, are not typically used for testing purposes. Testing whether experts have views that differ from special interests is not of interest here; to pursue that line of inquiry would require large numbers of cases. Rather, the purpose of the categories in Table 29.3 is to inject diversity into the P set so that if four separate perspectives exist in the population there will be reasonable opportunity to detect them. The Q-sample structure (Table 29.1) serves the same function—i.e., not to provide a basis for testing in a narrow sense but as a mechanism for minimally assuring that the statement set is sufficiently diverse so to permit the investigator to detect whatever different perspectives are in circulation.

29.2.1.4 Correlation

Notwithstanding the subjectivity inherent in Q sorting, responses can still be rigorously compared, and this comparison is usually accomplished through the application of correlation and factor analysis. Table 29.4 displays the calculations involved in correlation, using the response in Table 29.2 as Q-sort 1 and correlating it with the Q sort provided by another faculty member. As shown, statement number 1 received a score of $+4$ in Q-sort 1 and a score of 0 in Q-sort 2. This difference of $d = 4$, when squared, produces $d^2 = 16$. The squared differences are then summed across all 40 statements, and the resulting figure ($\Sigma d^2 = 458$) is entered into the formula for correlation. (The formula for Pearson's r shown in Table 29.4 assumes equal means and standard deviations for all Q sorts.) The correlation coefficient can range between ± 1.00 with 0.00 signifying an absence of relationship; consequently, the calculated value of $r_{1,2} = 0.05$ indicates that persons 1 and 2 are uncorrelated and do not share the same perspective about courses of action that would be beneficial to their department. Sometimes they are in agreement with one another and sometimes they are not as an inspection of Table 29.4 reveals.

For illustrative purposes, it is unnecessary to display the entire correlation matrix for all 11 Q sorts, the matrix for only five of which is shown in Table 29.5. Note the correlation of $r_{1,2} = 0.05$ as calculated above. However, the magnitude of the correlation between Q-sorts 1 and 3 ($r_{1,3} = 0.57$) suggests that these two individuals have similar views about which courses of action would be most beneficial for their department. Q-sort 2, which is unrelated to the other two ($r_{1,2} = 0.05$, $r_{2,3} = 0.00$), appears to have a considerable amount in common with Q-sort 4 ($r_{2,4} = 0.55$). This raises the specter of factionalism, with colleagues 1 and 3 entertaining one vision for their department and 2 and 4 a different vision; colleague 5 could prove pivotal inasmuch as this person's preferences bridge both groups, or at least the correlations alone suggest as much.

Attention rarely focuses on the $n \times n$ correlation matrix (where n equals the number of Q sorts), which is merely a temporary state through which data pass on the way to revealing their structure. On some occasions, however, it can be important to determine if two Q sorts are significantly correlated. (Were number 5 the department chair, for instance, interest might focus on which colleagues agreed significantly with the chair and which disagreed.) For determinations of this kind, reliance is placed on statistical criteria. For instance, the standard error of a zero-order correlation is given by the expression $\sigma_e = 1/\sqrt{N}$ where N is the number of Q statements. In the instant case, $\sigma_e = 1/\sqrt{40} = 0.16$, and under the normal curve, 99% of randomly generated responses would fall between $2.58\sigma_e = 2.58(0.16) = \pm 0.41$. In Table 29.5, Q-sort 5 is shown to be significantly correlated with number 2 ($r_{2,5} = 0.43$, $p < 0.01$) and with number 3 ($r_{3,5} = 0.50$, $p < 0.01$), both of which are in excess of .41.

TABLE 29.4
Correlation Between Q sorts

Statements	Q sorts 1	Q sorts 2	d^2
1	4	0	16
2	2	4	4
3	4	2	4
4	−1	−2	1
5	0	2	4
6	−3	3	36
7	−2	4	36
8	3	4	1
9	−1	3	16
10	−2	−3	25
11	0	1	1
12	1	−1	4
13	−2	1	9
14	0	−4	16
15	−1	2	9
16	1	0	1
17	1	0	1
18	−2	1	9
19	4	1	9
20	−3	1	16
21	0	−4	16
22	3	−2	25
23	1	−2	9
24	0	−4	16
25	−4	−4	0
26	−4	−2	4
27	3	3	0
28	2	0	4
29	−4	−1	9
30	−4	0	16
31	4	2	4
32	−2	−3	1
33	−1	3	16
34	−3	4	49
35	1	−3	16
36	0	−1	1
37	−1	−1	0
38	3	−3	36
39	2	−1	9
40	−3	0	9

$$\sum d^2 = 458$$

$$r_{1,2} = -\frac{\sum d^2}{2N\sigma^2} = 1 - \frac{458}{(2)(40)(2.46)^2} = 1 - \frac{458}{484} = 1 - 0.95 = 0.05$$

TABLE 29.5
Correlations Among 5 Q sorts (from original 11 × 11 matrix)

	Q sorts				
	1	**2**	**3**	**4**	**5**
1	—	0.05	0.57	0.17	0.34
2	0.05	—	0.00	0.55	0.43
3	0.57	0.00	—	0.12	0.50
4	0.17	0.55	0.12	—	0.24
5	0.34	0.43	0.50	0.24	—

29.2.1.5 Factor Analysis and Factor Rotation

Q methodology is an outgrowth of factor theory as it developed in the early decades of the twentieth century. In fact, Stephenson, the inventor of Q methodology, was the final doctoral student to study under Charles Spearman, the inventor of factor analysis, when both were at the University of London in the late 1920s. Space precludes going into technical details, which are covered elsewhere.[*] Suffice to say that factor analysis examines a correlation table such as the one shown in Table 29.5 and determines the number of subgroups (referred to as *factors*) that are present. If all 11 participants ranked the 40 items in essentially the same order—i.e., had there been general agreement about which courses of action would be most beneficial to the department—then only a single factor would be in evidence. On the other hand, were each person's view unique, then there would be 11 separate factors (and no hope of locating a consensus).

Table 29.6 shows the factor-analytic results for the situation under consideration, and three perspectives are in evidence (Factors A, B, and C).[†] The same standard error procedures previously explained apply to the factor loadings in this matrix: With $N = 40$ statements, loadings in excess of 0.41 are considered to be significant. So it can be seen that Factor A is defined by participants 2, 4, and 8; that is, these participants have ranked the statements in highly similar patterns and presumably share a common understanding of those courses of action that would be beneficial to their department. Similarly, Factor B is defined by participants 1, 6, and 11 who share an understanding of their own; and Factor C is defined by participants 5, 9, and 10 who share yet a third perspective. Participants 3 and 7 are *mixed* cases, which means that they have expressed viewpoints that share something in common with more than one of the three subgroups. Although not in evidence in this study, *null* cases are also possible; i.e., persons who express views that have nothing in common with the other participants and hence are not saturated significantly with any factor.

Conventional factor-analytic studies examine the relationships among traits and variables; hence, they usually go no farther than the matrix of factor loadings. In Q methodology, interest does not primarily center on which persons group together in the factors; rather, it is in gaining access to those belief and preference systems that underlie the factors. What is the character of that

---

[*] For simplified presentations of factor analysis, consult Adcock (1954), Brown (1980, 208–224) and Kline (1994). It is currently less necessary to possess substantial knowledge about factor analysis than was the case two decades ago given the availability of software packages such as PQMethod (Schmolck and Atkinson, 2002) and PCQ (Stricklin and Almeida, 2004), which are dedicated to Q data.

[†] The factor solution in Table 29.6 was reached using the principal components method followed by varimax rotation, and these are the most conventional of the alternatives available for purposes of factor extraction and rotation. In Q methodology, however, factor extraction is often accomplished using the centroid method. Factor rotation is increasingly pursued on the basis of theoretical considerations (Brown and Robyn, 2004), both of which are rarely used outside Q methodology.

TABLE 29.6
Matrix of Factor Loadings

	Factors		
Ps	A	B	C
1	16	**84**	29
2	**62**	−17	38
3	−14	**68**	45
4	**87**	07	12
5	12	13	**86**
6	37	**64**	−03
7	**54**	19	45
8	**66**	17	13
9	26	10	**79**
10	39	18	**62**
11	−01	**69**	01

Decimals to two places omitted; significant loadings ($p < 0.01$) in boldface.

perspective shared by participants 2, 4, 7, and 8 in Table 29.6; how does that perspective differ from the one shared by persons 1, 3, 6, and 11?

To answer these questions, the Q sorts of those persons who define a factor are merged to form a single Q sort, although this merging gives greater emphasis to some Q sorts compared to others just as variables are weighted differently in multiple regression analysis. Factor weights are calculated using the expression $w = f/(1 - f^2)$ where f is the person's loading on a factor and w is the weight. For the purely defining Q-sorts comprising Factor A, the weight calculations are as follows:

$$Q\text{-sort } 2: \quad f_2 = 0.62 \quad w_2 = 0.62/(1 - 0.62^2) = 1.01$$

$$Q\text{-sort } 4: \quad f_4 = 0.87 \quad w_4 = 0.87/(1 - 0.87^2) = 3.58$$

$$Q\text{-sort } 8: \quad f_8 = 0.66 \quad w_8 = 0.66/(1 - 0.66^2) = 1.17$$

Consequently, Q-sort 4, which is more saturated with Factor A than are Q-sorts 2 and 8, counts more than the other two combined in the process of their merger.

29.2.1.6 Factor Scores and Interpretation

The end result in this instance is three separate factor Q sorts (in the same format as shown in Table 29.2) that epitomize the views of the individuals comprising the respective factors. Representative factor scores for Factors A, B, and C are shown in Table 29.7, and their presentation and interpretation constitute the final step of any Q-methodological study.

Statements 6, 19, and 28 are statements that distinguish the three factors from one another. These statements, in conjunction with the scores for all 40 of the statements, lead to the conclusion that Factor A is mainly concerned with boosting the volume of publications ("Any publication is better than nothing"), that Factor B is interested in altering departmental routines so to provide more discretionary time for research ("teach overloads in the fall semester in exchange for light teaching loads in the spring..."), and that Factor C is interested in departmentally sponsored faculty-renewal programs. (Space precludes other than these facile factor interpretations, which

TABLE 29.7
Factor Scores for Select Statements

		A	B	C
	Distinguishing Statements			
6.	Any publication is better than nothing. Don't be vain.	+4	−3	−4
19.	Permit faculty to teach overloads in the fall semester in exchange for light teaching loads in the spring to increase research time.	0	+4	0
28.	Initiate in-service series for faculty renewal to increase exposure to new ideas.	−1	+2	+4
	Consensus Statements			
1.	Establish a faculty colloquium to share research and get feedback on pre-publication written work.	+4	+4	+4
8.	Hold internal competitions to fund conferences with awards going to those whose proposals are most likely to result in edited books.	+2	+3	+4
31.	Maintain reduced course loads for the most productive faculty in the department.	+4	+4	+3

are normally based on detailed consideration of all statement scores in each of the factors.) Keeping in mind that this particular department had been in a prolonged state of conflict, what was of particular interest were the proposals that achieved a high degree of consensus across the board—to establish a colloquium series (Statement 1 in Table 29.7), to establish a program of funding competitive projects leading to conferences and publications (statement 8), and to reduce course loads for the most productive members (Statement 31).[*]

The output from the factor analysis and factor rotation includes a matrix showing the scores for each statement ($N = 40$ in this illustration) in each factor. Also, the output from the PQMethod or PCQ programs provides additional information such as the factor loadings of each person completing a Q-sort (Table 29.6 is an example) to assist with the interpretation. Using information about the scores for each statement and the factor loadings of each person completing the Q sort, the researcher can identify the characteristics of the Q sorters associated with each perspective.

29.2.2 SUMMARY

Before turning to summaries of the application of Q methodology to various decision making situations, it is worth condensing the main ideas presented to this point. Around any decisional situation are volumes of communicability, much of it subjective in character (i.e., matters of opinion and conjecture). From this concourse of communicability is taken a Q sample for purposes of experiment, and this sample is administered in the form of a Q sort to relevant participants who represent their own individual points of view. The factor analysis of these Q sorts reveals a small number of decision structures (i.e., perspectives that recommend courses of action). The factors are functional in nature and may or may not correspond to the traits and variables typically relied upon in explaining decision making behavior.

---

[*] It is noteworthy that this department, which had been chronically riven, promptly implemented these proposals at its next meeting once it was recognized that none of these suggestions was opposed by any of the factions.

29.3 Q METHODOLOGY TO STUDY AND CONTRIBUTE TO DECISION MAKING

As noted in the Introduction and shown in the examples cited in the previous section, Q methodology is relevant to decision making not only because it provides a general approach for the study of subjectivity in any and all of its manifestations (Brown, 1980, 2004; Brown, Durning, and Selden, 1999; McKeown and Thomas, 1988; Robbins, 2005; Stephenson, 1953) but also because of its utility in facilitating decision making. In this part of the chapter, how Q methodology has been employed for both purposes is further examined.

29.3.1 RESEARCHING DECISION MAKING WITH Q METHODOLOGY

Consider a decision made by a college board of trustees to abolish its graduate degree program in Latin. The decision was made, after much debate, by a vote of nine trustees in favor of abolishing the program, five opposing, and two not voting. As a result of this decision, two faculty members and one staff member will lose their jobs, and resources will be moved elsewhere.

If there was a desire to understand why the trustees made this decision, then a study of them from a variety of perspectives would take place. Political scientists might want to examine what variables influenced their votes (i.e., what characteristics of the trustees were associated with a "yes" vote), or how the leader of the effort was able to gather a winning coalition (i.e., what deals were made). Sociologists might be interested in the group dynamics and power relationships that led to the decision. Economists might examine how the costs and benefits were calculated to understand the balance of opportunity costs and willingness to pay for the Latin program.

Another way of researching this decision would be to seek to understand what was going on in the minds of the trustees when they voted on the issue: What was the configuration of values, beliefs, interests, and information that influenced each vote (the person's decision) on whether the degree program should be eliminated? Such research would be designed to understand the decision structures that led the individuals to decide how to vote on the issue.

The term *decision structures* refers to the influences of different judgments on individual decisions.[*] Stephenson (1973) suggested that influences on individual decisions (multi-valued choice) include judgments about (1) the relative importance of different facts that have been collected (named "reality judgments" by Vickers (1965)), (2) personal values, (3) instrumental considerations (requirements for effecting a course of action), and (4) the relative significance of reality judgments, personal values, and instrumental considerations (Stephenson, 1973, 18).[†]

These judgments are all subjective, and Q methodology provides a means to identify the various judgments of each decision maker and their relative influence on the decisions—in other words, it can reveal an individual's decision structure. Thus, Q methodology can assist researchers in understanding what values, information, interests, and ideology influenced the decisions of the trustees when they voted to abolish the Latin program.

29.3.2 TYPES OF RESEARCH TO IDENTIFY DECISION STRUCTURES

Researchers have employed Q methodology in at least four different ways to identify decision structures, which is discussed in more detail below: (1) How professionals make decisions—their mode of thought and the factors that have had the greatest impact on their decisions; (2) the factors

---

[*] The term *decision structure* is borrowed from Harold Lasswell (1963, 221); also see Stephenson (1987) and Brown (1998). The operant factors resulting from a Q methodology analysis have also been described as "coherent schemata" (Stephenson, 1973), "frames" (Dayton, 2000), "narratives" (Webler et al., 2003), and perspectives, among other things.

[†] Similarly, Weiss (1983) maintained that individuals form their positions on decisions to be made through an interaction of interests, ideology (beliefs), and information related to the issue being considered. The I-I-I configuration of a person can be understood as that person's decision structure related to a particular issue.

that have influenced decisions by a specific set of decision makers on a particular issue (e.g., the trustees' decision to end the Latin program); (3) the dominant decision structures related to a particular issue, e.g., how decision makers and groups of stakeholders are influenced by different factors (values, beliefs, interests, knowledge) when taking a position on or making a decision concerning an issue such as global warming or banning the burning of the U.S. flag; and (4) the decision structures of single individuals who have found themselves in a position to choose a course of action relative to a public issue or a private undertaking.

29.3.2.1 How Professionals Make Decisions

Q methodology has helped researchers identify the decision structures of professionals in diverse areas. Two examples of this type of research are by Brown (2002), who used Q methodology to compare how four different types of professionals make decisions in complex and ambiguous situations; and by Wong, Eiser, Mrtek, and Heckerling (2004) who identified shared subjective influences on clinical decision making among participant physicians facing cases with common ethical issues.[*]

Brown's (2002) research showed that Q methodology provides a superior *functional* alternative to the *structural* approach used by Fernandes and Simon (1999) who wanted to understand how different types of professionals (architects, physicians, engineers, and lawyers) with different professional educations and experience reach understandings and make decisions in complex and ambiguous situations. To do so, Fernandes and Simon asked two members of each profession to contemplate a paradoxical case; they then summarized the results in terms of professional categories. The hypothetical case was as follows:

> "As a senior policy maker in your country you are called upon to advise an international organization about what is needed to solve a specific policy problem in a country called Hungeria. Please explain what other information you might need to solve this problem and then what your recommendations would be.... Hungeria, with a population of 26 million, has nearly four million people who exist below the poverty line and around one million people who are undernourished and hungry because they do not have sufficient food to eat. In estimating the numbers of people going hungry the Food and Agriculture Organization of the United Nations (FAO) uses as its criterion the energy intake level at which a person can barely survive, which is a daily calorie intake below 1.2 basal metabolic rate (around 2100 calories). Hungeria has a gross domestic product (GDP) of $638 billion and is a net food exporting country. The birth rate in Hungeria is 15 per thousand and the death rate is 8 per thousand." (231–232)

Fernandes and Simon collected the responses, queries, observations, assertions, and recommendations of each person participating in the study. They then categorized and counted the frequencies of each, using the categories established prior to the interviews. Based on their statistical analysis, they concluded (among other things) that professionals use actions more often than meta-actions; lawyers and engineers are more inclined to issue recommendations, and architects tend to rely more on queries and evaluations.

As an alternative, Brown constructed a Q sort comprised of the queries, observations, assertions, and recommendations that Fernandes and Simon elicited from the participants in their study supplemented by additional interview responses. This Q sort was then administered to 37 persons, some in the target professions and others not, who were asked to place the statements in an array from $+4$ (very much on my mind when making the decision) to -4 (far from my mind when making the decision) in a quasi-normal distribution. The Q sorts were factor analyzed as usual, and the five factors that emerged, contrary to the assumptions of Fernandes and Simon, were not dominated by any one of the professions. For example, medical personnel, an engineer, and lawyers clustered together on one of the factors. In sum, through the use of Q methodology, the

---

[*] Another example is Babcock-Lumish (2004) who shows how individuals in the "innovation investment community" (e.g., entrepreneurs and venture capitalists) perceive decisions to make risky investments in "early stage investments."

subjectivity intrinsic to the participants was allowed to reveal itself rather than being constrained by an imposed structure based on professional training.

In the same fashion, Wong et al. (2004) conducted research to identify the factors that influence physicians involved in ethical decision making. The researchers formulated four hypothetical case studies involving urgent decision making near the end of life. Then they asked 35 physicians and house staff at a Midwestern academic health sciences center to read each case and to select one of three clinical actions they would take for that case. The following is an example of one of the four scenarios placed before the participants:

"Mr. J. is 85 years old, living in a nursing home because of advanced dementia. You cared for Mr. J for many years prior to his dementia. He has now developed pneumonia and is transferred to an acute care hospital. Despite treatment with antibiotics, his clinical status deteriorates and his CO_2 is elevating and his O_2 is desaturating. A decision to intubate Mr. J. or not needs to be made. His next-of-kin, a nephew, lives out west and is unavailable for comment....

As his attending physician, you would:

(a) Intubate and ventilate Mr. J. and move him to the ICU. [aggressive]
(b) Provide comfort care after consulting another physician who concurs that treatment would be futile. [supportive]
(c) Consult an ethicist or ethics committee concerning the decision. [advice seeking]"

After selecting the preferred choice, participants were asked to complete a Q sort with 25 statements focused on possible influences on their recommendations, such as "My knowledge of the patient's wishes prior to the illness," "What the law requires," and "What I feel is most moral." These statements were sorted from -4 (least influential) to $+4$ (most influential). After the Q sorts were completed, the researchers conducted an interview with each participant to assist in understanding the person's thought processes during the Q sorting.

Factor analyses of the four separate correlation matrices (four Q sorts from each of 35 participants) identified a total of 17 factors, which were then reanalyzed using a second-order factor analysis (i.e., a factorization of all of the case-based factors). The second-order analysis resulted in three decision structures (representing underlying ethical perspectives), which were labeled (1) patient-focused beneficence, (2) a patient- and surrogate-focused perspective that included risk avoidance, and (3) best interest of the patient guided by ethical values. The authors found that decisions were not influenced substantially by their economic impact on the physician, their expediency in resolving the situation, or the expense of medical treatment. They concluded with two interesting subjective findings—that the decision strategies captured in the factors were context-bound and reflected well-known bioethical principles, and the complexity apparent in the many factors associated with the four scenarios could be reduced to only three second-order factors accounting for a large proportion of the variance.

29.3.2.2 Decisions Made by Specific Decision Makers

In addition to research on how professionals make decisions, Q methodology can also be used to identify the decision structures of decision makers in the process of addressing specific problems examples of which are studies conducted by Webler et al. (2003) and Donahue (2004). Webler et al. used Q methodology to explore factors influencing local government officials in New England to participate or refuse to participate in regional collaborative environmental policymaking on watershed management planning. The authors created a sample of 52 statements based on interviews, and the Qsort was administered to 39 local government officials in New Hampshire, Massachusetts, and Connecticut where these planning processes were active. Analysis resulted in five factors, which were interpreted by the authors as coherent narratives (i.e., decision structures) that captured basic perspectives of the local officials toward the opportunity to participate in a watershed management planning process—one factor centered on calculations influencing outcomes, a second weighing on interests and time, a third on assessing community benefits, a fourth on rooted personal environmental ethics, and a fifth that attempted to match skills and experiences with the requirements of the policy endeavor. The authors concluded that local government officials made their decision to participate or not based on three general considerations: if they felt that they could make a difference, if they saw working on the problem as consistent with their environmental ethic, and if they viewed their participation as in their community's interest.

Donahue (2004) used Q methodology to identify the factors affecting the decisions of fire chiefs about the level of fire protection that their local fire departments would provide. The study was motivated by a model suggesting that fire chiefs' decisions are influenced by the managerial environment, which is defined as internal and external pressures measured in terms of five dimensions: professional, social, fiscal, political, and technological. Managerial activities and decisions involve the making and implementing of decisions with respect to the use and mix of production inputs (firefighters, tools, trucks), which leads to outputs (fire prevention and suppression activities) and to outcomes (annual losses of property and lives).

To understand how fire chiefs perceive their managerial environments, Donahue interviewed a large number of them about the topic and attended several meetings of fire chiefs' groups. On these occasions, she recorded statements and from them, she extracted a sample of 40 to comprise the Q sort, which was administered to 32 fire chiefs in 20 counties in central New York. The P set included 18 full time and 14 volunteer fire chiefs, and the fire departments represented included 13 with full time staff members, 12 with volunteer staff members, and 7 with combinations of full time and volunteer. Analysis revealed four factors that were distinguished by whether the external and internal environments were perceived to be harsh or mild. As shown in Table 29.8, 10 of 14 volunteer fire chiefs, but only 2 of 16 full-time chiefs, were part of the low-pressure factor. Conversely, 12 of 16 full-time fire chiefs, but only 2 of 14 volunteer chiefs, were in Factors 2 and 4, which are characterized by harsh external environments. Donahue concluded that although these results cannot be generalized, they do suggest patterns that could guide future research.

29.3.2.3 Decision Structures Related to Policy and Other Issues

An additional use of Q methodology in understanding decision structures focuses on the values, beliefs, interests, and knowledge that underlie the competing positions of decision makers, stakeholders, and issue publics. Issues can be in either private or public realms, but the best documented examples are related to broad public policy areas (e.g., environmental policies) or specific controversies (e.g., abortion). Studies of this type have addressed a variety of issues, including forests (Clark, 2002; Steelman and Maguire, 1999), land use (Swaffield and Fairweather, 1996), water

TABLE 29.8
Four Managerial Environments

Factor		External Environment	Internal Environment	Managerial Style	Full Time Chiefs	Volunteer Chiefs
1	Low Pressure	Mild	Mild	Very Centralized	2	10
2	Moderate Pressure	Harsh	Mild	Centralized	8	0
3	High Pressure	Mild	HarshD	Very Participatory	2	2
4	Very High Pressure	Harsh	Harsh	Participatory	4	2

Source: From Donahue, A.K. *Administration and Society*, 35, 717–746, 2004.

resources (Focht, 2002), coastal zone management (Shilin, Durning, and Gajdamaschko, 2003), nature restoration (Woolley and McGinnis, 2000), wolf management (Byrd, 2002), biotechnology in Mexico (Galve-Peritore and Peritore, 1995), food security (Pelletier, Kraak, McCullum, Uusitalo, and Rich, 1999; Wilkins, Kraak, Pelletier, McCullum, and Uusitalo, 2001), corrections policy (Baker and Meyer, 2002, 2003), and diversity in New Zealand (Wolf, 2004).

Illustrative of these types of studies are Hooker's (2001) study of how stakeholders think about the relationship of individuals and society to forests, and Deitrick's (1998) research on how stakeholders in Pittsburgh perceive the issue of how brownfields should be redeveloped. Hooker sought to illuminate the competing concepts of preservation, conservation, and development that influence individual perspectives on forest policy. To this end, she created a 60-statement Q sort from hundreds of propositions taken from the literature on forest and natural resource policy, and she administered these in the form of a Q sort to a select group of diverse participants, including forest landowners, government officials, forest industry representatives, trade association representatives, scientists, leaders of conservation groups, academics, and public interest group representatives. Hooker's analysis identified five factors (i.e., five perspectives, or decision structures) that influence the positions that people take on forestry issues—labeled New Stewards, New Conservationists, Individualists, Traditional Stewards, and Environmental Activists—which she interpreted in terms of different but sometimes overlapping views on policies regarding the use of forests.

The purpose of Deitrick's (1998) research was to determine the different stakeholder views on proposals to redevelop brownfields in Pittsburgh. Consequently, she constructed a 24-statement Q sort from interviews with stakeholders (people with a direct interest in the brownfields issue), newspaper articles, letters to the editor, and other published materials. She then asked stakeholders from the private, public, and non-profit sectors plus community activists in the areas affected by brownfields to represent their views as Q sorts. Analysis identified three perspectives, or decision structures, related to this issue, which she labeled (1) the development perspective, (2) the community-environmental nonprofit/activist perspective, and (3) the technical perspective.

29.3.2.4 Decision Structures Using Single Cases

In his article on "How to Make a Cup of Tea," Stephenson (1987) explained how and why Q methodology can be used to identify decision structures through examination of single cases, asserting that "The $n = 1$ methodology for subjective science can provide authentic decision structures..."(44). Several studies have used Q methodology for this purpose (see Baas, 1997; Brown, 1998; Brown and Kil, 2002; Taylor, Delprato, and Knapp, 1994). An example of this genre explicitly focused on decision making is presented by Brown (1993–1994), who tested Downs's (1957) hypothesis that the rational voter "approaches every situation with one eye on the gains to be had, the other eye on costs, a delicate ability to balance them, and a strong desire to follow wherever rationality leads" (7–8).[*]

The concourse was drawn from newspaper accounts of current government activities from which was selected a representative Q sample structured in terms of Lasswell's eight value categories (Lasswell and McDougal, 1992)—e.g., reduce taxes (wealth), legalize prayer in the schools (rectitude), subsidize the arts (enlightenment), etc. In all, four statements were selected for each of the eight values for a Q sample of size $N = 32$ statements.

---

[*] Formally, Downs (1957) states that the rational voter compares the utilities expected from Party A (U^A) with those expected from Party B (U^B), both before the election (t) and, as a matter of expectation, after the election ($t+1$) with the difference ($U^A - U^B$) being the expected party differential (38–39). Among the yardsticks employed to determine a performance rating is knowledge of a party's policies, which are compared against the voter's conception of the ideal government in a good society (46).

On successive days, the Q sort was administered to a single person (Ms. X) who was asked to sort the 32 statements according to the following experimental conditions sponsored by Downs's theory:

1. *Self*: arrange these policies from those that you personally prefer $(+4)$ to those you oppose (-4).
2. *Gain*: from those policies from which you would personally stand to gain the most $(+4)$ to those from which you would stand to lose the most (-4).
3. *Cost*: those that would cost you most $(+4)$ to least (-4).
4. *GOP$_t$*: those policies that the incumbent Republicans are emphasizing/de-emphasizing during the current election.
5. *Dem$_t$*: those that the Democrats are emphasizing/de-emphasizing.
6. *GOP$_{t+1}$*: those policies that the Republicans are apt to pursue if elected.
7. *Dem$_{t+1}$*: and the same for the Democrats.
8. *Good society*: policies that would be enacted/opposed in a hypothetical good society.

Ms. X's sorts were correlated and factor analyzed, and the factors were theoretically rotated to explore whether Downs's hypothesis could explain the decisional stance taken by Ms X. As the rotations progressed, it was noted that contrary to theoretical expectations, Ms. X's personal policy preferences (*Self*) were not associated with either costs or gains as shown in Table 29.9, which demonstrates that Ms. X's policy preferences (Factor I) are not governed by considerations of gains (Factor II) or costs (Factor III), at least on the surface; rather, her preferences are connected to normative considerations of the good society, which she sees as also aligned with the way in which the Democratic Party (with which she identifies) would conduct itself following the election. The campaign dynamics, as X experiences them, are also apparent: Both the Republicans (Q-sort 4, Factor I) and Democrats (Q-sort 5, Factor I) are making appeals that are compatible with her personal preferences (Q-sort 1, Factor I). To some extent, the Republicans favor policies that would benefit her personally (Q-sorts 2 and 4 on Factor II). However, her expectation is that following the election, the Republicans will seek to implement policies that are the reverse of her own preferences (Q-sort 6, Factor I-negative).

Table 29.10 displays some of the scores for Ms. X's factors and provides more insight into her way of thinking. As demonstrated, she favors increased social security payments (Factor I, policy *a*), the retraining of the jobless (*d*), and reduction of pollution (*e*), even though she would only benefit from the latter. (At age 40, economically well off, and not subject to social security, she was nevertheless concerned about aging parents and the poor and jobless more generally.) And although

TABLE 29.9
Ms. X's Factors

		Factors		
		I	II	III
1	Self	88	28	−23
2	Gain	02	45	−19
3	Cost	−05	−16	79
4	GOP$_t$	61	64	14
5	Dem$_t$	61	−02	26
6	GOP$_{t+1}$	−55	11	22
7	Dem$_{t+1}$	48	−21	35
8	Good society	67	28	−10

TABLE 29.10
Factor Scores (Ms. X's Factors)

	I	II	III
(a) Increase social security payments.	+4	−4	−3
(b) Reduce taxes.	−3	+3	−3
(c) Fund more missiles.	−4	−1	+4
(d) Retrain the jobless.	+3	−3	+3
(e) Reduce pollution.	+2	+3	+4

she is aware that she would benefit from tax reductions (policy *b*, +3 on Factor II), she opposes them (−3 on Factor I) so social programs (such as retraining the jobless) can be paid for because these programs are apt to be expensive (+3 on Factor III). Pollution reduction (*e*) is regarded as beneficial (+3 on Factor II) and so it was embraced (+2 on Factor I) despite the fact that it will be costly (+4 on Factor III). In short, Ms. X has a *rationale* even though she might not be judged *rational* in Downs' sense.

At the beginning of this chapter, it was asserted that Q methodology runs parallel to quantum theory in many respects, and this is most clearly seen in relation to single cases as in the case of Ms. X above. Factors I, II, and III are intrinsic to Ms. X and are brought to light through administration of the eight experimental conditions shown in Table 29.9, but the number and nature of the factors that emerge cannot be known in advance, which is to say that they are indeterminate and characterized by *uncertainty*. Moreover, the factors are also in a relationship of *complementarity* (i.e., they are all aspects of X), but each emerges under separate experimental conditions. Similarly, the probability that certain policy preferences will surface varies with conditions: Reduce pollution, for instance (see Table 29.10), is consistently embraced, yet fund more missiles runs into interference under certain conditions, comparable to the interference effects of wave mechanics. The similarities between Q methodology and quantum theory are not mere analogy; however, as Stephenson (1983; 1994) has made clear, but are rooted in the same mathematics. The uncertainty underlying Table 29.9 is irresolvable, for instance, as is the difference between waves and particles. The complementarity among X's factors emerges as a function of her measurements.

29.3.3 Providing Information to Decision Makers

Decision makers often seek information and recommendations to assist them in distinguishing among choices and in finding compromise solutions for controversial issues. The advice can come from many different sources, including objective advice provided by analysts and researchers, opinions of diverse stakeholders both within and outside the organization, and public opinion.

Researchers and policy analysts have suggested that Q methodology can be used to assist decision makers in different ways. For example, Byrd (2001) found that policy analysts can employ Q methodology to (1) analyze stakeholder perceptions, (2) reframe (or redefine) an issue, and (3) evaluate policy options. In addition, based on their use of Q methodology to investigate national forest management, Steelman and McGuire (1999) concluded that Q methodology can help policy analysts to (1) identify important internal and external constituencies, (2) define participant viewpoints and perceptions, (3) provide sharper insight into participant-preferred management directions, (4) identify criteria that are important to participants, (5) explicitly outline areas of consensus and conflict, and (6) develop a common view toward the policy.

In this section, how Q methodology has been used to assist decision makers in three main ways is shown: to clarify the context of a decision (what are the decision structures of decision makers and stakeholders?); to understand competing problem definitions and solutions; and to identify innovative problem-solution combinations and fashion compromises, and to build winning coalitions.

29.3.3.1 Understanding a Decision Framework and Context

This first use of Q methodology to assist decision making closely resembles the research designed to identify the dominant decision structures related to particular issues as described in the previous section of this chapter. The main difference is that the focus of social science research is to identify and describe decision structures, whereas policy research emphasizes how that information can be used by decision makers. Some research, such as that published by Hooker (2001) and Deitrick (1998), provide both social science insights and analytic advice. As previously summarized, Hooker identified decision structures related to forest policy and Deitrick researched stakeholders' perspectives on brownfields redevelopment. Both of these studies provided novel social science knowledge about decision structures related to these issues, and both studies also offered decision makers information about the rival views of contending groups. Hooker's study gave decision makers a clearer picture of the clashing views on the use of forests, and Deitrick's study helped local decision makers better understand the differing perspectives on this difficult issue.

In her article, Hooker (2001) not only identified the decision structures at issue, but she also suggested how that information could be used. For instance, she proposed that knowledge of the four different perspectives, especially information on the views they have in common, would be a good starting point for structuring beneficial interactions between factors. As she wrote, "Conversations among analysts and members of the public who are interested in forest policy can use the new framework of beliefs identified in this study to redefine a policy agenda as well as commence facilitating dialogue" (174). She also suggested that the results of her study could be used to assist efforts to "structure a more effective public involvement strategy" (174), arguing that citizen participation should be set up so that all four perspectives were represented in the discussions. By including representatives of the four main perspectives in public hearings and advisory groups, policy makers could make sure that all of the competing views are heard.

Deitrick (1998) concluded that "planning and policy" could benefit from understanding the three perspectives that her study identified. She agreed with Hooker that knowledge of these three perspectives should improve public participation by insuring that each of the three perspectives be represented when brownfields issues are discussed. She also pointed out that the study identified not only disagreements among the three factors, but also ways in which they agreed. Thus, conversations among people with different perspectives could start with areas of agreement.

29.3.3.2 Identifying Competing Problem Definitions and Related Solutions

Decision makers must often act on controversial issues that are deeply divisive within organizations, and it may be useful to explore in depth the basis for the conflict. This can frequently be done by identifying the competing definitions of the problems facing the organization and the solutions evoked by each. As the examples below illustrate, Q methodology provides a penetrating method for understanding different definitions of organizational problems.

Maxwell and Brown (1999) provide an example of how Q methodology can be used as a consulting or organizational tool to help organizations make decisions in response to complex problems. The case concerned a middle school where faculty members disagreed on how best to deal with increasing levels of student misconduct, and consultants were brought in to help the school manage the conflict and to find solutions that would be widely accepted.

As their first step, Maxwell and Brown conducted a Q-methodological study to determine how members of the organization understood the nature of their problems. They began by interviewing teachers, staff members, and administrators, asking them for their thoughts on the problems facing the school. Through these open-ended interviews, they compiled a list of 44 problems, of which the following are examplary:

Too many office detentions are given.
The kids don't want to put in the effort.
Teachers don't know how to punish kids effectively.
The parents don't respect the teachers.
Kids have too many rights.

With these 44 problem statements comprising the Q sort, 20 faculty and staff members were asked to array the statements from $+4$ (most important) to -4 (least important), and the subsequent analysis showed that most participants loaded on one of two factors. Participants loading significantly on the *Resentment* factor expressed the view of most teachers and staff who had complaints against students, parents, administrators, and the school board, all of whom were viewed as unsupportive of school personnel, hence "placing them in an untenable position" (38). While the resentful were largely concerned with *inter*-group relations, the *Differentiating* factor was more concerned with *intra*-group relations, taking the view that the school contained both helpful and harmful elements; i.e., this group made distinctions among students (those needing support as well as those needing discipline) as well as among teachers (those who punish effectively and those who do not). The consultants presented the results of this first phase of the study, showing the participants those statements that represented sources of disagreement, but they also pointed out statements where they agreed, likening this process to "holding a mirror up to the teachers and staff... so that they might see themselves and co-workers more clearly" (40).

In the second phase of the study, the same participants were interviewed to elicit their proposals to solve the problems that had been identified, and they generated 35 potential solutions, which became the Q sort subsequently completed by 28 faculty and staff members. The condition of instruction asked the participants to sort the proposed solutions from $+4$ (apt to be most effective) to -4 (least effective), and factor analysis revealed three different overall strategies—(1) *punish* (i.e., solve the discipline problem by imposing harsher penalties), (2) *quarantine* (use special programs to separate problem children from the others), and (3) *coordinate* (encourage teachers and staff to work together more effectively through cooperation and coordination).

In addition to these competing approaches to solving the problem, the Q sorts identified actions that all three groups agreed should be implemented. For example, all three groups agreed that actions should be taken to (a) establish a procedure for parents to sign an agreement about the rules of conduct and the consequences for misconduct that will apply to their child; and (b) consistently follow rules and regulations already in existence such as the Student Conduct Code. Based on the results of their Q-methodological research, the consultants informed participants about the differences of opinion regarding the causes of student misconduct and the differing preferences for actions to address the problems. They identified the actions that were agreeable to all three factors as well as those unanimously opposed.

Other studies have reported a similar approach to identifying competing problem definitions and solutions for other policy issues. For example, a paper by Mattson, Byrd, Rutherford, Brown, and Clark (2006) describes a two-day workshop that had as its goal to improve practices and to establish some common ground amid the controversies and conflicts surrounding carnivore management. At the beginning of this workshop, 30 participants with different and, in some respects, opposing points of view (e.g., ranchers, environmental activists, scientists, and state and federal government managers) brainstormed about the nature of problems associated with carnivore conservation. The almost 300 problems associated with carnivore conservation that were identified by the group were recorded, and a sample of 51 of them was incorporated into a Q sort, which led to identification of four different decision structures on the issue of carnivore management.

On the second day of the workshop, the researchers elicited opinions from participants about possible solutions to the problems that had been identified during the previous day's session. The solutions were recorded, and 40 of them were incorporated into a Q sort, which was administered to the same group of participants. Analysis produced four factors, each a different pattern of recommendations about how the problems associated with carnivore conservation should be addressed. As in the case of the middle school study, this workshop on carnivore management identified a subset of policy actions that would be supported (or at least be unopposed) by the four groups, and these points of consensus are good starting points for policy makers. That is, by identifying both differences and commonalities in decision structures, Q methodology provides policy makers with information that can help them put together a winning coalition to support policy actions.[*]

An article by Gargan and Brown (1993) presents yet another case showing how Q methodology can clarify "the perspectives of decision makers" and, in conjunction with other procedures, can ferret out "prudent courses of action" (348). According to these authors, the special contribution of Q methodology to decision making is that "it helps overcome the limitations of the mind in dealing with complexity, and also serves to locate elements of consensus (if they exist) that might otherwise go unnoticed in the emotional turmoil of political debate" (348–349). The case in point concerned the formation of a strategic plan by a Private Industry Council (PIC), a local nonprofit agency primarily responsible for implementing the federal Job Training Partnership Act in a rural Midwestern county. The program's goal was to improve the employment chances of people having difficulty gaining employment by providing them with training and skill development.

The PIC Board of Directors decided to develop a strategic plan to respond to opportunities and challenges it faced during the lean years of the Reagan Administration. First, the Board used nominal group technique and idea writing to identify major issues and problems facing the agency by responding to the following prompt: "What issues and problems must be considered as most important and of highest priority for Private Industry Council over the next two to four years if the employment needs of the hard-to-serve are to be effectively dealt with?" (349). A total of 33 answers were generated and were incorporated into a Q sort used by the 10 Board members in response to the following condition:

> "Since all of the issues raised cannot be addressed simultaneously, some priorities must be established. To do this, you need to rank order the statements from those that you think should be the most important for PIC to deal with in the next two to four years ($+4$) to those that should be considered least important (-4)." (351)

The Q sorts were correlated and factor analyzed as usual, and three factors emerged representing different preferences for PIC implementation.

Gargan and Brown noted that the different policy preferences revealed in the Q sorts sometimes converged while at other times they sharply conflicted. Sometimes, two of the groups (e.g., Factors A and B) agreed on various statements while Factor C disagreed. In other instances, A and C agreed with Factor B disagreeing. On some proposed policy actions, all three agreed; on others, all three disagreed. By identifying the underlying conflicting perspectives and views regarding different courses of action, Q methodology provided valuable information to the Board members who were committed to forging a strategic plan. Brown and Gargan concluded by suggesting three ways decision makers could use the information from a Q study such as this: Create a

---

[*] It is worth noting that (as consultants and mediators know) simply pointing a way out of contentious relationships provides no guarantee that those involved will take it. As Maxwell and Brown (1999) reported in their middle school study, once the factions were shown an exit strategy for their discontents, they shelved the study and returned to the same disgruntled acrimony that had led to a request for outside help in the first place. In contrast, the members of the decision making group that produced the consensus shown in Table 29.7, despite their conflictual history, immediately took advantage of this insight and moved to implementation (see Note, p. 548).

committee comprised of representatives from each of the three groups to write the group's strategic plan; adopt policies for which there is consensus support; and use insights from the study to help formulate mutually beneficial deals and to build coalitions to support a set of actions.

29.3.3.3 Identifying Solutions to Intractable Problems

The two studies summarized in the previous section illustrate how decision makers could use the results of Q methodology to help with decisions on important issues. They have shown, for instance, that Q methodology provides information about (1) consensus statements with which all of the factors agree, (2) statements with which some but not all factors agree, and (3) statements showing the greatest disagreements among the factors. Information of this kind can be employed in different ways to assist decision makers to render good choices.

Other research has shown how Q methodology can be innovatively used to help decision makers who face seemingly intractable problems. In a demonstration of the utility of Q methodology to help "recast intractable problems" to make them tractable, Van Eeten (2001) presented a case study where, as a consultant to the Dutch government, he was involved in reframing a policy debate concerned with expansion of Amsterdam's Schipol Airport.[*] When discussing with stakeholders the controversial addition of a fifth runway, Van Eeten encountered bipolar positions with proponents advocating expansion as necessary for the economic benefits expected to accrue and others resisting expansion on the basis of environmental costs.

Doubting the simplicity of a business-environmental polarity as the sole dynamic at issue, Van Eeten collected 200 statements about expansion of the airport from media archives, advocacy papers, interviews, and transcripts of several stakeholder meetings. From these statements, he extracted a Q sample of 80 that were administered to 38 stakeholders selected to reflect the distribution of views on the expansion issue, including people who worked for airlines, airport management, different levels and sectors of government, national environmental organizations, local citizens, environmental groups, and commercial or regional economic interests. Analysis identified four factors containing five policy arguments that were labeled as follows:

Argument A: Societal integration of a growing airport
Argument B1: Expansion of aviation infrastructure as a necessity in the face of international competition
Argument B2: Expansion of civil aviation as an unjustified use of public funds
Argument C: Ecological modernization of the civil aviation sector
Argument D: Sustainable solutions to a growing demand for mobility

Policy arguments B1 and B2 captured opposite ends of a bipolar factor and the main (and irreconcilable) public debate on the issue, rendering it intractable. However, the study also identified three other policy arguments (A, C, and D) that are not captive of the intractability of the B1 vs. B2 debate. As he wrote:

"Arguments A, C, and D... each state that there is more to the problem than what key stakeholders are now considering. Although these arguments are habitually collapsed into and treated as part and parcel of the positions for or against growth, the analysis indicates that they are, in fact, relatively independent. Instead of conflating the alternatives in A, C, and D into B1 or B2, the data insist that they can be sensibly viewed as relatively independent from (indeed orthogonal to) the continuum for-or-against further growth." (404)

---

[*] Also see Dayton (2000) who suggested how Q methodology could be used to assist dialogue about intractable issues such as global climate change (cf. Focht and Lawler, 2000).

Van Eeten recommended that the alternatives corresponding to policy arguments A, C, and D should be placed on the policy agenda and be decoupled from the B1–B2 arguments, presenting a "richer package of proposals" that would enable decision makers to "address the expansion proposal by defining the problem more tractably as something in which decision makers can intervene in real and important ways" (406).

29.4 CONCLUSION

In their noble effort to bring rigor to the study of decision making, the behavioral sciences have increasingly focused on objective conditions and assumptions such as rationality and institutions and have left the decision maker dangling from the strings of transindividual variables and forces as if bereft of mind and intent. In part, this state of affairs is methodological: Having acclimated over the decades to an absence of ways for dealing effectively with intentionality, the student of decision making has become accustomed to examining the objective world outside the person as a basis for inferring the world inside. Objective conditions are important because they place constraints on viable alternatives, but decision makers typically endeavor to take limiting circumstances into account and to conceive of alternatives that will enable them to overcome obstacles. In this regard, the observer who has more direct access to the actor's vantage point will have an improved vista from which to view this struggle.

Q methodology contributes to the study of decision making by providing the means to account systematically for the outlooks, values, and thinking of actors as they strive to achieve desired outcomes. Consequently with Q methodology, the internal dimension of decision making can be examined with as much rigor as the external dimensions have been. Moreover, opportunities now exist for dealing with decision making in functional as opposed to those categorical terms that are characteristic of research strategies that rely on demographics and other traits. As shown in the aforementioned presentations, Q methodology can provide insights into decision making that are generally inaccessible via traditional methods. With Q methodology, researchers can now explore the subjectivity of decision makers, stakeholders, and the public, and they can benefit from results that illuminate the beliefs, values, interests, and information that converge and interact to influence individual views and decisions.

REFERENCES

Adcock, C. J., *Factorial Analysis for Non-Mathematicians*, University Press Melbourne, Melbourne, 1954.

Baas, L. R., The interpersonal sources of the development of political images: an intensive, longitudinal perspective, *Operant Subjectivity*, 20, 117–142, 1997.

Babcock-Lumish, T. L., *Venture capital decision making and the cultures of risk: an application of Q methodology to US and UK innovation clusters*, Working Papers in Economic Geography (WPG 04-20), Oxford University, http://www.geog.ox.ac.uk/research/wpapers/economic/wpg04-20.html, 2004 (accessed September 15, 2005).

Baker, R., and Meyer, F., *Women and Support for Correctional Reform*, Paper presented at the American Political Science Association annual conference, Boston, 2002.

Baker, R., and Meyer, F., *A Community Economic Elite and Support for Correctional Reforms*, Paper presented at the meeting of the Midwest Political Science Association, Chicago, 2003.

Brim, O. G., Glass, D. C., Lavin, D. E., and Goodman, N., *Personality and Decision Processes: Studies in the Social Psychology of Thinking*, Stanford University Press, Stanford, CA, 1962.

Brown, S. R., *Political Subjectivity: Applications of Q Methodology in Political Science*, Yale University Press, New Haven, CT, 1980.

Brown, S. R., The structure and form of subjectivity in political theory and behavior, *Operant Subjectivity*, 17, 30–48, 1993–1994.

Brown, S. R., *Decision Structures*, Paper presented at the meeting of the Brunswik Society (in conjunction with the Judgment and Decision Society), Dallas, 1998.

Brown, S. R., Structural and functional information, *Policy Sciences*, 35, 285–304, 2002.

Brown, S. R., Q methodology, In *The SAGE Encyclopedia of Social Science Research Methods*, Lewis-Beck, M. S., Bryman, A., and Liao, T. F., Eds., Vol. 3, Sage, Thousand Oaks, CA, pp. 887–888, 2004.

Brown, S. R., Durning, D. W., and Selden, S., Q methodology, In *Handbook of Research Methods in Public Administration*, Miller, G. J. and Whicker, M. L., Eds., Marcel Dekker, New York, pp. 599–637, 1999.

Brown, S. R., and Kil, B. O., Exploring Korean values, *Asia Pacific: Perspectives* [On-line serial], 2(1), 1–8. Available at http://www.pacificrim.usfca.edu/research/perspectives/brown_kil.pdf, 2002.

Brown, S. R. and Robyn, R., Reserving a key place for reality: philosophical foundations of theoretical rotation, *Operant Subjectivity*, 27, 104–124, 2004.

Byrd, K., Review of the book *Social Discourse and Environmental Policy*, *Operant Subjectivity*, 24, 154–158, 2001.

Byrd, K., Mirrors and metaphors: contemporary narratives of the wolf in Minnesota, *Ethics, Place, and Environment*, 5(1), 50–65, 2002.

Clark, A. H., Understanding sustainable development in the context of emergent environmental perspectives, *Policy Sciences*, 35, 69–90, 2002.

Dayton, B. W., Policy frames, policy making and the global climate change discourse, In *Social Discourse and Environmental Policy*, Addams, H. and Proops, J., Eds., Edward Elgar, Cheltenham, UK, pp. 71–99, 2000.

Deitrick, S., *Examining Community Perceptions of Brownfields Revitalization in Pittsburgh, Pennsylvania*, Paper presented at the meeting of the Association of Collegiate Schools of Planning, Pasadena, CA, 1998.

Dick, M. J. and Edelman, M., Consequences of the budget crunch: using Q methodology to prioritize subscription cancellations, *Journal of Nursing Education*, 32, 181–182, 1993.

Donahue, A. K., Managerial perceptions and the production of fire protection, *Administration and Society*, 35, 717–746, 2004.

Downs, A., *An Economic Theory of Democracy*, Harper & Row, New York, 1957.

Dryzek, J. S. and Holmes, L. T., *Post-communist Democratization*, Cambridge University Press, Cambridge, UK, 2002.

Fernandes, R. and Simon, H. A., A study of how individuals solve complex and ill-structured problems, *Policy Sciences*, 32, 225–245, 1999.

Fisher, R. A., *The Design of Experiments*, Oliver and Boyd, Edinburgh, UK, 1935.

Focht, W., Assessment and management of policy conflict in the Illinois River watershed in Oklahoma: an application of Q methodology, *International Journal of Public Administration*, 25, 1311–1349, 2002.

Focht, W. and Lawler, J. J., Using Q methodology to facilitate policy dialogue, In *Social Discourse and Environmental Policy*, Addams, H. and Proops, J., Eds., Edward Elgar, Cheltenham, UK, pp. 100–122, 2000.

Galve-Peritore, A. K. and Peritore, N. P., Mexican biotechnology policy and decision makers' attitudes toward technology policy, In *Biotechnology in Latin America*, Peritore, N. P. and Galve-Peritore, A. K., Eds., Scholarly Resources, Wilmington, DE, pp. 69–95, 1995.

Gargan, J. J. and Brown, S. R., "What is to be done?" Anticipating the future and mobilizing prudence, *Policy Sciences*, 26, 347–359, 1993.

Goldman, I., Communication and culture: A Q-methodological study of psycho-social meanings from photographs in *Time* magazine, Doctoral dissertation, University of Iowa, *Dissertation Abstracts International* 45:2683A, 1984.

Good, J., William Stephenson and the quest for a science of subjectivity, *Revista de Historia de la Psicología*, 19, 431–439, 1998.

Good, J., William Stephenson and the post World War II bifurcation of British psychology, *Operant Subjectivity*, 23, 116–130, 2000.

Good, J., Stephenson, William (1902–1989), In *Dictionary of Modern American Philosophers*, Shook, J. R., Ed., Thoemmes Press, Bristol, UK, 2005.

Grosswiler, P., The convergence of William Stephenson's and Marshall McLuhan's communication theories, *Operant Subjectivity*, 17, 2–16, 1994.

Hall, P. A. and Taylor, R. C. R., Political science and the three new institutionalisms, *Political Studies*, 44, 936–957, 1996.

Hooker, A. M., Beliefs regarding society and nature: a framework for listening in forest and environmental policy, *Operant Subjectivity*, 24, 159–182, 2001.

Kim, J. H., Kim, B. I., and Kim, J. K., Olfactory factors in aroma uses, *Journal of Human Subjectivity*, 1(2), 157–176, 2003.

Kline, P., *An Easy Guide to Factor Analysis*, Routledge, London, 1994.

Lasswell, H. D., *The Future of Political Science*, Atherton Press, New York, 1963.

Lasswell, H. D. and McDougal, M. S., *Jurisprudence for a Free Society*, Martinus Nijhoff, Dordrecht, The Netherlands, 1992.

Logan, R. A., Complementarity, self and mass communication: the contributions of William Stephenson 1902–1989, *Mass Communications Review*, 18, 27–39, 1991.

Mattson, D. J., Byrd, K. L., Rutherford, M. B., Brown, S. R., and Clark, T. W., Finding common ground in large carnivore conservation: mapping contending perspectives, *Environmental Science & Policy*, 9, 392–405, 2006.

Maxwell, J. P. and Brown, S. R., Identifying problems and generating solutions under conditions of conflict, *Operant Subjectivity*, 23, 31–51, 1999.

McKeown, B. F. and Thomas, D. B., *Q Methodology*, Sage, Newbury Park, CA, 1988.

Midgley, B. D. and Morris, E. K., Subjectivity and behaviorism: Skinner, Kantor, and Stephenson, *Operant Subjectivity*, 25, 127–138, 2002.

Morçöl, G., *A New Mind for Policy Analysis: Toward a Post-Newtonian and Postpositivist Epistemology and Methodology*, Praeger, Westport, CT, 2002.

Newman, T. D., Links between ethics and public policy: a Q methodological study of physician assisted suicide and euthanasia, Doctoral dissertation, Kent State University, 2005.

Pelletier, D., Kraak, V., McCullum, C., Uusitalo, U., and Rich, R., The shaping of collective values through deliberative democracy: an empirical study from New York's North Country, *Policy Sciences*, 32, 103–131, 1999.

Robbins, P., Q methodology, In *Encyclopedia of Social Measurement*, Kempf-Leonard, K., Ed., Vol. 3, Elsevier, San Diego, 2005.

Root, J., A partisan/nonpartisan schematic approach to interpreting political cartoons, *Operant Subjectivity*, 18, 94–107, 1995.

Schmolck, P. and Atkinson, J., PQMethod (Version 2.11) [Computer software]. Available at http://www.rz.unibw-muenchen.de/~p41bsmk/qmethod/, 2005.

Shilin, M. B., Durning, D., and Gajdamaschko, N., How American ecologists think about coastal zone environments, In *Values at Sea: Ethics for the Marine Environment*, Dallmeyer, D., Ed., University of Georgia Press, Athens, pp. 239–259, 2003.

Smith, N. W., *Current Systems in Psychology: History, Theory, Research, and Applications*, Wadsworth/Thomson Learning, Belmont, CA, 2001.

Steelman, T. A. and Maguire, L. A., Understanding participant perspectives: Q methodology in national forest management, *Journal of Policy Analysis and Management*, 18, 361–388, 1999.

Stephenson, W., *The Study of Behavior: Q-technique and its Methodology*, University of Chicago Press, Chicago, 1953.

Stephenson, W., Applications of communication theory: III. Intelligence and multivalued choice, *Psychological Record*, 23, 17–32, 1973.

Stephenson, W., Concourse theory of communication, *Communication*, 3, 21–40, 1978.

Stephenson, W., Quantum theory and Q methodology: fictionalistic and probabilistic theories conjoined, *Psychological Record*, 33, 213–230, 1983.

Stephenson, W., How to make a good cup of tea, *Operant Subjectivity*, 10, 37–57, 1987.

Stephenson, W., *Quantum Theory of Advertising*, Stephenson Research Center, School of Journalism, University of Missouri, Columbia, 1994.

Stricklin, M. and Almeida, R., PCQ for Windows (Academic Edition) [Computer software]. Available at http://www.pcqsoft.com, 2004.

Swaffield, S. R. and Fairweather, J. R., Investigation of attitudes towards the effects of land use change using image editing and Q-sort method, *Landscape and Urban Planning*, 35, 213–230, 1996.

Taylor, P., Delprato, D. J., and Knapp, J. R., Q methodology in the study of child phenomenology, *Psychological Record*, 44, 171–183, 1994.

Trahair, R., A psychohistorical study of political cartoons using Q-method, *Journal of Psychohistory*, 30, 337–362, 2003.

Van Eeten, M. J. G., Recasting intractable policy issues: the wider implications of the Netherlands civil aviation controversy, *Journal of Policy Analysis and Management*, 20, 391–414, 2001.

Vickers, G., *The Art of Judgment*, Basic Books, New York, 1965.

Wacholtz, L. E., *The Country Music Audience: A Q-technique Portrait of Seven Listener Types*, Paper presented at the meeting of the International Society for the Scientific Study of Subjectivity, Columbia, MO, 1992.

Watts, S. and Stenner, P., Doing Q methodology: theory, method and interpretation, *Qualitative Research in Psychology*, 2, 67–91, 2005.

Webler, T., Tuler, S., Shockey, I., Stern, P., and Beattie, R., Participation by local governmental officials in watershed management planning, *Society and Natural Resources*, 16, 105–121, 2003.

Weiss, C. H., Ideology, interests, and information: the basis of policy positions, In *Ethics, the Social Sciences, and Policy Analysis*, Callahan, D. and Jennings, B., Eds., Plenum Press, New York, pp. 213–245, 1983.

Wilkins, J. L., Kraak, V., Pelletier, D., McCullum, C., and Uusitalo, U., Moving from debate to dialogue about genetically engineered foods and crops: Insights from a Land Grant university, *Journal of Sustainable Agriculture*, 18, 167–201, 2001.

Wolf, A., The bones in a concourse, *Operant Subjectivity*, 27, 145–165, 2004.

Wong, W., Eiser, A. R., Mrtek, R. G., and Heckerling, P. S., By-person factor analysis in clinical ethical decision making: Q methodology in end-of-life care decisions, *American Journal of Bioethics*, 4, W8–W22, 2004.

Woolley, J. T. and McGinnis, M. V., The conflicting discourses of restoration, *Society and Natural Resources*, 13, 339–357, 2000.

30 Methods of Assessing and Enhancing Creativity for Public Policy Decision Making[*]

Göktuğ Morçöl

CONTENTS

30.1 Introduction..565
30.2 Problem-Solving and Creativity..566
30.3 What Is Creativity?..567
30.4 A Personal Construct Theory of Cognitive Complexity and Creativity.......................568
    30.4.1 Constructs, Elements, and Personal Construct Space..569
    30.4.2 Differentiation, Integration, and Cognitive Complexity....................................570
    30.4.3 The Creativity Cycle..571
30.5 Measuring Cognitive Complexity 572
    30.5.1 Mapping Cognitive Constructions with Repertory Grids...................................572
    30.5.2 A Comparison with the Q-Methodology...576
30.6 Methods of Facilitating Creativity 577
    30.6.1 Facilitating the Creativity Cycle with Repertory Grids.....................................577
    30.6.2 A Comparison with Other Cognitive Mapping Methods 578
    30.6.3 Other Methods of Facilitating Creativity...580
30.7 Summary and Conclusions...582
References...583

30.1 INTRODUCTION

Public policy problems are complex, and complex problems require creative solutions, as Lasswell, (2000) points out. In the following sections, I will discuss the relevancy of creative thinking for problem-solving in general, and public policy-making in particular. I will also summarize the findings of the psychological research on creativity and describe several methods of measuring and facilitating creativity. Not all aspects of the creative thinking process are known, but the advances in psychological research have shed some light on it. A general understanding of the creative thinking process has evolved, and methods have been developed to measure the creative potentials of individuals and to facilitate their creative thinking.

The methods of creativity measurement and facilitation described and discussed in this chapter are based on different theories, but they share some similar conceptualizations. I will describe

---

[*] Segments of this chapter are adapted from the material used in, Morçöl (2002, pp. 226–239), as indicated later in the text. The material is used here with the permission of the copyright owner (Greenwood Publishing Group).

methods of measuring and facilitating creativity with their theoretical underpinnings. Among these methods are the ones I adapted from George Kelly's (1955) personal construct theory and Repertory Grid methodology. I will give more detailed accounts of Kelly's theory and others', as well as my applications of his methodology.

30.2 PROBLEM-SOLVING AND CREATIVITY

Sternberg and O'Hara (1999, 258) point out that problem-solving is similar to the creative process in some aspects, and different in others: Problem-solving is an organized cognitive process that aims to generate correct solutions to specific problems, whereas the creative process generates goodness in thinking (e.g., a good formulation of a problem). The findings of the psychological research on creativity and problem-solving support Sternberg and O'Hara's assertion. The research in cognitive psychology shows that creativity is an important component in the discovery or definition of the problem and that the quality of a problem definition may, in part, determine the quality of solutions (Runco and Sakamoto, 1999).

The theoretical differentiation made between well and ill structured problems in the 1970s and 1980s (see, for example, Rittel and Webber, 1973; Van Gundy, 1988; Voss and Means, 1989) also contributed to our understanding of the significance of creative thinking in problem formulation. According to Voss and Means, a problem is well structured when its various components (e.g., constraints and goals thereof) are well-specified and known to the problem solver. Well-structured problems have solutions upon which people can agree. The problems in mathematics and geometry are of this kind. Well-structured problems may require some creativity, but not as much as ill-structured problems do. Because the goals, solutions, and constraints of ill-structured problems are not agreed upon, there is much more room and need for creative thinking in attempting to solve them.

Simon's (1973) research and conceptualizations showed that there is actually no boundary between well-structured and ill-structured problems. Any problem-solving process will appear ill-structured, if "the problem solver has access to a very large long-term memory of potentially relevant information, and/or access to a very large external memory that provides information about the consequences of problem solving actions" (181). He goes on to argue

[D]efiniteness of problem structure is largely an illusion that arises when we systematically confound the idealized problem that is presented to an idealized (and unlimitedly powerful) problem solver with the actual problem that is to be attacked by a problem solver with limited (even if large) computational capacities. If formal completeness and decidability are rare properties in the world of complex formal systems, effective definability is equally rare in the world of large problems.

In general, the problems presented to problem solvers by the world are best regarded as ill-structured problems. (186)

Simon's insight is particularly relevant to public policy problems: The problems the world presents to policy analysts and policy makers are always ill-structured. A policy problem may become well-structured in the policy making process, if only a small number of the aspects of the problematic situation are intentionally and selectively included in the problem formulation (Dunn, 1988). Dunn points out that in the practice of policy analysis, most of the problems remain ill-structured, because their boundaries are not easily known and they require complex analytic methods for solutions.

The ill-structuredness of policy problems is actually a reflection of their complexity, according to Dunn (2004, 75–76). He points out that policy problems are complex because they are interdependent, dynamic, subjective, and artificial. These characteristics of policy problems make it necessary to structure them carefully and with the participation of stakeholders. Dunn emphasizes that problem structuring is the most important aspect of policy analysis and creative thinking plays a crucial role in the structuring of policy problems (82).

Particularly because of the subjective and socially constructed nature of policy problems, it is important to understand the role of creativity in the formulation of policy problems. Creativity, as discussed in the next section, is a complex process that involves both cognitive and social construction processes. There are two main theoretical positions on the nature of social and public policy problems. The first, objectivist, position is that problems are social facts to be discovered and solved with scientific methods. The second, constructivist, position is that problems are social and/or cognitive constructions, not objective facts.

Merton's (1976) and Mani's (1976) works are examples of the objectivist position. They both argue that there are real social conditions that could be judged objectively as detrimental to the wellbeing of a society. According to Merton, "Social problems result from identifiable social circumstances, so it can be said that the very structure of society is a source of social problems" (40). Social problems may be latent or manifest according to Merton. "Manifest social problems are those generally recognized as problems. Latent social problems are conditions not widely identified as problems even though in fact they are at odds with people's interests and values" (41). According to Manis, social problems are either social conditions or social values that are detrimental to the wellbeing of human societies and that are identified by science. The problems identified by individuals or groups are only perceived social problems, and they may be real or spurious (4).

Constructivists argue that problems are either cognitive or social constructions, or both (see, for example, Fuller and Myers, 1941; Blumer, 1971; Spector and Kitsuse, 1973; Eden et al., 1983; Dery, 1984). According to Blumer, "social problems have their being in a process of collective definitions" (298). "Social problems are not the results of an intrinsic malfunctioning of a society, but are the results of a process of definition in which a given condition is picked out and identified as a social problem" (301). Dery points out that problems do not exist and that they are not objective entities on their own right. He goes on to argue: "the very notion of problem definition suggests a constructivist rather than an objectivist view" (p. xi).

Newell and Simon's (1972) work supports the position that all problems are cognitively constructed. According to Newell and Simon, the problem solver transforms information into a "problem representation," which is a symbol structure, not a mere reflection of external reality. Problem representations are formed within the cognitive structure of the problem solver, prior to receiving information; information is absorbed into (or shaped by) the previous cognitive structure (73–82). In this sense, problem representations are not direct representations (mirror images) of external realities; they are "internal" to the cognitive system of the problem-solver. It is important to understand these internal problem representations, because they dictate the means that can be used by a problem solver and determine the boundaries of the area of a cognitive system (e.g., human mind) in which alternative ways of action can be found (84). In other words, a problem representation constitutes a framework in which problems are defined. A problem definition is nothing but a specific and refined cognitive symbol structure (91–92).

If problem definitions were mere reflections of problematic situations (i.e., external realities), and could therefore be defined objectively, as Merton and Manis assume, a decision maker would need only to collect the correct information to solve a problem. Creativity would not then be necessary, nor would problem definition be an important aspect of policy or decision making. Creative thinking is necessary, because public problems are socially and cognitively constructed. Additionally, creativity is an inherent quality of the complex workings of the human mind, as Newell and Simon (1972) demonstrate. The creative process takes place within the cognitive medium they describe and involves processing cognitively-generated symbols.

30.3 WHAT IS CREATIVITY?

The creative process is still not understood in its entirety, but researchers agree that it is a multifaceted phenomenon. It is fostered or hindered by both environmental (social) and personality factors (Halpern, 1996, 378–380). Feldman (1999, 171–172) reports that researchers identified seven sources of creative thinking: cognitive processes, social/emotional processes, family environment, formal and informal education, history and characteristics of a particular field of study in which creative thinking occurs, culture of societies, and historical forces. Some families and cultures encourage creative thinking more than others. In science, creative breakthroughs are expected, welcome, and encouraged. In times of major social changes, people are more receptive to innovative artistic products, scientific breakthroughs, and creative policy solutions.

Although the social and cultural aspects of creative processes are very important, a detailed discussion of these aspects is beyond the scope of this chapter. I will focus mainly on the cognitive aspects of creativity, but, as the reader will see in the following sections, the social aspects of creativity are incorporated into the process in the form of social (group) interactions in many methods of facilitating creativity.

The earlier studies on creativity (in the late 19th and early 20th centuries) focused on possible connections between creativity and intelligence (Brown, 1989, 8). Some of these studies showed that there is a circumscribed relationship between intelligence and creativity. Getzels' and Jackson's classic study (1962) indicated that intelligence and creativity are correlated up to an IQ of 120; beyond that they diverge (cited in De Bono, 1992, 41).

More recent studies showed that the relationships between creativity and different modes of thinking are more important than the relationship between creativity and intelligence. Guilford's (1950, 1956, 1967) works set apart two modes of thinking—convergent and divergent—and showed that there is a closer relationship between divergent thinking and creativity. This is because, according to Dowd (1989), divergent thinking is an exploration of new ideas; it is tentative, exploratory, and oriented toward the development of possibilities than data, speculations than conclusions. Convergent thinking, on the other hand, brings in relevant data and arrives at a conclusion based on these data; it tends to be deductive, rather than inductive.

Guilford's theory inspired others to develop tests of creativity that essentially measure divergent thinking (e.g., Torrance, 1965; Wallace and Kogan, 1965). Tests of divergent thinking remain the most popular methods of measuring creativity today (Plucker and Renzulli, 1999, 36–39). These tests are not problem-free, however. Vernon (1989, 98–99) points out, for example, that they have low reliability.

The research findings in the U.S. and Britain in the last few decades indicate positive relationships between creativity and divergent thinking (McRae, 1987; Runco and Okuda, 1988; Brophy, 1998). McRae concludes from his own research that openness to experience is a common characteristic of creative individuals and that openness to experience and divergent thinking may interact as mutually necessary conditions for creativity, the former providing the inclination and the latter providing the aptitude for original thinking. Brophy cites the research findings that divergent thinkers are more likely to process diverse stimuli, organize thoughts flexibly, seek knowledge about varied subjects, and form intuitions; they are more intrinsically motivated to solve problems creatively. He points out, however, that creativity is not merely divergent thinking; a complete creative problem solving process requires periods of divergent ideation alternating with convergent evaluation and the ability to judge when each is appropriate.

Kelly's (1955) personal construct theory, which I used in developing the methods I describe later in this paper, includes conceptualizations that are parallel to the distinction between divergent and convergent thinking. In the next section, I summarize his theory and its implications.

30.4 A PERSONAL CONSTRUCT THEORY OF COGNITIVE COMPLEXITY AND CREATIVITY

Kelly (1955) articulated a comprehensive theory of personality and a method of eliciting personal constructs (the Repertory Grid Technique). Kelly's theory and method are still relevant, as their numerous applications in a variety of areas in the last five decades indicate. In their search of the literature, Woehr, Miller, and Lane (1998) found more than 1000 published studies that had applied Kelly's theory and method. Several statistical and computerized Repertory Grid-based cognitive mapping techniques have been developed in the last three decades (see, for example, Slater, 1977; Shaw and Gaines, 1982; Morçöl and Asche, 1993; Bezzi, 1999; Hankison, 2004).

Kelly's (1955) philosophy and theory are constructivist. As mentioned earlier, constructivism provides a cogent justification for the need for creativity in problem-solving. If problems were facts, as objectivists would assume, then there would be no, or very little, need for creative thinking; a mere discovery of facts would suffice to solve a problem. If reality is a cognitive or social construct, however, there is room and need for different (novel, divergent) ways of thinking. At the core of Kelly's constructivism are the ontological assumptions that the universe is essentially active and everchanging, and that the reality of universe is an essential continuity; i.e., it is not divided into independent events (19 and 20). The knowledge of such a universe cannot be gained objectively by an independent observer; it is constructed, and the superordinating view of the theorist, not the information coming from reality, determines the nature of construing. Therefore, in Kelly's philosophy, reality is subject to many alternative constructions, but among the "various ways in which the world is construed, some of them are undoubtedly better than others" (Maher, 1969, 15).

30.4.1 Constructs, Elements, and Personal Construct Space

Humans use cognitive tools to construe reality. Kelly (1955, 8 and 9) calls these tools constructs and elements. A construct is a bipolar dimension—a reference frame, or template—through which a person sees the continuous reality and brackets, or frames, it (e.g., good—bad; inclined—not inclined; things that I like—things that I do not like). Constructs are abstractions. Elements are more concrete, and they can be placed on construct dimensions (e.g., *ice cream* is a thing that I like, while *broccoli* is a thing that I do not like).

According to Kelly (1955), every person has a construct system—or, what Kelly calls a personal construct space—which is composed of a finite number of constructs and elements. A personal construct space is a hyperdimensional geometric space whose dimensions are constructs. The constructs and elements of this space can be analyzed mathematically and represented geometrically.[*]

In the applications of Kelly's theory, only a segment of a person's construct space that is pertinent to the context (e.g., a person's perception of a public policy problem area) are elicited. In the illustration of his method in the next section, for example, participants' constructions of environmental problems were elicited.

Each person's constructs are his/her own (they are not generic), and Kelly's Repertory Grid Technique is essentially idiographic. Each person's Repertory Grid—a matrix of his/her ratings of elements on construct dimensions—is meant to be evaluated individually. However, there are some commonalities among individuals in their constructions of events: "To the extent that one person employs a construction of experience which is similar to that employed by another, his psychological processes are similar to those of the other person" (Kelly, 1955, 90). And, "To the extent that one person construes the construction process of another he may play a role in a social process involving the other person" (95). These assumptions allow for comparisons between individuals' Repertory Grids. In the illustration in the next section, both individual Repertory Grids are analyzed and comparisons are made between them.

---

[*] Kelly's conceptualization and methodology has several similarities with Lewin's "life space" and Osgood's "semantic space," as he acknowledges (Kelly, 1955, 279).

30.4.2 Differentiation, Integration, and Cognitive Complexity

In Kelly's theory, there are two countervailing tendencies in a person's construct system: integration and differentiation. In the words of Adams-Webber (1970):

> From the standpoint of personal construct theory, all psychological development involves not only progressive differentiation among subsystems, but also increasing integration of constructs both within and between subsystems. Differentiation serves the specialization of subsystems, whereas integration serves the unity of each subsystem and that of the entire system as an operational whole. (51)

Kelly's notions of differentiation and integration parallel Guilford's ideas of divergent and convergent thinking. The tendency to differentiate is the basis of exploratory, speculative, and innovative thinking. The integration process is the same as converging new ideas (new constructs in one's personal construct space) into conclusions (a new configuration of one's construct space).

Kelly's followers used the notions of differentiation and integration to develop a comprehensive understanding of the complexity of a person's construct space. The initial conceptualizations of complexity took only differentiation into consideration. It was thought that a more differentiated set of constructs would constitute a more complex construct system. It was realized later that this initial conceptualization mixed up cognitive complexity with cognitive confusion or schizophrenic thought. Landfield (1979, 142) points out that a high degree of differentiation in the absence of integrative skills points to confusion rather than healthy complexity. According to Fransella and Bannister (1977, 61 and 62), the construct system of a schizophrenic is largely random in its organization, and randomness is considered to be the most complex mathematical state of affairs. They argue that "consistency" has to supplement differentiation in the definition of complexity. This would separate "complex normals" from schizophrenics. Complex normals will repeat the pattern of their structure when tested on a second occasion, while disordered schizophrenics will not.

Crockett (1965) posits that constructs are integrated hierarchically at different levels and that complexity of a construct system can be defined at these levels. He argues that the "structural complexity" of a person's cognitive system can be viewed as a function of both its degree of differentiation (the number of constructs) and its level of hierarchical integration (patterns of logical relationships between constructs and the extent which subsytems are interrelated by superordinate constructs).

A cognitively complex person is capable of construing broader aspects of reality and reconstruing it in more innovative ways. A number of researchers, including the proponents of Kelly's personal construct psychology (e.g., Bieri et al., 1966; Adams-Webber, 1969) and others (e.g., Piaget as cited in Dowd, 1989; Brophy, 1998) suggest that cognitive complexity is the basis of creativity. In Piagean terms, structural differentiation, which characterizes the development of every person, may proceed in a more complex fashion and involve many layers in creative people, (Dowd, 237). According to Brophy, cognitive complexity does not by itself assess creative performance, but shows the breadth of categorization, which is essential for creativity (133). Bieri and his colleagues point out that complexity involves construing social behavior in a multidimensional way, and a more cognitively complex person should have more cognitively complex constructs available for perceiving the behaviors of others. Adams-Webber suggests that a cognitively complex person will exhibit more skills than a cognitively simple person in inferring the personal constructs of others in social situations.

The conceptualization of cognitive complexity in terms both of differentiation and integration and its links to the creative process constitute the bases of the methods of measuring and mapping creative potentials of individuals, which will be discussed in the next section. The concepts of differentiation and integration help us take "snapshots" of one's cognitive complexity at a given moment; such snapshots show one's potential for creative thinking. Kelly's theory has another pair of concepts—"loosening" and "tightening of construction"—that are about the dynamic aspects of creativity. These two correspond roughly to the differentiation and integration. They are also the phases of the creativity cycle, according to Kelly. As such, they can be used in constructing a method of facilitating creativity.

30.4.3 THE CREATIVITY CYCLE

In Kelly's theory, the complexity of a person's construct system is not a stable state; it changes as the person interacts with his or her environment. Most definitions of creativity involve freedom from being "stimulus bound"—the individual's ability to hold his constructs "loosely," to see a problem differently from what a first sight might capture. This is the state in which a person's personal construct space is differentiated. Loosening of construction is only half of the creative process. In the other half, the first impressions evolve into meaningful statements, which Kelly calls the tightening of construction (Gendlin et al., 1968). Finally, the creativity cycle is completed. In this cycle, the relationships between a person's elements and constructs are rearranged, and new constructs may have been introduced to the construct system. In Kelly's (1955) words:

> [P]roductive thinking follows a Creativity Cycle. There is a shift to a new topic. The thinking about that topic becomes loose and fluid. The shifting conceptualization begins to fall into place under some new forms of superordinate construction. Now the conceptualization begins to become more precise, more tight. The person begins to construe more explicitly. The constructs become more stable. Elements in the construct contexts become identifying symbols, standing not only for themselves but for the classes of which they are constituent members, or the properties which bind the class into the group. (p. 1050)

According to Kelly (1955), in the loosening phase, a person may recall some events that were neglected before. New elements come into his field of attention. This makes constructs more "permeable" (i.e., more open to change through accepting new elements on their dimensions). The person may "shuffle some ideas into new combinations" (p. 1030). In the tightening phase, the construct system stabilizes in a new configuration (p. 1063). In other words, both the reconstruction of reality in person's mind and his preferences pertinent to that reality become "clear" in the tightening process.

Bannister, Adams-Webber, Penn, and Rodley (1975) explain why both loosening and tightening are necessary. A person loosens his construction of events in the face of "repeated predictive failure." Bannister and his colleagues call this phenomenon "serial invalidation." If a social theory fails to predict certain outcomes, then the theory is invalidated. For instance, Marxist theory's prediction that capitalist system would collapse because of its inner contradictions has not turned out to be correct. In this case, the theory itself must be invalidated. Under such conditions, according to Bannister and his colleagues, the theorist needs to loosen the relationships among his constructs in order to minimize the "reverberatory" impact of further invalidation. Marxist theory should be revised by excluding some of its elements and including others, for example. Alternatively, the theorist may replace the Marxist theory in his mind with another one. Bannister and his colleagues point out that the loosening of construct relationships is essentially undertaken to conserve the system; "progressive loosening," without corresponding integration, eventually would lead to the collapse of the entire conceptual structure. The person cannot keep loosening his constructions indefinitely. The Marxist theorist in the example could not keep progressively loosening his construct system, because then he would end up losing his sense of theoretical understanding and reach the conclusion that nothing in society is related to anything else. Instead, he should reintegrate his constructs to modify his theory or to reformulate a new one.

The ability of a person to loosen and tighten his constructions has something to do with the level of his/her cognitive complexity. According to Adams-Webber (1981), "persons with relatively monolithic (or 'cognitively simple') conceptual structures will tend to resist change in the face of ambiguity in order to avoid further confusion and anxiety.... [E]ven minor changes in a tightly organized construct system can present a prospect of impending chaos" (p. 55).

30.5 MEASURING COGNITIVE COMPLEXITY

Bieri (1955) was the first to develop an index of cognitive complexity. His index aimed to measure the extent to which subjects used different constructs independently of each other. Adams-Webber (1996, 234) points out that Bieri's index is essentially a measure of differentiation between constructs; it does not measure the level of integration of a construct system. Bieri and his colleagues (1966) acknowledged that Bieri's method aims to measure differentiation only. They pointed out that this is because the methods were theoretically grounded more in Kurt Lewin's theory of "life space" than in George Kelly's "personal construct space." In Lewin's theory, a person's life space is differentiated at varying degrees and it can be measured with the number of elements in it. Bieri's method uses two measures of differentiation: number of constructs elicited from a person and matches (commonalities) between constructs. The higher the number of constructs, the more differentiated—and complex—a person's construct system. The higher the number of matches between constructs, the lower the degree of a person's cognitive complexity (the matches indicate that seemingly different constructs do not, in fact, constitute different dimensions in cognition).

Bieri's method is still popular among some researchers. Woehr and his colleagues (1998), for example, report using a specialized computer program that is based on Bieri's score matching method, but makes some modifications in calculations. Another approach in measuring complexity is using factor analytic methods.[*] Unlike Bieri's pairwise comparisons of constructs, factor analytic methods compute composite correlations between constructs. Bieri and his colleagues (1966) recognize that factor analytic methods can also be used in measuring cognitive complexity and that factor analytic methods yield results similar to Bieri's. Principal components analysis has the capability of reflecting both the differentiation and integration in a person's construct space, as the following example illustrates.

30.5.1 MAPPING COGNITIVE CONSTRUCTIONS WITH REPERTORY GRIDS

I used George Kelly's Repertory Grid Technique in a research on the constructions of environmental problems in Turkey. The research involved six mid- and high-level bureaucrats at the Ministry of Environment, four environmental activists, and three university students. I first conducted Repertory Grid interviews with each individual; then. I analyzed their Grids to determine the degree of each individual's cognitive complexity and made comparisons among them.[†]

In the Repertory Grid interviews, the first step is to ask an interviewee to make a list of elements that are pertinent to the topic of the interview (in my research, those were the elements of environmental problems) or to provide them with a list of elements.[‡] In my interviews, I provided the interviewees with a common list of elements of environmental problems, which I had adapted from a list published in a Turkish daily newspaper. These elements are plotted on the cognitive maps below.

---

[*] I use the term "factor-analytic methods" to include both common factor analysis and principal components analysis here. Although the two are somewhat different in their computational algorithms, they both aim to reduce data to a smaller number of interpretable dimensions—factors or principal components. The details in the differences between the two are not directly relevant to my discussions here. For a detailed discussion of the similarities and differences between the two methods, see Hair, Anderson, and Tatham (1987).

[†] The details of the procedures I used are presented in, Morçöl (2002, pp. 226–239). The following discussion is summarized from this original, with the permission of the copyright owner.

[‡] The elements of a Repertory Grid can also be developed in a group, using a structured group process, such as brainstorming or the nominal group technique. See Morçöl and Asche (1993) for an application of these techniques.

The second step is to elicit the interviewee's constructs that are pertinent to the problematic situation under discussion. The method of "triad elicitation" is used in this step. Three of the elements are selected randomly and the interviewee is asked: "Which two of these three constructs are similar and which one is different? Why?" The similarity and difference identified by the interviewee are noted as the two poles of a dichotomous construct. The procedure is repeated with randomly selected triads of elements until it becomes apparent that the limits of the interviewee's personal construct space have been reached.

Once the constructs of an interviewee are elicited, its poles are written on both sides of the rows of a grid. Elements are placed as the columns of the same grid. Then the interviewee is asked to rate each element on each construct dimension. The ratings in a completed grid constitute a matrix that can be analyzed using principal components analysis (Bezzi, 1999), hierarchical cluster analysis (Shaw and Gaines, 1982; Mörçöl and Asche, 1993), or multidimensional scaling (Van Der Kloot, 1982). In my study, I used principal components analysis.

The results of the principal components analyses of the matrices of only two of the participants—one bureaucrat and one activist—are presented here. One of the measures of cognitive complexity is the percentage of variance accounted for the first component in principal components analysis (Adams-Webber, 1996). The percentages of variance accounted for the first three principal components in the analyses of the bureaucrat's and activist's Repertory Grids are presented in Table 30.1. I conducted two analyses for each individual: one for the matrix with elements as columns and another one with constructs as columns (i.e., transposed matrix).

Table 30.1 shows that the bureaucrat's percentages of variance accounted for the first principal components are relatively high for both elements and constructs (between 46.8% and 50.8%). This means that the bureaucrat's cognition of environmental problems is not highly complex. The activist's percentages of the variances accounted for the first principal components are considerably lower and the distributions of percentages among the three principal components are more equal, which indicates multidimensionality in thinking. However, before reaching any conclusions on the dimensionality of thinking in these two individuals, their cognitive maps should be interpreted.

The theory and applications of generating cognitive maps based on the factor loadings in principal components analysis are explained in detail by Slater (1977). The plotting of elements is straightforward: The coordinates of an element are the factor loadings on the first and second principal component. In Figure 30.1 and Figure 30.2, the elements are represented by their names. For each dichotomous construct, two points should be plotted to represent its two poles. Those two points are connected with a straight line. I did not plot the names of constructs, because that would overcrowd the figures, making interpretations more difficult. Instead, the two poles of each construct are represented by numbers with positive and negative signs, which are listed under each figure. The positive end represents the actual factor loadings of the construct, while the negative end represents the inverse of those loadings. Only the first two components are represented in Figure 30.1 and Figure 30.2. Although the third components are also important (the variances accounted for the third components are between 13.7% and 15.9%, as shown in Table 30.1),

TABLE 30.1

Percentages of Variance Accounted for the Principal Components in the Analyses of Repertory Grids

	Analyses of Elements				Analyses of Constructs			
	1st PC	2nd PC	3rd PC	All 3	1st PC	2nd PC	3rd PC	All 3
Bureaucrat	50.8	20.3	15.3	86.4	46.8	15.9	15.4	78.1
Activist	38.1	24.1	13.7	75.9	39.8	20.6	15.9	76.3

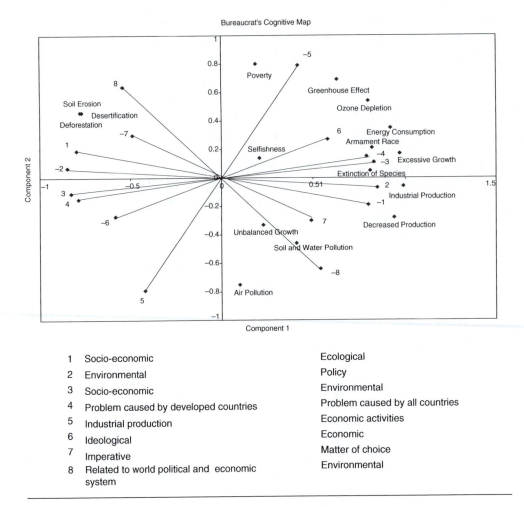

FIGURE 30.1 Bureaucrat's cognitive map.

because of the difficulties in plotting three dimensional data on a two dimensional plane and in interpreting three dimensional charts, they are omitted.

The bureaucrat's map (Figure 30.1) does not display a coherent and meaningful grouping of elements or construct dimensions. Most of the elements are scattered on the right side of the map without apparent or meaningful associations with the construct dimensions. What is significant in this map is that despite the smallest number of constructs elicited (only 8) and the large percentages of variance accounted for the first principal components (see Table 30.1)—both of which are considered as the indicators of cognitive simplicity—the bureaucrat's constructs are not tightly bundled. The map indicates a high degree of differentiation among the constructs. Since the constructs are not meaningfully bundled in groups, however, the degree of integration is not high. Therefore, this should not be considered as the map of a cognitively complex person.

The activist's map (Figure 30.2) is qualitatively different from the bureaucrat's. The constructs are meaningfully differentiated and integrated. Roughly three bundles of construct dimensions are discernable in his map. The first bundle includes the constructs 3 and 10. This metadimension associates the construct poles of causing international conflicts (10) and affecting some nations (−3) with poverty and decreased production. On the other side of the map, greenhouse effect,

Activist's Cognitive Map

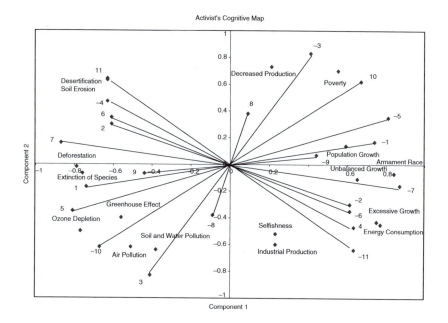

Construct #	PositivePole	NegativePole
1	Cause of the destruction of natural resources	Result of the destruction of natural resources
2	Problem for underdeveloped countries	Problem for developed countries
3	Affects all nations	Affects some nations
4	Using natural resources today	Preserving natural resources for tomorrow
5	Deterioration of natural conditions	Increase in material wealth
6	International cooperation would be effective	International cooperation would not be effective in its solution
7	Affects individuals directly	Does not affect individuals directly
8	Effects can be felt quickly	Effects will be felt in the long term
9	Easy to solve	Not easy to solve
10	May cause international conflicts	Not likely to cause international conflicts
11	Material poverty	Material wealth

FIGURE 30.2 Activist's cognitive map.

ozone depletion, and the pollution of the soil, water, and air are associated with the construct poles of not causing international conflicts (−10) and affecting all nations (3). In other words, this metadimension counterposes national and conflictual issues against global and non-conflictual ones.

The second discernable metadimension associates the elements of deforestation, extinction of species, ozone depletion, greenhouse effect with the construct poles of affecting individuals directly (7), being results the destruction of natural resources (1), and deterioration of natural conditions (5). On the other end of this metadimension are population growth, armament race, and unbalanced growth. These elements are associated with deterioration of natural resources (−5), being the cause of the destruction of natural resources (−1), and not affecting individuals directly (−7). This dimension seems to represent a thinking of the negative impacts of human and national activities on the environment.

The third metadimension associates excessive growth and energy consumption with the construct poles of being the problem of developed countries (-2), international cooperation not being effective (-6), using natural resources today (4), and material wealth (-11). Desertification and soil erosion are associated with material poverty (11), preserving natural resources for tomorrow (-4), international cooperation being effective in solutions (6), and being problems for underdeveloped countries (2). This metadimension seems to dichotomize the shortterm actions of the wealthy, developed countries against the problems that mainly affect the poor, underdeveloped countries and that can be remedied by international cooperation.

The cognitive map of the activist is both more differentiated (it has a moderate number of constructs and the least amount of percentage explained by the first principal component) and most integrated (it has three meaningful bundles of constructs) compared to the bureaucrat's map. It can be concluded that the activist has a higher level of cognitive complexity. Therefore, it can be argued that he has a higher potential for creative thinking.

30.5.2 A COMPARISON WITH THE Q METHODOLOGY

Kelly's Repertory Grid method is similar to the Q Methodology, which is presented by Durning and Brown in their chapter in this volume, in their philosophies and applications, but they differ in some aspects of their applications. Durning and Brown point out that Q methodology is an intensive methodology designed to study the subjectivity of an individual or a group of individuals and to identify individual preferences that may influence decision situations. Repertory Grids are used to elicit individual subjectivities and preferences as well. Q methodology is not designed to measure or facilitate creativity, but it can be used to analyze and interpret the preferences (i.e., cognitive constructions) of groups of individuals. As the authors point out, it can also be used generate innovative ideas (facilitate creativity), which is the topic of the next section.

There are two main differences between the Kelly's Repertory Grids and the Q methodology. Repertory Grids employ a more elaborate procedure to elicit a person's constructs (elicitation of elements and using triads of elements to elicit constructs). In Q methodology, these constructs are collected from a group of people. In the example of mapping environmental cognitions, I took a shortcut and collected elements from a group of people, but I elicited constructs individually. To the extent that individuals share common elements, they will be able to rate them on their known constructs; if they do not share the elements to begin with, then the Repertory Grids will have validity problems (see Morçöl and Asche, 1993 for a discussion of the validity problems in Repertory Grids). Q Methodology takes a short cut in developing statements (constructs). By doing so, it ignores a potential problem: whether or not a particular statement (construct) is within a person's construct space. However, it also avoids the practical problems in eliciting elements and constructs using Repertory Grids. The Repertory Grid construct elicitation process is long and cumbersome; participants seldom have the time and willingness to go through the process.

The second main difference is that whereas Repertory Grids are analyzed and cognitive maps are generated individually, Q methodologists combine individual sorts in correlation matrices and analyze these matrices to understand groupings of statements collectively. In Q methodology, factor analysis is used to analyze combined matrices to group participants on the basis of their commonalities in sorting statements. The Repertory Grid method is idiographic, and Kelly's personal construct theory would caution against using combined matrices, because in the process of combining matrices, individual constructions may be artificially melded together. In my application of Repertory Grids to develop environmental cognitive maps, I intentionally took a more idiographic and qualitative approach and analyzed and mapped each person's construct system individually.

TABLE 30.2
Final List of Elements (Goals) in the Virginia Tech Case

E1	Closer working relationships with business and industry
E2	Adequate facilities
E3	Change degree to Ph.D.
E4	Broadened, research-oriented program
E5	Increase in interdisciplinary approach
E6	Faculty development
E7	Program instructors teach more grad courses
E8	Globalization
E9	Emphasis on excellence
E10	Socio-political and philosophical connections in the division

30.6 METHODS OF FACILITATING CREATIVITY

The key assumption underlying the methods of facilitating (enhancing or stimulating) creativity is that creativity is "not a single trait that people either have or do not have" (Halpern, 1996, 365 and 366). Halpern points out that research in psychology shows that creativity can be understood best in degrees and that it is a complex cognitive and social process. Individuals' creative capabilities can be enhanced and social (group) environments can be designed to foster creative thinking. In the applications of Repertory Grids that I describe in this section, I utilized groups to enhance creativity.

30.6.1 FACILITATING THE CREATIVITY CYCLE WITH REPERTORY GRIDS

Kelly's (1955) Repertory Grid method can be used to facilitate the creativity cycle. I used the Repertory Grid Method with six graduate students in the Division of Vocational and Technical Education at Virginia Tech to facilitate their formulation of strategic goals for the division.[*]

The Repertory Grid procedure I used in this case was similar to the one I described earlier (the case of measuring cognitive complexity). I elicited elements from the students using the nominal group technique in a group session. Then, I elicited constructs from each student in individual sessions and facilitated the construction of their individual cognitive maps. In the end, in a group session, students generated a group cognitive map. Generating a list of elements in a group setting "loosens" the construction of a situation by group members by facilitating the acquisition of new elements by their construction systems. These new constructs allow individuals to see the problematic situation from different perspectives and consequently facilitate creative thinking. The results of this process are presented in Table 30.2.

In the second phase, I elicited each student's constructs and helped them construct their individual hierarchical maps of elements using a specialized computer program (an earlier version of Dickey, 2000). The constructs of one of the students (Jackie, pseudonym) are shown in Table 30.3. The software groups elements using a hierarchical cluster analysis algorithm and allows participants to name clusters of elements in a hierarchical manner. The names given to the clusters at the most meaningful clustering stage are used to develop a model of the problem (or a hierarchical system of goals) by utilizing a procedure called "laddering" (Ten Kate, 1981). This technique aims to elicit superordinate and subordinate constructs in a person's construction system. Superordinate constructs are elicited by asking the question "Why?" and subordinate

---

[*] The following description of the case was published in Morçöl (2002, pp. 235–239) and reprinted here with the permission of the copyright owner.

TABLE 30.3
Constructs Elicited from Jackie

C1	Changes within the area—External issues
C2	Involves national and international ties—Emphasis on research only
C3	Excellence—Specific to industry
C4	Knowledge within the area—Broader knowledge
C5	Knowledge within the program—Global
C6	Micro development—Macro development
C7	Expansion of working relationships—Specific to manpower
C8	Improvement of the program manpower—Specific to instruction

constructs by the question "How?" As the participant sets up the connections between his or her superordinate and subordinate constructs in developing a model, he or she stabilizes his or her construction and organizes the constructs in an ordinal relationship through "tightening" (Kelly, 1955, 1063). Jackie's model is presented in Figure 30.3.

In the final phase of the process, I facilitated a group meeting to develop a group map (see Figure 30.4). The group members merged the elements in their individual maps into the group map by rewording some of them and supplementing them with new ones. Personal construct theorists Shaw and Gaines (1982) see group discussions like this one as processes of "validation of constructs in the social context." In the Virginia Tech case, the constructs that were included in the group model were validated by being accepted by all the members of the group.

30.6.2 A COMPARISON WITH OTHER COGNITIVE MAPPING METHODS

My applications of Kelly's Repertory Grid method in the cases of the environmental constructions in Turkey and Virginia Tech students are examples of cognitive mapping. There are many other methods of cognitive mapping developed in the last few decades. The advances in computer and information technologies and in the applications of multivariate statistical methods enabled this development. Most of these methods have been used to facilitate creative problem solving or decision/strategy making, in a manner similar to what I did in the Virginia Tech case. The uses of cognitive mapping for analytical purposes, such as in measuring cognitive complexity, are rare.

The applications of cognitive mapping to facilitate creative problem-solving and decision/strategy making are too numerous to list here. Some of the most recent applications include the works by Tegarden and Sheets (2003), Ahmad and Ali (2004), Khan and Quaddus (2004). Khan and Quaddus's application of "fuzzy cognitive maps" is particularly interesting and important, because it is based on the recent theory of *fuzzy sets*, or *fuzzy logic* (Kosko, 1993), which has found many technological applications in diverse areas, such as improving the performances of automobile transmissions and household appliances and controlling the operations of mass transit systems (Mcneill, 1994). Fuzzy logic may have some impact on decision making methods through works like Khan and Quaddus' in the future.

Trochim's "concept mapping" method (Trochim, 1989; Trochim and Cabrera, 2005) has some similarities with my application of the Repertory Grid in facilitating the creativity cycle. Trochim uses a combination of statistical and group interaction techniques to help participants develop a collective concept map. As in the applications of Q methodology, Trochim's participants develop a set of statements in a brainstorming session and then each individual sorts them into groups. Again as in Q methodology, individual matrices of sorts (ratings) are combined mathematically into a group matrix. The statistical methods Trochim uses to analyze the group matrix (multidimensional scaling and cluster analysis) are different from the one Q methodologists use (factor analysis; see the Durning and Brown chapter in this volume). In Trochim's method, the resultant concept maps

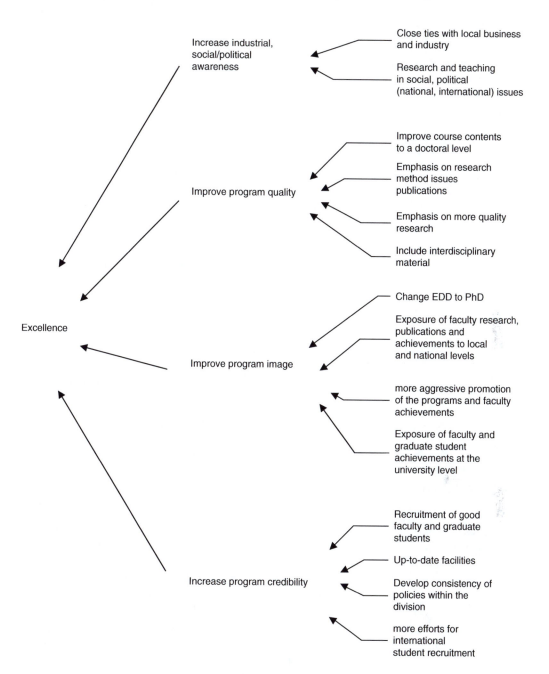

FIGURE 30.3 Jackie's model.

are interpreted by the group members. The logic of Trochim's procedure has some similarities with that of the Repertory Grid, but the two differ in two major ways. First, in Trochim's method, group members generate statements to be sorted later. In the Repertory Grid method, elements and constructs are generated (elicited), which is a more elaborate and analytical approach. Second, in Trochim's method, individual matrices are merged into a group matrix quantitatively and then a group map is developed quantitatively (using multidimensional scaling and cluster analysis). In my

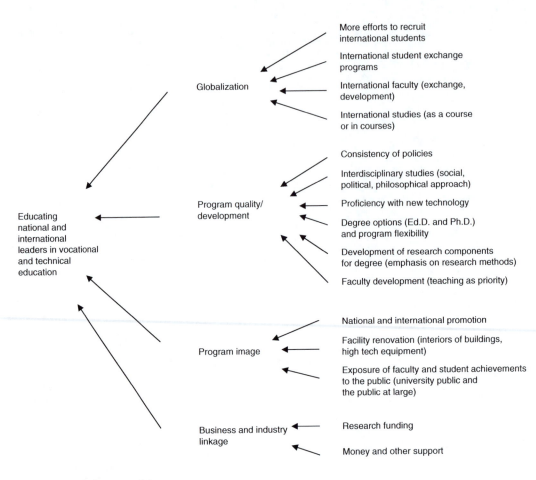

FIGURE 30.4 Group model.

application of Repertory Grids, I facilitated to merge individuals' maps in to a group map in a qualitative manner. As I mentioned earlier, this latter approach is more in tune with Kelly's theory.

Colin Eden and his colleagues' works on cognitive mapping deserve special mention, because they contributed significantly to the literature on strategic decision making and management over the last three decades (Eden, 2004; Eden and Ackermann, 1998, 2004; Eden et al., 1983). Eden and Ackermann's book (1998) is particularly noteworthy. The authors describe the applications of strategy making utilizing the Decision Explorer (1996) cognitive mapping software. The method they developed was inspired by Kelly's personal construct theory and has similarities with the Repertory Grid applications described in this chapter. Their method is designed to develop hierarchical models like the ones in Figure 30.3 and Figure 30.4, but avoids the labor intensive and time consuming aspects of Repertory Grid applications (elicitation of elements and constructs). The Decision Explorer software they use enables users to manipulate and analyze these models effectively and easily.

30.6.3 OTHER METHODS OF FACILITATING CREATIVITY

There are several other methods that were developed to facilitate creative thinking. Among the most well known of these methods are brainstorming, the nominal group technique (which I used in my creativity cycle case), and the Delphi. The rationale and applications of these methods are described and discussed in detail by Van Gundy (1988).

These methods, and most others I will mention in this section, are based on the two basic assumptions about creativity: (1) that creativity involves both divergent and convergent thinking (loosening and tightening), and (2) that it can be fostered by creating appropriate social environments. Brainstorming, the nominal group technique, and the Delphi are all group methods of generating innovative ideas. In all three of the methods, divergent thinking is fostered by encouraging participants to generate their ideas without restraint or criticism in initial phases. These ideas are later valuated and screened to select the most useful and relevant ones (convergent thinking).

Two types of cognitive tools are commonly employed in most creative thinking methods: association of words and association of images. Both word and image associations are based on the cognitive scientific understanding that analogical thinking underlies "much of our everyday thinking, our artistic expressions, and scientific achievements" (Halpern, 1996, 374). Indeed, recent studies in cognitive science show that analogical thinking (or, more appropriately called "metaphorical thinking") is essential to human cognition (see, for example, Lakoff and Johnson, 1980; Lakoff, 1993; Gibbs, 1993; Rumelhart, 1993). Lakoff and Johnson argue that our conceptual system is metaphorically structured (56). Lakoff points out that the metaphors are not mere linguistic devices, but their sources are in our cognition (203 and 204). Rumelhart observes that metaphorical thinking is ingrained in us from the beginning, when we were born. Gibbs suggests that the foundation of human consciousness is based on metaphors; this is why we employ metaphors in our everyday conversations and find them easy to understand (252 and 253).

Creative thinking methods utilize this natural human propensity to make metaphorical associations. All the creative thinking methods Halpern (1996, 381–388) describes (brainstorming, creative ideas checklist, attribute listing, and relational algorithm), for example, use word associations to stimulate creativity. The creative thinking methods that were created by De Bono (1973, 1985, and 1992) and the ones that are described in Van Gundy's comprehensive books (1988, 1995, 2005) are based on the principle of metaphorical (associational) thinking as well, although the authors do not specifically mention this. Most of the methods Van Gundy describes also follow the logic of Kelly's creativity cycle: loosening and tightening of construction.

De Bono (1973, 1985, and 1992), a well known inventor of a group of methods of facilitating creative thinking, popularized the term "lateral thinking" (in essence, divergent thinking or loosening of construction). DeBono (1973) argues that there are mainly two methods of thinking: vertical and lateral thinking. Vertical thinking is systematic, linear thinking; it involves using the same pattern (e.g., problem-solving algorithm) over and over again. Although vertical thinking is necessary, it will foster rigidity if overused—excessive patterning of information processing (i.e., clichés). Thus, an excessive use of vertical thinking becomes a major impediment to creative thinking. To avoid rigidity in thinking, one needs to go "sideways," take detours from the accustomed paths, or algorithms. Although lateral thinking by itself is not creative thinking, it is the most important component of creativity (1992, 55). Creative thinking must generate new and unusual ideas, but new ideas also have to be useful, valuable (3). Vertical thinking is needed to make them so.

De Bono (1992) describes a series of methods of stimulating creativity that involve mainly challenging and provoking accepted modes of thinking to divert participants' thinking into unusual patterns. The methods described in De Bono's book use verbal concepts and images to challenge and provoke thinking. Essentially, they utilize the metaphorical (associational) thinking capabilities of the human mind.

His method of "six thinking hats" (De Bono, 1985) deserves specific mentioning, because it adds another dimension to stimulating creative thinking: role playing. Participants in his creative thinking sessions use hats in six different colors in sequence to play the roles predefined for each color. Each of the six colored hats represents an aspect of the creative thinking process, according to De Bono: the white hat, dispassionate collection of facts and figures; the red hat, letting emotions making connections; black hat, thinking about negative consequences of actions (why it cannot be done, why it is costly); yellow hat, letting optimism take over; green hat, generating more and more diverse ideas; and blue hat, controlling and organizing information. By wearing the hats in a particular sequence, a participant generates ideas and screens them for usefulness and validity in a comprehensive manner.

Van Gundy's books (1988, 1995, 2005) include the most comprehensive compilations of creative problem-solving methods (over a hundred methods) that are available. The methods Van Gundy (1988, 1995) describes involve either word or image associations to stimulate creative thinking.

An important aspect of Van Gundy's books is the way he classifies the methods. He first divides them into individual and group methods. The individual methods use stimuli to facilitate word or image associations. Group methods also use word and image associations and take advantage of the thought stimulating atmosphere of social interactions. Ten Kate (1981, 73–75) further divides group methods into two: brainstorming and brainwriting methods. Brainstorming methods evolved from the classical brainstorming, which was invented by Alex Osborn in the 1940s. In brainstorming methods, verbal interactions among the members of a group are the primary tools of generating new ideas. The interactions are directed and facilitated by a facilitator. Brainwriting involves silent generation of ideas (writing down individual ideas separately). The ideas generated individually are shared with other group members at different degrees and in systematic and controlled ways. The nominal group technique and the Delphi are the most well known examples of brainwriting. Van Gundy (1995) points out that several studies show that brainwriting methods are more effective (more ideas are generated with them) than brainstorming methods.

Another important contribution by Van Gundy (1988) is his classification of the methods according to the phases of problem-solving and decision making: methods of redefining and analyzing problems, idea generation techniques, and techniques of evaluating and selecting ideas. One can see in this classification that it follows the logic of the creativity cycle (loosening and tightening, or divergent and convergent thinking). In the redefinition and analysis of problems, one's construct system is loosened to think in new ways. It is not left loosened, however; the construct system is tightened to redefine the problem. Idea generation is simply about loosening of ideas. The techniques of evaluating and selecting ideas help tighten them to make them useful and applicable.

30.7 SUMMARY AND CONCLUSIONS

The premise of this chapter is that creative thinking is needed in public policy analysis and decision making, because policy problems are typically ill-structured and complex and such problems require creative thinking for their solutions. Creativity, by definition, involves construing different facets of a problematic situation in a broad and novel perspective and formulating problem representations that generate innovative and useful solutions. Creativity is usually associated with divergent thinking, as opposed to convergent thinking, which has some validity, but a better understanding of the creativity process should include both modes of thinking. George Kelly's personal construct psychology provides a comprehensive and coherent conceptualization of the creativity process (particularly his conceptualizations of differentiation and integration and the creativity cycle) and the tools to measure creative potentials of individuals and to facilitate creative thinking.

The case of the environmental cognitions of Turkish individuals I described was an application of Kelly's Repertory Grid method in measuring and mapping cognitive complexity and creative potentials of individuals. The case of Virginia Tech students, on the other hand, illustrated an application of his creativity cycle conceptualization in the facilitation of creative thinking. Both applications are examples of cognitive mapping, which has become a popular approach in facilitating creative decision making and problem-solving in recent decades. The advances in the computer and information technologies and applications of multivariate statistical techniques enabled this development. I discussed, specifically, Eden and his colleagues' and Trochim's methods of cognitive (or concept) mapping and Q methodology and compared them with my applications of Repertory Grids. In addition, I briefly discussed some of the other well-known methods of facilitating creative thinking. I mentioned De Bono's techniques specifically, and also summarized the conceptual framework of Van Gundy's comprehensive compilations of creative problem solving methods.

The developments of creative thinking methods have contributed not only to the betterment of the business and public policy decision making processes, but they have also helped us understand the creativity process better. Creativity is not a mystery, nor is it a dichotomous or innate property of a select group of individuals. Creativity is a complex cognitive and social process, one which is not known in its entirety. However, it is known that creativity can be triggered or stultified by stimuli and social environment. Cognitive science has helped us understand human cognition better in recent years (see Gardner, 1985; Pinker, 1997; Lakoff and Johnson, 1999). Likely developments in the future will help us understand human cognition better and help enhance the creative potentials of individuals.

REFERENCES

Adams-Webber, J. R., Cognitive complexity and sociality, *British Journal of Social and Clinical Psychology*, 8, 211–216, 1969.

Adams-Webber, J. R., Actual Structure and Potential Chaos: Rational aspects of progressive variations within a personal construct system, In *Perspectives in Personal Construct Theory*, Bannister, D., Ed., Academic Press, London, 1970.

Adams-Webber, J. R., Empirical developments in personal construct theory, In *Personal Construct Psychology: Recent Advances in Theory and Practice*, Bonarius, H., Holland, R., and Rosenberg, S., Eds., St. Martin's Press, New York, pp. 53–67, 1981.

Adams-Webber, J. R., Cognitive complexity, In *Encyclopaedia of Psychology*, Corsini, R. and Auerbach, A. J., Eds., John Wiley and Sons, New York, pp. 234–235, 1996.

Ahmad, R. and Ali, N. A., Performance appraisal decision in Malaysian public service, *The International Journal of Public Sector Management*, 17(1), 48–59, 2004.

Bannister, D., Adams-Webber, J. R., Penn, W., and Rodley, A., Reversing the process of thought disorder: A serial validation experiment, *British Journal of Social and Clinical Psychology*, 14, 169–180, 1975.

Bezzi, A., What is this thing called geoscience? Epistemological dimensions elicited with the repertory grid and their implications for scientific literacy, *Science Education*, 83, 675–700, 1999.

Bieri, J., Cognitive complexity-simplicity and predictive behavior, *Journal of Abnormal and Social Psychology*, 51, 263–268, 1955.

Bieri, J., Atkins, A., Briar, S., Leoman, R. L., Miller, H., and Tripodi, T., *Cognitive Structure and Judgement*, John Wiley and Sons, New York, 1966.

Blumer, H., Social problems as collective behavior, *Social Problems*, 18, 298–306, 1971.

Brophy, D. R., Understanding, measuring, and enhancing individual problem-solving efforts, *Creativity Research Journal*, 11, 123–150, 1998.

Brown, R. T., Creativity: what are we to measure, In *Handbook of Creativity*, Glover, J. A., Ronning, R. R., and Reynolds, C. R., Eds., Plenum Press, New York, pp. 3–32, 1989.

Crockett, W. H., Cognitive complexity and impression formation, In *Progress in Experimental Personality Research*, Maher, B. A., Ed., Vol. 2, Academic Press, London, pp. 13–28, 1965.

De Bono, E., *Lateral Thinking: Creativity Step by Step*, Harper, New York, 1973.

De Bono, E., *Six Thinking Hats*, Little, Brown and Company, Boston, 1985.

De Bono, E., *Serious Creativity: Using the Power of Lateral Thinking to Create New Ideas*, Advanced Practical Thinking Training Inc. Publications, Des Moines, IA, 1992.

Decision Explorer [Computer software]. Scolari (Sage), Thousand Oaks, CA, 1996.

Dery, D., *Problem Definition and Policy Analysis*, University Press of Kansas, Lawrence, KS, 1984.

Dickey, J., *Cyberquest*, [Computer software], Blacksburg, VA, 2000.

Dowd, E. T., The self and creativity: several constructs in search of a theory, In *Handbook of Creativity*, Glover, J. A., Ronning, R. R., and Reynolds, C. R., Eds., Plenum Press, New York, pp. 233–242, 1989.

Dunn, W. N., Methods of the second type: coping with the wilderness of public policy analysis, *Policy Studies Review*, 7, 720–737, 1988.

Dunn, W. N., *Public Policy Analysis: An Introduction*, 3rd ed., Pearson Prentice Hall, Upper Saddle River, NJ, 2004.

Eden, C., Analyzing cognitive maps to help structure issues or problems, *European Journal of Operational Research*, 159(3), 673–685, 2004.

Eden, C., Cognitive mapping expert views for policy analysis in the public sector, *European Journal of Operational Research*, 152(3), 615–626, 2004.

Eden, C. and Ackermann, F., *Making Strategy: The Journey of Strategic Management*, Sage, Thousand Oaks, CA, 1998.

Eden, C., Jones, S., and Sims, D., *Messing About in Problems: An Informal Structured Approach to their Identification and Management*, Pergamon Press, New York, 1983.

Feldman, D. H., The development of creativity, In *Handbook of Creativity*, Sternberg, R. J., Ed., Cambridge University Press, Cambridge, UK, pp. 169–186, 1999.

Fransella, F. and Bannister, D., *A Manual for Repertory Grid Technique*, Academic Press, London, 1977.

Fuller, R. C. and Myers, R. R., The natural history of social problems, *American Sociological Review*, 6, 24–32, 1941.

Gardner, H., *The Mind's New Science: A History of the Cognitive Revolution*, Basic Books, New York, 1985.

Gendlin, E. T., Beebe, J., Cassens, J., Klein, M., and Oberlander, M., Focusing ability in psychotherapy, personality, creativity, In *Research in Psychotherapy*, Schlien, J. M., Ed., Vol. 3, American Psychological Association, Washington, D.C., pp. 230–256, 1968.

Gibbs, R. W., Jr., Process and products in making sense of tropes, In *Metaphor and Thought*, Ortony, A., Ed., 2nd ed., Cambridge University Press, New York, pp. 252–276, 1993.

Guilford, J. P., Creativity, *American Psychologist*, 5, 444–454, 1950.

Guilford, J. P., The structure of the intellect, *Psychological Bulletin*, 53, 267–293, 1956.

Guilford, J. P., *The Nature of Human Intelligence*, McGraw-Hill, New York, 1967.

Hair, J. F., Jr., Anderson, R. E., and Tatham, R. L., *Multivariate Data Analysis*, 2nd ed., Macmillan, New York, 1987.

Halpern, D. F., *Thought and Knowledge: An Introduction to Critical Thinking*, 3rd ed., Lawrence Erlbaum, Mahwah, NJ, 1996.

Hankison, G., Repertory grid analysis: an application to the measurement of destination images, *International Journal of Nonprofit and Voluntary Sector Marketing*, 9(2), 145–153, 2004.

Kelly, G. A., *The Psychology of Personal Constructs*, W.W. Norton and Company, New York, 1955.

Khan, M. S. and Quaddus, M., Group decision support using fuzzy cognitive maps for causal reasoning, *Group Decision and Negotiation*, 13(5), 463–481, 2004.

Kosko, B., *Fuzzy Thinking: The New Science of Fuzzy Logic*, Hyperion, New York, 1993.

Lakoff, G., The contemporary theory of metaphor, In *Metaphor and Thought*, Ortony, A., Ed., 2nd ed., Cambridge University Press, New York, pp. 202–251, 1993.

Lakoff, G., *Philosophy in the Flesh: The Embodied Mind and its Challenge to Western Thought*, Basic Books, New York, 1999.

Lakoff, G. and Johnson, M., *Metaphors We Live by*, University of Chicago Press, Chicago, 1980.

Landfield, A. W., Exploring socialization through the interpersonal transaction group, In *Constructs of Sociality and Individuality*, Stringer, P. and Bannister, D., Eds., Academic Press, London, pp. 133–152, 1979.

Lasswell, H., Cultivation of creativity, *Creativity Plus*, 2(1), 16–19, 2000.

Maher, B. Ed., *Clinical Psychology and Personality: The Selected Papers of George Kelly*, John Wiley and Sons, New York, 1969.

Manis, J., *Analyzing Social Problems*, Praeger, New York, 1976.

Mcneill, D., *Fuzzy Logic: The Revolutionary Computer Technology that is Changing our World*, Simon and Schuster, New York, 1994.

McRae, R. R., Creativity, divergent thinking, and openness to experience, *Journal of Personality and Social Psychology*, 52, 1258–1265, 1987.

Merton, R. K., Social problems and sociological theory, In *Contemporary Social Problems*, Merton, R. and Nisbet, R. A., Eds., Harcourt Brace, New York, 1976.

Morçöl, G., *A New Mind for Policy Analysis: Toward a Post-Newtonian and Postpositivist Epistemology and Methodology*, Praeger, Westport, CT, 2002.

Morçöl, G. and Asche, M., The repertory grid in problem structuring: a case illustration, *The International Journal of Personal Construct Psychology*, 6, 371–390, 1993.

Newell, A. and Simon, H. A., *Human Problem Solving*, Prentice Hall, Englewood Cliffs, NJ, 1972.

Pinker, S., *How the Mind Works*, W.W. Norton and Company, New York, 1997.

Plucker, J. A. and Renzulli, J. S., Psychometric approaches to the study of human creativity, In *Handbook of Creativity*, Sternberg, R., Ed., Cambridge University Press, Cambridge, UK, pp. 35–61, 1999.

Rittel, H. and Webber, M. M., Dilemmas in a general theory of planning, *Policy Sciences*, 4, 155–169, 1973.

Rumelhart, D. E., Some problems with the notion of literal meanings, In *Metaphor and Thought*, Ortony, A., Ed., 2nd ed., Cambridge University Press, New York, pp. 71–82, 1993.

Runco, M. A. and Okuda, S. M., Problem discovery, divergent thinking, and the creative process, *Journal of Youth and Adolescence*, 17, 211–220, 1988.

Runco, M. A. and Sakamoto, S. O., Experimental studies of creativity, In *Handbook of Creativity*, Sternberg, R. J., Ed., Cambridge University Press, Cambridge, UK, pp. 62–92, 1999.

Shaw, M. L. G. and Gaines, B. R., Tracking the creativity cycle with a microcomputer, *International Journal of Man-Machine Studies*, 17, 75–85, 1982.

Simon, H. A., The structure of ill-structured problems, *Artificial Intelligence*, 4, 181–201, 1973.

Slater, P., *The Measurement of Intrapersonal Space by Grid Technique*, Wiley, London, 1977.

Spector, M. and Kitsuse, J. I., Social problems: a re-formulation, *Social Problems*, 21, 145–159, 1973.

Sternberg, R. J. and O'Hara, L. A., Creativity and intelligence, In *Handbook of Creativity*, Sternberg, R. J., Ed., Cambridge University Press, Cambridge, UK, pp. 251–272, 1999.

Tegarden, D. P. and Sheetz, S. D., Group cognitive mapping: a methodology and system for capturing and evaluating managerial and organizational cognition, *Omega*, 31(2), 113–127, 2003.

Ten Kate, H., A theoretical explication of Hinkle's implication theory, In *Personal Construct Psychology: Recent Advances in Theory and Practice*, Bonarius, H., Holland, R., and Rosenberg, S., Eds., St. Martin's Press, New York, pp. 33–61, 1981.

Torrance, E. P., *Rewarding Creative Behavior*, Prentice-Hall, Englewood Cliffs, NJ, 1965.

Trochim, W. M. K., An introduction to concept mapping for planning and evaluation, *Evaluation and Program Planning*, 12(1), 1–16, 1989.

Trochim, W. M. K. and Cabrera, D., The complexity of concept mapping for policy analysis, *Emergence: Complexity and Organization*, 7(1), 2–10, June 2005.

Van Der Kloot, W., Multidimensional scaling of repertory grid responses: two applications of HOMALS, In *Personal Construct Psychology: Recent Advances in Theory and Practice*, Bonarius, H., Holland, R., and Rosenberg, S., Eds., St. Martin's Press, New York, pp. 90–121, 1982.

Van Gundy, A. B., *Techniques of Structured Problem Solving*, 2nd ed., Van Nostrand Reinhold Company, New York, 1988.

Van Gundy, A. B., *Brain Boosters for Business Advantage: Ticklers, Grab Bags, Blue Skies, and Other Bionic Ideas*, Pfeiffer and Co., San Diego, CA, 1995.

Van Gundy, A. B., *101 Activities for Teaching Creativity and Problem Solving*, Pfeiffer and Co., San Francisco, CA, 2005.

Vernon, P. E., The nature-nurture problem in creativity, In *Handbook of Creativity*, Glover, J. A., Ronning, R. R., and Reynolds, C. R., Eds., Plenum Press, New York, pp. 93–110, 1989.

Voss, J. F. and Means, M. L., Toward a model of creativity based upon problem solving in the social sciences, In *Handbook of Creativity*, Glover, J. A., Ronning, R. R., and Reynolds, C. R., Eds., Plenum Press, New York, pp. 399–410, 1989.

Woehr, D. J., Miller, M. J., and Lane, J. A. S., The development and evaluation of computer-administered measure of cognitive complexity, *Personality and Individual Differences*, 25, 1037–1049, 1998.

Wallace, M. A. and Kogan, N., *Modes of Thinking in Young Children: A Study of the Creativity-Intelligence Distinction*, Rinehart and Winston, New York, 1965.

31 Participatory Decision Making: Using Conflict Management Theories, Methods, and Skills to Overcome the Rational and Irrational Sources of Conflict

Susan Summers Raines

CONTENTS

31.1 Introduction..587
    31.1.1 Sources of Conflict...588
    31.1.2 Psychological Barriers to Rationality in Decision Making..............................589
    31.1.3 Attribution Bias 590
    31.1.4 Losing, Building, and Repairing Trust 592
    31.1.5 Procedural Barriers to Rationality in Decision Making 593
31.2 Methods and Skills for Participatory Decision Making 595
    31.2.1 Methods for Group Decision Making 596
    31.2.2 Large-Group Decision Making Methods...597
    31.2.3 Skills for Group Decision Making..599
31.3 Conclusions..603
References...604

31.1 INTRODUCTION

The existence and rapid growth of the field of conflict management stands as an implicit challenge to many of the assumptions of economic and utilitarian models of decision making. Academics and practitioners in the field of Conflict Management and Alternative Dispute Resolution (ADR)[*] assume that decision making is an often messy process that involves egos and other psychological biases, potentially clashing communication styles, leadership inadequacies, economic and non-economic incentives, and limitations on the ability of individuals and groups to obtain and process information. In fact, if decision making were as straight forward as traditional models argue, we would predict that conflict would occur less often and only as the direct result of

---

[*] Alternative Dispute Resolution refers to those processes used as alternatives to dispute resolution through the courts such as mediation, arbitration, regulatory-negotiation, and many others.

mutually-exclusive or non-overlapping utility functions. Yet, we know from simple observations that conflict occurs even when two or more negotiators have common interests and would be better off cooperating. As Fisher and Ury (1981) succinctly observe: "Negotiators are people first" (18).

Rational and utilitarian explanations for the occurrence of conflict in decision making fail to account for many, if not most, of the causes of conflict during the process of participatory decision making. This chapter will draw on literature from economics, psychology, communications, political science, and negotiation to demonstrate that traditional economic-utilitarian theories explain only a minority of the conflicts that occur during the process of group decision making. Then, it will discuss methods and skills for overcoming these obstacles in order to improve decision making in a group environment, using concrete examples and ideas for skill building. It is important to keep in mind that collaborative decision making is not suited to all situations. Serious time constraints, low salience of the issue to the group, the existence of statutory guidelines that prohibit the delegation of decision making authority to a group, all complicate collaborative decision making. However, in those situations where group decision making is warranted (Elangovan, 1998) it is important that decision makers have the knowledge and skills necessary to reach optimally efficient decisions through processes that improve, rather than damage, relationships among decision makers and those impacted by group decisions.

It is clear that the application of conflict management theories, methods, and skills to decision making is a sufficiently weighty topic that warrants a much deeper investigation than space constraints allow. Therefore, this chapter will serve merely as an introduction to these ideas, with plenty of citations provided to lead the reader to more detailed information, if desired.

31.1.1 Sources of Conflict

Rational choice theorists generally focus on conflicts surrounding the objective substance of the dispute, with conflicts between the interests of the decision makers generally thought of in economic terms and exchange theory. Economists, sociologists, and political scientists have built rational choice theory on the fundamental assumption that human behavior is "rational" and that individuals make decisions after carefully weighing the costs and benefits of various choices. Pure rational choice theory denies that human behavior is motivated by familial or societal obligations, emotions such as revenge or laziness, habits that may result in irrational outcomes, or norms of reciprocity. Rational choice theorists have come to accept the fact that cognitive limitations often result in "satisficing" behavior, in which decision makers often accept the first, best, option rather than exhaustively researching all possible choices (Simon, 1981; also see the Mingus chapter in this volume). Many other factors that could mitigate purely rational behavior remain topics for heated debate. A number of scholars have examined psychological constraints on rationality, including the impacts of time pressures, the level of perceived threat or the importance of the decision involved, and the impact of recent decision making failures on the ability to make effective current decisions (Janis, 1982; Janis and Mann, 1997). Elinor Ostrom's work (1998) has also examined behavioral impacts on rational choice theory, recognizing the importance of cultural norms that impact individual and group decision making. While work in this area is very promising, it remains under development and controversial among adherents to traditional rational choice theory. One of the strengths of rational choice theory is its simplicity and relative utility. Understandably, as the number of variables examined by the theory increases, its parsimony and simplicity decrease, leading to debates about which variables are the most worthy of inclusion.

In contrast to rational choice theorists, experts in conflict management tend to see rational, substantive conflicts of interest as only one of three possible sources of conflict. In addition to conflict arising from *substantive* differences in goals or desired outcomes, unproductive conflict also arises from the "emotional" or *psychological* needs of the decision makers and from concerns over the fairness and efficiency of the *processes* used for decision making. Conflict managers often

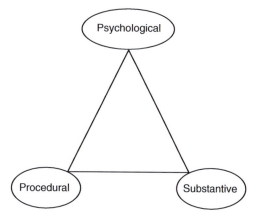

FIGURE 31.1 The conflict management triangle.

use the heuristic of a conflict triangle to explain the relative importance of these additional sources of conflict (Figure 31.1).

Almost any sustainable and effective decision requires decision makers to address all three sides of the conflict triangle. For example, if one addresses the substantive issues in dispute, but uses a decision making process that is seen as illegitimate, then it is more likely that the disputants will be dissatisfied with the outcome and this can make implementation difficult. Alternatively, if the decision does not take into account the ego needs of others, the importance of nurturing positive relationships with those impacted by the decisions, or the concerns of other decision makers, then the desired outcome may not be achieved, or may come at an unacceptably high cost. In other words, the substance of the dispute may be only one piece of the puzzle—but it is the piece examined by traditional rationalists almost to the exclusion of the other two pieces.

Group decision making occurs when two or more individuals or groups are involved in a decision making process. However, these theories and prescriptions also have merit when a single individual makes decisions that require the assistance of others to be implemented or enforced. A wise decision is one that is implementable, durable, efficient, and effective (Fisher and Ury, 1981). To achieve decisions that meet these criteria, it is important for decision makers to consider both the prescriptions of rational choice theorists, but also take into account a host of considerations outside of the scope of this body of theory.

31.1.2 PSYCHOLOGICAL BARRIERS TO RATIONALITY IN DECISION MAKING

Conflict and defection can and do occur, even in situations where it would be rational for individuals or groups to cooperate. People and many other animals survive and thrive due to the ability to cooperate (Kurzban, 2003). With the ability to cooperate comes advanced communication skills (to facilitate cooperation) and the ability to judge when others are not cooperating or playing by the rules. The extent to which these statements are true, and the reasons why they are true, are just beginning to be understood by social and biological scientists. In a recent study at Emory University's Yerkes National Primate Research Center, Capuchin monkeys were given a cucumber slice in exchange for a small pebble. When the monkeys in an adjoining cage were given grapes, which are more desired by monkeys, in exchange for the same pebble, the monkeys in the first cage would show displeasure at the unfairness by rejecting the cucumber and sometimes even throwing it out of the cage. "Monkeys rarely refuse food, but in this case they appear to be pursuing an even higher value than eating: fairness" (Cohen, 2003, 10; for more detail on this study see also Brosnan and de Waal, 2003). Here is an explicit example of a monkey choosing to reject food out of a concern for fairness; a behavior that most economists would not have predicted nor labeled as "rational," at least not in the short term and not at the individual level. Researchers found:

> Monkeys refused to participate if they witnessed a conspecific obtain a more attractive reward for equal effort, an effect amplified if the partner received such a reward without any effort at all. These reactions support an early evolutionary origin of inequity aversion. (Bronson and deWaal, 2003, 297)

Much of human decision making involves complex trade-offs between short and long term needs, the needs of the individual and the group, and the need to ensure an appropriate process for decision making and fairness, none of which have been adequately explained through existing rational choice models. Research, such as that being carried out at the Yerkes Center, may provide the data necessary to expand and improve upon rational choice theory in the future. While this data is being gathered at the individual level, it certainly has an important impact on our ability to understand group decision making, since an understanding of individual interaction within groups is at the heart of group decision making.

One of the problems with traditional rational choice theories is that they tend to give greater weight to rather short-term individual economic and material values over other values such as face-saving, justice, relationship preservation, communal welfare, social norm reinforcement, "doing the right thing," etc. As Steve Smith indicates, game theory (which assumes a rational choice model) leaves a lot to be desired because, "it treats interests and identities as given ...and we know nothing of the [parties'] prior relationship" (2004, 502). Yet, our identities, where they come from, and how they shape our relationships are indispensable to understanding how humans interact and make decisions (Coy and Woehrle, 2000). In other words, it is not simply the objective reality of a situation that influences human behaviors, but how that reality is perceived and understood by individuals and groups. These understandings are filtered through our identities. To complicate matters even more, our ability to communicate our perceptions and our needs is highly influenced by our cognitive abilities, communication skills, personalities, and many other factors not well accounted for by rational choice theory. This section of the chapter will examine a host of these psychological and sociological barriers to rational and optimal decision-making.

31.1.3 ATTRIBUTION BIAS

Understanding attribution bias is key to comprehending the roots of unproductive conflict and poor group interactions. Successfully dealing with attribution bias is vital to the resolution of conflict, fruitful group decision making, and efficient decision implementation. Attributions are motivational interpretations ascribed to behaviors.

Attribution bias is best explained by way of example: John just walked in late to an important company meeting. Because he was late, all of the chairs at the rear of the conference room were taken and he had to step over people in order to get to a vacant seat near the front of the room, causing significant noise and disruption. John's co-worker, Betty, was already upset with John because she just found out that he earns more than she does even though she has been with the company longer and has the same job duties. Betty *attributes* his tardiness to sleeping-in late and sees it as a reflection of John's poor work ethic. On the other hand, the speaker at the front of the room is John's boss, Steve. Steve *attributes* John's tardiness to the fact that John was most likely taking a last-minute call from an important customer, thereby reflecting John's strong work ethic and ability to prioritize. The strength or weakness of their previous relationship with John influenced the attributions made by Betty and Steve.

When we try to understand the motivations behind someone's actions, we rely on attributions. If we have a positive relationship with the actor and a high level of trust, then we generally attribute negative behaviors (such as tardiness) to circumstances beyond the actor's control rather than to dispositions. In this example, Steve has a generally positive relationship with John, who therefore attributes the tardiness to something outside of John's control. If the attributor has a negative relationship with the actor or no relationship at all, or a high level of suspicion or distrust, then she or he is likely to assume the behavior was the result of a disposition rather than being due to circumstances beyond the control of the actor. Then the behavior is likely to be seen as a sign of disrespect, laziness, or some other negative dispositional quality. Clearly, these cognitive short cuts can lead to sub-optimal group decisions, even when the objective circumstances would seem to predict mutually-beneficial exchanges or collaboration. Using an economic or utilitarian model of decision making one might overestimate the chances for positive outcomes if unaware of the relationship history or the negative attributions held by one or more of the negotiators.

In the example above, Betty demonstrated *accuser bias* when she assumed that John's negative behavior is a result of dispositional factors rather than to circumstances outside of his control. Research from the field of psychology has shown that humans have a tendency to over-attribute the behavior of others to dispositions rather than to circumstances (Ross, 1977). This tendency is called *fundamental attribution error* and is at the root of many unproductive conflicts and poor decision making at both the individual and group levels.

While humans tend to over-attribute behaviors of others to negative dispositions rather than circumstances, they do the opposite in relation to themselves. This tendency is most pronounced when one group's identity is perceived to be significantly different from the group with which they are interacting (Coy and Woehrle, 2000). People and groups tend to under-attribute their own negative behaviors to dispositions rather than to circumstances. In other words, people rationalize their own behaviors. This is related to the psychological concept of "denial." For example, if Betty had been late because she drank too much the night before and didn't want to get out of bed on time, she might under-attribute her behavior (i.e., lateness) to a disposition (e.g., irresponsibility) and over-attribute it to circumstances beyond her control, such as heavy traffic on the way to work.

This tendency toward fundamental attribution error is highly common between "in-groups" and "out-groups" and is known to sociologists as *intergroup attributional bias* (Hewstone, 1988). Intergroup attribution bias is most likely to occur when groups have mutually exclusive or conflicting interests and a history of conflict (Allred, 2000). When groups have a history of conflict, they often develop rigid, negative stereotypes of each other that are then applied to all members of the other group; regardless of individual variation and characteristics (Fisher, 2000, 171). These biases reduce the efficiency and accuracy with which individuals and groups process information and make decisions; resulting in sub-optimal, even irrational, outcomes.

Exactly how are attributions formed and maintained? First, the attributor seeks to know whether the actor's behavior is consistently applied under similar conditions. Second, they investigate whether this behavior occurs under a variety of circumstances. Third, the attributor seeks to discern whether others would likely behave similarly under the same circumstances (Allred, 2000, 240). Kelley and Michela (1980) describe this process of information gathering as very rational. However, the psychological biases against out-groups and the tendency to rationalize our own behaviors encourage the filtering out of information inconsistent with previously held attributions. These cognitive filters can lead to irrational conclusions, often resulting in behavior that escalates conflict and results in poor interactions and ineffective decisions. If one takes into account the existence of previously held attribution biases, then such behavior may be viewed as rational and predicted accurately. However, traditional models of rational choice have difficulty fully incorporating and weighing these biases.

Attributions matter because they can cause individuals and groups to filter out information that is inconsistent with their pre-existing beliefs, provoke anger in others, escalate conflict, and result in a lack of cooperation even when the objective conditions seem to favor collaboration. "Emotion is the critical link between attribution and the behavioral response; certain kinds of attribution arouse discrete emotions, such as anger or sympathy. It is these emotions, in turn, that elicit such responses as retaliation or helping behavior" (Allred, 2000, 241). Attributing negative behavior to an internal cause (e.g., laziness, greed) instead of to external causes (e.g., traffic, bad luck) tends to arouse anger and retribution. As the final section of this chapter indicates, it is possible to at least partially overcome these tendencies toward cognitive bias through education and training, and through the use of appropriate framing skills.

31.1.4 Losing, Building, and Repairing Trust

There are many factors that can lead to poor decision outcomes or a lack of cooperation when objective circumstances would seem to favor it. One of these factors includes a lack of trust between individuals working to make group decisions, or among groups negotiating with or against each other to reach decisions. Different cultural groups tend to place variable values on the importance of building rapport and trust before negotiating. Also, trust can be built through repeated successful interactions between decision makers who may have been initially wary of each other.

Game theory has dealt extensively with the issue of trust (Ostrom and Walker, 2003); particularly as it impacts behavior in iterative games versus one-shot games (Selton, 1991). It is assumed that defection (which is a breach of trust) is more likely to occur in one-shot games or in the last round of multi-round games. This prediction highlights the importance of ongoing relationships as a guarantor of cooperative behavior and follows logically from the assumptions of rational choice theorists (Axelrod, 1981). While great strides have been made in recent years (Ostrom and Walker, 2003), rational choice theorists generally have difficulty weighting the importance of trust building, face saving, and strong relationships as a resource in decision making and implementation when building economic and game theoretic models designed to predict behavior (Olson, 1965). Therefore, brief discussions about the importance of trust building and trust repair in the service of group decision making are in order.

Trust has been defined in many ways, but for our purposes it will be defined as "an individual's belief in, and willingness to act on, the basis of the words, actions, and decisions of another" (Lewicki, McAllister, and Bies, 1998, 440). This definition implies three basic factors as influences on trust: an individual's chronic disposition toward trust (i.e., how cynical are they?), situational parameters, and the history of the relationship (Lewicki and Wiethoff, 2000, 87). Dispositional factors are best addressed by literature from the field of psychology, while situational factors are generally addressed well by rational choice theorists (e.g., economists, political scientists, etc). This chapter will focus primarily on relationship issues as they have an important and often underestimated impact on both individual and group decision making.

Relationships occur either in a personal or professional arena, although these arenas seem to be increasingly blending. Professional relationships tend to be focused on achieving goals external to the relationship, whereas personal relationships are more focused on strengthening and improving the social-emotional benefits derived from the relationship (Lewicki and Wiethoff, 2000). However, research on decision making and conflict management indicates that in some situations attention to task to the exclusion of relationship results in poor decisions and difficulty with the implementation of decisions (Bush and Folger, 1994; Elangovan, 1998).

Trust can be broken down into two main types: calculus-based trust (CBT) and identification-based trust (IBT). In CBT, individuals do what they promise to do or what is clearly expected of them out of a desire to avoid unpleasant penalties (Lewicki and Wiethoff, 2000). This has also been called deterrence-based trust. In order for the deterrence to be effective, the punishment for defection must be higher than the reward for non-cooperation and the likelihood that punishment will occur must be high. To strengthen CBT, monitoring and sanctioning mechanisms must exist and function well.

> This kind of trust is an ongoing, market-oriented, economic, calculation whose value is determined by the outcomes resulting from creating and sustaining the relationship relative to the costs of maintaining or severing it. Compliance with calculus-based trust is often ensured both by the rewards of being

trusting (and trustworthy) and by the "threat" that if trust is violated, one's reputation can be hurt through the person's network of friends and associates. Even if you are an honest person, having a reputation for honesty is a valuable asset that most people want to maintain. (Lewicki and Wiethoff, 2000, 88–89)

Since CBT functions are based on the analysis of positive and negative incentives and rational calculation, rational choice theorists have done a great deal of research in this area (Oliver, 1980; Heiner, 1990).

Identification-based trust (IBT) is rarely discussed by rational choice theorists and is based on identification with the other's needs and desires (Lewicki and Wiethoff, 2000). This is the ability to empathize with another and to act in their best interests out of a sense of kinship or emotional closeness. "It is not enough to know they see things differently. If you want to influence them, you also need to understand empathetically the power of their point of view and to understand the emotional force with which they believe in it" (Fisher and Ury, 1981, 23). To strengthen IBT group members should strive to develop a collective identity, spend time together in both work and non-work settings, create joint goals or missions, and develop or commit to jointly shared values (Deutsch, 2000, 89).

Rational choice theories of decision making do not fully take into account the impact of culture on the building and maintaining of trust or its impact in complicating communication between individuals and groups. However, cultural norms about trust are crucial to efficient decision making; especially when different cultural groups take part in joint decision making or negotiations. Due to different cultural emphases on the importance of task accomplishment versus relationship building, many non-western cultures place a greater emphasis on the development of IBT over CBT (LeBaron, 2003). For example, Japanese and Middle Eastern negotiators typically spend a great deal of time getting to know their negotiating counterparts on a personal level before commencing the actual negotiations. The idea is that personal relationships must be built so that one can determine the trustworthiness of the other and develop empathy for them, in order for negotiations to be productive and for agreements to be implemented smoothly. Western negotiators, with their greater emphasis on CBT, tend to view this as wasted time or an evasive tactic on the part of their negotiating counterparts. Cultures relying on CBT create elaborate and legally binding contracts which lay out the expectations of each party and the penalties for not meeting those expectations. Cultures relying on IBT tend to have contracts (if they have them at all) that are more vaguely worded, since the negotiators can rely on the strength of their relationships to work out any problems that arise or to change the agreement as circumstances dictate.

Many researchers have worked to amend traditional rational choice models to account for human limitations on the ability to process, analyze and use information for decision making (Simon, 1981). In addition to the obstacles posed by limitations on the ability to process and analyze information; attribution bias, conflict orientations (discussed later), and attitudes toward trust building and repair clearly influence the ability of groups to successfully make and implement decisions. While not discussed herein, many other psychological factors influence the efficacy of group decision making, including: the impact of stress on decision makers, the level of risk aversion among decision makers, the power dynamics within the group, the perceived importance of the decision, etc., (Janis and Mann, 1977; Deutsch and Coleman, 2000). The next section of this chapter examines the importance of procedural barriers to rational decision making.

31.1.5 PROCEDURAL BARRIERS TO RATIONALITY IN DECISION MAKING

Process matters. More precisely, whether or not people view the process as fair and transparent really matters. Collaborative processes can heighten participants' perceptions of fairness by insuring that the process is representative, participatory, legitimate, and that accountability is maintained (McCreary et al., 2001). This section will examine the importance of decision making procedures by asking the following questions: when should collaborative processes be used for decision making? How do process decisions impact outcomes and implementation? and What decision making processes are likely to produce superior outcomes?

Procedural justice theorists argue that organizational decisions are more likely to be accepted and implemented if the processes by which they are achieved is perceived as fair (Lind and Tyler, 1988). Perceptions of process fairness are heightened when individual decision makers felt they had a sense of control over the process, they participated actively in the process, and they were treated with respect during the decision making process (Bingham, Kim, and Raines, 2002). Even when participants have been disappointed with the outcomes of a decision, they are often willing to accept the decision and implement it if they felt that the process for decision making was fair (Bingham, 2002; Pruitt et al., 1993). In fact, when weighing the importance of a fair process versus a fair outcome, individuals generally show a more pervasive concern for fair processes (Deutsch, 2000, 44). This finding is not generally predicted by traditional rational choice theory, as it is more focused on outcomes than processes. In some instances, it is impossible to know what a fair outcome would be at the outset of the decision making process. Therefore, decision makers must strive to create a process by which a fair outcome can be created, trusting that a good process will result in a good outcome.

According to Katz and Block (2000) when people are focused on the outcome of a negotiation or decision, they tend to get locked into positions early and display reticence to change their positions in light of new data. However, when decision makers focus toward a process goal (such as creating and using a process that all agree is fair), they:

> ...focus mainly on formulating and mastering the best strategy leading to successful resolution of the conflict. They tend to focus on constructive processes to resolve the conflict. Initial preoccupation with achieving a positional goal and final outcome is less likely to lead to constructive conflict resolution than an initial focus on process and strategy, which identifies basic needs and interests. The latter focus facilitates developing the strategies, the trust, good communication, and effective problem solving necessary to resolve difficult conflicts. (Katz and Block, 2000, 283)

Therefore, effective group decision making is more likely to occur when participants maintain a process focus, rather than an outcome focus. They need to trust that an optimal decision outcome will be the result of a process that is viewed as fair, efficient, and inclusive of stakeholder input.

According to Deutsch, "one wants procedures that generate relevant, unbiased, accurate, consistent, reliable, competent, and valid information and decisions as well as polite, dignified, and respectable behavior in carrying out the procedures" (2000, 45).

For these reasons, it is often useful for groups to make decisions collaboratively, using an agreed-upon process, rather than having a superior unilaterally impose a decision in top-down fashion. This is true, even if the actual outcome of the group decision making process is identical to the outcome that would have occurred through a unilateral decision. In her work on organizational decision making, Elangovan discusses the variables that should be considered when managers decide whether to retain control over a particular decision making process and outcome or to relinquish some control in favor of a collaborative decision making processes involving employees (1998). She concludes that managers should retain control when there is a strong time pressure, when the outcome is vital to company functioning, when the saliency of the decision is low for employees, or when the employees involved in the decision will not have any long-term interactions in the future. Adversely, when sufficient time exists, when employee cooperation is necessary for decision implementation, and when the decision is important to employees, they should be incorporated into the decision making process.

Some would disagree with Elangovan's finding that decisions vital to the company should be made solely by CEOs and managers (Carpenter and Kennedy, 1988; Costantino and Merchant, 1996). Taken to its logical extreme, this could mean that only symbolic or unimportant decisions are appropriate for group decision making. This could lead to an environment of cynicism and a disregard for the utility of collaboration. Instead, collaboration is most called for when individuals or groups have information or knowledge to bring to the negotiating table that may lead to a superior decision, when buy-in from affected stakeholders is necessary to secure smooth implementation of a decision, and when sufficient time exists to engage in a collaborative process (Costantino and Merchant, 1996).

Collaborative decision making processes are increasingly used in the area of public policy decision making. Public policies are generally made in a group context. Policies about education, housing, healthcare, environmental regulations etcetera deeply impact how people live their daily lives. Therefore, decisions on these issues often leave people feeling threatened. When people feel threatened they are more likely to stray farther from the predictions of rational choice theory by staking out and sticking to apparently irrational and extreme positions. In their research on public policy, Gordon and Arian found, "The more people feel threatened, the more their policy choice tends to maintain or intensify the conflict—that is, the more incendiary the policy choice is" (2001, 196). Creating processes for decision making that are transparent and allow for democratic participation can bring final decisions back into the realm of the rational and efficient. It should be noted that some public policies must be made by an individual executive or a small group of elected or appointed decision makers due either to time constraints, issues surrounding privacy or security risks posed by information used for decision making, or by explicit legislative or constitutional guidelines.

Why do participatory processes for public decision making often yield better, more implemental results? Ananda and Herath (2003) state that public involvement in the process of forestry policy making can reduce distrust between the stakeholders and government (for more information on this topic see also Tanz and Howard, 1991). Good public decision making involves stakeholders, elicits their input and any data they may have to bring to the table, improves transparency and therefore trust, can accommodate multiple objectives and perspectives, and leads to the careful evaluation of various outcome options rather than the premature selection of one outcome over another (Ananda and Herath, 2003). Investigations of conflict during decision making suggest some specific ways in which this relationship between conflict management and decision making might occur. Putnam argued that a conflict managed effectively can improve decision making by "expanding the range of alternatives, increasing close scrutiny of decision options, fostering calculated risks and enhancing cohesiveness. When managed ineffectively, conflict results in dysfunctional behaviors and low group productivity" (Kuhn and Poole, 2000, 562).

Additionally, Van Ninjatten (1996) notes that multi-stakeholder consultation can help to overcome the typical fragmentation of the decision making process that often occurs during the creation of public policy. By getting all of the affected groups together, both governmental and non-governmental, it is possible to make more than small tweaks to existing rules and regulations, but to instead create broader change in a coordinated fashion. Processes such as mediation and facilitated dialogues can heighten participants' feelings that the process was representative, participatory, legitimate, and that the process will result in greater accountability (McCreary et al., 2001). This is true in other complex decision making arenas as well.

There are many ways to ensure that processes are fair, allow participants a voice, and result in maximally efficient outcomes in terms of both subjective and objective concerns. The next section discusses specific ways to create processes that meet these criteria.

31.2 METHODS AND SKILLS FOR PARTICIPATORY DECISION MAKING

Now that we have discussed the potential benefits of collaborative decision making and many of the psychological and procedural barriers to sound group decision making, it will be useful to delineate some specific methods for group decision making. After the discussion of group decision making methods, specific skills for group decision making will be examined, including problem framing and maintaining a cooperative orientation to conflict.

31.2.1 METHODS FOR GROUP DECISION MAKING

Fisher and Ury's book *Getting to Yes: How to Negotiate Agreement Without Giving In* (1981) is somewhat akin to a holy book in the field of conflict management. Most practitioners and theorists in the field have read it and can quote from it by memory. While it specifically addresses negotiation and decision making at the individual level, the basic process that it lays out can be well applied at the group level. This process is also regularly applied by public policy facilitators. First we will offer a brief introduction to *Getting to Yes'* core concepts and methods for process creation. Then, we will examine how this process can be combined with techniques specifically designed to facilitate efficient and effective group decision making.

The basic problem solving and decision making process contains five steps: (1) Separate the people from the problem; (2) Focus on interests, not positions; (3) Invent options for mutual gain; (4) Insist on using objective criteria; and (5) Craft the agreement. The first step is very important. In order to maintain a cooperative orientation to conflict it is important to attack the problem, but not the person. When faced with the prospect of making a difficult decision, decision makers and negotiators often become competitive in orientation. They often assume that the decision represents a zero-sum situation where there will be winners and losers. However, this is the case much less often than is thought. Assuming a competitive orientation to conflict is likely to result in an escalation of the conflict. When conflict escalates, people "dig in" to their positions, even before they have done enough research to be absolutely sure that their positions are accurate or in their best interests. In a competitive orientation, people compete against each other to "win" the outcome they seek over the outcome sought by their adversary. When this happens decision makers tend to personalize the conflict and attack each other rather than attacking the problem.

In a cooperative orientation, decision makers focus on solving the problem together as a team, rather than on "winning." A cooperative orientation to conflict and decision making ensures more productive long term relationships between decision makers, a decision that is more likely to meet the needs of all parties, and less acrimony overall. Fisher and Ury call this an "integrative" style of negotiation because it integrates the needs of all parties. An integrative conflict management style should improve decision making because it encourages greater cooperation among group members, involves a more open and full discussion, and results in group synthesis of the information to reach a common solution (Kuhn and Poole, 2000, 562).

In the second step, it is important to focus on interests, not positions. A position is what we typically hear in negotiations and it sounds like a demand. For example, local citizens may demand that city officials reject the zoning request that would allow a Wal-Mart to come into their neighborhood. Their position is: "No Wal-Mart," or "Say no to the zoning request." There is only one way to meet those demands. They give very little room for negotiation. Additionally, positional statements tend to escalate conflict, as they leave negotiators with no way to save face or compromise—they either give in completely or hold their ground completely. Interests underlie positions. They tell us why the demand is being made. In this example, local citizens may wish to avoid increased traffic, protect local businesses, or preserve the character of the existing neighborhoods. There are many ways to meet these interests that may or may not include the granting of the zoning request. Once decision makers learn about the core interests of the parties, it becomes more likely that decisions can be made that will meet the interests of all involved.

The third step involves inventing options for mutual gain. Once the interests of the decision makers are known, it is a good idea to brainstorm all options that may meet those interests. It is important to separate this task from the task of evaluating the options. If each option is torn apart and criticized as it is made, it is likely that some participants may feel reticent to share their ideas. The brainstorming of options should include all possible options, including those that may provide incentive for further cooperation. For example, in a labor-management dispute, one option is for a strike to be held. This is an option in which both sides stand to lose a great deal. It is a "reality check" so to speak. Listing this option may help participants to understand the importance of creating additional options for mutual gain. When making decisions as a group it is important to manage the individual interpretations of the problem and its possible solutions in a way that does not stifle input or cohesiveness (Putnam, 1986).

For the fourth step, participants should set about to find objective criteria by which to evaluate or narrow the options. For example, when selling a used car in the United States and Canada, the Kelley "Blue Book" provides an objective price range for each type of car. This book can provide the range within which the negotiations will be confined. For public decision making, there are often statutes or administrative rules that can set the parameters for the discussion. If no clear objective criteria exist, it is possible for decision makers to create their own. For example, in a negotiation between labor and management over a contract dispute, both parties can agree that the eventual agreement will maintain the financial competitiveness of the company while improving the material conditions of the employees. Then, negotiators would look for options that can accomplish both goals. They can also look to the wages and benefits provided by other companies in the industry to ensure that competitiveness is maintained.

The last step involves reaching the agreement and discussing implementation plans. Each option is weighed against the objective criteria and decision makers work together to find a solution that meets their mutual needs. It is important to consider any obstacles to implementation of the agreements at this stage. Agreements based on calculus-based trust will often have enforcement provisions contained within them. For example, an American labor union contract with management will typically include penalties for the company and for individual employees for failure to abide by the contract provisions. Rules for monitoring and enforcing the contract will generally be spelled out explicitly in the contract, along with provisions for dispute resolution, such as an arbitration agreement. However, in identification-based trust, the implementation of the agreement rests more so on the strength of the relationship between the parties. When implementation issues arise, the parties will meet to discuss them and work them out in an ad hoc fashion. They trust that any future change in circumstances for the parties may result in a change in the agreement. The reliance on CBT versus IBT is largely culturally based, although it is increasingly common for international negotiators to build strong relationships and then codify them in explicit contract language.

31.2.2 Large-Group Decision Making Methods

The problem-solving process steps just discussed can be applied to most problems, regardless of the number of decision makers present. However because large groups provide greater logistical challenges ensuring the integrity and efficiency of the process may fall to a facilitator. Facilitators may be hired externally, or they may come from the ranks of the decision makers themselves. Regardless of their source, facilitators have developed a number of specific techniques to aid in the process of group decision making.

As opposed to a private negotiation involving only two parties, large groups of decision makers may be involved in decisions concerning public policies (as in a negotiated rulemaking process), strategic planning for businesses, or the creation of new programs or processes within public and private organizations. These methods work well with groups from 10 to 1000 and have been used in even larger groups. An example of a large group decision making process is the "Listen to the City" project in New York. This public discussion and consensus project was used to help decision makers decide how to undertake rebuilding after the 9/11 terrorist attacks (Conflict Resolution Center, 2004). As mentioned previously, when people have an opportunity to participate in the decisions shaping their lives and work, they are more likely to accept changes they might otherwise have resisted.

Open Space Technology (OST), one method of decision making designed for a group environment, is propounded by professional facilitator Harrison Owen (1997). For this process to work well, participants must feel strongly about the decisions being made. If the issue under discussion lacks salience, either few will participate, or the output will be of lower quality. Anyone in the organization, or anyone affected by the decision, is welcome to participate in the decision making process. This means that organizational leaders must be willing to relinquish and share ultimate control over the outcome. OST workshops can last from one to three days and involve as many as hundreds of people. Participants control the agenda and any decisions that result from the consensus-based discussions.

On the morning of the first day, participants are presented with a question around which the workshop will be focused, such as: "How can we improve transportation planning for Metro Atlanta?" or "What can our company do to maintain competitiveness?" Then, individuals are asked to write down a topic for break-out group discussions. Individuals must be willing to facilitate the discussion on the topic they suggest. Participants may then place these topics on a time/space matrix listing the time of day and the room number in which this discussion will take place. It is no problem to have two sessions on the same topic, if sufficient demand exists to do so. At the end of the day, each group leader will report out to the group to summarize the discussion and recommendations of their group. At the end of the workshop these summaries will form the options from which participant-decision makers will develop final agreements. When issues are complex, or additional data gathering is necessary, participants may use their OST time to create a longer-term process for data gathering and future decision making.

The group ideally strives for consensus, but it can agree at the outset to a less than 100% decision rule. In large groups, a 100% consensus rule can be unrealistic and it gives "spoilers" a great deal of leverage to control the outcome. Therefore, the group may agree to rules such as: consensus minus 1 (or 2, or 5 per cent, etc); or a supermajority rule (75 per cent or 60% per cent). There is a danger in settling for something less than nearly unanimous consent, especially if dissenters are powerful enough to hamper the implementation of the agreement, challenge it in court, or otherwise make moving forward difficult.

A number of other large group methods can be used for the creation of action agendas for organizational or systemic change and the processes necessary to achieve desired outcomes. For example, a Future Search Conference (Emery and Emery, 1989) involves the following steps:

1. The sponsors open the gathering with a problem statement, such as "How can we reduce crime in our community?"
2. Participants, sitting at round tables, are asked to review summaries of the history of the problem and their role in the problem. They become educated about the data and their place in relation to the problem and then decide which are the most important events in this history, from their perspectives.
3. Participants at each table are asked to analyze a specific time period in the history of the problem and then look for patterns in that period that they write onto butcher block paper that is posted on the walls of the room.
4. Participants are asked to examine the capacities of the organization(s) involved in this problem.
5. Participants are asked to envision the future they seek.
6. Finally, participants are asked to work together to decide what steps are necessary to reach that future. Generally, action planning groups are formed, agendas for action are created, and tools for evaluating progress are designed (Bunker, 2000).

Many other models for group decision making exist, with each targeted toward specific tasks, such as the creation of mission and vision statements within organizations, reorganizing the distribution of work, or achieving cultural change within dysfunctional organizations (Bunker, 2000). These large-group methods tend to be effective for the following reasons: they focus on common ground and areas of shared interests; they rationalize conflict in decision making by acknowledging and clarifying conflict rather than attempting to deny it; they avoid tackling issues that are not up for negotiation or cannot be addressed within the allotted time frame; they challenge participants to take a broader view of the conflict and to acknowledge the needs of other stakeholders as well as their own; they acknowledge the history and path dependence of the conflict; they treat the views and needs of all with respect, which tends to de-escalate conflict and reduce emotionality; and they increase democratic equality by reducing hierarchy and bringing decision making down to the level of individual stakeholders (Bunker, 2000, 566).

31.2.3 SKILLS FOR GROUP DECISION MAKING

The first skill to be discussed involves addressing attribution bias and framing problems constructively rather than destructively. As discussed earlier in this chapter, human beings tend to over-attribute the negative behaviors of others to dispositions rather than to circumstances, especially when there is a history of distrust or the absence of a positive relationship between the parties or groups. Attribution bias acts as a cognitive barrier to efficient information processing. It can lead to statements and behaviors that escalate conflict, and can contribute to inefficient decisions. The way people frame a problem, in their own minds and to others, impacts the way they go about problem solving and decision making. There is a great deal of research suggesting that the way people define problems highly influences the choices they make in attempting to address them (Kahneman and Tversky, 1979; Tversky and Kahneman 1981). The first moments of a conflict interaction can set the scene for a constructive or a destructive conflict (Folger, Poole and Stutman, 2001). "Attributing another person's behavior to causes within his or her control tends to arouse anger toward that person" (Allred, 2000, 242). Anger often results in punishing behavior, which escalates conflict and leads to irrational decisions (Weiner, 1995). When the original attribution is rooted in misperception, inefficient outcomes are most likely. This can result in a negative cycle of retaliation in which both parties rationalize their own behavior as justified in light of the other's actions.

How can individuals overcome the tendency toward attribution bias and the cycle of anger and defensiveness that often results in inefficient decisions? First, individuals and groups can benefit from learning about attribution along with other cognitive biases that impact information processing and decision making. "One experiment found that participants who were educated about attributional information were significantly less prone to that error" (Allred, 2000, 250; for more information on this topic see also Chen, Froehle, and Morran, 1997). It is also important for individuals to learn to accept feedback regarding their own behavior and use it as constructively as possible, in light of the tendency for individuals to rationalize their own behaviors. Additionally, decision makers need to be encouraged to take the perspective of the other(s) and to increase their empathetic abilities. Third party neutrals, such as facilitators or mediators, are often trained to assist decision makers as they try to accurately process information and communicate with those who may hold opposing views.

While these techniques may reduce the incidence of inaccurate attributions, it is also possible to manage anger more productively when negative attributions are correctly identified. When an actor has acted in a way that has harmed others the "victim" can vent anger in a way that escalates the situation, or, they can attempt to explain their perspective, discuss the harm incurred, and work with the actor to find ways to take responsibility. These actions attempt to repair any harm done and ensure that the infraction does not occur again. In this instance, the parties, again, are working together to solve a problem, rather than working against one another in a competitive manner. Negative outcomes become learning opportunities rather than fodder for escalated conflict.

This brings us to the issue of apologies. Like the Capuchin monkeys, human beings often behave irrationally when they feel that someone has violated a societal norm or that injustice has occurred. In her research into commercial disputes arising from Ebay transactions, Raines (2005) found that approximately 8 per cent of mediated disputes between buyers and sellers involved a demand for an apology. While this seems like a small percentage, it is important in explaining one recurring obstacle to conflict resolution and efficient decision making. In most cases, disputants paid more for the mediation service than the objective amount in dispute in the transaction. Disputants claimed that solely recouping their financial losses was an inadequate remedy when they felt they had been wronged. They often insisted on an admission of wrongdoing, an apology, and a pledge that the behavior would not be repeated. These behaviors would not be predicted under most rational choice models. An apology can be a very powerful force in improving working relationships between decision makers, defusing anger, and rebuilding broken trust (Weiner, Graham, and Zmuidinas, 1991).

When one asserts his or her needs and concerns to others, in the process of conflict resolution and decision making, it is important to state those concerns in a way that does not cast blame, include attribution bias, or personalize the dispute. Doing so invariably leads to defensiveness on the part of the listener and then to escalated conflict, emotionality, and inefficient decision outcomes. In other words, how you say what you need to say matters as much as the substantive content of the statement itself. "Framing" refers to the way in which a speaker phrases his or her assertions to the decision making partner. A great deal of knowledge about these skills and their impact on conflict escalation or de-escalation comes from the fields of psychology and communication.

Specific skills to encourage positive framing can be learned in order to enhance the quality of communication and likelihood of productive outcomes. When discussing a problem or providing constructive criticism, it is important to avoid statements that cast blame against the other person or group. For this reason, psychologists often recommend "I" statements over "you" statements. A "you" statement implies blame, such as *You* forgot to take out the garbage." In contrast, an "I" statement is focused on relaying the feelings of the speaker: "*I* am frustrated because the garbage is overflowing and making a mess." The first statement is more likely to incite defensiveness, whereas the second statement is more likely to invite cooperation and assistance in problem solving.

When attempting to frame feedback in a way that is less likely to cause defensiveness and escalation, a simple formula to remember involves first showing empathy to set a cooperative tone, then pin-pointing the problem with specific details, and lastly, asking for problem-solving ideas or input from the other person. For example, when an employee has not met an important deadline, the manager could say: "You need to stop fooling around and get your work done on time." This includes a "you" statement which implies a negative attribution in that the manager assumes the work was not done on time due to a personal failing of the employee. Alternatively, he could frame his statement in a way that is less likely to cause defensiveness or hostility: "I understand that you have been busy lately (showing empathy). *I* am under pressure to get the reports in on time and I cannot do that without your contribution (uses an "I" statement instead of a "you" statement). What can be done to ensure that the work is finished on time in the future? (Encourages productive joint problem solving)." Framing skills are fundamental to the process of productive communication and collaboration and can be enhanced through education and practice.

The second skill to be examined involves the maintenance of a cooperative psychological orientation to conflict, rather than a competitive orientation. Individuals with highly developed conflict management skills are able to choose the most appropriate response to conflict situations that occur during decision making. Those with less developed skills tend to rely on their existing habits of conflict management and apply them unreflectively to various types of conflict without differentiation. By analyzing the source and type of conflict, the conflict's salience, the players, and the timeline for decision making, individuals and groups can make better decisions. Rational and utilitarian models of decision making do not generally recognize that most people have conflict management habits and skills that are not adequately developed to allow them to consciously choose among all of the possible modes or orientations toward conflict before acting.

There are many models that describe individual orientations to conflict, but none more widely used than the Thomas–Kilmann Conflict Mode Instrument (Thomas and Kilmann, 1978).

Using 30 pairs of statements, this instrument helps individuals become more aware of their own conflict management behaviors and orientations. Thomas and Kilmann describe five common responses to conflict: competing, compromising, collaborating, accommodating, and avoiding. Individuals usually display higher scores in one or two areas, but occasionally individuals will score relatively evenly across all five categories. It is important to remember that there is no category that is more desired than others, but that individuals should be aware of their own tendencies and the costs and benefits of using one or two orientations to conflict to the exclusion of others. Each conflict is likely to have one type of orientation that is most effective at addressing the particular conflict. The goal is to be reflective about one's conflict style, learn to match the appropriate orientation or response to any particular conflict, and work well with others who may have differing orientations to conflict.

Like individuals, organizations (including families) tend to develop orientations to conflict that exhibit one or two of these modes as well. Clearly, an organization that consistently ties to avoid addressing conflicts is likely to reach sub-optimal outcomes more consistently than an organization that reacts proactively to problems as they arise. Alternatively, some organizations develop a very competitive culture or a competitive orientation to dealing with disputes with customers or clients, when a collaborative culture and approach might be more conducive to building positive relationships and outcomes.

One common source of unproductive conflict is related to the trade-offs between a competitive versus a collaborative orientation to conflict. According to Morton Deutsch, almost all conflicts are a mix of cooperation and competition. The make up of that mix is what, in part, determines the outcome of the conflict and the efficiency of decision making (Deutsch, 1973; Deutsch and Coleman, 2000). However, research shows that maintaining a cooperative orientation to conflict, as opposed to a competitive orientation, greatly increases the likelihood that negotiation will result in a mutually satisfactory resolution in most circumstances (Deutsch, 2000). A competitive orientation assumes a win-lose outcome and places the negotiators or disputants in adversarial roles. Competitive orientations assume that the negotiators' preferences are mutually exclusive and that resources are fixed, even when this may not be accurate.

Deutsch (2000) has elaborated a theory examining the importance of a cooperative orientation to conflict in terms of achieving optimal outcomes during negotiations or group decision making. Deutsch states that cooperative relations are more likely to exhibit: effective communication; friendliness, helpfulness, less obstruction, coordination of effort, division of labor, orientation to task achievement, orderliness in discussion, high productivity, consensus regarding beliefs and values, willingness to enhance the other's power, and the definition of conflict as a mutual problem to be solved through collaborative efforts (25).

Competitive orientations often escalate conflicts and exhibit "autistic hostility, self-fulfilling prophecies, and unwitting commitments" (Deutsch, 2000, 26). Autistic hostility involves the breaking off of contact between actors, resulting in an increased likelihood for misunderstandings and negative perceptions of one another. Self-fulfilling prophecies occur when one engages in hostile behavior in an effort to reduce vulnerability to the hostile actions of others. This is related to attribution theory (discussed earlier) and is summed up well by Fisher and Ury: "People tend to assume that whatever they fear, the other side intends to do" (1981, 25). As conflict escalates, actors often over-commit themselves to rigid positions and negative views of the other(s) which become difficult to back off from later. It also becomes difficult to switch to a more cooperative mode of communication once one has characterized the other party as evil, dishonest, or unworthy of respect (Deutsch, 2000, p. 27). In conclusion, Deutsch states:

> There is reason to believe that a cooperative-constructive process of conflict resolution leads to such good outcomes as mutual benefits and satisfaction, strengthening relationship, positive psychological effects, and so on, while a competitive-destructive process leads to material losses and dissatisfaction, worsening

relationship, and negative psychological effects in at least one party (the loser if it is a win-lose outcome) or both parties (if it is a lose-lose outcome). (27)

Efficient group decision making should exhibit cooperative rather than competitive orientations in most situations. Regardless of one's predispositions toward dealing with conflict, to the extent possible, conflict should be viewed as an opportunity to work together with one's negotiating partner (not viewed as an opponent) in an effort to conduct joint problem solving. In other words, it is the negotiators working against the problem, rather than against each other. Competitive orientations to conflict are best applied when there is a need to determine which side is more powerful, but not when the goal is to build or preserve relationships, encourage cooperation during decision implementation, and maximize joint outcomes. Maintaining a cooperative orientation to conflict can help to ensure that decision makers work well together, build or enhance positive relationships, reduce the likelihood of attributional biases, bring collective wisdom and expertise to the negotiating table, enhance participant satisfaction and commitment to intragroup norms, and result in better decisions overall (Alderton and Frey, 1986; O'Connor, Gruenfeld, and McGrath, 1993; Pelled, Eisenhardt, and Xin, 1999; Sambamurthy and Poole, 1992; Wall, Galanes, and Love, 1987; Wall and Nolan, 1986; 1987; Kuhn and Poole, 2000).

While Thomas and Kilmann, (1978) discuss five basic styles or orientations to conflict, latter work by Kuhn and Poole (2000, 560) condense these further into three main categories at the individual and organizational levels: avoidance, distributive, and integrative. "An individual *conflict style* is a behavioral orientation and general expectation about one's approach to conflict. This conception of style does not preclude the individual from changing styles or enacting behaviors not typically associated with a particular style, but asserts that individuals choose (though often not consciously) a pattern of principles to guide them through episodes of conflict" (559–560). Research shows that "groups that develop integrative conflict management styles made more effective decisions than groups that utilized confrontation and avoidance styles. Groups that never developed a stable style were also less effective than groups with integrative styles" (558). The evolution of group norms depends on a number of factors, including the styles of the individuals within the group, the exigencies of the group situation, and the particular skill sets of individual members (Kuhn, 1998).

Avoidance indicates that groups and individuals prefer not to explicitly acknowledge the existence of conflict, in favor of maintaining the appearance of harmony among group members. Avoidant groups and individuals use a combination of unassertiveness and uncooperativeness in the problem solving endeavor in their efforts to ignore problems whenever possible. Sometimes this desire to ignore problems or deny their existence can result in passive-aggressive behaviors. In avoidant group cultures it is not acceptable to explicitly acknowledge the existence of problems, which can lead to passive-aggressive behaviors in an attempt to subtly signal displeasure. These behaviors may include pouting, door slamming, the "silent treatment," etc. Conflict that remains unaddressed may grow until it becomes a crisis that can no longer be avoided. When conflict avoiders are no longer able to avoid, they tend to exhibit anger, hostility, and irrational decision making leading to sub-optimal outcomes. Avoidance is appropriate and rational when a problem is inconsequential to a decision maker, when one lacks the authority or power to influence the final decision, or when preserving relationships through accommodation is valued above securing a particular substantive outcome.

A *distributive* style indicates a competitive, confrontational, win-lose orientation to conflict. In this style, individuals and groups aggressively fight for their positions in an effort to "win" the argument or battle, rather than focusing on problem solving in a cooperative manner. This orientation is useful when there is inadequate time to reach a decision through collaboration, when the decision maker has adequate authority to justify unilateral decisions, and when the decision maker has the power to ensure that the decision is implemented at lower levels. When these variables are absent, the distributive style is seen as overbearing, unnecessarily harsh, and is often met with either passive or active resistance.

An *integrative* style indicates a willingness to acknowledge the existence of problems (unlike avoidance), and a desire to work cooperatively with others to solve them through consensus, collaboration, or at worst mutual compromise. The goal here is to preserve or enhance relationships while ensuring outcomes that are favorable, or at least palatable, to all stakeholders. This approach has a heavy emphasis on the use of appropriate processes for reaching resolution. A process that takes into consideration all parties' needs, gives each party a voice, and is considered "fair" by all would be considered appropriate. This is not a preferred method for conflict resolution when time is short, when the decision is seen as relatively unimportant by stakeholders, or when those in positions of authority are unwilling to share decision making control.

Kuhn and Poole posit that integrative groups will have the highest level of effectiveness, with distributive groups coming in second and avoidant groups coming in last. The higher the level of task complexity, the better the integrative style worked.

> Interactional norms formed in conflict situations can influence decision making, even when decisions do not involve conflict... Development of either an integrative or distributive style will cultivate the group's ability to surface key issues, which should contribute to problem analysis and critical evaluation of options. An integrative style should help the group establish interactional norms that promote inclusive, consensual goal-setting and the ability to analyze problems and propose solutions through a critical discussion that incorporates several perspectives, and therefore fosters positive subjective performance outcomes. In contrast, a distributive style should promote norms that militate against collaborative goal setting and analysis because it creates a 'win-lose' mindset. Avoidance is likely to inhibit all three functions because it encourages suppression of differences and either fast, unreflective decisions or indecisiveness. (Kuhn and Poole, 2000, 563)

So how can decision makers foster integrative approaches to conflict and decision making within their organizations? Training decision makers in the processes and skills of integrative bargaining and decision making is an important first step (Fisher and Ury, 1981). Additionally, organizations can train internal facilitators to assist groups as they make complex and important decisions, or hire them externally. Third party neutrals are experts in the *process* of collaborative decision making. They can help lead productive discussions, coach individuals and teams to enhance their own decision making skills, and offer process suggestions to maintain a focus on process rather than outcome (as discussed earlier in the chapter). Mediators and facilitators can "encourage the sides to focus on finding common ground, developing mutual understanding, empowering one another, and understanding the other's needs and emotions" (Katz and Block, 2000, 285). Lastly, organizations can "walk the talk" by increasing the extent to which they incorporate stakeholder input into decision making processes, when appropriate.

31.3 CONCLUSIONS

While traditional rational choice theorists focus primarily on the substantive goals and needs of decision makers and their incentives or disincentives for reaching agreement, this chapter examined many non-substantive sources of conflict in the decision making process. In addition to substantive differences in preferred outcomes between decision makers, outcomes are also influenced by the psychological needs and limitations of decision makers, along with the choice of procedures and skills used for decision making. This chapter began with a discussion of psychological and procedural barriers to rational and efficient decision making including: attribution bias; issues related to trust building and repair; and the importance of creating fair, transparent, and participatory processes for decision making. Then, the chapter summarized a number of specific methods to facilitate effective large-group decision making through the use of collaborative processes when appropriate. Finally, the chapter included a discussion of the specific skills useful for effective decision making, including: ways to overcome attribution bias; framing skills; and methods to encourage an integrative, rather than distributive or avoidant, orientation to conflict within groups of decision makers.

It is clear that the obstacles to efficient decision making come from both rational and irrational sources. However, the latter can be overcome through the conscious application of skills and knowledge from the field of Conflict Management in order to enhance the outcome of decision making processes.

REFERENCES

Alderton, S. M. and Frey, L. R., Argumentation in small group decision-making, In *Communication in Group Decision Making*, Hirokawa, R. Y. and Poole, M. S., Eds., Sage, Beverly Hills, pp. 157–173, 1986.

Allred, K. G., Anger and retaliation in conflict, In *The Handbook of Conflict Resolution: Theory and Practice*, Deutsch, M. and Coleman, P. T., Eds., Jossey-Bass, San Francisco, 2000.

Ananda, J. and Herath, G., Incorporating stakeholders values into regional forest planning: a value function approach, *Ecological Economics*, 45, 75–90, 2003.

Axelrod, R., The emergence of cooperation among egoists, *American Political Science Review*, 75, 306–318, 1981.

Bingham, L. B., Self-determination in dispute system design and arbitration, *Miami Law Review*, 56, 873–903, 2002.

Bingham, L. B., Kim, K., and Raines, S. S., Exploring the role of representation in employment mediation at the USPS, *Ohio State Journal on Dispute Resolution*, 17(2), 341–377, 2002.

Brosnan, S. F. and de Waal, F. B. M., Monkeys reject unequal pay, *Nature*, 425, 297–299, 2003.

Bunker, B. B., Managing conflict through large group methods, In *The Handbook of Conflict Resolution: Theory and Practice*, Deutsch, M. and Coleman, P. T., Eds., Jossey-Bass, San Francisco, 2000.

Bush, R. A. B. and Folger, J. P., *The Promise of Mediation: Responding to Conflict Through Empowerment and Recognition*, Jossey-Bass, San Francisco, 1994.

Carpenter, S. and Kennedy, W. J. D., *Managing Public Disputes*, Jossey-Bass, San Francisco, 1998.

Chayes, A. and Minow, M., Eds., *Imagine Coexistence: Restoring Humanity After Violent Ethnic Conflict*, Jossey-Bass, San Francisco, 2003.

Chen, M., Froehle, T., and Morran, K., Deconstructing dispositional bias in clinical inference: two interventions, *Journal of Counseling and Development*, 76, 74–81, 1997.

Cohen, A., What the monkeys can teach humans about making America fairer, *New York Times*, September 21.

Conflict Resolution Center, "Listening to the city," University of North Dakota. http://www.und.edu/dept/crc/facilitation-group.htm. (accessed December 9, 2004).

Costantino, C. and Merchant, C. S., *Designing Conflict Management Systems: A Guide to Creating Productive and Healthy Organizations*, Jossey-Bass, San Francisco, 1996.

Coy, P. G. and Woehrle, L. M., *Social Conflicts and Collective Identities*, Rowman and Littlefield, Boston, 2000.

Danesh, H. B. and Danesh, R., Has conflict resolution grown up? Toward a developmental model of decision making and conflict resolution. *International Journal of Peace Studies*, Spring/Summer, 2002.

Deutsch, M., Cooperation and competition, In *The Handbook of Conflict Resolution: Theory and Practice*, Deutsch, M. and Coleman, P. T., Eds., Jossey-Bass, San Francisco, pp. 21–40, 2000.

Deutsch, M., *The Resolution of Conflict: Constructive and Destructive Processes*, Yale University Press, New Haven, 1973.

Deutsch, M. and Coleman, P. T., Eds., *The Handbook of Conflict Resolution: Theory and Practice*, Jossey-Bass, San Francisco, 2000.

Elangovan, A. R., Managerial intervention in organizational disputes: testing prescriptive model of strategy selection, *International Journal of Conflict Management*, 9(4), 301–336, 1998.

Emery, F. E. and Emery, M., Participative design: work and community life, In *Participative Design for Participative Democracy*, Emery, M., Ed., Centre for Continuing Education, Australian National University, Canberra, 1989.

Fisher, R. J., Intergroup conflict, In *The Handbook of Conflict Resolution: Theory and Practice*, Deutsch, M. and Coleman, P. T., Eds., Jossey-Bass, San Francisco, 2000.

Fisher, R. and Ury, W., *Getting to Yes: Negotiating Agreement Without Giving in*, Penguin Books, New York, 1981.

Folger, J., Poole, M. S., and Stutman, R. K., *Working Through Conflict: Strategies for Relationships, Groups, and Organizations*, 4th ed., Addision Wesley Longman, Inc., New York, 2001.

Gordon, C. and Arian, A., Threat and decision making, *Journal of Conflict Resolution*, 45(2), 196–215, 2001.

Heiner, R. A., Rule-governed behavior in evolution and human society, *Constitutional Political Economy*, 1, 19–46, 1990.

Hewstone, M., Attributional biases intergroup conflict, In *The Social Psychology of Intergroup Conflict: Theory, Research, and Applications*, Stroebe, W., Ed., Springer-Verlag, New York, 1988.

Hirokawa, R. Y. and Rost, K. M., Effective group decision making in organizations: Field test of the vigilant interaction theory, *Management Communication Quarterly*, 5, 267–288, 1992.

Janis, I., *Groupthink: Psychological Studies of Policy Decisions and Fiascoes*, Houghton Mifflin, Boston, 1982.

Janis, I. L. and Mann, L., *Decision Making: A Psychological Analysis of Conflict, Choice and Commitment*, Free Press, New York, 1977.

Jehn, K. A., A multimethod examination of the benefits and detriments of intragroup conflict, *Administrative Science Quarterly*, 40, 256–282, 1995.

Katz, T. Y. and Block, C. J., Process and outcome goal orientations in conflict situations, In *The Handbook of Conflict Resolution: Theory and Practice*, Deutsch, M. and Coleman, P. T., Eds., Jossey-Bass, San Francisco, pp. 279–288, 2000.

Kahneman, D. and Tversky, A., Prospect theory: an analysis of decision under risk, *Econometrica*, 47, 263–291, 1979.

Kelley, H. H. and Michela, J. L., Attribution theory and research, *Annual Review of Psychology*, 31, 457–501, 1980.

Kilmann, R. H. and Thomas, K. W., Interpersonal conflict-handling behavior as reflections of Jungian personality dimensions, *Psychological Report*, 37, 971–980, 1975.

Kilmann, R. H. and Thomas, K. W., Developing a forced-choice measure of conflict-handling behavior: the 'MODE' instrument, *Educational and Psychological Measurement*, 37, 309–325, 1977.

Kuhn, T., *Group process and group performance: A qualitative, longitudinal study of conflict in decision making*, Paper presented: 84th Annual Meeting of the National Communication Association. New York, 1998.

Kuhn, T. and Poole, M. S., Do conflict management styles affect group decision making?, *Human Communication Research*, 26(4), 558–590, 2000.

Kurzban, R., Biological foundations of reciprocity, In *Trust and Reciprocity: Interdisciplinary Lessons from Experimental Research*, Ostrom, E. and Walker, J., Eds., Russell Sage Foundation, New York, pp. 105–127, 2003.

LeBaron, M., *Bridging Cultural Conflicts: A New Approach for a Changing World*, Jossey-Bass, San Francisco, 2003.

Lewicki, R., McAllister, D. J., and Bies, R. J., Trust and distrust: new relationships and realities, *Academy of Management Review*, 23, 438–458, 1998.

Lewicki, R. J. and Wiethoff, C., Trust, trust development, and trust repair, In *The Handbook of Conflict Resolution: Theory and Practice*, Deutsch, M. and Coleman, P. T., Eds., Jossey-Bass, San Francisco, 2000.

Lind, E. A. and Tyler, T. R., *The Social Psychology of Procedural Justice*, Plenum Publishing, New York, 1988.

McCreary, S. et al., Applying a mediated negotiation framework to integrated coastal zone management, *Coastal Management*, 29, 183–216, 2001.

O'Connor, K. M., Gruenfeld, D. H., and McGrath, J. E., The experience and effects of conflict in continuing work groups, *Small Group Research*, 24, 362–382, 1993.

Oliver, P., Rewards and punishments as selective incentives for collective action: theoretical investigations, *American Journal of Sociology*, 85(6), 1356–1375, 1980.

Olson, M., *The Logic of Collective Action*, Harvard University Press, Cambridge, MA, 1965.

Ostrom, E., A behavioral approach to the rational-choice theory of collective action, *American Political Science Review*, 92, 1–22, 1998.

Ostrom, E. and Walker, J., Eds., *Trust and Reciprocity: Interdisciplinary Lessons from Experimental Research*, Russell Sage Foundation, New York, 2003.

Owen, H., *Open Space Technology: A User's Guide*, Berrett-Koehler, San Francisco, 1997.

Pelled, L. H., Eisenhardt, K. M., and Xin, K. R., Exploring the black box: an analysis of work group diversity, conflict, and performance, *Administrative Science Quarterly*, 44, 1–28, 1999.

Pruitt, D. G. et al., Long-term success in mediation, *Law and Human Behavior*, 7(3), 313–330, 1993.

Putnam, L. L., Conflict in group decision-making, In *Communication in Group Decision Making*, Hirokawa, R. Y. and Poole, M. S., Eds., Sage, Beverly Hills, 1986.

Raines, S. S., Can online mediation be transformative? Tales from the front, *Conflict Resolution Quarterly*, 22, 4, 2005.

Ross, L., The intuitive psychologist and his shortcomings: distortions in the attribution process, In *Advances in Experimental Social Psychology*, Berkowitz, L., Ed., Academic Press, Orlando, 1977.

Sambamurthy, V. and Poole, M. S., The effects on variations in capabilities of GDSS designes on management of cognitive conflicts in groups, *Information Systems Research*, 3, 224–251, 1992.

Selton, R., Evolution, learning, and economic behavior, *Games and Economic Behavior*, 3(3), 24, 1991.

Simon, H., *Sciences of the Artificial*, 2nd ed., MIT Press, Cambridge, 1981.

Smith, S., Presidential address: singing our world into existence: international relations theory and September 11, *International Studies Quarterly*, 48(3), 499–516, 2004.

Stein, J. G., Image, identity, and the resolution of violent conflict, In *Turbulent Peace: The Challenges of Managing International Conflict*, Crocker, C., Hampson, F. O., and Aall, P., Eds., United States Institute of Peace, Washington, D.C., 2001.

Tanz, J. S. and Howard, A. F., Meaningful public participation in the planning and management of publicly owned forests, *Forestry Chronicles*, 67(2), 125–130, 1991.

Thomas, K. W. and Kilmann, R. H., Comparison of four instruments of conflict behavior, *Psychological Report*, 42, 1139–1145, 1978.

VanNinjnatten, D., Environmental governance in an era of participatory decision making: Canadian and American approaches, *Canadian Review of American Studies*, 26(3), 405–424, 1996.

Wall, V. W., Galanes, G. J., and Love, S. B., Small, task-oriented groups: conflict, conflict management, satisfaction and decision quality, *Small Group Behavior*, 18, 31–55, 1987.

Wall, V. W. and Nolan, L. L., Perceptions of inequity, satisfaction, and conflict in task-oriented groups, *Human Relations*, 39, 1033–1052, 1986.

Wall, V. W. and Nolan, L. L., Small group conflict: a look at equity, satisfaction, and styles of conflict management, *Small Group Behavior*, 18, 188–211, 1987.

Weiner, B., *Judgments of Responsibility: A Foundation for a Theory of Social Conflict*, Guilford Press, New York, 1995.

Weiner, B., Graham, S., Peter, O., and Zmuidinas, M., Public confessions and forgiveness, *Journal of Personality*, 59, 281–312, 1991.

32 Narrative Policy Analysis for Decision Making

Emery Roe

CONTENTS

32.1 Introduction 607
32.2 Conventional Policy Analysis and Narrative Policy Analysis.........................609
32.3 The Problem of Evaluation..611
32.4 Globalization 611
32.5 Framework...614
32.6 Framework for Evaluating Policy Narratives...616
32.7 The Framework Applied: Overpopulation...619
32.8 Conclusion...623
References 624

32.1 INTRODUCTION

Policy narratives are the rules of thumb, arguments, crisis scenarios, "war stories," and other accounts about how policy and management have, can, and should proceed in ways that enable decision makers to take action, be they policymakers, managers, their analysts, or others. More formally, policy narratives are scenarios (stories and arguments) that stabilize decision making for issues of high complexity, uncertainty, incompleteness, and conflict. Each narrative has a beginning, middle, and end (or premises and conclusions, if offered as an argument) and revolves around a sequence of events or positions in which something is said to happen or from which something is said to follow. A key question, then, is how to analyze and evaluate the narratives when their truth-value cannot be determined or is disputed. Narrative policy analysis has been developed as an approach to answering that question.

Analysis and evaluation are no easy matter, as there are all manner of policy narratives. Some narratives are really nonstories, in that they do not have their own beginnings, middles, or ends. Classic examples of nonstories are (1) policy critiques that rebut other arguments without telling their own stories and (2) circular arguments whose beginnings, middles, and ends are by definition difficult to parse. Other narratives come to us as condensed stories. There are adages: the best is the enemy of the good; the opposite of good is good intentions; perfectionism is a kind of idleness gone bad. There are analogies. Some are explicit: the abortion of a human zygote no more destroys life than burning a Home Depot destroys houses; government is best thought of as an insurance company with an army (Holland, 2003, 247). Other analogies are more implicit: environmental activists who in the name of the environment assert that they cannot be asked to put a price on nature sound remarkably like those corporations who in the name of shareholder value assert that they cannot be asked to put a dollar amount on corporate responsibility. Finally, speaking of responsibility, is it not odd that when the physicist Alan Sokal deceives a peer-reviewed cultural studies journal it is called a "hoax," but when another physicist does the same in peer-reviewed science journals, it is called "fraud"?[*]

A great many policy narratives come to us as reversals of conventional wisdom. It is too soon to say, replied Chou-en-Lai when asked about the significance of the long-past French Revolution (Bogdanor, 2003). In the U.S., corporations are treated as fictive persons for the purposes of the law; yet one psychiatrist, relying on the World Health Organization's Manual of Mental Disorders, concludes: "In many respects, corporations are the prototypical psychopath" (Dugan and Berman, 2004, B1–B2). Many Americans take pride in the fact that the U.S. has not taken a direct hit during wartime since the early 1800s; yet the United States' continuing inability to safely store nuclear waste from its weapons arsenal reveals the Cold War to be the first war in modern times where the United States has indeed taken direct hits from an enemy. Planners in California's Central Valley or Holland's Randstad view urban sprawl as a threat to adjacent agriculture. But is the problem not the opposite—one of agricultural sprawl with its subsidized water for subsidized crops?

The fact that reversals in conventional wisdom are frequent underscores a key feature of policy narratives; namely, that they bring with them counternarratives. All narratives have counternarratives; in semiotic terms, a story is marked by what it is not, be that a nonstory or counterstory. (Which is louder, the full fifteen seconds of astonished silence after the last note has sounded or the thunderous applause that follows?) Counterstories with opposing arguments and conclusions are incredibly important in policy and politics. In contrast, critiques and circular arguments on their own serve only to undermine a policy narrative rather than replace it with a counternarrative having its own beginning, middle, and end (from this point on counterstory and counternarrative are used interchangeably). The only real issue is whether the counternarrative is known or recognized. The dominant narrative has you dipping strawberries into cream; but have you ever dipped them in balsamic vinegar and coarsely milled pepper? One side of a debate speaks of the preconditions for good governance as a free press, a secure judiciary, and respect for human rights; the other side tells us good governance lies in having secure property rights, respect for the law, and free markets (compare Salim, 2004, to Haber, North, and Weingast, 2003). You say x; I say counter-x; and unsurprisingly, both assertions, and many in between, subsist and thrive alongside each other for those amalgam issues of uncertain, complex, incomplete, and disputed merits. I return to the topic below.

Some policy narratives, although different in their merits, share similar structures. What crisis narrative is this? The earth releases gases into the atmosphere that are then triggered by sunlight and lead to droughts, tidal waves, storms, and other natural disasters. This refers not to global warming, but rather to Aristotle's theory of comets (Tinniswood, 2002, 108). A newspaper reports, "Some environmentalists have warned that the fledgling science [of nanotechnology] has the potential to unleash hordes of minute machines—'nanorobots'—that would self replicate exponentially until

---

[*] On the Sokal hoax, see http://www.physics.nyu.edu/faculty/sokal (accessed July 29, 2004). The other physicist is Jan Henrik Schön (Service, 2002). In 2001, Schön averaged one scientific paper every eight days; in 2002, seventeen of his papers, a handful published in Nature and Science, were found to contain fictional results (Chang, 2002). An inquiry concluded: "None of the most significant physical results was witnessed by any co-author or other colleague" (Economist, 2002, 74). It can be argued that the two cases are very different. Although both intended to deceive, Sokal also intended to make his deception public whereas Schön presumably did not. If so, we can then dismiss as nostalgia the view of the editor of Science, Donald Kennedy. For him, the peer-review process cannot work without reviewers assuming the intention to deceive is not being committed on the part of the submitter. "Dr. Kennedy said the peer review system that underlies scientific publications is not designed to catch fraud. 'I don't think it's ever been expected to detect fraud wherever fraud occurs,' he said" (Chang, 2002, A20). If, however, the intent to deceive is important to a determination of fraud, note that Schön had his doctoral degree revoked because of his fraud, even though the university concerned did not find he had committed scientific fraud in his doctoral research (Chang, 2004). Princeton appears not to have done the same in Sokal's case.

a 'grey goo' covered the earth" (Welland, 2003). Similar concerns were expressed regarding recombinant DNA experiments at Harvard in the 1970s, the genetically engineered "ice-minus" bacterium for strawberry fields in the 1980s, and the genetically engineered crops (and weeds and insects) of the 1990s. Grey Goo I has been followed by Grey Goo II, III, and now IV.[*]

Crisis narratives are frequently linked. For many, Africa is the seriatim crises of epidemics, droughts, refugees, underdevelopment, desertification, deforestation, failed states, declining incomes, and constant famine. Closer to home, there are cities in which one would not choose to live. The reasons are similar: unaffordable housing, crime, inadequate public education, traffic, inner city, too much growth, too little of the right kind of growth—all of these reasons are significant. You counter: Just because it is a narrative does not mean it is not true. Crime is high, you insist; desertification is happening. The problem is the persisting uncertainty, complexity, incompleteness, and conflict over the issue in question. Now they tell us that our perceptions of high crime in the city are not borne out by the crime statistics there; now they tell us that the desertification in the Sahel was not caused by overgrazing and deforestation but global sea surface temperatures and possibly global climate change (e.g., Zeng, 2003).

The most condensed narratives are pictures, and they can tell many different stories. Yes, Trotsky did stand near to Lenin in that very famous picture, notwithstanding Stalin's airbrushing him out of the photograph later. Maps that were a major way to exploit natural resources are increasingly used to save them (Crane, 2004, 9). But policy issues are even less "clear-cut". Greenpeace releases contrasting pictures from 1928 and 2004, showing the dramatic reduction in the Patagonia Upsala glacier and crediting global warming for the change. A letter to the editor of the *Financial Times* claims that the reasons for the retreating crater lie with the increasing size and shifting movements of neighboring glaciers (Vestergaard, 2004). An article in *Science* on 63 glaciers in the Patagonian icefields (Rignot, Rivera, and Casassa, 2003) notes that those neighboring glaciers are advancing, but they are also thinning, while many of the other glaciers are retreating.

The policy narratives of interest to narrative policy analysis are the ones whose merits are not clear-cut. In the wicked and ill-structured issues of concern, reality is not clear, perceptions become multiple and competing and, not unexpectedly, different narratives are used to authorize decision making. Speaking of women with breast cancer and the controversy over its environmental causes, an epidemiologist tells us, "Their perception is very different from the scientific perception. They live day to day with the fear that's out there and I live with the scientists, knowing that the majority of scientists don't believe there is an environmental cause to cancer" (Kolata, 2002, A23). The analysis and evaluation of policy narratives are most acute when the narratives in question admit rather than deny the uncertain, complex, unfinished, and conflicted.

32.2 CONVENTIONAL POLICY ANALYSIS AND NARRATIVE POLICY ANALYSIS

While narratives are deservingly ubiquitous in politics and policy, you will not find "policy narrative" as an index entry in our leading textbooks on how to analyze, manage, and make decisions

---

[*] One report in *Science* is as follows:

> "God knows what's going to crawl out of the laboratory!" exclaimed the mayor of Cambridge, MA, in 1976, when the local government passed a moratorium on the technology, while a review committee evaluated the danger of Harvard's petri dishes might pose to the townspeople.
>
> Of course, what eventually "crawled out of the laboratory" was a series of life-saving and life-enhancing medications and vaccines, beginning in 1982 with recombinant insulin and soon followed by human growth hormone, clotting factors for hemophiliacs, fertility drugs, erythropoietin, and dozens of other additions to the pharmacopeia. Last fall brought the approval of a recombinant product for severe, life-threatening sepsis, the first drug approved for this condition. (Feldbaum, 2002, 975)

in politics and policy. The irony of course is that the policy analysis textbook, as with holy books in general, are themselves the stories we tell our people. We may disagree over whether or not "Rand Corporation begat...," "PPBS begat...," or "economics (no, public administration!) begat policy analysis, which begat implementation analysis, which begat public management, which begat the new governance theory...," but these creation myths are constantly retold in our graduate schools of public policy and management.

Myths? The American policy analyst and manager will in his or her graduate career come across the story that policy analysis rose from the ashes of failed public administration programs. Our European counterparts, in contrast, know—repeat, know—that public administration begat policy analysis and that public administration has always been the welcoming parent to its prodigal children, be they now calling themselves implementation, management, or governance. Most graduate schools do not treat such foundation stories as myths—and with good reason. If they were simply the stories we told our people, then what sense would there be to our claims that that *these*, rather than *those*, are the better methods for policy analysis and public management? If our house is built on sand, what purchase is there in saying one remodeling lasts longer than another? Without the link between PPBS and what we have learned since, how would we justify an eight-fold or six-fold or four-fold path to policy analysis? After all, who can doubt that analysis begins in problem definition and ends—and ends in what, precisely?

For its part, narrative policy analysis begins and ends in stories we tell to make sense of and act upon issues that are all too often uncertain, complex, incomplete, and conflicted at the same time. The issues are uncertain when causal processes are unclear or not easily comprehended. They are complex when the issues are more numerous, varied, and interdependent than before. They are incomplete when efforts to address them are interrupted and left unfinished. They are conflicted when different people can and do take different positions on them precisely because of the uncertainty, complexity, and unfinished business. Policy narratives are one major way to underwrite and stabilize our decision making in the face of any such amalgam of contingencies.

Because many of the issues analysts and managers are asked to address are ill-structured problems, the stepwise policy process they conventionally summon to guide and justify their course(s) of analysis and action must itself be a narrative. It should also go without saying that the terms, "uncertainty, complexity, and conflict," are themselves narrativized to differing degrees depending on the issue. Take something as central to social science as "interdependence." The concept is notorious for its lack of agreed-upon empirical measures (see La Porte, 1975). Undertake a thought experiment. What if instead of interdependence we had all along been talking about, say, the Taoist notion of *resonance* (kan-ying, ganying; see Loewe, 2003; Le Blanc, 1985)? Instead of things being interdependent, they resonate with each other. Instead of being interrelated, things move and act in response to and in concert with other things. Even the slightest divergence in a foundation narrative can ramify its development and application thereafter.

Exactly how does its own narrative go when it comes to narrative policy analysis? The terminology has varied and the process is by no means as mechanical as the following passage reads, but four steps are involved in a narrative policy analysis. First, the analyst identifies the dominant policy narrative(s) for the issue in question. Second, she identifies the narratives that run counter to the dominant account. Third, she compares the dominant policy narratives with the counternarratives to determine if there is metanarrative that can reconcile or accommodate these multiple, conflicting perspectives without slighting any of the oppositions in the process. The last step is to determine if and how a metanarrative recasts the issue in such a way that it is more tractable to conventional policy analytical tools of microeconomics, statistics, organization theory, law, and public management practice than were the original narratives which the meta-narrative embraces. If told the policy narrative is one where $a \rightarrow b \rightarrow c$, can you imagine a plausible counternarrative, where $(\text{not-}a) \rightarrow (\text{not-}b) \rightarrow c$ or where $a \rightarrow b \rightarrow (\text{not-}c)$? The conditions under which both the narrative and counternarrative can hold *at the same* time constitute the metanarrative. Metanarratives will be discussed further later in this chapter.

In this way, narrative policy analysis begins each analysis not with the conventional policy analytical question, "What's the problem?" but rather with "What's missing?" or "What am I, an analyst or manager, not seeing or understanding?" What is there in this ill-structured issue that could explain how the opposing positions could all be the case at the same time? What are the initial conditions, which, if I knew them better, connect the opposing elements in the narratives so that they are no longer mutually exclusive?

Note what has *not* been said in the preceding paragraphs. It is not claimed that all policy problems are wicked and all management issues ill-structured. It is not claimed that there is no such thing as power and that everything is relative. It is not claimed there will always be a metanarrative, that it will always be just one metanarrative, and that it will always recast the problem more tractably. It is not claimed that narrative policy analysis is the only or the best way to treat amalgam issues of high contingency. Such policy issues require triangulation from very different directions (you need only to look to the other chapters of this *Handbook* to see that) and narrative policy analysis is only one of the possible tacks.

32.3 THE PROBLEM OF EVALUATION

After my *Narrative Policy Analysis* (Roe, 1994) was published, two methodological issues came to the fore about the approach: Just how does one disclose, uncover, or otherwise make visible a metanarrative? Also, just how does one evaluate what is the better policy narrative in the absence of a metanarrative?

The first question has been dealt with at length in *Taking Complexity Seriously* (Roe, 1998). Because of space limitations and because of the importance of the second, remaining question, material that can be found elsewhere is not repeated here. The reader is referred to *Narrative Policy Analysis*, *Taking Complexity Seriously*, and *Except-Africa* (Roe, 1999) for case material—on global climate change, animal rights controversy, the tragedy of the commons, budgeting, disposition of Native American burial remains, and ecosystem management, among others—illustrating the importance of narratives and metanarratives for better decision making.

The rest of the chapter focuses on the question of how to determine the better narrative among several competing ones. To that end, it presents an evaluative framework for making such determinations. To focus the discussion and interrogate the issues in the detail they require, the chapter moves beyond short, condensed narratives to a case study of one set of interrelated and extremely important policy narratives, namely those around globalization, sustainable development, and overpopulation.

As originally conceived, determination of what was the better policy narrative took place around three connected features. The preferred narrative was one that: (1) took seriously the fact that development is genuinely complex, uncertain, unfinished and conflicted; (2) moved beyond critique of other narratives; and (3) told a better story, i.e., a more comprehensive and parsimonious account that did not dismiss or deny the issue's difficulty but which was amenable to policymaking and management. Narratives for and against globalization provide a current example of the strengths and limitations in this initial approach.

32.4 GLOBALIZATION

Readers scarcely need be told that the policy narrative in favor of the economic globalization of trade is a dominant scenario in numerous decision making arenas, as witnessed by the many calls for trade liberalization as a way of expanding economic growth. There are various counternarratives (counter-scenarios or counter-arguments) to the globalization narrative. For our purposes, we will focus on the opposing arguments to globalization put forth by environmental proponents of sustainable development. This opposition can be roughly divided into two camps: a "green" counternarrative and an "ecological" one (Roe and van Eeten, 2004).

The green counternarrative assumes that we have already witnessed sufficient harm to the environment due to globalization and thus demands taking action now to restrain further globalizing forces. It is confident in its knowledge about the causes of environmental degradation as they relate to globalization and certain in its opposition to globalization. In contrast, the ecological counternarrative starts with the potentially massive but largely unknown effects of globalization on the environment that have been largely identified by ecologists. Here enormous uncertainties over the impacts of globalization, some of which could well be irreversible, are reason enough not to promote or tolerate further globalization.[*] Where the green counternarrative looks at the planet and sees global certainties and destructive processes definitively at work, those ecologists and others who subscribe to the ecological counternarrative know that ecosystems are extremely complex, and thus the planet must be the most causally complex ecosystem there is. The ecological counternarrative opposes globalization because of what is not known, while the green counternarrative opposes globalization because of what is known. The former calls for more research and study and invokes the precautionary principle—do nothing unless you can prove it will do no harm. The latter says we do not need more research or studies to do something—take action now—precisely because we have seen the harm.[†]

---

[*] Any number of publications illustrate the green counternarrative. It features strongly in anti-World Trade Organization meetings. According to International Forum on Globalization's primer produced before the 1999 WTO Seattle meetings:

> Economic globalization is the number one threat to the survival of the natural world. National governments are losing the ability to regulate the globalization process and its effects on the environment...

> [G]lobalization is inherently destructive to the natural world because it requires that products travel thousands of miles around the planet, resulting in staggering environmental costs in the form of unprecedented levels of ocean and air pollution from transport, increased energy consumption and fossil fuel emissions (furthering climate change), increased use of packaging materials, and devastating new infrastructure developments—new roads, ports, airports, pipelines, power grids—often considered in formerly pristine places...

> Given the current climate change, atmospheric ozone depletion, ocean pollution, dwindling supplies of clean fresh water, habitat loss, and species extinction, the WTO is pursuing a course of action [i.e., trade liberalization] that will bring on a global environmental collapse. (Barker and Mander, 1999, 13–14).

"Economic globalization accelerates the causes of climate change: global deforestation and the use of fossil fuels. Either we stop this immediately or the next century will bring unimaginable disaster" declares the sub-headline of an advertisement against globalization and trade liberalization at the time of the WTO conference" (Global Warming, 1999, A16). The green counternarrative counsels: Stop corporations and public officials in this headlong rush to globalization. Promote an amalgam of policies and interventions that support local communities, business and democratic decision making.

[†] There are as well many publications for the ecological counternarrative. The well-known *Science* Policy Forum article, "Economic Growth, Carrying Capacity, and the Environment," by Kenneth Arrow and a group of ecological economists had this to say about the environmental impacts of economic liberalization policies:

> Environmental damages, including loss of ecological resilience, often occur abruptly. They are frequently not reversible. But abrupt changes can seldom be anticipated from systems of signals that are typically received by decision-makers in the world today. Moreover, the signals that do exist are often not observed, or are wrongly interpreted, or are not part of the incentive structure of societies. This is due to ignorance about the dynamic effects of changes in ecosystem variables...[G]iven the fundamental uncertainties of ecosystem dynamics and the dramatic consequences we would face if we were to guess wrong, it is necessary that we act in a precautionary way so as to maintain the diversity and resilience of ecosystems. (Arrow et al., 1995, 93).

In practice, the two environmental counternarratives are conflated. For instance, it is often argued that agricultural biotechnology should not be promoted until we know it will not cause environmental harm (Mann and Plummer, 2002)—and anyway, you certainly can not trust biotech companies, can you? Conflation, however, in no way reconciles the substantive contradictions between the opposing environmental narratives.

Unfortunately, neither the green nor the ecological counternarrative meet all three features for a better narrative. Clearly, the ecological counternarrative is preferable over the green version in terms of the first feature. The ecological counternarrative takes uncertainty and complexity seriously throughout, while its green counterpart goes out of its way to deny that any dispositive uncertainties and complexities are at work. Does this then mean the ecological version is the better environmental counternarrative? The answer depends on the other two features, and here problems arise. Plainly, the ecological counternarrative is open to all manner of critique, if simply because of its reliance on the precautionary principle, e.g., I can no more prove a negative than I can show beforehand that application of the precautionary principle itself will do no harm in the future (see Duvick, 1999). That said, from the narrative policy analysis framework, critiques against the precautionary principle, or for that matter against the ecological counternarrative, are of little decision making use if they are not accompanied by alternative formulations that better explain how and why it makes sense to be environmentally opposed to globalization. Critiques discredit rather than replace. In fact, proponents of the dominant globalization narrative have taken critiques of the ecological counternarrative as just another reason why they are right and the rest of us are wrong. In reality, problems with the precautionary principle no more "support" the dominant globalization narrative than do the critiques of that narrative's inverted U-curve "support" either environmental counternarrative.[*]

What about the third feature? Is there at least one metanarrative that explains how it is possible to hold, at the same time and without being incoherent or inconsistent, the dominant policy narrative about globalization, its ecological counternarrative, and other accounts, including critiques of both? Readers may have different metanarratives in mind, but the one I am most familiar with is the metanarrative about who claims to have the best right to steward the planet. The proponents of globalization and the proponents of the ecological counternarrative disagree over what is best for the environment, but both groups are part and parcel of the same techno-managerial elite who claim they know what is best for us. According to this metanarrative, we need free trade or the precautionary principle or whatever because we—the unwashed majority—cannot better steward our resources on our own. While we may bristle against the condescension of these elites—who elected either group to steward the earth?—it is patent that the metanarrative does not take us very far in deciding what to do instead. We are still left with the question: What is the better policy (meta)narrative?

Fortunately, it is now possible to provide a fuller evaluative framework of policy narratives. We know more than we did in the early 1990s about what it takes to ensure reliable development services taken to be critical by the human populations concerned, and in that knowledge can be found the better policy narratives. As one might expect, the evaluation is contingent on who is doing the evaluating, but at least now we have clearer alternatives than we did earlier.

The next section lays out the evaluative framework. The section thereafter demonstrates how the framework applies to policy narratives, particularly for those trying to realize sustainable development. Thereafter, that *bête noire* of globalized sustainable development, worldwide over-population, is analyzed and evaluated in terms of the framework. The chapter concludes with directions forward in the next generation of research on policy narratives.

---

[*] The inverted U-curve asserts there that as a country's per capita income initially increases so does its pollution but that after a point when incomes have become sufficiently high, declines in pollution occur. There is a considerable and lively debate over whether the data support such a conclusion (e.g., Arrow et al., 1995).

32.5 FRAMEWORK

Assume any system—technical, agricultural, social, ecological, or the one you have in mind now—has as a priority the aim of providing reliable critical services. It may not be the only aim, but it is a priority. The critical services may be crops, water, transportation, or electricity, among others. "Reliable" means the critical services are provided safely and continuously even during peak demand periods. The lights stay on, even when generators could do with maintenance; crop production varies seasonally, but food supplies remain stable; and we have clean water because we have managed our livestock so as not to contaminate the aquifer. The challenge to maintain reliable services is daunting, as these critical service systems—technical, agricultural, social, *and* ecological—are tightly coupled and complexly interactive. The generator goes off, and the knock-on, cascading effects are dramatic.

The wider literature my colleagues and I have been contributing to (Schulman, Roe, van Eeten, and de Bruijne, 2004; Roe, van Eeten, Schulman, and de Bruijne, 2002; Roe, Schulman, van Eeten and de Bruijne, 2005; see also Roe, 2004) tells us that the drive to high reliability management in such systems can be described along two dimensions[*]: (1) the type of knowledge brought to bear on efforts to make the system reliable, and (2) the focus of attention or scope of those reliability efforts. The knowledge bases from which reliable performance is pursued can range from formal or representational knowledge, in which key efforts are understood through abstract principles and deductive models based upon the principles, to experience, based on informal, tacit understanding. Knowledge bases, in brief, vary in their mix of induction and deduction, and thus their assembly of differing arguments and scenarios into policy narratives.

At the same time, the scope of attention can range from a purview which embraces reliability as an entire system output, encompassing many variables and elements, to a case-by-case focus in which each case is viewed as a particular event with distinct properties or features. Typically, scope is articulated in policy narratives as the different scales, ranging from specific to general, that must be taken into account. The two continua of knowledge and scope define a conceptual and perceptual space (Figure 32.1), where high reliability can be pursued (defined again as the continuous and safe provision of the critical service even during periods of stress). Four nodes of activities and the domain of the reliability professional are identified.

At the extreme of both scope and formal principles is the macrodesign approach to reliable critical services (the "macrodesign node"). Here formal deductive principles are applied at the system-wide level to understand a wide variety of critical processes. It is considered inappropriate to operate beyond the design analysis, and analysis is meant to cover an entire system, including every last case to which that system can be subjected. At the other extreme is the activity of the continually reactive behavior in the face of real-time challenges at the microlevel (the "micro-operations" node). Here reliability resides in the reaction time of the system operators working at the event level rather than the anticipation of system designers for whatever eventuality. The experiences of crisis managers and emergency responders are exemplary.

But designers cannot foresee everything, and the more "complete" a logic of design principles attempts to be, the more likely it is that the full set will contain two or more principles contradicting each other (again, prove beforehand that application of the precautionary principle will itself do no harm). On the other hand, operator reactions by their very nature are likely to give the operator too specific and hasty a picture, losing sight of the forest for the trees in front of the manager or operator. Microexperience can become a "trained incapacity" that leads to actions undermining reliability, as the persons concerned may well not be aware of the wider ramifications of their behavior.

What to do then, if the aim is reliability? Clearly, "moving horizontally" across the reliability space directly from one corner across to the opposite corner is unlikely to be successful. A great

---

[*] I thank Paul Schulman for the original framework, though he bears no responsibility for my adaptation and application.

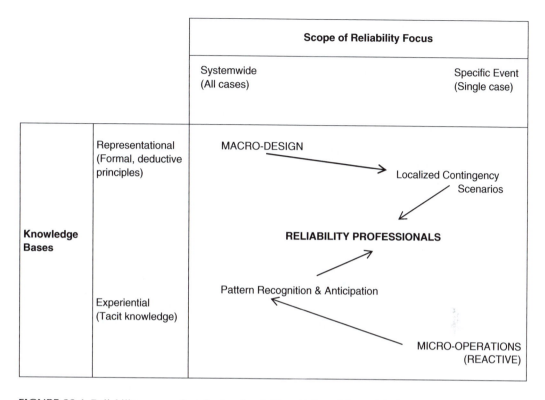

FIGURE 32.1 Reliability space of professional activities. (Adapted from Schulman, P.R. et al., *Journal of Contingencies and Crisis Management*, 12, 14–28, 2004.)

deal of our research has found that attempts to impose large-scale formal designs directly onto an individual case—to attempt to anticipate and fully deduce and determine the behavior of each instance from system-wide principles alone—are very risky when not outright fallacious (variously called the fallacy of composition in logic or the ecological fallacy in sociology). That said, reactive operations by the individual hardly constitute a template for scaling up to the system, as management fads demonstrate continually.

Instead of horizontal, corner-to-corner movements, Figure 32.1 indicates that reliability is enhanced when *shifts in scope are accompanied by shifts in the knowledge bases.* To be highly reliable requires more and different knowledge than found at the extremes of *a priori* principles and phenomenological experience. We know from our research that reliability is enhanced when designers apply their designs less globally and relax their commitment to a set of principles that fully determine system operations. This happens when designers embrace a wider set of contingencies in their analyses and entertain alternate, more localized (including regional) scenarios for system behavior and performance (the "localized contingent scenarios node" in Figure 32.1). From the other direction, reactive operations can shift away from real-time firefighting toward recognizing and anticipating patterns across a run of real-time cases (the "pattern recognition and anticipation node"). Operator and managerial adaptation—recognizing common patterns and anticipating strategies to cover similar categories of micro events or cases—arises. These emerging norms, strategies, and routines are likely to be less formal than the protocols developed through contingency analysis or scenario building.

It is in this middle ground where worldviews are tempered by individual experience, where discretion and improvisation probe design, where anticipated patterns mesh with localized scenarios, and where shared views are reconciled with individualized perspectives. Our research tells us that sustaining critical services in a reliable fashion is not really possible until the knowledge bases have shifted from what is known at the macro, micro, localized scenario, and pattern recognition levels. The four nodes are important only to the extent that designs, scenarios, personal experience, and empirical generalization can be translated into reliable critical services across the scales of interest. The translation is interpretative rather than literal—that is why new or different knowledge is generated.

The middle ground is, in our phrase, the domain of the reliability professional. These are the people who excel at cross-scale, context-dependent case-by-case analysis. They are the middle level managers and operators in the control rooms of our technical systems; they are the medical staff in our hospital emergency rooms; they are the firefighters who know when to drop their shovels and run for it; they are the farmers who decide to plow now before the first rains, the pastoralists who move their herds only after the first rains, the experienced extension agent and researcher who does not turn away from the villager they have worked with the minute she asks, "But what do *we* do now?"

32.6 FRAMEWORK FOR EVALUATING POLICY NARRATIVES

As we shall see, the policy narratives deployed by reliability professionals are different than those found populating the four nodes of macrodesign, localized contingency scenarios, pattern recognition and anticipation, and microoperations in much of the published literature. This is to be expected because the knowledge bases used in the narratives are different. Reliability professionals and the arguments they make have of course always been there, decade after decade. To be thoroughly arbitrary, we read about them in Albert Hirschman's *Development Projects Observed* (1967), Robert Chambers' *Managing Rural Development* (1974), and Jon Moris's implementation-oriented *Managing Induced Rural Development* (1981)—and that only touches the tip of a literature on reliability professionals in development. Hindsight, a facility for other languages, and greater respect for the fugitive literature would easily chronicle other archaeologies.

What has changed since the 1990s is that the reliability space and the differences in policy narratives around the nodes and in the middle are more obvious than before. The changed state of affairs is especially evident in recent publications. One example will have to suffice.

The Science of Sustainable Development, by Jeff Sayer and Bruce Campbell (2004), has plainly been written by and for the reliability professionals working in the middle of the development and the environment arena. The book, authored by two development practitioners with strong research and administrative *bona fides*, seeks to demonstrate how integrated natural resource management happens in practice. Through case studies from Borneo, Zimbabwe, and the Ecuadorian Andes combined with a very broad synthesis of the literature, the book "aims to demystify the sometimes obscure science of natural resources management, interpreting it for the benefit of those who need to deal with the day-to-day problems of managing complex natural resources" (i). That word, "interpreting," is more path-breaking than on first notice, because it is directly tied to the translation function that reliability professionals provide. In this way, the book reflects a major shift that has taken place over the years away from conventional development and environment narratives based solely or primarily on designs, contingency scenarios, personal experience, or major trends.

It is important to underscore how different the Sayer and Campbell discussion of "sustainable development" is from that which still takes place at the four nodes. It would be easy enough to critique their book from the nodes looking into the domain the authors occupy—one can already hear the critics. From the macrodesign node: "But the book doesn't have a chapter on the foundations and principles of sustainable development..." From the scenario node: "But the book doesn't have any discussion on the model that hunter-gatherers offer for contemporary sustainable development ..." From the microexperience node: "But the book doesn't tell us what the lived daily experience is really like for a peasant under 'sustainable development'..." From the pattern recognition node: "But the book has no discussion of global trends in per capita consumption and population growth rates that affect sustainable development ..."

The crux is not that these narratives from the outside are irrelevant. On the contrary, they could be very important—if and when they can be translated and interpreted into the different knowledge bases required for sustainable (aka reliable) development across multiple scales from the global to the specific. For example, the book is mercifully free of the *de rigueur* macronarrative about sustainable development as managing resources today so that the future has a chance to manage them tomorrow. It is not that this Bruntland Commission definition is "wrong," but that it never has been specific enough for management purposes. For Sayer and Campbell (2004, 57) as well as many others (this author included), the better narrative—that is, one which interprets Bruntland in reliability terms—is: sustainable development is about creating human opportunities to respond to unpredictable change across the scales humans find themselves interacting. That narrative is difficult enough to realize, but at least unpredictability and uncontrollability move center stage where they must be if sustainability is to be taken seriously.

Sayer and Campbell write decidedly from within the reliability space looking out to the nodes beyond. The two authors make it patent that sustainable livelihoods will not be possible until new and different knowledge bases are brought to bear across the scales from case to system. (In fact, one cannot talk about multiple scales for sustainability without shifting from knowledge bases.) The authors' call for more participatory action research (PAR), scaling out (rather than up or down), and use of "throwaway" models is especially apposite because those approaches at best help information gatherers become information users. At worst, PAR and formal models can be made as formulaic as the project log frame at the macrodesign node, as the authors are quick to point out.

Sayer and Campbell's call for more science-based integrated resource management can also be understood in the same light. When "Science" comes to us in a capital "S"—a set of must-do's (e.g., random assignment groups and controls)—it is far too rigid for translation by reliability professionals working in the middle. Yet Sayer and Campbell are correct to insist that small-"s" science has a major contribution to make. Science, when understood as one tack from the four nodes to the middle—that is, to "make sense of" principles, scenarios, the ideographic, and livelihood patterns—is crucial. We see the tacking in increasing calls for more "evidence-based" medicine and science, i.e., science that works best is the one that carries with it the means to translate all manner of scenarios and trends as well as principles and experiences.

The implication for evaluating policy narratives is as dramatic as it is straightforward. In terms of the above framework, the more useful way to evaluate the narratives in Sayer and Campbell's *The Science of Sustainable Development* is not from the outside looking in, but from the inside looking out along with other reliability professionals.

What precisely are the policy narratives deployed by reliability professionals such as Sayer and Campbell? They are not alone among development practitioners in making much of the importance of complexity and uncertainty, flexibility, experimentation, replication, integration, risk, learning, adaptive management, and collaboration to the work of development. The terms and the narratives they reflect are very much the common currency of many writing from the middle. When narrativized, however, the terms can render the insights from the middle banal and seemingly self-evident to any 17-year-old undergraduate: "Take uncertainty into account." Awesome! "You must be flexible in your approach." Too right!

In actuality, once the terms are probed further, they retain their unique insights. Again, we are in the presence of few studies but a great deal of practice. What seems to be the case is that when reliability professionals say we need more learning, what they are often talking about is a very special kind of learning from samples of one case or fewer, as in the cases of simulations (see March, Sproul, and Tamuz, 1991). When they say we must recognize and accommodate complexity and uncertainty, what they really mean is that this amalgam of the uncertain, complex, unfinished, and conflicted must be particularized and contextualized if we are to analyze and manage natural resources case by case (Roe, 1998). When they say we need more findings and better science that can be replicated across a wide variety of cases, what they really are calling for is identifying greater equifinality in results; that is, finding multiple but different pathways to achieve the similar objectives given the variety of cases (cf. Belovsky, Botkin, Crowl, Cummins, Franklin, Hunter, Joern, Lindenmayer, MacMahon, Margules, and Scott, 2004).

What reliability professionals mean by calling for greater collaboration is not just more team work or working with more stakeholders, but rather that the team members and stakeholders "bring the whole system into the room" for the purposes of making the services in question reliable (see Weisbord and Janoff, 1995). When they talk about the need for more integration, what they really mean is the need to recouple what have been all too decoupled and fragmented development activities in ways that better mimic but can never fully reflect the coupled nature of the environment around them (van Eeten and Roe, 2002). When they call for more flexibility, what they mean is the need for greater maneuverability of the reliability professionals in the face of changing system volatility and options to respond to those changes (Roe et al., 2002).

If reliability professionals say we need more experimentation, they decidedly do not mean more trial and error learning, when survival demands that the first error never be the last trial (see Rochlin, 1993). So when they call for more adaptive management, what they often are asking for is greater case-by-case discriminations in management alternatives that can range from self-organizing to command-and-control options, depending on the particulars (Roe and van Eeten, 2001a). What they really mean is that operators must juggle error tolerance and error intolerance together if reliability is to be achieved, e.g., they set bandwidths (limits, safety margins, tolerances) and manage adjustments within and around them (Roe and van Eeten, 2002). In this way, reliability professionals talk less about the macroapplication of the precautionary principle than about the need to take precautions by narrowing and "hardening" the bandwidths so as to better control and stabilize the adjustments in resource use within them.[*] Similarly, when others talk about objective risks associated with tightly coupled, complexly interactive systems, reliability professionals instead mean not so much the frequencies and hazards discernable through pattern recognition, as the risks that emerge out of and co-evolve with developing the unique knowledge bases to reliably manage the systems in question. In this and the other ways, activities in the middle domain have not become "more certain and less complex," but rather that the operating uncertainties and complexities have changed with the knowledge bases. Policy narratives are still needed, but they are decidedly different than those claiming priority at and around the four outer nodes.

Such distinctions can be multiplied, but the point here is that too many exist for them to be incidental. We must realize that those around the four nodes use narratives about "risk," "coordination," "learning," and the like differently than many of those in the middle. If we fully appreciated the differences, longstanding development controversies, such as that of "planning versus implementation," would have to be substantially recast. If you look closely at Figure 32.1, you see we are talking about professionals who are expert not because they "bridge" macroplanning and microimplementation, but because they are able to translate that planning and implementation into the reliable critical services.

Much more work is needed on the policy narratives in the middle already there. This chapter will have achieved 90% of its aims if even a handful of its readers followed up that challenge.

---

[*] A longer chapter would have more to discuss about bandwidth management by reliability professionals. The well-known ecologist Brian Walker (1995, 147) argues: "Species richness per se in an ecosystem has little ecological significance, but having a range of species with different environmental tolerances within important functional groups is a strong component of ecosystem resilience." A recent Policy Forum in *Science*, "Ecosystem-Based Fisheries Management" (Pikitch, Santora, Babcock, Bakun, Bonfil, Conover, Dayton, Doukakis, Fluharty, Heneman, Houde, Link, Livingston, Mangel, McAllister, Pope, and Sainsbury, 2004, 346–347), asserts "[m]aintaining system characteristics within certain bounds may protect ecosystem resilience and avoid irreversible changes" and argues for "safety margins," "reference points," and "community and system-level standards" within which to manage. Our own work on large water and hydropower systems describes formal bandwidth management in detail and its parallels to ecosystem-based resilience, resistance and recovery (van Eeten and Roe, 2002; Roe et al., 2005).

Until that time, we will have to make due with the framework itself as an evaluative device. Fortunately, even in its rough form, the framework allows us to evaluate notorious policy narratives in fresh ways. We now shift the analysis to that that great enemy of globalized sustainable development, worldwide overpopulation.

32.7 THE FRAMEWORK APPLIED: OVERPOPULATION

Arguably, the world's most famous policy narrative is that about global overpopulation and overcrowding. The crisis narrative is familiar: Human population numbers—now over 6.3 billion people on the planet with a net increase of 77 million a year (Wolf, 2003a) threaten the globe with massive, unprecedented overcrowding, environmental degradation, and all manner of resource-based conflicts. We are fast approaching, if we have not already passed, the sustainable limits of our key resources—water, air, and energy. Without population control (so the narrative goes), including but not limited to birth control and growth limits on our settlements and resource utilization, the planet is hardwired for rapid and irreversible decline into an urbanized clash of too many people chasing too few resources.

If the narrative sounds baldly grim, we are told to just look at the numbers. In the early 1950s, the global population was predicted to be 3.6 billion by 2000; the actual figure was more like 6.1 billion (Cooper and Layard, 2002, 8). The planet's population is expected to increase up to 12 billion by 2050 (9). FAO figures for forest loss are huge, i.e., a net loss of 6.4 million hectares lost between 1990 and 1997 alone (Kaiser, 2002, 919). In the current decade the majority of the world's population is becoming urban; a mere hundred years ago urban populations represented just 14% of the total (Crossette, 2002). Energy and water use projections augur horrific depletions (e.g., Brown, 2002, 926). Surface temperatures have risen over the last hundred years, and global climate change continues apace (Ramanathan and Barnett, 2003). The world's greatest problem is population growth, according to the DNA discovers, Watson and Crick (Daugherty and Allendorf, 2002, 284). As two conservationists recently put it in *Science* (Wright and Okey, 2004, 1903), "One word sums up the overall and long-term problem [in creating a sustainable future]: overpopulation. We wonder how any sane person could disagree."

Here is how a sane person can disagree. First, the numbers are disputed. The UN has revised it global population projections dramatically downward; it is now estimated the total will be nine billion by 2300 (United Nations, 2003). Other UN estimates indicate the world's population will peak at ten billion and possibly decline thereafter (Crossette, 2002). A more recent study indicates a forest loss in the same period of 20% less than the original FAO estimates, while water use projections have been fabulously overestimated (Kaiser, 2002; Brown, 2002). It has been repeatedly said that the most certain thing about global energy projections is that they are wrong. Surface temperatures have been increasing, but a vigorous dispute continues over just what this means or is caused by (e.g., Ramanathan and Barrett, 2003). And frankly, with all due respect to Watson and Crick, just what makes them reliability professionals on population growth?

Other problems with the data (and methodologies) are considerable and must be noted. There are strong taxonomic biases in conservation research (Clark and May, 2002), estimates of biodiversity losses are highly disputed, and there are those who consider some global phenomena, particularly urbanization, as having net benefits precisely when it comes to controlling total population numbers (e.g., family size and birthrates tend to drop when people live in cities; Revkin, 2002). We must, however, tread very, very carefully here. Just because the numbers are open to critique does not mean that we can conclude the counternarrative holds, i.e., there is nothing really to worry about by way of overpopulation. Does this mean then that analysts are stalled between two or more conflicting narratives with respect to population and crowding, waiting for evidence to shift more one way than the others? Figure 32.1 suggests how to evaluate the narratives.

Explicit in the call for population restrictions, including limits on growth and births, is the macrodesign concept of a global carrying capacity, a limit to the total number of people the planet can support without it tipping into environmental collapse. This limit is set, in theory, by principles of what is or is not sustainable. This too is disputed. The notion that we can derive the level of sustainable population from a notion of global carrying capacity and global calculations to that end is contentious even among ecologists. Which global carrying capacity limit do we use? Here the only certain number is 69. That is number of past studies reviewed in the recent meta-analysis of the widely divergent estimates for global carrying capacity. The meta-analysis found the lower and upper population bounds were between 0.65 billion and 98 billion people, with the best point estimate of 7.7 billion (van den Bergh and Rietveld, 2004). If such a range is not troubling enough, many ecologists also doubt whether there is such a thing as a "carrying capacity" for arid and semi-arid lands, which constitute much of the surface area of the planet (Roe, 1999; also Scoones, 1996).

So too for the other extreme. The microoperations of overcrowding are open to all manner of qualification. What feels overcrowded to someone in OECD countries need not be so to someone living in Asia. What feels overcrowded to a rural resident may not be experienced as overcrowded to an urban resident in the same country. Even if both sets of residents agreed that their areas were overcrowded in the same ways, one set may say the answer is not fewer people or animals as much as better education and technology. Even if everyone agreed that their areas were overcrowded and held similar reasons accounting for this, it is simply inconceivable that anyone knows enough, no matter how expert they are about the globe, to recommend what the actual population levels should be. It is difficult enough for a long-term resident of an area to make those estimates for his or her locality, let alone the most complex ecosystem there is, the globe.

Another way of putting this is that, as one moves from macro-design and individual experience, one draws on and adds to the knowledge bases about issues of population, age structures, crowding, and related factors. We have already seen how different global trends and empirical generalizations are when compared to the dominant macronarrative about global overpopulation. So too when one moves from macrodesign to localized contingency scenarios. Only a handful of the world's countries, notably India, China, Pakistan, Bangladesh, and Nigeria, account for the major increases in population (Wolf, 2003a). Equally important, just what are the carrying capacities of those specific countries? If one considers Europe alone, the problem there is one of *shrinking* population levels and declining fertility (Lutz, O'Neill, and Scherbov, 2003; Ringen, 2003). Global climate modeling has long moved to developing and improving regional climate models, and there are certainly regional differences in climate changes and their effects, such as effect on species (e.g., see Myers and Pimm, 2003).

Now plot the positions in a reliability space for the issue of global overpopulation (Figure 32.2).

This plotting of standpoints leads us to ask: Who specifically are the "reliability professionals" in this issue—that is, who are the people who tack from and translate positions around the four other nodes into reliable service provision? Who are these reliability professionals on overpopulation and overcrowding, and what does it mean to focus on them rather than the other four positions? The dimensions and plot of positions in Figure 32.2 help identify them.

Whoever the reliability professionals are, they have different knowledge bases than those represented by regional scenarios and system-wide pattern anticipation. The unit of analysis must lie somewhere between the endpoints of "region" (localized contingency scenarios) and the global (pattern recognition). Moreover, we would expect the professionals are already there—i.e., they do not have to be created. For highly contentious policy narratives as the one for overpopulation, all points in the reliability space can be assumed to be filled. To remind ourselves: Why are we interested in reliability professionals? Not because they have the "solution" to overpopulation, but because their policy narratives are the ones that have to translate the narratives at the four nodes, if they can be translated at all, into knowledge for providing more reliable services in the face of population pressures.

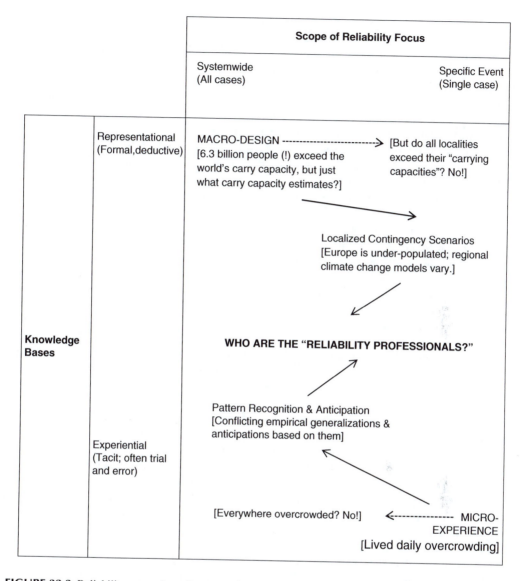

FIGURE 32.2 Reliability space for policy narrative on global overpopulation and overcrowding.

Return to Figure 32.2 and tack to the middle from the localized scenario and pattern recognition nodes. What is between a large region, such as Europe, and the globe? One obvious answer: the nation state. Pick two countries whose human populations share the same pattern recognition and localized scenarios, i.e., residents say they are overpopulated and overcrowded now and increasingly so in the future (this way they share the system-wide features purported to exist in the dominant policy narrative). Choose, for example, The Netherlands and Singapore. The population densities are perceived to be very similar between the highly urbanized western Netherlands—the Randstad—and Singapore (see Roe and van Eeten, 2001b). Then ask about sustainability as viewed from within rather than outside the middle: Based on experience and familiarity with the two countries, what policies enable its citizenry to increase human opportunities to respond to unpredictable change they find themselves in (i.e., the preceding Sayer and Campbell narrative about sustainable development)? From this vantage point, a country is overcrowded and overpopulated when its government and/or civil society—the domain of its reliability professionals—have few ideas about how to keep people residing, employed, and productive there.

Indeed, countries can move in and out over(under)population and over(under)crowding, depending on the livelihood strategies followed. A country that is not now overcrowded can become so, even if population numbers do not change. Its policies need only change for the worse. This suggests that an explicit goal of economic and social policy should not necessarily be one of preventing people from coming into the country, but rather one of retaining and sustaining people already there. The Netherlands and Singapore risk becoming truly overpopulated and overcrowded only when growing numbers of residents there want greater well-being but choose to leave even when they do not know for certain their greater well-being lies elsewhere. They are pushed, rather than pulled, to another place.

The reliability professionals who deploy this translated version of an overpopulation and overcrowding policy narrative vary from country and country. Nor are they macroeconomic, strategic planners there. Again, the reliability professionals searched for are those who excel at cross-scale, context-dependent case-by-case analysis. When it comes to sustainable development at a country level, they are the ones who are able to learn from few cases, they are adept at finding multiple ways of achieving the desired developmental ends, they bring into meetings those who are key to managing the development in question, they seek to recouple more effectively what has been decoupled through disciplinary specialization and agency fragmentation, they are constantly searching for ways to avoid loss of maneuverability, they believe tolerating error has to be balanced by error intolerance when survival is at stake, they distrust other's estimates of risk when it is not based on or reflects intimate knowledge of the system they are managing, and they frequently work within bandwidths that give them some flexibility but never all that they want to provide the reliable services key to what they take to be development.

It should be clear by this point that the middle's policy narrative about overpopulation and overcrowding contrasts starkly with the dominant narrative about global overpopulation. In this new policy narrative, no claim is made that overpopulation and overcrowding are not a problem, but then again no claim is being made that one country's mix of policies for addressing population and crowding will or could work in any other country. The dominant narrative instead bypasses the middle domain of professionals and offers nothing more than top-to-toe designs that promise reliability by bridging the outer nodes directly. They insist that the trends are this way, *therefore* the macrosolutions must be that way. But there is no "therefore." The knowledge bases important for ensuring reliability in what matters by way of critical services must be tacked to, not leaped over; they have to be taken into account, not willfully ignored or studiously avoided.

The analysis of Figure 32.2 and its reliability space for the overpopulation narrative also illustrates other points about how to evaluate differences between competing narratives. First, the figure shows the folly of believing that difficult issues can be solved at any one node. Dealing with the issue of overpopulation requires knowledge that exists beyond the four outer nodes. True believers who insist that one node is more equal than the others offer the surest route to failure when the goal is reliable critical services. So many environmental issues involving population-stressed resource utilization are taken to be primarily measurement problems in pattern recognition, when in fact they call upon a constellation of nodal and middle knowledge bases. What is the real carrying capacity of the earth? How do you count the amount of CO_2 a tree soaks up and what if the tree that stores the most carbon is not the best tree for the local ecosystem (Ball, 2003)? If genetic testing shows that a mouse listed under endangered species legislation is identical with a plentiful species not listed, why should you not delist that mouse and replace it by a more threatened species (Johnson, 2004)? We think these questions have answers, when in reality we are asking for the knowledge within which to make sense of the questions.

Second, Figure 32.2 suggests that a more comprehensive or compelling policy narrative is one about how conflicted the issue really is at the macro and micro levels and how the drive to say or do something reliable about population and crowding requires us to disaggregate at the global level and aggregate across the micro level. Third, even when we tack to localized contingency scenarios from the macrodesign and to pattern recognition from microoperations, there is no reason to believe that there will be consensus over the scenarios and the patterns observed. In contrast, in tacking to the new nodes, we would expect to see differences among scenarios and the data analysis. Why? The number and heterogeneity of the knowledge bases have increased in both cases.

Fourth, some policy and management issues are notable precisely for the lack of differentiated and conflicting positions around the four nodes. The classic "thin" policy narrative is "Except-Africa," as in "development works… except in Africa." When I first wrote about Except-Africa, I argued: "Africa, the basket-case?—better to say, Africa the twenty-first century's reservoir of new democracies" (Roe, 1999, 5). At the time I first posed the question, two nations were classified as free; now six are. Has that increase changed the Except-Africa narrative? Not a whit. If you want to find sober counternarratives to Except-Africa, do not expect them to come from the nodes but from the work of reliability professionals in these and other African nations.

The fifth and last observation brings us back to where the analysis began: the green and ecological counternarratives to globalization. In actuality, differences between the two are reducible to claims as to who best speaks for macrodesign and pattern recognition when it comes to environmental opposition to globalization. There are of course times when ecologists and environmentalists agree. The bitter debate over Bjørn Lomborg's *The Skeptical Environmentalist* (2001) can be seen in just this light. It appears to be a debate between the advocates of Lomborg and his ecological and environmental critics. In reality, it was a battle over who had the right to speak for the macrodesign and pattern recognition nodes when it came to the environment and sustainability. In the process, neither the Lomborg critics nor his advocates really took any interest in what those in the middle, such as Sayer and Campbell (2004), have to say about the issues.[*]

32.8 CONCLUSION

Just because they are all narratives does not mean that all policy narratives are equal. Just because policy narratives can be found doing battle with each other and across the nodes does not mean that the stakes are higher there. Nor does it mean these nodal narratives are the better ones because the shouting and waving is more frantic there, at least when it comes to underwriting and stabilizing decision making over critical services whose reliability matters to society and the public.

Readers must not be too sanguine that those at the nodes will take account of those in the middle domain. No matter what professionals such as Sayer and Campbell (2004) or all the other reliability practitioners have to say, there will be the economist who all but pats us on the head, saying, "Well, obviously the prices aren't right." Or the regional specialist who sighs, "Obviously, it's because… well, it's Africa, after all." Or the ethnographer who counters, "You don't know what these villagers are telling me!" Or the numbers expert who says, "Nor do you know the latest global trends." To adapt the useful phrase of Robert Chambers (1988), "normal professionalism" has all but been equated with those who claim to speak for and hold expertise at the four nodes.

The problem is not that such responses are irrelevant, but rather they too often do not carry with them their translation into the knowledge bases from which to strive for sustaining livelihoods over the scales of interest, including but never limited to the global scale. Who then is responsible for that translation and interpretation?

In an ideal world, the burden of proof rests with the affirmative. You say that *these* and not *those* big ideas, big scenarios, big people, or big trends set the future for reliable water supplies, crop yields, household incomes, and governance. Well then, make the case for that assertion. You do the translation. It scarcely will do for you to skirt the middle, leap from node to node, culling one

---

[*] For a flavor of the Lomborg debate, compare the op-ed piece by Martin Wolf (2003b) to the letters from Stuart Pimm (2003) and Paul Ehrlich (2003) in response.

story here and another there, and then call the potpourri "free trade" or "sustainable development." The willful avoidance and studied indifference just marked only serve those who expect others to simplify sustainability and population issues along with them.

But we do not live in an ideal world, and those at the nodes looking into the middle could well make the case that it is sheer hubris of reliability professionals to believe that they can round the circle, have their cake and eat it too, or as Sayer and Campbell argue, alleviate poverty and save the environment at the same time.

Perhaps. The fact of the matter is that we have very little research on reliability professionals and more than ample study of the nodes. Almost all the airtime in "doing development" has been given to the short-cut metaphysics of dominant policy narratives. If only we had full cost pricing, or sufficient political will, or had publics that could solve Arrow's voting paradox on their own, then everything would be okay. We can, they promise, jump from macro to micro and back again when it comes to reliability. These dominant narratives assign to anyone but their proponents the responsibility of translating design and experience into sustainable livelihoods. That is the real hubris and its costs are for all to see (for example, on "mega-projects," see Flyvbjerg, Bruzelius, and Rothengatter, 2003). In contrast, the middle is very much *terra incognita* if only because it has no real value to those who already know, after a fashion, the Answer. Reliability professionals—be they villagers or control room operators—are very much the marginalized voices to whom *Narrative Policy Analysis* recommended we give more attention. For in this middle are to be found the alternative narratives to the ones that dominate the nodes. The framework presented in this chapter is intended to help make that assessment and evaluation.

To get to the middle is daunting, but it is the way ahead. For far too many of our long-lived debates have been at the extremes of the reliability space, haven't they? Planning versus Markets. Markets versus Hierarchy. Science versus Technology versus Politics. Which way Africa: Kenyatta or Nyerere? Which way Latin America: Structural Adjustment or Basic Human Needs? Which way the world: Globalization or Anti-Globalization? We might as well be talking about who is more likely to be in Heaven, Plato or Aristotle.

REFERENCES

Arrow, K., Bolin, B., Costanza, R., Dasgupta, P., Folke, C., Holling, C. S., Jansson, B. O., Levin, S., Maler, K. G., Perrings, C., and Pimentel, D., Economic growth, carrying capacity, and the environment, *Ecological Economics*, 15(2), 91–95, 1995.

Ball, J., If an oak eats CO_2 in a forest, who gets emission credits?, *Wall Street Journal*, A1, A12, December 10, 2003

Barker, D. and Mander, J. 1999. *Invisible government—the World Trade Organization: Global government for the new millennium?* Primer prepared for the International Forum on Globalization, San Francisco.

Belovsky, G. E., Botkin, D. B., Crowl, T. A., Cummins, K. W., Franklin, J. F., Hunter, M. L., Joern, A., Lindenmayer, D. B., MacMahon, J. A., Margules, C. R., and Scott, J. M., Ten suggestions to strengthen the science of ecology, *BioScience*, 54, 345–351, 2004.

Bogdanor, V., Instant history, *Financial Times*, W6, December 13/14, 2003.

Brown, K., Water scarcity: forecasting the future with spotty data, *Science*, 297, 926–927, 2002.

Chambers, R., *Managing Rural Development: Ideas and Experience from East Africa*, Scandinavian Institute of African Studies Publications, Uppsala, Sweden, 1974.

Chambers, R., *Managing Canal Irrigation: Practical Analysis from South Asia*, Cambridge University Press, Cambridge, UK, 1988.

Chang, K., Panel says Bell Labs scientist faked discoveries in physics, *New York Times*, A1, September 26, see also p. A20, 2002.

Chang, K., Researcher loses Ph.D. over discredited papers, *New York Times*, D2, June 15, 2004.

Clark, J. A. and May, R. M., Taxonomic bias in conservation research, *Science*, 297, 191–192, 2002.

Cooper, R. N. and Layard, R., Introduction, In *What the Future Holds: Insights from Social Science*, Cooper, R. N. and Layard, R., Eds., MIT Press, Cambridge, MA, pp. 1–15, 2002.

Crane, N., Serious mappers, *TLS*, 9, February 27, 2004.

Crossette, B., Experts scaling back their estimates of world population growth, *New York Times*. http://www. nytimes.com (accessed September 29, 2005), 2002.

Daugherty, C. and Allendorf, F., The numbers that really matter, *Conservation Biology*, 16(2), 283–284, 2002.

Dugan, I. J. and Berman, D. K., Familiar villain emerges in a dark documentary film, *Wall Street Journal*, B1–B2, May 6, 2004.

Duvick, D. N., How much caution in the fields?, *Science*, 286, 418–419, 1999.

Economist, Scientific fraud: outside the Bell curve, *Economist*, 73–74, September 28, 2002.

Ehrlich, P., Front-line science does not stand still. Letter to the editor, *Financial Times*. http://www.ft.com (accessed January 20, 2003).

Feldbaum, C., Some history should be repeated, Policy Forum, *Science*, 295, 975, 2002.

Flyvbjerg, B., Bruzelius, N., and Rothengatter, W., *Megaprojects and Risk: An Anatomy of Ambition*, Cambridge University Press, Cambridge, UK, 2003.

Global warming—How will It end? [an advertisement], *New York Times*, (December 13):A16, 1999.

Haber, S., North, D. C., and Weingast, B. R., If economists are so smart, why is Africa so poor?, *Wall Street Journal*. http://www.wsj.com (accessed September 29, 2005), 2003.

Hirschman, A. O., *Development Projects Observed*, Brookings Institution, Washington DC, 1967.

Holland, M., Science statement, *Science*, 300, 247, 2003.

Johnson, K., Debate swirls around the status of a protected mouse, *New York Times*, 14, 2004, June 27.

Kaiser, J., Satellites spy more forest than expected, *Science*, 297, 919, 2002.

Kolata, G., Breast cancer on Long Island: no epidemic despite the clamor for action, *New York Times*, A23, August 29, 2002.

La Porte, T. R., Ed., *Organized Social Complexity: Challenge to Politics and Policy*, Princeton University Press, Princeton, NJ, 1975.

Le Blanc, C., *Huan-Nan Tzu: Philosophical Synthesis in Early Han Thought: The Idea of Resonance (Kan-Ying) with a Translation and Analysis of Chapter Six*, Hong Kong University Press, Hong Kong, 1985.

Loewe, M., Nothing positive, *TLS*, 28, June 27, 2003.

Lomborg, B., *The Skeptical Environmentalist*, Cambridge University Press, Cambridge, 2001.

Lutz, W., O'Neill, B. C., and Scherbov, S., Europe's population at a turning point, Policy Forum, *Science*, 299, 1991–1992, 2003.

Mann, C. and Plummer, M., Forest biotech edges out of the lab, *Science*, 295, 1626–1629, 2002.

March, J. G., Sproul, L. S., and Tamuz, M., Learning from samples of one or fewer, *Organization Science*, 2(1), 1–13, 1991.

Moris, J. R., *Managing Induced Rural Development*, International Development Institute, Indiana University, Bloomington, IN, 1981.

Myers, N. and Pimm, S., The last extinction?, *Foreign Policy*, 135, 28–29, 2003.

Pikitch, E. K., Santora, C., Babcock, E. A., Bakun, A., Bonfil, R., Conover, D. O., Dayton, P., Doukakis, P., Fluharty, D., Heneman, B., Houde, E. D., Link, J., Livingston, P. A., Mangel, M., McAllister, M. K., Pope, J., and Sainsbury, K. J., Ecosystem-based fishery management, Policy Forum, *Science*, 305, 346–347, 2004.

Pimm, S., Lomborg overlooked compelling information that did not fit thesis, Letter to the editor, *Financial Times*. http://www.ft.com (accessed September 29, 2005), 2003.

Ramanathan, V. and Barnett, T. P., Experimenting with Earth, *Wilson Quarterly*, 27(2), 78–84, 2003.

Revkin, A. C., Forget nature, *New York Times*, D1–D2, August 31, 2002.

Rignot, E., Rivera, A., and Casassa, G., Contribution of the Patagonia Icefields of South America to sea level rise, *Science*, 302, 434–437, 2003.

Ringen, S., Fewer people: a stark European future, *TLS*, *TLS*, 9–11, February 28, 2003.

Rochlin, G. I., Defining "high reliability" organizations in practice: a taxonomic prologue, In *New Challenges to Understanding Organizations*, Roberts, K. H., Ed., Maxwell Macmillan International, New York, pp. 11–32, 1993.

Roe, E., *Narrative Policy Analysis*, Duke University Press, Durham, NC, 1994.

Roe, E., *Taking Complexity Seriously: Policy Analysis, Triangulation, and Sustainable Development*, Kluwer Academic Publishers, Boston, 1998.

Roe, E., *Except-Africa*, Transaction Publishers, New Brunswick, NJ, 1999.

Roe, E., Real-time ecology, Letter to the editor and interchange, *BioScience*, 54(8), 716, 2004.

Roe, E. and van Eeten, M. J. G., Threshold-based resource management: A framework for comprehensive ecosystem management, *Environmental Management*, 27(2), 195–214, 2001.

Roe, E. and van Eeten, M. J. G., The heart of the matter: a radical proposal, *Journal of the American Planning Association*, 67(1), 92–98, 2001.

Roe, E. and van Eeten, M. J. G., Reconciling ecosystem rehabilitation and service reliability mandates in large technical systems: Findings and implications of three major US ecosystem management initiatives for managing human-dominated aquatic-terrestrial ecosystems, *Ecosystems*, 5(6), 509–528, 2002.

Roe, E. and van Eeten, M. J. G., Three—not two—major environmental counternarratives to globalization, *Global Environmental Politics*, 4(4), 36–53, 2004.

Roe, E., van Eeten, M. J. G., Schulman, P. R. and de Bruijne, M., *California's electricity restructuring: The challenge to providing service and grid reliability*, Report prepared for the California Energy Commission, Lawrence Berkeley National Laboratory, and the Electrical Power Research Institute, Palo Alto, CA: EPRI (Electric Power Research Institute), 2002.

Roe, E., van Eeten, M. J. G., Schulman, P. R., and de Bruijne, M., High reliability bandwidth management in large technical systems: findings and implications of two case studies, *Journal of Public Administration Research and Theory*, 15, 263–280, 2005.

Salim, E., The World Bank must reform on extractive industries, *Financial Times*, 15, June 17, 2004.

Sayer, J. A. and Campbell, B. M., *The Science of Sustainable Development: Local Livelihoods and the Global Environment*, Cambridge University Press, Cambridge, 2004.

Schulman, P. R., Roe, E., van Eeten, M. J. G., and de Bruijne, M., High reliability and the management of critical infrastructures, *Journal of Contingencies and Crisis Management*, 12(1), 14–28, 2004.

Scoones, I., Ed., *Living with Uncertainty: New Directions in Pastoral Development in Africa*, Intermediate Technologies Publications, Exeter, Great Britain, 1996.

Service, R., Bell Labs fires start physicist found guilty of forging data, *Science*, 298, 30–31, 2002.

Tinniswood, A., *His Invention So Fertile: A Life of Christopher Wren*, Pimlico, London, 2002.

United Nations, Department of Economic and Social Affairs, Population Division. World Population in 2300: Highlights, New York: United Nations, 2003.

van den Bergh, C. J. M. M. and Rietveld, P., Reconsidering the limits to world population: meta-analysis and meta-prediction, *Biosciences*, 54(3), 195–204, 2004.

van Eeten, M. and Roe, E., *Ecology, Engineering and Management: Reconciling Ecosystem Rehabilitation and Service Reliability*, Oxford University Press, New York, 2002.

Vestergaard, F., Letter to the editor: Pictures showing retreat of South American glacier cannot be accepted as evidence of global warming, *Financial Times*. http://www.ft.com (accessed September 29, 2005), 2004.

Walker, B., National, regional and local scale priorities in the economic growth versus environment trade-off, *Ecological Economics*, 15(2), 145–147, 1995.

Weisbord, M. and Janoff, S., *Future Search*, Berrett-Koehler Publishers, San Francisco, 1995.

Welland, M., Don't be afraid of the grey goo, *Financial Times*. http://www.ft.com (accessed September 29, 2005), 2003.

Wolf, M., People, plagues and prosperity, *Financial Times*. http://www.ft.com (accessed September 29, 2005), 2003a.

Wolf, M., A fanatical environment in which dissent is forbidden, *Financial Times*. http://www.ft.com (accessed September 29, 2005), 2003b.

Wright, B. A. and Okey, T. A., Creating a sustainable future? Letter to the editor, *Science*, 304, 1903, 2004.

Zeng, N., Drought in the Sahel, *Science*, 303, 999–1000, 2003.

Index

A

Action, 13, 81–96, 289–298
   see also Karma
Activation, networks, 321
Actors
   budgeting, 420–421
   e-government, 408–411
   Geographic Information Systems,
      531–532
   governing policy networks, 169, 174–175
Adaptation
   nonlinear decision making, 228, 232–239
   political decision making, 352–356
   punctuated equilibrium, 146
Adaptive conservatives, 54–56
Administration
   administrative behavior, 61–77, 81–96
   democratic theory, 158
   e-government, 395–414
   metropolitan areas, 348
   nonlinear decision making, 227–228
   political decision making, 355
   punctuated equilibrium, 134–135
   Simon, 61–77, 81–96
   see also Public administration
ADR *see* Alternative Dispute Resolution
Agency capture, 23–26
Agent-based models, 209–210
Aggadic material, 304
Aggregation, 8–9
Air quality, 46–47
Akrasia, 93
Algebraic linear programming, 498–499,
      504–505
Alternative Dispute Resolution (ADR), 587
Alternative strategic planning, 449–452
Ambiguity, 184
American war with Iraq, 51
Analects, 275, 276, 284
Analytical philosophy, 213–218
Ancient Greeks, 82–84
Approval, budgeting, 420, 426, 428
Arbitration, 175
Aristotelian practical reasoning, 82–87, 94–96
Arjuna, 293–294
Arms control, 46–47
Arthritis pain drugs, 461
"As-if", 114–115
Assumptions in interdisciplinary studies,
      248, 250–251, 256–260
Attribution bias, 590–592, 599
Audits, 420, 426, 429–430

Authority
   charismatic, 105
   discourse as, 99–115
   legal-rational, 105
   modern, 11, 99–115
   Q-methodology, 543
   Rabbinic decision making, 303–304, 310–311
   Rabbinic sages, 303–304
   traditional, 101–104
Autonomy, 272–273
Avoiding conflict, 602

B

Bacteria, 379
Bandwidth management, 618
Barnard, Chester, 62, 68–69
Barriers to decision making, 238, 589–590, 593–595
Bataille, Georges, 294, 297
Bay of Pigs invasion, 350
B/C *see* Benefit cost ratio
Beaufret, Jean, 289–290
Behavioral revolution, 61–77
Being-at-doing, 296–297
Benefit cost ratio (B/C), 488
Bhagavad Gītā, 293–294
Bhakti, 294
BIDs *see* Business improvement districts
Bifurcation diagrams, 198, 199
Biodiversity, 372
Boolean networks, 205–207, 209–210
Bottom-up theory, 158–159, 466
Boundaries, 213–214, 236–237, 249
Bounded rationality
   behavioral model, 7, 11, 61–77
   cognition, 122, 129
   evolution, 122, 129
   modern authority, 99
   organizational influence, 61–77
   political decision making, 349, 351
   public management networks, 335
   Simon, 7, 11, 61–77
Brain development, 74
Brainstorming, 580–581
Breakthrough policies, 48
Brokering, 321, 334
Buddhism, 13, 273–274, 289–298
Budgeting, 15, 417–430
   constraints, 495–496, 505–507
   evolution, 421–422
   execution, 420, 426, 428–429
   formulation, 420, 426–428

instrumental actions, 419–421
punctuated equilibrium, 135–136, 139–140
pre-preparation, 426–427
routines, 423, 425–430
rules, 423, 425–430
stages, 425–430
Bureaucracy
cognitive complexity, 573–576
democratic theory, 155–156, 158
drug trafficking, 364–365
e-government, 401, 403–405
public choice analysis, 23–26, 29–33
punctuated equilibrium, 142–143, 146, 147
Business improvement districts (BIDs), 356
Business-level strategic planning tools/techniques,
        438–439

C

Calculus-based trust, 592–593
Calendars, budgeting, 418
Cali networks, 363
Camus, Albert, 295
Capital intensity, 447
Cardiovascular risks, 477–479
Cartography, 530
Causal inferences, 92–96, 460, 462–463
Causal theory, 146
Cause and effect, 227
CBA see Cost-benefit analysis
Centralized decision hierarchies, 363–364
Chaos theory, 201–202, 205–207, 228–229
Childcare, 374–375, 466
Chinese philosophy, 265–286
Choice theories, 42, 120–121, 127–128, 369, 593
        see also Public choice analysis
Cholera, 528
Chung, 283
Citizen engagement, 355, 358
Civil society, 405, 407–409
Classical management, 176
Classification of ICT, 377–378
Clean air bill, 46–47
Clinger-Cohen Act (1996), 397
Cluster coefficients, 203
Cocaine, 363–369
Coda, 127
Codification, 301, 305
Cognition and decision making, 11–12, 119–129
        cognitive complexity, 565–583
        cognitive creativity, 565–583
        cognitive mapping methods, 572–576, 578–580
        cognitive psychological researchers, 6–7
Coherence, 232, 240–241
Collaboration
        collaborative decision making, 587–604
        conflict management, 587–604
        policy narratives, 618
        public management networks, 321–323, 333, 337,
                341, 343
Collective action, 172

Collective decision, 348, 353–354, 418–430
Columbian narcotics enterprises, 361–369
Common ground, creating, 257–260
Communication see Information and communication
                technology
Complexity
        analytical philosophy, 213–218
        boundaries, 213–214
        creativity, 568–572
        definition, 190–191, 194–196
        discrete systems, 203
        governing policy networks, 173, 176, 184
        interdisciplinary studies, 246–263
        nonlinear decision making, 224–242
        philosophy, 213–218
        political decision making, 356–358
        themes, 191–194
        thinking, 12, 189–218
Complex networks, 211–212
        control implications, 211–212
Complex systems, 12, 189–218
        Boolean networks, 205–207
        nonlinear systems, 194–212
Compliance measurement of, 465–467
Comprehensive rational model see Rational
                comprehensive model
Comprehensive understanding, 261–262
Computers
        complex systems, 210–211
        e-government, 395–414
        rise of power, 380–381
Concept mapping, 578–580
Concourse, 539–542
Condensed narratives, 609
Conflicts
        interdisciplinary studies, 255–257
        management, 17, 587–604
        participatory decision making, 17, 587–604
        policy making, 44–45
        policy networks, 180–181
        sources, 588–589
Confucian decision making, 13, 265–286
        integrity, 266–272
        intimacy, 266–269, 272–274
Conscience, 301, 309, 313–314
Consciousness, 107
Consensual objectives, 44–45
Consensus building, 321
Constraints of facility planning, 493–508
Constructs, 568–572
Contexts of decision making, 8
        budgeting, 15, 417–430
        drug trafficking, 14, 361–369
        e-government, 14–15, 395–414
        ICT, 14–15, 347–358, 371–393, 395–414
        institutional practices, 15, 417–430
        metropolitan areas, 14, 347–358
        political decision making, 14, 347–358
        public management networks, 14, 319–343
        Q-methodology, 556
        strategic planning, 15, 433–452

Contingencies, 301, 445–449, 451–452
Conventional policy analysis, 609–611
Cooperation
    bacterial networks, 379
    governing policy networks, 172–173, 175,
        177–181, 183
    participatory decision making, 601–602
Corporate-level strategic planning tools/techniques,
        439–440
Corporatists, 159–160
Correlation/correlation matrices, 539, 544–546
Cost-benefit analysis (CBA), 16, 63, 483–490
Counternarratives, 608, 611–613
Creativity
    cognitive mapping, 572–576, 578–580
    critiques, 567
    cycles, 571–572, 577–580
    definition, 567–568
    enhancing, 565–583
    facilitating, 577–582
    measuring, 572–577
    problem-solving, 566–567
    public policy decision making, 17, 565–583
Crisis
    management, 231, 235
    modern authority, 11, 99–115
    narratives, 609, 619
    nonlinear decisions, 231, 235
Critical pluralists, 193–194
Cuban missile crisis, 350
Cycle of death and rebirth, 291–292

D

DARE *see* Drug Abuse Resistance Education program
DARPA *see* Defense Advanced Research Agency
Dasein, 295, 296
Data driven methods, 331
Davidson, Donald, 92–96
D-decisions, 162–163
DEA *see* Drug Enforcement Administration
Decentralization, 113–114, 171, 172
Decision on the exclusion, 112–114
Decision hierarchies, 363–365
Decision premises, 66–67
Decision science
Defense Advanced Research Agency (DARPA),
        379
Degree distribution, 203
Deliberation, 82–89, 94–96
Delphi, 580–581
Demand constraints, 493–508
Democratic knowledge, 351
Democratic theory, 12, 151–164
    challenges, 154–163
    democratic institutions, 154, 155, 157, 160
    discourse theory, 152, 154–157, 163–164
    governance theory, 152, 157–164
    scope expansion, 163–164
    traditional approaches, 153–154, 157
Department of Defense (DoD), 386–391

Derrida, Jacques, 103–104, 112
Descartes, René, 270, 271
Descriptive models, 43–49
Destination maps, 198–200
Deterministic chaos, 201–202
Deterministic solutions, 514–515
Development narratives, 609–613, 616–619, 621–623
Devotion, 294
Dewey, John, 269
Difference, 106–107
Differentiation, 557, 570–571
Digital divide, 335
Digital government, 395–414
Disciplines, 245–263
Discounting, 487
Discourse theory, 99–115, 152, 154–157, 163–164
Discretion, 447
Disjointed incrementalism, 10–11, 39–58
Disputes *see* Conflicts
Distributions
    conflict management, 602–603
    degree distribution, 203
    punctuated equilibrium, 137–138
    queuing theory, 516–517, 519–520
DNA microarray technology, 379–380
DoD *see* Department of Defense
Dōgen, 293
Doublets, 99–115
Drug Abuse Resistance Education program (DARE),
        460–462, 464, 471, 474
Drug Enforcement Administration (DEA), 363
Drugs
    experiments, 459–462, 477–479
    trafficking, 14, 361–369
Dualisms, 99–100, 270–271
Dual solution, 501–503

E

East Asian perspectives, 13, 289–298
Ecological counternarratives, 612–613, 623
Economic globalization, 611–612
Economic man, 63
Economic Value Added (EVA), 440
Ecstatic decision, 13, 196, 289–298
Education, 472, 476
    see also Learning
Effective nonincremental changes, 45–47
Efficiency, public administration, 349–351
E-government, 14–15, 395–414, 525
    actors, 408–411
    cultural factors, 403–405
    force fields, 403, 405–408
    influencing factors, 405–408
    policy networks, 411–412
    projects, 396–397, 400–403, 410, 411
    roles, 411–412
E-Government Act (2001), 397
Electronic decision techniques, 331–336
Electronic government *see* E-government
Email, 333–336

Emergence
  definition, 208–209
  e-government, 407
  nonlinear decision making, 227, 235
Empowerment, 164
Emptiness, 297–298
Enlightenment, 101–102, 115, 127–128, 265, 270
Environmental factors, 361–369, 405, 445–447,
    575–576
Equilibrium theory, 12, 133–148, 210, 234–236
Ethics
  complexity, 216–218
  Nishitani on time and karma, 290
  nonlinear decision making, 237, 239
  practical reasoning, 84–85
  Rabbinic decision making, 309–310
  Simon, 66–67
Etzioni, Amatai, 64
European Union (EU), 406, 409, 411, 413
EVA *see* Economic Value Added
Evaluation
  budgeting, 420, 426, 429–430
  governing policy networks, 181–183
  narrative policy analysis, 611, 613–623
  policy narratives, 616–623
Evolution, 11–12, 119–129
  budget decision making, 421–422
  complex systems, 210–211
Exclusion, 112–114, 183
Existentialism, 272–274
Exit, queuing theory, 513–514
Experiments and quasiexperiments, 15–16,
    459–479
  ancillaries, 465–469
  case example, 476–479
  challenges, 473–476
  findings assessments, 473–476
  justification, 461–465
  medicine, 459–461, 471, 474, 476
  refinements, 465–469
Experts, 543
Explanatory networks, 178–180
Ex-post satisficing, 182–183
Exposure, 465–467
Extension techniques, 258–259
External contingencies, 445

F

Facilitation, governing policy networks, 175
Facilities
  creativity, 577–582
  planning, 492–508
Facta bruta, 292
Factor analysis, 539, 546–547, 572
  factor interpretation, 539, 547–548
  factor rotation, 539, 546–547
  factor scores, 539, 547–548
Factual premises, 66–67

Fact-value dichotomy, 62, 67
Failure of institutions, 112–114
Falsifiable hypotheses, 139
Fantasy, 109–110
Fast heuristics, 75–76
FDA *see* Food and Drug Administration
Feasibility zone, 494–498, 500–503
Federal budget, 139
Federal policy processes, 141–142
Feedback, 146, 203, 600
Financial constraints, 495–496, 505–507
Five-forces model, 438
Flat hierarchies, 364–365
Flexibility in decision making, 301
Food and Drug Administration (FDA), 477–479
Force fields, 386–391, 403, 405–408
Formulaic procedures, 330–331
Foucault, Michel, 105–108
Foundational authority, 105–108
Freedom of information, 397
Frugal heuristics, 75–76
Fuzzy cognitive maps, 578

G

Games, 174–175, 233, 512
Game simulations, 522
Game theory, 592
Garbage Can Model, 350, 399–403, 449, 451
Gemora, 302
Gene expression, 379–380
Geographic Information Systems (GIS), 16, 525–534
  background, 526–528
  democracy, 533
  industrial use, 526, 527
  interdisciplinary studies, 249
  maps, 528–534
  problem solving, 529–530
  public participation, 533
  science of, 531
Globalization, 611–613
Global overpopulation, 619–623
Golden Rule, 283
Google, 378
Governance
  democratic theory, 152, 157–164
  models, 170–172
  policy networks, 12, 169–184
  political decision making, 347–358
  public management, 170
Government, 27–33, 464–465
  see also e-government
Great Compassion, 297–298
Great Death, 297–298
Green counternarratives, 612–613, 623
Grounded theory, 320, 323
Group decision making, 587–604
Group discussion/exchanges, 330
Groupthink, 350
Guttmann scale, 325, 328

H

Habitual crisis management, 231
Halacha, 304–307, 309–310, 312–313
Halakhic decision making, 301
Hedonic pricing, 486, 487
Hegemony, 109
Heidegger, Martin, 289–292, 295
Heuristics, 75–76, 125–128, 522
Hierarchies, 170–172, 320, 363–365
Hinduism, 290, 292
Historic reviews, 13, 299–314, 436–437, 491–492
Hölderlin, Friedrich, 295
Hollow state, 350
Homeostasis, 234–235
Homo ludens, 297–298
Horizontal pluralism, 215–216
Hostility, 233, 361–369
Housing, 493–508
Human autonomy, 272–273
Human dynamics, 68–70
Humanities and interdisciplinary studies, 249–252,
        256–258, 261
Human nature, 122–127
Human temporality, 294–295
Humean practical reasoning, 82, 87–92
Hume, David, 94

I

ICT *see* Information and communication technology
Idealized models, 246–247
Ideal vs. practical considerations, 312–313
Identification-based trust, 592–593
Ideologues, 49–56, 412
IDS *see* Interdisciplinary studies
Illegal drug markets, 361–369
IMF and e-government, 410
Imperative functions, 90–92
Implementation factors, 158–159, 382–386, 465–467
Implication assessments, 474–476
Imposed use, 471–472
Incentives, 172, 179
Incompressibility, 195
Incrementalism
    cognition, 121, 129
    critiques, 54
    descriptive models, 43–49
    disjointed, 10–11, 39–58
    effective operation conditions, 57
    e-government, 399–403
    evolution, 121, 129
    ideologues, 49–56
    Lindblom, 10–11, 39, 134–135
    policy making, 39–58
    policy processes, 43–45
    pragmatists, 49–56
    prescriptive models, 49–57
    punctuated equilibrium, 134–136

rationality, 40–43
    Simon, 64
    strategic planning, 449
Individual decisions, 8–9
Inductive assessments, 466
Industry life cycle, 439
Information
    definition, 373–375
    public management networks, 322–323, 332–336,
        340–341
    Q-methodology, 555–560
    quantity, 376
    sources, 375–376
    transformation, 231
    see also Geographic Information Systems
Information and communication technology (ICT),
        371–393
    application, 378–380
    change over time, 380–381
    classification, 377–378
    e-government, 395–414
    examples, 378–380
    implementation factors, 382–386
    joint total asset visibility, 386–392
    public management networks, 332–336, 340–341
Information technology (IT), 371–393, 525–534
Informed decision making, 233–234
Insights, 253–257, 310–311
Institutional theory
    budgeting, 15, 417–430
    e-government, 405
    institutional design, 176–178
    institutional failure, 112–114
    public choice analysis, 25–26
Instrumentalism, 82, 95, 419–421
Integer programming, 16, 491, 508–510
Integration, 248, 258–260, 570–571, 603
Integrity, 266–272
Intellectual design, 175
Intentionality, 228–230
Interactions, 178, 321
Interactive policy networks, 174
Interdependencies, 170, 172, 173, 175
Interdisciplinary studies (IDS), 13, 245–263
    assumptions, 248, 250–251, 256–260
    concepts, 248, 250–259
    definition, 245–246
    discipline determination, 250–252
    holistic, 260, 263
    integration, 248
    patterns, 249–250, 254, 257–262
    perspectives, 245–262
    problem identification, 249–250
    steps, 248–262
    subsystems, 250, 261
Internal contingencies, 447–449
Internalism, 88–89
Internal rate of return (IRR), 488
Internet, 378, 396–397
    see also ICT
Interorganizational networks, 174, 319

Intervention, experiments, 465–467
Intimacy, 266–269, 272–274
Intractable problems, 559–560
Iraq, American war, 51
IRR *see* Internal rate of return
Isomorphism, 407
Israel, 299, 300
IT *see* Information technology

J

Jargon *see* Terminology
Jewish history, 13, 299–314
Jigsaw puzzles, 255
Johnson, John Thomas, 363
Joint image building, 175
Joint learning systems, 343
Joint total asset visibility (JTAV), 386–392
JTAV *see* Joint total asset visibility
Judaism, 13, 299–314
Junzi, 275–277, 284–286
Justification, 92–93, 215

K

Kant, Immanuel, 100, 102, 128, 307
Karma, 13, 227, 289–298
     see also Action; Causal…
Kasulis, Thomas, 266–268, 270, 271
Kelly's Repertory Grid Technique, 568–583
Knowledge
     information, 374–375
     interdisciplinary studies, 253–255
     management, 322–323
     policy making, 44–45
Krishna, 293–294
Kurtosis, 138, 141

L

Lacan, Jacques, 103–104, 111
Language, 103–104, 146, 256–257
Lateral thinking, 581
Law enforcement, 362–363
Leadership, 404, 459
Learning
     governing policy networks, 179, 181–183
     public management networks, 320–321, 329–332,
          343
     Simon, 74
Lefort, Claude, 108–110
Legal codification, 301, 305
Legal constraints, 495–496, 505
Legal formalism, 308, 310
Legality, 301, 305, 308–310
Legislatures, 67
Levi-Straus, Claude, 112
Li, 275–282, 284
Liberals, 54–56
Life cycle of issues, 48–49

Likert Scale, 390
Lindblom, Charles, 10–11, 39, 134–135
Linear programming, 16, 491–510
     algebraic form, 498–499
     examples, 492–508
     facility planning, 492–508
     mathematical solutions, 501
     prison planning, 504–508
Linkage identification, 260–261
Literal meaning, 308–309
Local government, 27–33, 140
Local public economies, 28–29
Logic
     of appropriateness, 351–352, 362, 365
     budgeting, 419–420
     of consequences, 348, 362
     of foundational authority, 105–108
     logical positivism, 62
     Rabbinic decision making, 310–311
Logistics maps, 198
Lorenz system, 198, 199
Lyapunov maps, 198, 199

M

McKinsey's seven-S framework, 439
Macrodesign nodes, 614–615
Majority opinion, 313–314
Management
     conflicts, 587–604
     network approach, 175–178
     public management networks, 319–343
Management information systems (MIS), 333
Man of Reason, 110–111
Mapping cognitive constructions, 572–576, 578–580
Maps, 528–534
March, James, 362, 366
Margin-dependent choice, 42
Market governance models, 170, 172
Mathematical linear programming, 501
Maturation, 461–462
Maximization problem, 503
Meaning making, 230–231, 240–241
Means and ends, 67, 399
Measuring cognitive complexity, 572–577
Measuring creativity, 572–577
Mechanical systems, 198–200
Medellín networks, 363
Media, 408–409
Mediation, 175, 180, 467–469
Meliorative liberals, 54–56
Mermelstein, Max, 363, 367–369
Merton, Robert, 66, 68
Meta-analysis, 469
Meta-governance, 161
Metaphors, 261
Metaphorticians, 192–193
Methods of decision making
     conflict management, 17, 587–604
     cost-benefit analysis, 16, 63, 483–490
     creativity for public policy, 17, 565–583

experiments, 15–16, 459–479
  Geographic Information Systems, 16, 249, 525–534
  integer programming, 16, 491, 508–510
  linear programming, 16, 491–510
  narrative policy analysis, 17, 607–624
  participatory decision making, 17, 587–604
  policy analysis, 17, 607–624
  public policy, 17, 565–583
  Q-methodology, 16–17, 537–560
  quasiexperiments, 15–16, 459–479
  queuing theory, 16, 511–523
  randomized experiments, 459–479
Metropolitan political decision making, 14, 27–33,
    347–358
Metropolitan public choice analysis, 27–33
Microarray technology, 379–380
Minimization problems, 503
Minimum wage, 52
MIS *see* Management information systems
Mishna, 302
Mixed scanning model, 64
Moderation, 467–469
Modern authority, 11, 99–115
  "as-if", 114–115
  exclusion, 112–114
  failure of institutions, 112–114
  foundational authority, 105–108
  language, 103–104
  Man of Reason, 110–111
  The Order of Things, 105–108
  political authority structure, 108–110
  relocation, 105
  representation, 105
  Simon's "concessions", 99–101
  social grammar, 103–104
  social relations, 110–111
  thought unhingement, 111–112
  tradition and authority, 101–103
Monkeys, 589–590
Monte Carlo simulations, 512, 522
Motivation, 90–92, 239
Mōksa, 292
Mu, 296
Multiactor governance models, 171, 172
Multi-phase queues, 513–514
Multiple qualitatively different behaviors, 198–199, 201
Mushin, 296
Myths, 610

N

Narcotics agents (narcs), 362–369
Narcotics enterprises, 361–369
Narcotraficantes (narcos), 362–369
Narrative policy analysis, 17, 607–624
  conventional policy analysis, 609–611
  evaluation, 611, 613–623
  globalization, 611–613
  overpopulation, 619–623
National Performance Review (1993), 396–397
National Science Foundation (NSF), 68

National Security Agency (NSA), 379, 381–382
Natural sciences, 246, 249, 252, 254, 256
NECG *see* Non-equivalent comparison group design
Needs of eternity, 311–312
Needs of the moment, 311–312
Negative exponential distributions, 516, 518
Negotiation, 159–160, 321–322, 330
Neighborhood councils, 355
Neo-corporatists, 159–160
Neo-reductionists, 191–192
Net present value (NPV), 488
Networks
  agreement processes, 328–329
  Boolean networks, 205–207, 209–210
  complexity, 203–212
  composition, 177
  cooperative bacterial networks, 379
  decisions, 320–321, 328–329, 332–343
  drug trafficking, 361, 363–364
  governance models, 12, 169–184
  interactions, 178
  management, 175–178, 181
  outcomes, 177–178
  public management, 14, 319–343
  public policy, 12, 169–184
  see also policy networks
Neurophysiology, 123, 125–127
New institutionalist theories, 25–26
New public management (NPM), 169, 170, 350–351
New sciences, 74–75
NGOs *see* Non-governmental organizations
Nicomachean Ethics, 84–85
Nietzsche, Friedrich, 291, 294, 295, 297
Nihilism, 295–297
Nishida, Kitarō, 291–298
Nishitani, Keiji, 13, 289–298
Nobel Prize, 64–65, 73
Non-binding constraints, 503
Non-equivalent comparison group design (NECG),
    463–464
Non-governmental organizations (NGOs), 319
Nonincremental changes, 45–49
Nonlinearity
  complex systems thinking, 194–212
  definition, 196–197
  interdisciplinary studies, 246, 248–250, 257,
    260–261
  sensibilities, 12–13, 223–242
    adaptation, 228, 232–239
    adaptive choice making, 237–239
    coherence, 232, 240–241
    complexity, 224–242
    praxis, 232, 240–241
    process habits, 241–242
    relationship dynamics, 225, 230–232
    timing, 235–236
Non-negativity constraint, 494
Nonstories, 607
Nostalgic conservatives, 54–56
NPM *see* New public management
NPV *see* Net present value

NSA *see* National Security Agency
NSF *see* National Science Foundation
Nuclear weapons, 46–47

O

Objective functions, 495–497, 500–501
Objective rationality, 65–66
Office of Management and Budget (OMB), 484, 489
Omniscient rationality, 11
Opportunity costs *see* Shadow price
Optimal choice, 495, 498–500, 508
Optimization, 232–233
Oral law, 302–314
The Order of Things, 105–108
Orejuela, Miguel Rodríguez, 363
Organizational behavior, 351
Organizational bureaucratization, 142–143
Organizational decision making, 12, 133–148
Organizational influence, 7, 11, 61–77
Organizational performance, 443–444
Organization integrative techniques, 259
Organization size factors, 448
Orientation factors, 448
Outcomes
    governing policy networks, 177–178
    measurements/variables, 473–476
    orientated studies, 397–398
Output orientated studies, 397–398
Overcrowding, 619–623

P

Paleontology, 136
Paperwork Reduction Act (1980), 396–397
Participatory decision making
    conflict management, 17, 587–604
    governing policy networks, 172, 175
    methods, 595–599
    nonlinear decision making, 235
    policy narratives, 617
    skills, 599–603
Path lengths, 203
Perceptions, 175–182, 225–228
Personal constructs, 568–572
Personal justifications, 464–465
Perspectives, 245–262, 449–452
Peshawar, Pakistan, 381–382
Phases
    Q-methodology, 539–548
    queuing theory, 513–514
Phase space, 198, 199, 202, 205–206
Philosophy, 191, 213–218
    Confucian decision making, 265–286
    integrity, 270–272
    intimacy, 272–274
    Nishitani on time and karma, 291–298
Plato's project, 270
Pluralism, 193–194, 214–218
PMN *see* Public management networks

Poisson distributions, 516–517, 519
Policy analysis, 12, 17, 189–218, 607–624
Policy change dynamics, 134, 137
Policy constraints, 495–496, 499
Policy controversies, 609, 611, 618
Policy decisions, 348
Policy narratives, 17, 607–624
Policy networks, 12, 160, 169–184, 411–412
    interests, 171–183
    objectives, 170, 173–176, 180–183
    problem-solving, 174–175, 178, 183–184
    strategies, 171–184
Policy processes
    disjointed incrementalism, 10–11, 39–58
    governing policy networks, 170, 172–173, 175,
        179–184
    incrementalism, 43–45
    punctuated equilibrium, 141–142
    Q-methodology, 552–553, 558–559
Politics
    authority structure, 108–110
    decision making, 14, 347–358
    democratic theory, 152, 155–163
    e-government, 411–412
    Humean practical reasoning, 90–92
    justifications, 464–465
    metropolitan areas, 14, 347–358
    negotiations, 330
    public administration, 349–351
    public choice analysis, 27–33
    strategic planning, 449–450
Polity, 154
Pollution, 46–47
Polycentric governance, 29
Population, 619–623
Porter's five-forces model, 438
Porter's value-chain analysis, 438–439
Portfolio management frameworks, 439–440
Positive framing, 600
Postmodernism, 113–114, 247, 251
Post-structuralism, 101, 103
Power, 153–154, 180–181, 335
PPGIS *see* Public participation geographic information
        systems
Practical reasoning, 81–96
Practical vs. ideal considerations, 312–313
Pragmatism/pragmatists, 49–56, 226
Pratītyasamutpāda, 292
Praxis, 232, 240–241
Precedents, 302, 305, 314
Pre-decision modes, 329–332
Predictive budget theory, 422
Pre-established procedures, 330–331
Prescriptive models, 49–57
Primals, 503
Principal–agent models, 25
Principal components analyses, 573–574
Priorities in nonlinear decision making, 225
Prison planning, 504–508
Private ICT firms, 408–410
Privatization, 171–172

Probability, 512, 516–523
Procedural barriers, 593–595
Process habits, 241–242
Process management, 176–178
Process norms, 183
Process orientated studies, 397–398
Process variables, 178–179
Professionals, decision-making, 550–551
Programming *see* Linear/Integer programming
Projects
    e-government, 396–397, 400–403, 410, 411
    selection, 488
P sets, 542–544
Psychological barriers, 589–590
Public administration
    democratic theory, 162
    e-government, 395–414
    political decision making, 349–351
    public choice analysis, 21–34
    rationality, 348–351
    Simon, 71–74
Public budgeting, 15, 417–430
Public choice analysis, 10, 21–34
    agency capture, 23–26
    bureaucracy, 23–26, 29–33
    classic studies, 22–23
    cognition, 120–121
    critiques, 29–31
    emergence, 22–29
    evolution, 120–121
    future directions, 31–34
    local government, 27–33
    metropolitan governance, 27–33
    new/neo institutionalist theories, 25–26
    outcomes, 23–29
    political institutions, 27–33
Public choice theory, 120–121
Public decision making, 595
Public economies, 28–29
Public management networks (PMN), 14, 319–343
    agreement processes, 328–329
    communication, 332–336, 340–341
    decision types, 323–328
    electronic decision techniques, 331–336
    ICT, 332–336, 340–341
    learning strategies, 329–332
    network management, 321–323
    policy networks, 169–170
    pre-decision modes, 329–332
    research agenda, 340–343
    value-adding functions, 337–341
Public policy, 17, 169–184, 565–583
Public-private partnerships, 355–356
Public service industries, 28–29
Public value, 320, 341
Punctuated equilibrium theory, 12, 133–148
    budgets, 139–140
    bureaucratization, 142–143, 146, 147
    challenges, 143–148
    characteristic distribution, 137–138
    falsifiable hypotheses, 139
    frontiers, 143–148
    policy processes, 141–142
    research conundrums, 134–137
    theoretical challenges, 145–148

Q

QCQ *see* Quantitative Cyberquest
Q methodology, 16–17, 537–560
    correlation, 539, 544–546
    essentials, 538–548
    factors, 539, 546–548
    frameworks, 556
    information provision, 555–560
    intractable problems, 559–560
    Kelly's Repertory Grid Technique, 576–577
    phases, 539–548
    P sets, 542–544
    research decision making, 549–555
    sample structure, 540–542
    sorting, 542–544
    special interests, 543–544
    structure, 540–542
Q sample structure, 540–542
Q sorting, 542–546
Qualitative factors, 201–203
Quantifying costs and benefits, 486–487
Quantitative Cyberquest (QCQ), 387–391
Quasiexperiments *see* Experiments and
        quasiexperiments
Queuing theory, 16, 511–523
    discipline, 517–518
    distributions, 516–517, 519–520
    elements, 512–519
    simulations, 16, 521–523
    solving a problem, 512–515
    structures, 513–514, 517–518

R

Rabbinic decision making, 13, 299–314
    Halacha, 304–307, 309–310, 312–313
    sages, 13, 300–304, 307–314
    seven dilemmas, 307–314
    text meaning, 307–309
    Torah, 304–307, 309–310
Randomized experiments, 459–479
    see also Experiments and…
Random numbers, 522–523
Ranking, 542–544
Rational choice theory, 120–121, 127–128, 593
Rational comprehensive model, 3–7
    cognition, 120, 127–128
    critics, 5–7
    e-government, 399–403
    evolution, 120, 127–128
    Simon, 6–7, 11, 63–64
Rationality
    breakdown, 40
    budgeting, 420–421

complex networks, 211–212
conflict, 588
democratic theory, 156–157
e-government, 399–403
incrementalism, 40–43
nonincremental changes, 45–47
procedural barriers, 593–595
psychological barriers, 589–590
public administration, 348–351
public choice analysis, 30–31, 33–34
strategic planning, 449–451
see also Bounded rationality
Reactive nihilism, 295–296
Reasoning, 81–96, 310–311
Recognition heuristics, 75–76
Redefinition techniques, 258
Redependency, 114
Regional economic planning, 353
Regional governance, 347–358
Regression-discontinuity, 462–463
Reinterpreted meaning, 308–309
Reinventing government movement, 396–397
Relationships
    ICT implementation, 386
    nonlinear decision making, 225, 230–232
    policy networks, 180–181
Reliability space, 617, 621
Relocation of authority, 105
Ren, 275, 277, 279, 281–284, 285
Rent seeking, 23, 31
Repertory Grid Technique, 568–583
Representation, modern authority, 105
Representative democracy, 151–164
Research
    agenda, 340–343
    psychological researchers, 6–7
    punctuated equilibrium, 134–137, 147
    Q methodology, 549–555
Resolving conflicts/disputes, 17, 587–604
Resource allocation, 417–430
Resources
    nonlinear decision making, 237–238
    policy networks, 170–181
Revolutionary Armed Forces of Columbia, 362
Rhetoric, 256, 258
Riddled basins, 202–203
Risk, 618
R methodology, 538
Robustness, 203, 207–208
Roles
    budgeting, 423, 425–430
    policy networks, 180–181
    politics, 411–412
    smuggling groups, 365–366
Roots, 173
Rotated factors, 539, 546–547
Routines in trafficking organizations, 366–369
Rule-based decision making, 369
Rules of drug trafficking, 361–369

S

Sages, 284, 300–304, 307–314
Sample constraints, 144–145
Sample structure, 540–542
Samskrita (being-at-doing), 296–297
Samsāra cycles, 291, 292
Sartre, Jean Paul, 291, 292
Satisficing
    budgeting, 420–421
        governing policy networks, 182–183
        political decision making, 349–350
        Simon, 62–64, 69
Satisficing man, 99
Saussure, Ferdinand de, 103
SBU see Strategic Business Units
Scaling, 236–237
Scenario analysis, 440
Schelling, Friedrich, 297
Schemata, 122–125
Science of complexity, 194–212
Scope factors, 249–250, 614–615
Search engines, 378
Second Temple, 299–314
Sehnsucht, 297
Self, 270–286
Self-organization, 210, 228–230
Self-organized brain, 228–229
Sensitivity, 201–202, 508
Service time, 518–519
Seven-S framework, 439
Shadow prices, 487, 501–503, 507–508
Shadow wage, 486
Shan, 277
Sheng, 284
Short decision hierarchies, 364–365
Shu, 283
Simon, Herbert
    administrative behaviour, 61–77, 81–96
    bounded rationality, introduction, 7, 11
    "concessions", 99–101
    decision making actors, 531–532
    political decision making, 349
    rational comprehensive model, 6–7, 11, 63–64
Simple nonlinear systems, 197–203
Simplex method, 492, 501
Simulations, 521–523
Single case decision structures, 553–554
Single-phase systems, 513–514
Size factors, 448
Skills, 599–603
Sliding of signifier, 103–104
Smugglers, 361–369
Snow, Dr Jon, 528
Social issues
    change, 164, 226–227
    changes, 164, 226–227
    dynamics, 68–70
    experimentation, 470
    grammar, 103–104
    preferences change, 499–501

problems, 174
punctuation, 104
reform advocates, 54
relations, 110–111, 155
responsibility, 227–228
sciences, 164, 249–258, 261
society-centred theories, 160
Social Security Act (1935), 48
Sociobiology, 124–125
Software, 334, 387–391, 411–412
Sokal hoax, 608
Sorting, 542–546
Sovereignty, 108, 149, 153–154, 158
Soviet Union, 381–382
Space constraints, 493–508
Spatial factors, 525–534
Species change dynamics, 134
Specificationism, 95–96
SPO *see* State Planning Organization
Stability, nonlinear decision making, 239, 240
Stakeholder analysis, 438
Stash houses, 367–369
State-centred theories, 159, 162
State of Israel, 299, 300
State Planning Organization (SPO), 400–403
Statistical analysis, 462–464
Stephenson, William, 537
Stochastic processes, 522
Stories, 607–624
Strategic Business Units (SBU), 436–437
Strategic games, 174–175
Strategic management, 15, 433–452
Strategic planning, 15, 433–452
    alternative perspectives, 449–452
    arguments against, 442–443
    arguments for, 441–442
    business-level tools and techniques, 438–439
    characteristics, 435–436
    concepts, 434–436
    contingencies, 445–449, 451–452
    controversies, 441–449
    corporate-level tools and techniques, 439–440
    definition, 434–435
    empirical evidence, 443–444
    future, 449–452
    historic reviews, 436–437
    organizational performance, 443–444
    techniques, 437–440
    tools, 437–440
Strict legality, 309–310
Structural considerations, 203–204
Structuralism, 101, 103
Structure
    public management networks, 321, 334
    Q-methodology, 540–542, 549–555
    queuing theory, 513–514, 517–518
Sub-Humean practical reasoning, 82, 87–92
Sub-regional economic partnerships, 354, 358
Substance abuse, 460, 461, 471, 474, 476
Substance assessments, 182–183
Substantive criterion, 181–183

Success factors, 178–179
Śūnyāta, 297–298
Supra-national organizations, 410–411
Surveillance, 525–526, 529, 533
SWOT analysis, 438
Syllogism, 85–87, 92–96
System coherence, 240–241
System dynamics models, 210
Systemic pragmatism, 226
System simulations, 521–522

T

TA2 *see* TextAnalysis2
Talmud, 305, 313–314
Tanabe, Hajime, 297
Taxonomy *see* Classification
Technicism, 100–101
Technology formats, 330–331
Terminology, interdisciplinary studies, 256, 258
TextAnalysis2 (TA2), 387–391
Text meaning, 307–309
Theology, 13, 265–286, 289–314
Theories
    administrative behaviour, 61–77, 81–96
    bounded rationality, 7, 11, 61–77
    cognition and decision making, 11–12, 119–129
    complex systems thinking, 12, 189–218
    Confucian decision making, 13, 265–286
    crisis of modern authority, 11, 99–115
    democratic theory, 12, 151–164
    discourse theory, 99–115, 152, 154–157, 163–164
    disjointed incrementalism, 10–11, 39–58
    evolution and decision making, 11–12, 119–129
    governance theory, 152, 157–164
    governing policy networks, 12, 169–184
    incrementalism, 10–11, 39–58
    interdisciplinary studies, 13, 245–263
    Judaism, 13, 299–314
    modern authority, 11, 99–115
    Nishitani's time and karma, 13, 289–298
    nonlinear decision making, 12–13, 223–242
    organizational decision making, 12, 133–148
    organizational influence, 7, 11, 61–77
    overviews, 10–13
    policy analysis, 12, 189–218
    policy making, 10–11, 39–58
    policy networks, 12, 169–184
    practical reasoning, 81–96
    public choice analysis, 10, 21–34
    punctuated equilibrium, 12, 133–148
    Rabbinic decision making, 13, 299–314
    theory of everything, 191–192
Thinking hats, 581–582
Thomas–Kilmann Conflict Mode Instrument, 600–601
Thought unhingement, 111–112
Threshold models, 146–147
Tian, 279
Time and karma, 13, 289–298
Timing, 235–236
Torah, 304–307, 309–310

Traditional democratic theory, 153–154, 157
Tradition and authority, 101–104
Trafficking, 361–369
Transformations, 152, 259–260
Travel cost method, 486, 487
Treatment, experiments, 465–467
    exposure, 465–467
Trochim's concept mapping, 578–580
Trust, 173, 179–180, 592–593
Turims, 306
Turkey, 14–15, 395–414, 572–576
Typology of networks, 323–328, 341

U

U-2 Spyplanes, 381–382
U-curves, 613
Umwelt, 123–124
Uncertainty
    e-government, 403
    nonlinear decision making, 224
    queuing theory, 512, 516–519
    strategic planning, 445–447
Undecidability, 114–115
Under-privileged interests, 181
UNDP *see* United Nations Development Program
Unilateral substantive criterion, 181–182
United Nations Development Program (UNDP), 397, 408,
        410–411
United Self-Defense Forces of Colombia, 362
United States National Science Foundation, 68
Unpredictability, 202–203
Urban Information Systems (URBIS) project,
        396, 397
Urban youth summer programs, 511
URBIS (Urban Information Systems) project, 396, 397
Utilitarian explanations, 588
Utopian visionaries, 54

V

Value adding, 337–341, 440
Value assumptions, 256–257
Value-based planning (VBP), 440
Value-chain analysis, 438–439
Value-maximixation, 41
Value premises, 66–67

Variables in ICT implementation, 382–386
Variables in nonlinear decision making, 233–234
VBP *see* Value-based planning
Vendor push concept, 407, 409–410
Vertical pluralism, 215–216
Vertical thinking, 581
Veto power, 181
VIGOR trial on Vioxx, 477–479
Vishnu, 293

W

Waiting times, 514–515
Waltman, Jerold, 50–52
War, weapons, 46–47
War on drugs, 361–369
Wei wu wei, 298
Wen, 275
Western context, 266–268, 270–272
What Works Clearinghouse (WWC), 472, 476
Wildavsky, Aaron, 135–136
Williams, Bernard, 88–89
Win-win situations, 182–183
Work force stabilization, 239
World Bank, 400–403, 408, 410
World Wide Web, 378, 396–397
Written law, 301–314
WWC *see* What Works Clearinghouse

X

Xin, 284

Y

Yi, 275, 277–278, 285–286
Youth summer programs, 511, 514–515, 519–520

Z

Zabludoff, Sidney, 364
ZBB *see* Zero-based budgeting
Zen mind, 296
Zero-based budgeting (ZBB), 63
Zero shadow price, 503
Zhong, 283
Zizek, Slavoj, 100, 109, 111, 113